AA Illustrated Guide to Britain

AA

ILLUSTRATED GUIDE TO BRITAIN

Published by Drive Publications Limited
for the Automobile Association
Fanum House, Basingstoke, Hants RG21 2EA

The publishers express their gratitude for major contributions by the following people:

AUTHORS

John Arlott	B. J. Hurren
Patrick Bailey	Brendan Lehane
F. R. Banks	Colin Luckhurst
J. C. Barringer	Eric Maple
Gerald Barry	Paul Martin
Vivian Bird	Geoffrey Moorhouse
David Bowen	Sylvie Nickels
John Burke	J. H. B. Peel
Max Caulfield	David Piper
J. P. Cushion	W. Gordon Smith
Arthur Eperon	John Street
John Gooders	James Wentworth Day
Anthony Greenbank	J. T. White

PHOTOGRAPHERS AND ARTISTS

Malcolm Aird	Chris Morris
S. R. Badmin	Patrick Oxenham
Christian Bonington	John Perkins
Martin Breese	Julian Plowright
John Bulmer	Michael St Maur Sheil
Tony Evans	Faith Shannon
Michael Hardy	Michael Taylor
Geoffrey Howard	Patrick Thurston
Anthony Howarth	Penny Tweedie
David Jefferis	Denis Waugh
Peter Keen	Michael Wells
Eric Meacher	Adam Woolfitt
Gordon Moore	Ian Yeomans

ILLUSTRATED GUIDE TO BRITAIN
was edited and designed by Drive Publications Limited
Berkeley Square House, London W1X 5PD
for the Automobile Association
Fanum House, Basingstoke, Hants RG21 2EA

Printed in Great Britain

Contents

THE MAKING OF BRITAIN

DISCOVERING BRITAIN

SPECIAL FEATURES

THE OUTDOOR LIFE

INDEX

THE MAKING OF BRITAIN

THIS PATCHWORK LAND

No country in the world is richer than Britain in its patchwork of natural beauty. It is a patchwork formed by the play of light and shade upon a landscape; by the tone which lichen and moss can give to stonework; by the placing of a church or a barn; and by the memories which have been stitched into this fabric of rivers and hills, forests and plains, marshes and coasts.

Even the British weather, changeable as it is in this sea-girt country, can be an ally. A wet and windy day is a day, above all others, to visit the Cambridgeshire Fens. The trees are permanently bent inland from the force of the wind, dramatic and dripping like clumps of witches' broomsticks. Wildfowl skitter over the marshes, and dikes stream away in straight lines as far as the eye can see. The landscape seems to stretch on flatly towards the end of the earth; and indeed there is little ground higher than this until the Steppes begin to slope upwards near Moscow, 1400 miles to the east.

Another experience for a wild and rainy day is to watch the Atlantic Ocean smashing in full force against the headlands of the Cornish coast.

From music-hall to Roman Wall

As with the weather, so with the land: there are endless surprises in this patchwork country. Few think of our time-blackened northern cities as centres for tourism, but a city such as Newcastle upon Tyne well repays a visit. From the Tyne Quay there is a dramatic view of buses, looking like tiny yellow beetles, crossing the bridges that are ranged one after another high in the air over the great canyon of the river. The city's Georgian terraces are as impressive as anything in Bath, and genuine Victorian music-hall is still performed at Balmbra's. Within a few miles of the centre of Newcastle upon Tyne is the start of Hadrian's Wall, which climbs and dips its way across the most magnificently unspoilt tract of land in England.

Even the grandeur of the Roman Wall country is surpassed in the west of Scotland. The famous 'Road to the Isles' from Fort William to Mallaig has mountains on either side, lochs every few miles, and deer rummaging below the scree. There are white sands at Morar, trawlers and oilskins in Mallaig and fabulous sunsets over Rhum. The area is rich in history as well, in the story of Bonnie Prince Charlie, who stepped into a French boat from this coast and left Scotland never to return.

Variety is the key to the abiding fascination of Britain. On a journey from London to the South-West, the landscape changes from the suburban neatness of the Home Counties to the charm of Hampshire, from the sweeping uplands of Wiltshire to the flat lands of Somerset, and finally to the haunted moors and bubbling river valleys of Devon. Along the route are fascinating places to explore at leisure: Winchester, where Alfred the Great had his capital; the mysterious Bronze Age sanctuary of Stonehenge; the plain of Sedgemoor, scene of the bloody battle in which the Duke of Monmouth's rebellion was crushed in 1685; Clouds Hill, where Lawrence of Arabia lived; and Buckfast Abbey, where the monks make their enormous vats of tonic wine.

Such varied scenes as these are to be found on a journey through Britain in practically any direction. At Tudeley in Kent is the only stained-glass window the French painter Marc Chagall ever designed in Britain. On the River Teifi in Wales there are men still using coracles. The first glimpse from the limestone floor of Ribblesdale, in North Yorkshire, of Pen-y-ghent and Ingleborough towering in the heavens is not easily forgotten; the temptation to follow a pipe band skirling down Princes Street during the Edinburgh Festival is hard to resist. Cobbled Durham City has its Miners' Gala in July, loud with the oom-pah of brass bands; by contrast, few places compare in tranquillity with Blythburgh Church in Suffolk, all whitewashed inside, or with the view over the estuary from Dylan Thomas's home at Laugharne in Dyfed, where the sands gleam silver, the tide fingers its way inland, and the gulls come to be lonely.

LAND OF WATER *The traveller in Britain is never far from the sound of running water. Wales is particularly rich in lakes, reservoirs and waterfalls: these falls are near the village of Ystradfellte, in Powys, where the River Mellte tumbles down a series of limestone terraces from its source high in the Brecon Beacons National Park*

THE MOULDING OF THE LANDSCAPE

The variety of Britain's scenery is due largely to the influence of the underlying rocks. These vary from some of the oldest rocks in the world, in the barren wilderness of West Sutherland, to new land surfaces still being formed on the shifting coastline of Dungeness, 600 miles to the south-east. Each region has its own distinctive story of development, but all rocks are of three principal types. Sedimentary rocks were formed by deposits laid down on the floors of oceans. Igneous rocks were formed when masses of molten material from the Earth's core were forced through the sedimentary rocks. Metamorphic rocks were formed when either sedimentary or igneous rocks were changed in character by heat or pressure.

The oldest rocks in Britain date back at least 3400 million years. No life existed then, nor has it existed for the greater part of Earth's history. This long period before any fossils were formed is known as the Pre-Cambrian phase. The oldest rocks tend to be the hardest and therefore to stand out as highlands. They include the splintery and contorted mountains along the north-west fringe of the Scottish Highlands and the Outer Hebrides. Further south, Pre-Cambrian rocks are exposed in Anglesey, the Malverns and The Long Mynd of Shropshire.

Earliest life under a huge ocean

Fossil evidence of life first appears in rocks of the Cambrian Period, about 570 million years ago. During this time, and the succeeding Ordovician and Silurian Periods, a great ocean trough lay between Norway and Ireland, with ancient land masses to its north-west in north Scotland, and to the south-east, where the English Midlands now exist. In this sea great thicknesses of mud accumulated, which were compressed under the weight of later sediments. From time to time, volcanoes poured ash and lava into the sea, and in Devonian times (395–345 million years ago) a high mountain range was pushed up from the deposits of the great basin. The north-east to south-west grain of these Caledonian mountains determined the line of Scotland's Great Glen and that of the Highland Fault which separates the Scottish Lowlands from the Highlands. This old, resistant rock forms many high peaks in Scotland, many of them little known because of their comparative inaccessibility. The peaks themselves are rocky and bare, but their slopes are being planted with forests of conifers.

The pressures that forced up the Caledonian ranges also thrust molten rock from the lower layers of the Earth's crust into the mountain roots. In this way, areas of granite and other igneous rocks were formed, and these hard rocks often stand out as hills when revealed by erosion. Snowdonia and the Lake District, the highest mountain areas outside Scotland, are both remnants of the Caledonian mountains.

Red soils from Devonian deserts

In the later part of the Devonian Period, the Caledonian mountains were worn down and much of Britain was a desert. The Old Red Sandstone was laid down in inland basins and lakes. Exmoor and the Brecon Beacons are formed from this rock, and its weathering produced the red soils of Devon. These Old Red Sandstones occur as far north as Caithness and the Orkney Islands.

The sea gradually drowned the Devonian deserts in the succeeding Carboniferous Period (345–320 million years ago). Thick layers of limestone were formed, which were covered in turn by the deltas of great rivers. As the deltas silted up and rose above sea level, muddy swamps formed on which thick forests flourished. The remains of these forests, when covered by more mud, were the origin of Britain's coalfields; and the new hill regions formed from these sediments include the Pennines and the mountains of South Wales. The coal deposits have been worn away on the high plateaux, where there are peat bogs and heather moors; but they survive as coalfields on the flanks of the hills.

Where man has 'improved' nature

One of the most important geological dividing lines in Britain is from the mouth of the Tees to that of the Exe in Devon. North and west of this line lie the geologically ancient mountain zones and hill areas of Britain, among which are nearly all the National Parks and Forest Parks. To the south and east are the lowlands of England, a more subdued landscape of ridges, vales and plains, consisting mainly of rocks formed after Carboniferous times. More fertile soils form in these areas than on the older rocks of the highlands, and they are more intensively farmed. The lowlands contain numerous

FERNS IN THE ROCKS *Much of Central Wales is formed of deposits laid down on the floor of a great ocean in Silurian times, 430 million years ago. The rocks, such as these at Craig Twrch, 5 miles east of Lampeter in Dyfed, were later folded and split by earth movements, and ferns grow in cracks widened by water and frost*

examples of the efforts of man to control and 'improve' nature by creating magnificent parkland settings for great houses.

Limestone formed in the Jurassic Period (195–136 million years ago) forms one long ridge from the North York Moors through the Cotswolds to the Isle of Purbeck. This ridge yields England's finest building stone and most of her iron ore. From Salisbury Plain, chalk uplands radiate north-east along the Chilterns and on to Flamborough Head in Humberside. To the south-east the chalk forms the North and South Downs. The chalk, made up of vast numbers of minute sea creatures and shells, was formed at a rate of 1 ft every 30,000 years in the Cretaceous Period (136–65 million years ago). Flints in the chalk provided early man with tools, and later generations with an important building material.

In west Scotland, the Tertiary Era (65–1 million years ago) was marked by a new phase of volcanic activity. Granites were formed in Skye, Rhum, Eigg and Arran, and lava flows cooled into hexagonal columns such as those at Fingal's Cave on the Isle of Staffa. In Tertiary times, southern England was on the edge of the great 'earth storm' which raised the Alps, and the limestone and chalk were folded up against the more resistant blocks to the north and west. The crests of these upfolds, such as that of the Weald, were later worn away by rivers to leave the steep slopes on the North and South Downs. In the broad basins between the upfolded chalk and limestone, new deposits were laid down during a fresh invasion of the sea over the English lowlands. These include the sands which form large areas of heathland around London, such as Bagshot Heath.

Melting ice that made an island

The last great moulding of the mountains and plains was due largely to the Ice Age, which

descended on Britain from the north-east about a million years ago. At its greatest extent, probably 200,000 years ago, a permanent ice-sheet, such as exists today in Greenland, covered much of Britain's land-surface as far south as a line from the Thames to the mouth of the Severn. Tongues of ice moved out from the highland areas on to the lowlands of south and east Britain. The deep, trough-like valleys of the Scottish Highlands, of the Lake District and of Snowdonia were all scoured out by the glaciers.

The vast amounts of material carried by the ice sheets were spread throughout the lowlands as hummocks of sand and gravel and as the great sheets of thick clay, rich in lime and other minerals, that plaster much of the English lowlands and, though difficult to work, supply a fertile, moisture-retaining soil. The immense mass of water resulting from the final melting of the ice sheets caused a rise in the sea level. Ultimately the rising waters broke through the narrow land-bridge in the south-east and, about 7000 years ago, finally separated Britain from mainland Europe.

The geological story is not yet finished. The hills are still being eroded. The rivers are still carrying material down to the lowlands, to the estuaries, and to the seas. The bed of the North Sea is slowly sinking under the enormous weight of newly deposited material. The coast-line of the south-east is still being attacked by the sea, and cliff-lines change with every winter gale, continuing a story that began 3400 million years ago, near the storm-battered cliffs of Cape Wrath at the north-west tip of Scotland.

REINDEER IN SCOTLAND *Winters are severe in the high mountain areas of Britain, and reindeer, widespread in Lapland and northern Sweden, have been successfully introduced to the Cairngorms in Scotland. A herd of 25, brought to Glen More in 1952, has increased to 100. The animals feed on mosses and lichens under the snow*

WHERE THE BRITISH CAME FROM

As the glaciers retreated from Britain for the last time, about 10,000 years ago, Stone Age men pushed trails through the virgin forests that advanced in the wake of the ice. These early Britons came across the land bridge that joined Britain to the Continent until the North Sea broke through, some 3000 years later. They were cave-dwellers at first, living in small bands by hunting, fishing and gathering wild plants. Their primitive stone tools and weapons have been found in gravel deposits and caves, particularly in the limestone regions of Derbyshire.

This way of life was replaced by that of the Neolithic (New Stone Age) invaders from Mediterranean lands. The Neolithic men, small, dark, long-headed and long-nosed, were the first farmers—herders of sheep and cattle, and growers of wheat and barley. They knew the art of pottery and their culture was based on the sophisticated use of stone. They worked flints in 'factories', such as Grime's Graves in Norfolk, and their burial places, marked by long barrows, are scattered on the downs.

Later invaders, *c.* 1800 BC, brought skills in the working of bronze and erected enormous stone circles, from Salisbury Plain to the Orkney Islands. It has been suggested that these 'henges' were gigantic 'calendars' for calculating seed-time and harvest by the position of the sun and moon. The many long-distance route-ways along hill ridges such as the Foss Way and the Icknield Way may have been first tramped by the traders of these early cultures.

Iron Age skills of the Celts

Britain at this time was known to the writers of the Classical world only as a faraway land at the uncertain frontier of the world, wrapped in mists and mystery. But soon these islands attracted many great migratory movements of peoples from the continental land mass.

About 500 BC came the first of a series of large-scale immigrations of a people who were moving west under the pressure of an expanding population in their homelands beside the Rhine. These were the Celts, who brought with them a new technology based on the working of iron. Later Celts were miners and traders, horse-breeders and cattle farmers. The strongest Celtic elements today are in the hill country of the North and West, the rugged lands into which these men of the Iron Age retreated when they were displaced from lowland England by later invaders. The Celtic language still lives in the Welsh tongue.

The Roman invasion which began in AD 43 was not a mass migration of peoples, but an occupation by a comparatively small group of highly organised conquerors. The Romans subjugated the natives, used their resources, and dominated them with superior force and administration. They built roads and left their mark in such place-name endings as '-chester', from the Latin *castra,* meaning a camp.

The native Celtic groups, in alliance with Germanic raiders from across the North Sea, finally broke the Roman hold after 400 years. The Anglo-Saxon peoples, who began their colonisation from the east coast, set up villages all over the English Plain, with place-name endings such as '-ing', '-ton' and '-ham'. These blue-eyed, fair-haired Anglo-Saxons were eventually converted to Christianity. Two of the best-preserved Saxon churches stand at Bradwell and Greensted in Essex.

Castles of the French Norsemen

The Anglo-Saxons, in turn, faced the onslaught of the Norse and Danish invaders. The Norsemen established bases in the Shetlands and Orkneys and spread down the west coast. They transplanted familiar names from their mountain homeland, such as 'fell' and 'beck', 'gill' and 'scar'; they cleared the forests and established settlements called 'thwaites'.

Another group of Norsemen, who had established themselves in that part of France which came to be known as Normandy, added French refinement to the hardiness of their Viking ancestors. The Saxons were no match for these Norman invaders, and after William's victory over Harold in 1066 the Normans overawed the population, then 2 million, by building a series of strongholds, many of which still stand today. Close links with the Continent led to the extension of monastic life, the building of new abbeys, the foundation of market towns and the emergence of great baronial estates.

With the Normans, the last successful military invaders of Britain, came the last major contribution to the evolution of a common language. The Latin and French elements combined with the Germanic and the Celtic to make the island tongue as complex in its origin as the physical characteristics of the people.

BARROW ON THE DOWNS *The Bronze Age, from 1800* BC *to 550* BC, *left many round burial mounds, or 'barrows', such as this one on the Marlborough Downs a mile east of Avebury. It is one of several on the Ridge Way, a track probably used by England's earliest settlers. The trees were planted on the barrow in the 19th century*

OUR CLIMATE AND ITS CAUSES

No one can accuse the British climate of being dull. The ceaseless pageant of blue skies, scudding clouds, mist, rain, frost, dew and snow, of windy days and still days, has inspired artists throughout the centuries and has helped to mould our green, rich countryside.

Britain lies between the land mass of Eurasia to the east and the Atlantic Ocean to the west, and our weather depends very much upon what happens over these neighbouring areas. When westerly winds blow they bring the relative mildness of the ocean atmosphere at any time of the year. Easterlies, however, bring different conditions according to the season. They reach Britain after blowing across a land mass which cools and heats more quickly than the sea. When the winter easterlies set in, the wind is knife-edged; yet the same airstreams in summer may bring heat waves.

Despite its reputation, Britain's climate and day-to-day weather is predictable to a limited extent. Over the Atlantic there is often a confrontation between cold airstreams moving south from the Arctic and warm, moisture-laden air moving north from the tropics. This produces depressions—pockets of low air pressure—which move eastwards or north-eastwards across the ocean, often crossing Britain or brushing its shores. Barometers fall, then rise again, as a mild, windy and wet period is quickly followed by a warm, dull spell or by squally, cool showers. At other times, the zone of high pressure centred over the Azores expands northwards. Then calmer air flows over Britain. Barometers rise and the weather is clear and sunny.

Where grass grows all the year

Spring is normally Britain's driest season, even though April is by tradition showery. Cold weather normally lasts no later than mid-April, and there are frequently some very warm days during the second half of the month. West-coast districts are popular for spring holidays because they are less vulnerable to rearguard actions from winter in the form of bursts of east or north wind. In parts of Cornwall and south Devon grass may grow throughout the year because of the absence of frost.

By late spring, daytime temperatures rise considerably, and the thermometer may even reach 21–24°C (70–75°F) over a wide area. In May and June, maximum day temperatures along the coasts normally exceed sea-surface temperatures by about 5–9°C (10–17°F). This difference, greater along the east coast, causes an alternation between off-shore and on-shore breezes—ideal for yachtsmen, and for holiday-makers who enjoy bracing air.

June is the brightest month of the year for Britain in general, and the average daily sunshine ranges from eight hours in the extreme south to about five hours in the north of Scotland. Rainfall tends to increase during July and August, partly because Atlantic depressions come nearer to our coasts during these months and partly also because air, as it becomes warmed, is capable of holding more moisture. When winds are ocean-borne and the weather is changeable, flat coastal areas have fewer showers than inland areas where there is high ground. But there may still be dry and sunny places inland, especially in the lee of high ground. East Wales and the Welsh Border country, for example, are comparatively dry on days of showery, south-westerly winds. In south-west England, when winds are northerly, visitors may find sunshine south of Dartmoor.

Beauty between the snows

Late summer is often noted for very warm weather, and this may continue into September. One advantage of a late holiday is that sea temperatures remain high because of the summer heat that the ocean has stored. Eastern resorts are particularly good for a late holiday because winds are then generally from the south-west and have lost some of their moisture by the time they have crossed the country.

The autumn winds eventually move round to the west and north-west, and the weather becomes less settled. The air is exceptionally clear during the sunnier spells. The bracken flourishes, and early frost can enhance the beauty of the landscape.

North and north-west winds often bring heavy falls of snow to north Britain during late October or November. But these are usually short-lived, and when the winds subside and the sky clears, the beauty of the countryside is unparalleled. Mid-winter snows are heavier and more prolonged; but even the winter months have their compensations when, during spells of east wind, the air clears and conditions become ideal for long walks and winter sports.

WARNING IN THE CLOUDS *The rays of a sinking sun strike through broken clouds on to the Atlantic off Morwenstow, in Cornwall. But there is a warning behind the evening glory. These are cumulus clouds, and when they begin breaking up like this, it means that showery weather—or at least changeable weather—is on the way*

HOW TO USE THE MAPS

Britain has been divided in this book into 13 main zones, each with an introduction describing the character of the area, its history and main attractions. If, for example, you plan a holiday in South-West England first refer to the map on the left. The figure 20 indicates that the introduction to the zone begins on that page.

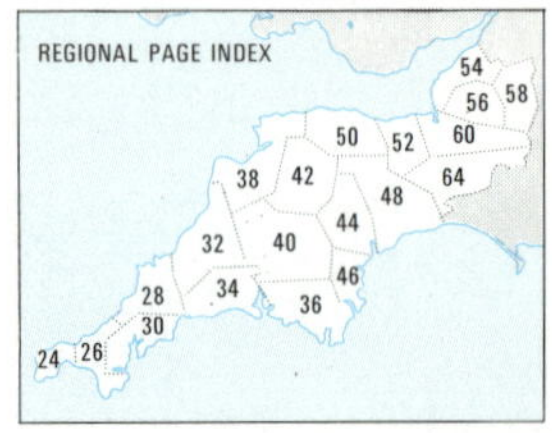

Two maps accompany this introduction. The first (above) shows that the South-West zone is divided into 20 touring regions—the number in each region indicating the page on which it is described in detail.

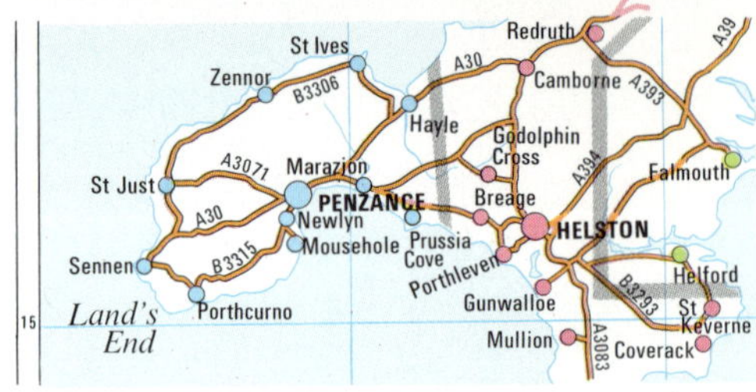

A larger-scale zone map, a section of which is shown above, indicates the best roads from one region to another. A suggested touring centre for each region is marked by a large coloured dot—in this section, Penzance and Helston. Smaller dots of the same colour show selected towns of interest within easy reach. Adjoining touring regions have dots of different colours and are separated by a grey line.

Each region has its own map giving details of places of interest such as cathedrals, castles, stately homes, and scenic spots, which are described in the gazetteer. Symbols used on these regional maps are explained in the key to the hypothetical region below.

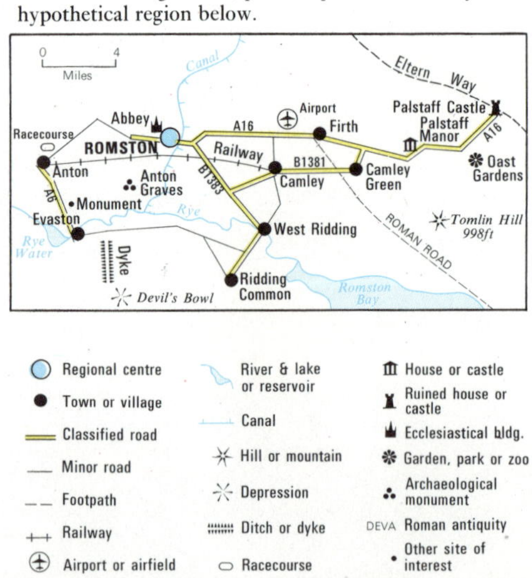

DISCOVERING BRITAIN

A DETAILED GAZETTEER OF OUR RICHLY VARIED COUNTRYSIDE

Nearly every town and village in Britain has something to offer the visitor—a stately home, a country church, a ruined castle or a village green—and the countryside which separates them is rich in riverside walks, picnic spots and fellside hikes. In this book, the entire country has been divided into 190 different touring regions, and people who know and love Britain have selected and described in detail the places most worth visiting in each area

Guidance on times when buildings and gardens in each area are open to the public is included, but these times can vary and to avoid disappointment visitors are advised to check for themselves before visiting an area. Further information on properties administered by the National Trust (NT), the National Trust for Scotland (NTS) and the National Gardens Scheme (NGS) can be obtained from these organisations, whose addresses are given on p. 530. Further information can be obtained from the local information centres listed. Advice on recreational amenities in Britain, in addition to that given separately for each region, will be found on pp. 529–31.

Britain in 13 zones: A JOURNEY OF DISCOVERY THROUGH

The 13 zones

SOUTH-WEST ENGLAND
20–65
Avon (south)
Cornwall
Devonshire
Somerset

SOUTHERN ENGLAND
66–103
Dorset
Hampshire
Isle of Wight
Wiltshire

SOUTH-EAST ENGLAND
104–149
Kent
Surrey
East Sussex
West Sussex

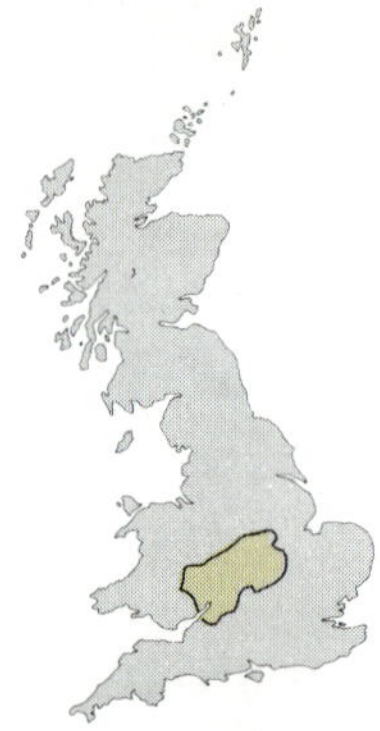

SOUTH MIDLANDS
150–187
Avon (north)
Gloucestershire
Hereford & Worcester
Leicestershire
Northamptonshire
Warwickshire
West Midlands (part)

HOME COUNTIES
188–223
Bedfordshire
Berkshire
Buckinghamshire
Hertfordshire
Oxfordshire

LONDON
224–261
Greater London

ENGLAND, WALES AND SCOTLAND

EASTERN COUNTIES
262–299
Cambridgeshire
Essex
Norfolk
Suffolk

WALES
300–335
Clwyd
Dyfed
Mid Glamorgan
South Glamorgan
West Glamorgan
Gwent
Gwynedd
Powys

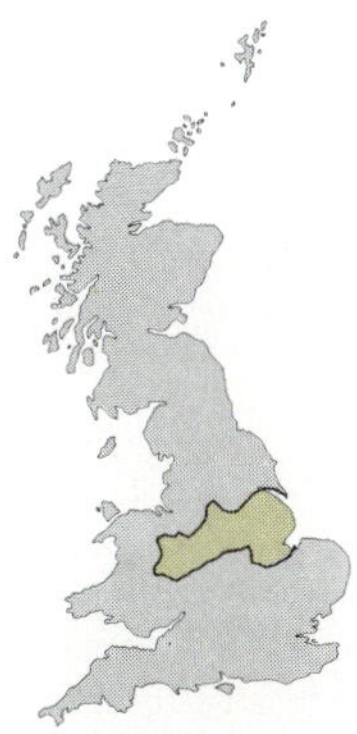

NORTH MIDLANDS
336–373
Derbyshire
Humberside (south)
Lincolnshire
Nottinghamshire
Salop
Staffordshire
West Midlands (part)

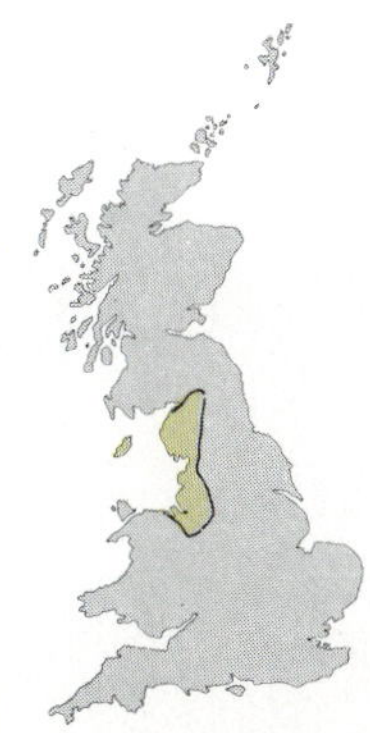

NORTH-WEST ENGLAND
374–405
Isle of Man

Cheshire
Cumbria (part)
Greater Manchester
Lancashire (part)
Merseyside

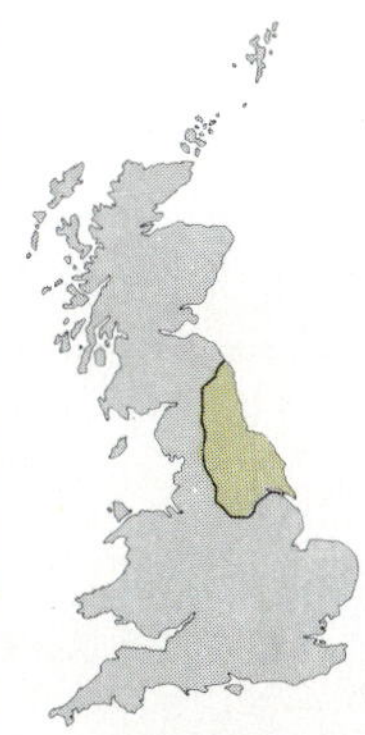

NORTH-EAST ENGLAND
406–445
Cleveland
Cumbria (part)
Humberside (north)
Lancashire (part)
Tyne & Wear
North Yorkshire
South Yorkshire
West Yorkshire

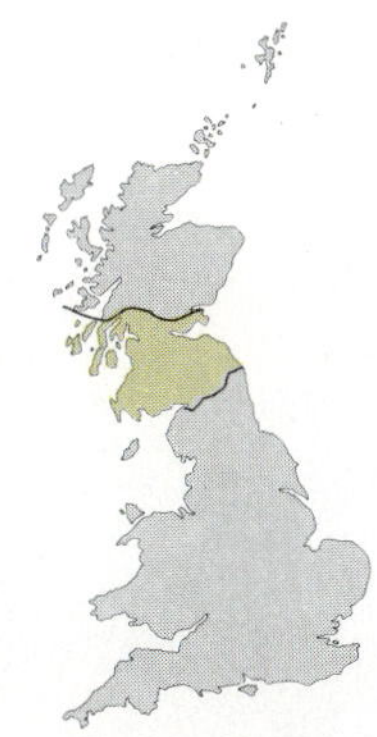

SCOTTISH LOWLANDS
446–487
Borders
Central (south)
Dumfries &
Galloway
Fife
Lothian
Strathclyde (south)
Tayside (part)

SCOTTISH HIGHLANDS
488–528
Central (north)
Grampian
Highland
Orkney Islands
Shetland Islands
Strathclyde (north)
Tayside (part)
Western Isles

SOUTH-WEST ENGLAND

The principal attractions that make the south-west of England Britain's most popular holiday region are its warm climate and its magnificent coastline. But inland, too, there are great riches: scenery grand or gentle, wild or pastoral; a switchback landscape of upland moors, rolling hills and steep river valleys; and the tangible remains of some 5000 years of history.

The Mendip Hills, riddled with many spectacular caves and gorges, have provided the limestone used in building Wells Cathedral and many other great Somerset churches. South-west of the Mendips, central Somerset dips like a basin to fenlands, drained in the Middle Ages, which are now rich pastures. Further west the land rises again, first to the heathery line of the Quantocks, then to the Brendon Hills, and finally to Exmoor where 1705-ft Dunkery Beacon is Somerset's highest point.

From brooding Dartmoor to a sub-tropical coast

Brooding over much of Devon are the great granite uplands of Dartmoor; but around these relics of volcanic upheaval 400 million years ago lies a great variety of scenery. The northern coast offers sandy beaches, stark cliffs and bracing winds. Inland there is a feeling of remoteness, among high, open roads and sunken lanes. Palm trees and sub-tropical flowers grow along the famous south coast, not far from the boggy, rock-strewn heights of Dartmoor. Cornwall is almost an island, for the River

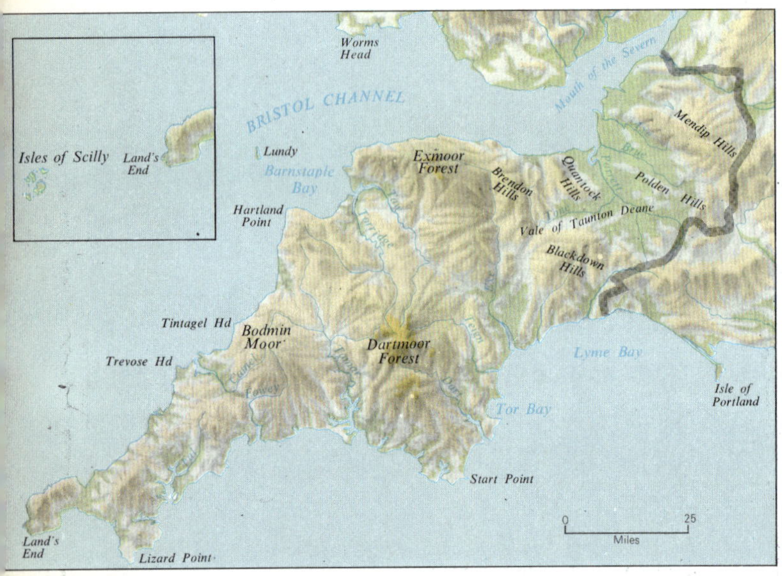

CLIFFS AND MOORS *The south-west peninsula is notable for its coastal cliffs and its upland moors drained by a network of rivers. The landscape is often hilly, and there are many lanes and several main roads which have 1-in-4 gradients*

Tamar flows along all but 5 miles of its border with Devon. It is a marine county, with the sea never more than 20 miles away. Its coves, bays, creeks and drowned valleys, interspersed with fishing villages and dramatic cliff scenery, are offset by the gentler landscape inland.

The earliest remains of man in the South-West date from the Neolithic Age, while the Bronze and Iron Ages have left barrows, cairns, standing stones and hut circles. The Romans left numerous remains in east Devon and Somerset, where their empire ended. Among them are the Foss Way that linked Exeter with Lincoln; the Mendip lead mines;

MID GLAMORGAN
SOUTH GLAMORGAN
Bristol Channel
Mouth of the Severn
Bridgwater Bay
Barnstaple or Bideford Bay
Lyme Bay
Tor Bay
AVON
SOMERSET
DEVON
DORSET
EXMOOR FOREST
DARTMOOR FOREST
BODMIN MOOR
Brendon Hills
Quantock Hills
Polden Hills
Blackdown Hills
Vale of Taunton Deane
Hartland Point
Start Point
Newport
Bridgend
Cardiff
Avonmouth
Portishead
Bristol
Clevedon
Abbots Leigh
Chippenham
Flax Bourton
Barrow Gurney
Queen Charlton
Yatton
Claverton
Monkton Combe
BATH
Hinton Charterhouse
WESTON-SUPER-MARE
Kewstoke
Congresbury
Churchill
Wrington
Burrington
Chew Magna
Combe Hay
Banwell
Charterhouse
Axbridge
East Harptree
Midsomer Norton
Norton St Philip
Trowbridge
CHEDDAR
Priddy
Chewton Mendip
Radstock
Downside
Mells
Frome
Burnham-on-Sea
Wookey
Wells
Croscombe
Nunney
Warminster
Lynton
Lynmouth
Ilfracombe
Brendon
Culbone
Minehead
DUNSTER
Watchet
East Quantoxhead
Stogursey
Holford
Nether Stowey
Meare
Shepton Mallet
Wyke Champflower
Witham Friary
GLASTONBURY
Arlington
Simonsbath
Stoke Pero
Exford
Crowcombe
Aisholt
Bridgwater
Street
Bruton
Braunton
Acland Barton
Barnstaple
North Molton
Winsford
Combe Florey
Broomfield
Keinton Mandeville
Castle Cary
Appledore
Swimbridge
Westward Ho
BIDEFORD
SOUTH MOLTON
Molland
Dulverton
Wiveliscombe
TAUNTON
Somerton
N Cadbury
Wincanton
Hartland
Clovelly
Rose Ash
Bampton
Langport
Compton Pauncefoot
Shaftesbury
Welcombe
Great Torrington
Wellington
Ilchester
Templecombe
Morwenstow
Burrington
Chulmleigh
Cruwys Morchard
Tintinhull
Montacute
Milborne Port
Sherborne
Ilminster
YEOVIL
Eggesford
Tiverton
Hinton St George
Crewkerne
Bude
Lapford
Morchard Bishop
Cullompton
Chard
Cricket St Thomas
Zeal Monachorum
Bickleigh
Blandford Forum
Holsworthy
Hatherleigh
Cheriton Fitzpaine
Crediton
Honiton
Axminster
OKEHAMPTON
EXETER
Ottery St Mary
Bridport
Dorchester
Axmouth
Beer
Branscombe
Chagford
Dunsford
Dunchideock
Moretonhampstead
SIDMOUTH
Launceston
Lydford
Powderham
East Budleigh
Altarnun
North Bovey
Exmouth
Budleigh Salterton
Weymouth
Postbridge
Chudleigh
Bolventor
TAVISTOCK
Widecombe in the Moor
Dawlish
Teignmouth
Princetown
Dartmeet
Callington
Calstock
Ashburton
Newton Abbot
St Cleer
St Ive
Buckland Monachorum
Buckfastleigh
Liskeard
TORQUAY
Paignton
St Germans
Saltash
Totnes
Stoke Gabriel
Brixham
LOOE
Antony
PLYMOUTH
Modbury
DARTMOUTH
Newton Ferrers
Stoke Fleming
Polperro
Kingsbridge
Salcombe
M4
M5
A48
A470
A420
A46
A36
A350
A39
A38
A361
A370
A371
A37
A303
A358
A373
A377
A396
A30
A3052
A376
A386
A388
A395
A3086
A35
A352
A354
A357
A31
A379
A381
A385
A387
A3359
B3130
B3133
B3223
B3224
B3226
B3227
B3181
B3212
B3357
B3210
B3207
60
75
90
105
120
135
150
45
30
15
REGIONAL PAGE INDEX
24
26
28
30
32
34
36
38
40
42
44
46
48
50
52
54
56
58
60
64
KEY TO MAP
Regional centre
Selected town or village
Regional boundary
County boundary
Major road
Minor road
Woodland
River and lake or reservoir

villas at Ilchester, East Coker and Camerton; and the baths of the Roman city of Aquae Sulis, now known as Bath. As the Britons were driven west by the invading Saxon tribes, Cornwall became, with Wales, a bastion of the old Celtic ways, and kept a separate Celtic language until the Middle Ages (it has recently been revived by students of Cornish history and traditions). The county remained virtually isolated from the rest of the country until modern times. By contrast, Devon people took the 'stage of history' in the reign of Elizabeth I, when Drake, Raleigh, Grenville and Hawkins, all sons of Devon, helped to fight off the might of Spain.

After the Civil War and the Monmouth Rebellion, peace and a new prosperity came to the region. The tin and copper mines of Devon and Cornwall flourished, while the fishing and ship-building trades were carried on in seaports which were among the finest in Britain. Quarries were opened in the Somerset hills, the cloth trade prospered, and local industries grew up—such as leather tanning and shoe-making at Street, printing at Frome, and lace-making at Honiton. Much of this industrial prosperity has now died away, and the tourist trade has become a most important element in the region's economy. But the South-West remains predominantly a region of farmers and fishermen, free from the blight of modern industrialisation.

Great buildings and famous people

Notable buildings are not lacking in this essentially rural setting. Bath, with its superb Georgian terraces and crescents, is justly renowned. Medieval building can also be seen at its finest in the cathedrals of Wells and Exeter; in Wells's unique moated Bishop's Palace; in spectacular St Michael's Mount off the Cornish coast; and in the great towers of Somerset's late-medieval churches. Outstanding domestic architecture includes Pendennis Castle, Montacute House and Cotehele House—one of the finest Tudor manor houses in England.

Writers such as Herrick, Blackmore, Wordsworth, Coleridge and Kingsley brought renown to the South-West; and among its other famous residents were Beau Nash, uncrowned king of Bath, and Sir John Millais, the Victorian artist, who used the beach at Budleigh Salterton as the setting for his *Boyhood of Raleigh*.

THE CLIMATE OF THE SOUTH-WEST

The combination of sea and a southerly latitude makes the South-West's climate the most mild and equable in Britain. Rainfall is heaviest on the highest parts of the moors—parts of Dartmoor have up to 82 in. a year compared with 31 in. in Exeter. The uplands have some 12 days of snow a year, compared with eight in central Somerset and two in the toe of Cornwall. The exposed parts of the south-west coast average 30 days of gales a year

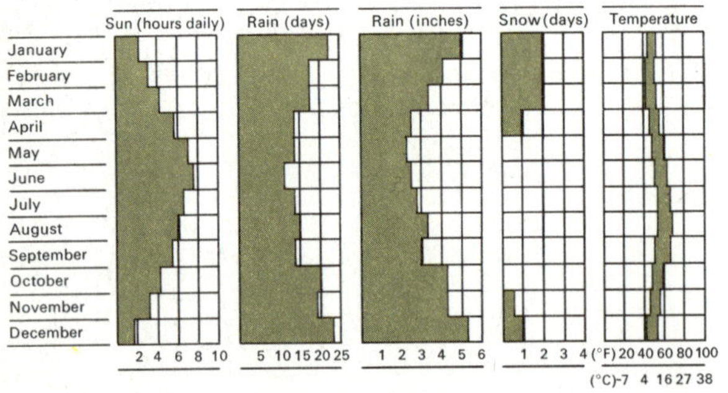

THE BATTLE AT HARTLAND POINT *Nowhere is it more evident that the sea has shaped the West Country than along the cliff-lined north coasts of Devon and Cornwall. At Hartland Point, humpbacked ridges of rock reaching out to where the coast used to be give evidence that the land is gradually receding under the Atlantic's endless attack*

The grandeur of Land's End

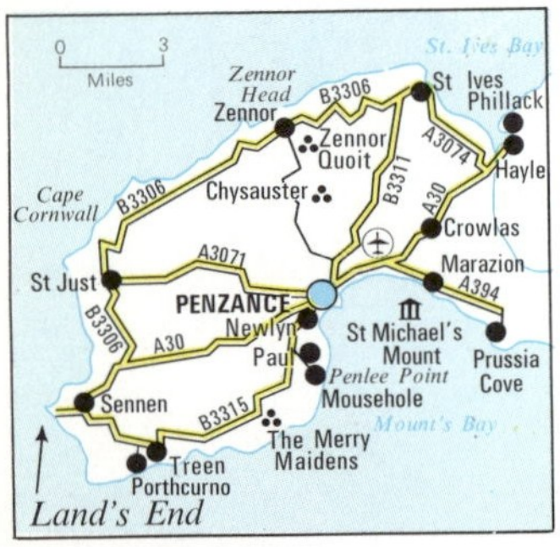

Angling Excellent shore fishing around the coast. Boats can be hired at Penzance for sea angling and shark fishing.

Water sports Surfing from Sennen Cove, St Ives and Hayle. Sailing and water-skiing at Penzance, Marazion and St Ives.

Places to see *Chysauster Ancient Village*: daily, except Sun. mornings Oct. to Mar. *St Michael's Mount* (NT); Mon., Wed., Fri. (guided tours only Nov. to Mar.); also Tues., July to Oct. *Trengwainton Garden* (NT), 2 miles west of Penzance: Mar. to Oct., Wed. to Fri. and Bank Hol. *Wayside Museum*, Zennor: daily, Whitsun to Oct.

Information centres Guildhall, St Ives. Tel. St Ives 6297. Alverton Street, Penzance. Tel. Penzance 2341. Town Hall, Hugh Town, St Mary's, Isles of Scilly. Tel. Scillonia 536.

FLOWER ISLANDS

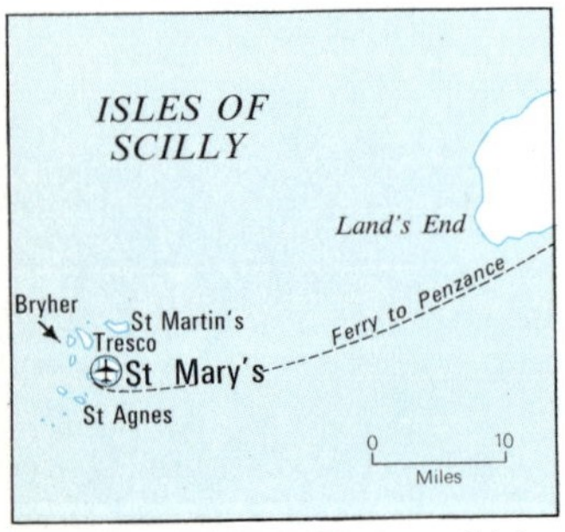

The climate of the Scillies is so mild that the islands are said to have only two seasons—spring and summer. Apart from tourism, flower-growing is the islanders' main source of income, and 'spring' flowers are often picked as early as November. Seabirds abound, and porpoises, dolphins and seals are common. St Mary's, the largest island, has the Scillies' only town—Hugh Town—and can be reached by boat or helicopter from Penzance

Land's End, the famous granite mass tumbling into the sea at the end of the Penwith Peninsula, is the furthest point west on the mainland of England. It is a place steeped in ancient lore and legend, in tales of shipwrecks, smuggling and strange happenings from the days when tin miners toiled in narrow tunnels under the sea. It attracts hordes of visitors each year. The neck of the peninsula is only about 5 miles wide, and in just over an hour a brisk walker can travel from the Channel shore, with its mild breezes, to the gale-swept Atlantic coast. In the south are sheltered coves where palm trees and camellias grow; in the north, black cliffs stand like bastions against the waves and blustering winds. Good roads follow most of the seaboard, and narrow lanes lead inland to scattered hamlets and lonely moors.

On a cliff at Porthcurno, plays can be seen at an open-air theatre overlooking the sea; on St Michael's Mount stands a famous castle-like mansion. Mousehole is one of the most picturesque fishing villages in the South-West. The area is rich in prehistoric remains; at Chysauster, near Penzance, there are the ruins of dwellings more than 2000 years old, evidence of one of the earliest mining settlements in Britain.

BEYOND LAND'S END *On a lonely Atlantic rock 1½ miles west of Land's End stands the Longships Lighthouse. Some 26 miles further out are the Isles of Scilly. Then there is nothing but ocean until the coast of America, some 3000 miles away*

Hayle
A port and industrial centre on the estuary of the River Hayle. Behind the sand dunes, locally known as 'towans', is a popular bathing beach. The bay sweeps round to Godrevy Lighthouse, which Virginia Woolf featured in her famous novel *To The Lighthouse*. Phillack, facing Hayle across the canal, has a 15th-century church with a 5th-century inscribed stone in its porch. Stretching north-east are 3 miles of beaches and dunes.

Land's End
The westernmost point of the English mainland; a mass of granite cliffs which plunge with dramatic steepness into the sea. Not even the crowds of people and the cars and coaches which bring them can dispel the fascinating atmosphere of the place. For those who want to breathe in the Celtic 'other-worldliness' of Land's End to the full, the best times are dawn and dusk. Especially fine is the view of the Longships Lighthouse, on a rock 1½ miles out to sea.

Marazion
A jumble of cottages set among winding streets and palm trees. The main road from Hayle runs through the village of Crowlas over a hill—and suddenly Mount's Bay comes into view. To the left, St Michael's Mount with its superb castle rises out of the sea, and to the right the bay curves past Penzance and Penlee Point. At low tide a causeway runs from Marazion to St Michael's Mount.

Mousehole
A place which keeps its flavour of an old Cornish fishing village; colour-washed and granite houses surround the small harbour, which is draped with nets and crowded with fishermen. Here, in 1777, died Dolly Pentreath, supposedly the last person to speak the ancient Cornish language as her native tongue. Her grave is at Paul, on a hill above the village.

Newlyn
A busy fishing port, with old cottages climbing up a steep hill. Artists first 'discovered' Newlyn about 100 years ago. Dame Laura Knight, Stanhope Forbes and Frank Bramley were painters associated with the place. About 3 miles south-west is a group of Bronze Age stones. According to legend, they represent maidens turned to stone as a punishment for dancing on a Sunday.

Penzance
This popular resort, facing St Michael's Mount across the beautiful sweep of Mount's Bay, has a climate so mild that

2000-YEAR-OLD VILLAGE *In the Iron Age village at Chysauster, the houses were roughly circular, and probably had roofs of stone or thatch, and open courtyards*

IN A DROWNED LAND *According to legend, St Michael's Mount is part of the lost kingdom of Lyonesse, where King Arthur's knights once rode*

palm trees and other sub-tropical plants thrive, particularly in the Morrab Gardens near the sea-front—*morrab* is the Cornish word for sea-shore. The town's two museums and library contain many records of Cornish history. Sir Humphry Davy, inventor of the miner's safety lamp, was born in Penzance in 1778, and a statue of him stands outside the market house in Market Jew Street.

Porthcurno

A pretty village, with a steeply shelving stretch of sand ideal for bathing. The cliff above the village belongs to the National Trust. On a cliff west of the beach is the open-air Minack Theatre, constructed in classical Greek style. Greek, Shakespearian and modern drama is performed at the theatre during the summer. On a headland south of Treen and east of Porthcurno is a 'logan' rock, estimated to weigh about 65 tons, which 'logs', or rocks, at the slightest touch. In 1824 a Lieutenant Goldsmith and a party of sailors pushed it over the cliff; the incident caused such an outcry that Goldsmith had to restore the rock to its original position at his own expense.

Prussia Cove

The cove, reached by a small track, was a notorious centre for smugglers, and John Carter, the leader, was known by his followers as 'The King of Prussia', after the hero of that time. In 1947 the battleship *H.M.S. Warspite* went aground and broke up on the rocks in the cove; shipwrecks such as this earned the peninsula its name Penwith, from a Cornish word meaning 'promontory of blood'. Just round the eastern headland are Praa Sands, a popular bathing beach with a caravan site.

St Ives

The picturesque cluster of gaily coloured stone cottages, which seem to tumble over each other in the narrow twisting streets, attracted first artists, then tourists. St Ives grew around a small chapel built by St Ia in the 6th century. It was once a busy fishing port, but today most of the fishing is done by holidaymakers. The artists James McNeill Whistler and Walter Sickert went to St Ives in the last century and set the fashion that made the town internationally famous as an artistic centre. The painter Ben Nicholson, the sculptress Dame Barbara Hepworth and the potter Bernard Leach made the town a 'workshop' of contemporary art and the Penwith Gallery, founded in 1949, has frequent exhibitions of their work. The former home and study of Dame Barbara Hepworth is now open as a museum and art gallery.

St Just

The westernmost town in England, standing 1½ miles east of Cape Cornwall, a fine rock headland. The town and its neighbourhood are rich in antiquities. In the large medieval church is a stone of the 5th or 6th century inscribed with the monogram XP, the first two letters of the Greek word for Christ, and two restored wall-paintings, one of which depicts Christ 'blessing the trades'. By Bank Square is a round amphitheatre, about 50 yds in diameter, called Plain-an-Gwarry, or the 'place of the plays', where miracle plays were performed in the Middle Ages and wrestling matches held in the 18th century. About 2 miles north, near Botallack Head, are the derelict workings of the 19th-century Botallack mines, which had shafts following tin and copper lodes far out to sea.

Sennen

The westernmost village in England, with a church which is partly 13th century. Tradition has it that King Arthur, leading the forces of seven Cornish chieftains, routed the Danes here. To celebrate the event, the victors held a banquet on a large rock which became known as the Table Men. The rock stands at the end of a footpath about ¼ mile north of the church.

Zennor

The village, named after St Senara, is a few hundred yards off the main road and less than a mile from the sea. The Norman church has a pew-end carving of 'the mermaid of Zennor', said to have come ashore to hear the squire's son sing and lured him back into the sea with her. The Zennor Quoit, half a mile south-east, is a Stone Age tomb. It has seven stones, each 10 ft high, capped with a slab 6 yds long.

A WEST COUNTRY POTTER TRAINED IN THE EAST

The Leach Pottery at St Ives was founded by Bernard Leach in 1920, after 11 years' study in Japan. No other western potter had ever been trained in the East; the style still influences his designs. A team of potters now works in the St Ives studio, producing a wide range of hand-turned domestic pots for sale, as well as exhibition pieces. The fish on the Leach Pottery tile is a John Dory

High cliffs of The Lizard

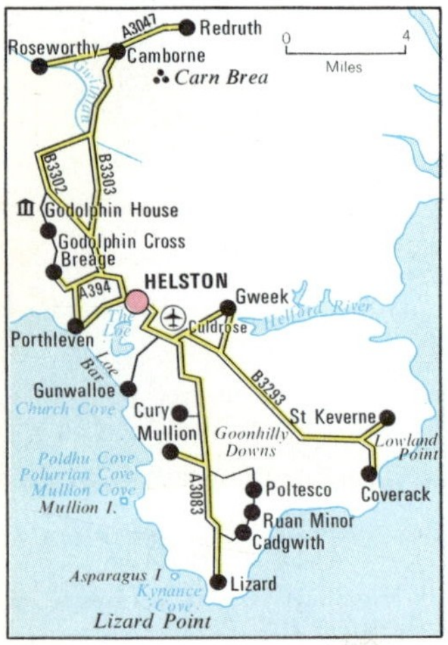

The Lizard, the southernmost part of England, takes its name from the Cornish *lis*, palace, and *ard*, high—appropriate words for this majestically beautiful coast, with its soaring cliffs and pinnacles of rock stretching down to Lizard Point. Its turbulent seas and treacherous reefs give the area another, more sinister, aspect: it is reckoned that more human lives have been lost in shipwrecks here than on any other part of the Cornish coast.

The Lizard is less crowded than the neighbouring regions to the east and west. Fishing villages of somewhat austere charm are found in the coves, and there are many fascinating spots to explore, such as the caves scattered about the beach at Kynance Cove.

Most of the peninsula inland consists of the Goonhilly Downs, famous for its satellite communications station with giant dish aerials. In May and June, the downs burst into life with golden gorse and the white blossom of the blackthorn. Cornish heath flowers on into early autumn and many rare clovers and rushes are found near the coast.

In winter, when gales are blowing or a shroud of sea mist appears, the land takes on a desolate, eerie quality. Walking along the lanes it is unusual to meet anyone except the occasional farmer or local tradesman. Only around Camborne and Redruth is there any large-scale industry. Several of the coastal villages sell ornaments that are made from the local serpentine stone, so called because its markings resemble those of a serpent's skin.

VOICES THROUGH SPACE *The aerials at Goonhilly Downs beam inter-continental communications through satellites 22,300 miles out in space. The satellites pick up the signal, increase its strength, and beam it back to earth. The boosting of the signal is vital, for when a voice on the telephone reaches the satellite it is 100,000 million times quieter than when it started*

Places to see *Camborne School of Mines Museum*, geological specimens: Mon. to Fri., except Bank Hols. *Cornish Engines* (NT), at Pool, 2 miles east of Camborne (giant beam winding and pumping engines): daily, Apr. to Oct. *Godolphin House*, Godolphin Cross: Thur. afternoon, June to Sept. *Helston Borough Museum:* weekdays, except Wed. afternoon. *Holman Group Museum*, Camborne, a collection of mining exhibits: Mon. to Fri., except Bank Hol.

Information centre Publicity Dept., Council Offices, Camborne. Tel. Camborne 712941.

Breage
An attractive village, quietly tucked away off the main road. The 15th-century Church of St Breaca has items of unusual interest: a Roman milestone, a Celtic cross and some finely restored wall-paintings, one portraying St Christopher, for centuries the patron saint of travellers. The paintings, probably done soon after the church was built, came to light in 1891. The church bell is the largest in Cornwall.

Cadgwith
A steep narrow lane winds down to a small cove, divided by a small rocky promontory. Thatched stone cottages cluster round the beach. The local fishermen catch mainly crab and lobster. A little south of the village is the Devil's Frying Pan, a huge basin of rock in the cliff which the tides enter. A cliff path leads about 1 mile north of Cadgwith to the pretty hamlet of Poltesco. By a cascading stream stands an old water-wheel, used to power machinery in the days when serpentine rock was quarried locally. The church at Ruan Minor, above Cadgwith, is partly built of serpentine stone.

Camborne–Redruth
The towns of Camborne and Redruth are joined in a continuous urban sprawl, forming the only large industrial area in western Cornwall. Camborne, once a centre of Cornwall's tin mining industry, has a world-famous school of mines; and the Holman manufacturing company exports mining equipment to many countries.

Outside Camborne's library stands a statue of the town's most famous son, Richard Trevithick (1771–1833), whose inventions revolutionised deep-shaft mining not only in England but throughout the world. Trevithick, who deserves to be at least as well known as George Stephenson, invented the first steam vehicle to carry passengers.

In Redruth, behind Druid's Hall, is the first house ever to be lit by gas—the Scottish inventor William Murdock (1754–1839) set up his own gas retorts there in 1792. Of the many tin mines in the district only two are working; the

THE PAST AND PRESENT OF CORNWALL'S MINES

A mineral field around Camborne was once the heart of an intensive tin-mining industry. This 1861 print of a mine at Carn Brea shows men washing the ore after it has been crushed in a stamping mill. At the industry's peak, 600 mines were active, but the import of cheaper Malayan tin forced most to close and only two survived. A gradual recovery in the tin market has revived interest in Cornish mining; new mines are being drilled and old ones re-opened

The castle-like ruins of stacks and engine-houses scattered throughout Cornwall are a reminder of the miners' constant battle against water. The giant pumps which drained the mines stood in these buildings

rest are derelict and their ruined buildings lend an odd romance of their own to the landscape. On the imposing hill of Carn Brea, 738 ft high, are the remains of a Roman fortress, an Iron Age camp site and a 15th-century castle.

Coverack

A picturesque seaside village, once a very active smuggling centre, where anglers can fish for bass and pollack. The cottages in the village are of stone and thatch; but with the addition of new housing, some of the place's traditional character has been lost.

Godolphin Cross

A pretty inland hamlet, about 2 miles north of Breage. It was named after the family of local squires, the Godolphins, who rose to eminence during the reign of Henry VIII. A member of the family, Sidney Godolphin, was Queen Anne's Lord High Treasurer. Godolphin House is largely 16th century, with Jacobean and later additions.

Gunwalloe

A tiny seaside resort. The main beach is Church Cove, so called because of the church which stands on the sands, and is now in danger of being washed away by the sea. Like so many places on the Cornish coast, Gunwalloe has its history of shipwrecks. In 1770 the beach was methodically 'mined' for treasure from the *Saint Andrew*, a Portuguese ship wrecked in 1525; a shipwreck in 1785 also attracted professional treasure-seekers in the mid-19th century. Treasure-seekers still visit the cove, but so far only a few coins have been found buried in the sand.

Helston

A market town, with steep streets whose attractive old stone houses jostle with modern buildings. Helston was an important port until a bank of sand and shingle, now called the Loe Bar, finally silted up the harbour mouth in the 13th century. Shipping was then diverted to Gweek, near Helford. Helston was also a Stannary town, where locally mined tin used to be weighed and taxed.

St Michael's Church was rebuilt in 1762 at the Earl of Godolphin's expense, the original church having been destroyed by lightning. The churchyard contains the grave of the inventor Henry Trengrouse (1772–1854), who pioneered the rocket-firing apparatus used by lifeboatmen and coastguards. A house in the town was the birthplace of 'Fighting' Bob Fitzsimmons, the only Englishman to become the world heavyweight boxing champion. He won the title from Jim Corbett in 1897.

Helston's most famous event is its annual Furry Dance, held on or near Flora Day, May 8, from 7 o'clock in the morning. The dancers, in formal dress, dance through the streets and in and out of the gaily decorated houses.

Just outside Helston, on the road to The Lizard, is the Royal Naval Air Station of Culdrose. Helicopters from the station have made some dramatic air-sea rescues in the past few years. The Loe is a pretty inland lake behind Loe Bar, 2 miles south-west of the town. According to local legend, Sir Bedivere cast King Arthur's sword Excalibur into the pool (a claim also made for Dozmary Pool on Bodmin Moor).

MULLION COVE *In the 18th and 19th centuries, Mullion was one of Cornwall's busiest smuggling centres. The secluded coves were ideal places to land contraband, or to sink it until it could be safely retrieved. The last attempt to smuggle in spirits there was in 1840*

Kynance Cove

This cove has some of the most spectacular scenery on the Lizard Peninsula. The cliffs are streaked with the red, purple and green of serpentine rock. Numerous caves, with such names as the Ladies' Bathing Pool and the Devil's Letter Box, surround the beach. Asparagus Island, just off-shore, is so-called because the plant grows there in abundance. It has a rock called the Devil's Bellows; the sea surges into tunnels at the base of the rock and spurts up through a crevice with a hissing noise.

Mullion Cove

A beautiful cove with immense, jagged cliffs, looking out towards Mullion Island. There is a small harbour, and the beaches here and at Polurrian Cove, $\frac{1}{2}$ mile north, are good for bathing.

Porthleven

The large inn and the Harbour House, both 18th century, and the 19th-century West Wharf, testify to the past importance of this seaport. The beach called Porthleven Sands, 2 miles long, is actually of shingle. The Wesleyan chapel, built in 1890, has an imposing façade, but was satirised in a local verse: 'They built the church, upon my word, as fine as any abbey; and then they thought to cheat the Lord and built the back part shabby.'

St Keverne

A small village near one of the most exposed parts of the Lizard coast. The spire of the 15th-century Church of St Akerveranus collapsed, and was rebuilt in 1770 as a landmark for shipping. The notorious rocks known as The Manacles, which lie off the coast, have taken a heavy toll of shipping over the centuries. Near the village, on the Goonhilly Downs, is the Post Office satellite communications station.

The rolling surf of Newquay

Angling Sea fishing at Newquay, on the Camel Estuary and from the beach at Perranporth. Shark-fishing trips can be arranged from Newquay.

Sailing On the Camel Estuary; there are clubs at Newquay, Padstow, Rock and Wadebridge. Harbour authorities should be consulted about offshore sailing.

Surfing Newquay is the main centre. Surf-boards can be hired on all main beaches. Championships are often held at Newquay.

Transport Daily flights from Newquay Airport to Heathrow. Also flights in summer to Scilly Isles, Channel Islands, Plymouth, Exeter, Brittany and Cherbourg.

Events Wadebridge Royal Agricultural Show is held in June. On May Day, a hobby-horse dances through the streets of Padstow.

Places to see *Trerice* (NT), near Newquay: daily, Apr. to Oct. *Trenance Gardens*, Newquay, a zoo in 6 acres of parkland: daily throughout the year. *Wheal Martyn Museum*, Carthew, 1½ miles north of St Austell, open-air working museum of the china clay industry: daily, Apr. to Oct.

Information centres Betty Pitman's Agency, Perranporth. Tel. Perranporth 3601. Information Centre, Morfa Hall, Cliff Road, Newquay. Tel. Newquay 2119. Council Offices, Station Road, Padstow. Tel. Padstow 532296.

For mile after mile from St Agnes in the south to Trevose Head in the north, the pattern is repeated: a black headland, a beach of golden sand, another headland leading to another beach and all the time the white-crested Atlantic rollers roaring in. The scenery is spectacular and the air exhilarating.

South of the inland moors, towards the white pyramids of china-clay waste near the Channel coast, a marked change takes place. The air becomes mild and the vegetation more rich and dense, as in the beautiful wooded valley south of Luxulyan.

Newquay is the region's principal resort, ideal for family holidays. Places of special appeal include Padstow, with its harbour and crooked streets and Perranporth with its miles of golden beaches. There is an Iron Age fort at Castle an Dinas. Two churches at Perranporth, half-buried in the sand, are dedicated to St Piran who, according to legend, floated over from Ireland on a millstone; and in many places Methodist chapels testify to the great influence John Wesley had on the Cornish people.

TREGEAGLE'S DILEMMA *Tregeagle, a Cornish spirit haunted by demons, is said to have fled to this 15th-century chapel crowning an outcrop of rock near Roche. But the holy words of the hermit who lived there were as hateful to him as the infernal screams of the demons on his heels*

FISHERMAN'S WATCHTOWER *Huer's House, near Newquay, recalls the town's pilchard-fishing days. Until the late 19th century, a man known as a huer cried 'Heva! Heva!' from the house as soon as the reddening of the sea told him pilchards were in the bay*

Bedruthan Steps
Some of the finest coastal scenery in the South-West. Cliffs, belonging to the National Trust, tower above a beach of sand and rock. There is a legend that the huge granite rocks were stepping-stones of the giant Bedruthan. Some of the rocks have unusual shapes, such as Queen Bess Rock, which is said to have a profile like that of Elizabeth I.

Newquay
The leading resort in this region. The 'new' quay dates from the 16th century, when it was found necessary to provide a new harbour for the prosperous fishing town of Towan Blystra. The town's livelihood depended on pilchards, and men called huers watched for shoals from cliff-top stations such as Huer's House on Towan Head. But tourism gradually replaced pilchard fishing after the arrival of the railway in 1876. Newquay's holiday pleasures include swimming, surfing, bird-watching, fishing and a zoo in Trenance Gardens. Trerice, 3 miles south-east, is a gabled, stone Elizabethan house, open to the public. It has fine plaster ceilings and latticed windows; the one in the main hall is made up of 576 panes of glass.

Padstow
A picturesque resort on the estuary of the Camel River. St Petroc is said to have founded a monastery here in the 6th century; hence the name Petrocstowe, which became Padstow. The 13th to 15th-century church contains a fine 15th-century carved font and several memorials to the Prideaux family who have been in continuous occupation of nearby Prideaux Place for nearly 400 years. The old town is a labyrinth of crooked streets sloping to the harbour, where there has been a ferry since at least the 15th century. Some of Padstow's houses date from the Middle Ages. On South Quay is 16th-century Raleigh Court, where Sir Walter Raleigh stayed

when collecting the dues to which he was entitled as Warden of Cornwall. During the annual festival of the 'Obby 'Oss, on May Day, a man dressed as a horse is led through the streets, and people dance in Market Square.

Perranporth
A village with 3 miles of beach now famous for surf-riding. There are three St Piran's churches here, two of which were once submerged by drifting sand. The first St Piran's, a tiny 6th or 7th-century church, was abandoned in the 11th century and rediscovered in 1835, buried in the vast tract of dunes north of the village, known as the Penhale Sands. At the time of its discovery the church contained three decapitated skeletons. In 1150 a second church was built on higher ground a quarter of a mile to the east—but the ground was not high enough; the building was abandoned in the 15th century but its site is still marked by an uninscribed 10th-century cross. The last St Piran's was built in 1804 at Perranzabuloe, $1\frac{1}{2}$ miles south-east—the name is a corruption of St Piran in Sabulo, meaning St Piran in the sand. In St Piran's Round, an ancient amphitheatre 130 ft wide, Cornish mystery plays were presented more than 300 years ago. They are still staged there with other plays in the summer.

Port Isaac
Slate-hung cottages line the steep, traffic-free streets which run down to the little fishing port. Cars have to be left on the hill above. The village has great charm and there are many fine walks from here; $2\frac{1}{2}$ miles south-east is a circular Iron Age fort called Tregeare Rounds.

St Agnes
A former mining village built on a steep hill about half a mile inland. Cornwall's most famous painter, John Opie, was born in 1761 at Harmony Cottage, $1\frac{1}{2}$ miles east of the town. From St Agnes Beacon, 1 mile west, the view takes in the Atlantic coast from St Ives to Trevose Head and Brown Willy on Bodmin Moor.

St Austell
A leading market town and the centre of the china-clay industry; also a good place from which to tour mid-Cornwall. The best-looking buildings in St Austell are the plain Georgian Quaker Meeting House (1829), the Italianate town hall (1844), and the 18th-century White Hart Hotel. Holy Trinity Church has some interesting carved figure-work in niches on the outside walls. On Carclaze Downs, north of the town, huge white mounds of sand and quartz—the mock-mountains of the china-clay mines—add a weird touch to the landscape.

Luxulyan, 4 miles north-east, is at the head of a wooded ravine overgrown with ferns and flowers and watered by streams made white by the washings of the nearby china-clay mines.

St Columb Major
A town noted for its church, which is one of the most impressive in Cornwall, with a four-tiered tower 600 years old. On Shrove Tuesday, crowds of townspeople take part in a local version of the game of hurling; it is traditionally played with an applewood ball covered with silver. Castle an Dinas, an Iron Age fort with three ramparts, stands $2\frac{1}{2}$ miles south-east of the town.

St Mawgan
A village in a wooded river valley which is a delightful retreat at the height of summer. The Church of St Mawgan (13th–14th century) is full of fine carvings, and a beautiful early-Christian cross stands in the churchyard. Next to the church is Lanherne, a fine Elizabethan building, now a nunnery.

St Wenn
A small, windswept place, one of the few villages on the remote downs which spread across the north of Cornwall between Padstow and Newquay. The 15th-century Church of St Wenna has a sundial inscribed 'Ye know not when'.

Trevose Head
The lighthouse here was put up in 1847. The view stretches from St Ives in the south-west to Lundy Island in the north-east. Just below to the south is Constantine Bay, which has a vast stretch of sand, while half a mile behind the bay there stand the ruins of a 14th-century chapel.

RELICS OF THE EVANGELISTS

When the Romans withdrew from the West Country in the 5th century, an invasion of saints began. They came from Ireland, Wales and Brittany, an army of evangelical Christians many of whom were soon surrounded by legend and immortalised in the names of churches or villages. St Feock, whose church stands by the River Fal, is said to have sailed from Ireland on a granite boulder. The hundreds of crosses still dotted about the Cornish landscape are a tribute to the impact of the saints and the fervour of the Celts. Some crosses marked graves, holy sites or places to pray by the wayside. Others were simply boundary stones or guideposts. This typical round-headed cross, St Piran's Cross (left), on the dunes near Perranporth, dates from AD 900

About a thousand years after the saints had swept into Cornwall, a new evangelist preached his way into Cornish history—John Wesley (left), the founder of Methodism. The Methodist 'cathedral' was Gwennap Pit (above), a natural amphitheatre caused by the subsidence of a mine. Wesley first preached in Gwennap in 1743, but it was not until 1762 that he discovered the pit, when a wild gale forced him and his congregation to shelter there. The pit was remodelled in 1806, with seating for 2000 people, and services are still held in it

The Cornish Riviera

Angling Sea fishing from pier, shore and rocks at Falmouth; also off-shore, especially over Manacles Rocks. Shark-fishing trips can be arranged with local fishermen.

Sailing The main centre is Falmouth, where there is a regatta in Aug. Boats can be hired at Falmouth, and tuition is available at St Mawes School.

Outings Sea and river trips from Falmouth Pier and Custom House Quay, Falmouth, to Truro, Helford River, and elsewhere along the coast; also from Lemon Quay, Truro, along the River Fal.

Places to see *Glendurgan Garden* (NT), a fine valley garden, 4 miles south-west of Falmouth: Mar. to Oct., Mon., Wed., Fri. *Pendennis Castle*, Falmouth: daily, except Sun. mornings Oct. to Mar. *Trelissick Garden* (NT), with views of the Fal Estuary, 4 miles south of Truro: weekdays and Sun. afternoons, Mar. to Oct. *Truro County Museum*: weekdays except Bank Hols.

Information centres Town Hall, The Moor, Falmouth. Tel. Falmouth 312300. City Hall, Truro. Tel. Truro 4555.

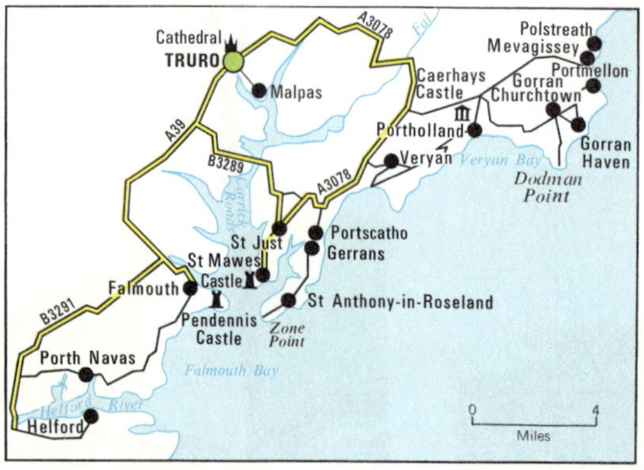

The label 'Riviera' which is applied to this part of south-west England is no mere gimmick dreamed up by the tourist industry. The resemblances to the continental Riviera will impress any visitor who has seen both places: the exceptionally mild climate which allows sub-tropical flowers and trees to flourish; the wide vistas of sparkling blue sea combining delightfully with a varied and luxuriantly coloured landscape; and the attractive little fishing villages and yachting resorts—some, such as St Mawes and Mevagissey, as inviting as any to be found on the shores of the Mediterranean.

Yet the essentially Cornish character of the region remains. It is in the sandy coves and the steep headlands which are gentler versions of the heights at Land's End and the Lizard. It is in the clifftop churches built of granite, and the tiny inland creeks which gleam unexpectedly out of thick overhanging woods. It is in the magic of names like St Just and Mevagissey, and the stirring reminders of past history in such buildings as Henry VIII's Pendennis Castle at Falmouth. The novelist and essayist 'Q', Sir Arthur Quiller-Couch, a Cornishman who loved this region, was not exaggerating when he said that its coves and other features are 'jewels in the diadem of a delectable Duchy'.

SLENDER MULLEIN This flower, one of the well-known Verbascum family, grows wild only in Devon and Cornwall, though it is occasionally grown in gardens in other parts of the country. It can grow up to 4 ft tall, and the clusters of large yellow flowers, 1 in. across, bloom from June to September

Falmouth
This leading holiday resort, popular all the year round, is noted for its superb setting. Its bay is an excellent yachting base and there are good bathing beaches. Cliff walks offer splendid views of the maze-like wooded river country inland and the rich blue waters of the Carrick Roads and Falmouth Bay. Boat trips can be made along the coast and up the Fal, Porthcuel and Helford Rivers. Some boats go as far up the Fal as Truro. Sub-tropical plants bloom and produce fruit in the genial climate, and in Queen Mary's Garden even bananas grow.

Falmouth is also an important port which caters for shipping from all parts of the world. Its harbour, Cornwall's largest, has a dry dock capable of handling tankers up to 90,000 tons. It was an obscure place until Sir Walter Raleigh, seeing its natural strategic advantages, recommended it for development as a port; his friend Sir Peter Killigrew took up the idea, laying the foundation for modern Falmouth. The opening of the railways in the 19th century led to its development as a resort.

The old town lies mainly near the harbour. Places of interest include the Church of King Charles the Martyr (Charles I), built in 1662; Arwennack House in Grove Place, which incorporates part of the Tudor mansion of the Killigrew family; and Pendennis Castle, built in the 1540's by Henry VIII on a knoll guarding the harbour entrance, and later extended by Elizabeth I.

Gorran Haven
A simple fishing village which has grown into a popular resort. The 15th-century church at Gorran Churchtown, 1 mile inland, has a granite tower 110 ft high, which is a landmark for shipping. A lane leads 1 mile south and then becomes a path to the headland of Dodman Point, a National Trust property overlooking Veryan Bay. There are traces of an Iron Age fort at the point. The Cornish author 'Q' used Dodman Point as the setting for his novel *Dead Man's Rock*.

Helford
A narrow road leads steeply down to an inn and a cluster of cottages. The village is beside one of the many beautiful wooded creeks which wind away from the estuary of the Helford River. In the 18th century, Helford's small harbour exported tin from the nearby mines to London; now it is popular with yachtsmen and anglers. Porth Navas, on a creek north of the river, has an oyster farm owned by the Duchy of Cornwall.

Mevagissey
One of Cornwall's most celebrated resorts, a fishing village whose simple beauty has attracted a number of writers and artists as permanent residents, and on which tourists descend in their thousands in summer. Fortunately for the sightseer, the village's streets are so narrow that heavy vehicles cannot enter them. On especially busy days during the holiday season the police close the village to all traffic, and motorists have to leave their cars just outside it. Boatmen take visitors on trips round the bay or on fishing expeditions, including shark fishing. There are good bathing beaches north at Polstreath and south at Portmellon.

LOW TIDE IN A DROWNED VALLEY *Millions of years ago the land mass of Cornwall subsided in the south, and the sea, running in among the woods and hills, drowned the river valleys. Silting is a common problem in these drowned valleys, and rivers like the Helford, which look broad and strong at high tide, become narrow channels winding between shining mudbanks when the tide is out*

TRURO CATHEDRAL *For eight centuries the See of Cornwall was united with that of Devon, and they shared a cathedral. In 1897 the Cornish See was reconstituted, and a new cathedral was built in Truro*

Portholland
A fishing hamlet with twin coves at the foot of tall cliffs, accessible only by one narrow lane through woods. Above the hamlet, a path leads through the woods for about ½ mile to Caerhays Castle, seat of the Trevannion family from 1390 to 1852 and still privately owned. It was restored by John Nash in the romantic 'Gothick' style in 1802. This mock-castle, with its backdrop of dark woods, is a striking sight from the cliff road.

Portscatho
The charming character of this small fishing village remains intact despite its increasing popularity. A steep lane from Gerrans leads down to the village, which has a tiny harbour and a promenade called The Lugger.

St Anthony-in-Roseland
A parish of scattered farms on the Roseland Peninsula. The word 'Roseland' has nothing to do with roses; it comes from the Cornish *ros*, meaning heath. From Gerrans, a tree-lined avenue passes an attractive 18th-century building called Trewince, now a hotel. At Zone Point, 2½ miles south-west, the National Trust property of St Anthony Head has fine views of Falmouth Bay. On the north side of the headland is a small beach from which the resort of St Mawes can be seen. Beside the beach is Place Manor, built in 1840, former seat of the Spry family and now a hotel. Near by stands the small Norman church of St Anthony-in-Roseland.

St Just
The church here was built in 1261, and its tower is 15th century. Its position on a hill above a wooded inlet off Carrick Roads—the famous waterway formed by the meeting of several rivers, including the Fal and Porthcuel—makes it one of the prettiest sights in the region. The hill slopes so steeply that the church's lychgate is level with its roof.

St Mawes
A fashionable yachting resort on the Roseland Peninsula, with a quality of breezy spaciousness, on the opposite side to Falmouth of the arm of sea called Carrick Roads. St Mawes Castle, built on a hillside overlooking the harbour, dominates the village. Henry VIII, fearing possible attack from the French, built this castle and Pendennis Castle at Falmouth as part of his system of coastal defence.

Truro
Cornwall's cathedral city and administrative centre. The cathedral, which has three spires, was completed in 1910, and was built on the site of the 16th-century parish church of St Mary. The church's south aisle was incorporated in the cathedral, whose impressive shape blends well with the dignified Georgian houses in the surrounding streets. Lemon Street is one of the best-preserved examples of Georgian architecture in Britain. In River Street is the County Museum and Art Gallery; its contents include a famous painting by Sir Godfrey Kneller (1648–1723) of a Cornish giant, and a collection of paintings by John Opie.

Veryan
A quiet village set among trees, 2 miles inland from Veryan Bay. Its name is a corruption of St Symphorian, to whom the church is dedicated. The Round Houses, built in the Regency period, are a well-known feature of the village. They were made round so that there would be no corners where the Devil could hide, and each building has a conical roof surmounted by a cross which was intended to drive away the Devil.

FROM PILCHARDS TO TOURISTS *Since Mevagissey's fishery declined and the tourist boom began, tourism has replaced pilchard-fishing as the village's major source of income*

Wild country of Bodmin

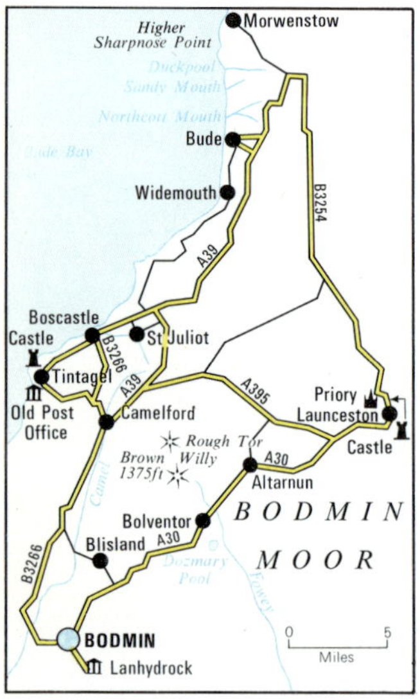

Angling On the estuary at Bude, and from the rocks and beaches all along the coast. Bude Canal is a noted coarse water. River fishing includes stretches of the Ottery, Inny, Camel and Tamar.

Surfing At Bude and Widemouth, frequent venues for the National Surfing Championships. Trebarwith Strand, about 1 mile south of Tintagel is good for ordinary surfing.

Events In Boscastle, a Floral Dance is performed once a week in summer. There is a Furry Dance at Bude most Wed. evenings.

Places to see *Ebbingford Manor*, Bude's oldest house: Tues., Wed. and Thur. afternoons, early June to mid-Sept.; also Sun. afternoon July, Aug. and Sept. *Historical and Folk Exhibition*, Bude: daily, Whitsun to Sept. *King Arthur's Hall*, Tintagel, built in 1933, with 73 stained-glass windows depicting Arthur's knights: daily, Easter to early Oct. *Lanhydrock* (NT), 2½ miles south-east of Bodmin: daily, Apr. to Oct. *Lawrence House* (NT), Launceston: weekday afternoons, Mon., Wed. and Thur. mornings, Apr. to Sept.; also Wed. afternoon, Feb., Mar., Oct., Nov. *North Cornwall Museum and Gallery*, Camelford: daily in summer. *Old Post Office* (NT), Tintagel: weekdays, Sun. afternoon, Apr. to Oct. *Tintagel Castle*: remains of 13th-century castle and of early Celtic monastery: daily, except Sun. morning Oct. to Mar. *Witches' House Museum*, Boscastle: daily, May to mid-Oct.

Information centre Old Railway Station, Bencoolen Road, Bude. Tel. Bude 4240 (seasonal).

The romantic north-west of Cornwall has a majestic coast, a wild and little-visited moor, and rich associations with the legendary world of King Arthur. There are no large towns, and most of the villages and hamlets preserve an air of seclusion which is becoming a rarity in the south-west as the summer invasions of tourists continue.

Just below Morwenstow, the northernmost parish in Cornwall, a great curve of cliffs stretches from the headland called Higher Sharpnose Point for 20 miles down to Tintagel. Here are stark cliff walls, with jagged rocks lying in tumbled heaps at their foot. The scenery has its softer touches as well. Between Morwenstow and the sandy beaches at Bude, the coast is laced with sheltered coves and with deep gorges through which streams tumble on their way down to the sea.

Bodmin Moor, about 12 miles from north to south and 11 miles from east to west, is crossed by only one major road, the A30 from Launceston to Bodmin. To the north of the road, Brown Willy (1375 ft) and Rough Tor (1311 ft), the moor's highest points, tower like mountains on the horizon. Few lanes enter the heart of the moor, and its most remote parts can be approached only on foot or on horseback.

THE BLEAK FACE OF BODMIN MOOR *Wind and rain have eroded the soil, littering the upland hillsides with granite boulders*

CORNISH SLATE—FROM QUARRY TO FARMHOUSE

DELABOLE QUARRY The slate quarry near Camelford is the largest in England. It has been worked continuously since Elizabethan times

SLATE HEADSTONE In Tintagel churchyard, headstones are buttressed against the wind

LOCAL FARMHOUSE Slate and granite are Cornwall's most important stones, and the typical Cornish building has a slate roof and granite walls, which are sometimes slate-hung

Altarnun
A moorland village above a stream on the edge of Bodmin Moor, and about 8 miles south-west of Launceston. The large 15th-century Church of St Nonna, known locally as the 'cathedral of the moor', has an imposing tower and a profusion of handsomely carved bench-ends.

Blisland
An unusual sight in Cornwall—a village set around a green flanked by trees. The church, dedicated to SS Probus and Hyacinth, has an early 15th-century brass commemorating one of its rectors. The local manor house incorporates a Norman archway and windows. In medieval times, the village was called Blisland-juxta-montem, or Blisland near the mountain—the 'mountain' probably being Brown Willy on Bodmin Moor, the highest hill in Cornwall.

Bodmin
The county town of Cornwall, though Truro is the administrative centre. Bodmin is steeply situated on the edge of Bodmin Moor; its main street, which is also a main road to and from the south-west, is often jammed with traffic, though in places it is wide enough for a market. The town's chief buildings include St Petroc's Church, rebuilt in 1469; remains of the Chapel of the Holy Rood; the early 19th-century cattle market; the Assize Court which was built in 1837; and the ruins of the 14th-century St Thomas à Becket's Chapel.

THE MOOR'S GENTLE SIDE *As well as high moorland—lonely, weather-beaten and littered with granite—Bodmin Moor has green fields, gently rolling hills, woods and hedgerows, flecked in summer with pink-purple foxgloves and the white flowers of yarrow*

The town was once noted for its holy wells; one of these, near St Petroc's Church, bears the date 1700 and an advertisement recommending the water as a cure for eye troubles.

Bodmin bears the brunt of incessant holiday traffic, but out of season it reverts to the normal life associated with a traditional town.

Bolventor
A tiny four-house hamlet beside the main road, in the middle of Bodmin Moor. Daphne du Maurier used its Jamaica Inn as the setting and title for her famous novel about smugglers. About $1\frac{1}{2}$ miles south-east is Dozmary Pool, a lonely expanse of water high on the moor. The pool is not bottomless, as legend claims—during one drought it dried up—but the magic of its reputed association with King Arthur's sword Excalibur still lingers around this eerie place. According to tradition, Sir Bedivere flung the sword into the pool at Arthur's command. According to a later legend, the ghost of Jan Tregeagle was set the endless task of emptying Dozmary Pool with a limpet shell.

Bude
Its fine surfing beaches have made Bude a popular resort in the last few years. The town was once notorious for its shipwrecks, and between 1824 and 1874 more than 80 ships were wrecked near it. South to Widemouth is a 3-mile cliff walk with breathtaking views.

Camelford
A busy little town between the Atlantic and the moor. According to local legend, King Arthur's Camelot was situated here; the legend also says that he fought his last battle at the ancient Slaughter Bridge, which crosses a stream a mile to the north. Just south of the village is a footpath which leads on to the moor.

Launceston
A hilly market town in the extreme north-east of the county, barely a mile from the Devon border. Portions of medieval Launceston remain: the two pointed arches of the South Gate from the old wall, much of the ramparts of a 13th-century castle, and a few relics of the Augustinian priory (1136). St Thomas's Church, built in 1182, has the largest font in Cornwall—Norman, with a bold, simple design. The Church of St Mary Magdalene (1511–24) is famous for the lavish carvings which completely cover its outside walls. New Bridge and St Leonard's Bridge are both 16th century. The 12th-century St Stephen-by-Launceston, which overlooks the town from a hilly suburb $1\frac{1}{2}$ miles north, was the town's first church. Most traffic bypasses Launceston's narrow streets, and the town retains its old-world character.

THE POET-PRIEST OF MORWENSTOW

Robert Stephen Hawker (left) the eccentric poet-priest who wrote the 'Song of the Western Men', was vicar of the turbulent parish of Morwenstow from 1834 until 1875. He campaigned vigorously in his church (right) against the wreckers in his parish, men who plundered ships wrecked on the cliffs near the village

THE LARGE BLUE

This butterfly is found only in the north of Cornwall. Its caterpillar feeds on thyme, and before becoming a chrysalis is adopted by ants, who take it to their nest and feed it in return for a honey-like liquid it secretes. The chrysalis lies in the nest throughout the winter, and hatches in the following June or July to produce a mature butterfly

Morwenstow
Cornwall's northernmost parish. Its church stands within a few hundred yards of the Atlantic, and behind it is the vicarage designed by the eccentric but well-loved parson, Robert Stephen Hawker (1803–75), who originated the Harvest Festival and wrote the poem 'Song of the Western Men', which includes the famous line 'And shall Trelawny die?'. The vicarage chimneys are copies of church towers which he admired in other parts of the country. One of the gravestones in the churchyard is a ship's figurehead, commemorating the wreck of the *Caledonia* in 1842. A path from the church leads past a driftwood building called Hawker's Hut, which Hawker used as a study, to cliffs which look down on surging breakers.

St Juliot
The church, known locally as St Jilt, was restored by Thomas Hardy, the novelist, in his apprentice days as an architect, and preserves a pen-and-ink sketch drawn by him. Hardy married the rector's sister, and wrote of the place as 'Endelstow' in his novel, *A Pair of Blue Eyes*. St Jilt stands on a slope above the trout-filled River Valency.

Tintagel
A village on the Atlantic coast famous for its association with Arthurian legend, which says that King Arthur had a castle here. The remains of a castle stand partly on the cliffs and partly on a narrow spit of land, but this was built for the Earl of Cornwall in 1145. It fell out of use about 300 years later and was already in ruins in Tudor times. The Old Post Office, a manor house restored to give it the appearance it had in Victorian times, when it was a letter-receiving office, is open to the public. Paths descend from the village to a shingle beach and Merlin's Cave.

Fishing villages of east Cornwall

Angling Looe is a centre for shark-fishing, and fully equipped boats can be hired. Sea and offshore fishing is good on the Fowey Estuary.

Sailing At Looe, Fowey and Polperro. Fowey and Looe have regattas in Aug., Polperro in mid-July.

Places to see *Antony House* (NT): afternoons, Tues., Wed., Thur. and Bank Hol. Mon., Apr. to Oct. *Cornish Museum*, East Looe: daily, May to Sept. *Cotehele* (NT): daily, Apr. to Oct. *Museum of Smuggling*, Polperro: daily, Easter to mid-Oct. *Old Guildhall Museum*, Higher Market Street, East Looe: mid-May to Sept., Mon. to Fri., also Sun. afternoons. *Restormel Castle*: daily, except Sun. mornings Oct. to Mar. *Woolly Monkey Sanctuary*, Murrayton, East Looe: Easter to Sept., daily.

Information centres Information Centre, Albert Quay, Fowey. Tel. Fowey 3320. Information Bureau, The Guildhall, East Looe. Tel. Looe 2072 (seasonal).

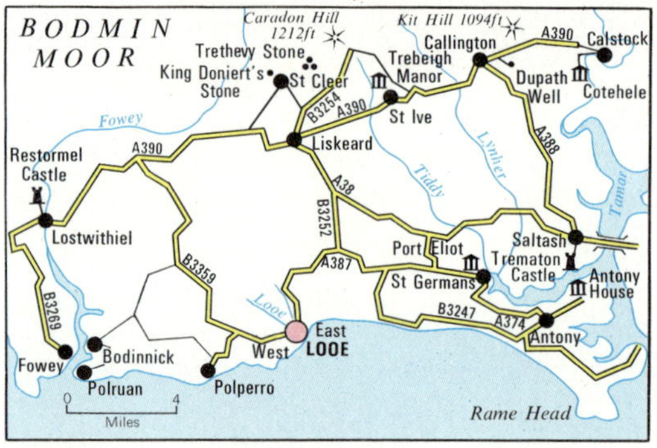

Before the coming of the railways and the motor car, Cornwall was a place apart from the rest of England, almost an island in itself. The isolated character of the county still lingers in the unfamiliar names of saints such as Probus, Hyacinth and Petroc, and in the vestiges of the ancient Cornish language still discernible in the dialect of local people. The separateness of Cornwall is emphasised by the broad River Tamar which almost completely divides it from Devon. Not only is this river the geographical boundary between the two counties, but it is also the frontier between two ways of life. At Saltash, two famous bridges span the river to provide the only links between the southern coasts of Cornwall and Devon.

It was the opening of the railways and roads which brought the tourists flocking to such picturesque resorts as Polperro and Looe, whose beauty and character no amount of commercialisation seems able to destroy. Except on its western side, overlooking Bodmin Moor, the region inland is green and thickly wooded—a world of small market towns and little-known, little-explored villages.

Some of Cornwall's finest houses are to be found here: Port Eliot at St Germans, Antony House north-east of Antony, Place House at Fowey, and perhaps the most beautiful of all, the Tudor mansion of Cotehele near Calstock, mostly built between 1485 and 1539.

Eastern Cornwall is rich in literary associations. Sir Arthur Quiller-Couch, writing as 'Q', lived in Fowey and made it the setting of his novel *The Astonishing History of Troy Town*; Richard Carew's 17th-century *Survey of Cornwall* remains a classic of regional history; and Daphne du Maurier has set a number of her novels in the area of Polruan and Fowey.

FROM DEVON INTO CORNWALL *At Saltash, two bridges over the River Tamar link Devon and Cornwall. The single-track railway bridge was built by the famous Victorian engineer Brunel and opened in 1859; the modern road bridge behind it was opened in 1961*

Antony
A village beside the St Germans or Lynher River Estuary, within strolling distance of the ferry to Plymouth. Antony House, $1\frac{1}{4}$ miles north-east, has been the home of the Carew family for over 500 years. Richard Carew (1555–1620) published his famous *Survey of Cornwall* in 1602; it is still an indispensable source of information on the county. The present house, simple and dignified, is believed to have been designed in 1721 by James Gibbs, architect of St Martin-in-the-Fields in Trafalgar Square, London.

Bodinnick
A much-used ferry connects Fowey to this picturesque place. A lane leading off the main street with its colour-washed cottages climbs a hill to give a fine view of Fowey and its estuary.

Callington
A quiet market town. St Mary's, a 15th-century church, has a fine alabaster monument to Lord Willoughby de Broke (1452–1502), who was Marshal of the Army under Henry VII. Kit Hill (1094 ft), dominated by a radio mast and the chimney stack of a derelict tin mine, gives views westwards to Bodmin Moor and eastwards to Dartmoor. A mile to the south-east is Dupath Well, a holy well in a 15th-century chapel.

Calstock
A small town on one of the loveliest reaches of the Tamar River, and a centre for the growing of strawberries, cherries and gooseberries. Just west of Calstock stands Cotehele, a gracious Tudor manor house, built round two quadrangles, with furnishings dating from the 16th century onwards.

Fowey
A network of narrow streets climbing the hills. New houses encroach, but the old waterside town still holds its own. The fierce Fowey seamen, nicknamed 'Fowey Gallants', who raided the coast of France throughout the Hundred Years' War, continued their raids even after Edward IV had made peace with the French king. Fowey's waterfront is crowded with seamen of all nations, whose ships move to an inner creek to collect cargoes of china clay. Near the 14th-century Church of St Fimbarrus stands Place House (1457), which has additions from the 18th and 19th centuries. It is privately owned. In a waterside house called The Haven lived Sir Arthur Quiller-Couch (1863–1944), author of some of the best tales written about Cornwall. For a time he was mayor of Fowey, which appears as 'Troy Town' in his novels.

Liskeard
A market town on a hill, with several handsome buildings, notably Webb's Hotel (1833) and the town hall (1859). The partly-Norman Church of St Martin is the second largest in Cornwall. A spring in Well Lane was reputed in medieval times to have healing properties.

Looe
East Looe and West Looe are joined by a Victorian bridge, built when the 15th-century bridge of 13 arches was demolished. West Looe clusters round the quayside Church of St Nicholas and has a 17th-century inn, The Jolly Sailor. East Looe has a 16th-century guildhall, now a museum. Looe offers good bathing, yachting, river and sea trips, and shark-fishing.

Lostwithiel
A pleasant market town, with attractive buildings such as the guildhall (1740), and the old grammar school (1781). There is a 15th-century bridge and by the River Fowey in Quay Street are remains of the medieval Stannary court which administered local laws in the tin-mining districts. A Civil War battle was fought near the town, and afterwards the Roundheads held a 'service' in the church in which a horse was used to represent King Charles. The church has a font with fine carvings. Lostwithiel was the capital of Cornwall in the 13th century.

Polperro
In spite of intense commercialisation, this very popular resort keeps the distinctive flavour of a Cornish fishing village. Strung along a narrow combe, the colour-washed cottages lead to a small harbour sheltered by two sea walls. One of the old cottages contains a smuggling museum in its cellar. West of the harbour is a swimming pool refilled daily by the sea at high tide.

POLPERRO HARBOUR *Polperro has all that a Cornish fishing village is supposed to have: lime-washed houses around a small harbour in a steep valley; streets so narrow that cars are banned from them; tales of smugglers; and a timeless sense of peace*

Restormel Castle
One of the oldest and most romantic ruins in Cornwall, standing a mile north of Lostwithiel. The considerable remains include the gate, keep, kitchens, great hall, private rooms and guest chamber. Below the castle is Restormel House, designed in 18th-century 'Gothic' style, with battlements.

St Cleer
A hilly village on the edge of Bodmin Moor, 700 ft above sea level. A 15th-century granite building near the churchyard of St Clarus houses a 'holy well'. The district is rich in ancient monuments. A mile north on the roadside is King Doniert's Stone, carved with Irish motifs; it is believed to record the death by drowning of a 9th-century Cornish king. Trethevy Stone, a mile north-east, is a massive Neolithic burial chamber, with seven upright boulders supporting a slab laid across the top. A path leads from here to Caradon Hill (1212 ft), offering views of Bodmin Moor and the English Channel.

St Germans
A village on a hill overlooking a small harbour. Colour-washed thatched cottages blend with a group of gabled almshouses. St Germans was Cornwall's cathedral city until 1043. For centuries it has been the seat of the Eliots, Earls of St Germans; their house, Port Eliot, can be seen from the churchyard. The famous church, partly rebuilt in 1592 on the site of the Saxon cathedral, has an unusually fine early Norman doorway. Inside the church is a monument to Edward Eliot, dating from 1722, by the Flemish sculptor John Rysbrack (1693–1770); there is also a window designed by the pre-Raphaelite painter Edward Burne-Jones (1833–98).

St Ive
Cottages encircle the 14th-century church. Trebeigh manor house stands on the site of a 12th-century hostel of the Knights Templar, who founded the church. One of the rectors was Jonathan Trelawny, who became Bishop of Bristol and was imprisoned by James II in 1688. The king's action inspired the famous refrain in a poem by R. S. Hawker, 'And shall Trelawny die?'.

Saltash
An attractive fishing port built on a steep hill above the banks of the Tamar, and the historic gateway between Cornwall and Devon. The 18th-century guildhall once stood on granite pillars, but the open area beneath is now closed in. The partly-Norman church next to it has a fine Tudor silver chalice, and 1½ miles to the south-west stands the roofless 13th-century keep of Trematon Castle.

A CORNISH TRADEMARK *Narrow streets like Lower Chapel Street in East Looe are typical of Cornwall's fishing villages*

RESTORMEL CASTLE *The ruined castle stands behind a 60 ft wide moat on a hill with artificially steepened sides. A castle was first built here c. 1100, and the circular wall was added later. Its defences were perfect, but Restormel saw little action*

Flowers in December in the South Hams

Angling Sea fishing at Dartmouth, Salcombe, Newton Ferrers and Plymouth. Freshwater fishing on rivers Dart, Erme, Avon and Plym.

Events Regattas at Plymouth (July/Aug.), Dartmouth and Salcombe (both Aug.). Plymouth has *Mayflower* celebrations in Sept.

Places to see *Cookworthy Museum*, Kingsbridge: Easter to mid-Oct., weekdays. *Dartmoor Wildlife Park*, Sparkwell: daily. *Dartmouth Town Museum*: weekdays, except mornings Oct. to Mar. *Elizabethan House Museum*, Totnes: weekdays, Mar. to Oct. *Plymouth Dockyard*: conducted tours Mon. to Fri. in summer. *Saltram* (NT): daily, Apr. to Oct. *Sharpitor* (NT), Salcombe: garden, daily; museum, daily Apr. to Oct.

Information centres Dartmouth Guildhall. Tel. Dartmouth 2281. Salcombe Town Association. Tel. Salcombe 2736. Plymouth Civic Centre. Tel. Plymouth 68000.

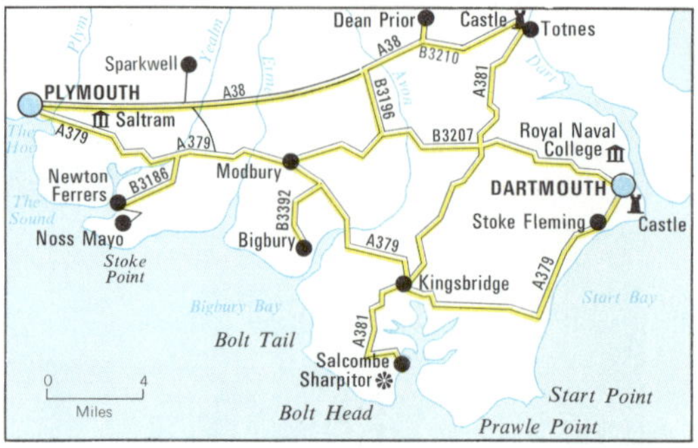

The rich agricultural region known as the South Hams extends from Totnes to Prawle Point and from Dartmouth to the eastern outskirts of Plymouth. *Ham* is an Old English word meaning an enclosed or sheltered place. The South Hams, the most southerly part of Devon, enjoys the mildest climate in Britain; the winds from the English Channel never blow so brashly as the Atlantic gales that batter north-western Devon. Honeysuckle lingers here until October, and even in December many flowers are still in bloom. For some visitors the climate is so mild that it has an enervating effect.

There are no industrial areas, apart from that centred on Plymouth at the edge of the region. The people of the South Hams are mainly an agricultural community, intent on making hay, and raising cattle and corn. Five rivers water the region—the Plym, the Yealm, the Erme, the Avon and the Dart—and the soil is unusually fertile.

The past and present prosperity of the South Hams is reflected in its architecture. The towns have large houses built in medieval and Tudor times by merchants and farmers; the villages are full of well-kept thatched cottages, coloured in washes of white, pink or ochre.

Much of the coastline has been built up in recent years, to cope with the rapid growth of tourism. But some parts remain delightfully rural—as at Blackpool Sands, near Stoke Fleming, where the famous local Red Ruby cattle bask on the beach.

A traveller named John Leland summed it up four centuries ago when he described the South Hams as 'the frutefullest part of all Devonshire'.

GEORGIAN ELEGANCE *The classical facade of Saltram looks out over a landscaped park, with views of Plymouth Sound. The house, originally Tudor, was redesigned in the 1740's, and its gardens have an orangery and summer house*

ELIZABETHAN CHARM *The Pilgrim Fathers set out from Sutton Pool, Plymouth, in the* Mayflower *in 1620. The rebuilding of Plymouth's city centre in recent years has left the tiny streets round the harbour little changed*

Dartmouth
A town of much historical and architectural interest about 1 mile from the mouth of the River Dart, superbly situated on a steep hill on the west bank of the river. It has been an important harbour since the Roman era. Many historic naval expeditions, including the fleet sent by Edward III to assist in the siege of Calais in 1347, sailed from here.

Dartmouth is a fishing port as well as a popular holiday resort. Boat trips along the beautiful estuary of the Dart are among the local attractions.

A waterside path leading to the open sea passes St Petrox's Church, rebuilt in the Gothic style in 1641–2. Alongside the church are the remains of a 15th-century cliff castle, which faces Kingswear Castle—also 15th-century—across the estuary. (Kingswear Castle is not open to the public.) The two castles were built in such a way that a thick chain could be stretched across the river to hold off enemy ships in time of war.

Other notable buildings in Dartmouth include the Butterwalk, a row of 17th-century houses on granite pillars with carved overhanging storeys, damaged by a bomb in 1943 and restored in 1954; the Castle Hotel, mostly 19th century, which incorporates a 17th-century coaching inn; Agincourt House, which dates from 1671; and the Customs House, built in 1739. Overlooking them all, from the crest of the highest hill above the town, stands the Royal Naval College, which has trained naval cadets since 1905. A car ferry plies across the river to Kingswear, the railway terminus.

THROUGH DEVON FIELDS FROM DARTMOUTH *The 11 mile long estuary of the River Dart offers a varied panorama of south Devon landscapes—from the urban scenery of Dartmouth on the river's west bank, to open views of woodland and fresh green fields*

Kingsbridge

This busy little market town, sometimes called the capital of the South Hams, stands at the head of the Kingsbridge Estuary. Among the town's interesting buildings are St Edmund's Church, with its 13th-century tower; the Shambles, a 16th-century market arcade largely rebuilt in 1796; and the 17th-century grammar school. William Cookworthy (1705–80), who discovered china clay in Cornwall and made the first true porcelain in England, was born here.

Modbury

Like many South Hams towns, Modbury is built on a steep hill. It is a picturesque market town with a number of Georgian buildings and several slate-hung houses, typical of this part of south Devon. The half-timbered Exeter Inn has been in use since Elizabethan times, and the church, imposingly sited astride the hill, has a tower with a medieval spire.

Newton Ferrers

Gabled houses and thatched cottages flank a steep lane above the wooded banks of the Yealm Estuary. Across the water, the village of Noss Mayo holds a traditional May Day procession each year. There is bathing on a sandy beach at Stoke, 1½ miles south of Noss Mayo.

Plymouth

With a population of just over 250,000, Plymouth is the largest city in the West Country. It was formed from the union of the old towns of Plymouth, Stonehouse and Devonport. It has one of the grandest sites of any city in Britain, lying mainly between the mouths of the Tamar and the Plym, which flow into the broad estuary of Plymouth Sound. Out to sea, past the fine headlands that enclose The Sound, or inland to Dartmoor and the Cornish hills, the views are superb.

The centre of the city was almost obliterated during the Second World War, and the crowded area around Sutton Pool represents virtually all that is left of old Plymouth, a noted seaport since the 13th century. During the Hundred Years' War, many ships sailed from here against the French, and later it was the port from which the Elizabethan sailors Hawkins, Raleigh and Frobisher embarked on their great voyages. Above all, it is the city of Sir Francis Drake, who played his famous game of bowls on the Hoe before setting out to destroy the Spanish Armada in 1588. The tale that he finished his game before turning his attention to the Spaniards is almost certainly true; but Drake's nonchalance must have been at least partly due to a shrewd assessment of the state of the wind and the tide, which would anyway have prevented him from sailing straight away.

The Pilgrim Fathers sailed from Plymouth to America in the *Mayflower* in 1620; and in 1772 James Cook departed from Plymouth on his great three-year circumnavigation of the world. From Plymouth, too, Sir Francis Chichester sailed on his single-handed voyage round the world in 1966–7.

Rebuilt since the war, Plymouth is a thriving industrial and naval centre with more recorded history than visible remains. The most notable historic building is the Citadel, at the east end of The Hoe; it commands the entrance to Sutton Pool and the Cattewater (the mouth of the River Plym). It was built in the 17th century by Charles II, on what were then the most advanced principles of fortress architecture.

Among the more recent attractions of Plymouth is the view which visitors can have from the roof of the Municipal Offices skyscraper. The view ranges from Dartmoor in the north-east to the distant Eddystone Lighthouse, which stands 14 miles out to sea.

Salcombe

The most southerly resort in Devon, with some of the finest scenery along the coast—especially 2 miles south-west, around Bolt Head (National Trust). The climate here is exceptionally mild, and orange and lemon trees grow beside the estuary; in summer the palm trees, bright sunshine and glistening white houses seem almost Mediterranean. Salcombe is a noted yachting centre, and offers good fishing and two sandy beaches. The tower of a ruined Tudor castle stands near North Sands beach.

Totnes

A charming old town set on a steep hill above the River Dart, with many interesting old buildings in Fore Street and High Street. It was settled and fortified by the Saxons, and medieval Totnes grew rich on the cloth trade.

At the north end of the town stands a castle, of which the 13th-century circular keep and some walls remain. The original castle dated from the 11th century. In the High Street are Elizabethan and 17th-century houses, some of them slate-hung in typical Devon style. Just off the High Street is the parish church of St Mary, a 15th-century building with a stone rood screen which is one of the finest in England. Near the church is the guildhall, dating in part from the 16th century and built on the site of medieval Totnes Priory; it is now a museum. The Butterwalk, in the High Street, is a row of houses with overhanging storeys. The King Edward VI Grammar School, founded in 1554, occupies an 18th-century building in Fore Street. Dividing Fore Street from High Street is the restored 15th-century East Gate, formerly the eastern boundary of the town.

ROAD TO THE ROCKS *The narrow, winding road sunk deeply into a mosaic of farmland in typical Devon style leads to Start Point—one of Britain's most rugged capes*

SOUTH DEVON COW *A Devon breed whose milk makes excellent clotted cream*

Grim rocks against the sea

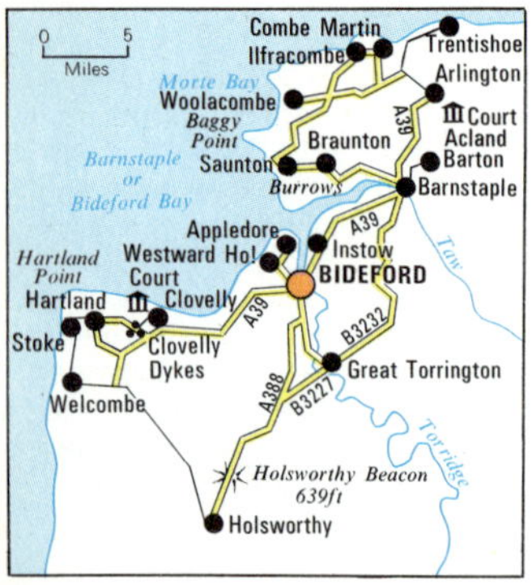

Angling Freshwater fishing on the Rivers Taw and Torridge at Barnstaple and Bideford; on the Gammaton and Jennets Reservoirs, Bideford, and on the Slade Reservoir, Ilfracombe.

Sailing In Bideford Bay and on the Torridge Estuary.

Surfing At Woolacombe Sands; Saunton Sands; and Westward Ho!

Steamer trips Trips to Lundy and South Wales and cruises along the North Devon coast from Ilfracombe, Easter and May to Sept.

Nature trails At Arlington Court, Arlington: daily except Sat., Mar. to Oct. There are two trails at Braunton Burrows: all year.

Events There are carnivals or fairs at Great Torrington in May, Holsworthy and Westward Ho! in July, Ilfracombe, Combe Martin and Braunton in Aug., Bideford and Barnstaple in Sept. The North Devon Show at Instow and the Devon Sheep Sale and Fair are both held in Aug.

Places to see *Arlington Court* (NT): daily, Apr. to Oct. *Burton Art Gallery*, Victoria Park, Bideford: daily, except Mon. afternoon. *Chambercombe Manor*, Ilfracombe: Easter to Sept., Mon. to Fri.; also Sun. afternoon. *Ilfracombe Museum*: daily. *Lundy Island* (NT): daily. *North Devon Athenaeum*, The Square, Barnstaple: weekdays, except Sat. afternoon. *North Devon Maritime Museum*, Appledore: Easter to Sept., Tues. to Sat. and Sun. afternoon. *St Anne's Chapel Museum*, Barnstaple: Whitsun to mid-Sept., daily.

Information centres Promenade, Ilfracombe. Tel. Ilfracombe 63001. Hall 70, Woolacombe. Tel. Woolacombe 553 (seasonal). The Quay, Bideford. Tel. Bideford 77676 (seasonal).

Devon's most spectacular stretch of coastal scenery extends from Welcombe on the west-facing coast, near the Cornish border, round to Trentishoe on the north coast—a chain of magnificent cliffs interrupted only by Woolacombe Sands and the long sand flats stretching southwards from Saunton. In some parts the cliffs drop sheer to the water's edge, as at Hartland Point; elsewhere they fall away to the sea in long, steep slopes. Dark grey rocks, crushed and folded, form peculiar zigzag patterns, as at the dramatic Gull Rock, just off Welcombe; but their grim beauty is softened by numerous coppices of thorn, oak and hazel which cling to the slopes, and by small waterfalls, such as the one at Speke's Mill Mouth, south of Hartland Quay.

The region has several popular seaside resorts, ranging from the holiday centre of Ilfracombe to the smaller coastal villages of Clovelly and Appledore. The north-eastern part of the region leads up to Exmoor; inland are small market towns of quiet charm such as Holsworthy, in remote country near Holsworthy Beacon, and Great Torrington, above the River Torridge. The most important centres of commerce and industry are Barnstaple and Bideford, which are linked by about 10 miles of mainly built-up road. The towns are near the estuary where the Rivers Taw and Torridge meet, and they were prosperous ports before the estuary silted up.

The climate of north-west Devon was well described by a local writer, the Victorian novelist Charles Kingsley, author of *Westward Ho!* 'It combines', he wrote, 'the soft warmth of south Devon with the bracing freshness of the Welsh mountains.'

NEAR HARTLAND QUAY *Along the north coast of Devon, promontories of grey rock, running steeply down to the sea, alternate with sheer, tall cliffs and long stretches of sand*

Acland Barton
A place in high wooded country north-east of Barnstaple. Nearly a thousand years ago a man named Acca had a farm here, so it was called Acca's land. On the site of the ancient farm stands the original house of the Aclands, for centuries one of the greatest West Country land-owning families, who took their name from the place. During the Second World War, the Aclands gave their entire estate in Devon to the National Trust. The house, built *c.* 1475, is still a private residence, a splendid example of a barton, or yeoman's residence, of the late medieval period.

Appledore
Here the Rivers Taw and Torridge meet before entering the sea about 2 miles away. This ideal site made Appledore a famous shipbuilding centre, and the industry has taken on a new importance since the largest covered shipbuilding dock in Europe was opened here in 1970. The best parts of the village are extremely picturesque—narrow streets climbing steeply from the quay; yachts coming and going at the slipway; trim cottages and gracious small Georgian houses; and everywhere lobster-pots, fishing nets and sailors in their blue jerseys. A ferry boat crosses the Torridge to the sandy beaches of Instow.

Arlington
Hidden amid tree-lined lanes, the hamlet lies beside Arlington Court, built 1820–3, one of the few great houses of north Devon, formerly the home of the Chichester family (whose most famous modern descendant was yachtsman Sir

ON THE CREST OF A WAVE *Breakers rolling in from the Atlantic make the sandy beaches at Woolacombe and other resorts along Devon's north coast ideal for surfing*

Francis Chichester). Arlington Court is now a National Trust property. The plainness of the house from the outside belies its rich interior. Among the treasures at Arlington Court is a watercolour by William Blake, *Cycle of the Life of Man*, discovered in an attic in the house in the 1950's. On the staircase is a display of dresses worn by the women of the family in the 19th century.

Barnstaple
An important marketing centre, and one of the oldest towns in Britain. It was an established borough, minting its own coins, as early as the 10th century. Barnstaple, for long the third-largest town in Devon (after Exeter and Plymouth), was an important harbour until the estuary of the Taw silted up. It was also an important 'staple', or market, for the wool trade. The town prospered greatly in the 18th century, and its centre is still largely Georgian.

The 18th-century Queen Anne's Walk, a pleasant colonnade, retains the Tome Stone, on which merchants set their money to make their contracts binding. St Anne's Chapel, dating from the 14th century, once housed the grammar school which educated the poet John Gay (1685–1732), author of *The Beggar's Opera*; the building is now a local museum. Off the High Street is the colourful Pannier Market, thronged with traders selling Devon produce on market days, Tuesdays and Fridays.

The fine Long Bridge over the River Taw, with its 16 arches, dates from the 13th century. Some of the original stonework can still be seen, though the bridge has been widened several times.

Bideford
The narrow streets of this busy town climb the steep hill on the west bank of the River Torridge, at the point where it begins to widen to form its estuary. The town's most famous sight is its bridge over the Torridge; it is 677 ft long, has 24 arches, and incorporates part of an original 15th-century stone bridge. An attractive street is Bridgeland Road, which has several 17th-century buildings. The town was the principal port of north Devon from the 16th century—when Sir Richard Grenville, captain of the *Revenge*, secured a charter for Bideford from Queen Elizabeth I —until the 18th century, when its overseas trade declined.

Braunton
This is locally claimed to be the largest village in England. Braunton's church has many features of interest, including a superb roof, and carved bench-ends which are among the finest in England. To the west lie the extensive sand dunes known as Braunton Burrows, a noted nature reserve. At Baggy Point, a little to the north, soaring cliffs offer stupendous views over Croyde Bay to the south, and Morte Bay to the north.

Clovelly
One of the show-places not only of Devon but of Britain. Cars cannot enter the village, and the cottages lining the steep main street are decked with flowers for most of the year. The village lies in a lush, narrow combe between steep cliffs. Clovelly Dykes near by is a large and impressive prehistoric hill-fort, consisting of three concentric banks separated by ditches; it probably dates from the Iron Age.

Great Torrington
This town, perched high on a steep hill above the River Torridge, occupies one of the finest sites in Devon. The distant views towards and from the town are superb. The little market square has considerable charm. Buildings of interest include the Georgian town hall, the early-Victorian market house, and the partly 17th-century Black Horse Inn.

Hartland
Formerly an important town, now a pleasant village 3 miles inland from Hartland Point, within easy reach of spectacular coastal scenery. St John's Church, built in 1839, contains one of the earliest pendulum clocks in Britain, made by John Morcombe of Barnstaple in the 17th century. The parish church, $1\frac{1}{2}$ miles west at Stoke, has one of the highest towers (128 ft) in Devon.

Ilfracombe
The largest seaside resort in north Devon, differing from most big resorts in being built around its old harbour. There are many good shingle beaches, two of them reached by tunnels through the rocks. The landscape along the coast and around the town is hilly and steep. Ilfracombe's many amenities include golfing, boat trips and fishing. There are coastal walks to several local viewpoints on each side of the town. The medieval Chapel of St Nicholas, which stands on a rock at the entrance to the harbour, was restored in the 1960s.

ISLAND OF BIRDS

Though only some 20 people now live on the island of Lundy, 12 miles north-west of Hartland Point, they still issue their own stamps. Lundy, now owned by the National Trust, is named after the old Norse word for puffin; and puffins still nest on the narrow cliff ledges, along with other birds. The island can be reached by steamer from Ilfracombe, the journey taking about 2 hours

Welcombe
This village, a short walk away from the Cornish border, is very Cornish in character. Its church is dedicated to the Celtic St Nectan; there is a holy well near by. A Cornish poet, the Rev. R. S. Hawker (1803–75), was curate here when he was vicar of Morwenstow, 3 miles away across the county border in Cornwall. From Welcombe Mouth, a 5-mile coastal lane leads north through striking cliff scenery to Hartland Quay.

Westward Ho!
An obscure spot until it was named after Charles Kingsley's famous novel (published in 1855). There are good bathing beaches, a fine golf course and the famous 2 mile long Pebble Ridge.

LANTERN HILL *Since the Middle Ages, a light has shone from the tiny Chapel of St Nicholas, patron saint of sailors, to guide boats into Ilfracombe harbour*

NO ROOM FOR CARS *Cars cannot drive through the narrow, cobbled main street of Clovelly, which drops 400 ft in a series of steps to an inn by the harbour*

Dartmoor's open wilderness

Angling On the moor, the Dart divides into the East and the West Dart. Sea trout fishing is good on the West Dart, while brown trout can be taken on both rivers. Salmon fishing is best about 3 miles upstream from Dartmeet. Anglers are advised to consult the angling guide published by the South West Water Authority.

Nature trails Bellever Forest Walk, Postbridge: all year. Trowlesworthy Warren, Dartmoor (5 miles south of Princetown): organised by the National Trust. Hembury Woods, 2 miles west of Ashburton: summer.

Events Ashburton has a carnival in late summer. The famous Widecombe Fair is held in Sept., and Tavistock Goose Fair is in Oct.

Places to see *Ashburton Museum*: mid-May to Sept., weekday afternoons, except Mon. and Wed. *Buckfast Abbey*: daily. *Buckland Abbey* (NT): Easter to Sept., weekdays and Sun. afternoon. *Castle Drogo* (NT), at Drewsteignton, 2 miles north-east of Chagford: Apr. to Oct., daily. *House of Shells*, Buckfast: daily, Easter to mid-Oct. *Lydford Castle*: daily. *Lydford Gorge* (NT): Apr. to Oct., daily; Nov. to Mar., daily as far as waterfall only. *Museum of Rural Industry*, Sticklepath: daily. *Okehampton Castle*: daily, except Sun. morning Oct. to Mar.

Information centres Dartmoor National Park, County Hall, Exeter. Tel. Exeter 77977. Seasonal centres at Postbridge, Tavistock, Haytor and New Bridge. Also a mobile caravan tours the area. Lower Car Park, Bovey Tracey. Tel. Bovey Tracey 832047 (seasonal).

Dartmoor, famous for its prison and for its rugged, desolate beauty, is the largest tract of open country left in southern England. Most of it lies in the Dartmoor National Park, which covers 365 square miles between Okehampton and Ivybridge, Tavistock and Christow. Within that area are mountains, moors, combes (valleys), dense woods, market towns, and remote villages. Two summits exceed 2000 ft (High Willhays, 2039 ft and Yes Tor, 2028 ft); several reach 1900 ft. Rainfall is heavy—as much as 80–100 in. annually at Princetown, compared with 35 in. at Exeter.

South of Okehampton an artillery range is in frequent use (live shells are used, so visitors should check at a local post office for details of firing days), and other parts are dangerously swampy; but the greater part of the moor remains accessible to all who enjoy solitude, stillness, and an invigorating blend of rough and smooth landscape.

The many prehistoric remains, including hill-forts, barrows, hut circles and standing stones, are mute reminders of the moor's earliest occupants, some from Brittany, others from Sussex and Kent. During the Middle Ages the moor was mined for tin, lead, copper and manganese. The miners ruled the industry firmly through their Stannary courts—the word 'stannary' derived from the Latin *stannum,* meaning tin—at the four Stannary towns of Tavistock, Chagford, Ashburton and Plympton, where the tin was weighed.

Today the moor is farming country, with sheep and cattle on the uplands and corn in sheltered regions.

COMBESTONE TOR *Though they look man-made, the granite rock-piles on Dartmoor owe their shape to erosion by the weather*

Ashburton
An attractive little town on a steep hill, in a setting of moorland and woods. Gabled houses, Regency villas, and the River Ashburn add to the charm of a place that is lively but not loud, restful yet not a museum-piece. The church's greystone tower is one of the most handsome in Devon. About 1 mile to the north is Boro Wood Camp, an Iron Age hill-fort overlooking the River Dart.

Buckfastleigh
Benedictine monks spent 30 years building the cathedral-size Buckfast Abbey, a mile north of the village. It was completed in 1938. Outside, the local limestone glows in the sunshine; inside there is rich modern stained glass, designed and made by the monks. At the nearby shop the monks sell their tonic wine and honey.

Buckfastleigh is the northern terminus of the Dart Valley Railway, privately run by steam-engine enthusiasts. Regular services from Easter to September take passengers to Totnes and back through a superb 7-mile stretch of the Devon countryside alongside the Dart.

Buckland Monachorum
Buckland 'of the monks' is a pleasant village with some 17th-century cottages. The abbey, founded in 1278, was converted into a mansion in 1541 and bought by Sir Francis Drake in 1581. It is now a maritime and folk museum, with relics of Drake.

Chagford
The name comes from Old English, meaning a ford in gorse-covered country. Chagford was a Stannary town until the late 16th century. Today it is a popular centre for touring northern Dartmoor. It has Tudor and Georgian houses and a 16th-century bridge over the River Teign. North-west is Gidleigh, with the remains of a small castle; the surrounding area is rich in prehistoric stone circles. Scorhill, west of Gidleigh, is one of the finest circles on the moor.

Dartmeet
The most famous beauty spot on Dartmoor, where the East Dart and West Dart rivers meet near the road from Ashburton to Two Bridges. A 'clapper' bridge, a rough-stone bridge typical of the West Country, crosses the bubbling, boulder-strewn East Dart a little way upstream from the modern bridge.

Lydford
This secluded village is dominated by the remains of its castle, which was built in 1195 to house offenders against forest and Stannary laws. Lydford Gorge offers a dramatic walk beside seething waters, through overhanging woods.

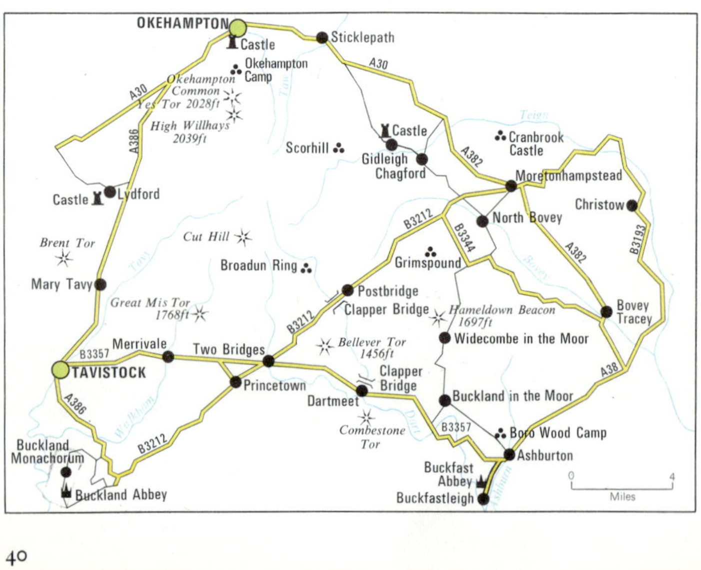

DARTMOOR PONY *Though ponies have run wild on Dartmoor for at least a thousand years, the ones there today are very tame. In autumn there is a round-up, and many of the ponies are sold*

DROVERS' BRIDGE *In the Middle Ages, the huge granite slabs littering Dartmoor were used to make bridges, such as the one at Postbridge, for trains of pack-horses bringing metal back from the mines*

RIDING COUNTRY *Few places in England offer riders so much open country as Dartmoor*

A MERCHANT'S THANK-OFFERING *According to legend, the 12th-century church crowning Brent Tor was built by a grateful merchant whose ship had narrowly escaped being wrecked*

PHOTOGRAPHER'S CORNER *A cluster of grey thatched cottages set against a thickly wooded hillside makes this part of Buckland-in-the-Moor one of the most photographed corners of England*

Moretonhampstead
A small market town with some fine old buildings. Of special interest are the two-storeyed granite almshouses dated 1637. This is a good centre for exploring the eastern part of Dartmoor. To the north-west of the town are the remains of Cranbrook Castle, an Iron Age hill-fort 1100 ft above the River Teign.

North Bovey
This is one of the prettiest villages in Devon. Its green is flanked by thatched stone houses; the church stands on a knoll above an 18th-century cottage now serving as a shop and post office. Grimspound, 3 miles to the south-west, is the site of a Bronze Age village, and has well-preserved remains of 24 huts. Grim was one of the names of Woden, god of the Anglo-Saxons, whom ancient legend credited with the building of many such prehistoric sites.

Okehampton
This market town, known as 'the capital of the northern moor', has the remains of a fine castle (the keep is Norman, the other parts are 14th century) in a beautiful setting above the River Okement. Some 4 miles to the east is the village of Sticklepath, notable for its interesting Museum of Rural Industry, which includes an early 19th-century iron foundry. South-east of Okehampton is Okehampton Camp, the remains of a hill-fort on a steep ridge. The camp was probably a frontier post during the Iron Age. South of the town, within the artillery range and often inaccessible to the public, are the highest tors (peaks) of Dartmoor—High Willhays and Yes Tor. From Yes Tor there is a wonderful view south over Dartmoor, west to Bodmin Moor, and north over most of Devon.

Postbridge
This hamlet, consisting of a few cottages and scattered farms, is famous for its stone clapper bridge, probably medieval, with three spans each of 15 ft. Broadun Ring, 1¼ miles north-west of Postbridge, is a prehistoric walled pound, 4 ft high in places, which encloses a group of hut circles. It stands on a slope from which there is a splendid view of the East Dart Valley. Just to the south of Broadun Ring is Broadun Pound, the largest known prehistoric enclosure on Dartmoor: 12 acres, walled, containing hut circles 9–15 ft across. More than 150 of these pounds have been discovered on Dartmoor; they were probably enclosures used to pen sheep and cattle.

Princetown
The largest town on the moor, and the bleakest, standing some 1400 ft above sea level and having more than its share of fog, rain, wind and snow. It was named after the Prince of Wales (later George IV), who gave land from the estates of the Duchy of Cornwall when it was decided to build a prison here to house the captives of the Napoleonic Wars. The foundations of the famous Dartmoor Prison were laid in 1806. Its use as a prison for criminals dates from the mid-19th century. Princetown is a good centre for exploring prehistoric remains. Bronze Age burial cists (hollowed-out stone coffins) and a row of standing stones are beside the road north-east to Lakehead from Two Bridges (1¼ miles north-east of Princetown). At Merrivale, 2 miles north-west of Princetown, are hut circles and one of the finest cists on Dartmoor. At Great Mis Tor, 1 mile to the north-east of Merrivale, a group of Bronze Age hut circles overlooks the River Walkham.

Tavistock
An important market town, traditionally regarded as the western capital of the moor. Tavistock grew up around its great Benedictine abbey, founded in the 10th century, traces of which survive near the parish church. From the 16th century the town belonged to the Dukes of Bedford. The town today has a largely Victorian character, reflecting the last great phase of its long-lived copper-mining industry. East Bridge and Vigo Bridge both date from 1773, and are handsome structures. Sir Francis Drake (*c.* 1540–96) was born at Crowndale Farm, 1 mile south of Tavistock.

Widecombe in the Moor
A picturesque village in a high fold of Dartmoor, with a large 14th-century church with a granite tower, sometimes known as 'the cathedral of the moor'. Tourists flock here in summer. Widecombe Fair, made famous by the 'Uncle Tom Cobleigh' song, is held on the second Tuesday in September. To the north-west of the village is Hameldown Beacon (1697 ft). On the west side of Hamel Down is a well-preserved group of Bronze Age barrows.

Through the switchback heartland of Devon

Angling Freshwater fishing in the Rivers Taw, Torridge, Bray and Mole; the best centre is South Molton. The Taw is noted for its salmon fishing, at its best from Mar. to May. Sea trout can be taken from July onwards. The Mole and Bray are good trout streams. The Torridge is at its best for salmon between Mar. and May, and for sea trout between July and Sept.

Riding Stables throughout the area.

Events South Molton Sheep Fair is held in Aug.

Arts Day, evening and residential arts and crafts courses are run by the Beaford Arts Centre. The centre promotes and sponsors entertainment over a large area of north Devon and has a small but well-established theatre group that tours the whole country. Details may be obtained from the Director, Greenwarren House, Beaford, Winkleigh, Devon.

Places to see *Museum and Guildhall*, Market Place, South Molton. Its contents include pewter, items relating to local history, a 1750 cider press and an interesting collection of old fire engines, including a manual pump which dates from 1736 and is one of the oldest fire-fighting appliances of its kind in the country: weekdays.

Information centre
The Quay, Bideford.
Tel. Bideford 77676 (seasonal).

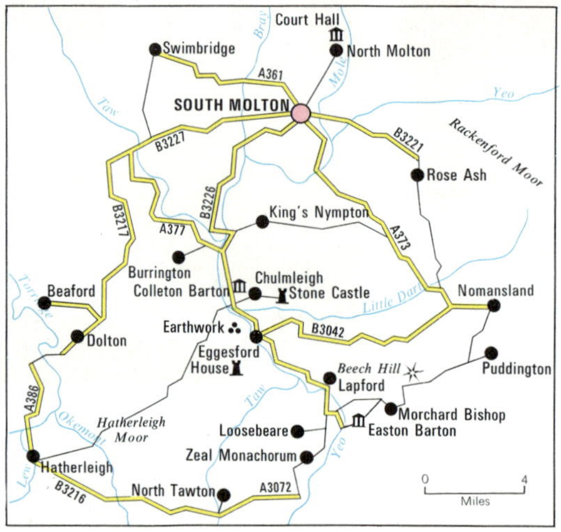

Central Devon lies between the heights of Dartmoor and Exmoor—an area bounded by South Molton, Morchard Bishop, and the hills west of Hatherleigh. It lacks any well-known show-pieces, but offers much quiet enjoyment to those who prefer to wander off the beaten track. Not that the area is without beauty spots and places of historical interest; few villages are more endearing than Rose Ash, few market towns more truly rural than South Molton. There are derelict iron and copper mines near North Molton, and ruined castles, impressive churches, innumerable thatched cottages and stone manor houses throughout the region. It is a country of farms, woods and orchards, a centre of Devon's ancient and famous cider industry.

Between South Molton and Morchard Bishop the country is high, lying between 500 and 900 ft above sea-level. The region is crossed by narrow, richly wooded valleys. There are many rivers and streams—the Taw, Mole, Lew, Yeo and Little Dart—trickling like blue threads across the land.

The 17th-century diarist Celia Fiennes, an intrepid woman who travelled the length and breadth of England on horseback, gave a description of the region which still applies. She remarked that 'these roads were much up and down'. Yet she enjoyed crossing 'a high ridge of hills which discovers a vast prospect on each side full of inclosures and lesser hills'. Typical of central Devon's remote and hilly character are the 2-mile footpath from Puddington to aptly named Nomansland, and the minor road from Tiverton across Rackenford Moor towards South Molton—some 15 miles of switchback without a single village.

Burrington
A charming village overlooking the River Taw, with woods all round. The church has a Norman font and a very fine carved screen. Burrington typifies the quiet, homely beauty of this region.

Chulmleigh
A small, hilly town above the Little Dart, long since bypassed by the main road. The large 15th-century Church of St Mary Magdalen is noted for its splendid rood screen and the 38 carved wooden angels on its roof. Another building of interest in the town is the Barnstaple Inn, dating from 1633.

According to local legend, a medieval Countess of Devon, Isabel, saved the seven children of a pauper at Chulmleigh who was so desperate that he was about to drown them. She brought up the children at her home, Stone Castle, 1 mile east of the town. The castle motte and bailey are still to be seen. About 1 mile west of Chulmleigh is Colleton Barton, built in the early 17th century, with a gatehouse which survives from a house built there in the Middle Ages.

Eggesford
A quiet spot among rolling hills. The church is full of impressive monuments to members of the Chichester family (ancestors of the round-the-world sailor Sir Francis Chichester). It stands in what used to be the park of Eggesford House, once a seat of the Chichesters, now a picturesque ruin. On the west side of the River Taw, which flows here in attractive curves beside wooded banks, are two prehistoric earthworks.

Hatherleigh
The peaceful market town, hardly larger than a village, stands on a hill away from the main holiday routes. In the steep main street stands the George Hotel, an inn probably dating from the 15th century. An annual fair and regular cattle sales are held in the town. Hatherleigh Moor is ideal for picnics and strolls. The obelisk on the moor was erected in 1860 to Lieut.-Col. Morris, a hero of the battle of Balaclava who survived the famous Charge of the Light Brigade. Anglers visit Hatherleigh to fish three local streams, the Lew, Okement and Torridge. A little way south of the town a footpath and track follow the Lew and Medland Brook for about 3 miles through wooded country.

Lapford
A village standing on a hill above the River Yeo, half a mile from the main road, with a steep street of thatched

TAIL-END OF A TRADITION *Though cider-making has been part of the Devon farmer's way of life for hundreds of years, it is now a dying art. Only a few farmers keep the old cider presses working, while the rest sell their apples to factories*

TURNING BACK THE CLOCK *Driving into the quiet market town of Hatherleigh is like returning to the past—most of the houses were built in the 19th century or earlier, and the George Hotel probably dates from the late 15th century*

THE PEACE OF A DEVON VALLEY *Flanked on one side by a thickly wooded combe and on the other by open meadows and a stream that is hardly more than a trickle, the remote valley road from Head Barton to King's Nympton seems as peaceful and ageless as the valley itself*

THE INDUSTRY THAT DIED *At Heasley Mill near North Molton, ivy-covered ruins and holes in the ground are all that remain of iron and copper mines derelict since the 1880's*

cottages and Georgian houses. The Church of St Thomas of Canterbury, dating mainly from the 15th century, but with a Norman doorway, has an exceptionally fine collection of carved woodwork. It is said to have been built by one of Thomas à Becket's murderers, William de Tracy, to expiate his crime. Bury Barton, 1 mile south of the village, is one of several attractive farmhouses in the area which date from the 16th and 17th centuries.

Morchard Bishop
A large village with thatched cottages and 18th-century houses, overlooking the River Yeo. It once belonged to the Bishops of Exeter. Easton Barton, half a mile to the south-west, is a good example of a late-medieval house; it was built *c.* 1500 and has been little altered since. There are fine views of Exmoor and Dartmoor from the church. A pleasant walk leads through woods to Beech Hill, 1 mile to the north-east.

North Molton
This small town is perched on a hill above the River Mole; the parish to which the town belongs is on the edge of Exmoor. The church has a fine medieval pulpit. Court Hall, built in 1553, was the seat of the Earls of Morley. The Tinners' Arms Inn recalls the neighbouring mines, now derelict. In R. D. Blackmore's novel *Lorna Doone* the ex-highwayman Tom Faggus is the blacksmith at North Molton.

Rose Ash
A high, remote village overlooking Exmoor. Ash trees abound, but 'Rose' is a corruption of Ralph, name of one of the de Esse family, who were granted the manor in 1221. The church was rebuilt in 1888, except for the tower; the interior has some fine Jacobean woodwork. Members of a single family, the Southcombs, were squires and rectors here from 1675 to 1948. Half a mile downhill from the church is a densely wooded combe beside a brook, crossed by the attractive Cuckoo Mill Bridge.

South Molton
A hilly market town, with a narrow island of shops in the High Street. West of the High Street is a broad road dominated by the 18th-century guildhall and the market house, built in 1863. A bust and plaque on the front of the guildhall commemorate Hugh Squier (1625–1710), a benefactor of South Molton, whose services to the town included the endowment of a grammar school in 1686. The intricate iron veranda above the shop at the western end of the central island is an eye-catching feature of this unusually attractive town centre.

The town has several fine Georgian houses, mainly in East Street. The 15th-century church overlooking the market place is set in an avenue of lime trees; it has a medieval stone pulpit and some handsome figure-carving in the nave and chancel. Almost every street in the town offers views across rolling hills, with Exmoor to the north-east.

Swimbridge
A village on the main road between Barnstaple and South Molton. Its name is said to be derived from Sawin of Birige, a priest in the time of Edward the Confessor. The church has a medieval spire and rich furnishings, including an elaborately ornamented font, a medieval stone pulpit and one of the finest screens in Devon.

Zeal Monachorum
This oddly named village is set in lonely country, 400 ft up, with a winding street of thatch-and-cob houses. Its name was formerly Sele Monacor, or the place among sallow, or willow, trees, belonging to the monks of Buckfast. A steep climb to the church at the top of the hill is worth making for the views of distant Dartmoor. There is also an enjoyable walk across the hills to the village of Loosebeare, 1 mile north.

THE PYRENEAN LILY Named after the range of mountains it first grew in, the lily now grows wild in the woods and hedgerows of north Devon. It blooms from the end of May to July before any other outdoor lily, and has 1–12 speckled greenish-yellow flowers, on a stem which grows up to 4 ft high and is covered with spear-shaped leaves. The fragrant flowers exude an unpleasant smell at close quarters

Around the South-West's ancient capital

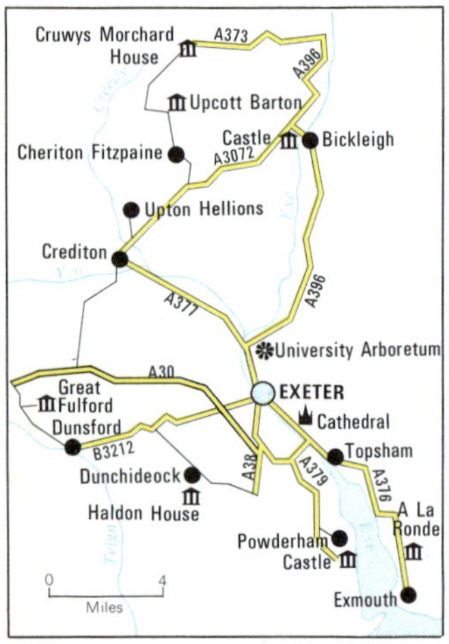

Events Devon County Show is held at Exeter in May, and Exeter Festival takes place in late May or early June. Exmouth Carnival and Exeter Air Day are in July.

Places to see *A la Ronde*, Exmouth: Easter to Sept., Mon. to Fri., Sat. morning and Sun. afternoon. *Exeter Maritime Museum*: daily. *Powderham Castle*: afternoons, mid-May to mid-Sept. *Rougemont House Museum*, Exeter: Tues. to Sat. *Royal Albert Memorial Museum and Art Gallery*, Exeter: Tues. to Sat. *Steam and Countryside Museum*, Exmouth: May to Oct., daily. *Underground Passages*, Exeter: Tues. to Sat. afternoons.

Information centre Tourist Office, Civic Centre, Paris Street, Exeter. Tel. Exeter 77888.

Exeter is the chief city of the South-West, and one of the most historic cities of Britain. Despite the severe damage it received in a single bombing raid in the Second World War, the city retains enough of its past to repay exploration. Its theatre, cinemas, shops and the bustle of a thriving modern city make an interesting contrast with the ancient cathedral and the secluded villages within walking distance of the city centre.

The present High Street was an ancient ridgeway when the Celtic people called the Dumnonii settled there between the second and third centuries BC. The site they chose was a dry plateau above the River Exe, at the lowest point at which it could readily be bridged, surrounded by grassy hills where their cattle could graze. These hills can be seen from the city's less built-up streets.

When the Romans came, in AD 50, they built walls round the city. The major portion of the walls can still be traced, and the best remains are those at Southernhay, Northernhay and Rougemont. The remains of one of the largest Roman bath houses found in Britain were excavated in the cathedral Yard.

The cathedral is Exeter's greatest glory. Its famous features include the two Norman towers, the magnificent west front covered with carved figures, the 59 ft high Bishop's Throne, the minstrels' gallery on the north side of the nave, and the astronomical clock in the north transept. Though designed on a grand scale, the cathedral is perhaps best remembered for its more intimate features: the detailed carving in wood and stone, and the numerous memorials to bishops and clergy.

Just opposite the cathedral, in the Close, is a building of obscure origin known as Mol's Coffee House, now an art shop. It has three floors, the first of which is fronted entirely by a huge double bay-window; above this is a painting of the coat of arms of Elizabeth I—a copy of the original carved version. Down towards the River Exe, opposite the Church of St Mary Steps in West Street, stands a group of 15th-century houses, including one which in 1961 was lifted intact and moved 50 yds from its original site.

During the Middle Ages, Exeter was the westernmost city in England, exerting a civilising influence throughout the South-West. The guildhall in the High Street is of medieval origin and is said to be the oldest municipal building still in use in England. Its distinctive architectural feature, dating from 1593, is the ornamental upper storey which rests on a row of granite columns. The 15th-century hall inside has a roof with gilded beams resting on bears holding staffs. The city's underground passages are worth a visit; they were dug in the 13th century to carry water from local springs. The passages can be entered in Princesshay.

An appealing aspect of Exeter is its nearness to water—the River Exe is only 5 minutes' walk from the High Street. Exeter was a flourishing port until 1282, when Isabel, Countess of Devon, built a weir across the river 3 miles downstream, which obstructed navigation. After three centuries of legal battles—during which time Exeter was served by the port of Topsham, 4 miles south-east— the weir was removed. But the river had become silted up by this time. A canal was dug in 1567, and extended in the 17th century. The Customs House was built on the Quay in 1681. This is a handsome two-storey brick building with a beautifully moulded plaster ceiling in the Long Room. Near by is the Exeter Maritime Museum, where visitors can inspect craft gathered from all over the world. The Quay itself is a quiet spot near a tree-shaded bend in the river, with the gracious Georgian Colleton Crescent flanking its east side.

COB COTTAGES IN DUNSFORD *Buildings made of cob (a mixture including clay and straw) last as long as a good roof and a solid plinth keep them dry. Damp makes them crumble—hence the old Devon saying: 'All cob wants is a good hat and a good pair of shoes'*

THE ORIGIN OF HIGH-BANKED LANES *High-banked Devon lanes may be a relic of Norman times, when Devon was made a royal forest and deer were protected as game for the king. To keep the deer off their crops, farmers banked or hedged-in their fields*

TWO SIDES OF EXETER *Though huge and imposing from a few yards away, Exeter Cathedral is almost hidden behind rows of tall shops and houses. Near by stands Mol's Coffee House (above), where Elizabethan sea-captains drinking by the galleon-style bay-windows on the first-floor could imagine themselves back on board ship*

The rapidly expanding University of Exeter has added a new dimension to the life of the city. Its impressive modern buildings are situated north of the city in 300 acres of beautiful grounds which used to be a private estate and are now open to the public. On the University campus are the Northcott Theatre, built in 1967, and an arboretum with 150 species of trees. Rougemont House Museum, in the lovely gardens in Northernhay, has a collection of items relating to local history, and old prints and paintings; much of interest is also contained in the Royal Albert Memorial Museum and Art Gallery in Queen Street.

The Exeter region as a whole contributes much to the popular idea of Devon. At Exmouth there are red cliffs, wide sandy beaches and blue sea; at Cheriton Fitzpaine, a landscape of windy, rolling hills; at Dunsford, thatched cottages and a wooded reach of river; and there is historic Exeter itself. Prehistoric remains are to be seen in the northern parts. The climate is mild, and drier than that of neighbouring Dartmoor. On the rich red earth of the region are farmed cattle and corn, and apples for the cider presses.

No other part of Devon has a greater variety of fine buildings—a cathedral, castles, abbeys, mansions, cottages, guildhalls and schools. Every type of holiday recreation is at hand—sightseeing, fishing, swimming and boating. But perhaps the greatest charm of the region lies off the holiday routes. A few minutes' walk from a busy main road will lead the visitor into the heart of quietness.

Bickleigh
A small, picturesque village under wooded hills beside the River Exe, with thatched, whitewashed cottages and rippling streams. Bickleigh Castle, dating from the 12th century, was reconstructed in the 17th century, but the sandstone gatehouse is medieval. Beyond the gatehouse, by the river, stands a Norman chapel. Following the Exe, between the road and Backs Wood, a 5-mile footpath leads to the town of Tiverton. (There is another Bickleigh in Devon, just outside Plymouth.)

Cheriton Fitzpaine
A village high in the hills, nestling among deep, winding lanes. There is a row of almshouses, built in 1594. Thatched cottages, built of typical Devon cob, cluster round the village church, which dates from the 15th century. The place has been changed to some extent by a new housing estate. Across the stream known as Holly Water a lane leads $1\frac{1}{4}$ miles north to Upcott Barton, a medieval house with Tudor and 17th-century alterations.

Crediton
A thriving market town on a main road. In Saxon times Crediton was a centre of Christianity and the See of a bishop. It has traditionally been regarded as the birthplace of St Boniface (AD 680–755), one of the first Christian preachers in northern Europe. The church, which was founded in Norman times, has the proportions of a cathedral. North of the town, a footpath beside the River Creedy leads to Upton Hellions.

Cruwys Morchard
A place which is ideal for solitary walks—a parish without a village, nearly 700 ft up, where the road runs through a beech wood. Holy Cross Church has a screen in classical Georgian style, considered to be the finest in Devon. Cruwys Morchard House stands near by; it is partly 16th century, with the west side rebuilt in 1732. The River Dart, a small tributary of the Exe, flows through the north of the parish.

OUT OF THE WOODS *No stretch of the River Teign is more beautiful than the wooded gorge that ends below Dunsford*

Dunchideock
A handful of cottages near a church, standing alone in a field. There is a medieval church house. The church, dating from the 14th century and much restored in the 19th century, is small and built of red sandstone. A few minutes' walk south is Haldon House, built in 1900. It is on the site of the 18th-century home of Sir Lawrence Palk, a governor of Madras. In 1788 Sir Lawrence built the tower called Haldon Belvedere (sometimes referred to as Lawrence Castle) on a hill near the house. The stairs are of marble brought from India. The tower, which is open to the public, offers wide views over a picturesque valley.

Dunsford
A charming village of thatch-roofed cob cottages, whose winding street climbs to a medieval church. Far below, the River Teign flows through a wooded gorge which is a noted beauty spot. Footpaths and a track follow the south bank of the river through Bridford Wood. Some 2 miles north-west of the village is Great Fulford, seat of the Fulford family since at least the 12th century. The present building, attractively set in a park with a lake, is mainly Tudor. In Dunsford Church stands a fine monument to Sir Thomas Fulford, erected in 1610.

Exmouth
The oldest seaside resort in Devon, renowned for its red cliffs and large bathing beaches. People from Exeter used it for bathing early in the 18th century, and it is from about that time that some of the town's finest buildings date. Worth seeing are the houses in the Beacon, a street where Lady Nelson lived. Exmouth offers the visitor good fishing, boating and golfing, as well as bathing. The town has a busy little harbour. Point in View is a picturesque group of almshouses with a chapel, built in 1811. The curious circular house A La Ronde, where the gallery and the staircase approaching it are decorated with thousands of sea shells, dates from 1798; it is open to the public in summer. A breezy cliff walk leads about 3 miles east to the resort of Budleigh Salterton.

Powderham
Here is one of Devon's most popular stately homes—Powderham Castle, principal seat and private residence of the Courtenays, Earls of Devon. The building is a blend of styles from the 14th to the 19th century. Its rooms are richly furnished, the fine picture collection includes portraits of the Courtenay family, and the park has deer.

Heart of the Devon Riviera

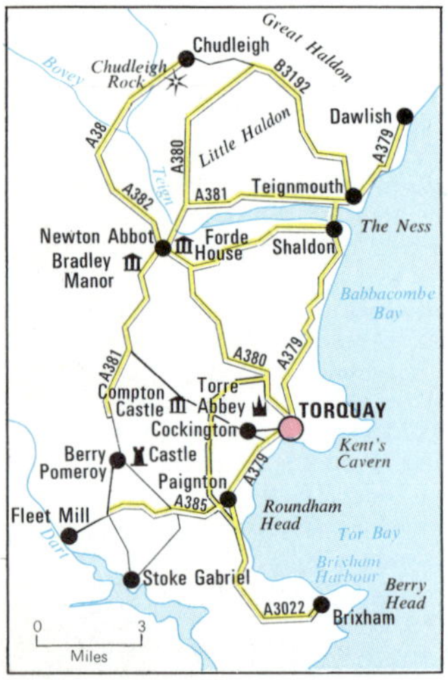

Angling Sea fishing at Teignmouth, Paignton, Torquay and Brixham (including shark fishing). Trout and salmon fishing in the upper reaches of the Rivers Teign and Dart.

Sailing At Paignton, Torquay and Brixham. Freshwater sailing on Decoy Lake at Newton Abbot.

Events Teignmouth Regatta, held in Aug., marks the start of Tor Bay fortnight, when each resort in turn has a regatta. There are carnivals at Dawlish and Teignmouth in Aug., and at Torquay and Paignton in June.

Places to see *Berry Pomeroy Castle*: daily. *Bradley Manor* (NT), Newton Abbot: Wed. afternoons, Apr. to Sept. *Brixham Aquarium* and trawling exhibition: daily, Whitsun to Oct. *Brixham Museum*: daily except Sun. mornings, mid-May to Sept.; Wed. and Sun. afternoons, Oct. and Apr. to mid-May. *Compton Castle* (NT), near Paignton, a 14th to 16th-century fortified manor house: Mon., Wed. and Thur., Apr. to Oct. *Kirkham House*, Paignton, built in the 15th century: weekdays and Sun. afternoons, Apr. to Sept. *Oldway Mansion*, Paignton, neo-classical, with Italian gardens: weekdays and Sun. afternoons in summer, Mon. to Fri. in winter. *Paignton Zoo*, Totnes Road: daily. *Torbay Aircraft Museum*: daily. *Torre Abbey*, Torquay: daily, except weekends in winter. *Torquay Natural History Museum*: weekdays.

Information centres Festival Hall, Esplanade Road, Paignton. Tel. Paignton 558383. Vaughan Parade, Torquay. Tel. Torquay 27248. The Den, Teignmouth. Tel. Teignmouth 6271 (seasonal). The Theatre, Brixham. Tel. Brixham 2861 (seasonal).

From Dawlish to Brixham the coast is noted for its colourful, luxuriant vegetation, its golden sands, the vivid blueness of sea and sky, and the continental atmosphere of its leading resorts, notably Torquay. Palm trees, luxury hotels with first-class cuisine, and bright-sailed yachts idling in the harbour or gliding over the sunlit waters of the bay show the resemblance to the Mediterranean. There are also extensive holiday camps and caravan parks, bed-and-breakfast establishments, typical English 'guest houses' and perhaps too much bungaloid growth for some tastes. No other part of Devon attracts so many summer visitors; no other part offers such variety of holiday attractions. The visitor can enjoy golfing, boating, fishing, miniature railways, underwater swimming and all the other usual seaside amenities.

When the coastal resorts seem too crowded and noisy, it is refreshing to escape into a countryside as deep and lush as any in the county; a farming land cultivated at least as far back as Celtic times, with few traces of urban industry. Here the earth is a vivid red, the air feels soft, even in winter, and the district is noted for its flower-growing farms.

The region as a whole has much of architectural interest: the ruins of a Norman castle at Berry Pomeroy, an abbey at Torquay, a charming cluster of cottages at Stoke Gabriel, Regency villas at Dawlish, and inland the typical thatched farmhouses of south Devon.

A SIDE-EFFECT OF WAR *Torquay's popularity as a resort dates from the 19th century, when the Napoleonic wars prevented many well-to-do people from taking their holidays on the Continent*

BERRY POMEROY CASTLE *The gatehouse dates from the 14th century, when the castle was built. It was burnt down in 1708*

HOME DURING THE ICE AGE *Prehistoric men and animals lived in Kent's Cavern, 1 mile east of Torquay, during the last Ice Age*

Berry Pomeroy
The village is named after the Pomeroys, a Norman family whose coat of arms is on the porch of the church. Near the church stand a medieval tithe barn and Berry House, dating in part from the 16th century. In a wooded valley, 1 mile north-east, are the romantically beautiful remains of Berry Pomeroy Castle. The towers date from the 14th century, when the castle was built by the Pomeroys. In the 16th century it was bought by the Seymour family, who spent a fortune building the living quarters around the courtyard.

Brixham
There are two parts to Brixham—the old village climbing a hill and the fishing harbour half a mile below. A stone on the quayside commemorates a key event in British history, the landing of William of Orange on November 5, 1688, which was the turning-point in the 'Glorious Revolution'. The pier was built in 1799–1804, and there are some early 19th-century houses round the harbour. Most of the town centre is early Victorian, recalling the time when the Brixham fishing fleet was the most prosperous in south Devon. There are several local caves which were inhabited from the Stone Age to Roman times, notably Windmill Hill cave, discovered in 1858 (open to the public). Henry Francis Lyte (1793–1847), poet and author, who wrote the hymn 'Abide With Me', was the first vicar of All Saints, the parish church of Lower Brixham.

Chudleigh
A small market town on the main Exeter–Plymouth road. It declined during the 19th century, losing much of its importance to nearby Newton Abbot. Chudleigh Rock, just south of the town,

TORRE ABBEY *The abbot's tower stands among the ruins of a 12th-century abbey*

BRIXHAM'S TRAWLERS *The fishermen who sailed from Brixham Harbour in the 18th century developed the art of trawling—dragging nets along the sea-bed—and this technique helped to make 19th-century Brixham the 'great fishery of the West'*

LURE FOR AN ARTIST *The harbour's beauty attracts artists to Brixham*

AT THE NETS *Mending the nets is part of every Brixham fisherman's routine*

JERSEY TIGER MOTH

August is the best month, and the countryside between Exeter and Teignmouth is the best place, to see this rare moth. These two colour variations occur

is a dramatic limestone outcrop containing prehistoric caves. In summer, local children carrying candles act as guides to the Pixies' Cave.

Dawlish
A pleasant town between the estuaries of the River Teign and the River Exe. Its architecture is partly Regency, partly Victorian. The town became a resort late in the 18th century. A picturesque feature is the Lawn, a landscape garden with a stream noted for its black and white swans. The Strand, a street created in the early 1800's, still keeps its elegant Regency character. Dawlish was a favourite of Jane Austen, and Dickens made it the birthplace of Nicholas Nickleby. The railway here—the main line to Penzance—is unusual in that it runs along the sea-front. Dawlish's bright red cliffs are well known, and to the north extend the broad beaches and sand dunes of Dawlish Warren.

Newton Abbot
This 'new town' is in fact seven centuries old. Part of it once belonged to Torre Abbey, from which came the 'Abbot' part of the name. First a market centre, then an important railway junction, Newton Abbot now relies on its usefulness as a tourist centre and on light industry. In the town centre stands the lone tower of St Leonard's Church; the rest of the building was demolished in 1836. The Courtenays, Earls of Devon, built Devon Square and the Italian-style Courtenay Park in the mid-19th century. The town's notable buildings include Forde House, built in 1610, and Bradley, a manor house built in 1419.

Paignton
A bustling seaside town, overlooking Tor Bay, with miles of caravan sites, holiday camps, hotels and guest houses. The resort has a zoo, children's playground, miniature railway and pier. The beaches are of shingle, gravel and sand. There are good views from Roundham Head, where there is a public garden. Paignton dates from Saxon times, when it was a small village half a mile from the sea.

Stoke Gabriel
A beautiful village built along a steep hill above a creek of the River Dart. New houses and bungalows have somewhat altered the character of the place. The medieval church with its Norman tower is reached by a cobbled walk beyond the local inn; the enormous yew tree propped up in the churchyard is believed to be about a thousand years old. A pleasant stroll through quiet farming land follows the lane towards Berry Pomeroy for about a mile. Then a track goes left to Fleet Mill, which stands beside a tributary of the Dart.

Teignmouth
One of Devon's oldest seaside resorts, with a long history as a fishing and ship-building centre. The town has many Georgian and early-Victorian buildings, including the Assembly Rooms, built in 1826, now a cinema. The golf course stands 800 ft above the sea, and there are good beaches, a pier and a fine esplanade by the Den, a 6-acre public garden. The 1700 ft long bridge across the estuary of the River Teign leads to the pretty village of Shaldon, where fine views can be seen from Ness Headland.

Torquay
The largest and most famous seaside resort in Devon. Its superb panoramic setting—high wooded hills overlooking the wide sweep of Tor Bay—its air of sophisticated yet friendly spaciousness, its luxurious hotels and stuccoed villas, the vivid colours of its sub-tropical trees and flowers make it the nearest thing to a French Riviera resort in Britain. It was created largely in the 19th century, and some parts of the town still preserve a distinctly Victorian character.

Torquay's attractions include theatres, a museum, art gallery, golf course and an underwater swimming club, as well as good beaches, such as Babbacombe to the north, cliff walks, parks and yachting. Cockington village is a well-known local showplace. Torquay has become an all-the-year-round resort because of its very mild climate.

Just east of Cockington are the ruins of 12th-century Torre Abbey and the nearby Chapel of St Michael, of unknown date. On the edge of the town, about 1 mile east of the harbour, is the famous Kent's Cavern, one of the oldest known human dwelling-places in Britain. It was occupied during the last Ice Age. Among the exhibits in the cave is the skull of a sabre-toothed tiger, and Torquay Museum contains other important finds from the site.

From white cliffs to red

Angling Sea fishing at Seaton and Sidmouth. Boats can be hired from the beach at Sidmouth. The best time for fishing at Seaton is between Sept. and Nov. for bass. Sidmouth Bay is best in spring and summer. Trout fishing on stretches of the Rivers Exe, Otter and Sid. Coarse fishing on the Exeter Canal.

Sailing In Sidmouth Bay and at Beer.

Other sports The annual Inter-County Tennis Championships are played at Budleigh Salterton. There are facilities for water skiing at Sidmouth. Speed hill-climbs are held at Wiscombe Park, Sidmouth.

Events The International Folklore Festival, Sidmouth, is held annually during the first week in Aug. Displays are given twice daily. The Honiton Glove Fair is at the end of July. Beer regatta is held in Aug.

Places to see *Bicton*, with woodland railway and countryside museum, East Budleigh: Easter to Oct., daily. *Cadhay*, Ottery St Mary: Wed. and Thur. afternoons, mid-July to Aug. *Farway Countryside Park*, 5 miles east of Ottery St Mary: daily, Easter to early Oct. *Fernwood* (NGS), Ottery St Mary: garden daily, Apr. to Sept. *Honiton and All Hallows Public Museum*, High Street, Honiton: weekdays, May to Sept. Killerton (NT), 6 miles south-west of Cullompton: Apr. to Oct., daily. *Knightshayes Court* (NT), near Tiverton: afternoons, Apr. to Oct. *Sidmouth Museum*, Hope Cottage, Sidmouth: weekdays and Sun. afternoon, Easter to mid-Oct.

Information centres (seasonal) Fore Street, Budleigh Salterton. Tel. Budleigh Salterton 5275. The Esplanade, Sidmouth. Tel. Sidmouth 6441.

Some of the most fertile grassland in Britain lies in east Devon; the cattle which graze on the meadows by the River Axe produce milk from which comes much of Devonshire's famous cream. Resorts such as Sidmouth attract holidaymakers in search of quieter pleasures than those found along the Devon 'Riviera', further west. The Rivers Otter and Sid are popular with anglers; and lovers of nature, especially bird-watchers, find abundant reward in exploring the unspoilt stretches of country along these waters.

East Devon is a region of contrasts: Beer Head, with its white cliffs, is the westernmost chalk headland along the Channel coast; not far south-west are the vivid red cliffs of Budleigh Salterton. In the north of the region the climate is brisk, but on the southern part of the coast it is mild enough for palm trees to be a common sight.

The traditional prosperity of the region was not based on agriculture alone. Tiverton and Cullompton were centres of the wool industry between the 15th and 18th centuries, and their handsome churches were endowed by rich local merchants. Honiton's Georgian houses recall its prosperity as a centre for the making of gloves and lace; Axminster's carpets were famous as long ago as the 18th century.

This quiet and largely rural corner of England has a surprising number of associations with great men. Sir Walter Raleigh was born near East Budleigh; the first Duke of Marlborough, ancestor of Sir Winston Churchill, near Axminster; the poet Samuel Taylor Coleridge at Ottery St Mary; and the Drake family were landowners in the region.

WHERE WALKERS NEED A HEAD FOR HEIGHTS *The 3-mile cliff walk from Branscombe to Beer offers sweeping views of the bay. The view is good, too, from the Beer Head caravan site*

Axminster
A small town on the River Axe, where the famous carpets are made. In 1755 a factory began to make the first carpets, but it went bankrupt in 1835 and its machinery was sold to a weaver at Wilton, in Wiltshire, now equally famous for its carpets. A new carpet factory was opened at Axminster in 1937, and visitors can see over it by appointment.

St Michael's Church at Musbury, 2½ miles south, contains an impressive monument to the Drake family.

MAKING LACE

Hand-made lace is still produced in Honiton. As many as 400 bobbins may be used to weave one intricate pattern

CREAM TEA

Devonshire cream is skimmed from milk which has stood overnight. It is then gently heated for several hours

Axmouth
An unspoilt little village; a cluster of cottages and farmhouses on the beautiful estuary of the Axe. To the east of the village, along the coast almost to Lyme Regis in Dorset, is the famous Dowlands Landslip, a section of cliff which collapsed on Christmas Day, 1839; 800 million tons of cliff are estimated to have fallen, leaving a gash 6 miles long.

Bampton
A market town on the River Batherm, with a graceful street of Georgian houses. There is an annual fair of sheep, cattle and Exmoor ponies in the last week of October. In the churchyard two handsome yew trees, about 500 years old, are encircled by stone seats. Chain Bridge, over the River Exe, 1½ miles south-west, is a charming old iron bridge.

Beer
A pleasant fishing village, in a small bay, once notorious for smugglers. A splendid cliff walk leads to Branscombe Mouth.

Beer Head, 426 ft high, has the westernmost chalk cliffs on the Channel coast. The Old Quarry, a mile west of the village, goes back to Roman times and was used until late in the 19th century; it provided white stone for many famous buildings, including Exeter Cathedral.

Branscombe
A village of unusual character and beauty. Houses of cob and thatch are sited irregularly on the steep wooded slopes of a combe, which widens out towards the sea. The attractive church has a Norman tower and nave, and 13th century transepts. In the north aisle is a monument to Joan Tregarthin and her two husbands; one of her children, Nicholas Wadham, founded Oxford University's Wadham College.

Budleigh Salterton
A quietly fashionable resort with red cliffs, a pebble beach and a fine sea view over Lyme Bay from West Down Beacon. The sea wall at Budleigh Salterton is the setting of the famous painting *The Boyhood of Raleigh* by the Victorian artist Sir John Millais.

Colyton
A small town full of narrow streets, with a history dating back to around AD 700. There are a number of fine Georgian houses, and the handsome church, largely rebuilt in the 15th century, has a tower crowned by an octagonal lantern. Inside the church are some of the finest monuments in Devon. The network of narrow, winding lanes linking the farms of Colyton parish makes the area ideal walking country.

Cullompton
A market town on a slope above the River Culm, noted for apple orchards which supply the local cider industry. Much of the town was burnt down in 1839; later Victorian additions blend with the few Georgian houses which survived the fire. The Manor House Hotel and Walronds House date from the early 17th century. The large and imposing parish church is noted for its splendid roof, well-preserved screen and large west tower. From Knowle Hill, 1 mile west of the village, there are good views to Exmoor, Dartmoor, the Blackdown Hills and Sidmouth Gap.

East Budleigh
A village just north of Budleigh Salterton. Thatched cottages climb a steep hill and footbridges cross a brook to houses lower down. The church has a great variety of carved bench-ends, and a memorial to the Raleigh family. Sir Walter Raleigh (1552–1618) was born at Hayes Barton, a beautiful Tudor building which is now a farmhouse 1 mile to the west.

The gardens at Bicton, 1 mile north, were designed by André Le Nôtre, who planned the gardens at Versailles. A narrow-gauge railway runs through the grounds, which include a pine wood.

SHELTERED BY THE CLIFFS *Gigantic red-sandstone cliffs, rising in places to over 500 ft, tower over Sidmouth's small fishing fleet. The fleet has to sail from the beach, for since Elizabethan times a long ridge of shingle has blocked the entrance to the Sid Estuary*

BRIDGE OVER THE EXE *In Tiverton, bridges replaced the two fords from which came the town's originial name of Twifyrde-tun*

SEATON BAY *The mile-long shingle beach at Seaton sweeps from high cliffs in the west to the mouth of the Axe in the east*

Honiton
The town's main street is chiefly late Georgian, the earlier town having been largely destroyed by fires in 1747 and 1765. The bypass, opened in 1966, has relieved Honiton of its once notorious traffic jams. The town has long been famous for its lace, produced since Elizabethan times; Queen Victoria's wedding veil was made of Honiton lace. The ancient glove industry is also well known, and Honiton still holds an annual fair in July which began in 1257.

The countryside around Honiton is ideal for walking. Within easy reach are Hembury Fort, the finest Iron Age hill-fort in Devon, which commands a magnificent view of the Devon countryside; the pleasant villages of Gittisham and Combe Raleigh; and St Cyres' Hill, with fine views of the Otter Valley.

Ottery St Mary
A town situated in beautiful farming country. It has an impressively large 14th-century collegiate church, modelled on Exeter Cathedral. The poet Samuel Taylor Coleridge (1772–1834) was born in the vicarage. About 1 mile north-west is Cadhay, a fine Tudor house built by a successful Devon lawyer.

Sidmouth
An unusually attractive seaside resort, full of Regency and early Victorian buildings. Much of the town has a quiet, residential character. The Duke and Duchess of Kent stayed there in 1819 with their infant daughter, later to be Queen Victoria, at Woolbrook Cottage, now the Royal Glen Hotel. Just east of the town a short path with fine views climbs Salcombe Hill Cliff.

Tiverton
Modern industry has encircled and partly dominated this town. Having declined as a wool centre, Tiverton revived during the 19th century after spinning looms had been established in the town by the Heathcoat family in 1816. There are remains of a 14th-century castle, which was once owned by the Courtenays, the Earls of Devon. The town's buildings include a spacious 15th-century church; the Waldron Almshouses and Greenway's Almshouses, both 16th century; and the famous Blundell's School, founded in 1604 by a rich local wool merchant. John Greenway, founder of the almshouses, added the richly carved south porch to St Peter's Church, in which can be seen representations of the ships that helped to make Tiverton prosperous.

The varied world of Exmoor

Angling Sea fishing at Lynmouth, Porlock Weir and Minehead. Freshwater fishing on Exmoor streams, on the River Exe at Exford and Dulverton and on the Lyn at Lynmouth, noted for its salmon.

Riding Exmoor has been called 'the riding playground of England', and horses or ponies can be hired from stables throughout the area.

Walks and nature trails There are 'way-marked' walks across Exmoor from Dunster, Minehead and Porlock. A coastal footpath runs between Minehead and Combe Martin, west of Lynton. Two-mile trail at Heddon Valley, Parracombe, south-west of Lynton: all year.

Events Minehead has a Hobby Horse Fair in May, an arts festival and a gala week in July, and a flower show in Aug. The Dunster Show and Brendon Show are in Aug.; horse trials at Dunster in Sept., and a pony fair at Brendon in Oct. The Lyn Festival, with morris dancing, is held at Lynton in May.

Places to see *Dunster Castle* (NT): mid-Apr. to Sept., daily except Fri. and Sat.; Oct., Tues., Wed., and Sun. afternoons. *Lyn and Exmoor Museum*, Lynton: Mon. to Fri., and Sun. afternoon, Apr. to Sept. *Watersmeet Cottage* (NT), 1½ miles east of Lynmouth: daily, Apr. to Oct.

Information centres Information Bureau, Market House, Minehead. Tel. Minehead 2624. Exmoor National Park Information Centre, The Parade, Minehead. Tel. Minehead 2984.

The boundaries of Exmoor have been altered many times since it became a royal forest a thousand years ago. Today the Exmoor National Park covers 265 square miles, from Combe Martin in Devon to Raleigh's Cross in Somerset. The region includes three types of landscape: coastal, pastoral moorland and heathland. From Minehead to Combe Martin a traditional seamanship is maintained by fishermen, pilots and lighthousemen. The pastoral moor is rich grazing country; the heathland is the home of red deer, grouse, ponies and sheep, the country of R. D. Blackmore's novel *Lorna Doone*.

Bronze Age people left their mark here, as at the burial site known as Chapman Barrows; and on Winsford Hill the Romans left an inscribed stone. But early settlers did not tame the moor. Not until the 19th century did John Knight, a Midlands industrialist, and his son Frederic, who between them put in some 60 years' work on the moor from their home at Simonsbath, just make a success of farming it.

Exmoor's many attractive villages include Parracombe, with its stone cottages, and Dunster, famous for its castle and medieval timbered houses. A road of formidable steepness follows the coast from Porlock to Lynmouth, and inland are many remote lanes—through Horner Woods, for example, or up to Trentishoe. But this is essentially a land for walkers and horsemen. They alone can reach the windswept Chains Barrows, or Dunkery Beacon, the highest hill, 1705 ft above the Bristol Channel with views of the Welsh mountains. On the summits the climate is brusque, but the valleys are mild and sheltered.

Smaller than Dartmoor, less bleak, more intimate, Exmoor combines the softness of Luccombe's pastures, the ruggedness of Brendon Common, and the grandeur of the cliffs above Heddon's Mouth. The heart of the moor—protected by the establishment of the National Park and by its own stern contours—remains little disturbed by modern life.

VIEW ACROSS EXMOOR *The wild expanse of Brendon Common sweeps south to the horizon from the valley of the East Lyn*

DUNSTER'S MARKET *The eight-sided Yarn Market is a reminder that Dunster once owed its prosperity to cloth-makers*

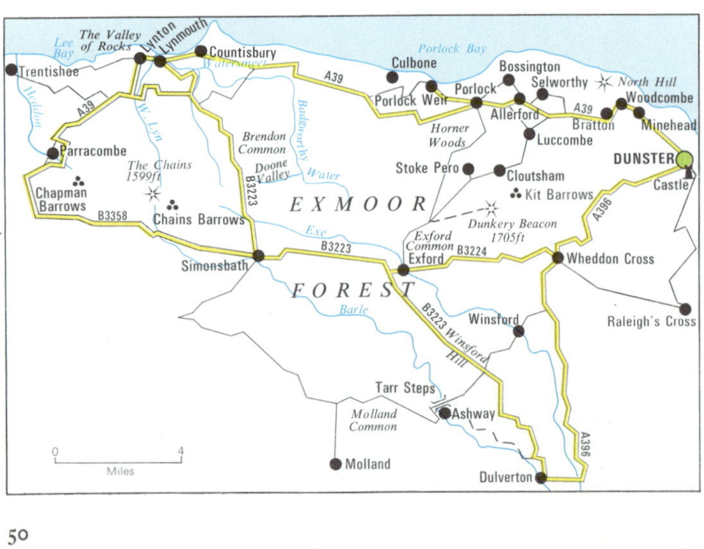

Brendon
One of Exmoor's showpiece villages, thatched and whitewashed, in a combe of overhanging woods, with a medieval packhorse bridge across the East Lyn River. A path leads south to Brendon Common and Hoccombe Coombe. The entrance to Hoccombe Coombe on the west bank of Badgworthy Water, is called Doone Valley because of its resemblance to the hideout described in Blackmore's novel. There is a memorial to Blackmore beside Badgworthy Water.

Culbone
This place is not accessible by car. The best approach is by a 2-mile footpath from Porlock Weir. The hills close in, the trees thicken, and suddenly the visitor is at the village with a small house, a small cottage and the smallest church in England in regular use.

Dulverton
Woods ring the horizon; the Rivers Barle and Exe flow near by. The market-place makes a friendly shopping centre. A track leads north-west to Ashway, birthplace of Sir George Williams, founder of the YMCA.

Dunster
Perhaps the most beautiful village on Exmoor, with a wide main street of old-world houses and the 17th-century Yarn Market. One end of the street is dominated by the tower on Conygar Hill, built in 1775, a landmark for shipping; at the other end stands the castle. Built by the Normans and enlarged down the centuries, Dunster Castle has been owned by only two families in a thousand years—the Mohuns and the Luttrells. Its gatehouse was built in 1421 by Sir Hugh Luttrell,

THE SMALLEST CHURCH IN ENGLAND *Culbone Church, just 12 ft wide, stands in woods where a colony of lepers lived in the early Middle Ages. The lepers followed services through a window*

MINEHEAD HOBBY-HORSE *On May Day morning, a colourful hobby-horse dances through Minehead. The custom is probably a survival of ancient fertility rites celebrating the coming of spring*

AN EXMOOR MYSTERY *No one knows when the Tarr Steps were built across the Barle, but they may be prehistoric*

LYNMOUTH AND LYNTON *Lynmouth's position between steep wooded hills and the sea enchanted the poet Shelley, who stayed there in 1812. It also checked the town's growth, and Lynton, crowning the dome-like cliff to the west of it, grew instead*

before the silting of the river destroyed Dunster's importance as a harbour. The church, once both Benedictine priory and parish church, is the largest and finest on Exmoor. It dates mainly from the 15th century, and has a magnificent rood-screen. The nearby Luttrell Arms Hotel is said to have been a residence of the medieval Abbots of Cleeve.

Exford

The stone bridge in the centre of the village is now used instead of the ancient ford that gave the place its name. Exford is a noted centre for stag-hunting and fishing, and an annual horse show is held on the second Wednesday in August. A footpath, about 5 miles long, leads north to Exford Common and so to Dunkery Beacon, the highest point of Exmoor (1705 ft).

Lynmouth

The town's picturesque small harbour and promenade are flanked by thatched houses and a narrow shopping street. In 1952 Lynmouth was struck by a torrential flood, following a freak storm over Exmoor, one of the most violent ever recorded in Britain. Nearly 100 houses and 28 bridges were destroyed or damaged, and 31 lives were lost.

From Lynmouth Harbour a steep road climbs more than 1000 ft to Countisbury. About $\frac{1}{4}$ mile below the Blue Ball Inn at Countisbury, a footpath on the right leads through wooded combes to beautiful Watersmeet Valley.

Lynton

Perched astride a dome-like cliff, Lynton is an endearing Victorian creation. Its small museum contains many interesting Exmoor curios. A cliff railway, opened in 1890, avoids the steep road down to Lynmouth. A $1\frac{1}{2}$-mile walk westwards leads to The Valley of Rocks, with its majestic skyline, beyond which a toll road continues to Lee Bay and Lee Abbey, a mock-Gothic Victorian mansion used as a Church of England centre for study courses and holidays.

Minehead

The most westerly town in Somerset, and also one of its most popular seaside resorts. Situated around a wide, curving bay in the mouth of the Bristol Channel, it is a place for enjoyable bathing—although there is a long walk to the sea at low tide. It also has a children's bathing pool on the sands and a well-equipped modern swimming pool. Another attraction is the Model Village, encircled by a miniature railway. Minehead has a cheerful, noisy atmosphere, in contrast with the stillness of nearby Exmoor. The oldest part of the town, known as Quay Town, rises to the slopes of North Hill, at the western end of the bay. Quay Town's harbour, dating back to 1616, is used by steamers making pleasure trips along the coast to Lynmouth and Ilfracombe.

North Hill, a little to the west of Minehead, offers a choice between the prehistoric mounds scattered about its crest and the charming hamlets of Woodcombe, Bratton, Selworthy, Allerford and Bossington, deep in the valleys on the landward side.

Molland

The hills all around are green, wooded and—in the distance—purpled by summer heather. The London Inn, thatched and cool, has a miniature zoo in its garden. The church, with its timbered roof, box pews, and three-decker pulpit, is noted for its unusually well-preserved Georgian interior.

Simonsbath

A village in an attractive setting on the Barle. A footpath opposite the inn follows the river into the heart of the moor. Across the bridge, a road climbs past the memorial to Sir John Fortescue (1859–1933), historian and librarian at Windsor Castle. On The Chains, 3 miles to the north-west, is the second-highest point (1599 ft) on Exmoor; a further $2\frac{1}{4}$ miles north-west are the prehistoric remains called Chapman Barrows.

Stoke Pero

A tiny hamlet with Exmoor's highest church, overlooking the Bristol Channel and the Quantock Hills. A 2-mile footpath through Cloutsham reaches Dunkery Beacon, passing Kit Barrows, a prehistoric burial site. From Dunkery are fine views as far as Bodmin Moor, the Blackdown Hills, and the Black Mountains of Wales. Cars can be driven to within $\frac{1}{4}$ mile of Dunkery Beacon on the minor road between Porlock and Wheddon Cross, while a 5-mile walk leads from Exford to Dunkery.

Winsford

A delightful village on the River Exe, with a hilltop church and a picturesque thatched inn. A lane leads 3 miles south-west to Tarr Steps, a stone clapper bridge across the River Barle. In the freak storm of 1952, the water ran so strongly that the ancient bridge was washed away and had to be rebuilt.

The Quantocks of Wordsworth and Coleridge

Angling Coarse and trout fishing on the River Tone at Taunton, Wellington and Wiveliscombe (on the A361 about 9 miles west of Taunton). Other good waters include the Taunton–Bridgwater Canal, the West Sedgemoor Drain and Clatworthy Reservoir.

Nature trails Quantock Forest Trail, 3 miles long, starts from Seven Wells Bridge, about 2 miles south-west of Nether Stowey: all year. The Neroche Trail, about 2 miles long, starts from Castle Neroche, 6 miles south of Taunton.

Events There are flower shows in Taunton in spring, early Aug. and autumn, and a carnival in Oct. Watchet has a flower show in Aug.

Places to see *Cleeve Abbey*, near Watchet: daily, except Sun. mornings Oct. to Mar. *Coleridge Cottage* (NT), Nether Stowey: afternoons, except Fri. and Sat., Apr. to Sept. *Gaulden Manor*, Tolland: May to Sept., Thur. and Sun. afternoons and Bank Hol. *Sheppy's Farm*, near Wellington, one of the few small farms still making and selling its own cider: daily. *Taunton Castle*, housing *County Museum* and *Somerset Light Infantry Museum*: weekdays, except Mon. Oct. to Mar. *Widcombe Bird Gardens*, Culmhead, 6½ miles south of Taunton: daily.

Information centre The Library, Corporation Street, Taunton. Tel. Taunton 84077.

The rolling, wooded Quantock Hills, home of the red deer, are to many people the most beautiful part of Somerset. The whole range, including foothills, extends only about 12 miles by 6. Unlike the gaunt Mendips, with their limestone gorges and underground streams, the Quantocks have gentle slopes fringed by small villages, pastures, heather-covered moorland and dark tangled woods, loud with running brooks and dense with flowers.

There are no towns or large villages among the inner hills; this is a realm of hamlets and scattered farms, reached by narrow lanes, churned into rivers of red earth after heavy rain. Churches, manor houses and cottages are chiefly of red sandstone, which contrasts pleasantly with the green of the surrounding pastures.

The best vantage-point from which to see the county is the crest of the Quantocks. The view takes in the point where the Severn Estuary meets the sea; eastwards it includes the Mendips and the low heartlands of Somerset, where the fens are crossed by drainage ditches, known locally as rhines; westward lies the magnetic horizon of Exmoor.

The Quantocks provided a home and an inspiration for the poet Samuel Taylor Coleridge, who settled at Nether Stowey with his wife and baby in 1796. During his stay there, which lasted less than two years, Coleridge wrote 'The Ancient Mariner', 'Kubla Khan', and the first part of 'Christabel'. Wordsworth and his sister also spent some time in the Quantocks, and accompanied Coleridge on many walks.

Because Taunton and Bridgwater are so near, any fine weekend sees the lanes filled with cars; but on weekdays it is possible to walk for miles with only the occasional tractor to recall the 20th century.

PAYING WITH THEIR LIVES *Judge Jeffreys hanged two of Monmouth's followers in the gateway to Cothelstone Manor after the duke's defeat at Sedgemoor in 1685. Earlier, during the Civil War, the manor was besieged, and its owner Sir John Stawell spent 14 years in prison. Both the manor and the gatehouse can be viewed by appointment*

Aisholt
A typical village of the Quantocks, with a small church and a few sandstone cottages midway up a wooded combe. From the top of the churchyard there is a fine view across the trees to Will's Neck (1261 ft), the highest point of the Quantocks. The poet Sir Henry Newbolt (1862–1938), whose best-known poem is 'Drake's Drum', lived at Aisholt; Samuel Taylor Coleridge had hoped to do so, but feared that his wife would find it too lonely. An attractive addition to the landscape is the new Hawkridge Reservoir, just outside the village.

Broomfield
Beech trees line the lane through the village; below, the Vale of Taunton Deane glows red and green throughout the year. All Saints Church is delightfully situated amid a cluster of trees. The village was the birthplace of Andrew Crosse (1784–1855), who pioneered experiments with electricity. The prehistoric Ruborough Camp, 1 mile to the north, was used by the Romans as a fort; the site is overgrown by trees.

Combe Florey
A beautiful sandstone village in the foothills. The manor house, chiefly 18th century but with a gateway built in 1593, was the home of novelist Evelyn Waugh. Another distinguished resident was Sydney Smith, described in his day as 'the wittiest man in England', who served as vicar (1829–45) and described country life as 'a kind of healthy grave'. At Cothelstone, 2 miles to the east, there is a fine Jacobean manor house.

Cothay
The manor house here (not open to the public) is one of the finest 15th-century country houses in England—gabled and buttressed, with mullioned windows and roughcast walls, approached by a formidable gatehouse, now converted into a chapel, and surrounded by splendid gardens.

Crowcombe
The best approach is by a steep lane from Nether Stowey which crosses a heath with, on the right, a view of the sea and the Welsh hills beyond. Then a steep hill (1 in 4) leads down to the village. The village church has handsomely carved Tudor bench-ends symbolising fertility—one of which depicts two men struggling with a dragon. Opposite the church is the Church House, partly Tudor, used as a school and almshouse until the 19th century. Crowcombe Court is early Georgian. On the lane leading to Stogumber stands an ancient tree, Heddon Oak, famed for its wide-spreading branches.

East Quantoxhead
A mile of lane from the Minehead road leads to this idyllic corner of Somerset—a cluster of cottages by a duck pond. Beyond the pond is the Court House, built of local stone and unaltered since

POETS' COUNTRYSIDE *In 1797 the poet William Wordsworth and his sister Dorothy came to live in the Quantocks, at Alfoxton House (left). Close by, at Nether Stowey, lived Coleridge. A portrait of the poet now hangs outside the cottage (above) where he wrote 'The Ancient Mariner'. The two poets and Dorothy enjoyed roaming the hills together, and the walk (below) leading through the woods was one of Wordsworth's favourites*

the east front was added in 1610. It is a seat of the Luttrell family, owners of Dunster Castle, who have lived in the district for 800 years.

Holford

A lane past the tiny church leads to Alfoxton House (now a hotel), which the poet William Wordsworth and his sister Dorothy rented in 1797. With Samuel Taylor Coleridge, they roamed the Quantocks, enjoying the incomparable countryside for a brief spell that produced some of Wordsworth's finest poetry—*Lyrical Ballads*, by Wordsworth and Coleridge, was published in 1798. Leaving Alfoxton House on the right, a track leads past some cottages to Holford Combe and a stream; a footpath then leads up through woods to the roof of the Quantocks. This was a favourite walk of Wordsworth's—'Upon smooth Quantock's airy ridge we roved'.

Nether Stowey

Bypassed in 1969 by a new main road, the village has returned to its former calm. For two years Coleridge lived here in a cottage now owned by the National Trust; the poems he wrote in it include 'The Ancient Mariner' and 'Kubla Khan'. Adjoining the local church is Stowey Court, a manor house dating in part from the 15th century, with a fine 18th-century gazebo (garden house). A stream flows down beside the road from the circular mound of a ruined castle, and the houses stand behind little bridges over the stream. Dodington Manor House, 2 miles to the north-west, dates from 1581. Above the village is Danesborough Camp, an oval high-banked prehistoric earthwork.

Stogursey

Formerly called Stoke Courcy, the *stoc* (estate) of William de Courci, a Norman knight. The only surviving part of the Benedictine priory that once stood here is the church, now the parish church of St Andrew, which contains some fine Norman work. Near the village stand the ivy-clad remains of a castle destroyed during the Wars of the Roses.

Taunton

The county town of Somerset; a lively commercial centre, but with much of interest for the tourist. It lies in the Vale of Taunton Deane, on the River Tone. The restored Norman castle (open to the public) is the grandest of the town's public buildings; it contains a museum, and its great hall, on the far side of the courtyard, was a scene of Judge Jeffreys's Bloody Assizes, in which vengeance was wreaked upon the Duke of Monmouth's followers after his defeat in 1685 at the Battle of Sedgemoor. Most of the rebels were deported to the West Indies; hundreds of others were hanged. The parish church, St Mary's, and the nearby Church of St James, are noted for their splendid towers (rebuilt in the 19th century). Other buildings include Gray's Almshouses (1635) in East Street; the old grammar school (15th and 16th centuries) which now forms part of the Municipal Buildings in Corporation Street; the Octagon Chapel in Middle Street, opened by Wesley in 1776; and a well-preserved medieval leper hospital marooned amid the traffic in Hamilton Road. On the outskirts of the town, Wilton has an attractive small church and Wilton House, the birthplace of Alexander Kinglake, author of *Eothen*, the famous Victorian book about travel in the East.

Watchet

For centuries this small harbour served the regions of Exmoor and the Quantocks. Coleridge chose it as the port of embarkation for his Ancient Mariner: 'Here', he told Wordsworth, 'is where he shall set out on his fateful voyage.' The harbour's importance declined in the 19th century, but it is still used by more than 100 ships a year; most of them bring wood and wood pulp from the Baltic and wine from Spain and Portugal, and export scrap metal and waste paper.

The town is also a quiet seaside resort, with fine cliffs to the west and a sandy beach. To the south-west are the remains of 12th-century Cleeve Abbey, with its fine refectory and gatehouse. On the road to Williton is the 13th-century parish church dedicated to St Decuman, who was said to have presided at the marriage of King Arthur.

Wellington

An attractive residential town, with some fine Georgian houses. It is noted for its ancient wool industry, which is still flourishing; cloths are exported from Wellington to places all over the world. The Squirrel Inn is nearly 400 years old and is now being converted for residential use; and The Three Cups in Mantle Street was first recorded in 1694. South of the town, on the highest point of the Blackdown Hills, an obelisk commemorates the Duke of Wellington, victor of Waterloo, who took his title from the town.

A resort in quiet country

Angling Sea fishing at Weston-super-Mare, either from the shore or from boats. Trout fishing on Chew Valley Lake, Blagdon Lake, Chew Magna and Barrow Gurney reservoirs.

Sailing At Pebble Beach, Clevedon, and at Weston-super-Mare.

Riding Over the downs at East Clevedon and on the sands at Weston-super-Mare. There are stables at both resorts.

Cricket A County Cricket Festival is held in early Aug. at Clarence Park, Weston-super-Mare.

Hockey An Easter Hockey Festival is held annually at Weston-super-Mare.

Steamer trips Trips from Weston-super-Mare to South Wales, North Devon and along the Bristol Channel.

Bowling The Clevedon Bowling Tournament, held in Aug., and Weston-super-Mare open tournaments in June and Aug., attract bowlers from all over the country.

Events Clevedon has a regatta and carnival in June, and a horse show and horticultural show in Aug. In Weston-super-Mare, there is power-boat racing in May, June, July, Aug. and Sept.; a carnival in July; a veteran car rally in June; and an Autumn Carnival in Nov. Motor speed trials are held there in Oct.

Places to see *Clevedon Court* (NT): Wed., Thur., Sun., and Bank Hol. afternoons, Apr. to Sept. *Museum and Art Gallery*, Burlington Street, Weston-super-Mare: weekdays.

Information centre Information Centre, Beach Lawns, Weston-super-Mare. Tel. Weston-super-Mare 26838.

This area contains some of the least-visited countryside in the south-west of England, as well as a seaside town which is a major holiday centre. Weston-super-Mare has all the advantages of a large sandy bay and a mild but bracing climate. The region inland is full of unspoilt hamlets and villages, and the secluded character of the countryside compensates for its lack of dramatic scenery or famous beauty spots.

The region is relatively flat, seldom more than 400 ft above sea level, but the landscape is undulating and not monotonous, and its highest points command fine views of the Welsh hills.

The villages and small towns are watered by many rivers and streams—the Yeo, Kenn, Oldbridge, Banwell and Chew—and there are lake-like reservoirs at Chew Stoke and Blagdon. The region does not figure much in the political history of England. It was, and it remains, a land of farmers and fishermen. But there are some fine historic houses—Churchill Court, the seat of Sir Winston's ancestors, and romantically beautiful Clevedon Court, built in the 14th century. The philosopher John Locke was born at Wrington, and much of Thackeray's *Vanity Fair* was written at Clevedon.

In the end, however, the visitor comes back to the quiet charm of the Severn Estuary and of the countryside inland—to such pleasures as the way through the woods at Bourton Combe (near Flax Bourton), the coastal lane from Weston-super-Mare to Kewstoke, or the footpath to Wrington Hill.

ISLE OF REFUGE *According to tradition, King Harold's mother Githa fled with the wives of other Saxon nobles to Steep Holme, this hump-backed island 5 miles out from Weston-super-Mare, after Harold's defeat and death at the Battle of Hastings. The Celtic historian Gildas went there in the 6th century in search of peace, but was disturbed by pirates*

Abbots Leigh
The village was once the property of the Abbey of St Augustine in Bristol. It is set deep in the shelter of Leigh Woods, with a track leading past Leigh Court to the banks of the River Avon. From Nightingale Valley there is a good view of the spectacular Clifton Suspension Bridge. Leigh Court, where Charles II sheltered from his enemies, was rebuilt in 1814 in classical Greek style.

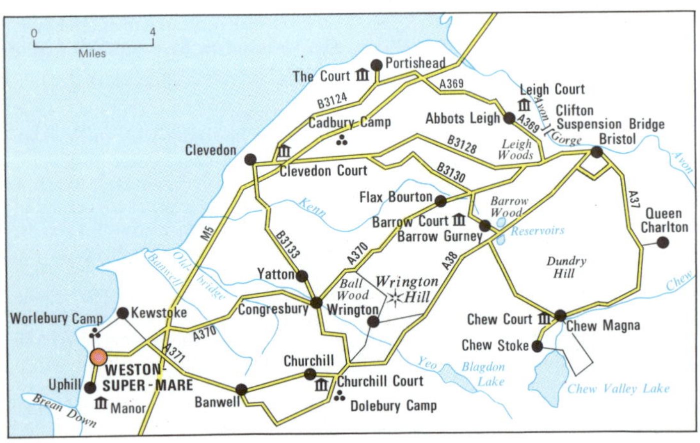

Banwell
This village was named after a millpond or well—no longer to be seen—that was said to possess healing properties. The church is among the finest in the region; it has some 15th-century Flemish stained glass, brought from Belgium in 1855. In 1824 a villager discovered Banwell Cave, in which have been found the bones of several wild animals, including a prehistoric cave lion. These are now in the County Museum, Taunton.

Banwell Court, also called The Abbey, was built by Bishop Bekynton of Wells in the 15th century, but has been much altered since; Banwell Castle, ¼ mile south-east of the village, is a Victorian folly. Both are privately owned. A village curio is an 18th-century fire-fighting pump, with two poles for pulling down burning thatch.

Barrow Gurney
Flanked by Barrow Wood and three reservoirs, Barrow Gurney Church incorporates part of a 13th-century Benedictine nunnery. Barrow Court is a Jacobean mansion, standing beside the church in a splendid garden. A footpath by the northern reservoir leads ½ mile to a hilltop wood called The Wild Country.

MONKS' STEPS *The flight of steps leading down into Kewstoke may have been made by pre-Roman inhabitants of the village*

Chew Magna
An attractive village, with several streams spanned by ancient bridges; the main street has a raised causeway. The fine bridge over the River Chew, south of the village, dates from the 15th century.

DONKEYS ON THE BEACH *Donkeys have been part of the scene on Weston-super-Mare beach since the mid-19th century. They are bred locally, take their first rider at the age of two and are retired after 14 or 15 years' work*

Near the church is a 16th-century building (open to the public) where manorial courts were held. Chew Tower, a castellated folly built *c.* 1770, stands on Dundry Hill, overlooking the village. A lane leads south from the village for 1 mile and follows the edge of a beautiful reservoir, Chew Valley Lake.

Churchill
This village of stone houses, just off the Bristol road, is dominated by privately owned Churchill Court, seat of some of the ancestors of the first Duke of Marlborough and of Sir Winston Churchill. South-east of the village, just beyond some traffic lights, a track 1 mile long leads to Dolebury Camp. The Camp is a large and magnificent Iron Age earthwork, with a stone-walled enclosure.

Clevedon
A small seaside resort on the Severn Estuary. Clevedon Court, now owned by the National Trust, was the home of Arthur Hallam, whose death inspired Tennyson's 'In Memoriam'. He is buried in St Andrew's Church. The novelist Thackeray worked for a time in this house, which retains some 14th-century features, including a chapel on the first floor. Clevedon is a good centre for walkers, standing as it does where two ranges of hills meet. One range runs northwards to Portishead, sloping to steep cliffs by the sea; the other, the larger of the two, runs inland towards Bristol, where it comes to an end at Leigh Woods, and the Avon Gorge, a good viewpoint.

On a hill 3 miles east of the town is Cadbury Camp, an Iron Age fortification (not to be confused with the more famous Cadbury Castle west of South Cadbury, in south Somerset).

Congresbury
Tradition has it that St Congar built a wattle church here and then, wanting shade, thrust a yew stick into the ground, where it sprouted like Joseph of Arimathea's staff at Glastonbury. The church which stands there today has one of the finest old vicarages in Britain, dating from the 15th century, with moulded beams. Just south of the AA box a footpath leads through Ball Wood to Wrington Hill, a 500 ft high viewpoint.

Flax Bourton
The village was once owned by Flaxley Abbey in Gloucestershire. The church has some good Norman features. A track leads south from the village to Bourton Combe, a wood of great beauty, nearly 600 ft up. At the southern tip of the combe the track swings round to the north and narrows into a footpath which leads back to the village.

Kewstoke
The most exciting approach is along the coastal toll-road north of the Knightstone Pavilion at Weston-super-Mare, which enters a steep wood overlooking the Severn Estuary. In 1852, in a recess in the church wall, a wooden cup was found, stained with human blood and said to have belonged to the martyred archbishop Thomas à Becket. The cup is now in the County Museum, Taunton. A series of stone steps, known as Monks' Steps or the Path of St Kew, leads to a hilltop from which the Welsh hills are visible across Sand Bay.

Portishead
A small resort and port on the Severn Estuary, sited on a wooded hillside near the mouth of the Avon. The old village, of which several houses survive, grew up around the church and the manor house, The Court. The high tides which sweep up the Severn Estuary, particularly at the Spring Equinox, are a feature of the coast upstream from Portishead.

CHEW VALLEY LAKE *This attractive beauty spot a mile south of Chew Magna is doubly attractive for fishermen—large trout run here, and fishing boats can be hired*

CLEVEDON COURT *Thackeray wrote part of* Vanity Fair *while staying in this 14th-century manor house. In his novel* Henry Esmond *he modelled 'Castlewood' on it*

Queen Charlton
A pleasant small village set around a green from which a stone cross rises on five steps. The first part of its name derives from Edith, the queen of Edward the Confessor, who owned the village.

Weston-super-Mare
Originally a small fishing village; now, after rapid growth in the last 100 years, one of the principal seaside resorts of the west coast. It has little of historical interest, but all the traditional features of a seaside town: piers, Winter Gardens, a Marine Parade extending for 2 miles, several parks and a wide sandy beach. There are regular boat trips from Birkbeck Pier at the north end of the front; donkeys, pony carriages and a Punch and Judy show on the beach. A coastal toll-road through woods leads to Worlebury Hill, site of an Iron Age camp, with a superb view across the Bristol Channel to the Welsh coast. Finds from the camp are in the museum in Burlington Street. Another fine view, north-west to Wales and south-west to the Quantocks, can be had from Brean Down, a headland 300 ft high reached by ferry across the River Axe from Uphill, a small village 1 mile south of Weston-super-Mare. There is a nature reserve at Brean Down. Uphill Manor is a picturesque Gothic mansion built early in the 19th century.

Wrington
The church has a fine tower, visible for miles around. The River Yeo flows near by, and wooded hills overlook the village from the north. Hannah More, the novelist and philanthropist, lived here for a time in a house called Barley Wood (½ mile north-east of the village) which she built in 1800. In the south porch of the church there are busts of her and of the philosopher John Locke, who was born here in 1632.

Yatton
The old village consists of a group of cottages, former almshouses and an old rectory clustered round a church, dating back to the 14th century. The church has a fine west front and the most elaborate south porch in Somerset. Its Perpendicular tower is visible for many miles around.

Where rivers honeycomb the hills with caverns

Angling Coarse fishing on the River Axe, noted for its bream, and the Cheddar Reservoir, noted for pike. Trout fishing at Chew Valley Lake.

Nature trails At Ebbor Gorge National Nature Reserve, near Wells, a 1½-mile nature trail starts from Deer Leap, near Wookey Hole.

Events The Royal Bath and West Show is held in May/June, and an Agricultural Show in Aug., at Shepton Mallet. There is a carnival in Wells in Nov.

Places to see *Bishop's Palace*, Wells: Easter, then May to Oct.; interior, Sun. afternoon; grounds and Chapel, Thur. and Sun. afternoons; daily in Aug. *Cheddar Caves Museum*: daily, Easter to Oct. *Cheddar Motor and Transport Museum*: daily. *Downside Abbey Church*: daily. *Gough's Cave* and *Cox's Cave*, Cheddar: daily, except in winter. *King John's Hunting Lodge* (NT), Axbridge: afternoons, Apr. to Sept. *Wells Museum*, near the cathedral: weekdays, Apr. to Sept.; afternoons, Oct. to Mar.; Sun. afternoon July to Sept. *Wookey Hole Caves*: daily. *Wookey Hole Museum*: daily.

Information centres Town Hall, Market Place, Wells.
Tel. Wells 72552 (seasonal).
Tourist Information Centre, Berrow Road, Burnham-on-Sea.
Tel. Burnham-on-Sea 782377.
The Library, Cheddar.
Tel. Cheddar 742769.

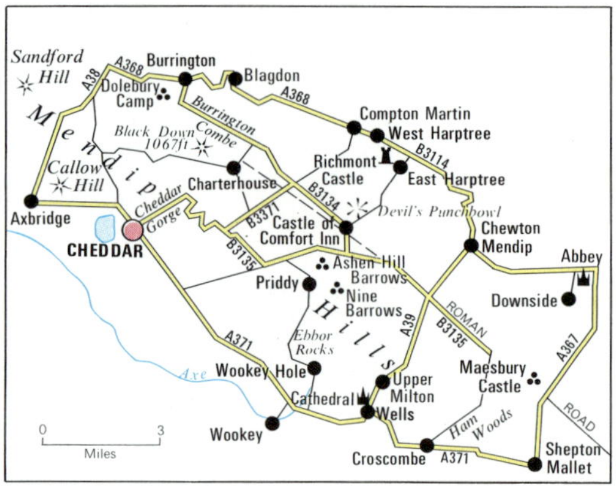

The Mendip Hills lie in a broad band across Somerset, from just outside Weston-super-Mare to the outskirts of Frome, 25 miles to the south-east. On their south-west side the hills drop abruptly to a low moor, while on the other side they slope more gently in a series of foothills. Because the Mendips rise from a low-lying plain, they appear higher than they really are; Black Down, the highest point of the range, is only 1067 ft above sea level.

The central and highest part of the Mendips is a bare upland region of lonely fields and greystone walls. The weather seems to jump between extremes: either there is brilliant sunshine and clear, sparkling air, or there is bleak, windswept gloom and driving rain. To the east, the hills are lower and the landscape gentler, gently sloping down to the lowlands. The western section consists of two ridges, whose hills include Sandford Hill, Banwell Hill and Bleadon Hill, which reach almost to the coast.

The Mendips are composed of limestone covering old red sandstone. The limestone accounts for the large number of drystone walls, the famous caves at Cheddar and Wookey, and numerous smaller caves and 'swallet holes'—small holes in the limestone which temporarily 'swallow up' streams.

Parts of the outskirts of the Mendips have been spoilt by new housing estates and caravan sites; but on the heights and along the byways the country is remote, the air bracing, the stillness profound. The Mendips offer splendid walks and leisurely driving.

Axbridge
An ancient town which became a borough before 1066. Its hub is a spacious square, off which there are many small old streets; the High Street contains several historic buildings, including King John's Hunting Lodge, an Elizabethan building that has no connection with King John. It houses a museum in which are preserved the old stocks, a 'bull anchor' used in bull-baiting until the 19th century, and a money-changer's table dating from 1627. A mile to the north, just beyond Rose Wood, a track narrows into a 2-mile footpath leading across Callow Hill and on to a lane that returns to the outskirts of Axbridge.

Burrington Combe
Burrington is approached along a dramatic gorge, a smaller version of Cheddar. In spring and summer, its cottage gardens are bright with flowers. There are many caves in the gorge, which were occupied in prehistoric times. Sheltering from a thunderstorm in a rocky cleft in the gorge, Augustus Toplady (1740–78), curate of neighbouring Blagdon, wrote the hymn 'Rock of Ages'. In Burrington churchyard is a huge hollow yew tree, 24 ft in circumference. Dolebury Camp, overlooking the gorge, is an oval Iron Age earthwork.

Castle of Comfort
An isolated inn, at the meeting of the roads from Priddy, Harptree and Chewton Mendip. It was patronised by the men who worked in the nearby lead mines, which are now disused. A mile to the north, on the lane to Compton Martin, a footpath leads east, past Spring Farm, within a few hundred yards of the Devil's Punchbowl, a notable swallet. In a field near the inn are traces of a Roman road from Uphill to Old Sarum; it is now a footpath, running south-east from Hill Grange to join the road ½ mile east of Rookery Farm. There is a series of four earthwork rings, the Priddy Circles, by the inn. Their origin is unknown.

Charterhouse
A lonely village on the heights, with the remains of Roman lead mines. All that can be seen now of the mines are patches of 'gruffy ground', where the 'gruffs', or hollows, are the filled-in shafts of old mines. A track adjoining Manor Farm leads to the heart of the former mining area, 1023 ft above sea level. Some 2 miles west of Manor Farm, a footpath leads north from Tyning's Farm across the summit of Black Down, from which the Welsh hills can be seen.

Cheddar
A village at the foot of the famous Cheddar Gorge; the finest views of the gorge are obtained by approaching from the north. There are more than 400 holes or caves in the area, and in the larger ones visitors can see stalactites and stalagmites rich in colour and fantastic of shape. Gough's Cave Museum has a collection of Old Stone Age tools and weapons and the skeleton, discovered in 1903, of a man who lived in the gorge some 12,000 years ago. At the foot of the gorge the Cheddar Motor and Transport Museum has a display of veteran cars and bicycles.

Cheddar cheese originated here more than 300 years ago. Today it is made in more places throughout the world than any other cheese.

Croscombe
A small village with two Tudor manor houses, the remains of a medieval cross at the foot of the church path, and a sky-

STATUES AT WELLS *Among the statues of the apostles on Wells Cathedral's west front, that of St Andrew (third from the right, top row) is taller than the rest—he is the cathedral's patron saint*

PENNILESS PORCH *The gateway leading from the cathedral green to Wells market-place is called Penniless Porch—beggars used to sit here collecting money from people making their way to the cathedral*

CHEDDAR GORGE *These towering limestone cliffs are one of Britain's most dramatic natural showpieces. They soar to about 450 ft—almost three times as high as Nelson's Column in London—and were probably cut by a stream which now runs underground*

THE GREAT CAVE OF WOOKEY HOLE *Visitors can reach the first three chambers of this complex of caves and grottoes which the River Axe has bored through the limestone of the Mendips. Cave explorers, equipped to travel under water, have reached 17 others*

line of steep and thickly wooded hills. Just north of the village, a lane leads into Ham Woods (600 ft). On a hill 1½ miles north of Ham Woods, stands Maesbury Castle, a large prehistoric earthwork consisting of two banks separated by a broad ditch.

Downside

A village noted for its nearby Roman Catholic abbey and school. A Benedictine community of English Catholics founded at Douai in 1607 moved to Shropshire during the French Revolutionary Wars in 1795 and finally settled at Downside in 1814. The present abbey, dating from the beginning of this century, is chiefly the work of Thomas Garner and Sir Giles Gilbert Scott, architect of Liverpool's Anglican Cathedral.

East Harptree

The scanty ruins of Richmont Castle are about ¼ mile south-east of the village church. The castle was besieged in 1138 when King Stephen captured it from Sir William de Harptree, a supporter of Queen Matilda's cause in the civil war between the king and queen. The castle was demolished by its owner, Sir John Newton, in the reign of Henry VIII; Sir John's huge, canopied tomb stands in the Norman porch of the church, which also contains a display of Roman coins found at East Harptree in 1887.

Priddy

A stack of disused hurdles on the green in the centre of this village high in the hills preserves the villagers' rights to have their 600 year old annual summer fair. But the most impressive sight around Priddy is Ebbor Rocks, a huge limestone cleft. A group of prehistoric grave mounds, Priddy Nine Barrows, dominates the village.

Shepton Mallet

The first part of the name is derived from the Old English *scaep tun*, an enclosure into which sheep were driven for safety. 'Mallet' preserves the family name of the post-Conquest owners of the manor. The town was an important wool market during the Middle Ages, and is now a centre for the cheese industry. The Church of SS Peter and Paul has a magnificent panelled roof. The market cross dominates the market-place, where the remains of the medieval Shambles, or meat market, a rare wooden shed of the 15th century, can be seen. A delightful feature of the town is the maze of little lanes that descend the hill to the north-west of the market-place.

Wells

The narrow and winding main street is noisy with cars and lorries, but the market square and cathedral precincts escape something of the din. Facing the spacious green is the city's famous cathedral. Its west front is one of the finest in Britain, originally embellished with nearly 400 statues of saints, angels and prophets; but many were destroyed in the 17th century. The cathedral was begun late in the 12th century and completed before the middle of the 14th. Its many features of interest include the majestic north porch; the inverted arches, added in 1338 to strengthen the base of the central tower; the Chapter House; the humorous carved pillar-capitals in the south transept; and the superb Lady Chapel. The Chain Gate, opposite the north porch, leads to Vicar's Close, a street of 14th-century houses.

Wookey

Some 2 miles north-east of this village is the famous group of caves known as Wookey Hole. (The name Wookey derives from the Old English word *wocig*, meaning a trap for animals.) The first three chambers of the caves are now floodlit; the River Axe flows through them before widening into a lake. A well-known feature of the caves is 'the Witch of Wookey', a huge stalagmite. The legend that a witch once lived in the caves was corroborated in 1912, when excavations revealed a woman's skeleton deep in the floor, close to a dagger, a sacrificial knife and a round stalagmite like a witch's crystal. Wookey Hole was occupied in the Iron Age, while nearby Hyena Cave was occupied by Stone Age hunters when rhinoceroses, mammoths, lions and bears roamed the Mendips. Finds from the caves are displayed in the local museum and in Wells Museum. From Wookey Hole a footpath leads east to Upper Milton and then south to Wells.

THE CHEDDAR PINK Cheddar Gorge is the only place where this rare flower grows wild. It was a favourite souvenir of Victorian tourists to Cheddar, which accounts for its rarity today. The sweetly scented flowers grow to a height of about 8 in. from a cluster of delicate leaves, and bloom in June or July

Prosperity from the waters

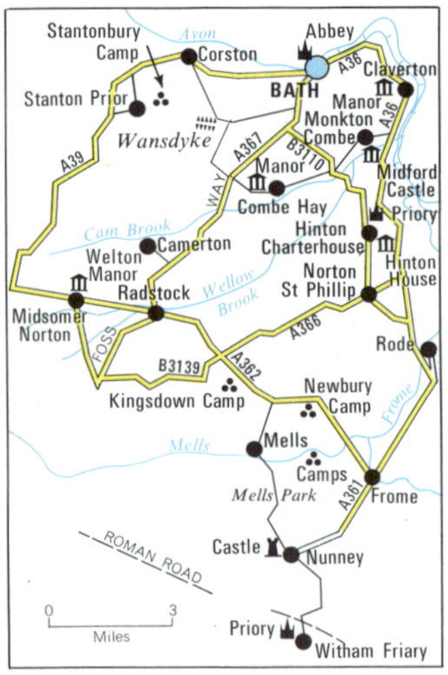

Angling Coarse fishing on the Avon, chiefly at Bath, and on the Kennet and Avon Canal.

Boating Boats for hire on Avon at Bathwick and Newbridge, Bath. At week-ends, a paddleboat travels along the Kennet and Avon Canal from Bathampton, 2 miles east of Bath.

Horse racing Bath Races are held at Lansdown, Bath, in the Flat season.

Cricket County cricket is played at the Recreation Ground, Bath.

Events In Mar. the Mid-Somerset Competitive Music Festival is held in Bath, and in June there is the internationally famous Bath Festival. Frome has a Cheese Show in Sept.

Places to see in Bath *Assembly Rooms* (NT), built *c.* 1771 and housing the *Museum of Costume*: daily. *Bath Carriage Museum*, Circus Mews: daily. *Burrows Toy Museum*, Milson Street: daily. *Exhibition Rooms*, Queen Square, geological display: Mon. to Sat. *Holburne of Menstrie Museum*: weekdays and Sun. afternoons. *1 Royal Crescent*: Mar. to Oct., Tues. to Sat., and Sun. afternoons. *Roman Baths and Museum*, Pump Room: daily. *Victoria Art Gallery*, Bridge Street: weekdays.

Places to see outside Bath *American Museum*, Claverton: afternoons except Mon., Mar. to Oct.; also Bank Hols. *Tropical Bird Gardens*, Rode: daily.

Information centre Abbey Churchyard, Bath. Tel. Bath 62831.

Bath is the most complete and best-preserved Georgian city in Britain. It is also one of Britain's oldest cities, famous since Roman times for its warm mineral springs.

Although the Wiltshire border lies only a few miles away, the Bath countryside is immediately and unmistakably part of the West Country. The splendour of Bath's stone-fronted houses is reflected in the neighbouring villages, in which the best stone cottages and manor houses hold their own against any in the country.

The city's history begins in AD 44 when it became an important Roman settlement, Aquae Sulis, or 'the waters of Sul', a Celtic goddess. The springs originate in the eastern Mendips, collecting mineral salts on the way, and reaching the surface again at Bath. In AD 973 King Edgar was crowned at Bath; in 1088 the See of Wells was transferred there. The defences of the medieval city may be seen at Borough Walls.

Bath was prosperous throughout the Middle Ages, but its modern renown dates from the 18th century. Early in the century, Dr William Oliver built a bath here for the treatment of gout, and his name is preserved in Bath Oliver biscuits. The creation of Bath as a showpiece of Georgian architecture was the work of the architect John Wood, who settled in Bath in 1727. His building schemes were backed by the Duke of Chandos and by Ralph Allen, a wealthy philanthropist and postal pioneer. The development of Bath as a place for high society owed much to Beau Nash, a talented dandy who brought the *élite* of London to the baths and to the balls and assemblies that made the city a byword for elegance and fashion. The 18th-century novelists Smollett and Fielding described Bath in their works, and it was still a favoured resort in the 19th century, when it appeared in the novels of Jane Austen and in Dickens's *Pickwick Papers*. Sam Weller declared that the waters tasted like 'warm flat-irons', and others have found comfort in the thought that medicine usually tastes nasty.

Bath today is mainly a residential town, but its celebrated architecture draws students from all over Europe. The waters are still sought for medicinal purposes and the city attracts many visitors who seek the pleasant country around it.

In the centre of the town the Roman baths (among the best-preserved Roman remains anywhere in England) adjoin the 18th-century Pump Room, and the abbey stands near by. There was an abbey at Bath in Saxon times; it was almost entirely rebuilt by Bishop Montagu in the 17th century, and much restored in the 19th century. North of this group of buildings and the main shopping street are the famous Circus, designed by John Wood, the equally famous Royal Crescent (the work of his son, John Wood the Second), and the Upper Assembly Rooms, one of Bath's grandest public buildings. The Pulteney Bridge, designed by Robert Adam, spans the River Avon, and fine Georgian buildings and streets abound.

SHOPPING OVER THE AVON *What looks from inside like a road lined with shops turns out to be a bridge across the Avon. Robert Adam designed Bath's unique Pulteney Bridge in 1771*

BATH ABBEY *The south side of the nave. The Perpendicular-style abbey was founded in 1499 by Bishop King, but was altered several times between the 17th and 20th centuries*

DUKE STREET *This fine Georgian street is typical of the area where the most fashionable people lived in 18th-century Bath*

Claverton
In the churchyard is buried Ralph Allen, one of the creators of Georgian Bath. The manor house (1820) is the home of the first museum of American life to be opened in Britain. The furniture as well as the exhibits have been brought from America, and there are especially interesting items dealing with the art of the Red Indians, with the religious sect called the 'Shakers', and with many aspects of American folk art.

Combe Hay
The lane plunges through woods, and between the trees there is a glimpse of a village of attractive cottages overlooking a stream, with a whitewashed inn standing on a knoll. Adjoining the church, the lawns of the Georgian Combe Hay Manor House slope down to an ornamental lake. Behind the inn a steep track offers a circular walk, about 2 miles long, passing Fortnight Farm and then dropping south via Week Farm back to Combe Hay.

Frome
A busy market town on the River Frome, full of steep and narrow streets, known to most summer motorists as a weekend bottleneck. Cheap Street (pedestrians only) is exceptionally quaint, and has a runnel of water down its centre. There are fine buildings of various periods including, at the approach to the bridge across the river, the early 18th-century almshouses. For the motorist who is in no hurry to move west, Frome is a good centre from which to explore Bath and Wells, Cheddar and many other places in eastern Somerset.

Hinton Charterhouse
A hilly village among woods, named after the 13th-century Carthusian priory 1 mile north-east of the village. This is the second-oldest Carthusian house in England, after Witham Friary, and the remains are more extensive than those at Witham. It is reached by a footpath north of Hinton House, an 18th-century mansion incorporating parts of the priory lodge and gatehouse.

Mells
One of the most beautiful villages in Somerset, appealing because it remains a workaday place, not a formal exhibit. Thatched cottages and stone houses are flanked by trees, and the village is graced with many small greens. The Tudor manor house, with gabled roofs and mullioned windows, was the seat of the Horner family, one of whom, steward to the last Abbot of Glastonbury, is said to have been the original of the nursery rhyme's 'Little Jack Horner'. There are four prehistoric camps near Mells. The nearest is Wadbury Camp, bounded by Mells stream and by ditches and stone walls. The others are Tedbury Camp, whose earth rampart is still as much as 15 ft high in places; Newbury Camp; and Kingsdown Camp, part Roman, part Iron Age.

THE
Pleaſant HISTORY
OF
JACK HORNER.

CONTAINING
The witty Tricks and pleaſant Pranks he play'd from his Youth to his riper Years; pleaſant and delightful both for Winter and Summer Recreation.

LONDON, Printed: And ſold by J. DREWRY, Bookſeller in DERBY.

LITTLE JACK HORNER

The rhyme of Little Jack Horner which first appeared in 1770 (left) is said to have been based on a fictitious story that the title deeds of Mells Manor (above), the 'plum', were sent to Henry VIII in a pie but were stolen on the way

Midsomer Norton
A small town which shares a coalfield with neighbouring Radstock. Its name is derived not from the River Somer, which flows through the town, but from Midsummer Day, the date of the festival of the church's patron saint, St John the Baptist. In the church is a statue of Charles II, said to have hidden in nearby Welton Manor during the Civil War.

Monkton Combe
A hamlet of ancient stone cottages in a deep wooded combe beside a small river, formerly a manor of the Bishops of Bath. It is overlooked from the north by Combe Down, which commands splendid views of Bath and the surrounding hills. There is an 18th-century stone lock-up in the village. Half a mile south-east is Midford Castle, beautifully set in wooded grounds. It was built *c.* 1775 to an unusual design—the shape of a clover-leaf—said to commemorate a gambling triumph of its owner, Henry Roebuck; his success was based on a lucky ace of clubs.

Norton St Philip
In this village is The George, a fine 15th-century inn of stone and timber, locally believed to be the oldest in England. Pepys admired the bells of the church, which he found 'mighty tuneable'. An attempt on the life of the Duke of Monmouth was made in the village during the rebellion of 1685; his would-be assassin fired a shot at him from a window as he was passing.

Nunney
A picturesque village on the eastern fringe of the Mendips. Best approached from Frome, its moated castle comes into view like a vision of the Middle Ages. The castle, dating back to 1373, is not large but it is the most impressive in Somerset. It is built on a narrow rectangular plan with a massive tower at each corner. The building was badly damaged when it was besieged during the Civil War.

THE LAST OF A VINEYARD *Terraces on a hillside near Claverton mark the site of a vineyard dating back to the early 19th century. Vines last grew there in the 1930's*

Wansdyke
The name given to an extensive earthwork, the longest of its kind in the British Isles. It stretches for some 50 miles from Hampshire across Wiltshire's Marlborough Downs and on across northern Somerset to Dundry Hill, south of Bristol; some people claim to have traced its length for another 30 miles. One of the best-preserved sections of Wansdyke is not far from Bath, south of the village of Corston.

The earthwork consists of a single bank with a ditch on the north side. Its exact origin and purpose are uncertain, but it undoubtedly dates from late in the Roman occupation or shortly after. It was probably built as a boundary between the Mercian people and the West Saxons. The name Wansdyke is in fact Saxon in origin—Woden's Dyke, or ditch. (One of the god Woden's functions was to be the god of tribal boundaries.)

On Stantonbury Hill, to the north of Stanton Prior and on the east of the road from Bath to Wells, is Stantonbury Camp, an Iron Age fortification whose north side is a section of Wansdyke.

Witham Friary
The first Carthusian monastery in England was founded here by Henry II, as a penance for the murder of Archbishop Thomas à Becket. The only remains are parts of the church and a dovecot that was converted into a village reading-room in the 19th century. A lane crosses the course of a Roman road, which probably went as far as the Roman lead mines in the Mendips. Its course can be traced westwards a few hundred yards to a copse, and eastwards for 2 miles into Marston Wood.

The Plain of Sedgemoor

Angling Coarse fishing on the River Parrett at Bridgwater, the River Brue at Burnham-on-Sea, and the Huntspill River. Pike fishing on King's Sedgemoor Drain and on the Bridgwater–Taunton Canal.

Sailing In Bridgwater Bay. There is a regatta every Aug.

Bird-watching At Brean Down, 6 miles north of Burnham-on-Sea, a National Trust bird sanctuary; and at the Bridgwater Bay Nature Reserve, about 5 miles north of Bridgwater.

Events In May, the Order of British Druids celebrates Beltane, the coming of spring, on Glastonbury Tor. On the last Sun. in May there is a Roman Catholic Pilgrimage to Glastonbury, and on the last Sat. in June there is a Church of England Pilgrimage. St Matthew's Fair, Bridgwater, and Glastonbury Tor Fair are in Sept. In early Nov., Bridgwater, Highbridge and Glastonbury have Guy Fawkes carnivals.

Places to see *Admiral Blake Museum*, Blake Street, Bridgwater: daily, except Tues. afternoons.
Chalice Well, Glastonbury: daily, except Thur., Mar. to Oct.
Glastonbury Abbey and *Abbot's Kitchen* daily. *Tribunal*, Glastonbury, housing *Glastonbury Lake Village Museum*: weekdays and Sun. afternoon.
Somerset Rural Life Museum, Glastonbury: weekdays and Sun. afternoon; also Sun. morning, Oct. to Easter.

Information centres Information Bureau, Burnham-on-Sea.
Tel. Burnham-on-Sea 782377.
Glastonbury Advertising Association, 7 Northload Street, Glastonbury.
Tel. Glastonbury 32954 (seasonal).
Tourist Information Centre, The Library, Cheddar.
Tel. Cheddar 742769.

Mid-Somerset is mostly low-lying, a land of willows and quiet streams, drained by the River Parrett and the River Brue, both of which flow into the Bristol Channel near Burnham-on-Sea. Through the centre of the region run the Polden Hills, which seldom rise above 300 ft but afford some fine views across the lowlands to the north and south.

This lowland region, known as the Levels, or the Plain of Sedgemoor, was once largely covered by water. It is intersected by a maze of drainage ditches, known as rhines, some long and straight like the King's Sedgemoor Drain, others narrow and winding.

Although several main roads cross the region, between them lies a vast tract of quiet countryside. This is a district of dairy farms, noted for the milk used to make the original Cheddar cheese.

Scarcely a mile from the main road at Bruton is Wyke Champflower, a village of charm, while at the other end of the region is Burnham-on-Sea, an attractive seaside resort. Glastonbury Tor, traditionally the place where the Holy Grail lies buried, is a landmark which is easily climbed, and near by are the remains of prehistoric lake villages whose inhabitants built their huts on artificial islands in the marshes.

GLASTONBURY ABBEY *Glastonbury and its ruined abbey are steeped in legend. The first Christian church in Britain is said to have stood here, and King Arthur was reputedly buried here. The abbey was one of the most powerful in Britain until Henry VIII dissolved it and hanged the abbot in 1539, leaving the magnificent walls to be broken up and used as building stone*

Bridgwater
An industrial centre and formerly a busy port on the River Parrett. A tidal bore sweeps up the river when the tide is flowing. The town was used by the rebel Duke of Monmouth as his headquarters before the Battle of Sedgemoor (1685). The duke was proclaimed king here as well as at Taunton. Robert Blake (1599–1657), Cromwell's great admiral, was born in Bridgwater; his house is now a museum. St Mary's Church, dating from the 14th century, is noted for its screenwork. Castle Street is worth seeing for its fine Georgian architecture.

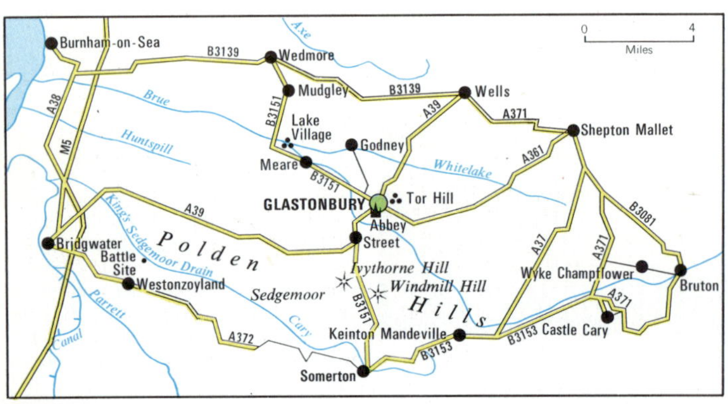

Bruton
A small town in the valley of the River Brue, which is crossed by a narrow packhorse bridge, known locally as Bruton Bow. R. D. Blackmore, author of *Lorna Doone*, was a pupil at King Edward VI's Grammar School, which stands on the site of an earlier school founded in 1520 by Richard Fitz James, Bishop of London. A Bruton stable boy, Hugh Sexey, who became the King's Auditor, founded Sexey Hospital in 1638; the carved wood and the triple windows are worth seeing. A three-storeyed dovecot on a hill above the town, owned by the National Trust, is all that survives of a 12th-century priory.

Burnham-on-Sea
A popular small seaside resort, with 7 miles of sandy beach and a sweeping view of Bridgwater Bay. The church should be visited for the 14th-century tower, 78 ft high and leaning some 3 ft out of the vertical, and for the reredos of the so-called 'Whitehall Altar'. This was commissioned by James II from Inigo Jones and Grinling Gibbons for the chapel of Whitehall Palace. The altar went from Whitehall to Hampton Court and then to Westminster Abbey; George IV gave it to Bishop King of Rochester, Vicar of Burnham, in 1820.

Castle Cary
The modern outskirts have little of interest, but the centre of this old town is worth exploring. The main street contains pleasant old shops and houses; behind the market hall stands a little circular lock-up, built in 1779 like a stone bee-hive, with gratings instead of windows. Castle Cary was the home of Parson Woodforde, whose diary, published as *Diary of a Country Parson,* is a classic of 18th-century country life.

Glastonbury
The town is famous for its great abbey, of which only fragments remain. Legend tells how Joseph of Arimathea came to convert the English; arriving at Glastonbury, he leant on his staff in prayer, whereupon the staff took root, a sign that the saint should settle and found a religious house. The holy thorn on Wearyall Hill, believed to have sprung from his staff, was destroyed during the Civil War, but a thorn in the abbey grounds is said to be a cutting from it. There is no historical evidence for the story of Joseph, but there was probably a religious foundation at Glastonbury as early as the 5th century. The abbey was the last of a series built on the site, the first being founded in AD 688; begun early in the 13th century, it was not

RECLAIMED FROM THE SEA *A great part of Sedgemoor lies below sea level, and though drainage schemes began around 1400, a report from the time of Charles I refers to parts of it as being covered by the sea for most of the year. Now the land is drained by a web of rhines, or ditches, dug between the 17th and 19th centuries*

completed until just before the Dissolution of the Monasteries by Henry VIII.

The Arthurian legend associates Glastonbury with Avalon, the place to which King Arthur was taken after his death. The Holy Grail which his knights sought is said to have been brought from Jerusalem by Joseph and to rest below the Chalice Spring on Glastonbury Tor, the steep hill which dominates the town.

Though best known for the legends long associated with it, the town itself is worth a visit. The George Inn is one of the few English inns to survive from pre-Reformation times. Other notable buildings include St John's Church and St Mary's Almshouses.

A series of mounds in a marshy valley a mile from the Tor are the only remaining evidence of one of several lake-villages that existed in this area before the Roman conquest. Articles found here, now in Glastonbury's Tribunal, include pottery, weapons and ornaments.

Keinton Mandeville

The village's main street of somewhat austere houses is interesting as the birthplace of Sir Henry Irving, the Victorian actor-manager; his house, marked by a plaque, is one of a row facing the baker's shop. Irving, the son of a local tradesman, achieved fame at the age of 33 when he played in *The Bells* at London's Lyceum Theatre. He was the first actor to be knighted, and his ashes are in Westminster Abbey.

Meare

The site of one of the lake villages built in the swamps during the Iron Age. The villagers' homes probably had timber foundations, daub and wattle walls and thatched roofs; and each building was supported by a central pole. Finds are in the County Museum at Taunton and the Tribunal at Glastonbury. In the Middle Ages the Abbots of Glastonbury owned Meare, and the manor house was their summer retreat. It dates from the 14th century, as does the curious Fish House, used by local fishermen who supplied the abbots with fish.

Sedgemoor

A low-lying, marshy region stretching from the Mendips to Taunton and Ilminster. Its willows are used for the local industry of basket-making. North-east of the village of Westonzoyland is the site of the Battle of Sedgemoor which ended the Duke of Monmouth's rebellion against James II in 1685. This fierce and bloody hand-to-hand struggle was the last major battle to be fought on English soil.

Somerton

A town attractively situated on the River Cary; the buildings round the market-place constitute one of the most appealing townscapes in Somerset. The church and some 16th-century houses on the north side of the market-place face the 18th-century former town hall and some houses built on the site of Somerton Castle; fragments of the castle are said to be incorporated in the White Hart Hotel. The octagonal market cross was rebuilt in 1673. West of the market-place are the Hext Almhouses, built in 1626.

Street

A busy little town just south of Glastonbury, on the slopes of the Polden Hills, where the Romans mined stone. There are good walks over the hills, with fine views across the moors to the Mendip and Quantock Hills and to the Bristol Channel. The view is outstanding from Ivythorn Hill, a 90-acre wooded estate owned by the National Trust, 3 miles south of Street. South-east of the town, on Windmill Hill, stands a tall monument to Admiral Lord Hood (1724–1816), who distinguished himself in naval actions against the French.

Wyke Champflower

Though lying scarcely a mile from a busy main road, this is a peaceful little place with a green flanked by beeches, elms and oaks. During the Middle Ages it was held by a knight from Champfleury in Normandy. The manor house stands near a church whose box pews have their own hat-pegs; on one wall are the armorial bearings of Henry Southworth, who built the church in 1623.

CROP OF SEDGEMOOR

The ditches of Sedgemoor yield an uncommon crop called withies—the young shoots of pollarded willow trees. They were first planted on a large scale in the early years of the 19th century, in West Sedgemoor, to cater for the Victorian passion for wickerwork; and they still provide work for deft-fingered local craftsmen

West Country legends

The Celtic gift for story-telling has left the West Country with a rich legacy of legends, some of them dating back to pre-Christian times. The demon dogs which are said to chase across Dartmoor followed by the Devil on horseback are a relic of the pre-Christian belief that hounds chased across the sky accompanied by the god Wotan. The stories have survived because of their vividness, or because the conditions which prompted them still exist. Stone circles and other prehistoric relics, which in the Celtic imagination became passports to a world of giants and demons, still brood over the Cornish landscape. The mists that swirl over the western moors and coasts can still people them in imagination with these and other supernatural beings.

THE LEGENDARY LAND OF KING ARTHUR

TINTAGEL IN LEGEND *In Tennyson's version of the Arthur story, Merlin found Arthur on the shore at Tintagel. That idea was Tennyson's, but the tradition that Arthur was born at Tintagel dates back to Geoffrey of Monmouth in the 12th century*

TINTAGEL IN FACT *Excavations have revealed that there was a British monastery at Tintagel about the time Arthur lived. Though no traces have been found of Arthur, and he is unlikely to have been born at the monastery, he may have visited it*

THE REAL KING ARTHUR *Most traditions make King Arthur a West Country man—born at Tintagel, holding court at Camelot and taken to die on the fairy Isle of Avalon. From study of historical sources, a real Arthur does emerge. He was probably a 5th or 6th-century British chieftain who led a successful Celtic rally against the invading Anglo-Saxons. The work of modern archaeologists supports the claim that the West Country was the real Arthur's home, and suggests that the place now known as Cadbury may have been his Camelot, and Glastonbury his legendary Avalon*

DOZMARY POOL *When the legendary Arthur lay dying after his last battle, he told Sir Bedevere to throw the sword Excalibur into a nearby lake. A hand rose from the lake and caught the sword. Dozmary Pool on Bodmin Moor is one of the places claimed as the resting-place of Excalibur*

GLASTONBURY TOR *In legend, Arthur visited Glastonbury at least twice: first to rescue Guinevere from Melwas, who had kidnapped her, and later to die. On the Tor, archaeologists have found traces of a settlement dating from Arthurian times—perhaps Melwas's fortress. In the grounds of Glastonbury Abbey is a site said to be Arthur's grave. All the evidence seems to support the claim. There is a case, too, for the belief that Glastonbury Tor is the fairy Isle of Avalon to which the dying king was carried. In the Dark Ages, the Somerset marshes covered much of the countryside around the Tor with water*

THE HOLY GRAIL *Joseph of Arimathea is said to have brought to Britain the cup Christ used at the Last Supper, and to have hidden it on Glastonbury Tor. In Arthurian legend, only Sir Galahad was granted a full vision of it. This pre-Raphaelite tapestry of Galahad's vision was designed by Sir Edward Burne-Jones and worked by William Morris. It can be seen in the Birmingham City Museum*

The ancient West

Many of the legends of the ancient West are linked with the stone circles and standing stones scattered over the region, dating mostly from the Bronze Age some 4000 years ago.

A stone circle called the Merry Maidens, near St Buryan in Cornwall, is one of the best-known sites associated with a legend common to many of the West's prehistoric relics. There are 19 stones in the circle, with two menhirs (single standing stones) near by. It is said that 19 maidens were dancing on the Sabbath to the music of two pipers. The Devil appeared among them and turned them to stone. The early Christian church may have encouraged this legend, in order to persuade the villagers to keep away from the stones as being 'evil', and so to break the influence of older beliefs.

Perhaps the strangest prehistoric relics in the West are the tolmens—huge stones with a hole cut through the centre. The Men-an-Tol, near Morvah, is one of the best examples. No one knows for certain what its purpose was, though it may be all that remains of the entrance to a tomb. Until about the 18th century, parents passed their children through the hole as a cure for rickets.

The great size of the prehistoric relics in the West forms the basis of widespread tales of giants and other supernaturally strong people. St Just is said to have visited St Keverne one day and stolen his host's chalice. St Keverne, in his anger, hurled three great boulders at St Just. The boulders still stand in a field near Germoe, on the road from Helston to Marazion.

Moorland legends

The West Country's high and windswept moors are a perfect setting for eerie tales of the supernatural.

When Sir Arthur Conan Doyle wrote *The Hound of the Baskervilles* he was drawing on one of the West's oldest stories. Demon dogs, known as wish hounds, yeth hounds or yell hounds, are said to chase along Dartmoor's Abbot's Way in search of unbaptised children. Sheep and ponies are said to flee from the hounds in terror, and any domestic dog hearing the hounds' baying is supposed to die of fear.

On the edge of Bodmin Moor, in an unmarked grave in St Breoc churchyard, lies the body of Jan Tregeagle, a steward to Lord Robartes at Lanhydrock in the 17th century. Tregeagle is said to have sold his soul to the Devil. But because he did one good deed during his life, the saints postponed his fate by setting his spirit endless tasks, such as emptying Dozmary Pool with a holed limpet shell or weaving a rope of sand. Demons are said to hunt Tregeagle over the moor, and Cornishmen have long said that the sighing of the wind is Tregeagle's moaning.

Sedgemoor in Somerset was the site of one of the last battles fought on English soil. The Duke of Monmouth and his rebels were defeated there in 1685. Ghosts are said to haunt the battlefield—vague, shadowy creatures which loom up over the marsh and quickly vanish again. At night, green blobs are said to glow over the battlefield, representing the unquiet spirits of Monmouth's slaughtered army.

Legends of the sea

According to tradition, a land called Lyonesse once stretched between Land's End and the Isles of Scilly. The Scillies were part of it, as was St Michael's Mount near Penzance. Lyonesse had many cities and some 140 churches, whose bells, it is said, can sometimes be heard tolling beneath the sea. Arthur's knights had many adventures in Lyonesse: Tristram, whose love affair with Iseult is part of the Arthurian legend, was born there.

Historically, it is quite possible that there was once a land beyond Land's End. In the Isles of Scilly, there is evidence that a single island has split into several islands at some time since the Bronze Age. Walls can still be seen in the sea between the islands.

Belief in mermaids was once widespread in the West Country, and reflected the reverence seafaring people felt for the imaginary gods and goddesses of the sea. Between Downderry and Looe in Cornwall is a small beach called Seaton Sands, said to be all that remains of a once-prosperous town. Some local sailors are reputed to have insulted a mermaid, who put a curse on the town. The sea swept in, and buried it under sand.

Other legends date back to the time when smuggling was part of many West Country men's way of life. Until the late 18th century, the sea near Gwennap Head in Cornwall was reputedly haunted by a ghost ship which occasionally took to the land. Cornish smugglers bringing contraband from Brittany may have given rise to this story, by painting their boats with luminous paint as a ruse to scare off intruders.

Saints and holy wells

There are some 100 holy wells in Cornwall, most of them named after Cornish saints. Many are reputed to have strange powers. According to legend, the holy well at St Cleer, on the south edge of Bodmin Moor, cures madness; the water from Ludgvan well, north-west of Marazion, ensures that children will never commit murder; showers of rain follow a wash in the water of St Constantine's well, near Trevose Head. St Keyne endowed the waters of her well, 5 miles north of Looe, with the power to make one partner in a marriage dominate the other, depending on who drank first.

The early saints made such an impression on the Celtic people whom they converted, that their very coming to the West Country was surrounded by tales of the miraculous. St Piran is said to have sailed from Ireland on a millstone, St Feock on a granite boulder and St Decuman on a bundle of twigs. St Decuman's teachings thrived in Devon until the saint met a martyr's death and was beheaded. According to legend, St Decuman retrieved his own severed head and walked away with it.

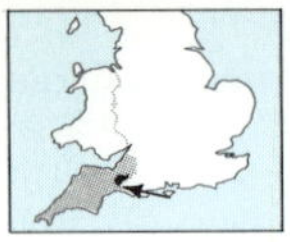

The green hills of south Somerset

Angling Coarse fishing on the Rivers Axe, Parrett and Yeo. Trout fishing on Sutton Bingham and Dunleigh reservoirs.

Bird-watching Sutton Bingham Reservoir, Yeovil, is a Wildfowl Trust observatory.

Local customs Punky Night, Hinton St George, near Crewkerne. On the last Thur. in Oct., children parade through the streets carrying lanterns carved out of mangel-wurzels, called punkies. The custom is said to commemorate an occasion when many of the village men were missing and their wives went out to search for them by the light of punkies.

Events Fairs at Crewkerne (Sept.) and Ilminster (Sept./Oct.). Carnivals in early Oct. at Yeovil and Chard.

Places to see *Burrington Court* (NT), Ilminster: Wed. *Brympton d'Evercy*, Yeovil: afternoons, except Thur. and Fri., May to Sept. *Bygones*, Cider Mills, Dowlish Wake: Mon. to Fri.; also Sat. and Sun. mornings. *Fleet Air Arm Museum and Concorde*, Yeovilton: weekdays, Sun. afternoon. *Lytes Cary* (NT), near Ilchester: Wed. and Sat. afternoons, Mar. to Oct. *Montacute House* (NT): Apr. to Oct., afternoons except Tues. *Stoke-sub-Hamdon Priory* (NT), 2 miles west of Montacute: hall only; daily. *Tintinhull House* (NT): Apr. to Sept., Wed., Thur., Sat. and Bank Hol. afternoons. *Wild Life Park*, Cricket St Thomas: daily. *Wyndham Museum*, Hendford Manor Hall, Yeovil: weekdays, except Thur.

Information centre Public Relations Office, 91 Preston Road, Yeovil. Tel. Yeovil 5272.

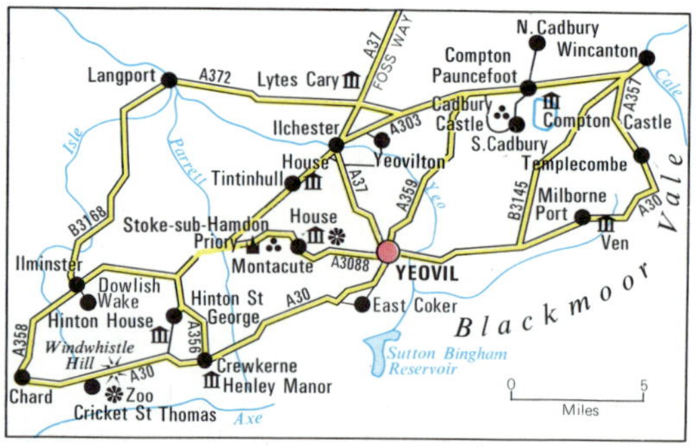

South Somerset, though lacking the contrasts found among the Mendips and the Quantocks, is not without surprises. There is the steep hill on which stands Cadbury Castle, said to be the site of fabled Camelot; and there is Windwhistle Hill, near Chard, from which can be seen on a clear day both the English Channel and the Bristol Channel. This is a region of remote villages and small country towns, rich with venerable houses and visible reminders of history. The only sizable industrial town is Yeovil, and even there the built-up area does not impinge too much on the surrounding green hills.

The low-lying, marshy lands in the north were once the home of the 'Seo-mere-saetan', the dwellers of the sea lakes from whom the county took its name. The Saxon *ea*, meaning island, is preserved as 'ey' in the names Muchelney and Athelney.

According to legend, the hill of Cadbury is the place from which King Arthur set out to find his sword Excalibur. For those with a taste for more certainty than the Arthurian legend can provide, a small obelisk at Athelney commemorates the desperate vigil of King Alfred in the winter of AD 878, before a battle at which the Danes were decisively beaten. At Ilchester is preserved one of the oldest maces in Europe, and by the village of Montacute stands Montacute House, a superb survival of the Elizabethan age. The Knights Templar, who fought for their faith at Jerusalem, are remembered at Temple Combe; and at Crewkerne and Cricket St Thomas are links with Horatio Nelson, the victor of the Battle of Trafalgar in 1805.

Cadbury
The attractive little villages of North Cadbury and South Cadbury are noted for the massive earthwork known as Cadbury Castle, which stands on a steep hill west of South Cadbury. The castle, believed to be the site of King Arthur's Camelot, is undoubtedly the finest prehistoric camp in Somerset, and one of the finest in England.

Chard
The highest town in Somerset, standing nearly 400 ft above sea level. There are superb views from nearby Windwhistle Hill (733 ft) and Snowdon Hill (709 ft). The town was first made a borough in 1234, and had a thriving wool industry until the 19th century, when people turned to making the net which forms the basis of machine-made lace. The 16th-century Court House, really a group of several Elizabethan houses, is Chard's most interesting sight, and the Church of St Mary has a 17th-century monument to William Brewer, a local doctor, and his family. The Choughs Hotel in the High Street has an Elizabethan interior, and the grammar school, founded in 1671, is partly housed in a building dating from 1583. Two streams flow along the High Street, one going north towards the Bristol Channel, the other south to the English Channel.

WILDLIFE IN THE PARK *Peacocks roam the grounds of Cricket House. The estate at Cricket St Thomas is now a wildlife park, where many birds and animals can be seen*

Compton Pauncefoot
This was the 'compton', or narrow valley, belonging to a Norman knight called Pauncefote ('Fat-bellied'). Opposite the village church is the Old Rectory, a pleasant Georgian house. Compton Castle is a Gothic fantasy built *c.* 1825, but the back part of the house is older, probably 17th century.

Crewkerne
This market town stands on a sheltered site on an east slope of the Black Down Hills, and has been a place of importance since before the Norman Conquest. The ancient craft of sail-making has been given new life through the modern interest in yachting. The Church of St Bartholomew, mainly 15th century, has an enormous west window. In Abbey Road is a Jacobean building which formerly housed the ancient grammar school, founded in 1499. Nelson's flag captain in the *Victory*, Captain Hardy, was a pupil there.

Cricket St Thomas
One of the most beautiful estates in the West Country. Cricket House is a Georgian mansion that belonged to the Bridport family, connected by marriage with Lord Nelson, who was a frequent visitor. The extensive grounds contain a wildlife park, open to the public; and the parish church of St Thomas also stands in the grounds.

Hinton St George
Cupped in a maze of narrow lanes, the village has a row of handsome stone houses and a medieval cross with a carving of St John the Baptist. The buttresses of the local church carry 'scratch' dials, a primitive form of sun-dial. Hinton House is a large, rambling building of various periods, the oldest parts dating from the 17th century.

Ilchester
Once a Roman town on the Foss Way, later a medieval town of some importance. Ilchester is now a busy road junction, but there are still many relics of its past around the village green. There are several Georgian houses, one of which is the town hall; it contains a 13th-century mace which is the oldest staff of office in England and one of the oldest in Europe. At the top of the 18th-century market cross is a sun-dial. Ilchester was the birthplace of Roger Bacon, one of the greatest scholars of the 13th century, who predicted the invention of submarines, aircraft and the telescope. Lytes Cary, a fine Tudor manor house 3 miles to the north-east, has a 14th-century chapel and a fine Elizabethan-style garden.

HAM HILL STONE *Intricate carving on the Church of St Bartholomew at Crewkerne highlights the beauty of Ham Hill stone. It was quarried from Hamdon Hill as long ago as Roman times, and builders in Somerset and parts of Dorset made continuous use of it from the 14th century, if not before, until the 19th century. Lichens thrive on it, giving the stone's colouring a mottled appearance*

CADBURY CASTLE *In the search for King Arthur's Britain, excavations have shown this hill to be the most likely site of Camelot*

Ilminster
A busy market town at the foot of the Black Down Hills, whose highest slopes (800 ft) look down at the town from across the River Isle. Several of the houses round the market square are 18th century, and the old grammar school (now a girls' school) dates from 1586. Where the High Street joins North Street, an old road climbs Beacon Hill, from which, it is said, 30 churches can be seen in fine weather. Barrington Court, 3 miles north-east of the town, was built in 1514–20 and is a fine example of an early Tudor manor house, with striking spiral chimneys.

Langport
An ancient market town on a hill beside the River Parrett, which flows below the main street. East of the church, an archway spans the road, carrying a small chapel, the Hanging Chapel, built for a medieval craft guild. Having served as a grammar school, it is now a meeting place of Freemasons.

Milborne Port
Once noted for the number of its mills, this small place was a port, or borough, returning two members to Parliament. The remains of a medieval cross stand in the centre of the village. The old guildhall, near the market hall, incorporates a Norman doorway, and the church is partly Saxon and early Norman. At the east end of the village, on the Salisbury road, stands a Queen Anne mansion, Ven, formerly the seat of the Medlicott family. On the lane to Milborne Wick traces of a prehistoric camp can be seen.

Montacute
The name comes from the Latin *mons acutus*, or pointed hill, a reference to St Michael's Hill, a conical knoll, topped by 60 ft St Michael's Tower, a folly built in 1760. The hub of the village is an open space, the Borough, flanked on two sides by old houses built of Ham Hill stone. Now the property of the National Trust, Montacute House is the best-known stately home in Somerset and one of the finest mansions in the west of England. It was built between 1588 and 1601 of Ham Hill stone by the Phelips family, and contains a valuable collection of furniture and china, portraits, tapestries, plasterwork and panelling. The gardens are a fine example of Jacobean planning, sloping from the house through a series of deep yew hedges and golden-stone terraces. In summer the grounds are scented by many-coloured roses. Some of the Atlantic cedars are 50 ft high.

Templecombe
The village takes its name from the Knights Templar, who held the manor in 1185. Scanty remains of their preceptory (the name given to an estate of the Templars) are preserved in Manor Farm; the large fireplace in the kitchen is the most interesting survival. The church contains some narrow upright seats which have been called 'the most uncomfortable in Christendom'.

STARTING THE DAY WITH CIDER

In the village of Dowlish Wake, a collection of Somerset curios owned by a local cider maker includes ancient pieces of farm machinery and a selection of old-fashioned cider jars and firkins—the barrel in the lower right-hand corner of the picture is a firkin. From the 16th or 17th century until *c.* 1950, it was customary for local farmworkers to be given a firkin full of cider in the morning to last them through the day. The firkin's size varied according to the age of the labourer, from a pint for the youngest to a gallon or more for the oldest men employed

Tintinhull
A pretty, old-world village, where the stocks may still be seen. Tintinhull House is a small and beautiful house built of Ham Hill stone in a delightful formal garden. It was built *c.* 1700, but a century later was given a new west front. The gardens have been laid out and developed since 1900.

Wincanton
A small but busy place, full of attractive stone houses. Its medieval name was Wincaleton, or the town on the River Wincawel (now the Cale). The town stands on a hill overlooking the Blackmoor Vale, a rich dairy district of varied and unspoilt scenery. Wincanton is a good centre for exploring this area.

Yeovil
A small market town until the 18th century, Yeovil is now a busy industrial centre. It is noted for its 300-year-old glove-making industry as well as its more recent industries, which include one of the world's largest helicopter constructors. To the west of the town, near Montacute, is the quarry of Hamdon Hill, long famed for the golden Ham Hill limestone, which has been used for so many of Somerset's villages and mansions. There is a large Iron Age fort on the hill. The museum in Hendford Manor Hall contains a noted collection of firearms, and also some remains of Roman mosaics. Yeovil's Nine Springs, at the bottom of Hendford Hill, are reached by a waterside walk through woods—huge beeches and shaded paths, with nine springs flowing into an enchanting lake.

SOUTHERN ENGLAND

The south of England, dominated by the chalk-lands of Salisbury Plain, is the country of white horses and other hill figures. Until the early years of this century the counties of Wiltshire, Dorset and Hampshire were closely alike in character and the accents of their people sounded similar to the ear of the stranger, for they all once spoke Saxon. This was the core of King Alfred's Wessex, a small, closely knit kingdom with its capital at Winchester, from which was to grow a vast empire.

Though mainly chalk-land, southern England has areas that are vastly different from the huge expanses of its plains and downs. The corner nearest to London shares the heathland and scrub of Surrey. The centre is dotted with water-meadows, and in the south the New Forest is a mixture of heathland, wooded country and pasture. The whole area is cut by the valleys of numerous rivers and streams, whose clear waters form a twisting network stretching down to the sea. The coast, flat in the east, rises gradually to Hengistbury Head in eastern Dorset, then runs in spectacular cliffs to the edge of Devon.

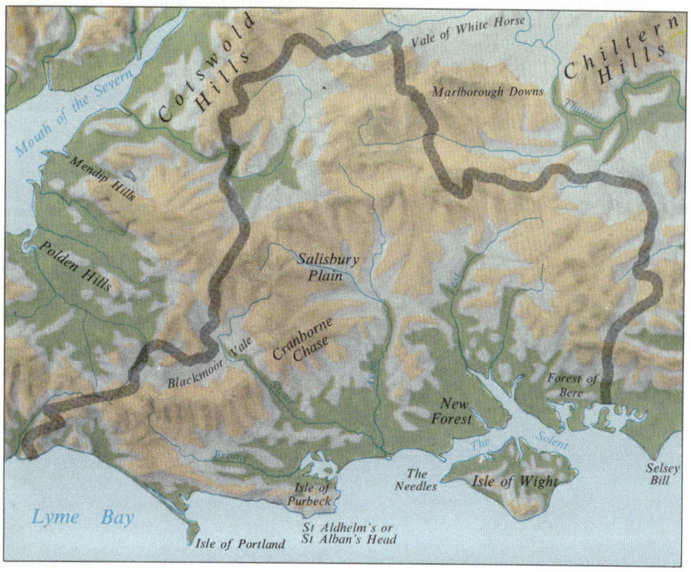

A LAND OF CHALK HILLS *The bare uplands of Salisbury Plain are the hub of southern England's chalk-lands. The Marlborough Downs spread north, and the hills of Dorset stretch south-west. The North and South Downs extend eastwards across Hampshire*

Saxon Wessex was predominantly farming country and, outside the towns, so it remains today. There are sheep and wheat on the hills; some fine dairy land in central Dorset and along the Hampshire river valleys; beef cattle in all the counties; hops in the east, round Alton; and strawberries in the Southampton–Portsmouth coastal belt. Apple orchards, though, are a rarity except for some in Dorset. Left to themselves the soils of southern England produce scrub and down grass, beech groves and yews (the yew is called the 'Hampshire weed'), birches and oaks.

The holiday activities of the south are centred on Bournemouth. Behind its 6 miles of sea-front is a broad swathe of hotels and boarding houses, and in the summer season its normal population of 150,000 is doubled by visitors. By contrast, the New Forest is a vast and virtually unspoilt tract of virgin land. It attracts thousands of summer visitors, even if surprisingly few of them venture far from the main roads. Southern England has its share of stately homes, but perhaps its greatest

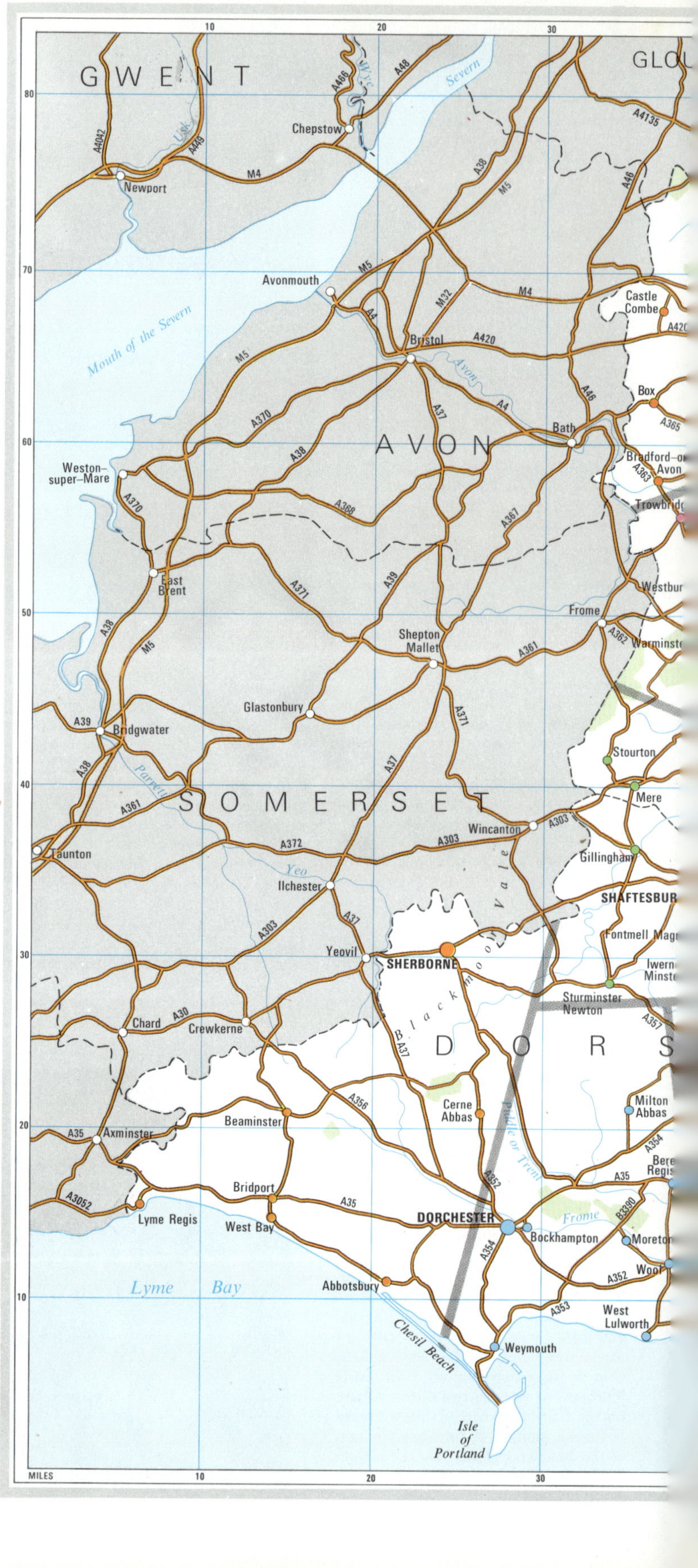

KEY TO MAP
Regional centre
Selected town or village
Regional boundary
County boundary
Major road
Minor road
Woodland
River and lake or reservoir
REGIONAL PAGE INDEX
OXFORD
BERKSHIRE
WILTSHIRE
HAMPSHIRE
SURREY
WEST SUSSEX
NORTH DOWNS
SOUTH DOWNS
SALISBURY PLAIN
NEW FOREST
ISLE OF WIGHT
Cirencester
Tetbury
Ashton Keynes
Cricklade
Highworth
Faringdon
Wantage
Harwell
Wallingford
MALMESBURY
Lydiard Tregoze
Swindon
Marlborough Downs
Aldbourne
Chippenham
Calne
Avebury
MARLBOROUGH
Ramsbury
Hungerford
Newbury
Reading
Staines
Lacock
Melksham
Devizes
Savernake Forest
Pewsey
Vale of Pewsey
Upavon
Highclere
Camberley
Sherborne St John
Basing
Basingstoke
Hartley Wintney
Farnborough
Aldershot
Odiham
Guildford
Hurstbourne Tarrant
Litchfield
Whitchurch
Ashe
Tufton
ANDOVER
Upper Clatford
Wherwell
Chilbolton
Bullington
Stonehenge
AMESBURY
Codford St Mary
Steeple Langford
Great Wishford
Wylye
The Wallops
Longstock
Crawley
Kings Worthy
Itchen Abbas
New Alresford
Alton
Selborne
Chilmark
Dinton
Teffont Evias
Tisbury
Wilton
SALISBURY
Stockbridge
Broughton
WINCHESTER
Avington
Tichborne
Britford
Alderbury
Mottisfont
Hursley
Twyford
Kilmeston
Hinton Ampner
Privett
Steep
West Meon
PETERSFIELD
Buriton
Midhurst
Ansty
East Meon
Breamore
ROMSEY
Rockbourne
Bishops Waltham
Soberton
Hambledon
Farnham
Cranborne
Cadnam
Fritham
Minstead
Southampton
Botley
Wickham
Moyles Court
LYNDHURST
Hythe
Hamble
Titchfield
Fareham
Forest of Bere
Chichester
Ringwood
Burley
Brockenhurst
Beaulieu
Buckler's Hard
PORTSMOUTH
Southsea
Hayling Island
South Hayling
WIMBORNE MINSTER
Lymington
Christchurch
BOURNEMOUTH
Hengistbury Head
The Solent
Spithead
Cowes
Ryde
Selsey Bill
Poole
Poole Bay
Yarmouth
NEWPORT
Carisbrooke
Freshwater
Calbourne
Mottistone
Foreland
Bembridge
Sandown
Wareham
Corfe Castle
Studland
The Needles
Brighstone
Shorwell
Godshill
Shanklin
Purbeck Hills
Isle of Purbeck
Swanage
Ventnor
St Aldhelm's or St Alban's Head
St Catherine's Point
Cranborne Chase
Thames
Kennet
Avon
Test
Itchen
Meon
Beaulieu
Stour
Nadder
Wey
Rother
Arun
M4
M3
M27
A4
A30
A31
A34
A27
A303
A338
A36

architectural wealth lies in the manor houses—some of them little more than prosperous farmhouses. There is one in almost every village. To this day most villages maintain their medieval structure, with a manor house, a church, a farm, often a village green and pond, and then the cottages—thatched and limewashed, looking as smart as ever.

Hampshire is the most diverse of southern England's counties, with sharp town and country divisions. Like all the south it is largely chalk country, but the county is rich also in trees, and in the south the spur of the South Downs running into Sussex is clad with 'hangers'—the hillside copses characteristic of the village of Selborne, which was immortalised by the writings of the 18th-century naturalist Gilbert White.

The Isle of Wight's resorts are charmingly set on a coastline of chalk downlands; but its inland villages such as Godshill, Bonchurch and Mottistone hold the essence of an island which visitors—'overners', as the islanders call them—do not always have time to appreciate.

Stonehenge and Woodhenge in Wiltshire, along with grave-mounds throughout the area, and Avebury on the Marlborough Downs, are the most important survivals of prehistoric Britain; it is hard to believe that these great bare uplands were once the main inhabited region of southern England and a place of European importance. By contrast, the county town of Salisbury lies among fertile water-meadows, and the sight of its cathedral spire rising above the trees was a compelling subject for John Constable and for hundreds of lesser painters.

The Wessex of Thomas Hardy's novels

Dorset averages a little more than 1 acre of land for each inhabitant. It has remained a private and rural county largely because it has not been lacerated by the construction of major roads. Even seaside resorts such as Weymouth, Swanage and Lyme Regis, have kept their Dorset character. Inland, Dorset remains a county of quiet villages tucked away in remote lanes, and of country towns like Dorchester, which have kept their traditions without conscious preservation because they are true to the character of place and people.

The quality of Dorset has never been caught more effectively than in the Wessex novels and poetry of Thomas Hardy. Readers of his works will recognise here the country of Tess, Jude, the Mellstock Choir and a whole gallery of not-so-fictitious people. For Hardy's characters were drawn from real life and their descendants live in Dorset today.

2000 HOURS OF SUNSHINE A YEAR

No other part of Britain combines high coastal temperatures with such an excellent sunshine record as southern England—2000 hours of sunshine can be recorded in some resorts during a year, with an average of 7 hours a day for the whole coast in June. Inland, the temperature can be as much as 6°C (10°F) warmer. Inland regions also have the widest range between day and night temperatures. The rainfall is low, averaging 28–30 in. a year

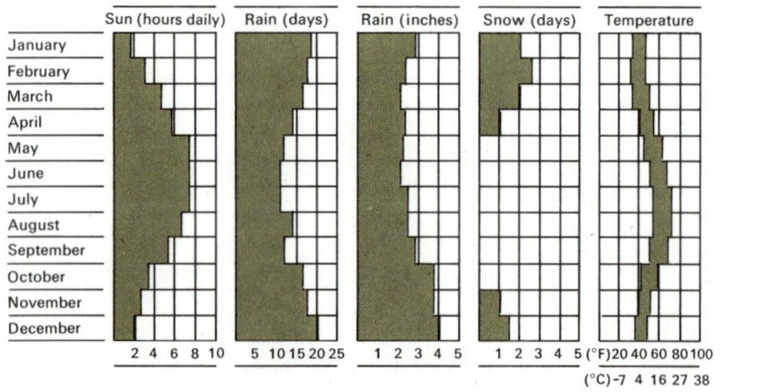

WHITE HORSE ON THE DOWNS *The Cherhill Horse, near Calne in Wiltshire, is 140 ft long. It was cut in 1780, the work of a Dr Alsop, of Calne, who is said to have stood more than a mile from his workmen, shouting instructions through a megaphone*

Where a giant's hills sweep down to the sea

Boats Sailing and water-skiing in Lyme Bay from Lyme Regis, West Bay and Portland. The *Daily Express* Power-Boat race passes off Portland Bill in Aug.

Folk customs Abbotsbury has a Garland Day on May 13 (if a Sunday then May 12). Garlands were once thrown into the sea, to ensure a good fishing catch.

Places to see *Abbotsbury Sub-tropical Gardens*: mid-Mar. to Sept., weekdays, Sun. afternoons. *Abbotsbury Swannery*: May to mid-Sept., weekdays; also Sun. if fine. *Bridport Museum and Art Gallery*: June to Oct., weekdays, except Thur. and Sat. *Melbury House* (NGS), 7 miles south-west of Sherborne: occasional Thur., June to Aug. *Philpot Museum*, Bridge Street, Lyme Regis: Easter to Sept., daily: Oct. to Easter, Tues. morning, Thur. afternoon., Sat. and Sun. *Portland Castle*: Apr. to Sept., weekdays, Sun. afternoon. *Portland Museum*, Avice's Cottage: daily, except Sun. and Mon. in winter. *Purse Caundle Manor*, 4 miles east of Sherborne: Wed., Thur., Sun. and Bank Hol. afternoons, Mar. to Oct. *St Catherine's Chapel*, Abbotsbury: weekdays, Sun. afternoon. *Sherborne New Castle*: Easter to Sept., Thur., Sat., Sun. and Bank Hol. afternoons. *Worldwide Butterflies* and *Lullingstone Silk Farm*, Over Compton, 3 miles west of Sherborne: Apr. to Oct., daily.

Information centre Town Council Offices, Lyme Regis. Tel. Lyme Regis 2138.

Rolling chalk hills stretch across west Dorset from south of Sherborne down to the sea at Lyme Regis. Their long crests look down on fertile valleys watered by the Rivers Cerne, Frome or Char, or by mere streams like the Wriggle, which twists its way around small prosperous farms. From Pilsdon Pen, at 908 ft the highest of Dorset's hills, there is a spectacular view over part of the Marshwood Vale, a huge bowl of gorse-scattered land.

Sherborne is an ideal base for exploring west Dorset. Within easy driving distance are the remains of ancient trackways and defensive earthworks cut from the shelves of chalk by Dorset's early inhabitants. The Cerne Abbas Giant was cut out of the turf about 1500 years ago.

The chalk hills end in huge cliffs at the sea-edge from Lyme Regis eastwards to Burton Bradstock, where there is an abrupt geological change to the shingle of Chesil Beach (*chesil* is Old English for shingle) which stretches as far as Portland. Beyond Portland Harbour is the Isle of Portland, famed for its stone.

Abbotsbury
A village with a long street of orange-tinged houses, interspersed with more typical Dorset thatched cottages. It has one of the largest and finest tithe barns in the country—276 ft long and 31 ft high, with a sturdy buttressed porch and hexagonal staircase tower. The barn was built in the 15th century by Benedictine monks, who also established Abbotsbury's famous swannery as a source of birds for their table.

Exotic plants and trees flourish in Abbotsbury's sub-tropical gardens, and late spring brings an abundance of camellias and heavily perfumed magnolias. To the north-west a path leads to White Hill, from which there is a superb view across to the 500-year-old stone-roofed Chapel of St Catherine, standing on another hill, with the Channel beyond.

A narrow, unsignposted road opposite The Ilchester Arms in Abbotsbury leads high up over Black Down Hill to the Hardy Monument—commemorating not Hardy the writer but Admiral Hardy, Nelson's flag captain at the Battle of Trafalgar. The car park by the monument is a fine viewpoint, commanding a huge panorama of the Dorset countryside. Miles of meadows, cornfields and coastline lie below, with not a blot on the landscape in any direction.

Beaminster
A small town set among steep farmland hills, much loved by Dorset's early 19th-century poet William Barnes, who wrote in the dialect of the county, and by the novelist Thomas Hardy, who made the town the 'Emminster' of his *Tess of the D'Urbervilles*. Its pinnacled market cross and prosperous 18th-century houses, built in the golden Ham Hill stone of the region, give the square an illusion of size; and the sparkling little River Brit, running along the side of the main street, adds charm.

Vivid green wooded hills descend close to the town on both sides, and there are rewarding walks in almost any direction. An enjoyable drive leads over Hackthorn Hill up the 800-ft rise of Toller Down, where there are secluded picnic spots with grand views.

Bridport
In spite of being intersected by the busy road to Exeter, the town retains a Georgian integrity, with wide streets and spacious pavements. The pavements were originally 'ropewalks' laid out for twisting and drying the cord and twine made in Bridport.

Cerne Abbas
Only part of the 14th-century tithe barn and 15th-century mullioned three-storeyed gatehouse remain of a former Benedictine abbey. The parish church has an imposing 15th-century buttressed tower, a late Norman chancel, early heraldic glass and, in a weathered niche in the west face of the tower, a well-preserved pre-Reformation Madonna.

Cut into the turf of the chalk hillside

THE TASTY VINNY

Dorset blue vinny (veiny) is an old variation of Stilton-type cheese, made from hand-skimmed milk. Dorset knobs are crisp rolls which are best eaten with the cheese

HUNTING AN ICHTHYOSAURUS

Mary Anning

Mary Anning, a carpenter's daughter, found a skeleton of an ichthyosaurus, a marine reptile which lived between 100 and 180 million years ago, in a cliff near Lyme Regis in 1811. Lyme Regis and Charmouth are a paradise for fossil collectors. The high and constantly crumbling cliffs are formed of shale and beds of limestone. In them are ammonites, sea animals with shells, which lived 100 to 320 million years ago. They can be broken out of some limestone beds, but may disintegrate if they are not given a coat of varnish or embedded in resin

A Dorset ammonite

The 21-ft ichthyosaurus found by Mary Anning

ABBOT'S GUEST HOUSE *This 15th-century house is one of the few buildings remaining from a Benedictine abbey at Cerne Abbas*

THE GOLDEN ARC *The pebbles at the Portland end of Chesil Beach are large, but they get smaller as the bank sweeps 16 miles west. Pebbles from here were used as ammunition by the Iron Age defenders of Maiden Castle*

NESTING TIME *Abbotsbury swans, feeding on the zostera grass, build more than 100 nests in the reeds in the breeding season*

north-east of the village is the Cerne Abbas Giant, the figure of a naked man holding a club. The figure, 180 ft tall, dates back about 1500 years and may be associated with ancient fertility rites; as late as the early 19th century, women believed that sleeping on the hillside could cure barrenness. From Dogbury Gate, 2 miles further north, the road westwards to Evershot climbs over Gore Hill, with incomparable views down to the prehistoric Cross and Hand, a weirdly shaped, weather-worn monolith, eerie and mysterious in its rugged, isolated setting. In Hardy's novel, Tess is made to swear an oath of fidelity on the stone.

Chesil Beach

A long, blue-clay reef extending for 10 miles from Abbotsbury to Portland. It is covered with an immense wall of shingle, in places 35 ft high and more than 150 yds wide. Stormy seas and strong currents have swept the pebbles from the Dorset and Devon coasts and piled them on the bank. The smallest pebbles are at the western end of the bank and they gradually increase in size going eastwards. At the Portland end the pebbles are a greyish colour, while to the west they are various shades of brown-yellow. This natural sea wall encloses a long, calm body of brackish water known as the Fleet.

The shingle is a good hunting ground for beachcombers—in the course of time the sea has cast up everything from whales to Spanish galleons—but swimming is hazardous because of treacherous currents. The simple pleasure of net fishing for mackerel, which come close to the shore, can be safely enjoyed.

Lyme Regis

A medieval port which became a seaside resort in the 18th century. It earned its royal title when Edward I used its harbour—sheltered by the massive breakwater known as the Cobb—during his wars against the French. The Duke of Monmouth landed here in 1685 to lead his ill-fated rebellion against James II. Smugglers used the town, until the fashion for sea-bathing restored it to respectability.

The resort was a favourite of the novelist Jane Austen, who set part of the action of *Persuasion* in Lyme Regis. There are fine views along the bay, dominated by Golden Cap, at 617 ft the highest cliff on England's south coast.

Portland

Thomas Hardy called this narrow, rugged peninsula 'the Gibraltar of Wessex'. All the level surfaces of the 2 mile wide mass of almost treeless rock are scarred with quarries; the light-brown, rough-textured Portland stone has been enhancing important buildings ever since Sir Christopher Wren used it to build St Paul's Cathedral.

Because of Portland's vulnerable position, two castles were built to fortify it. The earliest, the Bow and Arrow Castle built by the Normans above Church Ope Cove, is now in ruins, but Portland Castle, built in 1520 by Henry VIII, has been well preserved and still stands on the northern shore.

Modern Portland is a major naval base, using a massive harbour and breakwater which were completed in 1872 after taking 23 years to build. From Church Ope Cove, there are some fine cliff walks with impressive views; Portland's highest point (496 ft) gives good views westwards along the Chesil Beach and eastwards to the Purbeck Hills. The old lighthouse on Portland Bill is now used as a bird-watching station. There is good bathing for careful swimmers from Church Ope Cove.

Sherborne

The imposing abbey of golden stone has one of the most graceful fan-vaulted roofs in England. Sherborne School, just beyond the restored south porch of the abbey, incorporates a good deal of the original monastic buildings. The school figured as the setting for the film musical *Goodbye, Mr Chips*. The 13th-century almshouse near by has a fine triptych, which is either German or Flemish; the brilliance of its colouring is due to the use of tempera—paint mixed with egg yolk—on oak.

The town abounds in old inns and 16th and 17th-century houses, built in the same golden stone as the abbey, and set in curving little streets. Sherborne Old Castle, where Sir Walter Raleigh lived for 15 years, is now a ruin. Sherborne New Castle is rich in art treasures.

West Bay

A small port town, popular with tourists for its fishing and sailing, as well as its dramatic sandstone cliffs. It is quite unspoilt and has two good bathing beaches, one of shingle and one of pebble. Old cottages and a slate-hung early 19th-century customs house, now a café, fringe the beach.

The wild heathland that Hardy loved

Angling Sea fishing at Weymouth, Lulworth, and Osmington Mills. Coarse fishing at Radipole Lake, Weymouth. Trout fishing on the Rivers Frome and Trent.

Car ferry Weymouth Quay to Cherbourg and Channel Islands.

Places to see *Athelhampton*, 1 mile east of Puddletown, battlemented 15th-century manor house with fine gardens: Wed., Thur., Sun. and Bank Hol. afternoons, Easter to Sept. *Bindon Abbey*: daily. *Clouds Hill* (NT): afternoons only: Sun.; also Wed., Thur., Fri. and Bank Hol., Apr. to Sept. *Dewlish House*, 8 miles north-east of Dorchester, Queen Anne House: Thur. afternoons; May to Sept. *Dorset County Museum*, Dorchester: weekdays. *Dorset Military Museum*, Dorchester: weekdays, except Sat. afternoons Oct. to June. *Hardy's Cottage* (NT): exterior, Mar. to Oct., daily; interior, by appointment with tenant. *Hyde Crook* (NGS), 4½ miles north-west of Dorchester, gardens only: Easter weekend and Sun. in Apr. *Maiden Castle*: daily. *Milton Abbey*, church: daily. *No 3 Trinity Street*, Weymouth, Tudor building: Easter to Sept., Wed., Sat. and Bank Hol. afternoons. *Tank Museum*, Bovington Camp, 2 miles north-west of Wool: daily.

Information centres Publicity Office, 12 The Esplanade, Weymouth. Tel. Weymouth 72444. West Dorset District Council, 58 High Street, Dorchester. Tel. Dorchester 5211.

DORCHESTER *A sign over a restaurant and shop marks Judge Jeffreys's lodgings in 1685 during the Bloody Assize. Opposite is St Peter's Church*

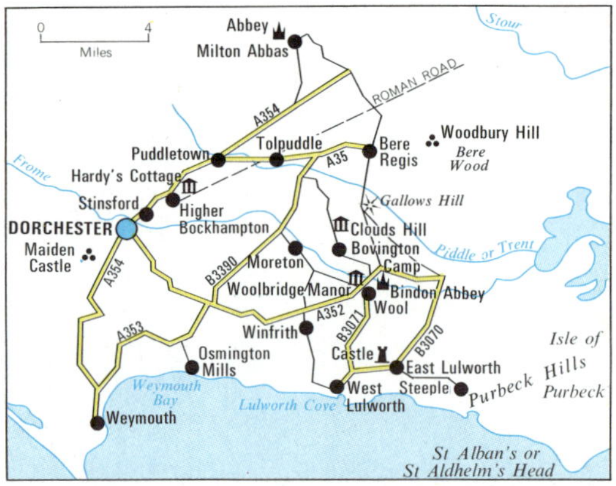

The wild heathland of mid-Dorset is Thomas Hardy country. The novelist lived all his life here and used the landscape as the memorable background to many of his novels. A re-reading of *The Return of the Native*, with its graphic descriptions of 'Egdon Heath', adds the pleasure of recognition to a visitor's exploration of this beautiful, if sombre, region.

Hardy was born in Higher Bockhampton, near Dorchester, and the village of Stinsford is the original 'Mellstock' of his novel *Under the Greenwood Tree*. Among the vast stretches of heathland, where brackens and rare wild flowers abound, are other towns which appear in his novels, such as Dorchester ('Casterbridge'), Weymouth ('Budmouth'), Bere Regis ('Kingsbere') and Puddletown ('Weatherbury').

South of Bere Regis, lonely hill country stretches to the sea; to the west is the fertile valley of the River Piddle, in which lies the famous village of Tolpuddle, home of the 'Tolpuddle Martyrs'. Here, in 1834, six farm labourers met to propose the formation of a trade union. They were arrested, charged as a 'secret society' and sentenced to seven years' transportation to Australia. After an outcry, they were pardoned two years later and offered a passage home.

South of the heathland is a region associated with another notable English writer; it was to a cottage north of Moreton that T. E. Lawrence, 'Lawrence of Arabia', moved in 1935 after he left the Royal Air Force, in which he had served as 'Aircraftman Shaw'.

The atomic energy station at nearby Winfrith seems to emphasise the solitude of this isolated yet not inhospitable countryside. Along the coast, by contrast, there are unspoilt chalk cliffs and the notable beauty spot of Lulworth Cove, one of the gems of the South.

THE BROODING WILDERNESS *Winfrith Heath is part of mid-Dorset's wild stretch of bracken and briars—Thomas Hardy's 'Egdon Heath'. In his novel* The Return of the Native *he describes it as 'majestic, watchful, haggard Egdon'. Amid its sombre beauty are rare wild flowers and many heathland birds, including the shy Dartford warbler, the red-backed shrike and the honey buzzard, which raids wasps' nests for food. The Winfrith (Celtic for 'happy stream'), rising in Winfrith Newburgh, flows past an atomic power station*

Bere Regis
The Saxon parish church was largely rebuilt by Cardinal Morton, Henry VII's Chancellor, and is noted for the painted timber roof of the nave. Its arches, supported by figures of the 12 apostles in 15th-century dress, bear the arms of the Cardinal's various offices. The church has become a place of pilgrimage for admirers of Hardy's novel *Tess of the D'Urbervilles.* Its heroine, Tess, was buried there, and a 15th-century window bears the lion rampant crest of the old Dorset family of Turberville on whom Hardy based his novel. On Woodbury Hill, just east of the village, stand the remains of an Iron Age fortification from which there are views across heath and river valleys stretching eastwards towards Poole.

Dorchester
A bustling county town and shopping centre. The lines of its main roads were laid down by the Romans, and there is an excavated Roman house in Colliton Park, near the county hall. Dorset County Museum has a good collection of Roman and pre-Roman finds, including the remains of an early warrior who, some experts believe, was dismembered after his death in battle at Maiden Castle. The museum also has a collection of Thomas Hardy manuscripts and a reconstruction of the novelist's study at Max Gate, his former home.

Maumbury Rings, south of the town, is the site of a Stone Age circle adapted by the Romans as an amphitheatre capable of seating 10,000 people. The site was used as late as 1767 for Hanging Fairs, or public executions.

Higher Bockhampton
Thomas Hardy was born in 1840 in this picturesque hamlet, in a neatly thatched cottage backed by bluebell woods. The raftered, whitewashed rooms of his cottage maintain the simplicity that Hardy loved, and the room in which he wrote has glorious views over endless miles of the heathland that inspired his novels. Hardy was buried in Westminster Abbey, but his heart was placed in a grave in the churchyard at nearby Stinsford.

Lulworth
A tourist spot of such renown that its real grandeur is best appreciated out of season. West Lulworth includes Lulworth Cove, where the chalk cliffs suddenly end and two arms of Portland and Purbeck stone almost encircle a lake-like body of water.

A not-too-arduous climb and walk westwards leads to the sheltered Man o' War Bay and to a huge limestone arch called Durdle Door, which juts out to sea. Walk along the beach on a wild, gusty day for a closer view of giant waves crashing through the arch.

East Lulworth, 2½ miles east of West Lulworth, is an attractive village dominated by the estates of the Weld family. Their castle, set in 600 acres of

COASTAL WALK *From Durdle Door, a natural arch of Purbeck limestone west of Lulworth Cove, a footpath leads westwards along 5 miles of spectacular chalk cliffs*

LULWORTH SKIPPER
This small brown-and-black butterfly, first recorded a century ago on the cliffs above Lulworth Cove, is seen in July and August. The skipper is extremely rare outside Dorset

rich woodland, was gutted by fire in 1929. The adjoining Rotunda, built in 1786, was the first Roman Catholic church built by royal permission after the Reformation; George III consented on condition that it did not look like a church.

The road eastwards to Steeple along the ridge of the Purbeck Hills gives superb views towards the coast across the beautiful Tyneham Valley. But this road is on Defence Ministry land, so watch for the notices indicating whether the area is open or closed.

Maiden Castle
One of the largest earthwork fortifications in Europe. It is more than 2 miles round the perimeter, and its terraced ramparts rise to more than 80 ft. Tools and pottery found beneath the ramparts indicate that the site was first occupied *c.* 2000 BC, then fortified in the Iron Age from 300 BC onwards, when the existing ramparts were constructed. The hill-fort was captured by the Romans under Vespasian in AD 43.

GATEWAY TO THE ISLES *Weymouth, a terminal for Channel Island ferries, was a port in Roman times, and grew important after Henry VIII developed the naval anchorage*

Milton Abbas
Thatched cottages line the street of this 18th-century 'model village'. The nearby Benedictine abbey church, which dates back to the 14th century, was sensitively restored by Sir Giles Gilbert Scott, who preserved the many splendid abbey monuments in this miniature cathedral. Milton Abbey, now a school, was built on the old site of the property given by Henry VIII to the lawyer who arranged his divorce from his first wife, Catherine of Aragon. There is a rewarding walk from the abbey up 100 grassy steps to St Catherine's Chapel above. The countryside around is quite unspoilt and incredibly peaceful.

Moreton
T. E. Lawrence—'Lawrence of Arabia'—was killed in a motor-cycle accident near here in 1935. His home, Clouds Hill, 2 miles north-east, was a gamekeeper's cottage when he found it. It is now owned by the National Trust and open to the public. Lawrence was buried in the churchyard of the small, cheerful church, which has chancel windows engraved by Laurence Whistler.

Weymouth
An ancient port and modern terminal for Channel Island steamers, as well as being a popular resort with sweeping, sandy beaches and safe bathing. Pleasant groups of Georgian and early Victorian houses, some with fine ironwork balconies, some bow-windowed, stretch in a line from the harbour to the end of the promenade. In Trinity Street, two Tudor cottages are now a museum, housing typical furnishings of an Elizabethan sea-dog's house. There are many unspoilt villages within easy reach, and a 4-mile walk eastwards to Osmington Mills can be rewarded by freshly cooked lobsters in any one of a number of little inns overlooking the sea.

Wool
A village of mellow charm on the River Frome, with one of the most beautiful 17th-century bridges in the county. The Elizabethan Woolbridge Manor was used by Thomas Hardy in *Tess of the D'Urbervilles* as the setting for Tess and Angel Clare's miserable wedding night. On the staircase of the manor, now a hotel, can be seen the faint tracings of two portraits of the real Turberville family; and the church where many of the family are buried is still standing. Half a mile east, the ruins of 12th-century Bindon Abbey stand among trees by the river. In its grounds is the open tomb in which, in Hardy's novel, Angel Clare placed Tess in his sleep.

The Blackmoor Vale

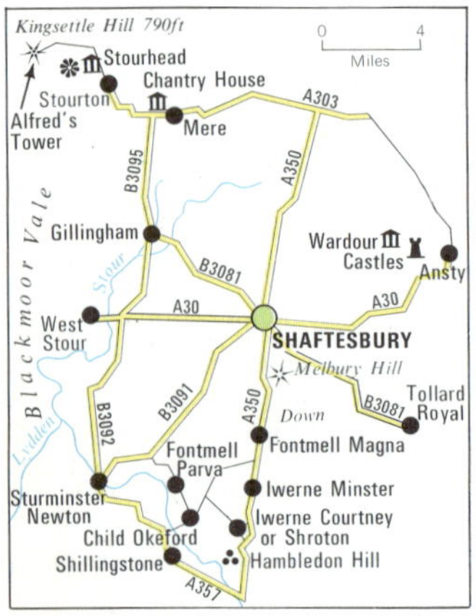

Angling On the River Stour and its tributaries at Shaftesbury and Gillingham. Some stretches are privately owned.

Archery Palladwr Bowman, Shaftesbury, is a noted club in north Dorset and the surrounding counties.

Canoeing It is possible to canoe on the River Stour from Gillingham and from Sturminster Newton to the upper reaches of the river.

Bowls Matches at the Green, Bleke Street, Shaftesbury.

Arts Plays are performed frequently at the theatre and art gallery at the Shaftesbury Club and Arts Centre, Bell Street; there are occasional concerts of chamber music.

Pilgrimages Every ten years Quakers from all over the south of England make pilgrimages to their burial ground in Ashmore, 2 miles west of Tollard Royal, to commemorate their persecution in the 17th and 18th centuries.

Places to see *Abbey Ruins*, Shaftesbury: daily. *Abbey Ruins Museum*, Park Walk, exhibits objects recovered from the excavation of the Benedictine nunnery, and a model of the abbey and the medieval town: Easter to Sept., weekdays, Sun. afternoon. *Shaftesbury Art Gallery*, Bimport: daily, except Mon., Easter to Sept. and Dec. *Stourhead* (NT), Stourton: grounds, daily; house, afternoons, except Fri., May to Aug.; Mon., Wed., Sat. and Sun. afternoons, Apr., Sept. and Oct.

Information centre Tourist Panel, Town Hall, High Street, Shaftesbury.
Tel. Shaftesbury 2420.

Undulating dairy country, well wooded, well watered and prosperous, spills over from north-east Dorset into Wiltshire. The little farming villages of the area are bordered to the south by the hills around Shillingstone, where moss is still gathered for sale in London's Covent Garden Market.

The landscape has the appeal of undisturbed rural tranquillity. In Shaftesbury, Dorset's most ancient hill-top town, 700 ft above Blackmoor Vale, there are frequent glimpses from old cobbled hill-streets across rolling fields and grazing meadows. On a fine day, the view extends right across the upper Stour and even as far as the distant hill of Glastonbury. Shaftesbury makes an excellent centre for exploring the region on foot or by car.

To the west lies the Blackmoor Vale, with rivers like the Stour, the Lydden and the Caundle Brook, which gives its name to many places along its course. The thickly wooded copses and gentle hills make ideal hunting country, and in winter the Blackmoor Vale Hunt, with its splashes of colour, turns the rolling landscape into a hunting print come to life.

PLANNED BEAUTY *The Pantheon at Stourhead's National Trust*

Ansty
A village in the heart of the farming country. Along a narrow lane out of Ansty is a signpost to Wardour Castle, once the home of the Arundel family and now a girls' school. The old castle was destroyed during the Civil War, and 1 mile away from its ruins is the present 18th-century castle. Adjoining this is one of the most beautiful baroque Roman Catholic chapels in England; its splendid interior, rich in art treasures, was designed principally by Sir John Soane, James Paine and Quarenghi.

Fontmell Magna
A village typical of many scattered Dorset settlements which have their ancient roots deep in the fertile soil. It is watered by the sparkling Fontmell Brook, flowing from the downs above. The area is rich in ash, beech and pine trees and has some particularly attractive thatched cottages. During the summer, open-air concerts are given in the pleasant rural setting of Springhead, a mill converted into a charming house with a romantic Venetian rotunda. It is reached by a narrow lane east of the A350, rising towards Melbury Hill and Fontmell Down.

Gillingham
A good shopping centre for tourists caravanning or camping in the dairy vale of Dorset. There are some fine Georgian houses to recall the time when the town and the countryside around it was acclaimed a beauty spot by the painter John Constable; the old silk mill was one of his subjects. The picture now hangs in the Tate Gallery. An old farmhouse beyond Wyke, on the main road north of the town, still has a lovely octagonal dovecot and a little stream flowing past its mellow brick-and-stone frontage. On the road to Mere is the old grammar school founded 450 years ago: the school itself has now been moved to the other side of Gillingham.

Iwerne Courtney
Sometimes known as Shroton, this is a charming village, well sheltered by the hills, on one of which, Hambledon Hill, is a prehistoric barrow. Child Okeford, 2 miles west, is a prosperous

FAMILY AFFAIR *Three thatchers, all in the same family, work on a Stourton roof*

HIGH OVER THE VALE *Cobbled Gold Hill in Shaftesbury runs steeply down towards the Blackmoor Vale. Many cottages on the steep 700-ft slope are built of green sandstone*

gardens is well framed by trees and shrubs

NATURAL BEAUTY *A typical farmhouse with a walled yard near Stourton, in the rich dairy lands on the Dorset–Wiltshire border*

farming settlement with thatched cottages, Georgian porticoed houses and an impressive manor. General Wolfe trained his troops here before the attack on Quebec in 1759.

Iwerne Minster
A prosperous-looking village with thatched cottages and an old timbered inn, The Talbot. The church is mostly Norman and 13th century, with modern additions, and its 15th-century spire is a rarity in Dorset. Just outside the village is the site of a Roman villa.

Mere
A village with two old coaching inns. The Old Ship has an interesting 18th-century sign associated with the badge of John Mere, a merchant adventurer who in the 14th century founded a chantry in the church for the singing of masses, and so gave the village its name. The Talbot is now modernised, but the old inn sheltered Charles II, in disguise, after the Battle of Worcester.

Just outside the pinnacled Perpendicular church, which has a rich and beautiful interior, is a Tudor chantry where the Dorset poet William Barnes had his own school. On the downland slopes outside the town are ridges which may have been Roman vineyards.

Shaftesbury
The town is built on the edge of a 700-ft plateau, giving fine views over the Blackmoor Vale. It figures under its old name, 'Shaston', in Hardy's novels. The town first grew up around a nunnery endowed in AD 880 by King Alfred. In the 18th-century Grosvenor Hotel, there is a famous Victorian sideboard, carved in 1862–7 by Gerrard Robinson from a single block of oak and depicting events in the 'Ballad of Chevy Chase'.

The town has some excellent grey-green, 18th-century stone houses, and the steep, cobbled Gold Hill is buttressed on one side and terraced like an Italian hill town on the other.

Stourhead
A stately home 2 miles north-west of Mere, built in 1722 by Colin Campbell in Palladian style for a banker, Henry Hoare. About 20 years later, Henry Hoare's son laid out pleasure gardens, lakes and temples in one of the finest landscape designs of the 18th century. The house, now owned by the National Trust, is crammed with art treasures: carved woodwork by Grinling Gibbons, paintings by Angelica Kauffman, work by the sculptor Michael Rysbrack, and furniture designed by Thomas Chippendale the Younger. The shores of the lake are edged with magnificent rhododendrons, beeches and tulip-trees.

There is a good $1\frac{1}{2}$-mile walk along footpaths from the 14th-century High Cross, which was brought from Bristol in 1765, down to the lake and across the bridge, then through the Grotto and past the Pantheon and up to the woodland-sheltered stone rotunda of the Temple of the Sun. The best views of the area are from the 790-ft Kingsettle Hill, with its triangular 160-ft tower built by the Hoares in 1772 to commemorate King Alfred's victory over the Danes in AD 879.

A STORE ON STILTS

Thatched-roof corn stores, raised on stone mushroom legs to keep out the rats, are typical of the region. They are often next to barns

Sturminster Newton
The market centre for the Stour farmlands. A graceful six-arched 15th-century bridge over the river carries the dire warning of 'Transportation for life' for those who damage it. The 17th-century town mill is still working, churning its waters into white-flecked foam. The wooden-porticoed Mill House on the road to Blandford Forum faces a thatched house of character. A little further on is Newton House; its Georgian façade, with a curious medallion frieze over the front door, hides its much greater age.

William Barnes, Dorset's 19th-century poet who wrote 'Linden Lea' and is noted for his use of the pure dialect of his county, was born at nearby Pentridge Farm. Thomas Hardy wrote *The Return of the Native* in a greystone mansion, Riverside, on the outskirts of the town.

Sturminster Newton is made colourful by many bow-windowed buildings of brick, stone and cob. There are also good thatched, timber-traced houses leading up to the pretty market square where, on Monday mornings, crowds of farmers and dairymen overflow into the station yard and surrounding streets. The thatched White Hart Inn is 18th century, and the Perpendicular church has been enriched by modern artists.

West Stour
An attractive village in the Stour Valley, with a restored 13th-century church. The village has associations with the 18th-century novelist Henry Fielding, who modelled the character of Parson Adams in *Joseph Andrews* on the vicar.

COOL WATER *This stone-walled well is in the village of Tollard Royal. Its age is unknown but it is still in working order*

Hills and heaths of east Dorset

Boats Sailing facilities and clubs at Poole, Swanage and Wareham.

Angling There is deep sea and shore fishing at Poole and Swanage and shark fishing off Poole.

Sports Poole Indoor Sports Centre caters for 27 different sports from archery to volleyball; visitors are welcome daily. Facilities exist for most sports in Swanage, including a sub-aqua diving centre on the pier.

Places to see *Brownsea Island* (NT), Poole Harbour, 500 acres of heath and woodland, guided tours of the Nature Reserve, which is run by the Dorset Naturalists' Trust: Apr. to Sept., daily. *Compton Acres*, Poole: daily Apr. to Oct. *Corfe Castle*: daily, Mar. to Oct. *Cranborne Manor Gardens*: Apr. to Oct., 1st Sat. and Sun. in each month and other occasional days. *Guildhall Museum* and *Maritime Museum*, Poole: both weekdays and Sun. afternoon. *Merley Tropical Bird Gardens*, Poole, over 100 species of exotic birds in outdoor aviaries: Apr. to Oct., daily. *Priest's House Museum*, Wimborne Minster: weekdays, Easter to Sept. *Scaplen's Court*, Poole: weekdays, Sun. afternoon.

Information centres The White House, Shore Road, Swanage. Tel. Swanage 2885. Civic Centre, Poole. Tel. Poole 5151.

Sharp contrasts characterise east Dorset—hills bleak and high, hills forested in beech and oak, fertile valleys, wild heathland and a cliff-edged coastline. There are frequent signs of ancient barrows and hill forts; from Pentridge, a *cul-de-sac* village north of Cranborne, the walker can follow a footpath leading to a prehistoric dyke garlanded with flowers.

South-west, towards Blandford Forum, the country becomes richly agricultural, with cornfields and pasturelands, then rolls eastwards towards Wimborne Minster past cultivated woodlands and peaceful dairy-lands along the valley of the River Stour. Wimborne Minster, built by the Kings of Wessex and beautified by medieval priors, makes a natural centre for touring east Dorset, with good roads radiating in all directions.

Southwards, the many chalk streams connected with the Rivers Piddle and Frome converge on Wareham, facing out to the almost landlocked harbour of Poole. Among the islands dotted in the harbour is Brownsea Island, the site of the first Boy Scout camp. The southern shore of the harbour is formed by the so-called 'Isle' of Purbeck, rich in marble quarries. The area, with its little stone hamlets, is criss-crossed with minor roads and tracks, some of which climb steeply south of Corfe Castle to give superb views across farmland towards the Channel.

IN THE MARSHES *East Dorset's wide variety of countryside includes bleak marshland and heath west of Poole Harbour*

Ashmore
The highest village in Dorset, 700 ft up in the chalk hills. From the top of an earthwork north of the village there is a fine view across Cranborne Chase to the Solent and the high land on the Isle of Wight. Surrounding a central duck pond are Georgian houses, cottages of flint, stone and brick and a church with a Norman font and a 17th-century altar table. The village is surrounded by beech and sycamore trees, and there is one especially abundant cedar.

Blandford Forum
This handsome Georgian town was practically burnt to the ground in 1731. Its new builders gave it the cool, classical proportions of early to mid-18th century planning. Nearly all the buildings in Market Place, East Street and Salisbury Street, including the period parish church, are well designed and built in pleasing red or rust brick and stone. The Corn Exchange is outstanding, as is the 200-year-old pump under a graceful Doric porch.

The nearby village of Bryanston, with its picturesque thatched cottages and well-known public school, lies beside a lovely bend of the Stour.

Signposts on the road from Blandford Forum to Salisbury point the way 'To 6*d* Handley'—the Saxon-named village of Sixpenny Handley.

COUNTING THE DAYS *On each side of the Wimborne–Tarrant Keyneston road are 365 beeches, one for every day of the year, planted by the Kingston Lacy Hall estate*

Corfe Castle
The village, with its tumbling and undulating stone roofs that cap grey-stone houses, has a quaint character of its own, but is dominated by the stark, spectacular fortress above it. Corfe Castle is a monument to centuries of cruelty, dating from the murder, in AD 978, of 18-year-old King Edward (later called 'The Martyr') by his step-mother Queen Aelfthryth. Cromwell besieged the castle in 1646, after which it was largely demolished and its stone used in local building.

Cranborne
Attractive brick-and-timber houses line the village's broad main street (it has several twisting by-ways). From AD 980 to 1102 it was the seat of the Chase Court—the official body controlling

CASTLE OF TREACHERY *The ruins of Corfe Castle stand starkly on a hill, in contrast to the mellowed stone and brick cottages in the village below. King Edward the Martyr was murdered here in* AD *978 and in the Civil War the castle was besieged by Cromwell*

hunting rights in Cranborne Chase forest—and had a grammar school, market and Benedictine abbey; but today it is only a village. Cranborne Manor, a mixture of medieval and Renaissance building, and its gardens, are occasionally open to the public. It has been in the family of the Cecils, Marquesses of Salisbury, since it was granted to them by James I.

The former royal forest of Cranborne Chase is now an area of beautiful rolling countryside with attractive villages separated by belts of woodland.

MISSING SPIRE *Wimborne Minster's spire fell from its Norman tower in 1600*

Poole

Dorset's largest town has a harbour with a miraculously untouched 18th-century atmosphere. Much of the tremendous natural harbour, about 95 miles round, seems little changed since the days of pirates—one almost expects to meet stocking-capped smugglers at the next corner. There are many 18th-century and early 19th-century houses, including delightful old inns like The Angel, and The Old Customs House, rebuilt in 1813 after a previous building had been burnt down.

A long line of harbour offices and ships' chandlers appears little changed since the days of prosperous timber trading with Newfoundland in the 18th and 19th centuries. Poole Pottery on the quayside is open to the public. There are two golf courses and from Compton Acres gardens there is a superb view over the harbour.

Studland

From a car park near the village a leafy lane leads straight on to a sandy and attractively secluded bathing beach. Its east-facing position protects it from aggressive westerly winds. From Shell Bay, at the north end of the broad Studland Bay, a car ferry crosses to Sandbanks, near Poole. At the southern end of Studland Bay a footpath over Ballard Down leads to Swanage, with a good view seaward to the crumbling chalk stacks of the Old Harry Rocks.

Swanage

The town, once a Saxon port, is referred to in the Domesday Book as 'Swanic'; and a granite column on the front commemorates King Alfred's naval victory over the Danish fleet in the bay in AD 877. Today it is a busy holiday resort, with a fine beach for bathing. The facade of the town hall was designed by Wren in 1670.

READY TO SAIL *The large natural harbour at Poole is a fine yachting centre. There are boat-building yards, and the port is used by coasters carrying grain, timber and coal*

Wareham

A market town of Saxon origin. After a fire in the mid-18th century, Georgian planners designed a spaciously wide main street, convenient in modern times for parking. Wareham, situated just above the Frome marshes, between the outlets of two rivers flowing into Poole Harbour, is a favourite resort for small-boat enthusiasts. The River Frome brings in a salty tang. Young fishermen can cast safely from its banks, and it is a pleasant place to picnic and watch the tall-masted boats.

In the Saxon Church of St Martin is a superb sculpture by Eric Kennington of Lawrence of Arabia, in Arab dress, lying with his head supported by a camel saddle. (Lawrence's home was in Dorset at the time of his death.) On St John's Hill, a small but interesting museum has numerous Lawrence relics. St Mary's Church, which contains the coffin of Edward the Martyr, gives views from its towers of the Old Quay.

Wimborne Minster

There is a splendid approach from Blandford to this little market town, down a long avenue of beeches, which skirts the triple-banked Iron Age defensive earthworks of Badbury Rings, centred in the heathlands of east Dorset, with five main roads radiating from it. Wimborne makes an ideal centre for touring the area. Its prosperity was formerly based on wool, but now comes from market gardening.

The twin-towered Church of St Cuthberga, one of the great churches of Dorset, embraces almost every style of architecture from Norman to late Gothic. On the west tower of the church is the Quarter Jack clock, which has the figure of a brilliantly clad grenadier to strike the quarter hours with a hammer. The Priest's House Museum has a collection of antiques and some of the best horse brasses in the country.

A spire soaring from the meadows

Angling Fishing in the Rivers Avon, Nadder and Bourne. The Avon is probably the best-known coarse-fishing water in the country.

Horse racing Four annual meetings are held during the Flat season at Salisbury Racecourse, on the Race Plain, 3 miles west of the city.

Boating Boats may be hired on the Avon. Best stretches between Castle Street and Stratford-sub-Castle.

Arts Salisbury Festival of Arts takes place in Sept. The Southern Cathedrals Festival is held at Salisbury Cathedral every third year —1982, 1985, etc.

Places to see *Church House*, Crane Street, Salisbury, 15th-century wool merchant's house: Mon. to Fri. *Mompesson House* (NT), Salisbury: Apr. to Sept., Mon., Tues., Wed., Sat., Sun. afternoons. *North Canonry*, Salisbury: afternoons, Apr. to Sept. *Old Deanery*, Salisbury: Tues. to Sat. afternoons in Aug. *Old Wardour Castle*, Tisbury: daily, except Sun. morning Oct. to Mar. *Philipps House* (NT), Dinton, 9 miles west of Salisbury: Wed. afternoon, Apr. to Sept. *Pythouse*, Tisbury: May to Sept., Wed., Thur. afternoons. *Salisbury and South Wiltshire Museum*, St Ann Street, Salisbury: weekdays; also Sun. afternoon, July and Aug. *Wardour Castle*, Tisbury, containing fine Adam staircase: mid-July to early Sept., Mon., Wed., Fri. and Sat. afternoons. *Wilton House*: Easter to early Oct., Tues. to Sat. and Sun. afternoon.

Information centre Information Bureau, Endless Street, Salisbury. Tel. Salisbury 4956.

ON THE LOOM *Wilton is famous for its carpets, which have been made in the town since the 17th century*

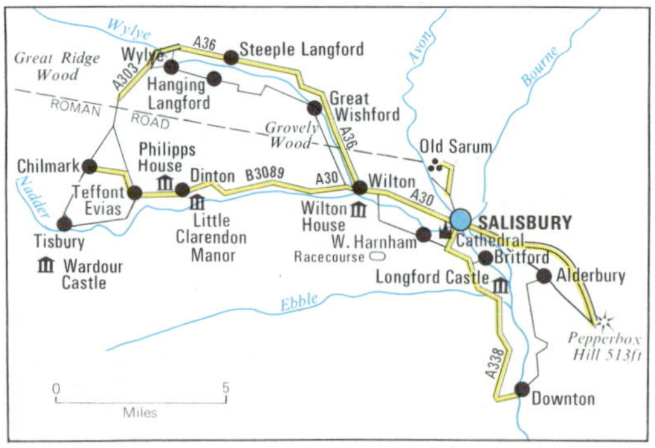

Salisbury, or New Sarum, built at the meeting-point of four river valleys and sheltered by downland, is one of the most beautiful cathedral cities in Britain. The first bishops laid out the town in the 13th century on a simple grid pattern, which has adapted well to the needs of modern traffic. The cathedral spire is the graceful centrepiece of a unified city in which buildings of all styles blend harmoniously —from medieval gabled houses, historic inns and market-places to stately pedimented Georgian houses and even a modern shopping centre.

Salisbury was founded in 1220 when Bishop Richard Poore abandoned the Norman cathedral built on the fortified hill of Old Sarum because it lacked a good water supply, and began to build a new cathedral about 2 miles south on flat, well-watered meadowland. The site of the new building was called 'New Sarum'. The cathedral is the only English medieval cathedral largely conceived and executed in a single style, rather than piecemeal over the centuries. Except for part of the tower and the spire, it is entirely Early English Gothic. The building was finished *c.* 1280, but the magnificent spire, at 404 ft the tallest in England, was not part of the original plan; it was added in 1334.

Columns of Purbeck stone appear dramatically throughout the cathedral's rich, spacious interior and there are many impressive tombs and monuments. In the north aisle of the nave a dial-less clock dates from 1386 and is probably the oldest mechanism in working order in the world. The miniature fan-vaulted roof in the grilled Audley Chantry is exquisitely designed, with ancient roundels, or decorative medallions, clearly visible in the high vaulting of the choir. The cloisters are the largest of any English cathedral, and the library over the East Walk contains one of the four original copies of Magna Carta.

The cathedral Close, still entered through medieval gateways, contains many notable houses dating back to the 13th century. The old deanery, built between 1258 and 1277, has its original timber roof; and Mompesson House, named after the wealthy merchant family who built it in 1701, has original panelling and plasterwork of graceful craftsmanship. Harnham Bridge over the Avon was built in the reign of Henry III and near it, at West Harnham, is an old watermill. Salisbury is an important market town and a good

Alderbury

A village with an inn, The Green Dragon, which figures in Charles Dickens's *Martin Chuzzlewit*. On a ridge 2 miles south-east is an extraordinary eye-catcher called Eyre's Folly, or 'The Pepperbox'. It is one of the oldest follies in the county, a slate-roofed, six-sided structure built in 1606. It stands on 73 acres of open downs covered with junipers, and is owned by the National Trust.

Trafalgar House, 2 miles south, was built in 1733 and presented by a grateful nation to Lord Nelson's family in 1814, when it received its present name. It contains a 'Ganges' room, panelled with timbers from the man o' war of the same name which fought with Nelson's fleet at the Battle of Copenhagen.

Britford

A village in the Avon water-meadows, with views of the spire of Salisbury Cathedral. It has charming old houses, including the 18th-century Bridge Farm and The Moat, a partly Georgian, partly Gothic Revival house.

Longford Castle, about 1 mile south, is largely 16th century and built to a triangular pattern. It has a notable collection of paintings.

Chilmark

A village with a wealth of 17th-century houses and cottages built with the beautiful cream-coloured Chilmark stone, which has been quarried near by since the Roman occupation and was used in the building of Salisbury Cathedral. The clear stream flowing through the village is crossed by delightful little stone bridges. The Early English church has a 'broach' spire, with stone pyramids at the corners of the tower instead of a parapet. The manor house is 17th century. Chilmark Common is a pleasantly shaded spot for a picnic.

Dinton

A delightful village built on a hillside and bordered by three beautifully landscaped houses. Philipps House, in Dinton Park, has an early 19th-century neo-Grecian white facade. Little Clarendon, just east of Dinton Church, is a handsome, creeper-covered, early Tudor manor house. Lawes Cottage, also close to the church, dates from the 17th century; it was the home of William Lawes, a composer and friend of John Milton, and some of his music for Milton's *Masque of Comus*, which was written in 1634, is said to have been composed there.

Great Wishford

Steeply roofed cottages, some dating from 1628, cluster around the parish church in the Wylye Valley. Built into the east wall of the churchyard is a record of the price of bread since 1800. The first price recorded is '3*s* 4*d* per gallon'—a reminder of the days when

FOR A CHURCH . . .

Chilmark stone, used for Salisbury Cathedral, is now quarried for churches

NEW FROM THE OLD *Some of the stone for Salisbury Cathedral was taken from Old Sarum (right) where only foundations remain*

touring centre, from which peaceful riverside drives radiate in every direction. The splendid Avon, which rises near Devizes, becomes navigable at Salisbury, after the waters of three other rivers have joined it.

East of the city the River Bourne winds through wooded downs and picturesque villages named after the river. To the west lie the valleys of the Wylye and the Nadder, separated by the wooded heights of Grovely Wood and the Great Ridge, along which can be traced the route of a Roman road plunging westwards towards Bath, the Roman city of Aquae Sulis.

The Wylye Valley delighted Izaak Walton, 17th-century author of *The Compleat Angler*, and the light reflected from its placid water-meadows inspired many of Constable's paintings. The Nadder Valley is fringed by the parklands of old country mansions, and along both valleys are many unspoilt little hamlets and prosperous farmlands, where well-fed cattle graze.

bread was sold in the semi-fluid state of dough.

To the south and west of the village are the forest downlands of Grovely Wood. Villagers keep up old customs. They exercise their ancient right to collect free firewood from Grovely Wood, and they dance on the lawns of Salisbury Cathedral every Oak Apple Day (May 29). They also lay oak boughs before the altar of the cathedral.

. . . OR A COTTAGE WALL

Cottages at Teffont Evias are built in warm, cream-coloured Chilmark stone

Old Sarum

The forerunner of modern Salisbury and site of the original Roman fortress of Sorviodunum. Though the site is deserted today there is still a strong atmosphere of its vanished glory. The huge circular mound of multiple earthworks, covering 56 acres, was probably first used as an Iron Age camp. The Saxons called the stronghold Searobyrg, meaning 'dry town'; in the Domesday Book, Salisbury is recorded as 'Sarisberie'. A small town grew up in Norman times and the first cathedral was completed by Bishop Osmund, a nephew of William the Conqueror. It was taken down when the See was moved to Salisbury, but the lines of the cathedral's foundations are still visible on the turf.

Old Sarum was one of the so-called 'rotten boroughs', abolished by the Reform Act of 1832, in which only ten voters returned two MPs: one was the constituency's most famous representative, William Pitt the Elder, the 18th-century Prime Minister, whose membership is commemorated by a plaque on the site, erected in 1931.

Steeple Langford

A village in the Wylye Valley with thatched brick cottages contrasting with the even older traditional chequered-flint houses. The Norman church contains a Purbeck marble Norman font and a 'squint' aperture in the wall. From the church there is an attractive short walk south-west across innumerable streams to join a minor road leading into Hanging Langford, a hamlet which seems to hang on to the lower ledges of the hills bordering Grovely Wood.

Teffont Evias

One of the most delightful villages in the Nadder Valley. Most of its houses are approached by little bridges over a swift-flowing stream. The old stone manor houses typify the obvious prosperity of the farming valley, and Fitz House is a particularly charming 17th-century farmhouse.

Tisbury

A village on a steep slope beside the Nadder. Its 200 ft long thatched tithe barn is one of the largest in England, and the church, which dates mainly from the 13th century, has a fine panelled and carved roof.

Wilton

This was once the capital of Saxon Wessex. The town's market-place has a severe yet pleasing early 18th-century market house. On one side a series of graceful, ruined arches leads to a compact Gothic church, restored by a former United States Ambassador in 1937 in memory of his namesake and ancestor, Robert Bingham, who was consecrated bishop here in 1229.

Wilton House, home of the Earls of Pembroke, stands on the site of an abbey founded by Alfred the Great. Much of the house was destroyed by fire in 1647, but it was reconstructed by Inigo Jones and his son-in-law John Webb. It contains a collection of paintings and furniture, as well as 7000 19th-century model soldiers. It is also noted for its elegant Double Cube Room, 60 ft long, 30 ft wide and 30 ft high. The park has fine cedars.

Wylye

An attractive village with the typical chequer-work stone and flint cottages of this part of Wiltshire. There is a restored Perpendicular church, with a Jacobean pulpit and fittings.

RICH PASTURES *Friesian cattle on the water-meadows of the River Wylye. The lush grass increases not only the yield but also the quality of the milk they produce*

Where man worshipped at the dawn of history

Angling Trout and coarse fishing on the River Biss at Trowbridge and on the River Wylye at Warminster; on the Kennet and Avon Canal at Devizes.

Golf Courses at Bishops Cannings, near Devizes, and at Warminster.

Boating Shearwater Sailing Club, Warminster, sail on the lake of the Longleat Estate. Licences are required for canoeing on the Kennet and Avon Canal. Paddle-steamer trips can be taken from Devizes.

Nature trails An educational nature trail runs 6 miles east of Devizes along the towpath of the Kennet and Avon Canal between All Cannings and Stanford Bridge. Guides are provided at the trail at Woodland Park, Brokerswood, which has a natural history centre.

Events The Devizes to Westminster Canoe Race starts on Good Fri. every year. A cattle and agricultural machinery market is held every Thur. in Devizes.

Places to see *Devizes Museum*, Long Street, containing the Stourhead collection of Bronze Age relics: Tues. to Sat. *Longleat House* and *Wildlife Park*, Warminster: daily, but house closed Christmas Day. *Phillips Countryside Museum*, Brokerswood: daily. *Stonehenge*: daily. *Wiltshire Regimental Museum*, Le Marchant Barracks, Roundway, 1½ miles north-east of Devizes: Mon. to Fri.

Information centres Redworth House, Amesbury. Tel. Amesbury 3255. Bramley House, Mere, Warminster. Tel. Mere 341. The Cedars, Bath Road, Devizes. Tel. Devizes 4911.

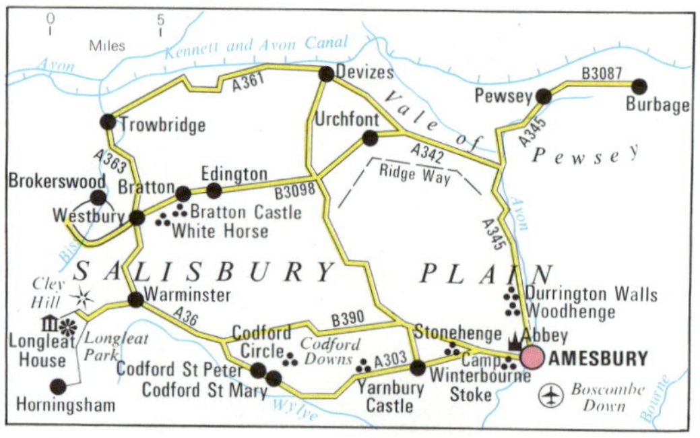

Stillness broken by the song of larks and lapwings across a vast, green expanse of undulating chalk downs, with an awesome atmosphere of prehistory—the landscape of Salisbury Plain has not changed greatly since John Evelyn, the 17th-century diarist, described it as a 'goodly plaine . . . and one of the most delightful prospects of nature'.

The plain, roughly 20 miles from west to east and 12 miles from north to south, stretches from the Vale of Pewsey southwards towards Salisbury, and is fringed by the attractive river valleys of the Avon, the Bourne and the Wylye. Some parts of the plain are given over to military use, but its essential grandeur remains. Modern farming has reclaimed large tracts of the land, using chemicals to turn the acid chalk hills into fertile soil for growing corn. The huge fields sweep unbroken to the horizon, and in the late summer the combine harvesters working against the skyline give a suggestion of the spaciousness of the North American prairies.

The average height of the plain is 450 ft, and it reaches its highest point of 755 ft on its north-west edge near Bratton Castle, a fine Iron Age hill fort. There are many superb views. One that best typifies the character of the plain is from the ancient earthworks of Yarnbury Castle, 2 miles west of Winterbourne Stoke on the southern fringe of the plain, from which downlands roll away into the distance.

The numerous other prehistoric sites on Salisbury Plain include Durrington Walls, Woodhenge and Vespasian's Camp as well as Stonehenge, which has the most complex history of any ancient monument in Europe. All these give evidence that there was civilised life in southern England more than 2000 years before the birth of Christ.

Amesbury
A town set in a bend of the River Avon, which is crossed by a five-arched bridge built in Palladian style. Amesbury Abbey is built on the site of the priory to which, according to Thomas Mallory, Queen Guinevere withdrew when she heard of King Arthur's death. West of the Avon, on the border of Amesbury Park, are the outlines of prehistoric earthworks which are named Vespasian's Camp after the Roman Emperor, but date from a much earlier age. The large military and R.A.F. camps near Amesbury include the important experimental flying base of Boscombe Down, where new aircraft are tested.

Codford St Mary
A typical small village of the Wylye Valley, on the edge of Salisbury Plain, joined by a single street to the even smaller village of Codford St Peter. The plain sweeps up behind the two villages towards the 617-ft prehistoric Codford Circle. Inside Codford St Peter's church is an unusually beautiful piece of stone carving, in the form of part of a 9th-century cross showing the figure of a man dressed in a short, draped tunic and performing a ritual dance.

Devizes
A pleasant old market town with some fine Georgian houses and a 19th-century castle that stands on the site of a Norman stronghold built by the Bishop of Salisbury. On the market cross is an inscription telling the salutary story of the sudden death in 1753 of one Ruth Pierce, after cheating at the local market. The museum has collections of finds from Neolithic, Bronze Age and Iron Age sites in Wiltshire.

Longleat House
One of Britain's great Elizabethan mansions, begun in 1568 for Sir John Thynne, an ancestor of the Marquess of Bath who owns it today. The lions roaming among visitors' cars in the park draw the weekend crowds; and the house itself—symmetrical except for its great hall at one side—has a rich collection of furniture, paintings and books. Near the park, which was landscaped by Capability Brown, is Heaven's Gate, a half-mile walk through woodlands bright with azaleas and rhododendrons in June, to a superb viewpoint looking down on Longleat in the valley below. In the village of Horningsham, 1 mile south, is a thatched Nonconformist chapel—one of the oldest in Britain—built in 1568 by the Scottish builders who worked on Longleat.

Pewsey
William Cobbett, in his *Rural Rides* published in 1830, was attracted to the Vale of Pewsey's 'villages, hamlets, large farms, towers, steeples, fields, meadows, orchards and very fine timber trees scattered over the valley'. Little has changed since Cobbett's day in the green valley of which Pewsey is the centre. Pewsey has a mixture of Wiltshire thatched cottages and Georgian houses, and at the crossroads a statue of King Alfred looks across the River Avon. Attractive villages surround the town, and prehistoric barrows line the high southern escarpment of the Marlborough Downs to the north.

Stonehenge
Viewed from the main road, the world-famous Bronze Age site appears minute against the vastness of Salisbury Plain. But once the visitor has walked, by a tunnel under the road, towards the first circular ditch, the whole perspective changes and human figures look like pygmies beneath the standing stones, the largest of which is 21 ft high. The outer ditch is the oldest part of Stone-

WILDLIFE AT LONGLEAT PARK

A cheetah and a herd of giraffes are among the wildlife in the park of Longleat, home of the Marquess of Bath. Fifty lions also roam free in a section of the park

THE LONGEST DAY AT STONEHENGE Companions of the Most Ancient Order of Druids keep a midnight vigil every June 21 before the midsummer sunrise over Stonehenge, where sunworshipping ceremonies are believed to have been held nearly 4000 years ago. The original avenue into Stonehenge was past the Slaughter Stone, top left; in spite of its name there is no proof that this stone was used for sacrifices. Round the perimeter are the 56 so-called 'Aubrey' holes, 16 ft apart and now filled with concrete. These holes were named after the 17th-century diarist John Aubrey who discovered them. South Barrow is the rough circle on the right of the site and North Barrow is at the left, near the present entrance path. In the centre of Stonehenge are two rings of sarsen stones which came from the Marlborough Downs. The fallen Altar Stone in the centre is one of 80 bluestones transported over 200 miles across land and water. The arrangement of the stones was changed at least twice between 1800 and 1500 BC, and two circles of holes between the centre and the perimeter are the traces of an earlier pattern of Stonehenge.

henge, probably constructed before 2150 BC. About 475 years later, a double circle was erected of 80 bluestones brought more than 200 miles from the Prescelly Hills in south-west Wales. It is believed they were floated on rafts across the Bristol Channel, then dragged over tracks of logs to Salisbury Plain. In 1650 BC the bluestones were taken down and two rings of sarsen stones (from 'Saracen', or 'foreign', though brought this time from no further away than the Marlborough Downs) were erected in the formation that survives today: an outer ring of standing stones, 14 ft high, with lintels across the top of them, and an inner horseshoe of five pairs of uprights with lintels. Later still, some of the bluestones were set up again in a line between the two rings of sarsens and in an inner horseshoe. The largest bluestone—the so-called Altar Stone—was set at the very centre, where it still lies. From the Altar Stone the eye is drawn towards the Heelstone, 256 ft away; it is over the peak of this stone that the sun rises on June 21, the longest day of the year, and this has led many experts to believe that the site had a religious purpose in connection with sun-worship.

Stonehenge, completed *c.* 1250 BC, retains a powerful atmosphere of mystery and awe. This sense is heightened when the sun casts the shadows of the huge upright stones towards holes near the outer ditch.

HATTED AND BOOTED

A Wiltshire cottage made of porous chalk blocks had to have a 'good hat and a good pair of boots' to keep out damp—thatch for the hat and sarsen foundations for boots

Trowbridge
The town was once a major settlement of Flemish weavers, who brought it great prosperity, and West of England broadcloth is still made here. In The Parade are some magnificent cream-coloured stone houses built by the 18th-century cloth merchants.

Warminster
A town at the head of the wooded Wylye Valley. Its prosperity as a wool town and corn market in the 18th century has left a heritage of beautiful houses and mullioned-windowed cottages, and two delightful inns.

Although the Army's School of Infantry is here, and there are many military camps near by, Warminster remains an attractive market town. Dr Arnold, headmaster of Rugby School, was a pupil at the Warminster Grammar School, which was founded in 1707. A 2-mile drive west of the town centre leads to the foot of Cley Hill, 800 ft, on the prehistoric Ridge Way which ran from South Devon to the Wash.

Westbury
A small weaving and glove-making town with a little market-place, good Georgian houses and an imposing town hall. Palace Green takes its name from the one-time residence of the Kings of Wessex. Cut into the chalk of Bratton Down, $1\frac{1}{2}$ miles north-east, is the most famous White Horse in Wiltshire. The existing figure was cut in the 18th century on the site of an earlier horse said to have commemorated King Alfred's victory over the Danes at the Battle of Ethandun in AD 878.

Woodhenge
A Neolithic earthwork older than Stonehenge was found here in 1925. Six concentric rings of holes, now marked by concrete posts, appear to have been made for wooden posts and positioned, like Stonehenge, to indicate where the sun would rise on Midsummer Day. Woodhenge, and the circular earthworks of Durrington Walls near by, together probably formed a single religious centre which was moved to Stonehenge *c.* 1800 BC at the end of the Neolithic period.

REBIRTH OF A CANAL *A total of 29 locks take the Kennet and Avon Canal up a hill west of Devizes. The canal, built in 1810, is being restored for recreational use*

The colourful fabric of the weavers' land

From medieval times until the Industrial Revolution, north-west Wiltshire made its wealth from weaving, and many fine houses in rich, cream-coloured Bath limestone remain from this affluent period. Indeed, the special charm of this area today lies in the character of its towns and villages, such as Charlton, Biddestone and Yatton Keynell.

The countryside, too, has the appeal of unspoilt rusticity. Low-lying agricultural land, watered by the Lower Avon, stretches south from Malmesbury to Chippenham and Melksham, and eastwards to Wootton Bassett. Westwards the land rises sharply or dips into wooded dells which shelter famous beauty spots such as Bradford-on-Avon and Castle Combe.

This is a land with its roots in history. The route of the Roman road from London to Bath passed just south of Calne, and along this route have been discovered the site of an important Roman settlement, Verlucio, and the remains of a villas. The medieval period, too, has left its mark in the number of fine churches that survive around Malmesbury and Chippenham.

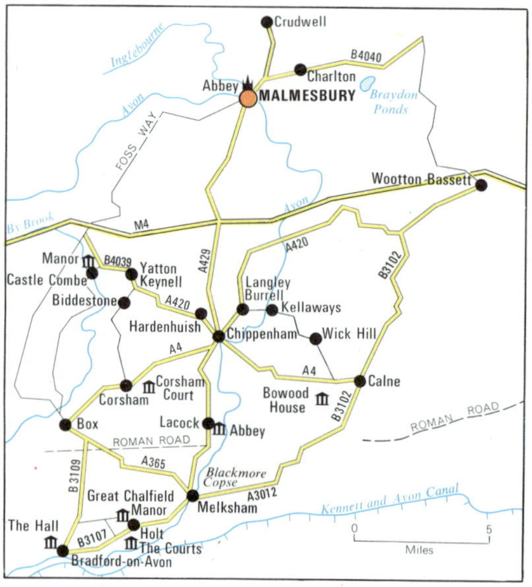

Angling There is trout and coarse fishing on the Bristol Avon at Melksham; the Avon and Frome at Bradford-on-Avon; the Marden and Avon at Chippenham; and the Kennet and Avon Canal at Semington, south of Melksham.

Boating On the Bristol Avon at Bradford-on-Avon, where a boating club holds a regatta in July. Sailing and canoeing on the Avon at Chippenham; canoeing at Melksham.

Golf Courses at Kingsdown, near Bradford-on-Avon and Chippenham.

Country park At Barton Farm, near Bradford-on-Avon.

Events A carnival is held in Malmesbury in the last week in Aug.

Places to see *Athelstan Museum*, Malmesbury: daily. *Corsham Court*, state rooms: Sun., Wed., Thur.; also Tues. and Sat., mid-July to mid-Sept. *Great Chalfield Manor* (NT), Melksham, moated manor house built *c.* 1480 in late Gothic style, with great hall and murals: mid-Apr. to late Sept., Wed. afternoon. *Lacock* (NT): house and grounds, afternoons only Apr. to Oct., but closed Mon. and Tues. in Apr., May and Oct.; open Bank Hol. Mon. *Malmesbury Abbey*: daily. *The Courts*, Holt, $2\frac{1}{2}$ miles north-east of Bradford-on-Avon: gardens (NT), Apr. to Oct., Mon. to Fri. afternoons. *Westwood Manor* (NT), 2 miles south-west of Bradford-on-Avon: Apr. to Sept., Wed. afternoon.

Information centre Malmesbury Town Hall. Tel. Malmesbury 2143.

Box

A large, straggling village with quarries that are still worked to produce the fine Bath stone. One of Isambard Brunel's masterpieces of Victorian railway engineering, the Box tunnel, nearly 2 miles long, links Box and Corsham.

Bradford-on-Avon

A town quite different in character from any other town in Wiltshire. Almost every route into the town is down a steep incline, and the Bath-stone houses have a unique beauty. The bridge across the Avon has two original medieval arches and a curious domed structure on one side—once a chapel where pilgrims from Malmesbury to Glastonbury stopped to pray, and which was converted in the 17th century into a lock-up.

The Saxon church in Church Street, with its simple stone roof, narrow arched porches and two sculptured angels, is almost certainly the Church of St Lawrence, founded by Bishop Aldhelm who died in AD 709. The church was hidden among houses and stables until a perceptive clergyman discovered it in the 1870's. Church House is a beautiful early 16th-century house built by a wealthy weaver, Thomas Horton, as a cloth hall. The Hall in Holt Road, built in 1610 by John Hall, is a fine example of Elizabethan architecture.

Bradford-on-Avon's tithe barn is one of the best-preserved in the country. It was built in the 14th century by the Abbess of Shaftesbury, and its massive timber joists and stone-tiled roof cover a granary more than 167 ft long by more than 30 ft wide. Some of the town's most beautiful houses date from the affluence of the 18th-century cloth merchants, and almost every climbing, spiralling street brings some interesting building or fine old inn into view. The many views of the Avon add a final touch of charm to the town.

Calne

Although at the centre of busy crossroads, Calne manages to retain the aura of an old market town, sheltered comfortably in the valley. Like so many north Wiltshire towns, it derived its original prosperity from weaving. When the Industrial Revolution killed its livelihood, it turned to bacon-curing and the making of sausages and pies.

The Lansdowne Arms, reconstructed in the 18th century, is on the site of an old inn dating back to the Middle Ages, and the original brew-house is still in the yard. The old almshouses in Kingsbury Street look across to the impressive parish church; its soaring nave arcades date from 1160, and much of the later 15th-century building was an offering by wealthy wool merchants of the time. Bowood House, 2 miles south-west, seat of the Marquess of Lansdowne, was partly designed by Robert Adam. The park of more than 1000 acres has a splendidly landscaped lake, with an Italianate cascade and shady walks.

Castle Combe

One of the most photographed villages in the country. The descent from the

KEEPING DRY FEET ON MAUD HEATH'S CAUSEWAY

This causeway recalls Maud Heath, who left her life savings in 1474 to build a 4-mile causeway from Wick Hill by way of her home at Langley Burrell to Chippenham, to replace the boggy path she used to take to market. The memorial pillar to her is at Kellaways

THE BUSY FORGE

Hunters, polo ponies and racehorses keep the Crudwell blacksmith busy

A SCENE SET FOR A PHOTOGRAPHIC PIONEER

William Henry Fox Talbot (above) carried out many pioneering photographic experiments at his home, Lacock Abbey (left). In 1833 he made the first photographic prints, for which he was awarded the Royal Society Medal. The house was built in 1540 on the remains of an abbey

ON THE BRIDGE *A chapel for pilgrims on a 14th-century bridge at Bradford-on-Avon became a lock-up in the 17th century*

wooded heights to this village-in-a-valley is dramatic. The twisting By Brook flows under a three-arched bridge with a turreted, towered church and gabled houses beyond.

Castle Combe was once a wealthy weaving centre. Its Weavers' House, where the villagers took the cloth after weaving it in their homes, still stands by the river. Mellowed cottages cluster about the stone-canopied market cross, while a short side road leads to the manor house, built in 1664 and now a hotel. There are only a few traces of the original castle, built by Walter de Dunstanville. His 13th-century effigy lies inside the parish church, which has some beautiful fan vaulting and a 13th-century font.

Chippenham

A stone-built town on the Avon, with an ancient market-place at its heart. The twin-gabled 15th-century town hall, with an unusual wooden turret, is probably the town's oldest building. The Hungerford Chapel of the parish church has many monuments of the 15th century, and some going back to the 13th century. The Grove was once the site of an early 18th-century spa, and Ivy House dates from *c.* 1730. At Hardenhuish (pronounced Harnish), just outside Chippenham, John Wood the Younger, of Bath, built the elegant Georgian church with its Venetian windows.

Corsham

A small town on the southernmost point of the Cotswolds. The Flemish-gabled cottages on the cobbled street and the honey-coloured, baroque-pedimented Hungerford almshouses all derive from its wealthy past as a weaving village. The school adjoining the almshouses has its original seating arrangement, with the master's pulpit desk of 1668 still in place.

Corsham Court, an Elizabethan mansion of 1582, has an impressive pedimented gateway. Capability Brown, the famous 18th-century landscape gardener, laid out the fine park with its elm avenue. The state rooms are filled with old masters and superb furniture.

Great Chalfield Manor

A moated, late Gothic house with Tudor overtones, $2\frac{1}{2}$ miles north-east of Bradford-on-Avon. The house is approached through an arched gateway, and its oriel windows reflect the sunlight on to the courtyard's polished yellow-grey stones. The great hall and screen remain as Thomas Tropenell built them in 1480. The house is owned by the National Trust.

Holt

Here, set in beautifully laid-out gardens, is The Courts, where local weavers, until the end of the 18th century, came to settle their disputes by arbitration. The elaborate façade dates from *c.* 1700, though the mansion itself is in the neo-Gothic style of a century later.

Lacock

One of the most beautiful villages in England. There is no building later than the 18th century in its winding streets of Gothic-arched, grey-stone houses and half-timbered cottages. There is a 14th-century barn, and the Perpendicular church, of St Cyriac, which has soaring aisles and a beautiful east window.

Lacock Abbey, which like most of the town is owned by the National Trust, still retains its 13th-century cloisters, sacristy and nuns' chapter house. It was the last religious house in England to be dissolved after the Reformation, and its conversion to a mansion was undertaken by Sir William Sharington who, *c.* 1540, built the curious octagonal tower overlooking the Avon. Later the abbey was the home of William Henry Fox Talbot (1800–77), a pioneer of photography: a stone barn near the gates houses a museum of his work.

Malmesbury

A town set high on a rocky hill between the River Avon and its tributary, the Inglebourne. It was a borough before the time of Alfred the Great. Water almost surrounds the base of the hill on which it stands, and no fewer than six bridges lead to the steep slope of the Market Square. Most of Malmesbury's streets are lined with golden Cotswold-stone houses built in the 17th and 18th centuries by its rich weavers. The spectacular octagonal Perpendicular market cross has stood in the busy Market Square since Tudor times.

The impressive late Norman abbey has a spacious nave and a superb south porch with fine romanesque carvings.

Melksham

An industrial town on the banks of the Avon. Only a few woods survive of forests which were once a favourite hunting ground of the Plantagenet kings. By the 17th century, Melksham was one of the great weaving towns of Wiltshire, and good 17th and 18th-century houses in Canon Square recall this period of prosperity.

THATCHED CHURCH *The timber-framed St Nicholas's Church at Sandy Lane, south-west of Calne, built in 1842, has a thatched roof—rare in Wiltshire churches*

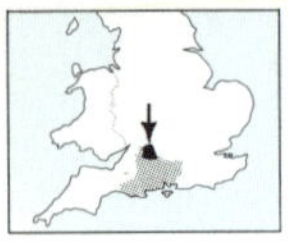

Hill of mystery on the downs

Angling Coarse fishing on the River Kennet, the Kennet and Avon Canal south of Marlborough, and Coate Water, Swindon.

Places to see *Avebury Manor*: afternoons, June to Aug.; also weekend afternoons May and Sept. *Avebury Museum* (NT): daily, except Sun. morning Oct. to Mar. *Great Western Railway Museum*, Faringdon Road, Swindon: weekdays and Sun. afternoon. *Lydiard Mansion and Park*, Lydiard Tregoze: weekdays and Sun. afternoon. *Richard Jeffries Museum*, Coate: Wed., Sat., Sun. afternoons. *Swindon Museum*, Bath Road: weekdays, Sun. afternoon.

Information centres Brunel Shopping Centre, Swindon. Tel. Swindon 26161. St Peter's Church, Marlborough. Tel. Marlborough 53989 (seasonal).

OGBOURNE ST ANDREW *Shortage of craftsmen probably led to brick nogging replacing decayed wattle and daub panels in this half-timbered house. Lime-washing gave a black and white effect*

The landscape of the extreme north of Wiltshire is one of quiet water-meadows cut by streams that run into the upper reaches of the River Thames. South of Swindon, however, the scenery changes abruptly as the rolling Marlborough Downs, with their dramatic, wooded heights, sweep southwards towards the Vale of Pewsey.

For prehistoric interest, this part of Wiltshire offers serious competition to the more famous stone circles of Stonehenge further south. The ancient track known as the Ridge Way runs along the crest of the Marlborough Downs; Avebury is regarded by many experts as the most important early Bronze Age monument in Europe; and, even after many excavations, the origins of the enormous man-made mound of nearby Silbury Hill still baffle archaeologists.

Swindon, the county's main industrial centre, is a town largely created by the coming of the railways, while Marlborough has the contrasting character of an ancient city on the borders of Savernake Forest, a royal hunting forest until the mid-16th century, and now leased to the Forestry Commission.

WHERE KINGS HUNTED *In medieval times Savernake Forest, with its beech and oak trees, was a favourite royal hunting ground*

Aldbourne
One of the prettiest villages in Wiltshire, set 700 ft up on the Marlborough Downs. By its village green are an old, weathered stone cross, a duck pond, and some thatched and colour-washed cottages. The church, which dates back to the 12th century, has a superbly executed alabaster tomb of a 15th-century priest. Two 18th-century fire engines are kept in the church. For more than 200 years until the early 19th century the village was famous for its bell foundries, as well as for rush and willow weaving. There are fine views from Baydon, just north of the village.

Ashton Keynes
A village set in the water-meadows of the upper reaches of the Thames. A stream runs beside the main street, and the houses are reached over separate small bridges. At the end of Church Walk, the stream widens in front of two mellowed stone houses, Brook House and Ashton Mill, to become recognisable as the infant River Thames.

Avebury
An attractive village with a partly Saxon, tree-sheltered church, a gabled Elizabethan manor house, and a thatched great barn, all linked by pretty garden-fronted cottages.

The village is ringed by one of the most important prehistoric monuments in Britain, the Avebury Stone Circle. This was set up by Bronze Age peoples *c.* 1800 BC, 200 years earlier than the main phase in the building of Stonehenge. About 100 great sarsen stones—local sandstone from Marlborough Downs—still stand, like a council of petrified old men, encircling an area 450 yds across. Many weigh more than 40 tons. Within the ring are the remains of two smaller circles of sarsen stones.

A 50 ft wide avenue of megaliths once led more than a mile beyond West Kennett to Overton Hill, and concrete posts show where the stones once stood. On Windmill Hill, 2 miles north-west, three concentric ditches mark the site of a Neolithic camp built *c.* 2500 BC.

Cricklade
The only town in Wiltshire on the River Thames, which at this point is merely a channel. The wide main street has good 17th and 18th-century houses, and just beyond the town is the 13th-century priory, now divided into small houses. The parish church of St Sampson has a cathedral-like turreted tower built by the Duke of Northumberland in 1553, some good Norman features and splendid carved heraldic work. A museum at the west end of the main street has a

IN A CENTURY LITTLE HAS CHANGED

19TH CENTURY *An 1860 engraving of Marlborough's wide, impressive High Street*

AVEBURY CIRCLE *Sarsen stones, meaning 'saracen' or foreign to the indigenous chalk, were set in groups by man in prehistoric times*

collection that illustrates the history of the town from the Roman occupation, through its Saxon period, when it had a mint, to the present day.

Highworth
A charming old town built on the crest of a 400 ft hill, with some superb 17th and 18th-century houses and fine views. Jesmond House Hotel and Highworth House are perhaps the best examples of this rich period in domestic architecture. The parish church has a monument to Lieutenant Warneford, V.C., who in 1915 destroyed the first German Zeppelin airship in the First World War.

Lydiard Tregoze
Lydiard Mansion, a Georgian house near Swindon owned by Thamesdown Borough Council, was once the home of the St John family. It was rebuilt in 1745 and in more recent years has been extensively restored. Its rococo ceilings are particularly beautiful. The church, standing in the parkland of the mansion, has a richly coloured triptych in a cabinet, some fine 15th-century Flemish stained glass, and a screen and monuments to the St John family. One of the most brilliant of the monuments is a gilded life-size figure of Edward St John, who was killed fighting for the Royalists at the second Battle of Newbury in 1645.

Marlborough
A town noted for having one of the widest main streets in the country. The broad, sloping High Street of splendid Georgian buildings and colonnaded shops obscures many fascinating back alleys with quaint, medieval, half-timbered cottages that escaped a big fire in 1653. The town has attracted tourists since the days of the stage-coach and has some excellent inns and hotels.

At each end of the High Street is a fine church. St Peter's has a well-proportioned, late-Perpendicular tower, where a curfew bell is rung every night; and St Mary's, also Perpendicular, has a Norman door, the rest of the church being restored after a fire in 1653. An enclosed, arched bridge at the western end of the town leads to Marlborough College, the public school built in 1843 on the site of an old castle. Near by is a mound called Maerl's Barrow, which gives the town its name; deer antlers dating from Neolithic times have been unearthed here.

A few minutes' walk south-east from the centre of Marlborough is a corner of the Savernake Forest. The Fyfield Down Nature Reserve, 3 miles west, contains some great sarsen stones.

IN MARLBOROUGH'S HIGH STREET

20TH CENTURY *Little has changed except the town hall (foreground), rebuilt in 1903*

Ramsbury
A picturesque village on a wide stretch of the River Kennet. The river flows through the park of Ramsbury Manor, built in 1680 by John Webb, the son-in-law of Inigo Jones. It was in this house that Cromwell laid his plans for the subjugation of Ireland. The town has many Jacobean and Georgian buildings, and an impressive parish church with Anglo-Saxon foundations.

Savernake Forest
A former royal forest now leased to the Forestry Commission, consisting of more than 2000 acres of rolling land richly covered with gnarled oaks and lofty beeches. Great avenues of trees open on to green glades of ferns and brackens. The Grand Avenue, with its cathedral-like arcades of beeches, is 4 miles long. Visitors can picnic by the roadside, or walk or ride into the forest where there are rare birds and wild flowers.

Silbury Hill
A huge, circular, flat-topped cone of a hill, built like an enormous sandcastle against the flat landscape. It is more than 130 ft high and 200 yds round the base—if it were set down in London's Trafalgar Square, it would practically fill the square and reach three-quarters of the height of Nelson's Column. Excavations have been undertaken at intervals since 1776, but the mystery of the purpose for which it was built is still unsolved. Recent excavations suggest that it was built *c.* 1600 BC, about the same time as the later stages of Stonehenge.

Swindon
The largest industrial town in Wiltshire, which owes the foundation of its prosperity to the old Great Western Railway works. Other industries have overtaken the railway's former dominance, but Brunel's famous railway village and its neighbouring railway museum just off the town centre have preserved some of the best of the age of steam. Old Swindon, situated on a hill overlooking the 'new' town, still retains a market-town atmosphere with its Georgian inns and houses.

THATCH PERCH

Thatchers show individual style in their treatment of gables, ridges and dormers—or even with thatch birds, such as these at Wanborough

Leafy lanes in northern Hampshire

Angling Coarse fishing on the Basingstoke Canal near Basingstoke, Farnborough, Aldershot, and also on the gravel pits at Charlton, 1 mile north-west of Andover.

Riding Stables for hire of horses at Andover. Good riding country on the downs to the west of the town.

Skiing The Stainforth Ski Centre, Hurst Road, Aldershot, has an artificial ski slope which is one of the largest in Europe.

Events The Aldershot Army Display, in mid-June, includes exhibitions of army activities, arena events, bands and a funfair. Andover Carnival is held in June and Basingstoke Carnival in July. The Farnborough International Air Show, the leading aircraft display in Britain, is held in early Sept. every two years (1980, 1982, etc.). The Aldershot Horse Show, one of the largest in the South, is held on Spring Bank Hol.

Arts Haymarket Theatre, Basingstoke, has frequent repertory performances throughout the year.

Places to see *Airborne Forces Museum*, Aldershot: daily. *Bladon Gallery*, Hurstbourne Tarrant: five annual exhibitions of paintings by leading artists, each lasting 10 weeks, music and poetry recitals: weekdays, except Mon. Oct. to May, and Sun. afternoon. *Gurkha Museum*, Church Crookham: Mon. to Fri. *Royal Army Dental Corps Museum*, Aldershot: Mon. to Fri. *Royal Army Medical Corps Historical Museum*, Aldershot: Mon. to Fri. *Sandham Memorial Chapel* (NT), Burghclere: daily. *Silchester (Calleva) Museum*, Rectory Grounds, Silchester Common: daily. *The Vyne* (NT), Sherborne St John: Apr. to Oct., afternoons, except Mon. and Fri. *Willis Museum*, Basingstoke: Tues. to Sat.; also Mon. afternoon.

Information centre Basingstoke District Council, 5 London Road, Basingstoke. Tel. Basingstoke 56222.

The Roman road called Portway once ran straight across northern Hampshire from Salisbury to the mighty Roman encampment at Silchester, on the Berkshire border. Traces of the route still survive, but modern main roads largely ignore it in favour of the new military and aircraft centres of Aldershot and Farnborough and the spreading modern town of Basingstoke.

The airfields at Farnborough and nearby Blackbushe stand on the sandy heathlands that spread into this corner of Hampshire from north-west Surrey. But west of Hartley Wintney the landscape, away from the main roads, changes to one of woods, streams and secluded villages.

Fast, straight main roads carry traffic to the West Country, leaving unspoilt a maze of leafy lanes lying between the main routes and repaying leisurely exploration. Andover is a good centre from which to tour this relatively undiscovered area. The road north-east towards Litchfield, for instance, follows a route that runs along Portway for 3 miles then rises through an avenue along the side of a hill, overlooking a pattern of woods and farmland. Near by, surrounded by wild flowers, are the two villages of Woodcott and Binley, of which the 19th-century traveller and writer William Cobbett said: 'I never saw inhabited places more recluse than these.'

South of Andover another attractive route follows the valley of the River Anton, then runs through a string of villages on the western bank of the upper River Test before returning westwards over the rolling green countryside of the Andover Downs.

Andover

A market town which declined in importance when railways replaced stage coaches. Later the motor car cluttered its streets; today a bypass has siphoned off much of the through traffic, but the town is renewing its life as the centre of one of London's 'overspill' schemes. There are several old inns, and relics of Iron Age encampments on the surrounding hills. Just south of the town there is scenic beauty along the little valley where the Pillhill Brook runs into the Anton, a tributary of the Test. Harewood Forest, 2 miles east, is crossed by numerous footpaths.

Basingstoke

Though the town is the focal point of numerous main roads, a bypass lets through traffic avoid its busy centre.

The delightful village of Basing, $1\frac{1}{2}$ miles east, is threatened today by the advance of industrial building from Basingstoke as it was threatened in the past by Cromwell's army. Basing House, a ruin with a 16th-century gatehouse and a dovecot, was the centre of a two-year siege in the Civil War, at the end of which, in 1645, the Marquess of Winchester and his Royalist followers were overwhelmed by Parliamentarian forces led by Cromwell in person. The famous

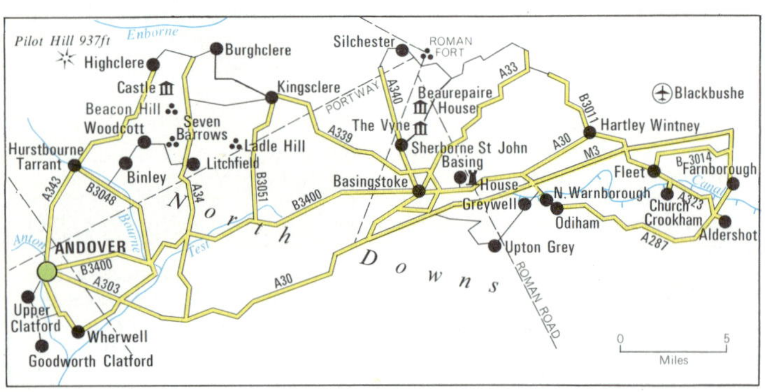

SPLASHES OF YELLOW *Fields of rape (Brassica napus) growing north of Hurstbourne Tarrant provide seed for sheep grazing. They are often mistaken for mustard fields*

architect Inigo Jones was among the prisoners taken. Basing Church has a brick tower and contains work of the Norman, Early English and later periods.

Farnborough
Famous as the home of the Farnborough Air Show, the town owes much of its importance to the development of the Royal Aircraft Establishment. The Empress Eugénie of France lived at Farnborough Hill in exile until her death in 1920. The house is now a convent.

Highclere
A village attractively ringed by park and woodland, and notable for Highclere Castle, once a country seat of the Bishops of Winchester and now the seat of the Earls of Carnarvon. The Carnarvon family had it rebuilt in 1842 by Sir Charles Barry, architect of the Houses of Parliament. On the 858 ft summit of Beacon Hill, 2 miles south-west of the village, is the grave of the 5th Earl of Carnarvon, who led the excavation of Tutankhamen's tomb in 1922. Tutankhamen was an Egyptian king who lived *c.* 1360 BC, and his tomb was of unparalleled splendour. During the excavations an inscription cursing any disturbers of the tomb was found, and the death of Carnarvon during the course of the excavations gave rise to superstitious fears of the wrath of the dead king. There is also an Iron Age fort on the hill. From Pilot Hill (937 ft), 2 miles west of Highclere, there are good views across a cluster of tiny villages nestling in the valley of the River Enborne.

At Burghclere, 2 miles east, is the Sandham Memorial Chapel, which has paintings by Stanley Spencer. A minor road leads 2½ miles further east to Kingsclere, largest of the three 'clere' settlements, a small downland town which was a royal manor under the Saxon kings. The restored church is largely Norman, and just to the south can be traced the route of the Roman Portway from Salisbury to Silchester.

Hurstbourne Tarrant
An L-shaped village on the Bourne Rivulet, a tributary of the Test. William Cobbett, author of *Rural Rides*, praised the village, and its surroundings as 'the pretty vale of Uphusband'.

Litchfield
A village bright with flowers in summer and set amid great, unhedged, agricultural rolling acres. The Seven Barrows, Bronze Age burial mounds, are 1 mile north, and there is an unfinished Iron Age fort on Ladle Hill, 2 miles north-east of the village.

Odiham
Flanked by the expanding towns of Aldershot and Basingstoke, Odiham almost miraculously retains a country-town atmosphere. Its wide main street is Georgian in character. There is a Tudor vicarage, a mainly 14th-century church of great beauty, an almshouse and a pest-house, built to house victims of the Great Plague in 1665. French prisoners were billeted there during the Napoleonic Wars.

HAMPSHIRE DOVECOTE *A 16th-century dovecot stands in the grounds of Basing House. It used to accommodate up to 1000 doves, which in the Middle Ages gave their owner a supply of fresh meat throughout the winter months*

At North Warnborough, 1 mile west by the Basingstoke Canal, are the ruins of Odiham Castle. From here King John set out on his historic journey to Runnymede in 1215, and a year later the castle was besieged by the Dauphin of France, whom the barons called in to support them.

Greywell, 1½ miles west, is an enchanting village, from which a minor road leads 2 miles south-west to the hamlet of Upton Grey, a circle of houses round a village pond.

Sherborne St John
This small place, with an old church, preserves a village atmosphere, though Basingstoke creeps nearer. A mile to the north-east, along the Bramley road, is The Vyne, a sumptuous Tudor manor house with later additions, built for Lord Sandys, Chancellor to Henry VIII. Its classical portico was added in 1654. The house and its grounds, with a lake, are owned by the National Trust, and are open to the public.

A mile further north along the same road is the moated manor house Beaurepaire, seat of the Brocas family. Near by a brook runs beneath the road.

Silchester
The site of the important Roman encampment of Calleva Atrebatum, at the north-east end of Portway, the Roman road from Salisbury. The shape of the defences and of an oval amphitheatre can still be traced on the ground, and a section of the wall, nearly 2 miles long, faces the medieval parish church. The Calleva Museum contains casts of archaeological finds made at the site, though the more important finds are now on display in Reading Museum.

Upper Clatford
The approach on the wandering little road from Andover is charming. Two small bridges cross the River Anton into the village. Swans sail by under the bridges, between which stands the small, partly Norman church, with its squat tower. Just west of the village is Bury Hill, on which stand the remains of an Iron Age fort. The road runs on southwards to Goodworth Clatford, another beautiful village which also has a river bridge and a church which is as simple in design as a child's drawing.

Wherwell
A Hampshire showpiece village of timbered and thatched cottages. The village is entered from the west down a steep hill which gives a fine vista of the Test Valley. Wherwell was well known in Saxon times, and there are traces of a priory founded by Queen Elfrida, the mother of Ethelred II.

BESIDE THE BOURNE *A thatched cottage in Hurstbourne Tarrant; the village's name comes from Tarrant Abbey in Dorset*

SILCHESTER—TODAY AND YESTERDAY

A Roman wall still surrounds the site of the encampment of Calleva Atrebatum

An artist's impression of Silchester during the 4th century. The only Roman town in Britain to have been completely excavated, it was already an important tribal capital more than 90 years before the Claudian conquest took place in AD 43. Its prosperity, which was based on wool, lasted until the end of the 4th century

Angling in the Test Valley

Angling Fishing for trout on the River Test and its tributaries, the Anton and the Bourne. Salmon can also be found on the lower reaches of the river, below Romsey. However, the fishing is almost all privately owned, and there are strict limitations on the number of fishermen allowed on the river at any time.

Events Romsey holds a carnival in July and an agricultural show is held in the town in Sept.

Folk customs The Courts Leet and Baron still meet at Stockbridge annually in Mar. The Courts are presided over by the Quondam Lady of the Manor and control the grazing rights on Common Marsh near the village. Among the officers appointed at the meeting is an official known as the Hayward, whose duties include the care of the common ground.

Nature trail At Danebury Hill a half-mile nature trail, open all the year, includes the site of an Iron Age fort among beech trees and woodland.

Places to see *Broadlands*, 1 mile south of Romsey: daily mid-May to late Sept.; but closed Mon. and Tues., June, July and Sept. *Hillier Arboretum*, Ampfield, 3 miles north-east of Romsey: Mon. to Fri.; also Sun., Easter to Oct. *King John's House*, Romsey, built between 1230 and 1240: Easter, then Tues. afternoon and Thur. to Sat., late May to Sept. *Mottisfont Abbey* (NT): grounds: Apr. to Sept., Tues. to Sat. afternoons; Whistler Room: Apr. to Sept., Wed. and Sat. afternoons. *Romsey Abbey*: daily.

Information centre Heritage Centre, Church Street, Romsey. Tel. Romsey 512200 (seasonal).

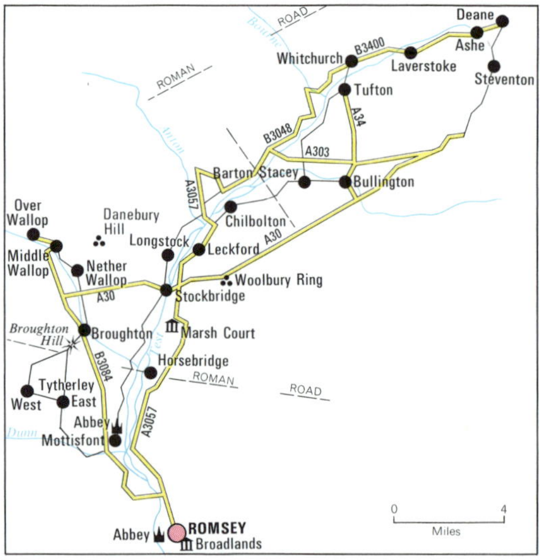

The broad valley of the Test, one of England's greatest trout rivers, is green and quiet countryside, where reeds and water-meadows fringe the river banks, and the peace is broken by little more than the plop of a fish leaping or the swish of a fishing line being cast.

The river rises near the village of Ashe and soon collects a handful of small tributaries. For much of its length the Test is not one stream but two, three or four separate channels running sweet and clear, sometimes merging to create broad, bright shallows. There are footpaths along parts of the river, but many stretches are reserved for expensive private fishing. On the upper reaches the trout rarely exceed 1 lb., but in the Stockbridge reaches there are four-pounders and the record is for an 18 lb. trout caught near Romsey. On the lower stretches between Romsey and Redbridge there are many salmon—the heaviest caught is recorded to have weighed 38 lb.

The river owes much to the chalk hills which border it and filter its waters; an unusual testimony to its clarity is the fact that the paper used for British bank notes is washed and processed in a paper mill at Laverstoke. In the valleys lie unostentatious little villages, with numerous farms and thatched cottages, while on the surrounding hills, barrows, tumuli and the remains of large Iron Age forts give plentiful evidence of earlier settlers in this green and fertile area.

PATIENCE AND PERSEVERANCE *Anglers at Longstock on the River Test can store their tackle in specially built thatched huts. Although private rights cost as much as £1000 a season, the fishing is so good that there may be a waiting list of applicants. The scoop-shaped nets across the river are lowered to catch eels*

HAMPSHIRE THATCH *Cottages dominate Nether Wallop; the village's name comes from the Old English for 'valley of the stream'*

SILENT SENTINELS *Pollarded lime trees form a 'guard of honour' along the paved walk to the medieval church at Bullington*

Ashe
An atmosphere of peace lies over this quiet village at the source of the River Test. There is one particularly beautiful house, a farm and a little church in a green hollow surrounded by yew trees. Jane Austen was born in 1775 at Steventon, $1\frac{1}{2}$ miles south-east, where her father was rector, and it was in a world bounded by the villages of Steventon, Ashe and Deane that she spent the first 23 years of her life.

Broughton
A village on the Wallop Brook, only 1 mile north of the Roman road that linked Winchester and Salisbury. The Romans' route is followed in part by

SPORTING FISH *Brown trout like these caught in a tributary of the River Test make good sport for anglers. The fish may vary from under 1 lb to more than 4 lb*

THRILL OF THE CATCH *A brown trout fights for its life against the pull of a fisherman's line on the River Test, a few miles above Romsey*

minor roads, but elsewhere only by footpaths. A Saxon warrior was found buried with his shield and sword on Broughton Hill, a mile south of the village.

The village has timbered houses decked with flowers, and well-kept old farmhouses surrounded by walls with thatched tops. In the churchyard of the mainly 13th-century Norman church is a round brick dovecot added in the 17th century. In 1841 Robert Owen, the social reformer, founded a socialist community at West Tytherley, 2½ miles south, but it was a failure.

Bullington
A handful of buildings beautifully sited beside a tributary of the Test. There is a fine Elizabethan house, a great barn and a church approached by a walk lined by pollarded lime trees. This village and its slightly larger neighbour Barton Stacey, which has an interesting old church mainly dating from the 12th century, lie in agricultural country which is unspoilt except for some areas used for military training. Two miles south of Barton Stacey are some Iron Age burial chambers.

Chilbolton
A picturesque village, with farmhouses, thatched cottages, a lovely Tudor house, and a church dating back to the 13th century, grouped on a quiet side-road just east of the Test.

Laverstoke
Behind high walls near this attractive village lie the paper mills at which the paper for British bank notes is produced. The mills were founded by Henri de Portal, a Huguenot refugee, who is said to have escaped from France hidden in a wine cask with his brother. He leased Bere Mill at Whitchurch in 1712, and the firm expanded to Laverstoke in 1724, when the Bank of England awarded them the paper contract which they have held ever since. Laverstoke House was built for the Portal family in 1796–8 by Bonami in the Classical style. The parish church dates from 1896.

Longstock
The Danes had a ship maintenance and construction yard here for their long ships, 15 miles up the Test from Southampton Water. The village is one of the most delightful in Hampshire, with one winding street, lined with period houses—colour-washed, timber-framed, with red brick and thatch. A minor road leads eastwards across the Test; at this point the river runs in separate channels, and along the banks stand circular thatched huts used by anglers. There is an important fish hatchery 1 mile upstream at Leckford, a village with a 13th-century church.

Mottisfont
A quiet cluster of houses on the fringe of the River Test flood plain. Mottisfont Abbey, approached by a wide straight drive, is an imposing 18th-century house incorporating the remains of a 12th-century Augustinian priory. It has paintings by Rex Whistler.

Romsey
An old market town built round its famous abbey, founded in the 10th century and retaining some traces of its Saxon beginnings. The cruciform church was enlarged by the Normans in the 12th century. Broadlands, an 18th-century house in a fine park, was the home of the statesman Lord Palmerston. Both house and gardens were remodelled by Capability Brown. It is now the home of Lord Mountbatten, and the Queen and Prince Philip spent part of their honeymoon there in 1947.

Stockbridge
The reaches of the Test near Stockbridge are the best for trout in southern England, and a rod may cost as much as £1000 a season. The town's wide main street has a bridge at one end, and the town hall, built *c.* 1810, has its clock in a turret. The Grosvenor Hotel, meeting point of the angling set, has a built-out porch where coach travellers could alight under cover. Marsh Court, 1 mile south, is by Sir Edwin Lutyens and is one of the few houses in England to be built of chalk. The lake beside the court is a haunt of water birds. There are fine walks over Stockbridge Down, owned by the National Trust, which lies to the east of the village.

ROMSEY ABBEY *The 12th-century church is all that remains of a great abbey which was sold for £100 at the Dissolution*

The Wallops
The three villages strung along the willowed Wallop Brook are an enchantment of framed thatched cottages. Nether Wallop has a 14th-century church raised a little above the village, and a mill. On Danebury Hill, 1½ miles north-east, are the remains of an Iron Age fort; from here a track crossing the Test by the bridge at Longstock leads to another hill fort, Woolbury Ring, 3½ miles away. The church at Over Wallop, to the west, has a fine 15th-century font. The pretty village of Middle Wallop links the other two villages.

KINGFISHER'S PREY *A kingfisher carries a minnow back to its nest to feed its young. The kingfisher often digs a nest 8 ft deep into the side of a river bank*

Whitchurch
Six roads converge on this small town on the upper Test, and their traffic somewhat overwhelms it. There is an old coaching inn, The White Hart, and a silk mill on the river, once water-driven but now powered by electricity. The mill stands on the site of a corn mill mentioned in the Domesday Book. A footpath from the village crosses the river twice on its way to the hamlet of Tufton, which has a manor house, two splendid barns still in use, watercress beds, a Norman church and a bridge which used to carry a railway over the river.

Saxon England's capital

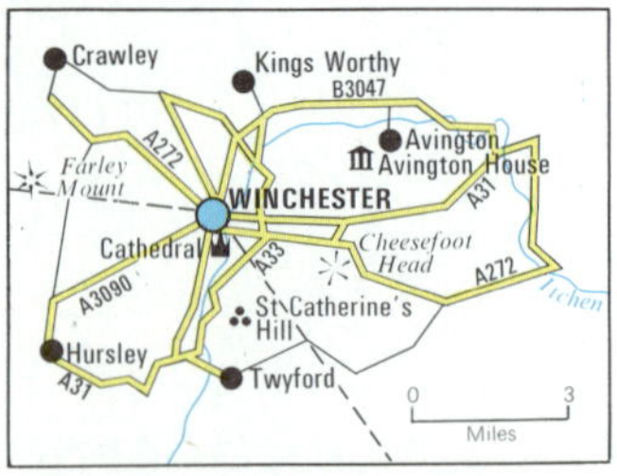

Angling Trout fishing on the River Itchen, though much is preserved.

Arts Frequent concerts are held in Winchester.

Places to see *Avington Park*, Avington: May to Sept., weekends and Bank Hol. afternoons. *Castle Hall*, Winchester: weekdays, except Sat. Oct. to Mar., Sun. afternoon. *City Mill* (NT), Winchester: Apr. to Oct., Tues. to Sat. afternoons. *Royal Greenjackets Regimental Museum*, Romsey Road, Winchester: Mon. to Fri.; also Sat. afternoon, Apr. to Sept. *Royal Hampshire Regiment Museum*, Southgate Street, Winchester: weekdays except Sat. *Hospital of St Cross*, Winchester: guided tours, weekdays. *Westgate Museum*, Winchester: weekdays, Sun. afternoon. *Winchester Cathedral*: *Library*, weekdays; *Treasury*, weekdays and Sun. afternoon, June to mid-Oct. *Winchester City Museum*: weekdays and Sun. afternoon.

Tours Guided tours of Winchester from the Guildhall, The Broadway, daily from May to Sept.

Information centre City Offices, Colebrook Street, Winchester. Tel. Winchester 65406.

The centre of Hampshire in every way is Winchester, for centuries the capital of Saxon and Norman Kings of England and still a city of history and charm, dominated by its long, grey-backed cathedral. Even when the Normans finally moved their capital to London, Parliament continued to meet often at Winchester and in 1485, Henry VII had his first son christened in the cathedral.

Long before King Alfred, whose statue today dominates the city's Broadway, made his capital at Winchester, the site on the downs on the west bank of the River Itchen was an important Belgic settlement. Under the Romans, Venta Belgarum became the fifth-largest city in Britain, and parts of the medieval city walls are of Roman origin.

The building of Winchester Cathedral was begun in 1079 on a site adjacent to that of an earlier Saxon church. Consecration took place in 1093, and extensions continued until about 1525. At 556 ft it is one of the longest cathedrals in Europe. Its design blends several styles, from the Norman transepts to the huge Perpendicular nave, transformed from its Norman original under Bishop William of Wykeham. Throughout the Middle Ages, Winchester and St Swithin's Shrine in its cathedral formed an important centre for pilgrims from the Continent on their way to Becket's Shrine in Canterbury.

The cathedral's treasures include no fewer than seven elaborately carved chantry chapels, endowed for the singing of special masses; mortuary chests enclosing the bones of ancient kings; medieval wall-paintings; 19th-century stained glass; and a square 12th-century black marble font with carved scenes from the life of St Nicholas. The cathedral library contains a 10th-century copy of Bede's *Ecclesiastical History* and the 12th-century Winchester Bible.

The grandeur of the cathedral is enhanced by the spacious lawns which set it well apart from the remainder of the city. In the cathedral Close are a deanery dating back to the 13th century, a Pilgrim's Hall, where pilgrims lodged in the Middle Ages on their way to Canterbury, and the half-timbered Cheyne Court, a Tudor building partly set into the medieval city walls.

THE CITY MILL *A youth hostel occupies the mill which was built in 1774; the building is preserved by the National Trust*

Winchester is rich in architecture from every period after the 13th century, and particularly in Queen Anne and Georgian buildings. The River Itchen flows swiftly through the city, fringed by attractive riverside walks and gardens, and the sight and sound of gaily running water is never far distant. Separated from the river by part of the old city walls are the remains of Wolvesey Castle, the former Bishop's residence, which stand next to the present partly 17th-century Bishop's Palace. South of the castle is Winchester College, founded by Bishop William of Wykeham in 1382 and one of the oldest public schools in the country.

Two of the five original gates into the city survive. Westgate, once used as a prison, is now a museum; near it stands the Castle Hall, a relic of the former Norman castle on the site, in which hangs a representation of the Round Table of King Arthur's

NATURAL AMPHITHEATRE *At Cheesefoot Head near Winchester, Eisenhower addressed Allied troops before the 1944 D-Day landings*

Avington
A village in the Itchen Valley, where the river fans out to make a lake behind the imposing mansion of Avington House. Nell Gwynne lived in the house when Charles II was staying at Winchester, and its later owners included the Dukes of Chandos and the Shelley family. Beside the park is an elegant 18th-century church, built by Margaret, Marchioness of Carnarvon. It preserves a squire's pew.

Cheesefoot Head
The site, 3 miles east of Winchester, of a great natural amphitheatre. Its earlier historical associations are obscure, but after a spell of dry weather the foundations of an oblong-shaped building, possibly Roman in origin, show through grass on the floor of the amphitheatre.

WAYFARER'S DOLE *Visitors to Winchester's Hospital of St Cross almshouses may request a traditional dole of bread and ale*

Knights, probably made in Tudor times. Kingsgate is beside the cathedral Close, and over it is the small medieval Church of St Swithin, recently restored.

A familiar sight in Winchester are elderly men in flowing gowns and ruffed caps. These are pensioners of the Hospital of St Cross, superb almshouses 1½ miles south of the city centre. At the 12th-century Hospital, visitors may ask for and receive the Wayfarer's Dole of bread and ale.

Two hills look down on Winchester. St Giles's Hill, on the east bank of the Itchen, is a public park from which there are fine views of the city. St Catherine's Hill, to the south, has an Iron Age earthwork, a clump of beech trees marking the site of a medieval chapel, and a 'miz-maze', or labyrinth, cut into the turf. One legend says that the maze was cut by an early Winchester College scholar who was kept behind during the Whitsun holidays. But the maze may even be of prehistoric origin, possibly connected with a religious dance ritual.

To the north of Winchester lies rolling country where plovers and skylarks fly, and through which the chalk stream of the Itchen flows southwards.

WINCHESTER CATHEDRAL *Seen from St Giles's Hill, the cathedral dominates the former capital of England*

Crawley
One of Hampshire's most charming villages, built almost entirely in the 16th century. A large pond flanks the manor house, and a pink, thatched cottage stands at the foot of a long hill of houses. Halfway up is an inn with bowed and latticed windows. The village is supposed to be the 'Queen's Crawley' of Thackeray's *Vanity Fair*.

Farley Mount
A viewpoint looking over the valleys of the Test and Itchen. There is a Bronze Age barrow, surmounted by a pyramid-shaped monument erected in 1795 to a horse which fell into a 25 ft deep chalk pit during a fox hunt without injury to itself or its rider. The Roman road from Winchester to Old Sarum and from there to Bath ran past this point.

Hursley
A one-street village, Tudor in character. Oliver Cromwell's son, Richard, lord of the Manor of Hursley, was buried in the old church, and there is a Cromwell monument under the tower of the present building.

Kings Worthy
A splendid church stands at the centre of a cluster of old cottages, with square-clipped yews to match the square 15th-century tower.

Twyford
A pretty village mainly noted for its associations with two famous people: Benjamin Franklin wrote portions of his autobiography at Twyford House; Alexander Pope was expelled from the school for lampooning his teacher.

THE TREES OF HAMPSHIRE

The conifer yew (left) flourishes on a chalk soil and has gradually spread over the entire county—hence its local name of the 'Hampshire Weed'. Beech 'hangers' (right) take their name from the fact that they appear to 'hang' on the hillside. When the trees are in leaf, their foliage is so thick that the soil beneath is often bare of other plant life. The leaves frequently remain on the tree in winter

In the New Forest

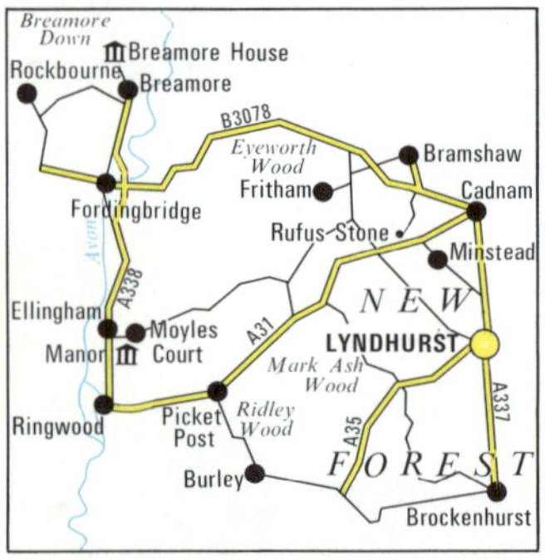

Riding There are stables throughout the area with mounts for riding and pony-trekking, particularly around Lyndhurst. Sales of New Forest ponies take place at Beaulieu Road, near Lyndhurst.

Angling Trout, salmon and coarse fishing on the Hampshire Avon at Ringwood. Some trout and coarse fishing on the many small lakes and streams of the forest.

Places to see *Breamore House,* Breamore: Easter to Sept., afternoons, except Mon. and Fri. *Furzey Gardens,* Minstead, with 8 acres of gardens: daily.

Camping On approved permanent sites in the New Forest.

Information centre Main Car Park, Lyndhurst.
Tel. Lyndhurst 2269 (seasonal).

For many people the New Forest is synonymous with Hampshire. Planted over 1000 years ago, it became a royal hunting preserve for William the Conqueror, whose treasury was at Winchester. The forest covers 90,000 acres, and two-thirds of it are open to the public. Besides the forest, there are great heaths golden with gorse or purple with heather in season; stretches of bogs and deep ponds, grazing lands, farms, little old churches and thatched cottages.

Few forests in Britain have such a variety of trees and such rich colouring. Beeches, oaks and birches predominate, but in season there is a riot of hawthorn and blackthorn blossom, while in the cultivated gardens of those who live in the forest—the 'commoners' as many of them are called—there are few British shrubs and plants that do not grow in abundance. In the vast woodlands, five varieties of deer run wild: red, roe, fallow, Japanese and Manchurian. There are also wild donkeys and some 2000 ponies.

A Court of Verderers administers the laws of the forest. These deal partly with such matters as the traditional forest rights covering the grazing of livestock, but some laws affect the general public. Wild animals, for instance, have priority on the forest roads, and there are strict regulations against the public feeding them.

The forest has football and cricket fields, excellent golf courses, and fine facilities for walking and riding. For the adventurous walker there is even the chance of coming across one of the 22 lost Saxon villages which, tradition says, have lain buried under the thick undergrowth since they were flattened by the Normans to create the hunting preserve, which remained a favourite resort for monarchs.

NEW FOREST PONIES *The forest is ideal riding country; the native*

THE PERFECT SERVANT

The 'Trusty Servant' inn sign at Minstead is modelled on a picture in Winchester College. The composite creature embodies a pig for unfussiness in diet—its snout locked for secrecy—an ass for patience, a stag for swiftness and a laden hand for hard work

Breamore (pronounced Bremmer)
The village, almost pure Tudor, is triangular in shape. At the base of the triangle are the big houses, at the apex a green with cottages and the narrow exit to the main road. An excellent Saxon church stands among trees a little apart from the village.

Breamore House, home of a single family, the Hulses, for over 200 years, was completed in 1583, and has an interesting collection of works of art, fine furniture and tapestries. On Breamore Down, north-west of the village, is a medieval miz-maze cut in the turf, possibly as the course of a religious ritual or folk dance.

Brockenhurst
A popular residential village, with a ford in the main street. The church is typical of the area, built on a mound in a mixture of Norman and Early English styles. A yew tree in the churchyard is said to be more than a thousand years old. On the outskirts of the village is a large hotel, the Balmer Lawn, where forest ponies approach close. Brockenhurst Manor Golf Club has one of the most beautiful heathland courses in Britain.

Burley
A pleasant, compact village off the main routes linking Southampton and Bournemouth. Though at its centre barely more than a street-and-a-half, it has an attractive inn, The Queen's Head, which has a display of hunting trophies. In the hunting season, a great concourse of forest dwellers turn out for the meet in Burley. A good walk leads northwards to Picket Post, and near by the route of an early smugglers' road can be traced among the fine beeches of Ridley Wood.

Cadnam
An important village at the hub of a network of roads, with an attractive thatched inn, The Sir John Barleycorn. Broad open commons, owned by the National Trust, cover 1½ square miles to the north and west.

Fritham
A scattering of houses and a hotel here typify the peace and seeming remoteness of the best New Forest villages. In Eyeworth Wood, near by, a large pond attracts wild life. In the surrounding area, Roman pottery and fossils of great antiquity have been found.

Lyndhurst
The administrative centre of the New Forest, beset by main-road traffic but surrounded by attractive woodland scenery. The Verderers' Court sits in the 17th-century Queen's House on the first or second Monday in January, March, May, July, September and November, to administer the forest laws.

There are impressive beeches in Mark Ash Wood, and the Knightwood Oak is about 600 years old, with a girth of more than 21 ft. The parish church, in Victorian Gothic style, has ornamentation by Millais, Leighton and Burne-Jones. In the churchyard is the grave of Alice Liddell (Mrs Hargreaves), the original of Lewis Carroll's Alice.

ponies, all privately owned, are thought to be the descendants of wild horses mentioned in the Norman forest laws

MEMORIAL TO A NORMAN KING

The Rufus Stone, near Minstead, was erected by Earl De La Warr in 1745 and marks the presumed spot where William II was killed by an arrow fired by Walter Tyrrell, while hunting on August 2, 1100. The killing was said to be accidental. The King's youngest brother, Henry, hearing of his brother's death, rode to Winchester, seized the treasury and had himself proclaimed king by the barons, forestalling the claims of his eldest brother, Robert of Normandy

Minstead
A village set in a maze of lanes, with a well-trodden track to an inn called The Trusty Servant. Minstead's 13th-century church, with rubble-and-daub walls and gabled windows, looks more like a row of cottages. Inside are a triple-decker pulpit, a double tier of galleries and a pew fireplace.

The Rufus Stone, 1 mile north-west, marks the spot where William II, called 'Rufus' because of his red hair, was killed by an arrow while out hunting.

Moyles Court
The hamlet takes its name from the manor house round which it grew. It is a true forest village, with soft, short turf growing right up to the walls of its houses, a few oaks, a ford, and ponies and cattle roaming around. The 17th-century manor house was the ancestral home of the Lisle family, until Alice Lisle became one of the first victims of Judge Jeffreys's Bloody Assizes for sheltering a fugitive after the Duke of Monmouth's 1685 rebellion, and the house became a ruin. Restoration has since been carried out and it is now used as a school. Alice Lisle is buried in Ellingham Church, 1 mile to the west, which also has a Lisle canopied pew that is still preserved.

Ringwood
A busy market town on the Avon, at the western end of the New Forest, and a centre for trout fishing. There are some attractive old houses. The Duke of Monmouth was taken prisoner near the town after the 1685 rebellion as he tried to reach the coast to flee the country.

Rockbourne
The village's one long street consists of Tudor and Georgian houses and splendid cottages, thatched and flower-bedecked. Those on the north side are reached across little bridges spanning a brook. At the far end of the village is a large farm incorporating a 13th-century manor house. The excavated site of a notable Roman villa lies half a mile south-east of the village.

VILLAGES OF THE NEW FOREST *The hamlet of Swan Green, near Lyndhurst, is at the heart of the New Forest. The thatched Tudor cottages set round its village green make up a scene which might belong to a former century in its seeming remoteness from the outside world. Around it are some of the most beautifully wooded parts of the forest, with footpaths among ancient oaks and beeches. The forest abounds in wildlife, including foxes, otters and badgers, as well as ponies and deer*

A royal hunting-ground

The word 'forest' has come to mean a densely wooded area, but originally it meant simply an area set aside for hunting, by the king or by powerful nobles. The Normans had some 80 such forests, and protected hunting rights in them with ferocious forest laws. Until the reign of Richard I (1189–99), who was more interested in crusading than in hunting, a man could be blinded merely for disturbing the royal deer.

Forests such as Savernake in Wiltshire, or Cranborne Chase and Powerstock in Dorset, have dwindled in size since the days when they were the playgrounds of hunting kings. But Hampshire's New Forest is still one of the largest areas of open land in the south, covering 145 square miles. It is the oldest of the great forests of England; but for William the Conqueror it was literally a new forest. He cleared away much of the ancient forest, destroying 22 Saxon villages it is said, and in 1079 decreed that the New Forest should be a royal hunting preserve.

The New Forest is full of the fascinating oddities of history, most of them arising from long-drawn-out disputes between the monarchs, intent on preserving hunting rights, and the commoners living in the forest. The commoners were forbidden by William to enclose land or to graze most animals for more than five months of the year; and for pigs the grazing season in the open forest was (and remains) only two months.

By the 17th century the forest that was founded because of a king's love of sport had taken on a new importance, as a source of timber for England's growing navy. But the old disputes about commoners' rights continued, and it was not until the 19th century that Parliament ended the monarch's right to keep deer in the forest and allowed commoners' cattle, ponies and donkeys to graze all the year.

Three Acts of Parliament this century have kept up with the ways of the forest. The most recent Act, in 1964, allowed camping sites and set aside land for the development of ornamental woods.

THE FOREST'S GUARDIANS *The men who keep law and order in the forest are called Verderers. Their officers, called Agisters, patrol the forest on horseback to watch over the welfare of the animals. Three Agisters are always on patrol. They have to mark every animal turned out in the forest by cutting its tail to show that dues have been paid. Any animal not marked may be impounded and its owner fined. The Agisters look after the general health of the animals, trace lost ones, report accidents and, in emergencies, destroy badly hurt animals. Their traditional uniform includes a green jacket and riding cap. The ten Verderers attend meetings of the Verderers' Court, which sits for one day a week during January, March, May, July, September and November. Anyone with a grievance may present his case, which the Verderers discuss. The court usually goes into committee during the afternoon, when the public are not admitted. The Verderers also play an important role in safeguarding the welfare of commoners' animals. By carefully selecting which stallions commoners can turn out in the forest, they have done much to improve the breed of the celebrated New Forest pony*

THE PANNAGE SEASON *The forest laws of the Norman kings allowed commoners living in the New Forest to turn out their pigs for pannage, or grazing on acorns, only from late September to November, as recorded in this 12th-century manuscript. Acorns are green during these months, and though excellent for fattening pigs they can poison other animals, including deer. Once the acorns turned brown, they were safe for deer and winged game to eat, so the pannage pigs had to be removed*

GRAZING IN THE FOREST *A pig feeds on forest acorns. The pannage season still applies, though commoners are now allowed, as a privilege, to graze breeding sows in the forest all year round*

THE VERDERERS' COURT *Foresters' grievances are heard in the court in Queen's House, Lyndhurst. The documents record grazing rights. In the background is the court's medieval dock*

MEDIEVAL POACHER *The Norman kings guarded their game with extraordinary ferocity. A poacher who killed a deer was put to death; for shooting at a deer he had his hands cut off; even for disturbing a deer he could be blinded. The Plantagenet kings were more lenient. Richard I abolished the penalties of death, blinding and maiming. Edward I decreed that only poachers who were caught red-handed could be prosecuted*

ENGLAND'S HUNTING KINGS *This 14th-century manuscript of the laws of England, which is in the British Museum, shows that King John was a hunting enthusiast, like his predecessors William the Conqueror and Henry II. The New Forest was John's favourite hunting-ground, and though during his reign (1199–1216) he sold forest land in other parts of the country, he extended the New Forest's boundaries. He also helped to preserve the forest by giving some 10,000 acres of forest land at Beaulieu to the Cistercian monks. According to tradition, John gave this land to the Cistercians shortly after ordering his horsemen to ride down some Cistercian monks in Lincoln. In a dream he was warned that he should repent. Beaulieu Abbey was to become a leading Cistercian foundation, a centre of advanced farming methods and a sanctuary for political refugees*

By Southampton Water

Sailing On Southampton Water, The Solent, Beaulieu River, Lymington and at Bucklers Hard.

Tennis Coca-Cola Hard Court Championships of Great Britain, Melville Park. Bournemouth Open Lawn Tennis Tournament is held in early Aug.

Places to see *Bargate Museum*, *Maritime Museum, Tudor House Museum*, Southampton: all Tues. to Sat. and Sun. afternoon. *Exbury Gardens*, Exbury: Apr. to mid-June, afternoons. *Maritime Museum*, Bucklers Hard: daily. *National Motor Museum*, Beaulieu: daily. *Rothesay Museum* and *Russell-Cotes Art Gallery and Museum*, Bournemouth: both weekdays. *Red House Museum*, Christchurch: Tues. to Sat., Sun. afternoon. *Zoological Gardens*, Southampton Common: daily.

Ferries Internal and external air services from Bournemouth (Hurn) Airport and Southampton Airport. Car ferries from Southampton to Isle of Wight, Cherbourg and Spain.

Information centres Information Bureau, Westover Road, Bournemouth. Tel. Bournemouth 291715. Town Hall, Christchurch. Tel. Christchurch 4321. Leisure Services Dept., Civic Centre, Southampton. Tel. Southampton 23855, ext. 615. Canute Road, Southampton. Tel. Southampton 20438.

The southern coastline from Bournemouth eastwards to the River Hamble on the eastern side of Southampton Water is a region of sharp contrast. Its two main centres vary widely in character: Bournemouth, the big seaside resort, has pine trees, gardens and steep ravines leading down to the sea, while Southampton, the major passenger port on the south coast, is dominated by its great docks for transatlantic liners.

Between these two big towns, the coastline changes from mile to mile. At Fawley, on Southampton Water, piers for servicing tankers visiting the vast oil refinery jut into the seaway, and metal structures probe skywards like a steel forest. Christchurch Priory is a fine monastic church that has survived the centuries; and in the former gatehouse of Beaulieu Abbey is a motor museum. The estuaries of the Hamble, Lymington and Beaulieu Rivers are polka-dotted in summer with craft of all kinds, while the Rivers Avon and Stour, banked with meadows, are quiet places to fish for grayling or trout, contrasting with the bustle of Southampton Water.

SEA, SAND AND SUN *The town of Bournemouth, facing Poole Bay, owes its rise to the development of the seaside holiday industry. Two centuries ago the area was worthless common land*

NIGHT INDUSTRY *The flare of Fawley oil refinery dominates Southampton Water*

Beaulieu
This small, attractive village near the head of the Beaulieu River is better known today for Lord Montagu's Motor Museum than for the abbey which it adjoins. The abbey was built by King John and destroyed by Henry VIII. The gatehouse, rebuilt in 1872 and now called Palace House, is Lord Montagu's home. The refectory of the abbey has been rebuilt as a parish church, and the lay dormitory is now a restaurant.

The National Motor Museum was founded by Lord Montagu in 1952 in memory of his father, the 2nd Baron Montagu of Beaulieu, a pioneer motorist. The museum contains more than 200 vintage and veteran cars—a 'veteran' must have been built before 1919 while vintage cars date from 1919 to 1930—as well as cycles and motor cycles.

Hatchet Gate, 1 mile west, is a pleasant picnic spot beside a deep pond and former mill house, now a private residence. To the south extends the lonely expanse of Beaulieu Heath.

Botley
This village, high up the navigable part of the River Hamble, has a reputation for locally grown strawberries. There are old houses on a wide main street, and a memorial to William Cobbett, the 19th-century author of *Rural Rides*.

Bournemouth
A town devoted to the holidaymaker, with superb sands, a mild climate and every kind of entertainment and open-air sport. Parks and gardens cover 2000 acres, or one-sixth of Bournemouth's total town area. There are two piers, and three lifts from street level to the beaches. The Bournemouth Symphony Orchestra, which has a world-wide reputation, plays in the Winter Garden.

Less than 200 years ago, the valley in which Bournemouth is situated was a wilderness of unused common land between the already flourishing boroughs of Christchurch and Poole. Many of the pine trees planted on this common land still survive to give the town an attractive

SHIPYARD FOR NELSON'S FLEET

Bucklers Hard became a shipbuilding centre in the 18th century, as it was near to the plentiful supplies of oak in the New Forest. The yards employed 4000 men and built 40 of the ships which fought under Nelson in the Napoleonic war

The *Agamemnon*, which Nelson called his favourite ship, was built at Bucklers Hard in 1781. The painting of her in action in the Mediterranean in 1794 is by Nicholas Pocock; it hangs in the National Maritime Museum, Greenwich

PLACE MILL *Corn was ground at this mill on Christchurch Quay up to the beginning of this century. The mill's origins go back to Saxon times. Originally it belonged to the Canons of Christchurch Priory, and was valued at 30 shillings in the Domesday Book. It is now owned by the Corporation and was used as a boathouse until 1970*

wooded setting. The 100-ft cliffs which circle the bay add to its charm and shelter the promenades and garden walks below them.

Bucklers Hard

A tiny village, on the lower reaches of the Beaulieu River, which through being near to the New Forest's plentiful supplies of oak, was a shipbuilding centre, founded by John, Duke of Montagu, until the 19th century. Huge stacks of timber used to stand for weathering in the unusually wide main street. The Master Builder's House Hotel was once the home of Henry Adams, who built ships for Nelson. There is a maritime museum, and some attractive Georgian cottages line the street that leads down to the river. Trips on the river can be made from the small landing stage.

Christchurch

An old town on the estuaries of the Rivers Avon and Stour, which grew up round a priory first built *c.* 1100. Behind Christchurch Quay stands the splendid priory church, its structure a blend of styles from Saxon times to the Renaissance. Its choir stalls are older than those in Westminster Abbey, and there is a monument to the poet Shelley. The town has the remains of a Norman house and castle, and the Red House Museum contains exhibits drawn from the geology and wildlife of the area. A 2-mile walk towards Bournemouth leads to Hengistbury Head, an observation point for bird migrations.

Hamble

This centre for yachting on the Hamble River is popular among summer visitors who come to watch the splendid array of yachts on the river—and to sample the local crab and lobster dishes. Hamble was a landing point for Saxon, Danish and French invaders. A fragment remains of the 12th-century priory, built by the Benedictines, which William of Wykeham rebuilt as a parish church in the 13th century.

Hythe

A small town, on the west bank of Southampton Water. It was once the point of departure for Imperial Airways flying-boat services to the Empire before the Second World War. The company was nationalised in 1939 to become BOAC (now part of British airways).

Lymington

An ancient town on the Lymington River, which has become a popular yachting centre. Its tidal harbour is usually crammed to capacity with yachts. Each Saturday a market is held along the main street. Lymington has a sports ground and a large open-air swimming pool. Pier Station is the departure point for car ferries to the Isle of Wight.

Southampton

The foremost passenger port for ships in Britain. It has an important modern university, the original buildings of which are literally 'red brick', and a great wealth of historic monuments, sites and remains. Although much damaged by bombing in the Second World War, the ramparts and medieval houses down by the Royal Pier are intact.

A worthwhile walk (best in the early evening) is along the ancient city walls, which bear many plaques and legends of historic events. The city is rich in seafaring history: armies sailed from here during the Hundred Years' War and the Pilgrim Fathers stopped here on the way from Boston in Lincolnshire to Plymouth, before setting sail for America. Southampton is a fine mixture of the old and the new, and has more than 1000 acres of open spaces, including parks, rock gardens and riverside walks.

Southampton Water provides a splendid, ever-shifting scene of shipping, ranging from the elegance of liners to bulky oil tankers. Ferries run from the Royal Pier in Southampton to Cowes, a journey of 55 minutes, and a pageant of ships can be seen on The Solent which, because of the 'buffer' made by the Isle of Wight, has four high tides a day.

The Isle of Wight

The Victorians adopted the Isle of Wight as a holiday island, and tourism has been its bread and butter ever since. The high chalk downs and the famous chines, or clefts, along the south coast appealed to the Victorians' sense of the picturesque; and the resorts they built have given the island a lasting appeal for lovers of Victorian architecture.

In the summer the island is crowded with visitors, its safe bathing and enviable sunshine record making it ideal for family holidays. The island, 23 miles from west to east and 13 miles from north to south, is far smaller than Greater London. Out of season, a morning's drive can cover most of the better-known places; one good road makes a complete circuit of the island round the coast, while an inland circular route passes through farmlands, villages and heaths. But when the roads are busy in summer it is never far to the nearest good picnic place or starting point for a ramble. The National Trust owns 4000 acres of the island, and there are numerous marked footpaths.

The Isle of Wight gives rise to an unusual double high tide in Southampton Water. The last of the flood running up the Channel sweeps round the east end of the island, where it meets the water already ebbing out of Southampton Water and drives it back in the form of a second high tide. This is a boon to shipping, and from the island's coast there is a constant view of passenger liners and oil tankers.

GODSHILL *Thatched cottages nestle in the shadow of the 15th-century church, perched on a hill above the village*

Sailing Cowes Week is held every year at the start of Aug., and Cowes is the starting and finishing point of the Round-the-Island Race in June and the Fastnet Race, which is held every two years. There are regattas at main resorts during the summer, and sailing schools at Yarmouth, Cowes, Newport and Wootton.

Places to see *Appuldurcombe House*, Wroxall: daily, except Sun. morning Oct. to Mar. *Arreton Manor*: Easter to Oct., weekdays, Sun. afternoon. *Bembridge Windmill* (NT): Apr. to Sept., daily. *Blackgang Chine and Wax Museum*: Easter to Oct., daily. *Carisbrooke Castle*, Carisbrooke: weekdays and Sun. afternoon. *Flamingo Park*, Seaview: Apr. and May, afternoons; June to Sept., weekdays and Sun. afternoon. *Museum of Isle of Wight Geology*, High Street, Sandown: weekdays. *Newtown Old Town Hall* (NT): afternoons only: Wed. and Sun., Apr. to Sept.; also Thur. and Sat., June to Sept.; daily in Aug. *Norris Castle*: Easter to mid-Sept., Sat., Sun. and Mon. *Nunwell House*, Brading: Spring Bank Hol. to Sept., afternoons except Sat. *Osborn-Smith's Wax Museum*, Brading: daily. *Osborne House*: Easter to mid-Oct., Mon. to Fri. *Robin Hill Country Park*, Arreton: Mar. to Oct., daily. *Smuggling Museum*, Ventnor: Easter to Sept., daily.

Ferries Hydrofoil, hovercraft or steamer services from Southampton, Portsmouth and Southsea, to Cowes and Ryde; steamers from Lymington to Yarmouth.

Information centres Isle of Wight Tourist Board, 21 High Street, Newport. Tel. Newport 524343. The Esplanade, Sandown. Tel. Sandown 3886.

Bembridge
A quiet seaside village with good bathing and wide, firm sands at low tide. The wide harbour makes Bembridge one of the island's most popular sailing centres. The four forts offshore are the relics of Victorian defences for Spithead.

Brighstone
A picturesque village with old thatched cottages and some inviting tea-gardens. The coast at Grange Chine and Chilton Chine is only 1 mile south, and there are good walks over Brighstone Down.

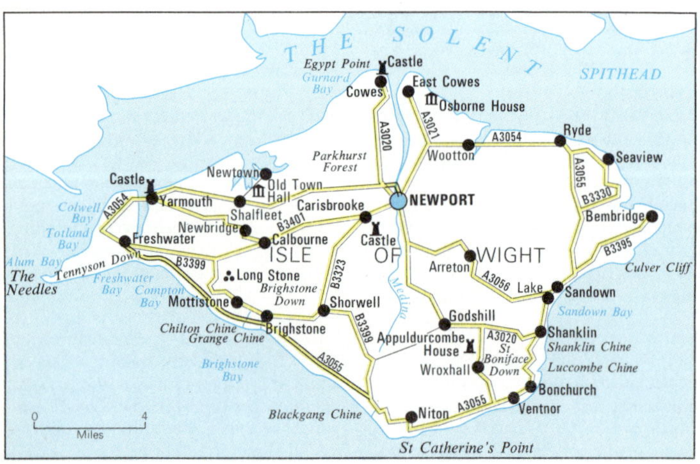

Calbourne
A showpiece village notable for its Winkle Street of low stone cottages, thatched or tiled. The church is Norman and Early English in period. It preserves a fine brass dating from 1380. There is a watermill, open to the public in summer.

Carisbrooke
The old capital of the island, with a mighty 12th-century Norman castle, built on the site of a Roman fort. Charles I was imprisoned here in 1647–8, and his son Henry and daughter Elizabeth came as prisoners in 1650. Visitors with a head for heights can walk all round the ramparts, from which there is a good view of the impressive castle remains on one side and, on the other, of green countryside. A 161 ft deep well in the castle has a 16th-century water-wheel once worked by prisoners and today by donkeys. One of the best walks on the island starts from Carisbrooke. At the west end of the village a lane climbs southwards to the downs and to an old Roman road leading to Shorwell, 4 miles away.

Cowes
There are two distinct towns, Cowes and East Cowes, separated by the River Medina. Cowes is Britain's yachting 'capital'; the Royal Yacht Squadron is housed in Cowes Castle, built originally by Henry VIII, and its 22 brass guns stand ready on Victoria Parade to start races and fire Royal Salutes. There is a good walk westwards past the castle to Egypt Point and the beginning of Gurnard Bay. East Cowes is the cradle and headquarters of the hovercraft industry of today.

Osborne House, 1 mile south-east, was Queen Victoria's home at the time of her death in 1901. Prince Albert and Thomas Cubitt together designed it as an Italian villa. Visitors can see the state and private apartments, furnished as they were in Queen Victoria's time. In the Swiss Cottage, a play house built for the Royal children, are the queen's writing-table and her personal collection of porcelain. Nearby is Norris Castle, where the young Princess Victoria frequently stayed with her mother.

Freshwater Peninsula
The western tip of the island ends dramatically in the huge chalk stacks known as The Needles. On the southern side of the peninsula, Compton Bay has good surfing and Freshwater Bay has a cave which can be explored at low tide.

Tennyson Down, leading to The Needles, is named after the poet who walked here every day from his home in Freshwater. Tennyson lived at Farringford—the house is now a hotel—from 1853 to 1867, and wrote much of his best work here, including 'Maud' and 'Idylls of the King'.

Totland Bay and Colwell Bay have firm sands and good bathing.

Godshill
A village on a steep hill, with a cluster of thatched cottages in apple-pie order nestling in the shadow of an early 15th-century church, well worth visiting for its paintings and effigies. Godshill and its many tea-gardens are extremely popular with summer visitors.

Appuldurcombe House, 1 mile to the south, is now a ruin, but the grounds laid out by Capability Brown are still pleasant to walk in.

Mottistone
A village for those who like old buildings and archaeology. It has a beautiful Tudor manor house and a 12th to 14th-century church, restored in the 19th century. A path by the lych gate leads to the Long Stone, a great pillar which is part of a long barrow which dates from between 2000 and 3000 BC.

Newport
'Capital' of the Isle of Wight, at the head of the River Medina. The town has an excavated Roman villa, some attractive 17th-century houses, and a guildhall designed by the 19th-century architect John Nash. The 1000-acre Parkhurst Forest, to the north-west near Parkhurst Prison, is the only big stretch of woods on the island.

WARNING BEAM *St Catherine's lighthouse, below the cliffs at Niton, warns shipping in the Channel of the coastline's dangers*

SUN TRAP *Ventnor, sheltered from the north by the huge mass of St Boniface Down, is one of the warmest holiday resorts on the island*

THE ISLAND'S FLOWER The wood calamint (*Calamintha sylvatica*) is found only on the Isle of Wight, on shady chalk banks from the west of Newport to Yarmouth. It flowers from August to October and sometimes even later. The calamint, 12–18 in. high, has a pleasant smell of mint

Ryde
One of the main gateways to the Isle of Wight. Ryde has a ½ mile long pier, built in 1813, and the electric railway added in 1880 was one of the first in the world. Ryde has 5 miles of sandy beach, excellent gardens on the esplanade, parks, heated outdoor swimming pools, and an amusement corner for children. Seaview, 2½ miles east, is a popular resort with good bathing sands and a flamingo park.

Sandown
The golden sweep of Sandown Bay extends for 6 miles between the chalk headlands of Culver Cliff in the north and Dunnose in the south. Sandown itself is a popular resort, with excellent sands, an esplanade and amusement parks. Lake, ½ mile south, is a secluded resort with a charm of its own.

Shanklin
Sheltered sands and a pier snuggle below the town centre, set on cliffs with a lift down to the beach. The Old Village has one of the prettiest inns on the island, The Crab. Shanklin Chine is a deep winding glen that is cool with ferns and foliage.

Shorwell
A picturesque village with thatched cottages. The local inn has a refreshment garden with dovecot, ducks, weeping willows and a babbling brook. The church is mainly 15th century; the large poppy-head pew ends, set at various angles, give the impression at first glance that the church is full of people.

Ventnor
A resort built on a series of terraces which zigzag down to the sea, giving a continental appearance. St Boniface Down, the highest point on the island (785 ft), shelters the town and its sandy beach from cold winds. In the Botanic Garden there is the only museum in the world devoted to smuggling. Bonchurch, east of Ventnor, is an old village with a beautiful pond, a tiny Norman church, and Victorian villas where Dickens, Thackeray and Macaulay stayed.

There is a good drive—or walk—westwards from Ventnor along the Undercliff, a ledge 6 miles long, formed by landslides, where palms, myrtles and cork trees grow. The Undercliff extends to St Catherine's Point, which has a lighthouse open to the public.

Yarmouth
The most continental of the island's resorts, small, clean, and bustling with yachts. The castle was built *c.* 1545. The ferry from Lymington is a picturesque way of reaching the Isle of Wight.

COLOURED SAND IN THE CLIFFS

The cliffs of Alum Bay are famous for their multi-coloured layers of sandstone. Island souvenirs (left), show their 12 distinct shades of sand. The cliffs were formed under water before the island emerged from the sea 50 million years ago

Hampshire's mighty naval base

Angling Sea trout can be found in the River Meon. Sea fishing at South Parade Pier, Southsea, and Portsmouth and Langstone Harbours.

Boats Sailing in Portsmouth and Langstone harbours, and at Fareham, Portchester, Gosport and Lee-on-the-Solent. Ferries from Portsmouth to Isle of Wight, Cherbourg, St Malo.

Events The Navy holds 'At Home' days during the late Summer Bank Hol. at H.M. Naval Base, Portsmouth.

Places to see *City Museum and Art Gallery*, Portsmouth: daily. *Cumberland House Museum*, Eastern Parade, Southsea: daily. *Dickens Birthplace Museum*, Old Commercial Road, Portsmouth: daily. *HMS Victory* and *Royal Naval Museum*, Portsmouth Dockyard: weekdays, Sun. afternoons. *Portchester Castle*: daily, except Sun. mornings Oct. to Mar. *Royal Marines Museum*, Eastney: Mon. to Fri.; also Sat. and Sun. mornings. *Southsea Castle Military Museum*, Clarence Esplanade, Southsea: daily.

Information centre Castle Buildings, Clarence Esplanade, Southsea. Tel. Portsmouth 26722/3.

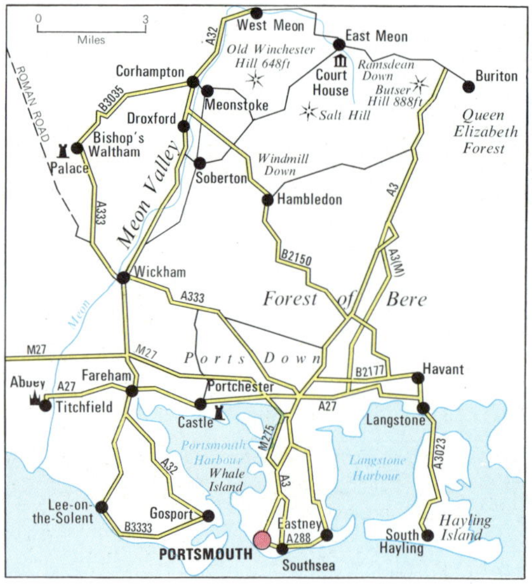

The River Meon, main river of south-east Hampshire, rises at a spring in the South Downs near East Meon and flows south to join the Solent just west of Portsmouth. Its green valley, rich in villages with churches dating back to Saxon times and sturdily square farmhouses in flint and brick, seems a world apart from the mighty naval base near its mouth.

Both worlds have played their part in British history. Hills like Ramsdean Down and Old Winchester Hill are capped by prehistoric earthworks and burial sites, while Portsmouth has been inseparably connected with Britain's days of naval greatness. Today the warships are more thinly scattered in Portsmouth's 300-acre dockyard. Many of them are reserve ships of the Home Fleet kept in 'mothballs', but the whole area remains a key part of Britain's defence network. Ports Down, the long ridge backing Portsmouth to the north, looks down on a vast conglomeration of airfields, barracks and training bases, stretching for 7 miles from the air base at Lee-on-the-Solent to the Royal Marine barracks at Eastney.

Inland, behind Ports Down, lie small villages in the much-diminished Forest of Bere, which is crossed by main roads but preserves patches of woodland and is bordered to the north by the green pastures of the Meon Valley. Traffic on the busy A32 thunders through the streets of many of the Meon villages; but at Corhampton an attractive minor road crosses the river and runs downstream for 5 miles.

THE VICTORY *Nelson's flagship, saved after Trafalgar, is preserved in the naval base at Portsmouth. The cockpit where Nelson died is kept as a memorial to Britain's naval hero*

PORTSMOUTH *Yachtsmen maintain the maritime tradition*

OLD PORTSMOUTH *In 1754 the Quebec House was built for sea bathers to change in*

NAVAL CITY *A reminder in Broad Street of Portsmouth's long naval history*

Bishop's Waltham
A town in the heart of Hampshire's strawberry-growing area. Its ruined 12th-century palace, part of the See of Winchester, was damaged in the Civil War when its royalist defenders were overcome. The buildings have state apartments, a cloister, a great hall and a four-storeyed tower.

Buriton
A quiet village where the historian Edward Gibbon (1737–94) spent his boyhood in the Georgian manor house which still stands. In the evening its large rectangular pond presents a memorable spectacle when the wild duck take wing. South of the village there are footpaths through Queen Elizabeth Forest, which covers the slopes of the South Downs and is now the Queen Elizabeth Country Park. Butser Hill, 888 ft, 1 mile west, is a viewpoint from which, on clear days, the sea can be seen beyond glorious countryside.

East Meon
An outstandingly beautiful village where Izaak Walton, the 17th-century author of *The Compleat Angler*, stayed to fish the River Meon which runs under and beside the village's main street. The village is still an important centre for trout fishing. The 14th-century Court House can be visited by appointment. To the south is unspoilt downland country, and there are good walks up Salt Hill.

Fareham
A residential town and shopping centre for Portsmouth commuters, but preserving some Georgian dwellings as an indication of its past. At the waterside a few small ships brave the passage up from Portsmouth Harbour.

Hambledon
This isolated village in aged red brick is renowned as the early home of cricket. The Hambledon Cricket club, founded in 1760, played on Broadhalfpenny Down, 2 miles north-east of the village, and gradually developed the laws of modern cricket. There is a monument to the club opposite the Bat and Ball Inn. A vineyard on Windmill Down, north of the village, produces excellent grapes.

Hayling Island
This freak formation divides the tidal waters of Langstone and Chichester Harbours, and is connected to the mainland at Havant by a bridge. The island, 4 miles square, is flat and liable to be very warm in summer, and its splendid stretch of beach makes it a popular holiday centre. There is excellent sailing on the Chichester Harbour side, and sea fishing is popular.

Portsmouth
Three of the seaport's four most famous 'ships' are the names of shore bases and will never go to sea. At Whale Island, is HMS *Excellent*, the Royal Navy's principal gunnery school. By Portsmouth Hard is HMS *Vernon*, the headquarters of torpedo experts. Across the harbour at Gosport is HMS *Dolphin*, a major submarine base. And in Portsmouth Naval Base itself, among sheds of red brick and concrete, stands HMS *Victory*, launched in 1765 and Nelson's flagship at the Battle of Trafalgar in 1805.

The city was badly damaged by bombing in the Second World War, though the cathedral preserves its 12th-century transepts and chancel. The Square Tower in the High Street dates from the time of Henry VII, and the Round Tower from 1417. Charles Dickens was born in a house in Commercial Road, now a museum. Buckingham House was the scene of the murder in 1628 of the first Duke of Buckingham, favourite of James I and Charles I; he was stabbed by a discontented soldier while planning an expedition to relieve French Huguenots besieged at La Rochelle by Cardinal Richelieu.

At Portchester, on the north side of Portsmouth Harbour, are the remains of the castle which Henry II built inside the walls of a Roman fort 1000 years older. Henry V marshalled his forces here for the victorious expedition to Agincourt in 1415.

Behind Portchester, the slopes of Ports Down present a good viewpoint for the whole of Portsmouth Harbour, the Solent and Spithead. On the down are four ruined forts and a monument to Lord Nelson, inscribed with tributes to Britain's most famous fighting admiral.

THE MEON VALLEY *South of Droxford, the Meon—praised by Izaak Walton in the 17th century for its fishing—flows placidly to the sea*

Soberton
A typical Meon Valley village, generating peace and quiet. Demons and gargoyles decorate the tower of the 16th-century church, which also has wall-paintings and a rare 17th-century altar cloth.

Southsea
The resort adjoining Portsmouth has a good sand-and-shingle beach and a wide range of holiday amusements. A military museum on the site of the 16th-century artillery fort, Southsea Castle, tells the history of the numerous fortifications in the area. Far out to sea from Southsea is a curious object called Nab Tower. This was originally a submarine detection station, but is now a signal point and marker for ships coming into Spithead. Southsea is a good starting point for a walk round Old Portsmouth to the west of the more modern town.

HOME OF CRICKET

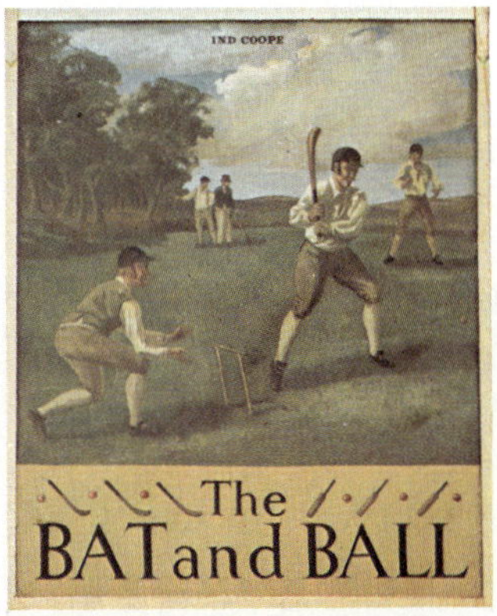

An inn sign at Hambledon marks the fact that cricket as played today started there in 1774, when the local team invented many of its laws

Titchfield
This little town, 2 miles from the mouth of the Meon, was once a seaport; today the river winds slowly across marshy Titchfield Haven to the Solent. Titchfield Abbey, dissolved in 1536, was adapted as a private dwelling by the Earl of Southampton, who changed its name to Place House. Charles I spent his last night of freedom here in 1647. The house has been a ruin since 1781. It is now preserved by the Ministry of Works. There are numerous 17th and 18th-century houses, and a Saxon church in a cul-de-sac by the river.

West Meon
A village sought by cricket enthusiasts for its associations with Thomas Lord, first owner of the ground famous as Lord's in St John's Wood, London, who died here in 1832 and was buried in the churchyard. Guy Burgess, the defector, is also buried there. The church has flint walls in which each stone is knapped and matched for size to present a perfect, even surface.

Wickham
A small town with many Georgian houses, which take on a mellow aura in evening sunlight. Wickham was the birthplace in 1324 of William of Wykeham, Chancellor of England and the founder of Winchester College and of New College, Oxford. About 500 years later the mill by the bridge was built from timbers taken from the American frigate *Chesapeake*, captured in 1813. To the east lies the Forest of Bere.

SMUGGLERS' MILL *The Old Mill at Langstone, reached by a causeway, was used by smugglers in the 18th century*

Country of Jane Austen

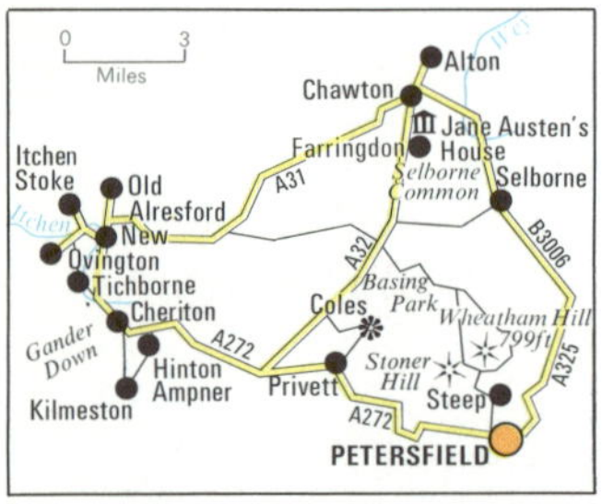

Angling Trout fishing on the River Itchen. Coarse fishing on the River Wey at Alton and on the lake at Petersfield Heath.

Golf Courses at New Alresford, Alton and Petersfield.

Gliding Lasham Airfield, 4½ miles north-west of Alton, is the largest gliding centre in the country and the frequent venue for national gliding championships.

Events The Tichborne Dole, which originated in the 12th century, is issued to the villagers of Tichborne and Cheriton on Mar. 25.

Places to see *Allen Gallery*, Church Street, Alton: weekdays. *Curtis Museum*, High Street, Alton: weekdays. *Jane Austen's House*, Chawton: daily, except Mon. and Tues. Nov. to Mar. *Gilbert White Museum*, and *Oates Memorial Library and Museum*, Selborne: relics of Gilbert White and Capt. L. E. G. Oates, who died on Scott's expedition in 1912: Mar. to Oct., afternoons except Mon.

The trunk road crossing Hampshire from south-west to north-east follows the route of the 'pilgrims' way' from Winchester to Canterbury. It passes through farming country where, on both sides of the ancient route, a maze of lanes connects scattered villages set about with streams and beech trees. There are watermills and watercress beds on the gentle River Itchen—a good trout river—and the area is rich in timber and hops for the hurdle-making and brewing industries centred on Alton.

This countryside still looks much as it did nearly two centuries ago, when the clergyman Gilbert White was making his studies of natural history at Selborne and the novelist Jane Austen was living and writing at Chawton. Near Jane Austen's former home are the streams, fed by springs, which merge to form the headwaters of the River Wey. The river flows north to Alton, then changes course to run north-east alongside the main road towards the Surrey border.

There is another riverside drive—along the Itchen from just west of Alresford through an enchanting string of villages starting at Itchen Stoke. The southern boundary of this area is formed by the remarkable A272 road, which passes not a single objectionable or ugly place on its cross-country route of over 70 miles across Hampshire and East and West Sussex, and is the lynchpin of the three counties.

TROUT STREAM *At Itchen Stoke, the River Itchen flows towards Winchester. The clear waters of this chalk stream offer the angler some of the finest trout fishing in the country*

Alresford

Old Alresford is a small village on one side of the River Alre, a tributary of the Itchen. It has an 18th-century red-brick church in which is buried Admiral Rodney, who defeated the Spanish off Cape St Vincent in 1780 and the French off Dominica in 1782. New Alresford lies 1 mile south, on the opposite bank of the river. It was a medieval wool town, and French prisoners were quartered there in the Napoleonic Wars; many are buried in the churchyard.

Today it is on the A31 and its main street suffers from heavy traffic; but Broad Street, lined with limes and colour-washed Georgian houses, retains its charm and dignity. The writer Mary Russell Mitford was born in Broad Street in 1787, but most of the material for her sketches of country life, *Our Village*, was based on Berkshire, where she lived later.

North of the town, Broad Street divides. The right fork passes by a mill stream and a dam built by Godfrey de Lucy, Bishop of Winchester, *c.* 1170, on its way to Old Alresford. The left fork leads to a footpath through watercress beds, passing a picturesque fulling mill spanning the river, then running alongside an idyllic stretch of the River Itchen for about 1 mile before leading back to a lane which joins the A31.

Alton

An old cloth-making and brewery town which the Roundheads captured from the Cavaliers during the Civil War. The fight ended in the Church of St Lawrence, where the Royalist leader, Colonel Boles, was killed.

At nearby Chawton is Jane Austen's last home, from 1809 to 1817. The house is now a museum.

Hinton Ampner

A pleasant, secluded place, with just a few small houses and cottages round the gates of Hinton Ampner House, a rebuilt 18th-century manor house which has armorial bearings on its gates and a church in its grounds. The village looks west to Gander Down and north to Cheriton, a battlefield in the Civil War.

ALRESFORD *A fulling mill spans a stream between the old and new towns. Fulling was a process used to harden cloth*

HAMPSHIRE'S NOVELIST

Jane Austen lived in the tiny Hampshire village of Chawton from 1809 to 1817. Her house (left) is now a museum and contains many of the novelist's personal belongings, including a portrait of her (right). Local society gave Jane Austen the models for the characters of many of her best-known novels which were written at Chawton, including *Emma*, *Mansfield Park* and *Persuasion*. She died at Winchester, and was buried in the Cathedral

The surrounding lanes pass by some fine Tudor farmhouses.

Kilmeston, 1 mile south, is a tiny and picturesque village. It has a manor house, a village green, brick-and-tile or pink-washed houses, dovecots and clipped yews—all in a picture-book village pattern.

Ovington
A small village attractively situated on the south bank of the River Itchen where it is joined by two other streams, the Candover and the Alre. Ovington Park has beautiful wrought-iron gates, and there is a 400-year-old inn with a low-ceilinged bar and huge log fireplaces at either end of it.

Petersfield
The town is seen by most people as merely a punctuation mark on the London–Portsmouth road; but it deserves better, for it has some splendid old houses in Sheep Street, Dragon Street and College Street, and an attractive bow-windowed inn. Stoner Hill, 2 miles north on the Alresford road, is well wooded and offers good views over the valley.

Privett
The village's large church has a 170-ft spire and a lych-gate made from ships' timbers, relics of Admiral Parry's 19th-century Arctic expeditions. The gardens of Coles, 1 mile north-east, are magnificent—26 acres of shrubs, borders, roses and a water-garden.

Selborne
The birthplace and home of Gilbert White (1720–93), the naturalist. Much of the village is as he knew it when he was a curate in the area in the 1750's. His house, The Wakes, where he wrote *The Natural History and Antiquities of Selborne,* published in 1789, is a memorial library and museum devoted jointly to Gilbert White and to Captain Oates (1880–1912), the Antarctic explorer. By the churchyard is a green called The Plestor, and inside the churchyard is a huge old yew tree surrounded by a seat. Pollarded lime trees interlace their branches in front of the butcher's shop. Selborne is a much-visited and venerated place. There is a good view of the village from Selborne Hanger, a steep, beech-covered hill on National Trust land west of the village. It is reached by a zigzag path which Gilbert White helped to make to one of his favourite haunts.

Steep
A minor road north of Petersfield winds between beech hedges to this village on a ledge. The partly-Norman church stands at the end of a tunnel of yew trees leading from the lych-gate. An attractive route leads northwards to Wheatham Hill, 1 mile north of Steep, then back down a long beechwooded hill to Petersfield, with scenic views into the valley throughout its length.

Tichborne
A village notable for the famous 'Tichborne Claimant' law case of 1871, when an Australian butcher was sentenced to 14 years' imprisonment for claiming to be Sir Roger Tichborne, heir to the local estates of the Tichborne family. The parish church, partly Norman, stands on a steep little hill overlooking Tichborne Park, the family mansion rebuilt in the last century. In the church's Tichborne Chapel is the 15th-century figure of Richard Tichborne, who died at the age of 14 months—in fulfilment, it is said, of a curse laid on him by a gipsy. The Tichborne Dole—formerly of loaves but now of flour—is distributed to villagers every year on March 25, maintaining a custom started in 1150 by Roger de Tichborne.

The dole originated in the deathbed request made by Roger de Tichborne's wife, that he should set aside the produce of some of his land for the relief of the poor. He agreed to grant as much land as she could crawl round during the time it took a brand to burn. She managed to crawl round 20 acres before dying, and to this day the land is known as 'the Crawls' after her feat.

PIONEER OF NATURAL HISTORY

The Rev. Gilbert White, 1720–93 (right), was a pioneer of natural history. As curate of Farringdon, near Selborne, he developed his records of wildlife into a book, *The Natural History and Antiquities of Selborne* (below), first published in 1789 and still one of the most engaging records of the English countryside ever written. The bird illustrated is the black-winged stilt, which White called the stilt plover. Gilbert White's 17th-century house, The Wakes, is now a museum, and visitors to the area can follow the footpath up Selborne Hanger (left) which White himself helped to make. This was the countryside in which Gilbert White made his studies of wildlife from 1751 until his death at the age of 73

THE TICHBORNE DOLE *The memory of Lady Mabella de Tichborne lives on in the annual dole she won for the villagers*

THE LYCH-GATE *Yews surround the lych-gate at All Saints' Church in Steep, near Petersfield. Lych-gates were built to shield the coffin and bearers from rain while awaiting the priest. The name comes from the Old English word* lich, *which means corpse*

SOUTH-EAST ENGLAND

The south-east corner of England juts boldly into the quick run of glittering tides. Its marshes, wide beaches and high chalk cliffs fronting the English Channel are backed by the rolling Sussex downs, the orchards of the Weald and the heaths of Surrey.

The Kent and Sussex shores have been the 'Gateway to England' through the centuries, and still bear the signs of successive waves of invaders. The Romans under Aulus Plautius landed there in AD 43 and left behind them the closest concentration of Roman shore-castles in Britain; their ruins survive today, sometimes incorporated in medieval castles. The Anglo-Saxons under Hengist and Horsa landed on this coast and later the Cinque Ports were created to stave off Danish intruders. The Normans landed there too, and set up a girdle of mighty fortresses such as those at Rochester, Dover and Canterbury.

Against this historic tapestry of war, the coast today has the longest stretch of holiday resorts in Britain. By contrast, the shoreline has also the lonely north Kent marshes, the windswept Isle of Sheppey, and the great empty acres of Pevensey Levels and Romney Marsh, where sheep graze among lonely churches. Along the shore of Romney Marsh were the secret landing-places of 18th-century smugglers, who took cargoes of brandy, tobacco, silk and lace far inland by secret forest tracks.

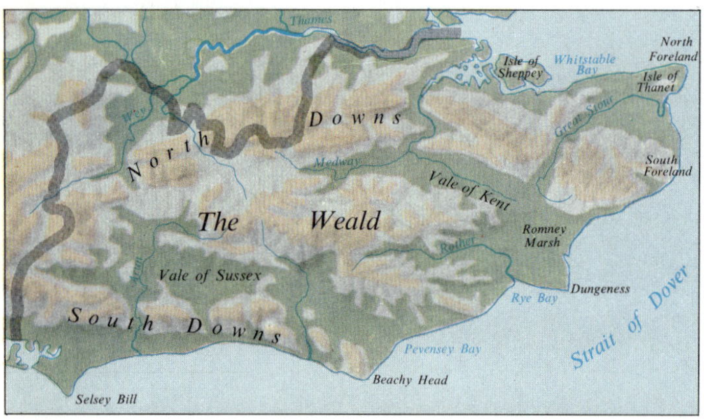

CHALK AND CLAY *Chalk hills with grassy slopes cross the South-East. The North Downs stretch through Kent and Surrey; the South Downs follow the Sussex coast, ending seawards in chalk cliffs. Forests once covered the Weald's clay soil*

The Sussex coast is backed by the South Downs. These grassy slopes are the land of skylarks and sheep—Southdown sheep are exported all over the world. The South Downs Way is 80 miles of Britain's finest riding and walking country, along ancient paths where primitive Stone Age man grazed his sheep 5000 years ago. Valleys cut through the chalk and are followed by rivers beloved of anglers—the Arun, the Adur, the Cuckmere and the Ouse—where there are reeds and water lilies, wild duck and snipe. These valleys flood in winter into long lakes alive with widgeon and teal. Amberley Wild Brooks is a sweep of 12 miles of cattle pastures and reedy dikes by the Arun, between Arundel and Pulborough. The steep escarpments of the North and South Downs face each other inwards across the Weald—once deep forests, today a countryside of enchanting villages, splendid mansions, rich farms, orchards and hop gardens with conical oast-houses. Here grew the oaks which built the

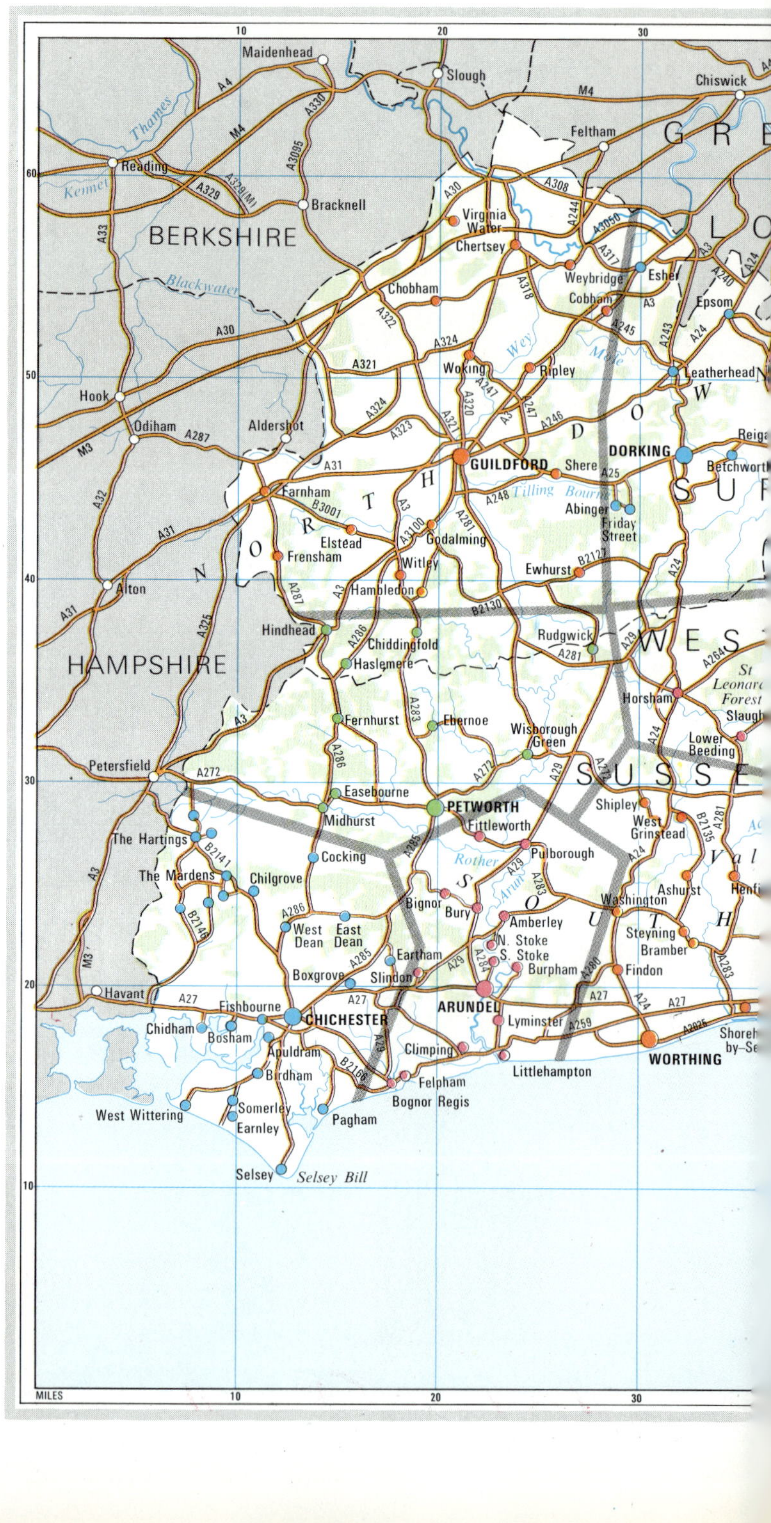

Thames
Tilbury
Isle of Grain
Sheerness
Cooling
Swanscombe
Gravesend
Sidcup
Hayes
Farningham
Eynsford
Cobham
Upnor
Gillingham
ROCHESTER
Chatham
Meopham
Hartlip
Lower Halstow
Newington
Eastchurch
Isle of Sheppey
The Swale
Whitstable Bay
Herne Bay
Reculver
Margate
Birchington
Broadstairs
North Foreland
Isle of Thanet
WHITSTABLE
Sarre
Minster
Ramsgate
Stour
Teynham
Lynsted
Fordwich
CANTERBURY
Sandwich
Wingham
Patrixbourne
Bishopsbourne
Selling
Chartham
Chilham
Godmersham
Barham
Barfreston
Deal
Walmer
St Margaret's at Cliffe
Alkham
Elham
Paddlesworth
DOVER
Folkestone
Hythe
Lympne
Aldington
Ashford
Wye
Hothfield
Charing
Pluckley
Lenham
Purley
Woldingham
Caterham
Godstone
Westerham
Redhill
Bletchingley
Outwood
Lingfield
Trottiscliffe
Wrotham
Wrotham Heath
Ightham
Sevenoaks
Birling
Aylesford
Allington
Offham
West Malling
East Malling
MAIDSTONE
Bearsted
Otham
Leeds
Mereworth
East Farleigh
Yalding
Loose
Boughton Monchelsea
Sutton Valence
Headcorn
Tonbridge
Chiddingstone
Hever
Penshurst
Bidborough
ROYAL TUNBRIDGE WELLS
Paddock Wood
Marden
Brenchley
Horsmonden
Goudhurst
Cranbrook
Sissinghurst
Biddenden
Benenden
Tenterden
Vale of Kent
Medway
EAST GRINSTEAD
Groombridge
Withyham
Tinsley Green
Crawley
Forest Row
West Hoathly
Wych Cross
Ashdown Forest
Eridge
Lamberhurst
HAWKHURST
Balcombe
Ardingly
Horsted Keynes
Cuckfield
Pilt Down
Mayfield
Etchingham
Burwash
Bodiam
Salehurst
Northiam
Robertsbridge
Brightling
Heathfield
Chailey
Chiddingly
Sedlescombe
Brede
Battle
Winchelsea
RYE
Rye Bay
Camber
Small Hythe
Appledore
Brookland
Ivychurch
Old Romney
New Romney
Lydd
Dymchurch
Romney Marsh
Walland Marsh
Dungeness
Strait of Dover
Ditchling
Barcombe
Plumpton
LEWES
Glyndebourne
Glynde
Upper Dicker
Hailsham
Herstmonceux
Pevensey Levels
Pevensey
Bexhill
HASTINGS
St Leonards
Falmer
West Firle
Alciston
Wilmington
Alfriston
Newhaven
Jevington
Westdean
Eastbourne
Eastdean
Seaford
Beachy Head
Pevensey Bay
Hove
BRIGHTON
Rottingdean
N O R T H   D O W N S
K E N T
T H E   W E A L D
E A S T   S U S S E X
REGIONAL PAGE INDEX
KEY TO MAP
Regional centre
Selected town or village
Regional boundary
County boundary
Major road
Minor road
Woodland
River and lake or reservoir

British Navy. Charcoal burners also felled them to smelt the Sussex iron; and gunpowder mills were set up in lonely wooded valleys, giving rise to the many hammer ponds, surviving today, which drove the water-wheels of forges and powder mills. Some of the ancient forest magic still lingers in the Wealden forests of St Leonards and Ashdown, where herds of deer roam wild. To the north-west, woods of pine and spruce and stag-headed oaks surge to the slopes of Black Down and Leith Hill, the two highest points in south-east England, which have views rivalling those from many a mountain peak.

Beyond, on the western fringe, poking their fingers in here and there among woods and downs, are the moorlands, wooded valleys and heather-covered hills of Surrey. These lands—Bagshot Heath, Chobham Common, Pirbright Common and Bisley Common—are so poor and acid in soil that it was never worth while, over the centuries, to enclose them for farming. A century ago, the sandy Surrey pine-and-heather country was as wild as parts of Scotland. Today, the mock-Tudor dwellings of the stockbroker belt are widespread; but there are still many commons and heaths—thousands of acres open to the walker and the picnicker.

The Weald that Kipling loved

The popularity of Kent as a place of residence near to London for great families in medieval times has left a legacy of stately homes—Penshurst Place, the semi-fortified 600-year-old birthplace of Sir Philip Sidney; Ightham Mote, half-timbered and moated, secretive in its Kent valley; and Knole, with its priceless treasures of furniture. Notable Sussex buildings include the restored 13th-century Michelham Priory, near Hailsham, which has one of the largest moats in the country; Petworth and Goodwood, classic 17th and 18th-century buildings; and the Royal Pavilion at Brighton, the Oriental extravaganza which was rebuilt for the Prince Regent by John Nash in 1822.

This rolling countryside has inspired some heroic English literature. Dickens lived and wrote in Kent. Defoe wrote *Robinson Crusoe* at Cranbrook. Kipling wrote of 'the wooded, dim blue goodness of the Weald'; G. K. Chesterton and Hilaire Belloc sang the praises of Sussex. The people match the land. They have a rich, soft dialect, a ruddy English look and a character which is as tenacious as Wealden clay. They, like their lovable land, are English to the backbone.

WHY THE AIR IS BRACING

The South-East has low rainfall and good sunshine records. Between 25 and 30 in. of rain fall each year—one-third less than in Devon and Cornwall—and the sun shines, on average, for 4½ hours each day. The low rainfall, and the considerable variation between day and night temperatures, account for the region's bracing air. March, April and May are the driest months of the year. Even January and February are drier than the late-autumn months

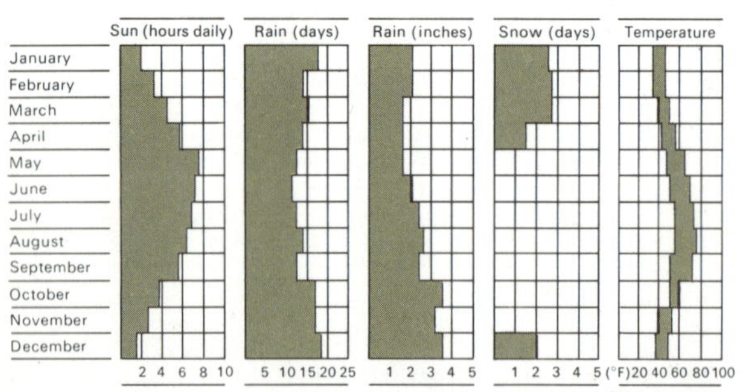

THE GOLDEN DOWNS *Valleys of bright barley cover the South Downs between Lewes and Brighton. On the downs are traces of the shafts from which Neolithic man mined flint arrow-heads, and the raised mounds of Iron Age hill forts*

A cathedral city near the sea

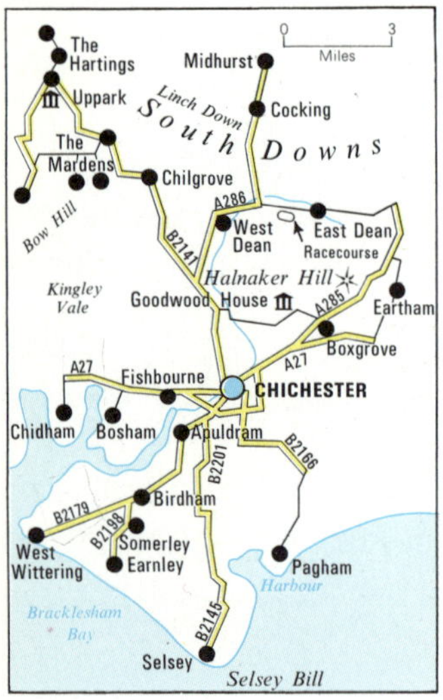

Chichester sits on a plain of rich farmland between the shining creeks, green islands and salt flats of Chichester Harbour, one of the largest semi-enclosed areas of tidal water in southern England, and the western rampart of the South Downs—the 'blunt, bow-headed, whale-backed Downs', as Rudyard Kipling described them.

The downs of West Sussex, heavily wooded, come within a few miles of Chichester. Hidden in their folds are little churches, many dating from the 12th and 13th centuries, and tiny villages with houses of flint, half-timbered brickwork and thatch. Many of the villages grew up under the protective wing of great estates such as Goodwood, which preserve large stretches of unspoilt downland countryside.

The area is rich in history. The downs are criss-crossed by ancient trackways, fine country today for walkers and horsemen. The South Downs Way runs along the downs north of Chichester at the start of its 80-mile course eastwards across four river valleys to Beachy Head. Chichester was already the site of an important settlement when the Romans arrived in AD 43 and made Cogidubnus, the reigning local king, their viceroy. The site of what may have been his palace is still being unearthed at Fishbourne. Four centuries later the Saxons encountered little resistance in this area; attractive seaside and downland villages like West Wittering and the Hartings preserve the Saxon suffix of *-ing,* meaning 'the people of'.

CHICHESTER *The 18th-century Deanery, with its small windows and large private garden, lies in the precincts of the Norman cathedral; it is framed by the garden's gates made of Sussex wrought iron. The medieval Deanery was destroyed at the siege of Chichester in 1642 during the Civil War*

Sailing Chichester Harbour has 27 square miles of navigable water, with yachting centres on numerous inlets. Bosham Sea School, and others, hire out boats. Regattas in the summer.

Angling Sea angling at Selsey and Bracklesham and from East Wittering beach.

Riding South Downs north of Chichester and the sands at Selsey.

Horse racing The 'Glorious Goodwood' meeting, starting on the last Tues. in July, is among the main events in the racing calendar.

Arts Chichester Festival Theatre is at Oaklands Park. Every seat in its six-sided auditorium is within 66 ft of the stage. Drama season from May to Sept.; concerts during winter. Chichester, Salisbury and Winchester choirs combine in July for the Southern Cathedrals Festival, held in Chichester in 1980, 1983, etc.

Places to see *Chichester District Museum*: Tues. to Sat. *Fishbourne Roman Palace*: daily, May to Nov. *Goodwood House*: afternoons only; Easter; also Sun. and Mon., May to Oct., and Tues. in Aug. *St Roche's Arboretum* (NGS), West Dean: daily early May and mid-June. *Uppark* (NT), South Harting: afternoons only; Apr. to Sept., Sun., Wed., Thur. and Bank Hols. *Weald and Downland Open Air Museum*, Singleton: Easter to Sept., daily except Mon.; Oct., Wed., Sat. and Sun.; Nov. to Mar., Sun. *West Dean Gardens*: Apr. to Sept., afternoons except Sat.

Information centre Council House, North Street, Chichester. Tel. Chichester 82226.

Apuldram
A parish on the Chichester Channel with a 13th-century church and a 15th-century manor house, Rymans, whose gardens are sometimes open to the public. There are waterside walks where wildfowl such as Brent geese, shelduck, wigeon and waders abound.

Birdham
A village on Chichester Harbour, attracting yachtsmen, artists and holiday-makers. Near Birdham, the painter J. M. W. Turner discovered the beauty of Chichester Harbour; his painting of it is on view in Petworth House. The parish church, built in 1545, has a low, narrow door through which, according to legend, the Devil was kicked out; then the door was blocked up so that he could not get in again.

Bosham
Cottages in soft colours stand on a little peninsula between two tidal creeks, with Quay Meadow at the seaward end. Harold, the Saxon, set out from here in 1064 on the voyage to Normandy which delivered him into the hands of William the Conqueror. The Bayeux Tapestry shows Harold on his way to mass in Bosham Church before the voyage. It was at Bosham that Canute is said to have commanded the tide to roll back.

BOSHAM *Beside the harbour is a Saxon church which appears on the Bayeux Tapestry*

Boxgrove
A straggling one-street village at the foot of the downs. The big surprise is the magnificent nave of the Priory Church, built between 1170 and 1220. Lord de la Warr, Lord of the Manor, stopped the church being pulled down after the Dissolution of the Monasteries in 1537 and converted it into a parish church.

Chichester
The site of the modern city was a settlement of the Regni tribe before the Romans built their new town of Noviomagus there. After the Romans left, the Saxon chieftain Aella gave the ruined city to his son Cissa, who called it after himself—Cissa's Ceaster or Castle. Viewed from any high point on the downs, Chichester is set amid fields, coloured woods, glimmering salt marshes and stippled harbour waters, with the thin cathedral spire pointing like a sword to heaven. The cathedral, begun *c.* 1091 by Bishop Ralph, the Norman, has a nave of soaring beauty. There is a magnificent window in the south transept, and the graceful, tapering spire,

277 ft high, dominates the West Sussex coastal plain. There are noble streets and homely corners of history in the town, a 15th-century market cross, some fine Georgian houses and long stretches of the original Roman wall.

Chidham
A Chichester Harbour village lying between two tidal creeks, with cottages, barns, a little church, a well-preserved farmhouse of 1759 and a manor house of the same century.

Chilgrove
A charming village in a valley, with a pub by a long green, just off the main road from Chichester to the Hartings. It is a good centre for downland walks, especially southwards to the ridge of Bow Hill, where two concentric ramparts mark the site of an Iron Age hill fort, Goosehill Camp. At Kingley Vale, 2¼ miles south of Chilgrove, there is a striking yew wood which is said to mark the graves of Danes killed in battle.

Cocking
The cottages have woodwork painted in the deep yellow used in all villages run by the Cowdray Estate. There are good walks through downland under Linch Down (813 ft) towards the Hartings. The red roofs of Cocking and Midhurst look gay from Cocking Down.

Earnley
A village of the Selsey peninsula, with a 14th-century church. There is a group of thatched flint barns at Marsh Farm, near the beach, and an old windmill at nearby Somerley. Offshore, low spring tides in Bracklesham Bay disclose unusual deposits of slate-coloured clays known as the Bracklesham Beds.

Fishbourne
One of the major Roman relics in Britain lies just west of Chichester, on a well-signposted side road. Excavations have disclosed an important Roman palace occupied during the 2nd and 3rd centuries AD, during the peak period of the Roman occupation; it may have originally been the palace of Cogidubnus, the Briton made viceroy by the Romans. Sections of the walls, baths and heating system are visible, but the most memorable feature of the palace is its superb mosaic floors. One intricate panel, 17 ft square, has as its central medallion a winged boy astride a dolphin. There is an adjoining museum devoted to the history of the site and an imaginative portrayal of life in Roman Britain.

Goodwood House
Seat of the Duke of Richmond and Gordon, with a beautiful racecourse high on the downs above it. The house, in Sussex flintwork, has a collection of Louis XV furniture and world-famous paintings. The Trundle, a 676-ft hill crowned by the earthworks of an Iron Age fort, is a natural grandstand from which to see the Goodwood Races.

A COUNTRY FOOTPATH THAT FOLLOWS A ROMAN ROAD

A section of Stane Street, the road built by the Romans in AD 70 from Chichester to London, can still be clearly traced on the downs near Eartham. A bridle path follows it for three miles over National Trust land, climbing to Bignor Hill

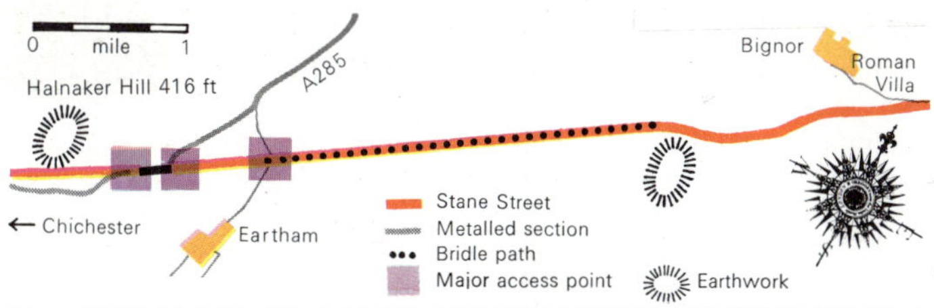

A mosaic floor in the Roman villa at Bignor shows Zeus as an eagle

The Hartings
Hamlets on the Hampshire border near Petersfield, with many downland walks. Uppark, on the downs a mile to the south, is a Queen Anne mansion where once lived Emma Hart, the second Lady Hamilton and Nelson's mistress. The downland hamlets of the four Mardens lie further south.

Selsey
The South Saxons landed at Selsey in AD 477. So did St Wilfrid, when he arrived in AD 681 to convert the Saxons to Christianity. He established a monastery, which later became a cathedral; its site is now submerged. Roman and early British coins have been found on the beach. From Selsey Bill, the southernmost point in Sussex, there are good views of the coast and across to the Isle of Wight.

West Dean
A charming downland village, with flint and half-timbered houses. It lies in the valley of the River Lavant, and has a park of beeches, horse chestnuts and elms, and a botanical garden of azaleas, magnolias and rhododendrons. At Singleton, 1¼ miles east, is the Weald and Downland Open Air Museum, an exhibition of ancient wooden buildings transferred from their original sites.

West Wittering
A former fishing village, tastefully developed into a small high-class residential and holiday resort. There are good modern houses and well-converted cottages, plenty of trees, and the remains of Cakeham Manor, once a palace of the Bishops of Chichester. East Wittering, near by, is a bungalow and chalet seaside village with sand at low tide.

SELSEY *The hard, sandy beach between Selsey and Bracklesham is good for riding, and the salt water helps to harden horses' fetlocks*

Water-meadows of the Arun

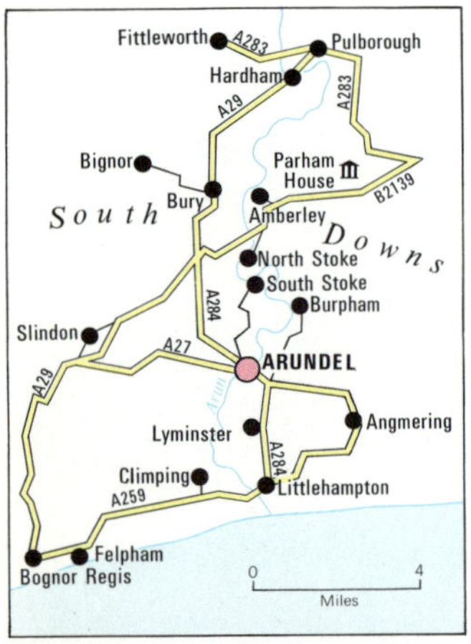

Sailing The mouth of the River Arun at Littlehampton is crowded with yachts at summer weekends. There are clubs and sailing schools at Littlehampton, Bognor Regis, Felpham and Pagham Beach. Bognor Regis holds a regatta in mid-Aug.

Angling Off-shore fishing is best from May to July. Good freshwater fishing in the Arun and the Rother.

Golf Courses at Bognor Regis, Littlehampton, Angmering and Pulborough.

Horse racing Fontwell Park racecourse, 4 miles west of Arundel, holds 14 National Hunt meetings during the year.

Cricket Bognor Regis Cricket Week is in the first week of Aug. at Nyewood Lane, Bognor Regis.

Tennis An Open Lawn Tennis Association Tournament, which includes the West Sussex championships, is held in Aug. at the Bognor Regis Lawn Tennis Club.

Bowls Greens at Bognor Regis.

Places to see *Arundel Castle*: Easter to late Oct., afternoons Mon. to Fri.; also Sun. afternoon May to Aug. *Bignor Roman Villa*: Mar. to Oct., Tues. to Sun. and Bank Hols.; also every Mon. in Aug. *Parham House*, Elizabethan house with long gallery: Easter to early Oct., Sun., Wed., Thur. and Bank Hol. afternoons. *Potter's Museum of Curiosity*, Arundel: Easter to Oct., daily; some afternoons in winter.

Information centres Belmont Street, Bognor Regis.
Tel. Bognor Regis 23140. Council Offices, Church Street, Littlehampton.
Tel. Littlehampton 6133.
61 High Street, Arundel.
Tel. Arundel 882268.

The valley of the River Arun is a place of impressive natural beauty. Rising in St Leonard's Forest, Sussex's longest river meanders south from Pulborough through peaceful pastures alive with birds and cattle, then cuts through the South Downs and past Arundel towards the sea at Littlehampton. Upstream the Arun is a good river for the angler, as pike, perch, chub and roach abound.

The Arun Valley was one of the six administrative divisions, or 'rapes', into which the Normans divided Sussex after the Conquest. Each rape had its own strip of coast, its own downland for grazing and clay farmland for cultivation, and to the north a strip of the ancient Wealden forest where kings hunted. The Normans built Arundel Castle to defend the valley against raiders; its successor still dominates the valley, and the town of Arundel at its foot, once a flourishing port, is a good touring centre. An attractive minor road, for instance, follows the river bank beside Arundel Park, which has noble trees, secluded dells and a fine lake. The road continues to an inn nestling beneath a wooded chalk escarpment right on the river bank.

The seaside resorts such as Bognor Regis and Littlehampton are bright and friendly places, and their happy marriage with the noble expanse of unspoilt farmland, woodland and downs behind them has a peculiarly English character to it.

AMBERLEY *At the foot of the downs above Amberley Wild Brooks, St Michael's Church stands beside the ruins of 14th-century Amberley Castle, once the home of the Bishops of Chichester*

Amberley

A village with a ruined castle, a Norman church, thatched cottages, and gardens bright with flowers in summer. Amberley sprawls on a low ridge overlooking the Amberley Wild Brooks—the name 'Wild' is derived from 'Weald'—which are 30 square miles of grazing marshes watered by the Arun, impassable for cars but ideal for walkers. The castle was built in 1380 for the Bishops of Chichester, and the ruined gatehouse and walls enclose an ancient manor house.

Arundel

The town climbs from the River Arun to the battlemented walls, massive keep and turrets of Arundel Castle, above which flies the flag of the Duke of Norfolk, Earl Marshal of England. The castle is flanked by the late 14th-century Church of St Nicholas and the Roman Catholic Cathedral of St Philip Neri, built by the 15th Duke of Norfolk in 1868–9. The entire view from across the river has a Gothic, fairy-tale effect.

The castle was built by Roger Montgomery, Earl of Shrewsbury, just after the Conquest, to defend the valley against sea raiders. It was added to in 1170 and 1190 and was almost ruined in 1643 by Cromwell's cannon fired from the steeple of St Nicholas's Church. The castle was rebuilt in the 18th century, and extensively restored in 1890. The Fitzalan Chapel, pictures, furniture, armour, State dresses, china, tapestries and other treasures deserve a day's study. The view from the 12th-century stone keep over the town, river marshes and downs is breathtaking.

People may walk freely in the 1100-acre park, which is open daily, but cars, motor cycles, bicycles and dogs are barred. In the park stands Hiorn's Tower, built in 1790 of flint and stone, in the style of a medieval hunting tower.

The town of Arundel is mostly Victorian but there are many 18th-century houses, and Mount Pleasant and Bond Street have many early 19th-century flint-walled cottages. Potter's Museum in the High Street was originally at Bramber, and is well known for its nursery rhyme tableaux incorporating stuffed animals. Dominating the High Street is the Norfolk Arms, a splendid 18th-century coaching inn.

Bignor

A village on the northern slope of the downs, famous as the site of one of the largest Roman villas in Britain. The villa, covering $4\frac{1}{2}$ acres, has fine mosaic floors, including one depicting Venus and the Gladiator, made of stones less than an inch square. In the village there is a fine half-timbered and thatched 15th-century shop.

WEATHER-BOARDING

Protection of houses against rain and gales by 'weather-boarding' was a common practice in late Georgian times, from 1800 to 1830. Oak boards were fixed horizontally to the walls of a house. The boards were 'chamfered' or cut at an angle of 45 degrees at the lower edge and 'feathered', or tapered, at the top edge for elegance

ARUNDEL CASTLE *From the heights of the town the fortress guards the Arun gap*

BOGNOR REGIS *Fishermen sell freshly caught cod at an informal beach market*

LITTLEHAMPTON *The East Beach has flat sands; west of the Arun lie grassy dunes*

Bognor Regis
Five miles of hard sand, safe paddling in shallow water, beach chalets, good sea-fishing, a pier and a holiday camp make Bognor a splendid family holiday centre. It began as a Saxon village, became a medieval fishing hamlet and then, from 1790, developed into a quiet and fashionable seaside watering place. Houses on the Steyne and in Waterloo Square have a Regency elegance. Hotham House is a Georgian mansion surrounded by acres of public woodland with a children's zoo. The 'Regis' was added to Bognor after King George V convalesced at nearby Aldwick in 1928.

Burpham
Scattered houses on grassy hillocks in the water-meadows of the Arun. The north wall of the church is Saxon, the arch to the south transept Norman, the vaulted chancel 13th century and the roof 15th century.

Bury
Hidden in narrow lanes, the village leads quietly down to the Arun. John Galsworthy, author of *The Forsyte Saga*, lived and died in Bury House. The river walks are still as Turner painted them.

Climping
A village on the western side of the Arun Estuary, with a hotel built this century in the style of a medieval manor. The village lies a mile inland from one of the rare stretches of undeveloped coastline in Sussex, and paths lead to the sea. There is a 13th-century church.

Fittleworth
A village of stone and timber-frame cottages. The narrow Stopham Bridge over the little River Rother is the best-looking medieval river bridge in Sussex. Stopham House is the seat of the de Stopham Barttelots, who came over with the Conqueror.

Littlehampton
A small, ancient, once-important port at the mouth of the Arun, now a good family seaside resort and popular yachting centre. Nine hundred years ago it was used by passengers to and from Normandy, and by vessels bringing stone from the quarries at Caen and returning laden with timber. Today, Littlehampton still has a pleasantly salty air about the harbour, a great green between the houses and the sea and a splendid expanse of sand; but only a little of the old town survives on the east bank of the Arun. There is also a promenade, a fun-fair, an 18-hole golf course which is reached by ferry across the river, and good fishing which is free on the towpath side of the river as far as Pulborough. Littlehampton seems made for children, small-boat enthusiasts and artists who sketch its old wharves. There are boats for hire, and daily motor launches up the Arun to Arundel. To the east, sea-shore holiday development continues in an almost unbroken line through East Preston, Rustington, Angmering-on-Sea and Ferring as far as Worthing. The gardens and promenades of these resorts have a fresh charm that attracts holidaymakers.

Lyminster
Its flint cottages, surrounded by flint walls, look like forts shutting out the sea-wind. There is a magnificent view from the church across the water-meadows to the skyline of Arundel.

Parham House
A beautiful Elizabethan mansion with walled gardens, set in a great deer park, with a church on the lawn. The house, with its superb period furniture and pictures, is very welcoming and lived-in and the view of woods, lake, bare downs and deer has not altered since Tudor times. Buses stop at the drive entrance, leaving a mile walk to the house; cars park by the house. Storrington, 2 miles east, is a good starting point for walks on the South Downs.

Pulborough
Fishermen flock to this village, which also has some of the best inland boating in East and West Sussex, on the little River Arun. There are prehistoric, Roman and Norman remains. Hardham Church, a mile south, has 12th-century wall paintings.

Slindon
A village of flint and brick buildings with views southwards to the sea and northwards to the woods, valleys and downs of Dale Park. The National Trust looks after the 3500-acre Slindon Park Estate, which includes much of the village and the beechwoods through which runs the Roman Stane Street.

North and South Stoke
The twin villages on either side of a great loop of the Arun give views across the water-meadows and up to the wooded hill of Arundel Park. Only a footpath connects the two villages. At nearby Houghton there is a 16th-century inn, The George and Dragon, where Charles II called in 1651 after the Battle of Worcester.

Landscapes that Turner and Tennyson knew

Point-to-point The annual meeting at Cowdray Park takes place on Easter Mon. The downs are good riding country, and there are several stables in the area.

Angling Good coarse fishing on limited stretches of the River Rother, a tributary of the Arun.

Golf Club courses at Cowdray Park and Hindhead.

Village games The unusual Sussex game of stoolball is still played on summer evenings at villages around Midhurst. Stoolball, first played in the 15th century, remained popular until the 18th century when it was supplanted by cricket. The games are similar, with 11 players each side; but in stoolball the ball is bowled underarm, the bat is like a table-tennis bat and the 'wicket' is a stool 1 ft square mounted on a stake 4 ft 8 in. from the ground. A stoolball player can be out 'body before wicket' as distinct from cricket's 'leg before'.

Arts Haslemere Music Festival, at which 16th and 17th-century music is played on authentic instruments of the period from the famous Dolmetsch Collection, is held during the last fortnight of July (box office open from Mar.). The Dolmetsch workshops can be seen by appointment. Concerts sponsored by the National Trust are held during the summer at Petworth House.

Places to see *Cowdray House*, Midhurst, ruins of Elizabethan mansion: daily. *Haslemere Educational Museum*: Tues. to Sat.; also Sun. afternoons, Apr. to Oct. *Petworth House* (NT): deer park, daily; house, Apr. to Oct., afternoons Wed., Thur., Sat., Sun. and Bank Hol. Mon.

Information centres Newlands, Pound Street, Petworth. Tel. Petworth 42241. North Street, Midhurst. Tel. Midhurst 2251. Bridge Street, Godalming. Tel. Godalming 4104.

POLO AT COWDRAY *Matches are played at weekends from April to August*

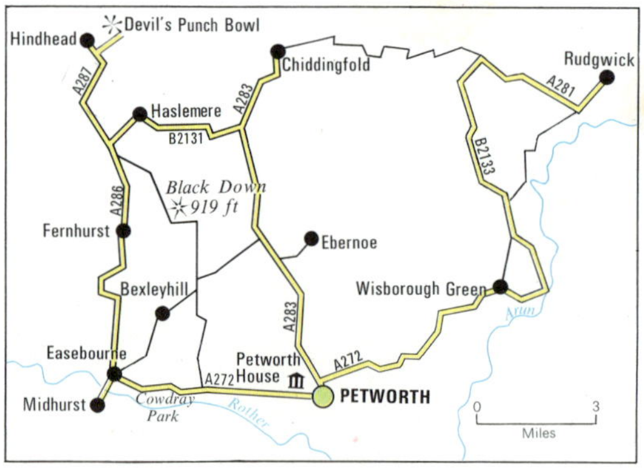

Two of the loveliest large estates in southern England—Petworth and Cowdray—lie along the winding valley of the River Rother just north of the South Downs. They adjoin Petworth and Midhurst, which retain their old character of small country towns and make good centres for touring the area. North of the River Rother, a maze of tiny streams waters the rich farmlands of the western Weald. The ending 'fold' in the names of a score of villages and farms such as Dunsfold, Chiddingfold, Ifold and Alfold, is a Saxon word meaning a clearing in a dense forest—the great Wealden forest which once covered most of south-east England.

Woodland still covers Black Down, the highest point in West Sussex—though today black fir and spruce predominate over the old Wealden oak, birch, ash and chestnut. Just across the county boundary are the wild heaths and heather-covered hills of Surrey around Haslemere and Hindhead, where thousands of acres are safeguarded by the National Trust. Hindhead stands on a sandstone plateau, crowned with commons of heather, gorse and fir trees; there are magnificent views across deep valleys like the Devil's Punch Bowl, which have been chiselled out of the hillsides by rain and wind over the centuries.

Miles of russet heathland stretch northwards from the Hindhead plateau, and though the busy London to Portsmouth road curls round the Devil's Punch Bowl, the wild grandeur of the view endures.

Black Down
The highest point in Sussex, 919 ft above sea level, is part of a plateau of nearly 500 acres covered with gorse, heather and trees, and owned by the National Trust. Several tracks lead to the top, including Tennyson's Lane, leading north to Haslemere. The poet used to walk here from his home, Aldworth House. Another path leads down the hill to Fernhurst.

Chiddingfold
One of the largest and loveliest of the Wealden villages, with a green, a pond of ducks and water-lilies, and one of the oldest and most picturesque inns in Surrey—the 14th-century Crown, where Edward VI stayed 400 years ago. The hotel has some good timbering and a great hall. St Mary's Church, facing the green, contains some locally made glass and a 15th-century bell.

EARLY INSTRUMENTS RE-CREATED

A lute (above) based on a 17th-century original is made at the Dolmetsch workshops in Haslemere. The harpsichord (right) was built in 1896 by Arnold Dolmetsch, who started the Dolmetsch Collection. On it lie genuine early musical instruments and an original Handel manuscript

Cowdray Park
A magnificent open space with beeches, oaks and chestnuts and the imposing ruins of Cowdray House, built *c.* 1530. The house was burnt down in 1793, and a week later its owner, Lord Montagu, was drowned in Germany—fulfilling, it is said, a curse laid on the family by a monk ejected from Battle Abbey by the first owner of Cowdray House after Henry VIII's Dissolution of the Monasteries. Picnickers in Cowdray Park are confined to the shores of Benbow Pond, near the east gate, where cars must be parked. The park is famous for its summer polo tournaments. An avenue of Spanish chestnuts is the start of a footpath to Bexleyhill, from which there are views across the valley of the Rother to the South Downs.

Ebernoe
A village famous for its medieval tradition, still maintained, of spit-roasting a horned sheep at a cricket match and fair on Horn Fair Day, July 25. The sheep is shared among spectators and a horn is given to the cricketer who makes top score in the match.

Haslemere
For centuries a centre for craftsmen in iron, glass, leather, paper and woodwork. The town is now developed for commuters but preserves some pleasing old buildings, including 17th-century tiled houses behind a raised walk. In the High Street is an Educational Museum of geology, zoology and human history, and the town is the home of the Dolmetsch family, who make harpsichords and other early musical in-

SAILOR'S STONE *A memorial on Gibbet Hill, Hindhead, marks the site where a sailor was murdered in 1786. At the nearby Royal Huts Hotel are the chains used to hang the murderers, and five paintings which tell the story of the crime*

struments and give recitals on them. Haslemere is at the centre of dense woods and heathery valleys, through which smugglers once brought their pack trains of brandy from Sussex beaches to the outskirts of London.

Hindhead
The highest village in Surrey, 850 ft up, is a relatively new village, developed late in the 19th century because of its superb scenery and good air. Gibbet Hill, to the north-east, is 45 ft higher still, and near it lies the spectacular Devil's Punch Bowl, a deep valley worn in the sandstone ridge on which Hindhead stands. In 1786 an unknown sailor was murdered here, and the murderers were hanged by the side of the Punch Bowl, where an inscribed stone recalls the event.

Midhurst
An old market town on the River Rother, full of attractive houses and several fine old inns, including the partly-15th-century Spread Eagle. Curfew is still rung at 8 p.m. every night at the parish church. It is said that a rider, lost in darkness, found Midhurst by following the sound of its church bell; in gratitude he bought a piece of land in Midhurst, now called Curfew Garden, and gave it to the town to pay for the nightly ringing of the bell.

Midhurst is the centre of one of the most beautiful regions of Sussex, and there are good walks west and east along the Rother, southwards towards the downs and northwards across the river to Cowdray Park. The Cowdray estate village of Easebourne lies just across the river to the north of the town; in its church is the tomb of the first Lord Montagu who, in 1591, entertained Elizabeth I at Cowdray House.

Petworth
The medieval town crowds up to the walls of Petworth House. It has many winding, narrow streets, especially round the tiny market-place, which has a plain arcaded 18th-century town hall. There are good half-timbered Tudor houses and some Georgian buildings, and the Somerset Almshouses, or Upper Hospital, were founded in 1746.

Petworth House was completed by the 6th Duke of Somerset in 1696, and it retains the 13th-century chapel of an earlier mansion. The Carved Room was decorated by Grinling Gibbons. The art collection includes a series of Turner landscapes, as well as paintings by Holbein, Rembrandt, Hals, Van Dyck, Gainsborough and Reynolds.

TENNYSON'S LANE *The poet used to walk this way to Black Down Hill where he described the view as 'green Sussex fading into blue, with one grey glimpse of sea'*

Rudgwick
A typical Wealden village on high ground north-west of Horsham, with tile-hung houses and good views to Chanctonbury Ring. There is beautifully carved tracery round the windows of the 14th-century church. Thick woodland surrounds the village, and the infant River Arun runs through the Roman Woods to the east of the village.

Wisborough Green
A tree-shaded village with a pond, a large green and an old barn with a deeply sloping roof. The partly-Norman church contains a notable wall-painting.

THE LAKE AT PETWORTH HOUSE IN TWO CENTURIES

DEWY MORNING, PETWORTH HOUSE *Turner added the tall-masted boats to his painting of 1831, to echo the vertical line of the spire of St Mary's Church behind Petworth*

PETWORTH TODAY *The 19th-century spire of St Mary's was replaced in 1953 by a pyramid-shaped cap, looking from the lake like a central dome on Petworth House*

Lakes and open heaths in commuters' Surrey

Boating The River Wey is navigable from Weybridge to Godalming. Sailing on Charlton Lake, Sunbury, and at Staines, Thorpe, Shepperton, Wraysbury and Frensham Ponds. Canoeing from Weybridge to Farnham.

Angling From sections of the Wey at Elstead, Tilford and Guildford, and stretches of the Thames downstream from Staines Bridge.

Golf Worplesdon Golf Club, near Woking, holds national tournaments, including the Mixed Open Foursomes in Oct. The Piccadilly World Matchplay Tournament is usually held at Wentworth Golf Club, Virginia Water, in Oct.

Shooting The National Rifle Association's Imperial Meeting is held at Bisley in July.

Arts The Yvonne Arnaud Theatre at Guildford has productions throughout the year.

Places to see *Albury Park*, near Shere: May to Sept., Wed. and Thur. afternoons. *Birdworld Zoo*, Oast House, Holt Pound, Farnham: daily. *Clandon Park* (NT): Apr. to mid-Oct., afternoons except Mon. and Fri.; open Bank Hol. Mon. (closed Tues. after). *Farnham Castle* keep: Apr. to Sept., daily. *Guildford Castle* keep: Apr. to Sept., daily. *Hatchlands* (NT): Apr. to Sept., Wed. and Sat. afternoons. *Loseley House*: June to Sept., Wed., Thur., Fri., Sat. and Bank Hol. afternoons. *Willmer House Museum*, Farnham: Tues. to Sat.; also Bank Hol. and Sun. afternoons. *Winkworth Arboretum* (NT): daily. *Wisley Gardens*: daily: Royal Horticultural Society members only Sun. mornings.

Information centre Civic Hall, London Road, Guildford. Tel. Guildford 67314.

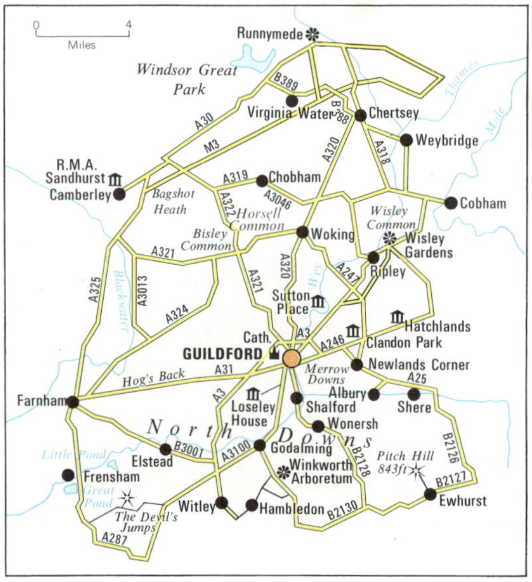

Surrey has managed to absorb a dense commuter population without sacrificing all its natural beauty. In the north of the county, towns like Woking, Camberley, Bagshot and Esher have become increasingly urbanised; yet around them there remain wide commons, sandy heaths and woodlands.

The towns themselves, sprawling as they often are, have not lost all their old-world features. Guildford is a county town full of well-preserved old houses; it is believed to take its name from a Saxon phrase meaning 'ford of the golden flowers'—the ford by which the Harrow Way, an ancient track along the North Downs, crossed the River Wey.

West of Guildford the downs narrow into the spectacular Hog's Back, and eastwards they broaden into wooded hills and commons, divided by the valley of the River Tillingbourne. There are attractive villages here—Shalford, Wonersh, Shere with its 'Silent Pool', and Albury—and stately homes vary from Tudor mansions such as Loseley House to the classical style of Clandon Park and Hatchlands.

Bagshot Heath
The heath, once notorious for highwaymen, extends south-east on to Bisley Common, famous for modern marksmen. Together they form a wide stretch of open country, with gorse, heather, pine and fir woods. Three miles south-west is the Royal Military Academy, Sandhurst, built in 1807.

Chertsey
A riverside town with wooded scenery, green fields, commons, including Chertsey Mead, and unspoilt woodland. There is a graceful seven-arched bridge over the river. A curfew bell in the church commemorates Blanche Heriot who, at the time of the Wars of the Roses, knowing that her lover was to be executed at curfew, climbed the church tower and hung on to the clapper of the bell until he was reprieved. Her courage inspired the ballad 'Curfew Must Not Ring Tonight' by the American poet Rose Hartwick Thorpe.

Elstead
A charming old village beside the River Wey, with a 14th-century church, a five-arched bridge, a Georgian watermill and a riverside walk to the ruins of Waverley Abbey, which inspired Sir Walter Scott's novel *Waverley*.

Ewhurst
An attractive village below the Surrey hills with some old houses, a church with a fine Norman doorway and an unusual village sign erected to mark the Coronation in 1953. The village is a good starting point from which to climb Pitch Hill, 843 ft, 1 mile to the north, or to explore the dense Hurt Wood.

Farnham
The most westerly town in Surrey, and one of the least spoilt. Here the so-called 'Pilgrims' Way' enters the county from Winchester. The route, still traceable in part along the southern edge of the Hog's Back, was used by Bronze Age traders long before medieval pilgrims, according to tradition, used stretches of it on their way to Canterbury.

William Cobbett, author of *Rural Rides*, was born in 1763 in what is now the Jolly Farmer Inn. The castle, built in the 12th century and belonging to the Bishops of Winchester until 1927, and then to the Bishop of Guildford until 1956, stands at the top of Castle Street, a broad street of gracious Georgian houses. Many kings and queens, from Edward I to Queen Victoria, have been entertained in the castle—and Cromwell besieged it. The castle is now used as a training centre, but the Norman keep, the most impressive part of the remains, is open to the public.

The town has gabled 17th-century almshouses, some half-timbered Tudor buildings, fine Georgian houses in West Street and a park of 308 acres. The road from Farnham to Guildford runs along the Hog's Back, a narrow 500-ft chalk ridge with long panoramic views of the Surrey countryside, north and south. There are several lay-bys for picnickers.

THE STORY OF TELEGRAPH HILL

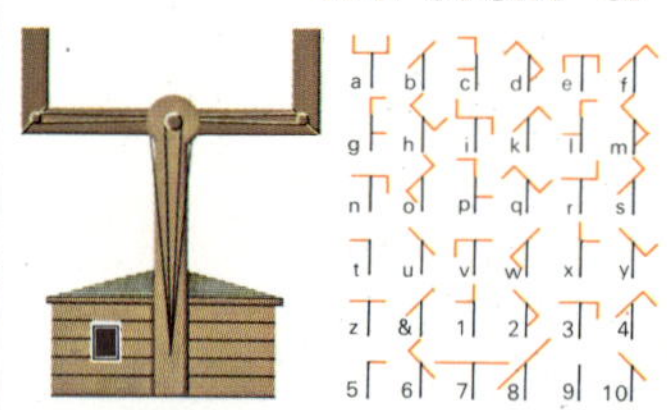

In the early 19th century the Admiralty used a line of 13 hilltop semaphore stations (below) to send messages to the Fleet at Portsmouth. One ruined signal post still stands at Telegraph Hill, Chatley Heath, Cobham (right)

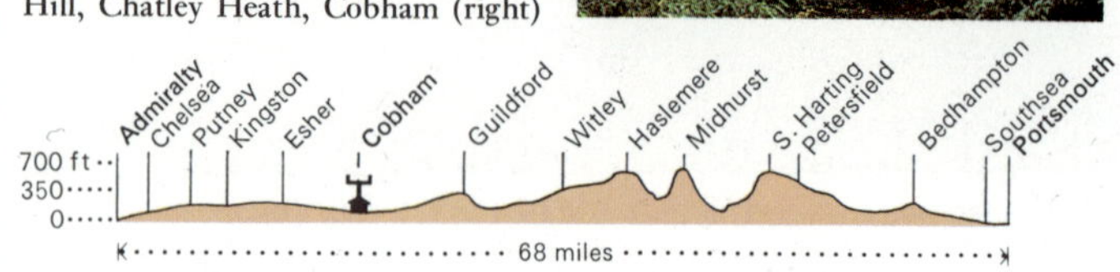

CYCLING THROUGH THE MUD *Bagshot Heath is a major venue for cyclo-cross, or cross-country cycling*

VIRGINIA WATER *The large artificial lake at the south-eastern corner of Windsor Great Park was laid out in George III's time by landscape gardeners Paul and Thomas Sandby. A colonnade of pillars from Leptis Magna, Tripoli, stands on the south bank, and a 100-ft totem pole commemorating the centenary of British Columbia was set up in 1958*

Frensham
The Great Pond at Frensham is one of the largest lakes in southern England, and even the Little Pond is far from little. Both are good for sailing, fishing and bird-watching, for many rare wildfowl visit them. Frensham Church has what is claimed to be a true witch's cauldron, 3 ft across, used by a Mother Ludlam who in the Middle Ages lived in a cave near Waverley Abbey. Views from the nearby Devil's Jumps—three curious hills, the largest of which, Stony Jump, belongs to the National Trust—are among the best in Surrey.

Godalming
This old wool town has narrow streets, half-timbered houses and inns of Tudor and Stuart days. The King's Arms had Peter the Great as a paying guest in 1698; and Tsar Alexander I of Russia and King Frederick William of Prussia dined there in 1816. Charterhouse School is on the north-west outskirts of the town. Winkworth Arboretum, 3 miles south-east, is a 95-acre hillside planted with rare trees and shrubs, with a lake and views over the North Downs. It was given to the National Trust in 1952. From here, there is a good drive west to the village of Hambledon, from which a footpath leads to Hydon Heath and its highest point, Hydon's Ball (586 ft).

Guildford
The town's architecture is a remarkable marriage of past and present—from the surviving keep of a castle built by Henry II, in Quarry Street, to the new cathedral, in simplified Gothic, which is a conspicuous landmark on Stag Hill, west of the town, and to the even newer buildings of the University of Surrey.

WISLEY GARDENS *Attractive walks among rock gardens clad with heather and alpine plants are a feature of the Royal Horticultural Society's 300-acre estate. The gardens are not only devoted to flowers, but are also used as experimental grounds for new varieties of fruit and vegetables and as a training centre for student gardeners*

Abbot's Hospital in the fine, steep High Street is a group of 17th-century almshouses, still inhabited. The Angel Hotel has an old wooden gallery and a coaching yard.

Loseley House, $2\frac{1}{2}$ miles to the south-west, was built in 1562 with stone from Waverley Abbey. The Elizabethan Sutton Place, $3\frac{1}{2}$ miles north-east, was one of the first non-fortified mansions built in Britain. Clandon Park, with its Palladian-style house, and Hatchlands, with a Robert Adam interior, are both on the road from Guildford to Leatherhead.

Ripley
An old-time coaching village of half-timbered houses and inns. Wisley, a mile to the north-east, has a pond beside the main road and acres of common land, good picnicking country. At Wisley are the 300-acre experimental gardens of the Royal Horticultural Society.

Runnymede
The broad meadow alongside the River Thames, where King John sealed the preliminary draft of Magna Carta in 1215, belongs to the National Trust. The unhurried pace of the cabin cruisers and smaller craft on the river makes a restful contrast to the bustle of traffic on the main road 20 yds away.

The domed Classical temple at the foot of Cooper's Hill, south of the road, is a Magna Carta Memorial, built by the American Bar Association. Halfway up the hill the John F. Kennedy Memorial stands on an acre of ground given to the United States. The Air Forces Memorial, at the top of the hill, commemorates 20,000 airmen who died in the Second World War with 'no known grave'; it commands a magnificent view of Windsor Castle and seven counties.

TEST PIECE *Refused permission to work in Guildford in 1683, John Aylward made this clock, gave it to the guildhall—and was allowed to set up shop*

Shere
An attractive village under the North Downs on the River Tillingbourne. One mile west is the romantic 'Silent Pool'. Legend has it that a peasant girl bathing there was frightened by King John and drowned. The gardens of nearby Albury Park, which are open to the public, were laid out by John Evelyn, the diarist, in the 17th century. From the large car park at Newlands Corner (567 ft), on the road to Merrow and Guildford, there are impressive views across the Weald to the South Downs.

Virginia Water
A haven of peace only 50 yds off the main road to the West Country. The lovely woodland lake, $1\frac{1}{2}$ miles long and part of Windsor Great Park, is an artificial lake, created in Georgian times from dammed-up marshy streams. Old stag-headed oaks mingle with beeches and dark conifers, and the water is alive with wildfowl and coarse fish.

Witley
The 600-year-old, tile-hung, steep-roofed White Hart is one of the oldest pubs in England, built on to a hunting lodge of Richard II. The Victorian novelist George Eliot wrote *Daniel Deronda* at Witley.

Riding country on the 'roof' of the South-East

Horse racing The Derby and the Oaks are run on Epsom Downs in early June, and there are other meetings at Epsom in Apr. and Aug. Lingfield Park has racing throughout the year except during Apr. At Sandown Park, near Esher, there is racing all the year except Aug. The countryside around Box Hill is good for pony trekking; there are stables on the hill, at Dorking and Abinger.

Golf There are 16 courses in the area.

Angling On stretches of the River Mole near Leatherhead and Dorking.

Arts Leith Hill Music Festival at Dorking Halls, Dorking, in Apr. Boxhill Music Festival, Cleveland Lodge, Dorking: June. The Thorndike Theatre, Leatherhead, has repertory productions all year. There is an open-air theatre season at Polesden Lacey in mid-July.

Fairs At Abinger Common, near Dorking, in mid-June. Antiques Fair at Dorking Halls, Dorking, in June.

Places to see *Claremont*, Esher, Palladian house: first Sat. and Sun. afternoons, Feb. to Nov. *Claremont Garden* (NT), south of Esher on the east side of the Portsmouth Road: daily. *Greathed Manor*, Dormansland, 5 miles south-east of Lingfield off B2028, Victorian House: May to Sept., Wed. and Thur. afternoons. *Outward Mill*: Sun. afternoons, Apr. to Oct. *Polesden Lacy* (NT): garden, daily; house, afternoons only; Mar. and Nov., Sat. and Sun.; Apr. to Oct., daily, except Mon. and Fri., but open Bank Hol. Mon.

Information centre Cheviot House, Monson Road, Tunbridge Wells. Tel. Tunbridge Wells 40766.

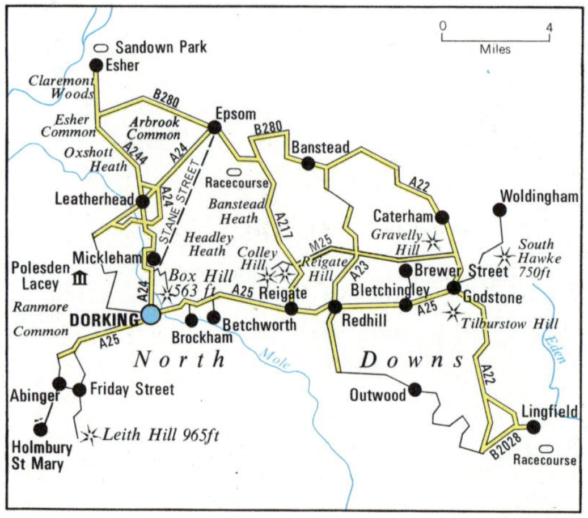

Some of the finest viewpoints in southern England lie only 20 miles from the heart of London, among the wooded hills that sweep across north Surrey. Their gentler, northern slopes form the rolling green downs of Banstead and Epsom, ideal riding country that is appropriately the scene of the world's most famous Flat race. The steep southern face has spectacular walks along chalk paths, with dramatic views southwards across the valleys of the River Mole and the River Eden towards the distant Ashdown Forest.

The ancient town of Dorking, situated where the Mole has cut a gap through the North Downs, is an ideal touring centre for the area. It has kept its charm, and the district around it is rich in beauty spots which can be reached by car or on foot. The sandstone escarpment of Leith Hill is the highest point in south-east England, with a view, on a fine day, stretching to the Channel coast.

Hidden among thick woods are attractive villages like Abinger, Friday Street, Holmbury St Mary and Peaslake. Even the narrow lanes that join the villages are hidden—sunk deep into the soft sandstone, with huge trees joining overhead to make a roof. Squirrels, foxes and badgers breed here unmolested.

North-east of Dorking, the downs rise spectacularly at Box Hill, one of the best viewpoints in Surrey, then stretch on towards Kent. Between the base of the downs and the West Sussex border is a landscape of winding lanes, country inns with attractive gardens and cricket on village greens at summer weekends.

Abinger
A village, in wooded hill country, which still has stocks and a whipping post, a partly-Norman church and many old houses. The nearby hamlet of Abinger Hammer recalls the forge 'hammers' of the 17th-century iron industry. Its village clock has a smith striking a bell; there is still a working smithy, and a tea-room beside watercress beds.

Betchworth
An attractive village on the River Mole east of Dorking, with wide views from Betchworth Clump. A 1½-mile walk along the river passes a weir on the way to Brockham, which has one of the prettiest village greens in Surrey.

Bletchingley
A village with a wide and picturesque main street, and the remains of a Norman castle. A mile to the north, at Brewer Street, is a 15th-century farmhouse; and 1½ miles to the east, Tilburstow Hill, 574 ft, is a good viewpoint.

Box Hill
One of the most popular viewpoints in southern England, so-called because of the ancient box trees on its flanks. It is an easy drive or walk to the 563-ft summit—the road up from near Burford Bridge ascends in a series of zigzags, like an Alpine pass. More than 800 acres of the woods and chalk downland now belong to the National Trust, and for the summer visitor there are good walks, picnic spots and a public swimming pool screened by trees.

North of Box Hill a narrow road through Little Switzerland, a beauty spot of hills and valleys, leads round the slopes of Mickleham Downs to the unspoilt village of Mickleham.

THE HORSE RACE THAT IS PART OF THE ENGLISH WAY OF LIFE

DERBY DAY, 1977 *The race is on, the fun of the fair forgotten*

DERBY DAY, 1858 *The horses took second place in William Frith's famous painting*

FRIDAY STREET *The tranquil lake on the north-west slopes of Leith Hill was used to power the bellows and forge hammers of iron works in the surrounding forests during the 17th century*

THE BOX TREES ON BOX HILL

Box Hill on the North Downs was a popular picnic spot as long ago as the reign of Charles II, when John Evelyn the diarist praised its yews and box trees, 'it seeming from these evergreens to be summer all the winter'. Many of the trees were cut down in the 18th century when box wood was in demand for the blocks from which wood engravings (left) were made. It is the densest English wood, and Thomas Bewick (1753–1828), famous engraver of birds and animals, claimed one of his blocks was sound after being used 900,000 times

Caterham
A modern town with many open spaces on its outskirts. Gravelly Hill (778 ft), on the downs just south of the town, offers good views across the Weald, and the line of the Pilgrims' Way crosses its slopes on its way to Kent.

Dorking
The town's High Street follows the route of the Roman Stane Street; the Saxons lived in Dorking and the Danes raided it. Charles Dickens stayed at the 400-year-old White Horse Inn, and the vanished King's Head is said to have been the 'Markis of Granby' in *The Pickwick Papers.* The hotel at Burford Bridge, 1 mile north, is where Lord Nelson finally separated from Lady Nelson in 1800, and where Keats, in failing health, completed 'Endymion' in 1818. A lane off the main road just south of the hotel leads to stepping stones across the River Mole and on to the slopes of Box Hill.

Epsom
Buildings in Church Street still recall the town's heyday in the 18th century, based on its medicinal spring. Today the town is more famous for its racecourse. The Derby has been run since 1780 on the downs south-east of the town, and early morning walkers can see horses at exercise. A bridleway stretches for 5 miles along an old Roman road leading to Box Hill.

Esher
Good surrounding open spaces—Esher Common, Arbrook Common and Oxshott Heath—resist the tides of suburban encroachment. Sandown Park Racecourse is just north of the town. There is a good afternoon's ramble round Claremont Woods where rhododendrons fringe a lake set in 50 acres of National Trust land, 1 mile south of Esher. The grounds were laid out by Capability Brown; the house they adjoin, built by Vanbrugh in 1708 and rebuilt for Clive of India in 1772, is now a school, preserving some fine interior decoration by Holland.

Friday Street
A tiny and lovely hamlet with a lake and pine-clad hills. Deep, narrow lanes lead there from Abinger. The inn, The Stephan Langton, is named after King John's Archbishop of Canterbury, born at Friday Street *c.* 1150. Beside the lake is the 60-acre Severell's Copse.

Godstone
A pleasant village in unspoilt North Downs country, which has a village green and pond and an Elizabethan inn, The White Hart.

Limpsfield, 2 miles east, is set in wooded countryside. The composer Delius is buried in the churchyard. To the north, the North Downs rise to 875 ft, one of their highest points; to the east are the High Chart woods.

Leatherhead
An attractive old town, with narrow streets and gabled houses. Its buildings range from the partly 12th-century church to the entirely 20th-century Thorndike Theatre, which opened in 1968. An open-air swimming pool just west of the town at Fetcham Grove is open to the public. Further west, Bookham Common and Banks Common have nearly a square mile of wooded land abounding in bird life.

Leith Hill
The summit is 965 ft high and there is a 64 ft tower on top, belonging to the National Trust and open to the public. The view from the top is a spectacular panorama of woods and farmland. The tower was built in 1766 by Richard Hull, who lived at nearby Leith Hill Place and is buried in the tower. There is a steep scramble up Leith Hill from the road immediately below it, or a gentler approach from 1 mile north on the Abinger road.

Lingfield
A Wealden village with buildings dating back to the 15th century and an unusual stone lock-up built in the 18th century and now a museum.

Outwood
On the east side of the village stands one of the country's oldest and best-preserved post-mills—a windmill in which the entire wooden body carrying the sails revolves around a central upright oak post, and is turned by hand to face the wind. It dates from 1665. Visitors can climb to watch the millstones at work, and buy the flour they grind.

Polesden Lacey
A lovely 19th-century house with a superb rose garden, owned by the National Trust and open to the public. The dramatist Sheridan once lived in a house on the site; the present house, built in 1824 and adapted in 1906, was the honeymoon retreat of King George VI and Queen Elizabeth.

Reigate
A spruce and commuterised town, with good open spaces. There is a picturesque early 18th-century market house and a castle mound under which there run medieval tunnels which can be visited by appointment. On Reigate Heath, to the west, is a converted windmill in which church services are held once a month. Colley Hill and Reigate Hill are fine viewpoints on the south-facing escarpment of the North Downs, and the Pilgrims' Way runs along their base.

Woldingham
A commuters' village, notable for splendid views from South Hawke, a lovely wooded tract $1\frac{1}{2}$ miles to the south owned by the National Trust. A mile further east, near Titsey Hill, the North Downs rise to a good viewpoint.

Where traces of the primeval forest survive

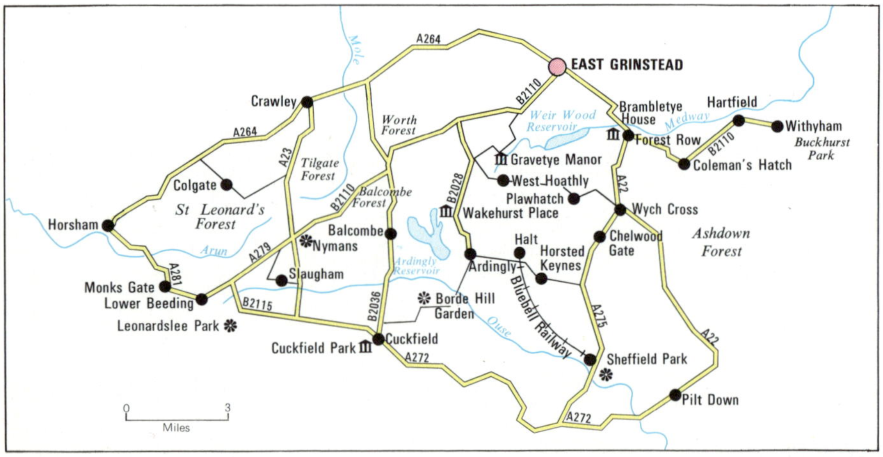

Riding Pony trekking near Crawley.

Sport centre The Crawley Sport-centre close to the town centre is open daily for public use.

Events The South of England Agricultural Society Show is held at Ardingly in June. There are donkey races at Cuckfield and at Wivelsfield, 4 miles south-east of Cuckfield, on Summer Bank Hol.

Places to see *Borde Hill Garden* (NGS): Easter to Aug., Sat., Sun., Wed. afternoons. *Horsham Museum*: Sat.; also Tues. to Fri. afternoons. *Leonardslee Park*, Lower Beeding: late Apr. to early June, Wed., Thur., Sat., Sun. *Nymans Garden* (NT): Apr. to Oct., Tues., Wed., Thur., Sat. afternoons; also Bank Hol. Mon. *Priest's House*, West Hoathly: Apr. to Sept., weekdays, except Fri., and Sun. afternoon. *Sheffield Park*, Tudor house near Uckfield: Easter to Oct., Wed., Thur. and Sun. afternoons. *Sheffield Park Garden* (NT): Apr. to mid-Nov., Tues. to Sat. and Sun. afternoon; also Bank Hol. Mon. *Spring Hill Wildfowl Park*, Forest Row: daily. *Standen* (NT), East Grinstead: Apr. to Oct., Wed., Thur. and Sat. afternoons. *Tilgate Park Nature Centre*, 1½ miles south-east of Crawley: daily except Fri. *Wakehurst Place Garden* (NT): daily.

Bluebell Railway Most weekends and Wed. during summer.

Information centres Mid-Sussex District Council, Oaklands Road, Haywards Heath. Tel. Haywards Heath 50301. Crawley Borough Council, Town Hall, The Boulevard, Crawley. Tel. Crawley 28744.

Along the forest ridge running through north Sussex are the last remaining tracts of the huge Wealden forest of Anderida, which in Roman times stretched for 120 miles in a broad swathe across south-east England.

The massive oaks were felled for the furnaces of the great Sussex iron industry which reached its peak in the early 17th century; the forest ponds, which were dammed to drive the forge hammers, are still a distinctive part of the Sussex scenery. Today, the forest is split up into separate patches of thick woodland in which are the sources of many rivers including the Ouse, the Arun and the Rother.

Ashdown Forest is the largest of these tracts of wild heath, moorland, rocky outcrops and woodland. From East Grinstead a maze of minor roads run southwards through the forest, with plenty of lay-bys and sign-posted picnic places. The village of Wych Cross is a centre for walks, with good views near by.

Many of the forest hamlets such as Chelwood Gate, Monk's Gate, Tilgate Forest, Coleman's Hatch and Plawhatch take their names from the old 'hatches' or gates to the forest. Names such as Hartfield, Boarshead and Buckhurst recall the game which was hunted when this was a royal forest; and the trees and bushes are remembered in such names as Ashurst, Bramblehurst, Bestbeech, Birchgrove and Oakleigh.

Other patches of the primeval woodlands survive further west in the forests of St Leonard's, Balcombe, Tilgate and Worth. These were once notorious haunts of smugglers, highwaymen and cattle thieves. Even today, especially in winter, they can be lonely, eerie places to walk through—but walking is the best way to see and to sense their wild beauty.

Ardingly

A village famous for its public school, Ardingly College, 1½ miles south. Wakehurst Place, 1½ miles to the north, is an Elizabethan mansion owned by the National Trust.

Its 120 acres of gardens and woods administered by the Royal Botanic Gardens, Kew, contain lakes and many exotic plants, trees and shrubs.

Crawley

One of the original new towns, Crawley is now an industrial community of more than 70,000. In its development it has swallowed the old coaching town and most of several nearby villages. The industrial estate is well separated from the town, which has a traffic-free shopping centre and well-planned open spaces which make the most of trees and green lawns. The main open space within the town boundaries is the wooded Tilgate Park, which has good picnic spots, and three lakes for rowing, sailing and fishing. Large tracts of the old Wealden forest survive just beyond the town to the south in Worth Forest, Tilgate Forest and Balcombe Forest. All are privately owned, but there are public footpaths.

Cuckfield

Two features of the 13th-century village which have resisted the suburban encroachment of Haywards Heath are the buildings of High Street and South

THE BLUEBELL RAILWAY

One of the few surviving steam railways in Britain runs through 5 miles of wooded country, carpeted with bluebells in early summer, between Horsted Keynes and Sheffield Park. The line was closed by British Rail in 1958, but the Bluebell Railway Preservation Society bought the track and rolling stock and re-opened the line some three years later, with a staff of mostly volunteers. There are now 20 locomotives, half of which belong to associated societies: the earliest dates from 1872, and some bear their original names, including *Bluebell, Coral Queen* and *Stepney*. Among the 30 coaches is the London, Brighton and South Coast Railway directors' saloon, built in 1914. Nearly a quarter of a million passengers each year indulge their nostalgia for the age of steam by taking a trip on the Bluebell Railway. The platform at Sheffield Park Station, headquarters of the line, is a good example of Victorian railway architecture, with its slender cast-iron columns and a collection of advertisements from a bygone age

Street, and the donkey races on Summer Bank Holiday. Near by are two notable gardens open to the public: the 30-acre Nymans, 3 miles to the north-west, at Handcross; and Borde Hill, $1\frac{1}{2}$ miles to the north-east, where there are rare trees and shrubs, with walks in the surrounding woodlands.

East Grinstead
A lively market town with a charter dating from 1221. It has a raised side-walk, old and new shops and a rose garden. Sackville College, founded by the Earl of Dorset as a home for the poor and disabled, was built in 1619 of local sandstone and is a beautifully preserved Jacobean building.

Forest Row
A village on a hillside above the River Medway in Ashdown Forest, and a good centre for walks or drives through the forest. To the north-west are the ruins of Brambletye House, whose owner, Sir James Richards, fled the country in 1683 when suspected of treason.

Horsham
A country market town which has kept its soul despite extensive development for London commuters and industries. The Causeway is a broad footway lined by old buildings, including the Tudor Causeway House, which is a museum. Horsham is a good base for walks through the 12,000 acres of St Leonard's Forest, where there are deep, wooded valleys and hills covered with gorse and heather. Colgate is an attractive hamlet in the highest part of the forest, at 480 ft. The forest has beds of lilies of the valley; according to legend they sprang from the drops of blood shed by St Leonard after fighting a mighty dragon.

ASHDOWN FOREST *The countryside south of Wych Cross is characteristic of the heaths and woods that cover 20 square miles of northern East and West Sussex. Nearly a quarter of the two counties is woodland, a legacy of the Roman forest of Anderida*

SHEFFIELD PARK Near the station are Capability Brown's landscaped gardens

Horsted Keynes
Tudor houses and two inns cluster round a village green. The wooded village is near the northern terminus of the Bluebell Railway.

Lower Beeding
Just north of the village set in parkland country there is a former hammer pond, used when iron was worked locally. Leonardslee Park, a mile south, has a chain of hammer ponds and gardens full of rhododendrons and camellias in the spring.

Another reminder of the 'iron days' of the Sussex Weald is to be found at Cuckfield Park, 6 miles west of Lower Beeding, where there is an Elizabethan house and gateway that were built by a local ironmaster.

Pilt Down
Notorious for the Piltdown Skull 'discovered' in 1912 by Charles Dawson, a solicitor and amateur antiquarian. It was regarded as a missing link between ape and man, about 150,000 years old, until 1953, when it was shown to be a hoax that had been contrived by adding the jaw and canine tooth of a modern ape to fragments of a genuine 50,000-year-old human skull.

Sheffield Park
National Trust garden with five lakes at different levels linked by cascades, among fine trees and shrubs. A mile away is a railway museum and the southern terminus of the Bluebell Railway, which runs through 5 miles of woodland to Horsted Keynes. The track, part of an abandoned Southern Region line from Lewes to East Grinstead, is operated by a private preservation company.

EAST GRINSTEAD *These restored timber-framed houses in the High Street, some now converted into shops, are typical of the Sussex style of hall house built in the 15th and 16th centuries*

Slaugham
The ruin in the valley is that of Slaugham Place, once the vast Elizabethan mansion of the Covert family. The original staircase is now in Lewes Town Hall. Slaugham Common overlooks the lakes on the estate of the old mansion. Tennyson lived at Warninglid, a village 1 mile south, before he became famous and built Aldworth House on Black Down, near Haslemere.

Weir Wood Reservoir
A man-made lake of 280 acres, beautifully set among woodlands 2 miles south of East Grinstead. There is no general public access, but permits are obtainable for trout fishing. The western end of the reservoir is a bird sanctuary and can be viewed from the road.

West Hoathly
A village in the heart of the Weald, founded in Saxon times and once a centre of the iron industry. Old houses include the manor house and the 15th-century Priest's House, which is now a museum. Smugglers used to signal down the valley from the church tower before meeting at the Cat Inn. They used the nearby Gravetye Manor, now a hotel, as their store for contraband.

Withyham
A hamlet built around a village green on the northern border of the Ashdown Forest. Withyham and nearby Hartfield are on the Buckhurst Park estate of Earl de la Warr, whose family, the Sackvilles, have lived here since 1200. The 17th-century Withyham Church is notable for its monuments, while 18th-century banners of the Dukes of Dorset hang in the Sackville Chapel.

By ancient downland tracks

Boats Yachts can be launched from the beach at various points; there are sailing clubs at Worthing and Shoreham and boating at Brooklands Pleasure Park, Worthing, where motor boats can be hired.

Angling Sea fishing from boats, beach and pier at Worthing and Shoreham; river fishing on the Adur and Arun.

Bowls Worthing is the site of the EBA National Championships each August and of many other major events.

Riding W. D. & H. O. Wills British Jumping Derby International is held in Aug., at Hickstead, 6 miles east of West Grinstead. Other jumping events are held at Hickstead during the spring and autumn. Riding on The Downs from Worthing.

Arts The Worthing Philharmonic and Symphony orchestras play at the Assembly Hall during winter. Worthing has an annual Competitive Music Festival at the end of Nov. and Sun. concerts all year round.

Sheep fair At Nepcote Green, Findon, second Sat. in Sept. The fair, established in 1790, includes the annual Southdown Sheep Society show.

Places to see *Highdown*, West Worthing: daily, Apr. to Sept. *House of Pipes*, Bramber: daily. *Marlipins Museum*, Shoreham-by-Sea: daily, May to Oct. *Shipley Mill*: May to Oct., first Sat. and Sun. afternoons in month. *West Tarring Cottages*, Worthing: Tues. to Sat. afternoons, Apr. to Oct. *Worthing Museum and Art Gallery*, Chapel Road: weekdays.

Information centre Town Hall, Chapel Road, Worthing. Tel. Worthing 204226.

The West Sussex seaside town of Worthing is a good centre from which to tour the middle part of the South Downs. At Findon, cottages with flint-walled gardens still preserve something of the downland village character despite the modern bungalows creeping nearer from Worthing.

Well-signposted footpaths follow ancient trackways across the chalk downs, along which lie mounds and earthworks that mark the sites of prehistoric forts and flint mines. The hump of Cissbury Ring and, further north, the clump of beech trees on Chanctonbury Ring, are landmarks for miles around.

The River Adur cuts a gap through the downs into a land of green pastures, cornfields, woods and leafy lanes north of Steyning. Truleigh Hill, on the east of the river, presents a fine panorama of the Adur Valley, whose broad water-meadows often fill with winter rains and spread to form a huge lake.

Further north the land rises towards Knepp Castle and West Grinstead Park, where generations of landowners have created a landscape of farms, orderly woods and a great lake from what was once wild Wealden forest.

CHANCTONBURY RING *Commanding views of Sussex can be seen*

THE SOUTH DOWNS WAY

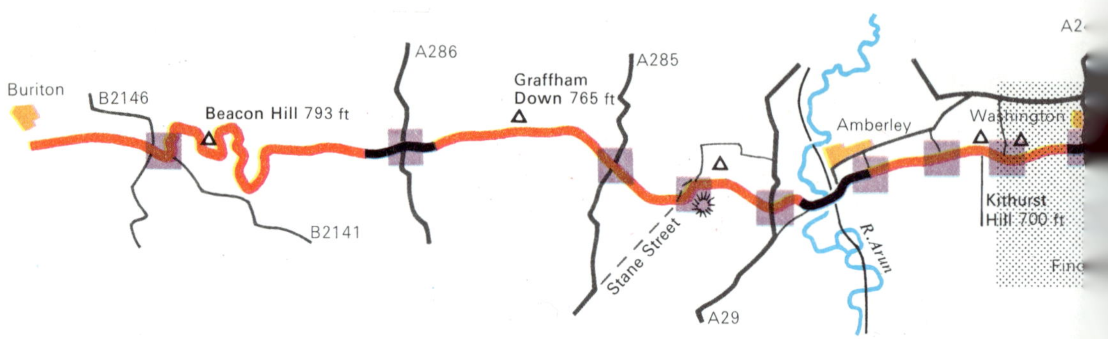

A long-distance footpath crosses four river valleys in its 80-mile course along the ridge of the South Downs from Buriton to Beachy Head. There are rights of access over nearly all the route, though detours are sometimes necessary to avoid crops. One particularly fine section starts from Chantry Lane, Storrington (right). A signposted track runs across the downs for 2 miles before dropping to Washington; the route then crosses the A24, before rising to Chanctonbury Ring. From here a path runs south to Cissbury Ring, but the South Downs Way continues 2½ miles eastwards to Steyning

CISSBURY RING The ramparts of the 60-acre camp, built in the Iron Age, were refortified in the 4th century AD against the Saxons

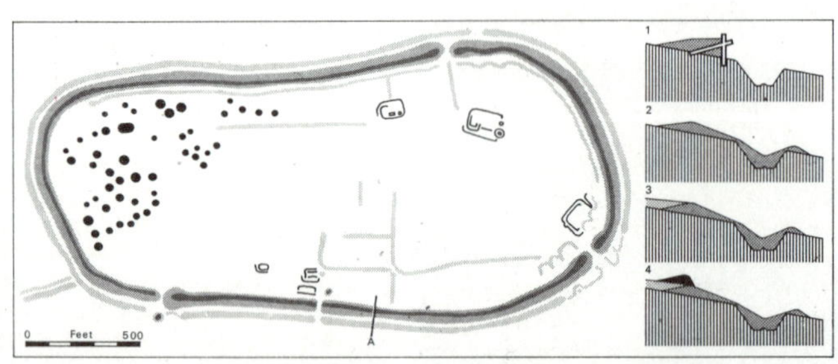

HILL FORT Excavations at Cissbury have revealed flint mines (dots), ploughing patterns (lines) and the sites of huts (rectangles). The rampart (right), first supported by timbers, fell and was strengthened by earthworks and a turf wall

from this Iron Age site. There are traces of an oval defensive mound among the beech trees

Ashurst
An unspoilt village with long views southwards to the downs. The farms near by have changed little in the last two centuries. Their fields are watered by the Adur, and many of their buildings are half-timbered, with hung tiles.

In the churchyard is the grave of Margaret Fairless Dowson, née Barber (1869–1901) who, under the pseudonym of Michael Fairless, wrote *The Roadmender*, a story of Sussex people. In it she described the Adur valley and the 'lean grey downs, keeping watch and ward between the country and the sea'.

Bramber
A 76 ft high fragment of the Norman castle wall, on a huge natural mound, recalls the days when the village was a provincial capital of William the Conqueror and a port on the River Adur. St Mary's, a 15th-century house built for the monks who were Wardens of the Bridge, is one of the few surviving examples of monastic inns. It is a splendid example of timber framing, but heavy traffic through the village in recent years has caused severe damage to the building.

Chanctonbury Ring
A footpath eastwards from the village of Washington leads, by a stiff 1½-mile climb, to the summit of Chanctonbury Ring, where a beech wood stands within the mounds of an Iron Age earthwork. There is a gentler but longer approach from the south side. The top is 783 ft high, and from it the view stretches for 30 miles over the surrounding country, north to Leith Hill in Surrey and south to the sea. In the wooded Wiston Park, a mile to the north-east, is an

ASHURST *A local writer praised 'the reeded waters of the sequestered pool'*

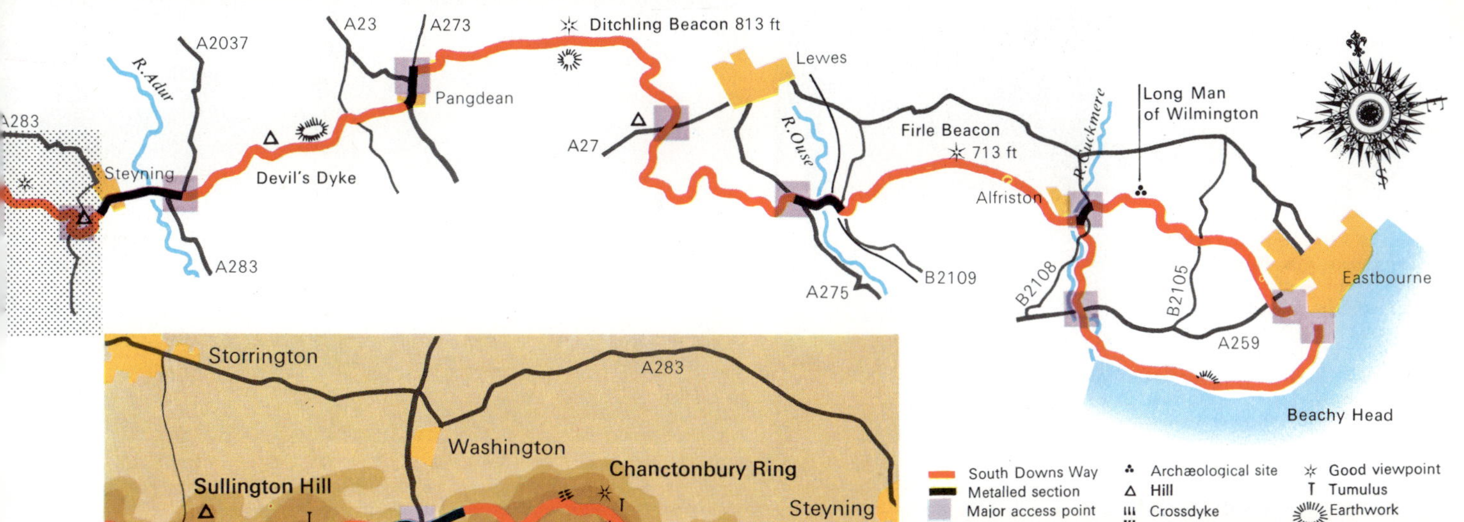

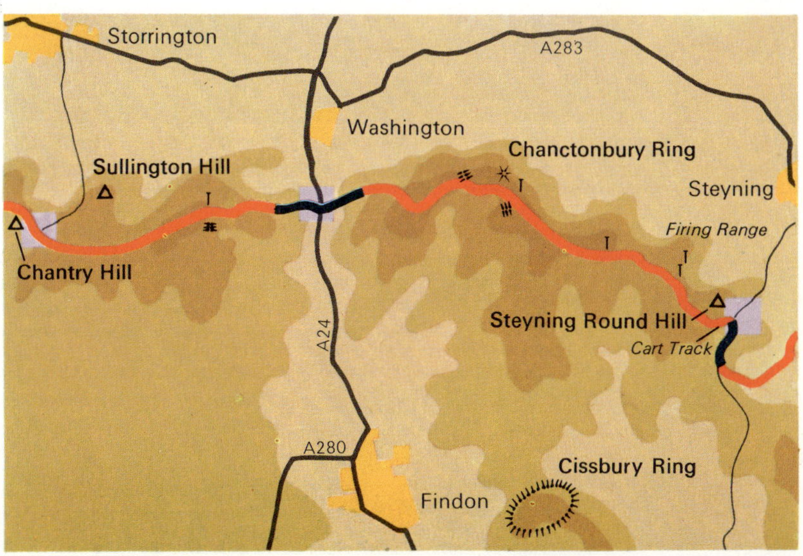

JOURNEY'S END At Alfriston, a branch of the South Downs Way turns south to run along the Seven Sisters. These cliffs end in the promontory of Beachy Head, with a lighthouse at its foot

Elizabethan mansion in which lived Charles Goring who, in 1760, planted the beeches on Chanctonbury Ring. The South Downs Way passes the Ring, and leads down to Steyning. Another path leads southwards to Cissbury Ring, 5 miles away across country.

Cissbury Ring
Two well-defined ramparts of an Iron Age fort, used from 300 BC to 59 BC, make these the largest and most impressive earthworks on the South Downs. The site, which has fine views, is maintained by the National Trust.

Henfield
A straggling village with a gorse-clad common, a peaceful river and water-meadow scenery. A 19th-century Sussex botanist, William Borrer, once counted 6600 varieties of plants in his Henfield garden, and his nephew, an ornithologist, saw 14 golden orioles on one thorn bush on Henfield Common.

Highdown Hill
A lone, conical hill, 266 ft high, which was the site of an Iron Age camp and a Saxon burial ground. Below the hill on the north side is Castle Goring, a beautiful white mansion of Italian design, built for the poet Shelley's grandfather.

Shoreham-by-Sea
A busy harbour at the mouth of the River Adur, ideal for small-boat sailors. It is a working port, and its long beach extends westwards to South Lancing and Worthing. The Marlipins Museum, built in the 12th century of chequered flint and Caen stone, is worth a visit for its paintings, historic ship models and relics of local history.

Steyning
A medieval, quietly prosperous town of old gabled houses. According to legend the village began in the 8th century, when St Cuthman pushed his invalid mother in a wheelbarrow from Devon. The barrow broke down at Steyning, so Cuthman stayed there and built a wooden church. The present church, dating from the 12th century, is one of the noblest in West Sussex. A track leads to the top of Steyning Round Hill, from which there is a fine view over the Adur Valley. Other walks climb the downs to Cissbury Ring and Chanctonbury Ring, where a beech wood, planted in 1760, stands in an oval prehistoric earthwork.

Washington
The American-sounding name of the village means, in fact, a Saxon settlement of the sons of Wassa. Hilaire Belloc's West Sussex Drinking Song—ending with 'the swipes they take in at Washington Inn is the very best beer I know'—is still sung by his admirers at the Frankland Arms on Washington Common, north of the village.

The parish church, rebuilt in the 19th century, retains its 15th-century embattled tower.

KNEPP CASTLE *Perched on an earth mound, or 'motte', a mile west of West Grinstead, a ruined keep is all that remains of a Norman castle dating from the 11th century. The ruin overlooks a fine stretch of parkland in the Adur Valley*

HOBBY HORSE *A museum at West Tarring, Worthing, has a hobby horse of a type used by 19th-century dandies*

SHOREHAM-BY-SEA *The Adur Estuary offers sheltered waters for canoeists and yachtsmen. Big boats use the harbour, too, and Shoreham is one of the largest privately owned ports in the country, handling 3 million tons of goods a year*

West Grinstead
This quiet village preserves much of its beauty despite the bustle of modern traffic. Its parish church is Norman, with a fine 15th-century timbered porch. West Grinstead Park is famous as one of the homes of the National Stud for breeding racehorses. The mill at Shipley, 2 miles west, belonged to Hilaire Belloc—who lived at nearby Kingsholm—and has been restored in the writer's memory.

Worthing
A popular holiday and residential town, with some Regency houses and squares and many London commuters' homes. It was a fishing hamlet until Princess Amelia, youngest daughter of George III, visited it in 1798. In the next 14 years, Worthing started to become the flourishing seaside resort it is today. It has safe sea bathing, a pier, 4 miles of promenades, concert halls and two good theatres.

Paintings in Worthing Museum include many early 19th-century and Victorian watercolours; and a half-timbered 16th-century house at West Tarring, on the north-west outskirts, has a collection of 19th-century 'bygones', and exhibits of local interest.

SUSSEX PLACE NAMES

Sussex was the 'land of the South Saxons' and there are traces of the conquerors in many place-names. The ending *-ing* meant belonging to a family or tribe; Worthing was 'Wurth's People'. The ending *-ton* meant an enclosure which developed into a village. Other derivations are: *-ham*, a hamlet; *-stead*, *-stock* or *-stoke*, a place; *-worth*, an enclosure; *-ley* or *-holt*, a wood; *-den*, a valley or a clearing for grazing animals; and *-burgh*, a fortified place

An extravaganza of pinnacles, piers and promenades

Angling Sea fishing from shore, pier and boats. Freshwater fishing on stretches of the River Ouse.

Sailing Brighton Regatta, in early June, includes sailing dinghy and rowing races.

Horse racing Flat racing at Brighton Racecourse, Apr. to Oct.; steeplechasing at Plumpton, Jan. to Apr., Aug. to Dec.

Sport Open-air arena with running track, at Withdean Stadium, London Road, Brighton, and King Alfred Sports Centre, at Hove. Cricket at the Sussex County Ground in Hove; football at Brighton and Hove Albion's Ground, Hove.

Events Veteran Car Run, London to Brighton: 1st Sun. in Nov. Historic Commercial Vehicle Club Run in May. British Coach Rally in Apr. Pioneer Motor Cycle Run: mid-Mar. Stock Exchange London to Brighton Walk: May. Antiques Fair in summer. Brighton Arts Festival two weeks Apr./May, and Brighton Carnival Week is in July or Aug.

Places to see *Aquarium*, Marine Parade, Brighton: daily. *Booth Museum of Natural History*, Dyke Road, Brighton: weekdays except Thur., Sun. afternoon. *Central Museum and Art Gallery*, Church Street, Brighton: weekdays except Mon., Sun. afternoon. *Newtimber Place*, Hassocks, near Clayton: May to Aug., Thur. afternoon. *Thomas Stanford Museum*, Preston Manor, Brighton: weekdays except Mon. and Tues., Sun. afternoon. *Royal Pavilion*, Brighton, Regency Exhibition, July to Sept. daily: State and private apartments, daily. *The Grange*, Rottingdean, museum containing a collection of toys: weekdays, except Wed., and Sun. afternoon.

Information centre Marlborough House, Old Steine, Brighton, East Sussex. Tel. Brighton 23755.

Brighton is an exhilarating town of spectacular contrasts. Graceful Georgian and late-Victorian houses co-exist with the extravaganza of the Royal Pavilion; oysters in the Lanes with cockles and whelks on the Pier; political party meetings with day-trippers' outings; bracing rides along the Promenade on open-deck buses with claustrophobic nights in the gambling casinos; antique shops with 'what-the-butler-saw' machines. The blend of culture and candy floss is Brighton's fascination.

It all began as a tiny fishing hamlet on the shore, with a farming settlement on the high ground behind. The fishing quarter was almost entirely swallowed by the sea and is reduced now to a few narrow lanes off Pool Valley. The farming village probably followed the intricate spider's web of narrow streets which today are called the Lanes and lined with antique shops.

The dual village of Brighthelmstone changed its face and character in the mid-18th century when Dr Richard Russell, a Sussex man, proclaimed the value of sea bathing and sea air and earned for the town its contemporary nickname of 'Doctor Brighton'.

The Prince of Wales, son of George III, visited Brighton in 1783 and commissioned Henry Holland to build him a Royal Pavilion there in Classical style, with a 'Chinese' interior. When the Prince became Regent in 1812 he engaged John Nash, the architect who laid out Regent's Park in London and the terraces round it, to enlarge the Pavilion into the present riotously extravagant building. As a

ROYAL PAVILION *An onion-shaped dome and minarets in the style of an Indian prince's palace adorn the Prince Regent's endearing creation at Brighton. 'The dome of St Paul's,' said Sydney Smith, a satirist of the time, 'must have come to Brighton and pupped'*

result of the Prince's interest, Brighton became the leading resort in England, despite derision from the Prince's contemporaries, who attacked the appearance of the Royal Pavilion; the author William Cobbett described it as a combination of 'a square box, a large Norfolk turnip and four onions'.

Modern Brighton is one of Britain's leading seaside resorts, with a shingle beach and three open-air swimming pools, one of the largest yacht marinas in Europe, a long promenade, two piers (only one of which is open), and an aquarium with dolphins. The $1\frac{1}{2}$-mile Volks Electric Railway runs from the aquarium to Black Rock swimming pool, with a stop on the way at a children's playground. Adjoining the Lanes is a modern piazza with seats, flower beds and a restaurant, which has tables outdoors in summer.

While Brighton puts itself out to attract holiday-makers during the summer season, it is a town that goes on living exuberantly through the winter, too. When the holiday visitors have gone home the conference delegates arrive, attracted by ease of transport from London and by the largest conference centre on the South Coast. All the year round 5000 businessmen and women living in Brighton commute daily by train to London and back. The University of Sussex, on the outskirts of Brighton, has added a new dimension to the town's life, including a modern theatre, the Gardner Centre. The students' lodgings, centred in the Kemp Town area east of the town centre, double as seaside holiday flats during the summer vacation.

Brighton has a flourishing cultural life, centred on the Theatre Royal, whose productions are of London standards and often, in fact, move on to the West End. There is an Arts Festival in May and a permanent concert hall, the Dome. The art gallery and museum in Church Street has a collection of English and European paintings and drawings, pottery and Sussex folklore, as well as one of the country's best collections of old English musical instruments.

THE ROYAL PAVILION

Brighton's proud centrepiece, the Royal Pavilion, was used in the first half of the 19th century by three monarchs—George IV (left), who completed it while he was Prince Regent, William IV and Queen Victoria. The Pavilion has been both praised and ridiculed. One phase of extravagant spending by the Prince Regent on the 'Chinese' interior decoration was attacked in Parliament and satirised by the caricaturist George Cruikshank in a famous cartoon of 1816, 'The Court at Brighton à la Chinese' (below). In it the Prince Regent, seated, grossly fat and dressed in Chinese style, is handing a document to Lord Amherst, British Envoy to the Emperor of China, inscribed 'Instructions for Lord Amherst to get fresh patterns of Chinese deformities to finish the decorations of the Pavilion'

Clayton
A village with a partly Saxon church, two 19th-century windmills, called Jack and Jill, and a spectacular folly, Tunnel House. This is a railwayman's cottage, still lived in, built in the shape of a castellated Tudor fortress with the trains on the London to Brighton line running through the middle of it. Clayton is a good starting point for a walk to Wolstonbury Hill to the west or Ditchling Beacon to the east, both famous downland viewpoints.

Ditchling Beacon
The 813 ft Ditchling Beacon is one of the highest points on the South Downs. A walker will enjoy the best views, for although a narrow road runs from Wick Farm, Westmeston, almost to the summit and down the other side to Brighton, a motorist will be too busy watching the difficult road to enjoy the scenery. The village of Ditchling, $2\frac{1}{2}$ miles north, has a 16th-century house given by Henry VIII to Anne of Cleves.

DEVIL'S DYKE *A V-shaped cleft in the downs gives long views across the Weald. According to legend the gap was made by the Devil who, to combat the growth of Christianity, started to dig a trench through which the English Channel would flood the Weald. A woman watching him held up a candle and the Devil fled, mistaking it for the rising sun*

Falmer
A village of flint, brick and timber, standing at the head of two valleys, one leading to Brighton and the other to Lewes. Stanmer, 2 miles north-west, has a picturesque church and a manor house built in 1724; Stanmer Park, former home of the Earls of Chichester, is the site of the University of Sussex.

Hove
A resort strictly classical in architecture and well-disciplined in character. It has many good parks and gardens. There is a floral clock in Palmeira Square and a scented garden in St Ann's Well Gardens. All Saints' Church is a splendid structure, noted for its richly carved screen and high altar. The church was designed by J. L. Pearson in 1890.

The King Alfred Sports Centre on the sea-front has two swimming pools, a restaurant, sports facilities and a children's playground. There is a lagoon for canoes, paddle-boats and yachts, and the beach has sand at low tide.

THE LANES *The fishermen's cottages of old 'Brighthelmstone' are today's antique shops*

ROYAL CRESCENT *Elegant terraces are a legacy of Brighton's Regency heyday*

VETERAN CAR RUN *Only cars built before 1904 are eligible for the run, which marks the abolition in 1896 of a law requiring a man with a red flag to walk in front of a car*

TELSCOMBE CLIFFS *Breakwaters at Saltdean protect the undercliff walk from the full force of the waves. Beyond, Peacehaven extends towards the mouth of the River Ouse*

HOME OVER THE TRAINS *This folly was built by the London, Brighton and South Coast Railway in 1841 as a home for the keeper of the Clayton Tunnel*

Plumpton
A downland village near one of England's prettiest racecourses. Plumpton Place is a fine 16th-century moated manor house, beautifully restored by Sir Edwin Lutyens in the 1920's. On the downs to the south is a V-shaped plantation of trees planted to commemorate Queen Victoria's Golden Jubilee in 1887.

Rottingdean
A village with an attractive High Street and green, where Kipling lived, at The Elms, until sightseers drove him to Burwash. There is a toy museum in The Grange. An open-top bus runs from Brighton's Palace Pier along the cliff-top coast road past Roedean girls' school. Rottingdean can also be reached from Brighton by the undercliff walk from Black Rock. This walk goes on past Rottingdean to Saltdean, a residential area with a sea-front and a new lido—a large swimming pool in a suntrap, with parking for 500 cars and a separate paddling pool for children.

UNIVERSITY OF SUSSEX *Sir Basil Spence's functional modern buildings in red brick and concrete contrast strikingly with the 200 acres of Stanmer Park in which they are set and the downlands sheltering them to the north. Sussex was the first of the new universities opened in the 1960's, and is noted for its courses in social sciences*

Chalk downs within sight and smell of the sea

Angling Sea fishing from shore and boats at Newhaven and Seaford; river fishing on certain sections of the Ouse, which is tidal from Newhaven to 4 miles north of Lewes.

Sailing Newhaven is a commercial port and an important yachting centre, with a marina. There are yacht races at weekends from Mar. to Oct. at Bishopstone and Seaford; or, when rough, on the River Ouse, 2 miles upstream from Newhaven.

Sports Seaford has an open competition for tennis, bowls, golf and sailing from the end of July to the end of Aug.

Events Glyndebourne's Opera season runs from the end of May to early Aug. Lewes has torchlight processions to celebrate Guy Fawkes night on Nov. 5.

Places to see *Anne of Cleves' House*, Lewes: weekdays, Feb. to Nov.; also Sun. afternoons, Apr. to Oct. *Barbican House Museum*, Lewes: weekdays; also Sun. afternoons, Apr. to Oct. *Beeches Farm*, 7 miles north-east of Lewes, 16th-century tile-hung house: gardens, daily; house, by appointment. *Bentley Wildfowl Gardens*: daily, Easter to Sept. *Charleston Manor*, Westdean: gardens, daily Apr. to Oct. *Clergy House* (NT), Alfriston: Apr. to Oct., daily; Nov. to late Dec., Wed., Fri., Sat. and Sun. *Drusilla's Zoo*, Alfriston: daily. *Firle Place*: Wed., Thur., Sun. afternoons, June to Sept. *Glynde Place*: May to Sept., Wed. and Thur. afternoons. *Lewes Castle*: weekdays; also Sun. afternoons, Apr. to Oct. *Michelham Priory*: daily, early Apr. to mid-Oct.

Cross-Channel ferries Car ferry from Newhaven to Dieppe all year by British and French Rail; more frequent services in summer.

Information centres 187 High Street, Lewes. Tel. Lewes 6151. 22 Roderick Avenue, Peacehaven. Tel. Peacehaven 2668.

BENTLEY *South American black-necked swan at the Bentley Wildfowl Gardens*

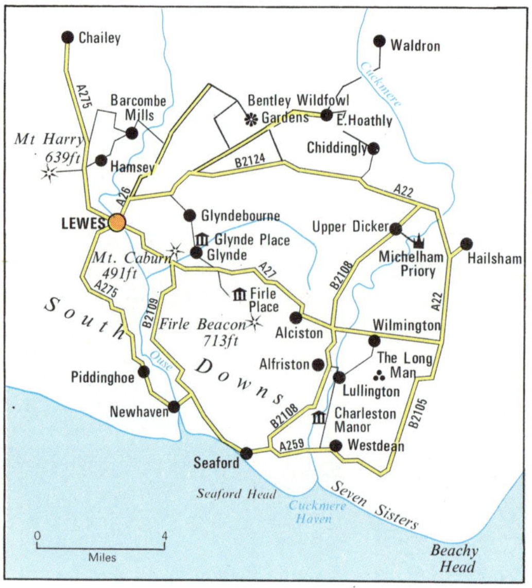

Near Lewes the South Downs rise to over 700 ft, in country for sheep, ramblers and pony-trekkers. Two beautiful rivers—the Ouse and the Cuckmere—cut wide valleys through the downs to the sea after meandering southwards across rich Wealden farmland and lush water meadows. Lewes, a friendly, old-fashioned county town on a hilly site by the Ouse, is a good centre for exploring the noble downs and valleys. Kingston, 2 miles south-west of Lewes, is one good starting point for a walk along the chalk ridges within sight—and smell—of the Channel.

Minor roads give constant views of downland country at its best. One, from Exceat, near Seaford, follows the slender River Cuckmere as it loops inland in flashes of silver through a green valley past Alfriston and Wilmington. Another road follows the more serene and pastoral Ouse, which at Piddinghoe, 2 miles from its mouth, already begins to smell of the sea.

Northwards from the downs, the two rivers enclose a land of small farms and grazing cattle, studded with small villages mentioned in the Domesday Book and little changed for three or four centuries. Still further north once lay the deep Wealden forests, largely cleared in the days of the Sussex iron industry. The first cannon to be cast in England was made at Uckfield in 1543, and iron furnaces belched out smoke over Sussex for another 200 years.

This broad, bright land is rich in history. On Mount Caburn are the ramparts of an Iron Age fort, 2000 years old; and The Long Man, cut into the chalk of Windover Hill, may date back to Saxon times. The Normans built a castle at Lewes, for defence against foreign raiders. But Lewes's biggest role in English history came when, in 1264, Simon de Montfort led the barons in revolt against Henry III and took him prisoner at the Battle of Lewes.

Alciston
A tiny hamlet with a 13th-century church and the remains of a 14th-century farm with a barn 170 ft long. It lies just off the main Lewes–Eastbourne road, and the top of nearby Firle Beacon (713 ft) gives an uninterrupted view to Beachy Head and the Channel.

Alfriston
A village in the Cuckmere valley, full of old houses—notably the Star Inn and the 14th-century Clergy House, the first building acquired by the National Trust, in 1896. Once a haunt of smugglers, it is a useful centre from which to explore the Cuckmere Valley down to Seaford or up to Hailsham and beyond. Lullington, just across the river, has one of England's smallest churches—only 16 ft square. There is a fine 5-mile walk along the top of the downs to West Firle.

Barcombe Mills
An angler's beauty spot on the River Ouse, signposted on a minor road from Hamsey, just north of Lewes.

Bentley Wildfowl Gardens
A collection of more than 100 varieties of swans, geese and ducks. Birds from the Arctic and Asia have become acclimatised in the 23-acre gardens.

TILE-HANGING: A TRADITION LIVES ON

Lewes is rich in tile-hung houses, which have been a feature of south-east England since the 17th century. Tiles were hung over wood-and-plaster houses to protect them against the weather. Curved and straight-edged tiles were sometimes combined in parallel strips. Some Sussex builders still hang tiles on the upper storeys of new brick houses

Mount Caburn
A 491-ft spur cut off from the rest of the South Downs by the River Glynde. The name derives from the Celtic name Caer Bryn, 'the fort on the hill', and the ramparts and surrounding ditch are still visible after more than 2000 years. The fort was first occupied in Iron Age times, and extended by the Romans. The top of Mount Caburn can be reached from Lewes or Glynde.

Chailey
The village is notable for a 13th-century church and for the smock windmill on its high, breezy common. Also on the common is the Heritage Crafts School for crippled children.

Chiddingly
There are magnificent views from the churchyard over the Weald towards the downs as far as Pevensey Level. In the church is an elaborate monument to Sir John Jefferay, Queen Elizabeth I's Chief Baron of the Exchequer, and further west are the remains of his Tudor mansion, Chiddingly Place. Lanes lead from here past Tudor cottages to East Hoathly and Waldron.

Cuckmere Haven
A secluded little bay, once used by smugglers, between Seaford Head and the scalloped edges of the Seven Sisters. There is a bracing walk along the Seven Sisters cliff path to Beachy Head.

THE SEVEN SISTERS *The South Downs end in seven dramatic chalk cliffs which rise to over 500 ft between Cuckmere Haven and Beachy Head and are criss-crossed by fine walking tracks. The depressions along the cliff edge are the valleys of ancient rivers, formed when the chalk extended further seawards and later cut off when the sea pounded the chalk away*

ALFRISTON *The wooden lion, one of several carvings at the Star Inn, is believed to be the figurehead from a Dutch ship wrecked in the Channel c. 1672. The timbering of the inn, like that of many other houses in the village, is 500 years old*

Michelham Priory
The River Cuckmere is diverted near Upper Dicker to form a $6\frac{1}{2}$-acre moat, one of the largest in England, around an Augustinian priory founded in 1229 and owned now by the Sussex Archaeological Trust. The priory has been restored, but the gatehouse dates from 1385.

Firle Place
The house is mainly Georgian, with an early Tudor core, and contains items brought from America by General Thomas Gage, British Commander at the start of the War of Independence. From the nearby village of West Firle a track leads to Firle Beacon.

Glynde
In this little village in 1778 John Ellman started strengthening the breed of the local sheep, and transformed them in a few years into the now famous black-faced Southdowns. The 16th-century Glynde Place has collections of pictures, bronzes and needlework, an aviary and a pottery. Nearby Glyndebourne Opera House was added to an original Tudor manor by John Christie in 1934.

Hailsham
A small, prosperous cattle market town 2 miles through woods from Michelham. The 15th-century church has eight bells which still ring a curfew at 8 p.m.

Lewes
A thousand years of history have left their mark on the county town of East Sussex. There are the remains of a Norman castle, a jumble of medieval streets and a variety of buildings in local materials, most of them Georgian. The downs rise over the town and the River Ouse runs through it. Barbican House, just outside the castle, is a museum. The Prince Regent, later George IV, stayed at Southover Grange, the big Elizabethan house in Keere Street. Anne of Cleves' House in Southover, now a folk museum with a collection of Sussex ironwork, was one of several houses given by Henry VIII to his divorced wife.

Inns in Lewes include The White Hart, which was praised by William Cobbett, the 19th-century traveller, in his *Rural Rides*. Bonfire night on November 5 is celebrated with some of the biggest bonfires and torchlight processions in Britain. There is a good walk to the north-west, past Lewes racecourse and along the crest of the downs to Ditchling Beacon—more than 6 miles of open country with fine views. The route leads past Mount Harry, site of the Battle of Lewes in 1264 when Henry III was beaten by the barons who rallied under Simon de Montfort.

THE LONG MAN *The figure on the downs above Wilmington may have been cut by the Saxons, for it resembles other Saxon finds. More than 700 concrete blocks were laid in 1969 to preserve the chalk outline*

MEDIEVAL DOVECOT *Doves were a delicacy in the Middle Ages; from these nesting holes in a ruined dovecot at Court House Farm, Alciston, the young birds were removed for the farmer's table*

Newhaven
The town became the 'new haven' after a storm in 1579 altered the course of the Ouse, which formerly flowed into the Channel at Seaford. It is a busy cross-Channel port, with a beach to the west and a long shingle bank to the east. Bronze tools of 900 BC and Roman coins of AD 285 have been found in the area.

Seaford
A breezy red-brick town, linked to Newhaven by a road across a marshy valley, which was once the course of the Ouse. Some medieval houses survive in Seaford's old town. There are long views of the Seven Sisters from Seaford Head, which also has the remains of a pre-Roman camp, and a short but exhilarating walk leads across Seaford Head to Cuckmere Haven.

Seven Sisters
A square mile of downland cliffs open to walkers. The sister cliffs—Haven Brow, Short Brow, Rough Brow, Bran Point, Flagstaff Point, Baily's Hill and West Hill Brow—undulate along the coast from Cuckmere Haven to Beachy Head. A track from Exceat Bridge on the Seaford road leads to the cliff path.

Westdean
A village of mellow cottages in bright gardens, with a steep walk over the hill to Exceat Farm and an attractive minor road up the Cuckmere valley. Charleston Manor, a mile to the north, is a blend of Norman, Tudor and Georgian architecture set beneath a wooded down. The Domesday Book records that the manor was owned by William the Conqueror's Cup-bearer under the name of Cerlestone. The restored tithe barn is one of the biggest in East and West Sussex.

Wilmington
The Long Man, cut into the downland turf of Windover Hill, is 231 ft tall. The figure, holding a staff in each of his outstretched hands, was first recorded in 1779, but it may date back to the 6th century. Another theory is that the figure represented King Harold of the Saxons, with a spear in each hand. The village has a ruined 12th-century priory.

Breezy clifftops and sun traps on the shore

Boating Boats for hire at sailing clubs in Eastbourne, Hastings, Bexhill and Pevensey Bay. Regattas at Hastings in Aug. and at Bexhill in Sept. Trips to Beachy Head lighthouse from Eastbourne.

Angling Sea fishing from pier and beaches at Eastbourne, Bexhill, Hastings, and some off-shore fishing. Freshwater fishing in Pevensey Haven and Sluice, River Cuckmere and streams and reservoirs in area. The International Sea Angling Festival is held at Hastings in Oct.

Tennis Rothmans Open Championships are held at Devonshire Park, Eastbourne, in June.

Arts Congress Theatre, Eastbourne: summer show season and visiting companies. Devonshire Park Theatre, Eastbourne: all-year repertory. The De La Warr Pavilion, Bexhill, has a festival of classical music in summer, a festival of light music in autumn, and frequent symphony concerts during the winter. Military bands play at Eastbourne's Grand Parade Bandstand in summer. There is a competitive Music Festival at the White Rock Pavilion, Hastings in Mar. and frequent concerts throughout the year.

Events Blessing of the sea at Hastings fish market at Rogationtide in early May; National Town Criers' Championship at Warrior Square Gardens, Hastings in mid-Aug.; International Chess Congress at Falaise Hall, Hastings, in Jan.; Sheep Dog Trials in Alexandra Park, Hastings in July or Aug.

Places to see *Battle Abbey*: daily, except Sun. mornings Oct. to Mar. *Battle Museum*: Easter to Oct., weekdays, Sun. afternoon. *Bexhill Manor Costume Museum*: Easter to Sept., Tues. to Fri. and weekend afternoons. *Country Park*, East Hill, Hastings: daily. *Fishermen's Museum*, Rock-a-Nore, Hastings: Apr. to Sept., daily. *Hastings Castle*: Easter to mid-Oct., daily. *Hastings Museum and Art Gallery*, Cambridge Road: weekdays, Sun. afternoon. *Museum of Local History*, Hastings: weekdays, Easter to Oct. *Pevensey Castle*: daily, except Sun. mornings Oct. to Mar. *St Clement's Caves*, West Hill, Hastings: daily. *Tower 73*, Eastbourne: Easter to Sept., daily. *Towner Art Gallery*, Eastbourne: weekdays and Sun. afternoon.

Information centres 4 Robertson Terrace, Hastings. Tel. Hastings 424242. Information Bureau, Lower Promenade, Eastbourne. Tel. Eastbourne 27474 (seasonal).

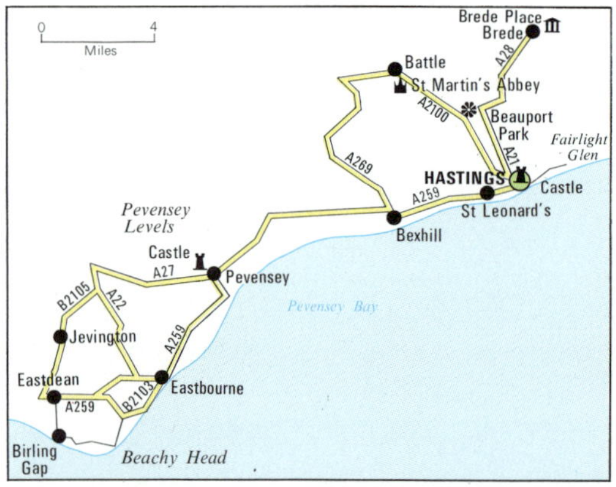

Unlike many of the most important holiday resorts on the Continent, built up deliberately for tourism by wiping out the old and starting afresh, Britain's major resorts have evolved gradually over the centuries. The whole story can be seen along a narrow strip of the Sussex coast between Beachy Head and Fairlight Glen.

Hastings is still, in part, the fishing village it was in Roman times. It is still also, in part, an old Cinque Port, set at the foot of a 13th-century castle built to protect the ancient harbour. In the 18th century arrived the health seekers, sent by doctors who had just discovered the value of sea air for chest troubles. The adjoining resort of St Leonards was laid out for them in fashionable Regency style in the early 19th century. Later still, the mass popularity of seaside holidays gave rise to a new Hastings superimposed on a thousand years of history—a resort with a 3-mile foreshore, a double-tiered promenade with sun-trap shelters, and every type of holiday entertainment.

Bexhill and Eastbourne have quite different origins. Bexhill was built for people who wanted to retire to the sea and live in peace, and it is still a peaceful and largely residential place. Eastbourne was developed by the 7th Duke of Devonshire when he inherited the small village in 1834. He wanted to build something totally different from the extrovert gaiety of nearby Brighton, and created an elegant place with fine parks and gardens, wide tree-lined roads and grass in long, trim stretches.

Between the resorts along this short strip of coast are downs and cliffs and inland villages on windy roads. This is breezy walking country for the active holiday-maker. Like the whole coastline, its greatest appeal is to people who like fresh air and have good appetites, rather than to those who want no more than to laze in the sun; for though this corner of England is sunny enough, the air is bracing.

Battle
The town and its abbey stand on the actual site of the so-called Battle of Hastings in 1066. Here, William the Conqueror and his invading Normans played their trick of pretending to flee from the field and then defeated Harold's English who chased them too carelessly. William swore he would build an abbey if he won, and kept his word. St Martin's Abbey, on the hilltop where Harold was killed, was consecrated in 1094 and dissolved by Henry VIII. Part of the remains are now incorporated in a girls' school, but the grounds and other buildings, including the fine 14th-century gateway, can be visited. Near the abbey are the Norman Church of St Mary and the Deanery, built in 1669. The gilded crown on the church spire indicates that the church is a Royal Peculiar and has the Queen as its patron.

The Pilgrims' Rest, once an almonry by the main gates of the abbey where the monks distributed alms to the poor and sick, is now a restaurant. A plaque in the centre of a car park marks the site of a bull-baiting ring that was in use up to the 18th century.

CONCERT ON THE PROM *Band concerts, traditional feature of a 'day by the sea', are given throughout the summer by military bands at Eastbourne's Grand Parade Bandstand*

Beachy Head
One of the highest cliffs on the south coast, towering 534 ft above the sea, with a lighthouse at its foot which sends its beam 16 miles across the English Channel. The view on a clear day stretches from the Isle of Wight in the west to Dungeness in the east; but on a blustery day sightseers may have to fight to keep their feet. An open-top bus goes to Beachy Head from Eastbourne, and there is a car park at the top.

There are many good walks over the springy turf of the downs; one is along the cliff track westwards to the old lighthouse Belle Tout, then on to Birling Gap and Eastdean, a total distance of 4 miles.

Beauport Park
On the Battle road near Hastings is a wooded estate of 900 acres with a fine Georgian mansion, used in the 18th century by General James Murray, Governor of Quebec. Now the mansion is a hotel, peacefully quiet within its own grounds of 33 acres. The rhododendrons and magnolias are magnificent.

HASTINGS PIER *The ruins of a Norman castle overlook the 600 ft long pier, opened in 1872. Champagne was 7s. 6d. a bottle at the opening ceremony. The pier was cut in two places during the Second World War when invasion was feared, but later repaired*

FISHMARKET *The net huts on the beach in Hastings Old Town, used to store fishermen's gear, date back to Elizabethan times and were built tall and narrow to reduce ground rent*

Bexhill
The pride of Bexhill is its De La Warr Pavilion, an entertainment centre built overlooking the beach, with restaurants, sun terraces, a ballroom, theatre and concert hall. The pavilion was designed in the 1930's in a bold modern style by two German architects, Mendelsohn and Chermayeff. More than half Bexhill's resident population are retired people.

Birling Gap
A freak cleft in the South Downs between Beachy Head and the mouth of the Cuckmere River. Steep steps to the sea were used by 18th-century smugglers.

Brede
Peter Pan's Captain Hook was invented here—based on the life of a pirate named J. W. Mahler who turned rector and was blackmailed by a man called Smith. J. M. Barrie heard the story when visiting Brede. Brede Place is an imposing Tudor mansion.

Eastbourne
The elegance intended by the 7th Duke of Devonshire when he designed the town in 1834 still survives. Along the 3-mile esplanade there are private houses, good hotels, banks of flowers changed with the seasons—but not a single shop, or even a newspaper kiosk. In the middle of the esplanade is the Wish Tower, once a Martello Tower and now a Coastal Defence Museum. The name Wish is a corruption of Wash, a stream that once flowed here. There are theatres and a bandstand with seats for 3000. In Motcombe Gardens, behind the parish church, is a lake formed by the stream, or 'bourne', which gave the town its name. From the western end of the esplanade a road leads to Beachy Head. From the Old Town a 3-mile walk across the downs leads to the village of Jevington.

Eastdean
A village in a hollow of the downs. There are walks seaward over the springy turf to Birling Gap 1 mile away, or inland to Jevington. The church has an 11th-century tower with walls 3 ft thick.

Hastings
A modern tourist resort which retains, at its eastern end, much of the character of its past as a fishing port and original member of the Cinque Ports. A warren of narrow streets, timbered houses and red-tiled cottages leads down to the harbour area, where fishermen unload their catch straight on to the beach and visitors can buy plaice, codling, lobster and crab. The tall wooden huts once used for drying nets still stand by the beach. A lift mounts the cliff face to the ruins of the 13th-century castle.

To the west is the centre of Hastings, mid-Victorian at heart, but with a number of unpretentious Regency terraces, good modern shops and an attractive cricket ground set right in the town centre. Further west still is St Leonards, laid out in the early 19th century by James Burton (his son, Decimus Burton, designed the Wellington Arch at Hyde Park Corner in London) and still mainly a residential area with small hotels and boarding houses. A continuous parade stretches for more than 3 miles along the sea-front, with every possible holiday amenity. For long stretches the parade has two tiers, with a covered underwalk beside the beach and underground car parks behind it.

St Clement's Caves, 3 acres in extent and used for centuries by smugglers, are entered near the castle. Hastings Museum and Art Gallery houses a good collection of Sussex ironwork. On display in the Town Hall throughout the year is the Hastings Embroidery, a modern 'Bayeux Tapestry' depicting 81 scenes from British history from the Battle of Hastings in 1066 to the present day. The Fishermen's Museum in the Old Town includes the last of the Hastings luggers built for sail.

There are magnificent cliff walks east of Hastings, with fine cliff views from East Hill, Ecclesbourne Glen, Fairlight Glen and the Fire Hills—so called because of the yellow blaze of gorse which covers them in the spring.

Pevensey
A village of quaint old houses, one of which, Mint House, was built *c.* 1342 on the site of a Norman mint. It is now a museum, with rooms once used by smugglers. The village is dwarfed by the immense fortress of Pevensey Castle, now in ruins, which covers 10 acres and was built between AD 250 and 300 by the Romans, as a defence against barbarian invaders. It used to stand on the sea-shore, and the long boats of the Roman legions came right to the gates; but the sea has now retreated, leaving the castle 2 miles inland. The Normans used masonry to build a more compact stronghold within the Roman walls. The fort continued to be garrisoned until the 14th century.

BRIDGE TO EUROPE *Low tides reveal off Little Galley Hill, Bexhill, the remains of a forest—part of the 'land bridge' which joined Britain and the Continent 10,000 years ago*

A quiet vale where iron furnaces once roared

HERSTMONCEUX *The castle was built of Flemish brick in 1441, partly demolished in 1777, and restored to its original plans in the early part of this century*

Angling River fishing in the Rother around Northiam, Bodiam, Robertsbridge and Etchingham; in the Teise around Lamberhurst; in Powdermill Pond, Battle; and in Great Sanders Reservoir, Sedlescombe.

Wine and cider-making Merrydown wine and cider are made at Horam Manor, 1½ miles south of Heathfield. The factory can be visited by prior appointment.

Folk customs Pancake race on some Shrove Tuesdays at Bodiam. Pancake making in this country dates back to before the Reformation. All eggs and butter had to be used up before Lent, so they were often used to make pancakes on Shrove Tuesday, the last day before Easter for general merrymaking, which included pancake races.

Places to see *Bateman's* (NT), Burwash: Mar. to Oct., afternoons except Fri.; also mornings Mon. to Thur., June to Sept. *Bedgebury Pinetum*: daily. *Bodiam Castle* (NT): daily, except Sun. Nov. to Mar. *Great Dixter*, Northiam: Apr. to mid-Oct., afternoons except Mon. *Heathfield Wildlife Park* and *Gibraltar Tower*: daily. *Herstmonceux Castle*, grounds only: Easter to Sept., Mon to Fri. afternoons, Sat., Sun. and Bank Hols. *Scotney Castle Garden* (NT), Lamberhurst: Apr. to Oct., afternoons except Mon. and Tues.; open Bank Hols.

Information centre Town Hall, Tunbridge Wells.
Tel. Tunbridge Wells 26121.

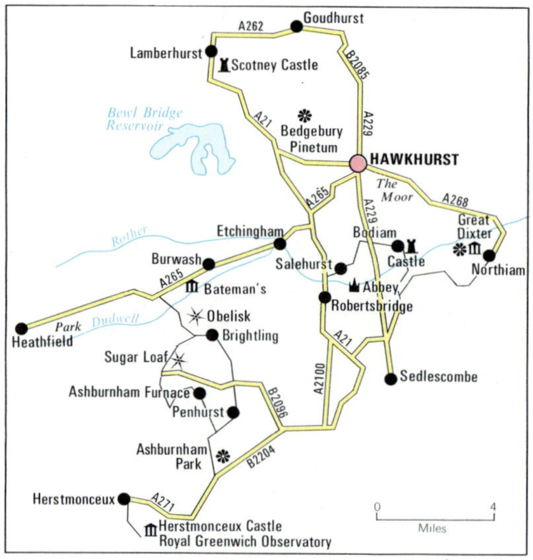

Inland from the heavily populated coast of East Sussex lie over 300 square miles of beautiful countryside with no large town and few settlements larger than villages. North of Heathfield, the River Rother winds slowly across its broad plain; to the south and west is a country of smaller valleys and tiny villages, joined by switchback roads over densely wooded ridges which rise to their highest point near Brightling. Channel breezes and the absence of urban smoke leave the air clear, which made Herstmonceux a natural choice as a new home for the Royal Greenwich Observatory when it moved from London in 1948.

There is a different panorama from each hilltop, seen at its best outside high summer when thick hedges and trees in leaf shorten the views. The area is closely associated with smuggling; in the 18th century the Hawkhurst Gang terrorised villages with organised crime. Before a great storm altered the course of the Rother the smugglers used flat-bottomed boats to bring their loot to the pack horses. Rudyard Kipling, who lived at Burwash, recalled their activities in his 'Smuggler's Song':

> Five and twenty ponies
> Trotting through the dark—
> Brandy for the parson,
> 'Baccy for the clerk;
> Laces for a lady, letters for a spy,
> And watch the wall, my darling, while
> the Gentlemen go by!

Local craftsmen still make fine wrought iron-work for tourists—a reminder that this was a centre of the Sussex iron industry from the 16th to the 18th century, when open-cast mining ripped gashes in the land.

BEDGEBURY PINETUM *Cedars, cypresses and other evergreens make this Forestry Commission park as attractive in winter as in summer. Many streams, often widening into lakes, wind through its 65 acres. The gardens were founded in 1924*

Ashburnham
Once at the heart of the Sussex iron industry, and the site of one of the last foundries to close, early in the 19th century. The forge still exists amid wooded and sparsely populated country on the north side of the 1000-acre Ashburnham Park; it is now a private house, with clinkers from the forge lining the flower beds. A track across the fields to Ashburnham Furnace passes the site of the huge ponds from which water was channelled to drive the forge hammers. The artificial channel still exists, and cannon balls made here have been found in the surrounding woods. The tiny nearby hamlet of Penhurst has a lovely 14th to 15th-century church with an Ashburnham family chapel.

Bedgebury
In a big park surrounding a Louis XIV-style mansion, a pinetum was planted when the conifers at Kew began to fall to London fumes. The mansion is now a girls' school, but most of the park is open for rambling and picnics. From the top of a hill there are views down grass slopes to dark green conifers—the largest collection in Europe—and a big pond where wild duck live.

Bodiam
A village at the edge of Bodiam Castle, a magnificent fortress built in

THE FOLLIES OF 'MAD JACK' FULLER

Two follies built in the early 19th century by Jack Fuller, a local squire and ironmaster, make unusual landmarks on the wooded hills near Brightling. The pagoda near Fuller's home in Brightling Park (above) was designed by Sir Robert Smirke to house an observatory; it has two storeys and a lead-covered dome. The 40 ft high 'Sugar Loaf' at Dallington (left), was built to win a bet. Friends challenged Fuller's claim that he could see the spire of Dallington Church from his home and proved him wrong; so he built a replica of the spire at Woods Corner, within sight of his house—'and no one', he said, 'can tell one from t'other'. Another pyramid, 60 ft high, stands over Fuller's grave in the churchyard at Brightling

1386 to discourage French raiders from sailing up the River Rother. The castle, with its beautiful lilied moat, is a hollow but romantic shell. Near by is the biggest hop farm in Britain, the Guinness estate, to which students crowd for work at harvest time in the autumn.

Brightling
A delightful village set in hilly country among stately beech trees. The view stretches north across the Rother Valley and south to the coast. The highest point, on Brightling Down, at 646 ft, is marked by an obelisk built by 'Mad Jack' Fuller, an ironmaster, squire and one-time MP for Lewes, who died in 1834. Fuller was noted for his eccentricities—he built two domes and two obelisks in the area; but he was sane enough to recognise the talent of a young painter, J. M. W. Turner, and to commission paintings from him.

Burwash
Rudyard Kipling lived in this outstandingly attractive village, spread along a ridge between the Rivers Rother and Dudwell. He described the surrounding countryside in *Puck of Pook's Hill*. Kipling's house, Bateman's, half a mile south of the village, is a fine Restoration period piece built by a Sussex ironmaster. There is an attractive drive across the Dudwell Valley to Brightling, through rich forest country whose firs screen valuable gypsum mines.

Etchingham
A village on the River Rother. Its church, built by Sir William de Etchyngham, is a perfect example of 14th-century Decorated architecture, with large, ornate windows, arches and doors, heavy external buttresses and a tall central tower.

Goudhurst
A beautiful village on a hill, with old inns, a duck pond and a 13th to 15th-century church which has marks on its walls said to have been made by archers sharpening their arrows before going to Agincourt with Sir John Bedgebury. The medieval Star and Eagle Inn, which was once joined to the church by a tunnel, was one base of the notorious Hawkhurst Gang of 18th-century smugglers. Spy-ways, the gang's sentry house with windows covering the main street in both directions, still stands. In 1796, the Goudhurst villagers routed the gang and hanged its leader, Richard Kingsmill, from a gibbet on Horsmonden Heath.

Hawkhurst
The largest village of the region, and a good centre for touring East Sussex. It is divided by a valley; the older part has a green called the Moor, while the newer part has 18th-century weather-boarded houses in its shopping centre.

Heathfield
A market centre on the ridge which dominates the area. There is a Sunday morning market for local produce by the Crown Inn. Gibraltar Tower was built in honour of General Eliott, who bought Heathfield Park with prize money gained in Havana and later commanded the garrison of Gibraltar in the siege of 1779–83. It houses a military museum and stands in a 200-acre wildlife park.

Herstmonceux
A small and unpretentious village. The moated castle lay in ruins for nearly 150 years after it was largely demolished in 1777. Since 1948 the rebuilt castle has been the home of the Royal Greenwich Observatory. The grounds are open to the public during the summer months.

Lamberhurst
Once an iron centre, now a small village on the London–Hastings road. Near by is Scotney Castle, a partial ruin set in woodland and waters, open to visitors in the summer.

Northiam
A long, straggling village where, by legend, Queen Elizabeth dined under an oak on the green in 1573. On the outskirts is Great Dixter manor house, a fine building dating back to 1460 and restored by Sir Edward Lutyens in 1911. It is open to the public and has exceptional gardens, noted for clematis.

Robertsbridge
A small town on the River Rother and the main London–Hastings road. It has several antique shops, and a cricket-bat factory, Gray-Nicolls, 1 mile west along the Brightling road, which can be visited by appointment. Bats have been made here since 1876. From the centre of Robertsbridge a lane leads eastwards to a good fishing spot on the River Rother. Salehurst, 1 mile north-east, has the ruins of a Norman abbey, and the abbey house next door contains a medieval loft, perfectly preserved and unique in southern England.

Sedlescombe
One of the prettiest villages in East Sussex, with many 16th and 17th-century houses among flowering gardens flanking a long triangular village green. Near by is the English Pestalozzi Children's Village for refugee children, which can be visited only by appointment.

TRUG-MAKING *Herstmonceux is one of many Sussex villages in which trug-making is a local tradition. The trugs, or baskets, are hand-made from broad bands of willow on an ash or chestnut frame*

The Garden of England

Kent has excelled in fruit growing since the Romans first planted orchards and vineyards there. Its fertile soil, mild climate and regular rainfall ensure top-quality fruit noted for firmness and succulence. London markets are within easy reach, and as a gateway to and from the Continent Kent has always been a natural place for growers to try out foreign varieties.

The apples the Romans grew, the pears introduced by the Normans and the fruit grown in the monastery gardens of the Middle Ages were different from most of the fruit grown in Kent today. Gardeners began creating new varieties by sowing pips from particularly fine specimens of their favourite fruit. In about 1830, Richard Cox is said to have planted one of these 'sport' pips in his Buckinghamshire garden, producing the first Cox's Orange Pippin, now England's most popular eating apple. The discovery in the 18th century that plants were male or female made it possible to breed new varieties on strict genetic lines.

In earlier centuries, when apples were eaten with a glass of port, the most popular varieties, such as Adam's Pearmain, were dry with a rather nutty flavour. Today, juicy and spicy apples are the favourites. The leading cookers have always been those with the most acid juice. Bramley's Seedling contains 1 per cent of malic acid—twice as much as a Cox's Orange Pippin.

Cultivation techniques have also changed. Once, large trees were planted in square formations, within which sheep could graze or currant bushes grow. Now many growers plant small trees close together in rows. In some cases, this has trebled the orchards' yield.

APPLE ORCHARDS IN BLOSSOM *There are more than 40,000 acres of apple orchards in Kent. Some 25,000 acres are planted with eating apples and the rest with cookers. The best time to see the orchards in blossom is usually mid-May. The traditional oast-houses in the background, for drying hops, are being replaced by oil-fired sheds*

PUTTING THE FLAVOUR INTO BEER

The hop *(Humulus lupulus)* was brought to England from the Continent in the 16th century. It quickly became established in the Kentish Weald, where today hop fields cover 10,000 acres. Hops are grown chiefly in the Medway Valley, from Tonbridge, Paddock Wood and Marden through to Staplehurst, and in a belt from Faversham to Canterbury. Bitter oils and resins such as lupulin are extracted from the fruit and used in brewing, to flavour, preserve and clarify beer. The vines grow rapidly (up to 6 in. in 24 hours) up strings set between posts to a height of 20–25 ft. They are picked from late August, then dried in oast-houses (right) or oil-fired sheds

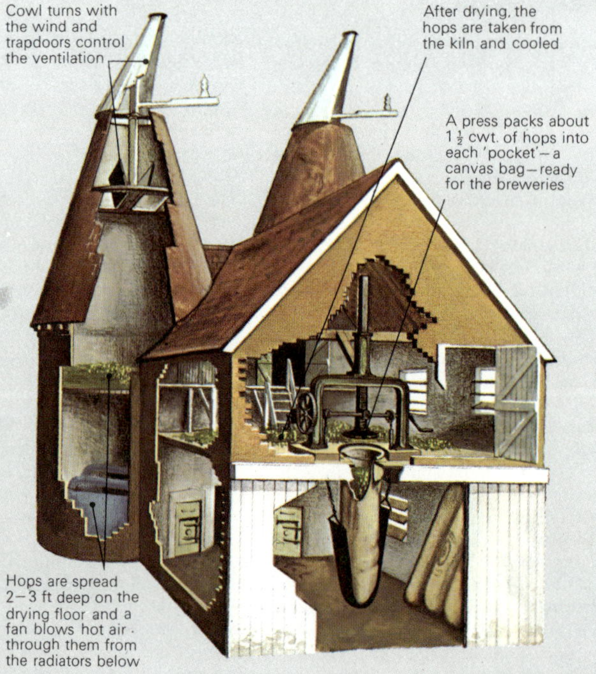

KENTISH COBS

Until the 20th century the cob nut or filbert, a variety of hazel nut which grows on small trees, was a major crop in Kent, and perhaps more characteristic of the county than any other produce. But during the last 50 years, imports from the sun-drenched orchards of southern Europe have made nut-growing in Kent unprofitable. Nevertheless, cob nuts are still grown in a few areas—notably between Mereworth and Wrotham and on the south bank of the Medway near Maidstone. The crop is harvested in October

Fruit grown in Kent

COX'S ORANGE PIPPIN *England's most popular eating apple, occupying some 13,000 acres of orchards in Kent. Other dessert varieties, such as Worcester Pearmain and Golden Delicious, are grown with Cox's for cross-pollination The apple is crisp, very juicy and has a slightly spicy flavour*

BRAMLEY'S SEEDLING *First grown in the early 19th century and now Kent's leading cooker. The trees have broad-spreading branches, and the apple is juicy and very acid*

WORCESTER PEARMAIN *The trees are usually planted with Cox trees, to act as pollinators. Nine Cox trees are planted to one Worcester, which is being replaced in some parts by Discovery and a new variety, Katcha. Worcester Pearmain is an early sweet apple with crisp white flesh*

CRISPIN *A new variety of apple, the same as Japan's Mutsu, developed from America's Golden Delicious. So far, it is too large to make an ideal dessert apple, but growers are trying to produce a smaller fruit*

GOLDEN DELICIOUS *About 1000 acres of Golden Delicious orchards have been planted in Kent, to meet foreign competition from the same variety. The apple has crisp, juicy flesh, and stores and travels well*

CONFERENCE *One of the two main varieties of dessert pear grown in Kent, first introduced towards the end of the 19th century. The fruit is juicy and sweet, and stores well. Pears are grown mainly in a belt stretching from Sittingbourne to Faversham, in many cases alongside dessert apple orchards*

DOYENNÉ DU COMICE *Its melting, slightly cinnamon-flavoured flesh has made Comice one of Kent's two most popular pears. Kent has some 8000 acres of pears*

WILLIAMS' BON CHRÉTIEN *First grown by a Berkshire schoolmaster c. 1770. The fruit is juicy and sweet, with a slightly musky flavour. Outside Kent, it is widely used for canning*

STRAWBERRIES *There are more than 3000 acres of strawberry beds in Kent, many on 'Pick your own' farms. The main varieties grown are Red Gauntlet, Favourite, Gorella and Vigour*

RASPBERRIES *This is an important soft fruit crop in Kent, particularly on the 'Pick your own' farms. The main varieties grown are Malling Jewel, Glen Cova and Malling Admiral*

CHERRIES *Kent is the main centre for English cherries. More important varieties include (from left) Napoleon, Early Rivers and Noir de Guben*

VICTORIA PLUM *About 4000 acres of orchards in Kent are occupied by plum trees, with Victoria, Czar and Marjorie's Seedling the main varieties*

CZAR *Imports have caused a decline in the English plum-growing industry, but Czar is still one of the best of the early cooking plums*

A royal spa at the heart of Kentish farmlands

Angling Coarse fishing on the River Medway in the Tonbridge area, at Tinker's Island, Tonbridge, and on stretches of the River Eden.

Boating On the River Medway at Tonbridge and in Dunorlan Park, Royal Tunbridge Wells.

Climbing There are good rock climbs at three sites near Royal Tunbridge Wells: Harrison's Rocks, Groombridge; High Rocks, 2 miles west of Royal Tunbridge Wells, headquarters of the Sandstone Climbing Club of Great Britain; and Bowles Rocks, Eridge. The Bowles Mountaineering and Outdoor Pursuits Centre at Eridge runs courses in climbing, skiing, canoeing and camping; casual visitors can picnic in the grounds for a small fee.

Riding Several riding stables in the area; good riding country. Horse shows and gymkhanas are organised throughout the year.

Golf The Nevill Golf Club at Royal Tunbridge Wells has an 18-hole championship course.

Cricket County cricket at the Nevill Ground, Royal Tunbridge Wells, in mid-June.

Hop gardens Whitbread Hop Farm, Beltring, Paddock Wood, is usually open to visitors during the first three weeks of Sept.

Arts Annual open-air art exhibition at The Pantiles, Royal Tunbridge Wells. The Royal Tunbridge Wells Symphony Orchestra performs at the Assembly Hall on Sun. in winter.

Places to see *Chartwell* (NT), Westerham: house, Mar. to Nov.: Tues., Wed., Thur. afternoons, Sat., Sun. and Bank Hol. Mon.; garden and studio: same days, Apr. to mid-Oct. *Chiddingstone Castle*: mid-Mar. to Oct., Sat. and Sun.; also afternoons Tues. to Fri. *Hever Castle*: afternoons only: Apr. to Sept., Tues., Wed., Fri., Sun., Bank Hol. *Ightham Mote*: Fri. afternoon. *Knole* (NT), Sevenoaks: Mar. to Nov., Wed., Thur., Fri., Sat. and Bank Hol.; also Sun. afternoon; park, daily. *Long Barn*, Weald, 2 miles south of Sevenoaks, reputed birthplace of William Caxton: Apr. to Sept., Wed. afternoon. *Penshurst Place*: Easter to Sept., afternoons except Mon. and Fri. *Quebec House* (NT), Westerham: Apr. to Oct., afternoons except Thur. and Sat.

Information centre Town Hall, Tunbridge Wells.
Tel. Tunbridge Wells 26121.

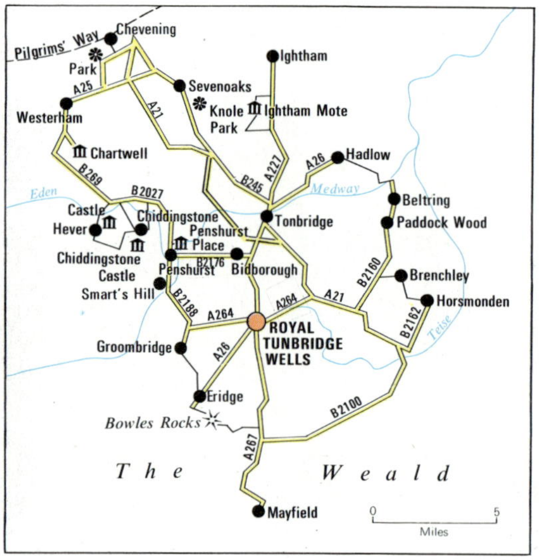

The Weald of western Kent is a fertile land. Scores of country lanes turn and twist round the Wealden hills, giving views, in season, of orchards where apples, pears, plums and blackcurrants grow, and fields of corn, cabbages or hops. The farms of the High Weald, with sandstone soil, are among the most productive in Europe. The Low Weald clay valleys between the hills are nearly as rich. Even the hedgerows are thick with food—blackberries, hazel nuts, sweet chestnuts and elderberries.

For centuries the men of this part of Kent came under the Jute law of Gavelkind which, even after the Norman Conquest, continued to divide a dead man's estates equally between all his sons. So instead of great estates owned by a powerful baron, there grew up in Kent numerous smallholdings and a race of prosperous yeoman farmers. Their descendants are still there today, fiercely independent, and many of their families have farmed the same land for centuries.

Though lacking vast estates, the Weald has more than its share of great houses. From medieval times, wealthy families who wanted to live outside London but within easy reach of Court and Parliament were attracted to the ridges of the High Weald. There they built fine houses, or converted older castles. The result today is the greatest concentration of famous houses—Penshurst, Hever, Knole, Ightham Mote—to be found anywhere in Britain, alongside neat villages and black-and-white timbered farmhouses.

It is not easy driving country, for lanes are narrow and winding; the AA signposts a blossom route during May. The Wealden smells are characteristic: in winter, log fires; in spring, fruit blossom; in summer, sun on lush meadows and wild honeysuckle; in autumn, the bitter-sweet smell of full-blown hops.

Bidborough
Twice named Kent's best-kept village, Bidborough has beautiful views over the Weald and North Downs. One of the best viewpoints is from the main road which climbs the ridge out of the village.

Brenchley
A village of Tudor cottages among Regency and Victorian houses. Orchards stretch to the main street, and an avenue of huge yew trees, 350 years old, leads to the door of the church. This was built in 1233, and has a screen added in 1536. Opposite the church is a well-restored row of cottages, once part of the Palace of the Duke of St Albans.

Chartwell
The country home of Sir Winston Churchill and its garden attract a constant stream of visitors. Westerham, where there is a bronze statue of Churchill, is the nearest centre; the route is well signposted. The interior of the house is preserved as a museum, with numerous souvenirs of the many roles in Sir Winston's life.

Chiddingstone
An Elizabethan village, almost intact, among groups of oast-houses, is kept to near-perfection by the National Trust. Perhaps it is even a shade too well groomed. The 19th-century neo-Gothic castle, originally a large 17th-century house, has an oriental collection and Stuart relics, and near by stands the village's original 'chiding stone'; according to legend, it was here that villagers used to chide any woman whose chatter annoyed them. There is fishing in the park lake for a small daily fee.

PENSHURST *Tudor cottages, timbered and tile-hung, enclose Leicester Square. The square is named after the Elizabethan Earl of Leicester, whose family still owns Penshurst Place*

SMART'S HILL *The Spotted Dog Inn in this village near Penshurst is a good example of weather-boarding, underlined by a wisteria. The inn was originally four cottages, built in 1480*

BOWLES ROCKS *The same sandstone formations which gave Royal Tunbridge Wells its mineral spring rise to a freak outcrop west of the town at Eridge. Here almost vertical ascents 70 ft high provide a good training ground for mountaineers*

Groombridge
In an area rich in attractive villages, Groombridge stands out, with its 18th-century tiled cottages round a triangular village green. The late 17th-century manor house, Groombridge Place, has been attributed to Wren.

Hever Castle
A moated manor house beside the River Eden, with all the fascination of a castle in miniature—a grand dining hall only 40 ft long, a tiny maze, a courtyard which would grace a country inn, and even a 'torture chamber' only 6 ft square. The house dates from the 13th century, but its great days were in Tudor times: Anne Boleyn spent her girlhood there, and Henry VIII was a frequent visitor.

When the Astor family bought Hever Castle in 1903 they enlarged it by building a miniature 'village' of single-storey Tudor-style houses across the moat. They also laid out an ornate Italian garden for their collection of Roman statues, ending in a piazza where today's visitors can have tea overlooking a 35-acre lake.

Horsmonden
In the old Gun Inn by the village green, huge joints are spit-roasted over apple logs four nights a week. In the same bar, the 17th-century gunmaker John Browne designed guns for Charles I and Cromwell, the British Navy and its Dutch rival. A cannon he cast for James I stands outside the inn.

Ightham
An attractive village on a busy road. Ightham Mote, 3 miles away but well signposted, is a perfect 14th–15th-century moated manor house, set among trees and meadows with peacocks in the gardens.

Mayfield
A busy village on a ridge, with wide panoramic views and a fine main street in which the principal attraction is the Middle House, dating back to 1576. There is an attractive 3-mile walk from the High Street through rural and riverside scenery to the hamlet of Broad Oak, crossing the valley of the River Rother.

Paddock Wood
A higgledy-piggledy village and centre for hop-growing and marketing. At Beltring, 2 miles north, is the Whitbread hop farm which has 25 oast-houses and the most modern equipment, and yet manages to look like a farm. Visitors are welcome at harvest time.

Penshurst
The village is dominated by Penshurst Place, where Sir Philip Sidney was born in 1554 and where his family have lived for 400 years. Penshurst stands in magnificent parkland grounds on the Rivers Medway and Eden. A descendant, Viscount De L'Isle, who won a V.C. at Anzio in 1944, lives there now. The Great Hall dates from 1340 and has a good art collection and a minstrels' gallery. In Penshurst village is the original Leicester Square, named after the Elizabethan Earl of Leicester. There is fine walking country round the village, with hills, woods and good fishing.

Royal Tunbridge Wells
One of the most elegant towns in the country. It was a rival to Bath as a spa in Regency days, when it was often visited by Beau Nash. The Pantiles, an 18th-century shopping walk shaded by lime trees, looks almost unchanged today. A walk across the common to the west leads to a sandstone outcrop among the trees called High Rocks, a picnic area since the 17th century. The 17th-century Church of King Charles the Martyr has an impressive wooden cupola and a white marble font. When Charles I was alive, the town was so popular that Queen Henrietta Maria, arriving with her court to take the spa waters, had to camp in tents on the common because so few houses had yet been built. There is a symphony orchestra, theatre and a county cricket ground in Nevill Park.

THE PANTILES *A colonnade of 18th and 19th-century houses and shops, with Italianate columns, lines the famous Pantiles at Royal Tunbridge Wells. At one end of the parade, in Bath Square, are the medicinal springs discovered by Lord North in 1606 which were quickly to make the town a fashionable spa and earn it royal favour. The waters can still be drunk. The 'pantiles' were laid in the early 18th century, but only 15 of the original tiles remain today*

Sevenoaks
A dormitory town. Knole Park, however, is good for picnics. Its mansion, Knole, begun in 1456 by Archbishop Bourchier and developed by Thomas Sackville in Elizabeth's reign, is one of the biggest private houses in the country.

Tonbridge
The town, part railway depot, part pleasant market town, is built on the River Medway. Motor cruisers are available for hire for trips on the river, which offers stretches of good fishing from its banks. Tonbridge School was founded in 1553 by a former Lord Mayor of London. Fire destroyed the first castle at Tonbridge in 1088, and the remains still standing of castle walls are of a later date. The gatehouse, with its four circular towers, is 13th century.

THE YEOMAN FARMER'S HOUSE

There was an abundance of oak in medieval times in Kent and the technique of timber framing was simple, so this type of house became a standard design for the prosperous farmer. Many examples survive throughout the area today. The house often included a central hall with a tall window under jutting eaves. These eaves are supported by diagonal bracing from the inner sides of the projecting upper storeys.

A pageant of shipping on the Thames Estuary

Angling There is sea fishing in the Medway Estuary; coarse fishing on stretches of the Medway upstream from Wateringbury.

Places to see *Cobham Hall*: Wed., Thur. and Sun. afternoons, Aug.; also Easter and Aug. Bank Hol. *Lullingstone Castle*: Apr. to Sept., Wed., Sat., Sun. and Bank Hol. afternoons. *Lullingstone Roman Villa*: daily, except Sun. mornings Oct. to Mar. *Owletts* (NT), Cobham: Apr. to Oct., Wed., Thur. afternoons. *Rochester Castle*: daily, except Sun. mornings Oct. to Mar. *Rochester Museum*, Eastgate House: weekdays. *Temple Manor*, Rochester: weekdays and Sun. afternoon.

Information centre Tourist Information Centre, 85 High Street, Rochester. Tel. Medway 43666.

Fast roads from London cross north Kent towards Canterbury and the coast. Relatively few motorists brave the tiny, wandering side-roads which twist between hills and lead down into valleys. Those who do so are well rewarded; so are walkers who are prepared to take to the hills. For among the North Downs lie rich farmlands, attractive villages perched on hillsides, and woods packed with bluebells and primroses in the spring.

Though only a few miles from the Greater London boundary, this is a world quite apart from the suburban sprawl which has reached further and further into north-west Kent.

Through the downs the River Medway winds its way out to the Thames Estuary, past the flatlands of the Isle of Sheppey and the Isle of Grain with its huge oil refineries. The big towns at the mouth of the Medway loom large in Britain's naval history: here, in 1667, horrified onlookers saw the Dutch fleet under Admiral van Ruyter crash through the chain boom protecting Chatham and sink four major ships of the line. Today the only hazards facing weekend sailors navigating the Medway in yachts or motor cruisers are tricky currents and shallows. Big modern ships pass close to the shore at Gravesend, as the Thames Estuary narrows to become London's river. By contrast, round the southern shore of the Medway Estuary the few surviving Thames barges with 80-ft masts and red sails are still sailed by preservationists.

This part of Kent has close associations with Charles Dickens and his novels, and visitors can follow the journeyings of Mr Pickwick to inns, orchards and cricket pitches. Dickens died at Gadshill, near Rochester, in 1870, in the house which as a small boy he had coveted when his father was a pay clerk in Chatham Dockyard.

CRICKET ON MEOPHAM GREEN *There is probably more cricket played on village greens in Kent, and there are more grounds on which the county side plays, than in any other county in Britain. Many of the inns on the edges of the greens are called The Cricketers' Arms. The modern sign of that at Meopham shows Kent and Surrey players in action*

Birling
An attractive village with a 12th-century church where nine members of the Nevill family are buried. With their armorial shields are two helmets. Sir Edward Nevill, a favourite of Henry VIII, used one of these helmets, weighing more than 15 lb., in the jousting at Greenwich in honour of the birth of a son to the first of Henry's wives, Catherine of Aragon. The baby died soon afterwards. There is a walk from the village centre up to the Pilgrims' Way, then westwards along the North Downs towards Trottiscliffe and Ryarsh—a bracing 3½ miles.

Chatham
A naval base developed by Elizabeth I from an unknown village. There is still an important naval dockyard here including a refitting base for nuclear submarines. There are several 18th-century houses in the town, and Dickens lived as a child at No. 2 (now No. 11) Ordnance Terrace.

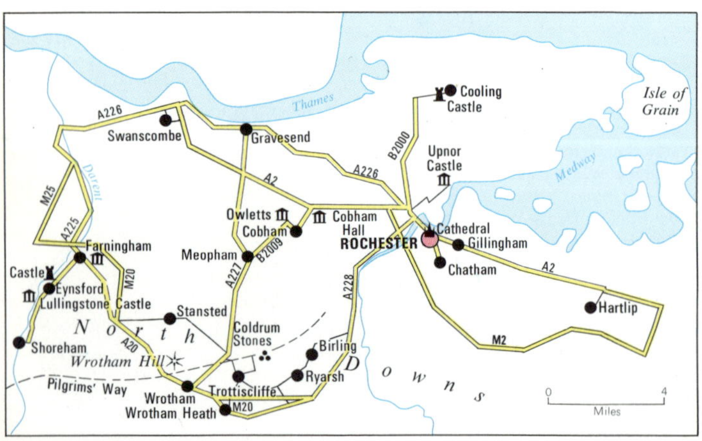

EYNSFORD *The River Darent at Eynsford is sometimes so low that motorists held up at the narrow 15th-century bridge can drive across the river to the 16th-century Plough Inn opposite. Elizabethan influences inspired the composer Peter Warlock (1894–1930), who lived at Eynsford, to write songs in the Tudor manner*

Cobham
A charming village, famous for its half-timbered Leather Bottle Inn, which figures in *The Pickwick Papers*. It was to The Leather Bottle that Tracy Tupman fled after being jilted by Rachel Wardle, and he was discovered here by Mr Pickwick. At Cobham Hall lived the Hon. Ivo Bligh, cricket captain of Cobham, Kent and England, who took a famous team to Australia in 1882. All the great Victorian cricketers, including W. G. Grace, played on the ground at Cobham Hall; today the Cobham team plays in the village on a pitch which was laid as a war memorial and is set against a background of apple orchards. The Hall, now a girls' school open to the public only in the holidays, has a part-14th-century great hall and Renaissance features by Inigo Jones and James Wyatt. On the fringe of the village stands Owletts, a large red-brick Restoration manor.

Cooling
The gateway of the 14th-century Cooling Castle stands in massive isolation on the Hoo Peninsula. It was the home of Sir John Oldcastle, hanged in 1417 as a Lollard—one of the supporters of John Wyclif, who believed that churchmen should live a life of evangelical poverty. Sir John was said to be the model for Shakespeare's Falstaff.

Eynsford
A charming village only 20 miles from London, with medieval houses and a 15th-century bridge over the River Darent, which flows on through meadows. On the outskirts stand the ruins of a castle with a defensive ditch and flint-rubble walls, the home of a Norman knight when Henry I came to the throne in 1100. Lanes and paths lead southwards, through attractive downland villages, to join the Pilgrims' Way near Wrotham.

THE DAYS OF STEAM *Gravesend is the point at which ships entering the Thames take on a river pilot for the journey upstream, and cutters ply back and forth all day between ship and shore. Tugs stand waiting to escort the larger vessels*

Farningham
One of the prettiest villages close to London with many 18th-century houses, a fine old inn and a weather-boarded mill by the River Darent. The river is rich in crayfish. The old manor house was once the home of Captain Bligh of the *Bounty*. From the hill above the river there is a minor road leading south to Eynsford; it is called Sparepenny Lane, because carters used it to avoid paying tolls on the main road.

Hartlip
A village on a ridge in cherry-orchard country, with attractive old houses, and new buildings in taste and harmony with the old. The church, restored in 1864, has Victorian stained glass.

Isle of Grain
Orchards of cherry trees have replaced the wheat fields that gave the island its name, and rows of poplars protect the cherry trees from the keen wind. The area is separated from the mainland by winding waterways.

Lullingstone
An 18th-century castle with a gateway dating from the reign of Henry VII and a dining-room used by Queen Anne. The lovely grounds include a herb garden and the Church of St Botolph, which was restored in the reign of Edward III.

Near the castle are the excavated remains of a Roman villa which was apparently occupied by Christians as early as the 4th century AD. It has a specially adapted private chapel, one of the earliest known places of Christian worship in Britain. There are good wall paintings and mosaics dating from the 1st to 5th centuries.

THE DAYS OF SAIL

Figureheads on display at Chatham Dockyard recall the days when ornamental carvings, originally national or religious emblems, graced the prow of every warship. Sometimes they represented notable men of the time: the likeness of the Marquis of Wellesley (centre), Governor-General of India from 1798 to 1805, appeared on a 74-gun ship built in Bombay. But more often they were symbolic figures. Britannia (left) adorned a 91-gun ship started at Chatham in 1859, and the Victorian-featured Nymphe (right) was for a sloop launched at Portsmouth in 1888

Rochester
The cathedral city of Rochester figures in the works of Charles Dickens, under its own and other names, more often than any other place except London. The cathedral was founded by the Saxon King Ethelbert, but the present building is Norman. The cathedral library is outstanding and contains the Textus Roffensis (1115–24), Coverdale's Bible (1535), the Great Bible (1539) and numerous ancient documents. Rochester is a pleasant but lively old town with a 17th-century red-brick guildhall. The great 125 ft high keep of the towering Norman castle, built in the reign of Henry I to defend the Medway crossing, is probably the finest in southern England. King John took the castle from his rebelling barons after a siege in 1215.

Swanscombe
Three fragments of a human skull found in a gravel pit at Swanscombe in 1935 and 1955 are thought to date back 200,000 years—making it one of the oldest skulls found in Europe. The site of the 'dig' is not open to the public. The 12th-century church has bricks from Roman times and a partly pre-Conquest tower, though late-19th-century restoration makes it difficult to detect the earlier parts of the building.

Trottiscliffe
A small village in wooded country at the foot of the North Downs and just off the Pilgrims' Way. About 1 mile east of the village are the Coldrum Stones, a megalithic Long Barrow estimated to date back to 2000 BC.

Upnor
The ruined castle dates from 1561 and was probably built from stones taken from Rochester's medieval walls. The castle saw action, ineffectively, when the Dutch sailed up the river in 1667. The Whittington Stone marks local fishermen's boundary rights.

ARTIST'S HOME *Samuel Palmer, painter and visionary, lived at Water House, Shoreham, for five years from 1825. Deeply influenced by the mystical poet and painter William Blake, Palmer produced landscapes of intense luminosity and drawings filled with detail. Many of the best pictures of Palmer's 'Shoreham period', including his* In a Shoreham Garden, *are in the Victoria and Albert Museum, London. He also won fame for his illustrations of Milton's works*

Wrotham
A charming village with a medieval church and an early 19th-century rectory. It lies in a hollow below Wrotham Hill, from which there are superb views across the Weald as far as the Fire Hills near Hastings. Some pleasant side-roads and tracks lead to remoter villages like Stansted, where each spring the banks are rich in primroses.

Along the River Medway

Angling Mote Park Lake, Maidstone; certain stretches on the Medway, Beult, Len and other local streams.

Boating The Medway is navigable from Tonbridge to Sheerness; there is canoeing on the estuary.

Cricket County matches at Mote Park, Maidstone; cricket week in July.

Events Kent County Agricultural Show is held at Detling, 2½ miles north-east of Maidstone, in July.

Places to see *Allington Castle*: afternoons. *Archbishop's Palace and Dungeons*, Maidstone: weekdays. *Aylesford Priory*: daily. *Boughton Monchelsea Place*: weekend and Bank Hol. Mon. afternoons, Easter to early Oct. *Chillington Manor House Museum*, Maidstone: weekdays. *Leeds Castle*: Tues., Wed., Thur. and Sun. afternoons, Apr. to Oct. *Maidstone Museum and Art Gallery*: weekdays. *Sissinghurst Castle Garden* (NT): daily, Apr. to mid-Oct. *Tyrwhitt Drake Museum of Carriages*, stables of Archbishop's Palace, Maidstone: weekdays. *Wool House*, Loose: Wed. afternoon, Apr. to late Sept.

Information centre The Gatehouse, Old Palace Gardens, Maidstone. Tel. Maidstone 671361.

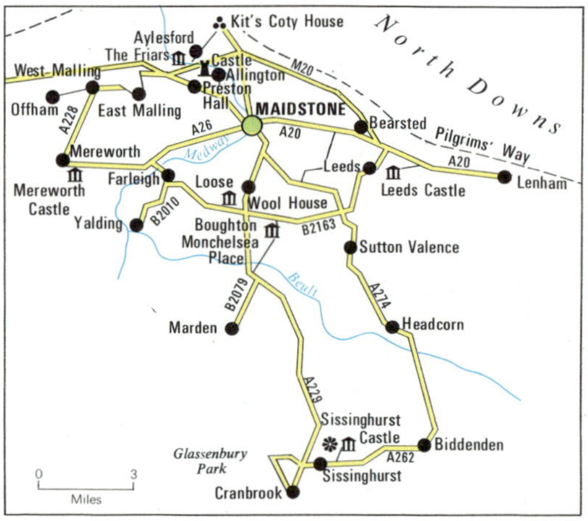

The River Medway has played a major role in Kentish history. For centuries barges carried timber, and later iron and guns, from the Weald downstream through Maidstone to the towns of the Thames Estuary. When hops were introduced from the Continent in the 16th century, the Medway provided water to make Maidstone the centre of the Kentish brewing industry. So fundamental a factor in the county's life did the Medway become that it is traditionally the dividing line between the 'Kentish Men' of the western bank and the 'Men of Kent' on the eastern side.

The coming of railway and road transport reduced the commercial importance of the river. Today the Medway and its tributary, the River Beult, wind peacefully through a mainly pastoral landscape of orchards, meadows and hop-gardens, with splendid fishing and good riverside walks.

Maidstone is Kent's county town, and a major marketing centre. The Medway still plays its part in the town's modern paper-making industry. Around the town lies rich orchard country where apple blossom forms a thick, heavy-scented canopy in the spring. The fruit is cultivated and marketed so intensively that even small villages like Marden have their own cold-storage facilities and packing stations.

When the trees are bare in winter, there can be seen from almost every road the black-and-white timbered houses of yeoman farmers of long standing. These are mellowed buildings, often set by a mill-stream, with a conical oast house beside their barns—though today many of the smaller oasts are being turned into dwelling-houses, as more and more hops are dried in large central oasts, equipped with moving belts and electrical heating.

The breezes which sweep across the Weald were once used to drive the vanes of many windmills for flour milling. Like the oast houses, many windmills fell into disuse and others became private homes; but at Cranbrook, a magnificent example has been preserved in full working order.

THE BIDDENDEN MAIDS *The village sign commemorates Mary and Eliza Chulkhurst, Siamese twins, born c. 1100, who lived for 34 years and left 20 acres of land to the village to provide an annual dole for the poor. The sisters' figures are stamped on cakes distributed free every Easter Monday*

LEEDS CASTLE *A golf course looks across the moat to the medieval castle, which has been used by many kings of England. French prisoners were housed there during the 17th century*

MAIDSTONE *The Archbishop's Palace, a manor house dating back to the 14th century, fronts the eastern bank of the Medway. Its rooms are now let to various organisations. The neighbouring All Saints' Church has one of the widest naves in England*

Allington
By a lock on the Medway is an inn, The Malta, dating back to 1784. Boats can be hired here for a leisurely cruise up the river to Maidstone and beyond. There is also a restored Norman castle, now a Carmelite friary.

Aylesford
An attractive village on the Medway with a medieval bridge and a rebuilt Carmelite friary, originally founded in 1284. It is noted for the pottery made by the monks. Admission to the friary is free, and pottery and souvenirs can be bought at a shop by the rose garden.

On the downs to the north is Kit's Coty House—three standing stone slabs, crowned by a fourth, which are the remains of a Neolithic burial chamber of *c*. 3500 BC. These downs were also the site of a great battle in AD 455 in which the Britons under Vortigern were decisively defeated by the Jutes. Just across the river from Aylesford is Preston Hall, a rehabilitation 'village' for invalid ex-servicemen established in 1921.

Bearsted
Although this attractive village is becoming a suburb of Maidstone, it is still enclosed by orchards. Alfred Mynn (1807–61), England's first fast round-arm bowler, played on its village green.

Biddenden
A beautiful village with weavers' cottages and a fine medieval cloth hall with seven gables. The village is noted for the story of the 'Biddenden Maids', Eliza and Mary Chulkhurst, who were Siamese twins joined at the hips and lived early in the 12th century.

Bethersden, 4 miles east on the A28, is a village famous for the marble which used to be quarried locally. The stone was used in Canterbury and Rochester Cathedrals. Bethersden church has a 15th-century tower.

Boughton Monchelsea
A village on a ridge, with a greystone Elizabethan manor house, Boughton Monchelsea Place. The manor, open in summer, has period furniture and tapestries and is set in a 79-acre deer park. The churchyard is famous for its roses.

Cranbrook
A busy, pleasant town with many 18th-century houses. Its fine medieval church has the honorary title of 'Cathedral of the Weald'. It has a porch, built in 1291, with a fine oak door. A splendid octagonal windmill, built in 1814, has been well restored and is kept in full working order. Glassenbury Park, 2 miles west, has a fine lime avenue leading to a moated 18th-century manor house.

Headcorn
A large village with magnificent timbered houses used as cloth halls by Flemish immigrant weavers in the 17th century. The church has good stained glass. A huge oak, 50 ft round at its base, is over a thousand years old and a survivor of the great forest of Anderida which once covered much of south-east England.

Leeds
The village has charming houses and a church with a massive Norman tower. But its fame rests mainly on the medieval castle east of the village—a majestic fortress, surrounded by a wide moat, which has seen many phases of English history since it was built in 1120. It was the home of Henry VIII's first wife, Catherine of Aragon, and Elizabeth I was a prisoner there before she became queen. The castle was restored in the 19th century and is now used largely for conferences, but it is open to the public on certain days.

Lenham
A village in the heart of the orchard country, with a fine square surrounded by medieval houses. There is a tithe barn, and the 14th-century church has some excellent wood carvings, wall-paintings and Elizabethan plate.

Loose
A village to explore on foot. A stream, once used to drive mills, runs through the heart of the village, and the sound of gently-running water is ever-present. There is a fine half-timbered Wool House, used in the 15th century for the cleaning of wool.

Maidstone
A busy market town which was already an active settlement as the original Medestane of the Domesday Book, when its chief activities were flour mills, eel fisheries and crystallising salt in primitive iron pans. There are trees, gardens and riverside walks alongside the Medway, on which cabin cruisers from Tonbridge glide peacefully downstream to Allington Lock. There is a museum of carriages opposite the 14th-century palace that was a residence for Archbishops of Canterbury until 1538. All Saints' Church is the largest in Kent. Bank Street, by the town hall, is a shopping area with guild signs displayed above ancient premises.

East and West Malling
Twin villages with strong Norman connections. West Malling has a fine main street, a market and some excellent 18th-century houses. There is an impressive Norman keep, known as St Leonard's Tower, built of Kentish ragstone by Bishop Gundulf of Rochester *c*. 1090. An inn named The Startled Saint, whose sign shows St Leonard with Spitfires circling within his halo, recalls the use of the nearby airfield during the Battle of Britain.

Mereworth
The village has a remarkable church, rebuilt in 18th-century neo-Classical style to match the nearby castle, and incongruous in its rural setting. Admiral Lucas, first recipient of the Victoria Cross is buried here. He won it in 1854, during the Crimean War. Mereworth Castle, outside the village to the south, is an 18th-century residence in Italian style, with a dome and pillared porticoes. The castle is privately owned.

Offham
On the green is a quintain, used in the days of jousting for practising with a tilt or lance. The target is on a pivot and can swing round and tip an inexpert tilter off his horse. The sport is revived each May Day.

Sissinghurst
In the Seven Years War, 3000 French prisoners were put into a medieval building 2 miles west of Sissinghurst; they called it the 'chateau'. Sissinghurst 'Castle' later became the home of the writer and poet Victoria Sackville-West and her husband Sir Harold Nicolson. The beautiful gardens, in which herbs are a speciality, are open to the public.

Sutton Valence
A village spread along a ridge with superb views southwards across the Wealden valleys. Its red-brick school, founded in 1576, is a landmark, but there is also a Norman castle ruin, some fine old houses and a windmill.

Yalding
A village notable for its old houses and its two 15th-century bridges built to cross the Medway and the Beult. Warde's Moat is a quaint moat-encircled vicarage.

THE LADY ORCHID Kent is rich in orchids, and one of Britain's most beautiful native species is rarely found growing wild anywhere except in Kent, among trees on chalk downs

One-time smugglers' paradise on a marshy coast

Angling Sea fishing, from beaches at New Romney, Dungeness, Denge Marsh, Galloways and Dymchurch. Freshwater fishing in the Rivers Rother, Brede and Tillingham, west of Rye, and in the Royal Military Canal.

Sailing There is a club at Rye Harbour, but conditions are difficult for the unskilled yachtsman.

Cricket Rye Cricket Club has its main week in Aug.

Folk customs Rye holds a Mayoring Day in May, when the mayor and councillors throw hot pennies from the town hall windows to children in the street; the tradition is said to commemorate the former minting of coins in Rye.

Markets in Rye There is a cattle market and a general market on Thur. off Cinque Ports Street.

Places to see *Lamb House* (NT), Rye: Apr. to Oct., Wed. and Sat. afternoons. *Martello Tower*, Dymchurch: daily. *Romney, Hythe and Dymchurch Railway*: daily, Easter to Sept.; Sat. and Sun., Mar., Oct. and Nov. *Smallhythe Place* (NT): Mar. to Oct., afternoons except Tues. and Fri. *Ypres Tower Museum*, Rye: Easter to mid-Oct., daily.

Information centre The Regent, Cinque Ports Street, Rye. Tel. Rye 2480.

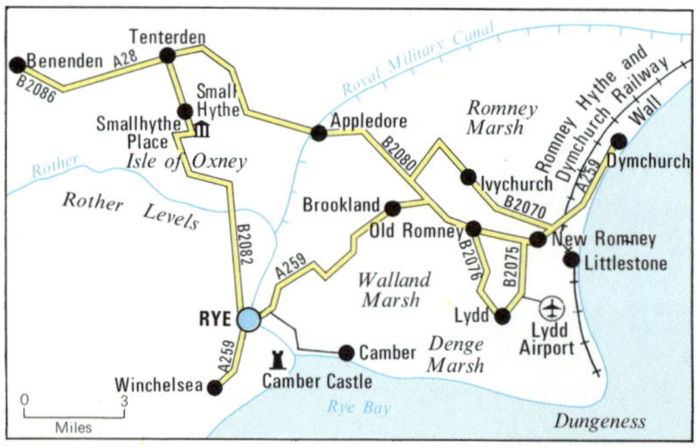

Richard Barham, the 18th-century curate of Ashford in Kent, wrote in his *Ingoldsby Legends* that 'the world is divided into five parts, namely Europe, Asia, Africa, America and Romney Marsh'. Even today the flat, misty marshes that jut into the Channel at Dungeness retain an air of mystery and secrecy which sets them quite apart from the wooded ridges of East Sussex and Kent which overlook them to the north.

Romney Marsh, and the adjoining Walland Marsh and Denge Marsh, make up a vast flat expanse of grazing land, carved across by deep dikes and dotted with the famous Romney Marsh sheep. Most of the area is barely above sea level and some is well below. There are splendid sunrises and sunsets. In the winter the marshes can be cold and dank with freezing fogs, and even in mid-summer, late evenings can bring a mantle of heavy white mist.

These marshes made an ideal area for smuggling until early in the 19th century, for only men born and bred there knew the routes through the maze of water channels. Even in the 1970's there are stories of illegal immigrants being landed there in the mist.

Inland, sheep graze among isolated villages, and tulip fields mark a new marsh industry. On the coast, beside beaches of pebble and sand, are little fishing hamlets now turned into quiet holiday resorts such as New Romney, Dymchurch and Littlestone. There are no big towns, but there are bungalows, chalets, caravans and a miniature railway for summer holidaymakers. In spring and autumn this is a splendid place to watch migratory birds, and at most times of the year the area is rich in seabirds.

A sea wall protects land reclaimed from the sea in past centuries and now cultivated. In medieval times Rye and Winchelsea stood on their hillocks as fortified seaports; but today they are 2 miles from the sea, and wide pastures stretch where French warships once sailed to attack them.

MINIATURE RAILWAY *The Romney, Hythe and Dymchurch Railway takes holiday passengers 14 miles from Dungeness to Hythe. Its steam engines are miniature replicas of historic locomotives*

Appledore
This peaceful village on a low ridge overlooking Romney Marsh was once, like so many other places in the area just inland from the coast, a flourishing port on the estuary of the River Rother. The Danes brought 250 ships up the river to winter here in AD 892. The course of the Rother was altered by a storm in the 13th century. Later the village became a market town. Its church was partly destroyed by the French in the 13th and 14th centuries and later rebuilt.

Benenden
This trim and secluded village, set among hopfields on a high spot of the Weald, is notable for its village green, with old timbered houses, chestnut trees and a cricket pitch. Hemsted Park is now the home of Benenden School for girls.

Brookland
A village which was once an island in Walland Marsh. Its church has an unusual three-tiered belfry, separated from the church and made of massive wood beams salvaged from coastal wrecks. Inside, the church has some unusual features, including a lead font bearing the signs of the zodiac.

Camber
One of the finest stretches of pure sand and sand dunes in England, with safe bathing. Camber remained little known for years because the sand was constantly shifting in the variable winds of this draughty corner of the coast. Now the sand is being held by grass planted by the Forestry Commission, and windbreaks are being grown, so the area is developing into a major holiday area. There are weekend bungalows and a 'village' for self-catering holidaymakers, with its own heated indoor swimming pool. Camber is a good place for spotting seabirds and migrants. Across the estuary of the Rother is the ruined 16th-century Camber Castle.

Dungeness
In complete isolation at the tip of Denge Marsh is a mammoth nuclear power station on a lonely, flat headland of shingle which the Channel tides are still extending. The structure 300 yds offshore is a sea-water intake for the power station. Fishing from the shore is excellent, but strong currents make bathing and boating hazardous. There is an old lighthouse and a new one, a 12,000-acre bird reserve and a bird observatory which has recorded more than 200 species in ten years.

Dymchurch
An old smuggling port, now a promenade with plenty of parking space flanking vast stretches of sand. One of the Martello Towers, built to guard the sluices that control the water level on the marsh, has been restored, complete with a cannon mounted on a rotating platform, for use as a museum.

THE MARSH FROG

The loud croaking of the marsh frogs is a familiar sound on the Romney Marsh in the spawning season from April to July. The marsh frog, which grows to 5 in. long, is the largest frog in Europe. The species was introduced to the area in 1935 when a zoologist, Percy Smith, who lived on the Marsh, set free 12 specimens imported from Hungary in a pond in his garden. The frogs escaped and soon spread throughout the marsh, but they are not found anywhere else in Britain, despite attempts to breed them

DRAINAGE DITCHES *Local landowners in the Romney Marsh area still pay for the upkeep of the dikes, which drain the marshland reclaimed from the sea over the centuries*

BEACH LUGGER *The boat's overlapping planks withstand hauling over shingly beaches*

IVYCHURCH *The 14th-century St George's Church, with a tower 100 ft high dwarfing the tiny village round it, is one of two so-called 'Cathedrals of the Marshes'*

Lydd
A busy small town whose 14th-century church is the second in the area to be known as the 'Cathedral of the Marshes'. It has a panel of mounted 16th-century brasses, and a 15th-century screen. The tower is 130 ft high. The town gave its name to the explosive lyddite, which was first tested on ranges near by in 1888.

New Romney
The largest town of the marsh, an ancient Cinque Port at the former sea outlet of the Rother, which changed its course during the 13th century to reach the coast near Rye. Old Romney is an unspoilt village 2 miles to the west. It has a 13th-century timber-roofed church. At New Romney are the headquarters and museum of the Romney, Hythe and Dymchurch Railway, built in 1929. Its engines are replicas, one-third full size, of London North Eastern expresses and other locomotives.

Rye
A lively but fairly unspoilt town, once a hill fort with formidable ramparts almost ringed by the sea and a target for attack by French raiders. The sea began to recede in the late 16th century, but the town has never lost its character and individuality. The steep cobbled street leading to the old Mermaid Inn, which opened in 1420, is a living survival of the past, when Rye was an important port.

The Church of St Mary, dating back to 1120, has a remarkable clock; few would suspect that its ancient-looking 'Quarter Boys'—cherubic figures which strike the quarter hours, but not the hours—were replaced by fibre-glass facsimiles in 1970. The originals, worn beyond repair, are on display inside the church. The 18th-century Lamb House was the home of Henry James, the novelist. The arcaded town hall dates from 1742, and there are numerous old houses in Mermaid Street, Church Square, Watchbell Street and High Street. Ypres Tower, once the home of the d'Ypres family and later a prison, is now a museum. From here and from the adjoining Gun Garden there is a good view across the marsh to the modern harbour of Rye—a few yachts, a chandler's shop and an inn on the shingle where the road ends.

Small Hythe
The exquisite half-timbered Smallhythe Place, built in 1480, was the home of the actress Ellen Terry, who died in 1928. She was a friend of the playwright Bernard Shaw, who wrote a part in *Captain Brassbound's Conversion* for her. The house is now a memorial museum containing costumes worn by the actress.

Tenterden
An attractive town on the edge of the Weald, important as a wool-trading centre in medieval times. The tall 15th-century church tower is a notable landmark, and there are many fine 18th-century houses in the wide, green-fringed main street. William Caxton, the father of English printing, is said to have been born in Tenterden in 1472.

Winchelsea
This is England at its best: an orderly and picturesque town with an air of complete peace, set on the opposite hill to Rye. Old houses have been neatly whitened, and huge climbing roses and gnarled branches of wisteria decorate tile-hung façades and trim porches. The original town (its name means 'the shingle island on the levels') was submerged in the 13th century, and a new town was built by Edward I on its present site.

The king laid out the town to a regular grid pattern—England's first town planning. As a result, there are none of the narrow streets which might be expected from the town's medieval origins, but instead wide avenues at right angles to each other. Three gates of the original walled town still stand; within them the original layout can still be traced, though only a fraction of the town Edward I planned was built. The nave of the present church was the chancel of the original minster which, because of repeated French raids, was never finished. On the new coastline, 2 miles south, there is a pebble beach where a wall keeps back the sea.

MERMAID INN *Rye's famous inn is the town's largest medieval building. As late as Georgian days smugglers used to sit drinking at the inn with their pistols on the table, unchallenged by the law*

DEFENDERS AND INVADERS

The south-east corner of England has been the invaders' gateway to Britain from pre-Christian times. Some six centuries before the Romans landed, Celtic tribesmen from northern Europe used this gateway. The Romans under Julius Caesar made two landings at Walmer in 55 and 54 BC, but soon left again. The legions invaded in force in AD 43, and stayed for 400 years. Towards the end of the Roman occupation, invading tribes of Angles and Saxons arrived, their landfall made easy by the coastline's many natural harbours. Later came Viking and Norman invasions. Each wave of newcomers threw up defences against the next likely invaders, and the area is rich in the remains of fortifications built to strengthen the natural barrier of the English Channel. In modern times the South-East has been the approach route for airborne raiders—the Luftwaffe—during the 1940 Battle of Britain.

ROMAN REMAINS *Richborough Fort (above) is the supposed landing-spot for the main Roman invasion of England, when the legions of Emperor Claudius under Aulus Plautius arrived in* AD *43. They thrust inland to Canterbury, and their fort at Richborough became a base for operations in the South-East. The Romans built two lighthouses at Dover during the first century* AD. *The lighthouses guided ships into the harbour and served as watchtowers against attack. One lighthouse or pharos (left) still stands*

PEVENSEY CASTLE *The Romans gave Britain her first defence system. Ten major forts were built to guard the main harbours, and each had a garrison and a detachment of the fleet based on it. Among them was a fort at Pevensey, of which the walls (foreground) still survive. The sacking of Rome by the Goths led to the recall of Roman troops in* AD *410, and the shore forts fell into disuse. A few of them, including Pevensey, were used by King Alfred during his struggle with the Danes in the 9th century. After the Norman Conquest, William the Conqueror realised the strategic importance of Pevensey and built a castle (background) within the walls of the old Roman fort. The prime purpose of William's chain of south-east castles was to overawe the native population*

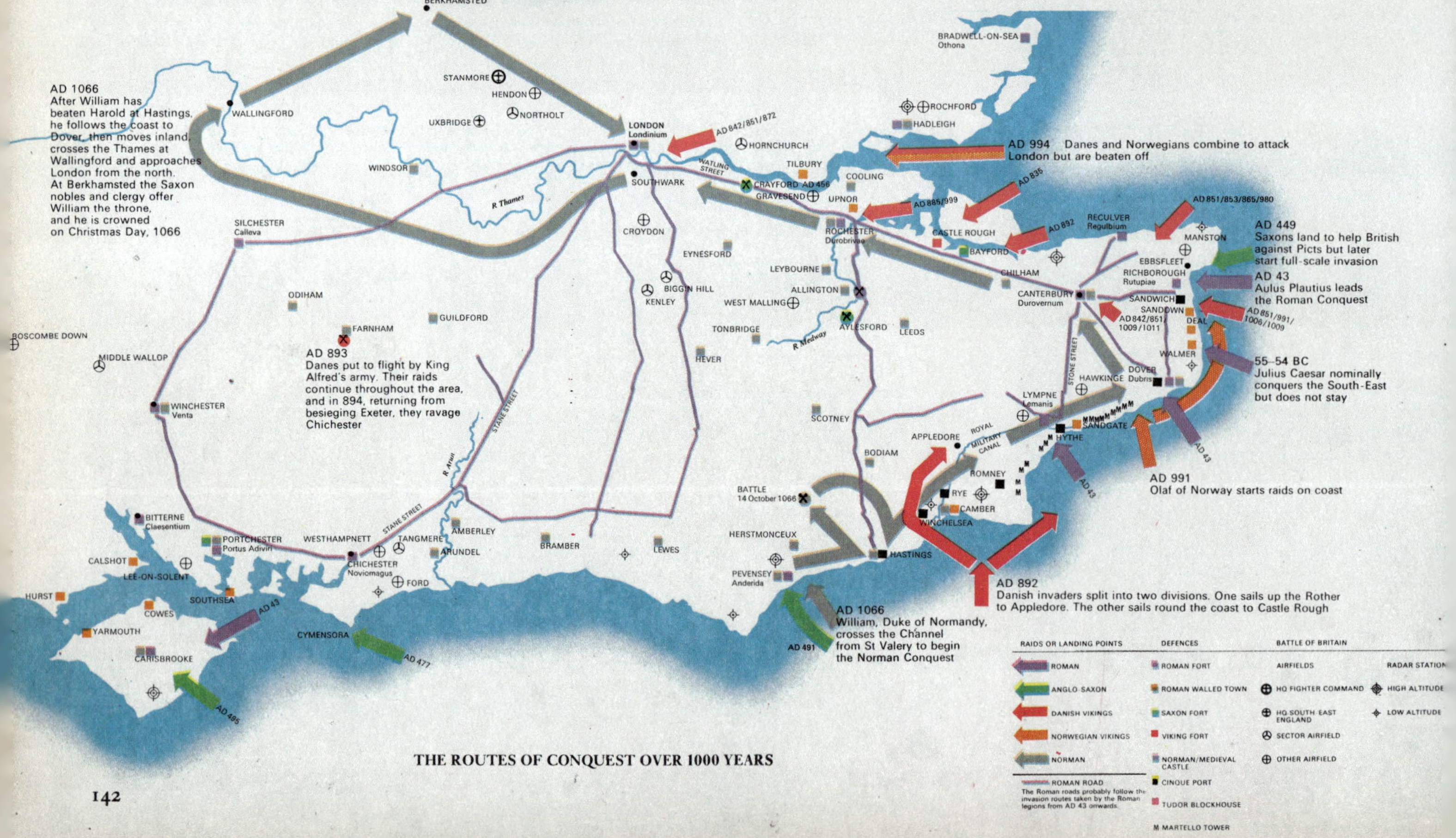

THE ROUTES OF CONQUEST OVER 1000 YEARS

HEVER CASTLE *From the reign of Henry II (1154–89) no baron was allowed to build a castle without permission from the king, and central government began to replace the feudal system introduced by the Normans. Nobles continued to build castles for prestige. In 1272, the year of Edward I's accession, Sir Stephen de Penchester obtained a licence to convert his house at Hever to a castle, and c. 1340 a licence to make further alterations was granted to William de Hever. In 1462 the castle was bought by the Boleyn family, who rebuilt much of it. Hever was the scene of Henry VIII's courtship of Anne Boleyn, his second wife and the mother of Elizabeth I. The main living quarters were over the entrance (above), which was defended by a drawbridge, three portcullises and two iron-studded doorways*

DEAL CASTLE *Henry VIII's break with Rome in 1531 brought fears that the great Roman Catholic powers in Europe might band together and invade Britain. As a result, some 20 powerful artillery forts were built along the south coast. The low-lying coastal area around Deal and the flanks of Romney Marsh were regarded as particularly vulnerable areas, and five castles were quickly built—at Deal, at Sandown near Deal, at Walmer, at Sandgate near Folkestone, and at Camber. Deal was one of the most powerful of these, and is among the best preserved today. It consists of a round, three-storey keep from which jut six two-storey bastions. These are ringed by six semi-circular one-storey bastions, on which the castle's main armament was mounted. The entire fortress is surrounded by a broad moat, which was not meant to hold water, of the same Tudor rose shape. The entrance was approached by a drawbridge and defended by a portcullis, and the entrance passageway had holes in its roof through which attackers could be fired upon from overhead. The basement of the outer bastions has a gallery pierced by more than 50 gunports from which guns could be fired at attackers trying to cross the moat*

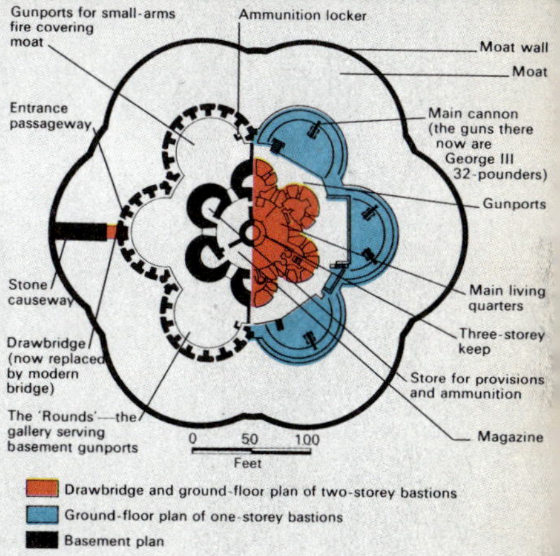

CINQUE PORTS *The seal confirming Hastings as one of the original Cinque Ports shows one of the sturdy, manoeuvrable boats which, in the 12th century, made Cinque Ports' seamen masters of the English Channel. Medieval kings relied on the coastal ports to provide ships and men to defend Britain's coasts. In return the ports were granted special privileges, such as the right to hold their own courts and to keep the revenue from fines. As well as Hastings, the original Cinque Ports were Sandwich, Dover, Romney and Hythe. Seamen from these ports, and other ports added later, sailed against the French and transported troops across the Channel to the kings' possessions in Normandy, Anjou and Aquitaine. From the 14th century onwards the Cinque Ports began to lose their power as their harbours silted up*

MARTELLO TOWERS *As a precaution against invasion by Napoleon in the early 19th century, 74 small forts were built along the coast from Folkestone to Seaford. Several still stand at the eastern end of the strip. Brick-built, with a gun mounted on a revolving platform on top (right), they were about 30 ft high, 25 ft in diameter, and had walls about 6 ft thick. The towers were two-storeyed; the lower part was for ammunition and general stores, and the upper part housed a garrison of about 24 men. Martello towers were named after a fort of this type at Cape Mortella in Corsica, which successfully held off a British attacking force in 1794. Napoleon never put to the test either the towers or the Royal Military Canal built at the same time, which zigzags behind Romney Marsh from Hythe to Winchelsea*

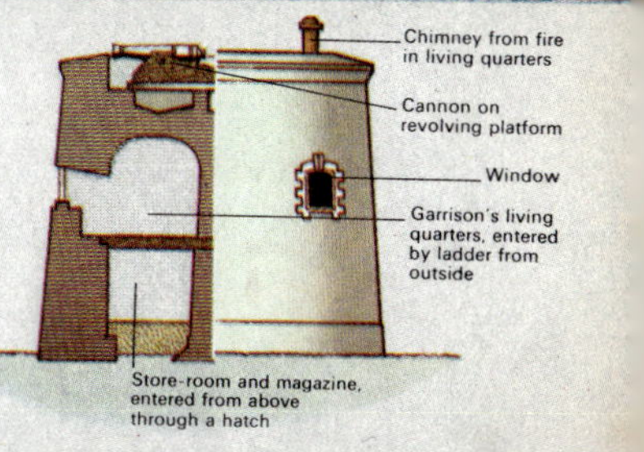

Coastline of the white cliffs

Angling Sea fishing at Folkestone, Deal and Dover.

Sailing Deal and Folkestone have sailing clubs. Regatta week at Deal is in mid-July and at Folkestone in the first week of July.

Walking Nature trails at Hothfield Common near Ashford (heath and bog) and at Wye and Crundale Downs.

Motor Sport Lydden Circuit, 5 miles from Dover on A2, has motor cycle or car racing most weekends.

Places to see *Crabble Watermill*, River: Easter; and Spring Bank Hol. to Sept., Wed. and Sat. afternoons, Sun. *Deal Castle*: daily, except Sun. mornings Oct. to Mar. *Dover Castle*: daily, except Sun. mornings Oct. to Mar. *Dover Museum*: weekdays except Wed. *Godinton House*: afternoons; Easter Sat., Sun. and Mon., also Sun. June to Sept. *Lympne Castle*, near Hythe: Apr., May, June and Oct., Wed. and Sun. afternoons; July, Aug. and Sept., daily. *Roman Painted House*, Dover: Mar. to Nov., daily except Mon. *Saltwood Castle*: June and July, Sun. and Bank Hol. afternoons; Aug., Tues. to Fri. and Sun. afternoon. *Walmer Castle*: daily, but closed Sun. morning, Oct. to Mar., and when Lord Warden is in residence.

Cross-Channel ferries Services from Dover and Folkestone to Boulogne, Calais, Ostend and Zeebrugge. Hovercraft car ferry, Dover to Calais and Boulogne. Coach-Air Services from Ashford Airport, near Lympne, to Ostend; to Beauvais, for Paris; and to Montpellier via Clermont-Ferrand.

Information centres Harbour Street, Folkestone. Tel. Folkestone 58594. Information Office, Town Hall, Dover. Tel. Dover 206941. Tourist Information centre, Townwall Street, Dover. Tel. Dover 205108.

The North Downs end at the sea in the famous white cliffs of Dover, looking out across the shortest sea route between Britain and the Continent. A coastline whose role for centuries was to present the first line of defence against invaders is today the gateway to Britain for tourists from overseas, for Britons returning from continental holidays—and even for French and Belgian day trippers.

Coastal ports, once fortified under a succession of rulers, now each go their own way. Dover is a huge passenger port, and thousands of people use its car ferry services to and from the Continent every week. Folkestone, also a ferry port, is adding light industry to its main business of providing for English holiday-makers; there are fine stretches of sand and shingle, and good shrimping and sea angling all along the coast. Deal is a Londoner's weekend retreat, and a splendid spot for shore fishing. Hythe stays quiet and dignified, catering, by tradition, for retired people seeking fresh air and rest.

Despite the surviving evidence of defence installations over the centuries and considerable modern development, there are still good coastal walks. There is good walking country, too, inland towards Ashford and Wye where the downs have a wealth of prehistoric remains and extensive views across rich valleys.

FOLKESTONE HARBOUR *Fishing vessels and cruisers find safe anchorage not far from the pier used by cross-Channel ferries*

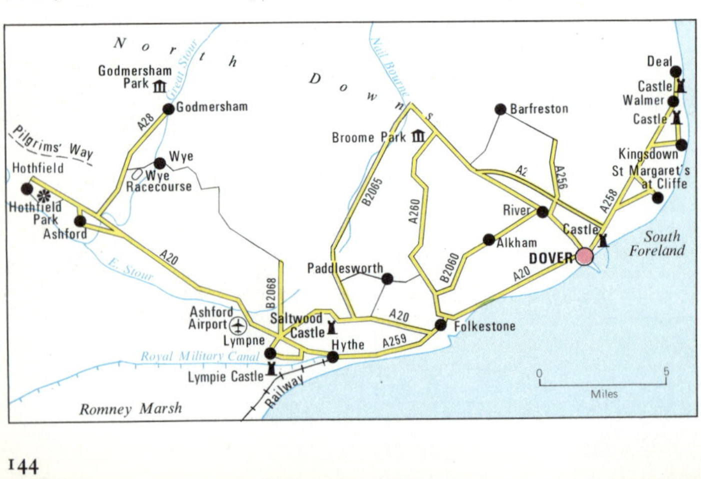

Alkham
A village in a quiet, secluded valley behind Dover, among elm trees and rolling chalk hills. It is notable for its 'nailbourne'—a stream which appears and disappears for no known reason. Legend says that disaster is imminent when it appears.

Ashford
A shopping centre which still has many medieval houses despite an expanding industrial area, based originally on the railway workshops. It is a central point for visiting numerous attractive villages. Godinton House, 2 miles north-west, has curved gables, stands in a park and dates from 1628.

Barfreston
The village church, built in 1080 of flint and Caen stone, is notable for the rich stone carvings on its interior walls. The carvings, which date from *c.* 1180, surround the doors and windows in long friezes of fantastic complexity, with leaves intertwining round angels, human heads and strange animals.

Deal
Its past importance as a Channel port is recalled by the endless pageant of ships visible from the sea-front as they pass close inshore to avoid the Goodwin Sands. The Sands are 5 miles offshore; waves can be seen breaking on them at low tide, and there are cruises out to them in summer. The town is a good centre for fishing, and has a pebble beach and many Georgian houses. Deal Castle, in the shape of a Tudor rose with rounded gun emplacements, was built by Henry VIII. A similar castle at Walmer, 1 mile south, is the official residence of the Lord Warden of the Cinque Ports. A plaque marks the spot where Julius Caesar is said to have landed in Britain in 55 BC. There is a bracing 5-mile cliff walk southwards to St Margaret's Bay; watch out for warning signs indicating dangerously crumbly stretches of the cliff edge.

Dover
Much of Dover has been rebuilt since the Second World War. It is an efficient port now, with handsomely built modern passenger terminals. Up by the castle, in what is left of old Dover, is a splendid park, a reminder of quieter and slower days.

The great castle was built by the Normans in the 12th century, using Roman foundation stones. They left intact the stone Roman *pharos*, or lighthouse—the earliest in Britain—which still stands today as a survivor of the Roman walled city of Dubris. The road to Canterbury still follows the route of the Roman Watling Street.

Crabble Mill, at River, two miles north-west of Dover, is a watermill that was built during the Napoleonic Wars to grind flour for the local garrison. It was recently restored to working order.

Folkestone
One of the most lovable of Britain's seaside resorts, and one of the prettiest. The Old Town is a picturesque harbour

CLIFF HOMES *Cranes work on East Cliff, Dover, to stop chalk from falling on to houses in Athole Terrace. The 200-year-old buildings have cellars cut back into the cliff*

DOVER SOLE

One of the best of all European flatfish takes its name from the Channel port, though the so-called Dover sole is caught widely in the southern North Sea. It is usually about 12 in. long, and a large fish can weigh 6 lb. The 'Lemon sole' is a different species, a member of the plaice family, found in deeper waters and identifiable by its larger size and its dark brown, orange or green markings. Local hotels make a speciality of sole dishes. French recipes abound, involving elaborate garnishes; but local people know that fresh Dover sole are delicious without additions and simply grill them

area with narrow cobbled streets, and the harbour is still a working harbour for cross-Channel steamers and fishing boats. The Leas, a beautifully laid-out cliff walk, is ablaze with colour whenever flowers can bloom.

In the Church of St Mary is a window in memory of William Harvey, the man who discovered how blood circulates, who was born in Folkestone in 1578. To the east is The Warren, a rugged landslip basin between high cliffs and the water's edge, with rare plants, hundreds of trees and shrubs, and fossils. From The Warren there are cliff paths eastwards to Dover.

Godmersham

An unobtrusive village on the River Stour with an early Norman church. Jane Austen often stayed with her brother at Godmersham Park and she used it as the background for her novel *Mansfield Park*. There are good walks through the park along the river bank.

Hothfield

A small village next to a 250-acre common with superb views—a natural picnic area and the starting point of a Nature Trail. The 13th-century church is in Hothfield Park, and contains a magnificent monumental tomb in

BLÉRIOT MEMORIAL *A granite shape in North Fall Meadow, Dover, marks the site where Louis Blériot landed on July 25, 1909 after making the first cross-Channel flight*

memory of Sir John Tufton who, in 1603, rebuilt the church after it had been destroyed by lightning in 1598.

Hythe

Hythe is a charming little town which reached its moment of importance as a Cinque Port and has been content since to rest and live well. There are attractive winding lanes and old houses perched on the hillside.

The crypt of St Leonard's Church contains a macabre mystery in the form of 600 human skulls and 8000 thigh bones which scientists say are of a different type from any found in Britain except in London's Spitalfields market. The Spitalfields' bones are of Roman date, while the Hythe bones date from the 14th and 15th centuries. Furthermore, these Hythe people were 3 in. shorter than the average for Englishmen.

Hythe today has a sea-front which is pleasant in good weather, but rough when the gales blow and the sea comes over the top. Through the town runs the Royal Military Canal, built to guard against Napoleon's expected invasion in the 19th century. The canal, lined in the town with trees and flowers, is popular for fishing, and a water pageant is held on it every other year.

At Saltwood, 1 mile north, are the ruins of an early Norman castle which was damaged by an earthquake in the late 16th century. The four knights who murdered Thomas Becket stayed at the castle on the night before the crime.

Lympne

The name is a corruption of the Roman name Lemanis, and this village was once a port used by the legions occupying the fortress now called Stutfall Castle, a ruin on high ground to the south. There is a 13th-century church with a massive Norman tower. The little airfield, a ferry terminus for planes to France, is now called Ashford Airport, though Ashford is 10 miles away.

Paddlesworth

The road from Folkestone climbs a steep slope to this little village behind the town, with wonderful views southwards over the coast in the Hythe area. It is a narrow road, but there are places for cars to pass. In the village is one of the smallest churches in Britain, measuring only 56 ft long by 11 ft wide and dating back to Saxon times.

St Margaret's at Cliffe

A cliff-top village, with weather-boarded houses and a fine Norman church which has early ships carved on some of its pillars. A steep lane, with a hairpin bend, plunges 400 ft down to the shore of St Margaret's Bay, the arrival point for cross-Channel swimmers. To the north is a memorial to the Dover Patrol, the destroyer fleet which during the First World War protected the supply routes of the British Army in France.

BARFRESTON *A bell in a yew tree calls worshippers to the church without a belfry*

Wye

This quiet market town bursts into life in the early spring for the Wye races. It is an attractive place, with fine old houses. Wye College, dating partly from the 15th century, is the agricultural college of London University, specialising in research to improve the standards of British farming. There is a good walk northwards to Olantigh. Olantigh Towers was originally a Georgian manor, dating from 1762, but it was burnt down in 1903 and subsequently rebuilt in the same style. The route continues along the River Stour to Godmersham, with views of the North Downs on both sides of the river valley.

Along the 'Pilgrims' Way'

BELL HARRY TOWER *Canterbury Cathedral's central tower, built in the 15th century, was named after the great bell it houses*

Angling There is sea fishing in Sandwich Bay, and freshwater fishing in Reed Pond and the River Stour at Sandwich, Canterbury and Fordwich. There are trout in stretches of the Stour north of Canterbury.

Cricket Cricket Week at the Kent County Club's main ground at Canterbury is in early Aug.

Events Canterbury Carnival is in late Aug., the Cathedral Festival Week in early June. Marlowe Theatre, Canterbury, has music and drama productions Apr. to Jan.

Places to see *Chilham Castle*, gardens and *Battle of Britain Museum*: afternoons, except Mon. and Fri., Easter to mid-Oct. *Howletts*, Bekesbourne: zoo park: daily. *Museum of Canterbury*, Poor Priests' Hospital, Stour Street, Canterbury: weekdays, but afternoons only Oct. to Mar. *Richborough Castle*, Roman site and Museum: daily, except Sun. mornings Oct. to Mar. *Roman Pavement*, Butchery Lane, Canterbury: weekdays, Apr. to Sept.; weekday afternoons, Oct. to Mar. *Royal Museum and Art Gallery* and *The Buffs Regimental Collections*, High Street, Canterbury: weekdays. *Westgate Museum*, St Peter's Street, Canterbury: weekdays, Apr. to Sept.; weekday afternoons, Oct. to Mar. The 'Invicta' steam engine, designed by Stephenson, is in Dane John Garden, Canterbury.

Information centre Sidney Cooper Centre, St Peter's Street, Canterbury. Tel. Canterbury 66567.

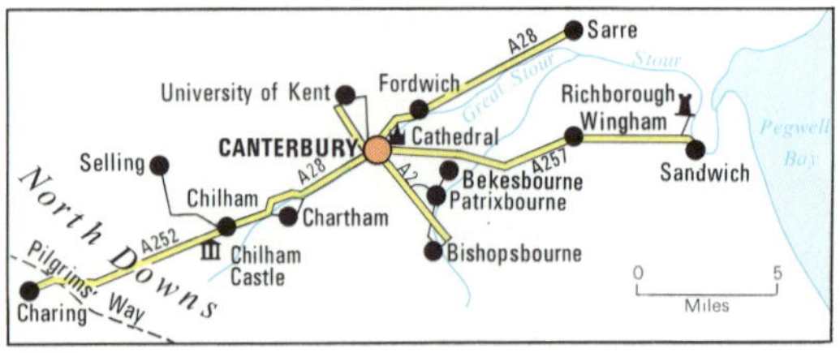

The city of Canterbury, cradle of Christianity in Saxon England, stands on a site that had already been occupied for 350 years when the Romans arrived there in AD 43. Advancing westwards from their landing point on the south side of Pegwell Bay, they found a settlement of the Belgae tribe at a key crossing point on the River Stour, and turned it into their encampment fortress of Durovernum.

The long grey cathedral that dominates the city is the Mother Church of Anglicans throughout the world. It dates from Norman times, and for 350 years after the murder of Thomas Becket in the cathedral in 1170 it was the destination of countless pilgrims. An ancient trackway dating from pre-Roman times runs along the high ridge of the North Downs. Traditionally the route has become known as the Pilgrims' Way, though modern historians doubt whether medieval pilgrims really used this route to travel from Winchester to Canterbury. Today the track is part of a long-distance footpath, the North Downs Way, and from its heights there is a wide view of rich pasture and cornfields northwards towards the coast on one side, and hops and orchards southwards through the Weald on the other.

Canterbury's first cathedral was built in AD 597, when St Augustine arrived from Rome in the Saxon town of Cant-wara-byrig—'the borough of the men of Kent'—to baptise King Ethelbert of Kent and so pave the way for the conversion of all England to Christianity. Nothing survives today of the cathedral that Augustine built, though there is Saxon as well as Norman work in the ruins of nearby St Augustine's Abbey. The present cathedral was begun in 1067, when Lanfranc, Abbot of Caen, was Archbishop of Canterbury. In 1174, four years after the murder of Thomas Becket, Henry II walked barefoot to the cathedral in penance; it was the king's words 'who will deliver me from this turbulent priest?' which had provoked four of his knights to commit the murder.

In the same year the choir was gutted by fire. Rebuilding began as pilgrims flocked to the shrine of the murdered Becket, and soon the great cathedral assumed its present majesty under the guidance of William de Sens, who designed the new choir and apse, and Henry Yevele, who designed the nave.

The cathedral remained a destination for pilgrims for more than 350 years until Henry VIII's Dissolution of the Monasteries when, in 1538, the shrine

CHARING *This town of timbered houses, probably once a halt for pilgrims, lies on the scenic 'route of the five Cs', which also passes Challock, Chilham and Chartham on its way to Canterbury*

CHILHAM *Tudor houses—including one with a bell tower, still called Pilgrims' Cottage—line the village street beside a 17th-century castle and an old inn once used by smugglers*

Bishopsbourne
A pretty village in the Stour Valley. The novelist Joseph Conrad lived in what is now the rectory, from 1919 until his death in 1924.

Charing
There are the remains of an Archbishop's palace where Cranmer lived and where Henry VIII stayed on his way to Calais in 1520 to negotiate with Francis I at the 'Field of the Cloth of Gold' in Artois. The tower of the parish church dates from the 14th century. There are good views across the Weald from the top of Charing Hill. From here the Pilgrims' Way can be followed for 10 miles to the north-west, past Hollingbourne and Thurnham to Detling.

COLLEY HILL *Yews line the way along the hillside near Redhill*

BOX HILL *The way across the Mole*

NORTH DOWNS WAY *A public footpath follows the crest of the North Downs for 141 miles across Surrey and Kent. The new route coincides in places with the traditional Pilgrims' Way*

of Thomas Becket was destroyed. The cathedral has suffered later blows, too. In the Civil War much stained glass and tapestry perished, and in the Second World War bombs fell on the cathedral precincts.

Canterbury Cathedral's surviving medieval stained glass is among the finest in the country, and there are modern windows, too, by the Hungarian artist Erwin Bossanyi. Among the cathedral's other principal features are the Norman crypt, the oldest part of the building and the largest Norman crypt in Britain; the Trinity Chapel, in which are the site of the original shrine of Thomas Becket and the tombs of Henry IV and Edward, the Black Prince; and the lovely 12th-century choir, with its 14th-century screen.

The city of Canterbury has preserved some of its medieval character. Long stretches of the town walls survive, built in the 13th and 14th centuries on Roman foundations, and there are some lofty overhanging houses in the lanes leading to the great Christ Church Gate, the main entrance to the cathedral. The King's School, one of the oldest in England, has an unusual exterior Norman staircase; and the 14th-century West Gate, the only survivor of seven former gates to the city, has a museum of arms and armour. The Marlowe Theatre commemorates the playwright Christopher Marlowe, who was born in the city in 1564 and educated at The King's School. From Tyler Hill, to the north, the University of Kent, founded in 1961, looks down on a city born 2000 years ago.

Eastwards, in the valley of the River Stour between Canterbury and the coast, the land changes dramatically to a flat area of rich farmland and narrow, almost forgotten roads. This is an area little known even to many Kent people; it has charming old boarded cottages, inns and barns, many of them thatched, and streams overhung with willows.

DUNN STREET *Near Charing the North Downs Way runs through tall beeches before one branch turns north-east towards Canterbury, 12 miles away*

Chartham
A village in the Stour Valley, a good centre for fishing and the site of a large paper mill. The 14th-century church has one of the oldest sets of bells in Kent. Bigbury Camp, 2 miles north, is the site of an Iron Age settlement.

Chilham
A picturesque village with a magnificent central square surrounded by timbered black-and-white Tudor houses, among which stand the impressive gates to Chilham Castle. The castle was built in 1616. Today it houses a Battle of Britain museum. The gardens, laid out by Capability Brown, contain a Norman castle keep built on Roman foundations. The 15th-century church has a white marble monument by the sculptor Sir Francis Chantrey (1781–1841), who left his fortune to found the art collection which is now in London's Tate Gallery. Paths through Perry Wood, 2 miles north-west, lead to the village of Selling.

Fordwich
A village on the River Stour which was once the port for Canterbury. Today, although the river is tidal at Fordwich, it is navigable only by canoes. Small cruisers can be used from Grove Ferry, 4 miles downstream near Sarre. The partly-Norman Church of St Mary has a sculptured tomb in which, it is said, St Augustine once lay; the ancient timbered town hall preserves a medieval ducking-stool, used to duck 'scolds'.

Patrixbourne
A village of old houses, whose excellent modern neo-Georgian close is a model of contemporary development, in harmony with its older surroundings. The Norman church has some 16th-century stained glass from Switzerland.

Richborough
When Thanet was separated from the mainland by the wide Wantsum Channel, the Romans built forts at each entrance—Regulbium (Reculver) to the north and Rutupiae (Richborough) to the south. The walls of Richborough Fort, dwarfed by the cooling towers of a new power station, now look over fertile land where the channel has silted up. The old harbour was used in the Second World War as a landing-craft base at which was made much of the prefabricated 'Mulberry Harbour', towed to Normandy for the 1944 invasion.

Sandwich
This ancient Cinque Port still has great charm and character, though the sea is now 2 miles away. There are many reminders of the Flemish weavers who poured into Kent towards the end of the 16th century and built superb timbered houses. The Barbican is a medieval conical-towered gate where, until 1977, a toll was collected for crossing the River Stour. Wingham, 5 miles west, has a fine row of half-timbered houses in a wide main street that is sheltered by trees.

Holiday coast of north Kent

Angling Sea fishing from shore and boats at Whitstable, Ramsgate, Margate, Broadstairs and Herne Bay. Coarse fishing in the River Stour and Seasalter marshes, near Whitstable.

Sailing On the Swale and in the Medway Estuary; clubs at Sheerness, Conyer's Creek, Mercer's Wharf, Faversham Creek and Broadstairs. Championship at Herne Bay in July. Ramsgate has a marina.
Whitstable has a yachting week and holds the National Merlin Rocket Championship meeting, both in Aug.

Arts Broadstairs holds a Dickens Festival for one week in mid-June and a music festival in July.

Events Blessing of the sea ceremony at Margate in early Jan., and at Whitstable in July. There are carnivals at Birchington and Ramsgate (late July), Broadstairs, Whitstable and Herne Bay (early Aug.). Broadstairs also has an Anglo-French Festival in May and a water gala in mid-Aug.

Places to see *Bleak House*, Broadstairs: Apr. to Oct., afternoons. *Dickens House Museum*, Broadstairs: afternoons, early Apr. to late Oct.; also Tues. to Thur. evenings, June to Sept. *Drapers Mill*, Margate: May to Sept., Sun. afternoon. *Fleur de Lis Heritage Centre*, Faversham: weekdays, except Thur. afternoon. *Maison Dieu*, Ospringe, Faversham: weekdays, Sun. afternoon. *Model Village*, Ramsgate: Apr. to Oct., daily. *Powell Cotton (Natural History) Museum*, Birchington: Thur.; also Sun. and Wed., late Mar. to late Sept., and Tues. and Fri. mid-July to early Sept.

Information centres Marine Terrace, Margate. Tel. Thanet 20241. Council Offices, Richmond Street, Herne Bay. Tel. Herne Bay 66031. Information Office, 1 Tankerton Road, Whitstable. Tel. Whitstable 272233. Seafront Offices, Sheerness. Tel. Sheerness 2395. Pierremont Hall, Broadstairs. Tel. Thane 68399. Queen Street, Ramsgate. Tel. Thanet 51086.

The holiday resorts of north Kent thrive on their good sands, safe bathing and an enviable record for long hours of sunshine and low annual rainfall. They are lively towns, mixing the graceful charm of Regency houses and terraces with the ornate perkiness of Victorian Gothic. There is plenty of modern entertainment—Margate's 'Dreamland' amusement park covers 20 acres—while quiet hotels with splendid high-ceilinged rooms still specialise in the traditional type of English family holiday. Breezes off the North Sea attract yachtsmen in summer but turn to strong gales, with high seas, in winter.

The opening of the Dartford Tunnel in 1963 increased the summer population of this coast by making it easier to reach by car or coach from the Midlands. Most of the north Kent coastal towns have also a strong core of permanent residents, for this has been an increasingly popular residential area since railway travel brought it within easy reach of London commuters, the journey taking about an hour.

To the west the land is flat, with marshes around the estuaries of the Medway and the Swale. Eastwards, the coast rises to cliffs around the North Foreland Peninsula, which is bounded by Margate on the north and Ramsgate, whose harbour faces south-east.

There are two 'islands' on the coast. Sheppey ('Isle of Sheep') is cut off from the mainland by the narrow Swale Channel, which is crossed only by the Kingsferry Bridge; the island is a home for modern industries and a feeding ground for fat sheep. Thanet is today an island only in name; but in Roman times, and later when the Saxons made their first permanent settlement here in the 5th century, Thanet was separated from the mainland by the Rivers Stour and Wantsum, together forming a safe anchorage with direct access to the Thames Estuary at high tide.

RAMSGATE *The yacht marina, opened in 1965, can hold 120 boats. Ramsgate's harbour faces south-east and its inner basin is further protected from North Sea gales by electrically operated gates which are opened and closed at each high water. Cargo boats and pleasure steamers make Ramsgate a busy harbour*

Birchington
An attractive residential town, loved by children for holidays as it has sandy bays for swimming and pools at low tide for shrimping and prawning. There are chalk cliffs. A museum in Quex Park, 1 mile south, is devoted to big game in African and Indian settings.

Broadstairs
A popular residential and holiday resort, with several miles of sand in small bays beneath chalk cliffs, and an old town, with buildings round the jetty, that recalls Dickensian days. Bleak House, named after the novel, is where Dickens lived while he was writing *David Copperfield*. The town holds a Dickens Festival in mid-June. From the North Foreland lighthouse, $1\frac{1}{2}$ miles north, there is a good view of ships entering or leaving the Thames Estuary.

Eastchurch
A lonely spot on the Isle of Sheppey where Lord Brabazon and the Hon. C. S. Rolls made many flights in the pioneer days of aviation. Leysdown-on-Sea, 2 miles east, is a resort with caravans and a holiday camp.

Herne Bay
An increasingly popular residential area, especially for retired people. It has excellent sea-angling and sailing, and there is a 5-mile walk along the cliffs to Reculver Towers.

Lower Halstow
An isolated village on a creek of the Medway Estuary, set among cherry orchards, with an 11th-century church. In certain lights, morning and evening, the view of the marshes, with Thames barges sailing alongside the dike wall, is something to remember.

Lynsted
A restful village with timbered houses in cherry-orchard country. In the church are 17th-century monuments by an early English sculptor, Epiphanius Evesham. Nearby Doddington has some pretty cottages.

Margate
Blackpool in Kent—but without quite so much noise and heartiness. The huge 'Dreamland' amusement park, intended for children, is equally attractive to older visitors; it includes a ballroom and a cinema. There are magnificent sands, floral gardens, a long promenade

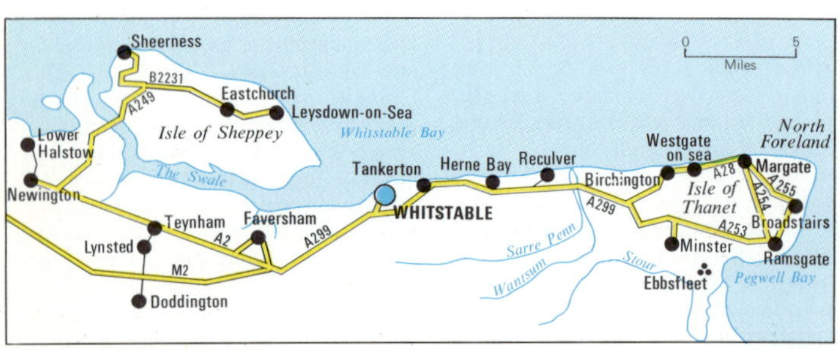

BLEAK HOUSE *Charles Dickens spent many summers at the castellated Fort House, once the home of captains of forts guarding Broadstairs harbour. The house, which Dickens called his 'airy nest', was later re-named Bleak House after his novel and is now a museum*

EBBSFLEET *The replica of a Viking boat, the Hugin, was sailed from Denmark in 1949. It rests at the site of 5th-century Saxon landings and near a new hovercraft terminal*

PEGWELL BAY *The wide sands stretching south of Ramsgate provide good hunting grounds at low tide for lug-worms, used as fishing bait, and for shrimps and cockles*

with a lido, and entertainments ranging from donkey rides to international wrestling. In the summer, there are 'no-passport' day trips to France. It was at Margate that the first bathing machines were used, as early as the middle of the 18th century when the town was called 'Bartholomew Fair by the Sea'. Neighbouring Westgate on Sea, more sedate, has two sandy bays. There is a good walk 3½ miles along the cliffs to Birchington.

Minster
Once an important market town, but now secluded and peaceful, set among fruit farms. It has one of the finest parish churches in Kent, including Norman work with Roman tiles and 15th-century choir stalls. There are the remains of an 11th-century abbey founded by monks from Canterbury.

Newington
Cherry growing is becoming more and more uneconomic, but there are still areas west of Canterbury where the cherry blossom is thick in the orchards; Newington, a village with a fine 15th-century church tower, is a good centre for a spring blossom tour.

Ramsgate
A holiday resort which lives in a state of intense but friendly rivalry with its neighbour Margate. The atmosphere of the two towns is quite different. Both have miles of safe sands and plenty of organised entertainment, but Ramsgate is more of an old-world and sea-going town. It is a major yachting centre, but its harbour surroundings still look like those of a small fishing port. Around its Royal Harbour and Yacht Marina the visitor can watch ships all day—including cargo boats as well as pleasure yachts and day-trip steamers. Sea-angling, from harbour or boats, is excellent; fishing boats can be hired for the day. There is a big open-air swimming pool by the sands, and a well-designed row of modern bathing chalets. At Ebbsfleet, on Pegwell Bay, 1 mile south, there is a hovercraft terminal, opened in 1969, and a modern replica of a Viking long boat of the type used by Saxon raiders who landed on this shore in AD 449.

Reculver
The twin towers of Reculver are a conspicuous landmark, deliberately preserved as a navigational guide for Thames Estuary shipping. They are the remains of a Norman church which was built on the site of a former Saxon church. Earlier still, *c.* AD 200, a Roman fort occupied the site, part of the defence camp of Regulbium at the northern end of the Wantsum.

Sheerness
The main town on the Isle of Sheppey and a naval centre since the time of Charles II, though modern changes in defence needs have reduced its importance. The sea front by Garrison Point provides a grandstand view of shipping in the Thames Estuary. A favourite naval inn, The Royal Fountain, is opposite the pier to which Nelson's body was brought home after Trafalgar.

Teynham
The first place in Kent where apples and cherries were systematically grown, in the reign of Henry VIII, and still a good starting place for a blossom-time tour through the Kent orchards in the spring.

Whitstable
A small port famous since Roman times for its oysters. Oyster dredgers are often at work, collecting the so-called 'Royal Whitstable Natives'. Whitstable has old streets, inns, shipyards and sail lofts, and is a good sporting centre for golf, fishing, swimming and sailing. Neighbouring Tankerton is a holiday centre with a mile-long parade and a long promontory of shingle and shell—'The Street'—uncovered at low tide.

SOUTH MIDLANDS

The South Midlands are at the heart of England. An ancient cross near the village of Meriden, just outside Coventry, marks the spot which many claim is the exact centre of the country. There is, however, none of the simple unity about the South Midlands that a central hub might imply. One viewpoint—the summit of the Worcestershire Beacon in the Malvern Hills—gives a clear impression of the contrasting themes which combine to form the South Midlands landscape.

South-west, the Cotswold Hills rise sharply. North-east, across the fields and villages of Warwickshire, a hazy skyline marks the sheep-grazing uplands of Northamptonshire and Leicestershire; and these, in turn, lead to fruitful fields and orchards. North are the fertile farmlands bordering Birmingham, the largest city in England after London. The panorama takes in slow-flowing rivers, and hills that just fail to attain the stature of mountains. One feature is common from eastern Leicestershire to southern Gloucestershire—the tall hedgerow elm, seen at its finest in Warwickshire where an ungrateful tradition has labelled it the 'Warwickshire weed'.

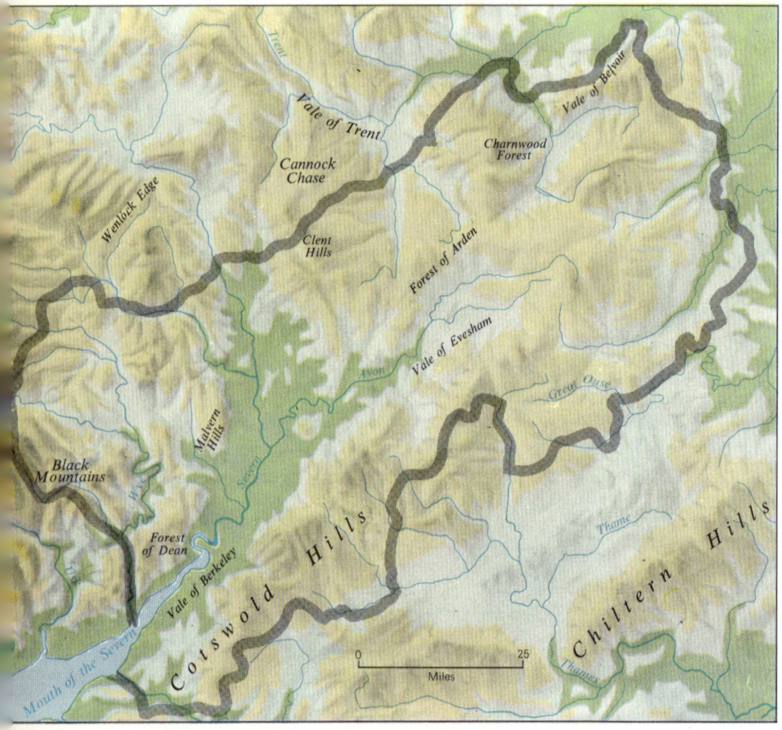

SHELTERING 'HORSESHOE' *The South Midlands vales are surrounded by a 'horseshoe' of hills and woodland. South-west are the Cotswolds; north, the forests of Arden and Charnwood; west, the Black Mountains, Malvern Hills and Dean and Wyre forests*

The South Midlands can justly claim to have played a leading role in shaping the destiny of the country—the many battles fought across its lands gave it the name 'Cockpit of England'. The Civil War began in a skirmish at Powick, near Worcester, and was ultimately settled by the victory of Cromwell's Ironsides in 1645 at Naseby, Northamptonshire, where an obelisk tells of 'the great and decisive battle fought in this field'. Two circular memorials mark the battlefield of Edgehill (1642) in Warwickshire. Other famous battles fought across the Midlands Plain

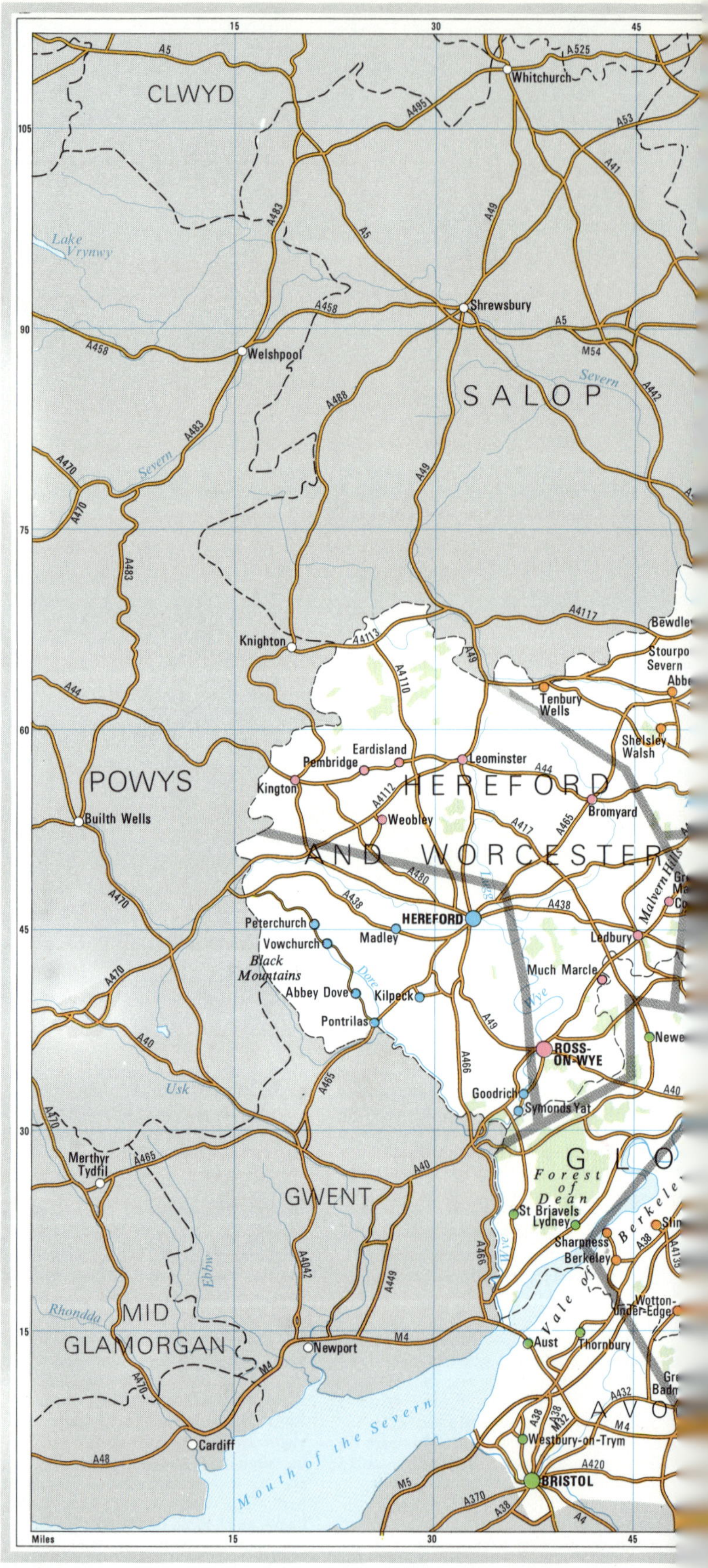

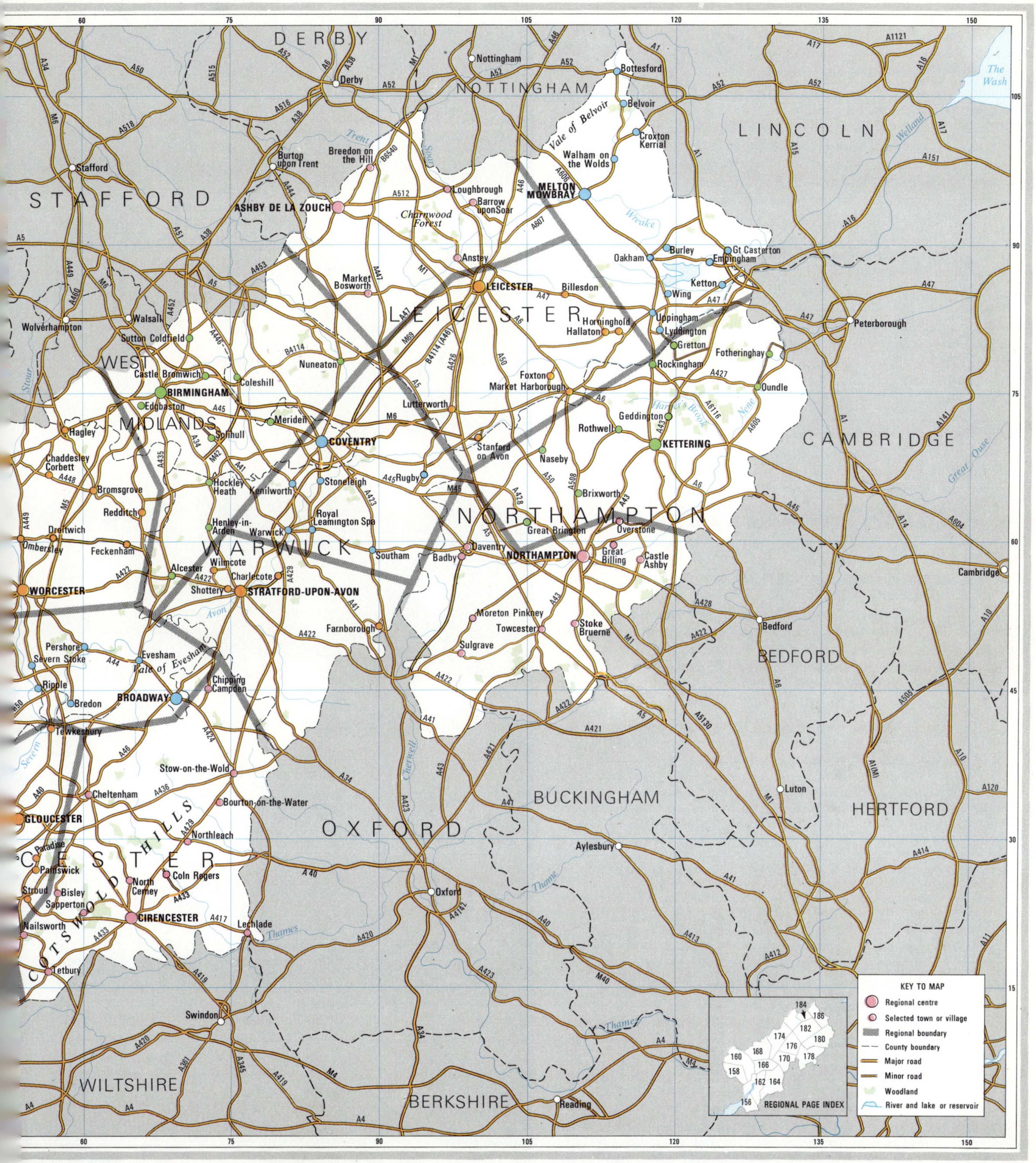

DERBY
NOTTINGHAM
STAFFORD
LINCOLN
LEICESTER
WEST MIDLANDS
WARWICK
NORTHAMPTON
CAMBRIDGE
BEDFORD
BUCKINGHAM
OXFORD
HERTFORD
GLOUCESTER
COTSWOLD HILLS
WILTSHIRE
BERKSHIRE
Nottingham
Derby
Stafford
Burton upon Trent
Breedon on the Hill
ASHBY DE LA ZOUCH
Loughbrough
Barrow uponSoar
Charnwood Forest
Anstey
LEICESTER
Market Bosworth
MELTON MOWBRAY
Bottesford
Belvoir
Vale of Belvoir
Croxton Kerrial
Walham on the Wolds
Wreake
Oakham
Burley
Gt Casterton
Empingham
Ketton
Wing
Uppingham
Lyddington
Gretton
Rockingham
Horninghold
Hallaton
Billesdon
Fotheringhay
Oundle
Peterborough
Foxton
Market Harborough
Geddington
Rothwell
KETTERING
Naseby
Brixworth
Nuneaton
Lutterworth
Wolverhampton
Walsall
Sutton Coldfield
Castle Bromwich
BIRMINGHAM
Edgbaston
Coleshill
Meriden
Solihull
Hagley
Chaddesley Corbett
Bromsgrove
Redditch
Hockley Heath
Kenilworth
COVENTRY
Stoneleigh
Rugby
Stanford on Avon
Royal Leamington Spa
Henley-in-Arden
Warwick
Droitwich
Ombersley
Feckenham
Alcester
Wilmcote
Charlecote
Shottery
STRATFORD-UPON-AVON
WORCESTER
Southam
Daventry
Badby
Great Brington
Overstone
NORTHAMPTON
Great Billing
Castle Ashby
Moreton Pinkney
Towcester
Stoke Bruerne
Sulgrave
Farnborough
Pershore
Severn Stoke
Evesham
Vale of Evesham
Ripple
Bredon
BROADWAY
Chipping Campden
Tewkesbury
Stow-on-the-Wold
Bourton-on-the-Water
Cheltenham
GLOUCESTER
Northleach
Paradise
Painswick
Coln Rogers
North Cerney
Stroud
Bisley
Sapperton
CIRENCESTER
Nailsworth
Lechlade
Tetbury
Swindon
Oxford
Aylesbury
Luton
Bedford
Cambridge
Reading
Trent
Soar
Avon
Severn
Stour
Cherwell
Thame
Thames
Welland
Nene
Harper's Brook
Great Ouse
The Wash
KEY TO MAP
Regional centre
Selected town or village
Regional boundary
County boundary
Major road
Minor road
Woodland
River and lake or reservoir
REGIONAL PAGE INDEX

include Evesham (1265), Northampton (1460), Tewkesbury (1471), Bosworth (1485) and Worcester (1651).

There are many other historical links. The boy king Henry III was crowned with his mother's bracelet in 1216 at Gloucester Cathedral, his father, King John, having lost the crown in The Wash. Forty-nine years later, in 1265, Henry III's forces killed Simon de Montfort, father of the English Parliament, in the battle of Evesham, which is commemorated by a monument in the grounds of Abbey Manor and by windows in St Lawrence's Church. A pillar opposite the Saxon mill at Guy's Cliff, near Warwick, shows where Piers Gaveston, a favourite and foster-brother of Edward II, was executed in 1312. The king himself was murdered in brutal fashion 15 years later at Berkeley Castle, where the death chamber is today a macabre showplace.

In November 1605, several of the Gunpowder Plotters fled from Dunchurch, in Warwickshire, crossed Worcestershire to Huddington Court, near Droitwich, and were eventually killed or captured at Holbeche House, near Dudley. Their picturesque 'Plot House' survives at Ashby St Ledgers, Northants. Battles of the Wars of the Roses are commemorated on inn signs at Tewkesbury, Gloucestershire; Mortimer's Cross, Hereford and Worcester; and Atherstone, Warwickshire.

Inn signs that record industrial history

Other inn signs throughout the South Midlands also recall a history—this time of local industry. At Hinckley, Leicestershire, where stockings are made, is The Golden Fleece; at Atherstone, Warwickshire, where hats are made, is The Hat and Beaver; at Worcester, famous for its glove-making, is The Glover's Needle. Alongside the car-manufacturing plants of Coventry and Birmingham there are other industries, too. Redditch, in Hereford and Worcester, makes needles and fishing-tackle, and Belbroughton makes scythes. At Loughborough, Leicestershire, is the largest bell foundry in Europe.

The eastern side of Leicestershire, one of the lesser-spoilt parts of Britain, is a beguiling place for the rambler, with walks in the shadows of great church spires at Langham and Ketton, and striking Norman work in several other churches, especially at Tickencote.

The Leicestershire countryside is notable for its red-brick villages, while Charnwood Forest's rugged outcrops suggest a 'little Wales'. The

HIGHER SUMMER TEMPERATURES THAN THE SOUTH

The South Midlands are relatively dry, with less than 175 rainy days each year against an average of just under 200 days for most of England. It has more frost and snow than the west, and spring comes late—temperatures do not reach 14–15°C (57–59°F) until April. But it is a warmer spring when it arrives. Summer temperatures are higher than in southern England, averaging 22°C (72°F) in July. They can reach 29°C (84°F) on the warmest day

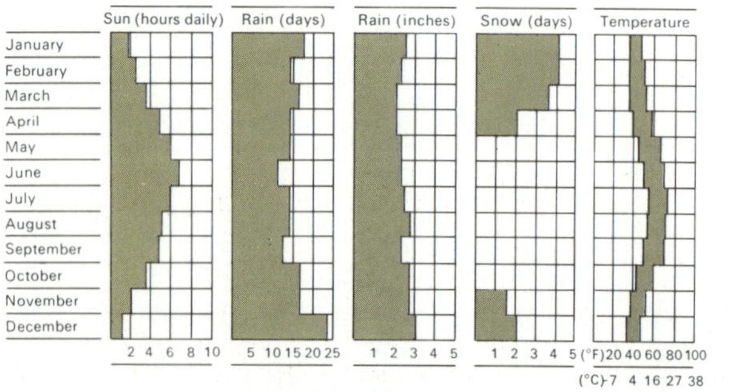

COTSWOLD PEACE *Idyllic Coln Rogers lies snugly among the meadowlands of the Coln Valley, in the Cotswolds. The village church, St Andrew's, is over 1000 years old and one of England's few surviving Saxon churches*

HOW THE MIDLANDS PLAIN BECAME THE 'COCKPIT OF ENGLAND'

A white rose grows in Bosworth Field where, nearly five centuries earlier, the White Rose of York was crushed in the final battle of the Wars of the Roses. Henry Tudor and a 10,000-strong army of Lancastrians were marching on London when, on August 22, 1485, Richard III and 12,000 Yorkists opposed them at Bosworth. The turning point in the Battle of Bosworth Field came when Lord Stanley, who was Henry Tudor's stepfather, deserted the king and threw in his forces on Henry's side. After two hours of hand-to-hand fighting the Yorkists were routed, leaving their king slain and 900 men dead or dying. Richard's crown was found in a thornbush. Stanley set it upon Henry's head and the Tudor dynasty was established. The battleground lies just west of the village of Sutton Cheney, 11 miles west of Leicester

bracken-clad Bradgate Park remains much as it was during the Middle Ages—a deer-inhabited moorland. The county has its own variety of gravestone—Swithland slate, the most durable of memorial stones. A memorial of another kind is the name of Robin-a-Tiptoe Hill, east of Leicester, which recalls the hanging of a sheep-stealer. The stately home of Staunton Harold shares lawns with a church beside a lake.

Forest setting used by Shakespeare

Northamptonshire was a county of windmills in less sophisticated days. Among its breezy pastures lies Sulgrave, where the stars and stripes of the American flag fly over the manor in which George Washington's ancestors lived for 100 years. Among Northamptonshire's oldest treasures are the Anglo-Saxon church at Brixworth, with its 13th-century tomb of John de Verdun, and the Norman castle at Rockingham.

Warwickshire is Shakespeare's county. The land south of his birthplace at Stratford-upon-Avon is known as the Feldon (from the Old English for open country) and the land to the north is known as the Arden (woodland). The Forest of Arden was the setting for Shakespeare's *As You Like It,* and in Packington Park modern Woodmen of Arden still practise the ancient skill of archery. Footpaths surround exquisite villages such as Welford-on-Avon and Aston Cantlow, where, according to tradition, Shakespeare's parents were married. Warwickshire's village churches hold many surprises, such as Ilmington's carvings of mice in the woodwork, Binton's memorial window to Scott of the Antarctic, and Temple Balsall's headstone to Henry Williams, composer of 'It's a Long Way to Tipperary'. Compton Wynyates is a Tudor house, seized by the Parliamentarians in 1644 during the Civil War and used as a garrison for 400 troops. After the war its owners, the Royalist Compton family, had to pay a £20,000 fine to get the house back.

The hardy villages of the Cotswolds

The Cotswold Hills dominate the eastern half of Gloucestershire and as far south as Bath in Avon. Sheltered, honey-coloured villages contrast with more exposed places such as Minchinhampton, with its common, and Stow-on-the-Wold, where, according to an ancient rhyme, 'the winds blow cold'. The Cotswold Edge is strewn with fossil shells deposited by the prehistoric sea that covered the Worcestershire Plain. But Gloucestershire is more than just the Cotswolds. To the west, the Vale of Berkeley leads seawards down the River Severn where fishermen trap salmon with outsize nets, and young eels are caught by the

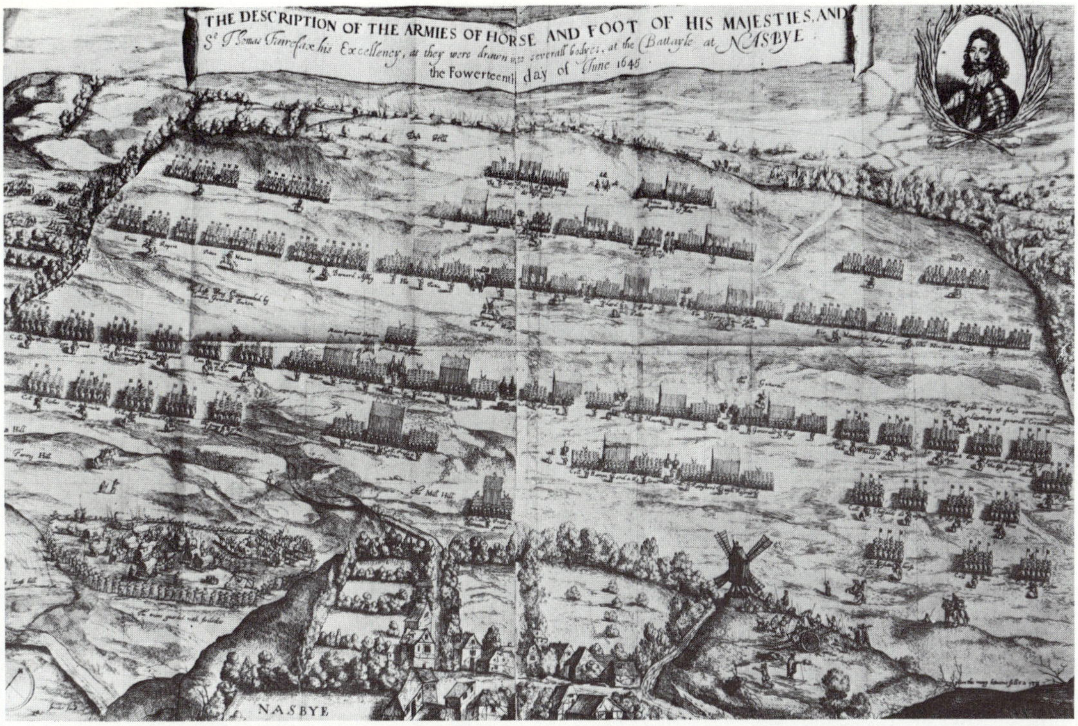

The destiny of England has more than once been decided on the fertile Midlands Plain, an area that became the 'Cockpit of England' because of its position across the approach route to London from the North. In the troubled Middle Ages, the Wars of the Roses (1460–85) were ended with Henry Tudor's victory at Bosworth Field. Later the Civil War (1642–5) was settled by Cromwell's victory on June 14, 1645, at Naseby, where a monument (top, right) marks the battlefield area. An engraving (above) made in 1647 shows the opposing forces—the Royalist army, commanded by Charles I and Prince Rupert at the top of the print, facing the Roundheads of Oliver Cromwell's New Model Army. The Royalists put 9000 men in the field against 13,000 Roundheads, but the battle went the king's way at first. Colonel Ireton's horse, on Cromwell's left, broke under the shock of Rupert's cavalry charge. But Rupert pursued Ireton's men for far too long, and by the time he returned to the battlefield, Cromwell had ordered a counter-charge which led to the Royalist infantry being trapped, and the day was won for Parliament. The king escaped, but his cause was doomed. A society known as the Sealed Knot adds an intriguing modern postscript to the Civil War. It recreates bygone battles (right), with its members wearing uniforms and carrying weapons modelled on those originally used

million. Beyond the Severn is the Forest of Dean, a little-known world of enchanting views and walks, with a tradition of iron-mining and charcoal-burning going back to prehistory.

Nature's mantle has fallen kindly on Hereford and Worcester. The orchards and market gardens of the Vale of Evesham, famous for Pershore plums, parade as tidy, regimented rows of trees and soft-fruit bushes—as pleasing to the eye as the hopfields of the fertile Teme Valley. Few English rivers offer such splendid cruising as the Severn and Avon, and the view of Bredon Hill from the Swan's Neck on the Avon is unparalleled in its tranquillity. The county has splendid towers at Worcester Cathedral, Evesham Abbey and Pershore Abbey; and it shares with Gloucestershire the 100 mile long Cotswold Way which gives a week of invigorating walking through a landscape that inspired Elgar to compose his *Introduction and Allegro for Strings*.

Apple orchards, woods and wild flowers

West of the Malvern Hills and the Worcester Plain the county stretches to the Welsh border. It is the country of the poet John Masefield, who was born at Ledbury; of half-timbered buildings in picturesque villages; and of cattle grazing in lush pastures. It is also an area of apple orchards—its cider industry rivals that of Devon and Somerset. The landscape almost everywhere is richly wooded, and in summer bright with flowers, including wild daffodils around Ledbury.

A network of waterways for cruising

Many of these counties are linked by canals—a means of communication that is of paramount importance to the South Midlands. Birmingham, at the crossroads of Telford's waterway system, has established a canal marina in the city centre, and there is a network of local waterways where cabin-cruisers can be hired, or holidays taken in the narrow-boats. Waterways include the Worcester and Birmingham Canal, which has the $1\frac{3}{4}$ mile long Wast Hill tunnel; the Oxford Canal; the Stratford Canal with its 12-mile southern section now in the care of the National Trust; the Staffordshire and Worcester Canal, joining the Severn in a picturesque basin at Stourport; and, striking through surprisingly remote country, the Leicester Canal from near Daventry to Leicester.

But whether a traveller is cruising the canals or rambling the hills, his eyes will invariably be drawn to the landscape that hovers invitingly to the west—the glorious border hills. It is a sight that inspired Housman to write 'A Shropshire Lad'.

Across the Severn to the Forest of Dean

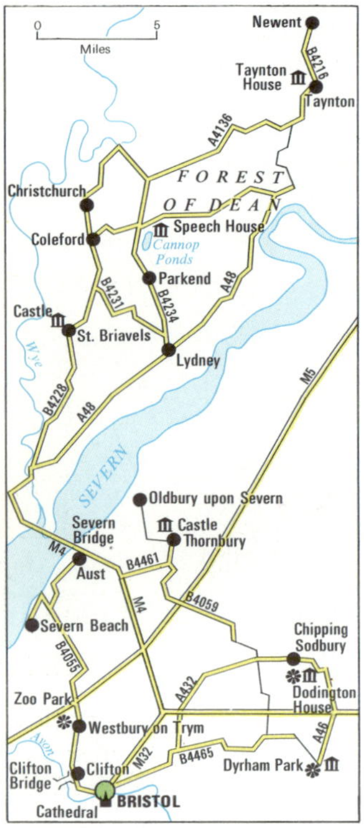

Sailing Clubs at Bristol, Oldbury upon Severn and Lydney.

Event On Easter Tues. buns known as Tuppenny Starvers are distributed to the choirboys of St Michael on the Mount Without, Bristol.

Places to see in Bristol *City Art Gallery* and *City Museum*, Queen's Road: both weekdays. *Blaise Castle House Museum*, Henbury: 18th-century house containing objects illustrating English life: weekday afternoons. *Cabot Tower*: daily. *Chatterton House*, Redcliffe Way; birthplace of the poet: by appointment. *Georgian House*, 7 Great George Street: weekdays. *Industrial Museum*: Sat. to Wed. *St Nicholas Church and City Museum*: weekdays. *SS Great Britain*, City Docks: daily. *Zoo*, Clifton: daily.

Places to see around Bristol *Dodington House*, Chipping Sodbury: early Apr. to Sept., daily. *Dyrham Park* (NT): park, afternoons; house and garden, Apr. to Oct., afternoons except Fri., but closed Thur. Apr., May and Oct.

Information centre Colston House, Colston Street, Bristol. Tel. Bristol 293891.

The magnificent suspension bridge across the Severn between Aust and Gwent, which was opened in 1966, has made near neighbours of the Forest of Dean and Bristol, two areas that once seemed miles apart. The tree-covered hills, winding valleys and fast-flowing streams of the great forest are now within comparatively easy reach of tourists in the south-west.

The forest covers an area of 27,000 acres, and 22,000 of them are clothed with an estimated 20 million trees, mostly oak and beech, but with birch, ash, conifers and massive hollies as well.

The people who live and work in and around the forest are known as Foresters and have traditional privileges granted to them centuries ago. The miners have the right to dig coal free and the quarrymen have the right to cut stone. Half the forest is fenced and the other half is grazed by the Foresters' sheep. Under the medieval right of pannage, they may also let their pigs feed among the oaks when the acorns fall. Charcoal-making, which traditionally used to go on in the forest, is now carried on in a factory near the Speech House; and little quarries producing grey and blue sandstone are scattered here and there.

Beneath the forest is a coalfield covering thousands of acres, and in a few places small mines are still worked. The roads which wind across the area provide delightful drives; even better are the hundreds of miles of forest paths for walkers, through ferns and patches of wild daffodils. Foxes and badgers abound, and for the bird-watcher there are kestrels, sparrowhawks, owls, ring doves, herons, snipe and hosts of smaller birds.

WILD WOAD Leaves of the woad (*Isatis tinctoria*), which grows on the cliffs of the Severn Valley, were used by early Britons to dye their bodies blue; the plant was used as a dye until the 16th century

Aust
This little village on the banks of the Severn is now dominated by the modern Severn Bridge which carries the M4 to Wales; but it will never lose its lure for people interested in history. Buried in the rugged clay and limestone cliffs, part of the 200-million-year-old Westbury Beds, lie the fossilised remains of countless prehistoric animals. Archaeologists have found Roman remains on the cliff tops.

PAYING 'ON THE NAIL'

Merchants put cash on flat-topped pillars ('nails') outside Bristol Corn Exchange to settle bargains

Bristol
An ancient and modern city, lively, contemporary and keeping up with fashion, but deeply soaked in history. It grew up around its harbour on the River Avon and as a result the city became a flourishing commercial port from the 10th century onwards. As a mark of its importance it was made a county in its own right in 1373, and after John Cabot set sail in 1497 from Bristol to discover Newfoundland and North America—a year before Columbus landed on the American mainland—it became known throughout the world. Here, too, was founded in 1552 the Society of Merchant Venturers, who did so much to lay the prosperous foundations of the Empire.

Bristol's cathedral started as an Augustinian monastery in 1148. The town has some good modern architecture, too, among the buildings erected to replace bomb damage from the Second World War. Rooftop views from the new Broadmead shopping area are as good as those from Cabot Tower, which was erected to commemorate Cabot's discovery of North America. The Theatre Royal, the oldest existing theatre in

MAGIC EYE *A painting over the door of Perrygrove House, in Coleford, is to ward off evil forest spirits*

England, built in 1766, is the home of the Bristol Old Vic Company, and in Broadmead is John Wesley's Chapel. He built it in 1739, and it is the oldest Methodist chapel in the world.

The Bristol Avon is a more attractive river than the Severn, and the Avon Gorge, where the river flows between steep cliffs of limestone, is spanned 245 ft above high water by the Clifton Suspension Bridge, designed by Brunel but not completed and opened until 1864, five years after his death.

In the old quarter of the city outside the 18th-century Exchange Building are four bronze pillars where merchants completed their transactions. The pillars are known as nails, and here originated the phrase 'paying on the nail'.

Towards Westbury on Trim are the Clifton and Durdham Downs, 442 acres of rolling downland.

Dodington House
A Palladian house, designed by James Wyatt in 1796 and completed in 1813, the year Wyatt died in an accident on his way from the house to London. The house is almost square; on the west side is a portico built so that a carriage could drive through to the main entrance. The grounds were laid out by Capability Brown in 1764.

Dyrham Park
A 17th-century house built by William Blathwayt, Secretary of State to William III. It is one of the National Trust's finest properties, and worth a visit for its gardens and tapestries alone. There is an orangery where oranges, grapefruit and mimosa grow.

Newent
Wild daffodils grow thickly around this old market town in spring; they have even colonised the central strip of the Ross Spur motorway. Near the town is a falconry centre where this ancient hunting art has been revived. The birds can be seen being handled, in ground training and at work in the sky.

The 16th-century timber-framed market hall is well preserved and there are several 18th-century houses and a medieval spired church. The lead was removed from the church roof by the Royalists in 1644 during the Civil War, to make bullets to repel Roundhead attacks, and after a heavy fall of snow in 1674 the roof collapsed, destroying the nave. It was rebuilt after Charles II made a grant of 60 tons of wood from the Forest of Dean. Taynton House, 3 miles south, has three interesting barns, one of which dates from 1695.

St Briavels
This splendid walking centre high above the River Wye has one of the best-sited and most interesting youth hostels in Europe, a medieval castle with several 700-year-old fireplaces. Early English kings stayed in the castle when they came to hunt deer and wild boar. From the castle there are wonderful views across the Forest of Dean. Opposite the castle is a Norman church with an unusual Whit Sunday custom of giving out bread and cheese after service.

THE VITAL LINK *The Severn Suspension Bridge, opened in 1966, replaced the ferry at Aust, which was for years the only way for motor traffic to cross the river estuary. The toll bridge, with a centre span of 3240 ft, is now an important link in the M4*

Speech House
A 17th-century house, built when the iron-founders moved into the Forest of Dean. It has a court-room used to settle disputes between them and the Foresters who lived by woodcutting and poaching. The court-room is now a hotel dining-room, but is still used ten times a year for official sittings of the Verderers' Court. The house stands in the centre of the forest near Cannop Ponds, which were dug in 1820 to provide a water supply for iron smelters.

From Speech House a road leads towards Parkend and Lydney, south through the forest, and after 2 miles it runs below Fancy Tip, the tip of an old colliery now pleasantly overgrown with grass and broom. It is well worth a scramble to the top for the magnificent view across the great forest.

Thornbury
The unfinished Tudor 'castle' of the Duke of Buckingham is one of the most imposing Tudor buildings in the west of England. The Duke was executed in 1521 before it was completed.

THE 'GREAT BRITAIN'—BRUNEL'S IRON MASTERPIECE RETURNS

A print of the 3443-ton *Great Britain*, designed by Brunel, being launched at Bristol by the Prince Consort in 1843. She was the first ship to rely primarily on screw propulsion

In 1886, the *Great Britain* was damaged and beached in the Falkland Islands. She remained there until 1970, when she was towed to Bristol to be restored for public viewing

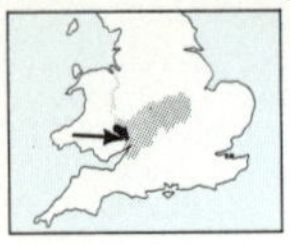

Hereford, cathedral city by the Wye

Angling There is coarse fishing on the River Wye above and below Hereford; also some trout fishing.

Boating At Symonds Yat. Canoeing at Ross-on-Wye.

Events The Three Choirs Festival is held at Hereford every 3rd year (1982, 1985, etc.).

Places to see *Abbey Dore Court*: garden only; daily. *Churchill Gardens Museum*, Hereford: afternoons. *Goodrich Castle*: daily, except Sun. morning Oct. to Mar. *Hereford Cathedral Chained Library*: weekdays, Easter to Sept. *Hereford City Museum and Art Gallery*: weekdays. *The Old House*, Hereford, half-timbered building of 1621, with Jacobean furniture: daily, except Sat. afternoon Oct. to Mar.

Information centre Town Hall, Hereford. Tel. Hereford 68430.

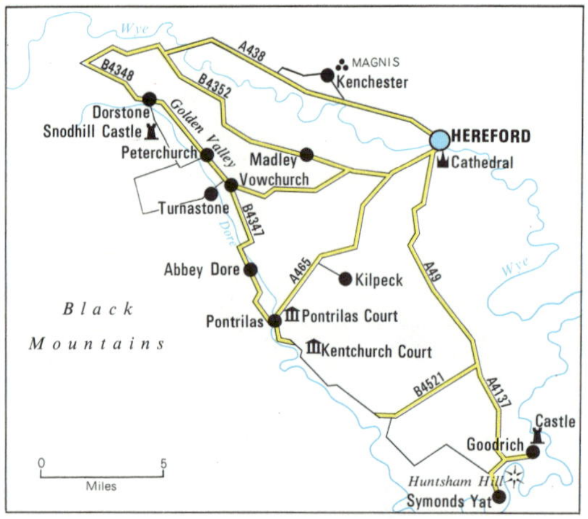

The country south-west of Hereford is not widely thought of as holiday country. It is tucked away in the shadows of the Welsh mountains to the west, and is off the main holiday routes. But for those who love walking among hills and meadows, or who enjoy motoring through villages and beside narrow, winding rivers, there are few places to compete with the peaceful countryside.

Two river valleys provide some of this area's finest scenery. To the south lies one of the most spectacular stretches of the Wye Valley, dominated by the scenic splendour of Symonds Yat. To the west the River Dore winds its way for 10 miles between Dorstone and Pontrilas along the beautiful Golden Valley, where cornfields, orchards and rich grass meadows are flanked by the Black Mountains on the west and gentle hills on the east.

In Saxon and Norman times Welsh raiders came down from the mountains and were challenged from the crags of Symonds Yat or at Goodrich Castle.

This is the land of the cider apple, and the world's largest cider factory is in Hereford, producing 60 per cent of Britain's consumption. The traditional cider-apple orchards of small farms and cottages are today gradually giving way to larger, more economical fruit farms. In spring they are a riot of blossom which can challenge Kent. In the older orchards, mistletoe berries hang from the trees in abundance in autumn.

GATEWAY TO BEAUTY *The Wye winds below Symonds Yat. The yat, Old English for gate, was once a pass through Iron Age fortifications on the 400 ft high crag*

Abbey Dore
Fine examples of Early English architecture can be seen in the parish church, which was built from the chancel of a Cistercian abbey. The magnificent oak chancel screen was designed for Lord Scudamore in the 17th century by John Abel. The stonework of the choir and the 13th-century presbytery are impressive. Near by is a 14th-century farmhouse, The Grange.

Goodrich
The magnificent ruins of Goodrich Castle stand on a wooded hill overlooking the River Wye. The castle is square, with a tower in each corner; round it is a deep moat cut out of solid rock. The oldest part of the castle is its greystone keep, built in the late 12th century. From the 14th century it was the home of the Talbots, Earls of Shrewsbury, until it was destroyed by Cromwell's troops in the Civil War. The destruction of the castle was due to a mortar called 'Roaring Meg', which fired 200 lb. balls, and this mortar has been preserved in Churchill Gardens, Hereford.

Hereford
Once the Saxon capital of West Mercia, Hereford is steeped in history. It is not simply a museum piece, however, but very much the administrative and social centre of the county. The city is surrounded by orchards and rich pastures, grazed by herds of red-and-white Hereford cattle which provide some of the finest beef in the world. One of the old inns famous for its beef is The Green Dragon, an old posting inn with panelling dating back to 1600.

High Town is the hub of Hereford, with its shops and market hall, and there is access to Broad Street with the cathedral at its south end. The art gallery and museum contains a Bronze Age burial and finds from Iron Age forts and from the Roman town of Magnis, now Kenchester, $5\frac{1}{2}$ miles north-west of Hereford.

Hereford Cathedral dates from the 12th century, but has been much altered in later years. It is mainly Norman, but changes through the centuries have left it a mixture of pink sandstone of many periods. The central tower is 14th century, as are the choir stalls. The cathedral contains the internationally famous Mappa Mundi, a map of the world drawn *c.* 1300. The chained library is the largest of its kind in the world, containing nearly 1500 books, each attached by a chain to rods on the 17th-century oak bookcases.

The River Wye flows through the city under a 15th-century six-arched stone bridge, just upstream from the cathedral. Near by, some of the medieval city walls still stand. A tablet in Gwynne Street marks where Nell Gwynne was born.

Kilpeck
This village has a beautiful Norman church, one of the finest remaining in Britain. The carved south door is a masterpiece, and the chancel carvings are a mixture of Norman and local Celtic, with a strangely modern effect.

DOG AND RABBIT *One of 74 decorative figures on the exterior of Kilpeck Church*

Madley
A village with some black-and-white houses, with a finely preserved parish church of mixed Norman and Gothic architecture. Its beautiful 14th-century stained glass in the east window is among the finest in Britain, and the present-day vogue for stained glass as an art form is making Madley an artists' shrine. Every June the parishioners hold a music festival in the church. Near by is a 16th-century timbered farmhouse.

Peterchurch
The village has a fine Norman church, and in the hills to the west are the ruins of the medieval castle of Snodhill. To the east of Peterchurch is stone-built Wellbrook Manor. One of the wings dates from the 14th century.

Pontrilas
This hamlet at the southern end of Golden Valley is notable for two interesting houses: Pontrilas Court, which is a 17th-century gabled stone house, and Kentchurch Court, 2 miles south-east, which has been the seat of the Scudamores since the 11th century; it was remodelled by John Nash in 1795 and has fine 17th-century wood-carving.

Symonds Yat
One of the most beautiful views of the River Wye; the word *yat* means a gate. The river winds its way through a narrow gorge, swinging round in a great loop for 5 miles, circling Huntsham Hill and then curving back to within a quarter of a mile of its original course. The best view of it is from Yat Rock on the Gloucestershire side of the river.

ROARING MEG *This locally made mortar, now in Churchill Gardens, Hereford, was used by Parliamentary troops to force Goodrich Castle to submit in the Civil War*

Vowchurch
This village with its stone bridge across the River Dore lies in the centre of the Golden Valley. The valley's name is thought to be due to a misunderstanding by the Normans, who translated *dwr*, the Welsh for water, as *d'or*, the French for 'golden'. The 14th-century parish church has a fine Jacobean screen and an unusual roof, supported by oak posts within the building instead of by the walls. Just across the river at Turnastone is another attractive church with a Norman doorway.

A narrow road leads westwards from Turnastone, past half-timbered farmhouses, into the hills with their marvellous views of the Golden Valley.

ROYALIST STRONGHOLD *Moated Goodrich Castle, built in the 12th century as a defence against Welsh raiders, was a Royalist bastion captured by Cromwell's men in 1646*

Along the Wye Valley

Events There is a distribution of Pax Cakes for Good Neighbours on Palm Sun. in Mar. to the residents of Sellack and Kings Caple, 4 miles north-west of Ross. An Agricultural Show is held on late Summer Bank Hol. at Leominster.

Places to see *Berrington Hall* (NT), Leominster, built 1778–81 by Henry Holland, park laid out by Capability Brown: Easter to Sept., Wed., Thur., Sat., Sun. and Bank Hol. afternoons; Oct., Sat. and Sun. afternoons. *Burton Court*, Eardisland: Whitsun to mid-Sept., Wed., Thur., Sat., Sun. afternoons. *Croft Castle* (NT), 5 miles north-west of Leominster: early Apr. to Sept., Wed., Thur., Sat., Sun. and Bank Hol. Mon. afternoons; Oct., Sat. and Sun. afternoons. *Dinmore Manor*, 6 miles north of Hereford: afternoons. *Eastnor Castle*, 2 miles east of Ledbury: late May to Sept., Sun. and Bank Hol. afternoons. *Eye Manor*, 4 miles north of Leominster: afternoons only: mid-Apr. to June. Wed., Thur., Sat., Sun.; July to Sept., daily. *Falconry Centre*, Newent, 8 miles east of Ross-on-Wye: Feb. to Nov., daily. *Hellen's*, Much Marcle: Easter to Oct., Wed., Sat. and Sun. afternoons. *Hergest Croft Garden and Park* (NGS), Kington: Easter weekend, then daily May to Aug. *Leominster and District Folk Museum*: Apr. to Oct., weekdays, Sun. afternoon; Nov. to Mar., Fri. and Sat. afternoons. *Lower Brockhampton* (NT), Bromyard: Feb. to Dec., Mon., Wed., Fri., Sat. and Bank Hol. Mon.; also Sun. morning.

Information centres Library, South Street, Leominster. Tel. Leominster 2384. Wyedean Tourist Board, Ross-on-Wye. Tel. Ross-on-Wye 2768. St Katherines, High Street, Ledbury. Tel. Ledbury 2461.

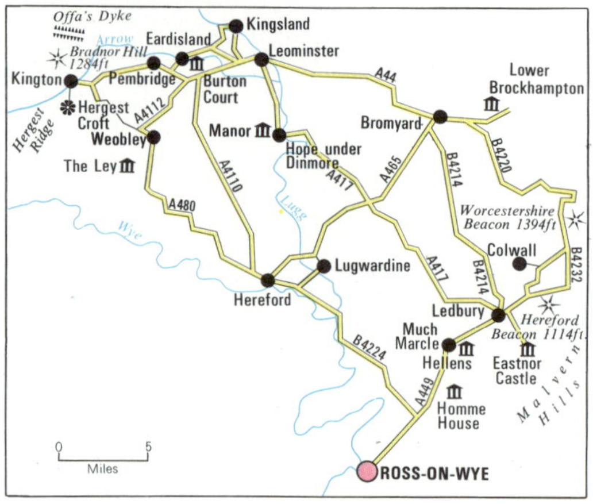

Broad plains between hills form the typical landscape of Hereford and Worcester east of the Wye, a countryside that is gently picturesque rather than grandly beautiful. The land grows more rugged towards the Welsh border, and the border hills are the beginnings of the Radnor Forest, while further south, Brecon's Black Mountains spill over the border into gentle hills.

The Wye, England's cleanest major river, runs through ever-changing scenery on its journey from the Cambrian Mountains to the sea over rocky beds, through gorges, meadows and woodland. Above and below Ross, the Wye Valley provides some of the most beautiful walks and views in the country. The river is a paradise for anglers, famous for its salmon; and in other rivers there are trout and grayling.

The land is well farmed, which adds beauty to the landscape. The farming ranges from hops and cider apples to pigs and sheep; but much of this area is grazed by the plum-red Hereford cattle, with their white faces, legs and chests, which still produce some of the world's best beef cattle for export.

For centuries this was a land of turbulence, and castles were built along the Welsh border in the 12th and 13th centuries to fight off raids. Now it is a land of peace, a quiet land of old timbered houses, market towns and villages steeped in history—a land for browsing.

ON HIGH *Tudor houses lead to Ledbury Church which, wrote John Masefield, has a 'golden vane surveying half the shire'*

DOWN CHESTNUT ROW *Spanish chestnut trees, which stretch for half a mile through Croft Castle park, are 350 years old*

CRUCK-FRAMED HOUSES

Cruck framing is one of the earliest styles of domestic building still seen in Britain. The 'crucks' are pairs of curved timbers from the ground to the ridge of the roof, best seen at the ends of the house. Other timbers, supported by the crucks, carry the walls and roof. There are many cruck-framed houses in the west Midlands and Wales. They were mostly built between the 11th and 16th centuries

Bromyard
A market town rich in old houses, notably the half-timbered Falcon Inn. Lower Brockhampton manor, 2½ miles east of Bromyard, is the sort of building which tells much about the way our medieval ancestors lived. It is a stout, timber-framed house built for a squire's family, with latticed windows, tilting timbers and a picturesque buckled roof of fine old tiles. It has a gallery in the dining-hall. The gatehouse over the moat was built in the 15th century and is especially well preserved.

Colwall
A good walking and touring centre on the Hereford side of the Malvern Hills. Footpaths lead north to Great Malvern and the Worcestershire Beacon or southwards to Hereford Beacon, which rises to 1114 ft and has a fine example of an Iron Age hill fort covering 44 acres.

Eardisland
A pretty village beautifully situated by the grass banks of the little-known River Arrow. Burton Court, an 18th-century house with a 14th-century Great Hall,

GREEN PASTURES *Sheep graze on the lush meadowlands at Brinsop, south-east of Weobley, and cattle rest in the shade. The Hereford breed, which has helped to improve the beef cattle of almost every country in the world, was developed in this well-farmed area*

houses a collection of European and Oriental costumes and curios. Its manorial records date back to 1332 and are kept in Hereford Library.

Kington
A small market town, set in pleasant hill country, where big autumn sales of Clun Forest and Kerry sheep are held. It is the essence of a border town, where visitors can still see the earthworks of Offa's Dyke, the defence wall between England and Wales built in the 8th century by King Offa of Mercia. There is good hill walking, with lovely views from Hergest Ridge and Bradnor Hill. Hergest Croft Gardens are rich in trees and shrubs and have a rainbow display of azaleas and rhododendrons in summer. The golf course has views across to the Black Mountains, Radnor Forest and the Malvern Hills.

Ledbury
England's small market towns can sometimes be as pretty and more engaging than its villages, and Ledbury, greatly loved by poets, is such a place. The Brownings and Wordsworth used to visit Ledbury; John Masefield was born there and said that the Hereford scene had a profound influence on his work. Ledbury has changed little over the centuries, and the October Hiring Fair is still held in the streets, although it is not now for hiring men, but simply a festival. The town is still as Masefield described it—'pleasant to the sight, fair and half-timbered houses black and white'. One of the most attractive buildings, inside and out, is the 16th-century Feathers Inn, and there is an arcaded 17th-century market hall supported on pillars of chestnut.

Ledbury is almost equidistant from Hereford, Worcester and Gloucester, and is set among pastures and streams, making it a good base for walking the Malvern Hills. In the fields around Ledbury, tiny wild daffodils grow; and behind windbreak hedges are Herefordshire's extensive hop gardens—second only to Kent in production. The 19th-century Eastnor Castle near by contains art treasures and is surrounded by a beautiful park.

Leominster
This old wool town lies in a beautiful valley at the junction of the River Lugg and Pinsley Brook, among hopfields and orchards of cider apples. It has produced fine-textured wool, known as Lemster Ore, since the 13th century, and from Leominster, Hereford cattle are exported all over the world. Just off Broad Street, with its fine Georgian buildings, stands the 11th-century Priory Church, which has three naves. Here, too, is a ducking stool, used up to 1809 to still the tongues of nagging women.

Six centuries ago the monks of Leominster bred in this countryside the Ryelands sheep, famous for their wool, which were later exported to Australia, New Zealand and South America. They can still be seen in Hereford and Worcester—hornless, wide-backed sheep with woolly forelocks. There are good trout in the River Lugg.

Much Marcle
This peaceful village near the Gloucestershire border has a famous herd of Hereford beef cattle and a cider factory. There are two well-known mansions here: Hellens, which partly dates from 1292 and has a 17th-century dovecot, and Homme House dating from 1623.

Pembridge
The 600-year-old church in this village of half-timbered houses has an attractive timber belfry tower, which was once a place of refuge for villagers when the Welsh raided from across the border. In the stone base of the tower are embrasures through which arrows were once shot. There are still seven of these detached towers in Herefordshire.

Ross-on-Wye
This steep-streeted town of Georgian houses stands on a bend in the river looking towards the Welsh Hills, and is the main tourist centre for the Wye Valley. Out of season Ross again becomes a peaceful market town, with its life centred around the 17th-century arcaded market hall.

A local philanthropist, John Kyrle (1637–1724), who was called 'The Man of Ross' by Alexander Pope, spent most of his 87 years here and left his mark on the town. His house in the High Street became an inn after his death, and 80 years later it was converted into two shops, which still stand. Kyrle laid out The Prospect, a public garden near the 14th-century church, from which there are magnificent views of the river and the hills. Kyrle's Walk starts from a stone arch at the south-west side of The Prospect. He is also remembered as the man who gave Ross-on-Wye its first public water supply, built the causeway to Wilton Bridge and built the pinnacles on the church spire.

Weobley
This black-and-white timbered village looks almost unreal, like a film set. But the Red Lion Inn has been there since the 14th century and the church since the 13th century. South-west of the village is The Ley, an eight-gabled, timbered farmhouse built in 1589 and one of the most attractive in Britain. It also has a priest's hole used for hiding Roman Catholic priests after the Reformation.

IN MEMORY OF THE MAN OF ROSS

A plaque over a Ross shop marks where philanthropist John Kyrle was born

This swan design, laid out in horses' teeth, is in John Kyrle's old garden behind the shop in Ross market-place

A gate leads to The Prospect public garden, given by Kyrle, who was Alexander Pope's 'Man of Ross'

The Vale of Gloucester

Angling Coarse fishing on the Gloucester and Sharpness Canal. Salmon on the Avon at Tewkesbury and trout on the Frome at Stroud.

Boating Rowing on the Gloucester and Sharpness Canal. Sailing on the Avon and Severn. Boats and cruisers for hire at Tewkesbury.

Events Three-day horse trial takes place at Badminton in Apr. The Three Choirs Festival is held every third year (1980, 1983, etc.) at Gloucester Cathedral, and the Gloucester Festival is held over 2/3 weeks early in Aug. Cheese rolling at Cooper's Hill, Brockworth, 2½ miles south-east of Gloucester, on Spring Bank Hol.

Places to see *Badminton House*: Wed. afternoon, early June to early Sept. *Berkeley Castle*: Apr. and Sept., afternoons except Mon.; May to Aug., Tues. to Sat. and Sun. afternoons. Oct., Sun. afternoons. *Bishop Hooper's Lodging*, Gloucester, a museum of folk life and regimental history: weekdays. *Gloucester City Museum*: weekdays. *Jenner Museum*, Berkeley: Apr. to Sept., afternoons except Mon. *Westbury Court Garden* (NT), Westbury-on-Severn: May to Sept., daily except Mon. and Tues.; Apr. and Oct., Sat. and Sun. *Westonbirt Arboretum*: daily. *Wildfowl Trust*, Slimbridge: weekdays and Sun. afternoons.

Information centre Gloucester Leisure Centre, Station Road, Gloucester. Tel. Gloucester 36498.

The Severn Valley from Tewkesbury to the sea starts in hilly country, then flattens out towards the estuary. Its shifting sands and flat grasslands seem in many places to have more seabirds and geese than people. But in the middle of the valley is the ancient and solid city of Gloucester—a busy manufacturing centre, with a hard-working port and a fine cathedral. East of the city the land rises towards the wooded slopes of the Cotswold Hills.

Gloucester was a meeting place of Roman roads and a rich agricultural centre in Roman times; but in the 6th century the Saxons destroyed the Roman buildings and routed the Christian communities of the West and Wales. Gloucester's new civilisation did not start until Ethelbert ruled in Kent. There is a suggestion, based on a passage by the Venerable Bede, that St Augustine travelled to Gloucestershire to meet the British bishops at Aust. As a result, the Christian faith regained its strength and the county became rich in abbeys and churches.

Gloucestershire is a great sporting county, famous for cricket, rugby football and horse racing. There is rowing on the Gloucester Canal, and sailing and water-skiing are becoming popular on gravel pits. Nine-pin bowling, the original English game of skittles, is played all over the county. In Gloucester alone there are more than 8000 registered skittlers.

WINTER VISITORS *Bewick's swans—named in honour of Thomas Bewick (1753–1828), an illustrator of birds—among ducks and geese at the Wildfowl Trust at Slimbridge, founded in 1946. The swans fly in from northern Europe in winter*

THROUGH THE ARCH *The pinnacled tower of Gloucester Cathedral is framed in the ruins of a stone arch, all that remains of the aisle of the 12th-century priory church*

Badminton

The impressive Palladian mansion, Badminton House, set in a 15,000-acre estate, has been the home of the Dukes of Beaufort for more than 300 years. The three-day Badminton Horse Trials are held there in April, and visitors can see the house and the kennels of the Beaufort Hunt. The house has a collection of Italian, Dutch and English paintings and much fine carving by Grinling Gibbons.

Berkeley

Berkeley Castle, built in the 12th century, stands in lovely grounds in a tranquil town where the liveliest noise comes from the hounds of the Berkeley Hunt in the kennels close by. In the park there are red and fallow deer and wild geese. The Berkeley family have occupied the castle continuously since the 12th century. Edward II was murdered in the dungeons in 1327.

The parish church has a superb east window of nine lights, filled with pictures of Christ healing the sick—a memorial to Edward Jenner, discoverer of vaccination, who was born in Berkeley and returned there before his death in 1823. He is buried in the chancel.

Berkeley is the centre of the Vale of Berkeley—thousands of acres of flat land stretching for 15 miles on the east bank of the Severn. Little watercourses form criss-cross patterns, with lanes crossing them on stone hump-backed bridges beside meadows of grazing cows. A canal passes through the Vale from Gloucester to Sharpness—a vital 17-mile waterway which links Gloucester with the sea.

Gloucester
This bustling manufacturing and market centre was once the Roman fortified town of Glevum, for centuries guardian of the routes to Wales that converged at the lowest crossing-point of the Severn. There are several interesting medieval buildings, including the New Inn, Fleece Inn and the 16th-century Greyfriars ruin.

But Gloucester is more of a commercial centre than a tourist attraction. The opening of the canal between Gloucester and Sharpness in 1827 made the city an important inland port.

The cathedral's east window measures 72 ft by 38 ft, and its area of stained glass is the largest in the country after York Minster's. It was made *c.* 1350 to commemorate Edward III's victory at the Battle of Crécy in 1344.

Painswick
This old wool town of greystone buildings dating back to the 14th century stands on a hill in the Cotswolds. In the parish churchyard there are more than 100 clipped yews, some of which have been there since 1714. Traditionally there were only 99 trees; it used to be said that every time the 100th was planted, the Devil removed it. The peal of 12 bells in the 15th-century St Mary's Church is one of the finest in the west, and by the churchyard wall there is a pair of iron stocks, shaped like a pair of spectacles.

On the Sunday following September 19, the church holds a Clipping ceremony—a medieval custom in which children join hands round the church while a hymn is sung. The ceremony, which has nothing to do with shearing sheep, was once an ale-swilling dance.

Paradise
A hamlet just north of Painswick. It was named by Charles I who, while bombarding Gloucester, stayed there and described it as the most delightful spot he had ever seen. The local inn, inevitably called The Adam and Eve, was at that time called The Plough.

Slimbridge
Five miles from Berkeley Castle and on the Berkeley Estate is the Wildfowl Trust, founded by Peter Scott. This has the world's largest and most varied collection of wildfowl, in beautiful surroundings. There are more than 2500 swans, geese and ducks of 160 species, and there are six flocks of flamingoes. The most spectacular sight is in winter, when thousands of wild geese find sanctuary in the Severn Estuary. From towers on the Wildfowl Trust land, the geese can be seen feeding.

Stroud
This little town at the junction of five valleys is being modernised yearly, and its quaint, steep streets are becoming fewer. It is an old wool town, still famous for its West of England cloth and dye trade; but it has other more modern industries. Above the town is Minchinhampton Common, a 600-acre National Trust property giving fine views over the Golden Valley.

Tewkesbury
An old town of timbered, black-and-white houses and good inns, where the Severn and Avon meet. The town is steeped in history. It was the site of a Yorkist victory in the Wars of the Roses in 1471. Parts of the bridge, which crossed the Avon in the 13th century, are included in the present-day King John's Bridge. Among the 13th and 14th-century inns are the Royal Hop Pole Inn, mentioned in *The Pickwick Papers*, the timber-framed Bell Inn, and The Black Bear. The 16th-century Tudor House, now a hotel, has a priest's hole (a hiding place) in the chimney of what is now a coffee room. The town's most impressive building is the abbey, with a magnificent 132 ft high Norman tower.

Westbury-on-Severn
Canals bordered by yew hedges string together the lakes at Westbury Court where the Dutch water garden, laid out between 1696 and 1705, is the only remaining one in England.

Westonbirt
The famous Westonbirt Arboretum, managed by the Forestry Commission, covers 117 acres and extends into Wiltshire. This tree collection was started in 1829 by the squire of Westonbirt, Robert Stainer Holford, and is one of the finest in the country. It is particularly beautiful when the leaves are changing colour in autumn. There are also large banks of rhododendrons, which are a mass of colour from spring to October.

Wotton-under-Edge
This old market town on the edge of the Cotswolds has some fine old buildings including a 14th-century school and a 14th to 15th-century church. Among the interesting treasures in the church are some fine brasses and an 18th-century organ built by Christopher Schrider for St Martin-in-the-Fields, London, and played by Handel at a time when George I attended services there. The Vicar of Wotton bought it when St Martin's discarded it. In Orchard Street is a house where Isaac Pitman (1813–97), a schoolmaster at Wotton, devised his system of shorthand. The almshouses date from 1632.

MAJESTIC TOWER *Over Tudor houses and a watermill rises the tower of Tewkesbury Abbey, one of the finest Norman towers in the country. From the top there is a view over the Severn and Avon Valleys and to the Welsh mountains*

THE ALPINE WOUNDWORT *Stachys alpina*, a hardy perennial, is rare in Britain, growing only in woods in the Cotswolds and in Clwyd. It puts out pale pink flowers from mid-June to late July

Mellow Cotswold villages

The minor roads through the Cotswold Hills and valleys are mazy and muddled, reeling around in eccentric patterns. This is perfect country for wanderers without watches, and it is as easy to tour on foot or on horseback as by car. The north Cotswolds are a well-known tourist area; the south Cotswolds, less well known, are equally attractive with their steep-sided hills, beechwoods as colourful in spring and autumn as in summer sunlight, and peaceful villages of mellow Cotswold stone.

In Shakespeare's day this was sheep country and the centre of England's wool industry. Many of the hills are still used for grazing, although most of Britain's raw wool now comes from Australia and is manufactured in Yorkshire. The rich wool merchants built most of the lovely churches and manor houses in the Cotswolds from the 15th to the 17th centuries.

Streams such as the Windrush, the Coln and the Evenlode, which run briskly through the countryside, are rich in trout and crayfish. The Thames starts as a muddy pool in a field just off the A433, 3 miles south-west of Cirencester, at a place called Thames Head. The walks in the varied scenery of the Cotswolds are of every type, short of scrambling. A 100-mile trail, the Cotswold Way, has been marked out by the Ramblers' Association, and there are rewarding walks of 3 or 4 miles, such as the one from Cranham through Cranham Wood to Birdlip Hill, with its magnificent view. Most of the Cotswolds is riding and hunting country, and point-to-point meetings are frequently held.

HOME OF THE WOOL MERCHANTS *The 14th-century buildings in the High Street of Chipping Campden, seen through the arches of the timber-roofed market hall. The town was a principal centre of the Cotswold wool trade in the Middle Ages*

Places to see *Arlington Mill Museum*, Bibury: Mar. to Oct., daily; Nov. to Feb., weekends. *Birdland*, Bourton-on-the-Water: daily. *Chedworth Roman Villa* (NT), 8 miles north-east of Cirencester: Mar. to Oct., Tues. to Sun. and Bank Hol. Mon.; Nov. to mid-Dec. and Feb., Wed. to Sun. *Cheltenham Museum*: weekdays. *Corinium Museum*, Park Street, Cirencester: Tues. to Sat., and Sun. afternoon; also Mon., May to Sept. *Hailes Abbey* (NT), 6 miles north-east of Cheltenham: weekdays, Sun. afternoon. *Hidcote Manor Garden* (NT), 4 miles north-east of Chipping Campden: Apr. to Oct., daily except Tues. and Fri. *Holst Birthplace Museum*, Cheltenham: Tues. to Sat. *Pittville Pump Room*, Cheltenham: May to Sept., weekdays, Sun. afternoon. *Sudeley Castle*, Winchcombe: afternoons, Mar. to Oct.

Information centres Cotswolds Publicity Association, Corn Hall, Market Place, Cirencester. Tel. Cirencester 4180.
Municipal Offices, The Promenade, Cheltenham. Tel. Cheltenham 22878.

PITTVILLE PUMP ROOM

Colonnaded façades and a pillared and balconied hall are among the outstanding features of this beautiful Cheltenham building

Bisley
This charming village high on a hill is called 'Bisley-God-Help-Us' by the locals because of the winter wind. It has much to interest the tourist, including spring-fed fountains, a 19th-century lock-up, a Saxon cross and the Bear Inn, which has two secret passages and a priest's hole. There is a riding school, 2 miles west, where ponies can be hired.

Bourton-on-the-Water
A beautiful village with the little River Windrush flowing down its main street under low bridges beside trees and lawns. The village becomes crowded in midsummer and on fine weekends; but at quieter times there are charming walks along roads lined by beautiful Cotswold stone houses.

Cheltenham
One of the foremost spas in England, and a lively centre of music, art and sport. The only alkaline springs in Britain run underground in the area and are drawn at the Pump Room where the waters can be taken.

The Promenade is a wide and spacious street with splendid Regency houses, trees and statues. The Pittville Pump Room, with its colonnade and dome, is the town's most beautiful building. The Cheltenham Music Festival was started in 1944 with the intention of fostering contemporary British music. First performances of works by Sir Arthur Bliss, Benjamin Britten, Sir Arnold Bax, Malcolm Arnold and many other British composers have been given there. There is also a fine cricket ground and a steeplechase course in Prestbury Park.

Chipping Campden
An old town of Cotswold stone houses nestling among the hills. The mainly 15th-century church has a 14th-century chancel and a stately 120 ft high tower. Inside there are excellent brasses. The town's finest building is the Jacobean market hall. Hidcote Manor Garden to the north-east, a most delightful garden, is open to the public.

HOUSES FROM THE NATURAL ROCK

Cotswold limestone is still quarried at Farmington (left), as it was in the 17th century when fine manor houses like the one above were built

Cirencester
A rewarding touring centre for walking, motoring or riding. The old town, called Corinium by the Romans, was, after London, the largest town in Britain in the 2nd century. Three Roman roads, Akeman Street, the Foss Way and one of the two Ermine Streets, radiate from Cirencester. The site of the old town has been excavated and there are many exciting Roman finds, including coins and mosaics, in the museum. The remains of an amphitheatre lie on Querns Hill, near the town centre.

Cirencester has blended old with new, and its more modern buildings fit in gracefully with the old houses of Cotswold stone. The 15th-century church, built when Cirencester was the greatest wool market in England, has a magnificent nave and screen and some fine brasses. There is a Tudor inn with an 18th-century façade, and a market, mentioned in the Domesday Book, which is busy on Fridays.

There are some lovely walks in 3000-acre Cirencester Park, containing woodland and farms, nearly all open to the public, and one of the world's finest polo grounds. Its trees include beeches and a 5-mile avenue of chestnuts. Within walking range of the park are switchback lanes and wooded hills, among which lie a dozen pleasant villages, including Sapperton and Bisley.

Lechlade
A pretty town of Georgian houses, taking its name from the River Leach which wanders into the Thames beside the Trout Inn just below St John's Bridge. Lechlade Bridge, known as Halfpenny Bridge, from the days when there was a halfpenny toll, is the highest navigable point on the Thames for cabin cruisers. Old wharves, now lined with pleasure-boats, once catered for barges carrying stone to London for St Paul's Cathedral in the 17th century.

The 15th-century church at Fairford, 4 miles to the west, has 28 fine windows of contemporary stained glass illustrating biblical scenes and stories.

Nailsworth
A town nestling in a wooded valley, noted for the Nailsworth Ladder—a chalky hill with a gradient of one in three in places, which is frequently used as a motor trials test hill.

North Cerney
This beautiful spot by the River Churn has some fine old houses and an unusual 12th-century church, with a Norman saddle-back tower, its roof gabled like an ordinary house, to which a belfry was latter added. The church has some fine Norman carving and a 14th-century cross in the churchyard.

Northleach
In the 15th century, Northleach was as important in the wool trade as Cirencester. It has remained a village with narrow, winding streets, changed little since the Middle Ages. There are some fine old buildings, including a group of almshouses from Tudor times and the Blind House, with no windows, once used as a prison. The 15th-century church is one of the finest left by the old wool merchants.

A PINNACLE RISING FROM THE HILLS *This 50 ft high limestone rock, known as the Devil's Chimney, is on Leckhampton Hill, near Cheltenham. The slim rock was left after centuries of quarrying had gone on around it. According to local superstition it rises from Hell*

Sapperton
The River Frome winds its way past this lovely village overlooking Golden Valley, which stretches from Sapperton to Chalford. The overgrown entrance to a 2½-mile tunnel which carries the now-derelict Thames–Severn Canal under the A419 is still visible. Daneway House is a stately greystone building with 14th-century walls. At nearby Chalford, along the valley, is a museum of canal lore in a round, tower-like, lock-keeper's cottage.

Stow-on-the-Wold
This quiet hill-top town in the Cotswolds was once a bustling centre of the wool industry. Its importance grew in the Middle Ages because it stood at the junction of several main roads. The market square is large, and is hemmed in by a cluster of old houses and inns arranged in higgledy-piggledy fashion. The local saying 'Stow-on-the-Wold, where the wind blows cold' probably explains why the buildings are bunched together. Stow Fair, for centuries one of the biggest livestock markets in Britain, is still held in May and October, but today it is mainly a show, although some trade in horses and farm equipment is still carried on.

Tetbury
An Elizabethan market town with fine old buildings. It is famous for its 17th-century town hall built on three rows of pillars, and for the Chipping Steps (Chipping is an Old English word meaning 'market') which lead to the old market. At Beverstone, 2 miles west, are a fine Norman church and the ruins of Beverstone Castle where King Harold stayed in 1051, and which was held by the Berkeleys when it was successfully besieged by King Stephen in 1145.

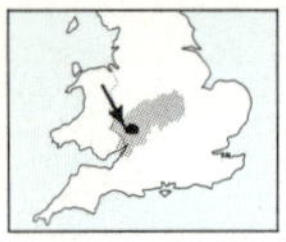

In the lee of the Malverns

Angling Salmon and coarse fishing at Ripple on the Severn; coarse fishing at Upton-upon-Severn and on the Avon at Pershore and Evesham.

Events There are regattas at Evesham and Upton-upon-Severn on Spring Bank Hol. The Three Counties Agricultural Show is held for three days in June at Malvern.

Places to see *Almonry Museum*, Vine Street, Evesham: Easter to Sept., afternoons except Mon. and Wed. *Bredon Tithe Barn* (NT): daily. *Buckland Rectory*, 2 miles south-west of Broadway, England's oldest rectory: Mon., May to July and Sept.; Mon. and Fri., Aug. *Little Malvern Court*, 14th-century Prior's Guesten Hall: May to Oct., Wed. afternoon. *Malvern Spa*, at St Ann's Well: daily. *Middle Littleton Tithe Barn* (NT), 3 miles north-east of Evesham: daily. *Snowshill Manor* (NT), Broadway; Tudor House containing collections of musical instruments, clocks, toys, bicycles: May to Sept., daily except Mon. and Tues.; also Bank Hol. Mon.; Apr. and Oct., Sat. and Sun.

Gardens to see Occasional days in summer (NGS). *Bell's Castle*, Bredon Hill, near Kemerton. *Court Farm*, Broadway. *Orchard Farm*, Broadway. *Overbury Court*, Overbury. *The Priory*, Kemerton. *Ripple Hall*, Ripple.

Information centres Information Office, 110 High Street, Evesham. Tel. Evesham 45944. Malvern Urban District Council, Winter Gardens, Grange Road. Tel. Malvern 4700.

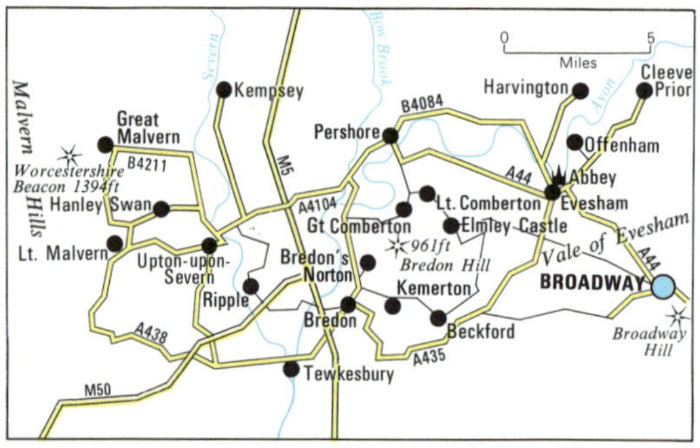

The River Avon, an anglers' river in which perch, chub and bream live, flows into Hereford and Worcester on the north side of Tewkesbury under arches of willow. Around Evesham it runs placidly through flat, featureless land with field after field of cabbages, lettuces, sprouts, beans and asparagus. The Avon then passes through orchards of plums, cherries and apples. In spring the orchards are a mass of blossom and present a magnificent sight.

Further south, the orchards give way to more hilly country with Cotswold stone walls, where cattle and sheep—the Welsh breeds of Clun Forest crossed with Kerry Hill—graze in the pastures. Here, the landscape of three counties, Hereford and Worcester, Gloucestershire and Warwickshire, runs unchanged across the border from one county to another.

The Avon twists its way round Bredon Hill from which, on a clear day, at least eight counties can be seen. To the west, across the River Severn, are the sheltering Malvern Hills; the rough commonland which fringes the slopes is excellent ground for walking, leading up through grass and bracken to the 1394 ft summit of the Worcestershire Beacon.

EVESHAM ABBEY *A 14th-century gateway in the market-place is all that remains of a once-famous abbey which was dissolved in 1539 by Henry VIII*

Bredon
A large, attractive village on the River Avon, which has a 14th-century tithe barn. Bredon Hill, 3 miles north-east, rises to 961 ft; there is a castellated Gothic folly on its slopes, and the remnants of prehistoric and Roman earthworks on its summit. From the folly there is a magnificent view of the Avon winding its way round the hill through large meadows, which are commonland, and across the plain of Malvern.

How many counties can be seen from Bredon Hill depends on the weather and on the viewer's imagination; some say eight, some say 14. Rewarding hours can be spent motoring or walking along the ribbon of narrow lanes through attractive villages like Bredon's Norton, Beckford and Kemerton.

Broadway
The beauty of the mellow, honey-coloured old stone buildings of Broadway has lured visitors since the last century—although in those days, before tourism became an accepted industry, the village was known as 'The Painted Lady of the Cotswolds'.

But Broadway is not known just for its pretty houses and tidy gardens. Some of the world's best modern furniture is designed and made there. The industry was started by the Gordon Russell family in 1904 to mend antique furniture for the village inn, the 16th-century Lygon Arms, a former coaching inn. Now its products are exported throughout the world to such places as Baghdad Palace, embassies in Moscow, and wealthy homes in Los Angeles. The North Cotswold Hunt meets outside The Lygon Arms, where winter visitors can film huntsmen, horses and hounds.

A Norman church, St Eadburgha's, is set among trees below nearby Broadway Hill. From the top of the hill there are fine views across the Vale of Evesham.

Elmley Castle
A pretty village at the foot of Bredon Hill. The castle has disappeared, but the village street has attractive half-timbered cottages. The 12th to 15th-century Church of St Mary has some fine English sculpture in the medieval tradition. In the park is a herd of fallow deer.

Evesham
This market town on the River Avon is the centre of the fruit-growing industry of the Vale of Evesham, which is noted for the mass of fruit blossom it displays in the spring. Despite great expansion the town keeps its elegance. Close to the ruined abbey by the river are fine Georgian houses and a few half-timbered buildings, the best of which is 15th-century Booth Hall, now restored and occupied by a branch of a national bank.

All that remains of the 14th-century abbey is a half-timbered gateway of Norman stone and the impressive Bell

CASTLE-TOP VIEW *On a fine day it is possible to see at least eight counties from the ramparts of Bell Castle, an 18th-century folly on the slopes of 961 ft high Bredon Hill*

HIGH ON THE COTSWOLDS *Beacon Tower stands on the top of Broadway Hill, high above the village of Broadway. It was built by Lady Coventry in 1797*

TITHE BARN *Bredon has one of the best-preserved tithe barns in the country. It was built in the 14th century to store grain which had been paid as taxes to the church*

Tower. There are two fine churches—All Saints', parts of which are 12th century, and St Lawrence's, which was rebuilt in the 16th century. An interesting little museum, the Almonry in Vine Street, has medieval remains and old agricultural implements. One of Evesham's main attractions is water sports on the Avon. Offenham, a riverside village, 2 miles north-east, is one of the few villages in England which still has a maypole.

Malvern
Sheltered by hills from the west wind, Great Malvern is an underrated holiday spa and a splendid walking centre. Apart from its spa it has an active Festival Theatre, for long associated with performances of the plays of Barrie and Shaw. It also has a heated outdoor swimming pool and lido, good boating and fishing, a nine-hole golf course, a concert hall, winter gardens and children's entertainments.

Above all, Malvern has the hills—not for mountain climbing, but for free, unfettered and untrammelled walking, easy enough for anyone who is reasonably fit. The hills provide magnificent views westwards towards Wales, and eastwards across garden-like, patchwork scenery to Warwickshire. The hills are protected by the Malvern Hills Conservators, who have planted trees and maintain the many footpaths.

Pershore
A market town, rich in well-kept Georgian buildings, set among woodlands and fruit farms where the delicious Pershore plums are grown. The town is reached from the east by crossing a 14th-century six-arched bridge over the River Avon. Parts of Pershore Abbey, originally Norman, survived the Reformation to serve as the parish church. The magnificent lantern tower was built *c.* 1330. Near by is St Andrew's Church, which contains 13th to 15th-century work.

Ripple
An attractive village grouped around a green. It has a half-timbered mid-16th-century manor house, 18th-century almshouses and some stocks. In the church are 15th-century misericords—carvings on seats in the choir stalls—depicting agricultural scenes.

COTSWOLD CHARM *The mellow, honey-coloured stone of cottages in Broadway is one reason why many visitors regard it as the most perfect of all Cotswold villages*

Farmland by the Severn

Angling There is salmon and coarse fishing on the River Severn at Worcester, Stourport-on-Severn and Holt Fleet, Ombersley. Trout and grayling on the River Teme at Tenbury Wells.

Boating Rowing, canoeing and cruising at Stourport-on-Severn and Worcester.

Events The Three Choirs Festival is held at Worcester Cathedral every 3rd year (1981, 1984, etc.).

Places to see *Avoncroft Museum of Buildings*, 3 miles south of Bromsgrove: daily, Mar. to Nov. *Bewdley Museum*: weekdays and Sun. afternoon, Mar. to Nov. *The Commandery*, Worcester. a pre-Reformation hospital: Tues. to Sat.; also Sun. afternoon, Apr. to Sept. *Dyson Perrins Museum of Worcester Porcelain*, Worcester: Apr. to Sept., weekdays; Oct. to Mar., Mon. to Fri. *Elgar Birthplace Museum*, Broadheath, 2 miles west of Worcester: afternoons except Wed. *The Greyfriars* (NT), Worcester: 1st Wed. afternoon of month, May to Sept. *The Guildhall*, Worcester: Mon. to Fri. *Hanbury Hall* (NT), Droitwich: early Apr. to Sept., Wed. to Sun. and Bank Hol. afternoons *Harvington Hall*: afternoons, Feb. to Nov.; also mornings Easter to Sept. *Hereford and Worcester County Museum*, Hartlebury Castle: Feb. to Nov., Mon. to Thur.; also Sat. and Sun. afternoons. *Spetchley Park*, 3 miles east of Worcester: gardens, Apr. to Oct., Mon. to Fri. and Sun. afternoon. *Worcester City Museum and Art Gallery*: weekdays.

Information centres Information Bureau, Norbury House, Droitwich. Tel. Droitwich 2352. The Guildhall, Worcester. Tel. Worcester 23471.

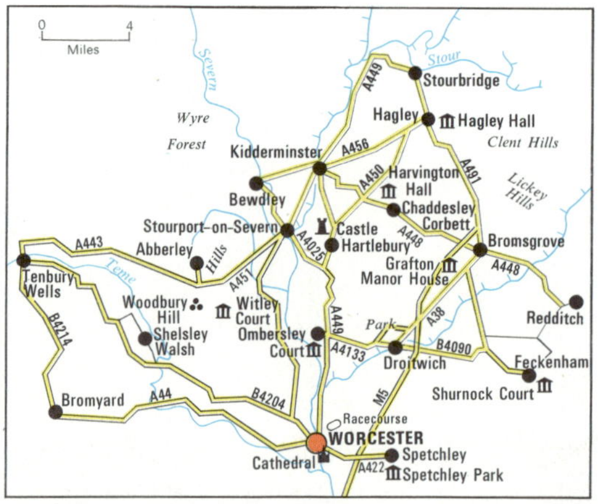

The eastern part of Hereford and Worcester has as much natural beauty as any area in England. The south has better scenery than the north, but even industrial towns of the Black Country are close to attractive countryside and have compensations in the form of beautiful old buildings and churches.

To the south-east of Stourbridge are the hills of Clent and Lickey, with woodlands, shrubs, pools and pleasant walking country rising to 1000 ft. There are farmlands between Redditch and Bromsgrove, and hills stretch along the Shropshire border to the west. Downstream from Stourport, pleasant dairy-farming land borders the River Severn as it widens on its way towards Worcester.

Just over a mile downstream from Worcester's magnificent cathedral, the Severn is joined by a sinuous stream called the Teme, one of the prettiest rivers in Britain, which winds its way through meadows, hop fields, woods, steep, lush green hills and orchards of cider apples and cherries. Beside its banks are bright green meadows; the soil is tinged with red sandstone, which dyes the water brick red when the river is in flood.

The farms grow hay, corn, apples and soft fruit, and the meadows are grazed by burly Hereford cattle. Hereford and Worcester is second only to Kent as a hop-producing county, and most of the hops grow along the Teme and westwards towards Bromyard.

FOUNTAINS AT WITLEY *Elegant classical fountains adorn the grounds of Witley Court, near Abberley. The house was burnt down in 1937, but a fine church stands beside the ruins*

OLD WORCESTER PORCELAIN

A porcelain bowl and saucer from the Dyson Perrins Museum, Worcester. They were made in the mid-18th century by the Worcester Porcelain Factory, now the Worcester Royal Porcelain Company. The cobalt-blue colouring became increasingly popular with 18th-century potters as it was the only colour that could be used under the glaze. The various forms of the letter W were marked on the factory's porcelain to indicate the exact date it was made during the Wall period (1751–76), which was named after Dr John Wall, one of the men who founded the company in 1751

RARE MOTH AMONG THE BIRCH TREES

The Kentish Glory moth, once abundant in the south of England, now survives in only a few districts—among them the Wyre Forest. It is, however, common in many parts of Scotland. The caterpillars feed on birch leaves

Abberley
A village which makes a good centre for walking and motoring tours of the Teme Valley and the thickly wooded Abberley Hills. At Great Witley, $2\frac{1}{2}$ miles southwards, Woodbury Hill is topped by ancient earthworks covering 20 acres, the largest in the county. An attractive Queen Anne house, The Elms, is now a hotel.

Bewdley
One of England's finest old towns, with a Georgian church and many 18th-century houses, especially in Load Street. Tickenhill House, on a hill above the town, has a brick façade added in 1738 to the remains of a Tudor royal palace. The town stands on the fringe of the Wyre Forest, and a $3\frac{1}{2}$-mile nature trail starts near the Duke William Inn.

Bromsgrove
Many fine buildings are to be seen in this town of light industries. Parts of the grammar school were built in 1553, and in the High Street there are several attractive Georgian houses. The sandstone Church of St John the Baptist has a 14th-century tower and spire. Grafton Manor, 2 miles south-west, has a Tudor chapel and a lake.

Chaddesley Corbett
A pretty village with half-timbered cottages and old buildings, notably the 14th-century Talbot Inn. The 14th-century church, dedicated to St Cassian who was murdered in the village, has a 12th-century font. Just north-west of the village is Harvington Hall, a manor house with a moat and secret passages.

Droitwich
Until recently, Droitwich was best known for the therapy treatment afforded by its brine water baths. The water was pumped from a lake over a bed of rock salt deposited 200 ft below ground, and as it contained 2½ lb. of salt in each gallon, 10 times more than sea water, it was extremely buoyant. Water is still pumped, with a reduced brine content, to an open-air pool in Droitwich Park.

Droitwich has the elegant atmosphere of Bath, and has some black-and-white timbered buildings, yet it is a lively market town. The Church of the Sacred Heart and St Catherine has walls and a ceiling covered with striking mosaics depicting the life of St Richard.

Feckenham
A charming village standing on what was a Roman road. It has several half-timbered and Georgian houses, and was once important for the manufacture of needles and fish-hooks—industries which are now centred in Redditch, 4 miles north. A mile east is 16th-century Shurnock Court, a whitewashed farmhouse with four chimneys, each built in the shape of an eight-pointed star.

Hagley
A large village notable for Hagley Hall, a Palladian building in a splendid landscaped park, with an Ionic temple, a rotunda and Gothic ruins. The mansion was built between 1754 and 1760 by Lord Lyttelton.

Hartlebury Castle
For centuries this has been the home of the Bishops of Worcester. Only the moat survives of the original castle, as the present red-sandstone mansion was built on its site in 1675. The mansion was completely restored in 1964. In the north wing is the Hereford and Worcester County Museum, which has exhibits of local crafts and industries.

Ombersley
A pretty village of half-timbered 16th and 17th-century houses and attractive old inns, the most picturesque being The King's Arms. Ombersley Court is a fine 18th-century mansion which was refaced early in the 19th century.

Shelsley Walsh
A tranquil village with leafy lanes set among hop fields and bordered by pleasant hills. On many weekends the air is filled with the roar of cars and motorcycles competing in sprint hill-climbs on a steep private road. The church has a late 15th-century screen.

WORCESTER CRICKET *Visiting Test sides by tradition play their first county match on the ground beside Worcester Cathedral*

Spetchley Park
A 19th-century mansion with ornamental gardens standing in a 20-acre park, containing red and fallow deer and a lake with many wildfowl. At Warndon, 3 miles north, is a church with a timbered tower and 15th-century font.

Stourport-on-Severn
Until the late 18th century, when the canals were built, Stourport was a quiet village. Then it became a bustling commercial centre, the busiest inland port in the Midlands after Birmingham. Today the canals are used mainly for pleasure boats. For the tourist on foot there are some fine Georgian houses and an iron bridge built in 1870.

Tenbury Wells
A market town on the River Teme, surrounded by apple orchards and hop fields. A saline spring was discovered there in 1839 and a pump room followed, but spas were going out of fashion and its popularity did not last long. The town has half-timbered and Georgian houses and a Tudor inn, The Royal Oak. The 18th-century church has several effigies and tombs, and a 12th-century tower with Norman windows.

Worcester
This ancient city, dominated by its magnificent cathedral, stands on the banks of the River Severn in the centre of a rich, fertile plain. It is compact enough for wandering in, and is rich in old buildings, including Greyfriars, a timbered Franciscan house of 1480. The Dyson Perrins Museum has one of the world's finest collections of Worcester porcelain and bone china. The splendid 18th-century guildhall displays Civil War armour used at the Battle of Worcester in 1651.

The cathedral was started in 1084 and has a beautiful crypt built by Bishop Wulfstan; the choir stalls were added in the 13th century, and the tower in the 14th century. Among the many monuments is the tomb of King John, including an effigy of his face. One of the best views of the cathedral is from the modern Giffard Hotel in the cathedral precincts. The cathedral overlooks one of the most peaceful and beautiful cricket grounds in England.

The Methodist Church of St Andrew has a very different setting, standing over a shopping arcade high above Pump Street. It was opened in 1968 and is reached by lift, or winding staircase beside a large, colourful stained-glass window in modern abstract style. All that remains of the 15th-century St Andrew's Church is a tower and spire 250 ft high above riverside gardens. Its local name is the Glover's Needle.

Beside the River Avon

Angling Coarse fishing on the Stratford Canal and on the Avon.

Boating Punts, canoes and rowing boats at Stratford-upon-Avon.

Nature trail Through Oversley Wood, starting from Alcester.

Horse racing Nat. Hunt meetings at Stratford-upon-Avon racecourse.

Events The Shakespeare Festival of plays at the Royal Shakespeare Theatre, Stratford-upon-Avon, lasts from Apr. to Dec.

Places to see in Stratford-upon-Avon *Hall's Croft*, Old Town: Apr. to Oct., weekdays, Sun. afternoons; Nov. to Mar., weekdays only. *Harvard House*: weekdays; also Sun. afternoons, Apr. to Sept. *Motor Museum*: daily. *New Place*: weekdays; also Sun. afternoons, Apr. to Oct. *Shakespeare's Birthplace*: daily, except Sun. mornings Nov. to Mar. *Theatre Picture Gallery*: Apr. to mid-Dec., daily; mid-Dec. to mid-Mar., Sat. and Sun. afternoons. *Tibor Tiatsa Collection*: weekdays.

Other places to see *Anne Hathaway's Cottage*, Shottery: daily, except Sun. mornings Nov. to Mar. *Charlecote Park* (NT): May to Sept., daily except Mon., but open Bank Hol.; Apr. and Oct., Sat. and Sun. *Compton Wynyates*: Apr. to Sept., Tues. to Sat. afternoons; also Sun. and Bank Hol. *Farnborough Hall* (NT): Apr. to Sept., Wed. and Sat. afternoons. *Mary Arden's House*, Wilmcote: Apr. to Oct., weekdays and Sun. afternoons; Nov. to Mar., weekdays only. *Upton House* (NT), Edge Hill: Apr. to Sept., Mon. to Thur. afternoons; also some Sat. and Sun. afternoons.

Information centre 1 High Street, Stratford-upon-Avon.
Tel. Stratford-upon-Avon 66175.

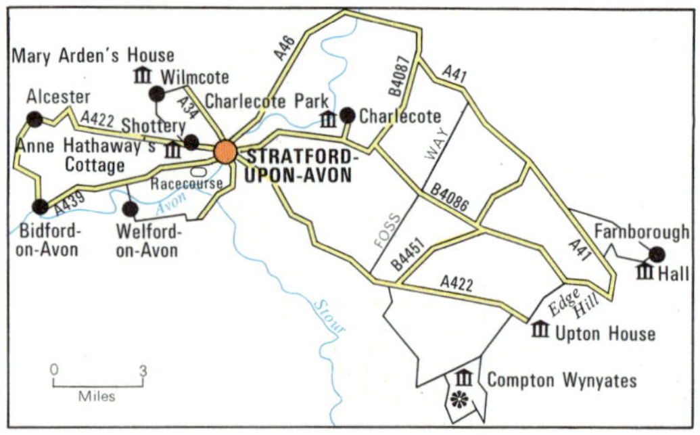

The countryside round Stratford-upon-Avon seems a world apart from the urban centres of the Midlands, and untouched by time. Much of its character is formed by the River Avon, edged with willows and flowing in a broad, peaceful valley through pasturelands where cattle graze. Mirrored by the water are the mighty battlements of Warwick Castle and the towers of humble village churches.

At Stratford-upon-Avon the swans gather round the arches of Clopton Bridge, and the view from the bridge of Holy Trinity Church in its riverside setting is one of the best-known in Britain. Boats can be hired, and the views from the water offer a different perspective of the town. Further downstream the river makes a broad loop round Welford-on-Avon and runs through Bidford-on-Avon, before crossing the border into Hereford and Worcester.

Little now remains of the great Forest of Arden of Shakespeare's day, but there are wooded walks and many quiet picnic spots on the river bank, not far from the places associated with Shakespeare's life. The gentle green countryside has few spectacular viewpoints, but Edge Hill is a dramatic exception. This high ridge gave its name to the first major battle of the Civil War. There is also a notable link with the more distant past in this corner of Warwickshire. A neolithic pillar, the King Stone, stands on its southern boundary. It is one of the Rollright Stones, a Bronze Age stone circle, the remainder of which lie in Oxfordshire.

VIEW FROM THE FOLLY *A tower built by a local eccentric in 1750 offers broad views over the countryside near Edge Hill*

Charlecote

A village with pleasing old cottages. The church was rebuilt in 1851, and in it can be found the Lucy family monuments, taken from the old church, the oldest dating from 1600.

An avenue of limes leads to Charlecote Park, a massive Elizabethan mansion set in fine, open parkland where deer roam. It was here that Shakespeare is said to have been caught poaching deer by the irate landlord. The story goes that he was birched and, in revenge, wrote lampoons on Sir Thomas Lucy, but when the authorship was discovered, fled to London, and so began his career. Charlecote, built by Sir Thomas Lucy in 1558, is now owned by the National Trust.

Farm buildings opposite the entrance to Charlecote Park have been converted into a restaurant, which has a walled garden where waterfowl, budgerigars and other birds are kept. Outside is a collection of historic carriages, including a phaeton that once belonged to Alphonso XII, the last king of Spain. Horse and carriage rides are available.

Compton Wynyates

One of the most beautiful houses in England—a superb example of Tudor architecture, little altered in later centuries. The stone and weathered brick of the exterior stand out against the dark green of the yews and hedges, which are tailored into neat, formal shapes. Behind the house, which has corkscrew Tudor chimneys, undulating countryside stretches away to the horizon. The name Compton recalls the family who built this house between 1480 and 1528. 'Wynyates' is Old English for 'valley through which the wind blows'.

The house was largely built of material salvaged by a member of the Compton family from the ruins of Fulbrook Castle, near Warwick. It contains a banqueting hall with a minstrels' gallery and a priest's hiding hole, skilfully concealed. An escape route used to lead from the hole out to the moat. But the house was captured by Cromwell's troops and returned to the Royalist Compton family on condition that the escape route was permanently blocked up.

Edge Hill

Magnificent beech trees line the road running along the top of the ridge, at the foot of which the first major battle of the Civil War took place in 1642. The castellated Edge Hill Tower, now part of the local inn, The Castle, was built as a folly by Sanderson Miller, a local squire and architect in the 18th century. There is a fine view from the top of the tower.

Farnborough Hall, built in Italianate style, lies in a hollow on the other side of the valley and is owned by the National Trust. The principal rooms contain Italian paintings and sculptures, and look out across an artificial lake to Edge Hill. The best view of the tree-lined ridge, however, is obtained from the top of a landscaped terrace which has two temples and an obelisk.

Shottery

The village is only a mile west of the centre of Stratford-upon-Avon, and Anne Hathaway's cottage is clearly signposted. The 'cottage' is in fact a thatched house of 12 rooms. The section

ANNE'S COTTAGE *This 15th-century thatched cottage at Shottery was Anne Hathaway's home until her marriage to William Shakespeare c. 1582*

WHERE THE AVON FLOWS QUIETLY TO THE WEST *A few minutes' walk upstream from Stratford lies a stretch of the River Avon which has remained unchanged since Shakespeare's time. The river rises at Naseby in Northamptonshire and finally flows into the Severn at Tewkesbury in Gloucestershire; the name Avon comes from afon, Welsh for river*

of the house furthest from the road was badly damaged by fire in late 1969, but it has now been fully restored. In the parlour is the uncomfortable narrow bench, or settle, where Shakespeare is thought to have courted his future bride. In spring and summer the typically English cottage gardens are ablaze with flowers, including some fine roses.

Stratford-upon-Avon

This old market town, the birthplace of William Shakespeare, has become one of the world's most famous tourist centres. From April to October it attracts thousands of visitors who come here to trace the poet's life from cradle to grave.

Stratford is best explored on foot, and the main centres of interest can be seen in a walk taking about two hours. From Shakespeare's birthplace, a half-timbered early 16th-century building in Henley Street, the route runs down Bridge Street to Clopton Bridge, built in the 15th century by Hugh Clopton, who became Lord Mayor of London and who built New Place in Chapel Street. From the bridge a road on the west bank passes the red-brick Royal Shakespeare Theatre, built in 1932.

The theatre gardens run down to the river bank. On the south side, a gate leads back to Southern Lane and to the tree-lined approach to Holy Trinity Church. This beautiful parish church, overlooking the river, is Shakespeare's burial place. His tomb and those of some of his family are marked by simple engraved stones in front of the altar.

Not far from the church is Hall's Croft, the home of Shakespeare's daughter, Susanna, who married Dr John Hall. The house has fine Tudor gables and a walled garden. From Hall's Croft, Church Street leads back to the centre of the bustling market town.

Many hotels and shops in Stratford-upon-Avon have been renovated in the accepted half-timbered style, with black beams criss-crossing whitewashed walls. Other buildings, including the properties that belong to the Shakespeare Birthplace Trust, have been carefully restored to their original colour, with the natural tone of the wood offset by a warm, cream-coloured wash.

A contrast to the Shakespearian emphasis in Stratford-upon-Avon can be found in the Tibor Tiatsa Collection of miniature model cars and the exhibition of textiles and ceramics which are kept on permanent display in a shop at 60 Ely Street.

Upton House

A William-and-Mary mansion owned by the National Trust. The gardens surrounding the house are laid out on gentle slopes against a background of woods. There is a large collection of paintings which includes works by the English artist George Stubbs and the Dutch master Peter Breughel, as well as a fine collection of Sèvres porcelain.

Wilmcote

The village where Shakespeare's mother, Mary Arden, was born. Her house, a well-preserved Tudor building, is a typical farmhouse of the period. Many old agricultural implements, known as Warwickshire bygones, can be seen in an exhibition in the converted buildings at the back of the house.

THE PLAYS *Viola and Olivia in a scene from* Twelfth Night *during the Royal Shakespeare Theatre season*

THE PLAYWRIGHT *A statue of Shakespeare stands in the garden of his birthplace in Henley Street. In the garden are trees, shrubs and flowers mentioned in his plays or poems, and the carefully preserved half-timbered house is furnished as in his day*

Shakespeare's Stratford

Shakespeare never lost touch with his home town of Stratford-upon-Avon, even at the height of his success in London, and much of the homely imagery in his plays derives from Stratford's busy streets and peaceful countryside. In Shakespeare's youth, Stratford was an important market centre, and market days gave the boy a chance to note the manners, dress and speech of its tradesmen, farmers, milkmaids, lawyers and 'poor market-folks that come to sell their corn', as he was later to describe them in *Henry VI*. Throughout his life Shakespeare remembered with delight the herbs and flowers in Stratford's gardens and fields: 'Hot lavender, mints, savory, marjoram; the marigold that goes to bed wi' the sun . . .'; and in *Love's Labour's Lost* he may have been thinking of winter visits to his grandparents' farm at Wilmcote as he wrote: 'When icicles hang by the wall, and Dick the shepherd blows his nail.'

TRAVELLING PLAYERS *Troupes of players from London regularly visited the provinces. When Shakespeare was five the Queen's Players came to Stratford, setting a fashion that soon made the town a centre for touring companies. In 1587, the year Shakespeare is thought to have left for London, at least five companies played in the town. Tradition has it that Shakespeare fled Stratford for London after being caught poaching Sir Thomas Lucy's deer in Charlecote Park (below); but it is more likely that he went to look for a job in the theatre, inspired by the plays he had seen in Stratford to become an actor 'who struts and frets his hour upon the stage'*

SHOEMAKER'S SHOP *As an important market town, Shakespeare's Stratford was a centre for many trades, most of them, like the crafts of the millers, tanners, wheelwrights, blacksmiths, weavers and shoemakers, closely linked with agriculture. Shakespeare's father, the son of a yeoman farmer from nearby Snitterfield, rose in the world to become a successful Stratford tradesman; he made gloves, traded in wool and hides and may even have been a retail butcher. In 1557 he married Mary Arden, the daughter of Robert Arden, a wealthy gentleman farmer from Wilmcote; and during his lifetime he held all the town offices from ale-taster to bailiff*

WORKING IN THE FIELDS *Peaceful fields and woodland lay close around Stratford's bustling streets, and on market days the town was thronged with farmers. Malting, the preparation of barley for brewing beer, was Stratford's principal trade*

TUDOR MILKMAID *In Stratford, most families had at least one cow, and a prosperous farming family such as the Ardens had several. When Shakespeare's grandfather Robert Arden died in 1556, he left seven cows and other livestock*

POET'S TOWN *The earliest known map of Stratford, made in 1759, shows the town still very much as it was in Shakespeare's day. The site of Shakespeare's mansion, New Place, is at 1 on the map, and at 2 is the guild chapel, guildhall and grammar school. Shakespeare's birthplace is at 3, and 4 marks the town's principal market-place, Rother Market.*

Stratford in Shakespeare's time was a centre for the marketing of corn, malt and livestock. Its malting trade, dating back to the Middle Ages, reached as far as Wales, Cheshire and Lancashire. Stratford's population of 1500, large for a country town in an age when London's population was only 200,000, made it a town of far more consequence in the Midlands than it is today. Stratford was also a centre of local government and of rural business, with one of the finest grammar schools in the country. The town itself was governed by a council, headed by a bailiff.

Some claim that Shakespeare could not have written the plays attributed to him because he was no more than a 'country bumpkin'. But the 'William Shakespeare gent' who was Stratford's leading citizen when he died in 1616 was actually, as the Shakespearian critic Ivor Brown put it, 'a country-town boy, which is quite a different thing from a country boy'. His father, a wealthy tradesman, had been bailiff of the town in 1568, and his mother was the daughter of a prosperous gentleman-farmer of an old Warwickshire family. Shakespeare himself, in the words of one who knew him, was 'a handsome, well-shaped man, very good company, and of a very ready smooth wit'. When he went to London, Shakespeare often played before Elizabeth I, rubbing shoulders with her aristocratic courtiers.

All of this went into his plays—the glitter of London, the solid virtues of his home town and the countryside around it. Above all, it was the ancient borough of Stratford, in the heartland of England, that shaped the man revered as the greatest poet of the English language

DINING AT HOME *A middle-class provincial family ate well, though their meals were less elaborate than in London. Justice Shallow, entertaining Falstaff to a country meal in Shakespeare's* Henry IV, *ordered: 'Some pigeons . . . a couple of short-legged hens, a joint of mutton.' This diet of meat often led to scurvy, especially in winter when there were no vegetables or fruit*

NEW PLACE *In 1597 Shakespeare bought New Place, one of the finest and largest houses in Stratford. He retired there in 1610, six years before he died. This sketch, drawn from memory by an engraver, George Vertue, in 1737, is the only known illustration of the house, which was demolished c. 1702*

SHAKESPEARE'S BIRTHPLACE *Shakespeare was born in 1564 in this house in Henley Street, Stratford. The house was his father's home and workshop, and in Shakespeare's lifetime it was two separate buildings. Built in the early 16th century, it has been restored and is now a tourist attraction. It is a typical middle-class dwelling of the period and, like most of the Stratford houses dating from Shakespeare's time, it is half-timbered, with the spaces between its strong oak framing filled in with wattle and daub*

SHAKESPEARE'S SCHOOL *The young Shakespeare was educated at the King's New Grammar School, in the upper floor of the long building to the left. Drawing on memories of his schooldays, Shakespeare was later to write, perhaps with some sympathy, of 'the whining schoolboy, with his satchel, and shining morning face, creeping like snail unwillingly to school'. Below the schoolroom was the guildhall, where touring players gave a performance for the town council before being licensed to play in the town*

Birmingham reborn

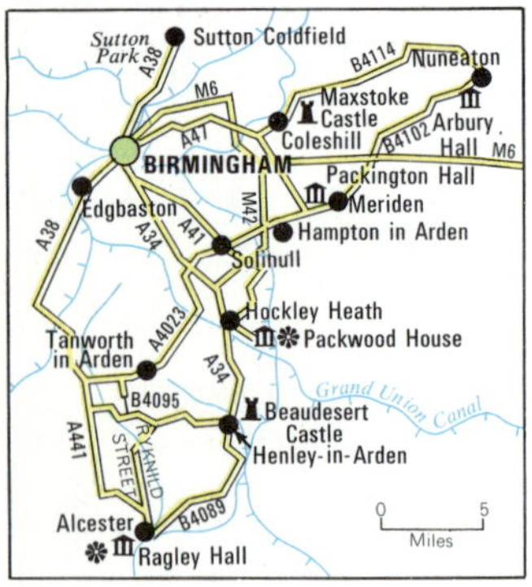

Places to see *Arbury Hall*: Easter to early Oct., Bank Hol. Mon. and Sun. afternoons. *Aston Hall*, Birmingham: weekdays and Sun afternoon, Apr. to Oct. *Botanical Gardens*, Edgbaston: daily. *City Museum and Art Gallery*, Birmingham: weekdays. *Coughton Court* (NT), 2 miles north of Alcester: afternoons only; May to Sept., Wed., Thur., Sat., Sun. and Bank Hol. Mon.; Apr. and Oct., Sat. and Sun. *Packwood House* (NT): afternoons only; Apr. to Sept., Wed. to Sun., and Bank Hol. Mon.; Oct. to Mar., Wed., Sat., Sun. *Ragley Hall*: early Apr. to Sept., afternoons except Mon. and Fri. *Sarehole Mill*, Hall Green: Wed. to Sat. afternoons. *Selly Manor*, Bourneville, 3 miles south of Edgbaston: Tues., Wed., and Fri afternoons. *Weoley Castle*, Birmingham: Wed. to Sat. afternoons.

Information centre Council House, Victoria Square, Birmingham. Tel. 021–235 3411/2.

The West Midlands county is dominated by the great industrial city of Birmingham and its suburbs, a sprawling area of factories and other buildings which have spread into the surrounding countryside. The population of the whole county is a little over $2\frac{3}{4}$ million, of whom a million live in the municipal area of Birmingham.

Hundreds of industries, large and small, are centred there. Despite the dirt and ugliness brought by the Industrial Revolution, there are many attractive features, mostly man-made—lovely buildings, beautiful parks and suburban streets lined with trees.

The massive rebuilding which has been going on in recent years has transformed Birmingham. The city is also the centre of Britain's canal system and, apart from the commercial use of its waterways, it is a fine place for beginning inland-waterway cruising into neighbouring counties and even to London along the Grand Union Canal.

In Shakespeare's day the thickly wooded Forest of Arden covered 200 square miles to the north and west of the Avon, but all that now remains of this great forest are widely scattered clumps of trees. Before coal was mined extensively in the Midlands, the trees were cut down as fuel for the iron works of the area.

The names of some villages in the area still serve as a reminder of the days when the land was covered by forest: Henley-in-Arden and Tamworth in Arden. Shakespeare is believed to have used Hampton in Arden as the scene for most of *As You Like It*.

CITY OF NATURE *The Botanical Gardens at Edgbaston, opened in 1832, include a house specially built for a giant Amazon water lily*

Alcester
An old market town standing at the junction of two Roman roads and where two rivers, the Alne and the Arrow, meet. Little remains of the Roman camp near the Roman Ryknild Street, but the town keeps its old-world look with timber-fronted houses, old windows, and its 17th-century, timber-topped town hall. Alcester has long been known for its cabinet making.

Ragley Hall, $1\frac{1}{2}$ miles south-west, has records going back to AD 710. It is the seat of the Marquess of Hertford, whose family have owned the land since 1591 and the hall, which contains some magnificent baroque plaster-work and many fine paintings, since it was built in 1680. It is surrounded by 8000 acres of farmland and woodland and a 400-acre park, including a lake, that was landscaped by Capability Brown.

CITY OF ART *Birmingham's Art Gallery in Congreve Street has a fine collection of pre-Raphaelite paintings, and Rodin, Epstein and Henry Moore sculptures*

Arbury Hall
The seat of the Newdegate family since the 16th century, Arbury Hall was built on the site of an Augustinian priory. It was originally Elizabethan, but in the 18th century was transformed into a Gothic-style mansion. It has large grounds and a landscaped garden. The novelist George Eliot (1819–80) was born at South Farm on the estate.

Birmingham
In Shakespeare's day, this was a market town lying in the heart of the English countryside, surrounded by forests and common land. But even then it was important for industry. Birmingham was noted for its large number of smiths who, using coal from the North Warwickshire mines as fuel, hammered out anything from door knockers to arms. During the Civil War they made more than 15,000 swords for Cromwell and the Parliamentary forces.

The Industrial Revolution caused a rapid expansion of trades and crafts, and Queen Victoria declared Birmingham a city. The expansion continued and Birmingham became one of the greatest industrial cities in the world, and the second largest city in Britain. The cost of this was much dirt and ugliness, shoddy, mock-Gothic buildings and back-to-back houses. Despite this it produced the best art galleries outside London, a university respected all over the world, a theatre, the Birmingham Repertory Theatre, where great actors have learnt their art, and one of Britain's leading orchestras.

Birmingham has been transformed. Whereas other city centres have been rebuilt from scratch after heavy bombing in the Second World War, Birmingham has been changed into a city of the future as it goes on living and working. Even New Street Station is new again—a gleaming, white-tiled place of bright

SERMON IN TREES *Yew trees planted at Packwood House represent Christ (the tallest tree), the four evangelists, the apostles and the multitude at the Sermon on the Mount*

HONEY FROM THE WALL *When the gardens of Packwood House were laid out by John Fetherston in the 17th century, 30 'boles', or niches, were set into the wall as bee hives*

lights. Many other things are new—the post office with its attractive tower, roads, houses, factories and schools.

The modernisation is most marked around the Bull Ring where new roads and office blocks have changed the face of this historic market-place. Markets have stood there since the 12th century, but none like the present one.

The best of the old remains. The town hall, the city's concert hall, based on the temple of Castor and Pollux in Rome, looks as elegant as ever among its new neighbours. The Cathedral Church of St Philip, in English Baroque of 1715, also remains. Aston Hall, a Jacobean mansion with fine carved fireplaces and needlework hangings, is in Aston Park—a museum now, but left just as it was when the Holte family lived there.

The city museum and art gallery has pictures by Van Gogh, Claude, Botticelli, Gainsborough and Constable, and a magnificent collection of sculptures by Epstein, Moore, Rodin and Hepworth.

Amid the old and the new, there is still Birmingham's network of canals, with signposts reading 'Liverpool' and 'Manchester', 'Coventry' and 'London', 'Nottingham' and 'Lincoln'.

Coleshill

As its name implies, this pretty village stands on the side of a steep hill above the River Cole, which is crossed there by a five-arched medieval bridge. Near the church, which has a 14th-century tower, are the pillory, village stocks and a whipping-post. Maxstoke Castle, 2 miles east, is a 14th-century building in red sandstone, with a great hall built by the Earl of Huntingdon in 1345.

Edgbaston

One of the prettiest suburbs of Birmingham which includes the university, the Warwickshire county cricket ground, and botanical gardens containing a large collection of trees and shrubs, an alpine garden, a palm-house, and a small zoo. The magnificent clock tower on the university building can be seen for miles.

Henley-in-Arden

This small market town is a fine walking centre, set in gently undulating country beside the River Alne in what used to be the heart of the Forest of Arden. The long main street is lined with oak-timbered buildings, mostly 15th, 16th and 17th century. There are two old inns, the 16th-century White Swan and the 15th-century Blue Bell, and a 15th-century guildhall. The church has magnificent roof beams and stone carvings. Near the earthworks, which are the sole remains of Beaudesert Castle, is a 12th-century church which has a Perpendicular west tower and a Norman chancel arch.

Meriden

This village claims that the medieval cross on its village green marks the centre of England. Just west of Meriden is 18th-century Forest Hall, the headquarters of the Woodmen of Arden, one of the oldest archery societies in England. The society was established in 1785, and its membership is restricted to 81 archers.

Packington Hall, 2 miles north-west, is surrounded by a 700-acre woodland park which has a herd of fallow deer. In the park is the Old Hall, dating from 1679, which incorporates an earlier house visited by Charles I in 1642.

Packwood House

In the grounds of this house is a remarkable 17th-century garden of shaped yew trees depicting the Sermon on the Mount. Trees representing four evangelists, the 12 apostles and the Lord are arranged on a great lawn, with another collection of yews representing the multitude. The house itself is a lovely example of a timber-framed Tudor building, built mainly between 1556 and 1560 by William Fetherston.

ENGLAND'S CENTRE *Meriden's medieval cross is said to mark the centre of England*

Solihull

Although Birmingham's sprawl has reached it, Solihull is a county borough in its own right with a population of 100,000. The buildings are a pleasant mixture of old and new with many examples of timber-framed Tudor houses and shops. Particularly attractive are the George Inn, the 15th-century Old Berry Hall, which still has part of its moat, and Solihull Hall. Solihull School was founded in 1560.

Sutton Coldfield

A medieval market town which is now a dormitory town for Birmingham, 7 miles away. Its main attraction is the magnificent 2400-acre park to the west of the town, one of the best natural parks in Britain. There are woods, valleys, open moors covered in gorse and heather, large lakes for boating, bathing and fishing, bird sanctuaries, and a championship golf course. Near the golf course is Old Moor Hall, the 15th-century home of Bishop Vesey of Exeter. Several of the stone houses built by him in the 16th century can still be seen in the town. The old Roman Ryknild Street runs through the park.

COLESHILL RELICS *A whipping-post and pillory are preserved at Church Hill*

Coventry – beauty from ruins

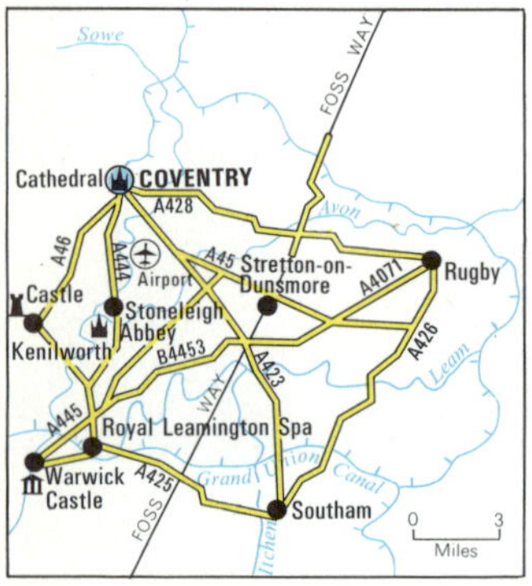

Angling Trout and coarse fishing on the Leam and Avon at Leamington, and on the Grand Union Canal at Warwick.

Horse racing Flat racing and steeplechasing at Warwick.

Flying Baginton Airport, Coventry.

Events The Royal Show is held in July at Stoneleigh. The Warwick Mop Fair is held in Oct.; originally a mop fair was held for the hire of servants but now it is a carnival. The Wroth Silver ceremony is held on Knightlow Hill, Dunchurch, in Nov. when tithes are paid to the Duke of Buccleuch.

Places to see *Herbert Art Gallery and Museum*, Jordan Wall, Coventry; weekdays and Sun. afternoons. *Jephson Gardens* and bird sanctuary, Leamington Spa: daily. *Kenilworth Castle*: daily, except Sun. mornings Oct. to Mar. *Leamington Spa Art Gallery and Museum*, Avenue Road: weekdays, except Wed. afternoon. *Lord Leycester's Hospital*, Warwick: weekdays. *Lunt Roman Fort and Museum*, Baginton, 3 miles south of Coventry: late May to Sept., afternoons except Mon. and Thur. *Oken's House*, Warwick: weekdays, Sun. afternoon. *Rugby Gallery and Museum*, St Matthew Street: daily. *St John's House*, Warwick, including *Museum of Royal Warwickshire Regiment*: weekdays except Tues.; also Sun. afternoon May to Sept. *Warwick Castle*: daily. *Warwickshire Museum*, Warwick: weekdays; also Sun. afternoons in summer. *Zoo Park*, Whitley Common, Coventry: daily.

Information centres Coventry Information Centre, Broadgate. Tel. Coventry 20084. Warwick Council Offices, Court House, Warwick. Tel. Warwick 42212.

The city of Coventry is a pleasant surprise in a mining and industrial area. The centre bears little outward sign of the city's industrial importance, or of the fact that at the end of the Second World War it was a mass of rubble. The modern shops, cinemas, restaurants and car parks at the heart of the city are set amid flowered public parks, and only the untouched shell of the old cathedral, alongside the new cathedral, recalls the wartime destruction when most of the centre of the city was levelled in one air raid.

Green open spaces surround the city, and the countryside to the south has variety and beauty, as well as historical interest. Kenilworth Castle, frequently visited by Elizabeth I and her court, is now in ruins, but is still an impressive sight. Warwick is dominated by another great castle, home of the Earls of Warwick until recent years. Royal Leamington Spa, in keeping with its name, is a town of graceful terraces, spacious gardens and riverside walks, while further south lies Shakespeare country.

To the north of Coventry the landscape is largely man-made. Open-cast mining has left its scars and slagheaps, and former villages have been engulfed by spreading towns. Yet even here there is still a trace of the original rural character of much of the rest of the county. Rugby today exhibits an almost totally industrial face, but it lives in history as the rural town of *Tom Brown's Schooldays,* and as the home of one of the most famous public schools in the country—which gave to the world the sport of Rugby football, though the rules have changed considerably since Thomas Hughes' famous description in his book.

PREPARING A PRIZEWINNER *A brewer's drayhorse is prepared for the ring at Stoneleigh Abbey, the National Agricultural Centre and permanent home of the Royal Show*

Coventry
An important city since the 14th century, with a history dating from Anglo-Saxon times. A nunnery destroyed by the Danes was replaced by a Benedictine monastery founded in the 11th century by Leofric, Earl of Mercia. It was his wife, Godiva, who is said to have ridden naked through the streets of Coventry in protest against the oppression of the people by Leofric. The original 'Peeping Tom' who came out to look is commemorated by three statues. One is a 17th-century wooden statue on the first floor of the Leofric Hotel, the second is above a shop-front on Hertford Street, and the third is on a clock overlooking Broadgate, the city's main square; as Lady Godiva crosses the clock, the head of Peeping Tom pops up. A statue to Lady Godiva stands in Broadgate.

On the night of November 14, 1940, 40 acres of the city centre were destroyed by German bombers. After the war, Coventry was rebuilt and a new cathedral was consecrated on May 25, 1962. The blackened ruins of the old cathedral form an approach to the new, and a wooden cross made out of two charred roof timbers has been placed on the original altar with the inscription 'Father Forgive' carved behind it.

The new cathedral, designed by Sir Basil Spence, is an exciting example of modern architecture. The exterior is of pink-grey sandstone in a series of massive vertical structures, stark and Gothic in their effect. Graham Sutherland's vast tapestry of 'Christ in Glory' dominates the nave, which is lit by slanted stained-glass windows throwing strips of light towards the altar.

A few of Coventry's medieval buildings remain—among them St Mary's Hall, once a merchant's guildhall; the Church of the Holy Trinity; St John's Church; St John's Hospital; and the lovely timbered houses in Priory Row. There are also some well-preserved old city gates. But primarily Coventry is a modern city, with well-planned shopping centres, a new civic theatre, the Belgrade, and fine parks and gardens. The University of Warwick is 4 miles south-west of the city.

Kenilworth
The dramatic ruins of the great castle stand on a gentle grass slope a short distance from the modern town centre. The main street of the original town winds away to the left of the main gateway. The castle was a stronghold for lords and kings of England in the 11th and 12th centuries, and re-modelled as a palace by John of Gaunt, the fourth son of Edward III, in the 14th century.

The Earl of Leicester entertained Elizabeth I at Kenilworth, but the castle has not been lived in since the Restoration. Its chief points of interest are the remains of the keep, and the pleasure gardens laid out by the Earl of Leicester, the outlines of which are still visible. The great 16th-century northern gatehouse still survives, as does much of John of Gaunt's banqueting hall. The castle is the setting for much of the action in Sir Walter Scott's *Kenilworth*.

Royal Leamington Spa
A spacious town on the River Leam, owing its fame to natural spring saline waters, the presence of which was first recorded in 1586. Queen Victoria granted the prefix 'Royal' to the town after a visit in 1838. Leamington has been a fashionable health resort ever since, and the mineral waters can be taken under supervision, at the Royal

FORTRESS HOME *The 14th-century Warwick Castle was converted into a house in the 17th century and was continuously inhabited by the Earls of Warwick until recently*

Pump Room in the town centre. The terraces leading off the main shopping street, The Parade, are fine examples of late Georgian architecture.

Rugby

A town noted for its important railway junction, called Mugby Junction by Dickens in a story in a special Christmas number of the magazine *All The Year Round*, and for its public school, founded in 1567. Rugby's distinguished ex-pupils include the poet Matthew Arnold, son of the school's most famous headmaster, Dr Thomas Arnold, who was described by Thomas Hughes, also an ex-pupil, in *Tom Brown's Schooldays*.

Rugby football originated at the school, and a tablet on a wall inside the close by the school buildings, which can be seen by appointment with the porter, describes 'the exploit of William Webb Ellis, who with a fine disregard for the rules of football as played in his time, first took the ball in his arms and ran with it, thus originating the distinctive feature of this Rugby game AD 1823'.

Southam

Market Hill, the main street of this old market town with a bridge over the River Itchen, makes a broad sweep past the 14th-century Church of St James, notable for its broach spire. The town has associations with the Civil War—Charles I stayed at the Manor House on Market Hill, now a chemist's shop.

An inn, originally called The Horse and Jockey, has been renamed The Old Mint, a reminder that in medieval times Southam 'tokens' were minted in the district. These were a form of local currency in small denominations—used because local people found normal coins too high in value for everyday use. Some Southam farthings are collectors' pieces or are in museums.

LADY GODIVA *A statue in Broadgate commemorates Lady Godiva, who rode naked through Coventry in protest at her husband's oppression of the citizens*

PEEPING TOM *Animated figures on a clock overlooking Broadgate in Coventry tell the story of Peeping Tom—the only man who looked at the nude Lady Godiva*

Stoneleigh

A compact village close to a former abbey, and approached across a stone bridge. In the village churchyard is buried the Duchess Dudley, who died in 1669 aged 98, and was the first woman to be created a duchess in her own right. Near the church are some half-timbered Elizabethan houses. There are also a few cruck-framed cottages, using curved oak beams as the main supports.

Part of Stoneleigh Abbey grounds are now the permanent site of the National Agricultural Centre, the site of the Royal Show and the centre of the British Show Jumping Association.

Warwick

The county town on the banks of the River Avon is best explored on foot. It is small and compact, and a pleasant blend of Georgian and Tudor architecture. Overlooking the river stands Warwick Castle, which was sold by Lord Brooke in 1978 after having been in his family's possession since 1605.

Mill Street, a cul-de-sac ending at the castle wall, has some attractive half-timbered houses. Oken's House, near the castle wall, contains the Joy Robinson doll museum, named after the woman who inherited and enlarged the collection of wood, china, metal and wax dolls and placed it in the museum in 1955.

Lord Leycester's Hospital in High Street has an exceptionally attractive half-timbered courtyard.

OKEN'S HOUSE *Thomas Oken was one of the principal citizens of Warwick in the 16th century. His house, which survived a fire in 1694, is now a museum of dolls*

Close to Shire Hall, the county's administrative headquarters, stands St Mary's Church, rebuilt in 1704 after a fire. The 15th-century Beauchamp Chapel, part of the old church, contains the tomb of Richard Beauchamp, Earl of Warwick, who died in Rouen in 1439. It is this Earl who is portrayed in Bernard Shaw's *St Joan* and who was largely responsible for her execution. Robert Dudley, the Earl of Leicester who entertained Elizabeth I at Kenilworth, is also buried here.

Northampton and the River Nene

Boating Boats can be hired on the Grand Union Canal and at towns along the River Nene.

Angling Coarse fishing on the Nene and its tributaries; Fawsley Park Lakes and Ashby Road Reservoir, Daventry; Castle Ashby Lakes; Sywell and Hollowell Reservoirs; Abington Park. Trout on Ravensthorpe Reservoir, north-west of Northampton.

Sports Golf: Borough Hill and Northampton. Swimming: Billing Aquadrome, Overstone Solarium and Northampton (open-air and indoor pools). Motor racing: Silverstone. National Hunt steeplechasing: Towcester.

Places to see *Abington Museum* and *Museum of the Northamptonshire Regiment*, Northampton: weekdays; also Sun. afternoon, Apr. to Sept. *Castle Ashby*: Apr. to Sept., Thur., Sun. and Bank Hol. afternoons. *Central Museum and Art Gallery*, Northampton: weekdays. *Museum of Leathercraft*, Northampton: weekdays. *Stoke Bruerne Waterways Museum*: daily, except Mon. Oct. to Mar. *Stoke Park Pavilions*, 3 miles east of Towcester, Inigo Jones pavilions and linking colonnades: June and July, Sat. and Sun. afternoons. *Sulgrave Manor*: daily except Wed., Feb. to Dec.

Information centre 21 St Giles Street, Northampton. Tel. Northampton 34881.

SULGRAVE MANOR *The arms of Washington's ancestors above the porch are said to be the origins of the American flag*

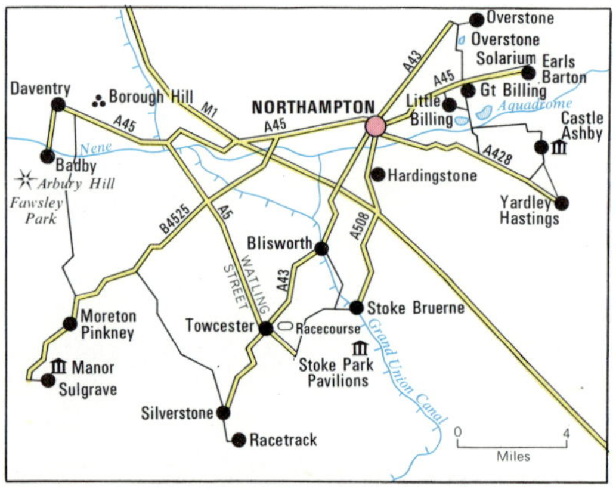

The scenery in the southern half of Northamptonshire is pleasant rather than spectacular. Away from the thundering traffic of the M1, which slices across the county, the industrial aspect of Northampton quickly gives way to broad landscapes broken by occasional farm buildings, especially to the south-west of the city. The switchbacks of the winding B4525 from Northampton towards Banbury in Oxfordshire reveal glimpses of stone houses and church spires that appear above the crest of a hill, only to disappear again between the folds of green slopes.

Though far from the sea, Northamptonshire offers ample opportunity for water sports. Its canals, rivers, lakes and reservoirs are used to capacity. There is cruising on the Grand Union Canal which connects with the River Nene. Using both waterways, it is possible to sail to the Wash. There is swimming and sailing at Billing Aquadrome, and fishing in many lakes and rivers.

This part of the county has close links with English history. The Battle of Northampton, fought at Hardingstone Fields in 1460, at which the Yorkists captured Henry VI, was a crucial battle of the Wars of the Roses. Two centuries later, during the Civil War, the Royalists camped at Northampton and Daventry before the two battles of Edgehill and Naseby, which were equally crucial for England. The county is also indirectly linked with American history and the American War of Independence, for at Sulgrave lived the ancestors of George Washington.

Badby
An attractive village on a hillside, with some thatched cottages and a wood, Badby Wood, which is carpeted with bluebells in spring. Arbury Hill, $1\frac{1}{2}$ miles south-west, is topped by the earthworks of a Roman camp.

Fawsley Park, 2 miles south, where Charles I hunted deer, has a chain of lakes, a ruined Tudor dower house, a 16th-century hall that was the home of the Knightley family for more than 400 years, and a medieval church in which there are monuments to the Knightley family and a magnificent 17th-century altar-tomb.

Castle Ashby
An impressive approach to the castle and its adjoining hamlet is along the minor road that runs from Yardley Hastings between avenues of stately trees. The castle, set in a large park landscaped by Capability Brown, is a splendid 16th to 17th-century mansion where the Compton family, who became Marquesses of Northampton, have lived since 1574. A parapet along the top balustrade has a carved Biblical inscription, and the interior of the house contains some fine decoration, furniture, tapestries and paintings.

Daventry
This small town's past stretches back to prehistoric times. Huge earthworks mark the site of an Iron Age fortified camp on Borough Hill, just east of the town. There are magnificent views from the top, despite the forest of radio masts of the Daventry broadcasting station.

During the Civil War the Royalist army camped round the hill before their defeat at the Battle of Naseby, and tradition has it that Charles I slept at the Wheatsheaf Inn. The town has a pleasant market-place and an 18th-century church and moot hall.

Great Billing
The village forms a semicircle, with two access points to the Northampton–Wellingborough road. The church is partly Norman, and there is a post office dated 1703.

At Little Billing, 1 mile south, is the Billing Aquadrome, a recreational centre set round five lakes, which are flooded gravel pits, in a 250-acre park. It contains a boating marina linked to the River Nene, lakes for anglers, an outdoor swimming pool, a working watermill and a miniature railway.

Earls Barton, $2\frac{1}{2}$ miles east, has a church with one of the finest Saxon towers in England.

Moreton Pinkney
The road through this pretty village is full of bends—made it is said, to avoid squatters' cottages on the green when the road was originally built. Some 17th and 18th-century houses have attractive stonework and thatched roofs. The 13th-century church has a beautiful chancel, restored in 1845.

Northampton
A lively county town on the River Nene, best known today for its shoe industry. Oak bark was extensively used to tan leather until about a century ago and tanneries were built along the banks of the Nene and its tributaries, close to the trees and water they required. Northampton became the main centre to which the treated leather was sent. During the Civil War, Northampton provided 1500 pairs of shoes for Cromwell's forces—and as a result its castle and town walls were destroyed by Charles II.

The Central Museum and Art Gallery in Guildhall Road has a display of shoes, past and present. These include the shoes worn by Queen Victoria for her wedding and, from later times, ballet shoes worn by Nijinsky and Margot Fonteyn. The most unusual exhibit is one of a set of boots made for an elephant in 1959 when the British Alpine Expedition re-enacted Hannibal's crossing of the Alps. There is also a cobbler's shop, dating from a century ago, complete with all its tools.

The town centre was rebuilt after a disastrous fire in 1675, but its old market square, one of the largest in England, is still in use. Two churches are particularly remarkable. St Sepulchre's, near the market-place, goes back to the time of the Crusades and is a circular replica of the original in Jerusalem. St Matthew's, in the Phippsville district on the Kettering road, was built in the Gothic revival style of the last century and has close associations with the High Church evangelical Oxford Movement of the early 19th century. This church has since become famous for commissioning paintings and sculpture. It has two important modern works of art—a Crucifixion painted by Graham Sutherland and a Madonna and Child

CASTLE ASHBY *Magnificent 18th-century iron gates guard the approach to the house, built in 1574 by the first Earl of Northampton, and later improved by Inigo Jones*

sculpture by Henry Moore. The late-Victorian Repertory Theatre in Guildhall Road houses the long-established Northampton Repertory Company in an ornate setting of gilt and red plush.

Overstone

A village built mainly of stone, as its name suggests. Overstone Hall, now a girls' school, is an extravagant Victorian building standing in a park with a lake. The church is Gothic, of rather pale stone for this area, and was rebuilt in 1807. It has some 16th-century stained glass, and two early 18th-century monuments by John Hunt.

Overstone Solarium, $\frac{1}{2}$ mile south, is a 'water playground' with two lakes, a swimming pool and a ballroom and conference centre decorated with furnishings taken from a nearby mansion, Horton Hall, demolished in 1936.

Stoke Bruerne

A village on the Grand Union Canal, which runs through a tunnel over a mile long between Stoke Bruerne and Blisworth. The Waterways Museum, housed in a former warehouse on the towpath, illustrates the period when the canals were extensively used in a landlocked county for transporting grain, coal and other cargoes to the ports.

Sulgrave

A small village surrounded by unspoilt farming land. Wide grass banks separate the main street from the cottages, many of which are thatched.

Sulgrave Manor is a compact, two-storey 16th-century manor house. The American flag flies over it, for the house was built in 1560 by Lawrence Washington, an ancestor of George Washington, whose coat and saddlebags are on display. The family coat of arms, which appears over the porch, is thought to have been the basis for the original Stars and Stripes. It consists of two bars and three stars, or 'mullets', named after the 'molette' or spiked disc at the end of a spur. The manor house is now a museum.

Towcester

A town that claims to be one of the oldest in the county. It has been an important road junction ever since the Romans built Watling Street. The Saracen's Head Inn figures in *The Pickwick Papers* as one of Mr Pickwick's stopping places, and the 13th to 15th-century church has a collection of interesting chained books.

On the outskirts of the town there is a racecourse, and the Silverstone motor-racing circuit, built around a disused airfield, is $4\frac{1}{2}$ miles south-west.

BOOT FOR AN ELEPHANT

This curio in Northampton Museum was used in 1959 in a reconstruction of Hannibal's crossing of the Alps

SILVERSTONE *The British Grand Prix is raced alternately at Silverstone, near Towcester (odd-numbered years), and Brand's Hatch, near Farningham in Kent*

Northamptonshire's squires, spires and ruined castles

Events Rothwell's summer fair is held during first week after Trinity.

Places to see *Alfred East Art Gallery*, Kettering: weekdays except Thur. *Althorp*: afternoons only; Easter to Sept., Tues., Thur. and Sun., but daily except Mon. in Aug.; Oct. to Easter, Sun. afternoon. *Boughton House*: afternoons only; late July to mid-Sept., Sat. to Thur.; mid-Sept. to late Oct., Thur., Sat., Sun. *Guilsborough Grange Bird Park*, Guilsborough: Mar. to Oct., daily. *Kirby Hall*: weekdays, Sun. afternoon. *Lamport Hall*, Lamport: Easter to Sept., Sun. afternoon and Bank Hol.; also Thur. afternoon, June to Aug. *Lilford Wildlife Park*, 1 mile east of Pilton: Easter to Oct., daily. *Lyveden New Bield* (NT), Pilton: afternoons. *Rockingham Castle*: afternoons only; Easter to Sept., Thur., Sun., Bank Hol. Mon. and Tues. *Triangular Lodge*, 2 miles north-east of Rothwell: weekdays, Sun. afternoon. *Westfield Museum*, Kettering: afternoons, Mon. to Fri.

Information centre Public Library, Sheep Street, Kettering. Tel. Kettering 82143.

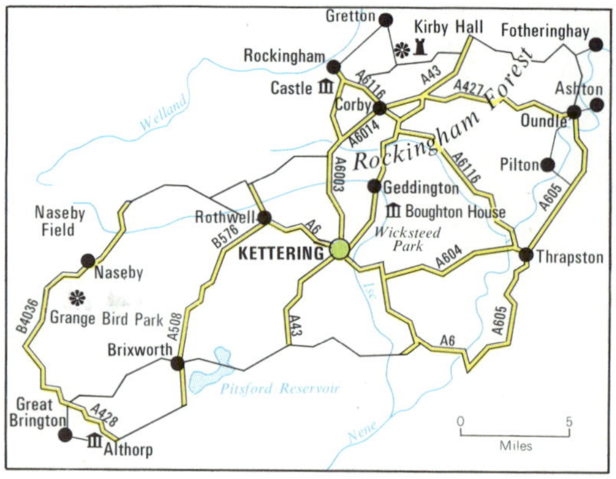

Northamptonshire has often been called 'the county of squires and spires'. In course of time squires have become fewer, but the graceful broach spires—forming a single unit with their towers, without a dividing parapet—are still familiar landmarks in the county, set amongst the trees of its rich pastureland. Despite some industrial development, the northern part of the county remains mainly agricultural. Cattle graze in the rich pastureland of the Nene Valley. Patches of woodland survive from the once-vast Rockingham Forest, where kings of England hunted the fallow deer. William the Conqueror's Rockingham Castle, near the Rutland border, still stands guard over the village at its foot.

Between Brixworth and Naseby, there are splendid panoramas across the uneven hills, some of which rise suddenly above acres of open ploughland like man-made earthworks. Boating and angling are popular on the River Nene, which is navigable through most of the county, and on numerous reservoirs, the largest of which is Pitsford Reservoir near Brixworth. The Nene flows past one tiny hamlet which played an unhappy role in history: at Fotheringhay, tranquil today in its riverside setting, Mary, Queen of Scots was executed in 1587 for conspiring against the English throne. Her hair had turned completely grey after her 19-year imprisonment. Her son, James VI of Scotland, was to become King of England in 1603.

Brixworth
The Saxon Church of All Saints, high on a hill, is one of the finest and largest in England. It has a stair turret built outside the tower, and many tiles dating from the Roman occupation have been found built into the arches. Lamport Hall, 3 miles to the north of Brixworth, has been occupied by the Isham family continuously since 1560.

Fotheringhay
A tiny hamlet where once stood the historic Fotheringhay Castle. It was in the banqueting hall of Fotheringhay Castle that Mary, Queen of Scots was executed. Here, also, the future King Richard III was born. The castle was gradually demolished during the 17th and 18th centuries, and all that remains of it today is a mound in the grounds of a farmhouse. The River Nene flows through the village under an attractive 18th-century bridge and past the Perpendicular parish church, which has a fine lantern-shaped tower.

Great Brington
A peaceful village with an old cross and a partly 12th-century church. Althorp, 1 mile to the east, the home of the Spencer family since 1508, has been remodelled over the years, lastly by Henry Holland in 1787. The mansion, clearly visible from the A478, has an extensive picture gallery with Dutch, Italian and English paintings, including portraits by Gainsborough and Reynolds. The house, but not the park, is open to the public, and there are picnic spots off the minor roads near by.

Gretton
A stone-built village, with stocks and a whipping-post which were last used in the mid-19th century. Kirby Hall, 3 miles south-east, is a partially restored 16th to 17th-century house that from the distance still appears habitable. In fact, the only surviving rooms are those first seen from the driveway; the rest is a shell. Kirby Hall and its gardens were once famous throughout England, but in the 19th century the house fell into ruin. The gardens have been restored and the remains of the house preserved.

ELEANOR CROSSES MARK A QUEEN'S LAST JOURNEY

The cross at Geddington is one of 12 set up by Edward I at the resting places of the coffin of his wife, Eleanor of Castile, on its journey from Harby to London in 1290. Two other crosses survive—at Hardingstone, near Northampton, and Waltham Cross, Hertfordshire

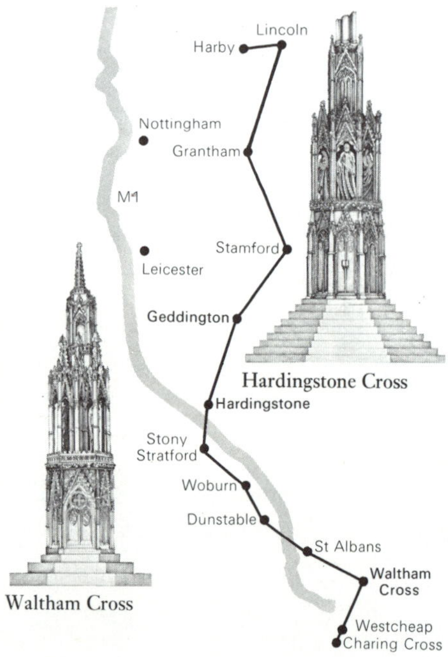

Hardingstone Cross

Waltham Cross

An effigy of Queen Eleanor lies on her tomb in a shrine in Westminster Abbey. The tomb is made of Purbeck marble, with shields suspended round it. The effigy was cast of gilded bronze by William Torel, a goldsmith, in 1291. Torel also cast the effigy of Henry III for the abbey

KIRBY HALL *Only the façade of Kirby Hall, near Gretton, remains, though it still looks habitable. It was begun in 1570 and added to in the 17th century by Inigo Jones*

Kettering
This footwear-manufacturing centre on the River Ise has a mainly 15th-century church with a 177-ft spire. Boughton House, a vast building 3 miles to the north-east, has been held by the family of the Duke of Buccleugh since 1528 and has suffered little change during the last 200 years.

Naseby
A village near the source of the Avon, the Nene and the Welland, and the site of the battle in 1645 in which the fate of Charles I was determined by Fairfax's victory. A stone column 1½ miles north of the village commemorates the battle. Another monument, south of the village, is thought to mark the site of the decisive cavalry charge led by Cromwell. In the churchyard is a huge metal ball retrieved from a building destroyed in the siege of Boulogne in 1544 and brought to England by Sir Gyles Allington, Master of Henry VIII's Ordnance.

Oundle
A delightful small country town surrounded on three sides by the River Nene, which is extensively used for sailing and cruising. The town has picturesque inns and old houses as well as its famous public school, the buildings of which are grouped about the partly 14th-century church. The Latham Almshouses date from the early 17th century.

Rockingham
A pretty village with a steep main street of stone houses. The church and former royal castle dominate the village from the top of the hill, where there are splendid views over the Welland Valley. Rockingham Castle, built by William the Conqueror, was in continual use as a fortress until the Middle Ages. By the end of the 15th century it had fallen into disrepair. Elizabeth I gave the castle to Edward Watson, the son-in-law of Lord Chief Justice Montagu, who restored it, and the castle has remained in the same family ever since. Charles Dickens was a frequent visitor, and the castle is the 'Chesney Wold' of his *Bleak House*. The castle contains fine furniture and a collection of paintings, and there is a portrait of Francis I of France, which is believed to have been given to Watson by the French king himself.

Rothwell
A small hillside town. The public library is one of several buildings in the county financed by Sir Thomas Tresham (grandfather of Francis Tresham, one of the conspirators in the Gunpowder Plot). Decorative friezes depict the coats of arms of many leading 16th-century families. In the crypt of Holy Trinity Church are thousands of bones and skulls, discovered by a sexton while digging a grave in 1700. Nobody knows how they came to be there.

Rushton Hall, 2 miles north-east, is an Elizabethan house, once the home of Sir Thomas Tresham and now a school for blind children. The Triangular Lodge in the grounds, reached by a separate entrance, was one of the reputed meeting places of the Gunpowder Plot conspirators. There are three gables, and the 33 ft long inscription carved around the building has 33 letters in each of three equal sections.

PITSFORD RESERVOIR *A tributary of the River Nene feeds this reservoir near Brixworth, opened in 1956. It is stocked with trout, and is popular for sailing*

Leicester and its canal

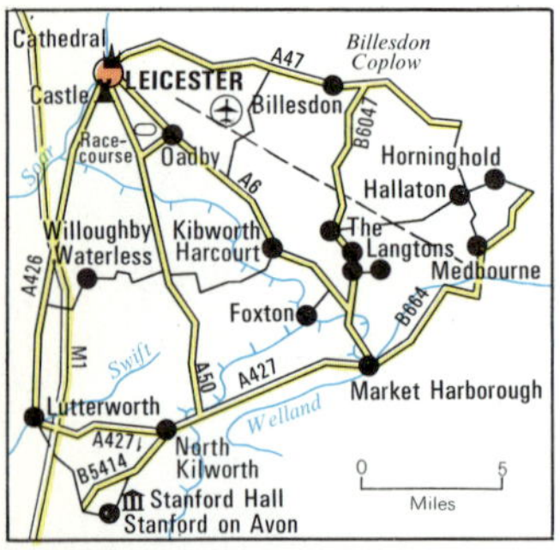

Angling Coarse fishing at Market Harborough on the Grand Union Canal and on the Soar at Leicester.

Flying From Leicester Airport.

Events The Hare Pie Scramble and Bottle Kicking take place on Easter Mon. at Hallaton. The City of Leicester Show is held at Abbey Park on late Summer Bank Hol. Mon. and Tues. Leicester has a week of Promenade concerts early in June.

Places to see *Beaumont Hall Gardens*, Leicester, botanic gardens: Mon. to Fri., except Bank Hols. *Belgrave Hall*, *Jewry Wall Museum*, *Leicestershire Museum and Art Gallery*, *Newarke Houses Museum*, *Royal Leicestershire Regiment Museum*, and *Wygston's House*, a costume museum, all Leicester: weekdays and Sun. afternoon. *Quenby Hall*, 7 miles north-east of Leicester: Sun. and Bank Hol. Mon. afternoons, early June to Sept. *Stanford Hall*, Stanford on Avon: Thur., Sat., Sun. and Bank Hol. Mon. afternoons, Easter to Sept.

Information centre 12 Bishop Street, Leicester. Tel. Leicester 20644.

BOTTLE KICKING *Three villages compete to kick casks of beer across a stream. Later they drink the beer at Hallaton's conical market cross*

Some of the richest grazing land in England lies between Leicester and Market Harborough, where the origins of the weekly cattle market can be traced back seven centuries. The pace of daily living in southern Leicestershire is as tranquil as the countryside itself. Secluded by-ways meander through a landscape of open fields, occasionally interrupted by the line of a canal or the curve of a river.

From Kibworth Harcourt, minor roads lead eastwards through the Langtons, a group of villages set in lush agricultural land, towards the lovely villages of Hallaton and Horninghold. From Kibworth, too, country lanes wind westwards across the main Leicester–Northampton road and on to Willoughby Waterless, a small village built mainly of brick in a county where stone predominates.

A branch of the Grand Union Canal joins Market Harborough to Leicester, making a sharp westward loop towards the multiple locks at Foxton. In the early 19th century the canal was extensively used by narrow boats carrying goods from the industrial Midlands to London. Today it is used for recreation and pleasure craft. For much of its length, the canal runs through open countryside, and the walks along the towpath are pleasant and peaceful.

THROUGH THE LOCKS *Spectators at Foxton help boat-owners to operate the series of locks on the Grand Union Canal*

Billesdon
A large, attractive village where remains of Iron Age earthworks have been found. Billesdon Coplow, a lovely wooded hill 600 ft above sea level, gives fine views of the Leicestershire countryside. There is a mainly 13th-century church (restored in 1860), and the school in the old part of the village dates from 1650.

Foxton
A village church, dating back to the 13th century, contains part of a Saxon cross, which suggests that it dates from pre-Conquest times; and the manor house near by is partly medieval.

The road from the village leads to the bottom of Foxton Locks, on the Grand Union Canal, which can also be reached by a ten-minute walk along the towpath. The locks are arranged in two tiers, each with five locks, and the two tiers are linked by a central meeting pool, the only place where there is room for two boats to pass each other. This series of locks raises the level of the water by 75 ft. The locks were built in 1811 to serve commercial barges, but today are used mainly by pleasure craft; there is no lock keeper, but the locks can easily be operated by weekend sailors.

Hallaton
An old village set in pleasant hill country. It has a quaint conical market cross, and a well-preserved terrace of 17th to 19th-century stone-built cottages. St Michael's Church, in a commanding position above the village, has a Norman west tower and an unusually ornate turret and good broach spire (a spire without a parapet) which were probably added in the 13th century.

On Easter Monday, two unusual rituals take place in Hallaton. One is the sharing among local residents of a large hare pie—originally a token rent for a field—which is traditionally provided by the village rector. In the other ritual, 'bottle kicking', the villagers of Hallaton, Horninghold and Medbourne compete to push two small casks of beer—or 'bottles'—over a local stream. Afterwards, the casks are opened by the villagers and the beer drunk.

Horninghold
A compact village in open country with pleasant walks to the Eyebrook Reservoir, 2½ miles east, on the Rutland border. Little remains of the original Norman settlement apart from the Church of St Peter, sensitively restored by Victorian craftsmen. The surrounding houses, some stone-built and others half-timbered, date only from early this century, but they were laid out to form a harmonious pattern and now look convincingly 'mellow'.

Leicester
The county town is a cathedral city, the home of a university, and much engaged in the traditional trades of hosiery and footwear, to which light engineering is a 20th-century addition. The city is built on the site of an old Roman settlement, Ratae Coritanorum. Traces of the Roman occupation have been found at the Jewry Wall.

There was a Bishop of Leicester in the 8th century, but the bishopric lapsed for centuries. It was revived in 1926, when the parish church of St Martin's was raised to the status of a cathedral. The centre of the city is marked by a Gothic clock tower dated 1868. The immense de Montfort Hall recalls the first Earl of Leicester, Simon de Montfort, a benefactor of the city, who led the successful revolt against Henry III, and whose Parliament, summoned in 1265, set a precedent for future relations between rulers and ruled. New Walk, where the old Victorian lamp-posts have been preserved, leads from the centre of the city to Victoria Park. It is accessible only on foot, offering a pleasant three-quarter-mile stroll through a part where, despite modern development, some reminders of a more leisured past remain.

Newarke Houses Museum, close to the castle ruins, provides a vivid illustration of the social history of the past 400 years. One of its most interesting features is a life-sized street scene from mid-Victorian days. The Magazine, an ancient city gateway, is now the museum of the Royal Leicestershire Regiment. The well-preserved timbered guildhall was built in the 15th century for the Corpus Christi Guild; and St Nicholas

GLASS AND ALUMINIUM *Leicester University is one of the city's modern landmarks. It includes this School of Engineering, housing 300 students. The building, designed by James Stirling and James Gowan in contemporary style, was completed in 1963; it won an architectural award for the use of aluminium in its construction*

Church, with Roman and Saxon stones evident in its structure, is one of the oldest churches in the country.

Leicester's market square just behind Gallowtree Gate is still in daily use, as it has been since the 13th century—a reminder that the city lies at the heart of an agricultural county.

Lutterworth
In the mail-coach days this small town was an important staging post, and its position beside the M1 bears out the fact that many of today's roads follow traditional routes. The parish church is the town's focal point. It was here that John Wyclif—rector from 1374 to 1384—preached against the abuses of papal politics. The church was considerably restored in the 19th century, and a massive tower has replaced the original spire. However, it still has some 15th-century wall-paintings. There are several well-preserved half-timbered houses here, and also an 18th-century bridge which spans the River Swift in a series of three arches.

Market Harborough
An attractive small town with a wide main square. A market was held here as early as 1203. A general market is still held on Tuesdays and Saturdays, and a cattle market on Tuesdays. Industrial development has not destroyed the town's wealth of fine Georgian architecture. The most famous building is the former grammar school, a timbered building built by Robert Smythe, the school's founder, in 1614. It stands on wooden pillars which raise it above street level, and pedestrians can walk underneath. The inn sign of the town's principal hotel, The Three Swans, is a magnificent example of 18th-century ironwork. The Church of St Dionysius, built in the 13th to 15th centuries, has fine window tracery and a broach spire.

Stanford on Avon
A village divided by the Avon between Leicestershire and Northamptonshire. Its church has an organ which was discarded by Cromwell from Whitehall Palace, as well as a pinnacled 15th-century tower, screenwork and old glass. Stanford Hall stands in an impressive setting of open pastureland. The present mansion, built on the site of an earlier one, dates from the reign of William and Mary. It has an imposing façade which matches well with its surroundings. The grounds are fenced, not walled, and the main entrance is approached along a tree-lined driveway. Inside the hall, a collection of costumes and period furniture is on display. The stables house a collection of vintage cars and a replica of an early flying-machine.

GUILDHALL TIMBERING *Leicester's 15th-century guildhall contains a fine medieval timbered hall, a mayor's parlour, a library and cells. It was the town hall until 1876*

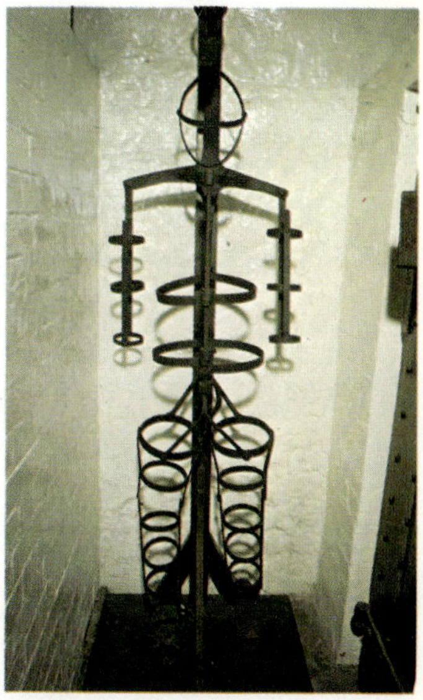

GUILDHALL RELIC *Gibbet irons, now in Leicester Guildhall, were last used in 1832*

Eerie crags of Charnwood

Angling There is coarse fishing for bream, dace, roach and perch on the River Soar.

Boating Holiday boating on the Grand Union Canal at Barrow upon Soar. Boats for hire at Mountsorrel Mar. to Nov.

Country parks Bradgate Park and Swithland Wood are open to walkers daily. Permits can be obtained for cars with invalid passengers to drive in Bradgate Park on certain days.

Events The Ashby Agricultural Show is held at Calke Park on the late summer Bank Hol. An athletics meeting between the Amateur Athletic Association and Loughborough Colleges is held annually, usually in June, at Loughborough. There are weekly concerts at Loughborough University during term. Loughborough holds a fair in Nov.

Places to see *Ashby de la Zouch Castle*: Mon., Tues., Fri. and Sat.; Sun. afternoon. *Bosworth Field Visitor Centre*: afternoons, Apr. to Oct. *Bradgate House*: Apr. to Oct., Wed., Thur., Sat. afternoons and Sun. morning. *The Carillon*, Loughborough: Easter to Sept., afternoons. *Kirby Muxloe Castle*: weekdays, except Tues. afternoon and Wed.; also Sun. afternoon. *Staunton Harold Church* (NT): Apr. to Oct., Wed., Thur., Sat., Sun. *Twycross Zoo Park*, 5½ miles north-west of Market Bosworth: daily. *Whatton House*, Hathern, 4 miles north-west of Loughborough: gardens open Sun. afternoon, Easter to Sept.

Information centre John Storer House, Wards End, Loughborough. Tel. Loughborough 30131.

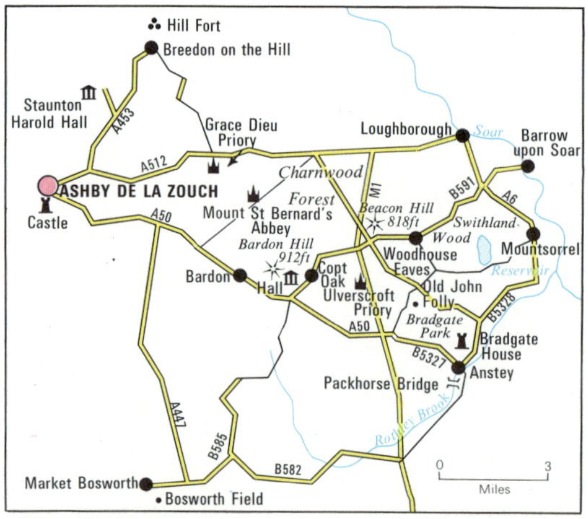

Charnwood Forest, once densely wooded, has suffered from centuries of felling, and presents today an extraordinary, almost eerie, panorama of open heath, rocky outcrops and uneven ridges, broken occasionally by an isolated clump of oak trees or the ragged edge of a former granite quarry. Charnwood contains some of the oldest rock formations in the country; they date from the pre-Cambrian period and are at least 570 million years old.

The area, once an untamed wilderness, but partially enclosed and laid with roads in 1829, covers about 30 square miles. Almost all of it can be explored by car or on foot, and the views from Bardon Hill and Beacon Hill are impressive. The craggy hills, with their fantastic rock formations, seem like miniature mountains, and it is hard to believe that they are less than 1000 ft high. The strange half-light that precedes a storm makes the landscape even more freakish and dramatic. For centuries Charnwood, originally called Cernewoda, from the Welsh *carn*, meaning rock, was an important source of wood for the charcoal industry. Gradual clearing of the forest over the years has revealed traces of Roman and Saxon settlements and the sites of several medieval abbeys, built there for seclusion. Older even than the abbeys are the quarries. The vast quarry in Mountsorrel, just beyond the village green, has given its name to a type of granite which has been extensively quarried in the area for nearly 1000 years. From Mountsorrel there are magnificent views over the valley of the River Soar which forms part of the course of the Grand Union Canal.

WHERE A KING DRANK *Richard III is said to have taken a drink from Dick's Well at the Battle of Bosworth*

Anstey
A village with some old cottages and a 14th-century, five-arched pack-horse bridge that is only 5 ft wide. Anstey has a close link with the Luddite Riots, which started in 1812, in the early stages of the Industrial Revolution. Ned Ludd, who was born in Anstey, became an apprentice in the local hosiery industry, and when the mechanisation of the early 19th century threatened unemployment, he opposed the innovations by smashing the stocking frames.

Ashby de la Zouch
The town's name marks the passing of an original Danish settlement into the hands of the La Zouch family, from Brittany. A grand terrace of houses in Classical style dates from the town's development as a spa in the 19th century. In the wide main street there are Elizabethan half-timbered houses standing alongside bow-fronted Georgian shops.

Behind the main street lie the ruins of a castle built in the 15th century by the first Lord Hastings. Ashby (the full name is seldom used locally) was the setting for the tournament in Sir Walter Scott's novel, *Ivanhoe*.

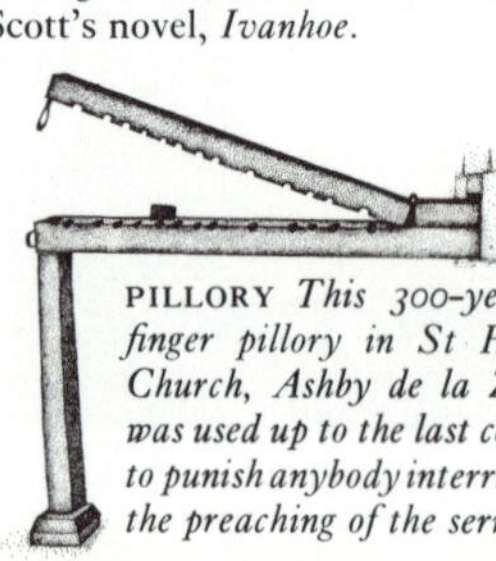

PILLORY *This 300-year-old finger pillory in St Helen's Church, Ashby de la Zouch, was used up to the last century to punish anybody interrupting the preaching of the sermon*

Bardon Hill
At 912 ft this is the highest point in Charnwood Forest. There is no road leading up to it, but a footpath 1 mile long from the village of Copt Oak leads past Bardon Hall to the summit, from which there are views over the forest.

Beacon Hill
From the top of the 818-ft hill, marked by a plinth, there are spectacular views over the landscape of Charnwood, and on the horizon, 3 miles to the north-east, the bell tower at Loughborough can be seen. A road from Woodhouse Eaves, 1 mile east, leads to a car park, from which it is only a short walk to the summit.

Bradgate Park
One of Leicestershire's main recreation areas is an enclosed stretch of land,

HILL OF SECLUSION *When Bronze Age men lived on Beacon Hill (foreground) forests spread to the horizon. In medieval times monks built their abbeys in clearings of Charnwood Forest and their sites can still be found among the strange rock formations*

OLD JOHN *A tower on a 700 ft high hill in Bradgate Park was built in 1786 by the 5th Earl of Stamford in memory of a retainer killed by a pole from a bonfire*

DOWN IN THE GLADE *Fallow deer roam in the woods of 850-acre Bradgate Park*

covering over 850 acres, which was presented to the city and county in 1928 by a private benefactor, Charles Bennion. In late spring and summer the park is an attractive place for walks. Bradgate is not a park of formal avenues and carefully planned vistas, but is an untouched stretch of moorland, woods, heath and rocky hills. There are fine cedars and oaks, and walks along paths beside the course of a tiny stream.

Bradgate House, now in ruins, was the home of Lady Jane Grey, uncrowned 'Queen' of England for nine days in 1553 until she was executed by order of Mary Tudor. Above the ruins, the turf sweeps up to a late 18th-century folly, a tower called Old John, built as a memorial to a retainer who was killed by a falling bonfire. From here there are extensive vistas over Charnwood Forest.

Breedon on the Hill

A village forming a small crescent round an Iron Age hill fort. The 200 ft high limestone hill has been partially demolished by quarrying over the ages.

A narrow road leads up to the Church of SS Mary and Hardulph. This contains friezes, panels, and a remarkable sculptured angel, 3 ft high, saved from a former Anglo-Saxon monastery on the site which was destroyed by the Danes in the late 9th century. The church is a local landmark and there are extensive views from it northwards over the valley of the River Trent.

The village has a curious conical stone lock-up, used in the 17th century.

Loughborough

A thriving town with a centre that is gay with coloured canopies twice weekly on market days, a modern shopping precinct, and an international reputation for sport and bell casting.

As a memorial to those who died in the First World War, Loughborough built a carillon of 47 bells, which is housed in a 150-ft bell tower in Queen's Park. Carillon recitals are given on Thursday and Sunday throughout the summer months.

The town has a University of Technology, many of whose students live in a specially designed village. A separate College of Education specialises in physical-training courses for teachers.

Market Bosworth

A tree-lined avenue leads into this small stone-built market town. The town was recorded in the Domesday Book, and markets have been held there since 1285. The Dixie family, who bought the local manor house in 1567 and are still in residence, have a royal charter allowing them to operate one of only seven privately owned markets in the country. The church, mainly 14th century, has 15th-century alterations and many memorials to the Dixie family.

Bosworth Field, 1 mile south, was the site of the decisive battle in the Wars of the Roses in 1485 when Henry Tudor defeated Richard III. The battlefield is now laid out with a battle trail and an interpretive centre.

THE BELL GRINDER

A bell is ground after being cast at the Loughborough factory of John Taylor, where bells for churches have been made for more than a century

Mount St Bernard's Abbey

Only ruins remain to recall the grandeur of many of Charnwood's former priories and abbeys, such as Grace Dieu and Ulverscroft. But Mount St Bernard's Abbey, at the western end of the forest, was founded as recently as 1835.

Staunton Harold

One of the most beautifully proportioned and situated great houses in Britain. It is a mainly Georgian structure with a Palladian façade and is surrounded by parkland, with woods and lakes. The 5th Earl of Ferrers designed and built the house in 1763; it incorporates the remains of an original manor house which had been in his family since the time of William the Conqueror. The hall was bought in 1955 by Group Captain Leonard Cheshire as a Home for the Incurably Sick.

Services at Staunton Harold Church, built in Cromwellian times, follow 17th-century custom, with men and women sitting on opposite sides of the aisles.

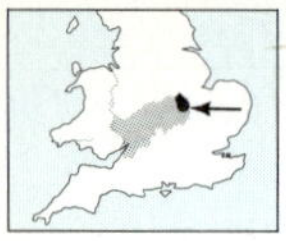

Belvoir and the wolds

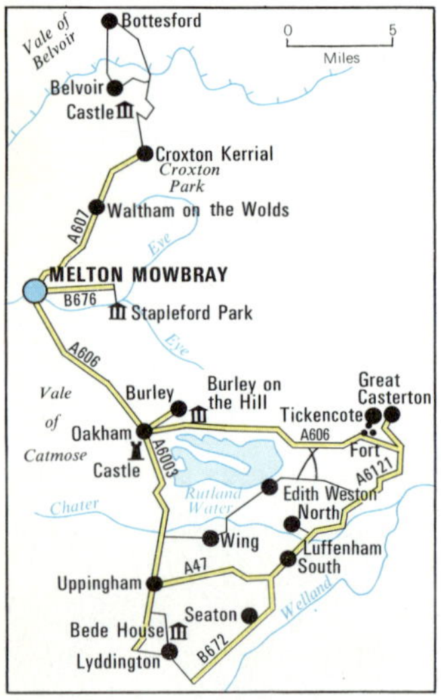

Rutland ceased to exist as England's smallest county in 1974, when it was merged with Leicestershire. Green hills undulate across the region, and sheep graze on open slopes broken by low hedges and occasional villages.

The wolds landscape is, in part, the work of man. In the last century the great landowners, realising they had some of the finest fox-hunting country in the world, planted small woods, or 'coverts', between the huge open fields for foxes to live and breed in. These coverts, many covering 100 acres or more, now blend in well with the surrounding countryside.

A maze of attractive roads dip and climb across the wolds between Melton Mowbray, in the valley of the River Eye, and the Vale of Belvoir in the north. There are fine views of the vale from many villages whose names indicate their position 'on-the-Wolds'.

From the roads there are splendid vistas across drystone walls and low hedges of a countryside that has the look of timelessness. Much of this is due to the weathered pink-brown Ketton stone traditionally used in so many buildings. In towns and villages, roofs of roughly shaped Collyweston slates contrast with the dumpy outlines of thatch.

Although records mentioning the town of Oakham go back to before Norman times, Rutland did not appear as a separate county until the reign of King John. However, the unusual village name of Edith Weston recalls this earlier period. Queen Edith was the wife of Edward the Confessor, who bequeathed to her the land that was then a royal domain.

ACROSS THE WELLAND VALLEY *The Harringworth Viaduct was built between 1876 and 1878 to carry the former Midland Railway across the valley. The viaduct, three-quarters of a mile long, has a span of 82 arches and is 70 ft high*

Angling There is coarse fishing on the River Chater at Luffenham, the Oakham Canal and River Wreake.

Events The Rutland County Show is held at Oakham in Aug.

Places to see *The Bedehouse*, Lyddington: weekdays; also Sun. afternoon, Apr. to Sept. *Belvoir Castle*: afternoons: Apr. to Sept., Wed., Thur., Sat., Sun.; Oct., Sun. *Oakham Castle*: daily, except Sun. and Mon. mornings. *Rutland County Museum*, Oakham: Tues. to Sat.; also Sun. afternoon, Apr. to Oct. *Stapleford Park*: afternoons; Easter to Sept., Sun. and Bank Hol. Mon. and Tues.; also Wed. and Thur. from May, and Tues. June to Aug.

Information centre Melton Carnegie Museum, Melton Mowbray. Tel. Melton Mowbray 69946.

Belvoir
The castle dominates the village from a high spur, and the approach road climbs steeply through dense woodland. The view from the terrace of the castle extends over the Leicestershire Wolds. In the 16th century the 11th-century castle ceased to be a fortress, and today it is the home of the Duke of Rutland. The house has been much added to and was last enlarged in the 19th century. There are painted ceilings in the Elizabeth Salon, and the family collection of art treasures includes Gobelin tapestries and paintings by Holbein and Gainsborough. Leicestershire is a traditional hunting county, and the Belvoir pack is one of the best-known in England.

Bottesford
A large, scattered village which has close historical links with Belvoir Castle. An avenue of trees leads to the parish church of St Mary-the-Virgin, where many former Masters of the Belvoir Hunt are buried. The church is crowded with magnificent tombs, some of which could be fitted in only by making alterations to the building. The monuments to the 7th and 8th Earls of Rutland are by Grinling Gibbons.

Burley
A village with some of the best views in this part of Leicestershire. To the south-west, 2 miles away, Oakham Church spire can be seen rising above the Vale of Catmose. The village manor, Burley on the Hill, stands on rising ground in beautiful parkland. The house was built in the late 17th and early 18th century by the Earl of Nottingham and was the third to be erected on this hilltop.

The church, originally Norman, was restored by John Loughborough Pearson *c.* 1870. Its chief object of interest is a kneeling white-marble figure, part of the monument to Lady Charlotte Finch, wife of the Earl of Nottingham, carved in 1820 by Sir Francis Chantrey.

BELVOIR CASTLE AND THE FOXHOUND THAT TOOK ITS NAME

The original castle, built in the 11th century by Robert de Todeni, standard-bearer of William the Conqueror, had fallen into ruins by the 16th century when it was presented to the Manners family, who later became Dukes of Rutland. They rebuilt the house several times, and the present building dates from the early 19th century, when James Wyatt was commissioned to convert the house into a sham medieval castle. The Belvoir foxhound (right) took its name from the castle, near which it was bred in the 18th century, when fox-hunting became popular. The hound is distinguished by its colour, which is the darkest of any pure-bred foxhound

Croxton Kerrial
A small, stone-built village. The site of the former Croxton Abbey, founded in 1150, has recently been revealed by excavations in the 800-acre Croxton Park, the one-time hunting seat of the Dukes of Rutland. Only the fishponds of the original abbey still exist.

Great Casterton
A village of particular interest to antiquarians. Recent excavations revealed the skeleton of a Stone Age man and the remains of a Roman fort and a villa, in which a cache of coins was buried. The Church of SS Peter and Paul is mainly 13th century, with a west tower added in the 15th century. There is a Norman font and a fine Early English chancel.

A mile to the west is the village of Tickencote. The interior of its restored 12th-century church is dominated by an elaborately carved chancel arch which has become slightly lopsided. Outside the church stands an old bell.

Lyddington
An attractive village stretching out along a main street, with a village green. St Andrew's Church has unusual altar rails, completely encircling the communion table. The 13th-century Bede House, originally built as a palace for the Bishops of Lincoln, was given by Elizabeth I to Lord Burghley and in 1602 converted into an almshouse. Its 15th-century hall has an elaborate ceiling.

Melton Mowbray
An old market town and unofficial capital of the hunting country, where three hunts meet—the Quorn, the Cottesmore and the Belvoir. Every hotel has prints and table mats recalling the heyday of hunting in the last century.

There are attractive walks in the parks and gardens along the banks of the River Eye. In the town centre, the main streets converge on the large market square. The church, with an imposing central tower, is one of the most beautiful in the county.

Oakham
A small, compact county town with a well-preserved market square, in which there is a set of stocks and an old butter cross. This used to stand on the roof of the market stall where butter was sold; today it stands on top of eight oak posts. The parish church of All Saints has a 12th-century Bible. Near by are the original 16th-century buildings of Oakham School and its modern War Memorial Chapel.

A 12th-century banqueting hall is all that remains of Oakham Castle, and the hall is now used as a magistrates' court. The castle belonged to the Earl of Ferrers, whose name means farrier or blacksmith. Close to it is a fine new county museum, opened in 1969.

Rutland Water, a new reservoir to the south-east, will be the largest man-made lake in Europe when filled.

Stapleford Park
A Tudor mansion and a modern safari park. The hall dates from 1500, but additions over the centuries have given it many different architectural styles. It was extensively restored in 1633, when Flemish gables were added to the original building, which is now a wing. Many rooms date from the Restoration, and some from the 19th century.

There are tapestries, pictures and a unique collection of Victorian Staffordshire pottery figures. It was not until after the First World War, when Thomas Balston, an author and painter, started to collect the statuettes of famous personalities, that attention was drawn to the value of these figures. His book on Staffordshire portrait figures was published in 1958 and his collection of more than 400 figures is in the house.

There is an exceptionally fine 18th-century church, a lake and an animal park in the grounds, which can be toured by a miniature railway.

OAKHAM CASTLE *The castle's walls are decorated with horseshoes paid as a toll by visiting peers since medieval times*

Uppingham
Uppingham School, in the centre, dominates the town with its 16th-century courtyards and quadrangles, together with later additions. Robert Johnson, its founder, also built Oakham School.

Waltham on the Wolds
One of the oldest inhabited villages in the region, where remains of Saxon coffins and Roman pavements have been found. Three landmarks show for miles around—the television transmitter masts, the spire of the church, and the black smock windmill, so called because the shape of its body resembles the smocks that were worn at one time by country folk.

Wing
A small village notable for its rare turf maze, 40 ft in diameter, which can be seen at the east end of the village. It may have been laid out in medieval times on the site where a prehistoric dance ritual took place.

HOME COUNTIES

The five counties to the north and west of London have a landscape that is as varied as any in England. There are windswept heights and dense, silent beechwoods; one river where holiday craft jostle through busy locks, and another that drifts in seclusion along willow-lined banks; historic houses that share the past with grassy tracks and hill-carvings of even older times. The towns are equally varied—ancient Oxford is famous for its scholars, Witney for its blankets, Luton for its cars. But within this patchwork are some unifying themes.

The pattern of the landscape is set by the three hill regions of the Chilterns, the Berkshire Downs and the Cotswolds, and by the rivers that wind through them—especially the Thames and the Great Ouse. Beechwood forests, so dense that they only rarely allow views across the countryside, cover most of the Chilterns, especially in Buckinghamshire. The Berkshire Downs, on the other hand, are bare and open. At Inkpen Beacon, in the southernmost corner of Berkshire, they reach almost 1000 ft, the highest point of any chalk downs in England, giving a sweeping vista across the River Kennet to the Lambourn Downs. The Cotswolds, which cut across the extreme north-west corner of Oxfordshire, are different again, presenting a landscape of green fields and grey

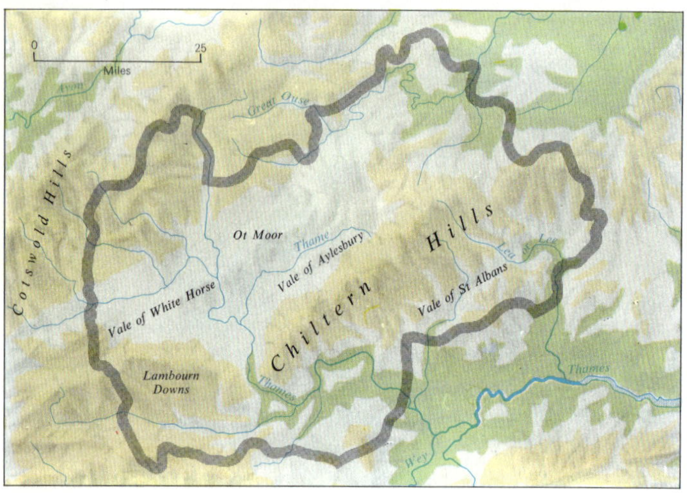

CHALK AND LIMESTONE *The two major hill ranges of the Home Counties are the chalklands of the Chiltern Hills in the east, and the Berkshire Downs in the south. Part of the limestone Cotswolds cuts across north-west Oxfordshire*

limestone. Walls, cottages, manor houses and churches are all built of this local stone which, around Banbury where the Cotswolds meet ironstone hills, takes on a honey-coloured tint.

The Thames from its source in the Cotswolds retains much of the atmosphere of Jerome K. Jerome's *Three Men in a Boat*. The locks may be easier to navigate today and the pleasure craft using them may have sleeker lines, but the riverside inns are as welcoming as ever, and fields lining the river banks are still a popular spot for weekend picnic parties. The River Ouse has an entirely different character. It rises east of Banbury, and on its winding journey through Buckinghamshire and Bedfordshire to The Wash it has no need for the elaborate system of locks necessary on the Thames. Instead, the Ouse runs for long stretches at its own natural level, setting an idyllic pace under willow trees.

Throughout the Home Counties are many prehistoric and Roman remains. One of the oldest links is the Ridge Way, a track across the

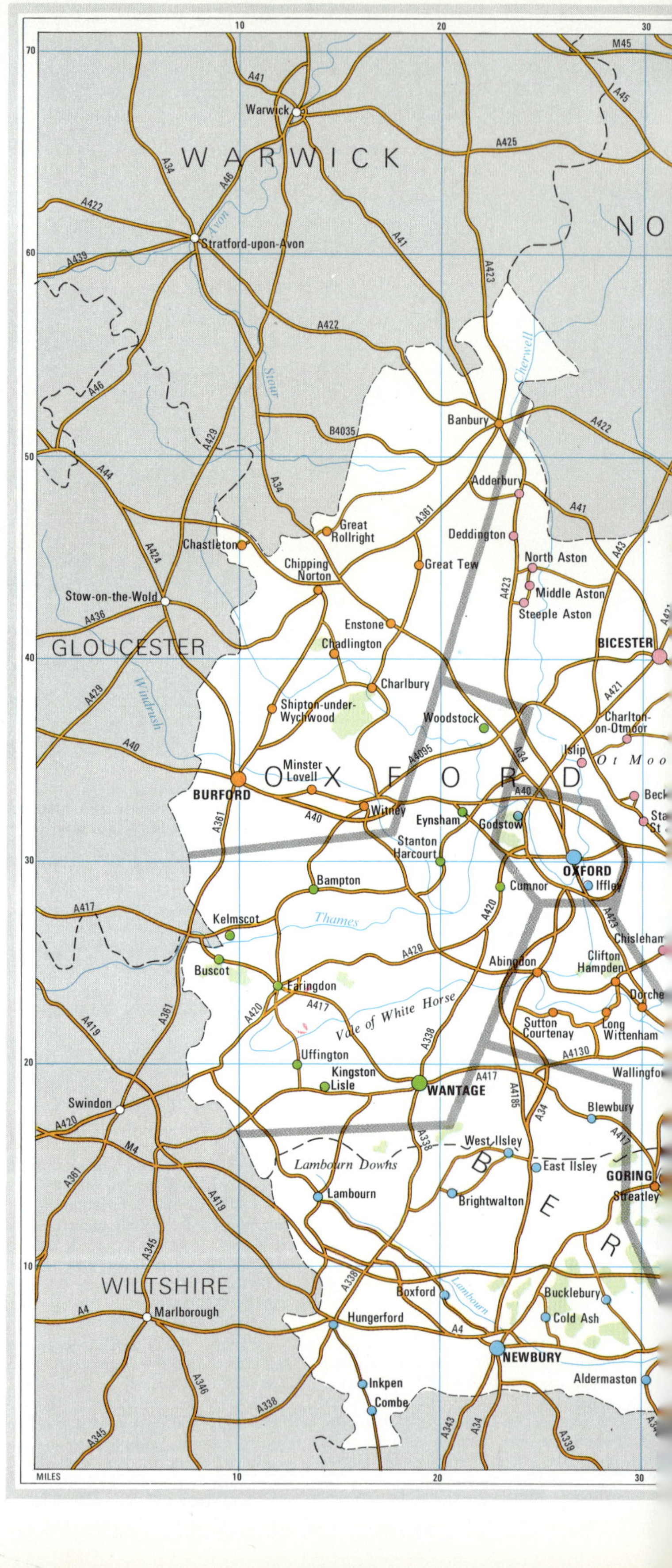

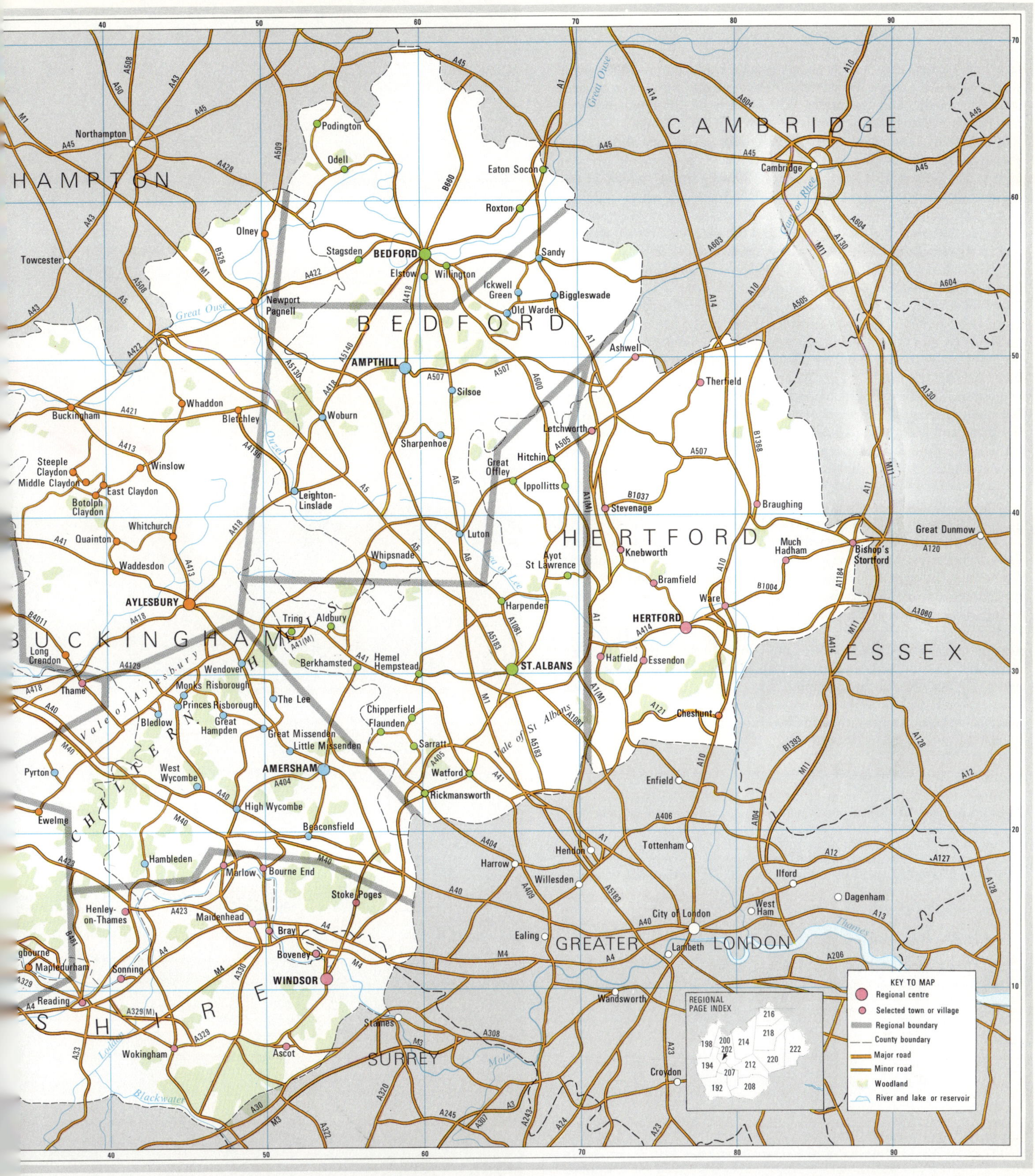

CAMBRIDGE
HAMPTON
BEDFORD
HERTFORD
BUCKINGHAMSHIRE
ESSEX
GREATER LONDON
SURREY
CHILTERN HILLS
Vale of Aylesbury
Vale of St Albans
Great Ouse
Ouzel
Lea or Lee
Cam or Rhee
Thames
Mole
Loddon
Blackwater
Northampton
Towcester
Olney
Podington
Odell
Stagsden
BEDFORD
Elstow
Willington
Eaton Socon
Roxton
Sandy
Ickwell Green
Old Warden
Biggleswade
Newport Pagnell
AMPTHILL
Silsoe
Woburn
Sharpenhoe
Whaddon
Bletchley
Buckingham
Steeple Claydon
Middle Claydon
East Claydon
Botolph Claydon
Winslow
Leighton-Linslade
Whitchurch
Quainton
Waddesdon
AYLESBURY
Cambridge
Ashwell
Therfield
Letchworth
Hitchin
Great Offley
Ippollitts
Stevenage
Braughing
Luton
Whipsnade
Ayot St Lawrence
Knebworth
Much Hadham
Bishop's Stortford
Great Dunmow
Bramfield
Ware
HERTFORD
Harpenden
Tring
Aldbury
Long Crendon
Thame
Wendover
Monks Risborough
Princes Risborough
The Lee
Berkhamsted
Hemel Hempstead
ST. ALBANS
Hatfield
Essendon
Cheshunt
Bledlow
Great Hampden
Great Missenden
Little Missenden
Chipperfield
Flaunden
Sarratt
Pyrton
West Wycombe
AMERSHAM
Watford
Rickmansworth
Enfield
Ewelme
High Wycombe
Beaconsfield
Hambleden
Marlow
Bourne End
Hendon
Tottenham
Harrow
Willesden
Ilford
Dagenham
Henley-on-Thames
Maidenhead
Stoke Poges
Bray
Boveney
City of London
West Ham
Ealing
Lambeth
Mapledurham
Sonning
WINDSOR
Reading
Wandsworth
Staines
Wokingham
Ascot
Croydon
M1
M4
M11
M40
A1
A1(M)
A5
A6
A10
A41
A45
KEY TO MAP
Regional centre
Selected town or village
Regional boundary
County boundary
Major road
Minor road
Woodland
River and lake or reservoir
REGIONAL PAGE INDEX
216
218
198
200
202
214
222
194
212
220
207
192
208

Berkshire Downs that was in use as a main trading route during the Bronze Age. St Albans is the site of Verulamium, one of the finest Roman towns in Britain; and the Great White Horse of Uffington, possibly carved in Iron Age times, is the oldest of Britain's hill figures.

The Home Counties are rich in other byways into history. At Wantage market-place a statue of King Alfred records his birth in the town in AD 849. Near Kingston Lisle there is the 'Blowing Stone', which Alfred is said to have used to summon his subjects to battle against the Vikings. In the 18th century, Thomas Gray composed his 'Elegy Written in a Country Churchyard' at Stoke Poges, and the notorious Hell Fire Club held its meetings at Medmenham Abbey, near High Wycombe.

Oxford's architectural treasure-house

There is a scarcity of medieval castles—probably because this part of the country, set so far inland, was considered safe in the Middle Ages. But the Home Counties have Vanbrugh's masterpiece, Blenheim Palace, and the royal residence of Windsor Castle, rich in work of every period since the Middle Ages. The greatest treasure-houses of medieval architecture are the colleges and other buildings of Oxford University. Outstanding examples of earlier architecture include the cathedral of St Albans and many fine parish churches such as St Mary's, Iffley, one of England's most famous Norman churches. The best examples of later architecture are the splendid Jacobean Hatfield House, in Hertfordshire; the 18th-century Woburn Abbey, in Bedfordshire; and many smaller houses such as Hughenden Manor, in Buckinghamshire, which was the home of Benjamin Disraeli from 1847 until his death in 1881.

Londoners' demands for recreation are met in the Home Counties in many varied ways. The steep slopes north of Luton are used for gliding; Whipsnade Zoo attracts visitors in their thousands; Ascot and Newbury racecourses are among the best in the land. There is pony-trekking among hills, and polo at Smith's Lawn, Windsor, patronised by royalty. There is coarse fishing from river banks, and trips along the Thames in pleasure boats, hired cabin-cruisers and punts. As this is part of the vast commuter country surrounding the capital, there are golf courses in plenty. By contrast, off the main highways there are numerous secluded villages which still preserve an unspoilt rural remoteness within the confines of their own green boundaries.

WIDE-RANGING TEMPERATURES

The mixture of hills and plains in the Home Counties creates a variety of weather patterns. Rainfall, generally moderate, increases in the west; sunshine is plentiful, but winds from the east, south-east and north can bring haze on warm days. There is a wide range between high and low temperatures. A valley in the Chilterns near Rickmansworth has the most extreme range in the country: 32°C (90°F) on the hottest day, —12°C (10°F) on the coldest night

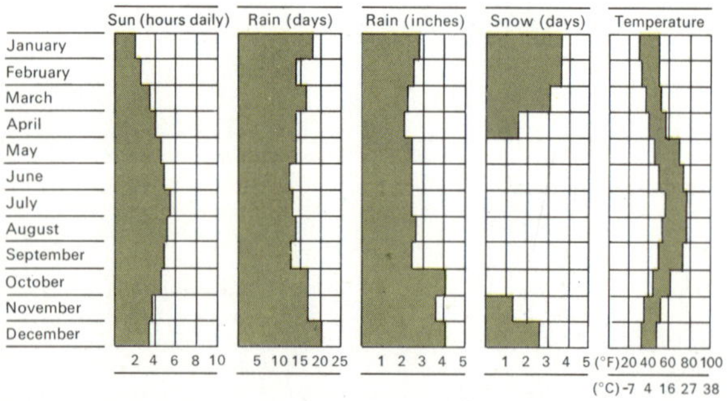

FOREST IN THE HILLS *A track leads beneath beech trees in the heart of the Chiltern Hills at Princes Risborough, Bucks. The Chilterns are wooded in the west and mainly bare in the east. Their highest point is 852-ft Coombe Hill, above Wendover*

Rolling Berkshire Downs

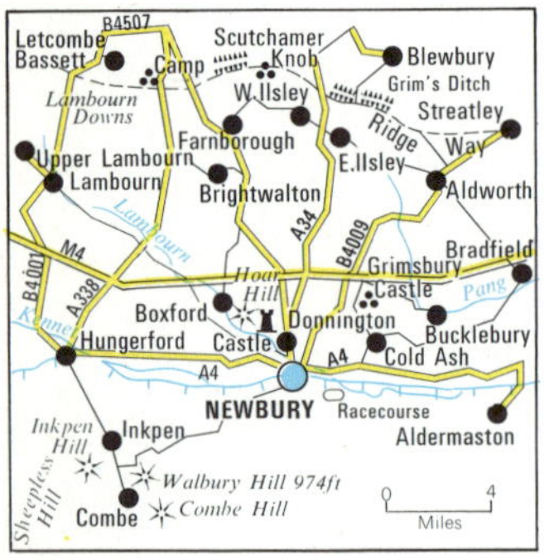

Angling River Kennet: the Old Mill Hotel, Aldermaston, issues permits; the Piscatorial Society has waters at Thatcham, Newbury and Kintbury. Canal fishing at Hungerford: Hungerford Canal A.A. Midgham, near Cold Ash, is a favourite anglers' haunt and there is trout fishing on the River Pang at Bradfield. Permission from Reading A.A.

Bird-watching On the Kennet and at gravel pits in the area.

Canoeing Information from the Kennet Valley Canoe Club, Newbury.

Horse racing Newbury Racecourse; hurdling and steeplechasing from Jan. to Mar. and Nov. to Dec.; Flat racing from Apr. to Oct.

Events Candle auction for charity in Aldermaston village hall in mid-Dec. every three years (1980, 1983, etc.). People bid to rent land for a year, and whoever is bidding when the candle has burned to a certain level wins the auction for the land.

Arts The Watermill Theatre, in a converted mill at Bagnor, near Newbury, holds a season of plays from May to mid-Oct.

Places to see *Alfred's Castle*, Iron Age hill fort near Ashdown House: daily. *Ashdown House* (NT), near Lambourn, late 17th-century house built for Elizabeth of Bohemia: afternoons only: Apr., Wed.; May to Sept., Wed. and 1st and 3rd Sat. in month. *Donnington Castle*: daily. *Newbury Museum*, Wharf Street, Newbury: weekdays, except Wed. afternoons Oct. to Mar. *Sandleford Priory*, near Newbury, former Augustinian priory now St Gabriel's School, with a 14th-century chapel, and gardens by Capability Brown: by appointment. *Stratfield Saye House* and gardens: daily, except Fri., Easter to late Sept.

Information centre Newbury District Council, The Wharf, Newbury. Tel. Newbury 42400.

The Berkshire Downs were once great sheep-lands. Even now, with most of the land under the plough, the downs still offer trackways of springy turf between the huge wheatfields, bracingly windblown, with wide views stretching to far horizons. This turf is the training ground of some of England's finest thoroughbred horses, and strings of them at exercise are a common sight on the downs.

Prehistoric tracks like Ridge Way and the Icknield Way cross this land of marvellous antiquity and give the energetic walker a chance to roam far. Notable sites are the great Iron Age hill fort of Segsbury Camp and the curiously named burial mound of Scutchamer Knob, and there are numerous round barrows and sections of the mysterious Grim's Ditch, the significance of which is still unknown.

Southwards, the land drops through great birch and oak woodland, then over commons of bracken and heather into the more populated Kennet Valley, a land of flat meadows, dotted with poplars and willows. South of the river the bold, chalk escarpments rise again towards Hampshire, with Inkpen Hill and Walbury Hill near by.

Scattered throughout the region are cottages and houses of flint and brick with thatched roofs, mostly of the 18th and 19th centuries. Old streets and attractive houses give an air of quaintness to towns such as Newbury, Hungerford and Lambourn.

A bridge has stood here on the Kennet at Newbury since Saxon times, but the present structure dates from 1769

Aldworth
The church has some fine 13th-century effigies of the de la Beches, a famous Berkshire family in the Middle Ages. There are good views from the steep hill leading eastwards to Streatley.

Aldermaston
The name is today more associated with the atomic research establishment sited near by, but it remains a delightful old village on a wooded hillside south of the Kennet. Its mainly 12th-century church is surrounded by magnificent cedars, yews, limes and elms.

Stratfield Saye House, seven miles to the south-east, is the seat of the Duke of Wellington. The house dates from 1630 and was bought, with the estate, by the first Duke of Wellington in 1817 with money voted to him by Parliament in recognition of his military achievements. Additions were made in Victorian times to the house, which now contains an extensive collection of material connected with the Duke's victories. In the grounds a stone marks the grave of Copenhagen, the charger ridden by the Iron Duke during the whole day at the Battle of Waterloo.

SITE OF SIEGES *The 14th-century gatehouse is all that remains of Donnington Castle, near Newbury, defended by the Royalists in three Civil War sieges*

Blewbury
In the old part of Blewbury there are narrow lanes between white cottages, old pubs, watercress beds and some old wattle-and-daub houses. The parish church is Norman, with a Perpendicular west tower; and a mansion, Hall Barn, is said to have been one of Henry VIII's hunting lodges. It is a good starting point for walkers heading for the downs.

Boxford
A quaint village of thatched roofs and weathered tiles, with a gabled mill beside a stream flowing under the road. There is a path up Hoar Hill, which is bare except for a clump of firs.

Brightwalton
Hidden amidst a labyrinth of lanes, the village is charmingly set among hills, with fine walks among great beechwoods.

Bucklebury
An old and pretty village lying in the valley of the River Pang with, near by,

STORY OF A CANAL

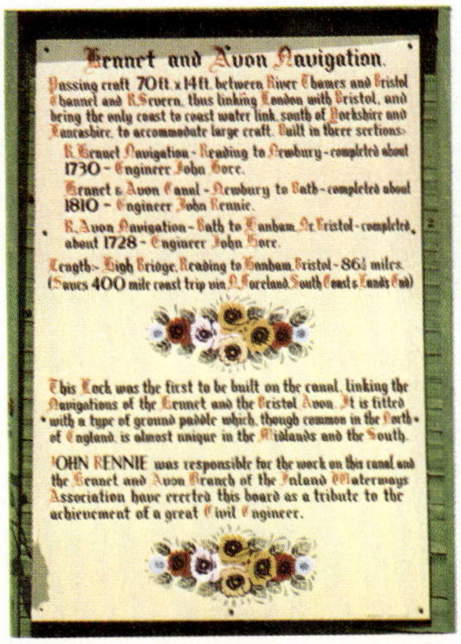

A decorative history at Newbury Lock

A warning notice at Newbury recalls the days of horse-drawn canal traffic

Along the Kennet and Avon Canal, used commercially in the 18th century, trippers now cruise in vessels like this. In Newbury, grooves can still be seen in the stonework of the canal, cut by the haulage ropes of old horse-drawn craft

5 square miles of common on which 20,000 Parliamentarian troops camped before the second Battle of Newbury in 1644. A feature is a mile-long avenue of oaks, planted in Queen Anne's reign.

Cold Ash
A good place for the walker, for it has a lovely common covered with gorse and furze. There are good views over the Pang Valley or, in the opposite direction, into Wiltshire. In nearby Fence Wood, there are the round ramparts of the old camp called Grimsbury Castle, which has a never-failing spring.

Combe
A lonely, tree-shaded village between three enormous downs—Walbury Hill, Combe Hill and Sheepless Hill. There are glorious views of the Kennet Valley from the downs.

Hungerford
This town, on the main London–Bath road, has long been famous for fishing. The best time to visit it is on Tuesday in Easter week, when the picturesque Hocktide ceremony is combined with celebrations marking the award of fishing rights to the town by John of Gaunt in the 14th century. The 'tutti-men', carrying a pole adorned with tutties, or nosegays of flowers, claim kisses from pretty girls; and a toast to 'the immortal memory of John of Gaunt' is drunk in 'ancient Plantagenet punch'.

The town hall has a horn that is said to have been given to the town by John of Gaunt.

East and West Ilsley
The twin villages are right in the heart of the downs. The walk from West Ilsley to Farnborough is superb, amid rolling cornfields often bright with charlock.

LONELY GIBBET *The sinister Combe Gibbet dominates the scenery from Inkpen Hill, part of the highest chalk downs in England, nearly 1000 ft above sea level*

Inkpen
Inkpen Hill, 954 ft, and nearby Walbury Hill, 974 ft, are the highest chalk downs in England. On the summit of Inkpen Hill is Combe Gibbet, one of the last of these grisly landmarks left in England, kept in repair by the tenants of Eastwich Farm. Felons and highwaymen were hanged from the gibbet up to the early 19th century. A short walk to the west is a Neolithic long barrow.

Lambourn
A quaint town with a 12th-century church and Victorian almshouses. Lambourn is the centre for some well-known racing stables, and every day the roads are filled with thoroughbreds walking in single file on their way to be exercised. The town is the best centre for exploring the downs, which are dotted with burial mounds and traces of field systems, some dating back to prehistoric times. The Seven Barrows are 2½ miles north of Lambourn. Segsbury Camp, an Iron Age hill fort at Letcombe Bassett, is 5 miles north-east.

Newbury
The fortunes of this prosperous racing centre were founded in the early part of the 16th century by Jack of Newbury, who was England's greatest clothier at one time. He also paid for the rebuilding of St Nicholas's church, which was used as a guardroom and hospital in the Civil War. The remains can still be seen of the house in Northbrook Street where he entertained Henry VII.

Beyond the small bridge over the Kennet lies the market-place with its old cloth hall, a marvel of Jacobean woodwork. A mile to the north are the ruins of Donnington Castle, which bears scars from the Civil War, when it was successfully defended three times by the Royalist Sir John Boys.

The Vale of the White Horse

Angling Some coarse fishing on the Thames, mainly near the Swan Hotel at Radcot Bridge; Tadpole Bridge; and Newbridge.

Boating Boats can be hired at Pink Hill Lock near Eynsham, and at Radcot, Buscot and Kelmscot.

Bird-watching Many rare birds can be seen round the gravel pits and on the open country of the downs.

Walking The great Ridge Way is one of the oldest highways in Britain. In this region it can be followed on foot from just south of Letcombe Bassett, across Whitehorse Hill to the point where the track crosses into Wiltshire, 3½ miles south-west of Woolstone.

Events There is a fair at Wantage in May. Woodstock has a carnival week in June and a fair in Oct.

Places to see *Blenheim Palace*: late Mar. to Oct., daily; park open daily throughout the year. *Buscot House* (NT): afternoons only: Apr. to Sept., Wed., Thur., Fri. and some Sat. *Buscot Old Parsonage* (NT): Wed. afternoons by appointment. *Great Coxwell Tithe Barn* (NT), 1½ miles south-west of Faringdon, 13th-century stone building with timber roof: daily. *Kelmscott Manor*: first Wed. in month, Apr. to Sept. *Oxfordshire County Museum*, Woodstock: weekdays, except Mon. Oct. to Apr., and Sun. afternoon.

Information centre Thames and Chilterns Tourist Board, 8 The Market Place, PO Box 10, Abingdon. Tel. Abingdon 22711.

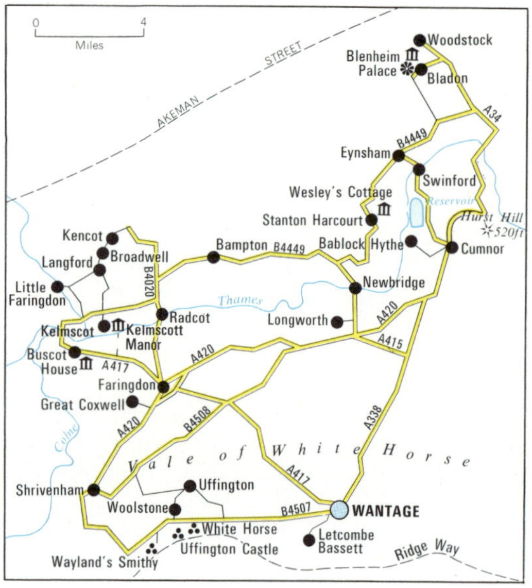

The gentle water-meadows of the infant River Thames form the boundary between Oxfordshire and Berkshire. South of the river lie the rich, flat farmlands of the Vale of the White Horse, named after the great chalk figure cut in ancient times into the bold escarpment of the Berkshire Downs which border the Vale to the south.

Most of the river bank can be walked; there is good fishing in the waters, which are popular too for small-boat sailing. The fame of Bablock Hythe, mentioned by Matthew Arnold in 'The Scholar-Gypsy', has brought riverside huts and caravans, but there is unspoilt charm higher upstream at two crossing points—Newbridge, and the triple-arched bridge spanning the river at Radcot—both of which are believed to have been completed by the 14th century. At Newbridge an attractive inn, The Rose Revived, provides a quiet patio from which to watch the river's mirror-like surface.

This is an area rich in literary associations. The poets William Morris, Dante Gabriel Rossetti, Alexander Pope and Matthew Arnold all lived here. So did Thomas Hughes, who wrote about the area in the first chapters of *Tom Brown's Schooldays*. Hughes also wrote a Victorian best-seller, *The Scouring of the White Horse*, in which he perpetuated the myths and local stories connected with the White Horse and with Alfred the Great, who was born at Wantage.

The abundance of myths is understandable in an area so much of which belongs to a very old England, with the prehistoric Ridge Way, a Roman road and relics of Celtic times and earlier.

Bampton
The village used to be called Bampton in the Bush, because there were no roads to it until the mid-18th century. It is now a fairly large village with stone cottages and Georgian facades. The church, with its 13th-century spire, has a magnificent exterior. On Spring Bank Holiday there is Morris dancing in the streets and the horse fair, held in August, dates from the reign of Edward I, though it is now more of a social occasion.

Buscot
This Thames-side village has a pump under a four-gabled roof. Buscot House, 1 mile south-east, is a National Trust property standing in a wooded park that contains three lakes.

Cumnor
The village is perched on the west side of 520 ft Hurst Hill. Its church is notable for a rare contemporary statue of Elizabeth I and an unusual 17th-century spiral staircase. Sir Walter Scott wrote in *Kenilworth* about the mysterious death at Cumnor in 1560 of Amy Robsart, the wife of Robert Dudley, Earl of Leicester. She was found with a broken neck at their home, Cumnor Hall, and her death seemed to pave the way for a projected marriage between the Earl and Elizabeth I. Nothing now remains of the house.

Eynsham
The road from Oxford crosses the Thames into Eynsham over the 18th-century toll bridge at Swinford. The town has a 14th-century cross, 20 ft high, and an arcaded hall in its square.

Faringdon
Alfred the Great is said to have had a palace here, and the town is mentioned in the Domesday Book. It is a pleasant grey-limestone market town, looking older than it really is, for almost nothing except its medieval church is earlier than the 17th century. The Folly, half a mile east of the A420 to Oxford, is a towering brick structure built by Lord Berners as recently as 1935 to relieve local unemployment.

Kelmscot
A straggling, greystone village where the poet William Morris lived, from 1871 until his death in 1896, in an impressive gabled Elizabethan manor

PLUM CAKE ON A SWORD

A plum cake is impaled on a sword and carried during the Spring Bank Holiday Morris dancing at Bampton. Pieces of the cake are sold and bring 'good luck' to all who eat them. A 'fool' also figures in the celebrations

HAND-STITCHED GLOVES

A woman hand-sews a glove at Woodstock, which is famous for its glove-making industry—a craft that has been carried on in this small town for more than 400 years. Townspeople make the hand-stitched gloves as a cottage industry

INSPIRATION FOR 'NEWS FROM NOWHERE'

The woodcut frontispiece from *News from Nowhere,* the tale by William Morris (1834–96) of a party of travellers whose journey ends at Kelmscott Manor, depicted in the drawing. The border design is by Morris, the designer, printer and writer, who is buried in Kelmscot churchyard

The stone path which led up to the old house still remains in this modern view of the Elizabethan Kelmscott Manor. To recreate the scene described by Morris, new trees were planted in 1968 by the Morris Society, and visitors can relive the experience of the book's travellers

house which backs on to the river, among fields and pollarded willows. Little Faringdon, 2 miles north-west, has an old mill, and a 3-mile drive to the north passes through the lovely villages of Langford, Broadwell and Kencot.

Stanton Harcourt

Wesley's Cottage, north of the churchyard, was so named because John and Charles Wesley and their sister Kezia used to visit the vicar there. Pope's Tower is one of the few remaining parts of the once great manor, original home of the Harcourt family, where in 1718 Alexander Pope completed the fifth volume of his translation of *The Iliad*.

Uffington

A village in the heart of the Vale of the White Horse, with good views of the horse cut into the chalk of nearby White Horse Hill. There is still dispute over when the strange figure of the White Horse, 374 ft long, was cut into the hillside, and what motivated the men who did it. One theory is that the horse was cut in Saxon times to commemorate a 9th-century victory by King Alfred over the Danes. But its semi-abstract style is similar to the art of the Iron Age Celts, who may have cut the figure as early as 350 BC to represent their goddess Epona, protectress of horses, who was known to the Romans. A path from Woolstone, 1 mile south of Uffington, leads to the horse, so life-like that it appears to be galloping across the downs.

Uffington Castle, which crowns White Horse Hill and stands on the line of the ancient Ridge Way, is an Iron Age camp, 250 yds long and nearly 200 yds wide. Its oval ramparts give views over five counties on a clear day.

Wayland's Smithy, 1½ miles south-west, is a famous long barrow. Excavations in 1919–20 revealed eight Stone Age skeletons and one possibly Iron Age or Romano-British burial. An earlier Stone Age barrow was afterwards found within the larger one. It had 14 more graves. Wayland the Smith figures in Scandinavian mythology as a maker of invincible weapons.

Wantage

A quiet town in the centre of a wide agricultural belt. A century ago it was notorious for thieves and ruffians who fought, stole and murdered after dark, or who baited bulls and badgers and got roaring drunk in local cock-pits. It has cobbled streets and 17th and 18th-century houses, and is a pleasant town for quiet strolling. The cobbles in the passage leading from Newbury Street to some 17th-century almshouses are made of sheep's knucklebones. There is a statue in the town square to Alfred the Great, who was born in Wantage. At the west end of the spacious square stands the Church of SS Peter and Paul, partly dating from the 13th century and containing, as well as some fine wood carvings, the tombs of some of the Fitzwaryn family, into which Dick Whittington married.

Woodstock

Until recently this was one of the most beautiful towns in the country, but much of its 18th-century elegance has been destroyed by modern building. However, Woodstock will continue to draw visitors because of Blenheim Palace, Sir John Vanbrugh's grandiose masterpiece built for John Churchill, the 1st Duke of Marlborough. Among the famous craftsmen who worked on the palace were Sir James Thornhill, who painted the ceiling in the great hall, Laguerre, Gibbons, and Rysbrack, the designer of the duke's monument in the chapel. The house was begun as a gift from a grateful nation to the duke after his victory over the French and Bavarians at Blenheim in 1704; but the Marlboroughs themselves had to pay £50,000 for its completion. One of its main attractions today is the room where Sir Winston Churchill, grandson of the 7th Duke of Marlborough, was born on November 30, 1874.

The park-like landscapes of the immense Blenheim Park were created by Capability Brown, who dammed the River Glyme to make Blenheim's fine lake. Bladon stands on the edge of the park, and in Bladon churchyard Sir Winston and his parents Lord and Lady Randolph Churchill are buried.

A GOD ON THE HILL *The White Horse at Uffington may have been made to represent a pagan deity able to take a horse's form*

Man-made landscapes

England's greatest contribution to the art of gardening was the 18th-century movement back to nature. The formal geometric patterns of the Renaissance, which had reached their zenith in the work of André Le Nôtre at Versailles for Louis XIV, now seemed unattractive to British gardeners. They began to cut down the formal avenues, break up the terraces and search for a kind of gardening that was uniquely English. In the words of Alexander Pope, who was talented as a gardener as well as a poet, they rejected gardens where 'Grove nods at grove, each alley has its brother, And half the platform just reflects the other'.

In their place they made gardens that reflected nature, using only the beauties of the countryside, the contours of the ground, the trees, rivers and lakes, and the contrasts of light and shade that each provided.

The enthusiasm of intellectuals and writers such as Pope, Joseph Addison, Horace Walpole, William Shenstone and Thomas Gray gave the landscape movement its initial impetus, and strong social and economic influences contributed to its success. The landowners were wealthy and could afford to develop their gardens on a grand scale, creating lakes and forests. The security of family estates and fortunes seemed assured. They could look comfortably into the future and plant for posterity.

Although the landscape garden was essentially English, it owed something to other lands. There was influence from China, through the paintings on Chinese porcelain that decorated fashionable drawing-rooms; and the original inspiration had come from French landscape painters. The result was as much graphic art as gardening—a style summed up by Walpole when he wrote of the men who made the English landscape: 'They leaped the fence and saw that all nature was a garden.'

THE LONG AVENUE, CLIVEDEN *Neat, geometrical lawns, parallel lines of trees, a long straight drive and formal statuary—these were some of the characteristics of the classic 17th-century garden. The men who made the natural English gardens of the 18th century rejected this style. Their inspiration was partly drawn from France, for in their search for what the artist William Hogarth called the 'wavy line of beauty', they followed French painters such as Claude and the Poussin brothers*

William Kent (1684–1748)

Kent, the first of the professional landscape gardeners, started work as apprentice to a coach builder in Yorkshire. He came to London to study art, and then spent four years in Rome where he became influenced by the new French landscape painting school. There he met the 3rd Earl of Burlington, who recommended him as the man to paint the murals and design the gardens of Kensington Palace. Kent's enthusiasm made him something of a laughing stock. He tried to make the gardens more natural by planting dead tree stumps 'to give the greater air of truth to the scene'. He was largely responsible for the design of the grounds of Stowe, in Buckinghamshire, and also the Vale of Venus at Rousham House in Oxfordshire

ROUSHAM HOUSE: THE VALE OF VENUS *Comparison of a contemporary print (above) with the Vale of Venus as it appears today (below), shows how well William Kent's original conception has survived. The Vale—and the whole layout of the estate—is typical of Kent's gardens, with a series of views like landscape paintings. Horace Walpole described it as the most engaging of all his works—the most 'elegant and antique'. It has been suggested that the poet and amateur gardener Alexander Pope had a hand in the design because he was a friend of the Dormer brothers who owned the property; but this is unlikely, as it is a close reflection of Kent's Grecian valley at nearby Stowe. It was probably this earlier work that prompted the owners of Rousham House to engage Kent to design a 'natural' valley*

Capability Brown (1715-1783)

Lancelot Brown is better known by his nickname 'Capability'. It derived from his habit of saying, when looking at the grounds surrounding a mansion, that they had 'capabilities of improvement'. He is the most outstanding of all the landscape gardeners of the 18th century, and it may be more than coincidence that he was originally a gardener —unlike the others. He began very humbly, in the kitchen garden at Kirkharle in Northumberland, becoming head gardener at Stowe and carrying out much of the work planned by William Kent. He set up as an independent designer of gardens in 1750, and a few years later to have a garden designed by Capability Brown was to be in the forefront of fashion

THE LAKE AT BLENHEIM PALACE *The lake Capability Brown created at Blenheim is considered to be his masterpiece. Brown's greatest power was probably his management of water, and he created many 'natural' lakes. Above is Brown's design for the bridge at the south end of the lake at Blenheim, near Bladon (where Sir Winston Churchill is buried). Below is the bridge that divides the lake. It was designed by Vanbrugh, the original architect of Stowe, where Brown worked as a gardener before he became nationally known as the 'Landscape Architect of England'*

Humphry Repton (1752-1818)

The name of Repton had become so much a household word by the end of the 18th century that he has the distinction of being mentioned in one of Jane Austen's novels, *Mansfield Park* (1814). He started life as a general merchant, but had no liking for commerce—his tastes were for painting, poetry and music. The idea of setting up as a landscape gardener, which came to him on a sleepless night in 1788, gave him an opportunity to use his talent for painting. In order to show his clients what he proposed, he prepared 'before and after' sketches to demonstrate the improvement. These were bound in red leather and became known as the Red Books. He often worked on gardens originally laid out by Capability Brown

WEST WYCOMBE PARK *Repton's Red Book technique, and his tactful manipulation of an open landscape, are shown in the two sketches he made showing how he proposed to open the vista in front of West Wycombe Park in Buckinghamshire. Below is the house today. An important aspect of his work was to provide a setting for a house that gave panoramic views over the garden from the principal windows*

Oxfordshire's Cotswolds

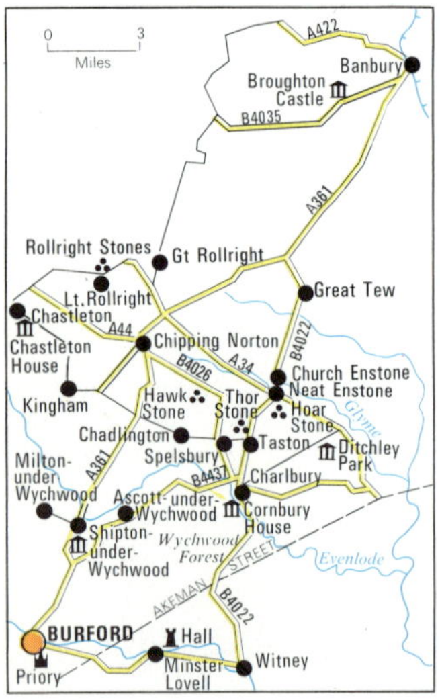

Boating On the Oxford Canal, which passes through Banbury.

Angling Trout at Chipping Norton; coarse fish and trout at Burford; fly fishing only at Minster Lovell.

Events Grass is strewn in Holy Trinity Church, Shenington, near Banbury, on Whit Sat., and the following two Sats. During the last week in June, Westminster Morris Men dance in the market-place at Chipping Norton. Banbury has a Cavalcade of Sport in early Sept. and a Michaelmas Fair is held there in mid-Oct.

Places to see Banbury Museum, opposite Banbury Cross: weekdays, except Tues. and Sat. afternoons. *Broughton Castle*, Banbury, moated 14th-century manor house with Elizabethan additions: Apr. to Sept., Wed. and Bank Hol. Sun. and Mon.; also Sun. afternoons, June, July and Aug. *Chasleton House*: daily, except Sat. and Sun. mornings and Wed. *Cotswold Wildlife Park*, near Burford: daily. *Minster Lovell Hall*: weekdays, Sun. afternoon. *Tolsey Museum*, High Street, Burford, 18th-century-style dolls' house and Cotswold stone display: afternoons Easter to late Oct.

Information centres Borough House, Marlborough Road, Banbury. Tel. Banbury 52535. Information Bureau, Guildhall, Chipping Norton. Tel. Chipping Norton 2341.

The Cotswold countryside of north Oxfordshire seems very much the English heartland. Here are sleepy villages clad in Cotswold grey limestone or golden ironstone; rich, solid farms; ridges grazed by sheep; undulating wolds and gentle streams such as the Windrush and the Evenlode.

In the Middle Ages, Cotswold wool was one of England's chief sources of revenue, and the rich Cotswold wool merchants built a series of magnificent churches and splendid stone manor houses. Against a background of wide, flat meadows and soft knolls crowned by clumps of trees, man has added soaring spires, delicate battlements, spiral chimneys, stone-mullioned windows, heraldic-emblazoned porches, stone dovecots and stone-roofed tithe barns.

A fragment of the once great royal hunting forest of Wychwood overlooks the valley of the River Evenlode, and gives its name to picturesque villages like Shipton-under-Wychwood, Milton-under-Wychwood and Ascott-under-Wychwood. In medieval times the forest was as large and important as the New Forest. Henry I used to keep a menagerie there, and in Tudor times hunting parties used to carouse in Burford. The surviving woodland, the highest peak of which reaches 509 ft, is beautiful countryside.

MINSTER LOVELL HALL *These ruins, standing in fields near the River Windrush, are all that remain of the 15th-century home of the Lovells, a family of power throughout the Middle Ages*

BANBURY CAKES

These cakes, made from flaky or puff pastry filled with dried spiced fruit, can still be bought in the town, although the original shop has been demolished. The making of Banbury cakes was first recorded in the 16th century, but they were probably made in earlier times

Banbury

Best known for its cakes and its celebrated cross, Banbury remains a pleasant town in spite of being a large industrial, marketing and shopping centre. It dates back to Saxon times, though few buildings survive from earlier than the 17th century. This is largely due to a kind of demolition frenzy among Banbury's inhabitants. In the 17th century, they petitioned Parliament to pull down their great castle so that they could use the stone to repair the damage caused to the town by two Civil War sieges. In the 18th century, they blew up their old church rather than restore it.

The original Banbury Cross was destroyed, too, in an upsurge of Puritanism three centuries ago. The present cross dates only from 1859. The 'fine lady' of the rhyme is believed to have been a member of the Fiennes family, who still live at nearby Broughton Castle. The ride to the cross was probably a May Morning ceremony.

Burford

An ancient town thought to have been the scene of a church assembly in AD 683, attended by the King of Mercia. The main street slopes down in a melody of Cotswold stone to the meandering River Windrush, marked by a picturesque bridge and the splendid Church of St John the Baptist — the second largest in Oxfordshire, with one of the county's most impressive spires. Tudor houses line the streets, interspersed with Georgian façades. A feature of the High Street is the Tolsey, an upper storey supported on pillars, which was where market and other tolls were collected. Restored in 1959, it is now a museum and council chamber.

Burford Priory was rebuilt in 1808, but many Elizabethan elements were retained, including over the door the coat of arms of William Lenthall who, as Speaker of the Long Parliament, defied Charles I. The Cotswold Wild Life Park is a zoo collection in an open park.

Chadlington

A pleasant village set on Chadlington Downs, an attractive area for walking. The 8 ft high Hawk Stone, which was probably put up in the Bronze Age, crowns a bare ridge 1 mile north of the village. Spelsbury, 1½ miles east, has 17th-century almshouses and a feudal atmosphere; and in the outlying hamlet of Taston stands a prehistoric monolith known as the Thor Stone.

Charlbury

A village looking across the Evenlode Valley to Wychwood Forest. The church dates from medieval times, and has a 700-year-old stairway and some fine stained glass. A row of stone-roofed houses near by has a 30-yd stretch of wisteria. Cornbury House was the home of the Earl of Leicester, favourite of Queen Elizabeth I; it is set amid a 600-acre deer park.

The 18th-century mansion of Ditchley Park, 2¼ miles north-east, is on the site of an earlier building used by James I when hunting in Wychwood Forest and later owned by the family of General Robert E. Lee, who fought for the South in the American Civil War and signed its surrender. It is now an Anglo-American conference centre.

Chastleton

The Jacobean Chastleton House, on land bought from Robert Catesby, a conspirator in the Gunpowder Plot, keeps a remarkable 17th and 18th-

WHERE HENRY VIII HUNTED *Wychwood Forest, where Tudor monarchs including Henry VIII hunted, now has a nature reserve in the 1500 acres which still survive*

century atmosphere. It is built in Cotswold stone, and much of the original furniture is still there. In the grounds there is a garden of box bushes, cut in fantastic shapes. The village has many stone-built thatched cottages.

Chipping Norton
The highest town in the county, at 700 ft. It was mentioned in the Domesday Book as Norton; the 'chipping' or 'cheapening', meaning 'market', was added to the name in the 13th century. Set at the junction of several roads, the town today is often too busy to provide the quiet charm expected in the Cotswolds; but when the traffic subsides, it recovers some of its genteel 18th-century atmosphere. The Crown and The White Hart were once coaching inns, and The Fox has a 16th-century fireplace. Near St Mary's Church is a row of 17th-century almshouses.

Enstone
Two villages, Church Enstone and Neat Enstone, face each other across the River Glyme. Here is one of the oldest tithe barns in the country, built in 1382, and a church containing Norman and Saxon masonry. A pleasant 1½-mile walk to the west leads to an ancient chambered tumulus. South of Neat Enstone is the Hoar Stone, a prehistoric monument.

STOCKS AT GREAT TEW *Early 17th-century stocks stand on the village green at Great Tew. Some of the stone cottages were built in the same century*

Great Tew
An unusually attractive village, in which honey-coloured 17th-century cottages, roofed with scalloped thatch, nestle amid woods. Lord Falkland lived there in the 17th century and his house was a centre for the brightest intellects of Oxford and London, including Clarendon and Hobbes.

Minster Lovell
The loveliest of the villages on the Windrush, with a 15th-century bridge and an inn, The Old Swan, which is also 500 years old. Across the fields are the ruins of a manor house to which are attached two tragic legends. One, the 'Mistletoe Bough' legend dating from medieval times, is of a young girl who, during a game of hide-and-seek on Christmas Eve, hid in a heavy chest and was trapped; her skeleton was found years later. The second legend concerns Francis Lovell, who supported the 15th-century pretender Lambert Simnel. He hid in a secret room to which only one servant had access; but the servant died suddenly and Lovell, unable to get out, died of starvation. In 1718, during alterations, a hidden chamber was revealed, with the skeleton of a man who had been sitting at a table.

Rollright Stones
The famous Bronze Age stone circle stands beside a road running along the windy ridge of the Cotswolds. The principal part consists of the King's Men—a 100 ft diameter circle of pitted and time-worn stones, varying from a few inches to 7 ft in height. On the opposite side of the road—across the county boundary in Warwickshire—is the King Stone. Bent in the middle, it looks like an old man, weary and failing.

Witney
A blanket-making town which preserves a Cotswold market-town atmosphere. To the south of a long and expansive green, set with lime trees, is the fine, wide main street. It has an unusual 17th-century Butter Cross, with a gabled roof crowned by a clock-turret and a sun-dial, all resting on 13 stone pillars. Opposite is the town hall, a room overhanging a piazza; and the old Blanket Hall has an unusual one-handed clock.

WORKING ON THE WOOL

Wool being sorted in the blanket-making town of Witney. Most other processes in this ancient industry are now carried out by machinery

A moorland in Oxfordshire

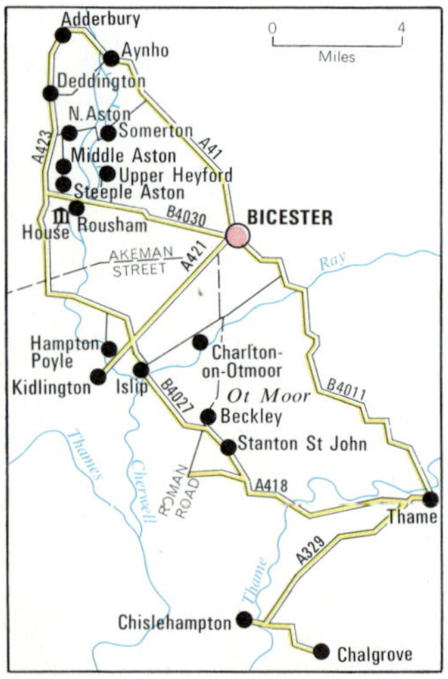

Angling Chub, roach, perch and pike on the River Cherwell to the north of Oxford, and on the Ray at Islip.

Boating Boats can be hired at Aynho Wharf, 2½ miles east of Deddington; there is canoeing on the Cherwell from Somerton to Oxford.

Places to see *Rousham House*: Apr. to Sept., Wed., Sun. and Bank Hol. afternoons. *Rycote Chapel*, 2½ miles south-west of Thame: weekdays and Sun. afternoon.

Gardens to see Occasional days in summer (NGS). *Barton Abbey*, near Steeple Barton; *Court Farm* and *Haseley Court*, Little Haseley, 6 miles south-west of Thame; *Rectory Farm*, Stanton St John.

Information centre Borough House, Marlborough Road, Banbury. Tel. Banbury 52535.

An area of far horizons, with vast cornfields and stretches of wilderness, extends down the eastern side of Oxfordshire. Much of this region is off the tourist track, and it is no accident that the Services have adopted it for a military airfield at Upper Heyford and a rifle range on Ot Moor.

Ot Moor is a curious phenomenon in this generally highly cultivated, domesticated part of Britain—a bleak, uninhabited expanse covering some 6 square miles, crossed by only two tracks; the north–south one is an old Roman road. A 15-mile road round the moor connects a ring of attractive villages, many of them with cosy thatched cottages and views across the sharply contrasting desolate moorland.

There are attractive villages, too, along the banks of the River Thame in the south and along the River Cherwell in the north, beyond which the country takes on the slightly sterner character of the Midlands. By the Cherwell near Bicester stands Rousham House, one of the finest Jacobean mansions in the country.

THE PUZZLING MAZE *This turf maze—one of only seven found in different parts of England—is preserved in the gardens of Troy Farm, 1½ miles east of Somerton, where it can be seen by appointment. It was probably made in medieval times*

Adderbury
A village with houses of warm stone and a gentle, elm-shaded green. Many of the houses are 17th century, among them Adderbury House, a fine, gabled building which was once the home of the Earl of Rochester, a dissolute Restoration poet who courted his insane second wife by pretending to be the Emperor of China. The 14th-century church has an imposing tower with a fine spire.

The Astons
North Aston, Middle Aston and Steeple Aston are three large villages on the west bank of the Cherwell. North Aston has great elms and a village green, while 1 mile south of Steeple Aston lies Rousham. Here, in peaceful seclusion, is a manorial village with wayside houses, a church and the great Rousham House. The house, built in 1635 by Sir Robert Dormer and used as a Royalist stronghold during the Civil War, was enlarged in 1738 by William Kent, who also surrounded it by a man-made landscape including Classical temples, cascades and statues in 30 wooded acres within a bend of the River Cherwell.

BEAUTY THAT GREW *The part-13th-century Thame Church shows a pleasing development of styles from Early English to Perpendicular. It is noted for its brasses*

Beckley
The Roman road north from Dorchester ran through this village on the edge of mysterious Ot Moor. The old road can still be traced as a hedged lane, too narrow for cars. Walkers, however, can use it to enjoy the great silence and solitude of the moor. The 400-ft ridge behind the village is a good spot from which to look over the bleak but fascinating 4000-acre expanse.

Bicester
An important hunting centre; and to prove that the horse is king here, the roads round the town have grass borders to make it easier on the hooves. Bicester is also a major centre for shopping and industry. The old market square, with some 16th-century buildings, is still the centre of the town, and there are other old buildings in Sheep Street and near the 12th-century church.

Charlton-on-Otmoor
Sitting on a knoll on the edge of a moor, this is a charming village with thatched 17th-century cottages and stone farmhouses. The best time to visit it is on May Day, when the local children perform country dances after morning service and decorate the church with garlands of clipped box leaves. Cromwell's men tore down the gallery and rood in the church.

Chislehampton
A small village with a long bridge over the Thame, which was crossed by Prince Rupert on his way to victory over the Roundheads at Chalgrove in 1643. From Chislehampton (*chisel* is Old English for gravel) there are many pleasant drives and walks, and most of the nearby villages are worth a visit.

Deddington
A quaint town with many large old houses of honey-coloured stone. It was called Daedintun by the Saxons, who built it on a hill commanding the valleys of the Sor and Worton Brook. Charles I slept at Castle House, which dates back to the 16th century, on the night after his victory at Cropredy Bridge in 1644. There are also two old inns and a fine market-place.

Islip
The best known of the villages on the edge of Ot Moor, with a charming, climbing main street of crooked stone houses, cottages and inns. St Edward the Confessor was born here *c.* 1004. A winding road along the Cherwell leads to Hampton Poyle, 1½ miles north-west, which has a church dating from the 13th century and some 16th and 17th-century cottages. There is a footpath to Hampton Gay, 1 mile north-west, which has some manor ruins. Another path from Hampton Poyle leads south to Kidlington Church.

Stanton St John
A village of stone, with some cottages dating back to the 16th century. Milton's grandfather lived here and a plaque marks the birthplace of John White, founder of Massachusetts.

WATER LILIES IN THE WILDS *Ot Moor is mostly a barren area, but here and there water lilies grow in streams that wind through a former marsh. There are villages on its fringe, but the moor is uninhabited and the Army has a rifle range there*

Thame

A market town that was old at the time of the Domesday Book. Its mile-long main street is so wide that a whole group of buildings, including the town hall, have been set down in the middle of the road. Every year this road is filled with stalls at the big autumn fair. The houses and cottages are like a Christmas-card picture—particularly the small gingerbread house near the top of the main street. Four of the inns date from the 15th century. One of them, The Bird Cage, is a gabled and timber-framed building, which is believed to have once been the local lock-up. Another inn, The Spread Eagle, was made famous by John Fothergill, a writer on country inns between the two World Wars, in *An Innkeeper's Diary*. There are fine brasses in the 13th-century church.

THE HOUSE THAT WILLIAM KENT ADORNED—AND THE FOLLY HE BUILT ON THE HILL

Kent built this sham castle gate, now known as the 'Rousham eyecatcher'

Rousham House was built in 1635 by Sir Robert Dormer but was much improved by William Kent (1684–1748). The garden is one of Kent's few surviving landscapes

The outbuildings of Rousham House contrast with the main building

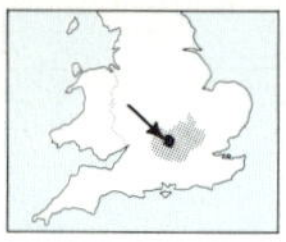

Oxford's unchanging beauty

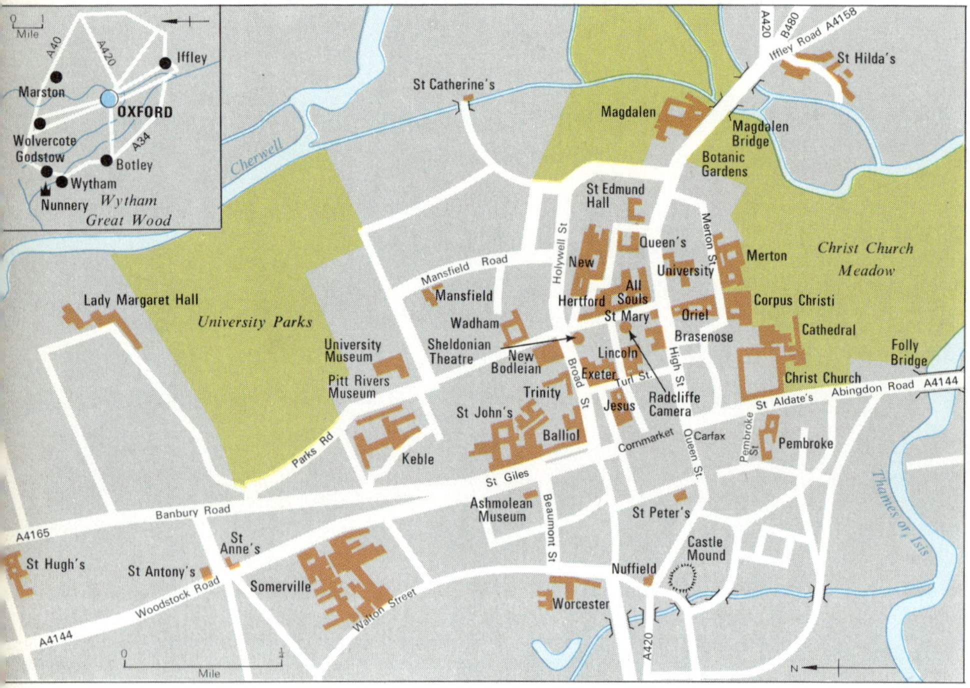

Angling On the Thames, Cherwell, Evenlode and Windrush.

Boating On the Thames at Folly Bridge and on the Cherwell at Magdalen Bridge and Bardwell Road.

Events The two principal university rowing races, Torpids and Eights, take place on the Isis in the last week of Feb. and May respectively. At dawn on May 1, the choir of Magdalen College sing from the top of Magdalen Tower. The English Bach Festival is held in the city in late spring or early summer, and the St Giles' Fair is held in Sept.

Places to see *Ashmolean Museum*: weekdays, Sun. afternoon. *Christ Church Library*: vacation weekday afternoons by appointment. *Christ Church Picture Gallery*: daily. *Museum of Modern Art*, Pembroke Street: Tues. to Sat., and Sun. afternoon. *Museum of Oxford*, St Aldate's: Tues. to Sat. *Museum of the History of Science*, Broad Street: Mon. to Fri. *Oxford University Museum*, Parks Road: weekdays. *Pitt-Rivers Museum*, Parks Road: weekday afternoons.

The colleges are usually open in the afternoons and in vacations.

Information centre St Aldate's, Oxford. Tel. Oxford 48707.

With its honey-coloured stones, noble lawns and dreaming spires, Oxford is part of man's cultural heritage. Factories and houses have sprawled across the suburbs, but the colleges at the heart of the city remain compellingly lovely. Within a single square mile, 653 buildings are listed as being of architectural or historic merit.

The city, originally called Oxnaforda, began with the foundation of St Frideswide's nunnery in the 8th century. A university was established by 1214 and by the end of the 13th century, four colleges had been founded: University, Balliol, Merton and St Edmund Hall. In the following century Exeter, Oriel, Queen's and New Colleges were founded. Lincoln, All Souls and Magdalen (in medieval times it was pronounced 'Maudalayne', and 'Maudlin' is its pronunciation today) are 15th century. Brasenose, Corpus Christi, Christ Church (the headquarters of Charles I during the Civil War), St John's, Trinity and Jesus all date from the 16th century; Wadham and Pembroke, from the 17th century; Worcester and Hertford from the 18th century; and Keble from the 19th century.

There are five women's colleges dating from the end of the 19th century—Lady Margaret Hall, Somerville, St Anne's, St Hugh's and St Hilda's. The most modern colleges are St Catherine's and Wolfson, both founded since the Second World War. St Antony's, Nuffield, Wolfson, Linacre and St Cross are postgraduate.

Most colleges are within an easy walk of the High Street, and all the colleges west of a line drawn through St Giles Street, Cornmarket Street and St Aldate's are 'modern', with the exception of Worcester and Pembroke. Christ Church is the largest, richest and noblest college; Magdalen the most beautiful; Merton has the oldest surviving buildings; and the gardens of St John's, Trinity, Worcester, New College and Wadham compete for the title of being the most lovely. Other historic buildings of the university are the Bodleian Library, the Radcliffe Camera (one of the reading rooms of the Bodleian), the Sheldonian Theatre, designed by Wren, and the new Ashmolean Museum.

The rivers help to make Oxford what it is. The city is on the Thames but here the great river, known to the Romans as Thamesis, is called the Isis—and exactly where the Thames becomes the Isis and then the Isis becomes the Thames again has never been defined. Meeting the Isis just south of Folly Bridge is the Cherwell (pronounced Charwell). Flowing through flat lands, bordered with pollarded willows, the rivers provide marvellous punting, boating, fishing and bathing. From Wolvercote, further north, the Isis meanders through the vast Port Meadow, owned by the city since before the days of the Domesday Book.

From Folly Bridge to Iffley Lock the river narrows, and here the college rowing eights train and the 'bump races' called Eights are held. The crew bumping the boat in front moves up a position until it holds pride of place at the 'head of the river'. May Eights are held over four days in late May, when spectators crowd the boathouses and riverside.

The River Cherwell forms a boundary to the spacious University Parks and there are pleasant walks of less than a mile within the city, through Christ Church Meadow, and along the river banks.

TURRETS AND TOWERS *The city centre, seen from South Hinksey, is dominated by the massive high-walled buildings of three of Oxford's colleges—Christ Church, Oriel and Merton*

ON THE ISIS *At the Eights Week races in May, each crew tries to catch up and bump the boat in front. The leading crew at the end of four days' racing is Head of the River*

OFF TO WORK *A scout cycles down New College Lane on his way to work. 'Scout' is the traditional name for a college servant assigned to look after undergraduates*

ALL SOULS COLLEGE The college was founded in 1438 as a memorial to the soldiers of Henry V who were killed at Agincourt, and in other battles. It has no undergraduates, all its members being Fellows who include authorities on law, history and social sciences. Sir Christopher Wren was a Fellow. There is a magnificent collection of legal works among the 300,000 books in the Codrington Library, which is built in the Italian style along the north side of the Great Quadrangle.

ASHMOLEAN MUSEUM Elias Ashmole founded the original museum in Broad Street in 1677 to house curiosities collected by the traveller and naturalist John Tradescant. It grew in size and importance and now, in its new home in Beaumont Street, has comprehensive collections of coins, paintings and European and Near Eastern antiquities. Among British relics are Guy Fawkes's lantern and the Alfred Jewel, of gold, enamel and rock crystal, which is believed to have been made in the 9th century for King Alfred.

THE BODLEIAN LIBRARY One of the most important libraries in the world. Henry IV's son Humphrey, Duke of Gloucester, founded the original library in 1480, and in 1598 Sir Thomas Bodley, a diplomat, re-formed it and gave it his own invaluable collection. The library was formally opened in 1602. Bodley also arranged with the Stationers' Company for a copy of every new book published in Britain to be sent to the library. There are now more than 2,500,000 books in the library. Among the manuscripts are the Codex Laudianus, a 7th-century manuscript of the Acts of the Apostles used by the Venerable Bede, an *Anglo-Saxon Chronicle* dating back to the 12th century, and an incomparable Oriental collection. Part of Duke Humphrey's Library and the old Divinity School, the oldest lecture room in the university, is open to the public. The neighbouring Radcliffe Camera, designed by James Gibbs in 1737, which has an underground store holding 600,000 books, is one of the university's reading rooms.

BRASENOSE COLLEGE The front facing Radcliffe Square dates from the college's foundation in 1509. A Brasenose Hall existed in the 13th century, and in 1333 a group of undergraduates, unhappy with conditions in Oxford, moved to Stamford in Lincolnshire, taking with them an ancient knocker in the shape of a nose—the Brazen Nose. In 1890 it was brought back to Oxford, and is now over the Brasenose High Table. Another 'nose' over the college gate is also believed to date back to the time the college was formed. The present college is built over the sites of nine old halls. The roof of the chapel and a kitchen-range off the hall are 15th century.

CHRIST CHURCH The college is always known as 'The House'. It was founded as Cardinal College by Wolsey in 1525 on the site of St Frideswide's nunnery. When Wolsey fell into disgrace it was renamed King Henry VIII's College, and in 1546 the college chapel became also the cathedral of the diocese and the college was then named Christ Church. The college's hall has 17th-century fan-vaulting and in Wren's Tom Tower is the bell Great Tom, which came from Osney Abbey. Part of the cathedral dates from the 8th century but it contains examples of numerous English architectural styles. The nave, choir and transepts are 12th century, the Lady Chapel 13th century, and the Latin Chapel 14th century. The college has a collection of fine portraits.

MAGDALEN COLLEGE The original buildings have changed little since they were built at the end of the 15th century. The square tower which dominates the part of the city near Magdalen Bridge over the River Cherwell has a peal of ten bells. At sunrise on May Day the college choir sings a Latin hymn from the top of the tower. The New Buildings, begun in 1733, blend beautifully with the original building. The hall has a fine Jacobean screen, and there are some valuable manuscripts in the library. The Magdalen Walks along the bank of the River Cherwell include one named after the essayist Joseph Addison, who was a Fellow of the college.

MERTON COLLEGE Walter de Merton, Bishop of Rochester, obtained a charter for a college at Malden, in Surrey, in 1264 until he found a suitable site in Oxford. The college moved to Oxford about ten years later. The old city wall encloses part of the college, and the original hall still remains, although it has been extensively altered. The Muniment Tower, which contains about 6000 documents, dates from the 14th century. The helmet of Sir Thomas Bodley, founder of the Bodleian Library, is in the college library. The chapel is renowned for its 14 windows with 13th and 14th-century glass.

ST MARY THE VIRGIN One of the best views of Oxford is from the tower of the university church, which is mentioned in the Domesday Book. The magnificent tower was built in the 13th century and the nave in the 15th and 16th centuries. In 1556 Archbishop Cranmer was chained to a pillar in the church to recant his 'heretical' views. But he refused, and before he died at the stake in what is now Broad Street he held out to the flames the hand which had signed his written recantation.

SHELDONIAN THEATRE The building was designed by Sir Christopher Wren like a Roman theatre and named after its benefactor, Archbishop Sheldon. University books were printed here in the 17th century, but now it is used for university functions and concerts. Allegorical pictures representing the victory of the Arts and Sciences over ignorance were painted on the ceiling by Robert Streater. On pillars outside, carved heads of philosophers have been replaced by modern replicas.

TRINITY COLLEGE The traditional rival of Balliol stands next door to it at the end of Broad Street. The college was founded in 1555 by Sir Thomas Pope, who is buried in an alabaster tomb in the chapel which was rebuilt in the 17th century. Parts of the 14th-century Durham College are incorporated in the present buildings. Wren designed the garden quadrangle, and the Lime Walk in the gardens dates from 1713.

UNIVERSITY COLLEGE According to tradition, Alfred the Great formed a community here in 872. Even though it

ALL SOULS *The college was founded in 1438 as a memorial to the dead of Agincourt. The tower bearing the college arms was designed by Nicholas Hawksmoor, a pupil of Wren*

ST MARY'S CHURCH *Carvings adorn the 13th-century tower of the university church. Cranmer was burnt at the foot of the tower for heresy in 1556*

GARGOYLE *A statue holding an owl as a symbol of learning stands in Magdalen*

OXFORD AT PLAY *Punting on the Cherwell is a traditional summer recreation for undergraduates, though many find a paddle easier to handle than a punt-pole*

THE OLD BODLEIAN *This window, like much of the Old Bodleian, has changed little since it was built in the 15th century*

TOM QUADRANGLE *The main quadrangle of Christ Church takes its name from the great bell in Tom Tower; the bell is dedicated to St Thomas of Canterbury. The quadrangle was built by Cardinal Wolsey in 1525 and was originally designed to be cloistered*

ARMS IN STONE *An early Bishop of Exeter helped build Corpus Christi*

is one of the oldest residential colleges in Oxford, founded in 1249 by William, Archdeacon of Durham, the present college buildings go back only 300 years. There is a memorial in the front quadrangle to the poet Shelley, who was 'sent down'—or expelled—for distributing his pamphlet, *The Necessity of Atheism*.

WADHAM COLLEGE Nicholas Wadham (1532–1609) planned the college, which was completed four years after his death. The chapel and hall are particularly well designed and the college gardens are noted for their beauty.

WORCESTER COLLEGE The college, which stands at the western end of Beaumont Street, was founded in 1714, but parts of its buildings are of an earlier date. The library contains original designs and drawings by Inigo Jones. The large gardens are noted for their lake.

Godstow

An attractive 3-mile walk crossing Port Meadow leads to Godstow with its bridges, weir and the Trout Inn. Near by are the ruins of a nunnery where Rosamund, the mistress of Henry II, was educated and is said to have been poisoned by Queen Eleanor. Slabs from the stone coffins of nuns were dug up when the lock was built and used to make a pavement across the fields to the village of Wytham (pronounced White-ham). West of the village, the 600-acre Great Wood extends to the river.

Iffley

A towpath along the west bank of the Isis leads to Iffley, now a suburb of the city, where a lock is the starting point of the Eights races to Folly Bridge. The Norman Church of St Mary is noted for its carvings and rich decorations, and its splendid west front.

OXFORD AT WORK *St Cross Building in Manor Road was opened in 1964 to house the law library, the English faculty library and the Gulbenkian lecture theatre*

Leafy banks of the Thames

Angling There is coarse fishing on the Thames at Pangbourne and Whitchurch (free fishing 1½ miles above and below Whitchurch Bridge), Goring, Moulsford, South Stoke, Appleford, Culham and Abingdon. There are trout in the River Pang.

Boating Boats can be hired at Abingdon, Wallingford, Goring and Pangbourne. There is canoeing on the Thame at Dorchester and on the Thames at Sutton Courtenay.

Events The election of the Mayor of Ock is held on the nearest Sat. to June 20, when there is also morris dancing.

Places to see *Abbey Buildings*, Abingdon; remains of a Benedictine abbey containing an Elizabethan-type theatre in which performances are given during the summer: afternoons, except Mon. Oct. to Mar. *Abingdon Town Museum*: afternoons. *Basildon Park* (NT), between Goring and Pangbourne: Easter to Oct., Wed. to Sun. afternoons. *Guildhall*, Abingdon: paintings and 16th to 20th-century silver plate: by appointment. *Long Alley Almshouses*, Abingdon; 13th-century almshouses still in use; open at any reasonable hour. *Mapledurham House*: Easter Sun. to early Oct., Sat., Sun. and Bank Hol. afternoons. *Milton Manor*, near Abingdon: Easter to early Oct., Sat., Sun. and Bank Hol. afternoons. *Pendon Museum*, Long Wittenham; railway exhibits and models of the countryside of 1930's: Sat. and Sun. afternoons. *Priory Cottages* (NT), Steventon: South Cottage only, Wed. afternoons. *Wellplace Bird Farm*, Ipsden: Sat. and Sun.; also Mon. to Fri. afternoons, Easter to Oct.

Information centre Thames and Chilterns Tourist Board, 8 The Market Place, PO Box 10, Abingdon. Tel. Abingdon 22711.

MAYOR FOR A DAY *Residents of Ock Street, Abingdon, elect their own mayor in a traditional ceremony. He holds office for only one day a year, in June*

The River Thames below Oxford has a gentle and very English beauty. From Abingdon to Wallingford there are long reaches mirroring green banks and trees, where the stillness is broken only by the occasional canoe or river launch.

Flowing at first through a flat countryside, the river offers glimpses of the high Berkshire Downs and, in the distance, the beech-clad Chiltern Hills. Below Wallingford the countryside is more varied. Hills and woods extend to the water's edge. There are attractive inns with their own moorings; picturesque locks; and the lawns, flowers and boat-houses of immaculate riverside houses. At last the river streams through the gentle gorge of Goring Gap, between the Berkshire Downs and the Chilterns, towards Pangbourne.

This is a historic waterway, particularly in its upper reaches. Great abbeys and monasteries lent it magnificence in the past, and in the Middle Ages its waters were so rich in salmon that even the very poor ate them as their staple diet. Earlier still, Celtic Britons built their camp on the twin hills of Sinodun (*dun* is Celtic for fort), south of Dorchester. At Dorchester the Romans built one of their most important camps; and ancient tracks such as the Icknield Way and the Ridge Way lead down to fords or bridges across the slow-flowing river.

THE PEACEFUL THAMES *There are fine views of Day's Lock and Weir at Little Wittenham bridge from the Wittenham Clumps*

Abingdon

A Thames-side town best approached from the river. A Benedictine abbey was built here in the 10th century and, though much of the abbey has disappeared since the Reformation, there are some interesting remains by the river. The granary contains a reconstruction of an Elizabethan theatre, and performances of Handel's operas are often given there during the summer. The Guildhall contains two Gainsborough paintings, and the County Hall, built when Abingdon was Berkshire's county town, is one of the most magnificent in the country. Many authorities believe that the building, completed in 1682, took its style from designs by Sir Christopher Wren.

At Steventon, 4 miles south, a former priory has been converted into two houses. One has the original Great Hall.

Dorchester

A beautiful town on the River Thame (pronounced Tame) near its junction with the Thames. The town's history goes back to before the Bronze Age, and it was an important Roman settlement. The old High Street, although now on the main road from Henley to Oxford, is winding and lovely, lined with half-timbered or brick houses.

The late-Norman abbey, 200 ft long and containing 13th-century glass, is one of the most splendid buildings in the Thames Valley. The prevailing style of the building is Decorated, and among its treasures are a 12th-century lead font, and a window and stonework representing the Tree of Jesse. Medieval miracle plays are sometimes acted here.

A path near the abbey leads through a Victorian lych-gate towards the river. Across the river are the Sinodun Hills, a fine viewpoint, crowned by a hill fort dating back to *c.* 1500 BC.

Ewelme

A small village where Henry VIII spent his honeymoon with Catherine Howard at the local manor house, which was then a palace. It was also the home of Alice, Duchess of Suffolk. Her 15th-century tomb in the local church is a fine example of medieval craftsmanship and is perfectly preserved. It escaped destruction by Cromwell's men because of the intervention of the local lord of the manor. The tomb has an effigy of the Duchess in court dress, with her head supported by four angels, while below, seen through tracery, is another effigy of the Duchess wrapped in a shroud. The church also has an interesting collection of brasses. Jerome K. Jerome, author of *Three Men in a Boat*, is buried in the churchyard.

Ancient almshouses built around a cobbled courtyard are still in use today, and the village school is one of the oldest in the country, in use since 1437. A clear stream packed with watercress beds runs beside the main street.

Goring

Attractively situated with the Chilterns at its back and the downs opposite, Goring was important in prehistoric times as the ford where the ancient Ridge Way and Icknield Way joined. The best way to see Goring is to approach it in a boat from up-river. The river widens, and separate channels diverge to Cleeve Mill on the left and to the picturesque Swan Hotel at Streatley, which lies on the right bank. The town has good hotels and restaurants, and boats can be hired and daily fishing tickets bought.

Long Wittenham

An attractive village and a good starting point for an exhilarating walk to the Sinodun Hills and the adjoining wooded hill known as the Wittenham Clumps. From Little Wittenham, a mile east, there is a half-mile footpath through Little Wittenham Wood to the summit. From here can be seen the Vale of the White Horse to the west and, to the east, the great undulating plains backed by the scarp of the Chilterns.

Mapledurham

A secluded hamlet right on the Thames and almost hidden among rolling hills and great woods. A few early 17th-century almshouses of rose-red brick cluster near the great 16th-century mansion, built by Sir Michael Blount, who entertained Elizabeth I here. Near

ABINGDON *An artificial ruin, which was built in the 19th century, incorporates stones from the destroyed abbey church*

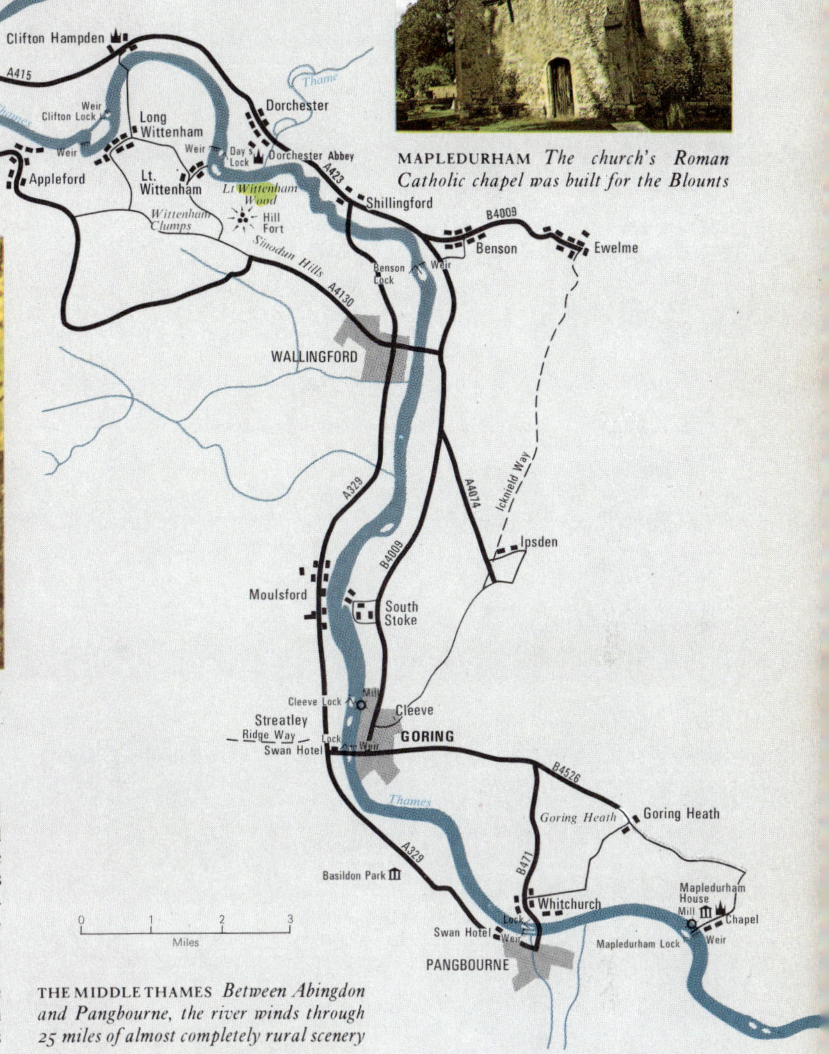

THE MIDDLE THAMES *Between Abingdon and Pangbourne, the river winds through 25 miles of almost completely rural scenery*

MAPLEDURHAM *The church's Roman Catholic chapel was built for the Blounts*

ST HELEN'S CHURCH *The 14th-century church spire dominates Abingdon*

WALLINGFORD *The part-13th-century bridge replaced a ford across the Thames*

by are an ancient water-mill and weir. The 14th-century church contains a Blount family chapel, and the Vicar is appointed by Eton College. Mapledurham was the country home of Soames Forsyte, the principal character in John Galsworthy's *Forsyte Saga*.

Pangbourne

Kenneth Grahame, who wrote *The Wind in the Willows*, lived and died here. Though now becoming a London commuters' town, it has considerable Edwardian elegance and it is a good centre for walks and drives through typical hilly, wooded Thames-side scenery. By the Swan Hotel, where the heroes of Jerome K. Jerome's *Three Men in a Boat* stayed, the water cascades over the weir. The town, which has some fine 17th and 18th-century buildings, is built on a little trout stream, the Pang, from which it takes its name.

Streatley

An unspoilt town on the west bank of the Thames opposite Goring. There are Georgian houses and a 19th-century malt-house, used as a village hall. Streatley Hill looms close behind the town. The route to the summit leads past St John's Church, turns left along the main road, then after 100 yds follows a public footpath to the top of the hill. It is a ten-minute climb, and from the summit looking upstream there is one of the best views of the Thames Valley.

Sutton Courtenay

One of the most elegant villages on the Thames. A long row of cottages and houses leads to a great open green. The church, Norman and Early English, has a 16th-century brick porch, and a one-handed clock on its tower. In the churchyard is the grave of the 1st Earl of Oxford and Asquith who, as Henry Asquith, was Britain's last Prime Minister of a Liberal Government, from 1908 to 1916. The manor house dates from the 15th century.

Wallingford

Romans, Saxons, Danes and Normans realised the importance of this Thames crossing point, the name being Saxon for 'ford of Wealh's people'. The town's charter dates from 1155 and was granted by Henry II, whose possession of the Throne was confirmed by the Treaty of Wallingford. The castle, a Royalist stronghold in the Civil War, finally surrendered to the Parliamentary army in July 1646, and was one of the last Royalist castles to fall. It was kept in use as a prison until 1652, when it was demolished.

Wallingford today is a market town and riverside resort, with swimming and paddling pools which in no way detract from the beauties of the towpath walks. There are many fine Georgian houses, and the 17th-century town hall, which stands on stone pillars, contains several portraits by Gainsborough.

ROWING *The Thames at Pangbourne is still as tranquil as when E. H. Shepard illustrated* The Wind in the Willows

CRUISING *Trees slope to the tow-path on a wide reach of the Thames below Goring Gap, popular for holiday cruising*

Downstream to Windsor Castle

Angling Good coarse fishing along the Thames from Sonning to Windsor and in Windsor Great Park ponds.

Boating Boats for hire at Henley, Hurley, Wargrave and Cookham.

Events The Royal Horse Show takes place at Windsor during May. There is polo in Windsor Great Park most weekends in summer. Windsor Festival of Music is held early in Oct. The Royal Ascot race meeting is in June and the Henley Royal Regatta is held June/July.

Places to see *Cliveden* (NT): Apr. to Oct., Sat. and Sun. afternoons; gardens only, Mar. to Nov., daily, except Mon. and Tues., and Bank Hol. Mon. *Eton College*: daily, except mornings during term time. *Greys Court* (NT), 3 miles west of Henley: Apr. to Sept., Mon., Wed., Fri. afternoons; grounds, weekday afternoons. *Henry Reitlinger Bequest*, Oldfield, Riverside, Maidenhead; pottery, paintings: Apr. to Sept., Tues. and Thur. and 1st Sun. of each month. *Household Cavalry Museum*, Windsor; Mon. to Fri., but closed Good Friday; also Sun., Apr. to Sept. *Savill Garden*, Windsor: Mar. to Oct., daily. *Stanley Spencer Gallery*, King's Hall, Cookham: Easter to Oct., daily; Nov. to Easter, weekends. *Stonor Park*, near Henley: Easter to Sept., Wed., Thur., Sun., Bank Hol. afternoons. *Windsor Castle*: precincts open daily. State Apartments weekdays unless Queen in residence, usually for two months starting a fortnight before Easter, for three weeks in mid-June, and for two weeks at Christmas and New Year. Queen Mary's Dolls' House, the Old Master Drawings and the Albert Memorial Chapel remain open when Her Majesty is in residence. St George's Chapel is open when no service is in progress, the Round Tower Tues. to Sat. *Windsor Guildhall Exhibition*, High Street; charters and documents associated with the Royal Borough, and portraits: afternoons, Easter to Sept. *Windsor Safari Park*, south-west of Windsor: daily.

Information centres Central Library, St. Ives Road, Maidenhead. Tel. Maidenhead 25657. Windsor and Eton Central Station (Easter to Sept. only). Tel. Windsor 52010. Civic Offices, Civic Centre, Reading. Tel. Reading 55911.

QUIET BACKWATER *Motor cruisers find peaceful moorings in the backwaters round Monkey Island, near Bray. An 18th-century lodge on the island has paintings of monkeys on the ceilings*

ROYAL RIVER *The wooded banks between Henley and Windsor line some of the favourite reaches of the river for pleasure cruisers and oarsmen*

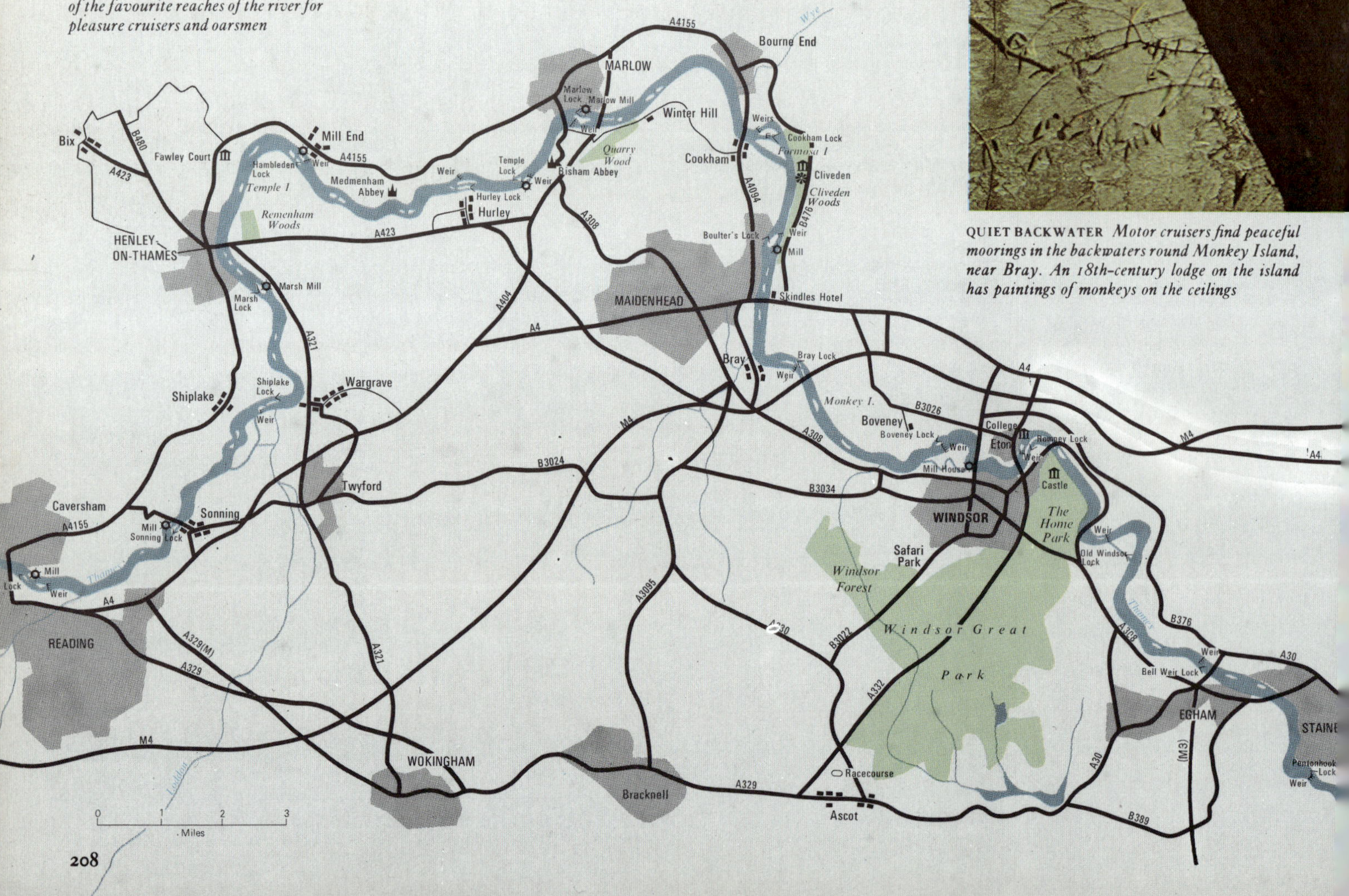

COOKHAM LOCK *Woods border the approach to Cookham Lock, which is separated from Cookham village by a large island. Beyond stretch the beech-clad slopes of Cliveden Reach*

From Sonning downstream past Henley and Maidenhead, and on to Windsor and Eton, the ever-widening Thames looks its finest. Great beechwoods roll down softly contoured hills to the water's edge, and along the river's course are pleasant meadows, islands, weirs, locks, historic houses and ancient abbeys. In summer a medley of rivercraft—launches, punts, skiffs and canoes—moves past houses with trim lawns and private boat-houses, and past inns and restaurants with their own moorings and well-tended lawns, gay with umbrellas.

At Marlow the riverscape is unmistakably rural, with fine views downstream to the foaming weir and upstream to wooded hills which were still remote country when Shelley lived and wrote there. Among the hills to be climbed within half a mile of Marlow is Winter Hill, from whose summit there are glorious views. Past Bourne End, a yachtsman's mecca where cattle graze on riverside pastures, lies Cookham, with its lock set among woods and attractive backwaters. Further downstream are the magnificent beechwoods overhanging Cliveden Reach, one of the most beautiful stretches of the Thames. The woods, ablaze with colour in the autumn, descend to the water's edge on the east bank, while facing them on the west bank are level meadows. Between the two, the river steers a straight and narrow course to Boulter's Lock, a beauty spot of cultivated prettiness which retains much of the 19th-century atmosphere described in Jerome K. Jerome's *Three Men in a Boat.* Through Maidenhead the river flows beneath two of the finest bridges on the Thames, and beyond it the rural scene returns briefly, around the red-brick and timbered cottages of Bray, the last real 'village' on the river.

Among the willows that fringe the bank downstream to Boveney are the immaculate velvet lawns of a score of private riverside houses built by the earliest 'commuters', in Edwardian times. Near Windsor the river is congested with launches, skiffs, motor cruisers, punts and steamers. Yet there is stateliness here, too. The ramparts of Windsor Castle, England's largest castle and an official residence of the Queen, dominate the busy town at their feet. On the north bank stands the historic town of Eton, with its famous school, founded in 1440, which Gladstone described as the 'queen of public schools'.

Ascot
A town of wide streets near the famous racecourse, and a good centre for drives and walks in nearby Windsor Great Park. The Royal Ascot race meeting in June was started by Queen Anne in 1711 but, like much of the town, all the racecourse buildings are modern.

Bourne End
A riverside commuting town with a fine sailing reach. Just below the town, the Wye stream enters the Thames, and attractive villas and gardens line the north bank downstream to Cookham.

Bray
The village is celebrated for its 16th-century turncoat vicar, Simon Aleyn, who lived through four reigns and adjusted his religious attitude to suit each one. It is hidden from the river, near which are old houses and an inn.

Monkey Island, half a mile downstream, has an hotel, set in extensive gardens, incorporating parts of an 18th-century fishing lodge built for the

3rd Duke of Marlborough. On its ceilings are paintings by Clèrmont of monkeys dressed in costume.

Cookham

A village of red-brick cottages facing a green. The painter Stanley Spencer (1891–1959) lived at Cookham; his painting of *The Last Supper* hangs in the church, which is partly 12th century, and other works by Spencer are displayed in King's Hall. Below Cookham Bridge are attractive backwaters with boat-houses, one of which is the office of the Keeper of the Royal Swans. Formosa Island is the largest island on the river, 50 acres of green woodlands concealing the remains of an 18th-century house.

One of the finest stretches of the Thames starts at Cookham Lock and runs downstream past Cliveden. Cliveden House was built by Barry in 1851. Once owned by the Astors, it was a meeting-place of politicians and international celebrities, the so-called 'Cliveden Set', before the Second World War.

Henley-on-Thames

The first river regatta in the world was held at Henley in 1839. The regatta is now held every July. Henley has a handsome 18th-century bridge with five arches, a square-towered Perpendicular church and timbered houses, including the 14th-century Chantry House. Its main street is wide and elegantly Georgian, and there is a fine view from the towpath downstream to Temple Island. Remenham Woods rise on the right bank, and a further mile round the curve of the river at Mill End are the picturesque Hambleden Lock and Mill. On the left bank is 17th-century Fawley Court, now the Divine Mercy College. At Grey's Court, just west of Henley, parts of the 14th-century fortifications to the house remain, and there is a donkey wheel, used in Tudor times for raising water.

SWAN-UPPING *Cookham Bridge is the background to Stanley Spencer's painting, now in the Tate Gallery, of the annual counting of Thames swans*

COOKHAM BRIDGE *The scene at the bridge has hardly changed since Stanley Spencer painted his picture in 1918. Spencer spent much of his life in Cookham, and used it as the setting for many of his paintings*

Hurley

The tree-lined banks of the river by the lock, weir and mill are popular with campers and picnickers. The village is about half a mile from the river. Bisham Abbey, 1½ miles downstream, has been rebuilt as a physical training school. Medmenham Abbey, a mile up the river, was built on the site of a Norman abbey by Sir Francis Dashwood in the 18th century. It is said to have been used by his Hell Fire Club for black-magic rites.

Maidenhead

'Maydenhythe', or the medieval 'maidens' landing place', is a large 'dormitory' suburb of London, but is a good centre for exploring the nearby countryside. The balustraded road bridge and Brunel's railway bridge, with its long brick-work spans and resounding echoes, are among the finest bridges on the river. Boulter's Lock, just upstream, has been a famous riverside spot since Edwardian days. Ray Mill Island is a public garden, and the mill is now a hotel.

Marlow

A busy riverside town with a wide and attractive main street and a fringe of modern houses. The town's outstanding feature is its elegant suspension bridge, completed in 1836 and renovated in 1966 after plans to replace it were defeated. It offers the motorist a fleeting glimpse of delightful riverside sights, particularly the lawns of The Compleat Angler Hotel, where the willow tree is said to have been planted by the Duke of Wellington. The hotel is named after the book on the delights of fishing written by Izaak Walton.

The riverside is dominated by the spire of All Saints Church. High Street and West Street still have many attractive Georgian houses, and in West Street is the house where Shelley wrote *The Revolt of Islam* and his wife Mary wrote *Frankenstein*. The weir, lock and lock-house stand picturesquely against the background of Quarry Wood. There are good walks along the riverside below Marlow Lock and in Quarry Wood. These beechwoods cover 25,000 acres; at their northern end Winter Hill, owned by the National Trust, is a fine viewpoint.

Reading

This industrial town 15 miles east of Newbury is noted for its university as well as its industry. Henry I lies buried here in the remains of a Norman abbey founded in 1121. Oscar Wilde wrote his famous 'Ballad of Reading Gaol' and 'De Profundis' during his imprisonment in the town.

Sonning

A village with three excellent inns, at a point where the river divides round several little islands. A mile downstream, St Patrick's Stream parts from the river, taking in the Loddon tributary before rejoining the Thames just beyond Shiplake. Below the confluence lies Wargrave, a good stopping place for motorists, walkers or river-users.

LEISURELY CRUISING *A steamer passes through Boulter's Lock, near Maidenhead, one of the busiest on the Thames*

STRENUOUS ROWING *The Thames attracts oarsmen from all over Britain, and frequent regattas enliven the river at summer weekends. Here two crews practise for the annual regatta held at Maidenhead on the Saturday before the late Summer Bank Holiday*

WINDSOR'S ROYAL SKYLINE *Windsor Castle, a favourite home of the Royal Family, is the largest castle in England, covering 13 acres. The site was chosen by William the Conqueror, but the oldest parts of the existing castle, including the Round Tower, date from the 12th century. Much of the castle visible from the river was built in the reign of George IV*

FISH ON GLASS *Pictures of the fish that Izaak Walton described are painted on the windows of The Compleat Angler Hotel*

ANGLING AT MARLOW *A fisherman waits for a catch on the Thames at Marlow. The river here was a favourite haunt of the 17th-century writer Izaak Walton. His famous book* The Compleat Angler, *first published in 1653, took him 40 years to compile*

WHITE WATERS *Canoeing is increasingly popular on the Thames, and canoeists vie with one another to brave the turbulent waters of its many weirs. The weir at Hambleden is one popular canoeists' venue. The white-boarded mill behind it, one of the most picturesque on the river, was originally built in the 14th century*

Windsor

A largely Victorian town which owes everything to its great royal castle. Near the hill on which it is built were once sited a fortress used by the ancient Britons and by Julius Caesar, and a palace used by Saxon kings. The castle, founded by William the Conqueror, first became a royal residence in the reign of Henry I, and incorporates additions dating from that time to the reign of Queen Victoria. Much of the castle visible from the river was built after 1824 by Wyatville. The Lower Ward contains St George's Chapel, the finest example of Perpendicular architecture in England. It owes much to Edward IV and Henry VIII, and is now the burial place of royalty. The Albert Memorial Chapel, built originally by Henry VIII, was converted into a shrine to the Prince Consort by Queen Victoria.

The Middle Ward of the castle contains the famous Round Tower, built in the reign of Henry II. The Upper Ward contains the State Apartments, dating from Edward III's time, as well as the Sovereign's private apartments. The castle is surrounded by good walking country in the 4800-acre Great Park, which also has a starling roost and a heronry. Windsor Guildhall was completed by Wren in 1689, after the death of the original architect. Its council chambers incorporate columns which do not reach the ceiling, a joke by the architect in response to the councillors' insistence on decorative columns.

Across the Thames is Eton, with its quaint old High Street. At the far end lies Eton College, founded in 1440 by Henry VI, and some buildings date from that time.

Stoke Poges, 4 miles north, is famous as the setting of the 'Elegy Written in a Country Churchyard' by Thomas Gray, who is buried in the churchyard.

Wokingham

A busy rural market town, now popular with London commuters. The by-ways have some Georgian houses and half-timbered cottages. The parish church still rings a curfew at 8 p.m. in winter.

Beechwoods of the Chilterns

Angling Coarse fishing on the Colne at Denham, 6 miles east of Beaconsfield; trout can be caught on the Chess at Chesham and Chorleywood.

Events Ceremony of Weighing the Mayors takes place in Apr. or May at High Wycombe; the outgoing and incoming mayors are weighed and the weights publicly proclaimed.

Places to see *Bekonscot Gardens*, Beaconsfield: daily; model trains run only from Easter to Oct. *Dorneywood Garden* (NT), Burnham Beeches: Aug. and Sept., Sat. afternoon by appointment. *Hughenden Manor* (NT), near High Wycombe: Apr. to Oct., afternoons except Mon. and Tues.; also Bank Hol. Mon. afternoon; Mar. and Nov., Sat. and Sun. afternoons. *Milton's Cottage*, Chalfont St Giles: Feb. to Nov., weekdays, except Tues., and Sun. afternoon. *Princes Risborough Manor House* (NT): May to Sept., Wed. afternoons. *West Wycombe Caves*, excavated in 1748 to provide chalk for road making: afternoons, early Mar. to late Sept.; also Sun. and Bank Hol. mornings late May to early Sept.; late Sept. to mid-Feb., Sat. and Sun. afternoons. *West Wycombe Park* (NT): afternoons only; June, Mon. to Fri.; July and Aug., Sun. to Fri. *Wycombe Chair and Local Industry Museum*, High Wycombe: weekdays, except Wed.

Information centres County Hall, Walton Street, Aylesbury. Tel. Aylesbury 5000. District Council Offices, Queen Victoria Road, High Wycombe. Tel. High Wycombe 26100.

MILTON'S COTTAGE *Milton escaped from the Plague of London in 1665 and lived at Chalfont St Giles, where a chance remark by a Quaker friend led to the writing of* Paradise Regained

Running across the southern half of Buckinghamshire is the low chalk ridge of the Chiltern Hills. Much of the ridge is covered with beechwoods —dense, green-gladed places, full of paths, mossy banks, running streams and blinks of sunlight. The northern escarpment of the hills falls suddenly from wooded heights into river valleys. In springtime it is a land of bluebells and cherry blossom, and in early summer of nightingales; and always there is the smell of beech leaves and cherry-wood.

Much of Buckinghamshire has become a commuting area for London, but many villages and the centres of some of the towns have kept their traditional Chiltern character, with brick-and-flint houses leading up wide streets to a Norman church. Industry has come to Great Missenden, Princes Risborough and High Wycombe; but arable and dairy farming at the foot of the hills and sheep rearing on the higher slopes go on much as they have done since Saxon times when yeoman farmers settled there.

The prehistoric track of Icknield Way can be traced across the region from Watlington in the south-west, through Chinnor and Bledlow to Great Kimble, and the pre-Roman Grim's Ditch with its earthwork ramparts runs north from Lacey Green to Great Hampden. This is walking country, with public footpaths leading across hills and woods, past prehistoric mounds and barrows and by cypress-guarded abbeys.

The region is rich in history. At Penn lived William Penn, founder of Pennsylvania, and at tiny Jordans, near Beaconsfield, there are beams that were part of the *Mayflower*, the Pilgrim Fathers' ship. At Great Kimble, the democrat John Hampden protested against Ship Money, a tax imposed by Charles I without the authority of Parliament. His refusal to pay the £1 tax caused his arrest and trial, and widened the breach between King and Parliament which led ultimately to the Civil War. West Wycombe has connections with the more raffish side of the 18th century, as it was the headquarters of the notorious Hell Fire Club, a group of rakes and gamblers who are said to have indulged in witchcraft orgies. Edmund Burke, the 18th-century political philosopher, is buried at Beaconsfield. Disraeli had a house at Hughenden, and he is buried in Hughenden churchyard.

Amersham

The old town has been well preserved; the Swan Inn surprises tourists by claiming that it was *rebuilt* in 1643. The High Street is broad and noble with Georgian houses, old gabled and timbered inns, and cobbled courtyards leading to thatched cottages. In the centre of the High Street is the 17th-century market hall, built on open arches. Near the market hall is an old cottage decorated with murals, including portraits of Julius Caesar and Hector of Troy, painted on the living-room walls about two centuries ago. There are some attractive old inns including The Crown, the gabled Elephant and Castle, and Mill Stream House, where the stream flows through the inn.

A monument on a nearby hillside commemorates many Lollards who were burnt at the stake in the 15th and 16th centuries. They were extremist followers of John Wyclif, the reformer who attacked the dogmas of the Church and the power of priests.

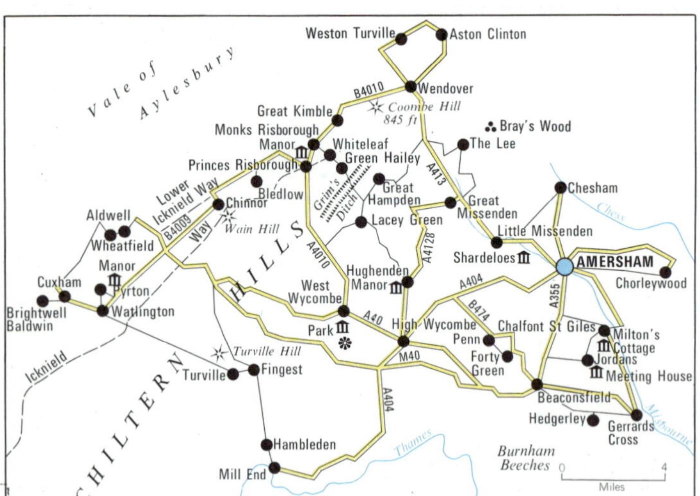

Beaconsfield

An elegant town with old inns, timbered cottages and many creeper-clad 17th-century houses. The surrounding countryside was at one time thickly wooded, and a haunt of highwaymen and footpads. It is claimed that sword cuts on the staircase of the George Inn were made by the highwayman Claude Duval while fighting off Bow Street Runners. Penn's Quaker Meeting House and the Mayflower Barn are at Jordans, a mile east of Beaconsfield, and a mile further on is Milton's cottage at Chalfont St Giles, where he wrote *Paradise Regained,* the sequel to *Paradise Lost.*

HELL FIRE 'CLUB HOUSE'

Ten members of the Hell Fire Club could meet in this ball, on the tower of a West Wycombe church

Bledlow
Beside the 13th-century church runs the Lyde stream, with watercress beds, and the village also has herringbone-brick cottages and a 17th-century inn, The Red Lion. The view from Bledlow Ridge is a typical Chiltern panorama of long rises, lush fields and woods of beech, cherry, lime and hornbeam. On Wain Hill is a cross cut into the turf, possibly in the 17th century.

Great Hampden
Hampden House, the 17th-century home of John Hampden, is now a school. The church, near by, dates mainly from the 13th century. Hampden, who, after his protest over Ship Money, fought for the Parliamentary Army and died after the Battle of Chalgrove, is buried in the churchyard. Grim's Ditch runs across the grounds of Hampden House, while the ancient Icknield Way passes through Great Kimble. In Kimble church is a Norman font and a copy of the parish report recording that Hampden and others refused to pay Ship Money. A road with one of the loveliest views in Buckinghamshire runs south-east along the crest of the hill from Monks Risborough past Green Hailey.

Hambleden
A good starting-point for exploring some of the most glorious valleys in the Chilterns. A narrow road from the village leads to Fingest, notable for its fine Norman church tower, and Turville, where a black-capped windmill stands on a high ridge. The 14th-century church at Hambleden has been described as a miniature cathedral. In front of it is the village square, with cottages and an inn, and a village pump beside a great chestnut tree. Down by the Thames at Mill End is a white-boarded mill, dating from 1338.

High Wycombe
A largely industrial town with only a few remaining old buildings such as the 18th-century town hall, the 17th-century little market house and the 13th-century church. To the north of the town is Hughenden Manor, Disraeli's old home which, with 169 acres, is now National Trust property.

West Wycombe Park, 3 miles west, the magnificent home of the Dashwood family, is a Palladian mansion set in grounds landscaped by Humphrey Repton. On a hilltop is an old church with an immense gilded ball on the top of the tower. The church was rebuilt in the 18th century by Sir Francis Dashwood, one of the leaders of the Hell Fire Club, otherwise known as the Medmenham Monks, taking this name from the ruined abbey at Medmenham, where they held many of their rites.

The Missendens
Great Missenden claims to be the heart of the Chilterns, but it has become industrialised and has lost much of its former charm. Little Missenden, however, is much quieter and the banks of the River Misbourne are coloured in season by marsh marigolds or orange monkey flowers. Two miles to the north of Great Missenden is The Lee, a village with a 700-year-old church and a green on which are two great boulders said to be relics of the Ice Age. A mile away to the north-east in Bray's Wood are the remains of British and Roman settlements. On the road to Lacey Green is the Pink and Lily Inn, a favourite of the poet Rupert Brooke.

Princes Risborough
Many timbered and thatched cottages remain in the centre of this rapidly expanding town. The brick market house, with its arcades, is crowned with a wooden cupola, and the 17th-century manor house is now owned by the National Trust. There is an easy walk along Icknield Way to Monks Risborough. On the side of the hills above are the tumbled thatched cottages of the hamlet of Whiteleaf and the 80-ft Whiteleaf Cross, which is believed to have been cut in the turf in the 17th century.

Just over a mile to the north-east is Chequers, the official country retreat of the Prime Minister, but it is not open to the public. Lord Lee of Fareham in 1917 created a trust enabling the 16th-century mansion to be used by British Prime Ministers.

Pyrton
A secluded village with some thatched and Georgian houses and a fine Elizabethan manor house. It is the centre of some interesting walks to villages such as Cuxham, which has a stream running beside the main street, and Brightwell Baldwin to the west. Wheatfield, 2 miles to the north, is little more than a Georgian church and a farm set next to Wheatfield Park in a lovely valley.

Wendover
A quaint old town with timbered fronts, but now on a busy road. The room in the half-timbered Red Lion where Cromwell slept in 1642 is kept much as it was in his time. A drive 1½ miles west leads to Coombe Hill, part of the Chiltern escarpment. From the summit, on which there is a monument to the men of the county who died in the South African War, there are long views over the Vale of Aylesbury to the north.

BURNHAM BEECHES *The 600-acre forest of Burnham Beeches is part of a vast forest that extended over the Chiltern Hills in prehistoric times. There are many footpaths through the huge beech trees, which look their best in spring and autumn*

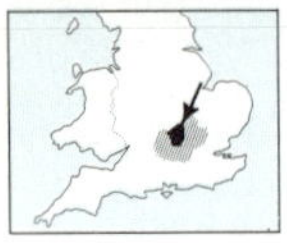

The Vale of Aylesbury

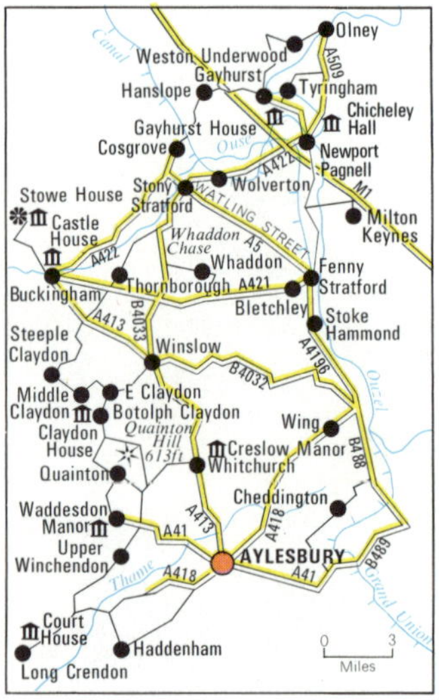

Angling Coarse fishing on the canal at Cheddington, Stoke Hammond and Fenny Stratford.

Boating Boats for cruising on the Grand Union Canal can be hired at Bletchley, Claydon, Stony Stratford, Wolverton and Cosgrove.

Customs Firing the Poppers, 18th-century ceremony at St Martin's Church, Fenny Stratford, Nov. 11; metal pots charged with powder are touched with a red-hot rod.

Places to see *Ascott* (NT), Wing: Apr. to Sept., Wed., Sat. and Bank Hol. Mon. afternoons; also Sun. afternoon July and Aug. *Chicheley Hall*, near Newport Pagnell: Easter to Sept., weekend and Bank Hol. afternoons; also Wed. and Thur. afternoons from end of May. *Claydon House* (NT): Apr. to Oct., afternoons except Mon. and Fri. *County Museum*, Aylesbury: weekdays. *Cowper and Newton Museum*, Olney: Tues. to Sat. *Dorton House*, Aylesbury, Jacobean mansion: May to July and Sept., Sat. and Sun. afternoons. *Flamingo Gardens*, The Manor, Weston Underwood: Easter to Sept., Wed., Thur., Sat., Sun. afternoons. *Hartwell House*, Aylesbury, Jacobean house: Wed. afternoon, early May to late July. *Waddesdon Manor* (NT): late Mar. to Oct., afternoons except Mon. and Tues.; Bank Hol. all day. *Wotton House*, near Aylesbury, built 1704: Wed. afternoon, July to Sept.

Information centres County Hall, Walton Street, Aylesbury. Tel. Aylesbury 5000. Milton Keynes Development Corporation, Wavendon Tower, Wavendon. Tel. Milton Keynes 74000.

The Chilterns divide Buckinghamshire suddenly and dramatically. To the south are chalk uplands clothed in scrub, bracken and beech. But to the north of the range lies the Vale of Aylesbury with a well-watered clay soil ideal for dairy farming and stock rearing.

The vale is one of England's richest agricultural regions; Creslow Great Field, at 300 acres, is the largest single pasture in Britain, and it has fattened beef for royal households since Tudor times.

North of the Vale of Aylesbury is the valley of the River Ouse, a quiet countryside described by the 18th-century poet William Cowper, who lived there and wrote in 'The Task' these lines about the Ouse:

'Slow-winding through the level plain
Of spacious meads, with cattle sprinkled o'er.'

The two big towns in the region, Aylesbury and Buckingham, have managed to retain a market-town atmosphere despite the tide of industry advancing from the north-east. A new city being built, Milton Keynes, will eventually incorporate the existing towns of Bletchley, Wolverton and Stony Stratford and have a population of 250,000.

There are many areas of undisturbed distinction. Round the Claydons, south of Buckingham, the land is especially quiet and lovely, and throughout the region the traveller comes suddenly on villages with ancient churches, little bridges and thatched cottages.

TICKFORD BRIDGE *This bridge at Newport Pagnell, built of cast ir*

WALLS MADE OF 'WICHERT' IN HADDENHAM

The village of Haddenham is famous for its wichert—a local building material. It is dug from a bed of chalky marl just below the surface near the village, then soaked in water, mixed with straw and used to form thick walls. Old wichert walls (top picture) are imitated by modern development (lower picture) using the same material in the same style

Aylesbury

The county town presents a daunting approach of roundabouts, ring roads and skyscrapers, but in the centre it is full of character and charm, with narrow Tudor alleyways, good 17th-century houses, especially in Church Street, and quiet pathways around the great churchyard of St Mary's. The church dates mainly from the 13th century, but was restored in 1848. A walk up Church Street following the curve round Parson's Fee leads to more 17th-century relics – Hickman's Almshouses and Prebendal House. The latter, now offices, was once the home of John Wilkes, the 18th-century politician. The market square is rich in alleys, courtyards and inns. The King's Head was founded in 1386 although the 'head' is Henry VIII's. This inn, which has the unusual distinction of being owned by the National Trust, is entered through a medieval gateway. Its lounge has a leaded window which was already old when the Tudors came to the throne. Two of its panes are now part of a window in Westminster Abbey and three others are in the British Museum. The hall of the inn has 15th-century stained glass. There is even a seat said to have been used by Oliver Cromwell when he stayed there in 1651 on his way to London after his victory at the Battle of Worcester.

Buckingham

A quieter town than Aylesbury, but still a notable centre. Alfred the Great made Buckingham a county town in AD 888, but after it had been partly destroyed by fire in 1725 it lost that distinction to Aylesbury. Lying amid the meadows of the Ouse, its centre is the long market-place with its ancient cattle-pens. The town jail, built in the 18th century in the form of a castle, is now an antique shop. The red-brick town hall is bordered by many fine old cottages and houses. The Chantry Chapel off the market-place has a Norman doorway, and up the hill is Castle House, where Catherine of Aragon stayed as Queen and, approximately a century later, Charles I presided at a war council. In the room where the council was held is a magnificent carved oak mantelpiece, reaching to the ceiling and dated 1619.

The Claydons

Steeple Claydon, Middle Claydon, East Claydon and Botolph Claydon were all manors once belonging to the 2nd Earl of Verney, who built Claydon House at Middle Claydon, one of the finest mansions in Buckinghamshire, in 1752. The house has a Chinese room and a series of rococo state rooms, one of which is a Florence Nightingale museum; her sister married a former owner, Sir Henry Verney, in 1858.

c. 1810, is one of the world's oldest iron road bridges still in daily use. It is unaltered apart from having had steel road plates fitted

Long Crendon
A village near the River Thame with a four-arched bridge, straggling streets and 17th-century cottages, often lost amid roses. Manorial courts were held in The Courthouse, which was given by Henry V to his wife Katharine and is now owned by the National Trust. Two other notable houses are the 15th-century Manor House and 19th-century Long Credon Manor with its arched gatehouse.

WINDMILL ON THE HILL *A view near Brill, with its 17th-century windmill on the skyline. The village, 4 miles north-west of Long Crendon, also has a manor*

Olney
A market town on the River Ouse, famous for its Shrove Tuesday pancake race—a tradition which started in the 15th century—and a good centre for exploring several attractive villages.

Weston Underwood, 1½ miles west of Olney, was the home of the poet William Cowper (1731–1800), whose house is still there. A stone gateway built in 1700 forms the entrance to the village, which has thatched cottages and barns and a great manor. A wildlife farm has many rare species of birds.

Gayhurst, 3½ miles south-west of Olney, is attractively situated in woodlands beside the Ouse; Gayhurst House once belonged briefly to Sir Francis Drake. It was a meeting place for Sir Everard Digby, Robert Catesby and Thomas Winter, who were leaders with Guy Fawkes of the Gunpowder Plot.

AYLESBURY'S DORMOUSE

The edible, or squirrel-tailed, dormouse was introduced into Tring Park in 1902, and is now breeding in the countryside near Aylesbury. These nocturnal animals were a favourite Roman delicacy, but are not eaten today. They live in deciduous woodland, and sometimes make their way into houses to hibernate

Beside Gayhurst House is a church dating from 1728, and a gatehouse which has been turned into an inn. Across the Ouse is the late 18th-century Tyringham Hall.

Quainton
A village with a spacious green, a pond, the remains of a medieval cross, an old windmill, Tudor cottages, gabled almshouses set up in 1687, an old rectory and a 14th-century church. To the north of the village is Quainton Hill (613 ft), a steep grassy rise. According to local stories, this is a region haunted by goblins and fairies, and at midnight horses with headless riders are supposed to gallop around. Along a track now called Gipsy Lane, which was an old Roman road, a stone dated 1641 marks the grave of a King of the Gipsies.

Stowe Park
More than 200 acres of parkland, laid out in the 18th century by Capability Brown and William Kent. The gardens are dotted with Classical temples and pavilions, and there is a long artificial lake. A great Corinthian arch frames Stowe House, once the home of the Dukes of Buckingham and Chandos and now a public school.

Waddesdon
A 19th-century village and manor house built by Baron Ferdinand de Rothschild. Set amid 160 acres of National Trust land, Waddesdon Manor stands on a hill 600 ft high and looks like a French château. The long, steep hill through Upper Winchendon, 2 miles south, ends in an escarpment overlooking the valley of the River Thame.

Whaddon
A village on a low plateau, where Roman legions once camped. The nearby Whaddon Chase was later a great hunting ground of kings of England. Now, only the woods called Thickbare, Thrift and Broadway remain of this great forest. The village of Thornborough, 4 miles west, has a green, thatched houses and a medieval bridge.

Whitchurch
A village of picturesque half-timbered cottages. Creslow Manor, now a farmhouse, is one of the oldest houses in the county. It was built *c.* 1300 with a tower, mullioned windows and a vaulted cellar, and its stable has a Norman doorway. Next to the manor is the 300-acre Creslow Great Field, which has been royal grazing land since Tudor times. It has remained intact and constitutes the largest single pasture in Britain.

Winslow
An old town rich in thatched cottages with overhanging gables. Winslow Hall was probably designed by Wren, and the town square has two notable inns: The George, with a balcony of intricate ironwork, and The Bell, said to have been a haunt of Dick Turpin.

Bedfordshire's green pastures

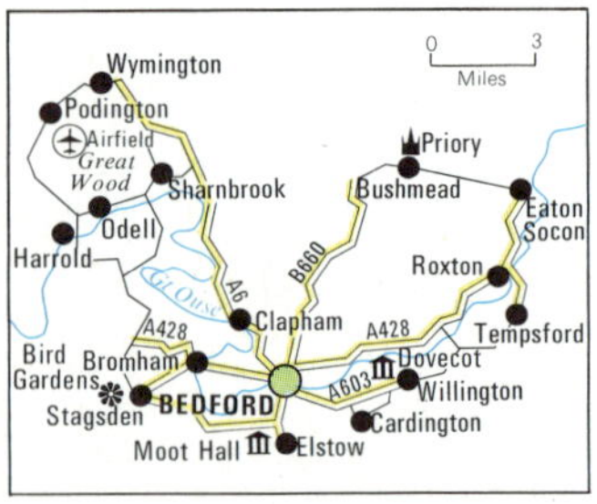

Angling Coarse fishing on the River Great Ouse in and around Bedford.

Boating On the Ouse at Bedford. A regatta is held in July.

Events May Day celebrations (not always on May 1) are held at Elstow, and at Ickwell Green.

Places to see *Bedford Museum*: Tues. to Sat.; also Sun. afternoons. *The Bunyan Collection*, Public Library, Bedford: weekdays. *The Bunyan Meeting Library and Museum*, Bedford: Tues. to Sat. afternoons. *Cecil Higgins Art Gallery*, Bedford: Tues. to Sat.; also Sun. afternoons. *Moot Hall*, Elstow: Tues. to Sat.; also Sun. afternoons. *Odell Castle Gardens* (NGS): occasional Sun. afternoons in summer. *Stagsden Bird Gardens*, 5 miles west of Bedford: daily. *Willington Dovecote and Stables* (NT): Apr. to Sept., by written appointment.

Information centre Town Hall, St Paul's Square, Bedford. Tel. Bedford 67422.

Wherever the eye turns among the rolling pasturelands of north Bedfordshire, it catches the glint of water. Most of this area is in the valley of the River Great Ouse, a broad, wandering river that enters the county from Buckinghamshire near Harrold, runs north-east past Odell, loops southwards to Bedford, then meanders in wide curves past Willington, Roxton and Eaton Socon towards the Huntingdonshire border. Tributaries flow through water-meadows to join it, their routes marked by willows and alders and lined by paths for anglers.

The fields are always under grass. Seventy per cent of the land is made up of clay soils but, in the south of the county, lighter chalky soils mingle with the clay and make good land for wheat.

This peaceful region has absorbed history rather than reacted to it. The farmers and their fields were largely undisturbed by Romans, Danes, Angles and Saxons alike. The Danes sailed up the Great Ouse as far as Willington, where they built a harbour and docks; and the Angles and Saxons, stolid farming people themselves, settled by the side of the original inhabitants.

The villages to the north of Bedford are lonely and unspoilt, linked to the outside world by broad lanes. Many of their houses have thatched roofs, and the churches around which they cluster are built in the Northamptonshire tradition, with stone spires and fine square-hewn masonry in brown ironstone. Outside these churches and on village greens John Bunyan was a frequent preacher.

Bedfordshire's quiet beauty also stretches east—to Roxton with its rush-roofed chapel, Cardington and its beautiful church, and to Bushmead where there are remains of royal stables and an Augustinian priory.

Bedford
The county town, straddling the River Great Ouse, is a pleasing mixture of periods. The Norman castle is now only a mound, but there are four old churches. On the north bank are St Peter's, partly Saxon and partly Norman, and St Paul's, built in the 14th and 15th centuries. On the south bank are St Mary's, which has a Norman tower, and St John's, dating from the 14th century. The town has four public schools, including Bedford Modern School, founded in 1566.

The town is proud of John Bunyan, who lived there from 1655 until his death in 1688—though nearly a third of this time, from 1660 to 1673, was spent in prison. Among many reminders of Bunyan are a statue on St Peter's Green, the John Bunyan Library in Harpur Street, and the Bunyan Meeting House and museum near by.

The Swan Hotel, designed by Henry Holland in 1790, has the staircase from Houghton House near Ampthill. There is a pleasant riverside walk along the tree-lined Great Ouse, overlooking Mill Meadows Island.

Cardington
A village recognised from far away across the flat countryside by its giant airship sheds, in one of which the R101 was built. She set off from Cardington on her maiden flight in 1930, only to crash in France with the loss of all but six of the 54 people aboard.

John Howard (1726–90), the great prison reformer, lived at Cardington, and his house is still there. His friend Samuel Whitbread, the brewer, bought the manor in 1769 and commissioned the village's present bridge from John Smeaton, the engineer of Eddystone Lighthouse. The church has a Wedgwood black basalt font—one of only two in England, the second being at Essendon in Hertfordshire.

Eaton Socon
This large village on the A1 and beside the Great Ouse was an early coaching town, and the White Horse Inn, partly 13th century, was visited by Pepys and Dickens, who mentioned it in *Nicholas Nickleby*. It is now part of the Huntingdonshire town of St Neots. There are miles of riverbank upstream open to walkers. The remains of the 12th-century Bushmead Priory, 4 miles west, are incorporated in a 16th-century building.

Elstow
Though almost a part of Bedford, Elstow retains its village identity. It is famous as the home of John Bunyan. He was born in Harrowden, a mile east of Elstow. His parents moved to Elstow and John, a tinker like his father, lived on there after he married until he moved to Bedford in 1655. He was converted while playing tip-cat, a ball game, when he heard a voice saying: 'Wilt thou leave thy sins and go to heaven, or have thy sins and go to hell?'

A nunnery was founded at Elstow by William the Conqueror's sister, but all that remains are parts of the cloisters and fishponds behind the Church of SS Mary and Helen, which is Norman and later. The 16th-century Moot Hall (market hall) on the green contains a good exhibition illustrating rural life in Bedfordshire in John Bunyan's time. May Day is celebrated by maypole dancing on the green.

Odell
The cottages of this village stand beside a bend of the Great Ouse. There was a castle here, and a new house, with attractive gardens, stands on the site. A gate near the church, which has a massive pinnacled tower, leads to an avenue of old trees. Odell Great Wood, near by, is a good place to spot wild flowers and butterflies. The water-filled gravel pits east of Odell are a good site for bird-watching.

Podington
This small village by a tributary of the River Nene, built in warm-looking Northamptonshire stone, is typical of unspoilt North Bedfordshire. The church dates from Saxon times. A well-signposted road leads east to Podington Airfield and its drag-racing track, used for one of the most spectacular of modern sports. The church at Wymington, 1½ miles north-east, built *c.* 1350, is a good example of the Decorated style of architecture and has some medieval wall-paintings of the Day of Judgment.

PILGRIM'S PROGRESS

John Bunyan was born in 1628 and spent his childhood in the village of Elstow, where the Moot Hall (above) now houses an exhibition of the rural life of Bunyan's time. The print (left), from the 1767 edition of his allegory *The Pilgrim's Progress,* shows Bunyan asleep in Bedford jail, dreaming of Christian's entry into Heaven

UP IN A BALLOON: TWO GENERATIONS OF LIGHTER-THAN-AIR TRAVEL

A balloon rises from the countryside of Bedfordshire, now a popular centre for the fast-growing sport of hot-air ballooning, revived after two centuries of neglect since the first experiments were made in France in the 18th century. A propane-fuelled burner (left) produces the hot air to inflate the nylon envelope. The balloon, with a crew of three, can travel at 500 ft, and stay aloft for two hours

Cardington is now a ballooning centre, but the huge 1000 ft long airship hangars which dominate the landscape recall an earlier age of lighter-than-air travel. From here the R101 airship left in 1930 on its ill-fated maiden voyage, when it crashed in France, on its way to India, with the loss of 48 lives. The RAF still use wartime barrage balloons at Cardington in the training of parachutists

Roxton
An old village near the busy A1, which crosses the Great Ouse here by Tempsford Bridge. The Church of St Mary dates from the 14th century, and has a fine Perpendicular screen, decorated with paintings of the saints. Thatched houses and barns stand beside the river. The Congregational Chapel is an impressive thatched building with two wings, converted from a barn in 1808 by Charles Metcalfe, the lord of the manor.

Stagsden
The Stagsden Bird Gardens cover 8 acres and contain 130 species of birds, including rare breeds of pheasants, brought together by a private collector, F. E. Johnson. There is also a large collection of roses.

Willington
A village which has several interesting antiquities. The Tudor manor house was bought by Sir John Gostwick, Cardinal Wolsey's Master of Horse, in 1529, but has been demolished. The present Manor Farm is on the site and two of the 16th-century buildings remain. They are now owned by the National Trust. The dovecot, a great building like a barn with a stepped façade, contains 1500 nesting boxes and is a reminder of the time when pigeons and their eggs were favoured foods. The second building, King Henry's Stables, is stepped to match the dovecot, though it may have been a dwelling when it was first built.

The church dates from the 16th century and is a good example of the late-Perpendicular style. But the oldest part of Willington is down by the River Great Ouse, where the conquering Danes cut a channel from the Great Ouse and built a harbour before the Conquest. The harbour could hold 25 long ships and had two slips for repairs. The shape of the docks can still be seen.

Woburn and the downs

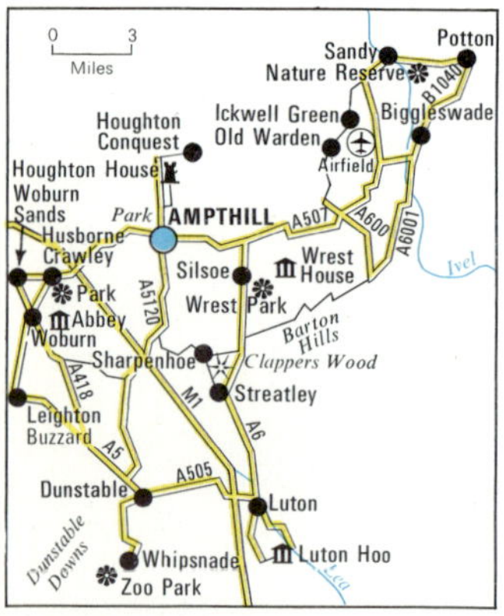

Places to see *Lodge Bird Reserve*, Sandy: Mon. to Fri.; also Sat. and Sun., Easter to Sept. *Luton Hoo*: Easter to Sept., weekdays, except Tues. and Fri.; also Sun. afternoons. *Luton Museum and Art Gallery*: weekdays; also Sun. afternoons, Feb. to Nov. *Shuttleworth Collection*, Old Warden Airfield: daily. *Whipsnade Zoo*: daily. *Woburn Abbey and Wild Animal Kingdom*: daily. *Wrest Park*, Silsoe: gardens only: Apr. to Sept., weekends and Bank Hol. Mon.

Information centres Central Library, Bridge Street, Luton. Tel. Luton 32629. Queensway Hall, Dunstable. Tel. Dunstable 603326.

The southernmost tip of Bedfordshire has the county's most varied scenery. The chalk Chilterns stretch north-east from Buckinghamshire, their steep slopes facing north-west and providing, at Dunstable Downs, an ideal launching ground for gliders. Further north is a lower ridge of sandstone, running from Leighton-Linslade in the south-west to Potton in the north-east. This ridge rises to its greatest height at Woburn and the landscape is one of low hills covered with pine trees, or open heathland.

Between the two ridges lies farming country, intensively cultivated. Fields of Brussels sprouts and potatoes stretch to the lower slopes of the hills, and many small farms offer tomatoes in season for sale to the passer-by. To the north-east, around Sandy and Biggleswade, the river-gravel soils are rich and there is much market gardening. Half the population of Bedfordshire lives in Luton and Bedford, and most of the rest of the county is left to the farmer.

If the happiest counties are those with a tranquil history, Bedfordshire must be counted happy, for it has seen few battles or revolts. Early man had settlements here: there are relics dating back to the Palaeolithic Age. The Belgic tribes settled along the sandstone belt, and the Romans conquered them with little trouble without setting up military posts in the county. Conquering Danes split the county into Danish and English territories, but neither the Norman Conquest nor the Wars of the Roses led to any major confrontations in Bedfordshire. In the Civil War the county was Parliamentarian, but still the area remained remote from serious conflict.

A GLIDER'S VIEW *A view from a glider 300 ft above Dunstable Downs. Whipsnade Zoo is on the far left. Flights can be arranged from the club on the downs, one of the many clubs to be started since the sport came to this country from Germany in the 1930's*

A PARK WHERE WILD DEER FROM ALL OVER THE WORLD ROAM FREE

Woburn Park was founded by the 11th Duke of Bedford in 1900 to save the Père David's deer from extinction. He started the herd with 18 deer from China; it has been increased by other species from all over the world whose survival was in danger. The Duke's family, the Russells, have lived at Woburn since the 17th century, and gave the land on which Whipsnade Zoo was built

MUNTJAC A small deer, which comes from South-East Asia. More than 400 live wild in England. The muntjac barks when alarmed

CHINESE WATER DEER One of two species of deer which do not have antlers; now rare even in China

MANCHURIAN SIKA A hardy deer which is a native of Central Asia. There are 140 in the grounds of Woburn

AXIS DEER Poaching has reduced its numbers in its native India, where it is also known as the chital deer

RUSA DEER A native of Java, and one of the rarest species of deer in Europe. There are 16 at Woburn, and the only others in Europe are in Moscow Zoo

Ampthill
An old town in the sandstone belt, sheltered by hills. Its connections with royalty began after Agincourt, when Sir John Cornwall built a castle here for his bride, Henry IV's sister. Henry VIII sent Catherine of Aragon, first of his six wives, to Ampthill while arranging to divorce her. In the 17th century the castle fell into ruin, but Charles II gave its Great Park to the Ashburnham family, and Lord Ashburnham built the present house in 1694. It is privately owned, but the 300-acre park, with its famous old oaks, is open to the public; an 18th-century cross marks the site of the castle. The avenue of limes on the road towards Woburn is named after the Almeida Avenue in Madrid.

Houghton House, 1 mile north, is the shell of another great house built on sandstone. It was John Bunyan's inspiration for 'House Beautiful' in *The Pilgrim's Progress*. The house was built *c.* 1615 for the Countess of Pembroke.

Ickwell Green
A typical English village, looking very much like an old engraving: low-eaved thatched cottages and a smithy, with noble trees towering above them, stand round the village green, with its striped maypole, where May Day is celebrated by traditional dancing. Thomas Tompion, the 'father of English watch-making', was born near Ickwell in 1639.

Luton
An industrial town set in a valley cut in the Chilterns by the headwaters of the River Lea. Luton still makes straw hats, but Vauxhall Motors started Luton's modern industrial prosperity in 1905, and since then the population has trebled. St Mary's Church is 12th and 14th century, and its tower of black-and-white chequered stonework is made from Bedfordshire clunch, a mixture of flint and clay.

Just south-east of the town, at a point where the Lea widens into an ornamental lake, lies Luton Hoo. Its park was landscaped by Capability Brown. The house, the home of the Wernher family, was built by Robert Adam in 1768 and remodelled after a fire in 1843.

Old Warden
The last Lord Ongley, who died in 1877, rebuilt the village in its present neat mid-Victorian form, as a model village for his tenants. The spacious cottages have thatched roofs arching over the upper windows.

Old Warden Airfield, also called Biggleswade Airfield, 1½ miles north-east, is the home of the Shuttleworth Collection of historic aircraft, flown during the summer, and vintage cars.

Sandy
The River Ivel, flowing north to join the Ouse, has brought down soil that makes the country around Sandy very fertile, and the town is a market-gardening centre. Some of the houses are of sandstone, and so is St Swithin's Church, partly 14th century. A mile to the east of the town, on the Potton road, lies a 104-acre nature reserve administered by the Royal Society for the Protection of Birds. A nature trail winds through wooded hills.

Sharpenhoe
The name of this tiny village comes from the steep spur of the Barton Hills that overlooks it (*ho* is Old English for 'spur of land'). The hill, crowned by Clappers Wood, is part of a 135-acre National Trust property. There is a footpath from the village—a steep climb—and the Streatley road passes near the crest. It is believed that these hills were the inspiration for the 'Delectable Mountains' in John Bunyan's allegory *The Pilgrim's Progress*.

PRIORY REMAINS *The magnificent Norman nave, dating from 1150, is all that survives of Dunstable Priory; the east end has disappeared since the Dissolution*

Silsoe
A pleasant village notable for Wrest Park, the estate of the de Grey family, first Earls, then Dukes, of Kent, from *c.* 1280 until the family died out. The present house, built *c.* 1835, is now an agricultural college. It has fine gardens, notable for their canals.

Whipsnade
A hamlet high on Dunstable Downs to which the world has been coming since 1931, when Whipsnade Zoo opened. The animals have a great deal of space and freedom, ditches often taking the place of bars. This means a lot of walking for visitors, but cars can be taken in, for a charge, and there is a minibus service. A steam-engined train takes visitors through the rhino enclosure.

Much of Dunstable Downs is owned by the National Trust. There is a wide common, woods and wild flowers, and views over nine counties. In the turf of the western slope is cut the white chalk Whipsnade lion.

Woburn
The Russell family, Dukes of Bedford, used to own a tenth of the county, and they gave their estate good churches, inns and private houses. Many of the cottages have a carved monogram 'B' under a coronet on their facades; some of them have no door at the front of the house, owing to the whim of an early Duke of Bedford who disliked seeing cottagers gossiping at their front doors.

The original Woburn Abbey was founded in 1145, but Henry VIII gave it to the Russells at the Dissolution. The present house was rebuilt by Henry Flitcroft in 1747–61 and remodelled by Henry Holland in 1787–8. The State Apartments have gilded ceilings and are filled with art treasures. In the 3000-acre park is the famous Wild Animal Kingdom, where visitors can drive among lions, giraffes and elephants.

In the village of Woburn, a fire in the 18th century made room for much Georgian architecture. Holland built part of the original Bedford Arms—then called The George—but it has been much altered since. Nearby Woburn Sands was created by the coming of the railway in the 19th century.

PÈRE DAVID'S DEER This species, now extinct in the wild, was discovered near Peking by a French missionary in 1865. The herd at Woburn is controlled at between 300 and 400

SWAMP DEER In its native India, this rare deer is called the barasingha—meaning '12-pointed', after the number of points on mature antlers. There is a herd of 25 in the park at Woburn

Leafy lanes in Bernard Shaw country

Angling There is coarse fishing on the Grand Union Canal at Berkhamsted, and at Rickmansworth, 8 miles south of Hemel Hempstead.

Boating Holiday cruising on the Grand Union Canal; boats for hire at Berkhamsted, also canoeing and sailing.

Golf There are 18-hole golf courses at Rickmansworth and St Albans.

Events A music festival is held at St Albans every Nov. An international model-boat regatta is held on Verulamium Lake on late Summer Bank Hol. weekend. A fête is held in Berkhamsted Castle grounds on Spring Bank Hol.

Places to see *Ashridge*, Berkhamsted: occasional days throughout summer. *Berkhamsted Castle:* weekdays, Sun. afternoon. *Gorhambury House*, St Albans: May to Sept., Thur. afternoon. *Hitchin Museum*, with *Hertfordshire Yeomanry Regimental Museum*: weekdays. *Moor Park*, Rickmansworth: Mon., except Bank Hol. *Piccotts End*, 1 mile north of Hemel Hempstead: daily, Mar. to Dec. *St Albans City Museum*: weekdays. *Salisbury Hall*, London Colney, 4 miles south-east of St Albans: Easter to Sept., Sun. afternoons and Bank Hols.; July to Sept., Thur. afternoons also. *Shaw's Corner* (NT), Ayot St Lawrence: Mar. and Nov., Sat. and Sun.; Apr. to Oct., daily except Mon. and Tues. *Tring Zoological Museum*: weekdays and Sun. afternoon. *Verulamium* near St Michael's Church, St Albans: Roman theatre, daily; museum, weekdays and Sun. afternoon.

Information centre Tourist Information Centre, Chequer Street, St Albans. Tel St Albans 64511.

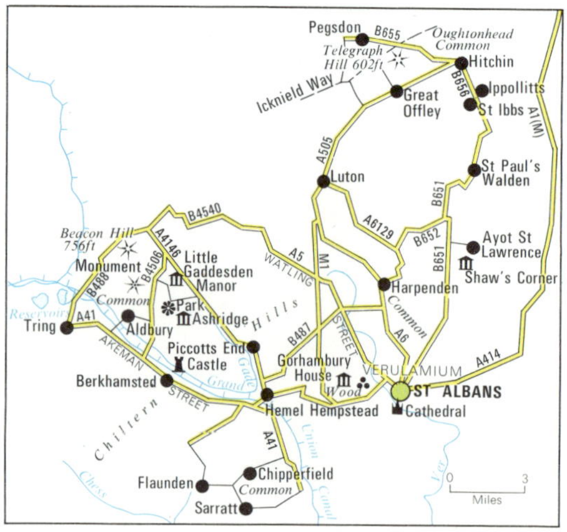

St Albans has been an important centre since the Romans chose it as the site of Verulamium, one of their finest towns in Britain. It was important to the Normans, too; and when they built their great abbey church, the present cathedral, they incorporated in its fabric a central tower of red brick from the earlier Roman town. The abbey was not a rich one, however, and because of the lack of abbey funds in the Middle Ages, the rest of west Hertfordshire's churches are serviceable rather than striking; most of them are crowned by a tower and a small spire, or 'Hertfordshire spike', like a candle snuffer.

Thatch, half-timbering, tiles and weather-boarding are the dominant styles in west Hertfordshire's villages. The county is lacking in durable stone for building as it consists mainly of undulating chalklands, such as the gentle eastern slopes of the Chiltern Hills—with some deposits of clay in the river valleys to the south. Delightful beechwoods cover the high ground around Ashridge Common near Little Gaddesden in the north-west.

Main roads—from the Romans' Watling Street to the modern M1—have always sliced through Hertfordshire. But between Hitchin and St Albans is a belt of unspoilt countryside that is typical of rural Hertfordshire. There are numerous scattered villages, such as St Paul's Walden where the Queen Mother was born in 1900 at a house called The Bury, home of the Bowes-Lyon family. Leafy lanes zigzag through the countryside only a few miles from two traffic-laden motorways; and large trees—reminders that Hertfordshire used to be densely wooded—soften the contours of grassy hills and steep little valleys.

ALDBURY *The old stocks were last used in 1835 to punish a drunken villager*

Aldbury
A pretty village around a green, with a duck pond, old stocks and a whipping-post. Up the hill to the east lies the Ashridge Estate, 6 square miles of National Trust property including woods and commons and extending north to Ivinghoe Beacon. The Beacon (756 ft), a notable viewpoint, is one of several beacon points established in the area during the reign of Elizabeth I to summon men in case of invasion from Spain. These beacons were not bonfires, but pans filled with pitch. The Bridgewater Monument, reached across Aldbury Common along a magnificent avenue of trees, commemorates the 3rd Duke of Bridgewater (1736–1803), who pioneered Britain's canal system. There are 172 steps to the top, which commands a good view.

Ashridge House, begun in 1808 in Gothic style by James Wyatt, is now a management training centre for industry. The surrounding parkland was laid out by Humphry Repton and Capability Brown.

Ayot St Lawrence
A small village shaded by huge old trees and reached by narrow, high-banked lanes. At its south end is Shaw's Corner, George Bernard Shaw's home from 1906 until he died there in 1950. It is a 20th-century building, now owned by the National Trust, and the contents remain as they were in his lifetime.

Shaw said that he chose to live at Ayot St Lawrence after reading the inscription on a gravestone in the local churchyard. This, recording the death of a woman who lived to 70, added the comment 'Her Time Was Short'. Shaw remarked: 'I knew that Ayot, where they call a life of 70 years a short one, was the right place for me.' Shaw lived to the age of 94. His ashes were scattered in the garden of his house.

A gate beside the 14th-century village church leads across a field to a beautiful little church with a Grecian front built by Nicholas Revett for Sir Lionel Lyde in 1778–9. It was commissioned when Sir Lionel's plans to demolish the 14th-century building, because it obstructed his view, were brought to a halt.

TRING MUSEUM *The museum at Tring has a fine collection of stuffed animals*

Berkhamsted
An attractive country town on the Grand Union Canal. There is a large church, parts of which are 13th century, where the father of the poet William Cowper was once rector. Cowper was born in Berkhamsted rectory in 1731. The Norman castle, now in ruins except for earthworks and a moat, was a favourite royal residence until Elizabeth I's time.

Chipperfield
A charming village on the edge of the Chilterns, with woods and heathland, 116 acres of common, and a 17th and 18th-century manor house. Apostles' Pond is set among 12 lime trees.

Flaunden, 1½ miles west, is a small village on high ground above Flaunden Bottom, a wooded side valley of the River Chess; these deep valleys, or 'bottoms', are characteristic of West Hertfordshire. Flaunden Church is Victorian, designed by Sir George Gilbert Scott, architect of the Albert Memorial in London.

Sarratt, 1½ miles south, has a church with Hertfordshire's only 'saddleback' tower—with a roof in the gabled shape of an ordinary house roof.

ST ALBANS ABBEY *The present-day cathedral incorporates an abbey built in the 11th century around the shrine of St Alban, executed in* AD *303 and the first Christian martyr in Britain. It has been added to or altered during every succeeding century*

Great Offley
A village on high ground with views over miles of countryside. At Pegsdon Beacon, 2 miles north-west on Telegraph Hill and accessible only on foot, a pitch-pan beacon was set up in Elizabethan days to give warning of a Spanish invasion. Offley, which has a partly 13th-century church, has a team of Morris dancers. Oughtonhead Common, 2 miles east, covers 43 acres of interest to botanists and ornithologists.

Harpenden
The old High Street has picturesque houses and shops, a reminder of the time when this present-day London commuters' town was an agricultural village. The common, off the High Street, slopes south and gives good views of the Harpenden Valley.

Hemel Hempstead
The old town is in a valley in the Chilterns formed by the River Gade, which is joined here by the Bulbourne. St Mary's Church is mainly Norman and there are some Tudor cottages and 17th and 18th-century buildings in the High Street. A sprawling new town was added to the old in 1947. The valley of the Gade, north of the town, makes a pretty drive. Nearly a mile along it is Piccotts End, a 14th-century house with wall-paintings. Little Gaddesden Manor, $5\frac{1}{2}$ miles further north, is Elizabethan.

Ippollitts
A small village with a magnificent church, mainly 14th century, dedicated to St Hippolytus, 3rd-century Roman martyr and horse doctor. Sick horses are said to have been led into the church in the Middle Ages in the hope of a miraculous cure.

FINDS AT THE EXCAVATED ROMAN CITY OF VERULAMIUM

The theatre (left) dates from the mid-2nd century AD and probably accommodated 5000–6000 spectators. The gangways which divide the terraced seats were used as entrances into the arena by actors, acrobats and gladiators. The central pillar is a modern reconstruction. The 2nd-century bronze figurine of Venus (centre) was found in the cellar of a timber shop. The plaster painting of a bird (right), also 2nd century, is from the corridor ceiling of a town house

St Albans
The city dates back 2000 years and is the third important town on the site. The Belgic tribes who spread through the area had a settlement here; there are earthworks in Prae Wood, $1\frac{1}{2}$ miles west of the town. The Romans built Verulamium beside the River Ver, to the west of the present city. It is thought from a reference in Tacitus, the Roman historian, that Verulamium may have been one of the few examples in Britain of a municipium, in which the inhabitants had the same rights as citizens of Rome. The Roman hypocaust, or heating system, and a theatre can still be seen, and there are other remains in the nearby museum. Just to the east is one of Britain's oldest inns, Ye Old Fighting Cocks, which was rebuilt in 1600 on medieval foundations. The 18th-century clock tower, 77 ft high, offers a fine view over the city.

The cathedral, St Albans Abbey, crowns a hill. Alban, a Roman soldier executed outside Verulamium in AD 303, was the first Christian martyr in Britain; the Saxons built an abbey on the supposed site of his martyrdom. The abbey was rebuilt by the Normans, and enlarged in the 13th century. It became a cathedral in 1877, when the bishopric was created. At the same time the Puritans' whitewash was cleaned from the piers of the long Norman nave, to reveal a series of medieval wall-paintings. More fine paintings have come to light during restoration in recent years.

Gorhambury House, 2 miles west, home of the Earls of Verulam, was built in 1777–84 near the ruins of the old Tudor manor house of Sir Nicholas Bacon. He was Elizabeth I's Lord Keeper and the father of Francis Bacon, the statesman and essayist, who is buried in St Michael's Church.

Off the market-place is French Row, where some buildings may be 14th century. Among them is the Fleur de Lys Inn, where King John of France is said to have been held after being captured at Poitiers in 1356.

Tring
A pleasant small town notable for its Zoological Museum, which became part of the British Museum in 1938 when Lord Rothschild left it the vast insect collection he had built up over the years.

Tring Church is mainly 13th and 14th century. Lanes to the north of the town lead to four reservoirs, now all part of a National Nature Reserve.

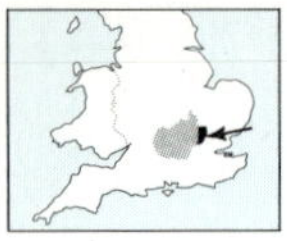

Garden cities of Hertfordshire

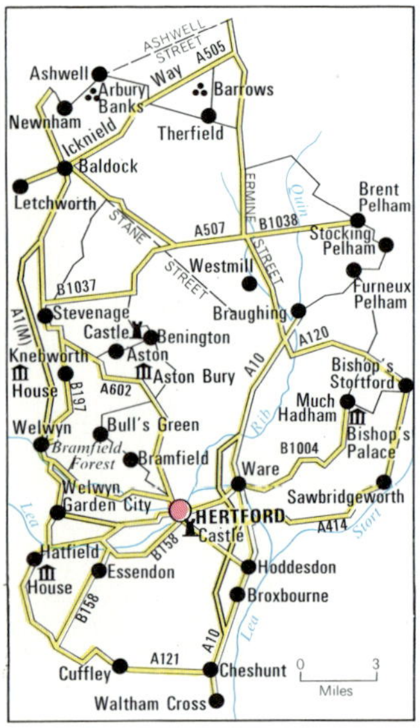

From ancient times, good roads from the coast through London have taken travellers hurrying across Hertfordshire on their way to the North. The Romans built Ermine Street, which ran from Pevensey to York, part of which is now the A10. The Great North Road (A1) became the backbone of the county, and divided it in half as effectively as a natural barrier. Modern motorways have taken the dismemberment of the county a stage further.

Between the main roads to the North, however, old villages remain unspoilt, with little traffic, and there are pleasant circuitous routes running from west to east. An exceptional number of Elizabethan and Jacobean houses were built in this area, which had the advantages of being near London and offering good hunting in the forests, which still survive in scattered patches of the county.

Many small rivers flow to join the River Lea, itself a main tributary of the Thames. Northwards, the land rises where the heavy clay of the Thames Basin is overlaid by chalk; the highest points are the easternmost humps of the Chilterns. There are well-signposted footpaths crossing the area and a maze of lanes leads through a landscape filled with the charm of a typical English rural scene.

The Industrial Revolution did not greatly affect Hertfordshire, as the county had no coal or iron: but the continuing growth of London has encroached a good deal. Britain's first garden city, Letchworth, was planned in 1903. The second was Welwyn Garden City (1920). Then came the new towns built round an existing nucleus in the 1940's and 1950's: Stevenage, Hatfield, and the further extension of Welwyn Garden City. There is a good deal of industry, both light and heavy, and the agriculture is also mixed. In the Lea Valley around Waltham Cross and Cheshunt there are 1000 acres of heated glass under which are produced a quarter of Britain's total salad crops.

Angling Trout and coarse fishing on the River Rib at Braughing, on the River Stort at Sawbridgeworth and the River Lea at Hertford. Coarse fishing on the River Lea Navigation Canal at Cheshunt Marshes and on the Brookfield Lane Reservoir (noted for carp) at Cheshunt, 5 miles south of Hoddesdon.

Boating Hertford and Ware are centres for pleasure cruising and sailing, and boats can be hired at Rye House, Hoddesdon. Sailing on the Windmill Lane gravel pit, Cheshunt.

Events The County Day Fair is held at Hertford every Spring Bank Hol. The Bakers versus Sweeps football match is held on Boxing Day at Waltham Cross.

Places to see *Ashwell Village Museum*: Sun. afternoons. *Hatfield House*: late Mar. to early Oct., house and gardens afternoons except Mon., but including Bank Hols.; park, daily. *Hertford Castle*: first Sat. morning of month, May to Sept.; gardens, daily. *Hertford Museum*: weekdays. *Knebworth House*: Easter to Sept., Tues. to Sun.; Oct., Sun. only. *Rhodes Memorial Museum*, Bishop's Stortford, 8 miles north-east of Ware: weekdays.

Information centres Vale House, Hertford. Tel. Hertford 54977. District Council Offices, The Campus, Welwyn Garden City. Tel. Welwyn Garden City 31212.

HATFIELD HOUSE *Robert Cecil, 1st Earl of Salisbury and Elizabeth I's Secretary of State, built this stately home between 1608 and 1612. His descendants still live there. The east wing, in the foreground, was designed as a guest wing*

VILLAGE PUMP ON THE GREEN *Tudor cottages stand between the green and the 12th-century church at Westmill, one of the most attractive villages in Hertfordshire. Charles Lamb, the essayist, once owned a cottage called Button Snap near the village*

Ashwell
The spacious planning of this village is due to its Roman origins. A group of handsome beamed cottages with decorative plasterwork, or pargeting, adjoins the 17th-century Hall of the Guild of St John in the High Street. The church is mainly 14th century, and on top of its tower is a small spire or 'Hertfordshire spike'. In its base is a 14th-century carving of the old St Paul's Cathedral. A spring, the source of the River Cam, or Rhee, surrounded by ash trees, gives the village its name.

Ashwell's history since the Stone Age can be traced in the tiny folk museum in the old Tythe House, Swan Street. The minor road from Newnham, 2 miles south-west, follows the course of an old Roman road, Ashwell Street, past Arbury Banks, the site of an Iron Age hill fort. North-east of Ashwell the course of the Roman road can be traced as a grassed-over track running eastwards into Cambridgeshire.

Bramfield
A village ringed by woodlands, which are remnants of the forests that once covered the county. There are numerous walks in the woods on either side of the road to Bull's Green, $1\frac{1}{2}$ miles north-west. Sally Rainbow's Dell is a deep chalk pit that shows a profile of the soils and rock strata. Thomas Becket was Rector of Bramfield in the 12th century, but his church was rebuilt in the 13th.

Braughing
An important village in Roman times, when it was the hub of seven Roman roads, including Ermine Street and Stane Street. It has a mainly 15th-century church and houses with half-timbering and 16th-century moulded plasterwork. The River Quin flows past the village green. Furneux Pelham, 3 miles north-east, has a 13th-century church with windows by Morris and Burne-Jones; and nearby Brent Pelham has medieval stocks and a whipping-post. Westmill, 2 miles north-west, has a 12th-century church, a cottage called Button Snap once owned by Charles Lamb and preserved by the Lamb Society, and a beautiful old barn.

Essendon
A village on a hill in unspoilt rural country. The village church was partly destroyed in 1916 by a German Zeppelin which was brought down at Cuffley, 4 miles south. The church has a rare Wedgwood black basalt font of 1780.

Hatfield
The population of this old coaching town has doubled since 1946, when a new town was built to the west of the A1000. But on the east the charming Georgian old town survives; steep Fore Street has a particularly lovely row of houses. The town climbs a hill which is crowned by the 13th-century St Etheldreda's Church, and the 15th-century Old Palace. Elizabeth I lived in the palace as a child and it was there that she heard the news of her sister Mary's death and her own accession in 1558.

The Old Palace is the threshold to Hatfield House, one of the finest Jacobean houses in Britain. It was built from 1608–12, in the shape of an E, by Robert Cecil, 1st Earl of Salisbury and Elizabeth I's Secretary of State. It contains mementoes of the queen. The house is the home of the present Marquess of Salisbury, and is surrounded by 1500 acres of parkland, with woods and some farmland.

PARGETING *Houses in Ashwell High Street, dating from 1681, are notable for their decorative plasterwork, more characteristic of East Anglia*

Hertford
The county town's situation, remote from main through roads, has left it comparatively unspoilt. There was a settlement on the site long before the Romans, and there are the ruins of a Norman castle on the site of an earlier Saxon stronghold, built to protect London from the Danes. The town centre has a Victorian Corn Exchange, handsome buildings and decorated plasterwork. The Shire Hall which stands in the middle of the town was built in 1769, and was designed by Robert Adam.

Knebworth
Knebworth House is mostly the work of the Lytton family. Sir Robert Lytton began building a Tudor mansion in 1492 on the site of an earlier castle. The 19th-century Lyttons, including the 1st Lord Lytton, novelist and politician, rebuilt this in Gothic style. The church, in the 260-acre park, was built in the 12th century and is full of 18th-century family memorials. The modern town of Knebworth lies to the east, across the A1 motorway. The Church of St Martin's was designed by Sir Edwin Lutyens.

Aston, 2 miles north-east, has a 16th-century mansion, Aston Bury, thatched cottages and barns and a 13th-century church. Benington, $1\frac{1}{2}$ miles further north-east, has 16th-century cottages beside the village green, a 14th-century church and the ruins of a moated Norman castle. A Georgian house, Benington Lordship, stands on the castle site.

Much Hadham
One of the county's showpieces. The village has impressive old buildings because it was for centuries the country seat of the Bishops of London. Their palace, near the originally 12th-century church, is mainly Jacobean. Much Hadham Hall dates from 1735, and the house called The Lordship has William and Mary stables and huge yew hedges. The 16th-century Morris Cottage was the home of William Morris's sister.

Therfield
A village on the crest of the Royston Downs, with a fine view overlooking the Cambridge plain to the north. It has the mound of a castle and a beacon of Elizabeth I's time. After 2 miles, the road to the north joins A505, the pre-Roman Icknield Way. On Therfield Heath, just south of the junction, are a Bronze Age barrow cemetery and a Neolithic long barrow.

Ware
The River Lea, on which the town is built, is now used by pleasure boats and anglers, but once carried heavy traffic from the local malting industry. The Great Bed of Ware, 10 ft wide and 11 ft long, mentioned in Shakespeare's *Twelfth Night*, was once in The Saracen's Head at Ware. It is now in the Victoria and Albert Museum. Ware is also famed as John Gilpin's destination on his runaway ride in William Cowper's poem. The church is mainly 14th and 15th century, with attractive monuments. Jane Grey was proclaimed Queen at Ware in 1553.

WELWYN VIADUCT *The 40 arches of the viaduct span the Mimram Valley. It was built in 1850 by the Great Northern Railway to link Peterborough and King's Cross*

LONDON

The capital which keeps on growing

It is London's sheer size which first strikes the visitor, an impression created by its density at the centre as well as by the fact that where inner London ends, the suburbs begin and run on for miles in every direction. Greater London today covers more than 620 square miles. It began around the twin areas of the City and Westminster, and along the meandering line set by the Thames. Over the centuries it has spread to annex scores of towns, villages and hamlets—and it is still spreading. It has also steadily increased in density, even spreading upwards with 'high-rise' building after the Second World War.

The picture has a brighter side. A wealth of open spaces—parks, squares and heathland—helps greatly to relieve the density. On the fringes, much real countryside has been preserved as a result of steps taken since 1938 to halt the suburban sprawl by the establishment of the Green Belt of open land around the city. The boundary of Greater London now encloses part of this belt on the chalkland edges of the shallow, saucer-shaped depression in which the capital lies. To the south, London stretches to the downs of Surrey and Kent; to the north-west it nears the fringes of the Chiltern Hills.

Londoners have benefited from another progressive measure besides the creation of the Green Belt. The Clean Air Act of 1956 has brought increased sunshine to the city—as much as 50 per cent more from November to January. Central London now averages 7 hours of sunshine a day in spring and early summer, compared with $7\frac{1}{2}$ hours in the suburbs.

Surprisingly, London's 25 in. of rain a year is less than in many parts of the Continent—Rome has 32 in., Nice 31 in. Central London's minimum temperatures are 2–3° C higher than in the surrounding countryside, because of the warmth from heated buildings.

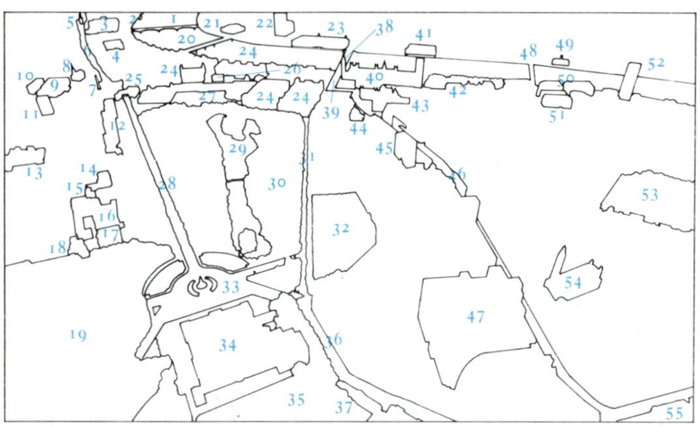

HEART OF LONDON *Key to aerial photograph on pp. 224 and 225: 1 Waterloo Bridge 2 HMS Discovery 3 Somerset House 4 Shell-Mex House 5 St Mary-le-Strand Church 6 Strand 7 Nelson's Column 8 St Martin-in-the-Fields Church 9 National Gallery 10 National Portrait Gallery 11 New Zealand House 12 Carlton House Terrace 13 St James's Square 14 Marlborough House 15 Queen's Chapel 16 St James's Palace 17 Clarence House 18 Lancaster House 19 Green Park 20 Hungerford Bridge 21 Royal Festival Hall 22 Shell Centre 23 County Hall 24 Government offices 25 Admiralty Arch 26 Banqueting House 27 Horse Guards 28 The Mall 29 Lake in St James's Park 30 St James's Park 31 Birdcage Walk 32 Wellington Barracks 33 Queen Victoria Memorial 34 Buckingham Palace 35 Buckingham Palace grounds 36 Buckingham Palace Road 37 Queen's Gallery 38 Big Ben 39 Westminster Bridge 40 Houses of Parliament 41 St Thomas's Hospital 42 Victoria Tower Gardens 43 Westminster Abbey 44 Central Hall, Westminster 45 New Scotland Yard 46 Victoria Street 47 Stag Place 48 Lambeth Bridge 49 London Fire Brigade 50 Thames House 51 Westminster Hospital 52 Vickers Building 53 Vincent Square 54 Westminster Cathedral 55 Victoria Station*

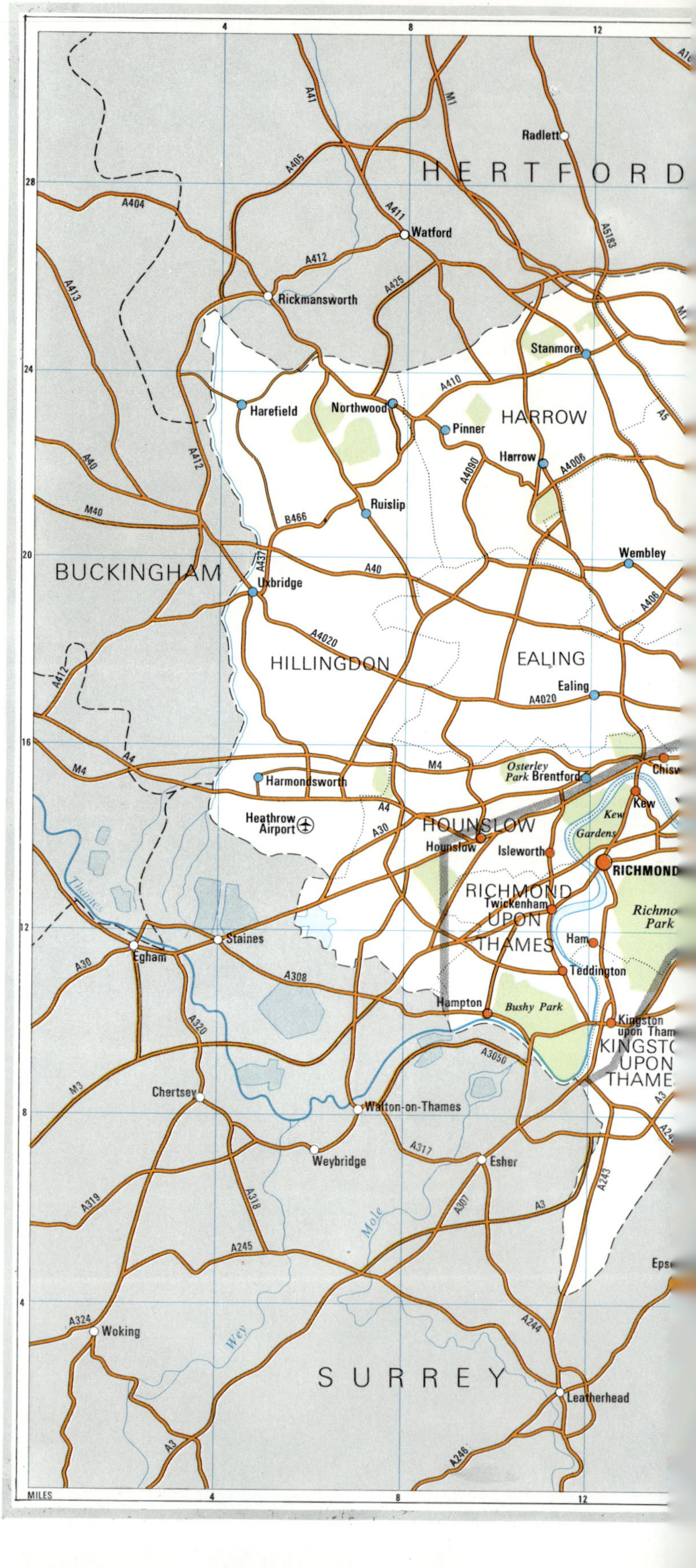

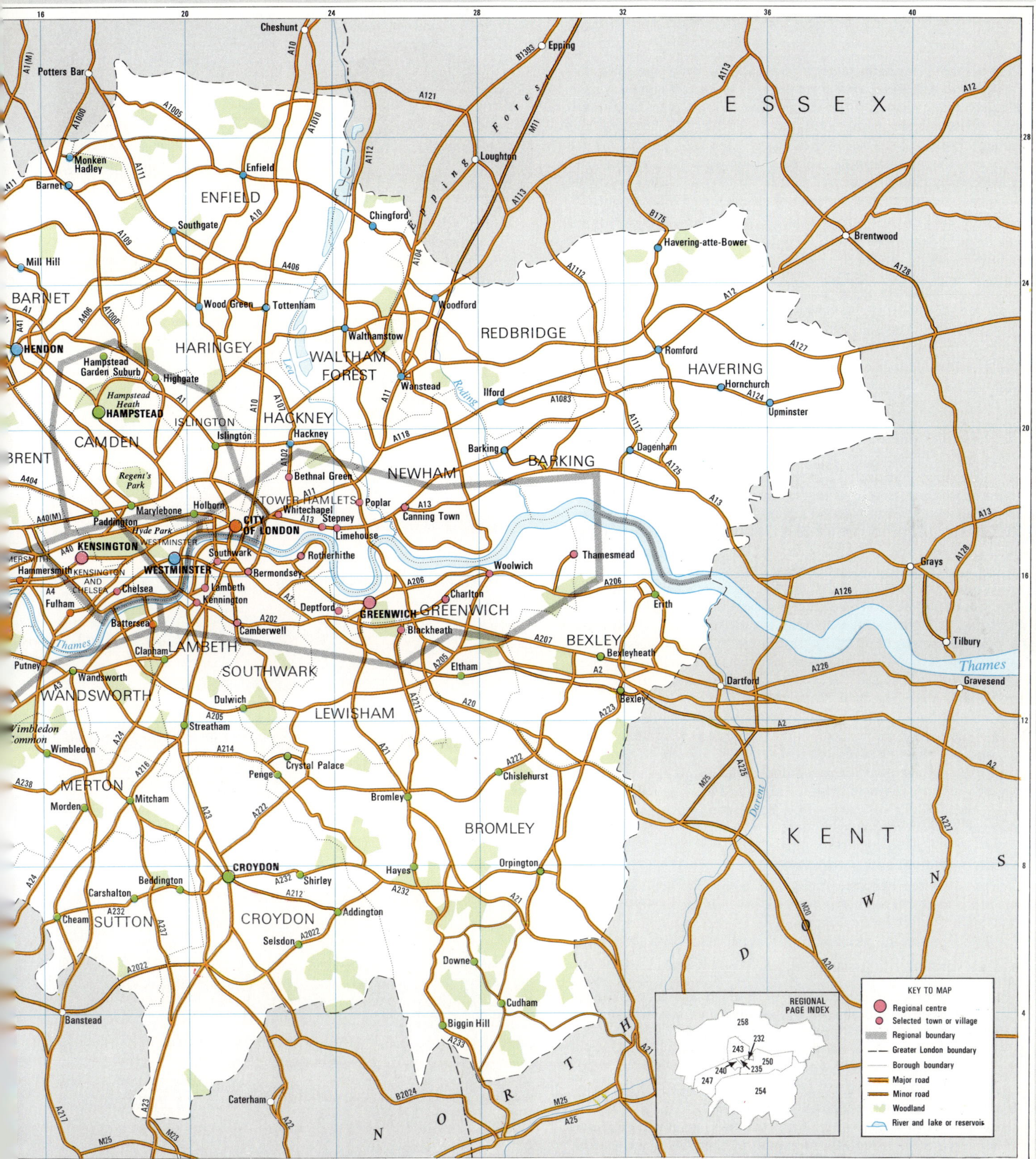
ESSEX
KENT
NORTH DOWNS
Epping Forest
Cheshunt
Epping
Potters Bar
Loughton
Monken Hadley
Barnet
Enfield
ENFIELD
Chingford
Southgate
Havering-atte-Bower
Brentwood
Mill Hill
BARNET
Wood Green
Tottenham
Woodford
REDBRIDGE
HENDON
HARINGEY
Walthamstow
WALTHAM FOREST
Romford
HAVERING
Hampstead Garden Suburb
Highgate
Wanstead
Hornchurch
Hampstead Heath
HAMPSTEAD
Ilford
Upminster
ISLINGTON
HACKNEY
Islington
Hackney
CAMDEN
Barking
Dagenham
BRENT
BARKING
Bethnal Green
NEWHAM
Regent's Park
TOWER HAMLETS
Poplar
Marylebone
Holborn
Whitechapel
Paddington
CITY OF LONDON
Stepney
Canning Town
Hyde Park
Limehouse
KENSINGTON
WESTMINSTER
Southwark
Rotherhithe
Thamesmead
Grays
Hammersmith
KENSINGTON AND CHELSEA
WESTMINSTER
Bermondsey
Woolwich
Chelsea
Lambeth
Kennington
Charlton
Erith
Fulham
Deptford
GREENWICH
Battersea
Camberwell
Blackheath
Tilbury
Thames
Clapham
LAMBETH
BEXLEY
Bexleyheath
Putney
Wandsworth
SOUTHWARK
Eltham
Dartford
Gravesend
WANDSWORTH
Bexley
Dulwich
LEWISHAM
Streatham
Wimbledon Common
Wimbledon
Crystal Palace
Chislehurst
Penge
MERTON
Bromley
Darent
Morden
Mitcham
BROMLEY
Orpington
Hayes
CROYDON
Shirley
Beddington
Carshalton
Addington
Cheam
SUTTON
Selsdon
Downe
Cudham
Banstead
Biggin Hill
Caterham
A1(M)
A1000
A1005
A10
A1010
A121
B1393
M11
A113
A112
A12
A111
A109
A406
A104
B175
A1112
A128
A1
A41
A127
A107
A11
A1083
A124
A118
A102
A1112
A125
A404
A40(M)
A13
A40
A4
A2
A206
A202
A207
A226
A126
A3
A205
A20
A223
A2212
A205
A214
A24
A216
A238
A21
A222
A23
M25
A225
A227
A232
A212
A237
A2022
M20
A20
A233
B2024
A22
A217
M23
A25
REGIONAL PAGE INDEX
258
232
243
250
240
235
247
254
KEY TO MAP
Regional centre
Selected town or village
Regional boundary
Greater London boundary
Borough boundary
Major road
Minor road
Woodland
River and lake or reservoir

London's 2000 years of history

London is the result of almost 2000 years' development, most of it uncontrolled. Attempts to impose a pattern on this vast organism have largely failed—notably Sir Christopher Wren's plan for the recreation of its ancient centre after the Great Fire of 1666, and the ambitious scheme of John Nash for beautifying the West End during the Regency era. Both men realised a part of their vision for London—the noble bulk of St Paul's Cathedral and the handsome Nash terraces in Regent's Park are evidence. But what is visible of their work is essentially the result of compromise, caused as much by shortage of money as by native dislike of anything too deliberately on the grand scale.

If London's growth over the centuries has been a largely haphazard affair, its creation was deliberate enough. The invading Romans in AD 43 wanted a site somewhere along the Thames which could be settled and fortified, and they chose the area which was later to become the 'square mile' of the City. The wall which the Romans put around London contained it for 1000 years after their departure. In the years following the Norman Conquest, the City spilt a little to the west to meet Westminster. The movement of population westwards was accelerated by the Great Fire, which devastated most of the City.

The parks which make London unique

After the fire, such planning as there was came from the big estate owners developing their land. Their main innovation was the square, an attractive open space, usually with grass and trees, and surrounded by terraces of houses. Most of London's squares were constructed between the Restoration and the late 18th century, and the typical flavour of the townscape of western inner London survives from then. From the 1630's onwards, the people of London benefited from the creation of the great parks, such as Hyde Park, St James's Park and Regent's Park. Once royal hunting grounds, these lovely stretches of grassland were gradually ceded to the public. It is the parks, more than any other feature, which make London unique among the world's great capitals.

London offers the visitor many superb vistas, as well as surprises round the corner. Though the view from Westminster Bridge has changed much since the poet William Wordsworth declared in his famous sonnet that 'Earth has not anything to show more fair', it is still a splendid experience to stand on the bridge and sweep the eye over 'Ships, towers, domes, theatres and temples'. The view today also takes in skyscrapers such as the Vickers building on Millbank, starkly elegant in the 20th-century idiom of glass, concrete and steel. Britain's tallest structure, the GPO Tower just north of Soho, offers a new panorama of London and the countryside on its doorstep.

Where the medieval pattern survives

The Victorian Prime Minister William Gladstone advised a group of visitors to London that the best way to see it was from the top of a bus. But walking may often be a quicker and more rewarding way in today's traffic-choked streets, especially in the West End, with its shops, restaurants, theatres, clubs and historic public buildings, interspersed with parks and squares. Here, and in neighbouring areas, is to be found the greater part of London's massive store of art and archaeological treasures, in the British Museum, the Tate Gallery, the National Gallery and the museums of South Kensington. The relative openness of the West End contrasts with the cramped and quirky density of the City, which has been built and rebuilt many times on the original Roman site. The streets and alleys of the City still reflect the old medieval plan.

London has often been described as a 'collection of villages'. This is true both of the city centre, where districts like Soho and Bloomsbury merge into each other yet remain unmistakably themselves, and also of the outer areas, where such places as Hampstead, Highgate, Greenwich and Richmond still keep much of their distinctive character.

ROMAN ORIGINS

The city of Londinium, founded by the Romans soon after AD 43, occupied roughly the same area as the modern City's 'square mile'. It was the furthest point up the Thames which sailing ships from the Continent could reach on the tide, and a suitable place for building a bridge, because of the gravelly soil. With these advantages, Londinium quickly became the leading port of Britain, as well as the main junction for the Romans' countrywide system of roads. After Queen Boudicca, or Boadicea, sacked the city in AD 60, the Romans enclosed it with a strong defensive wall, which was nearly 2 miles long, about 20 ft high and 9 ft thick. The wall was built of tiles and mortar and Kentish ragstone. A gold medallion (above) commemorated the recovery of Londinium by Constantius Chlorus in AD 296, after he had defeated Allectus, a Roman who had usurped the imperial authority in Britain. Chlorus, mounted on a charger, is being hailed as *Redditor Lucis Aeternae* (restorer of eternal light) by a grateful citizen kneeling at the gates of the walled city. A well-preserved remnant of the Roman wall is in Cooper's Row, beside the modern Midland House (above). The upper part, with its rounded openings, is a medieval addition, possibly of the 12th century

CONQUEROR'S TOWER

During its long and often sombre history the Tower of London (below) has been a fortress, palace and prison. One of the earliest prisoners was Charles, Duke of Orleans, captured at the Battle of Agincourt in 1415. A 16th-century illustration (right) shows him seated in the central tower—which became known as the White Tower after the exterior was whitewashed in 1241—with Traitors' Gate in the foreground and London Bridge in the distance. The White Tower is the oldest and most impressive of the present buildings. It was started soon after 1066 by William the Conqueror, and built of stone from Normandy

PROSPERITY AND PERIL IN THE 17th CENTURY

London *c.* 1616, as seen in the panorama by the Dutch artist Claes Visscher, was a bustling, prosperous capital, with buildings on both banks of the river and on London Bridge. Old St Paul's on the north bank, and Southwark Cathedral ('St Mary Church') on the south, dominated this city of churches. Entertainment flourished on the south bank at such theatres as the Globe, where Shakespeare's tragedies had recently been staged for the first time. Citizens crossed the river by boat or over London Bridge, which was a street in itself, with shops and houses. Holborn's Staple Inn (left), with its picturesque timbered front, oriel windows and overhanging gables, gives an idea of what much of the city looked like at the time. Built in 1586, it is the only surviving example of domestic Elizabethan architecture in London. A fire caused by an overheated baking oven in a similar timbered building in Pudding Lane started the Great Fire of London on September 2, 1666. Over 13,000 buildings were destroyed, but only four people were killed. A law passed after the fire required all new buildings to be of brick or stone

FIRE OF LONDON, 1666 A contemporary painting of the Great Fire shows London Bridge and Old St Paul's in flames, with the Tower of London on the right

GRACIOUS LIVING AFTER THE RESTORATION

The square was London's most important architectural innovation between the Restoration in 1660 and the late 18th century. Most of the early squares were created by noblemen who had turned to property speculation. One of the pioneers was the Earl of Southampton, who built Bloomsbury Square, on the estate where he had his own residence—it was the first square to be called a square. With their orderly lay-out and simple yet dignified buildings, the squares were intended to reproduce the style of gracious country living in a city grown crowded and noisy. The first square to be built in the West End was St James's Square (*c.* 1665), shown above as it was in the early 18th century and as it is today. The Earl of St Albans created it as a fashionable quarter, and it has remained fashionable. But whereas it was once the home of dukes and earls, it is now occupied mainly by clubs and commercial firms. The ornamental pond in the centre has gone, and the private garden is now for the use of people who work in the square. John Bacon's equestrian statue of William III among the plane trees was erected in 1807. The much-restored St James's Church, beyond in Piccadilly, was designed in the 1680's by Sir Christopher Wren, who regarded it as his most successful parish church

COUNTRY RETREATS OF THE 18th CENTURY

As far back as the mid-18th century, building speculators began to exploit the market for 'country in town' dwellings in unspoilt areas such as Clapham and Blackheath, south of the Thames. They built houses in long terraces, in the simple uniformity of style based on Classical examples which is today described as Georgian—a style which proved as economical as it was pleasing and elegant. Notable surviving examples include the houses on the north side of Clapham Common, seen in their original state in an 18th-century print (above left); the Church of the Holy Trinity also survives today. The celebrated crescent at Blackheath called the Paragon (detail, above right) consists of seven buildings linked by colonnades. It was built by Michael Searle in the 1790's, and still stands in an unspoilt setting. Clapham had become a suburb by Thackeray's time (about the mid-19th century). He wrote: 'Of all the pretty suburbs that still adorn our metropolis there are few that exceed in charm Clapham Common.' In the previous century the common, like many open spaces around London, had been notorious as a place for highwaymen. Today both Clapham and Blackheath are very much part of London, yet they retain a good deal of their country-like character

PROGRESS AND DEFIANCE IN MODERN TIMES

St Pancras Station, built 1868–74 as the London terminus of the Midland Railway, shows in spectacular style the romantic Victorian attitude towards material progress. In John O'Connor's painting of 1884 (above left), the vast building beyond Pentonville Road seems to dissolve in the glow of sunset, looking more like a fairy castle than a railway station. St Pancras today (above right) presents a less fairy-tale appearance, its surface blackened by soot and grime. The station was the work of Sir George Gilbert Scott, a leader of the Gothic Revival in architecture, which sought inspiration in medieval forms. His aim in designing it was to show that 'Gothic would admit of any degree of modernism'. Scott and his fellow revivalists left a profound imprint on London's architecture, the most notable example besides St Pancras Station being the Houses of Parliament by Barry and Pugin. The scale and dynamism which transformed London in Victorian times has been matched by the massive rebuilding of London after the destruction caused by bombing in the Second World War. The famous photograph of St Paul's standing intact during the second Great Fire of London, the blitz of December 29, 1940, became a symbol of London's faith in itself (below). There was colossal devastation around the cathedral from the fires caused by over 10,000 incendiary bombs. Many historic buildings, including Wren churches, were destroyed

FIRE OF LONDON, 1940 A press photographer stood on a City roof to take this picture, one of the most famous of the war, of St Paul's Cathedral ringed with flames

The square mile where London began

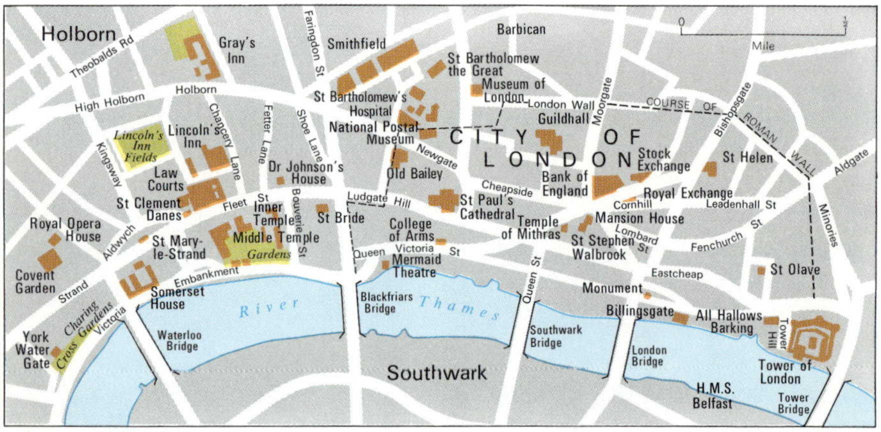

Events The Butterworth Charity's presentation of hot cross buns takes place on Good Fri. at St Bartholomew the Great, Smithfield. An open-air art exhibition is held in early May in Victoria Embankment Gardens. The election of Sheriffs of the City of London is held in June at Guildhall. Bound Beating of the Tower takes place on Ascension Day every three years (1981, 1984, etc.). The ceremonial road-sweeping procession of the Vintner's Company from St James Garlickhythe is held in July. The City of London Festival is held during July in even-numbered years. Christ's Hospital 'Bluecoat' march takes place in late Sept. The opening of the Law Courts procession is held about Oct. 1. The Lord Mayor's Procession and Show takes place on the second Sat. in Nov. From May to Sept., bands play on some afternoons in Victoria Embankment Gardens and on the steps of St Paul's Cathedral; also during lunchtime in the Tower gardens.

Places to see *Dr Johnson's House*, Gough Square: weekdays. *Gray's Inn*: grounds, Mon. to Fri. afternoons May to July; Mon. to Fri., all day, Aug. and Sept.; buildings, on application. *HMS Belfast*, near Tower Bridge: daily. *Lincoln's Inn*: buildings and gardens by appointment. *Monument*: Apr. to Sept., weekdays and Sun. afternoon; Oct to Mar., weekdays. *Museum of London*, London Wall: Tues. to Sat. and Sun. afternoon. *National Postal Museum*, King Edward Street: Mon. to Fri. *Old Bailey*: trials open to the public Mon. to Fri. *St Bride's Crypt Museum*, Fleet Street: daily. *Sir John Soane's Museum*, Lincoln's Inn Fields: Tues. to Sat. *Stock Exchange*, gallery: Mon. to Fri. *Tower of London*: weekdays; also Sun. afternoons Mar. to Oct.

The famous 'Square Mile' of the City of London is the original Londinium, contained within the 2nd-century Roman wall which defined the city for almost 1000 years on its twin hills by the Thames. Ludgate Hill, once known as Ludhill, is now dominated by St Paul's Cathedral, while on Cornhill is the modern business, banking and insurance area which includes the Bank of England, the Royal Exchange and the Mansion House. London's early history can be seen in fragments of Roman brick, bonded with Kentish ragstone, which were part of the Roman wall, on Tower Hill and in the Tower of London. The giant, squat bulk of the White Tower was begun by William the Conqueror in the 11th century. To the east of the Tower rise the cranes where the great dock system begins on the widening Thames—the river which was for centuries the lifeline of London's world-wide commercial power.

For the visitor the initial impression of the City is of a largely modern landscape with banks and tall office blocks, creeping massively towards Sir Christopher Wren's great dome of St Paul's. But closer inspection reveals older survivals, including more than 20 churches built by Wren after the Great Fire of 1666. Outside the area destroyed by fire, and survivors, too, of Second World War air raids, are a few splendid medieval churches—St Bartholomew the Great, All Hallows Barking, St Helen's, and St Olave's, the church often mentioned by Pepys.

The noise and bustle of the City is accentuated by the fact that modern building still follows the dense medieval street plan. It is an area best seen on foot, because off the main canyons between the buildings narrower streets lead to smaller alleys, hidden taverns and minute churchyards. From Ludgate Hill westwards the towering buildings of finance give way to the quieter, mellowed Inns of Court—legal London, divided into two by the bustle of Fleet Street. Then, in the Aldwych and the Strand, theatres and hotels seem like the first outposts of the West End. The river, too, changes its character, as only low-lying barges, oil tankers or pleasure craft can go under bridges further upstream than London Bridge.

TOWER GUNS *These French 6-pounder guns pointing over the River Thames were captured at the Battle of Waterloo*

TOWER RAVENS *According to legend, if the ravens disappear the Tower will fall*

Bank of England

The Bank was founded in 1694, but its present fortress-like building was rebuilt between the wars. It stands on the north side of an open space known as 'the Bank', the commercial centre of the City. Since the Gordon Riots of 1780, when the Bank was threatened, it has been protected each night by a detachment of the Brigade of Guards.

To the south of the Bank is the 18th-century Mansion House, official residence of the Lord Mayor of London, and hidden away behind it is the fine Wren church of St Stephen Walbrook. The former Royal Exchange, founded originally by Sir Thomas Gresham, the Elizabethan financier, is on the east side of the Bank, and north-east of this is the new skyscraper Stock Exchange building, where a public gallery overlooks the brokers and jobbers at work.

Barbican

Named after a barbican, or watch-tower, built into the city wall, the area was levelled by bombing in the Second World War and is being rebuilt. The development scheme, begun in 1962, aims to bring back residents to the heart of the City, which hitherto died every night when office workers commuted to the suburbs. Eventually the Barbican will house 6500 people. Office buildings are now connected by raised walkways, and the residential area will include a concert/conference hall, a library, art gallery and theatre providing a new home for the Royal Shakespeare Company.

Just outside the limit of the Barbican is the new Museum of London, with exhibits ranging from Roman busts to every-day items of the recent past and forming a comprehensive picture of the city's life and history.

Billingsgate

The principal fish market in London is named after a former river gate in the City wall. Five o'clock in the morning is the best time to see the fish porters, who sometimes carry a hundredweight of fish at a time in baskets on their flat hats made of leather and wood.

Covent Garden

For 300 years the chief market for fruit, vegetables and flowers in London—but congestion in the surrounding streets necessitated transfer of the market to a new site at Nine Elms, south of the Thames. The name was originally Convent Garden, from an old garden that had belonged to the monks of

THE MAJESTY OF A MASTERPIECE *Sir Christopher Wren designed St Paul's as a noble building that would dominate London. Though modern City blocks now tower higher than St Paul's, the domination envisaged by Wren can still be seen from the river*

Westminster Abbey. The 4th Duke of Bedford obtained a royal charter for the market at the time he was planning a residential quarter there. He wanted a church on the west side but did not want to spend much money on it, so he told Inigo Jones that it was to be like a barn. The architect's reply was 'It will be the handsomest barn in Europe'—and he built St Paul's Church. It has many connections with the theatre, and plaques commemorate famous actors, actresses and impresarios.

To the east is the Royal Opera House, often called simply Covent Garden, the home of international opera in Britain. There have been four theatres on the site since 1733, and the present building dates from 1858.

Fleet Street
The centre of London's newspaper industry, named after the River Fleet which flows under it to the Thames. Fleet Street and the streets leading off it are at their liveliest after 10 p.m. when the papers are coming off the presses in Fetter Lane, Shoe Lane and Bouverie Street, and vans are rushing them to railway stations. In Gough Square, to the north, is Dr Johnson's house, a fine 17th-century house, and on the south side of Fleet Street is St Bride's Church, one of Wren's most beautiful churches, with a soaring 'wedding-cake' spire.

Gray's Inn
One of the four Inns of Court, or corporate legal societies, which already existed as a school of law in the 14th century—the others are Lincoln's Inn, Middle Temple and Inner Temple. A 17th-century gatehouse leads into Gray's Inn from High Holborn. In the gardens, which are open to the public, is a catalpa tree said to have been planted by Francis Bacon, a treasurer of the inn, from cuttings brought back from America by Sir Walter Raleigh.

Guildhall
The seat of the Corporation of London, which governs the City, and the centre of much of its pageantry. The sheriffs for the coming year are elected here at a colourful ceremony on Midsummer Day, and in November the new Lord Mayor gives a banquet at which the Prime Minister is the main speaker. When it is not in use the public are allowed into the main hall, which was mostly rebuilt in the 15th century and was restored after being badly damaged in the Second World War.

The library, containing a house deed of sale signed by Shakespeare, is one of the most comprehensive in the country.

Lombard Street
The financial centre of London since the Middle Ages. Many banks there still display signs, similar to inn signs, in the medieval way. The street takes its name from merchants from Lombardy, in Italy, who settled there as money-lenders in the 12th century.

WHERE THE FIRE BEGAN *The Monument, with 311 stairs to a look-out platform, was designed by Wren to commemorate the Great Fire of 1666 which started in nearby Pudding Lane*

OLD CURIOSITY SHOP *The 16th-century antique shop in Portsmouth Street is often claimed to have been the model for the book by Charles Dickens, who used to visit a friend near by*

APOTHECARIES' HALL *An archway off Blackfriars Lane leads to the charming courtyard of the Hall of the Apothecaries' Company. The 17th-century building was altered in 1779*

THE MERCHANT'S SIGN *Grocers from the 16th to the 19th century displayed the sign of three sugar loaves. This merchant's shop in Creechurch Lane also adds the firm's sign of a crown*

LINCOLN'S INN *This tree-shaded square surrounded by barristers' chambers is the heart of Lincoln's Inn, one of the four Inns of Court, which is entered from Chancery Lane through a 16th-century gatehouse. The Inn's 17th-century chapel is by Inigo Jones*

BRONZE GRIFFIN *London's heraldic beast in the Strand marks the boundary between the cities of Westminster and London*

Queen Victoria Street
A street opened in 1871 to link the Bank with the Victoria Embankment. Here is the 17th-century College of Arms, or Heralds' College, which deals with heraldry and genealogy. The Mermaid Theatre, opened in Puddle Dock in 1959, was the first theatre built in the City since the 16th century.

Near to Bucklersbury House are the reconstructed walls of the Roman Temple of Mithras, which was discovered in 1954 when foundations were being dug for an office building.

St Paul's Cathedral
Sir Christopher Wren's masterpiece has now been cleaned of decades of London soot so that the warm-coloured Portland stone glows as it did when the cathedral was first begun in 1675, nine years after the medieval St Paul's was destroyed in the Great Fire. The vast scale of the cathedral's interior has been enhanced since the Second World War by the replacement of bomb-damaged stained glass with clear glass, as originally specified in Wren's designs. On the inside of the dome are paintings by Sir James Thornhill. In his later years Wren loved to stand in the cathedral and look up to the dome. Above is the climb to the Whispering Gallery, which picks up a whisper from the other side of the dome, then to the Stone Gallery, giving a view out over the city, and higher to the Golden Gallery at the top of the dome and finally into the Golden Ball. The crypt of St Paul's is almost a cathedral in itself, with massive tombs of Nelson and Wellington and Wellington's 18-ton funeral carriage, which carried his body to St Paul's in 1852.

Smithfield
The largest meat market in the world is on the site of a medieval tournament ground. St Bartholomew's Hospital, south of Smithfield, is the oldest hospital in London; it was founded by a courtier of Henry I in 1123. In the nearby church of St Bartholomew the Great, built at the same time, is the font where the artist Hogarth was baptised in 1697. Further south rises the dome of the Central Criminal Court, the Old Bailey, with its bronze figure of Justice, built in 1902 on the site of Newgate Prison. The street here was widened to take the crowds who watched executions; Michael Barrett, an Irish nationalist hanged at Newgate in 1868 for causing an explosion at Clerkenwell, was the last person publicly executed in England.

Strand
The Victorian Gothic building of the Law Courts, with its pinnacles, spires and statues, is at the east end of the Strand. Public galleries are open for the hearing of civil cases.

Near by is the Wren Church of St Clement Danes, the St Clement's in the 'Oranges and Lemons' nursery rhyme and now the official church of the Royal Air Force. Further west are St Mary-le-Strand, a masterpiece of James Gibbs, built in 1714; and Somerset House, where the registers of all births, marriages and deaths in England and Wales were kept from 1837 until 1974.

Temple
A secluded island of barristers' chambers, ancient halls and great lawns between the roar of traffic in Fleet Street to the north and the Embankment to the south. It is reached from Fleet Street by 17th-century gateways and shaded alleys and consists of the Inner and Middle Temples, two of the great Inns of Court. The buildings, much restored after war damage, include noble assembly and dining-halls—where a prospective barrister must eat three dinners a term for 12 terms before he can qualify—and the beautifully restored 12th-century Temple Church.

Tower of London
William the Conqueror's magnificent bastion tells the history of England over almost 1000 years. William began the White Tower, and further building went on until the 19th century.

It was the Royal Mint from the 13th century to 1834, and a prison from its early years. Traitors' Gate, leading to and from the river, and the site of the execution block on Tower Green, within the walls of the Tower, recall the times when Anne Boleyn, Lady Jane Grey, the Earl of Essex and the Duke of Monmouth were executed in the Tower.

The Crown Jewels are shown in a new top-security setting, and the Armouries house a comprehensive collection of weapons and armour, including a full-size suit of armour for an elephant, used at the Battle of Plassey, in India, in 1757.

The centre of government and fashion

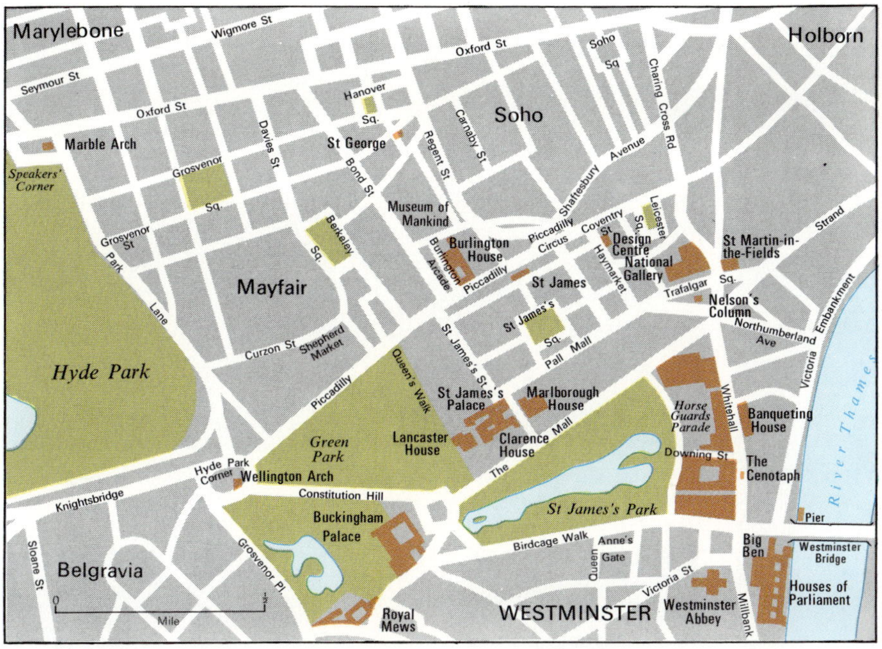

There are less than 4 square miles of land to the historic district of Westminster; but within this narrow compass, decisions have been taken which have shaped the destiny of Britain. For Westminster contains the nation's law-making and administrative nerve centre. The grand fretted silhouette of the Houses of Parliament rises beside the river; leading up to Trafalgar Square is Whitehall with its Ministries; and off Whitehall, at No. 10 Downing Street, stands the unpretentious house where the Prime Minister lives and the Cabinet meets.

Old Westminster and its modern extension into London's West End contribute many other strands to national life. There is the pageantry of Buckingham Palace, home of the monarch, and Westminster Abbey, burial-place of kings and stage for coronations; there is Soho's night life; the high fashion of Mayfair; the elegant club life of St James's; and the famous department stores of Oxford Street and Regent Street.

A guide book of 1851 commented that 'Westminster loves to spend lavishly what London has laboriously earned'. As far as spending goes, this is still true. For the West End contains not only the shopping centre of Britain, but many of London's leading hotels, restaurants, night-clubs, cinemas and theatres.

River trips From Apr. to Sept. there are boat trips from Westminster Pier to Hampton Court, stopping at Putney, Kew and Richmond; four hours each way.

Events Changing the Guard takes place at Buckingham Palace daily at 11.30 a.m. Mounting the Guard is at Horse Guards Parade at 11 a.m. on weekdays and 10 a.m. on Sun. The Trooping the Colour ceremony takes place at Horse Guards Parade usually on the second Sat. in June. The State opening of Parliament is in late Oct./early Nov. Remembrance Day Service at the Cenotaph is on the second Sun. in Nov. Military and brass-band concerts are held in St James's Park on weekday afternoons in the summer; there are lunchtime concerts on Mon. and Tues. in St. Martin-in-the-Fields. Frequent art exhibitions are held at the Arts Council, 105 Piccadilly, open Mon. to Fri. The Royal Academy of Arts, Burlington House, Piccadilly, holds a Winter Exhibition from Jan. to Mar. and a Summer Exhibition from May to early Aug. The Maundy Money is presented in London on Maundy Thur. every 3rd year. The Royal Horticultural Society Spring Flower Show is held at the Society's Hall, Vincent Square, in mid-Apr. The Antique Dealers' Fair and Exhibition is at Grosvenor House, Park Lane, mid-June. The Costermongers' Harvest Festival is held at St Martin-in-the-Fields on first Sun. in Oct. Trafalgar Day service and parade at Nelson's Column on Oct. 1. There is carol singing most evenings, from about Dec. 14 to Christmas Eve, round a decorated tree in Trafalgar Square.

Places to see *Banqueting House*, Whitehall: Tues. to Sat., and Sun. afternoon. *Design Centre*, Haymarket: weekdays, and Wed. and Thur. evenings. *Houses of Parliament*: public galleries; after 2 p.m. Mon. to Fri. during sessions; tours on Sat. *Jewel Tower*, Old Palace Yard: weekdays. *Lancaster House*: Easter to mid-Dec., Sat., Sun. and Bank Hol. afternoons; closed during conferences. *Marlborough House*, Pall Mall: by appointment. *Museum of Mankind*, Burlington Gardens: weekdays, Sun. afternoon. *National Gallery*, Trafalgar Square, and *National Portrait Gallery*, St Martins Place, both weekdays and Sun. afternoon. *Queen's Gallery*, Buckingham Palace: Tues. to Sat. and Sun. afternoon; also Bank Hol. Mon. *Royal Mews*: Wed. and Thur. afternoons; closed Royal Ascot week. *Tate Gallery*, Millbank: weekdays and Sun. afternoon. *Westminster Hall*: Mon. to Thur. mornings when Parliament in session; other times Mon. to Sat.

Buckingham Palace
The principal home of the sovereign since the time of Queen Victoria. Built in 1703 for the Duke of Buckingham, it was remodelled by John Nash for George IV, but the dignified classical façade was added only in 1913.

Grosvenor Square
This large square is dominated by the massive United States Embassy, built in 1960 and designed by the Finnish-American architect Eero Saarinen. A building on the north side has a plaque commemorating the fact that General Eisenhower planned the invasion of Europe at his headquarters in the square. In the gardens is a memorial statue of President Franklin D. Roosevelt.

Houses of Parliament
Officially the New Palace of Westminster, Parliament stands on the site of the principal royal residence from the time of Edward the Confessor to that of Henry VIII. The old palace, which had long been a meeting-place of parliament, was almost entirely destroyed by fire in 1834, except for the moated 14th-century Jewel Tower, the chapel crypt and the magnificent Westminster Hall. The present Houses of Parliament, a majestically rambling and elaborate group of buildings in the Gothic style, were built between 1840 and 1860 by Sir Charles Barry and A. W. Pugin. The House of Commons, destroyed by fire in an air-raid in 1941, was restored after the war to its old character. The chamber preserves the intimate scale of the original building, as recommended by Sir Winston Churchill, who felt that a small space favoured 'good House of Commons speaking'. The Clock Tower by the House of Commons is famous for its bell, Big Ben, named after the first Commissioner of Works, Sir Benjamin Hall. In the tower are cells where MPs can be confined for a breach of Parliamentary privilege. The last occasion was in 1880, when Charles Bradlaugh, MP for Northampton and an advocate of free thought, was imprisoned for refusing to take the oath.

Mayfair
Much of the 18th-century layout of streets and squares is still to be seen, as in Berkeley Square and Grosvenor Square; but the huge modern blocks of offices, flats and hotels are now much more prominent than the older buildings. Curzon Street retains some beautiful old houses, notably Crewe House, a Georgian mansion built for Edward Shepherd, an architect whose name was given to Shepherd Market, a 'village' of narrow streets close by. The name Mayfair comes from a traditional fair which was held in the market every May, on a site now marked by a plaque.

Oxford Street
The most popular shopping street in London, famous for its multiple stores. Marble Arch, at the west end, was

LONDON'S HEARTBEAT *Piccadilly Circus is traditionally the heart of London's West End. All the principal theatres are within walking distance of Eros, and the centre of London's cinema world, Leicester Square, is but a short distance along Coventry Street*

TRAFALGAR SQUARE *The spacious square was laid out in 1829–41 to commemorate Nelson's naval victory of 1805. Around Nelson's Column and Landseer's four bronze lions swirl the familiar London pigeons, which are fed by sightseers*

WESTMINSTER FAÇADES *St George pursues the Dragon every hour over Liberty's store in Regent Street. Pillars grace the entrance to the Haymarket Theatre (centre), rebuilt by John Nash in 1820. In St James's Street is the 18th-century façade of Boodle's Club*

designed by John Nash in 1828, and was originally intended to be the entrance to Buckingham Palace. Speakers' Corner, just inside Hyde Park near Marble Arch, is an open space where anyone may exercise his right of free speech with no hindrance except the ordeal of heckling. Debating is at its liveliest on Sundays, when large crowds gather.

Pall Mall
This broad thoroughfare took its name from 'paille-maille', an old French game resembling croquet which was introduced in the reign of Charles II. It is the centre of London club life. Many famous clubs, such as The Athenaeum and White's, are in or near the street.

St James's Square was laid out in the 17th century as a fashionable quarter, mainly for the aristocracy. Most of the houses in the square have been rebuilt; No. 14 is the London Library, and No. 10, Chatham House, is the Royal Institute of International Affairs.

Piccadilly
The street is said to have taken its name from Piccadilly Hall, a house built near by in the 17th century by a maker of 'piccadils', a neckwear popular at the time. On the south side is St James's Church, built *c.* 1684 by Wren and his only surviving church in the West End. On the north side is Burlington House, home of the Royal Academy of Fine Arts. Burlington Arcade, close by, is an elegant Regency shopping promenade.

Piccadilly Circus is the hub of London's entertainment world, lit up at night by huge advertising signs. In the centre is the memorial fountain to the 7th Earl of Shaftesbury, the Victorian philanthropist, topped by a winged archer which everyone knows as Eros, but which the sculptor, Sir Alfred Gilbert, intended as the Angel of Christian Charity. It was unveiled in 1893. Radiating from Piccadilly Circus are Regent Street and Piccadilly; Shaftesbury Avenue and the Haymarket, famous for their theatres; and Coventry Street, which leads to the centre of London's cinema world, Leicester Square.

Regent Street
A popular shopping street, first constructed by John Nash in 1820–3 as part of a boulevard designed to connect the Prince Regent's house overlooking St James's Park with his newly acquired property of Regent's Park. The houses in the street have largely been rebuilt since that time, though the curved section of the street north-westwards from Piccadilly Circus follows the bold sweep envisaged by Nash.

Hanover Square, to the west, was laid out in 1717; the contemporary church of St George's, Hanover Square, has long been noted for fashionable weddings. Lady Hamilton, Shelley, Disraeli, and George Eliot were married in the church. East of Regent Street is Carnaby Street, famous for its lively clothing shops for young people.

St James's Palace
This rambling brick mansion, built for Henry VIII, was the official residence of the sovereign until the time of Queen Victoria. Sentries of the Brigade of Guards parade each day in front of the picturesque Tudor gatehouse. A courtyard accessible to the public leads to the Chapel Royal, built *c.* 1532. Clarence House, to the west, built in 1825 by Nash for the Duke of Clarence (later William IV) and enlarged in 1873, is the London residence of the Queen Mother.

St James's Park
One of the smaller royal parks, and one of the most beautiful. The island in the lake is preserved as a breeding-place for water-fowl; the pelicans are particular favourites with Londoners.

The Mall, on the north side, forms a grand ceremonial approach to Buckingham Palace. The wide boulevard, with its double avenue of plane trees, makes a wonderful processional avenue for State

SHOPPING ARCADE *The Royal Opera Arcade, off Pall Mall, is the earliest London arcade. It was built in 1817*

COUNTRY IN THE TOWN *Queen's Walk, on the east side of Green Park, typifies the peaceful green spaces in central London*

BIG BEN *The clock tower of the House of Commons, at the north end of Westminster Bridge, is named after its bell. In the background to its right are the twin towers of Westminster Abbey and, further right, the tower of Westminster Cathedral*

BUTTON COSTUMES *The street traders' Pearly King and Queen attend a Harvest Festival at St Martin-in-the-Fields*

MODERN SKYLINE *The modern office block of Millbank Tower, 34 storeys high, rises beyond a Victorian street lamp*

pageants, and the Queen drives this way to open Parliament, to attend the Trooping the Colour ceremony, and during State visits. Queen Anne's Gate, to the south, is a quiet close built in 1704 and the most charming street in London dating from the reign of that queen.

Soho

A bustling district of narrow, rather dowdy streets, famous for its foreign restaurants and shops—and its brash night-life. It became the principal foreign quarter of London after 1685, when thousands of French Protestant refugees began to flee across the Channel because of the revocation of the Edict of Nantes. The name is said to have come from the rallying cry 'So-ho', used by followers of the rebel Duke of Monmouth, who lived in the area, but it was more probably a hunting call. In Soho Square, which was laid out after the Restoration, there is a statue by C. G. Cibber of the Duke's father, Charles II.

Trafalgar Square

London's most famous square was laid out to commemorate Nelson's great naval victory of 1805. Dominating it is Nelson's Column; with its 17 ft high statue of the admiral at the top, it reaches a height of nearly 185 ft above the ground. At its base are four bronze lions by Sir Edwin Landseer.

The National Gallery, which houses one of the world's richest collections of paintings, overlooks the square from the north side, and to the north-east is the Classical church of St Martin-in-the-Fields, built in 1726 by James Gibbs.

Westminster Abbey

The most beautiful Gothic church in London, founded by Edward the Confessor in the 11th century. Among its features are Poets' Corner, where some of England's greatest writers are buried; the tomb of the Unknown Warrior, which commemorates the British servicemen who gave their lives in the First World War; and the Coronation Chair in Edward the Confessor's Chapel. All the coronations of the English sovereigns since that of William the Conqueror in 1066 have taken place in the church, and most of the sovereigns from Henry III to George II are buried there. The rebuilding of the church was begun in 1245, in the Early English style, for Henry III; the nave was not rebuilt until after 1376.

Whitehall

The street was named after a royal palace, of which nothing but the Banqueting House remains. The broad street, lined by many government offices, is the administrative centre of the country. Off Whitehall is Downing Street, unimposing in appearance in spite of its place in British life. No. 10 has been the official residence of the Prime Minister since 1732, when Sir Robert Walpole moved in after George II had offered the premises to him.

The Banqueting House, on the other side of Whitehall, designed by Inigo Jones and completed in 1622, was the first example in England of the new Classical style introduced from Italy. The magnificent ceiling was painted by Rubens. The Cenotaph was unveiled in 1920 on the anniversary of Armistice Day and now commemorates the British Empire and Commonwealth servicemen who died in the two World Wars. Wreaths are laid at its base at the Armistice Day ceremony each year.

Horse Guards, on the west side of Whitehall, is a picturesque 18th-century building with a clock tower, on the site of an old guard-house. Two mounted troopers of the Household Cavalry are posted there, and Mounting the Guard takes place every morning. Through the archway is the Horse Guards Parade, a broad parade ground, where in June, on the Queen's official birthday, the spectacular ceremony of Trooping the Colour is performed.

Pageants and ceremonies of the nation's capital

CHANGING THE GUARD

The guard at Buckingham Palace is changed at 11.30 a.m. daily. Usually it is formed from one of the regiments of Foot Guards—the Grenadier Guards, Coldstream Guards, Scots Guards (left), Irish Guards and Welsh Guards. A band leads the new guard from Wellington or Chelsea barracks to the Palace forecourt and after the ceremony it leads the old guard back to their barracks

CEREMONY OF THE KEYS

The Chief Warder (above) of the Yeoman Warders (left), with his escort, locks the gates of the Tower of London at 10 p.m. every day. By the Bloody Tower a sentry challenges them: 'Halt! Who goes there?' The Chief Warder answers, 'The keys.' 'Whose keys?' 'Queen Elizabeth's keys. God preserve Queen Elizabeth.' The sentry replies, 'Amen'

FIRING A ROYAL SALUTE

Gun salutes mark anniversaries such as that of the Queen's Accession on February 6 and her birthday on April 21. They are fired by the King's Troop of the Royal Horse Artillery in Hyde Park (above and right) and by the Honourable Artillery Company at the Tower

QUIT RENTS CEREMONY

A billhook, a hatchet, and six horseshoes and nails are handed by the City Solicitor to a representative of the Queen at the Law Courts in the Strand on October 26. The City pays this quit rent (rent in lieu of services) for land in Shropshire

MOUNTING THE GUARD

Mounting the Guard, the cavalry term for changing the guard, takes place at 11 a.m. on weekdays and 10 a.m. on Sundays at the Horse Guards, a square facing Whitehall with buildings designed by William Kent c. 1745 and built in the 1750's. The guard is formed by units of the Household Cavalry—the Life Guards and the Blues and Royals. When the Queen is in London, an officer, a corporal of horse, 16 troopers and a trumpeter on a grey horse take part in the ceremony

The Blues and Royals (above) can be identified by the red plumes on their helmets and by their blue uniforms. The Life Guards (right) wear white plumes and red tunics. Both wear cuirasses, or armour to the waist

THE GLORIOUS PAGEANTRY OF TROOPING THE COLOUR

Trooping the Colour on Horse Guards Parade is such an impressive pageant that it draws crowds even to the rehearsals before the ceremony proper on the second Saturday in June. The Trooping marks the official birthday of the Queen and each year the colour, or flag, of one of the five regiments of Foot Guards is displayed to the music of massed bands

The five regiments of Foot Guards can be identified by the plumes in their caps, or bearskins, and by the spacing of the buttons on their tunics. The Grenadier Guards have white plumes and evenly spaced buttons; the Coldstreams, red plumes and buttons in pairs; the Scots Guards, no plumes and buttons in threes; the Irish Guards, blue plumes and buttons in fours; the Welsh Guards, white-and-green plumes and buttons in fives. At the Trooping, the Foot Guards line up to await the Queen, who is in uniform and riding side-saddle. The colour is then 'trooped' or displayed before her

THE BARGE MASTERS

The role of the Thames in London's history is recalled by the ceremonial Barge Masters still appointed by the Queen and four of the City Companies, or trade guilds (above, left to right, Vintners', Fishmongers', the Queen's, Watermen's and Dyers'). The Queen's Barge Master attends the State Opening of Parliament. The Fishmongers' Barge Master starts the annual Doggett's Coat and Badge race for Thames watermen, which is rowed from London Bridge to Albert Bridge in late July. The race was begun in 1715 by Thomas Doggett, a London theatre manager, to mark the anniversary of George I's accession. The winner receives an orange-coloured coat, and a silver arm badge (right) embossed with the white horse of Hanover

BEATING THE BOUNDS

The custom of beating the bounds, or walking round the parish boundaries, began in the Middle Ages when there were few maps of England and it was necessary for officials to point out the extent of each parish. The custom is followed on Ascension Day every three years (1978, 1981, and so on) at the Tower. It starts with a service at the Chapel of St Peter ad Vincula; then choirboys go round beating the boundary stones with willow wands

OPENING OF THE COURTS

A service at Westminster Abbey marks the start of the Legal Year in October. All the judges and leading barristers in England and Wales are invited to attend the service, and after it they walk in procession (above) to the House of Lords for the traditional Lord Chancellor's Breakfast. The Michaelmas law sitting which begins in October is the first of the year's four sittings; the others are Hilary (starting in January), Easter, and Trinity (May)

THE DAY A PROUD CITY FÊTES ITS LORD MAYOR

The Lord Mayor's Show is London's great gesture of pride in its history and strength as a world commercial centre. It is a defiant gesture, too, for the ceremony is always held on the second Saturday in November, when the city is often wrapped in mist or rain. The pikemen in their half-armour (above) accompany the newly elected Lord Mayor in his gilded coach from Guildhall, past St Paul's Cathedral, down Fleet Street to the Royal Courts of Justice, where he takes his oath of office before the Lord Chief Justice. On the following Monday evening, the Lord Mayor gives a splendid banquet at Guildhall; this has two traditions—a first course of turtle soup and a speech from the Prime Minister. The Lord Mayor's Show began about 600 years ago as a waterborne procession with ornate barges sailing down the River Thames. One of the most distinguished of London's Lord Mayors was Dick Whittington (d. 1423), who held office four times

TRADITIONAL ROADSWEEP

The road is swept for the Vintners when their Grand Master is installed in July

THE SWAN-UPPERS

Ownership of swans on the River Thames is shared by the Sovereign and two City Companies—the Dyers and Vintners—a right going back to the Middle Ages when swans were a table delicacy. Swanmasters of the Queen and the companies go out in boats in July to lift and mark the birds

BLUE COAT BOYS' MARCH

Boys of Christ's Hospital, Horsham, West Sussex, wear 16th-century dress as they march, in late September, to a service at St Sepulchre's, Holborn

ROYAL MAUNDY MONEY

Specially minted silver coins are distributed by the Sovereign in London on Maundy Thursday every third year The custom goes back to the Middle Ages when the monarch washed the feet of the poor and gave them alms

The Lord Mayor's coach, weighing 4 tons and pulled by six horses, was built in 1757 and was painted by Giovanni Cipriani, a Florentine historical painter and engraver. A bodyguard of members of the Company of Pikemen and Musketeers (below right) marches beside the coach with its liveried coachman and attendants. Beadles (below left), who were once civic officials, are among many in the procession who wear traditional costumes. Each year a theme relating to London life or history is chosen, and floats carrying tableaux on this theme precede the Lord Mayor's coach. The Lord Mayor, who is also the City's Chief Magistrate, is selected by the liverymen of the City Companies, and the Show and banquet are only the beginning of his busy and expensive year. He goes to four or five dinners a week and makes at least one speech a day during the week—although he takes weekends off. He receives an allowance (£27,000 in 1973) from City funds to help with his expenses, but he must supplement this with a considerable sum from his own pocket. He pays half the cost of the banquet and the other half is met by the two Sheriffs. But a Lord Mayor regards such financial sacrifices as worth while because of the prestige, since in his year of office he is second in importance in the City only to the Sovereign. The Lord Mayor entertains at the partly 15th-century but greatly restored Guildhall, which was damaged both in the Great Fire of 1666 and the Blitz. His official residence, the Mansion House, was originally designed in Palladian style by George Dance the Elder in the 18th century, but has been altered since

Mews and museums

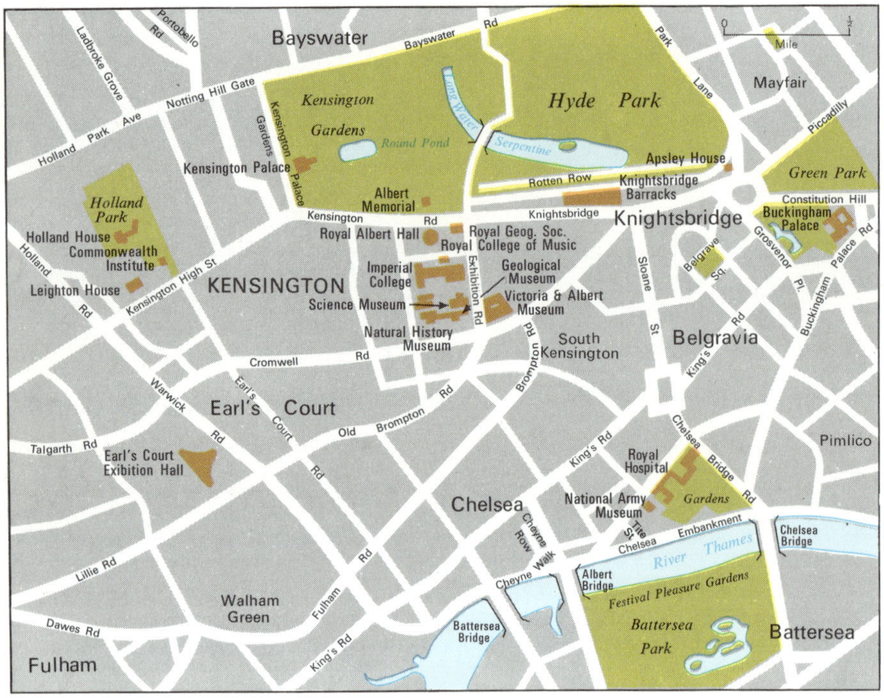

HOMAGE TO THE ARTS *Beyond the figures of sculptors on the Albert*

Angling There is coarse fishing at the south-east end of the Serpentine in Hyde Park.

Boating Sailing and rowing on the Serpentine, where there are boats for hire. Model yachting on the Round Pond in Kensington Gardens.

Horse riding On Rotten Row in Hyde Park. There are several riding schools in the area.

Events Earl's Court Exhibition Hall is the scene of the International Boat Show early in Jan., and of Cruft's Dog Show in mid-Feb. The English Folk Dance and Song Societies Festival is held at the Royal Albert Hall in Feb. The Chelsea Flower Show is held in the grounds of the Chelsea Royal Hospital in late May. The Royal Tournament is in July at Earl's Court. The Henry Wood Promenade Concerts are given at the Royal Albert Hall from late July to mid-Sept., and the European Brass Band Contest is held there in Oct. The Fine Arts and Antiques Fair is held in June, the biennial Motorfair (1979, 1981, etc.) for two weeks in Oct., the International Caravan and Camping Exhibition in Nov., and the Royal Smithfield Show during the first week of Dec. at Earl's Court.

Between Hyde Park and a bend in the Thames lies one of the most fashionable parts of London, combining Kensington, Chelsea, Knightsbridge and Belgravia. Here are two contrasting worlds—a select, conservative world of quiet Georgian squares, 'village' streets and mews (formerly stable-alleys) lined with smart white houses, antique shops and old inns; and a younger, livelier world of exotic restaurants, artists' studios, boutiques and discothèques.

The broad green stretches of Kensington Gardens and Hyde Park extend to the busy shopping streets of Kensington High Street and Knightsbridge. Near by is the great enclave of buildings erected by the Victorians to promote the arts and sciences—the domed Albert Hall, home of the 'Proms', and the ornately towered museums along Exhibition Road and Cromwell Road. Further south runs the King's Road, where brightly attired young men and girls buy and wear the latest fashions.

Until the 19th century, Kensington was a separate village outside the city limits. Its growth began in 1689 when William III bought a house there and made it into his Kensington Palace. He commissioned Wren to improve it, and designated about 26 surrounding acres as private grounds. Knightsbridge was then a hamlet, named after a bridge over the River Westbourne on which two knights, according to legend, duelled to the death. Belgravia was swampland, abounding in cut-throats and thieves; and Chelsea was a secluded riverside village. The growth of population in the 18th and 19th centuries swallowed these areas into inner London.

TOWER FOR TROOPS *Knightsbridge Barracks, designed by Sir Basil Spence, are the quarters of the Household Cavalry*

Memorial stands the Royal Albert Hall, with a frieze honouring the Arts and Sciences

OLD SOLDIERS *Army pensioners raise their three-cornered hats during a parade at Chelsea Royal Hospital on Oak Apple Day (May 29), the anniversary of the restoration of Charles II, who founded the hospital for veteran and invalid soldiers in 1682. The pensioners' uniforms are adapted from those of the Duke of Marlborough's armies in the early 18th century. Sir Christopher Wren designed the hospital building*

TOWER FOR A MUSEUM *The Natural History Museum was built in 1873*

Belgravia

A stately, opulent district, laid out in a spacious grid of crescents and squares, with solid, cream-coloured stucco mansions in Regency style. Belgrave Square was designed by George Basevi and built by Thomas Cubitt in 1825. Senior servants of the recently established Buckingham Palace moved there, and by 1860 it had become the residence of baronets and dukes. Today the square is partly occupied by embassies and professional societies.

Chelsea

In some places, Chelsea is a village, in some a booming, fashionable centre, and in others a cherished relic. Its main artery, the King's Road, was once a footpath through fields and later a private coach road for Charles II. Since the 18th century Chelsea has been a favourite haunt of writers and artists. It achieved a colourful notoriety in Victorian times as a result of the 'Bohemian' style of life of such residents as Whistler and Oscar Wilde. Today it has an abundance of boutiques, thronged by cosmopolitan, mainly young, customers. At its western end, where the street is less brightly painted, lie the houses, antique shops and junk shops of World's End. Here, and at the west end of the parallel Fulham Road, are found Chelsea's long-resident 'villagers', who put out the flags when their soccer team has won high honours. To the east lies the Chelsea Embankment, a fine Thames-side promenade with views of Battersea Park and the Festival Gardens on the opposite bank. On the west side of Chelsea Bridge, stretching from the Embankment, are the gardens of the Chelsea Royal Hospital, where each May the Chelsea Flower Show is held. The hospital, built by Sir Christopher Wren, was founded in 1682 by Charles II for veteran and invalid soldiers. A bronze statue of the king, by Grinling Gibbons, stands in the central quadrangle of the mellow brick buildings. About 500 army pensioners are lodged and boarded in the hospital. They can be seen wearing scarlet frock coats in summer, dark blue overcoats in winter, peaked caps for daily wear and three-cornered hats for ceremonial occasions. A National Army Museum was opened beside the Royal Hospital in 1971.

Cheyne Walk, separated from the Embankment by a line of gardens, is a row of fine early 18th-century houses, many with wrought-iron fences and gates. Several 19th-century authors and artists lived here, including the novelists George Eliot and Henry James; Whistler and Turner, both of whom painted scenes of Chelsea's river and bridges; and D. G. Rossetti, a leader of the Pre-Raphaelite movement in poetry and painting. Cheyne Row, off Cheyne Walk, is a quiet street of modest, unspoilt terraces built in 1708. The author Thomas Carlyle, known as the 'Sage of Chelsea', lived for 47 years at No. 24. The house still contains his manuscripts and personal possessions. J. S. Sargent, the painter, lived at 31 Tite Street and Oscar Wilde at No. 34.

Earl's Court

A busy cosmopolitan and residential area, best known for its exhibition hall, opened in 1937. The hall covers 18½ acres and can accommodate 20,000 people. Earl's Court also has a centre for Commonwealth visitors and an Overseas Visitors' Club. The lively Earl's Court Road has a wide variety of foreign food shops and restaurants.

Holland Park

The park once formed the private grounds of Holland House, a Jacobean mansion which was a meeting-place for Whig politicians in the 18th and early 19th centuries. The surviving east wing was restored after being bombed in 1941. Open-air concerts and plays are given in the gardens in summer.

The Commonwealth Institute, founded in 1887 in honour of Queen Victoria's Jubilee, was transferred in 1962 to the south end of Holland Park. Leighton House, built in 1866 for the artist Lord Leighton to his own design, has an Arab Hall decorated with Oriental tiles and elaborate stained-glass windows.

Hyde Park/Kensington Gardens

The two adjoining open spaces together make up the largest public park in central London—630 acres of grassland, flowers and trees, with a rural walk of about 4 miles around the perimeter. Hyde Park and Kensington Gardens belonged to Westminster Abbey until the Dissolution of the Monasteries in 1536, after which Henry VIII made the area a royal deer park. In 1635, Charles I opened it to the public and it became fashionable for carriage-driving and riding. In 1730 Queen Caroline, the wife of George II, ordered the creation of a lake by damming ponds fed by the now-vanished River Westbourne. The Kensington Gardens side of the lake was called the Long Water, and the Hyde Park side was called the Serpentine. Boating, sailing and bathing have been popular there ever since. The bridge crossing the lake marks the boundary between the two parks, and gives a delightful view of distant Westminster Abbey and the Houses of Parliament. Rotten Row, perhaps a corruption of 'Route du Roi', is a sandy, shady track south of the Serpentine, used by horse-riders. Kensington Gardens, first laid out in the reign of William III, were extended by Queen Anne and later by Queen Caroline. The Round Pond near the centre attracts model yachtsmen, and the statue of J. M. Barrie's character Peter Pan, near the Long Water, stands in the gardens.

The Albert Memorial was built in Hyde Park in 1876 as the national memorial to the Prince Consort. A statue shows the prince, underneath a huge Gothic canopy, with the catalogue of the Great Exhibition of 1851 which was held in Hyde Park. The memorial faces the Royal Albert Hall, an immense oval amphitheatre with a glass dome, built in 1871. The famous Promenade Concerts are held there in summer.

ROTTEN ROW *A carriage-and-pair take a jog-trot down Rotten Row, the sandy riding track stretching nearly a mile on the south of the Serpentine. The paths on either side were a fashionable rendezvous after church on Sunday mornings for Victorian society*

CHELSEA'S SAGE *A memorial to the writer Thomas Carlyle (1795–1881) stands near 24 Cheyne Row, home of the 'Sage of Chelsea' for 47 years. His manuscripts are still in the house*

FLOATING HOME *This converted barge at Chelsea Reach is one of the Thames houseboats whose owners combine a Chelsea address with a life afloat. Moorings at Chelsea are limited to 50*

Kensington
The east end of Kensington High Street is famous for its large and elegant department stores. West of Kensington Gardens and north of the High Street is Kensington Palace Gardens, a tree-lined street of great 19th-century mansions leading to Palace Green, where the novelist W. M. Thackeray died in 1863. In South Kensington the streets are narrower, the inns and cafés more intimate. Workers' cottages, in mews and back streets, have now become luxurious white-fronted residences. The mews used to be stables; the first stables to be called mews were the royal stables at Charing Cross, which stood on the site where once the royal falcons were kept in mews, or moulting cages.

The great museums of Kensington, which make this a centre of culture and science, were developed from the profits of the Great Exhibition of 1851. The Victoria and Albert Museum, behind its immense Renaissance-style façade, houses the national museum of applied arts, with treasures from all over the world. Across Exhibition Road stands the Natural History Museum, a great Romanesque palace which was built in 1880. Further up Exhibition Road are the Science and Geological Museums.

Kensington Palace
This was originally the country home of the Earl of Nottingham. In 1689 it was acquired by William III, who commissioned Wren to enlarge the palace. Further enlargements were made by William Kent for George I, and Kensington Palace remained the residence of the reigning sovereign until the death of George II in 1760. The State apartments contain magnificent rooms by Wren and Kent and a collection of portraits, paintings and costumes.

WHEN THE MUSEUMS ARE OPEN

Apsley House, Wellington Museum, Hyde Park Corner: Tues., Wed., Thur., and Sat.; also Sun. afternoons. *Carlyle's House* (NT), Cheyne Row: weekdays except Mon. and Tues.; also Sun. afternoons. *Commonwealth Institute*, Kensington High Street: weekdays and Sun. afternoons. *Geological Museum*, Exhibition Road: weekdays and Sun. afternoons. *Leighton House*, Holland Park Road, art gallery and museum: weekdays. *National Army Museum*, Chelsea: weekdays and Sun. afternoons. *Natural History Museum*, Cromwell Road: weekdays and Sun. afternoons. *Science Museum*, Exhibition Road: weekdays, Sun. afternoons. *Victoria and Albert Museum*, Exhibition Road; weekdays except Fri.; also Sun. afternoons.

From Bloomsbury to London's northern heights

Angling There is coarse fishing in the Hampstead Heath Ponds.

Boating There are boats for hire on Regent's Park Lake. During the summer there are boat trips on the Grand Union Canal and Regent's Canal from Little Venice. The Zoo waterbus leaves Little Venice hourly on weekdays and Sun. afternoons, from Mar. to Oct.

Cricket The season at Lord's Cricket Ground, St John's Wood, is from mid-Apr. to early Sept.

Swimming In the Hampstead Ponds, Highgate Ponds, Parliament Hill Lido and the Oasis, Holborn.

Events Camden holds a festival of the arts for two weeks in Mar. The London Cart-horse Parade is held in Regent's Park on Easter Mon., and the Open Air Theatre in Regent's Park presents a season of plays during the summer. The Hampstead open-air art exhibition is held in Heath Street every weekend from June to mid-Aug. A fair is held on Hampstead Heath on the late Summer Bank Hol. Military and brass-band concerts are held in Regent's Park on Sun. and Bank Hols. during the summer. From early June to late July, lakeside orchestral concerts are held on Sat. evenings at Kenwood. Sun. evening recitals are held in Kenwood House, end of Apr. to early June.

Places to see *British Museum* and *The British Library*: weekdays and Sun. afternoons. *Courtauld Institute Galleries*, Woburn Square: weekdays and Sun. afternoons. *Cricket Memorial Gallery*, Lord's Cricket Ground, St John's Wood: open on match days. *Dickens House*, Doughty Street: weekdays. *Fenton House* (NT), Hampstead: Jan. to Mar. and Nov., Sun. afternoon and Sat.; Apr. to Oct., Wed. to Sat., and Sun. afternoon. *Foundling Hospital*, Brunswick Square, art gallery: Mon. to Fri. *Iveagh Bequest*, Kenwood House: daily. *Jewish Museum*, Woburn House: Mon. to Thur. afternoons, Fri. and Sun. mornings. *Keats House*, Hampstead: weekdays, Sun. afternoons. *London Zoo*: daily. *Madame Tussaud's*: daily. *Percival David Foundation of Chinese Art*, Gordon Square: Tues. to Fri.; also Mon. afternoon and Sat. morning. *Planetarium*: daily. *Pollock's Toy Museum*, Scala Street: daily except Sun. *Wallace Collection*, Manchester Square: weekdays, Sun. afternoon. *Wellcome Institute for the History of Medicine*, Euston Road: Mon. to Fri.

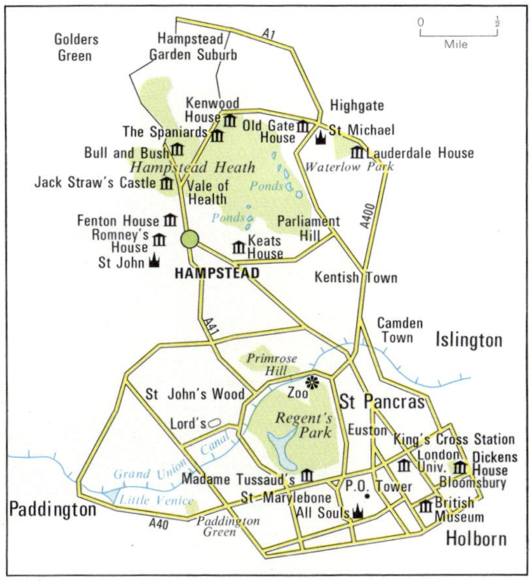

London's northward spread is the result of a progression which countless Londoners have made over the last three centuries—a withdrawal from the noise and bustle of the inner city to rural retreats within easy travelling distance of the centre. The areas just north of Oxford Street were first built up in the 18th century on the estates of profit-minded aristocratic landowners such as the Russells (Dukes of Bedford). These areas have a fine regularity of basic layout, from Bloomsbury in the east to Paddington in the west. Their grid of streets holds several famous squares, such as Bedford Square, the best-preserved of all London's squares, and is interrupted by the occasional delightful irregularity of a captured village. There is the meander of Marylebone High Street between the development of the Portman and Harley-Cavendish estates, or Paddington Green, which keeps something of its restful rural character in spite of the massive new road developments in the area.

Further north, a generally glum district is relieved by Regent's Park, with its dreaming white terraces. Just north-east of the park are Park Village East and Park Village West where, in the early 1800's, John Nash first experimented with little villas in varying styles, ancestors of much of the suburban architectural development of Greater London in later years. This is a district of odd contrasts, echoing with the cry of gibbons and roar of lions from the nearby Zoo, and the calling of trains driving north from the great railway termini at Euston, St Pancras and King's Cross. From here the ground begins to rise towards Hampstead and Highgate. These unusually attractive suburbs stand on steep hills, two of the northern heights of London, looking out over the Thames basin in one direction, and in the other across the great plain once covered by the forest of Middlesex. Between them stretches London's most famous open space, Hampstead Heath. Both Hampstead and Highgate have long been fashionable places to live in, especially in artistic and literary circles. Past residents include Constable, Keats, Coleridge, A. E. Housman and the author of *The Forsyte Saga*, John Galsworthy.

Bloomsbury
A district noted for its handsome squares, among them Russell Square, Bloomsbury Square and Bedford Square. Bloomsbury in the 18th century was fashionable as a place of residence for rich merchants and aristocrats. It is now dominated by two great institutions of learning and scholarship—the British Museum, which contains The British Library, and the widely scattered University of London, whose main building is the bulky Senate House, with a tower 200 ft high. The museum's vast and growing collection of treasures includes the magnificent Elgin Marbles from the Parthenon in Greece and the Sutton Hoo Ship Burial. The British Library, formed in 1973 mainly from collections held by the British Museum, has more than 8 million volumes, and among its manuscripts are two of the four extant copies of Magna Carta.

Bloomsbury is rich in associations with intellectual and artistic figures, especially the members of the 'Bloomsbury Group', who lived there in the early 1900's. Among them were the novelists E. M. Forster and Virginia Woolf and the economist J. M. Keynes.

Euston
For many years a shabby, nondescript quarter, Euston has been almost completely rebuilt and now forms one of the most impressive areas of modern London. In Euston Road are three of the world's most famous railway stations. The enormous St Pancras Station, completed in 1874, has a Gothic façade displaying the grandiosely ornate style beloved of the Victorians. Long reviled by critics as hideous and revolting, it has now come into favour as a 'period piece', and in the late 1960's a move to demolish the façade stirred up a vociferous and successful protest. St Pancras serves the central Midlands and Yorkshire. King's Cross, near by, serving the eastern Midlands and the north, has a front which has been praised as more 'functional', while Euston Station, serving the western Midlands and the north, was completely rebuilt during the 1960's in uncompromisingly plain modern style.

Hampstead
The suburb was no more than a country village until the 18th century, when the discovery of a mineral spring led to its becoming a resort of high society. Many of the streets and houses of this period have survived unspoilt, and it is these, together with the magnificent Heath, which give Hampstead its special character. Church Row is Hampstead's most enchanting street, with the earliest terraces built *c.* 1720. It leads from Heath Street to St John's, the 18th-century parish church of Hampstead. The painter John Constable (1776–1837), for long a local resident, is buried in the churchyard. Three of his Hampstead paintings, including one of the Heath, are in the Tate Gallery. Well Walk and Flask Walk recall Hampstead's days as a popular spa. The reputedly healing waters (no longer used) were taken from a local well and sold in flasks to visitors.

Keats Grove is noted for its fine Regency houses, including Keats House, where the poet John Keats (1795–1821) lived from 1818 to 1820, during his most creative period. In the house are many personal relics of the poet.

The oldest house in Hampstead is Fenton House, a beautiful brick mansion of *c.* 1693, enclosed by a delightful walled garden. It stands in Hampstead

RESTAURANT IN THE SKY *A revolving restaurant crowns Britain's highest structure, the GPO's 620-ft telecommunications tower, which was completed in 1964*

Grove, in a quarter which still preserves its old village atmosphere, a network of narrow passages, intricate alleys and tiny squares. In Holly Bush Hill, lower down, is the weatherboarded Romney's House, built in 1797 for the artist George Romney. Hampstead Grove leads up to the Heath, but it is worth turning off first to see the Admiral's House, in Admiral's Walk. A painting of the house, by Constable, is in the Tate Gallery. The painter's first home in Hampstead was 2 Lower Terrace. At Grove Lodge, near by, the novelist John Galsworthy lived from 1918 to 1933.

Hampstead Heath

An area of unspoilt heathland about 790 acres in extent. It is hard to realise that this is only a few miles from the heart of London. The Heath spreads itself over sandy hills and into secluded valleys; there are broad stretches of grass and gorse, and trees in rich variety. It is a great breathing space and pleasure ground for Londoners, offering many delightful walks and other open-air attractions. In summer, the visitor can bathe, fish, ride, fly kites and take part in various games; and in winter there are skiing and tobogganing if enough snow is on the ground. On Bank Holiday weekends, a fair takes place near the 'hamlet' known as the Vale of Health (possibly so-called because its inhabitants were unaffected by the Great Plague of 1665).

By the Whitestone Pond, where the poet Shelley is said to have sailed paper boats for children, is a flagstaff which marks the highest point on the Heath. Close by is Jack Straw's Castle, an inn known to Dickens and Thackeray and thought to be named after one of Wat Tyler's men in the Peasants' Revolt of 1381. The inn was bombed during the war, and rebuilt in battlemented, mock-medieval style. The Spaniards Road runs along a ridge through the Heath to the Spaniards Inn, an 18th-century tavern with a weatherboarded front and attractive garden, near the gates of Kenwood House; the building was possibly the home of a Spanish ambassador in the 17th century. According to legend, the highwayman Dick Turpin frequently visited the inn.

Kenwood House, whose beautiful grounds merge with Hampstead Heath, is a charming Georgian mansion rebuilt in 1769 by Robert Adam for the 1st Earl of Mansfield. The house, with its superb art collection, was bequeathed to the nation in 1927 by the 1st Earl of Iveagh, the brewer.

Highgate

The older part of Highgate, which stands on the top of the twin hill to Hampstead, retains, like its neighbour, the flavour of an 18th-century village. The centre of the old quarter is South Grove, which leads from the High Street to the Old Hall, built in 1691, and to St Michael's, the parish church of 1832, whose landmark of a spire is visible from central London. The most delightful street in Highgate is The Grove, which has houses of the late 17th and early 18th centuries. The poet Samuel Taylor Coleridge (1772–1834) lived in a friend's home, 3 The Grove, from 1816 until his death.

At the junction of Hampstead Lane with High Street, the highest point in Highgate, is the Old Gate House, an inn named after a vanished tollhouse. North Road, which starts near by, has some 18th-century houses, but its most famous buildings are the Highpoint flats, a landmark of the area as well as in the development of modern British architecture. The flats, designed in 1936 by Lubetkin and Tecton, were praised by the French architect Le Corbusier as a 'vertical garden city'.

The poet A. E. Housman (1859–1936) lodged at Byron House in North Road and wrote 'A Shropshire Lad' there. The oldest and finest house in Highgate is Cromwell House, in Highgate Hill

HAMPSTEAD HEATH *Contrasting with the green peace of London's best-loved open space*

A VIEW OF THE 'VILLAGE' *Beyond a mist-filled stretch of Hampstead Heath rises Highgate, twin 'village' to Hampstead. Many charming houses cluster on the hill*

CHURCH ROW *This famous Hampstead street dates from c. 1720. The houses are in a variety of styles, and the street has a row of trees down the middle*

is the skyline of the city centre 4 miles away

KEATS HOUSE, HAMPSTEAD *Keats wrote his 'Ode to a Nightingale' here*

KENWOOD CONCERT *The lakeside at Kenwood is an idyllic setting for music*

opposite Waterlow Park. Built *c.* 1637, in a warm red brick and with an attractive stone doorcase, it is now a hostel for Roman Catholic students for the priesthood. Near the foot of Highgate Hill the Whittington Stone marks the spot where Dick Whittington, a mayor of London in the Middle Ages, is supposed to have rested with his cat when he heard Bow Bells recalling him to the City.

Waterlow Park, reached from the High Street, is a secluded retreat on the slopes of a hill above the valley which runs up towards Kenwood House. It has several small lakes, attracting a varied bird life. Lauderdale House, owned after 1660 by the 1st Duke of Lauderdale, a minister of Charles II, stands on a terrace just inside the park, surrounded by a pleasant garden. Near the park is Highgate Cemetery (now closed) where several famous people are buried, including Karl Marx and the novelist George Eliot (1819–80).

Islington

A favourite place of residence in the 18th and early 19th centuries, as it is again today. Many streets and terraces built during its earlier prosperity have been attractively renovated.

The centre of the old part was Islington Green, near which is the picturesque Camden Passage, an alley noted for its market and antique shops. Canonbury Square, built *c.* 1800, is characteristic of late-Georgian Islington. The tall Canonbury Tower, now part of a theatre, was built *c.* 1595.

Marylebone

The district was laid out as a select residential quarter in the 18th century and it has many streets and squares with complete terraces of that period. Marylebone Road was built in 1756 as part of a new thoroughfare connecting Paddington and Islington. Today, its buildings show a curious mixture of styles. The 16-storey Castrol House, built in 1959 opposite Marylebone Town Hall, is one of the earlier and more successful examples of the modern 'match-box' style. Madame Tussaud's Museum of Waxworks, the Planetarium, and the Edwardian building which houses the Royal Academy of Music, contribute to the variety. The upper part of Gloucester Place, alongside, leads to Dorset Square, which has unspoilt terraces of the early 19th century.

Baker Street is famous as the home of the first great detective in fiction, Conan Doyle's Sherlock Holmes, who shared rooms with Dr Watson at '221B'. Other famous streets in the district are Harley Street, home of fashionable medical practice; Wigmore Street, with its small concert hall where musicians traditionally make their London début; and Wimpole Street, where the poetess Elizabeth Barrett Browning (1806–61) lived for 10 years with her family.

Portman Square, which lies behind Selfridge's store in Oxford Street, was laid out after 1761. The finest of its

LITTLE VENICE *Some of London's canals, largely fallen into disuse since their heyday in the 19th century, have been revived with the introduction of pleasure trips. Colourful barges ply between Little Venice, a basin of the Grand Union Canal, and the Zoo*

ZOO AVIARY *The aviary at London Zoo, its angles reflected in a placid reach of Regent's Canal, was designed by Lord Snowdon and opened in 1965*

NASH TERRACES *Gleaming white stucco and Classical decoration are features of the elegant terraces in Regent's Park, which John Nash laid out in the Regency era*

surviving houses of that period is Home House, built by Robert Adam and now occupied by the Courtauld Institute of Art, part of the University of London. Manchester Square, to the east, was completed in 1788. In the square is Hertford House, the home of the Wallace Collection, the richest privately formed art collection in London and now the property of the nation; a famous picture in the collection is Frans Hals's *The Laughing Cavalier*.

Paddington

Most of this district was laid out to a regular pattern during the first half of the 19th century, and it has now come into popularity again as a residential district. Along wide boulevards like Westbourne Terrace, families are moving back into tall Victorian houses which have been split for years into single-room apartments. Paddington's huge railway station was built by Isambard Brunel, the famous Victorian engineer. Little Venice is a secluded basin of the Grand Union Canal, from which trips can be taken to the Zoo.

Regent's Park

One of the largest parks in London and the most complete, with everything a park should have: acres of playing fields, shady avenues, an attractive lake for boating and sailing, a smaller boating pond for children, beautiful gardens, and a charming open-air theatre. On its north side is London Zoo, which has the most representative collection of animals in the world. The park was laid out in the early 1800's by John Nash for the Prince Regent, who contemplated taking one of the country villas to have been built there. But the scheme fell through, and in 1838 the park was opened to the public. Nash also designed the great series of terraces which surround three sides of the park.

Riverside home of kings

Boating There is sailing and rowing on the Thames above Putney and boats can be hired at Richmond and Kingston; also boating at Battersea Park. The Oxford and Cambridge Boat Race, from Putney to Mortlake, and the Head of the River Race are held on a Saturday in late Mar. or early Apr. The Schools' Head of the River Race, from Hammersmith to Putney, is held in Mar. and the Wingfield Sculls from Putney to Mortlake in May. Regattas are held in the summer at Putney, Hammersmith, Richmond, Twickenham and Kingston.

Angling There is coarse fishing on the River Thames upstream from Kew; also on Pen Ponds in Richmond Park and at Battersea Park.

Horse riding There is riding in Richmond Park. Polo is played by the Roehampton Club in Richmond Park.

Rugby International, club and Services Rugby Union matches are played at Twickenham.

Events Cruft's Dog Show is held at Earl's Court in mid-Feb. The *Daily Mail* Ideal Home Exhibition is at Olympia or Earl's Court in Mar. There is a parade on Easter Sun. in Battersea Park. The national final of the Greyhound Derby takes place on the 4th Sat. in June at the White City stadium. The Improve Your Home Exhibition is held at Olympia in Sept., and the Camping and Outdoor Life Exhibition in Dec./Jan.

Places to see *Chiswick House*: Apr. to Sept., daily; Oct. to Mar., Wed. to Sun. *Festival Gardens*, Battersea Park: gardens daily; children's zoo, daily, Easter to Sept. *Ham House* (NT), Petersham: afternoons daily, except Mon. *Hampton Court Palace*: daily; closed Sun. morning, Oct. to Apr.: park, daily. *Hogarth's House*, Chiswick: weekdays, except Tues. in winter; also Sun. afternoon. *Kew Bridge Beam Engines*, north of Kew Bridge: Sat., Sun. and Bank Hol. Mon. *Kew Palace*: Apr. to Sept., daily. *Marble Hill House*, Twickenham: daily, except Fri. *Osterley Park House* (NT): afternoons, except Mon. *Royal Botanic Gardens*, Kew: daily. *Syon House*, Isleworth: house: Sun. to Thur. afternoons, Easter to Sept.; gardens: daily.

Before the River Thames reaches Fulham and the riverside factories, it passes from Hampton Court through a leisurely world of waterside inns and promenades. This stretch has traditionally provided out-of-town homes for English monarchs. When the Thames was still a main thoroughfare, kings of England built their palaces and planted their gardens along its banks, at Richmond, Kew and Hampton Court, on the way to Windsor. Most of Richmond Palace has gone, but its park, the Old Deer Park, remains. Hampton Court, built by Cardinal Wolsey and handed on to the cardinal's monarch, Henry VIII, survives in its extensive grounds, as does the more modest palace, built by the early Hanoverian kings, at Kew in its world-famous botanic gardens.

Aristocrats followed their kings and built riverside mansions in the region, some of these surviving with their cunningly contrived landscape gardens—such as the 17th-century Ham House, and the late 18th-century elegance of Robert Adam at Syon and Osterley. Less ostentatious houses were also fashionable, like Horace Walpole's Strawberry Hill, which set the pace for the Gothic revival in domestic architecture. Richmond Hill, with its views over the valley, became sought after, and retains its 18th-century terraces of Georgian and Queen Anne houses.

Though the Thames Valley is now built up as far as Kingston upon Thames and beyond, it still has frequent open spaces, thanks partly to the survival of these once-private estates. The river itself is still the most attractive route from which to see the many and varied aspects of the valley—starting from the lights at Battersea, along the Hammersmith and Chiswick Malls with their inns and boathouses, and on between tree-lined banks through a series of riverside villages.

ACTOR'S GARDEN *A temple built by Capability Brown stands near the riverside villa at Hampton where David Garrick lived*

Chiswick

A fashionable place of residence in the 17th and 18th centuries; some of the atmosphere of that period still survives. Chiswick Mall, easily reached on foot from Hammersmith Mall, is a riverside street lined with delightful houses, including Kelmscott House, built *c.* 1780 and once the home of William Morris, the pre-Raphaelite artist and author, who died there in 1896.

The 17th-century Hogarth's House was for 15 years the summer home of William Hogarth, the artist. Chiswick House, further west, is one of the finest of the smaller aristocratic mansions in London. It was built in 1729 by the 3rd Earl of Burlington, patron of architects. His protégé William Kent decorated the rooms and also laid out the gardens.

Fulham

A street market in North End Road still sells fruit and vegetables in a district once famous for market gardens. Fulham Palace was the private residence of the Bishops of London for more than 1000 years: the site of the old moat surrounding it is now a public garden.

Ham

An attractive residential area between Richmond Park and the river. Its older part is scattered round the gorse and bracken of Ham Common, which also has an attractive duck pond, and a playing field with an inn at its corner. A bridle path from the common leads to Ham House, a charming 17th-century brick mansion famous for its decorative work carried out by continental artists and craftsmen for the Duke of Lauderdale, favourite of Charles II. There are beautiful grounds, and tea is served under the trees in the walled rose garden. A polo field lies just outside the grounds, beside a path to the riverbank.

Petersham village, on the road from Ham to Richmond, consists almost entirely of 17th and 18th-century houses. Petersham Meadows run down to the Thames, and there is a superb view along the river towards Richmond from the foot of River Lane, where cows graze by the riverbank and small-boat sailors launch their craft.

Hammersmith

Five main roads converge at Hammersmith Broadway; but the riverside, only a few hundred yards away, provides a quiet walk right through to Chiswick Mall. The bank opposite is lined with trees, and the towpath itself is dotted with 18th-century houses, inns and boat-houses. Hammersmith Bridge, a suspension bridge built in 1887, shows Victorian lavishness at its most blatant. It has now become a period piece, with its gilt turrets and elaborate decoration.

Hampton Court Palace

In a park bordered by the Thames stands the magnificent palace begun in 1514 by Cardinal Wolsey, which became

THAMES AT RICHMOND *A view of the Thames beloved by countless artists over the centuries: the wooded Terrace Gardens sweep down from Richmond Hill to the Thames as it flows between Petersham Meadows (left) and Marble Hill Gardens on the Twickenham bank*

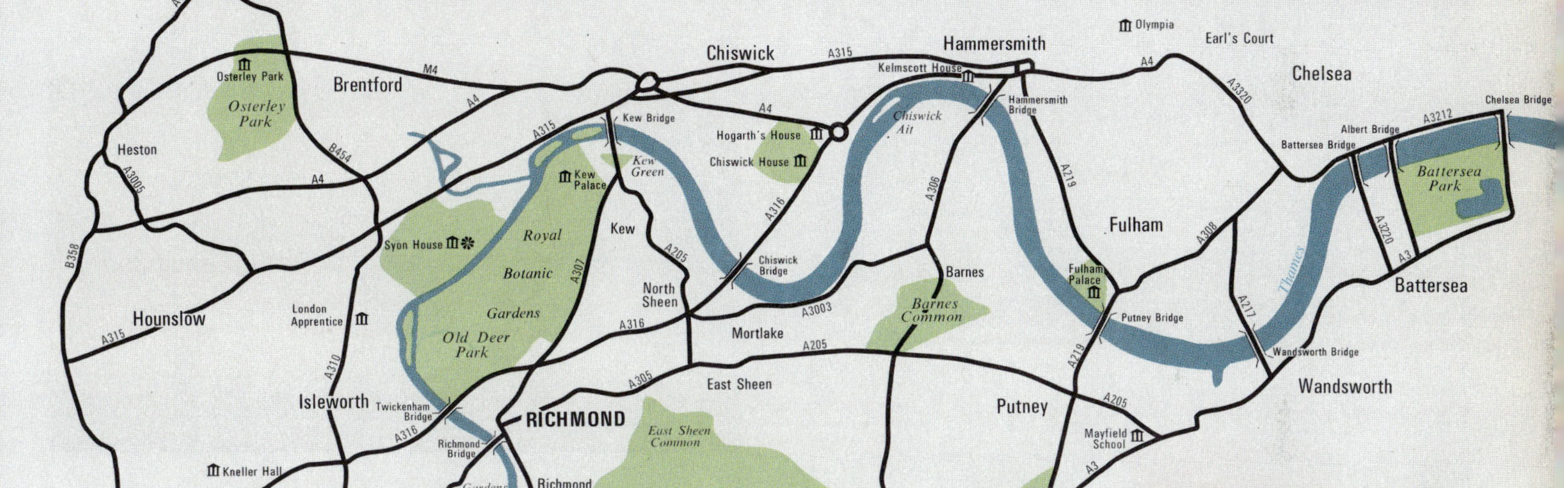

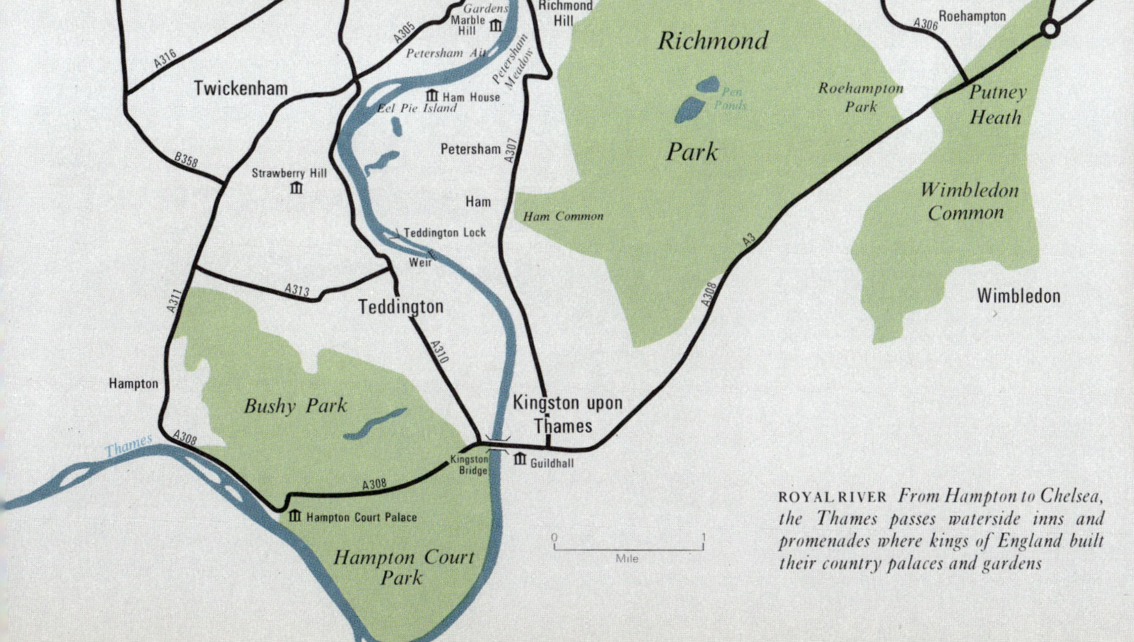

ROYAL RIVER *From Hampton to Chelsea, the Thames passes waterside inns and promenades where kings of England built their country palaces and gardens*

ROYAL BEAST *The lion is one of ten heraldic figures at Hampton Court Palace entrance. It bears the Arms of Henry VIII and appears on the Royal Standard*

CHISWICK MALL *Dinghies sail past Chiswick's riverside street of Georgian houses*

KEW GARDENS *The curved-glass Palm House has a gallery where visitors can walk inside*

the favourite country home of Henry VIII. Henry enthusiastically played Royal Tennis—a different game from modern lawn tennis and still played as 'real' tennis—in the closed court adjoining the palace, and jousted where the Tiltyard Gardens are now situated. Five of his wives lived here and the ghosts of two of them, Jane Seymour and Catherine Howard, are said to haunt the rambling palace. One of its most important features is the Great Hall, renowned for its hammer-beam roof.

The principal façades, overlooking the gardens, date from the accession of William III in 1689, when Sir Christopher Wren was commissioned to enlarge and improve the building. The great gatehouse, at the other end of the palace, is of Henry's time. Anne Boleyn's Gateway is an excellent example of Tudor brickwork, surmounted by a splendid astronomical clock made for Henry VIII. The great vine, planted in 1769, is noted for its black grapes. The grounds are beautifully laid out, and the maze is a perennial attraction.

Isleworth
The nucleus of the old village lies by the river. The London Apprentice, near the parish church, is an 18th-century inn. Syon House, founded in 1415, was given to the Earl of Northumberland by Elizabeth I in 1594, and was reputedly repaired by Inigo Jones in 1632. Catherine Howard was a prisoner here before her execution. The grounds were laid out in the 18th century by Capability Brown, and part of them is now the National Gardening Centre, a display of British horticulture.

Kew
The early Hanoverian kings built a palace here and brought high society with them. The triangular Kew Green, with its parish church of 1714, was the village centre, and the 18th-century houses around it still convey the elegant style of that time.

In 1759 Princess Augusta, mother of George III, laid out a private botanic garden in the grounds of Kew Palace. The grounds, landscaped by Capability Brown, were opened to the public in 1841, and are today the Royal Botanic Gardens, with more than 45,000 species and varieties of plants. The principal purpose of the gardens is the study of horticulture and botany. But shaded walks and fine floral displays are the attractions for ordinary visitors. The 165 ft high Chinese pagoda was designed by Sir William Chambers in 1761, and the great Palm House was completed in 1848 to a design by Decimus Burton.

Kingston upon Thames
The administrative centre of Surrey, a thriving market town and Royal Borough, now surrounded by modern industries and new housing estates. Near the guildhall, built in 1935, is the Coronation Stone, said to have been used at the crowning of at least six Saxon kings.

Putney
A popular rowing centre, and the starting-point of the Oxford and Cambridge boat race. Mayfield School, built in 1955, is an excellent example of modern school architecture. Putney Heath was notorious in the 18th century as the haunt of highwaymen and vagabonds. Nearby Barnes has Regency riverside terraces, and a cluster of attractive houses round the common.

Richmond
The town stands on the slopes of a hill rising from the Thames. It takes its name from a palace rebuilt by Henry VII, previously Earl of Richmond in Yorkshire. Elizabeth I died in the palace in 1603, but little remains of it today except a brick gatehouse beside the attractive green. Maids of Honour Row has some well-preserved old houses.

The Terrace, on top of the famous Richmond Hill, gives sweeping views of the Thames and leads to the main gate into Richmond Park—2400 acres of open land where 600 deer roam, and where there are shady walks and rides, open heaths and azalea plantations.

ROYAL PARK *Fallow bucks graze beneath the trees in Richmond Park—2400 acres of plantations and heathland in which 600 deer roam free where Tudor kings once hunted*

KEEPING THE WATER IN *To stop the Thames at Richmond from dwindling to a muddy ditch at low tide, sluice gates near Twickenham Bridge are lowered after high water*

the dome, above a tropical 'forest'

THE BOAT RACE *One of London's popular attractions is the annual 4¼-mile race between Oxford and Cambridge from Putney to Mortlake*

ALBERT BRIDGE *The web of Albert Suspension Bridge is lit up at night. Built in 1873, it is one of the less sturdy London bridges; a notice warns marching troops to break step when crossing. The chimneys are those of Battersea Power Station, built in 1932*

Twickenham
Headquarters of Rugby Union football in Britain since 1907, and venue for major international matches. There are several fine old houses such as Marble Hill House, built in 1728 for George II's mistress, Henrietta Howard, and now restored. Montpelier Row and Sion Row are unspoilt terraces of the early 18th century. The poet Alexander Pope is buried in the churchyard.

At Strawberry Hill, just to the south, is a Gothic Revival villa, built between 1750 and 1776 for Horace Walpole, the author, and now a teachers' training college. The National Physical Laboratory, one of the most important scientific research centres in Britain, is at nearby Teddington, where the weir above Teddington Lock is the end of the tidal section of the Thames.

Down-river to Woolwich

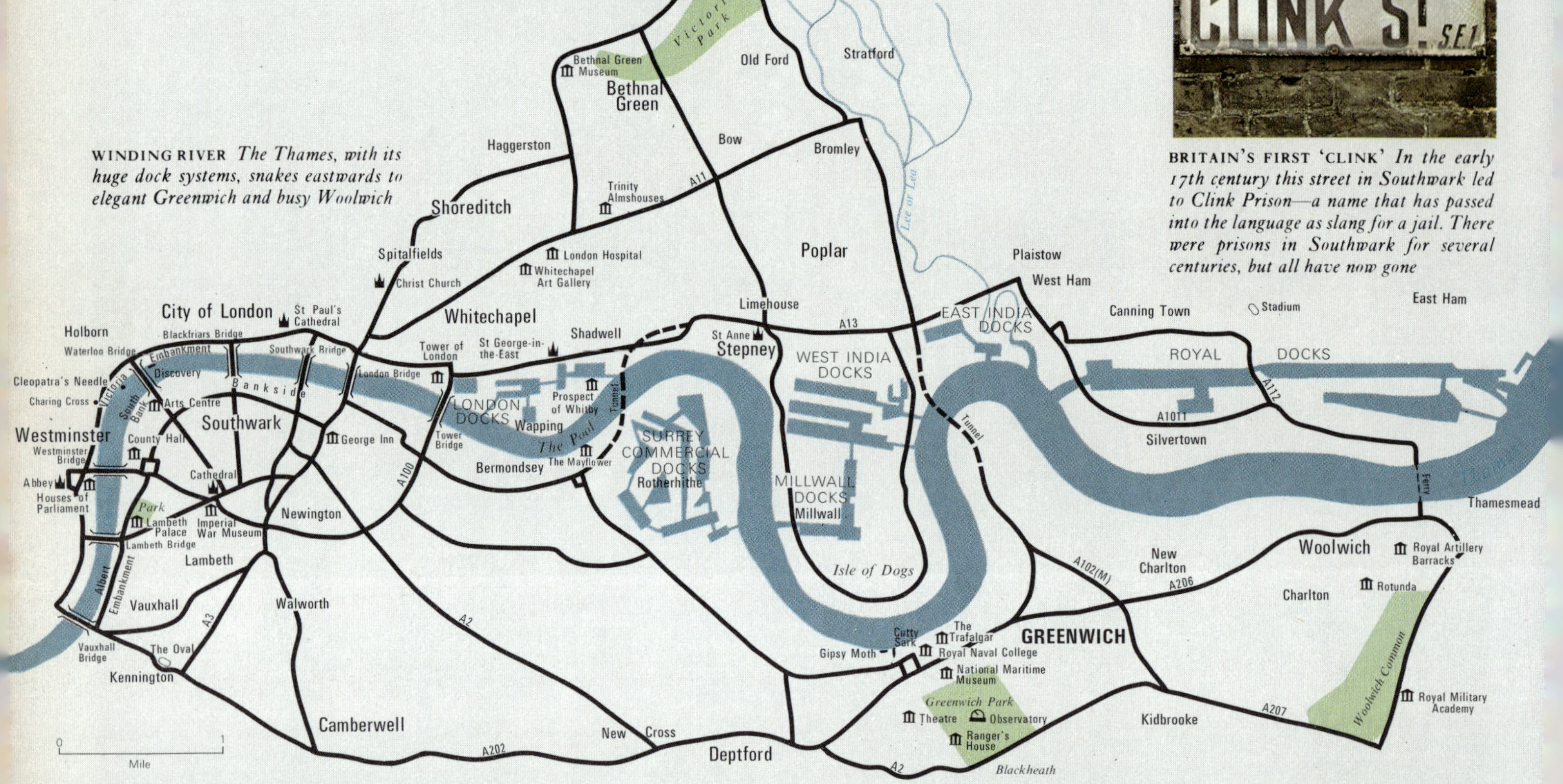

WINDING RIVER *The Thames, with its huge dock systems, snakes eastwards to elegant Greenwich and busy Woolwich*

BRITAIN'S FIRST 'CLINK' *In the early 17th century this street in Southwark led to Clink Prison—a name that has passed into the language as slang for a jail. There were prisons in Southwark for several centuries, but all have now gone*

River trips There are river trips from Charing Cross Pier to Greenwich every 45 mins., and to the Tower of London every 30 mins.; also from Tower Pier to Westminster and to Greenwich every 20 mins., Apr. to Sept. Circular cruises from Charing Cross Pier to Greenwich and back, and from Westminster Pier to Hampton Court and back, with stops at Putney, Kew and Richmond.

Cricket The season at the Oval, Surrey County Cricket Ground, is from Apr. to early Sept.

Events The Southwark Shakespeare Festival is held in the courtyard of the George Inn, Borough High Street, on Sat. afternoons from late May to July. Swan Upping starts at London Bridge in mid-July. The Doggett's Coat and Badge Race, the Thames watermen's rowing race from London Bridge to Chelsea, is held in late July or early Aug. There are concerts of military and brass band music in Greenwich Park on Sun. and Bank Hols. in summer.

Places to see *Bethnal Green Museum*: weekdays, except Fri., and Sun. afternoon. *Cuming Museum*, Walworth Road: weekdays. *Cutty Sark*, Greenwich: weekdays. *HMS Discovery*: afternoons. *Geffrye Museum*, Kingsland Road, Shoreditch: Tues. to Sat., Sun. afternoon. *Imperial War Museum*: weekdays and Sun. afternoon. *National Maritime Museum*, Greenwich: weekdays, Sun. afternoon. *Old Royal Observatory*, Greenwich: weekdays and Sun. afternoon; performances at the Caird Planetarium at published times. *Queen's House*, Greenwich: weekdays, Sun. afternoon. *The Rotunda Artillery Museum*, Woolwich Common: Mon. to Fri.; also Sat. mornings and Sun. afternoons. *Royal Naval College*, Greenwich: afternoons, except Thur. *South Bank Arts Centre*: regular concerts at the Royal Festival Hall, Queen Elizabeth Hall and Purcell Room (Tel. 01-928 3191); and frequent art exhibitions at the Hayward Gallery (Tel. 01-928 3144). *Southwark Cathedral*: daily. *Whitechapel Art Gallery*, Whitechapel High Street: daily, except Mon.

SCOTT'S SHIP *Beside the Victoria Embankment is the* Discovery, *the polar-research ship that took Captain Scott on his first expedition to the Antarctic in 1901–4*

POOL OF LONDON *The river which made London a port in Roman times still teems with cargo ships. The twin arms of Tower Bridge are raised to let tall vessels through*

CATHEDRAL AND MARKET *Southwark Cathedral, overlooking Borough Market, was developed out of a church founded in 1106*

The Thames east of Southwark is a working river, with shipping constantly moving in and out of the huge dock system. Southwark itself is a bleak tangle of warehouses, railway viaducts and breweries, relieved only by its fine Gothic cathedral. To its west, between Waterloo Bridge and County Hall—the impressive headquarters of the Greater London Council—lies the South Bank, a handsome stretch of riverside and a cultural centre including the Royal Festival Hall and the National Theatre. Between Waterloo and Kennington lies Lambeth, part of Cockneyland and home of the 'Lambeth Walk' dance. Here, slums mingle with handsome late Georgian and early Victorian terrace streets.

Eastwards, the districts on both river banks, badly damaged in the blitz, are a mixture of docks, industry, slums and experimental post-war housing developments. Much of the lively traditional character of the East End survives, notably in its pubs, some of which offer entertainment in music-hall style.

Downstream, the Thames widens towards Greenwich where, heralded by the delicate rigging of the *Cutty Sark*, stands the river's architectural masterpiece, a group of buildings which includes the Royal Naval College, the work of Sir Christopher Wren. Greenwich Park rises behind the college towards the Old Royal Observatory, with Blackheath beyond.

Bankside
A district on the south bank of the Thames between Blackfriars Bridge and London Bridge which offers splendid views—particularly at sunset—of the dome and towers of St Paul's Cathedral rising above warehouses and the river. Theatres and amusement gardens stood here in the 16th and 17th centuries. Among them was Shakespeare's Globe Theatre, the site of which is marked by a tablet on a brewery wall in Park Street. The picturesque Anchor Inn was used by Dr Samuel Johnson.

Bethnal Green
The district, once known for its silk-weaving, is now engaged largely in the furniture and leather trades. Bethnal Green Museum, opened in 1872, incorporates the iron-and-glass roof designed originally for the Victoria and Albert Museum in South Kensington. Close by is the remarkably large expanse of Victoria Park, known as the 'playground of the East End' because of its many facilities for sport and recreation.

Deptford
A district once famous for its great naval dockyard, established by Henry VII in 1485 and closed in 1869, and for

the Royal Naval Victualling Yard, opened in 1745 and closed in 1961. Some of the Victualling Yard's buildings still stand, but most of the site is now covered by a housing estate. A quayside walk commands a fine view across the river to the Isle of Dogs and downstream to Greenwich.

Greenwich

A town intimately connected with British sea-power. Near the pier, preserved in a dry dock, is the famous clipper *Cutty Sark*, launched in 1869; below decks is a collection of ships' figureheads, and paintings and prints of the sea. Close by is berthed *Gipsy Moth IV*, in which Sir Francis Chichester sailed single-handed round the world in 1966–7.

The Royal Naval College, formerly known as Greenwich Hospital, is a complex of superb buildings, largely designed by Sir Christopher Wren and opened in 1705. They include the Painted Hall, whose walls are decorated to give the illusion that columns support the roof. Behind the college lies the National Maritime Museum, which by means of models, paintings and manuscripts surveys British naval history from Tudor times. The oldest part of the museum is the Queen's House, designed by Inigo Jones for Anne of Denmark, consort of James I. It was completed in 1635, and is the earliest English example of Palladian architecture.

Behind these buildings rises Greenwich Park, which provides a splendid panoramic view of East London. It was laid out for Charles II by Le Nôtre, landscape gardener to Louis XIV of France and designer of the park and gardens at Versailles. On the summit stands the former Royal Observatory, now part of the Maritime Museum. (The work of the Observatory was transferred in 1950 to Herstmonceux, in Sussex.) A brass strip on the path outside marks the zero meridian of longitude, as recognised by most countries. Near by is the Caird Planetarium, opened in 1965. On the western side of the park are several fine 17th and 18th-century houses, including Ranger's House, once the home of Lord Chesterfield and now used for Sunday evening concerts during the summer. The Greenwich Theatre, which has an art gallery attached, was converted from an old music hall in 1967.

Lambeth Palace

The London home of the Archbishops of Canterbury for the past 750 years, and a picturesque survivor of the great medieval and Tudor mansions that once flanked both banks of the Thames. Begun in the early 13th century, the palace has been added to many times over the centuries. The gatehouse, built in 1490, is a noble red-brick structure, but the finest building is the Great Hall of 1660, with its magnificent 70 ft high Gothic roof. Archbishop's Park, reached from Lambeth Palace Road, is open to the public. The Albert Embankment, a promenade which passes the front of the palace, provides a fine view of the Houses of Parliament on the opposite bank, with the towers of Westminster Abbey rising behind.

Southwark

Southwark's cathedral is second only to Westminster Abbey as London's finest Gothic building. It is mostly 13th century although the nave was reconstructed in the last century. Borough High Street has been one of the South's great highways since the Middle Ages, when Chaucer's pilgrims rode down it towards Canterbury; and Borough Market claims to be London's oldest fruit and vegetable market. The George Inn, built in 1677, is the only surviving galleried tavern in London.

'E' FOR EXECUTION *This warehouse in the Pool of London stands on the site of Execution Dock, where bodies of pirates were hanged in the river on chains. One victim was Captain Kidd, hanged in 1701*

PALACE ENTRANCE *Beyond Morton's Tower, one entrance to Lambeth Palace, is the Great Hall, now a library*

GREENWICH *The Royal Naval College was built in 1705 as a hospital*

OVER THE THAMES *The Woolwich Free Ferry, for passengers and cars, has been in operation since 1889. Paddle-steamers gave way to diesel boats only in 1963*

UNDER THE THAMES *One of the two road tunnels under the river in London is the Rotherhithe Tunnel. The 'gun-barrel' effect is caused by the pattern of the tiles*

'CLIPPER' PRESERVED *The* Cutty Sark, *at Greenwich, was one of the last and fastest of the clipper ships which brought tea to England from China in the 19th century*

Stepney

A district at the heart of the East End, where tall blocks of flats have replaced most of the slums. The Highway, Stepney's main street, was once notorious for its seamen's drinking dens. Two picturesque 16th-century inns are The Town of Ramsgate, close to which the infamous Judge Jeffreys was arrested in 1688, and The Prospect of Whitby, an old smugglers' haunt. In pre-war days Stepney's Limehouse area was known as Chinatown because of its large Chinese population. It is still visited for its Chinese restaurants. St Anne, Limehouse, is one of three great East End churches designed by Nicholas Hawksmoor (1661–1736). The others are St George-in-the-East, Stepney, and Christ Church, Spitalfields.

Thamesmead

A 'new town' of London which will provide housing for 60,000 people when completed around 1983. The project, started in 1968, involves reclaiming part of the Erith Marshes, 3 miles east of Woolwich. Its ambitious design won international awards for architecture.

Whitechapel

A district inhabited chiefly by traders and craftsmen, many of them descendants of late 19th-century Jewish refugees from Russia. It was in the Whitechapel area that Jack the Ripper claimed his victims in 1888. London Hospital, beside the Whitechapel Road, is the largest general hospital in England. The Trinity Almshouses, a picturesque group of cottages, were founded in 1695 for 'decay'd masters and commanders of ships or ye widows of such'. The Whitechapel Art Gallery has become renowned for its enterprising exhibitions of work by contemporary artists.

Woolwich

A mainly industrial district, long noted as a garrison town. The Royal Artillery Barracks, built in 1776, face Woolwich Common. The nearby Rotunda was erected in St James's Park for a visit by the allied sovereigns after Napoleon's abdication in 1814, and was moved to Woolwich in 1819. It has a roof by John Nash, and now houses an artillery museum. Plumstead Church, to the east, has a 17th-century brick tower.

RIVERSIDE INNS *The Mayflower (left) near the southern end of the Rotherhithe Tunnel, stands on the site of a 16th-century tavern, The Shippe—said to have been used by the Pilgrim Fathers. At Greenwich is The Trafalgar (right), built in 1847. It once had landing steps to the veranda for customers arriving by water*

A 'green belt' around the southern suburbs

Angling There is coarse fishing at the Eagle Pond, Clapham Common; Wandsworth Common; and Crystal Palace boating lakes.

Motor sports and cycling Cycling events are held at Crystal Palace and Herne Hill. Motor and motor-cycle racing at Crystal Palace. Speedway at Wimbledon and stock-car racing at New Cross and Wimbledon.

Swimming Open-air swimming pools at Eltham Park and Tooting Common. Swimming and diving pools at the National Sports Centre, Crystal Palace.

Events All England Lawn Tennis Championships are held at Wimbledon during the last week of June and the first week of July. International and national athletic meetings are held at Crystal Palace throughout the season. The Greater London Horse Show is held on Clapham Common on the late Summer Bank Hol. There are fairs at Blackheath at Easter and the Spring and late Summer Bank Hols; lakeside concerts at Crystal Palace from July to Aug.; and concerts throughout the year at Fairfield Halls, Croydon.

Places to see *Chessington Zoo*: daily. *Children's Zoo*, Crystal Palace Park: Apr. to Oct., daily. *Down House*, Downe: afternoons, except Mon. and Fri. *Dulwich College Picture Gallery*: weekdays, except Mon.; also Sun. afternoon, Apr. to Sept. *Eltham Palace*: Thur. and Sun. *Hall Place*, Bexley: weekdays; also Sun. afternoon in summer; gardens, daily. *Horniman Museum*, Forest Hill: weekdays, Sun. afternoon. *Lawn Tennis Museum*, Wimbledon: Tues. to Sat.; also Sun. afternoon. *Ranger's House*, Blackheath: daily.

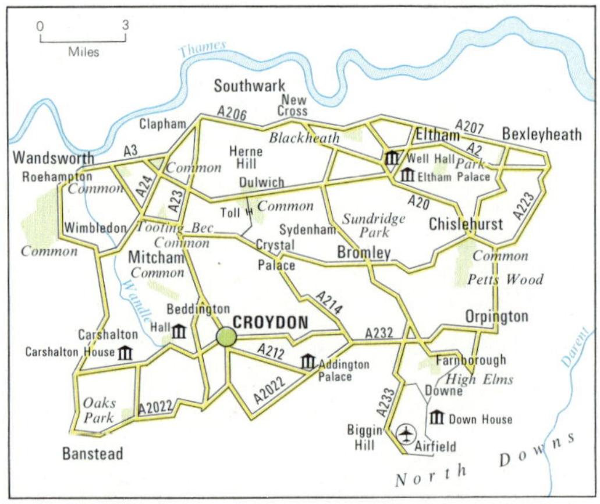

Until the middle of the 18th century, London south of the Thames meant only one area—Southwark. This was because London Bridge, with Southwark as its bridgehead, was the city's only river crossing. But in the 1750's there began a spate of bridge-building, and London started its seemingly inexorable advance to the south. The rate of growth was accelerated in the mid-19th century by the development of railways, and again, after 1918, by the growing popularity of the motor car.

A tide of suburban bricks and mortar flooded the ground rising towards the North Downs in Kent and Surrey, largely engulfing the old country towns and villages such as Blackheath, with its common fringed by elegant houses; Eltham, with its surviving fragment of a royal palace; Dulwich, with its splendid art gallery; and Mitcham, with its historic cricket green.

The growth has reached the point that some of London's suburbs now have suburbs of their own; Croydon's mushrooming office blocks are fast making it a twin of the City. Yet within this great built-up area there still remain districts like Banstead, which seem almost pure country. The creation of 'green belts' round London, with the passing of the Green Belt Act in 1938, has played a large part in protecting such areas of natural beauty from further urban development and in providing 'lungs' for the city.

Addington
A village on the North Downs with a cricket club founded in 1743 and surrounded by excellent golf courses. Addington Palace was a hunting lodge of Henry VIII. Rebuilt in 1770, and a home of the Archbishops of Canterbury in the 19th century, it now houses the Royal School of Church Music.

Beddington Park
This well-wooded park, watered by the River Wandle, contains two fine buildings. The Church of St Mary the Virgin, basically 14th and 15th century, has a Norman font, an Elizabethan pulpit, and good brasses. Nearby Beddington Hall was the seat of the influential Carew family from 1349 to 1762. Sir Francis Carew grew the first English oranges here in the early 17th century; the wall of the orangery, with its heating ducts, remains.

Biggin Hill
A sprawling village on a plateau of the North Downs, with a famous Battle of Britain airfield. A chapel commemorates 453 pilots stationed there who died in the war. St Mark's Church was built almost single-handed by its vicar between 1955 and 1959, with material from the derelict All Saints' Church, Peckham, which he personally dismantled. The Westerham road has a fine view over the Darent Valley.

Blackheath
A suburb surrounding an open common, the remnant of heathland once frequented by highwaymen. Here, golf was introduced into England from Scotland by James I in 1608. Grouped about the common are attractive houses, of which the finest example is the Paragon, a crescent of late 18th-century villas connected by colonnades.

Bromley
An outer suburb, formerly a market town. The charming red-brick Bromley College—almshouses founded in 1666—has fine wrought-iron gates. Bromley Palace, now a teachers' training college, was the home of the Bishops of Rochester from 967 to 1846. In the High Street a plaque commemorates the site of H. G. Wells's birthplace. Sundridge Park, to the north-east, has a golf course and a rambling white 18th-century mansion built by John Nash.

Carshalton
The older part of this suburb is pleasantly grouped around two ornamental ponds. It includes the 18th-century Greyhound Inn and several old houses whose attractive grounds are open to the public. Carshalton House was built in 1704 for Sir John Fellowes, a governor of the South Sea Company. On the downs, 2 miles south, is a public park with fine trees—once the grounds of a mansion, The Oaks, destroyed in an air-raid in 1944. It was the home of the 12th Earl of Derby, who founded two great horse races, one named after himself, the other after his house.

Chislehurst
A residential area built around a large wooded common. At the Elizabethan Camden Place, now the golf clubhouse, the exiled French Emperor, Napoleon III, and Empress Eugénie came to live in 1871. On the common stands a memorial to their son, the Prince Imperial, who died fighting for the British against the Zulus. Chislehurst Caves are underground chalk galleries of unknown

LAST OF 'THE FEW' *A Spitfire (foreground) and a Hurricane stand at the entrance to Biggin Hill RAF station, in tribute to the fighter pilots who, in planes like these, won the Battle of Britain*

CRYSTAL PALACE *A national sports centre was opened at Crystal Palace in 1964. As well as its diving-pool and Olympic-length swimming-pool, it has an 18,000-seat sports stadium*

age used as air-raid shelters in the Second World War. At Petts Wood, between Chislehurst and Orpington, is a stone sundial showing only British Summer Time in memory of William Willett, a local resident who founded the Daylight Saving system in 1908.

Croydon
Surrey's largest town before its absorption into Greater London. It is a fast-expanding commercial centre, busy shopping town and popular residential area. Old and new buildings mingle here. Brick almshouses, built in 1599 and scarcely changed since, nestle among tall office blocks; and the surviving portions of the medieval Palace of the Archbishops of Canterbury contrast with such fine modern buildings as Fairfield Halls, used for concerts. The Halls also contain the Ashcroft Theatre and the Arnhem Gallery.

Crystal Palace
A high plateau named after the immense structure of glass and iron designed by Sir Joseph Paxton as a hall for the Great Exhibition of 1851 in Hyde Park, and re-erected near Sydenham in 1854. The hall was destroyed by fire in 1936, except for two tall towers which were demolished in 1940. Part of the area is now a public park, containing a boating lake, children's zoo, and prehistoric monsters in plaster—sole survivors of the 1851 exhibition. Close by is a BBC television transmitting mast, over 700 ft high. International athletic matches and other major competitions are held at the National Sports Centre, which has a covered hall, four swimming and diving pools, squash courts, a stadium and an artificial ski slope.

Downe
An attractive, secluded village, mainly of flint cottages, on a ridge of the North Downs. Down House, to the south, was the home of Charles Darwin for 40 years until his death in 1882; it is now owned by the Royal College of Surgeons, and has been restored as it was in Darwin's time. Between Downe and Farnborough are the grounds of a large 19th-century house, High Elms, now a public park and golf course.

Dulwich
One of London's quietest suburbs, retaining much of its old rural atmosphere. Dulwich College Picture Gallery, London's first public art gallery, founded in 1814, houses a splendid collection, including works by Rembrandt, Raphael, Rubens, Canaletto and Watteau. To the south is Dulwich College itself, a public school whose old boys include P. G. Wodehouse, the creator of Jeeves. Dulwich Village is a street of fine Georgian houses. College Road, climbing to Crystal Palace, passes through the only remaining toll-gate in London. Dulwich Park is best visited in early summer when the azaleas and rhododendrons are in flower.

CENTRE COURT *The All England Lawn Tennis Championships were started at Wimbledon in 1877. New courts were opened in 1922*

Eltham
A residential town south of the main London–Canterbury road, with a palace which was the favourite country residence of English kings from Henry III to Henry VIII. The palace, although rebuilt in this century, retains a magnificent 15th-century oak roof in the banqueting hall and a fine stone bridge over the moat. In a small public park is Well Hall, the surviving wing of an Elizabethan manor house.

Mitcham
A suburb noted for its cricket, played on the green since 1730, and its fair, held on the open space known as Three Kings Piece during the second week of August. Near the green are two fine 18th-century buildings, Eagle House and the King's Head Inn.

Wimbledon
A residential area world-famous for its international tennis championships. The 1045-acre common, on which stands a windmill built in 1817, is a gorse, bracken and tree-covered plateau, excellent for both walking and riding. It is still patrolled by the official conservators. On the south-west corner is the mound of an Iron Age fortification. This is known as Caesar's Camp, although scholars believe it has no connection with the Romans. In summer, model yachts glide across the ponds on the common; in winter there is skating.

On the common's western edge, at Roehampton, lies the Alton Towers estate. Tall blocks of flats are set on wooded slopes, and the estate is considered one of the country's most handsome post-war housing developments.

HORNIMAN MUSEUM *The museum, at Forest Hill, is devoted to man and his world*

THE MARKETS OF LONDON

Onion-seller, 1710: 'Buy my four ropes of hard onions'

Travelling musician playing a tune on the fiddle

Rag and bone merchant: 'Any old iron take money for'

London has always been a market-place before anything else, and its markets are as various as they are colourful and fascinating. They range from the humble street markets, where you can buy anything from an African parrot to a Victorian wardrobe, to the great wholesale markets which daily feed the city's millions. Even street pedlars, whose traditional cries were once so much a part of the London scene (right), have not yet entirely disappeared from the city's streets.

BILLINGSGATE—A BYWORD FOR BAD LANGUAGE

Many writers in the 17th century referred to the rowdy behaviour of the fish porters and fishwives of Billingsgate, and it was at this time that the name of the market became synonymous with abusive language. The 19th-century artist Thomas Rowlandson captures the bustle of Billingsgate life in his aquatint (left), in which fishwives can be seen squabbling on the quay. The market (right) lies just west of Tower Bridge, on the north side of the Thames. Its name traditionally derives from Belinus, a Celtic king of the 4th century BC who built a wooden quay on this site, with a water-gate to guard it. The present market building was erected in 1875. Fish sold at Billingsgate come from ports as far away as the north of Scotland and Norway. Billingsgate is used by 130 firms, and there are about 2500 employees, including 500 licensed porters

PETTICOAT LANE—WHERE THE POOR BOUGHT CLOTHES SECOND-HAND

Rag Fair, depicted by Rowlandson in the early 19th century, was in Rosemary Lane, now Royal Mint Street. It vied with nearby Petticoat Lane as a market for second-hand clothes, most of them stolen

The famous market in Petticoat Lane—actually Middlesex Street—originated as a place where the local poor could buy old clothes and cast-offs of the rich. Today the market attracts tourists

WHERE ANTIQUES CAN BE BOUGHT AT BARGAIN PRICES

A display of handbags in Portobello Road Market, open on Saturdays

Antique clocks decorate a stall in Camden Passage, Islington

London is today the world's largest market for art works and antiques. Names of dealers such as Christie's and Sotheby's appear frequently in the headlines, with sales of masterpieces and rare objects which can fetch huge sums of money. But much activity in London's antiques world goes unrecorded. Every Saturday all kinds of 'junk'—knick-knacks, curiosities and minor antiques—are sold at markets like the one in Kensington's Portobello Road. People buy junk mostly on a whim, or because they want to decorate their homes; some are lured on by stories of obscure objects being bought for a song and re-sold for a small fortune

'I sweep your chimneys clean, O, sweep your chimneys clean, O!'

Pudding-pieman: 'A pudding, a pudding, a hot pudding, bake as I go'

'Coals ten-pence a bushel, buy them and try, small coal!'

'Clean your boots, Sir! Shoeblack, your Honour! Black your shoes, Sir!'

'Any knives or scissors to grind? Bring them out my pretty dears. I'll make them look like new!'

Stall-holders at Covent Garden in the early 19th century: 'All a-growin', all a-blowin''

NEW COVENT GARDEN, WHICH COMES ALIVE WHILE LONDON SLEEPS

For more than 300 years London's principal wholesale market for vegetables, fruit and flowers operated in and around Covent Garden, just off the Strand, where lorries were unloaded and loaded in the public streets and handcarts threaded their ways across busy pavements and roads. Increasing numbers and sizes of lorries inevitably led to congestion, and in 1974 the market was moved to a self-contained 68 acre site just south of the Thames, at Nine Elms, Battersea. Lorries from the Continent and market gardens all over England start arriving in the small hours of the morning. By 5 o'clock they have unloaded their crates, wholesalers have made bulk purchases, and porters are busy loading produce for distribution in all directions. Some of this activity can be seen from a public gallery, but most trading is finished long before the commuter trains start to pass through the site.

SMITHFIELD—THE WORLD'S LARGEST MEAT MARKET

Before its modernisation in the 1860's, Smithfield (originally 'smooth field') was a market for sheep, horses, cattle and hay. In Rowlandson's picture, cattle are seen in pens around the market centre

Smithfield's Central Meat Market Arcade, built in 1866, can receive up to 400 truckloads of meat at a time. It is the world's largest wholesale meat market, famous for the quality of its beef, pork and lamb

THE BUSTLE AND COLOUR OF OPEN-AIR STREET MARKETS

London has more than 100 street markets, many of them in the suburbs. The large markets offer every kind of article for household use, but the emphasis is usually on market produce. Even in these days of 'streamlined' shopping at supermarkets, the street markets are still immensely popular, with their colourful displays of flowers, fruit and vegetables, and their cheery hoarse-voiced Cockney traders, whose characteristic patter is a mixture of ironic flattery and shrewd appeal to self-interest. Among the best-known suburban markets are Brixton Market, dating from the 1870's, and Kingston Market, established in the 17th century

Fruit at Brixton Market brings an extra dash of colour to London

Fruit, flowers and vegetables are sold in Kingston's market

Woodland on London's northern border

The northern stretches of outer London for centuries contained hunting country of heath and wood, as well as rich farmland. To the north-east, the fields and moors extended to the edge of the great Essex Forest, a fragment of which remains at Hainault, along the Greater London boundary, and a much larger portion in the beautiful Epping Forest, just beyond the boundary in Essex.

London has now covered much of this countryside with suburbs and factories. Flyovers and motorways march dramatically on huge concrete legs across acres of residential avenues and gardens; and jet aircraft thunder overhead on their way to or from Heathrow, the world's busiest international airport. Yet pockets of an older way of life survive, and old houses mark the centres of once-rural villages or small towns. Open spaces remain, as at Osterley Park, with its fine Georgian house, and Stanmore Common. Visitors to Harrow School are often surprised, after climbing up from the suburbs, to find teashops and old, winding streets on Harrow Hill. The sweeping views from this hill give an impression of just how enormous the London conurbation has grown. Less dramatic, but more rural, is the fine walking country on the fringes of outer London, such as Hadley Common, near Barnet.

The eastern extremities of outer London border on the marshy Thames Estuary, but there has been expansion here too, and drained areas have been filled with residential and industrial building. Dagenham, for instance, has the world's largest housing estate planned as a single unit; it was designed between the wars for some 90,000 people employed in local industries, including the giant British Ford factory.

Angling There is coarse fishing on King George's Reservoir at Chingford, on the Grand Union Canal at Uxbridge, and at Enfield.

Boating Sailing and rowing on the Welsh Harp, where a regatta is held on the Spring Bank Hol.

Motor racing There is stock-car racing at Harringay and speedway at Hackney Stadium.

Events at the Empire Stadium and Pool, Wembley The Football League Cup Final is held on the third Sat. in Feb. The All England Badminton Championships are in the last week of Mar. The FA Cup Final is on the second Sat. in May, the Rugby League Cup Final the following Sat. There is a bi-annual Military Musical Pageant (1981, 1983, etc.) at the end of June. The Royal International Horse Show is at the end of July, the Horse of the Year Show in Oct. An Ice Show opens the week before Christmas and continues until the end of Feb.

Places to see *Battle of Britain Museum*, Hendon: weekdays, Sun. afternoon. *Bruce Castle Museum*, Tottenham: weekdays, except Wed. *Church Farm House Museum*, Hendon: daily, except Tues. afternoons and Sun. mornings. *Eastbury Manor House*, Barking: Tues. *Forty Hall*, Enfield: daily except Mon. *Gunnersbury Park Museum*, local history and transport: afternoons. *Osterley Park* (NT): house, afternoons except Mon.; gardens, daily. *Queen Elizabeth's Hunting Lodge*, Chingford: afternoons, except Mon. and Tues.; also Bank Hol. Mon. *Royal Air Force Museum*, Hendon: weekdays, Sun. afternoons. *Vestry House Museum*, Walthamstow: weekdays. *William Morris Gallery*, Walthamstow: weekdays; also first Sun. of each month.

WATER PLAYGROUND *The tree-fringed Ruislip Lido, formerly a reservoir, is a centre for bathing, small-boat sailing and water-skiing*

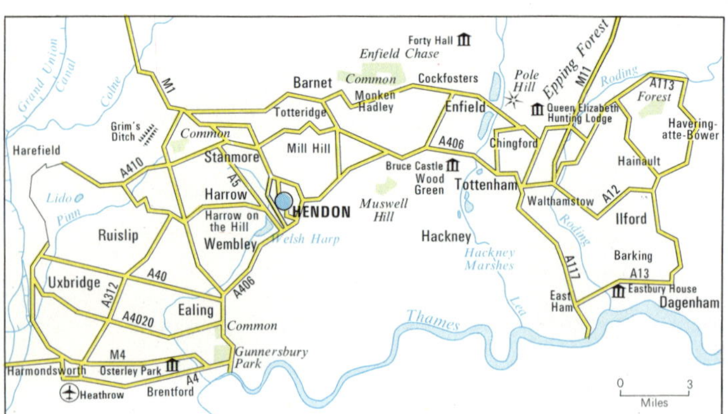

Barking

An ancient market town, now joined to neighbouring Dagenham, Ilford and East Ham by continuous housing, but improved in recent years by handsome new shopping parades. Like much of outer London, the area contains patches of quiet wilderness, such as the creeks and mud-flats where the River Roding becomes Barking Creek during its passage to the Thames.

Barking was famous in the Middle Ages for its wealthy abbey. Today only the 15th-century gate-tower survives. Eastbury House, a brick Tudor building which is now owned by the National Trust, stands a mile to the east, surrounded by a large housing estate.

Barnet

This borough includes some of London's most attractive residential areas—the select village of Totteridge, for instance, and Mill Hill, high on its green ridge with its old weather-boarded houses, and famous for the Nonconformist public school, Mill Hill. There are pleasant rural walks on the semi-wild Hadley Common, part of the old Enfield Chase. The common's woodland and undergrowth stretch nearly 2 miles, from the still-rural village of Monken Hadley in the west to Cockfosters in the east.

Hadley Green, at Monken Hadley, is surrounded by 18th-century houses and cottages. An obelisk set on the green in 1740 marks the site of the Yorkist

TITHE BARN *At Harmondsworth, near Heathrow Airport, a 500-year-old tithe barn is still used for storing grain. The imposing building is 190 ft long*

victory of 1471 at the Battle of Barnet. The nearby church has on its tower a unique copper cresset of the 18th century; this was filled with oil and lit as a beacon in times of crisis.

The modern suburb of Hendon, to the south, contains the nucleus of an old village around the parish church. At West Hendon is the Brent Reservoir, better known as the Welsh Harp—a name taken from a nearby inn—a popular spot for sailing.

Brentford

Narrow central streets recall Brentford's heyday as a market town and former county town of Middlesex. South of the town, down Dock Road or Catherine Wheel Road, lie the boats and waterside sheds where the Grand Union Canal meets the Thames. In the large and attractive Gunnersbury Park, north of the Chiswick Flyover, is an early 19th-century house of the Rothschilds, the international banking family.

Osterley Park, a mile to the west in fine grounds, was built in 1577 for Sir Thomas Gresham, founder of the Royal Exchange in the City. The corner

HUNTING LODGE *Near the southern end of Epping Forest stands the Tudor timber-framed Queen Elizabeth's Hunting Lodge, now a museum of the forest's history*

towers are of Gresham's time, but the house was largely rebuilt between 1761 and 1780 by the architect Robert Adam.

To the north lies the residential district of Ealing, its large grassy common crossed by the old Oxford road out of London. In Walpole Park, near Ealing Broadway, stands Pitshanger Manor, a house rebuilt in 1801 for his own use by Sir John Soane, the architect who founded the Soane Museum at No. 13, Lincoln's Inn Fields. Pitshanger Manor is now a public library.

Chingford

A residential town near the southern end of Epping Forest. To the north is Queen Elizabeth's Hunting Lodge, a picturesque timber-framed Tudor building which contains a museum illustrating the natural history and archaeology of the forest.

A public golf course near by slopes up to Chingford Plain and Pole Hill, which offer superb views over the forest and east London. To the west lie large reservoirs fed by the River Lea, winding through built-up areas to Hackney Marsh recreation grounds.

Enfield

A town containing fine old houses, especially in Gentlemen's Row, near the church. Forty Hall, on the northern edge of the town, is a charming house, built in 1632 for Sir Nicholas Raynton, Lord Mayor of London, and now a cultural centre and museum. It faces a park containing tall cedars and a lake.

Harefield

A village in one of the most rural parts of Greater London, where agriculture is still the main employment. The local church is famous for its monuments, which include the 17th-century monument of Alice, Countess of Derby. The picturesque almshouses close to the church were founded by the countess.

Harrow

The 18th-century houses of Harrow on the Hill, the older part of the large borough of Harrow, stand on a hill rising high above the Middlesex plain. Clustered near the parish church, with its 13th-century spire, are the bulky Victorian buildings of Harrow School, whose famous ex-pupils include Sir Robert Peel, Lord Byron, John Galsworthy and Sir Winston Churchill.

To the north the land rises to more than 500 ft on Stanmore Common, the highest point for miles around. Near by is Grim's Ditch, or Dyke, an earthwork constructed in Saxon times and probably intended to mark the boundary of Offa's kingdom of Mercia.

Havering-atte-Bower

Still a rural village, set among elms round a large green, on a hill from which there is a view right across the Thames Basin. Close by is the Round House, an unusual oval-shaped building which was built about 1800.

Uxbridge

An old market town on the River Colne which has become the centre of a rapidly growing residential district. In the High Street are the market house, built in 1789, and the Crown and Treaty Inn, which dates back to the 16th century. The inn incorporates a building called the Treaty House, where the Commissioners of Charles I met

SCHOOL SHOP *Two Harrow boys, wearing traditional boaters, window-shop outside the school stores on Harrow Hill. The school tuck-shop is part of the stores*

representatives of Parliament in 1645 to sue for peace, without success.

Ruislip, a newer residential district to the north-east, still contains some 16th and 17th-century timber-framed houses. To the north is Ruislip Lido, a popular centre for water sports and recreation, originally a reservoir built to feed the Grand Union Canal.

Wembley

A residential area notable for the colossal Empire Stadium, built for the British Empire Exhibition of 1924–5 and now used mainly as a sports arena. The stadium can accommodate 100,000 spectators, and is at its liveliest on the Football Association's Cup Final Day.

Wood Green

Alexandra Palace, a famous landmark of this hilly district, is a huge building whose long terrace commands views right across London to the North Downs. Opened in 1873 for concerts and assemblies, it was burnt down almost immediately, and was rebuilt in 1875. Since 1935, parts of the building have been used as BBC studios.

HADLEY COMMON *Woodlands that were once part of the ancient forest of Enfield Chase stretch for nearly 2 miles eastwards from the village of Monken Hadley*

GENTLEMEN'S ROW *Enfield preserves the atmosphere of the country town it once was. Charles Lamb stayed in this 18th-century house, 17 Gentlemen's Row, in 1827*

London through the eyes of the French Impressionists

(1870-1900)

Victorian London was a city of bustling streets, dark alleyways, odd characters and imposing, grime-encrusted buildings. It was the London of Charles Dickens, a city pulsating with energy but paying the price, in the squalor of its slums, for the headlong rate at which it was growing. This was the city to which, in 1870, the year that Paris fell to the Prussians and also the year that Dickens died, came the French Impressionist painters Claude Monet and Camille Pissarro. They saw London as it had never been seen by any artist before, because they looked with fresh eyes.

Monet, at the age of 30, and Pissarro, aged 40, came as refugees from the Franco-Prussian War. They stayed until the middle of the following year, when peace returned to their country, Monet living in the West End and Pissarro in Norwood, a quiet suburb in south London. In 1874, the year the Impressionists held their first group exhibition in Paris, a third member of the group came to London from France—Alfred Sisley.

Even to the French art public, the Impressionists were unacceptably rebellious, with their search to capture fleeting impressions made by the interplay of light and shade, sun and cloud. In London, their names meant even less than in Paris, and the few paintings they exhibited during their stay went almost unnoticed. Pissarro disliked the English, and wrote to a friend: 'One gathers only contempt, indifference, even rudeness . . . Here there is no art; everything is a question of business.'

But Pissarro and Monet were fascinated by London, and both returned in the 1890's. Unlike most of their English contemporaries, whose work was either grandiose or sentimental, the Impressionists painted simple, informal views—often just of rivers, roads and trees. After the first shock of their originality had worn off, their art became popular. They succeeded where English painters had failed, in opening English eyes to the charm and beauty of the landscapes of late-Victorian London.

ROAD AT HAMPTON COURT Alfred Sisley (1839–99) painted this view while he was working in London in 1874. The painting is now in a Munich art gallery. Sisley went to Hampton, then a quiet village and now a densely populated suburb in south London, not to paint its chief attraction, the great Tudor palace, but to look for the kind of river landscape, with water sparkling under a summer sun, which he had already painted in France. Rivers flowing to a vague horizon were a common motif in Impressionist paintings, not only because of the shimmering of light on water, but also because rivers, like roads and pathways, made a useful backbone for loose, informal compositions. Sisley was the most conservative of the Impressionists, with a simple vision and a preference for plain technique. He returned to England twice in the 1890's to paint. Back in France, he died in poverty, unrecognised as an artist.

THE HOUSES OF PARLIAMENT Claude Monet (1840–1926) painted the Thames and the Houses of Parliament many times. He first tried the subject in 1871, but his most evocative Thames paintings, like the one on the right, now in a Paris art gallery, were done between 1899 and 1904. The London which Monet saw—a place of elusive, shifting colours and insubstantial forms—has now partly disappeared. The Clean Air Acts of 1956 and 1968 banished London's smogs, and destroyed many of the effects which Monet tried to capture on his canvasses. To record the changing patterns of London's light and colour, Monet worked on several canvasses at the same time, and completed some of them in his studio in France. He hoped to exhibit his Thames paintings in London, but a showing was never arranged—the paintings were too original for the conservative tastes of that time.

ROAD AT UPPER NORWOOD Camille Pissarro (1830–1903) painted this view of a suburban road (left) in 1871. The painting is in the Neue Pinakothek, Munich. Pissarro found Norwood 'a charming suburb'; but he thought the English inhospitable, and the few paintings he exhibited in London in the 1870's aroused no enthusiasm among Londoners. The houses he painted were typical of those being built in London suburbs to house the middle classes of the capital. Not far from this road was one of the most remarkable buildings of 19th-century Europe, the Crystal Palace. Pissarro gave it only an incidental place in another painting of a street of modest villas. Like Sisley, he preferred the simple to the grand or picturesque.

EASTERN COUNTIES

The eastern counties present a green, brown and yellow vista of farmlands, more extensive than anywhere else in the British Isles, some rolling over low, whalebacked hills, others fading into infinity across the dark, flat land of the East Anglian Fens. The land is a rumpled counterpane—a patchwork that is flattened along its seaward rim and in its fenland heart, and rises in other places into colourful ridges, never gaudy but full of subtle shadows and changes of hue.

A FLAT COUNTRYSIDE *Two plateaux stand out above the generally flat countryside of the eastern counties. One extends across inland Suffolk; the other separates the low-lying Fens from the popular cruising waterways of the Norfolk Broads*

There are gentle, undulating hills; little, domesticated valleys; rolling heathlands; dominant church towers that often appear too large for their villages; and towns which perch on hummocks, or nestle by rivers and streams. This is a breezy part of Britain, too, especially in the area of the Norfolk Broads. Even on the hottest day, the sunbather may need to shelter from the wind. But there is consolation—long hours of sunshine and the lowest annual rainfall in Britain.

The roads, too, are generally easy to travel. Away from the busy A1, the country around Huntingdon is full of leisurely lanes; away from the A12, Suffolk is expansive and unspoilt. Even the large towns such as Peterborough, Chelmsford, Cambridge and Norwich are reasonably accessible out of rush hours for visiting motorists.

By many a roadside there are flowers, fruit and vegetables for sale. Around Wisbech, root crops grow alongside orchards. Beyond, bulb fields run on into Lincolnshire. The twisting Norfolk and Suffolk lanes open out suddenly above spacious levels of pastureland and glide into warm-hued villages. The very flatness of the Fens emphasises a variety of skylines, and the sparseness of trees gives prominence to the most insignificant wind-hunched clump. The skies everywhere seem to take on an importance of their own. On a summer's day they can offer a dizziness of untainted blue or, in a single afternoon, a dozen variations in the weather—dazzling sun in one quarter, the rainbow-arc of a shower in another, a mounting storm on the far horizon. There are no dawns like those over Winterton, Southwold and The Naze; no sunsets like those across the shimmering Fens.

The light in the eastern counties is incomparable, too. There is hardly a trace of industrial pollution in the air, apart from the brick haze outside Peterborough. To make up for that, Peterborough has one of the great Norman cathedrals, companion to Norwich and Ely cathedrals.

Land of the North and South Folk

The kingdom of East Anglia was originally made up of the North Folk (Norfolk) and the South Folk (Suffolk). Its boundaries were once almost as impregnable as nature could make them—the sea to the north and east; the swamps of the undrained Fens to the west; a barrier of oak forest cutting off Saxon Essex to the south. Over the years the forests were thinned from the banks of the Stour, and the Fens were drained. When main roads were cut through the defensive earthworks across the Newmarket causeway, the boundaries of the counties began to blur—so much so that, today, the tortuous inlets of the Essex coast and much of its urban countryside, together with the Fens and the upland fringes of Cambridgeshire, which now includes the former county of Huntingdonshire, are all loosely classified as being parts of East Anglia.

Successive waves of invaders, including the Angles themselves and the marauding Vikings, swept in from the sea and left their mark on the countryside. Everywhere are Roman remains, Saxon burial grounds, and names and word-endings such as the Danish *by* (meaning a town or settlement) and the Old English *ea* and *ey* (signifying an island). Later came more peaceful infiltrations. Icelanders from the cod-fishing trade settled in the coastal towns. Flemish weavers brought their skills to the wool towns and also set up as brewers—notably in Woodbridge and Ipswich from where they exported beer to their former homeland.

The Dutchman who turned a dream into reality

The Dutch contributed to the architecture and agriculture of the land. Until the coming of the Dutchman, Cornelius Vermuyden, in the 17th century, the drainage of the Fens remained an improbable dream. Other Dutchmen, for a brief span in the mid-17th century, posed the first serious threat of invasion since William the Conqueror. Today, there is a brisk holiday and commercial trade with the Danes, Dutch and Germans in and out of Harwich, Felixstowe, Great Yarmouth and King's Lynn—ports whose trading significance in the past can be assessed by the richness of their merchants' houses, customs houses and exchanges. Later contributors to the welfare of the counties were the Scottish tenant farmers who came there during the depression years between the two World Wars and, shocked by the impoverishment and neglect of the land, set to work and revitalised derelict holdings.

Much of England's history was influenced by the people of the eastern counties. The names of great men and women—soldiers, sailors, noblemen and reformers—are remembered not just on tombstones, but in historic buildings.

Hereward the Wake, Nelson and Wolsey belong to East Anglia; Boadicea ruled there, Mary Tudor lived there before she was Queen, and Catherine of Aragon died there. Oliver Cromwell came from Huntingdon. Among the powerful Dukes of Norfolk was Thomas Howard, who

LINCOLN
CAMBRIDGE
NORFOLK
SUFFOLK
ESSEX
BEDFORD
HERTFORD
GREATER LONDON
KENT
The Wash
The Fens
Bedford Levels
Breckland
The Broads
The Sandlings
Blakeney Point
Orford Ness
The Naze
Foulness Point
Thames
Sleaford
Boston
Spalding
Wisbech
Thorney
PETERBOROUGH
Whittlesey
March
Stilton
Ramsey
Lt. Gidding
HUNTINGDON
Brampton
Buckden
Kimbolton
St Ives
Hemingford Grey
Godmanchester
St.Neots
Madingley
CAMBRIDGE
Gog Magog Hills
Duxford
Bedford
Letchworth
Luton
Hertford
St Albans
Watford
Waltham Abbey
London
Staines
HUNSTANTON
Heacham
Brancaster
Holkham
Wells-next-the-Sea
Blakeney
Cley next the Sea
Sheringham
CROMER
Felbrigg
Glandford
Holt
Overstrand
Mundesley
Happisburgh
Lt.Walsingham
Sandringham
Fakenham
Castle Rising
King's Lynn
Castle Acre
Swaffham
East Dereham
NORWICH
Hickling
Horning
Potter Heigham
West Somerton
GREAT YARMOUTH
Breydon Water
Reedham
Downham Market
Stoke Ferry
Hingham
Wymondham
East Wretham
Santon Downham
Brandon
THETFORD
Euston
Bressingham
Diss
Harleston
Bungay
Beccles
Lowestoft
Kessingland
The Saints
Ely
Soham
Mildenhall
Swaffham Prior
Newmarket
Moulton
BURY ST EDMUNDS
Walsham le Willows
Hoxne
Eye
Woolpit
Stowmarket
Debenham
Earl Soham
Framlingham
Coddenham
Blythburgh
Heveningham
Southwold
Walberswick
Yoxford
Dunwich
Snape
ALDEBURGH
Wickham Market
Orford
Woodbridge
IPSWICH
Felixstowe
Shotley
Harwich
Clare
Cavendish
Long Melford
LAVENHAM
Kersey
Hadleigh
Sudbury
Polstead
Stratford St. Mary
East Bergholt
Flatford
Nayland
Dedham
Manningtree
Bures
Ashdon
SAFFRON WALDEN
Wendens Ambo
Castle Hedingham
Finchingfield
Gt Bardfield
Lt. Bardfield
Thaxted
Lt. Maplestead
Stebbing
Stansted Mountfichet
Gt Dunmow
Braintree
Coggeshall
COLCHESTER
Wivenhoe
Brightlingsea
St Osyth
Clacton on Sea
Walton-on-the-Naze
Frinton
The Layers
Gt Canfield
The Rodings
CHELMSFORD
Danbury
Maldon
Goldhanger
Bradwell-on-Sea
Chipping Ongar
Ingatestone
Brentwood
Burnham-on-Crouch
Paglesham
Gt Wakering
Leigh-on-Sea
Southend-on-Sea
Rochester
Chatham
Gillingham
Ramsgate
MILES
REGIONAL PAGE INDEX
KEY TO MAP
Regional centre
Selected town or village
Regional boundary
County boundary
Major road
Minor road
Woodland
River and lake or reservoir

was the uncle of Henry VIII's second wife Anne Boleyn and grandfather of his fifth wife, Catherine Howard. He helped to destroy both Wolsey and Thomas Cromwell. Elizabeth Fry, the prison reformer, and Thomas Clarkson, who in the early 1800's strove for the abolition of slavery, were both born in East Anglia.

Tranquillity that inspired Constable

The eastern counties also have a proud association with the arts. Many writers have passed through the halls of Cambridge, learning or teaching —men as different in time and style as Hakluyt and Rupert Brooke, Rider Haggard and Cowper, Borrow and Pepys. Among the painters inspired by the tranquillity of the countryside were Constable and Gainsborough. The area's links with music range from the sardonic folk-song 'The Foggy, Foggy Dew' to the compositions of Benjamin Britten, and to the music festivals which are held at Aldeburgh, King's Lynn and Norwich.

For the naturalist, the eastern counties are a delight. The multitude of creeks are a vast sanctuary for birdlife. The Fens, the Broads and the coastal marshes provide the finest opportunities for bird-watching in the British Isles. Though some of the wildlife and nature reserves have had to be protected from careless intruders, there are still numerous conservancy areas to which visitors are welcomed.

With the exception of booming Southend, Clacton and Yarmouth, the seaside resorts are small, intimate places, rarely harassed by streams of traffic, and ideal for the family. There are no sumptuous cliffs, and only a few sheltered coves. But there are magnificent skies, unbroken highways of sands and lovely, unspoilt tracts of heathland.

Flower festivals and county shows

The River Great Ouse is navigable for cruisers between Denver Sluice in Norfolk and Tempsford in Bedfordshire, and also along its offshoots to Cambridge, Mildenhall and Stoke Ferry. Huntingdon and St Neots have sailing regattas during the summer and there are also races and regattas on the Broads and Broadland rivers. Coarse fishing is excellent. Everywhere are agricultural shows, county shows, flower festivals, fairs and traction-engine rallies. Many of these events sound parochial. It is remarkable, though, how many are worth a detour and a visit—and in this, they are very much like the villages and towns that foster them.

THE DRIEST VILLAGE IN BRITAIN

The eastern counties are the driest part of the country. Less than 20 in. of rain fall each year on the Essex coast bordering the Thames Estuary; and Great Wakering, a village near Southend, is the driest spot in Britain, with 18·4 in. Summer temperatures reach 29°C (84°F) on the hottest days, but sea breezes bring coastal temperatures down sharply. The winter climate is moderate. Norfolk has the worst of East Anglia's winter, with snow on 15 to 18 days

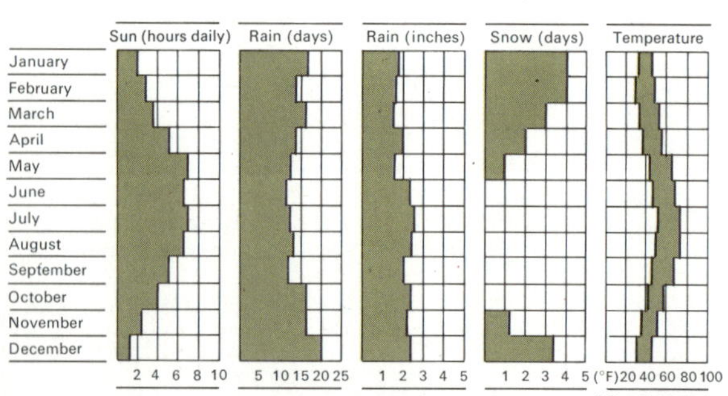

UNCLAIMED FENLAND *Reeds thrive in Wicken Fen, part of fenland's original undrained area. The Fens were first reclaimed by the Romans, then by the Dutch. Some 700 windmills drained the Fens until 1820, when steam pumps were introduced*

Three faces of Essex

Boating On the estuaries of the Crouch, Roach and Blackwater, and at Southend.

Sailing On the Blackwater Estuary; at Burnham-on-Crouch; and off the coast at Southend (8 yacht clubs). Yacht marina at Wallasea Island.

Angling Sea fishing from pier and boats at Southend; at Creeksea on the River Crouch, 1 mile west of Burnham. Coarse fishing in Priory Park Lakes, Southend; South Weald Lakes, Shoebury Park Lake and Epping Forest ponds; on the Rivers Chelmer, Can and Blackwater. Trout at Hanningfield Reservoir, Chelmsford.

Sports Greyhound racing at Southend and football (Southend United) at Roots Hall Stadium. Southend has a multi-nation swimming gala in June and a cricket week in July.

Events Southend's Whitebait Festival—the blessing of the fish—is held at the end of Sept. Southend has a flower festival in Apr./May, a vintage bus rally in June, and a carnival week in Aug.

Places to see *Beecroft Art Gallery*, Westcliff: weekdays, Sun. afternoon. *Chelmsford and Essex Museum*, Chelmsford: weekdays and Sun. afternoon. *Ingatestone Hall*: mid-Apr. to early Oct., Tues. to Sat.: also Bank Hol. *Prittlewell Priory Museum*: weekdays; also Sun. afternoon Apr. to Sept. *Southchurch Hall*, Southend: weekday afternoons and Sat. morning; also Sun. afternoon, Apr. to Sept. *Thurrock Riverside Museum*, Tilbury: Tues. to Sat., except Thur. afternoon. *Tilbury Fort*: weekdays and Sun. afternoon. *Waltham Abbey*: daily.

Information centre Civic Centre, Southend-on-Sea. Tel. Southend 49451.

Essex between London and Chelmsford has three faces. Epping Forest, covering 5600 acres on the fringe of Greater London, is the remnant of a great 60,000-acre hunting ground of Saxon, Norman and Tudor monarchs. It is a place of sunlit glades, of rough heaths and great hornbeam trees. The motorist, rambler or rider can explore the forest by roads, footpaths and bridleways.

Utterly different is the built-up Thames-side fringe from Purfleet to Shoeburyness. This one-time marshland and farmland is industrialised and suburbanised, with docks, oil-storage tanks, factories and new building estates. Southend, with its pier and illuminations, is London's own Blackpool.

Peculiar to Essex is the region's third aspect—the coastal belt of reclaimed marshes sweeping north from Shoeburyness to the Blackwater Estuary. It includes Foulness, Havengore, Potton and Wallasea Islands, parts of which are accessible today only with military passes. This great prairie, reclaimed from the sea in the 17th century by Dutch engineers, has wide horizons, the sharp tang of the sea and sharper winds. It is a lonely kingdom of wild geese and curlews, wildfowlers and oystermen, marsh farmers and cattle. Outside the sea-walls lie miles of mud-flats, treacherous saltings, remote islands, and lonely creeks, a paradise for wildfowl and small-boat sailors.

FOULNESS *The largest island in the Thames Estuary has an estimated*

Bradwell-on-Sea
A nuclear power station dominates the broad estuary of the Blackwater, but 2½ miles east stands the tiny chapel of St Peter-on-the-Wall, which St Cedd built in AD 654 from the stones of the great Roman fort of Othona. The fort's walls can be traced in the grass, and the chapel, one of the earliest shrines of Christianity on the English mainland, stands astride the entrance. For centuries it was a smugglers' hide-out, then it became a beacon tower, a barn and a cattle-shed; in recent years the surviving Saxon nave has been reconsecrated, though no services are held there.

Bradwell Lodge, in the village, is a Tudor and 18th-century building. There are good inns, and a tiny lock-up set in the churchyard wall. From the chapel it is possible to walk 12 miles or more along the lonely sea-wall southwards to Burnham-on-Crouch and scarcely see a house or a human being.

Brentwood
Despite increasing commuter development, this is an excellent centre for walks through unspoilt rural country and spacious parklands within 25 miles of St Paul's Cathedral. South Weald has a 400-acre park containing lakes and deer. Thorndon Park has two lakes, oak trees, and well-signposted walks.

Burnham-on-Crouch
A homely town, famous for yachting, oysters, smuggling yarns and long sea-wall walks. The Quay is a mixture of red, white and yellow colour-washed houses and cottages of former sea captains. There are boat-builders' yards, clap-board cottages, old inns, a smell of ropes, tar and salt water, and a forest of masts bobbing on the tide. There is a 6-mile walk up the Crouch to the waterside hamlet of North Fambridge, with its low-ceilinged Ferry Boat Inn.

Chelmsford
With increasing popularity, Essex's county town has lost much of its rural peace to residential development and light industry. But some early buildings survive; the Church of St Mary the Virgin, which became a cathedral in 1914, has a 15th-century tower.

Writtle, only 2 miles west of the centre of Chelmsford, has one of the loveliest greens in Essex, with a duck pond, Tudor and Georgian houses, a church at one corner and an inn on the other. The High Woods come almost up to the village. Near the church is the 400-acre Hylands Park, which includes a large mansion, woods and lakes.

Chipping Ongar
The wide High Street has houses dating from 1642, and the 50 ft high castle mound north-east of the church is impressive. Round the town lies pleasant farming country—*ongar* is an Anglo-Saxon word meaning 'grazing land'.

The little church, a mile west at Greensted, dating from 1013, is the only surviving Saxon church with a nave wall built of logs. The oak logs are split and set upright in an oak sill.

Danbury
The town crowns a 400-ft hill, with wide views over gorse-clad commons and, to the east, the sails of barges and yachts on the Blackwater Estuary. The stately church is 600 years old and has some notable wooden effigies of knights. The timber-framed Griffin Inn dates from the 16th century. Danbury Palace, built in 1832, stands in a large park.

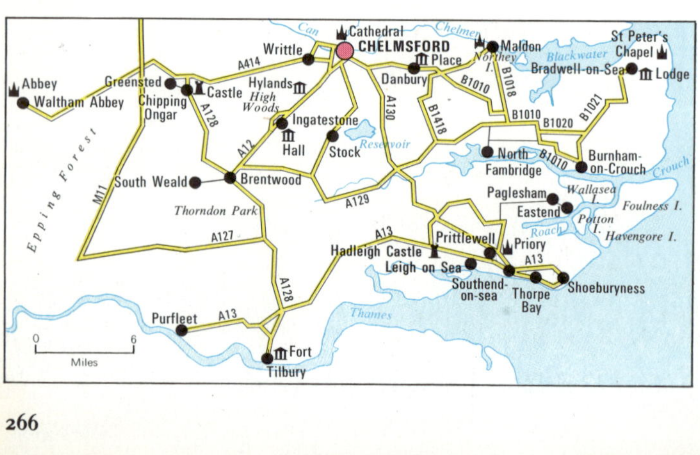

10,000 *Brent geese on its marshes in winter*

FOREST GLADE *Epping Forest was bought by the Corporation of the City of London with private funds for public use in 1882*

Ingatestone
Tudor, Georgian and Victorian houses are splendidly set off by the noble red-brick tower of St Peter's Church. A footpath from the church leads to the Hall, an E-shaped Tudor house with stepped gables built by Sir William Petre, *c.* 1545, and now the home of Lord Petre. In the north wing the Essex Records Office holds annual exhibitions of historical interest. The first-floor gallery contains good pictures.

SPANISH WOOD *Beams for the belfry at Stock came from Spanish galleons*

Leigh-on-Sea
The resort was an old fishing and smuggling village when Southend was a mere hamlet, and it still retains much of its old-world charm. There are cockle-boats and sheds, sailors' inns and clapboard cottages, and ships moored offshore. The cliffs provide fine sea views.

The font in the church at Hockley, 6 miles to the north-west, was made from three huge blocks of Purbeck marble, nearly 900 years ago, and is a fine example of early-English craftsmanship.

Maldon
One of the least-spoilt old towns in Essex. It stands on a hill where, in the summer of AD 991, Brythnoth's Anglo-Danish troops were defeated by the Viking invaders camped on Northey Island. The battle, which lasted three days, is commemorated in an epic 10th-century poem 'The Battle of Maeldune'. The triangular tower of the 13th-century All Saints' Church is the only one of its kind in England. Fishing boats and Thames barges cluster at the picturesque Hythe at the east end of the town.

Paglesham
A village that keeps its aura of salty individuality amid flat fields, elm-bordered, between the estuaries of the Roach and the Crouch. The neighbouring hamlet of Churchend has a neat little red-brick hall, an ancient inn, some attractive cottages, mostly clapboard, and Tudor farmhouses. Across the fields, at Eastend, the Georgian Plough and Sail Inn proclaims the background of the village's inhabitants.

Southend-on-Sea
One of the biggest seaside resorts in Britain, with the longest pleasure pier in the world – $1\frac{1}{3}$ miles long – and a 60 ft floral clock. There are fairs, cliff gardens and 7 miles of seafront.

WALTHAM ABBEY *The sound of the abbey bells inspired Tennyson's poem 'The Bells'*

Southend began as a humble hamlet called the South End of Prittlewell. By 1933 it had grown to its present size and swallowed up Leigh-on-Sea, Westcliff, Prittlewell and Thorpe Bay. When the crowds are not there, it retains a glimmer of the faded elegance of the select watering-place to which 'Prinny', the Prince Regent, relegated his Princess Caroline to stay in what is now Royal Terrace.

Tilbury Fort
A handsome fort with a triumphal arch, built in 1682 to stop the French or Dutch from coming up the Thames. The arched watergate has a handsome, lavishly decorated entrance.

Waltham Abbey
An old, small abbey, once grand, kingly and powerful, on the edge of Epping Forest. King Harold built a religious college there, and gave it riches. It is said that after he was slain at Hastings he was buried at Waltham—a plain slab is believed to be his tomb. Henry II built a great abbey, a majestic offering to God to expiate the murder of Thomas à Becket. Much has gone, destroyed in the Reformation, but what remains is magnificent. The great Norman nave has been compared with Durham Cathedral, and there are fine monuments and stained glass. Tennyson lived at nearby Beech Hill Park from 1837 to 1840.

Oysters and Roman remains at Colchester

Sailing Clubs all along the coast, and ample facilities for visiting craft.

Golf Courses at Clacton; Colchester; Frinton; and Harwich.

Excursions Air trips from West Road, Clacton, in summer. Cruises from Harwich on Rivers Orwell and Stour; around Harwich Harbour; and across to Felixstowe.

Events There are regattas at Clacton in Aug., and Harwich in June; Pyefleet Week (yacht racing) is at Brightlingsea in Aug. There is a carnival at Clacton in Aug., and at Harwich in Nov. The Oyster Feast at Colchester is held in Oct.

Places to see Colchester: *Bourne Mill* (NT), Wed., Sat., Sun. and Bank Hol. afternoons, Apr. to Sept. *Colchester and Essex Museum*, The Castle, with remains of a Roman Temple: Apr. to Sept., weekdays, Sun. afternoon. *Museum of Social History and Natural History Museum*: both weekdays. *The Minories*, art gallery: weekdays, except Mon., Sun. afternoon. *Zoo*: daily. *Layer Marney Towers*, Layer Marney: Thur. and Sun. afternoons, Apr. to Oct.; also Tues. afternoons July and Aug. *Paycocke's* (NT), Coggeshall: Wed., Thur., Sun. and Bank Hol. Mon. afternoons, Apr. to Sept. *St Botolph's Priory*, Colchester: daily. *St Osyth's Priory*, St Osyth, chapel and Abbot's tower: Easter, and daily May to Sept.

Information centres 4 Trinity St., Colchester. Tel. Colchester 46379. Central Seafront, Clacton-on-Sea. Tel. Clacton-on-Sea 23400.

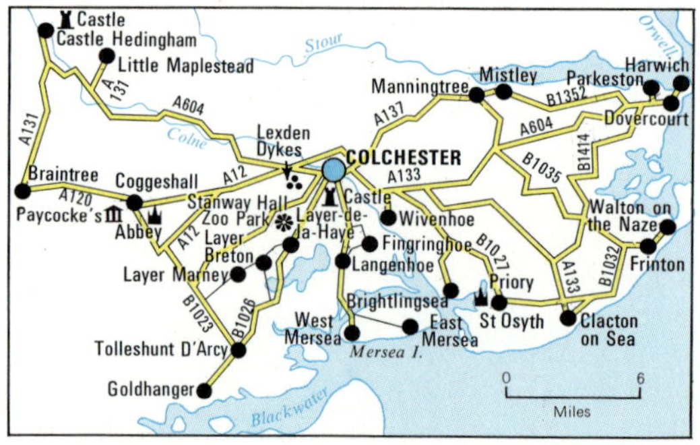

North-east Essex, bounded by water-meadows, willows and noble churches along the River Stour, is a region of beauty and peace, with its roots deep in English history. Colchester was one of the greatest Roman fortress-cities in England after London. Traces of Anglo-Saxon occupation exist in names along shining creeks—Langenhoe, Fingringhoe and Wivenhoe. The Normans came later, and Norman-French names linger in village names such as Tolleshunt D'Arcy, Layer Breton and Layer-de-la-Haye. There is a rare Knights Templar church at Little Maplestead; the ruins of a mighty Norman castle stand at Castle Hedingham; and Colchester has one of the largest Norman keeps in Europe.

The coast is a maze of opalescent mud-flats and winding creeks, tide-washed islands of green samphire (an edible marsh plant) and purple sea-lavender, the 'heather' of the sea. The tides creep in like silk through uninhabited marshes where wild duck, sheep and cattle abound, and only curlews and redshanks break the summer silence. Smugglers came up the creeks where the Vikings were before them. Today yachtsmen, small-boat sailors and smacksmen sail the waters which the long-ships sailed.

Inland, along the Colne Valley, is a different world of open heaths, deep woodlands and the rich brown earth of farming country, with former spinning and weaving villages—a region blending history with beauty, and as yet little spoilt by development.

MANNINGTREE *The harbour, popular with weekend sailors, was once a flourishing port for barges, carrying mixed cargoes down the coast to London*

Braintree
A bustling town which made its fortune out of wool more than 400 years ago but now depends largely on the manufacture of silks, an industry founded by the Courtaulds, and steel window-frames. Few towns combine the old and the new so well. Even the modern town hall is in harmony. Every street has ancient houses, and the partly medieval Swan Hotel has a striking courtyard.

Brightlingsea
An old fishing and yachting port at the mouth of the Colne Estuary. Jacobes Hall, the best medieval house in the town, is now a hotel. The splendid church tower, 94 ft high, is one of the finest in East Anglia. Inside the Perpendicular church is a series of wall plaques dedicated to seamen killed in battles or drowned on the fishing grounds.

Castle Hedingham
A great Norman castle keep, 100 ft high, built in 1140 by the mighty de Veres, Earls of Oxford, dominates the little medieval town. A Norman church and a Georgian squire's house huddle beneath the great castle mound.

Clacton-on-Sea
A cheerful Victorian-Edwardian seaside town with pier, pavilion, promenade, sandy beaches, public gardens and a holiday camp. The attractive pseudo-medieval Moot Hall is skilfully adapted from a medieval barn.

Coggeshall
A small medieval wool and lace-making town on the route of the old Roman Stane Street, now the A120. The many fine old houses include Paycocke's, a well-known wool merchant's house of 1500, heavily beamed and panelled. Even older and equally lovely is the Woolpack Hotel. The remains of a 12th-century abbey are set beside a fast mill-stream.

Colchester
Almost the perfect marriage between old and new, standing on a hill in rolling country. First it was the capital city, probably wooden and stockaded, of 'Old King Cole', the ancient British chieftain Cunobelin who reigned over much of south-east England. Then a great Roman city was built on the site by Claudius in AD 49–50. Boadicea, Queen of the Iceni, sacked it in AD 60 in a rising against the Romans. The Normans gave it a great castle. Cromwell's army besieged the town in 1648, after which the two Royalist commanders of the defences were executed as rebels.

COLCHESTER CASTLE *William I used stone from the Roman fort to build the castle. The Norman keep is the largest in Europe*

ST OSYTH'S PRIORY *The remains date from the 12th to 16th centuries; best preserved are those of the gatehouse*

BUILDING OF LIGHT *The library of Essex University, built in 1967 to a design by Kenneth Capon, is reflected in the waters of one of the three lakes in Wivenhoe Park, Colchester. The well-wooded grounds of the university overlook the Colne*

and are the last remnants of an attempt by Richard Rigby, MP, Paymaster General of the Forces in 1762, to build an elegant little 18th-century spa town. There are many pleasant Victorian, Georgian and older houses, and a large stone swan admires itself in a fountain.

Mersea Island
An island famous among small-boat sailors. West Mersea is overcrowded with houses and boats, but attractive old fishing cottages survive in the old town. The White Hart Inn stands opposite the Norman and 14th-century church; the Victory Inn overlooks the yacht anchorage. East Mersea is set amid relatively unspoilt farmland and grazing marshes.

St Osyth
The most imposing range of monastic buildings in Essex. The priory, which dates largely from the 12th century, was founded by St Osyth, wife of a 7th-century East Anglian king, who was beheaded by the Danes in AD 653. The buildings were extended by successive owners, notably Lord Darcy. The gatehouse is magnificent and there are lovely gardens. The waterside village still has considerable charm.

Walton on the Naze
The Naze juts into the North Sea south of Harwich, with its great Naze Tower to warn mariners of the West Rocks off shore. Behind the Naze and town lie broad salt-marshes and islands, a paradise for bird-watchers. The town has bungalows, chalets, caravans, a beach and an 800 ft long pier. There is safe bathing, the sea fishing is excellent, and lobsters can be bought.

Wivenhoe
A village with a busy shipyard on the wooded reaches of the Colne. Its church was damaged by earthquake in 1884. The older houses include one in East Street that has fine pargetting, or decorated plasterwork. Essex University, standing in Wivenhoe Park, is functional, with tower blocks, concrete and glass—and a lake which saves the scene.

Over the centuries, Colchester has been a great centre for weaving and the heart of the oyster trade in Britain. The annual oyster feast is unique. The main streets still follow the Roman plan and parts of the Roman walls remain, including the high Balkerne Gate. The Norman castle keep, the largest in Britain, is on the site of the Roman temple founded by Claudius and has magnificent collections of Roman relics. The modern town hall, Italianate and elegant, is topped by a bronze statue of Helena, mother of Constantine, regal with a sceptre and cross, her face turned towards Jerusalem.

Colchester is a bright, clean town with a repertory company, museums and art galleries, and 180 acres of public parks and gardens, including the beautiful Castle Park. There is an open-air zoo at Stanway Hall, 3 miles south-west.

Frinton
A trim, neat, self-consciously exclusive resort, born in the 1890's, with good sands, a sloping cliff and some modern skyscraper flats.

Goldhanger
A rash of modern building has scarcely touched the attractive heart of this farming and fishing village. A wheel-turned pump still raises water. The Chequers Inn, *c.* 1500, has a manorial court-room which was also used for medieval marriage feasts. There are pleasant walks along the sea-wall, west and east, and Goldhanger Creek is full of small boats, oysters and wading birds.

Harwich
The busy continental car ferry to the Hook of Holland sails from Parkeston, 2 miles west. Harwich faces the meeting-place of the broad Stour and Orwell Estuaries, a fortified port that has seen the comings and goings of every sort of ship for ten centuries. The pattern of the narrow, cobbled streets is medieval and the atmosphere sea-faring. Neighbouring Dovercourt is a quiet family resort, Edwardian in flavour.

The Layers
Layer Breton has a great heath with a church in the middle of it, an old inn and cottages. Layer-de-la-Haye, 2 miles north-east, also has attractive houses and cottages, and fine views over the 1200-acre Abberton Reservoir, winter haunt of some 20,000 wildfowl.

Layer Marney, 1½ miles west of Layer Breton, has a splendid red-brick tower gatehouse of *c.* 1520 and a red-brick church of 1524.

Little Maplestead
The main feature of the village is the 14th-century round church of the Knights Templar. There are only four others like it in England.

Manningtree
An attractive little port famous for its swans, its maltings for fermenting barley, and its sailing barges. At neighbouring Mistley, the two great towers of the church were designed by Robert Adam

PAYCOCKE'S *The house in West Street, Coggeshall, takes its name from its 16th-century builder, John Paycocke, a wool merchant. It contains a collection of period furniture*

North from The Rodings

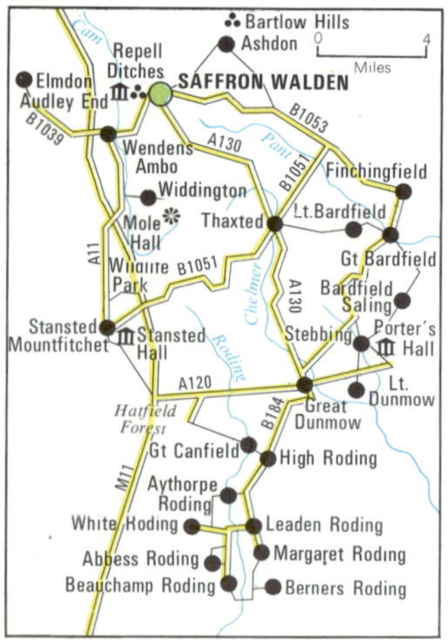

Boating Boats for hire on Hatfield Forest Lake. Canoeing on the Chelmer.

Places to see *Audley End House*: early Apr. to Oct., daily except Mon. and Good Fri.; also Bank Hols. *Great Bardfield Cottage Museum*: Apr. to Oct., Sat. and Sun. afternoons. *Mole Hall Wildlife Park*, Widdington: daily. *Saffron Walden Museum*: weekdays; also Sun. afternoons in summer. *Stansted Windmill*: Apr. to Oct., first Sun. in month.

Information centres Information Bureau, 4 Bene't Street, Cambridge. Tel. Cambridge 358977/319189. Town Hall, Princes Street, Ipswich. Tel. Ipswich 55851.

Countryside of quiet charm, little changed for centuries, comes right up to the edge of Saffron Walden, itself dating from the Middle Ages and one of the most attractive small towns in East Anglia. The nearby great park of Audley End surrounds one of the finest and largest Jacobean mansions in Britain. There are other equally attractive, ancient little towns, such as Great Dunmow and Thaxted.

The countryside is mainly rolling and wooded in the east, while westwards from Saffron Walden lies the loneliest part of Essex, a countryside of low chalk hills on the Cambridgeshire border. Round the village of Elmdon is a maze of by-roads little known to the average motorist, with breezy landscapes and a feeling of wide open spaces.

The Rodings, to the south, are a group of villages among rich farmland, intersected by the pretty little River Roding. The villages have an 18th-century charm and are rich in half-timbered houses, moated manor farms and ancient churches, some with wooden spires. Roads wind past farms, many of them still with high hedges, scattered woods and glimpses of water-meadows. This is the picturesque England which the 18th-century artist George Morland painted and the Victorian novelist Anthony Trollope loved.

VILLAGE OF HROTH *Leaden Roding is one of a group of eight Esse*

Ashdon

A village with a timber-framed guildhall near the church of *c.* 1500, and an inn, The Rose and Crown, which is probably 300 years old. The Bartlow Hills to the north are the site of the best Romano-British burial grounds in the country. There were seven, four of which remain in good order. When they were excavated, in 1832–40, walled graves were uncovered, full of glassware, enamels and bronzes, obviously the treasures of men of high rank. The superb collection was taken to Easton Lodge, but was destroyed there in a fire in 1847.

Audley End

The house is approached by a stately Adam bridge over the River Cam. Built in 1603 for Thomas Howard, 1st Earl of Suffolk, who became Lord High Treasurer, the house was originally far larger and prompted James I to remark that it was 'too big for a king, but might do for the Lord Treasurer!' What is left is nonetheless immense, and includes a magnificent entrance hall and staircase. There is much fine Adam work, lovely 18th-century furniture, and a notable collection of stuffed birds.

Red-brick Tudor stables flank the house, and in the grounds are a round temple by Robert Adam, a Palladian bridge carrying a summer-house, a Temple of Concord (1781), several decorative lodges and the tall Springwood Column (1774). The village is a well-planned estate, mainly Georgian, with Jacobean almshouses.

The Bardfields

The picturesque villages of Great Bardfield, Little Bardfield and Bardfield Saling are flanked by the little River Pant. The Hall at Little Bardfield dates from *c.* 1580, and St Katherine's Church has a Saxon tower and an organ of *c.* 1700. Great Bardfield, once a market town, has many medieval and Georgian houses, a restored windmill, and a mainly 14th-century church, St Mary's, notable for its fine stone screen. The village has a picturesque High Street, and its inhabitants include many artists. A 16th-century museum houses an exhibition of historic Essex farming maps, books and pottery, and has 'corn dollies' for sale.

JACOBEAN ELEGANCE *Audley End House was begun in 1603 by Thomas Howard, 1st Earl of Suffolk. The present interior and grounds are largely the late-18th-century work of Robert Adam, who took care to preserve their Jacobean elegance*

GREAT DUNMOW TOWN CRIER

Great Dunmow's town crier, seen on the steps of Thaxted Town Hall, opens official functions all over East Anglia

villages which have the affix 'Roding'. The name comes from the Old English 'Hrothingas', meaning 'a settlement of Hroth's people'

Finchingfield
A much-photographed village, with a church on a hill, a stream with a duck-pond and a green. Houses of all shapes, sizes and periods are enhanced by the timber-framed long white guildhall. All combine to produce a haphazard grouping which makes for striking beauty. The little bell-turret on top of the church crowns the scene.

THAXTED MORRIS MEN

Thaxted's Morris dancers hold a festival in the town every June and tour the area at Easter and Spring Bank Holiday

Great Canfield
A neatly beautiful village on a by-road. The great castle mound—50 ft high, with a dry moat 45 ft wide—is the majestic tree-clad relic of the once-mighty castle of Aubrey de Vere, Great Chamberlain of England 800 years ago. It dominates the churchyard and the village. Hatfield Forest, $3\frac{1}{2}$ miles west, is a 1000-acre National Trust open space of woodland and grassland, with a lake for boating and fishing.

Great Dunmow
The town lies at a junction of Roman roads and has a picturesque timbered guildhall, an old inn, called The Saracen's Head, and a pond, the 'Doctor's Pond', which was the scene of the first lifeboat experiments, carried out by Lionel Lukin in 1785.

Every four years Great Dunmow is the scene of the famous 'trial' at which a flitch of bacon is presented to any married couple 'who have not had a brawl in their home nor wished to be unmarried for the last 12 months and a day'. It is an old Breton custom brought to Little Dunmow by the Fitzwalters and revived by Harrison Ainsworth, the historical novelist, in 1855. The ceremony, with bewigged amateur judge and counsel, is conducted with mock seriousness, and is unique in England.

The Rodings
Eight farming villages lie along the valley of the River Roding, most of them picturesque with old churches, moated halls, clapboard or half-timbered cottages and set in rolling sweeps of ploughland, grassland or woodland. This is a curiously individual agricultural world of its own, with enchanting old houses. Anthony Trollope, the Victorian novelist, loved 'the Roothings', as Essex people call them, and hunted there each winter. They are: Abbess Roding; Aythorpe Roding; Beauchamp Roding; Berners Roding, with a church in the Hall's yard; High Roding; Leaden Roding, with a picturesque Hall and outbuilding; Margaret Roding, with a fine white Georgian house facing the road behind its moat; and White Roding.

Saffron Walden
Only 40 miles from London, yet an unspoilt small town with superb medieval houses—of which the youth hostel at the corner of Myddelton Place is one of the best. The town got its wealth from wool and from its crop of saffron, which was a medicine as well as a dye. The saffron industry is commemorated in the name of the town. The High Street has many late Georgian houses, and medieval houses and cottages are scattered throughout the town, particularly in Myddelton Place, Castle Street, Church Lane and at the junction of Church Street and Market Hill.

A great earthwork at the west end of the town, in which 200 Saxon skeletons were discovered, is known as Repell Ditches and attracts archaeologists.

Stansted Mountfitchet
Stansted is nationally famous as the hub of the fierce battle to prevent the third London Airport from being situated there in a sweep of country said to contain 540 buildings of architectural or historic interest, other than churches. The town is noisy with traffic, but side streets contain old houses of charm. Stansted Hall stands in a great park with a lake. There is a medieval church, the site of a Norman castle and a 65 ft high red-brick tower windmill built in 1787 and restored in 1966.

Mole Hall Wildlife Park, at Widdington, 4 miles north-east, includes wallabies, chimpanzees and a variety of birds.

Stebbing
Good half-timbered houses line the sloping village streets. Porter's Hall is a big 16th-century manor house ringed by a moat, and the clapboarded watermill on the Stebbing Brook is one of the most attractive in the country. The Great Mount, 225 ft wide, like a gigantic molehill, is believed to be the site of a castle built by Ranulf Peverel *c.* 1086.

Thaxted
A small town with a magnificent part-14th-century cathedral-like church and a tower windmill. A little street of timber-framed, overhanging houses behind the 15th-century timbered guildhall leads to almshouses and a double row of dormered, gabled and colour-washed cottages on the road out to Cutler's Green. Clarance House is an 18th-century gem opposite the church.

Wendens Ambo
A tiny village hiding up a by-road near Audley End Station, unforgettably lovely and much photographed. The lane to the church has enchanting cottages on the left and the Hall Barn on the right.

EAST ANGLIAN CORN DOLLY

Corn dollies are ornaments plaited from straw after the harvest. It is believed they evolved from the bound sheaves of corn which pre-Christian peoples used as thank-offerings to their gods. The first dollies were probably in the form of either a goddess or a cornucopia. They are still made in country districts in England, and their shape varies from region to region. One example of the East Anglian corn dolly (left) is plaited round a wooden core and trimmed with decorative braid

Villages among the fenlands

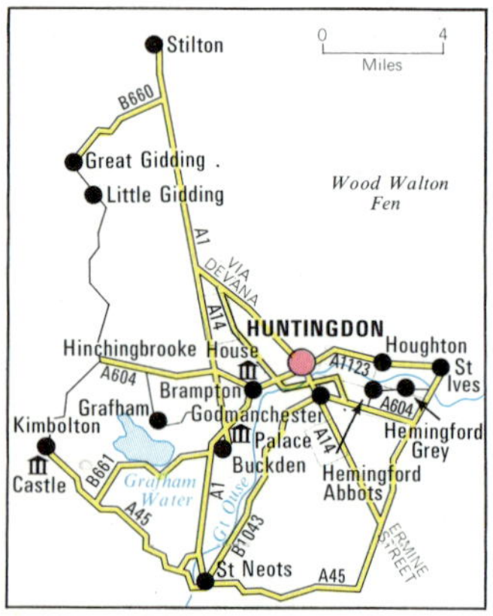

Angling Coarse fishing on the Great Ouse; trout fishing on Grafham Water.

Boating Pleasure cruising at Huntingdon, St Ives and St Neots, where there are boats for hire. Sailing on Grafham Water and the Great Ouse.

Horse racing Steeplechasing during the winter at Huntingdon.

Events On Tues. after Spring Bank Hol. at St Ives, six children receive Bibles under a will made in 1675 which stated that the Bibles were to be allocated by casting dice. There are carnivals at St Neots in Aug. and at Huntingdon in Sept.

Places to see *Buckden Palace*: July, Aug. and Sept., Sun. afternoon. *Cromwell Museum*, Huntingdon: weekdays except Mon.; also Sun. afternoon. *Hinchingbrooke House*, Brampton: Sun. afternoon in Mar., Apr., May, July and Aug.; also Bank Hols. *Kimbolton Castle*: Spring and Late Summer Bank Hol.; also Sun. afternoon mid-July to Aug. *Norris Museum*, St Ives: Tues. to Fri., and Sat. afternoon; also Sun. afternoon, May to Sept.

Information centre County Library, Princes Street, Huntingdon. Tel. Huntingdon 52181.

PEPYS'S HOUSE *A 15th-century farmhouse at Brampton was the family home of the diarist Samuel Pepys*

The flat countryside in the north-east of Cambridgeshire (which now takes in Huntingdonshire) gives an impression of far horizons, for most of it is fenland where cattle graze on drained pastures. To the south is a mellow corner which was the childhood home of one of the most powerful men in British history—Oliver Cromwell, who was born at Huntingdon in 1599.

He was a farmer and Member of Parliament there, and many of the buildings, including the church in Huntingdon where he was christened and the grammar school which he attended, are still much as he knew them. Here, too, Samuel Pepys went to school for a year before he was sent to St Paul's, London, in 1640.

The market towns of Huntingdon, St Ives and St Neots are linked by the River Great Ouse, and the best way to see them is from the river. Boats can be hired at Huntingdon to explore south-west to St Neots or east to St Ives. The river journey to St Ives offers perhaps the lovelier route, with stops at flower-bright Houghton, and at the twin villages of Hemingford Abbots and Hemingford Grey.

THE RIVERSIDE SCENE AT HEMINGFORD GREY *The village, with its thatched cottages and timbered houses, has changed little since the 18th century. St James's Church stands on the Great Ouse; its steeple has been truncated since 1741, when the top section was swept into the river in a violent storm. The remains of it are believed to be still lying on the river bed*

Brampton
A village of dusky red and yellow cottages, including the home of Samuel Pepys's family. It was here, according to legend, that Samuel buried his money when a Dutch invasion was feared. The 13th-century church has a fine font, an oak screen, and three finely carved choir stalls of the 14th century.

The road to Huntingdon passes Hinchingbrooke House. The finely sculpted gatehouse is believed to have been brought here from Ramsey Abbey in the 16th century, but the mansion was built by Oliver Cromwell's prosperous great-grandfather, Sir Richard Cromwell, around the remains of a nunnery. After the Restoration the 1st Earl of Sandwich added to the west side of the court. A serious fire in 1830 did extensive damage, but the house was meticulously restored and it is now a school that is open to public view at certain times during the summer holidays.

Buckden
A village of brick-and-timber houses near Bishop's Palace, which was for centuries the fortified home of the Bishops of Lincoln. Henry VIII sent Catherine of Aragon to live there before moving her to Kimbolton. The inner gatehouse has some intricate brickwork and attractive windows.

Grafham Water
A reservoir, covering 6 square miles, supplying towns within a 20-mile radius and best approached up a sweeping arc of road from the A1 at Buckden. There are extensive picnic areas, and some grassy walks round the lake. Sailing is for club members only and fishing rights are for ticket-holders only.

Hemingford Grey
A village of timber, thatch and mellow brick cottages with a thick-walled 12th-century manor, which is still lived in. The church stands on a curve of river, fringed by willows. The upper section of its spire came down in a gale in 1741 and is locally believed to be at the bottom of the river. The village links up with Hemingford Abbots, which has two attractive meres.

Huntingdon and Godmanchester
In Roman times Godmanchester was an important settlement on the crossroads of the Via Devana, which ran from Colchester to Chester, and Ermine Street, which linked London with York. It retained its importance and became one of the earliest boroughs, receiving its charter in 1213, but is now amalgamated into one borough with Huntingdon. Between them stretch the 300-acre meadow of Port Holme on one side of a 17th-century raised causeway, and West Side Common on the other, both crossed with pleasant footpaths and loops and runnels from the Great Ouse. The Elizabethan grammar school is near the causeway and there are many old buildings with a variety of gables, dormer windows and colour washes.

The Huntingdon end of the causeway has a pedestrians' bridge parallel to the beautiful 13th-century road bridge.

Huntingdon, formerly a county town, is more cramped than Godmanchester but has some unspoilt corners with several fine Georgian houses. Oliver Cromwell was born in a house close to Ermine Street, its site marked by a plaque on the Huntingdon Research Centre. He was baptised in All Saints' Church, which is partly 11th century. His father is buried there. About 1610, Oliver attended the old grammar school, a basically Norman building, where Samuel Pepys was also a pupil. It was opened as a Cromwell Museum in 1962 by the then Speaker of the House of Commons. The George Inn, once the property of Cromwell's grandfather, has an inner courtyard overlooked by a gallery where Shakespearian plays are produced occasionally.

Kimbolton
A red-roofed village with a 13th-century church and a medieval castle where Catherine of Aragon spent her last four bitter years. The castle was greatly extended by Henry Montagu, a Lord Chief Justice, who bought it in 1620, two years after sending Sir Walter Raleigh to the scaffold. The most distinctive of further renovations to the castle are those of Vanbrugh at the end of the 17th century, with later additions by Robert Adam, including the outer gatehouse and north gateway. The castle is now a school. Montagu became the 1st Earl of Manchester, and there are impressive monuments to the Manchester family in the 13th-century St Andrew's Church, which also has a 16th-century screen partially decorated with paintings of kings and angels.

Little Gidding
A cluster of buildings with a long and interesting history. In 1625 Nicholas Ferrar, the son of a prosperous merchant family, turned his back on worldly things, brought his mother and many relatives here, and vowed to lead a life of prayer and good works. The family rebuilt the Church of St John the Evangelist, which had been used as a barn and pigsty, established a small local school, and tended the poor and ailing. In spite of their wish for seclusion the Ferrars began to attract both respectful and suspicious attention.

Charles I came to visit them—the third time, in 1646, in search of a hiding place from Cromwell's forces. Word of this last visit leaked out later, and the house and church were sacked by the Roundheads as a reprisal. The church was rebuilt in the early 18th century and added to in the 19th and 20th centuries. The Society of the Friends of Little Gidding, formed in 1946, makes an annual pilgrimage to the church on the second Saturday in July. The beliefs and practice of Ferrar's community inspired the last poem in T. S. Eliot's sequence 'Four Quartets'.

ICE SKATING AT ST IVES

A primitive ice skate (above) from St Ives museum recalls the time when the Great Ouse used to freeze in winter. The picture of skating at St Ives bridge, also in the museum, was painted by Charles Whynter in 1891. The tall bridge chapel, built with the bridge in the 15th century, was then in use as a house

The chapel on the 15th-century bridge at St Ives is one of only four medieval bridge chapels surviving in England. It was converted into a house in the 19th century, when an extra storey was added, but this was later removed

St Ives
A market town originally called Slepe, but which changed its name after a priory dedicated to St Ivo was built there in 1050. The 15th-century bridge has a chapel in its centre bay. Oliver Cromwell had a farm near by and his statue, in which he is depicted booted and wearing an unpuritanically rakish hat, stands in the market-place.

St Neots
A pleasant market town on the Great Ouse with a history dating back to the 10th century. One side of the huge market square backs on to the river. The 15th-century Perpendicular church tower rises nobly beyond the square, with wonderful interior roof carvings of angels, birds and animals.

Stilton
A village on the edge of the Fens with the reputation for a cheese that it has never produced. The 17th-century Bell Inn was once an important staging post beside what was the Great North Road, which is now diverted around the village. Leicestershire farmers took their produce to the inn for collection and delivery by coach to London, where the cheese became known as 'Stilton'.

BUTTERFLY OF THE FENS

The large Copper butterfly, *Lycaena dispar batarus*, takes its name from the copper bands on its wings. It is found only in Wood Walton Fen, where it is protected. The butterfly was brought to England from Holland in 1927 to replace the native British species, extinct since 1848. The male and female can be distinguished by their upperside markings

The glories of Cambridge

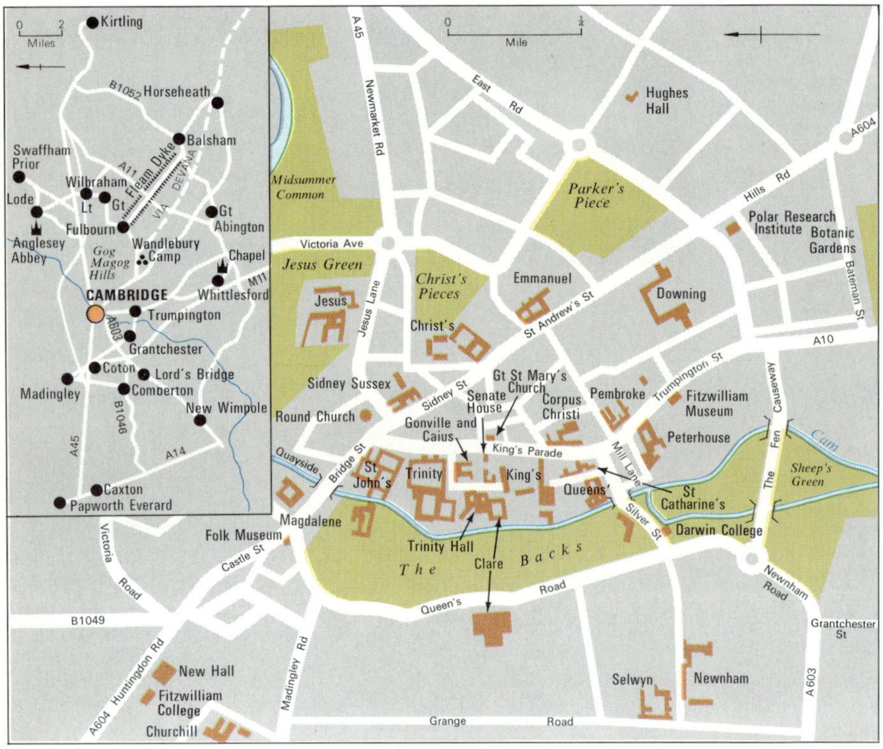

Angling There is coarse fishing for bream and chub on the River Cam.

Nature trail At Wandlebury, 2 miles south of Cambridge.

Events The Lent Bumps (rowing contest) take place in Feb. May Week is held for 10 days from the end of May to the 2nd week in June. Cambridge has a Midsummer Fair in June, a Folk Festival in late July and Festival of the Arts in that month.

Places to see *Anglesey Abbey* (NT): Apr. to mid-Oct., afternoons except Mon. and Fri. *Cambridge University Botanic Gardens*: weekdays. *Cambridge and County Folk Museum, Fitzwilliam Museum*: both Tues. to Sat. and Sun. afternoon. *Duxford Airfield*, 8 miles south of Cambridge: Apr. to Sept., daily; Oct., Nov., Mar., weekends. *Scott Polar Research Institute* and *University Museum of Archaeology and Ethnology*: both weekday afternoons. *Sedgwick Museum of Geology*: Mon. to Fri., Sat. morning. *Wimpole Hall* (NT), 8 miles south-west of Cambridge: mid-July to mid-Oct., afternoons except Mon. and Fri., but open Bank Hol.

Information centre 4 Bene't Street, Cambridge.
Tel. Cambridge 358977/319189.

A Roman town was established by AD 70 on a hill overlooking the River Cam, which the Romans knew as the Granta. The name of the site, where the Saxons settled after the Romans had left, evolved gradually from Grantacaester to Grantabric, Cantabridge and finally to the modern Cambridge. Part of the Cam near the city is still called locally by its old Roman name.

When the university was established early in the 13th century, students made their own lodging arrangements and grouped around the religious and lay teachers whose ideas most appealed to them. It was 1284 before the first true college, Peterhouse, was founded by the Bishop of Ely. Discipline was slack and the behaviour of students led to a 'town and gown' conflict which went on into the 18th century.

Cambridge was a busy commercial centre even before the university was established, and today its industries include radio and electronics, cement-making, flour milling and the manufacture of scientific instruments. The university itself is a major scientific research centre, with its Cavendish Laboratory—where Rutherford split the atom and established the science of nuclear physics—the Observatories, the Scott Polar Research Institute and the University Chemical Laboratory.

Visitors can go into college courtyards, chapels, dining halls and certain gardens at most times. There are public tennis courts on Christ's Pieces—the name 'piece' in Cambridge means open space—and on Jesus Green. Punts or boats can be hired at Magdalene Bridge for a trip past the Backs, the lawns sloping down to the riverside, or at the bottom of Mill Lane and Silver Street for a choice between the Backs and the Granta. Good walks include footpaths across Jesus Green and over Midsummer Common to the college boathouses.

Visitors should particularly try to see Rubens's *The Adoration of the Magi*, bought in 1962 for £275,000 and presented to King's College, where it now forms the Chapel altar-piece; the Old Court of Corpus Christi; the President's Lodge of Queens'; and the Wren Library of Trinity. Much good modern building includes the Erasmus Building in Queens', opened by Queen Elizabeth the Queen Mother in 1961; New Hall for women, 1954; Fitzwilliam College, 1963; and the History Faculty Building, 1968.

SOARING PINNACLES *The tower of the 19th-century gateway of King's College rises among the pinnacles along King's Parade*

OVER THE COLLEGES *An aerial view of Cambridge, showing King's College Chapel, left centre, Clare College to its left and St John's and the Bridge of Sighs in the background*

THE OLD GRANARY *This was part of 19th-century Newnham Grange, once owned by Charles Darwin. The house and the granary are now incorporated in Darwin College*

BOTANIC GARDENS Covering more than 40 acres at the junction of Trumpington Street and Bateman Street, the gardens are second only to Kew in importance. Although primarily designed as a botanical teaching and research aid for the university, they have much to offer the casual visitor. The gardens are best visited in the afternoon, when the plant houses are open.

CLARE COLLEGE The beautifully proportioned building was designed not by an acknowledged architect, but by Thomas and Robert Grumbold, who described themselves as master masons, and by 'bricklayer' John Westley. It is the third oldest Cambridge college after Peterhouse and Michaelhouse, which later became incorporated into Trinity. A college was founded here in 1326 but was destroyed by fire and was refounded in 1338 by Lady Elizabeth de Clare. Another fire, in 1521, destroyed what was then known as Clare Hall, and the present buildings were begun by the Grumbolds in 1638. The gardens are noted for their variety and beauty.

FITZWILLIAM MUSEUM The museum was founded in 1816 by Viscount Fitzwilliam, who left it £100,000 together with his own library and collections. The building was designed by George Basevi, who was killed in a fall at Ely and did not see the museum completed. Outstanding among later benefactors have been the Courtauld family. There are extensive Egyptian, Greek and Roman collections, illuminated manuscripts, and one of the most comprehensive displays of English pottery and

DOWN THE LANE *Windows of Trinity College look on Trinity Lane, which backs on to the college's Great Court, built c. 1600*

EDWARD'S PASSAGE *A typical back-lane bookshop for students*

CORPUS CHRISTI *A 16th-century glass figure of Fortune*

MARKET DAY *Cambridge market is held six days a week in the large square in front of the 15th-century Great St Mary's Church*

WITHOUT A NAIL *The wooden bridge over the Cam at Queens' College was built in 1749 on mathematical principles so that no nails were needed. Etheridge, its designer, received a fee of 20 guineas. It was rebuilt to exactly the same design at the beginning of this century*

porcelain. Paintings, covering major European movements from the Middle Ages to the present, include works by Titian, Rembrandt, Gainsborough, Hogarth and Turner.

FOLK MUSEUM A domestic museum of town and country over the last few centuries, preserving articles of daily use including furniture, cooking equipment and tools which might otherwise disappear. It was converted in 1936 from the old White Horse Inn.

GREAT ST MARY'S CHURCH The university church, originally called St Mary's-by-the-Market, is 15th century with a 17th-century tower. The market is still held in the square in front of the church. Galleries had to be installed in the 18th century to cope with the large congregations. There is some fine Georgian screenwork. Visitors can climb the tower (inside, rather than in emulation of the traditional undergraduate steeplejacks) from which there are wide views of town and countryside.

KING'S COLLEGE CHAPEL With the superb fan tracery in its soaring stone roof, this is one of the most magnificent examples of Perpendicular architecture in England. It was begun by Henry VI in 1446, but work was interrupted by the Wars of the Roses and it was not completed until 1515. Flemish craftsmen took the next 26 years putting in the glass of brilliant reds and blues and subtle greys and yellows. Among the chapel's other glories is *The Adoration of the Magi* by Paul Rubens, which was presented to the college in 1962. The chapel looks splendid at any time, but particularly when seen in spring with daffodils covering the meadows. Every Christmas Eve the famous Festival of Nine Carols and Lessons is held, and at other times the University Musical Society performs the Bach Passions.

MAGDALENE (pronounced Maudlin) Founded in 1542 by Baron Audley of Walden, a courtier of Henry VIII, Magdalene has two small but charming courts and the Pepysian Library, to which Samuel Pepys bequeathed his engravings and books—leaving instructions on how the books were to be arranged in the bookcases that he had provided. The manuscripts of his Diary, written in shorthand, are also in the library.

PETERHOUSE COLLEGE The oldest college in Cambridge, founded in 1284 by Hugh de Balsham, Bishop of Ely. He left some money towards the building of the hall which, although often renovated, still keeps some original masonry. The woodwork was removed in the last century and the painted panels showing masters and benefactors date from the 17th century. The poet Thomas Gray was a fellow at the college and had a room overlooking Little St Mary's Church. Gray was afraid of fire and had a ladder permanently attached to his window. In 1742 undergraduates hoaxed him by shouting 'Fire' under his window and Gray, in his nightshirt, went down the ladder into a tub of water put there by the undergraduates. He was so angry that he left and went to Pembroke.

QUEENS' COLLEGE The college is named after two queens—Henry VI's wife Margaret of Anjou, who founded it in 1448, and Edward IV's wife Elizabeth, who refounded and endowed it in 1465. Elizabeth built the Second Court, with its cloisters and half-timbered President's Lodge. The wooden Mathematical Bridge gives a fine view of the college, the Backs and the river. This bridge was built without a single nail in 1749 and was reconstructed in its original form at the beginning of this century.

ROUND CHURCH The Church of the Holy Sepulchre is one of the few round churches in England. Its circular Norman nave was supplemented by chancel and north aisle in the 14th century, and all too drastically restored in the 19th, though without robbing the interior of its warmth and intimacy.

ST JOHN'S COLLEGE The impressive Tudor gateway, with its turrets and gilded heraldry, is a fitting introduction to the splendours of St John's. Inside is the early 16th-century First Court, with the college dining hall. The second or Shrewsbury Court has a 187 ft long Combination Room, or Fellows' Common Room, built in 1598. The third square, completed in Restoration times, is connected with New Court on the

TIMBER LANTERN *The hall of St John's College was built in 1516, but this hexagonal wooden lantern was not added until 1703. It was built by Abraham Silk and carved by Francis Woodward*

MILTON'S TREE

The poet and author John Milton (1608–74), whose portrait (above) is in London's National Portrait Gallery, studied at Christ's College, Cambridge. He is said to have planted the mulberry tree (right) in the Fellows' Garden. In his day, mulberries were planted for silk worms to feed on their leaves, as part of a national plan which had been launched by James I to expand the silk industry

THE BRIDGE OF SIGHS *The enclosed stone bridge over the River Cam at St John's College is properly New Bridge, but it has been known as the Bridge of Sighs since it was built in 1831 because it follows the style of the 16th-century Bridge of Sighs in Venice*

UNDER THE DOME *New Hall, a women's college opened in 1954, was designed by Peter Chamberlin, and has a concrete dome over its first-floor dining-room. There is a large barrel-vaulted library and the startling, white-brick buildings are set among trees*

other side of the river by the 19th-century Bridge of Sighs, with its traceried windows. Sir George Gilbert Scott built the chapel during extensive renovations in the last century.

SENATE HOUSE An 18th-century classical conception of James Gibbs, who was architect of the Fellows' Building for King's. Fortnightly assemblies of the Senate, the University's 'Parliament', are held here during term-time, framing rules and conferring honorary degrees on distinguished public figures. The New Library was built from designs of Sir Giles Gilbert Scott in 1934.

STOURBRIDGE CHAPEL A richly moulded Norman chapel, a mile east of Cambridge on the A45. It was once a leper hospital. King John granted it the tolls of annual Stourbridge Fair on the Common, for centuries one of the largest fairs in Europe. The last was held before the Second World War. Near by is the 13th-century Abbey Church.

TRINITY COLLEGE The most spacious college in Cambridge. Its oldest buildings surround the 2-acre Great Court, which is claimed to be the largest university court in the world. Henry VIII founded Trinity in 1546 by amalgamating a number of earlier colleges and adding his own endowments. On the chapel tower of the Great Court, which was designed by Thomas Nevile, Master of the College, in 1610, is a gilded clock which strikes each hour twice. In first-floor chambers near the Great Gate, Sir Isaac Newton worked on his Laws of Motion. Francis Bacon, Byron, Thackeray, Tennyson and Macaulay were among the many illustrious men who studied at Trinity. The library, in Nevile's Court, was started by Wren in 1676 and contains 10th-century illuminated manuscripts, a 15th-century Roll of Carols and manuscripts of Milton, Tennyson and Thackeray. The chapel was built in the 16th century and the wall and roof-paintings were added in the last century.

POINTING TO THE WIND *The post mill at Great Chishill, 7 miles south-west of Whittlesford, was built in 1819. The fantail turns the mill on a central post*

GRANTCHESTER *The clock immortalised in Rupert Brooke's poem is set into the 15th-century tower of the Church of St Andrew and St Mary*

Grantchester

A serene little village of thatch, timber and plaster, loved by so many generations of tutors and undergraduates that it has become almost an integral part of Cambridge. It can be reached by crossing the floodgate at the bottom of Mill Lane, branching from the towpath towards Newnham Road, through Grantchester Street and Grantchester Meadows and then by a footpath across the meadows. In the old vicarage the poet Rupert Brooke lived and wrote before the First World War. Just outside the village, on the Trumpington road, is a signpost pointing to Byron's Pool. The muddy cut, by which sat not only Byron but predecessors such as Chaucer, Spenser, Milton and Dryden, is less attractive than the paths to it through the coppice, rustling with squirrels. In the Church at Trumpington is the brass of Sir Roger de Trumpington dated 1289—the second oldest in Britain.

Two miles to the south-west of Grantchester, the eight giant saucers of the world's largest radio telescope can be seen from the A603 at Lord's Bridge.

Fulbourn

A village from which a footpath leads east to the 3 mile long Fleam Dyke, a massive 7th-century earthwork built to defend East Anglia from the Mercians. Other footpaths go north-east to Great Wilbraham, and a direct footpath from Fulbourn to Little Wilbraham passes a gleaming windmill converted into an attractive home. One end of the great dyke is near Balsham, whose church has a 13th-century tower and inventive 14th-century choir stalls carved with grimacing animals and men, or possibly demons. Until the middle of the 19th century the church had its own band, and a few old instruments are kept in a glass case by the south door.

Gog Magog Hills

Although they are only 300 ft above sea level, the Gog Magog Hills offer some fine views of the towers and spires of Cambridge. Wort's Causeway, off the road to Great Abington, is crossed by the Roman Via Devana, which runs parallel with the main road and offers a wonderful 9-mile walk south-east to Horseheath. Footpaths just south of the Gog Magog Hills lead from the Roman road to Wandlebury Camp, an Iron Age fort rebuilt later by the British tribe, the Iceni. This is a weekend recreation area for Cambridge.

At Whittlesford, 4 miles west of Great Abington, the road bypasses the railway station, and white railings have replaced a one-time level crossing, sealing off Duxford Chapel in a cul-de-sac beside the old Red Lion Inn. The chapel was founded soon after 1200 as a hospital. In the 14th century it became a 'free chapel' until dissolved by Edward VI. It was a tollhouse for the bridge before being converted into a barn for the inn.

Sawston Hall (not open to the public), a mile north-east of Whittlesford, dates from the mid-16th century and has always been in the hands of the Roman Catholic Huddleston family. Mary Tudor sheltered there when her claim to the throne and her life were threatened by Lady Jane Grey's supporters. The first Village College, founded there in 1930, provided advanced education for children on lines specially suited to a rural environment, and also further education for adults.

Kirtling

A village close to the Suffolk border. The red-brick, turreted gatehouse with its mullioned windows is all that remains of the 15th-century mansion of Lord North, Henry VIII's Chancellor, who made great profits out of monastic confiscations and was for a time the respectful jailer of Elizabeth I before she became queen. His tomb is in the flint-walled Church of All Saints.

Madingley

From the uplands surrounding the American Military Cemetery and from the byroads between the A45 and Comberton or Coton there are many glimpses of Cambridge between long rollers of undulating farmland. Papworth Everard, in the wooded lanes further west, has an enlightened village settlement for the handicapped. Caxton, near by, has a fine old coaching inn and a pebbly 15th-century church. At New Wimpole an elm avenue leads to the county's greatest mansion, Wimpole Hall (not open), which was built by Sir Thomas Chichele *c.* 1640 and considerably altered in the 18th century by the 1st Earl of Hardwicke. A sham castle in the park was built about the same time.

Swaffham Prior

A Fenland village with two churches in one churchyard, the result of a parish amalgamation in 1667. St Cyriac's is derelict, its empty windows looking into a mess of rubble and even its clawing creeper largely dry and dead, while St Mary's has been admirably restored. Anglesey Abbey, 3 miles south-west beyond Lode, is a 13th-century Augustinian foundation assimilated into a country house in the 17th century. The house and extensive gardens are now run by the National Trust.

A cathedral 'lantern' high over the Fens

Events Three-day fairs are held at Ely at the end of May and Oct. The Burghley Three-Day Horse Trials take place in Sept.

Places to see *Burghley House*: Apr. to Oct., weekdays, except Mon. and Fri., Sun. afternoon; open Bank Hol. *Peckover House* (NT), Wisbech: Apr. to mid-Oct., Tues., Wed., Thur., Sat., Sun. and Bank Hol. afternoons. *Ramsey Abbey Gatehouse* (NT): Apr. to mid-Oct., daily. *Stretham Old Beam Engine*: daily. *Thorney Wildlife Park*: Easter to Oct., daily. *Waterfowl Gardens*, (Wildfowl Trust), Peakirk, 7 miles north of Peterborough: daily. *Wicken Fen Nature Reserve* (NT): daily. *Wisbech and Fenland Museum*: Tues. to Sat.

Information centres Town Hall, Peterborough (Peterborough 63141). Council Offices, Ely (Ely 3311).

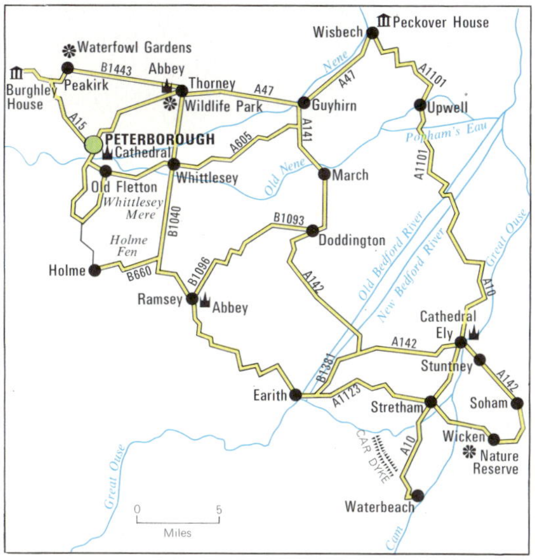

The vast, hedgeless fields of the Fens change dramatically through the year—sometimes bright with flowers or golden grain, and at other times darkened by spreads of sugar beet, potatoes and cabbages. Thousands of years ago there were great forests, and their remains are still ploughed up in the warped shape of bog oak—which may have been any type of tree, not necessarily oak.

The formation of the peat is believed to have choked the trees, then the low-lying land flooded and either turned gradually into a morass or suffered at some stage a cataclysmic subsidence. What are now hummocks above the fields, supporting the few substantial towns and villages, were once islands which survived the inundations. They are identified by the suffix *ea* or *ey*—Old English for island. In other place-names derived from Old English, *mere* denotes a lake now reclaimed for agriculture; *lode* is a navigable cut through what was once swamp; *drove* is also a cut, but with a path along its bank; and *hythe* is a quay.

MEDIEVAL TRIUMPH *Alan de Walsingham's octagonal lantern for Ely Cathedral, replacing a tower which collapsed in 1322, was one of the finest engineering feats of the Middle Ages*

Burghley House
One of England's greatest Elizabethan houses, and the home of the Exeter and Cecil families for more than four centuries. The house, begun in 1552 by Sir William Cecil, is square, built around a central courtyard with rounded corner towers topped by turrets. The grandest room in the earliest part is the great hall, with a double hammerbeam roof and a large fireplace. The Marble Hall, the Scagliola Hall and the Andromeda Hall were completed in 1587, after Cecil had become Lord Burghley and Lord High Treasurer.

Little of the original decoration remains, but there is carved woodwork by Grinling Gibbons, and much wall-painting, the subjects of which give their names to the Hell Room and the Heaven Room. There are more than 700 works of art, and the house is also noted for its painted ceilings, fine furniture and tapestries, silver fireplaces and a rose garden.

Ely
The word means Eel Island, a reference to the staple diet of the Saxons who lived there. The administrative area of the Isle of Ely, which is now absorbed into Cambridgeshire, was an island when Hereward the Wake held out against the Normans. The island disappeared when the Fens were drained in the 17th and 18th centuries.

Ely Cathedral, a magnificent sight for miles from any direction, was begun in 1083 on the site of a 7th-century Benedictine abbey. The Norman nave once led to a chancel beneath a central tower. When this tower collapsed in 1322 it was replaced by the wonderful octagonal lantern of Alan de Walsingham, who also designed the choir stalls.

The Ely Porta is a three-storey gatehouse to the original abbey. King's School, founded by Henry VIII, claims descent from the monastic school which Edward the Confessor attended. There is an enjoyable walk from the cathedral to Cherry Hill Park, along the bank of the River Ouse.

March
A large railway junction straggling beside the River Nene. The 15th-century Church of St Wendreda has a double hammerbeam roof, with about 200 angels carved in oak, their wings open in flight instead of being folded back as in most 'angel' roofs.

APPLE PICKING *Fruit is grown extensively round Wisbech and in spring 'blossom routes' are signposted through orchards*

Peterborough
The Soke (Old English for an administrative area) of Peterborough was once under the jurisdiction of Northamptonshire, then of Huntingdonshire, but now forms part of Cambridgeshire. The city is a market town and an industrial centre. New factories and tower blocks cluster round the cathedral and partly hide its glory, the triple-arched west front. An earlier church was sacked by Hereward the Wake and the Danes, an alliance of old enemies hoping to defeat William the Conqueror. The present building is largely the work of the Norman victors, their massive columns of local Barnack stone rising to the roof with its finely painted ceiling. The 15th-century apse has an efflorescence of fan tracery. An epitaph for Robert Scarlett, the grave-digger who buried both Catherine of Aragon (in the north aisle) and Mary, Queen of Scots (later removed to Westminster Abbey by her son, James I), records that, in his day, he interred twice as many people as the total population of Peterborough.

There are remains of Civil War fortifications outside Old Fletton, now a southern suburb of the city; and Peterborough's guildhall is a market cross with an upper chamber, dating from 1671, set in gardens which were once the market place.

Ramsey
A market town for an area which is intensively productive of cabbages, leeks and celery. The remaining 13th-century Lady Chapel of a medieval abbey has been incorporated in the Abbey Gram-

THE LONG BATTLE TO DRAIN THE FENS

The Romans were the first to raise causeways above the treacherous surface of the Fens. They also opened drainage channels to divert water and to carry food to garrisons further north. The remains of one such channel, Car Dyke, can be seen near Waterbeach. After their departure, most of their work fell into disrepair.

From the 13th century onwards there were sporadic attempts to set up comprehensive drainage schemes. A 14-mile cut from Peterborough to Guyhirn diverted the waters of the River Nene and still plays an important part in the modern system. Sir John Popham, Lord Chief Justice under James I, gave his name to Popham's Eau, which carried water to King's Lynn outfall. The 4th Earl of Bedford, whose family had been given the abbey estates of Thorney and Whittlesey after the Dissolution, was empowered by Royal Charter to turn the wastelands into good summer grazing grounds. He and his 'Adventurers' (their name is preserved in such areas as Adventurers' Fen) engaged the Dutch engineer Vermuyden to straighten out the wayward rivers and sluice them against tidal inflow. The first attempt was a failure, largely because of Charles I's lack of money, but eventually the canal known as the Old Bedford River was constructed, supplemented in 1649 by the New Bedford.

The basic idea had been simply to assist the downhill dispersal of water over the lower-lying seaward silts, or flats. But soon there was no downhill. Paradoxically, the more effective the drainage the more the spongy peat contracted so that eventually it was lower than the silts, and the water flowed back. How this happened can be seen today by comparing the Nature Reserve at Wicken Fen, which is largely undrained and is higher than surrounding peatlands, with Holme Fen, which has shrunk because of drainage.

Natural drainage did not work, so hundreds of pumping windmills had to be installed to move the water into the main outlets. When the tide was out, the surplus was discharged into tidal rivers. When the tide began to return, the sluices were closed to keep the waters out. The practice today is the same, but diesel and electric pumps have replaced windmills

THE WILD FEN *Marsh plants flourish and wildfowl abound in Wicken Fen, which the National Trust keeps in its natural state. As it is largely undrained, it is higher than the shrunken, drained peatlands around it*

mar School, which is not open to the public. The gatehouse, dating from *c.* 1480 and owned by the National Trust, can be visited.

Soham

Felix of Burgundy founded a monastery here, but like many others in the region this was destroyed by the Danes. The cruciform church, begun in the 12th century but much added to, has a mighty tower with a peal of ten bells. The Village College holds a lively festival every May, with exhibitions, discussions, music and dancing.

Thorney

A village with peaceful, ochre-coloured houses which give the appearance of a minster close. The 7th-century monastic settlement was ravaged by the Danes and rebuilt by the Normans. Part of this abbey is now incorporated in the parish church, which was restored in the 17th century. French names and epitaphs on gravestones recall the generosity of a 17th-century Duke of Bedford who offered help to refugees from Louis XIV's religious persecution in their establishment of a community in Thorney. A short walk up the Whittlesey road from the church is Thorney Wildlife Park, with elephants, monkeys, birds and a miniature railway.

BANKER'S HOME *Peckover House (left), over the River Nene at North Brink, Wisbech, was built by Jonathan Peckover, a wealthy banker, in 1722 and contains fine rococo decoration in both wood and plaster. The house is now owned by the National Trust*

Whittlesey

An industrial and market town with a forest of tall brickwork chimneys stretching westwards towards Peterborough. Until the 19th century, Whittlesey Mere was a 1900-acre lake, much broadened during floods. In winter it froze hard enough for skating, which was not only a major Fenland sport, but one of the fastest and most reliable ways of getting about. The last great drainage scheme of 1851 used a massive centrifugal pump to remove the water. This drove away many species of wildfowl, but also banished the agues and rheumatics which had plagued the fen-dwellers.

Wisbech

A flourishing centre of a rich flower and fruit-growing area. The town, surrounded by bulb fields and orchards, is at its loveliest in blossom time and is full of activity during the fruit-picking season. Architecturally, Wisbech is the region's most distinguished town outside Cambridge. North Brink, above the River Nene, is a series of impeccable Georgian houses, no two alike but all the best of neighbours. The bridge is noisy by day but is a fine vantage point in the evening. Close to it is Peckover House, owned by the National Trust. It was built in 1722 by Jonathan Peckover, a Quaker who founded a bank later incorporated in Barclays. In the centre of the town the lovely Crescent, Union Place and Ely Place embrace the castle, now a compact private residence embodying remains of successive castles from Norman times. On the north-east outskirts are two attractive marshland churches at Walsoken, which is mainly Norman, and West Walton, which has a detached 13th-century tower. At Tydd St Giles, 5 miles north, Nicholas Breakspear (*d.* 1159), the only Englishman to become Pope, as Adrian IV, is said to have been curate.

LURE FOR BIRDS *This mere was dug to attract duck and other water birds to the Nature Reserve at Wicken Fen. Insects abound in the Fen*

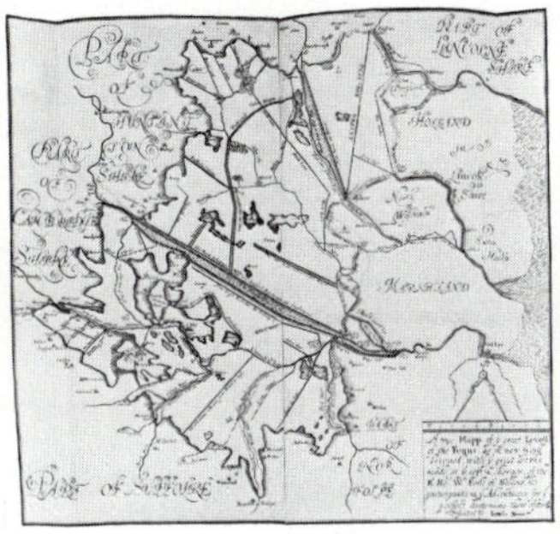

DUTCH PATTERN *A 17th-century map shows the plan of the Dutch engineer Vermuyden who was engaged to drain the Fens by the 4th Earl of Bedford. Though the plan was never completed, two canals were constructed*

THE NEW BEDFORD RIVER *Vermuyden built this drain parallel to the Old Bedford River in 1651 and made a large area fit for summer pasture; but the scheme was not a complete success until windmills assisted drainage in the next century*

INSIDE WICKEN MILL *The vertical shaft, turned by the windmill's sails, drives the large wheel. This operates an outside scoop-wheel to drain the Fenland*

MODERN POWER *The Fens have been drained in turn by windmills, steam pumping engines and now by electric and diesel-powered pumps. This diesel engine is at Mepal, near Earith*

WHEN STEAM ENGINES REPLACED WINDMILLS

Early in the 19th century, steam engines began to replace windmills for fen drainage. One of the few surviving beam pumping engines (diagram, far right) was built at Stretham in 1831 by the Butterley Company of Derbyshire. The huge horizontal cast-iron beam was raised and lowered like a seesaw by steam power, to drive the flywheel below it (right). This in turn drove a scoop-wheel, 37 ft in diameter, which could lift water a height of 12 ft into a dike at 124 tons a minute. In 1925 a diesel engine took over, but the steam engine has since been called on in emergencies. The Stretham Engine Preservation Trust maintain it in perfect order, and visitors may inspect it. The engine-house also contains, on an upper floor, a collection of peat and bog oak samples and fragments of Roman pottery dug from the Fens

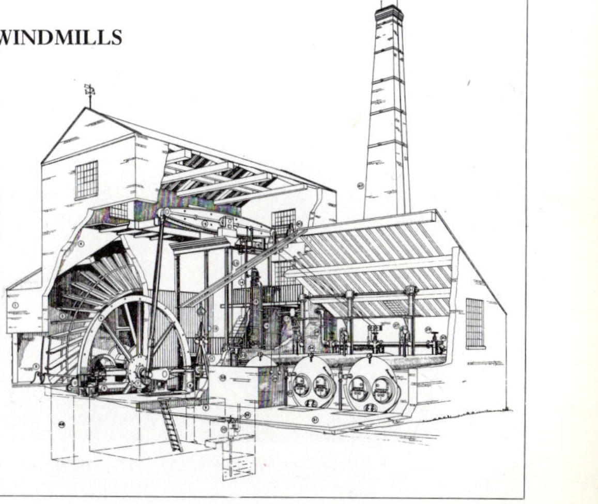

The saltings of north-west Norfolk

Angling There is good coarse fishing on the Great Ouse from King's Lynn south to Denver Sluice.

Sailing There are centres along the coast of the region at Snettisham, Hunstanton, Brancaster Staithe and Wells-next-the-Sea.

Events King's Lynn has a week-long 'Mart', or local fair, in mid-Feb. In the last week of July there is an annual Festival of the Arts centred at The Fermoy Centre, King's Lynn. Wells-next-the-Sea has a gala fortnight in early Aug.

Places to see *Castle Rising Castle*: daily, except Sun. mornings Oct. to Mar. *Holkham Hall*: late May to late Sept., Thur.; also Mon., July and Aug. *Houghton Hall*, 7 miles west of Fakenham: Easter to early Oct., Sun. afternoon, Thur. *King's Lynn Museum*: weekdays. *St. George's Guildhall* (NT), King's Lynn: Mon. to Fri., and Sat. morning, when not in use. *Sandringham* (closed when Royal Family in residence): house, grounds and car museum: mid-Apr. to mid-Sept., Tues., Wed. and Thur.; also Sun. afternoons and Mon., May to Aug. *Sandringham Church*: weekdays. *Scolt Head Island* (NT): when sea-crossing conditions suitable (tidal boat service from Brancaster Staithe). *Shirehall Museum*, Walsingham: May to Sept., daily; Oct., Sat. and Sun. *Trinity Hospital*, almshouses, Castle Rising: Tues., Thur., Sat. *Walsingham Abbey*: Wed.; also Sat. and Sun. afternoons, May to Sept., and Mon. and Fri. afternoons in Aug.

Information centre Le Strange Terrace, Hunstanton.
Tel. Hunstanton 2610.

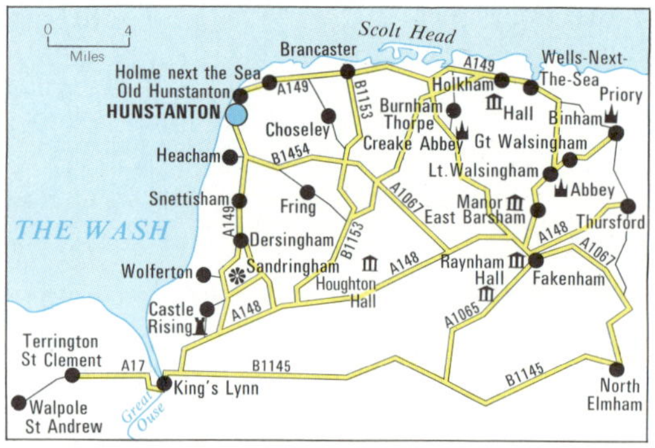

The north-west Norfolk coast, sweeping towards The Wash, consists mainly of a long stretch of sand and low cliffs, exposed saltings and tidal inlets, with cliffs only at Hunstanton. The title 'next-the-sea' attached to many village names tells the story of this coastline over the past few centuries—for the waves have long retreated from these once-busy little ports. Pebble flint predominates in their buildings, but carr stone—a brown sandstone quarried at Snettisham—gives a warmer, softer look to cottage walls around Sandringham.

Marshland begins around King's Lynn, stretching westwards into Lincolnshire. The last imposing outpost of western Norfolk is the church of Terrington St Clement, with a separate tower which may originally have been planned as a central tower for the cathedral-like building, a plan abandoned because the soft ground would not bear the weight. Near by is Walpole St Andrew, from which the unlucky King John sent his baggage train across The Wash in October 1216. The ponderous wagons, carrying the royal treasure, were trapped in quicksand and sank without trace.

Lord Nelson was born at Burnham Thorpe in 1758 and in the Church of All Saints there are several mementoes of him, including a lectern and a crucifix made of timbers from his flagship, *Victory*.

Brancaster
A red-roofed village with a 14th-century church, from which a mile-long lane leads to the beach through thickets of tall reeds and across the saltings. Although the sandy beach is large and attractive, tides make swimming dangerous. From Brancaster Staithe, 1½ miles east, there is a boat service to Scolt Head Island, a bird sanctuary and nature-study area a mile to the north.

Castle Rising
A former port from which the sea has long withdrawn. The impressive Norman castle of William de Albini, who became Earl of Sussex on marrying Henry I's widow, stands within ditches and ramparts probably built by the Romans. Here Edward III installed his scheming mother, Isabella, after he had decreed the death of her lover and accomplice, Roger Mortimer. In 1544 the castle was granted by Henry VIII to the Duke of Norfolk, and remained in the Howard family until 1958. It is now administered by the Department of the Environment. It is approached through a ruined gatehouse. The hall-keep has a great stone staircase leading up to a fascinating sequence of rooms, galleries and minor staircases.

Fakenham
A market town with a partly 15th-century church and some Georgian buildings. Three miles to the north, the road to Great Walsingham tops the brow of a steep hill, suddenly revealing East Barsham Manor, a sumptuous Tudor red-brick mansion. Raynham Hall, 3 miles south-west of Fakenham, was the home of the early 18th-century agriculturalist and politician the 2nd Viscount Townshend. He was known as 'Turnip Townshend' because he encouraged the growing of turnips and, more important, evolved the system of crop rotation. The hall is still the home of the Townshend family.

Heacham
The village sign and a tablet in the church recall Pocahontas, the Red Indian princess who married John Rolfe, of Heacham Hall, in Virginia in 1614. She was only 22 when she died, three years later; but she left a son, Tom, who returned to America and has since been claimed as the ancestor of many famous families. The hall was destroyed by fire during the Second World War.

Caley Mill, on the main King's Lynn–Hunstanton road, is a packing and dispatch centre for lavender. The lavender fields around Heacham and at

SEA HARVEST *Whelks are boiled before being sold at Wells-next-the-Sea*

THE STRIPED CLIFFS OF HUNSTANTON *Centuries of erosion by the sea have undermined the cliffs north of Hunstanton, revealing multicoloured layers of rock in stripes of white chalk, red chalk, and carr stone, a form of brown sandstone*

KING'S LYNN CUSTOM HOUSE *The Custom House was built in 1683 by Henry Bell for Sir John Turner, a local vintner*

Choseley Farm, 5½ miles east, are at their best during July and early August, when the crop is picked and taken to a small distillery in a barn at Fring, 4 miles south-east. The mill and distillery, where lavender water is made, are open to the public.

Holkham Hall
A huge, dun-coloured early 18th-century Palladian hall, the home of the Earl of Leicester. The manor of Holkham was bought in 1610 by Edward Coke, the famous jurist who became Lord Chief Justice. The 1st Earl of Leicester built the present mansion in 1734. When the direct line failed, the estate passed to the agricultural reformer, Thomas Coke (1752–1842), 'Coke of Norfolk' as he was called. He became Earl of Leicester and transformed a wasteland in which 'two rabbits fought for every single blade of grass' into a scientifically cultivated, fertile region. The Hall contains an impressive art collection including works by Leonardo da Vinci, Raphael, Rubens, Van Dyke and Gainsborough. Across the park, which has deer and a long lake, is a garden centre which specialises in alpine plants and shrubs.

Hunstanton
The largest of the west Norfolk resorts and the only East Anglian seaside town which faces west. There are great stretches of sand, and though the funfair and caravan park are an integral part of the waterfront, they do not disturb the town's essentially Victorian atmosphere. Old Hunstanton, half a mile north, is a residential village with beach huts nestling in the dunes. Holme next the Sea, a further 1½ miles north-east, has a bird observatory, and migrant birds throng the coast in autumn.

King's Lynn
An ancient market town, an important port and a growing industrial centre. In spite of recent growth the town—always known to local people simply as 'Lynn'—has many buildings from the medieval to Georgian periods. The Tuesday Market, founded in the 12th century, is held in a spacious square which is a car park on other days. The even older Saturday Market is held at the southern end of the High Street. The part-14th-century Clifton House, its little garden courtyard reached between barley-sugar pillars, was a merchant's house. Now it is the Borough Engineer's office, but some sections are open to the public, including a 16th-century brick watch-tower.

The 15th-century guildhall dazzles with chequered flintwork, and is well balanced by the 19th-century town hall built on to it in the same style. One of Lynn's most graceful buildings is the square Custom House built by Henry Bell, an architect and mayor of Lynn, in 1683. The names of nearby buildings—the Hanseatic Warehouse, the Greenland Fishery House—are reminders of the town's trading history.

Little Walsingham
A tiled, brick-and-timber village notable for its Shrine of Our Lady of Walsingham. In 1061 Lady Richeld, the lady of the manor, had a vision in which she was commanded by the Virgin Mary to establish a *Santa Casa*, a replica of the Nazarene House of the Annunciation. The shrine she built was soon added to by Augustinian and Franciscan foundations. Henry VIII made a pilgrimage to Walsingham from East Barsham, although years later, after his quarrel with the Papacy, he had the shrine destroyed. The slipper chapel at Houghton, where pilgrims would take off their shoes before completing their journey to the shrine barefoot, is still a place of pilgrimage. Between 1931 and 1937 Anglo-Catholics established a new Italianate shrine. The grounds of the original priory, also destroyed by Henry VIII, contain an imposing archway in a remnant of the east wall.

Sandringham
A 7000-acre estate owned by the Royal Family and taking in seven parishes, although there is no village of Sandringham. The house was bought by King Edward VII, when Prince of Wales, in 1861, from Duchy of Cornwall revenues accumulated while he was a minor. The grounds and an exhibition of Royal cars are open during the summer if no member of the Royal Family is in residence, and a good entry for a drive through the luxuriant woods is along the road from Castle Rising, emerging towards Dersingham.

Wells-next-the-Sea
A town now inland rather than next-the-sea, but with a gay quayside. Its sprats are famous and delectable, and it does a brisk trade in whelks. The major surprise is the dignified rectangle of the Buttlands, a green surrounded by houses, the name of which probably derives from an area allocated for long-bow practice in the 16th century.

HOUGHTON *The Slipper Chapel, where early pilgrims removed their slippers before walking to the Shrine of Our Lady of Walsingham, became a Roman Catholic shrine in 1934*

LAVENDER PICKING *Caley Mill, at Heacham, is the centre of the local lavender industry. After harvest in July the essence of the plant is distilled*

Where Norfolk battles against the hungry sea

Angling Coarse fishing on the River Bure at Blickling and Aylsham; best after Oct. when there is less weed in the river. Lake fishing at Gunton Park, 4 miles south of Cromer. Sea fishing at Cromer and Sheringham, from the pier or at sea in a crab boat.

Golf Eighteen-hole courses at Cromer and Sheringham.

Sailing Club at Blakeney.

Sub-aqua Club at Sheringham.

Events On Sat. afternoons at the Church of St Mary, Wiveton Green, 1 mile south-east of Blakeney, money is distributed to pensioners under the terms of the will of Ralph Greneway, who died in 1558. Sheringham has a Little Theatre repertory season during the summer, and there are carnivals at Cromer and Sheringham in Aug.

Places to see *Baconsthorpe Castle*, 4 miles south-east of Holt: weekdays, Sun. afternoon. *Blickling Hall* (NT): late May to Sept., daily except Fri.; also afternoons Easter to late May and early Oct. *Cromer Museum*, Tucker Street: weekdays and Sun. afternoon. *Felbrigg Hall* (NT), house and gardens: Apr. to early Oct., Tues., Wed., Thur., Sat., Sun. and Bank Hol. Mon. afternoons. *Glandford Shell Museum*, near Blakeney: Mon. to Fri., and Sat. afternoon; also Sun. afternoon, May to Sept. *Kelling Park Aviaries*, Weybourne Road, Holt: daily. *Sheringham Hall*: park, daily; gardens, Fri. afternoon May to Sept. *North Norfolk Railway Museum*, Sheringham: daily, Easter to late Oct.

Information centres North Lodge Park, Cromer. Tel. Cromer 512497. Station Road, Sheringham. Tel. Sheringham 824329 (seasonal).

The coastal strip of Norfolk curving from Happisburgh in the south-east to Blakeney in the north-west is heavily fortified against the never-ending assault of the sea. At Happisburgh, the defences take the form of sloping walls surmounted by ladders; at Bacton there are zigzag breakwaters; at Overstrand, a concrete-packed palisade; and at Sheringham, huge switchback promenades.

The long coast road links the main resorts, and also offers easy access to the Broads. Between Cromer and Weybourne, the tourist has the choice between the seaside and an inland ridge of heath and woodland. Towards the west, flint is so widely used in building that some towns and villages look from a distance as though quantities of pebbles have been shovelled up and starkly mortared together.

Different areas along the coast have their various seafood specialities. Lowestoft and Yarmouth are famous for herring; crab and lobster are not so much a delicacy as a staple diet from Bacton to Sheringham; and Stiffkey has its cockles, known as 'Stewkey Blues'. At most resorts enthusiasts can fish from the shore or from hired boats; cod, dab, plaice, mackerel and whiting are plentiful.

Daffodils are especially associated with Fenland; but even as far east as Ingham and Lessingham there are many large daffodil farms which in spring look as dazzling as mustard fields.

LANDING THE CATCH *A tractor hauls a fishing boat on to a north-east Norfolk beach. Crab fishermen must use the open beaches because there is no harbour on this coast*

RICH HARVEST *Cromer is the centre of the thriving crab industry in Norfolk*

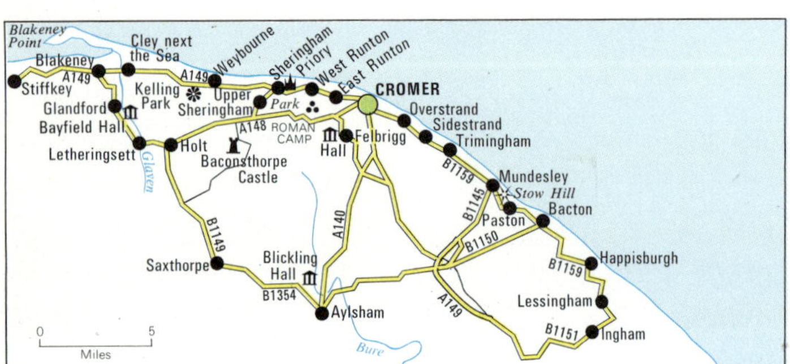

Blakeney

A boating centre with a main street of brick-and-flint houses, and a waterfront crowded with yachts and cruisers. A few public seats give a view over the quay and the twisting inlet of the River Glaven. A boat service goes to Blakeney Point Nature Reserve, a wildfowl breeding ground. From the Point, a 4-mile boat trip north-west from Blakeney, seals may occasionally be seen.

Blickling Hall

The house—with its Jacobean facade, cupolas, turrets, chimneys and shaped gables framed between two yew hedges—is beside a church and an inn on the road between Aylsham and Saxthorpe. The estate was at one time owned by the Boleyn family; it is said that Anne Boleyn was born and spent her childhood in an earlier house on the site. The present building was not begun until 1616. Later it was the home of the 1st and 2nd Earls of Buckinghamshire, and it is now owned by the National Trust.

Cley next the Sea

A village which, in spite of its name, is a mile from the sea because of land reclamation in the 17th century. The village street of flint houses leads to a quay with a fine windmill. A road crosses the saltings to a long, shallow beach of shingle—but swimming here is dangerous. Much of the marsh is a bird sanctuary, continuing north-west along the spit to Blakeney Point, which is a 5-mile walk from Cley.

Cromer

A bustling family holiday resort with a zoo, a pier, a boating lake, a good sandy beach, and large hotels and boarding houses. The narrow streets of the old town twist around the 160-ft tower of SS Peter and Paul, the tallest church tower in Norfolk. The crab fishermen prepare their baits on the eastern end of the beach. A cliff path leads half a mile east to the lighthouse.

Paths westwards from Cromer lead to East Runton, a mile away, and to West Runton, a mile further on, where there are large camping and caravan sites. A footpath leads 2 miles inland from Cromer to the earthworks of a Roman camp near Beacon Hill, the highest point in Norfolk.

Felbrigg

The Danish name means a 'plank bridge'. Historians believe that the original village clustered around its Perpendicular church, in the grounds of Felbrigg Hall, a mile to the east of the present village. In the church are some fine 14th-century brasses of Simon de Felbrigg and his wife, the first owners of the original hall. The present Jacobean mansion was built in the early 17th century.

Glandford
A village of flint and red-brick houses. Its museum has a display of sea-shells based on the collection of Sir Alfred Jodrell of Bayfield Hall, an 18th-century house a mile to the south. At the beginning of this century, Sir Alfred also restored St Martin's Church and incorporated typical features of Norfolk, including a copy of the Seven Sacraments font at Walsoken, bench-ends and a rood screen. The church's carillon plays hymn tunes every three hours.

Happisburgh
The tower of St Mary's Church is as important a landmark to mariners as the red-and-white striped lighthouse, half a mile to the south, in warning them of the position of treacherous sandbanks. The sea close to the beach, however, is shallow and safe for bathing. Shrapnel from German bombs dropped in 1940 can still be seen embedded in aisle pillars of the 15th-century church. The octagonal font of the same period is carved with figures of lions and satyrs or 'wild men of the woods'. There are good views inland from the churchyard.

Holt
A market town where Sir Thomas Gresham, who founded the Royal Exchange in London, was born in 1519. He founded Gresham's School in 1555. Its Tudor-style building of 1858 is in the town square, although the school moved to its present building, half a mile along the Cromer road, in 1900. This road runs through avenues of beech and pine, broken up by expanses of heather and bracken, to Sheringham. The road to Cley next the Sea, 4 miles north-west, passes through rolling fields and woodland patches above saltings. Just over a mile to the west, the road to Blakeney crosses the attractive River Glaven, which runs through the gardens of 18th-century Letheringsett Hall. Baconsthorpe Castle, south-east of Holt, is a moated 15th-century ruin. Kelling Park, 2 miles along the Weybourne road, has a display of tropical birds.

Mundesley
A quiet holiday village with sands and safe bathing. The waters are shallow, and yet between Mundesley and Trimingham, 2½ miles north-west, they have eroded away much of the cliffs, fields, houses and even breakwaters in the last century. At Paston, 1½ miles south-east, lived the influential family of the same name, whose collection of letters gives a vivid picture of violence and intrigue during the reigns of Henry VI, Edward IV and Richard III. The steep-roofed Paston barn remains near the village, and the mill on Stow Hill, half a mile south of Mundesley, still referred to as the 'Paston mill', commands good views.

MARSHES STAINED BY THE SEA *On the flat north-east coast of Norfolk, seas sweep unchecked across the marshes, then retreat leaving salt deposits such as these at Stiffkey. Salt flats are common along this coast, but the deposits are not rich enough for commercial use*

Overstrand
A holiday resort, with a good sandy beach, built near crumbling cliffs. In the 14th century its church fell into the sea and the present Church of St Martin was built—although this, too, had to be restored after the roof collapsed in the 18th century. At Sidestrand, a mile further east, the 15th-century church was in danger of falling over the cliff as well; so in 1881 it was taken down and rebuilt inland, on its present site.

Sheringham
Upper Sheringham is on the hill and Lower Sheringham is the old fishing village which became a holiday resort at the end of the last century. There is a ridge of pebbles at high tide, but the ebb tide reveals extensive, clean-washed sands. Fishing boats are launched down a precipitous slipway below a concrete bridge joining east and west promenades. An indoor railway is open during the summer, and occasionally off-season.

Upper Sheringham once depended on agriculture but is now a residential district. Sheringham Hall has splendid rhododendrons in its park, designed by Humphry Repton. Just under a mile to the east are the ruins of 13th-century Beeston Priory, where the surrounding common has a fine spread of wild flowers from spring to autumn. On the inland slopes, the justifiably named Pretty Corner offers views of heath, woodland and sea.

PATTERNS IN FLINT

Pebbles have been used for building in Norfolk since Saxon times. In a chequerboard design, as in the end wall of the house on the near right, alternate sections of flint and stone were used. In other designs, as in the Sheringham house on the far right, a complete wall was faced with pebbles but the doors and windows were 'squared off' with brickwork

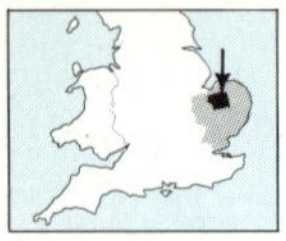

The wilderness and solitude of Breckland

Angling There is coarse fishing on the Little Ouse and River Thet at Thetford. Also on the Little Ouse at Brandon and Lakenheath, and on the Great Ouse and tributaries at Downham Market. There is trout and coarse fishing on the River Lark and the local dikes at Mildenhall.

Boating There is a sailing club near Denver on the Great Ouse. Boating on the Lark at Icklingham Bridge, 3 miles south-east of Mildenhall. Canoeing and rowing on the Little Ouse from Brandon to Thetford.

Nature trail The Santon Downham Forest Walk starts at the car park beside the Forestry Commission headquarters in Santon Downham. The walk is open all the year.

Events Swaffham holds a carnival on the late Summer Bank Hol. Joint celebrations are held every third year with Swaffham's French and German twin towns of Couhé Verac and Hemmoor (1980, 1983, etc.).

Places to see *Ancient House Museum*, Thetford: weekdays, Sun. afternoon. *Castle Acre*, bailey gate and priory: daily, except Sun. morning Oct. to Mar. *Euston Hall*: May to Sept., Thur. afternoon. *Grime's Graves*: daily, except Sun. morning Oct. to Mar. *Kilverstone Wildlife Park*, near Thetford: daily. *Oxburgh Hall* (NT): Apr. to mid-Oct., Tues., Wed., Thur., Sat., Sun., and Bank Hol. afternoons. *Thetford Castle*: daily. *Thetford Priory*: daily, except Sun. morning Oct. to Mar. *Weeting Castle*, near Brandon: daily.

Information centre Ancient House Museum, Thetford. Tel. Thetford 2599.

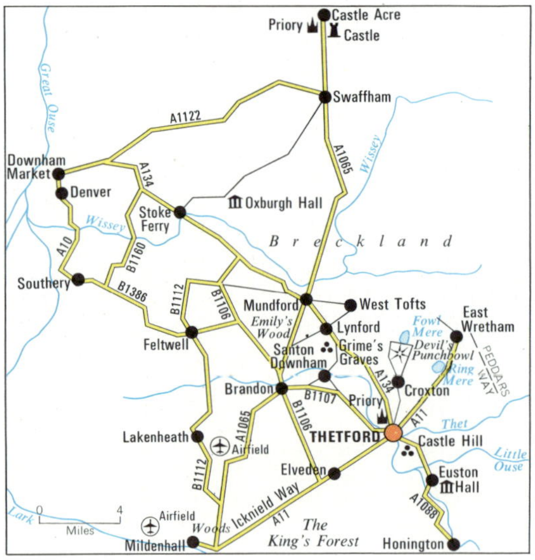

The name of Breckland, an area of about 300 square miles shared between Norfolk and Suffolk, derives from its 'brecks' or 'brakes', tracts of heath spasmodically broken up for cultivation by early man, but allowed to relapse into wilderness. Though Breckland is today one of the least densely populated areas in the country, it was not always so. Early man found the dry soil and climate good for simple farming. Streams and meres provided adequate water, and flints for making tools and weapons were plentiful. These settlers have left many mementoes of their existence: tumuli of the ancient dead rear like whalebacks out of heath and ploughed field, and arrowheads and domestic implements can still be found embedded in paths and patches of scrub. There is a comprehensive picture of Breckland history and wildlife in the Ancient House, Thetford, a Tudor merchant's home converted into a museum.

The Forestry Commission has altered the original character of the terrain by adding mainly coniferous plantations which have introduced an element of sombre mystery. Deciduous trees have been planted more imaginatively in recent years, and on roads around Croxton and Mundford there is a striking contrast between frowning barricades of Scots pine and the varied hues of beech, birch and lime.

Much of the heathland is given over to airfields and battle-training areas, but there remain extensive open spaces. Even unclassified roads are usually well surfaced. There are picnic sites with scope for woodland strolls in Mildenhall Woods, Emily's Wood between Mundford and Brandon, and The King's Forest between Elveden and Bury St Edmunds.

Brandon
The town stands on flint, is largely built of flint, and was for long the home of England's oldest industry, flint knapping. Arrowheads and prehistoric tools were hammered out of mined slabs. Gun flints were supplied from Brandon to the British Army during the Napoleonic wars. Demand for gun flints from Africa and from muzzle-loading enthusiasts in America has been so great that knapping has been moved from behind The Flintknappers' Arms to a bigger yard on the Bury St Edmunds road.

MOATED HOUSE *Oxburgh Hall, with its 80 ft high gate tower, is one of Norfolk's finest medieval buildings. It was built for the Bedingfelds, whose descendants still live there*

Castle Acre
A village on the old Peddars Way, which joined Holme next the Sea to the Roman garrison at Colchester. It is enclosed by the earthworks of the castle of William de Warenne, son-in-law of William the Conqueror and first Earl of Surrey. A steep village street leads into it through an imposing 13th-century bailey gate. De Warenne founded the Cluniac priory, whose ragged remains in their beautiful landscape clearly show their original shape and dimensions. The west front has one of Britain's finest surviving tiers of Norman arcading. Some of the prior's rooms are still intact and contain displays of medieval masonry found during excavations.

Downham Market
A small, congested market town on a hill from which roads lead out to the scattered Breckland–Fen border villages. Around Stoke Ferry, Southery and Feltwell the 'breck' gives way to black fenland soil. Denver, a mile south of Downham Market, has a tower windmill, and masts of yachts and dinghies rise above the banks of the sluices. This drainage scheme was started by Charles I's Dutch engineer, Vermuyden, in an attempt to bring agricultural prosperity to the area and provide a foundation for a market town to be called Charlemont. Repeated flood-tides ruined the project, but modern drainage techniques are now achieving some success. The old vicarage at Denver has a seven-branched decorated chimney. Oxburgh Hall, 8 miles east, is a magnificent 15th-century moated dwelling which was owned by one family, the Bedingfelds, for almost 500 years.

East Wretham Heath
This area contains all the eerie, fascinating aspects of the true 'breck' countryside, including reed-fringed meres which may be dry one season, dark and deep the next, so that trees sprouting from their beds sometimes appear like the rigging of drowned ships. Ring Mere is set in the Norfolk Naturalists' Trust Nature Reserve beside the open road to East Wretham village; there are parking areas. Fowl Mere, a haunt of wild birds protected by wire, trees and nettles, faces the more accessible Devil's Punchbowl, which has a picnic area. Shattered farm and village buildings reduced to ghostly husks by battle training may be glimpsed on forbidden Ministry of Defence ground beyond West Tofts.

Euston
A street of black-and-white timber, thatch and tile, flint and brick houses. The Hall has for centuries been the home of the Dukes of Grafton, who once hunted widely over the then unfarmed, unbombed heaths. The church is within the park gates, and a sleepy

NORMAN PRIORY *The 15th-century tower of Castle Acre Church, seen from the ruins of the priory founded in the 11th century*

CARVED WOODEN SIGNS *The village sign of Castle Acre shows the priory as it was in Norman times, and Swaffham's sign depicts John Chapman, the 14th-century 'Pedlar of Swaffham'. These, and more than 100 other village signs in Norfolk, were carved by Harry Carter, the cousin of Howard Carter, a leader of the expedition that discovered Tutankhamen's tomb in 1922. The Castle Acre sign, carved in 1951 to commemorate the Festival of Britain, was made of oak taken from the belfry of the village church. The Swaffham sign was carved in 1925 to replace one erected in 1912. Most of the money for these village signs was raised by the Women's Institutes.*

tributary of the Little Ouse meanders through the grounds. The stream, bridge, cedars, beeches and parkland are best seen from the road to Ixworth, which also passes through Honington, birthplace of Robert Bloomfield, whose long poem 'The Farmer's Boy' is a lasting record of 18th-century rural life; it brought him international fame in his own lifetime, but he died a pauper.

Grime's Graves

In 1870 one of the craters, which are believed to have existed here for 4000 years, was excavated to reveal the shaft and cramped tunnels of a Neolithic flint mine. Antler picks were found abandoned in a gallery, and later a chalk figurine, probably of a fertility goddess, came to light. It is believed that about 700 or 800 shafts must have been dug. One pit is usually open to the public; explorers of the tunnels are advised to wear old clothes and carry a torch.

Mildenhall

The name will always be associated with a rich treasure of 4th-century Roman silverware. Over 30 pieces were ploughed up in 1946 and are now displayed in the British Museum.

In 1780 the lord of the manor, Sir Thomas Bunbury, tossed a coin with Lord Derby to decide which of their names should be given to a proposed horse race. If Lord Derby had lost, there would have been a Bunbury Day at Epsom instead of a Derby Day.

The north porch of the church is the largest in Suffolk. Arrowheads and small shot fired by Cromwell's supporters have been found embedded in the woodwork of the angel roof of the nave.

Santon Downham

A foresters' community above the Little Ouse. From a car park beside the Forestry Commission headquarters begins a well-defined 2-mile walk, with seats at intervals, through the forest plantations of beech, pine, poplar and willow. Both the forest walk and the secluded road which eventually joins the Thetford road run through a magnificent lime avenue, maintained and extended by felling and replanting 90-yd sections every ten years.

Swaffham

The 18th-century 'market cross' in the huge market-place is in fact a rotunda built by the 4th Earl of Orford, Horace Walpole. An 18th-century spire blends in well with the 16th-century church tower. The north aisle is associated with John Chapman, 'the Pedlar of Swaffham', also commemorated by a monument in the market-place. In the 14th century he is said to have gone to London in search of treasure seen in a dream. On the way he met a man who spoke of having dreamt of a treasure buried in the Swaffham pedlar's garden. Chapman hurried home to find that under his tree there was a pot of money, which he used to build the church aisle.

Thetford

Vigorous post-war industrial expansion has not spoilt the old town, which is one of the few in Britain to have Saxon remains. It was the See of East Anglian bishops until 1091, and it is surrounded and interwoven by fragments of religious foundations, the most substantial being the ruins of Thetford Priory.

The Bell Hotel is largely Elizabethan, with a modern extension overlooking a riverside promenade and three-way bridge. Behind Nether Row, older arches cross weirs and waterways at the meeting of the Rivers Thet and Little Ouse, leading to leisurely riverside Spring Walks and Nun's Bridges. This crossing-point of the Icknield Way, the oldest trade route in England, is overlooked by Castle Hill, steep Iron Age earthworks developed and fortified by the Normans and now a park.

A gilded bronze statue was installed in 1964 in front of the King's House in honour of Thomas Paine, the author of *The Rights of Man*, who was born in White Hart Street in 1737.

STONE AGE FLINT MINE

Grime's Graves, named after the Anglo-Saxon god Grim, or Woden, are hollows in the ground on the sites of shafts sunk into the chalk in Neolithic times. About 4000 years ago, men of the late Stone Age dug the shafts to extract flints from the chalk beds about 20 ft below ground. The excavated flints were 'knapped', or struck with another stone to chip them into arrowheads, axes, scrapers and other implements. Archaeologists have unearthed chalk carvings of ritual significance, including a figurine of a pregnant woman (above), probably a fertility goddess

Norwich–where wealth and beauty flourish

Angling The River Wensum above Norwich contains roach, perch, dace, grayling and pike. There are roach at Wymondham on the River Bass, a tributary of the River Yare, and there is coarse fishing on the River Waveney around Harleston.

Events The Royal Norfolk Agricultural Association has a two-day Show in Norwich on the last Wed. and Thur. in June. The Norfolk County Music Festival is held in May in the Assembly House, Norwich. Norwich also has a Triennial Festival (1979, 1982, etc.), when local art societies put on exhibitions and shows.

Places to see *Banham Zoo*, near Diss: daily. *Bressingham Hall Gardens and Steam Museum*: early May to Sept., Sun. afternoon; also Thur., late May to early Sept. and Wed. in Aug. *Bridewell Museum of Local Industries*, Norwich: weekdays. *The Mustard Shop*, Bridewell Alley, Norwich, a museum devoted to the production of mustard: weekdays. *Norfolk Wildlife Park,* Great Witchingham: daily. *Norwich Castle Museum*: weekdays, Sun. afternoon. *Royal Norfolk Regiment Museum*, Britannia Barracks, Norwich: Mon. to Fri. *Rural Life Museum*, Gressenhall: mid-July to mid-Sept., daily except Mon., but open Bank Hol. Mon. *St Peter Hungate Church Museum*, Norwich: weekdays. *Stranger's Hall Museum of Domestic Life*, Norwich: weekdays.

Information centre East Anglia Tourist Board, 14 Tombland, Norwich NOR 07P. Tel. Norwich 20679/23445.

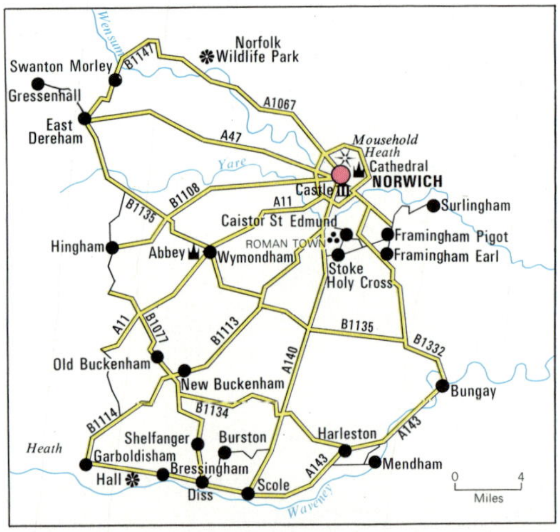

For almost 900 years Norwich has been the See of East Anglian bishops, and now it is a cathedral city, county borough, port and industrial centre. It has prospered through the weaving of worsted cloth (named after the village of Worstead, 11 miles north-east of the city) and later by the manufacture of shoes, mustard and chocolate. Norwich is within easy reach of the Broads, the central and southern farmlands and the arc of the north-east Norfolk coast.

The finest view of the city is from Mousehold Heath, a tract of furze and heather much loved by John Crome—founder, with John Sell Cotman, of the Norwich School of painters in the early 19th century. From the heath can be seen the towers of more than 30 medieval parish churches, dominated by the cathedral spire soaring to 315 ft.

There are three attractive approaches to the Cathedral of Holy Trinity. From the predominantly Georgian square of Tombland, named after the Saxon *toom*, meaning an open market-place, the way lies either through the ornate 14th-century Ethelbert Gate or else through the 15th-century Erpingham Gate, which is ornate with statues and heraldry. The approach from the east is through the watergate by the River Wensum; joined to the watergate is a house known as Pull's Ferry—though there is now no ferry.

The cathedral has a superb Norman nave and tower, to which the present stone spire was added in the 15th century. In recent years the buttresses, tower and spire have been extensively restored. Edith Cavell, who was executed in Belgium in 1915 for helping British prisoners to escape from the Germans while she was a nurse in Brussels, is buried below in Life's Green at the eastern end of the cathedral, and there is a bust of her near the Maid's Head Hotel.

The Norman keep of Norwich Castle stands on the most substantial of the city's hills, surrounded by a moat converted into steep, attractive walks and gardens. The castle has a well-organised museum with some imaginative tableaux of historical scenes and Norfolk wildlife. The Norwich School is well represented in the art gallery. Other good museums are the Bridewell, featuring local industries and building methods, and Strangers' Hall (said to be named after the Flemish 'strangers' who settled here to weave in the 16th century), with its rooms furnished in the styles of different periods.

Near Strangers' Hall is the Maddermarket Theatre, reconstructed after the First World War from a chapel and warehouse into a replica of an Elizabethan playhouse, where an adventurous repertory company of amateur actors stages works under professional producers. Cobbled Elm Hill is the best known of the quaint and colourful streets, and at the top is the little Church of St Peter Hungate, rebuilt in 1460, which has been turned into a museum of ecclesiastical treasures from all over Norfolk. The outskirts of

TWIN TOWERS *After a 14th-century dispute, monks built the octagonal tower of the Church of SS Mary and Thomas at Wymondham and townspeople built a square tower*

Bressingham
Gardens of alpine plants and perennials are lavishly displayed at Bressingham Hall during the summer. A growing number of old engines draw passenger trucks on a tour of the nursery gardens; a glittering roundabout is accompanied by its brassy steam organ; and there is a growing collection of traction and other steam engines in the museum.

Diss
A town with attractive shops and a mixture of Tudor, Georgian and Victorian houses stacked up around a wide mere, with streets twisting out narrowly at the head of the sloping market-place. The town is at its busiest and most jolly on Friday, market day. The roads towards Burston, 2 miles north-east, and Shelfanger, 2 miles north, are particularly bright, with a frieze of houses in differing styles, some with gay plaster.

TRIBUTE TO STEAM

This handsome tank locomotive, 2500, built in 1934 for the London, Midland and Scottish Railway, is among 35 railway and other steam engines at Bressingham Hall. Engines take visitors on tours of the extensive gardens and nurseries

STORY IN STONE *St George prepares to fight the dragon on the 14th-century St Ethelbert's Gate in Norwich Cathedral Close*

FROM THE CLOISTER *Norwich Cathedral's Norman tower, with its fine 15th-century spire, is framed in a cloister arch. The arches, begun in 1300, took 130 years to complete, and their tracery varies in style*

Norwich have their charm, too. To the south are little rural communities—still too individual to be called suburbs—such as Surlingham, Stoke Holy Cross with its weatherboarded mill, which is now a restaurant, and Caister St Edmund, whose church is inside the walled town of the Iceni and Romans, once known as Venta Icenorum. According to legend the town was part of Boadicea's capital but there is no proof of this. Swells of arable land towards Bungay and the Burlinghams are often crowned with round-towered churches, some with octagonal tops. They are sturdy rather than splendid and their flintwork is usually more starkly functional and less decorative than that of Suffolk.

To the west of Norwich the hollows often flood; along the roads, signposted warnings of fords are common, and some display depth indicators. Few of the villages are especially picturesque, but there are scattered rich manor houses and a great deal more sumptuous parkland than many visitors expect.

East Dereham
St Withburga founded a nunnery here in the 7th century. The unusual town sign spanning the narrow entry to the market-place from the south depicts the legend of two does which, in answer to St Withburga's prayers during a famine, came to the nunnery to give their milk. St Nicholas's Church, partly Norman with a detached 16th-century bell tower, stands on the site of the nunnery. In the churchyard is St Withburga's Well. The melancholic poet William Cowper, who died in 1800, is buried there, with a monument and window to his memory. Bishop Bonner's cottages, named after a 16th-century rector who became Bishop of London, have plasterwork ornamented with flower and fruit designs. The cottages house an archaeological museum.

The author George Borrow (1803–81) spent much of his childhood at Dumpling Green, a mile south of East Dereham, in a house now known as Borrow Hall.

Great Witchingham
A parish with a part-13th-century church and the Norfolk Wildlife Park. Otters, bears, deer and other animals roam in natural surroundings, and visitors can walk inside the aviaries.

Harleston
A village with a few Georgian houses and a mellow old market-place. It is a good centre for leisurely exploration of one of the most attractive stretches of the River Waveney—from the great 17th-century red-brick Scole Inn, 7 miles to the south-west, to Bungay, 7 miles to the north-east. In summer, the great spread of a rose nursery blazes from the green slopes just outside Harleston. The valley is a froth of blossom in the spring, and in summer is a sparkle of cottage gardens. The painter Sir Alfred Munnings (1878–1959), a past President of the Royal Academy, was born in the pretty hillside village of Mendham, 2 miles away over the river.

Hingham
A pleasing medley of Georgian houses clustered about a larger and a smaller square, with most front doors opening straight out on to the broad road. The town maintains a connection with Hingham in Massachusetts, which was founded in the early 17th century by Robert Peck, a disputatious rector who left to seek freedom in America. He was later joined by Samuel Lincoln, whose family originated from Swanton Morley, 10 miles to the north, and whose direct descendant was Abraham Lincoln. The 15th-century tomb of Lord Morley is in the 14th-century St Andrew's Church.

Wymondham
An ancient, shapely town centred on a 17th-century market cross which has an octagonal chamber raised on arcades. The Abbey Church of SS Mary and Thomas has two huge towers, the result of a 14th-century dispute over the shared use of the church by townspeople and monks from the priory. The monks built for themselves the present octagonal tower, and at the same time put up a thick wall to seal off themselves and the high altar from the parishioners. In retaliation, the townspeople built the square west tower larger than that of the monks' tower.

Kett's Rebellion—a peasants' revolt in 1549 against encroachments on common land—began in Wymondham. The rebels, under Robert Kett, captured Norwich before the revolt was crushed; Kett was hanged in Norwich and his brother in Wymondham.

The Norfolk Broads

Angling There is coarse fishing at Horning on the River Bure and on Salhouse Broad; at Potter Heigham on the River Thurne and on Hickling Broad; on the River Waveney at Lowestoft, also on Oulton Broad and at Beccles. There is sea fishing at Great Yarmouth and Lowestoft.

Boating Boats can be hired at Oulton Broad, Horning, Acle, Wroxham, Beccles and Potter Heigham. A school at Martham teaches sailing.

Nature trail Hoveton Great Broad Trail, reached only by boat, starts from the entrance to Salhouse Broad, 2½ miles downstream from Wroxham: May to mid-Sept., daily Mon. to Fri. and Sun. afternoons.

Events There is a regatta at Lowestoft during the 2nd week of July. Frequent sailing meetings and power-boat races take place on Oulton Broad during the summer. Lowestoft has a sea-angling festival in late Oct. or early Nov. Oulton Broad Regatta Week is in late Aug. Beccles has a town regatta in Aug. and a festival of sport is held during Sept.

Places to see *Berney Arms Windmill*, Reedham: Apr. to Sept., daily. *Burgh Castle*, 3 miles south-west of Great Yarmouth: weekdays and Sun. afternoons. *Caister Castle*, with motor museum: mid-May to Sept., daily except Sat. *Elizabethan House Museum, Maritime Museum for East Anglia*, and *The Tolhouse Museum*, all Great Yarmouth: Mon. to Fri.; also Sun., June to Sept. *Old Merchant's House*, Great Yarmouth: Apr. to Sept., Mon. to Fri. *Roos Hall*, Beccles: by appointment. *Somerleyton Hall*, 5 miles north-west of Lowestoft: Easter to Sept., Thur., Sun., and Bank Hol. Mon. afternoons; also Tues. and Wed. afternoons, July and Aug. *Transport Museum*, Carlton Colville, 5 miles east of Beccles: weekends only, May and June to Sept.

Information centres Blyburgate Library, Beccles. Tel. Beccles 714073. 14 Regent Street, Great Yarmouth. Tel. Great Yarmouth 4313. Central Marine Parade, Great Yarmouth (summer only). Tel. Great Yarmouth 2195. The Esplanade, Lowestoft. Tel. Lowestoft 65989.

A CRAFT REVIVED *Reeds are collected at Ranworth for thatchers.*

Within the triangle of Norwich, Lowestoft and Sea Palling lie more then 30 Broads, or open expanses of water with navigable approach channels. Together with linked rivers, lakes, streams and man-made waterways, they provide about 200 miles for sailing and motor-boat cruising.

It was long believed that the formation of the Broads was the freakish aftermath of glacial action; but research during the past 20 years has established that most of these shallow lakes—broadening out from the Rivers Yare, Bure and Waveney, and their tributaries the Ant, Thurne and Chet—were man-made diggings for peat or turf, an activity recalled in the village name of Barton Turf. Peat is no longer widely used on fires; but a revival in thatching has renewed the demand for reeds, another product of the Broads.

For long stretches, the waterways are below the level of the flat countryside, and are often revealed only by sails apparently scudding through fields. The real character of the Broads can be appreciated only from a boat, and craft can be hired and boat trips joined at centres such as Wroxham, Potter Heigham or Horning. A day trip can be made in a hired boat from Potter Heigham taking in Horning before lunch and Hickling Broad in the afternoon. This Broad, part of a nature reserve, is noted for its varied birdlife; spoonbills can be seen in summer.

The Bure and its tributaries thread most of the lakes together. The Yare carries cargo and pleasure boats through Thorpe into the heart of Norwich. Small craft can go through to the yacht marina on the River Wensum. The Waveney, with many attractive stretches, links up with the northerly Broads only by a circuitous route via Breydon Water and the Bure. All the rivers feed into Breydon Water and so into the sea. There are fine windmills at Horsey and Reedham and the smock mill, shaped like an old smock, at Herringfleet by the Waveney is still in working order.

BOATING HAVEN *The Norfolk Broads are a haven for sailing and motor-boat enthusiasts. The five major Broads are Wroxham, Barton, Hickling, Ormesby and Filby*

LARGEST BRITISH BUTTERFLY

The Norfolk Broads are rich in butterflies. Among them is the Swallow Tail, at 3 in. across the largest butterfly in Britain

Thatching today is big business—reeds are even exported, particularly to America

Beccles
This mellow old town is best seen from the River Waveney and tow-paths. Gardens run down to the water, fringed with boat-houses and landing-stages. The 14th-century detached bell-tower of St Michael's Church dominates the meadows. The tower is 97 ft high and has a peal of ten bells.

Great Yarmouth
This busy summer resort also prospers from frozen-food packaging and from its various supply services to the North Sea gas-drilling rigs. Fairgrounds include a well-planned area for children and there are two piers, cinemas, a model village and indoor and outdoor model railways. South Quay has Elizabethan House, furnished as a merchant's home and open as a museum. Two other museums are Old Merchant's House and the Tolhouse in Tolhouse Street. There is so little left of the old town that the Yarmouth scenes in the 1969 film version of *David Copperfield* had to be shot in Southwold to achieve an authentic atmosphere.

The neighbouring town, 3 miles to the north, is Caister-on-Sea, with an extensive sandy shore and the ruins of the 15th-century moated castle of Sir John Fastolf, who appears in Shakespeare's *Henry VI*. The castle has a museum of veteran and vintage cars.

Hickling
A village to the north of Hickling Broad, one of the widest stretches of water in Norfolk. The village is best approached by the Pleasure Boat Inn, whose 'staithe', a Broadland term for a quay or landing-stage, is known to every regular voyager on these waters. The Norfolk Naturalists' Trust has observation hides on Hickling Broad.

Horning
A village in woodland, with private inlets from the River Bure leading, like miniature Venetian canals, up to attractive houses and gardens. Hoveton, 2 miles west, has a nature trail, which is open during the summer only.

The neighbouring village of Wroxham is a prosperous community of bungalows with close-cropped lawns, and a Broad worthy to be sailed on rather than chugged across by motor boat.

Lowestoft
A town much bombed during the Second World War, Lowestoft has a dour, courageous tradition of fishing, maritime trade and defiance of the sea. Its lifeboat station was founded in 1801, 23 years before the Royal National Lifeboat Institution came into being. The town's traditions are best summed up by the monument, in gardens near the lighthouse, to the men of the Royal Navy Patrol Service who 'have no grave but the sea'. Lowestoft Ness is the most easterly point in Britain. Beyond the inner harbour and Lake Lothing is Oulton Broad, scene of yacht, dinghy and motor-boat racing, with extensive moorings, boat-yards and hire facilities. The Broad is flanked by a park with a swimming-pool, bowling greens, and a children's playground.

Potter Heigham
A village with shops, a supermarket and clustering sheds to provide almost anything that the holidaymaker afloat is likely to need. A modern road bridge has recently bypassed the old single-lane hump-backed bridge, below which yachtsmen must still lower their masts and their heads.

Reedham
The chain ferry provides the only crossing for vehicles over the River Yare and marshes between Norwich and the coast at Great Yarmouth. On the outskirts of the village is a taxidermy firm which does a brisk trade with museums, theatres and film companies. Visitors can see work in progress, inspect the display of stuffed birds and animals, and also watch feathers being fashioned into ornaments and gifts. In the grounds are live peacocks, monkeys and other wildlife.

A few miles over the marshes, overlooked by Burgh Castle, the ruined Roman fort of Gariannonum, is Berney Arms, where a late-19th-century drainage windmill-pump—70 ft high and in complete working order—is open to the public during the summer.

Rollesby
The Norman church in the village has a round tower which has had 14th-century upper stages added. The village is 1 mile north-west of the 200-acre Rollesby Broad which is linked to the deep Ormesby and Filby Broads. The A149 between Ormesby and Rollesby gives some of the best views found anywhere in Broadland. Navigable dikes in the group of Broads have been closed by sluices to reduce the risk of flooding. Archaeological excavations have produced evidence that around 2000 BC a community of Beaker Folk, so-called because of the pots they made, lived in the area.

West Somerton
A quiet village at the eastern end of Martham Broad, with a weedy reach good for angling. Drainage of the marshy surroundings, carried out through a maze of streams and dikes reaching the sea near Yarmouth, was once powered by windmill-pumps, most of them now shorn of their sails. In the 18th century, smugglers are said to have landed cargoes in Somerton Gap, working to instructions provided by the windmill sails, which were set at agreed angles to issue warnings of Revenue men and transmit messages.

A PATTERN IN THATCH

English thatching can be seen at its best in Norfolk. It is a skilled craft, handed down from father to son. The way a thatcher lays and cuts the reeds (top picture) produces a distinctive surface pattern for each roof

—AND A GIANT RODENT

The Cream-bordered Green Pea is a small moth common in the Fens and the Broads. The larva feeds on willows, especially osier

In 1930 several 2 ft long coypus escaped from a Norfolk fur farm. Their descendants now thrive in East Anglia

CLEANING THE CATCH *Fish unloaded at Lowestoft are filleted at the harbour. Organised tours of the harbour and fishing industry are available on selected days.*

Thoroughbreds on the heath

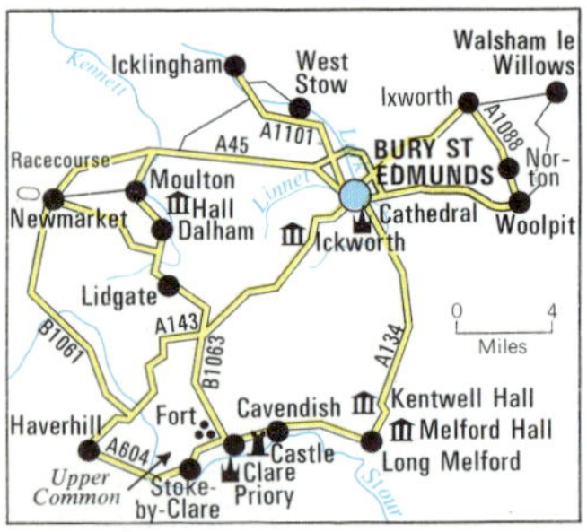

Horse racing National Stud, Newmarket: Sun. afternoons, Apr. to June, and mornings on race days.

Nature trail West Stow.

Events A Cake and Ale Ceremony follows the service in St Mary's Church, Bury St. Edmunds, on Thur. after the 2nd Mon. in Jan.; cake, ale and money are distributed to the poor of the parish. Suffolk County Harvest Festival is held in Bury St Edmunds Cathedral in Oct. A Bach Festival is held in Melford Hall and Holy Trinity Church, Long Melford, in mid-Sept.

Places to see *Angel Corner* (NT), Bury St Edmunds: weekdays. *Clare Priory*: gardens, daily. *Ickworth* (NT): Apr. to mid-Oct., Tues., Wed., Thur., Sat. and Sun. afternoons. *Ixworth Abbey*: May to mid-Aug., Tues., Thur., Sun. afternoons. *Kentwell Hall*, Long Melford: afternoons only; Easter to Sept., Wed., Thur., Sun.; also Sat., July to Sept., and Fri., July and Aug. *Melford Hall* (NT), Long Melford: Apr. to Sept., Wed., Thur., Sun. and Bank Hol. afternoons. *Moyse's Hall*, Bury St Edmunds: weekdays. *Norton Bird Gardens*, Bury St Edmunds: Apr. to Oct., daily; Nov. to Mar., Sat. and Sun.

Information centres Abbey Gardens, Bury St Edmunds. Tel. Bury St Edmunds 64667/63233. Public Library, Rookery Precinct, Newmarket. Tel. Newmarket 61216.

Edmund, King of East Anglia, was murdered by the Danes at Hoxne in AD 870. After many years and many temporary resting-places, his body was eventually brought to a burial place which became known as St Edmundsbury—now Bury St Edmunds. A magnificent abbey built there became a place of pilgrimage. The powerful abbots of St Edmundsbury held sway for centuries, but frequently they provoked resentment. Local women once beat tithe collectors with their distaffs, and in 1327 the townspeople pulled down the abbey gate and looted the abbey—but the town paid to rebuild the gate in the early 15th century.

Today, roads reach out in all directions and Bury St Edmunds is an ideal centre for touring East Anglia. To the west are the beginnings of the Fens. Northwards the roads run through sand and scrub—country which, until the First World War, was used almost exclusively for hunting but which is now a mixture of plantations, military airfields and battle-training areas. To the south, the rich undulations of highest Suffolk reach their peak at Rede, 420 ft above sea level. Flowing into Bury St Edmunds are the charming streams of the Lark and Linnet, and all around are the estates of the Suffolk nobility.

Across the centre of the county are the relics of the old mid-Suffolk railway line, closed in 1952—old wagons transformed into farm sheds, crossing-keepers' cottages and platelayers' huts peeking up from the fields, and abandoned station platforms. Just below the surface are even older relics—Palaeolithic and Neolithic implements have been found in great numbers. In 1954 Romano-British pewter was unearthed at Icklingham; and, more recently, the Roman cemetery found there is second in size only to that at Poundbury in Dorset.

IN THE RING *The public is admitted to the bloodstock sales held during the autumn and winter at Park Paddocks, Newmarket*

Bury St Edmunds

This town was no more than the monastery of Beodricsworth when a shrine was built for St Edmund's corpse in the 9th century. At the great altar in 1214 the barons vowed to extract from King John the concessions set out in Magna Carta. Cathedral extensions among the abbey ruins were completed in 1970, to mark the 1100th anniversary of Edmund's death. There is still controversy over the future of the west front, which has Tudor, Georgian and Victorian houses built into its remains.

The sloping plain before the abbey is known as Angel Hill. On it is the Angel Hotel, well known for its Dickensian associations. Here Mr Pickwick stayed and received the news of the commencement of the breach of promise action against him by Mrs Bardell. Also on Angel Hill is a Queen Anne house, owned by the National Trust, which has a collection of clocks, given by Frederic Gershom-Parkington, a musician known for early radio broadcasts, in memory of a son killed in the Second World War.

Moyse's Hall, a rare 12th-century house in Cornhill, escaped conversion into a fire station in the late 19th century and is now an unusual museum with the death mask of William Corder, Maria Marten's murderer in the Red Barn at Polstead, and a book bound in his skin. The Nutshell is one of the smallest inns in the country, and has a collection of Victoriana and other bric-à-brac.

Ickworth, a freakish rotunda 3 miles south-west, is owned by the National Trust and houses an impressive array of silverware and Regency and 18th-century French furniture. Its park was landscaped by Capability Brown.

Cavendish

The expansive slope of the green, with its village sign, is set off by the pink wash of admirably restored thatched cottages below a church with a jutting stair-turret. A son of Sir John Cavendish, the Chief Justice, stabbed Wat Tyler at Smithfield in 1381. A vengeful mob descended on Sir John at Cavendish, whereupon he hid his valuables in the church belfry and fled—only to be caught near Lakenheath and killed.

Clare

The railway station once aroused indignation because it cut through the remains of Clare Castle; but it is now itself abandoned below the castle keep, which is choked by trees. Streets here

THE RISE AND FALL OF PARGETING

Suffolk has some fine examples of half-timbered houses with the raised ornamental plasterwork known as pargeting; the two usually went together. Pargeting was first used in Elizabethan times; it developed in the 17th century, then declined as this style of half-timbering went out of fashion

MORNING GALLOP *An everyday scene on Newmarket Heath as strings of horses exercise*

THE WINNER *A painting by George Stubbs (1724–1806) of Newmarket Heath shows Gimcrack, a winner of many races, remembered by the annual Gimcrack Stakes at York*

BY THE GREEN *The battlemented wall of an Elizabethan almshouse, and the tower of Holy Trinity Church, form a stately background to the green at Long Melford*

should be strolled along rather than driven through. The 15th-century priest's house at the churchyard corner has an exuberant flourish of pargeting, and there is a colourful swan and foliage sign outside the Swan Inn. Bridewell Street leads to Upper Common and to an enclosure of earthworks identified by some authorities as an Iron Age fort and by others as a Danish stronghold.

Clare Priory, converted into a house in 1604, is now again the property of the Augustinian Friars. Clare College, Cambridge, was named after the family of the Earl of Clare; Elizabeth de Burgh, sister of the 10th Earl, gave money to help refound the college in the 14th century.

Neighbouring Stoke-by-Clare once had a Benedictine priory, the remains of which are now incorporated in a private school. The Tudor tower on the curve of the village street looks like a decorative gatehouse but is, in fact, a dovecot.

Long Melford

The most impressive single thoroughfare in Suffolk—long and wide, with houses of dignity and shops of charm. Holy Trinity, has the finest proportions and flushwork—a form of decoration using flints—of all Suffolk churches; the Lady Chapel is cool and elegant, and still has a children's multiplication table on one wall as a memento of its days as a schoolroom from 1669 to 1880.

On all sides there are sweeps of parkland and great manors, including the Tudor red-brick Melford Hall, which was restored in the 19th century, and the moated Kentwell Hall, built in 1564, which is approached along a superb avenue of limes.

Moulton

A village with a packhorse bridge so narrow and hump-backed that traffic must now follow the by-road through a ford which is sometimes completely dry and sometimes swirling with water. The River Kennett, which follows the Cambridge border, links Moulton to Dalham and Lidgate. The Duke of Wellington lived for some years at Dalham Hall; Cecil Rhodes bought it for his retirement, but he did not live to retire.

Newmarket

The headquarters of horse racing in Britain since the 17th century, when James I played a part in starting racing there. Notices along the roads warn the motorist that strings of horses are likely to be crossing, and the landscape of the heath is dotted with the cupolas and turrets of studs and stables. The National Stud is next to the racecourse, just south-west of the town.

In the High Street is the home of the Jockey Club, the controlling body of British racing, built in 1772 and much enlarged over the years. The public is allowed in during the six annual bloodstock sales in the autumn and early winter; a record price of 202,000 gns was paid for a yearling in 1975. At the junction of the Milton-Chippenham

HOUSE IN THE WALL *Tudor, Georgian and Victorian houses have been built into the ruins of the west front of the 11th-century Abbey Church at Bury St Edmunds*

road with the former A45, there is a gipsy boy's grave on which hopeful punters lay flowers.

One of the most famous inns in Newmarket is The Rutland Arms—part of which dates back to Charles II—which has kept some rooms exactly as they were in the 1850's. Newmarket, the landward outpost of Suffolk, was protected from invasion by the Mercians in the 7th century by the Devil's Dyke.

Walsham le Willows

This village justifies its name, but there are splendid limes and beech trees too. The village is set in the heart of parkland, and draws together roads and lanes from surrounding villages. There are weather-boarded and timber-framed cottages, and a fine confusion of eaves and roof levels.

The name of the Six Bells Inn derives from the bells of the church tower. Inside the church hangs a 'crant', a medallion used to mark the pew seats of unmarried girls who have died; until the 19th century the 'crants' were hung with wreaths by young men on each anniversary of the deaths.

Woolpit

The name derives not from the wool trade but from a Saxon wolf-pit, into which captured wolves were thrown and destroyed. Its coaching inn stands beside a neat little green, once on a busy main road, now bypassed. Woolpit white brick was once used in much East Anglian building but proved to weather badly; the brickworks were abandoned after the Second World War. The church tower and spire are 19th century. The porch might almost be a castle gateway and the nave roof is adorned with carvings of angels. On the far side of the A45 are a moat and spring known as Lady's Well, whose waters were believed in the 14th century to cure any ailment.

By the Stour in Constable country

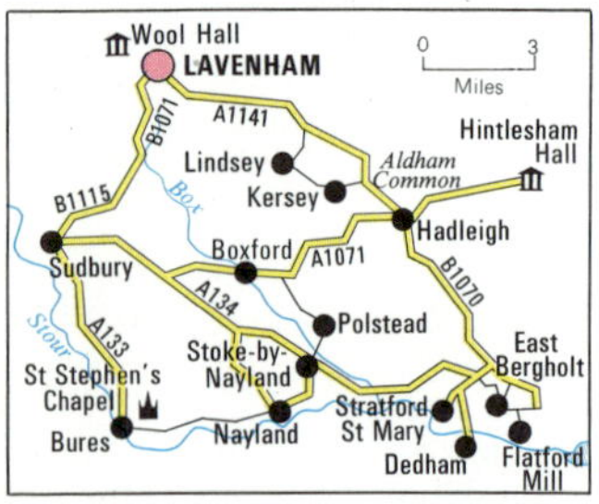

Angling Coarse fishing on the Stour at Dedham, Nayland and Bures.

Boating Sailing on the Stour below Brantham. Canoeing downstream from Sudbury.

Places to see *Castle House*, Dedham: afternoons only; Wed., Sun. and Bank Hol. Mon., mid-May to mid-Oct.; also Thur. and Sat. in Aug. *Gainsborough's House*, Sudbury: Tues. to Sat. *Lavenham Guildhall* (NT): daily, Mar. to Nov., but closed Fri., Mar. and Nov. *Little Hall*, Lavenham, headquarters of Suffolk Preservation Society: Easter to mid-Oct., Sat., Sun. and Bank Hol. afternoons.

Information centre Sudbury Library, Market Hill, Sudbury. Tel. Sudbury 72092.

The River Stour, running through chalky lowlands, formed a natural boundary between the kingdoms of Essex and East Anglia in Anglo-Saxon times. Today willows, elms and poplars fringe paths and ditches through the water-meadows, and the river from Flatford to Sudbury is spanned by a succession of agreeable bridges which join Suffolk to Essex.

John Constable (1776–1837) was born in a house above this vale. His father owned two windmills near East Bergholt, and watermills at Flatford and Dedham. Millwheels, locks, sluices and the riverside trees enchanted the young artist's eye and mind. As he put it: 'Painting with me is another word for feeling, and I associate my careless boyhood with all that lies on the banks of the Stour; those scenes made me a painter.' Constable learnt from what he saw in boyhood and used what he learnt in his realistic approach to Nature. It is impossible now to follow the course of the Stour, or to explore its hinterland, without seeing the cottages, steeples, water and sky in the way he has taught us to see them. 'As long as I am able to hold a brush, I shall never cease to paint them,' he wrote.

Prosperity came to much of the region not from agriculture but from the rise of the wool trade in the 14th century, which left a legacy of sumptuous architecture, with especially splendid churches in towns and villages which now seem too small and remote to support such magnificence.

Bures
A diminutive township straddling river and border, across which Hugh Constable, the painter's great-grandfather, came from Essex early in the 18th century to make his first home in Suffolk. Edmund, East Anglian king and martyr, was crowned at the age of 15 on Christmas Day, AD 855, in a chapel above the town. The chapel, consecrated by Archbishop Langton in 1218 and well restored in this century, stands not on St Edmund's Hill but on a crest at the end of a lane signposted 'Chapel', half a mile out of Bures on the road that leads to Boxford.

Dedham
The High Street has fine upper storeys and roof-lines above shop fronts, two spacious inns and the splendid brickwork of the Elizabethan Free Grammar School. The tower of the 16th-century church is in many of Constable's paintings. The combined insignia of the Guilds of Weavers and Millers, who richly endowed the church, is among heraldic shields on the roof of the nave. Pews include one with medallions commemorating the first Moon landing in July, 1969. The artist Sir Alfred Munnings lived in Castle House, where many of his canvases are on show.

East Bergholt
Constable's birthplace is still an unspoilt village of fine large houses, some Elizabethan plastered cottages, and luxuriant gardens embowered in trees along an erratic ridge above the River Stour; the Anglo-Saxon name Bergholt means 'wooded hill'. Constable's parents are buried in the churchyard and there is a memorial on the inner north wall to his wife Maria, granddaughter of the rector. The church tower was never finished—supposedly because there were no funds after Cardinal Wolsey's downfall—so the bells hang in a 16th-century wooden cage. The grounds of the late Randolph Churchill's home have been re-landscaped as the Stour Garden Centre.

Flatford Mill
The Constable family mill is now such a target for tourists that there are one-way lanes, a car park, cafés, a souvenir shop, and boats for hire. Willy Lott's Cottage, one of Constable's most celebrated subjects and the home of a friend of the painter, has been meticulously preserved. Cross the wooden bridge to the Essex towpath, and in a few minutes the world is once more that of the paintings: ash and willow, shimmering meadows, and the winding stream—sometimes slow, sometimes turbulent and muddy after heavy rain.

Hadleigh
The long High Street offers every kind of Suffolk domestic architecture—timber, plasterwork with or without the decoration known as pargeting, pillars and noble doorways. Overall House was named after Bishop John Overall, one of the men who translated the magnificent Authorised Version of the Bible for James I. Church Square has a glowing 15th-century guildhall, and a gateway, the Deanery Tower, which is all that remains of the original deanery.

A bench-end in the church shows a wolf holding a human head by the hair,

REED HARVEST *Tall reeds cut by hand on the River Stour near Nayland are used for making baskets and furniture*

WEALTH FROM WOOL *The fine buildings at Lavenham reflect the wealth that came to Suffolk from wool in the Middle Ages*

representing the legend of the recovery of St Edmund's head after his martyrdom by the Danes. Guthrum the Dane is said to be buried below the south aisle, but his supposed tomb canopy dates from long after Guthrum's death.

On Aldham Common, outside the town, is a memorial to Dr Rowland Taylor, the Protestant Vicar of Hadleigh, who was burnt at the stake in 1555 during Bloody Mary's reign. Hintlesham Hall, 4 miles east, was the home of the Timperley family, who built the original Elizabethan house. It was much altered in the 18th century, and the façade dates entirely from that period.

Kersey
One of the prettiest villages in Suffolk. Approached from either end, the street of dark-timbered and pastel-tinted houses runs through a watersplash where ducks take precedence over cars. The sign of a horse's tail hanging from the eaves of a nearby house is the old trade emblem of a vet. Like nearby Lindsey, the village gave its name to a type of woollen cloth once produced here as a cottage industry.

Lavenham
This is the most resplendent of the Suffolk wool towns, with fine medieval timber houses. The market square is dominated by a 16th-century cross and a guildhall which has been a prison, workhouse and almshouse and is now owned by the National Trust. The Wool Hall, which was in danger of being dismantled early this century, is now incorporated in the extensive Swan Hotel. Inside is preserved behind glass a section of the bar-counter scored with signatures of American airmen who were based in the district during the Second World War.

The church and its massive tower were largely endowed by John de Vere, 13th Earl of Oxford, and by Thomas Spring, a rich clothier who asked for forgiveness from Henry VII for his profit from 'usurious covenants, illicit sales, and deceptions in measuring cloth'.

Constable was at school here, and he enjoyed visiting the Taylors of Shilling Old Grange where Jane Taylor, a contemporary of the painter, wrote 'Twinkle, Twinkle, Little Star'.

SYMBOL OF A MARTYR

Legend says that after St Edmund was killed by a Danish arrow in AD 870, the body was decapitated and the head thrown into a thicket. St Edmund's followers found the head being guarded by a grey wolf. The legend inspired this 14th-century bench-end in Hadleigh Church

Nayland
After the decline of the weavers' trade, Nayland continued as a little market town. The church spire was found to be unsafe and was removed in 1834, and an earth tremor shook the remaining tower in 1884. A facsimile spire was put up during reconstruction in 1963. One of Constable's only two religious paintings hangs above the altar. The other is in the Church of St Michael at Brantham, 2½ miles south-east of East Bergholt.

Stoke-by-Nayland's parish church has an imposing brick tower, and near by stands a much-photographed row of timbered houses.

Polstead
Trim cottages and compact gardens perch on a cluster of little hills overlooking the River Box and Polstead Pond. There are well-marked footpaths and several walks across the common, and the climb to the church gives an awe-inspiring view of Stoke-by-Nayland on the other side of a valley.

The gravestone of Maria Marten, who was murdered in 1827 by her lover, William Corder, in the now-demolished Red Barn, was stolen piece by piece by souvenir hunters and has now been replaced by a notice-board.

Stratford St Mary
The main London–Yarmouth road bypasses the village, leaving its church isolated on a mound on the far side of the dual carriageway. A white, tomb-like building is a pumping station, but otherwise the buildings, which include old coaching inns, are mellow and welcoming. By-roads lead through villages set in attractive countryside.

Sudbury
The birthplace of the painter Thomas Gainsborough, whose statue looks out over a square choked by stalls on market day. His father's original Tudor house, with an added Georgian front, is now a museum and a lecture and exhibition centre, with an attractive garden. The town is 'Eatanswill' in *The Pickwick Papers*. The 15th-century St Peter's Church, on Market Hill, has painted screen panels and the 'Sudbury Pall', a wonderful piece of 15th-century embroidery on velvet.

THE UNCHANGING SCENE THAT CONSTABLE PAINTED

The scene at Flatford has changed little since John Constable painted Willy Lott's Cottage, early in the last century. Today's scene has the same completely English peace as in Constable's painting, which is now in the Christchurch Mansion Museum at Ipswich. Constable's self-portrait (left) is in the National Portrait Gallery in London

The open farmlands of central Suffolk

Angling Coarse fishing on the River Gipping at Ipswich and the River Deben at Wickham Market.

Sailing There are clubs near Ipswich at Bourne Bridge, Pin Mill and Woolverstone.

Riding Stables at Ipswich.

Events There are Spring Bank Hol. Mon. Fairs at Framlingham and Needham Market. The Suffolk Agricultural Show takes place in Ipswich in May or June.

Places to see *Christchurch Mansion*, Ipswich: weekdays, Sun. afternoon. *Easton Farm Park*, Wickham Market: daily, mid-Apr. to early Oct. *Framlingham Castle*: daily, except Sun. morning Oct. to Mar. *Framlingham Museum*: Tues., Thur., Sat. afternoons. *Glemham Hall*: 3 miles north of Wickham Market: Easter to Sept., Wed., Sun. and Bank Hol. afternoons. *Helmingham Hall*, moated gardens and deer park: Sun. afternoons only, Easter and late May to Sept. *Heveningham Hall*: Apr. to early Oct., Wed., Thur., Sat., Sun. and Bank Hol. afternoons; also Tues. afternoon, May to Sept. *Ipswich Museum*: weekdays, Sun. afternoon. *Museum of East Anglian Life*, Stowmarket: Apr. to Oct., weekdays and Sun. afternoon. *Otter Trust*, Earsham: daily, Mar. to Nov. *Saxstead Green Windmill*: weekdays.

Information centres Information Bureau, Town Hall, Princes Street, Ipswich. Tel. Ipswich 55851. East Anglia Tourist Board, 14 Museum Street, Ipswich. Tel. Ipswich 214211.

BUNGAY WEATHERVANE *The black dog is said to haunt the coastal marsh*

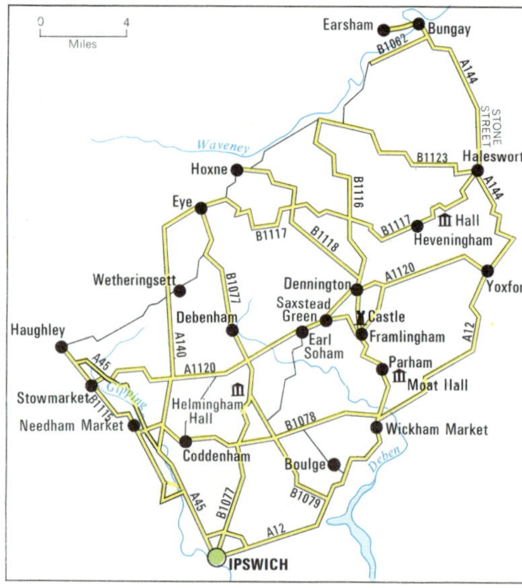

Suffolk's central plateau was once clothed by widespread forests; but now it is open farmland with little shelter from trees or hedges. The farms are extensive—many are as large as 3000 acres—and, in this bleak landscape, villages cluster around greens which originated in the Middle Ages as clearings in the woodland. Water-towers and silos overshadow church steeples and moated farmhouses. The moats were sometimes dug for defence, but often they resulted from the removal of clay for building, and were then adapted for water storage—vital on land which has a low average rainfall of 20–30 in. a year. In winter the soil is dark and bare; in summer there is a shimmer of wind-stroked barley, wheat and oats. Sugar-beet is widely grown and, in summer, pea lorries block the lanes and scatter pulp over the roads on their way to the frozen-food packaging centres at Lowestoft and Great Yarmouth. Most of the county's trade is channelled through Ipswich at the head of the Orwell Estuary, where farmland, industry, main roads and railways meet the major inlet from the sea.

Suffolk has produced much violence, intrigue and rebellion. In the 12th and 13th centuries, the quarrelsome Bigod family were continually building, losing and rebuilding their castles for and against their kings. Bloody Mary raised her standard at Framlingham, marched on London, and set about burning at the stake people who disagreed with her religious views. William Dowsing, the iconoclast Puritan of Laxfield, later went about as Cromwell's emissary, smashing stained glass, hurling down religious statues, and disfiguring the beauty of fonts and roofs. Remarkably, in spite of the Danes, Dowsing and Victorian restorers, there is still much left that is worth seeing.

Bungay

The odd name possibly derives from 'bongue', a good ford, or 'le bon eye', a spit of land thrusting out into the river. Castle ruins seep through part of the town as alley walls and fragmentary lumps of masonry, and The White Lion stands on part of the old fortifications. A fire in 1688 destroyed most of the original houses and melted St Mary's church bells. The most rewarding streets lie beyond the churchyard and above the River Waveney. Bungay Stone, west of the north porch, is said to be a Druid relic 2000 years old. The butter cross once had a cage in which wrongdoers were exposed to public mockery.

One of the largest collections of otters in the world can be seen at the Otter Trust, Earsham, 1½ miles south-west of Bungay.

Coddenham

This mellow village hidden below sheltering hills was once Conbretovium, on an old Roman road. The 18th-century school was opened to teach 30 children reading, writing, costing of accounts, 'and the girls knitting and sewing also'.

Debenham

The first trickles of the River Deben run beside the gently sloping main street and weave in and out of the town. The appropriately named Water Lane is almost permanently submerged. Rush-weaving is carried on in a building beside the bridge, and looms can be seen through the street window. The surrounding farmlands are sometimes desolate at first sight, but time and familiarity add lustre to the hamlets, including Wetheringsett, where Richard Hakluyt, a 16th-century rector and geography lecturer, wrote his scientific and patriotic book, *Principall Navigations, Voiages and Discoveries of the English Nation*, first published in 1589.

Earl Soham

An oasis of beech, poplar and elm in an unexpected hollow of the farming plateau. It has a timber-framed inn, Regency houses and shops, plastered cottages with frontages festooned with creeper, steep thatches, and Earl Soham Lodge, a moated manor. From its knoll the 15th-century church looks down on these different but never-conflicting styles of architecture. The village sign on the green is an oak carving of a falconer, presented by the Women's Institute to mark the Queen's coronation in 1953. At Saxtead Green, a mile to the north-east, a post-mill, which revolves on a central post, is kept in working order by the Department of the Environment. Visitors may climb up a wide wooden ladder to its 'buck', or body.

Eye

The centre of one of the largest electoral divisions in the region, but itself sleepy and faded. The railway between Stowmarket and Norwich, opened in 1849, was to have gone through Eye. But it went to Diss, across the border in Norfolk, when Eye's local squires refused to have it on their land. The 15th-century church has a 100-ft tower and a fine rood screen. The White Lion has a ballroom, with a musicians' gallery, across the old stable yard. It was once a centre for military, political and farming festivities; it now holds jazz evenings.

Framlingham

A market town dominated by the castle of the treacherous Bigods. There are attractive old almshouses within the castle, which has been partly restored and also has a walk linking nine of the towers, two ditches, and a lower court beside an artificial lake.

A helmet which belonged to Thomas Howard, who was made Duke of Norfolk after his defeat of the Scots at Flodden, is in the church, together with the splendid Howard tombs. There are antique shops, pleasant side streets, and roads leading to such attractive villages as Dennington, 2 miles north, with its wonderful 14th-century church, and Parham, 2 miles south-east, with its romantic moated hall.

SAXTEAD GREEN *The post-mill on Saxtead Green, near Framlingham, dates from the 18th century but was rebuilt in 1854. The mill was turned on a central post to catch the wind*

Heveningham
The Hall was built in the 18th century and overlooks parkland laid out by Capability Brown. The interior contains the best surviving work of James Wyatt, particularly in the entrance hall, which has a semi-circular vaulted ceiling, and in the dining-room, which was restored according to the original plans after a fire in 1949. The Hall belongs to the Department of the Environment. Its grounds include an orangery.

Hoxne
From earliest times this has been a religious centre and it is generally accepted as the place of St Edmund's martyrdom in AD 870, though some authorities deny this. The king is said to have sheltered under Goldbrook Bridge, and to have been betrayed to the pursuing Danes by a bridal party. He laid a curse on the bridge, and to this day no girl will cross it on her wedding day.

Ipswich
The county town of East Suffolk and a thriving port on the River Orwell. Cardinal Wolsey was born here and the gate of his uncompleted college stands forlorn beneath dockland offices and warehouses. Christchurch Mansion, in a spacious park, is a lively domestic museum with furniture, fine panelling, model ships, dolls' houses and children's toys from the past, and an art gallery with some local scenes by Gainsborough and Constable. There is elaborate plasterwork on the Ancient House in the Butter Market. Dickens stayed at The Great White Horse when he was a reporter, and the inn provided him with the setting for Mr Pickwick's misadventure when he went into a lady's bedroom by mistake.

Stowmarket
A market and small industrial town with roads radiating to all parts of central Suffolk. Abbot's Hall, on the site of a rest-house formerly belonging to the monks of St Osyth's, Essex, incorporates a largely open-air museum of rural life. It preserves records and specimens of country crafts, and is gradually increasing its collection of old farming implements, machinery and vehicles. The Soil Association carries out experiments in organic farming at Haughley, 2 miles to the north-west.

Wickham Market
A straggling village on the upper reaches of the River Deben. At Boulge, 2½ miles south-west, Edward FitzGerald, translator of *The Rubaiyat of Omar Khayyam*, is buried. On his grave is a rose bush which came from Omar Khayyam's grave in Iran.

Yoxford
A village known as 'the garden of Suffolk' because of its lush setting between stretches of parkland. Its lanes and cottage gardens are golden with primroses and cowslips in spring.

'CRINKLE CRANKLE' WALL *The garden wall of Heveningham Hall takes its name from its snake-like shape. The style is typical of Suffolk, which has 45 surviving examples*

PARGETED WALL *The Ancient House in the Butter Market, Ipswich, built in 1567, has fine pargeting, a form of decorated plasterwork seen at its best in East Anglia*

East Anglia's crumbling coastline

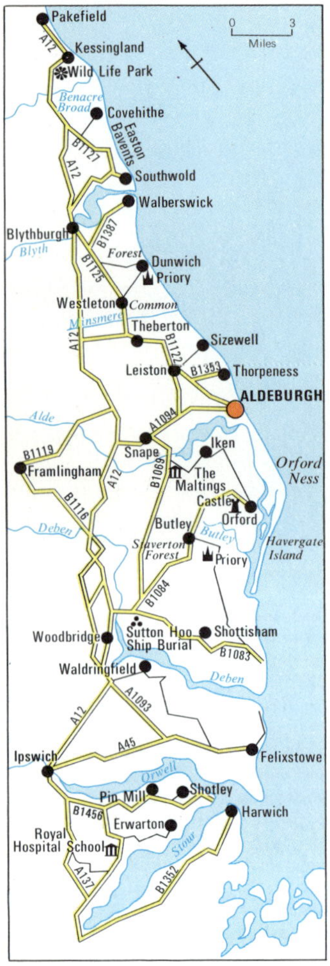

The coastline from Felixstowe in the south to Kessingland in the north has been invaded in turn by Romans, Angles and Danes—and always it has been assaulted by the sea. The shelly sand offers little defence against treacherous tides and savage storms. Whole towns have disappeared below the water, which has flooded inland to inundate wide areas.

Remorseless erosion has made it impracticable to build a through road along these shores. Separate roads lead out to each of the seaside towns and villages from the main Ipswich–Lowestoft road; but a more attractive link-road runs from Woodbridge through Leiston, Theberton and Westleton to Blythburgh—over rolling expanses of broom and heather, with side turnings into dark, coniferous woods or above winding estuaries haunted by the cries of wildfowl.

Bird-watchers will find this one of the most rewarding regions in Britain. There is good sailing from Aldeburgh, Southwold, Orford and Woodbridge, though the entrances to the Rivers Blyth and Deben require some skill in navigation. Thorpeness has a tranquil mere with boats for hire, and the sea around Sizewell is safely warmed by water from coolers at the atomic power station. Fish are plentiful, and even on the coldest night the fishermen's lanterns gleam along the shore.

It is a dry, sunny but breezy coast, with great cloudscapes. When the tide is 'making', it can deposit a deep layer of sand on the beaches; when it is 'scouring', the shingle reappears. Beachcombers can occasionally find amber or, more frequently, the flesh-coloured stone, cornelian.

Events The Chairman's charter ceremony opens Southwold Trinity Fair in May or June. The Aldeburgh Festival takes place in June with concerts at Aldeburgh and Snape Maltings.

Places to see *Aldeburgh Moot Hall*, restored 16th-century timber building: early June to Sept., most afternoons; also mornings mid-July to mid-Sept. *Kessingland Wildlife Park*: daily. *Leiston Abbey*, near Aldeburgh: weekdays and Sun. afternoon. *Orford Castle*: daily, except Sun. morning Oct. to Mar. *Woodbridge Tide Mill*: late May to June, weekend mornings; mid-July to late Sept., daily; late Sept. to Oct., weekend afternoons.

Information centres 91 Undercliff Road West, Felixstowe. Tel. Felixstowe 2122/3303. Town Hall, Southwold. Tel. Southwold 722366.

Aldeburgh

A flourishing town with good hotels and mixed architectural styles, which grew up after the prosperous medieval fishing and ship-building centre of Slaughden was destroyed by the sea. Slaughden was still prosperous when the Rev. George Crabbe lived and worked there at the beginning of the 19th century before writing *The Borough*, a collection of tales which was the inspiration for Benjamin Britten's opera *Peter Grimes* which is set in the village. Aldeburgh's world-famous music festival is held every June. The River Alde, its banks bright with small craft, cuts in close behind the yacht club and divides the mainland from a long, marshy spit. The river passes Orford Ness, with its unapproachable radar installations, and Havergate Island, nesting-place of the avocet, before joining the River Ore.

Two miles to the north, Thorpeness is a gay mock-Tudor extravaganza with a water tower disguised as a house and known as 'The House in the Clouds'.

Blythburgh

In the 15th century Blythburgh was a thriving port, but it declined as the Blyth became too shallow for big ships. Its large 15th-century church stands above the common and the bird-haunted mudflats; pillars retain the marks of tethering rings from the days when Cromwellians used the nave as a stable.

Dunwich

In medieval times a large port, and a bishopric with many monasteries and churches. King John granted the borough a charter, with all rights over wrecks on its shores, for an annual payment of 5000 eels. Now its many religious foundations are beneath the sea; the last fragments of All Saints' Church went over the crumbling cliffs in this century. The cliffs continue to flake away, occasionally revealing shreds of bone from the old graveyard. Hens now run around in the shell of the priory, and the smell of smoked sprats drifts from the little fishermen's huts on the beach.

There is a Forestry Commission picnic place in Dunwich Forest beside the byroad from the Hinton crossroads on the B1125. Dunwich Common, a National Trust property, offers a wide vista of the sea, Sizewell atomic power station and the reedy marshes of Minsmere Nature Reserve. There are extensive walks along cliff, shore and dike to Walberswick, 3 miles north.

THE MALTINGS *The Aldeburgh Festival hall at Snape is on the site of a malt store*

Felixstowe

A bustling seaside resort with no historic mansions, no pretensions, and much brash good cheer. It became fashionable after a visit by the German Empress Augusta and her children in 1891.

The wide arc of the sea-front road stretches right round the bay for more than 2 miles and is separated from the promenade by floral gardens and lawns. With its multi-storeyed houses, it is a familiar sight to voyagers bound from Harwich for the Hook of Holland or Denmark. The cranes and activity of neighbouring Harwich form part of wide panoramas seen from old fortifications below The Dooley, a historic inn with many doors used in the past to facilitate escape from press gangs and Revenue men.

Kessingland

A conglomeration of caravans and holiday bungalows which are reaching out towards the holiday camps of Pakefield, 2½ miles to the north, but fading to the south into the tranquillity of Benacre Broad, Covehithe and Easton Bavents. Church towers at Kessingland and Covehithe have long been navigational marks for mariners. The Wild Life Park,

AVOCET *A rare British bird which breeds only on Minsmere and Havergate Island*

DUNWICH—THE TOWN THAT VANISHED BENEATH THE NORTH SEA

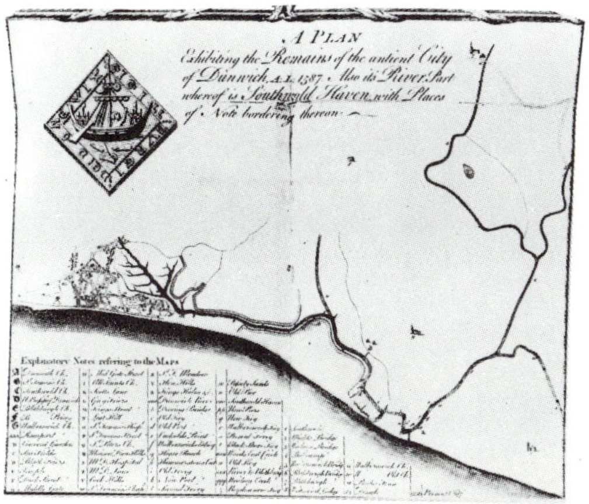

Dunwich, the Roman town of Sitomagus, and once a flourishing port trading with France, has now vanished beneath the sea. In the 6th century it was the seat of the first Christian Bishop of East Anglia, Felix of Burgundy, who crossed the Channel to convert the heathen inhabitants of East Anglia to Christianity. Its prosperity continued until long after the Norman Conquest. In 1215, King John granted a charter to the town. Disaster struck Dunwich in January 1326, when 400 houses and three of the town's nine churches were washed away in a great storm. The map (above) shows the town as it was in 1587, after the sea had destroyed many of the medieval buildings. The Corporation seal is in the top left hand corner. The crumbling cliffs at Dunwich (right) are still being eroded by the sea. Now only a few houses and part of an old graveyard remain, but the town's memory lives on through the preservation of King John's charter and many of the historical records of the medieval Dunwich Corporation

standing in several acres of woodland at the junction with the Lowestoft road, is richly stocked with animals. It also has aviaries and a children's zoo.

Orford
A winding road to Orford skirts conifer woods and passes through gnarled, ancient Staverton Forest in which sits the huge surviving 14th-century gatehouse of Butley Priory. The heraldic carvings on the gatehouse include national emblems and baronial family devices.

There are oyster beds in the River Butley, and salmon, eel and trout are smoked locally. Orford Castle's 18-sided keep, with good views to the Ness and its lighthouse, was built by Henry II.

THAMES BARGES *Preserved barges at Pin Mill are now used only for races*

Shotley
The tip of the promontory was formerly occupied by HMS *Ganges*, the Royal Navy training establishment. A road westward gives glimpses of the Stour estuary and leads to the imposing Royal Hospital School at Holbrook, for sons of members of the Royal Navy and Royal Marines, active or retired.

Snape
The Maltings concert hall became the centre of the Aldeburgh Festival in 1967. It was burnt down on the first night of the 1969 season, and was rebuilt in time for the 1970 Festival. It is used throughout the year for antique fairs, jazz concerts and television and recording sessions. A 3-mile tow-path walk leads south-east to the mound of Iken Church.

Southwold
The elegant little town, once congested, was rebuilt around wide greens after a devastating fire in 1659. Gun Hill, with its Tudor cannon, and North Parade, lined by Victorian terraces, look down on rows of jaunty beach huts with an Edwardian atmosphere. Church services begin after 'Southwold Jack', the 15th-century oak figure of a man-at-arms, has struck his bell. The track of the long-abandoned railway provides an attractive route through gorse and blackberry bushes to a bridge over the River Blyth and on to Walberswick, a mile south.

Walberswick
This once-flourishing port has weathered gracefully into a pleasant residential community with large houses and well-tended gardens. The Church of St Andrew stands within the ruins of its larger medieval predecessor. The shore is much more sandy than most beaches on this coast, and there are gay, lopsided holiday houses among the extensive dunes planted with marram grass. Attempts have been made to bind these perpetually shifting sea defences with plastic seaweed, to avoid a repetition of the 1953 floods; but results so far have been discouraging. The village offers the best view of Southwold across the River Blyth—only a mile to the north yet 8 miles by car.

Woodbridge
A lively town set on slopes above the Deben at its loveliest point. Its prosperity was based on sailcloth, rope-making and boat-building. Shire Hall on Market Hill was built, like so many local treasures, by Thomas Seckford, in the 16th century. Woodbridge has one of the country's few surviving tide-operated mills. A mile away, on the opposite bank of the Deben, is the site of the Sutton Hoo ship-burial where excavations in 1939 revealed the remains of a Saxon ship, and a vast treasure hoard.

'SOUTHWOLD JACK' *St Edmund's services start when this figure rings its bell*

WALES

Wales: a land of mountains, lakes and legends

Medieval Welsh folklore abounds in stories of heroes who leap on to bubbles without breaking them . . . of missionary saints who sail the seas on leaves. These legends are the product of a land whose remote mountains, lakes, windswept cliffs and languid sands still have the power to unfetter the imagination.

There are more tangible remains of the past. The rocks of Anglesey are pre-Cambrian, the first to be formed more than 3000 million years ago as the molten earth began to harden at its crust. Worn by time and ages of slowly moving ice, Anglesey is today rather flat. It grows crops, rears sheep, has an attractive coastline and good bathing and sailing facilities, and boasts a splendid view of Snowdonia.

The Cambrian rocks of the mainland to the south-east sprout into the highest peaks in Britain south of the Scottish border—the Snowdon range and the once-volcanic mountains of south Gwynedd (Merioneth). This is the most dramatic area of Wales, over 800 square miles of National Park lands, rich in forest, with steep slopes topped by 3560-ft Snowdon itself. There are attractive waterfalls, pretty villages, and a gloriously wild stretch of coastline with miles of rocky shore and broad, sandy flats. To the east—in what was Flintshire but which now, together with Denbighshire, forms the county of Clwyd—are two popular resorts, Rhyl and Prestatyn. Southwards run the Cambrian Mountains, the long backbone of Wales. The natural highland barrier of woods and moorlands, settled in the west by the Celts, made invasion difficult for successive waves of intruders—Roman, Norman and Plantagenet.

MOUNTAIN BACKBONE *The Cambrian Mountains are the backbone of Wales, linking the Snowdonia and Clwydian ranges in the north with the Brecon Beacons and Black Mountains in the south. The highlands are cut by the gorges of numerous rivers*

Hills where Wales is at its remotest

The northern part of the county of Powys—which now comprises the former counties of Montgomery, Radnor and Brecon—blends with England as the Severn descends to a land of black-and-white houses, border castles and Hereford cattle, where English is the common language. But further west, Welsh ousts the English language, sheep outnumber cattle (here mainly Welsh Blacks), timber gives way to stone and slate, and farms become smaller. The Welshness is unmistakable. This is Wales at its most remote, with few inhabitants and a mountain landscape that is softer than Snowdonia.

Southwards, in central Powys, the population is sparser than anywhere in England and there are no industrial towns. This quiet grandeur continues in south Powys, notable for the Brecon Beacons National Park, with its gorges, caves, waterfalls and lakes—some of them used as reservoirs to supply the more densely populated south. Between the broad valleys of the Wye and Usk, the Black Mountains mark the end of Wales and the beginning of England. There is good pony trekking here and skiing on the snow-covered slopes in winter.

The occupations change from farming to mining and industry as the land drops to the Glamorgans, Gwent and the Bristol Channel. Gwent's east is flat and pastoral, and its coast is mainly silt, clay, sand and gravel. But the Glamorgans—Mid, South and West—despite heavy industrial growth, have rolling landscapes and coastlines with sandy resorts. Sailing is a popular sport in Swansea Bay, and the Gower Peninsula gives opportunities for caving.

Seabirds and seals on weather-beaten shores

The grandeur of the coastline heightens in south Dyfed (Carmarthen and Pembroke). The shores here are often wild and weather-beaten—a series of dramatic capes and headlands that abound with seabirds and seals. Inland, Mynydd Prescelly—where the blocks for Stonehenge were quarried—has a peak that rises to 1760 ft. But generally this is the flattest part of Wales, busy with dairy farming and bright with a patchwork of colour-washed farmsteads and cottages.

In north-west Dyfed (Cardiganshire), Welsh is spoken by three out of every four people. The Cambrian Mountains stretch across its east side, while the west has lovely wooded valleys cut by rivers such as the Teifi and Rheidol. Dotting the landscape are the many castles with which Welsh history is closely linked. First came the Romans, who built roads into the interior and forts to defend them—the finest Roman legacy in Wales is the legionary base which covered more than 50 acres at Caerleon on the Usk in Gwent.

The period that followed was the most colourful in Welsh history. Arthur, the legendary king of the Britons, led Celtic resistance to the Saxons during the 6th century, and South Wales is rich in Arthurian sites. They extend to the north, too, for according to various accounts that mingle fact with fiction, he killed monsters both at Aberdyfi and in Snowdonia. A little later, Celtic saints sailed to and from Ireland, busying themselves with souls, animals, and all kinds of miracles, and snubbing

LONELY LAKE (overleaf) *Llyn Llydaw is ringed by the wild peaks of Snowdonia, dominated by 2947-ft Y Lliwedd*

KEY TO MAP
Regional centre
Selected town or village
Regional boundary
County boundary
Major road
Minor road
Woodland
River and lake or reservoir
REGIONAL PAGE INDEX
330
324
326
322
332
334
320
316
318
306
308
314
312
310
MILES
20
40
60
80
100
GWYNEDD
CLWYD
POWYS
DYFED
WEST GLAMORGAN
MID GLAMORGAN
SOUTH GLAMORGAN
GWENT
SALOP
HEREFORD AND WORCESTER
CAMBRIAN MOUNTAINS
Cardigan Bay
Caernarfon Bay
Carmarthen Bay
St Bride's Bay
Mouth of the Severn
HOLYHEAD
Holy I.
Cemaes Bay
Amlwch
Moelfre
Penmon
Beaumaris
Llangefni
Menai Bridge
Bangor
Llanfair PG
Newborough
CAERNARFON
Llanberis
Bethesda
Llanfairfechan
Penmaenmawr
Conwy
Llandudno
COLWYN BAY
Abergele
Rhyl
Prestatyn
St Asaph
Holywell
Flint
Denbigh
Mold
Hawarden
Chester
Birkenhead
Liverpool
Ruthin
Wrexham
Llanrwst
Capel Curig
Betws-y-coed
Betws Garmon
Beddgelert
Blaenau Ffestiniog
Clocaenog Forest
Cerrigydrudion
Corwen
LLANGOLLEN
Chirk
Overton
Whitchurch
Nefyn
Criccieth
Porthmadog
Portmeirion
PWLLHELI
Abersoch
Aberdaron
Bardsey I.
Lleyn Peninsula
Harlech
Bala
Llanarmon Dyffryn Ceiriog
Llanrhaeadr-ym-Mochnant
Dyffryn Ardudwy
Barmouth
DOLGELLAU
Dinas-Mawddwy
Llanfyllin
Shrewsbury
WELSHPOOL
Llanfair Caereinion
Cemmaes
Tywyn
Aberdyfi
Machynlleth
Dyfi Valley
Montgomery
Caersws
Newtown
Kerry
Borth
Llanidloes
ABERYSTWYTH
Devil's Bridge
Rhayader
Knighton
Radnor Forest
New Radnor
Presteigne
New Quay
Aberaeron
Tregaron
LLANDRINDOD WELLS
Builth Wells
Leominster
Lampeter
Llanwrtyd Wells
Llangammarch Wells
Aberedw
Clyro
Hay-on-Wye
Hereford
Strumble Head
Cardigan
Cilgerran
Nevern
Llandyssul
Pumpsaint
Fishguard
Mynydd Prescelly
Newcastle Emlyn
Mynydd Eppynt
Crychan Forest
Llandovery
St David's Head
St David's
Ramsey I
Trecastle
BRECON
Black Mountains
Brecon Beacons
Tretower
Grosmont
HAVERFORDWEST
CARMARTHEN
Llandeilo
Fforest Fawr
Crickhowell
Abergavenny
MONMOUTH
Broad Haven
Skomer I.
Skokholm I
Dale
Milford Haven
St Ann's Head
Pembroke
Tenby
Manorbier
Bosherston
St Govan's Head
Amroth
Pendine
Laugharne
Llanstephan
Llanelli
Ystradfellte
Ebbw Vale
Abertillery
Raglan
Usk
Chepstow
Caerleon
Newport
Vale of Neath
Aberdare
Rhondda
Neath
Swansea
Gower
Worms Head
Port Talbot
Pontypridd
Caerphilly
Bridgend
Porthcawl
CARDIFF
Penarth
Llantwit Major
Barry
Bristol
Vale of Conwy
Vale of Clwyd
Clwydian Range
Berwyn

the Christians from Canterbury, and even St Augustine himself, by refusing to submit to Rome. They and their troublesome Welsh princes were eventually contained behind the Dyke, built by Offa, the Saxon king, at the end of the 8th century down the east of the country from the north coast to Hereford and Worcester.

Next came the conquests of Wales—made, not by kings and large armies, but by a handful of adventurous Norman lords, commissioned by William, and inspired by his promise that they could rule what they won in battle. One of these lords was Robert Fitzhamon, who captured the old Roman fortress of Cardiff in an attack from the sea, establishing a castle there which can be seen today.

Fortresses that defied Llewellyn the Great

Other Norman lords built castles at strategic points in the lowland areas to safeguard their successes. One of these, with a rectangular keep, is at Chepstow; another, with the more advanced and less vulnerable circular keep, is at Pembroke. The rise of the Welsh prince Llewellyn the Great in the late 12th and 13th centuries, and his fierce attacks on the domains of the Border Lords, led to the building of a double, and sometimes triple, line of fortresses along the border—Gwent's Grosmont, Skenfrith and White castles are examples.

By 1282, Edward I had broken the power of the Llewellyns by defeating Llewellyn the Great's grandson, Llewellyn ap Gruffydd. To mark his conquest he built massive fortresses throughout Wales—at Builth Wells, Aberystwyth, Flint, Rhuddlan, Conwy, Caernarfon, Harlech and Beaumaris. These 'Edwardian' castles, famous throughout Europe for their military architecture, combined palatial living quarters with highly sophisticated defensive designs.

The castles remained virtually impregnable until the introduction of cannon in the 14th century. It was these weapons, firing cannon balls 22 in. in diameter and larger than the shells used in 20th-century battles, that helped Owen Glendower, hero of Welsh nationalism, to take Harlech in 1401 during the last great Welsh rebellion. His rebellion failed. The Welsh became involved in the Wars of the Roses and when Henry V died, a descendant of Llewellyn the Great married Henry's widow. Their grandson, Henry Tudor, supported by the Welsh, defeated Richard III at Bosworth Field to become Henry VII—the first of the Tudors—thus giving Wales a sense of victory over England.

It was left to Henry VIII to pass the Statute of Union in 1536 that joined Wales to England for good. In the Civil War, Wales was on the king's side, despite its discontent at the indifference to Wales of both the Tudors and the Stuarts. A tradition of dissent grew up which, fanned by the forerunners and followers of Wesley, developed in the 18th century into Methodism. This religion swept Wales and left an enduring mark on the country. In the following century came the Industrial Revolution, and the development of the coalfields, metal industries, and the railway.

Haven of the polecat and pine marten

In many parts of the country, industry has intruded only slightly upon Wales's natural beauty, which supports a unique population of plants and animals. Colonies of seabirds thrive on islands such as Caldy, Bardsey, Skomer, famous for Manx shearwaters, and Grassholme, with its gannetry. Inland there are black grouse, a few breeding pairs of kites and peregrines, occasional hobbies, and in the north, a few hen-harriers. Animals include the red squirrel, otter, grey seal—a large colony breeds off Ramsey Island—deer and wild pony. But there are greater rarities: the polecat of the north which was almost extinct a few years ago; some colonies of American mink along the Teifi banks; and the beautiful pine marten. Herds of white cattle at Dynevor in the south and Vaynol in the north are said to be descended from Roman cows.

The country is rich in plant life, too. Thousands of acres of hillside have been planted with new trees, and the moorlands change colour

THE WELSH LANGUAGE

It is estimated that a quarter of the population of Wales speak Welsh as naturally as they do English—and there are a few thousand people who speak Welsh only. The basic vocabulary of present-day Welsh is Celtic, but it includes a sprinkling of Latin and English. It is a lyrical-sounding language, but very tongue-twisting for outsiders. The Welsh alphabet omits the consonants j, k, q, v, x and z. It has the one 'f' (pronounced 'v') and adds a double 'ff' (pronounced as the ordinary English 'f'); a double 'dd' (pronounced as 'th' in 'then'); and a double 'll' (almost impossible for an outsider to pronounce correctly; to get near to the sound, put the tongue at the back of the roof of the mouth and say 'hl'). Welsh place names, often mystifying at first, become easier to understand when it is realised that they are often made up by joining together a number of separate word elements. When the word 'bryn', for example, appears in a place-name it usually denotes a hill; 'llyn' a lake; and 'ynys' an island. Other meanings of elements in Welsh place names are:

aber estuary	*cwm* or *dyffryn* valley	*pen* headland
afon river	*dol* meadow	*pistyll* waterfall
bach or *fach* small	*fawr* or *mawr* large	*pwll* pit or pool
bont bridge	*glan* or *lan* shore	*rhiw* slope
bwlch pass	*gwyn* white	*rhos* moor or marsh
caer or *gaer* fort	*llan* church	*traws* cross
capel chapel	*maen* boulder	*tre* town
coed wood	*mynydd* mountain	*ty* house
coch or *goch* red	*ogof* cave	*ystwyth* winding

CASTLE BY FLOODLIGHT *Edward I laid the foundations of Caernarfon Castle in 1283. In 1969 it was the majestic setting for Prince Charles's investiture as Prince of Wales*

through the year as heather, bilberry and bog asphodel bloom and die. The warm and damp climate of the south-west encourages exotic flowers normally seen in Mediterranean countries.

The other richness of Wales is in its people. The Welsh claim to sing, speak, write, dance and dream with more artistry than their Anglo-Saxon neighbours in the east. And they make good their claim by producing more leading actors and singers for the size of their population than any other nation. From its reservoir of talent, Wales has produced men of world rank: the poets W. H. Davies and Dylan Thomas; the painter Augustus John; the composer Vaughan Williams; and David Lloyd George, the 'Welsh Wizard' who was as great a national leader in the First World War as Winston Churchill was in the Second.

The explorer H. M. Stanley was born in Denbigh; Lawrence of Arabia at Tremadog; the infamous Judge Jeffreys near Wrexham; the Labour politician Aneurin Bevan at Tredegar; the actress Mrs Siddons at Brecon; and the social reformer Robert Owen at Newtown.

The Welsh tradition is best exemplified in the many eisteddfods held every year—the best known at Llangollen. These contests in music and verse, many of them conducted in the Welsh language, express the tradition of *hywl*, or fervour, which generations of preachers have led a chapel-going people to expect from those who deal in the spoken word.

MILD WINTERS ON THE COAST OF NORTH WALES

The mountains bring a variety of weather to Wales. Coastal regions have 175–200 days of rain a year; the mountains, 200–225 days. This can mean well over 100 in. of rain in Snowdonia, compared with only 26 in. at Rhyl. Because it is so well protected by hills, the North Wales coast has mild winters: 6°C (43°F) at Llandudno in January, which is comparable to England's south coast. The entire Welsh coast averages almost $4\frac{1}{2}$ hours of sunshine a day for the year. Summer temperatures along the north coast compare favourably with England's south coast. Llandudno's average highest temperature is around 27°C (81°F)

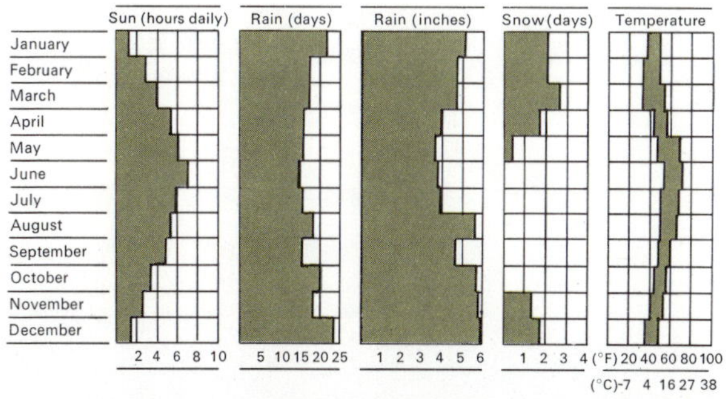

The rugged headlands of St Brides Bay

Angling Trout and salmon in River Teifi: Thornton Reservoir, Milford Haven; Pembroke Town Mill Pool; on the Rivers Cleddau and Nevern. Pike in Bosherston Pools. Sea-fishing at Fishguard, Pembroke Dock, Tenby. Tope off Caldey Island.

Boating Sailing at Broad Haven, Dale, Fishguard, Milford Haven, Tenby and Saundersfoot.

Sports There is aqualung tuition and hire at Tenby, water-skiing at Neyland and Tenby.

Events There is a river pageant at Haverfordwest in June. Coracle races are held on the Teifi at Cilgerran in Aug.

Places to see *Caldey I. Priory and Monastery*, by launch from Tenby: Spring Bank Hol. to Sept., Mon. to Fri. *Carew Castle*: Spring Bank Hol. to Sept., daily. *Castle Museum*, Haverfordwest: weekdays. *Cilgerran Castle* (NT): weekdays, Sun. afternoons. *Graham Sutherland Gallery*, Picton Castle: Easter to Sept., daily except Mon. and Fri.; Oct. to Easter, Sat. and Sun. afternoons. *Tudor Merchant's House* (NT), Tenby: Easter to Sept., Mon. to Fri.; also Sun. afternoons.

Information centres Wales Tourist Board and Pembrokeshire Coast National Park: 40 High Street, Haverfordwest. Tel. Haverfordwest 3110 (seasonal); Kingsmoor Common, Kilgetty. Tel. Kilgetty 813672.

The sea cliffs and sandy bays of south-west Dyfed form such a spectacular part of Britain that in 1952 almost all the coastline was designated as The Pembrokeshire Coast National Park. Around St Brides Bay, rugged cliffs rise majestically from the shores. The headlands have a dramatic grandeur when lashed by the great Atlantic waves, and between them are numerous sheltered coves. Small resorts have grown up around some of these coves, but others are accessible only by steep cliff paths.

It is a sunny coast, but a windy one too, which explains the scarcity of trees along the moors near the sea. Offshore, several islands are the safe breeding grounds of seals and of thousands of seabirds, including razorbills, guillemots, fulmars and gannets.

Despite its impressive sea cliffs, south-west Dyfed as a whole is the least mountainous part of Wales, except for Anglesey. In the north, the land rises eastwards from St David's Head in a series of moorlands towards its highest point of only 1760 ft in the Prescelly Hills. These rolling uplands, cut by deep river valleys, are rich in prehistoric relics, and it was from here that Bronze Age Britons are thought to have dragged huge blue dolerite stones to Milford Haven to be floated across to the Bristol Avon on their 240-mile journey to Stonehenge on Salisbury Plain.

The countryside around Haverfordwest is rich farmland which has much of the mellow charm of the English West Country; this area is often called 'Little England beyond Wales'. This is not only because its scenery is gentler than most of Wales, but also because, after the Norman Conquest, English-speaking settlers by-passed Glamorgan and Carmarthenshire to settle in Pembrokeshire, and gave to their settlements the English names that distinguish this region from the rest of Wales today.

Bosherston
A village noted for its three-pronged lake—nearly 3 miles of water covered with white water-lilies in summer. The arms of the lake were originally the mouths of three rivers, later cut off from the sea by a sand bar. A footpath leads 1½ miles south-east to a fine bathing beach at Barafundle Bay.

St Govan's Head, 1½ miles south, is famous for the tiny chapel of St Govan, only 20 ft by 12 ft, perched half-way down the cliffs and approached by a steep flight of steps. The chapel dates from the 13th century or earlier. Huntsman's Leap, half a mile west, is a great fissure in the cliffs. According to legend a horseman once jumped the narrow gap, 130 ft above the sea, but died of fright after the feat.

There is a spectacular walk along the cliffs 2 miles further west to Elegug Stack, a massive limestone pillar covered with seabirds in the breeding season. Much of the countryside is part of the Castlemartin tank firing range; there are notices warning of times during which firing will be in progress.

Broad Haven
An attractive little resort on St Brides Bay, with a smooth, sandy beach at low tide and good sea fishing. Little Haven, another resort with a long sandy beach, lies in a narrower bay half a mile south, surrounded by fine cliff scenery.

Cilgerran
A large village beside the River Teifi, with impressive remains of a late 11th-century castle built on a high bluff overlooking a deeply wooded ravine; a painting of the ruins by Turner hangs in the Tate Gallery. The village is a popular salmon and trout-fishing centre.

Dale
A village in a sheltered bay, and a popular yachting centre. The beach is shingle, but there is a stretch of sand at West Dale, half a mile across the narrow peninsula of St Ann's Head, where Henry Tudor landed in 1485. A minor road leads 2 miles south to St Ann's Head Lighthouse at the tip of the promontory.

Marloes, 2 miles north-west, has a mile-long stretch of flat sands, backed by rugged cliffs. A minor road from the village church leads to the top of the cliffs, but there is still a half-mile scramble down to the beach which, as a result, never becomes overcrowded.

Fishguard
A picturesque port, with a fine bay, surrounded by steep cliffs. An inscribed stone recalls the last invasion of British soil. A party of French, sent to seize Bristol, were driven north by the wind and landed near Fishguard in 1797. They mistook red-cloaked women onlookers for guardsmen, and surrendered.

Haverfordwest
Formerly the historic county town of Pembrokeshire. St Mary's Church was built in the 13th century and there is a museum within the ruins of the 12th-century castle walls.

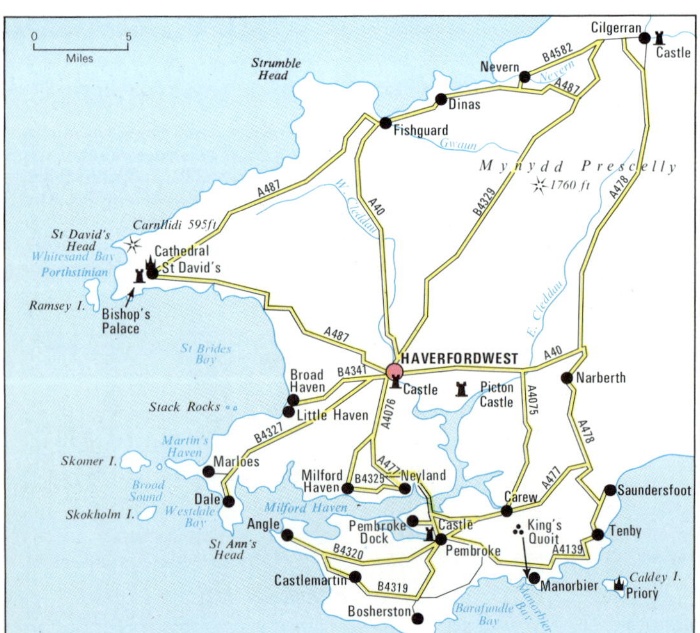

WORK AND PLAY *Milford Haven harbour runs nearly 20 miles inland from St Ann's Head, and is ideal for sailing. It is one of the largest natural harbours in Britain and oil-tankers of up to 250,000 tons are able to use its 150 ft deep channel*

CLIFFSIDE CHAPEL *The simple building set into the cliff at St Govan's Head is a 13th-century chapel, but the altar and a seat were cut into the stone much earlier*

ST DAVID'S CATHEDRAL *Local sandstone was used to build the 12th-century cathedral, which has a fine nave with an Irish oak roof and a 14th-century stone screen*

Manorbier
A village built round the ruins of an impressive, moated Norman castle overlooking a beautiful bay of the same name. The great Welsh scholar and topographer Giraldus Cambrensis was born here *c.* 1146. About half a mile to the south-west lies King's Quoit, a prehistoric group of standing stones capped by a stone 15 ft long and 9 ft wide.

Milford Haven
An important port and oil-refining town, with a splendid harbour 20 miles long. The deep-water channel admits oil tankers of over 250,000 tons. The port was founded at the instigation of Sir William Hamilton, and Nelson stayed there with him and Emma, Lady Hamilton in 1801. Though fishing is not as important as it was, the return of the local fishing fleet is still a spectacular sight. The trawlers spend between ten days and three weeks at sea.

Nevern
A village in a picturesque setting, with a medieval bridge, a few cottages and a Norman church restored in the 19th century. The so-called 'Bleeding Yew' near the church drips a blood-like sap. The church has a Norman tower and two stones carrying inscriptions in the 5th-century Gaelic script known as Ogham. St Brynach's Cross, in the churchyard, has notable Celtic carvings, and near by are a wayside cross cut into the rock face and a kneeling place—a relic of the 6th century when this was a stopping-place for pilgrims to St David's.

ATLANTIC GREY SEAL

Grey seals are comparatively rare, and most breed on Britain's western coasts, particularly around the islands off south-west Dyfed, such as Ramsey and Skomer. The seals arrive from their Atlantic feeding-grounds in September and the breeding season lasts into October. Calves are born with a white woolly coat which changes to slate-grey after three weeks. After four weeks the mother leaves them to find their own way to the sea, and within days the calves become expert at catching their own fish. A bull may grow to 8 ft long and can weigh as much as 600 lb. Grey seals are intelligent and have been taught in captivity to obey words of command

Pembroke
A small town with one of the largest and most impressive Norman castles in Britain, surrounded on three sides by water. The outer wall has seven bastion towers, and the keep is 75 ft high. Henry VII was born in the castle in 1457. It was allowed to fall into ruin after the Civil War. The vast limestone Wogan Cavern is entered from the northern hall inside the castle.

St David's
Britain's smallest cathedral city, named after St David, patron saint of Wales. The cathedral, set in a hollow below the town, is mainly 12th century. Near the cathedral are impressive ruins of the medieval Bishop's Palace.

A mile south of St David's are several good bays, with sand and cliff scenery. They include St Non's Bay, named after St David's mother and thought to be the Saint's birthplace (*c.* AD 500), Caerbwdi Bay and Caerfai Bay. From Carnllidi (595 ft), above Whitesand Bay, one of the finest in the area, Ireland can be seen on a clear day.

Ramsey Island, half a mile off the coast, is a privately owned and farmed nature reserve where more than 30 species of birds breed. Boat trips round the island can be made from Porthstinian, near St David's. Grassholme Island, 12 miles west of St David's Head, is a nature reserve and one of the largest gannetries in the world, with more than 15,000 pairs of gannets.

Skomer Island
Boats from Martin's Haven carry 4000 visitors a year to the island nature reserve 1½ miles off the coast. It contains more than 30 species of birds, including 25,000 pairs of Manx shearwaters.

Tenby
An attractive resort with narrow streets, and houses, shops and cafés built against the ruins of the 13th-century town walls. Set on a rocky promontory, the town overlooks two great bays, both sandy. There is a picturesque harbour.

Caldey Island, 2½ miles out from Tenby and reached by launch, has an ancient priory church and a modern monastery. The Cistercian monks there produce perfumes that are sold on the island and at Tenby.

SOLVING A RIDDLE

The inscriptions on this 7 ft high stone pillar at St Dogmaels, 3 miles north-west of Cilgerran, helped scholars in 1848 to decipher Ogham, a 5th-century Gaelic script

The land of Merlin the wizard and Dylan the poet

Angling There is salmon and trout fishing on the River Teifi at Newcastle Emlyn and on the River Taf at Whitland, 6 miles north of Pendine; also at Carmarthen on the River Tywi and on the River Gwilli, and at Llandeilo on the Tywi. There is trout-fishing on the River Cennen at Llandeilo and on the Gwendraeth Fawr at Kidwelly. There is sea fishing from Burry Port and Ferryside.

Boating There are sailing centres and boats for hire at Laugharne and Burry Port. Annual regattas are held at Burry Port and Ferryside during Aug.

Events United Counties Agricultural Show is held at Carmarthen in the second week of Aug. There is also an agricultural show at Llandeilo in Aug. A pilgrimage service is held in the churchyard at St Clears, 4 miles north of Laugharne, on the last Sun. in July. The Dylan Thomas Festival is held every three years (1981, 1984, etc.) at Laugharne; it usually includes a performance of *Under Milk Wood*.

Places to see *Boat House*, Laugharne: daily except Mon. *Carmarthen County Museum*: Mon. to Fri. *Carreg-Cennen Castle*: daily, except Sun. mornings Oct. to Mar. *Kidwelly Castle*: daily, except Sun. mornings Oct. to Mar. *Parc Howard Museum and Art Gallery*, Llanelli: weekdays and Sun. afternoons, Mar. to Nov.

Information centre Wales Tourist Board, Old Bishops' Palace, Abergwili. Tel. Carmarthen 31557 (seasonal).

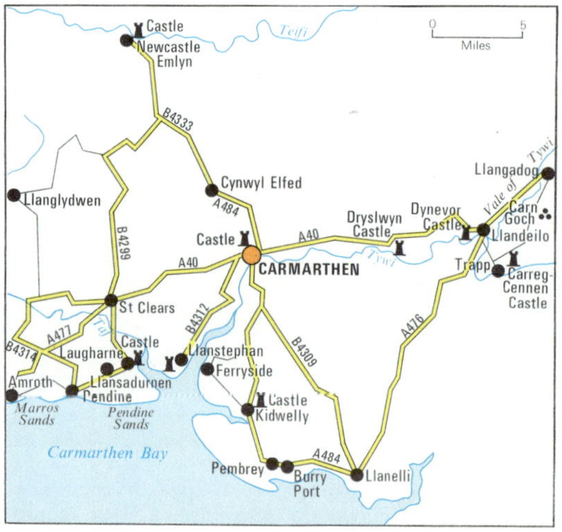

South-east Dyfed (formerly Carmarthenshire) has a distinctive scenic beauty of its own, more serene in character than the dramatic coastline to the west, or the Brecon Beacons which border it to the east. Many visitors enjoy the picturesque countryside beside the River Teifi, which used to mark the northern boundary of Carmarthenshire, while to the south-east the Vale of Tywi passes from wild and sparsely populated country down through the rich agricultural valleys around Carmarthen to the sea. The Black Mountain rises to 2632 ft in the east, and along the coast are several good beaches, including Pendine's 5-mile strip of sand, famous for early motor speed trials.

Above all, this is a land of romantic legends and ruined castles. In the historic town of Carmarthen, the rotting stump of an oak tree is determinedly protected because according to legend Merlin, the magician of Arthurian tales, cast a spell saying that when it fell, Carmarthen would fall too. Carreg-Cennen, near Llandeilo, is the most impressive of the numerous castles, while south-west of Llangadog, in the Vale of Tywi, lies Carn Goch ('Red Cairn'), the largest Iron Age hill fort in Wales—half a mile across.

Fishermen still use coracles from which to net salmon on the Teifi and the Tywi, as they have done in this region since before the Romans. Other specialities of the area are its laver bread, made from seaweed, and the cockles gathered at Ferryside at the mouth of the Tywi. The poet and playwright Dylan Thomas lived at Laugharne for 16 years.

Amroth
A resort on a sand-and-shingle beach. At very low tides, stumps of petrified trees and other relics of a forest buried under the waves 1000 years ago can be seen among the sands. Amroth is the starting point of the Pembrokeshire Coast National Park footpath—167 miles of spectacular cliff scenery.

Wiseman's Bridge, about 1 mile west, was the site of a full-scale rehearsal for the 1944 D-Day invasion of Normandy, attended by Winston Churchill.

NEOLITHIC TOMB *A chambered tomb dating back to the Stone Age stands 1½ miles west of Llanglydwen. Such tombs were originally covered by earth mounds*

Carmarthen
A town on a bluff above the Tywi, dominated by the ruined Norman castle. There are some narrow streets reminiscent of medieval times, but the town has been refashioned in modern times.

The Welsh name for Carmarthen is *Caerfyrddin*, meaning 'Merlin's City'—the great wizard was allegedly born here. The famous tree trunk, upon which he put a spell: 'When Merlin's oak shall tumble down, Then shall fall Carmarthen Town', lies in Priory Street, embedded in concrete and wrapped in iron bands to keep it from falling.

In 1843, Carmarthen was the scene of the Rebecca Riots when 'Rebecca and her Daughters'—400 men dressed as women—attacked the jail in protest at tolls charged at the town gates. They took their name from the Biblical verse which says of Rebekah, 'be thou the mother of thousands of millions, and let thy seed possess the gate of those which hate them' (Genesis XXIV 60).

Carreg-Cennen Castle
Seen from the road up from the little hamlet of Trapp, this great 14th-century fortress looks the perfect setting for King Arthur's knights. Surrounded by fertile valleys, it stands 900 ft above sea level, with a 300-ft sheer precipice below its walls. A subterranean passage 150 ft long leads down into the bowels of the cliff, where there is a spring. Openings cut in the cliff-face to let in light give dramatic views of the Black Mountains.

Laugharne
Parts of this ancient town are still charming, with an old harbour and castle and splendid sea views of the Taf and Tywi Estuaries. The town's charter, granted by the Normans in 1307, is kept in the small but elegant town hall, which was rebuilt in 1746. Local government is still conducted under this charter, and meetings of the Court Leet and Court Baron, held on alternate Mondays, are presided over by an official known as a Portreeve.

Dylan Thomas lived at the Boat House, in Cliff Walk, just behind the castle. He is buried in the local churchyard. Half a mile south are Sir John's Hill, which is featured in one of Thomas's poems, and the remains of Roche Castle at the foot of the hill.

Llandeilo
A pleasant, hilly town on the north bank of the River Tywi, and a market and fishing centre. The poet Edmund Spenser, in his *Faerie Queene*, sites Merlin's cave among the wooded hills around Llandeilo.

In a walled park stands Dynevor Castle, seat of Lord Dynevor (spelt *Dynefwr* in Welsh), whose family has held it since the days of the Welsh chieftain Roderick the Great in the 9th century. The present castle dates from the 17th century, but the ruined keep of the original castle, which dates from the 11th century, still stands on a cliff above the river.

IMPREGNABLE FORTRESS *Carreg-Cennen Castle, near Trapp, was completed in the 14th century on the site of a Norman building. It withstood a siege by Owen Glendower*

Llanelli
The largest town in south-east Dyfed, with a population of more than 28,000, is largely an industrial centre which rose in importance during the later stages of the Industrial Revolution, in the 19th century. Its great industries of coal and tin-plate are now dead, but it remains prosperous mainly because of the presence of nationalised steelworks. It has a sandy beach, a 110 ft long swimming-pool and a civic park. A mansion in the park, Bryncaerau Castle, is now the Parc Howard Museum and Art Gallery.

Llanstephan
A beautifully situated village on the peninsula between the Rivers Taf and Tywi. It has a ruined Norman castle, with gatehouse and keep. A boat can be hired to cross the Tywi to Ferryside, near which lies Kidwelly, which has an immense 13th and 14th-century castle, ruined but still splendid, with a semicircular moat and an inner courtyard with a circular tower at each corner.

Llansadurnen
A village sited on a limestone bluff notable for Coygan Cave, in which fossil relics of mammoths, woolly rhinoceroses and other animals have been found.

Newcastle Emlyn
One of the centres of the 'Rebecca Rioters' and now a busy little market town on the River Teifi. The first Welsh printing press was set up here in 1718. On the east side of the town are remains of the 15th-century castle, called New Castle to distinguish it from the older Cilgerran Castle further down the river.

Pembrey
A village linked with the larger town of Burry Port, and lying behind 5 miles of firm sands and dunes, the Pembrey Burrows. Part of the Burrows has been planted with trees by the Forestry Commission. The dunes, wild and undeveloped, have been the scene of controversy over plans to use the area for Government research work. The nave and chancel of the 13th-century church have a fine timber barrel roof. There is a memorial in the churchyard to the crew and passengers of a French sailing ship, *Jeanne Emma*, which foundered on the sands at the mouth of the Tywi Estuary in 1828. Among those drowned was a niece of Napoleon's wife, Josephine.

Amelia Earhart landed near Burry Port in 1928 to become the first woman to fly the Atlantic—she accompanied the pilot and co-pilot in a crossing from Newfoundland that took 20 hr., 40 min. In 1932 she became the first woman to fly the Atlantic solo.

Pendine
A resort between dunes and hills, notable for its 5-mile stretch of firm, smooth sand. In the 1920's Pendine Sands were used by car drivers in speed-record attempts; in 1924 Sir Malcolm Campbell broke the current world record with an average 146·16 mph.

LAUGHARNE, WHERE DYLAN THOMAS WROTE POETRY IN A GARDEN SHED

The poet Dylan Thomas (1914–53) lived for 16 years in the Georgian Boat House, perched on the steep bank of the River Taf at Cliff Walk, Laugharne. Thomas wrote many of his poems in a shed in the garden. The charcoal portrait of Thomas (right) was drawn when he was 36 by his friend Michael Ayrton and is now in the National Portrait Gallery, London. The fictitious town featured in Thomas's play *Under Milk Wood* is believed to have been based on the town of Laugharne and its people, although the poet vigorously denied this

The greener Rhondda

RHONDDA'S GOLDEN VOICES *The singing of the Treorchy Male Voice Choir has become world-famous*

Angling On the upper reaches of the River Taw. Coarse fishing at Roath Park Lake, Cardiff. Sea fishing at Penarth, The Mumbles, Barry, and off the Gower coast.

Sailing There are clubs at Swansea, The Mumbles, Porthcawl, Barry, Penarth, Cardiff and Newport.

Events The ten-day Llandaff Festival is held at the cathedral in June. Military tattoo at Cardiff Castle, alternate years (1979, 1981, etc.).

Places to see *Afan Argoed Country Park*, Cymmer, 6 miles north-east of Port Talbot: daily. *Caerphilly Castle*: daily, except Sun. morning Oct. to Mar. *Cardiff Castle*: daily. *Ewenny Priory*, Bridgend: Mon. to Fri. *Maritime and Industrial Museum*, Swansea: weekdays. *National Museum of Wales*, Cardiff: weekdays, Sun. afternoon. *Oystermouth Castle*, Swansea: weekdays, Sun. afternoon. *Swansea Museum*: weekdays. *Welsh Folk Museum*, St Fagans: weekdays, Sun. afternoon. *Welsh Industrial and Maritime Museum*, Cardiff: daily.

Information centre Wales Tourist Board, 3 Castle Street, Cardiff. Tel. Cardiff 27281.

Only a century-and-a-half ago, the great series of valleys running down from the edge of the Brecon Beacons still kept their natural beauty. Today, such names as Mountain Ash, Pontypridd, the Rhondda, Neath and Swansea are linked with the starkness of coal and iron mines.

But not all of this area is industrially ravaged—the coastline running from Barry to Porthcawl and Port Talbot has many fine beaches and resorts; and the Gower Peninsula, which runs for 14 miles west of Swansea, also has beaches, coves and numerous fishing villages. Caerphilly has a majestic 13th-century castle, the largest in Wales, and the quiet, leafy Vale of Glamorgan, running for 20 miles west of Cardiff, displays beautiful landscapes and seascapes.

Even the mining valleys themselves have new interest and character. In the last century there was no relief from the monotony of their strung-out coal and iron workings, their belching chimneys, their railway lines, and their long, mean strings of terraced houses. Now, a drive down the Rhondda Valley gives a different impression. There is still much industry, but the hills above are green and the little houses neat and clean, their doors and windows colourfully painted. As the old heavy industries of coal and iron die out, brighter, cleaner factories take their place, and in the Vale of Neath a million young trees sprout from the cleared tips and former industrial sites.

IN SEARCH OF SHELLFISH *At first light the cockle gatherers of Penclawdd drive across the sands to the Loughor Estuary*

Aberdare
Since much of the coal-mining is carried on in side valleys, Aberdare has managed to escape the worst scars of mining. It has excellent views of the Brecon Beacons. A statue commemorates the Aberdare Great Choir, which sang at the Crystal Palace in 1872.

Barry
A village of only 85 inhabitants in 1880, which expanded at a furious pace after becoming a coal-exporting port. Barry Island, joined to the mainland by a causeway, has a good sandy beach and an amusement park which is one of the largest in Britain. A pebble beach stretches 2½ miles westwards to Porthkerry.

Bridgend
An old market town with a 12th-century castle that includes a Norman doorway. Ewenny Priory, 1½ miles south, is a splendid example of a monastery with military defences. It was founded in 1141 as a cell of the Benedictine abbey at Gloucester. Coity Castle, 1½ miles north-east, is 12th to 14th century. It was abandoned in the 16th century.

Caerphilly
The town was noted until the beginning of the century for the crumbly cheese of the same name, which is now made elsewhere. Its massive, 13th-century, partially restored castle, with a moat and buttressed wall, covers 30 acres. The castle has a fragment of a round or 'drum' tower, which leans about 12 ft out of the perpendicular, because of an attempt to blow it up during the Civil War.

Cardiff
This great seaport city on the Bristol Channel has been the capital of Wales since 1955. Its prosperity began with the opening of Bute West Dock in 1839 and today the docks at Cardiff, Penarth and Barry have between them 7 miles of quays. The docks and factories lie mainly south of the city.

The spacious Civic Centre in Cathays Park contains the offices of civic and national institutions. Cardiff Castle dates from 1093 and is built on the site of a Roman fort, although a great part of it was built during the last century when the family of the 3rd Marquess of Bute carried out extensive modifications.

Llandaff Cathedral is 2½ miles north-west of Cardiff; the city of Llandaff was incorporated into Cardiff in 1922. The first church, built in the 6th century, was of wood, replaced in the 12th century by Norman stone. Extensively damaged during the Second World War, it was reconstructed and re-opened in 1957 and the interior of the nave is dominated by an aluminium sculpture by Epstein of Christ in Majesty.

On the banks of the River Taff, near the city centre, is the National Stadium, the famous Rugby football ground. The city is the home of the University College of Cardiff and of the National Museum of Wales, which houses Welsh archaeological, art, industrial, zoological and other collections.

The Welsh Folk Museum, which has a section devoted to fishing through the ages, is at St Fagans, a village of thatched cottages on the western outskirts of Cardiff.

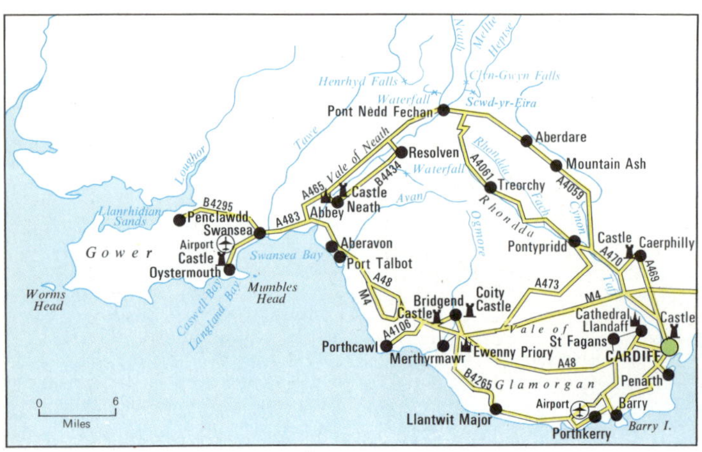

BLEAK BEAUTY *The lonely northern coastline of the Gower Peninsula looks out over salt-marshes to the treacherous sands of the silted-up Loughor Estuary off Carmarthen Bay. The peninsula's empty spaces, fringed with cliffs and caves, provide a restful escape from the expanding suburbs of industrial Swansea to the east*

Gower
A peninsula stretching for 14 miles from Mumbles Head on Swansea Bay to its tip at Worms Head, and almost unspoilt. Starting from The Mumbles, there is a cliff walk to Langland Bay and on to Caswell Bay. From Penclawdd—meaning 'head of the dike'—on the northern coast, cockle gatherers drive their ponies and donkeys across the Llanrhidian Sands to the cockle-beds of the Loughor Estuary.

Neath
An industrial town, with a history going back to Roman times; its Roman fort of Nidum was recently unearthed. There are ruins of a Norman castle and of an abbey founded in 1130. Today its immediate environs are scarred with collieries, and steel and engineering works, but there is attractive countryside in the Vale of Neath which runs north-east towards the Brecon Beacons.

At Resolven, 6 miles north-east, is the lovely 80-ft waterfall of Melin Court. At Pont Nêdd Fechar at the head of the valley, the scenery becomes even more spectacular, with gorges, torrents, wooded glens and waterfalls. The Scwd-yr-Eira ('spout of snow') Fall on the River Hepste is more than 50 ft high, and the flow is propelled outward from its cliff with such force that it is possible to walk behind the arc of water.

Porthcawl
A popular seaside and residential resort with a good promenade, two fine beaches and a large amusement park at Coney Beach. On fine days the tors of Exmoor can be seen beyond the Bristol Channel.

Rhondda
The valleys of Rhondda Fawr, or 'large', and Rhondda Fach, or 'small', form one of the most famous coal-mining regions in Britain. Until 1850, this was wild country, without roads; but with the sinking of the coalpits, miners' cottages, interspersed with Nonconformist chapels and workmen's institutes, spread along the slopes until, 80 years later, the strings of little mining townships had raised the population to more than 140,000. The great musical tradition of the Rhondda valleys, established in the 19th century, continues through numerous brass and silver bands and the world-famous Treorchy and Pendyrus Male Voice Choirs.

Swansea
The second-largest city in Wales, after Cardiff, is set at the mouth of the River Tawe on the great curve of Swansea Bay. Before the 18th century it appeared to have a future as a picturesque watering place; but the intense development of copper and other metals decided its fate. Swansea is now an important port, with 6 miles of quays, an industrial centre and the home of the University College of Swansea. In the Royal Institution of South Wales are many prehistoric finds from caves on the Gower Peninsula. The new guildhall has panels by Frank Brangwyn.

Oystermouth and The Mumbles are seaside resorts within Swansea's boundaries. Oystermouth has an 11th-century castle, and in the local churchyard is buried Thomas Bowdler, who at the beginning of the 19th century published an expurgated edition of Shakespeare's works, so giving the word 'bowdlerise' to the English language.

Port Talbot, to the south-east, has the mighty Margam and Abbey steelworks—4½ miles of blast furnaces and rolling mills, forming Britain's biggest steelworks, with a big new tidal harbour for ore-carriers.

PORT TALBOT *South-east of Swansea, the smoke stacks and cooling towers of Port Talbot, home of one of Europe's largest steelworks, rear against the South Wales hills*

Border castles beside the Wye

Angling Coarse fish and trout in rivers Wye, Monnow and Usk. Trout in Llandegfedd Reservoir.

Boating There is sailing on the Llandegfedd Reservoir, Pontypool, and on the Rivers Wye and Severn at St Pierre.

Pony trekking At Cwmyoy, Abergavenny, Monmouth, Whitebrook.

Forest drive A 7-mile scenic drive through Ebbw Forest starts from Cwmcarn, 4 miles south of Llanhilleth: daily, Easter to Aug.

Places to see *Abergavenny Museum*: weekdays and Sun. afternoon, Mar. to Nov. *Caldicott Castle*, 4 miles south-west of Chepstow: afternoons, Easter to Oct. *Chepstow Castle*: daily, except Sun. morning Oct. to Mar. *Legionary Museum*, Caerleon: weekdays, Sun. afternoon. *Llanfihangel Court*: afternoons only; 1st and 3rd Sun. in June; every Sun. July and Aug.; also Bank Hol. Sun. and Mon. *Monmouth Museum*: weekdays and Sun. afternoon. *Newport Museum*: weekdays. *Raglan Castle*: daily, except Sun. morning Oct. to Mar. *Skenfrith Castle* (NT), Monmouth: daily. *Tintern Abbey*: daily, except Sun. morning Oct. to Mar. *White Castle*, 7 miles north-east of Abergavenny: weekdays and Sun. afternoon.

Information centres Wales Tourist Board, Tintern Abbey Car Park. Tel. Tintern 431 (seasonal). Torfaen Borough Council, Gwent Square, Cwmbran. Tel. Cwmbran 67411.

FORTIFIED BRIDGE *The bridge over the River Monnow at Monmouth has a gatehouse with a portcullis, built in 1260*

Gwent—as Monmouthshire is now called after the ancient Welsh kingdom of that name—glories in the Wye Valley, its wooded river frontier with England. West of the Wye lies quiet pastoral countryside, set against the dramatic western backcloth of the beginnings of the Welsh hills. The area has a turbulent past. In this Border country, the Silures tribe under Caractacus provided tough opposition to the Roman invaders, and in a later age the Normans had to build strong castles to maintain control over their territory. Today the English tourist will find nothing more foreign here than a strange mixture of Welsh and English place-names.

From Monmouth, roads to the south wind through the deep, wooded valley of the lower Wye past Tintern Abbey to Chepstow. The M4 leads west through the region, but the older A48 main road offers the more attractive drive westwards to Newport, following the line of the road built by the Romans to link their walled civilian town at Venta Silurum, near modern Caerwent, with their military fortress at Caerleon. Picturesque roads to the north follow the winding Usk, whose pure waters offer some of the best salmon fishing in southern Britain, towards the ruined 15th-century Raglan Castle.

Within half an hour's drive from the pastoral charm of eastern Gwent lies the edge of the South Wales coalfield; here the countryside is ribbed into valleys whose towns of tightly packed houses grew on foundations of coal, iron and steel.

Abergavenny
A market town on the River Usk, set in a bowl surrounded by mountains called Sugar Loaf, Ysgyryd Fawr and Blorenge, each rising to more than 1500 ft. Abergavenny is the gateway to the Brecon Beacons National Park, and a starting point for the Heads of the Valleys road which runs westwards across the heads of the great industrial valleys of South Wales. There are buildings dating from Tudor times. An 11th-century castle, now in ruins and housing a museum of local farm equipment, was the scene of a notorious massacre by William de Braose in 1177. Llanfihangel Court, 4 miles north-east, is an Elizabethan manor house with fine gardens. From Campston Hill there are views of Grosmont and Skenfrith Castles.

Abertillery
An industrial town, dominated by its long stretches of pitheads, factories and terraced houses. Though few mines have been worked since the 1930's, new industries have been brought in and the town, with its tilted streets and mountain horizons, has a moderately prosperous look.

Caerleon
Modern Newport encroaches on Caerleon, destroying some of its character. The name means 'Camp of the Legion', and here are the remains, covering more than 50 acres, of the amphitheatre and barracks of Isca, where 6000 troops of the Roman 2nd Augustan Legion established a stronghold in AD 80 to subdue the inhabitants of the area.

Caerwent, 8 miles east, was the site of Venta Silurum, a civilian city built as part of the Roman policy of pacification and fraternisation. The town's walls and gates are still visible, and there are Roman relics in the parish church.

Chepstow
A historic fortress town, built on limestone cliffs at the lowest crossing of the Wye. The great Norman castle, built on a spur of rock overlooking the river, has a 13th-century chapel and looks down on Chepstow's steep medieval streets. Remains of the wall that enclosed the town can still be seen in places, and there is an impressive 16th-century west gate. A graceful bridge, built by John Rennie, spans the Wye on the site of a Roman ford.

Ebbw Vale
The mining town is inseparably associated with the name of Aneurin Bevan, the Labour MP for this constituency for 31 years without a break, from 1929 until his death in 1960. He was born at 32 Charles Street in nearby Tredegar, and three large stones now stand at Waun-y-Pound, 1 mile out of Tredegar on the A4047, in memory of him. Ebbw Vale has one of the most spectacular industrial sights in Britain—the 2½ mile long steel sheet and tin-plate works of the British Steel Corporation.

Grosmont
An old-world town on a hillside. It is noted for angling in the nearby Monnow, and for the ruins of a Norman castle, one of three built to guard this part of the borderland against Welsh raids. Owen Glendower was defeated at Grosmont by Henry of Monmouth, later Henry V.

Skenfrith, 4 miles south-east, was the smallest of the three castles. The castle is rectangular, with round, or 'drum', towers at each corner and a circular keep within the walls.

The ruins of the third castle, White Castle, stand 5 miles south-west of Grosmont and Skenfrith, at the apex of the defensive triangle covering the approaches to the Welsh mountains.

Monmouth
A town with several Tudor and Georgian buildings and a network of old streets. Three rivers flow round the town, the Trothy, Monnow and Wye. Once a Roman settlement, Monmouth later had Breton lords. There is an 11th-century castle, where Henry V was born in 1387. The castle ruins and the well-preserved 17th-century Great Castle House, with splendid decorative ceilings, remain. In the town are the Shire Hall, built in 1724, several fine old inns and a museum with a collection of Nelson relics, including his fighting sword and models of his ships. Nelson visited the town in 1802. Outside Shire Hall, in Agincourt Square, Henry V's statue stands alongside that of C. S. Rolls,

MINING COMMUNITY *Llanhilleth, a small town lying south of Abertillery, has steep rows of terraced houses set beneath wooded hills. The homes were built for miners and their families during the expansion of the South Wales coalfield in the last century*

ROMAN RUINS *The great Roman garrison of Isca, established at Caerleon in* AD *80, was used for almost 300 years*

ROYALIST STRONGHOLD *Raglan Castle, built in the 1400's, was the last castle to fall to Cromwell in the Civil War*

CISTERCIAN ABBEY *A farmyard adds a domestic touch to the ruins of Tintern Abbey, rebuilt by Cistercians in 1288*

pioneer airman and the 'Rolls' of Rolls-Royce, whose father, Lord Llangattock, lived near Monmouth.

Among Monmouth's attractions is the Monnow Bridge, the only Norman fortified bridge surviving in Britain. Its gatehouse was built in 1260 as one of four medieval gates into the town.

South-east of the town, a bridge leads to Kymin Hill (800 ft), which is National Trust land and has views over the Monnow and Wye Valleys.

Newport

A busy industrial town and seaport on the estuary of the Usk. There is a splendid view of port derricks and ships' masts from 240 ft up on the catwalk of Newport's unusual Transporter Bridge, which carries six cars and 100 passengers at a time across the Usk in a carriage slung like a cable-car below a moving trolley.

The Cathedral of St Woolos dates back 1400 years but did not become a cathedral until 1949. It has Norman arches and a medieval tower. The magnificent east window was erected in 1963. In the art gallery adjoining Newport's museum is Epstein's bust of the town's famous son W. H. Davies, the 'tramp poet', whose best-known lines are 'What is this life if, full of care, we have no time to stand and stare?'

Raglan

A quarter of a mile north of the main road skirting the village stands the ruined Raglan Castle, a 15th-century fortified house. It was used as a fortress in the Wars of the Roses, and later became the home of the Earls of Worcester. During the Civil War the 5th Earl held out for ten weeks before surrendering to Cromwell's troops.

Tintern Abbey

The abbey, one of the finest relics of Britain's monastic age, owes almost as much of its beauty to its splendid setting—a quiet meadow in a bend of the Wye overlooked by wooded hills—as to the graceful beauty of its roofless walls. The abbey was founded in 1131 by the Cistercians, and suppressed by Henry VIII in 1536. Its abbey church, with soaring east end and rose window, is almost intact. The Anchor Inn was probably the abbey's watergate; a 13th-century arch links it with the slipway.

Usk

An old market town, and a splendid centre for angling. The ruins of a Norman castle overlook the river, and the town also has a 13th-century church with a Tudor screen, a 13th-century priory gatehouse and an 18th-century bridge with five arches.

Cefntilla Court, 2 miles north-east, the home of Lord Raglan, was built in 1616 and restored in 1856. There are pictures, porcelain and relics of the Peninsular Campaign and the Crimean War; the 1st Baron Raglan commanded the British troops in the Crimea.

Where Brecon Beacons flared

CYLINDRICAL TOWER AND KEEP *Tretower Castle was last garrisoned in 1403*

Pony trekking Centres include the YHA Pony Trekking Centre, Capel-y-ffin, in Llanthony Valley. Also Crickhowell and Llangorse.

Angling Trout in River Usk and tributaries around Brecon, and River Tywi near Llandovery. Coarse fishing in Llangorse Lake and Canal.

Canal cruising On Monmouthshire and Brecon Canal.

Places to see *Brecknock Museum*, Brecon: weekdays. *Brecon Beacons Mountain Centre*: daily. *Dan-yr-Ogof*: Apr. to Oct., daily. *South Wales Borderers Regimental Museum*, Brecon: daily. *Tretower Court and Castle*: weekdays, Sun. afternoon.

Information centres Brecon Beacons National Park, Glamorgan Street, Brecon. Tel. Brecon 2763 (seasonal). Brecon Beacons Mountain Centre, near Libanus. Tel. Brecon 3366.

The 519 square miles of the Brecon Beacons National Park contain a wide variety of scenery. There are bare, contoured hills and sheer mountainsides; high moorlands grazed by sheep and free-roaming ponies; tall trees shadowing rocky gorges; great cascades of foaming water; a wonderland of underground caves; lakes often as unruffled as a looking-glass; and always, never far away, some ruin or symbol of the past.

The National Park extends from the Black Mountain of south-east Dyfed in the west to the Black Mountains, divided between south-east Powys and the county of Gwent, in the east. The actual 'Beacons', rising to 2906 ft at Pen y Fan, take their name from their use as sites for signal fires. The windswept crests of the Beacons can be reached only on foot, and the views from the summits are awe-inspiring. Near at hand are sheer precipices, falling 600 ft, that have been likened to the crests of great waves about to break; below them are immense semicircular valleys, or cwms. Further off, heather uplands slope southwards to the edge of the South Wales coalfield, while to the north lies the unmarred beauty of the high peaks of the mid-Wales mountain ranges.

The Park is ideal countryside for the walker, the geologist and the naturalist. Some of the rocks date back 300 million years. There are relics of the Neolithic and Bronze Ages, and inscribed stones dating from the 5th and 6th centuries when this was the Irish principality of Brycheiniog. There is also an extraordinary richness of wild plants, animals and, especially, of bird life. Around Llangorse Lake are the nests of great crested grebes and of coots; elsewhere can be seen little grebes, goosanders, kingfishers, herons and red and black grouse.

ROCKY RIVER BED *The River Wye, which flows through three Welsh counties on its 130-mile journey to the Severn Estuary, travels a rocky path through the Brecon countryside. The river has some of the best salmon fishing in the country*

Brecon

An old market town of narrow streets, at the confluence of the Rivers Honddu and Usk, with many country crafts and antique shops, two notable museums, the ruins of a medieval castle and a partly-13th-century fortified cathedral. The cathedral contains a fine Norman font and the largest preserved cresset

MANOR FORTRESS *Ducts above the gatehouse of Tretower Court, now preserved as an Ancient Monument, were used to pour molten lead over attackers. The 14th-century building is one of the best examples of a fortified manor house in Wales*

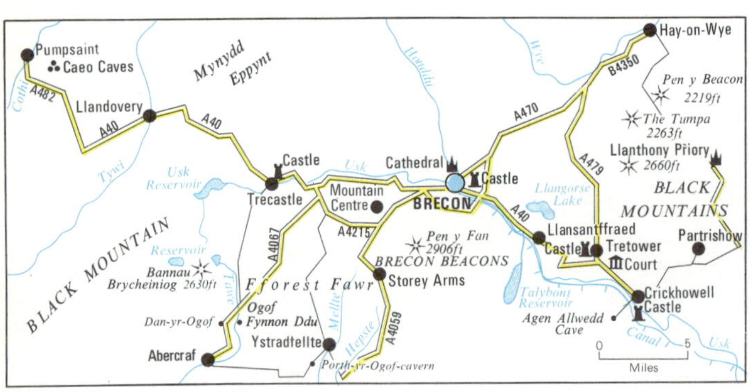

stone in Wales; the cresset was an ancient stone which had 30 cups containing oil for lighting the cathedral.

Brecon is a convenient centre for exploring the National Park. The Mountain Centre, reached by a turning off the Merthyr Tydfil road, about 3½ miles from Brecon, provides information on fishing, hikes, geology, flora and fauna. From the Storey Arms Youth Centre, 7½ miles south-west of Brecon, there is a winding climb to the summit of the Beacons at Pen y Fan. From the top, the whole glory of the Beacons lies spread out below, with views of the Malvern Hills, the Bristol Channel, the mountains of North Wales and the industrial region to the south.

SOARING PEAKS *Pen y Fan marks the 2906-ft summit of the Brecon Beacons. The top, which takes about an hour to reach from Storey Arms Youth Centre, gives fine views that take in the Malvern Hills, the Bristol Channel and the South Wales industrial area*

Crickhowell
A pleasant and small town lying in the Usk Valley, at the foot of the Black Mountains. Some visitors are puzzled by the arches of its long bridge—12 one side, 13 the other—which were made unequal for structural reasons. The town has some fine Georgian houses, fragments of a castle, the gateway of a long-vanished manor house and a 14th-century church, with elaborate tombs.

The 14-mile Agen Allwedd cave, 2¼ miles south-west, is one of the longest caves with a single entrance in Britain. The Usk valley is lushly beautiful and walks in any direction are worth while. Partrishow, 5 miles north-east, has a small church with a fine rood screen.

Dan-yr-Ogof
A maze of natural limestone caverns, 1½ miles in extent, in the Tawe Valley to the north of Abercraf. Another cave, Ogof Fynnon Ddu (*ogof* is the Welsh for 'cave'), lies to the east. There are stalactites and stalagmites, grotesque rock formations and underground lakes.

Hay-on-Wye
A small market town set high above one of Britain's most enchanting rivers, the Wye, with the Black Mountains, at their steepest and grandest, looming near. Only the gateway of the Norman and later castle survives. There is a walk of about 3½ miles along the ridge tracks of the Black Mountains; and gentle ascents to Pen y Beacon and The Tumpa. A road southwards over 1778-ft Gospel Pass leads through the Black Mountains to the ruins of Llanthony Priory.

Llandovery
George Borrow, the author of *Wild Wales*, published in 1862, described Llandovery as 'about the pleasantest little town in which I have halted in the course of my wanderings'. Today it is a busy market town with a cobbled square and a fishing centre. It is a good point for exploring the north-west corner of the Brecon Beacons National Park.

Pumpsaint
A hamlet by a bridge over the River Cothi. *Pump* is Welsh for five; the 'Five Saints' stone, on a road near Ogofan Lodge to the south-east, is the spot where legend says five saints, who were born at one birth, once rested their heads. The local church is dedicated to them. About a mile east is an ancient gold mine, worked since Roman times, now owned by the National Trust.

Trecastle
A quiet village with the site of a 12th-century castle which provides the largest motte and bailey in the Park. It is a centre for exploring south-east Dyfed's Black Mountain, its summit Bannau Brycheiniog and the great Usk Reservoir. There is a fine mountain road running below the peak which, at 2630 ft, is the second highest mountain in South Wales after the Beacons themselves. The northern face of this mountain is deeply scarred with precipices, below which lie two small lakes.

Tretower
A circular keep surrounds a cylindrical tower in the ruins of the Norman castle. It was built to defend the valley of the Usk, and was in use as late as 1403 during the revolt of Owen Glendower. Tretower Court is a Welsh fortified manor house where the 17th-century poet Henry Vaughan is said to have lived. It was built in the 14th century complete with arrow slits, and apertures over the gatehouse through which molten lead could be poured on to attackers.

Ystradfellte
A village on the River Mellte in the heart of Fforest Fawr, once a royal hunting-ground. The surrounding countryside abounds in caves, streams and waterfalls on the Mellte and Hepste rivers; at one point the Mellte disappears underground into Porth yr Ogof.

Moorlands around Cardigan Bay

CORACLE ON THE TEIFI *The coracle of the Welsh fisherman is made of canvas stretched over a wickerwork frame. Its design has not changed since the Iron Age, when early Britons used hides to cover the craft*

Angling Trout and salmon on Rivers Aeron, Rheidol, Taifi and Ystwyth, streams Arthand Wyre, and at Devil's Bridge. Trout in Nant-y-Moch Lake and in Teify Pools, Strata Florida.

Nature trail There is a 3-mile trail with viewing shelters and hides in Cardigan Wildlife Park.

Events Aberystwyth has an Agricultural Show, a Yacht Club Regatta, a Donkey Derby, and a Sea Angling Festival during the summer.

Places to see *Ceredigion Museum*, Aberystwyth: Mon. to Sat. afternoons. *Llwernog Silver-lead Mine*, Ponterwyd: Easter to Oct., daily. *Nanteos Mansion*, 2 miles south-east of Aberystwyth: June to Sept., afternoons. *National Library of Wales*, Aberystwyth: weekdays. *Strata Florida Abbey*: weekdays, Sun. afternoon. *Vale of Rheidol Narrow Gauge Railway*: daily, mid-Apr. to early Oct.

Information centre Tourism Dept., 6 Park Avenue, Aberystwyth. Tel. Aberystwyth 617911.

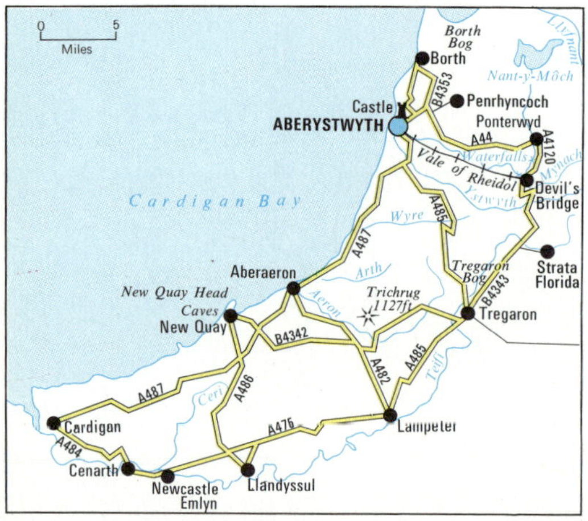

The countryside of south-west Dyfed (Cardiganshire) gives a sense of space and size. Inland there are great sweeping moorlands, rising to mountain masses 2000 ft or more high and interspersed with marshes. Views are wide, horizons far; the wind sweeps freely across the vastness, and skylarks and meadow pipits sing. Other birds to be found are peregrines, golden plovers, merlins, teals and even red kites, now reduced to about a score of breeding pairs in the whole of Britain. There are red grouse among the waving heather, and kestrels among the rocks at the valley heads.

There are few signs of human habitation—this region is one of the most sparsely populated in Britain, outside the remoter parts of Scotland. Only in the thickly wooded valleys of the Rivers Aeron, Ystwyth, Leri, Llyfnant and Rheidol is the sense of space temporarily lost—soon to be recaptured along the 40 miles of splendid coastline. Here are some of the finest beaches in Britain, and although there are many caravan sites and towns they do not, in the main, detract from the beauty of cliffs and coves.

Railway enthusiasts can ride on the narrow-gauge steam railway which runs for 12 miles from Aberystwyth up the Vale of Rheidol to the falls at Devil's Bridge, one of the greatest of Welsh tourist attractions. For anglers the valley of the Teifi is renowned for salmon and trout, and at Cenarth the ancient art of fishing from coracles is still practised.

South-west Dyfed is proud of its lobsters, though the bulk of its income comes from milk and livestock produce. There are few industries, but traditional craftsmen include blacksmiths, potters, weavers, wood-turners, cabinet-makers and wood-carvers.

Aberaeron
A quiet resort town with two beaches, and rock pools full of prawns and shrimps. The port had a busy ship-building industry in the 19th century. Today it is the base of a fishing fleet, and an expanding sailing centre. There is magnificent touring and walking country in the vicinity. Six miles of the enchanting Aeron Valley and 10 miles of the Teifi Valley lie within Aberaeron's rural district boundary. Parts of the Aeron Valley are richly wooded, and the view from Trichrug Mountain is well worth the ascent to the 1127-ft summit.

Aberystwyth
A town that contains a university and the National Library and has a promenade fronting Cardigan Bay. In 1969 the Prince of Wales was a student at the University College of Wales at Aberystwyth; the university's buildings are spread throughout the town and provide important landmarks. Visitors are permitted to view the lecture rooms and laboratories at certain times by applying for permission to the head porter of each building.

There are pebble and sandy beaches for bathing, and on the seafront are the ruins of a castle, the precincts of which are laid out as public gardens. The College Museum has a rich collection of pottery, glass, china and folk objects, and the National Library of Wales houses some Welsh literary treasures. Among them are the manuscript of the Black Book of Carmarthen (one of the earliest in Welsh, dating from the late 12th century), the White Book of Roderick, and the Book of Taliesin. The library, which took from 1873 to 1955 to establish, contains more than 2 million printed works and $3\frac{1}{2}$ million Welsh historical records.

WELSH CRAFTS

Wood-carving and weaving are two ancient crafts still practised in many parts of Wales. Love-spoons (left), traditionally carved from a single piece of wood, were made by young men as gifts for girls they were courting. The custom still lives on, though today spoons are also made for tourists. Factories for woollen goods have largely taken over from hand-weavers. But even machine-made blankets (right) owe much to tradition. The turned-down blanket shown uses a traditional design and dyes; the other uses the same design in colours adapted for the modern market

SEAFRONT MUSEUM *The original building of the University of Wales, established in 1872, dominates the promenade at Aberystwyth. Within its walls is a museum*

Borth
A village resort consisting mainly of one street of picturesque cottages, set on a pebbly beach looking towards a 3-mile stretch of golden sand. There is another broad stretch of sand northwards at the head of the Dyfi Estuary, with a dramatic background of mountains; but it is not a safe place from which to swim. Borth Bog, which is just inland, contains many rare plants.

Cardigan
A pleasant country town approached by an ancient seven-arched bridge over the River Teifi. Near the bridge are two towers and some walls, all that remains of a castle partly demolished in 1645. A wide variety of plants, animals and birds can be seen in the 200-acre wildlife park just outside the town.

Devil's Bridge
One of the most popular tourist attractions in Wales. The 12th-century Devil's Bridge is the lowest of three bridges built close together over the River Mynach, where it meets the River Rheidol in a series of spectacular waterfalls, the highest of which is 300 ft.

Lampeter
Set at the meeting place of several little valleys on the north bank of the Teifi, which at this point separated the former counties of Cardiganshire and Carmarthenshire, this is an important market centre. A horse fair is held annually in May. St David's College was founded here in 1822 to educate youths for the Anglican church ministry in Wales.

Llandyssul
A pleasant little market town, prettily situated on the River Teifi. The ancient restored church, which has a battlemented tower, seems to stand guard on the river bank. The town makes a good centre for visiting Henllan Bridge, with its picturesque rapids, Newcastle Emlyn and other parts of the Teifi Valley.

New Quay
One of the prettiest of seaports on Cardigan Bay, climbing in terraces from splendid sands and a tiny harbour to a background of wooded hills overlooking this fine bay. New Quay Head rises to 300 ft over the harbour and gives glorious views. There are several interesting caves here, including Ogof Ddauben, 'the two-headed cave', and a rock which is a sanctuary for sea-fowl.

Tregaron
A small market town in the middle of a great stretch of mountain and moorland, and one of the most popular pony-trekking centres in Wales.

About 1 mile north lies Cors Goch Caron, or the Bog of Tregaron. At 4 miles long, it is the largest in England and Wales and it is still extending. The bog is a nature reserve containing many rare plants, such as sundews, bog rosemary, bladderworts and sedges.

DEVIL'S BRIDGE *The first stone bridge over the River Mynach to bear the name of Devil's Bridge was built in the 12th century; a second was later built over it and both are now spanned by a steel bridge. Just beyond, the Mynach plunges down through a deep gorge*

Hills and 'dingles' in Radnor Forest

Angling On the River Ithon near Llandrindod Wells for trout and chub. Coarse fishing in town lake at Llandrindod Wells; on the Wye and tributaries near Presteigne, Builth Wells and Rhayader, and Elan Reservoirs. Trout on the River Irfon at Llangammarch Wells and Llanwrtyd Wells.

Pony trekking There are centres at Builth Wells; Llanwrtyd Wells; Presteigne; and Rhayader.

Events The Royal Welsh Show is held at Llanelwedd Hall grounds, Builth Wells, in mid-July. The Sheep Market is on Mon. at Builth Wells. In May there is a drama festival at Llandrindod Wells. An eisteddfod is held at the Albert Hall, Llandrindod Wells, in Oct.; concerts are held at the town's Church Hall on Suns. from June to Aug. Bowling festivals are held in Llandrindod Wells in June and Aug.

Places to see *Abbey of Cwmhir*, Llandrindod Wells, remains only: daily. *Automobile Palace*, Llandrindod Wells, cycle collection: weekdays. *Monk's House*, Monaughty, a Tudor mansion 4 miles south-west of Knighton: weekdays in summer. *Llandrindod Museum*, Temple Street: Mon. to Fri.; also Sat. mornings, May to Sept. *Welsh Craft Centre*, Llandrindod Wells: daily.

Information centres Town Hall Gardens, Llandrindod Wells. Tel. Llandrindod Wells 2600. Old Swan, West Street, Rhayader. Tel. Rhayader 810591 (seasonal).

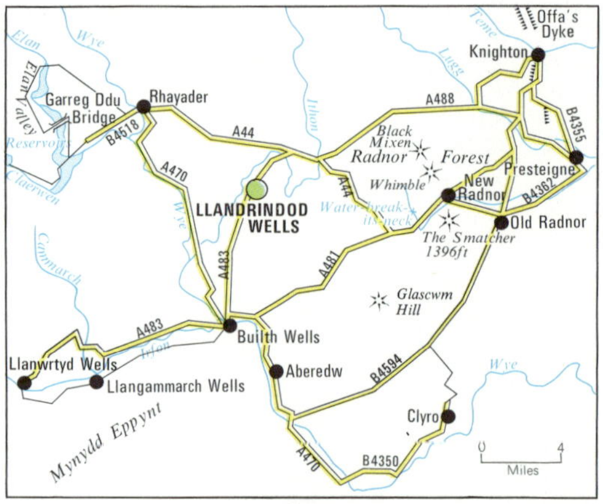

Central Powys (Radnorshire) is sparsely populated with few means of livelihood except hill-farming, forestry and tourism. To the north-west are hills merging into the great moorlands beyond the Elan Valley. East of the moorlands, steep and narrow valleys divide a succession of rounded hills stretching to the English borderlands. The landscape is less dramatic than much of Wales, but it has a quiet beauty of its own, particularly in the valleys of the Rivers Teme and Lugg, and along the Wye.

A distinctive feature of the region is the huge, mysterious, rock 'dome' called Radnor Forest, which can be seen from as far away as Worcestershire. This has never been a great wood in the modern sense; in medieval times 'forest' meant any unenclosed land used only for hunting. Radnor Forest consists of several rolling hills, all about 2000 ft high, and a series of deep valleys, locally called 'dingles', which are the haunts of badgers and other wildlife.

Like the rest of Wales, this countryside is rich in symbols of the past—Bronze Age tumuli, cairns and standing stones, Roman remains, and fragments of border castles sacked by Prince Llewellyn or by Owen Glendower in their efforts to achieve Welsh independence. Central Powys is a region of water, the land of old Welsh spa towns, and of the four great reservoirs, built to serve Birmingham, which have drowned the lovely, if lonely, Elan Valley, where the poet Shelley lived in the early 1800's.

Aberedw
A pretty village near the Wye, here overhung by trees and great dramatic crags. A natural terrace formation runs for a mile above the river. Aberedw has a restored 14th-century church, with a fine porch, and the remains of a castle which once belonged to the Baskerville family. A mile south-east, high among rocks, is Llewellyn's Cave, where Llewellyn ap Gruffydd, the only Prince of Wales born on Welsh soil, hid before being caught and killed in nearby woods in 1282.

Builth Wells
A market town which has an 18th-century bridge with six arches over the River Wye. In Victorian times, the great era of spas, its two springs, one saline, the other sulphur, were said to have great healing effects. The local wells are no longer in use. The town was destroyed by fire in December 1691, and the rebuilt town has little left of its early days. The Royal Welsh Show is held every July in the grounds of nearby Llanelwedd Hall. The town is an excellent centre for exploring a lovely stretch of the Wye Valley. The river flows south-west through a steep-sided valley and turns into cascading rapids at the narrowest point a mile below the village of Aberedw.

Clyro
An attractive village near the Wye where the Rev. Francis Kilvert, the diarist, was curate in the 19th century. His writing vividly portrays life in the area in his day. There are the traces of a Roman camp and a Norman castle. The village has a good modern pottery.

Elan Valley
A beautiful area around a chain of lakes built as reservoirs between 1892 and 1952, and now piping almost 60 million gallons of water a day to Birmingham. Just to the west, in the Claerwen Valley, is a dam 184 ft high, the highest gravity dam in Britain, which holds 10,000 million gallons of water. There is a road up the valley to the Claerwen Reservoir, opened by the Queen in 1952.

Knighton
A small agricultural town in the valley of the River Teme, and a centre for easy hill-walking in the lovely borderlands. The Welsh name for Knighton, Tref-y-Clawdd, 'Town on the Dyke', refers to the earth bank and ditch built *c.* AD 784 by Offa, King of Mercia, to defend his lands against the Welsh. The dyke is 30 ft high near Knighton. A long-distance footpath partly following the line of the dyke was opened in 1971.

SHEEP CENTRE *Rhayader is a town near moorland grazing and has sheep fairs and butchers' shops specialising in mutton*

OLD SHEEP TRAIL *A shepherd takes the old drove road over Glascwm Hill along which sheep were once driven to England*

A TOUCH OF ENGLAND *Half-timbered Tudor houses in Presteigne are built in a style characteristic of nearby Herefordshire*

WATER FOR BIRMINGHAM *The Penygarreg Dam, one of a series begun in 1892 and completed only in 1952, holds back the water of the River Elan for piping to the Midlands*

Llandrindod Wells
Once the largest and most popular of the Welsh spas. Its waters first became famous in the reign of Charles II, and at the height of its popularity in late Victorian times it used to draw 80,000 visitors a year The town, on a 700 ft high plateau overlooking the River Ithon, has wide streets and good 19th-century architecture.

Today, it is the county's administrative centre and an inland resort with facilities for bowls, golf, angling and boating. It is a favourite touring and conference centre all the year round.

Just over a mile north of the town are the well-preserved ruins of a Roman fort known as Castell Collen.

Llangammarch Wells
The River Cammarch merges with the Irfon at this small spa, making it an excellent place for salmon and trout fishing. In the grounds of the Lake Hotel is a spring which contains barium chloride, which was widely advertised at one time as a cure for diseases of the heart. The spring is no longer accessible to the public.

Llanwrtyd Wells
Nobody 'takes the waters' here any more, but this small spa remains an attractive, well-sited village, with splendid views of the desolate hills of Mynydd Eppynt, over which drovers once herded their Welsh Black cattle to English markets. It is a pony-trekking centre, and offers good angling in the Irfon. Rare kites soar over the wild hills to the west.

New Radnor
In spite of its name New Radnor is seven centuries old and has the ruins of a castle 200 years older. It is beautifully placed at the foot of Radnor Forest, with a 1396 ft high hill, The Smatcher, rising opposite. On the south side of the forest is a waterfall with the quaint name of 'Water-break-its-neck'.

Old Radnor lies 2½ miles east, on a hill-spur 840 ft high. The church, one of the finest in Wales, claims that its organ case (*c.* 1500) is the oldest in Britain. The font is formed from what is believed to have been a Bronze Age altar stone.

Presteigne
An ancient little town situated on the south bank of the River Lugg, which here divides Wales from England. It has several black-and-white timbered cottages and Georgian houses, and no fewer than 30 of its present buildings were once inns. The partly timbered Radnorshire Arms has a priest's chamber, or hiding place, dating from Tudor times, and secret passages.

With hills rising gently to 1000 ft before sweeping away to Radnor Forest, the town is a good starting point for hillside rambles and pony trekking.

Rhayader
Several roads converge on this quiet market town on the upper Wye, which has become an angling, pony trekking and touring centre. The shops offer local products: Welsh dressers, pottery and other crafts. It is also the nearest town to the Elan Valley Reservoirs, 3½ miles west.

DROWNED VALLEY *Submerged beneath rippling waters are the few stones that remain of Shelley's house, one of many covered by the waters of the Elan Valley Reservoirs*

The mountains of Berwyn

Angling There is coarse fishing in the Severn at Welshpool, and trout fishing on Lake Vyrnwy.

Pony trekking At Newtown and Cefn Coch, near Llanfair Caereinion.

Events Welshpool holds a large fatstock market every Monday, including Bank Holidays.

Places to see *Montgomery Castle*: daily. *Powis Castle* (NT): Easter to early Sept., afternoons except Mon. and Tues.; also Bank Hol. *Powysland Museum*, Welshpool: weekdays, except Wed. in winter. *Robert Owen Memorial Museum*, Newtown: afternoons. *Welshpool and Llanfair Light Railway*: Easter to mid-Oct., weekend afternoons; also daily mid-June to Sept.

Information centres Vicarage Garden Car Park, Welshpool. Tel. Welshpool 2043. Great Oak Street, Llanidloes. Tel. Llanidloes 2605 (seasonal).

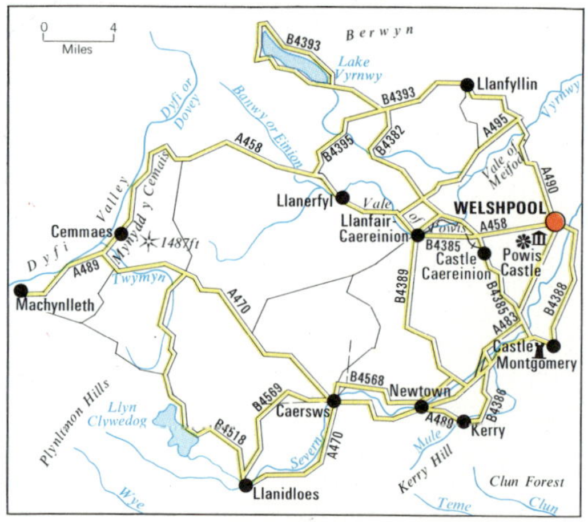

North Powys (Montgomeryshire) lies south of the Berwyn Mountains; although less well known than the neighbouring counties, it has its own grand vistas of mountains and deserted moorlands. From the Berwyn Mountains in the north-west, the land rolls southwards in a succession of uplands and river valleys. In some places the landscape seems totally uninhabited, particularly in the barren area that stretches from Machynlleth to Llanidloes.

It is only along the English border to the east and in the mild and lovely Severn Valley that there are clusters of towns and villages. Large tracts of land are wild and lonely, although re-afforestation is bringing lushness and variety to the scenery. The Wye and Severn rise among the Plynlimon Hills in the south-west to begin their journeys to the Severn Estuary.

There are many half-timbered houses, and churches rich with fine wood-carvings, and the countryside around them has an abundance of wildlife: foxes, otters, polecats, badgers, pine martens, buzzards and rare red kites. North Powys is as rich in historical associations as any other part of Wales. The great Owen Glendower, fighter for Welsh independence, made Machynlleth his capital and called his first parliament there in 1404, when he was proclaimed king. From Newtown came Robert Owen, a fighter of a different kind—campaigner for the reform of working conditions in factories in the early 19th century. He was born in the town in 1771 and buried in the churchyard in 1858. Surviving associations with Owen include a 19th-century weaving factory and the Robert Owen Memorial Museum.

POWIS CASTLE *This red limestone castle near Welshpool dates from the late 13th and early 14th centuries. The formal gardens have the same form they had when laid out more than 250 years ago, with long terraces sloping down to a parkland that is renowned for its trees, including a 181 ft high Douglas fir, the tallest tree in Britain*

Caersws
A former Roman military station that is now the centre of the agricultural area of the Upper Severn Valley. Maes-Mawr is a fine old half-timbered house. There are good walks across the surrounding hills and moors.

Cemmaes
The River Dyfi is good for salmon fishing in the vicinity of this undisturbed village. There are fine walks, particularly along a path starting at the local inn and leading to the highest point of the plateau Mynydd y Cemais (1487 ft). There are enchanting views eastwards to the River Twymyn, as it forces its way through a narrow gorge, and of the Dyfi Valley to the west. The varied birdlife includes herons, buzzards and curlews.

Kerry
A village near the English border, which is a good centre for not-too-difficult walks. There are fine views from the wild and lonely Kerry Hill, 2½ miles south, and from near the Anchor Inn on the Clun road, 3 miles south-east. The hills are criss-crossed with rivers, including the Teme, the Clun and the Mule, and grazed by fat Kerry sheep.

Llanfair Caereinion
A largely 18th-century town, once the site of a Roman fort on the River Einion, or Banwy. It is an ideal centre for exploring the great lonely regions of north Powys. The town is also the starting point of the Welshpool and Llanfair Light Railway, which runs for 5½ miles to Sylfaen and back and is being gradually extended towards its original terminus at Welshpool. In the churchyard at nearby Llanerfyl, a Latin inscription on a gravestone suggests that this was the site of a Romano-British Christian burial ground.

Llanfyllin
This town was once famous for its inns; 'Old ale fills Llanfyllin with young widows', ran the saying. Now only two inns survive but it is still a pleasant town noted for its blend of Georgian and Regency architecture.

Lake Vyrnwy, 9 miles west, is easily accessible by road through beautiful hilly country, or by a fairly stiff walk across the hills. The lake, a reservoir which supplies Liverpool with water, is well known for its fishing and there is a 12-mile road round its shores.

Llanidloes
A relaxed little town clustered round the fine half-timbered market house, built in 1609. It is a good centre for climbers or walkers touring the Plynlimon heights, which rise at the back of the town, or making for the sources of the Wye and Severn. The road north-west to Machynlleth winds over the spectacular scenery of the Plynlimon moors and past Llyn Clywedog, a 6 mile long reservoir completed in 1967.

MARKET ARCHES *Llanidloes Market House, the arches of which were built to shelter stallholders, overlooks the half-timbered houses across the market-place*

Machynlleth
One of the most agreeable of all Welsh towns, particularly for its enchanting position in the Dyfi Valley, one of the great natural features of mid-Wales. It has been an inhabited site since the early Iron Age. Owen Glendower made it the capital of Wales, and he was proclaimed king here at a parliament in 1404. The present Owen Glendower Institute is traditionally his Parliament House. Because of Machynlleth's position at the junction of several old coach roads, and as a great sheep-trading centre, the town had 24 inns in the 19th century. Four inns, the haunt of anglers fishing the Dyfi, still cluster round the clock tower which marks the centre of the town. There are 17th, 18th and 19th-century houses in the street called Maen Gwyn; and near the clock tower is Royal House, where the future Henry VII is said to have stopped in 1485.

Montgomery
Nominally the county town (though the administrative offices are in Newtown and Welshpool), but in reality little more than a village of some 1000 inhabitants. It has some fine half-timbered and Georgian buildings. The ruins of a 13th-century castle overlook the town from a steep hill. This was the home of the Herbert family, of whom the best known is George Herbert, the 17th-century clergyman-poet.

Newtown
The second largest town in north Powys, and an important agricultural and sheep-raising centre. It is cradled among hills alongside the River Severn, with fine views and access to some excellent countryside.

RARE ROCK FLOWER The rock cinquefoil *Potentilla rupestris* is found only rarely, growing on rocky ground in north and central Powys. It looks like a large strawberry plant, with stems 1–2 ft tall and white, rose-like flowers up to 1 in. across

Welshpool
A bustling market town with a great deal of Georgian architecture. The glory of the town is Powis Castle.

The Powysland Museum has many interesting relics of the region, the most notable of which is an Iron Age shield.

MAN-MADE LAKE *Lake Vyrnwy was made in 1881 when the valley of the River Vyrnwy was flooded to make a reservoir. It is 5 miles long and nearly a mile wide, one of the largest man-made lakes in Wales. The dam at its lower end carries a road across the valley*

The Vale of Llangollen

Angling There is coarse fishing in lakes and streams of the Denbigh hills, also around Llangollen on the Shropshire Union Canal. There are salmon, grayling and trout on the River Clwyd in the Ruthin area, and on the Dee and Ceiriog.

Boating Trips from Llangollen by horse-drawn boats, and longer trips to the Horseshoe Falls and Chain Bridge.

Pony trekking Centres near Llangollen, Ruthin and Glyn Ceiriog.

Events The International Musical Eisteddfod is held at Llangollen in early July. Each Wed., from Spring Bank Hol. to Sept., is 'Medieval Day' in Ruthin: townspeople and shopkeepers dress up, and there are displays of spinning, dancing, etc.

Places to see *Chirk Castle*: Easter to Oct., Wed., Thur. and weekend afternoons; also Wed. and Thur. mornings, June to Sept. *Denbigh Castle*: daily, except Sun. morning Oct. to Mar. *Erddig* (NT), 1 mile south of Wrexham: Apr. to Oct., afternoons except Mon. *Geological Museum of North Wales*, Bwlchgwyn: weekdays; also Sun. in summer. *Llangollen Canal Museum*: daily, Easter to Sept. *Plas Newydd Museum*, Llangollen: May to Sept., daily. *Valle Crucis Abbey*: daily, except Sun. morning Oct. to Mar.

Information centre Town Hall, Llangollen. Tel. Llangollen 860828.

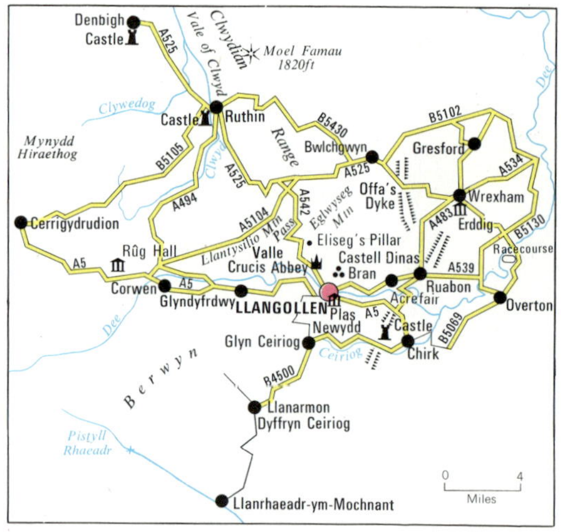

Some of the most spectacular scenery in Wales lies along the Vale of Llangollen, threaded by the River Dee. Northwards, the Horseshoe Pass thrusts between Llantysilio Mountain and Eglwyseg Mountain towards the level country south of Ruthin. No fewer than five of the traditional 'Seven Wonders of Wales' are in the county of Clwyd (formerly Denbighshire and Flintshire). The full list, as named in a traditional Welsh folk rhyme , is

'Pistyll Rhaeadr and Wrexham steeple
Snowdon's mountain without its people,
Overton yew trees, St Winifred's Wells,
Llangollen bridge and Gresford bells.'

Mountain ranges, with peaks over 2000 ft high, overlook lush fields in the valleys of the Rivers Clwyd and Dee. Chirk Castle is famed for the exquisite 18th-century wrought-iron gates by the brothers Robert and John Davies. The waterfall of Pistyll Rhaeadr vies for attention with the Pont-Cysyllte Aqueduct carrying the Shropshire Union Canal across the Dee.

Canoeists can brave the foaming Dee at Llangollen, and anglers can fish for salmon, grayling and trout. The Clwyd, too, is excellent for fishing. There are mountains and moorlands for climbing and walking, attractive winding lanes round Glyn Ceiriog, 5 miles south of Llangollen, and an industrial estate at Wrexham, the main centre of population.

HORSESHOE FALLS *Telford built the falls on the River Dee above*

OVER THE DEE *The Pont-Cysyllte Aqueduct at Acrefair, built by Telford between 1795 and 1805, is seen through an arch of the Bont Bridge, which dates from Roman times*

Chirk
A village surrounded by mountain, river and woodland scenery at the eastern end of the Vale of Ceiriog. Chirk Castle, 2 miles west, is set in a park rising from the river valley. The castle has been occupied since 1310, when it was built by Roger Mortimer, and since 1595 it has been the home of the Myddleton family. The massive rectangular castle has round 'drum' towers at each corner and a fifth tower over the gateway; the battlements are wide enough to allow two people to walk abreast along them.

In 1718, Sir Robert Myddleton commissioned two Welsh brothers, Robert and John Davies, to make wrought-iron gates for Chirk Castle. Their handiwork, completed in 1733, is a design of striking complexity and delicacy. The castle contains many 16th-century decorative features and some fine Stuart portraits including those of Charles I and Charles II. In the park are traces of Offa's Dyke, the rampart built by Offa, King of Mercia in the 8th century.

Corwen
A market town on a stretch of the Dee renowned for its trout, salmon and grayling. There are fine walks in the Berwyn Mountains. The area has many associations with Owen Glendower, the 15th-century hero who led the Welsh in rebellion against Henry IV and, in 1404, summoned his own parliament, before the revolt failed. He took his name—Glyndwr in Welsh—from one of his estates at what is now Glyndyfrdwy, 4 miles east of Corwen.

Denbigh
An ancient market town overlooking the Vale of Clwyd, and a good touring and fishing centre. The impressive castle, built by the Earl of Lincoln in 1282, stands on a hilltop 467 ft high. Eight

Llangollen in 1795 to dam water for his aqueduct carrying the Shropshire Union Canal

IN THE HILLS *A windswept field of barley emphasises the isolation and remoteness of the mountains rising to the south-west of Llangollen*

of its great towers and the gatehouse still stand. There are remains of the old town wall, with a gatehouse. Leicester's Folly is the name given to the ruined wall of a church intended to replace St Asaph's as the diocesan cathedral after the Reformation. The church was never finished.

Below the castle walls once stood the cottage where H. M. Stanley, explorer of Africa and the man who found Dr Livingstone, was born in 1841, and there is a model of the cottage in a museum in the castle. The town hall dates from the 16th century. It was enlarged in 1780. The Bull Inn has a splendidly carved staircase and some 17th-century outbuildings.

Llanarmon Dyffryn Ceiriog
A tongue-twisting name, meaning 'Church of St Armon in the Vale of the River Ceiriog', for an enchanting little village in the depths of the Berwyn Mountains. It is a good centre for exploring the 15 miles of the lovely vale, and for fishing in the river. On the high hills enclosing the vale are numerous burial sites and ancient encampments.

Llangollen
The town, named after the Celtic St Collen, lies at the head of the beautiful green Vale of Llangollen, famous as the scene of the International Musical Eisteddfod, the contest for folk dancers and singers held every summer since 1947. The town's 14th-century stone bridge over the Dee, built by a Bishop of St Asaph, is one of the traditional 'Seven Wonders of Wales'. Though Llangollen was once a centre for slate quarrying and now has some light industry, the countryside in the 7 mile long vale is largely unspoilt by industrial development.

Plas Newydd, an 18th-century black-and-white house, was for 50 years the home of the famous 'Ladies of Llangollen'. In 1778 two independent-minded Irish aristocrats, Lady Eleanor Butler and Miss Sarah Ponsonby, came to live in Llangollen with their maid, Mary Carryl. Their mannish clothes attracted a good deal of attention, but their reputation for wit and hospitality was widespread. Among their numerous distinguished guests were William Wordsworth and the Duke of Wellington. The interior of the house is decorated with carved oak and contains a large collection of wood-carvings.

A mile to the north-east across the Dee, a footpath climbs 100 ft to the remains of Castell Dinas Bran, an 8th-century castle. Behind it the massive limestone cliffs of Eglwyseg Mountain run northwards for 3 miles.

The remains of Valle Crucis Abbey, a Cistercian abbey founded in 1202, stand $1\frac{1}{2}$ miles north-west of Llangollen. Eliseg's Pillar, just to the north of the abbey, commemorates a battle fought in AD 603 by Eliseg, a Celtic Prince of Powis, against the invading Saxons. The pillar was broken during the Civil War and replaced in 1779. Past the pillar and the abbey ruins the road climbs to the famous 1300-ft Horseshoe Pass from which there are fine views, especially towards Eglwyseg Mountain 2 miles to the east.

At Acrefair, $3\frac{1}{2}$ miles east of Llangollen, is the Pont-Cysyllte Aqueduct, built by Telford between 1795 and 1805 to carry the Shropshire Union Canal 120 ft above the Dee Valley on its way to Llangollen. The aqueduct is 1007 ft long and has 19 arches.

Llanrhaeadr-ym-Mochnant
A village on the eastern slopes of the Berwyn Mountains, from which a minor road leads $3\frac{1}{2}$ miles north-west to the 240 ft high waterfall of Pistyll Rhaeadr, the highest in Wales and one of the traditional 'Seven Wonders'.

COLOURFUL COSTUMES *People from all over the world wear their national dress at Llangollen's International Eisteddfod, a summer folk festival*

Overton
In the churchyard of this peaceful town is the splendid group of yew trees, another of the 'Seven Wonders of Wales' commemorated in verse.

Ruthin
An old market town in the fertile Clwyd Valley, ringed by wooded hills, many of them over 1000 ft high. It was once a fortified town, garrisoned for the Lancastrians in the Wars of the Roses and for the Royalists in the Civil War. The curfew has been rung nightly at 8 o'clock since the 11th century. The 18th-century Castle Hotel incorporates an adjacent 14th-century timber-framed building. In the market-place is the Maen Huail, a stone where by tradition King Arthur had Huail, brother of Gildas the historian, beheaded as a rival in love. Two banks are housed in other half-timbered buildings: Exmewe Hall, built in 1500 by a former Lord Mayor of London, and the 15th-century courthouse, which still has part of a gallows used to hang a Jesuit priest in Elizabeth I's reign. The parish church has magnificent wrought-iron gates made by the brothers Robert and John Davies in 1727.

Ruthin Castle was built in the 19th century on the site of an original medieval castle. It is now a hotel, where nightly banquets based on Tudor recipes are served to the accompaniment of the music of the Welsh harp and a choir.

Wrexham
The industrial centre of North Wales, with collieries, steelworks and chemical, brick and tile factories. It is also an important market town. St Giles's Church, finished in 1472, has a soaring 135-ft pinnacled steeple—one of the traditional 'Seven Wonders of Wales'—and lovely wrought-iron gates built by the Davies brothers. In the churchyard is the tomb of Elihu Yale, one of the Pilgrim Fathers, after whom Yale University in the United States is named.

Gresford, 3 miles north, has a fine church whose peal of 12 bells is another of the traditional 'Seven Wonders'.

Castles and beaches of the North Wales coast

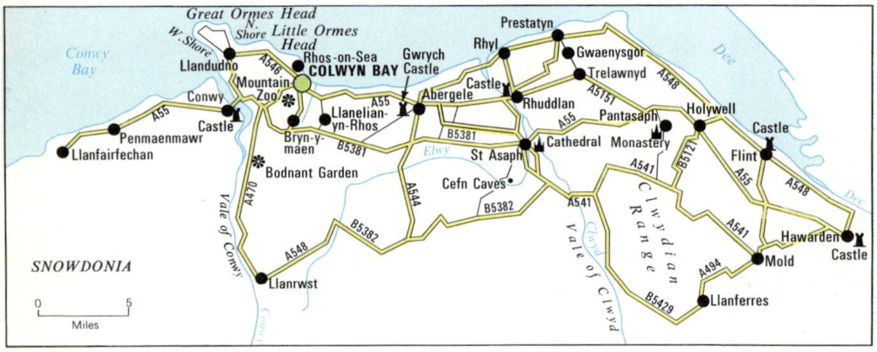

Boating There are clubs at Colwyn Bay, Conwy, Llandudno, Prestatyn and Rhyl. Boat services run from Llandudno to Liverpool and the Isle of Man.

Angling Sea fishing from the pier and boats at Llandudno; shore and boat fishing at Rhyl and Colwyn Bay. Freshwater fishing on Rivers Clwyd and Elwy, and lakes and streams in the Clwydian Range.

Events There are sheep-dog trials in mid-Aug. at Llanarmon-yn-Ial, 3 miles south of Llanferres. The North Wales Art Societies Exhibition is held at the Civic Centre, Mold, at the beginning of June. The Harlequin Puppet Theatre, Rhos-on-Sea, stages shows from the end of June to mid-Sept. Trelawnyd Male Voice Choir rehearses on Sun. and Tues. at the Memorial Hall, Trelawnyd, near Prestatyn; visitors are welcome.

Places to see *Aberconwy House* (NT), Conwy: Apr. to Oct., daily except Wed. in Apr., May and Oct. *Bodnant Garden* (NT): late Mar. to Oct., daily. *Conwy Castle*: daily, except Sun. morning Oct. to Apr. *Doll Museum*, Llandudno: Easter to Sept., weekdays, Sun. afternoon. *Flint Castle*: weekdays, Sun. afternoon. *Great Orme Cable Railway*, Llandudno to Great Ormes Head: daily, Easter to Sept. *Plas Mawr*, Conwy: daily. *Rapallo House Museum and Art Gallery*, Llandudno: Apr. to Nov., Mon. to Fri. *Rhuddlan Castle*: daily, except Sun. morning Oct. to Mar. *Royal Floral Hall*, Rhyl: Easter and daily, Whitsun to late Sept. *St Asaph Cathedral and Museum*: daily. *St Winifred's Well*, Holywell: daily. *Welsh Mountain Zoo*, Upper Colwyn Bay: daily.

Information centres Publicity Department, Town Hall, Rhyl. Tel. Rhyl 31515. Chapel Street, Llandudno. Tel. Llandudno 76413.

For more than 18 miles the North Wales coast runs in long, sandy stretches, broken only by the occasional headland. Along this holiday coastline are a variety of developed resorts, from Llanfairfechan and Penmaenmawr in the west, through Conwy, Llandudno, Rhos-on-Sea, Colwyn Bay and Rhyl to Prestatyn in the east. In addition to the organised resorts, there are many small bays and stretches of sandy beach, all easily reached from the main road which skirts the coast.

Inland, by contrast, runs the lovely valley of the Clwyd, described by Gladstone as 'The Eden of Wales', where the craggy Snowdonia landscape gives way to softer-contoured hills, green uplands, moorlands and woodland. This is good country for lazy exploration, for some of the most picturesque villages in Wales nestle in the folds of these hills. Further west, the River Conwy flows past Llanrwst and seawards to the estuary guarded by Conwy Castle.

To the east, along the Dee Estuary, lie the borders of County Clwyd, until recently Flintshire, with attractive towns such as Holywell, Hawarden and Mold. Here, as well as the unchanging natural beauty of the waterfalls, there are many reminders of the past: prehistoric caves used by Neanderthal man, towns visited by medieval pilgrims, and castles built to subdue the Celts. There are many inns too, where in the evenings the traveller can hear Welsh songs.

Colwyn Bay

A safe, sandy 3-mile stretch of bay with all the usual seaside amusements for children and adults. On a wooded hillside just above the town is the Welsh Mountain Zoo, where there are daily displays by free-flying birds of prey.

A 2-mile walk up the Nant-y-Glyn Valley leads to Christ Church, known as 'The Cathedral on the Hill', at Bryn-y-maen. The church tower offers a panoramic view of the district. At Llanelian-yn-Rhos is another fine church with a rare rood loft.

Conwy

A town unforgettable for its massive castle above the River Conwy and the medieval walls which still surround it. The entire defensive complex is in a good state of preservation. It is still possible to walk along the castle's 15 ft thick walls, which were built in the shape of a Welsh harp and are half a mile in length, with eight great drum-towers and 21 semicircular towers at regular intervals. The castle was begun in the 13th century for Edward I and, like Caernarfon, was involved in the turbulent history of the Middle Ages and the Civil War. The delicate ironwork of Telford's suspension bridge over the Conwy makes an effective contrast with the solidity of the castle. Robert Stephenson's tubular bridge, on one side, was built in 1848, and the road bridge, on the other, was finished in 1958.

Bodnant Garden, $3\frac{1}{2}$ miles south-east, is one of the most beautiful gardens in Britain. Its 7 acres slope down to the River Conwy, with the peaks of Snowdonia as a backcloth.

Flint

The town which gave its name to the former county was superseded by Mold as county town of Clwyd. Flint Castle, now in ruins, was the first of a chain of medieval castles which included Conwy, Denbigh, Rhuddlan, Caernarfon, Beaumaris and Criccieth. In Flint Castle Richard II surrendered to Henry Bolingbroke in 1399.

Hawarden

William Ewart Gladstone, four times Prime Minister of England, came to the castle in 1839 to marry a Welsh heiress, Catherine Glynne. The castle, built in 1752 on the original medieval site, was his home until his death in 1898.

One of Gladstone's favourite recreations was chopping down trees in Hawarden Park. Chairs carved from

CALM WATERS *At Penmaenmawr, Welsh for 'large stone head', the swell of Conwy Bay is flanked by high cliffs through which tunnels carry the road and railway*

BESIDE THE BEACH *A 2-mile terraced promenade lines Llandudno sea-front*

BRIDGE OVER THE CONWY *The suspension bridge built by Thomas Telford in 1826 is still used by pedestrians. The battlements of its supporting towers match the medieval turrets of Conwy Castle, one of the fortresses built throughout Wales more than 500 years earlier by Edward I to defend his newly won territory*

these trees are believed still to exist. When Gladstone received the note from Queen Victoria in 1868 summoning him to Windsor to become Prime Minister for the first time, he read it, then continued his tree-felling before going to Windsor. Gladstone left his entire library to St Deiniol's Library in Hawarden, which was opened in 1908.

Holywell
The town is known as the 'Lourdes of Wales' and St Winifred's Well has long been the goal of many pilgrimages. St Winifred was a 7th-century girl beheaded by Prince Caradoc for resisting his advances. A spring gushed where her head fell. The well water is still supposed to retain medicinal properties. At Pantasaph, 2½ miles west of Holywell, there is a model of the Grotto of Lourdes in a disused quarry behind the Franciscan monastery.

Llandudno
The largest of all Welsh holiday resorts, but one which in spite of its size has managed to retain considerable character. The principal beach, North Shore, consists mainly of a magnificent crescent bay, with good bathing and firm sand. It is enclosed by two headlands, Great Ormes Head and Little Ormes Head. There are four ways to the top of 679-ft high Great Ormes Head—by road, cable car, funicular tramway, or on foot through the delightful Happy Valley. A 5-mile Marine Drive is cut into the side of the cliff.

Little Ormes Head is only 464 ft high, but its cliffs are craggier than the other head. West Shore offers fine views of Conwy Bay and Snowdonia. The Lewis Carroll memorial on the West Shore marks the fact that the author of *Alice in Wonderland* stayed in the town with the Liddells, parents of Alice, the girl for whom Carroll wrote his famous story.

HILLSIDE GARDEN *A footpath to the top of the Great Ormes Head at Llandudno passes through the Happy Valley, notable for its rare flowers and trees*

Mold
The county town of Clwyd, and the centre of the North Wales coalfield, is a busy market town. Interesting features are the High Street's picturesque buildings, the 15th-century church containing a remarkable fresco of animals and the new County Civic Centre buildings in the parkland setting of Llwynegrin, 1 mile north of the town. Llanferres, 4 miles south-west, is on the foothills of the Clwydian Range and a good viewpoint for the surrounding country.

Prestatyn
A popular holiday resort with plenty of entertainment and sport and 4 miles of fine beaches. The hills behind the town on the way to Gwaenysgor and Trelawnyd are good walking country. There is a Norman font in the church at Gwaenysgor. Prestatyn was the northern end of Offa's Dyke, an earthwork which extended from the River Dee in North Wales to the River Severn near Chepstow; it marked the boundary between England and Wales and was built by Offa, King of Mercia in the 8th century.

Rhyl
This seaside resort has two of the largest funfairs in North Wales, as well as the usual holiday entertainments, including cycling and roller-skating tracks.

At Rhuddlan Castle, begun in 1277, Edward I is said to have proclaimed his infant son Prince of Wales.

St Asaph
A village-city with one of the smallest cathedrals in Britain, founded in AD 573. The building is partly Norman, but most of it is 15th century. It was considerably restored *c.* 1870 by Sir George Gilbert Scott. At Cefn Caves, 2 miles south-west, relics of prehistoric man and the bones of bears, bison and reindeer have been found. Some experts consider that they could be 50,000 years old.

Grandeur of Snowdonia

Climbing The chief centres are rock faces at Llanberis Pass and Nant Ffrancon Pass. Plas y Brenin, the National Mountaineering Centre, is at Capel Curig.

Angling Rivers Seiont and Conwy have salmon and brown trout. Bethesda, Beddgelert, Ogwen, Padarn and Peris lakes have trout.

Boating Sailing clubs at Conwy, Caernarfon, Deganwy, Llanfairfechan, Penmaenmawr and Port Dinorwic.

Walking Beddgelert Forest Trail starts just north-west of Beddgelert, Gwydyr Forest Trail starts 3 miles west of Betws-y-coed.

Places to see *Bangor Art Gallery* and *Museum of Welsh Antiquities*: weekdays. *Bible Garden*, Bangor: daily. *Bryn Bras Castle*, near Llanrug: Apr. to Sept., afternoons; also mornings, mid-July to Aug. *Caernarfon Castle*: daily, except Sun. mornings Oct. to Mar. *Dolbadarn Castle*, Llanberis: daily, except Sun. mornings Oct. to May. *Encounter Wildlife Museum*, Llanrwst: daily, Mar. to Dec. *Hafodty Gardens*, Betws Garmon: daily. *Llanberis Lake Railway*: Easter to Sept., daily. *North Wales Quarrying Museum*, Llanberis: Easter to Sept., daily. *Penrhyn Castle* (NT), Bangor: Apr., May and Oct., afternoons; June to Sept., daily. *Segontium* (NT): weekdays and Sun. afternoon. *Ty Mawr* (NT), Dolwyddelan, 3½ miles south-west of Betws-y-Coed: Easter to Oct., daily except Sat.

Information centres (seasonal) Slate Quay, Caernarfon. Tel. Caernarfon 2232. Community Centre, Llanberis. Tel. Llanberis 765.

The Welsh call Snowdonia the 'Eagles' Nesting Place', and even though eagles no longer fly here the grandeur of the name is still appropriate for a region that is scenically one of the glories of Britain. The Snowdonia National Park is a region of wild mountains, notched in places like a battlemented tower, with high passes and craggy peaks. Sheer precipices plummet into valleys which sparkle with wood-fringed lakes and cascading waterfalls.

At the centre of the range is Snowdon—3560 ft above sea level and the highest mountain south of the Scottish border. Its attendant peaks are all about 3000 ft high, and near by are other peaks of the Glyder and Carnedd ranges.

This is ideal country for the climber—the first men to conquer Everest trained in Snowdonia—and for the walker, the angler and the motorist. Among the splendid sights are the passes of Nant Ffrancon, Nantgwynant and Llanberis, where rock climbers can often be seen at dizzy heights. These rugged mountains and wild passes ring with the ancient history of Wales and Britain; there are relics and legends of the Bronze Age and Iron Age, of the Celts, the Romans, the Normans, the two Llewellyns—Llewellyn the Great and Llewellyn ap Gruffydd—and Owen Glendower.

MOUNTAIN RIDE *A rack-and-pinion railway, opened in 1896, runs up Snowdon from Llanberis. The 5-mile track has gradients of up to 1 in 5 and, on its way to the summit, the train runs along the edge of the precipice Clogwyn du'r Arddu*

Bangor

The cathedral and university city of North Wales is said to derive its name from the protective fence or 'bangor' of a monastic settlement there in the 6th century. The present cathedral, on the site of the early church, was built in the 19th century to a design by Sir George Gilbert Scott, architect of the Albert Memorial in London.

Penrhyn Castle, a mile to the east, was built between 1827 and 1840 with a marble exterior in neo-Gothic style. Its boundary wall is 7 miles long. The castle now belongs to the National Trust and contains stuffed birds and animals, early locomotives, a collection of more than 1000 dolls, and a slate bedstead weighing 4 tons. In the castle grounds is the Llanfair-ym-Muallt Pottery, which has items for sale.

Beddgelert

Three valleys meet in this little village, which is near the Beddgelert Forest and surrounded by the splendours of Snowdonia. According to legend the village was named after Llewellyn the Great's dog, Gelert, killed by the prince in a fit of temper; but modern research has revealed that an 18th-century innkeeper, David Prichard, invented the story and passed it on to a contemporary ballad writer. If the motive was to attract trade, Prichard's idea has been successful, for the 'Grave of Gelert' draws thousands to visit it. A forest trail starts at Beddgelert, and there are many other walks in the surrounding woods and mountains. On the route up to Aberglaslyn Pass there is a magnificent view of the Glaslyn, a mountain torrent. There is a car park near the bridge.

Bethesda

Although it is a byword for slate, the town has more to commend it than its 1000 ft deep quarries. It is situated in one of the most spectacular parts of Snowdonia and is a starting point for the ascent to the Nant Ffrancon Pass, a high road with views of awesome splendour. The tortuous route runs between the bare flanks of Carnedd Dafydd (3427 ft) and the peaks of the Glyders.

At the head of the pass is Llyn Ogwen, from which a path leads south to Llyn Idwal, rich in wildlife, and to the so-called Devil's Kitchen, a huge rock-walled chasm north of Glyder Fawr. All around are rock climbs of varying degrees of difficulty, among which 3010-ft Tryfan, just south of Llyn Ogwen and the A5, is renowned.

Betws Garmon

A village notable for Hafodty, a rock and water garden, near the Nant Mills waterfalls, where in season masses of azaleas and hydrangeas bloom. This is a good centre for walking the Snowdonia foothills, which include Moel Eilio and Mynydd Mawr, both over 2000 ft.

Betws-y-coed

This village, nestling in the densely wooded hills of the Gwydyr Forest, was

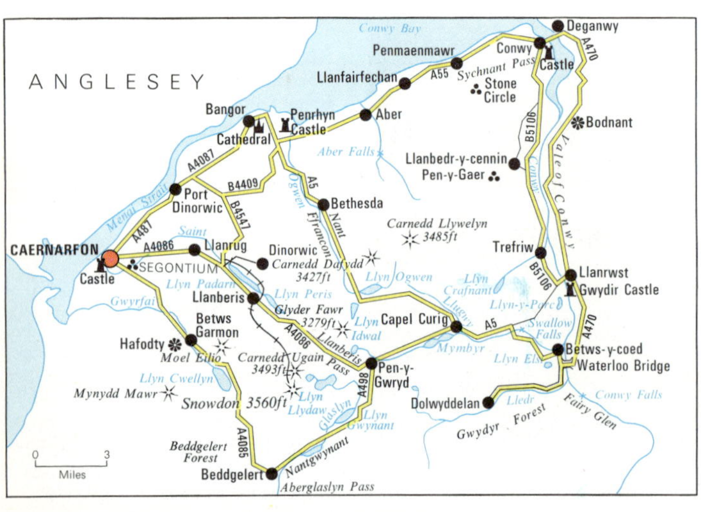

popularised by the painter David Cox in the early 19th century. The name means Chapel, or Sanctuary, in the Wood. It stands at the junction of the Conwy, Llugwy and Lledr Rivers and their valleys. In this ideal walking country the Swallow Falls, 2½ miles west, and the Fairy Glen and the Conwy Falls, 2 miles south, are magical.

Caernarfon
An ancinet town, overlooking the Menai Strait, and the ceremonial capital of Wales. The magnificently preserved castle dominates the town. In it was born the son of Edward I, who became the first English Prince of Wales in 1284; and in 1911 the Duke of Windsor (then Prince Edward) and in 1969 Prince Charles were invested there as Princes of Wales. Many episodes in the long history of revolt against English rule took place in the castle, and in the Civil War it was one of Cromwell's strongholds.

At Segontium, half a mile east, is the site of a Roman military settlement, finds from which are on display in a museum on the site. Rome also left its mark on Caernarfon in the parish church at Llanbeblig, where some say the grave of Constantine the Great's father was unearthed during rebuilding.

Capel Curig
A mountain village in the shadow of the Snowdon range, and an excellent climbing and fishing centre. It sits between two mountains both nearly 3000 ft high. There is a mountaineering centre, Plas y Brenin, run by the Central Council of Physical Recreation, near the village. A National Nature Reserve at Cwm Glas Crafnant, 2 miles north of Capel Curig, has numerous Arctic and Alpine plants and flowers. The lake of Mymbyr near by is good for trout fishing, and the mountain inn at Pen-y-Gwryd was used by Sir John Hunt's team while practising for their 1953 ascent of Everest.

Llanberis
The village is the starting point for the railway ascent, and the easiest walk, to the summit of Snowdon. A narrow-gauge railway along the eastern shore of Llyn Padarn, opened in 1971, gives fine views of Snowdonia. The road south-eastwards up Llanberis Pass runs dramatically between Snowdon and the huge rock slabs of the Glyders.

Llanfairfechan
A modern resort with fine beaches and the usual seaside amusements. Snowdonia rises behind the town, and the Afon Ddu tumbles down the hills through the town to the sea. There are many good walks; one of the most rewarding is to Aber Falls, 4½ miles south, where the 150-ft falls, broken by jutting rocks, make sparkling cascades.

Llanrwst
An old market town in the Conwy Valley, where the river is crossed by a handsome stone bridge with three arches, attributed to Inigo Jones. Trefriw, 3 miles north-west, is a tiny spa with rich sulphur and iron waters.

Penmaenmawr
A modest seaside resort, with a 3-mile stretch of sand, between the two headlands of Penmaen-bach and Penmaenmawr at the base of the Snowdonia foothills. Walkers on the moorland behind the town can sometimes find flints—the residue, probably, of an important Stone Age flint workshop near the Stone Circle, about 1½ miles from the town. There is a steep walk with rocky scenery across the Sychnant Pass over the mountains to Conwy.

TWO RARE FLOWERS The spotted rock-rose, *Tuberaria gultata* (left), is a late-spring plant occasionally found in dry places near the North Wales coast. It is related to the true rock-rose. The slender mountain spiderwort, *Lloydia serotina* (right), has delicate white flowers which appear during June. This plant is found only in Snowdonia, and even there it is very rare

Snowdon
Monarch of all mountains in England and Wales. There are numerous walks and climbs to the summit from villages that encircle the mountain. The easiest walk is from Llanberis, up the track that follows the railway line. The most attractive time to walk is during September, when the harvest moon illuminates the route for those setting off at midnight to see the unforgettable sunrise from the summit.

Three routes start from the top of Llanberis Pass. The easiest is the Miners' Track, which climbs from the shore of Llyn Llydaw; copper was once mined in the vicinity. The Pig Track passes Llyn Llydaw, 300 ft higher up, and although rough in parts it is a more interesting path. A third route, over Crib Goch, is dangerous for the inexperienced.

On the west side of Snowdon there are two well-marked paths. The first but hardest walk is the Beddgelert Track, starting from a point 2 miles north of the village. The Snowdon Ranger path starts from a Youth Hostel on the shores of Llyn Cwellyn.

Starting from Nantgwynant on the south side of the mountain lies the Watkin Path—the most rewarding of all the routes to the summit, through woods and thickets of rhododendrons and past waterfalls. The last section is very steep and needs climbing experience.

GATEWAY TO THE PASS *The wild River Ogwen is bridged at the village of Bethesda, gateway to the Nant Ffrancon Pass*

'UGLY HOUSE' *A 15th-century cottage of boulders 3½ miles west of Betws-y-coed is named Ty-hyll, meaning Ugly House*

WILDLIFE IN WALES

A long and varied sea coast, extensive mountain and moorland regions and a small population make Wales one of the last refuges for some of Britain's rarest Birds and animals. Among the survivors are red kites, which nest near Gwenffrwd in central Dyfed, and polecats, which have been mercilessly hunted for centuries and now have one of their last strongholds at Tregaron Bog, inland from Cardigan Bay.

Wales is more than just an outpost for declining populations of rare animals. It is rich, too, in birds, wild animals and plants which were never common anywhere. Welsh cliffs and islands are famed for their seabird colonies. Thousands of guillemots, razorbills, kittiwakes and fulmars cling to breeding sites on the great headlands of the Pembroke coast and the Lleyn Peninsula. Skomer and Skokholm, islands off the Pembroke coast, are havens for many thousands of Manx shearwaters. Grassholme Island has one of the four largest gannetries in the world.

Less spectacular, but no less delightful, are the oak woods that cling to the steep Welsh hillsides. Between the lichen-covered oak trees—an ideal habitat for wood warblers and pied flycatchers—the ground is covered with wild flowers, such as primroses, anemones and bluebells. The woods in north-west Gwynedd support the pine marten, and the meadows near Tenby, on Carmarthen Bay, are the only home of the Tenby daffodil. Otters hunt and play in the tumbling Welsh streams; dippers and grey wagtails flit along them. On the mountain screes of Snowdonia there are choughs and ring ouzels, and feral goats (wild animals descended from escaped domesticated stock) may be seen fleetingly. And buzzards soar on splayed wings in the sky overhead, looking like small eagles.

NATIONAL PARKS

SNOWDONIA NATIONAL PARK The Snowdon massif, the eroded remains of a mile-high pile of rocks thrown up by volcanic eruptions more than 450 million years ago, is the mountainous heartland of the Snowdonia National Park. Its peaks and scree-strewn slopes harbour the sure-footed feral goat. The rare Snowdon lily is found only in Cwm Idwal, a lake valley with high cliffs reaching to 3200 ft, which is a National Nature Reserve, an area of high scientific interest. On the eastern border of the park, along the Conwy River Valley, is the Gwydyr Forest, the Welsh refuge of the rare pine marten. Further south, Bala Lake is famed for the gwyniad, a white fish reaching 9–11 in. long that is found nowhere else in the world. In Merioneth, the bleak Cader Idris (2927 ft) has many Arctic/Alpine plants on its heights. Choughs, which survive in small numbers in Wales, breed in Merioneth's old slate quarries. The coastal estuaries of the park are rich in

PEMBROKE COAST *Storm waves pound the sandstone cliffs of St Ann's Head*

SNOWDONIA NATIONAL PARK *The Gwydyr Forest on the north-east fringe of the park*

NATURE'S SURVIVORS AND RARITIES IN WALES

FERAL GOAT *The high mountain screes of Snowdonia are the main stronghold of this shy and once much-hunted animal*

SKOMER VOLE *A creature unique to Skomer, easily observed because of its tameness*

POLECAT *The polecat's last British breeding ground is in central and north Wales*

RED KITE *In the Middle Ages, kites were common in Britain, and even scavenged in London. Now only a few pairs remain, breeding in remote Welsh valleys*

birdlife, and part of the Dyfi Estuary is a nature reserve. Just outside this area is a bird sanctuary at Ynys-hir, owned by the Royal Society for the Protection of Birds (information can be obtained from them at The Lodge, Sandy, Bedfordshire). The birds of Snowdonia include buzzards, kestrels, ravens, jays, magpies, ring ouzels, woodpeckers and dippers. Polecats breed in the park and can sometimes be seen in woodland glades.

PEMBROKESHIRE COAST NATIONAL PARK This park is one of the outstanding regions in Great Britain for natural beauty. Rugged cliffs fall hundreds of feet to the sea, and seabirds flock round them. The islands of Ramsey, Skokholm, Skomer and the remote Grassholme are nature reserves that can be visited for day trips or longer stays with special permission. Ramsey Island, a reserve of the RSPB, has choughs, guillemots, razorbills, gulls, cormorants, shags, fulmars and peregrines. Skokhom also has seabirds, including 20,000 pairs of shearwaters; but it is better known as an observatory for studying bird migration. Skomer is the jewel of the four islands, with a large and varied seabird population, including storm petrels and thousands of Manx shearwaters. It has grey seals and its own race of vole, the Skomer vole. Due to its geographical isolation, this creature has evolved as a totally separate sub-species of the mainland bank vole. It differs not only in colour and shape from the mainland animal, but also in its habits, particularly its tameness which makes it one of the easiest of British small mammals to observe. The island of Grassholme, an RSPB reserve managed by the West Wales Naturalists' Trust (WWNT), is a colony for thousands of gannets. Boats sail round the island in the summer, but landings are difficult and have to be arranged through the WWNT (4 Victoria Place, Haverfordwest, Dyfed). The Tenby daffodil is a Welsh speciality which grows near Tenby, on the west side of Carmarthen Bay.

BRECON BEACONS NATIONAL PARK The moors of the Brecon Beacons are the home of grouse and merlin, and in their valleys can be seen most of the typical Welsh birds. Llangorse Lake has many species of duck, as well as great crested grebes, reed warblers and wagtails, with ravens and buzzards overhead. On the cliffs of Craig y Cilau, one of the National Nature Reserves within the park, and at other limestone sites, are found varieties of the whitebeam shrub unknown outside Wales.

OTHER PLACES TO VISIT

ANGLESEY There are bustling seabird colonies on the island's coast, which has been officially designated as an Area of Outstanding Natural Beauty—an area where development is restricted.

BARDSEY ISLAND A bird observatory off the Lleyn Peninsula, ideal for watching spring and autumn migrants. Choughs, Manx shearwaters and storm petrels breed on the island.

GOWER A peninsula designated an Area of Outstanding Natural Beauty. Its south coast has limestone cliffs with sandy and rocky bays. In the north are sandflats and the Whitford Burrows National Nature Reserve, which swarms with Brent geese and other wildfowl and waders.

GWENFFRWD An RSPB reserve in central Dyfed, the only authorised spot for seeing red kites, which breed there.

GREAT ORMES HEAD Cliffs famous for plants, birds and butterflies, including the dwarf grayling.

NEWBOROUGH WARREN A National Nature Reserve with many birds including curlews, whimbrels, godwits, stints, sandpipers and oystercatchers.

TREGARON BOG This National Nature Reserve is a 'raised bog'—a huge mound of marshland plants. It is a refuge for polecats.

BRECON BEACONS NATIONAL PARK *Beyond rolling hills gleam the Neuadd Reservoirs*

DWARF GRAYLING *This rare butterfly lives on the cliffs of Great Ormes Head*

ROSY MARSH MOTH *Long thought extinct, this moth still lives in Wales*

WELSH FLOWERS *Two specialities: the Snowdon lily (left) and the Tenby daffodil*

The coves and rugged cliffs of Anglesey

Sailing There are clubs at Beaumaris, Menai Bridge, Traeth Bychan and Holyhead. Races twice a week at Holyhead in summer. The Straits Regatta Fortnight is held late July/early Aug.

Angling Sea fishing at Bull Bay, Malldraeth, Menai Straits and Moelfre. Trout fishing (fly only) on local lakes.

Events Plays in Welsh are performed at the Welsh National Drama Festival in the first week in Oct. at Llangefni. The County Agricultural Show is held in the second week in Aug. near Mona Airfield.

Places to see *Anglesey Column*, between Llanfair P.G. and Menai Bridge; daily. *Beaumaris Castle*: daily, except Sun. morning Oct. to Mar. *Cemlyn* (NT), 2 miles west of Cemaes Bay, bird sanctuary: daily. *Museum of Childhood*, Menai Bridge: Easter to Oct., weekdays and Sun. afternoon. *Plas Newydd* (NT): afternoons except Sat., Easter to Oct. *South Stack Lighthouse*: clear weekday afternoons, at discretion of Principal Keeper. *Tegfryn Art Gallery*, Menai Bridge: daily.

Information centre Isle of Anglesey Tourist Association, Coed Cyrnol, Menai Bridge. Tel. Menai Bridge 712626.

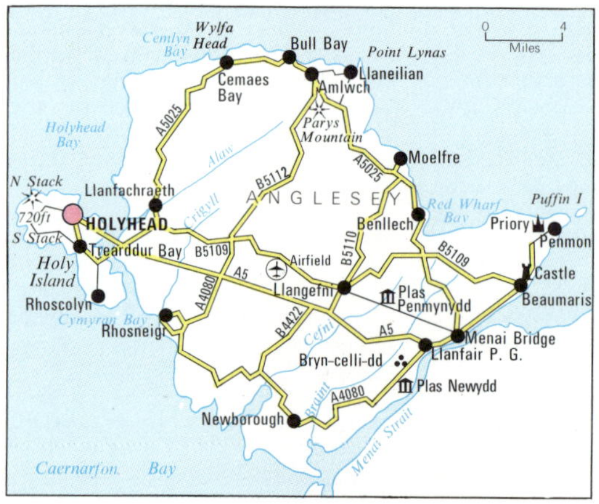

Anglesey, in north Gwynedd, is a non-mountainous island; its highest point, Holyhead Mountain, is just over 700 ft above sea level. From *c.* 150 BC it has been a centre of Celtic culture and religion—and even today it has a high proportion of Welsh-speaking people. The island is still remembered in Welsh history as the place where the Druids made the fiercest stand against their Roman conquerors. Plas Penmynydd was the ancestral home of the Tudors, while the nearby village known as 'Llanfair P.G.' is renowned for having the longest place-name in Britain.

Anglesey was originally thought to mean 'Isle of the English', but it is now believed to mean 'Isle of the straits'—from the old Norse word *ongull* meaning 'strait'. Its landscape derives from rugged, twisted rocks that are among the oldest in Wales. There are small farms and charming stone-walled villages, glorious beaches and sandy coves.

Inland, there are four excellent trout lakes, an abundance of interesting old churches, prehistoric cromlechs, tumuli and chambered cairns, centuries-old manor houses and a fine castle built by Edward I at Beaumaris, which still retains its ancient dock where boats tied up in the sea-flooded moat. Telford's famous suspension bridge, opened in 1826, carries road traffic over the Menai Strait. The railway runs over what was Robert Stephenson's Britannia Tubular Bridge, opened in 1850: but the tubes had to be removed following extensive damage by fire in 1970.

Amlwch
An important port for the copper-mining centre at nearby Parys Mountain during the 19th century. The industry was started by the Romans. Today it is a quiet resort with good cliff and coastal scenery. The beach at Bull Bay has little sand but there are rocky, sheltered coves for safe bathing and fishing. A 2½-mile walk east, along a road with rocky outcrops and splashes of gorse, leads to Llaneilian, which has a medieval church built on the site of a 5th-century one. On a hill at nearby Point Lynas stands an old semaphore signalling station which formed part of a chain between Holyhead and Liverpool and enabled mid-19th-century shipowners to obtain news of the arrival of their ships.

Beaumaris
The name is derived from the Norman *beau marais* meaning 'beautiful marsh'. Today this little town is one of the most attractive in Wales, with early Victorian terraces designed by Joseph Hansom, of cab fame, half-timbered houses and a splendid medieval moated castle. The 15th-century Old Bull's Head Inn has a good collection of china. The Tudor Rose, of the same period, houses a small museum, and the 17th-century Court House is reputed to have been the scene of one of Judge Jeffreys's assizes. A mile north of the town, at Friars Road, is a barn called The Fryars, which is on the site of a 13th-century monastery.

Cemaes Bay
Several sandy beaches and coves provide good bathing. There is a picturesque stone quay, and there are plenty of cliff walks over land belonging to the National Trust. The nuclear power station at nearby Wylfa Head, one of the largest in the world, could well be mistaken for a 20th-century fortification.

Cemlyn Bay
A deep bay with a long, well-sheltered beach, which is safe for bathing, though pebbly. There are clifftop walks and a car park. Two miles of coastline are owned by the National Trust and protected as a sanctuary for migrant wildfowl. Visitors can view the sanctuary from the road.

SHORE FORTRESS *Beaumaris Castle was built by Edward I in 1295 to guard the Menai Strait. The castle's outer or 'curtain' wall, with 12 towers, surrounds a higher inner wall protecting the main part of the stronghold. Small boats could once dock in the sea-fed moat*

SOUTH STACK *The lighthouse on South Stack, a rocky island off Holyhead Mountain, was built in 1809. The island is joined to the mainland by an iron bridge, at the foot of a zigzag path with 400 steps cut into the rock. South Stack is indented by caves where seals breed, and seabirds nest on ledges in the steep cliffs*

Holyhead
The town is on Holy Island, which is joined to Anglesey proper by a causeway. Holyhead's most striking building is the cruciform Church of St Cybi, with a 13th-century chancel, but the place of greatest interest is Holyhead Mountain. From the top of the precipitous cliffs there are panoramic views of the Isle of Man, the mountains of Cumbria, Snowdonia—and Ireland.

As early as 2000 BC, Holyhead was busy with boats discharging quantities of axes from Ireland, and 500 years later the town handled the importing of Irish mined gold. At the foot of Holyhead Mountain is South Stack, a small rocky promontory with a lighthouse, caves inhabited by seals, and rocky ledges where seabirds nest. The island can be reached by a bridge.

On the south-west slope of Holyhead Mountain are the remains of a collection of circular and rectangular dwellings. Some believe that these hut circles date back to the time of the Irish axe and gold trade; others, however, believe they are the remains of a village founded here between the 2nd and 4th centuries AD.

North Stack has great caverns, one with an arch 70 ft high called The Parliament House because of the continuous chattering of the birds in summer. Large colonies of gulls, razorbills, cormorants and guillemots nest here and on South Stack.

MENAI BRIDGE *The original arches at the ends of Telford's suspension bridge carry Anglesey's only road to the mainland*

Llanfair P.G.
Even the Welsh have found it necessary to shorten the original name to Llanfair P.G. The full name, the longest in Britain, is Llanfairpwllgwyngyllgogerychwyrndrobwllllantysiliogogogoch, which means 'the church of St Mary by the hollow of the white aspen, over the whirlpool, and St Tysilio's Church close to the red cave'. Extra-long platform tickets can be obtained at the station, where the name, displayed at full length, is a magnet for photography-minded tourists. There is a 2-mile woodland walk to the south-west to Bryn-celli-ddu, where a Bronze Age burial chamber has been uncovered.

Llangefni
This is the administrative centre of the island, and the scene of a lively open-air market every Thursday and livestock sales every Wednesday. Plas Penmynydd, 2 miles to the east, was the birthplace of Owen Tudor, grandfather of Henry VII.

Moelfre
A quaint old fishing village with a shingle beach and a lifeboat station renowned for its rescues. However, during a catastrophic storm in 1859 the *Royal Charter* was wrecked in the bay with the loss of some 460 lives. Bullion and other valuables worth more than £400,000, on the way from Australia, were recovered from the wreck. Charles Dickens used the story in his essay *The Uncommercial Traveller*.

Newborough
The Warren National Nature Reserve at Newborough covers 1500 acres of open dunes where wildfowl and wading birds abound. Among species to be seen are curlews, oystercatchers, peregrines, redshanks and sandpipers.

Penmon
From the pebbly beach there are fine views of Snowdonia and the Great Orme at Llandudno. Inland are the remains of a 12th-century priory, the Church of St Seiriol, and a 16th-century stone dovecot whose walls are lined with about 1000 nests. The wishing well—the holy well where St Seiriol baptised converts—is a great attraction. A mile offshore is Puffin Island, also called Priestholm after a hermit who built a cell there *c.* AD 540. It is a sanctuary for seabirds, and also has the fragments of a late Norman church and tower.

Where Lleyn drops to the sea

Boating There are sailing clubs at Porthmadog, Abersoch, Nefyn and Pwllheli, with tuition at Pwllheli. Regattas are held during the first week of Aug. at Pwllheli, Criccieth and Abersoch. There is a powerboat club at Pwllheli and races are held at Abersoch.

Angling Sea fishing at Pwllheli, Criccieth and Abersoch.

Pony trekking At Criccieth, Pwllheli and Llanystumdwy.

Water sports Water-skiing at Abersoch and Pwllheli.

Events There is an open-air market every Wed. at Pwllheli, a Spring Fair in May and an Autumn Fair in Nov. Sheep-dog trials throughout the area in late summer and early autumn.

Places to see *Brynkir Woollen Mills*, 3 miles north of Criccieth: weekdays except Bank Hols. *Criccieth Castle*: daily, except Sun. mornings Oct. to Mar. *Festiniog Railway Museum*, Porthmadog: Feb. to Oct., daily. *Festiniog Narrow Gauge Railway*, oldest passenger-carrying light railway in the world, built over 130 years ago. Frequent services between Ffestiniog and Porthmadog: mid-Feb. to late Mar., weekends; Apr. to Oct., daily. *Lloyd George Memorial Museum*, Llanystumdwy: May to Sept., Mon. to Fri. *Maritime Museum*, Porthmadog: daily, Apr. to Sept. *St Cybi's Well*, Llangybi, 4 miles north of Pwllheli: daily.

Information centre Festiniog Railway Station, Porthmadog. Tel. Porthmadog 2981 (seasonal).

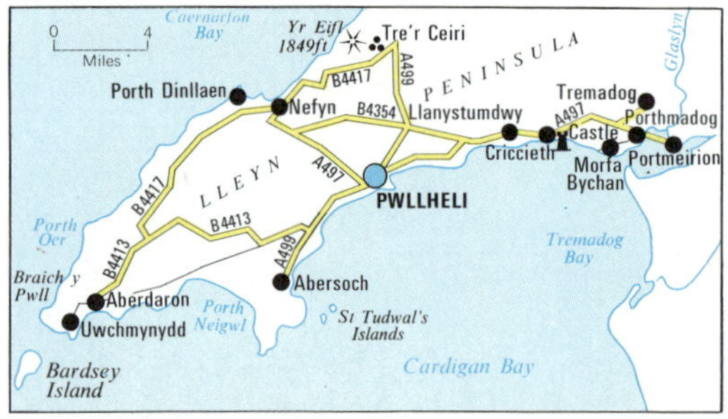

The landscape of the Lleyn Peninsula is quite unlike that of the rest of North Wales. It has distant horizons broken by dramatic mountains falling sheer to the sea; rocky coves, wide bays and enticing beaches; whitewashed cottages amid small fields or on top of round-backed hills; and charming fishing villages. Trees are scarce on this windswept peninsula, but it is ablaze with gorse and heather.

Lleyn was one of the earliest inhabited parts of Wales. There is ample evidence of prehistoric man. On the easternmost peak of Yr Eifl—literally meaning 'The Forks' but called 'The Rivals' by the English—is Tre'r Ceiri, popularly known as Town of the Giants, one of the most important hut circle clusters in Wales.

But the early Christian churches have made an even greater impression on this peninsula. Everywhere there are reminders of Gallic and Celtic saints. Two miles off the coast lies Bardsey Island, once a place of pilgrimage where, it is said, many holy men lie buried. There is also a legend that the Welsh wizard Merlin lies in an enchanted sleep on the island, with the golden throne of Britain and other treasures, waiting for the reappearance of King Arthur. Other famous Welshmen from the Lleyn were David Lloyd George, whose home was at Criccieth, and T. E. Lawrence, Lawrence of Arabia, born at Tremadog.

RUGGED COASTLINE *Massive boulders perched high on the cliffs*

ITALY IN WALES *A campanile is one of Portmeirion's architectural fancies*

Aberdaron
A remote, charming village of narrow, winding lanes, with an inn noted for its giant crabs and lobsters. Aberdaron was once the point of embarkation for pilgrims to Bardsey. They crossed to the island—Ynys Enlli or 'Isle of the Eddies'—from Braich y Pwll, 2½ miles west of Aberdaron among the cliffs at the 'Land's End' of North Wales. Today it is possible to drive or walk south along the winding road to Uwchmynydd, a wild headland owned by the National Trust where there is a superb view of Bardsey and the boiling sea around it.

Abersoch
One of the most attractive villages on this coast. The harbour and estuary are full of colourful craft and sails, and lively with people who love 'messing about in boats'. There are fine sandy beaches, and there is plenty of sea fishing, especially

RURAL PEACE *Whitewashed cottages, placid cattle and poultry dot gently sloping fields at the foot of the eastern slopes of Yr Eifl, near Llanaelhaearn*

above *Caernarfon Bay, north of the peaks of Yr Eifl ('The Forks'), typify the rugged northern shore of the Lleyn Peninsula*

for mackerel. Offshore lie the privately owned St Tudwal's Islands, famous for seabirds, deep sea caves and great lobsters. Boat trips round the islands start from Abersoch.

The next great bay, Porth Neigwl or Hell's Mouth, where powerful tides and eddies have destroyed many ships, is one of the most impressive in Wales; it is said that in heavy gales the grinding of the pebbles shakes nearby houses. There are 4 miles of beach here, reached by steep and difficult footpaths down the almost sheer face of the cliffs.

Criccieth

A small, still unspoilt seaside resort, facing south and more sheltered than most on the peninsula. It has two excellent sand-and-shingle beaches which provide first-class bathing. Lloyd George (1863–1945) is the local hero. He was brought up at the nearby village of Llanystumdwy by his uncle, and later he married a Criccieth girl and lived just outside Criccieth for part of his life. He is buried at Llanystumdwy, where there is a Lloyd George Museum.

ABERSOCH *Sailing boats crowd the sheltered harbour on Cardigan Bay*

The ruins of a 13th-century castle stand high on the headland, between two bays which can be reached easily on foot. From the castle there is a magnificent view that takes in Snowdonia and, to the south-east, the sweep of Cardigan Bay and Harlech Castle.

Nefyn

An ancient town which has become a popular resort with good beaches and excellent cliff walks. The town has many historical and mythological associations. It is said that the British chieftain Vortigern, who invited Saxon mercenaries into England, found refuge here when he had to flee to Wales. In 1284, Edward I staged a tournament at Nefyn as part of the celebrations to mark the final defeat of Llewellyn ap Gruffydd. The site of the tournament lists can still be seen. Nearby Porth Dinllaen was a famous 18th-century smuggling port. Four miles north of the town, on the lowest of the triple peaks of Yr Eifl, lies Town of the Giants, an Iron Age encampment which consists of more than 100 hut circles. The ruins of the walls which once surrounded the site still rise to 15 ft in places. The walk to the top is rewarded by magnificent views.

Porth Oer

A beautiful white beach, famous for its whistling sands. The whistle is caused by the grinding together of the very fine particles of sand when walked on. There is good bathing and fishing.

Porthmadog

With its twin town of Tremadog, Porthmadog is the gateway to the Lleyn Peninsula. Both towns, at the mouth of the River Glaslyn, were built on reclaimed land in the 19th century by a local MP, William Alexander Madocks. The harbour is picturesque and filled with sailing boats and yachts. Near by are the delightful sandy beaches of Borth-y-Gêst and Morfa Bychan.

Shelley is believed to have written part of *Queen Mab* in Tan-yr-allt, near Tremadog. There is a local story that Shelley was shot at by peasants who were angered by his habit of putting sick sheep out of their misery without first finding out if they could be cured.

The Welsh prince Madoc, son of Owain of Gwynedd, is said in a 15th-century poem to have sailed from Borth-y-Gêst to America in the 12th century.

Portmeirion

One of the show-places of Wales and a superb product of the imagination and enterprise of one man, the architect Clough Williams-Ellis. Starting in 1926 he began to create in the heart of wild Wales a showpiece type of village similar in spirit to Portofino in Italy. On a little tree-clad peninsula between the Rivers Glaslyn and Dwyryd, Williams-Ellis rebuilt a sumptuous hotel, planted cypresses, palms and eucalyptus, and introduced many architectural fancies, among them an Italianate campanile, castle and lighthouse. The wild gardens, full of exotic plants, are some of the most splendid in Wales.

Portmeirion has been used as a film-set, and Noël Coward wrote his comedy *Blithe Spirit* there.

Pwllheli

The view from Penygarn, the hill behind Pwllheli, shows the two different sides of the town. One part is the old town, the other a modern seaside resort centred on the great 5-mile sweep of South Beach, which is both sand and shingle. The town's outer harbour is filled with yachts and powerboats and there is excellent fishing in the area for bass, mackerel, pollack and flatfish.

Cader Idris, the 'chair of Arthur'

Sailing There are clubs, with good estuary sailing, at Aberdyfi and Barmouth; Bala Lake is a sailing centre and has tuition courses.

Climbing Snowdonia National Park includes Cader Idris summit, 3 miles south-west of Dolgellau. The Moelwyn Mountains are an hour's walk north-west of Ffestiniog, for rock climbing of all grades.

Pony trekking At Arthog, Bontddu, Dolgellau, Ffestiniog and Tal-y-bont, 4 miles north of Barmouth.

Angling Mullet and mackerel at Barmouth. Sea bass in the Mawddach Estuary and Harlech Strand. Lobster and crab between Llwyngwril and Afon Dysynni.

Events Sheep-dog trials are held in Aug. at various centres. Fairs are held in several towns, including Bala, Blaenau Ffestiniog and Dolgellau in spring and autumn.

Places to see *Dolwyddelan Castle*, 4 miles north of Blaenau Ffestiniog: daily. *Fairbourne Railway*, from Fairbourne north to Penrhyn Point: Easter; also Whitsun to Sept., daily. *Festiniog Railway*: mid-Feb. to late Mar., weekends; Apr. to Oct., daily. *Harlech Castle*: daily, except Sun. mornings Oct. to Mar. *Llechwedd Slate Cavern*, Blaenau Ffestiniog: Easter to Oct., daily. *National Park Centre*, Aberdyfi: Easter, and daily late May to Sept. *Talyllyn Narrow Gauge Railway*, operates from Tywyn to Abergynolwyn: daily, mid-May to Sept.

Information centres Snowdonia National Park Information Service, Maentwrog, Gwynedd. Tel. Maentwrog 274. Phone only: Aberdyfi 321, Bala 367, Blaenau Ffestiniog 360, Harlech 658, Dolgellau 422888.

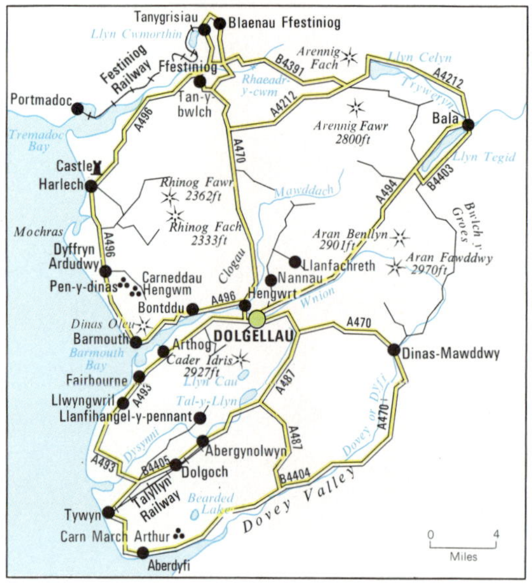

The craggy mountains of south Gwynedd, crowned by Aran Fawddwy and Cader Idris, both nearly 3000 ft high, combine with its mirror-like lakes to make landscapes of compelling beauty. Much of this land lies within the Snowdonia National Park. Some peaks are bare, some pine-forested. There are streams, waterfalls and two romantic river valleys, the Dyfi and Mawddach. Exhilarating passes include Bwlch y Groes, the Pass of the Cross, at 1790 ft the highest road in Wales, linking Bala and Dinas Mawddwy. This is a green land of hill-farms and of glens. It is a place for the walker, the rock-climber and the pony-trekker, while its pure waters are rich in salmon, trout, perch and eels.

The mark of history is on the land in its ruins and in its legends. Races more ancient even than the Celts have left their burial-chambers. There are Iron Age forts; Roman roads and fortresses; Irish relics of the 4th to 6th centuries, when this land was part of the Kingdom of East Ireland; and splendid Norman castles such as Harlech.

Aberdyfi
An attractive little port at the mouth of the Dyfi, and a relaxing holiday centre. There are miles of fine, sandy beaches backed by dunes, with a good golf course. The sunken tree trunks just discernible in the sands at low tide are the relics of a time, 7000 years ago or more, when much of what is now Cardigan Bay was still land. According to legend, the 'Bells of Aberdovey' can be heard ringing in the sea swell from a drowned city when trouble threatens.

The ridges of the south Gwynedd mountains rise steeply on the north side of the estuary, and there are many excellent walks. A steep climb from the centre of Aberdyfi leads to a ridge a mile north of the town from which, on a clear day, the view extends southwards across the Dyfi Estuary and northwards across the so-called Happy Valley towards the towering summit of Cader Idris. The hilltop track leads 2½ miles east to the Bearded Lake, and to the nearby Carn March Arthur, where a mark on the fallen cairn is said to be the giant hoofprint of King Arthur's horse.

SHEEP MARKET *Dolgellau has a regular sheep market that attracts many farmers from surrounding hill villages wishing to buy and sell*

Bala
A sleepy town at the northern end of Llyn Tegid, or Lake Bala, which at 4½ miles long and nearly a mile wide is the largest natural lake in Wales. It is an excellent sailing and fishing centre. One of the rarities among its fish is the gwyniad, a white-scaled salmon which lives about 80 ft deep and can be caught only in a net. There is a legend that a drowned palace lies beneath the lake. The town is famous as a centre of Methodism and as the original home of Welshmen who migrated to South America in 1865 to found a colony in Patagonia. Some of their descendants still speak Welsh as well as Spanish.

Bala is a magnificent walking and driving centre, at the heart of some of the wildest hill country in Wales. To the west the River Tryweryn flows between the two peaks of Arennig Fawr (2800 ft) and Arennig Fach (2259 ft). To the south loom Aran Benllyn (2901 ft) and Aran Fawddwy—at 2970 ft the highest Welsh mountain outside the Snowdonia range.

Barmouth
A modern seaside resort, with 2 miles of sandy beaches. The Panorama Walk, a series of terraced paths overlooking the Mawddach Estuary, rises just east of the town from a path on the north side of the Dolgellau road. The 4½ acres of cliffs known as Dinas Oleu, just beside the town, became in 1895 the first property to be acquired by the National Trust.

The surrounding hills are full of interesting archaeological remains: Carneddau Hengwm, 3 miles north, has two chambered tombs, and Pen-y-dinas, half a mile further north-west, has the remains of an Iron Age camp.

Blaenau Ffestiniog
A town noted for its slate quarries, which press close on all sides. In some places the bluish slate crags even overhang the houses in a menacing way. But the bleakness is relieved by the splendour of the setting. The countryside is ideal for walking and fishing, and at least 15 lakes are within easy reach. A steep path from the post office at Tanygrisiau, a mile south-west, leads northwards alongside a mountain stream to waterfalls near Llyn Cwmorthin. The Stwlan hydro-electric dam on the Tanygrisiau Reservoir is one of the longest in Britain. Ffestiniog, 2½ miles south, is a fine walking centre, at the head of the Vale of

CENTURY OF STEAM *The Talyllyn Railway was built in 1865, to carry slate*

CLIFFTOP FORTRESS *Harlech Castle, built by Edward I c. 1283, stands on a crag protected by the sea on one side and a wide moat on the other. Beyond it stretch the peaks of Snowdonia*

ENDURING SLATE AND STONE

Welsh buildings have been constructed of local slate and stone for hundreds of years. Where possible, early builders incorporated natural outcrops of rock in foundations for the walls. This 18th-century farmhouse is built of masonry laid in courses, bound together with rubble and mortar and reinforced at the corners with large dressed stones. The small barn has drystone walls, laid in very rough courses. All the roofs have courses of dressed slates

ARTHUR'S CHAIR *The massive 2927-ft summit of Cader Idris, a name which means 'the chair of Idris' or Arthur, dominates the skyline south of Dolgellau. Its steeper faces present a challenge to experienced climbers*

Ffestiniog. A spectacular 200-ft waterfall, Rhaeadr-y-Cwm, is 3 miles east of the town. There is a good view of the lower part of the vale from the narrow-gauge Festiniog Railway, built to carry slate from the Blaenau Ffestiniog quarries to Porthmadog. It was re-opened for passengers in 1954 and has a run of 12¼ miles between Porthmadog and Tanygrisiau.

Cader Idris
South Gwynedd's most famous mountain, though at 2927 ft it is topped by the 2970 ft of Aran Fawddwy. Myth has it that anyone who sleeps the night on Cader Idris wakes either blind, mad or a poet. The easiest route to the top starts from Llanfihangel-y-pennant, 3½ miles south-west. The toughest begins at the eastern edge of Tal-y-llyn and climbs past Llyn Cau, reputedly a bottomless lake with a Loch Ness-type monster; only experienced climbers should attempt this ascent. There are also two routes from Dolgellau, on the north side: the Foxes' Path, 4½ miles, and the Pony Track, 6 miles.

Dinas Mawddwy
One of the most attractive of all Welsh villages, with excellent fishing for salmon and trout in the River Dyfi. Footpaths above the village lead to magnificent waterfalls, and Dinas is a base for climbing the peaks of Aran Fawddwy, 4½ miles north, and 2901 ft Aran Benllyn, 1½ miles further on.

Dolgellau
The small town of Dolgellau lies in the long valley-rift of the Mawddach. It is a picturesque, brooding town, with buildings made from the local dark slate. The so-called Precipice Walk circles a high ridge 2 miles north of the town and gives fine views across the Cambrian Mountains, including the Aran peaks and the rugged north face of Cader Idris. The walk, which runs through woodlands and meadows, is reached from a signposted track starting from a car park north-east of Dolgellau on the Llanfachreth road.

A shorter walk from Dolgellau starts from the north side of the bridge over the River Wnion and climbs to the golf course near Hengwrt, from which there is a fine view of the five peaks of Cader Idris. The Torrent Walk runs for a mile up the River Clywedog, a tributary of the Wnion 2 miles east of the town.

Dyffryn Ardudwy
A village separated from the sea by wide sand dunes and surrounded by 2000-ft mountains studded with Neolithic and later remains. There are beaches and good walks. The dunes terminate to the north in Mochras, or Shell Island, where specimens of rare shells can be found on the beach.

Harlech
This town on Tremadog Bay is dominated by its castle, built by Edward I *c.* 1283 on the site of an early Celtic fortress. It was here that Owen Glendower's wife and family were captured by Henry V. The song 'Men of Harlech' was composed to commemorate the bravery of the Lancastrian Dafydd ap Einion, who held the castle during a siege in the 15th-century Wars of the Roses, although the first written version of the song dates only from the 18th century. Harlech was the last North Wales stronghold to hold out for the Lancastrians, and also the last castle held by the Royalists in the Civil War. Marvellous views of the Snowdon range, the Lleyn Peninsula, Tremadog Bay and the mountains to the south can be seen from Harlech. Herds of wild goats roam the Rhinog Mountains on the 991 acres of a nature reserve.

Tywyn
A seaside town at the base of the hills of the Cader Idris range. The parish church contains St Cadfan's Stone, with an inscription, probably dating from the 7th century, which is thought to be the oldest written example of the Welsh language, although no satisfactory translation has been made.

The narrow-gauge Talyllyn Railway, from Tywyn to Abergynolwyn, was built in 1865 for the transport of slate. It is now maintained by a Preservation Society. There is a halt at Dolgoch, near the magnificent Dolgoch Falls which drop a total of 125 ft.

NORTH MIDLANDS

A wide range of scenery is contained within the five counties which stretch across England from Salop (Shropshire), on the Welsh border, to Lincolnshire on the North Sea coast. The designation 'North Midlands' may suggest to many in the South a picture of red-brick houses huddled together in rows of identical streets, stained with the grime of the Industrial Revolution. This impression is far from the truth, for the North Midlands have broad expanses of rural landscape.

Salop, the westernmost of the five counties, is a land of stock-rearing and dairy-farming, scattered with orchards. Neighbouring Staffordshire has the heath and woodland of Cannock Chase and acres of lush farmland, while Derbyshire has the Peak District—a landscape of moorland, deep green valleys and rough stone crags.

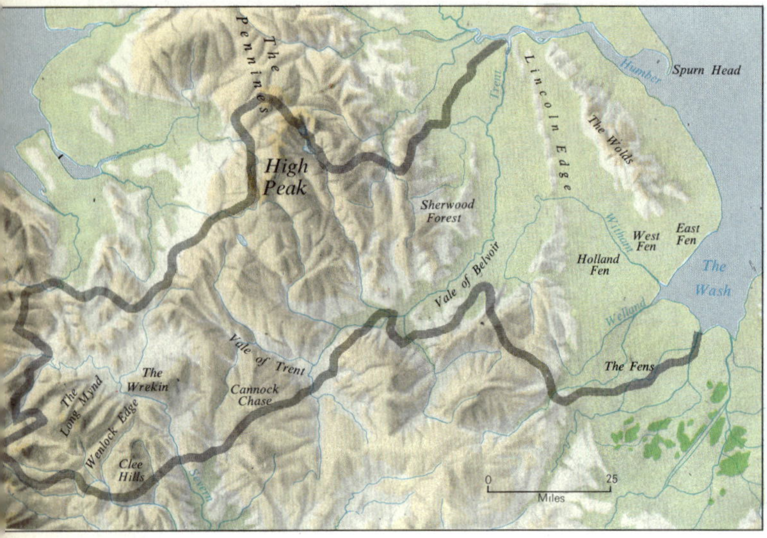

THE CENTRAL PEAKS *The gritstone uplands of the Derbyshire Peak District are at the centre of the North Midlands. To the west are the extreme fringes of the Cambrian Mountains, and to the east the land drops to the Lincolnshire Fens*

In Nottinghamshire, the contrast ranges from coalfield slag heaps to pasturelands and acres devoted to mixed farming. The county has an area of intensive rose cultivation south-east of Nottingham, and the green woodlands of Sherwood Forest, home of the legendary Robin Hood. The rich, dark fenland soils to the east make Lincolnshire Britain's largest agricultural county, with huge acreages of wheat, potatoes and barley, and a concentrated market-gardening industry.

Two major rivers divide the North Midlands—the long River Severn that drains to the Bristol Channel from its source in the Welsh hills and, on the east, the River Trent, carrying much of the pollution of the industrial heartland to the Humber Estuary.

Inspiration for novelists and poets

Two hundred years of industrial growth have obviously left their mark—especially in Nottinghamshire and Derbyshire, where colliery winding gear and slag heaps frequently line the horizon. But the importance of the industrial North Midlands is not only economic. The area has made its contribution to the cultural heritage of the nation, too, for the mining town of Eastwood in Nottinghamshire was the home and inspiration of D. H. Lawrence; and Arnold Bennett, whose novels portray life in the

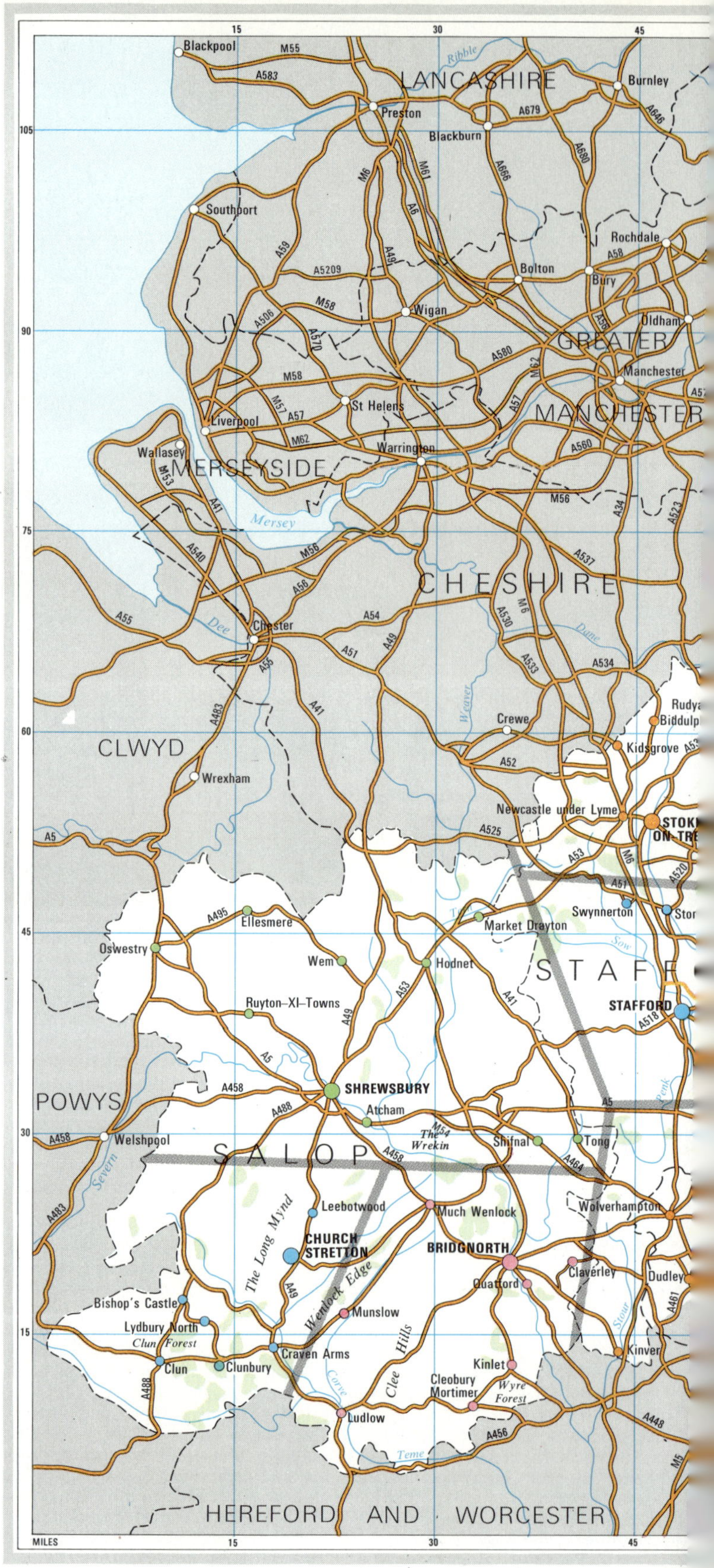

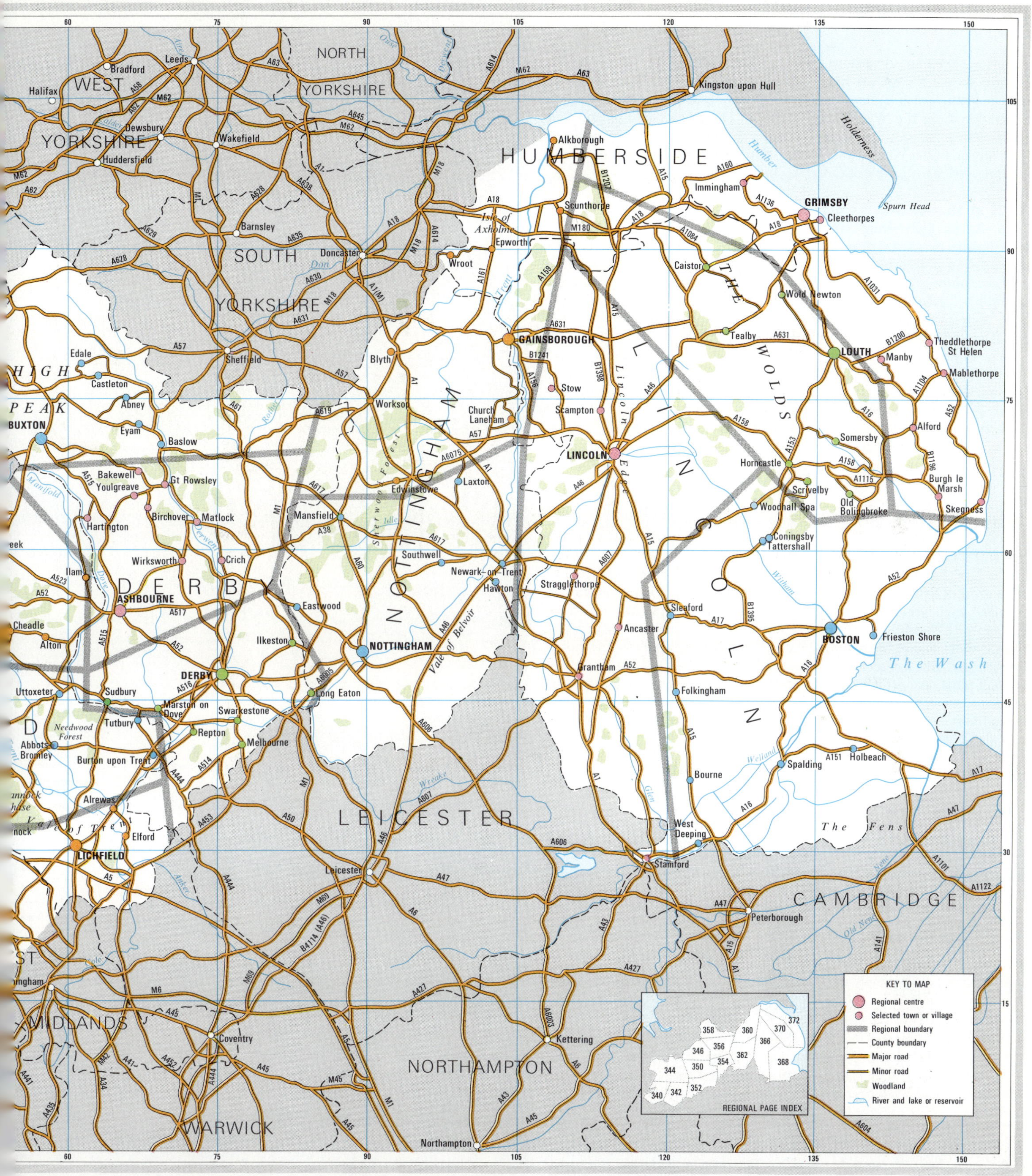

NORTH YORKSHIRE
WEST YORKSHIRE
SOUTH YORKSHIRE
HUMBERSIDE
HIGH PEAK
DERBY
NOTTINGHAM
LINCOLN
THE WOLDS
LEICESTER
CAMBRIDGE
NORTHAMPTON
WARWICK
MIDLANDS
Leeds
Bradford
Halifax
Dewsbury
Wakefield
Huddersfield
Barnsley
Doncaster
Sheffield
Kingston upon Hull
Alkborough
Scunthorpe
Immingham
GRIMSBY
Cleethorpes
Spurn Head
Holderness
Humber
Isle of Axholme
Epworth
Wroot
Caistor
Wold Newton
Tealby
GAINSBOROUGH
LOUTH
Theddlethorpe St Helen
Manby
Mablethorpe
Edale
Castleton
Abney
Eyam
BUXTON
Baslow
Blyth
Worksop
Stow
Church Laneham
Scampton
LINCOLN
Lincoln Edge
Somersby
Alford
Horncastle
Scrivelby
Old Bolingbroke
Burgh le Marsh
Skegness
Woodhall Spa
Coningsby
Tattershall
Bakewell
Youlgreave
Gt Rowsley
Birchover
Matlock
Hartington
Edwinstowe
Laxton
Mansfield
Sherwood Forest
Crich
Wirksworth
Southwell
Newark-on-Trent
Hawton
Stragglethorpe
Ilam
ASHBOURNE
Eastwood
Cheadle
Alton
Ilkeston
NOTTINGHAM
Vale of Belvoir
Ancaster
Sleaford
BOSTON
Frieston Shore
The Wash
Grantham
Folkingham
DERBY
Uttoxeter
Sudbury
Marston on Dove
Swarkestone
Long Eaton
Tutbury
Repton
Melbourne
Needwood Forest
Abbots Bromley
Burton upon Trent
Bourne
Spalding
Holbeach
Alrewas
Elford
Vale of Trent
LICHFIELD
West Deeping
The Fens
Stamford
Leicester
Peterborough
Coventry
Kettering
Northampton
KEY TO MAP
Regional centre
Selected town or village
Regional boundary
County boundary
Major road
Minor road
Woodland
River and lake or reservoir
REGIONAL PAGE INDEX

Potteries, lived at Stoke-on-Trent in Staffordshire. The Midland counties have other literary links: Somersby, in the Lincolnshire Wolds, was the birthplace of Tennyson; and another poet, A. E. Housman, drew inspiration from the Wenlock countryside. The history of England is reflected everywhere: Danish place-names are common in Lincolnshire —an aftermath of Viking raids—and Salop, where the Welsh influence is strong, has many people of Celtic stock.

A village that braved the plague

Eyam is the Derbyshire village where, in 1665, the Rev. William Mompesson persuaded people not to flee from the plague, brought to the village in an infected box of clothes. Five out of every six inhabitants died, including Mompesson's wife, but the plague was prevented from spreading. In 1643, during the Civil War, a major battle at Slash Hollow, near Winceby in Lincolnshire, ended in defeat for the Royalist forces and fame for a rising cavalry commander named Oliver Cromwell.

The cathedral at Lincoln, dominating the skyline for 20 miles around, and the 'village cathedral' at Southwell, Nottinghamshire, are among the best ecclesiastical architecture in the North Midlands. Derbyshire's stately homes at Chatsworth, Haddon and Kedleston owe much to the mellow beauty of the yellow and grey building stones of the county. This use of local raw materials by masons of centuries past has left a rich variety of ordinary domestic buildings throughout the counties—stone-and-slate farmhouses along the Welsh border, honey-coloured limestone villages in Lincolnshire, and the Tudor 'magpie' style of darkened timber over whitened plaster walls seen in villages to the west.

Sea walls that shelter holiday sites

The holiday locations of the North Midlands, though fewer than in some other areas of Britain, are becoming increasingly popular. Thousands are attracted each year to the vast caravan and chalet sites that dot the Lincolnshire coastline, protected from the bracing east winds by dunes and sea walls, and to the booming resorts of Skegness, Mablethorpe and Cleethorpes. But for scenery and natural beauty, the Derbyshire Peak District must take pride of place. Here, among bracken clinging to rock outcrops, are opportunities for the energetic to enjoy rock-climbing, or for ordinary travellers to enjoy the mental relaxation of hill-walking.

DRY WEATHER IN THE LOWLANDS

Most of the North Midlands, with the exception of central and north Derbyshire, has a low rainfall, averaging 26 in. each year in the west and decreasing eastwards to as little as 22·4 in. at Skegness on the coast. Buxton, affected by the hills of the Peak District, has 48·5 in. The central counties and the Lincolnshire lowlands have more thunderstorms than most parts of the country, with 12 thundery days a year at Nottingham and 16 over Lincolnshire

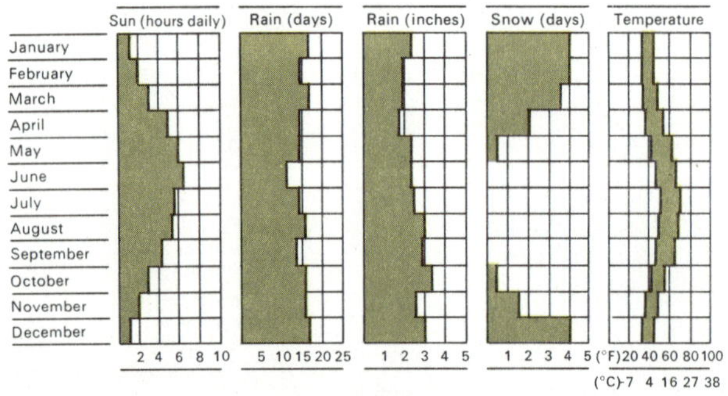

DOVE DALE *Green hills rise on the east bank of the River Dove, just north of Thorpe, in Derbyshire. Footpaths follow the 2-mile Dove Dale gorge, one of the most attractive stretches in the gentler, southern part of the Peak District National Park*

Rich green hills by the Severn

Angling There are trout in a tributary of the Onny, 2 miles north of Craven Arms, and on the River Clun in Old Castle Gardens at Clun; pike in Stokesay Pool; carp in Bache Pool near Craven Arms; coarse fishing at Walcot Hall Lake near Lydbury North.

Boating and water-skiing There are facilities on Marton Pool, near Westbury.

Gliding Asterton, on Long Mynd, is a centre for gliding.

Nature trails Earl's Hill, Pontesbury, 1½ miles north-east of Minsterley, all year. Edge Wood, Westhope, near Craven Arms, and Old Rectory Wood, Church Stretton, from May.

Events The Severn Valley Motor Club holds Speed Hill Climbs at Loton Park in Apr. and autumn. There is a 2-weeks Arts Festival at Church Stretton in July. A Traction Engine Rally takes place at Bishop's Castle on late Summer Bank Hol. Mon. Clun Show and Carnival take place in Aug., and at Purslow there is a show, gymkhana and motor-cycle scramble on late Summer Bank Hol. Mon.

Places to see *Acton Scott Working Farm Museum*, 2½ miles south of Church Stretton: Apr. to Oct., daily. *Clun Town Trust Museum*, Town Hall: Easter to Nov., Tues. and Sat. afternoons. *Stokesay Castle*, Craven Arms: daily, except Tues.

Information centre Shropshire Hills, Church Street, Church Stretton. Tel. Church Stretton 2535.

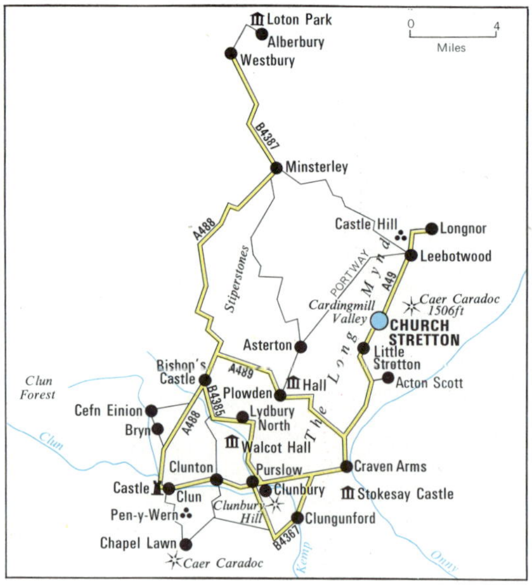

Country houses owned by long-established county families stud the rich green countryside south of the River Severn. Their well-tended grounds, such as those of Loton Park at Alberbury, stretch alongside the main roads. West and south the hills rise dramatically towards the wild heathlands and moors of the Welsh border country.

There is a local legend that on the 1700 ft high rocky Stiperstones, 4 miles south of Minsterley, devils gather on Midwinter Night to choose their leader. To the east of these sombre rocks rises The Long Mynd, a 10 mile long ridge of bleak hills between 2 and 4 miles wide, which commands magnificent views.

West of Bishop's Castle the bare hills of Clun Forest, crossed by the River Clun, extend to the borders of Powys. Welsh place-names abound here—for example, Bryn and Cefn Einion. This fascinating border country was described by Shropshire-born novelist Mary Webb in *The Golden Arrow* and *Gone to Earth*. Her fictional 'Shepwardine' is based on the little market town of Church Stretton, which nestles in a picturesque valley at the foot of The Long Mynd. The valley contains a branch of Watling Street, built by the Romans when they were constructing garrison towns to keep out Celtic marauders.

FARM NEAR CLUN *Clun Forest sheep, which take their name from the area in which they were bred, are popular with lowland farmers for their fine, dense fleeces*

ANCIENT FORT *A ditch beside an oval earthwork near Clun is said to have been dug by King Caractacus and defended against the Romans in* AD *50*

Bishop's Castle
A border town in rich sheep-farming country on the edge of Clun Forest. In the late 8th century, Egwin Shakehead, lord of the manor at nearby Lydbury North, was cured of palsy at St Ethelbert's shrine—on the site of which Hereford Cathedral now stands. He bequeathed all his territory to St Ethelbert. Over 300 years later the Normans interpreted this as a bequest to the Bishop of Hereford, and in 1127 they built a fortified castle for the bishop near Lydbury North, to protect his land. Around this castle the present town grew up. The bishop's successors, with their chief tenants, the Walcots and Plowdens, governed the town until 1570. A bowling green at the top of the town now stands on the castle's fragmentary remains. The 18th-century town hall, at the top of the steep High Street, contains two silver maces, hallmarked 1697. The Three Tuns Inn dates back to 1642, and there are three Tudor houses: the Old Hall, the Old Market Hall and the House on Crutches, whose overhanging upper storey is supported by posts.

Church Stretton
A cluster of red-roofed houses makes up this small resort and market town; it was granted a Market Charter by King John in 1214. The parish church is partly 12th-century Norman and partly 17th century, with a 14th-century nave roof. Over the bricked-up Norman north door, known in the past as the Corpse Door because the dead were taken through it, is a well-worn Saxon fertility figure. Little Stretton, 1 mile south, has a charming 17th-century timber-framed manor house. Its 20th-century church is unusual in having a thatched roof.

Spectacular scenery rises west and east of Church Stretton and Little Stretton. Cardingmill Valley, which provides a splendid walk to the heights of The Long Mynd, begins on the northern outskirts of Church Stretton.

Another fine walk leads to the oval summit of Caer Caradoc, 2 miles north-east. Halfway down the heather-clad western slope of this 1506-ft hill is a cave where the British chieftain Caractacus made his last, unsuccessful stand against the Romans in AD 50.

Clunbury

A village whose much-restored Norman church retains its original nave, with two round leaded windows. On Clunbury Hill, half-a-mile south, is a prehistoric menhir, or upright monumental stone, known locally as the Fairy Stone. The stone was left by Ice Age glaciers.

Craven Arms

A quiet little market town, named after its modernised Georgian inn. The town comes to life during its sheep auctions, held from late August until late October. Stokesay Castle, three-quarters of a mile south, is a perfectly preserved 13th-century fortified stone manor, which consists of two sturdy stone towers joined by a great gabled banqueting hall with tall Gothic windows. The black-and-white Elizabethan gatehouse has a stone roof and overhanging upper storey. The nearby church, separated from the manor by a moat, has a Norman doorway, rebuilt in the 17th century.

Leebotwood

An attractive village with some picturesque 17th-century half-timbered houses. The thatched Pound Inn, the oldest house, has an outside beam dated 1650 and is finely panelled inside. The attractive 13th-century church stands on a rise among trees just west of the village. Its box-pews incorporate some 17th-century woodwork. North-west of the church, on Castle Hill, is a 260 ft long mound that was probably an early Saxon fortification built over a prehistoric barrow.

At Longnor, $1\frac{1}{2}$ miles north-east, is a 17th-century red-brick manor house with a watermill in working order. Chinese wallpaper recently found in the dining-room is probably the oldest wallpaper in England.

FORTIFIED MANOR *Stokesay Castle is one of the finest fortified manor houses in England. It takes its name from the de Sayes, its earliest occupants, who fortified it against Welsh marauders. They are believed to have built the tower, now surmounted by a 16th-century timber storey (right). The other tower (left), built by the Ludlows, is 13th century*

Clun

The westernmost of the four communities in the valley of the River Clun, immortalised in a verse of A. E. Housman's 'A Shropshire Lad':

'Clunton and Clunbury,
Clungunford and Clun
Are the quietest places
Under the sun.'

The people of Salop claim that this rhyme is older than Housman's poem and that in earlier versions the adjective varied from 'quietest' to 'prettiest', 'drunkenest', or 'wickedest'.

Discoveries during the past 100 years have shown that Clun originated in the Bronze Age and is one of the most ancient settlements in the country. The town is dominated by a keep on a hill above the river, the remains of a castle built by the Normans in the early 12th century to defend the Welsh border. The late 18th-century town hall contains a museum of local prehistoric relics.

At Pen-y-wern, about $1\frac{1}{2}$ miles south-east, the ruins of an early Bronze Age stone circle crown a 1258 ft high hill. Chapel Lawn, a further $1\frac{1}{2}$ miles south-east, has an oval earthwork, possibly used by Caractacus during his final struggle against the Romans. Its 25 ft high ramparts enclose a 12-acre camp.

The Long Mynd

A 10 mile long ridge of bleak hills, whose 4530 acres of heath and moorland, owned by the National Trust, provide some of the finest walking country in all Salop. A track of unknown age, The Port Way, runs the entire length of its crest and commands superb views across the surrounding country. Barrows and prehistoric defence earthworks abound. The Midland Gliding Club has its headquarters at Asterton, on the western edge of The Long Mynd. On fine days there are good views of the gliding.

Lydbury North

A quiet village whose great Norman parish church is rich in beautiful medieval carving; the high altar's candlesticks, dated 1640, are particularly fine. The 18th-century Walcot Hall, 1 mile south across the River Kemp, was the home of Clive of India. Plowden Hall, 2 miles north-east, the ancestral home of the Plowden family, was built for the lawyer, Edmund Plowden. It is a half-timbered Elizabethan manor with Jacobean additions, incorporating a hidden passage and chamber.

Castle above the Teme

Angling There are trout and coarse fish in the Teme at Ludlow; and in Ledwyche Brook, 1½ miles east. Also coarse fishing on the Severn at Bridgnorth, Coalport, Iron-Bridge and Buildwas.

Horse racing National Hunt meetings at Ludlow.

Events The Ludlow Summer Festival of Drama, Music and Art lasts for two weeks in June/July.

Places to see *Benthall Hall* (NT); Easter to Sept., Tues., Wed. and Sat. afternoons. *Bridgnorth Castle*: daily. *Buttercross Museum*, Ludlow: Apr. to Oct., daily. *Ironbridge Gorge Museum*: daily. *Ludlow Castle*: daily. *Midland Motor Museum*, Bridgnorth: daily, except weekday mornings Oct. to Apr. *Much Wenlock Guildhall*: Apr. to Sept., Tues. to Sat.; also Sun. and Mon. afternoons. *Much Wenlock Museum*: Apr. to Sept., weekdays, Sun. afternoon. *Wenlock Priory*: weekdays, Sun. afternoon. *The White House Museum of Buildings and Country Life*, Aston Munslow: Wed. afternoons and Sat., Apr. to Oct.; also other afternoons in June, July and Aug. *Wilderhope Manor* (NT), 7 miles south-west of Much Wenlock: Apr. to Sept., Wed. afternoons.

Information centres Bridgnorth Library, Listley Street. Tel. Bridgnorth 3358. Guildhall, Much Wenlock. Tel. Much Wenlock 727679 (seasonal). Castle Street, Ludlow. Tel. Ludlow 3857 (seasonal). The Iron Bridge Tollhouse, Ironbridge. Tel. Telford 882753.

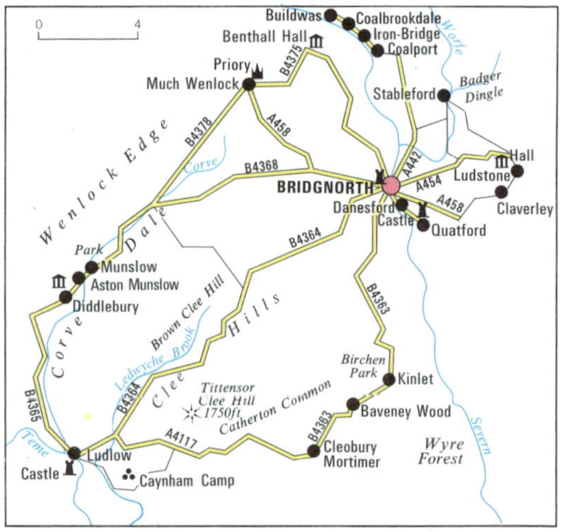

The rich agricultural land of south-east Salop (Shropshire) is dominated by the limestone ridge of Wenlock Edge, which the poet A. E. Housman described in 'A Shropshire Lad':

'On Wenlock Edge, the wood's in trouble;
His forest fleece the Wrekin heaves;
The gale, it plies the saplings double;
And thick on Severn snow the leaves.'

Between Wenlock Edge and the twin hills of Titterstone Clee and Brown Clee to the south-east, the River Corve winds through beautiful Corve Dale, which has a wealth of attractive 15th and 16th-century manor farms. The Corve joins the valley of the River Teme near Ludlow, where the ruins of the massive 11th-century sandstone castle stand out high above the river like a picture in a child's story book.

Ludlow is a perfect centre for exploring the hill and valley country around. Just outside the town Tinker's Hill, a foothill of the Clee Hills, is surmounted by the earthworks of Caynham Camp. In the south-east corner of Salop, the River Severn flows down from the Wyre Forest past old manors and farmhouses to the attractive town of Bridgenorth.

BORDER STRONGHOLD *Ludlow Castle was built in the 11th century*

To the north, the Severn flows through the Iron-Bridge Gorge, one of the major centres in Britain's Industrial Revolution. The 200-ft bridge, built in 1779 and still used by pedestrians, marked the first use of iron in industrial architecture; its designer, Abraham Darby, used woodworking joints, not understanding the use of bolts and rivets. Darby's grandfather, 70 years earlier, was the first man to smelt iron with coke; his furnace can be seen in the Ironbridge Gorge Museum that extends from Coalbrookdale to Coalport.

ASTON MUNSLOW *Ruins of a Norman dovecot stand in the White House grounds*

Bridgnorth
An ancient market town on a red sandstone ridge. The Low Town is connected to the High Town by a winding main road, a cliff railway and flights of steep steps. The Low Town, on the banks of the Severn, has some attractive old houses, including Diamond Hall, built in the late 17th century by Colonel Roger Pope with the winnings of his horse Diamond.

The High Town has a foreign air about it, with stepped streets lined by red-tiled houses with tall chimneys. The tower of the late Norman castle keep leans at 17 degrees from the perpendicular—three times the angle of the Leaning Tower of Pisa. There are views across the Severn from the walk around the castle grounds. The High Street has many 18th-century houses and inns, as well as earlier buildings. The Italianate parish church of St Mary Magdalene was built in 1794 by Thomas Telford, best remembered for his bridge engineering. It stands among Georgian houses in East Castle Street. The town hall was built in 1652 and incorporates materials from an ancient barn.

Claverley
A village rich in the black-and-white cottages that are typical of Salop. The parish church was built by the Norman knight Roger de Montgomery. Its murals are reminiscent of the Bayeux Tapestry: knights fight between formalised trees, and one knight is upside-down after being unhorsed. There is a wealth of fine Crusader tombs, and around the plinths are sculptured scallop-shells, the emblem of medieval pilgrims. The cross now in the churchyard was erected in 1349 as a memorial to victims of the Black Death.

To the north of the village the lane crosses a little trout stream, then passes between steep cliffs on its way to Ludstone, 1 mile north-east. Ludstone Hall, an early Jacobean manor house, stands on the site of an ancient monastery and is surrounded by a moat which is still filled with water.

Cleobury Mortimer
A market town which derives its name from the great Norman family of Mortimer who established themselves here in 1086. Hugh de Mortimer built a fortress in 1160 which Henry II later demolished; the earthworks can still be seen near the church. In front of the mid-16th-century Talbot Hotel, once a

to repel Welsh raiders. It was later extended, then finally abandoned in the 18th century

HERMITAGE CAVE *One of the caves in Bridgnorth's sandstone ridge is believed to have been the retreat of the 10th-century hermit Ethelred, King Athelstan's brother*

coaching inn, are the remains of an ancient market cross, where the body of Henry VIII's brother Arthur was laid during the journey from Ludlow to Worcester Cathedral, where he is buried.

Half-timbered and 18th-century houses line the tree-shaded main street. It is believed that William Langland, author of 'Piers Plowman', was born here in the 14th century and the church has a window in his memory.

Catherton Common, 3 miles west, is a good picnic spot. A prehistoric camp crowns 1750-ft Titterstone Clee Hill.

CLIFF RAILWAY *The track linking High and Low Bridgnorth has a 1 in 1½ gradient*

Kinlet
An unspoilt village, and an excellent centre for walking on the edges of the Wyre Forest. The partly Norman church, set in parkland, has memorials recalling that two ancient families of Salop, the Blounts and the Childes, once lived at Kinlet. Kinlet Hall, built in 1729 as the seat of the Childe family, is now a school. A path from the church leads through Birchen Park; another walk leads 2 miles south-west to a hamlet called Baveney Wood, which is on the edge of a pine forest.

Ludlow
The approach to Ludlow across the attractive Ludford Bridge and the steep slope of Broad Street gives an immediate impression of the town's mellow beauty. Roger Montgomery, Earl of Shrewsbury, built the massive red-sandstone keep and castle in 1085. Norman, Plantagenet and Lancastrian kings and princes developed, destroyed and rebuilt the castle. Here the two sons of Edward IV were sent for 'safe keeping' until they were taken to their deaths in the Tower of London. Henry VIII's elder brother Arthur came to the castle with his wife, Catherine of Aragon. His death in Ludlow a few months later changed the course of English history. Henry became heir apparent and later married Catherine. The terraced walk round the castle was laid out by Arthur for Catherine. John Milton saw the first production of his masque 'Comus' in the castle hall in 1634.

The sandstone Church of St Lawrence has cathedral-like grandeur. Its Perpendicular-style tower dominates castle and town. Most of its graceful interior dates from the early 15th century. The large east window depicts, in brilliant colours, the life of St Lawrence, Ludlow's patron saint. In the churchyard are the ashes of the poet A. E. Housman (1859–1936).

Near by is the Reader's House, a medieval building which has Tudor additions and a three-storey Jacobean porch. The town has several ancient inns, including the 17th-century Feathers Hotel in The Bull Ring, and the 300-year-old Angel, where Lord Nelson once stayed. There are alleyways with little antique shops, and rewarding walks can be taken along paths by the River Teme.

Much Wenlock
An old market town, granted its first charter in 1468, with many black-and-white cottages. Its half-timbered Gaol House was built in 1577. The church has a Norman doorway and the guildhall is built on sturdy wooden pillars. The priory was founded by St Milburga in the 7th century, destroyed by the Danes and rebuilt by Lady Godiva and her husband, Leofric. Benthall Hall, 4 miles north-east, is a 16th-century stone house with mullioned windows.

Munslow
A charming black-and-white village at the foot of Wenlock Edge, in the attractive Corve Dale. It has two gabled and half-timbered inns, and a Norman church with 14th-century stained glass. Aston Munslow, less than 1 mile to the south-west, has a 14th-century manor, The White House, with an agricultural museum and an attractive garden.

Quatford
The ancient castle and church look part of the rocky eminence on which this village is built. Quatford Castle is a folly with sham battlements, built in 1830. At Danesford, just to the north, are the earthworks of a Danish camp.

THE STURDY BOX-FRAMED HOUSES OF SALOP

Box-framed houses in Salop have three distinctive features—a base of the local red sandstone; an extravagant use of wood in intricate patterns; and a roof of slate from nearby Welsh quarries. Slate has been used in Salop since the Middle Ages. Its use helped to dictate the style of houses because its weight demanded stronger beams than would have been needed under a thatched roof. Because of this sturdy construction many survive today

County town on the Severn

Angling There is salmon and coarse fishing on the Severn, trout and coarse fishing on the Tern at Crudgington and on the Shropshire Union Canal at Market Drayton.

Events The Shropshire and West Midland Agricultural Show takes place in May at Shrewsbury. There is a regatta at Shrewsbury in June, and a Flower Show in mid-Aug.

Places to see in Shrewsbury
Clive House, College Hill, art exhibits, furniture, and regimental museum of 1st Queen's Dragoon Guards: Tues. to Sat.; also Mon. afternoons. *Rowley's House*, Barker Street, museum with Roman exhibits: weekdays. *Shrewsbury Castle*: weekdays; also Sun., Easter to Oct.

Places to see around Shrewsbury
Attingham Park (N.T.): Easter to Sept., afternoons except Mon. and Fri., but open Bank Hol. *Boscobel House*: weekdays, Sun. afternoons. *Coleham Pumping Station*, Longden Coleham, 5 miles south-west of Shrewsbury; beam engines and housing: Wed. and Fri. afternoons. *Haughmond Abbey*, 2 miles north-east of Shrewsbury: weekdays, Sun. afternoons. *Hodnet Hall Gardens*: Easter to late Sept., afternoons. *Viroconium Museum*, Wroxeter: daily, except Sun. morning Oct. to Mar. *Weston Park*, Shifnal: Easter to July, afternoons except Mon. and Fri.; every afternoon in Aug., weekend afternoons only in Sept.

Information centre The Square, Shrewsbury. Tel. Shrewsbury 52019.

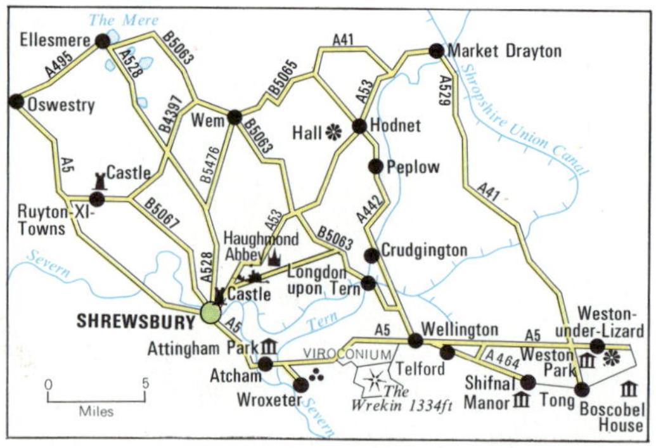

A broad, level plain lies north of the winding River Severn. Its rich arable farming land is well-watered by the Severn and its many tributaries; and charming black-and-white timbered villages reflect the prosperity of many centuries. The plains are broken by patches of hill country, the most notable of which is the Wrekin, a spectacular isolated rock mass, rising to 1334 ft south-west of Wellington. From the Wrekin peak there is a splendid view of the lush surrounding countryside.

Shrewsbury, ornamented by its pink-sandstone castle, is a historic and attractive county town on the banks of the Severn. To the south-east, beyond Wellington, the landscape is scarred by 19th-century industrialisation; but the whole area has been re-planned as a vast new town, linking several industrial centres and absorbing a population of about 250,000.

The new town has been named after Thomas Telford, the engineer and architect. In the 18th century Telford was Surveyor of Public Works for Shropshire, and the aqueduct he designed to carry the Shropshire Union Canal at Longdon upon Tern is the oldest cast-iron aqueduct in the world. It dates from 1794.

CANAL CRUISE *Goldstone Wharf is a boat centre on the Shropshire*

HILL OF THE BEACON *The cone-shaped Wrekin, rising to 1334ft beyond the Severn near Wellington, was the site of a beacon which warned of the coming of the Spanish Armada*

Atcham
A village on a horseshoe bend of the Severn, through which the river flows swiftly under a fine seven-arched bridge built in 1768. Parts of the mainly 13th to 16th-century church, the only existing one dedicated to St Eata, were built with stones from the ruins of Roman Viroconium, the modern Wroxeter.

The Mytton and Mermaid, a delightful Georgian inn, faces the lodge of Attingham Park, a mansion built in 1785 for Lord Berwick and now owned by the National Trust. Its most notable features are the south portico, which ascends through three storeys, and the fine interior decoration. John Nash designed the picture gallery and Humphry Repton laid out the grounds.

Ellesmere
A small market town with some old streets, mellow Georgian houses, half-timbered buildings and a parish church, St Mary's, which has a remarkable 15th-century wooden chancel roof.

Seven attractive small lakes, rich in bird life, make this Salop's own 'Lake District'. The Mere, at the east end of the town, covers 116 acres and is popular for boating, fishing and picnics.

Hodnet
A small hill town, rich in black-and-white half-timbered houses. St Luke's Church, mainly 14th century, has a battlemented octagonal tower and a chained Nuremberg Bible printed in 1479. A tile in the chancel commemorates a 19th-century rector, Reginald Heber, who wrote 'From Greenland's Icy Mountains' and other hymns.

Hodnet Hall, a 19th-century mansion in Tudor style, is surrounded by 60 acres of wooded gardens with a chain of pools. The house is not open to the public, but visitors to the gardens can have tea in a 17th-century barn.

Union Canal, near Market Drayton

Market Drayton
The birthplace in 1725 of Robert Clive—Clive of India—and today an attractive market town; its Wednesday ma.ket has been held for 700 years. There are many good half-timbered houses dating from the mid-17th century. In the 14th-century parish church there are several Norman features, particularly a carved capital depicting William Rufus and his court. From the sturdy tower—said to have been climbed by the youthful Clive—there are fine views across the valley of the River Tern. The 16th-century grammar school where Clive was educated stands near the church, and has a desk carved with his initials.

Oswestry
A picturesque market town set between pastureland and wild hill country, and for centuries the scene of warfare between the English and the Welsh. The town was largely rebuilt in the 19th century, but part of the Norman church survived and so did the early 15th-century grammar school, which is now divided into three cottages.

There are a number of good 17th-century houses; among them is the Llwyd Mansion, with its double-headed eagle crest granted by the Holy Roman Emperor to the Lloyds of Trenewydd for outstanding service in the Crusades. The Croeswylan, or Weeping Stone, in Morda Road, is the pedestal of a cross set up in 1559 during a plague which killed one person in seven. Ruined Oswestry Castle is in a public park.

Ruyton-XI-Towns
This red-sandstone village received its name in 1301 when 11 small hamlets united. As a result its village street stretches 1 mile—making it one of the longest in the country. The church, with its massive battlemented tower, has an engraved antique mace, and a chalice of finely hammered silver. By the church are the remains of a 14th-century castle keep, with walls and foundations more than 8 ft thick.

Shifnal
A market town, which has fine half-timbered and Georgian houses, and was described by Dickens in *The Old Curiosity Shop*. St Andrew's Church, originally Norman, was one of the few buildings to escape a great fire in 1591 which destroyed most of the town. The church, built of local sandstone, has 16th and 17th-century monuments, and two chancels, one original and the other built in the 14th century.

Shifnal Manor, a mile south, is a moated farmhouse by a stream. At Weston-under-Lizard, 5 miles north-east, is the entrance to Weston Park, a splendid post-Restoration mansion owned by the Earls of Bradford but open to the public. The great house, built in 1674, has a superb collection of furnishings and paintings, and a deer park laid out by Capability Brown.

WALL PULPIT *A 'pulpit' built by the 19th-century eccentric George Durant in the grounds of a ruined castle at Tong*

WHERE ELIZABETHANS WALKED *Houses in Grope Lane, Shrewsbury, are typical of the town's numerous half-timbered buildings, little changed since the days of Elizabeth I*

Shrewsbury
A county town beautifully situated within a loop of the Severn. Everywhere are superb black-and-white buildings in plaster and weathered timber, including Abbot's House (1450); the tall gabled Ireland's Mansion (1575); and the early 16th-century Rowley's House, which has a museum of Roman remains.

St Mary's Church dates back to the 12th century and has a lofty stone spire, fine medieval carving and stained-glass windows. The circular St Chad's, designed in 1792 by George Steuart, stands in a prominent position overlooking the Severn. It is one of the country's few round churches and has a strangely shaped tower which looks like a minaret topped by a dome.

The town's library is now housed in the original early 17th-century buildings of Shrewsbury's public school. The naturalist Charles Darwin, who was born in Shrewsbury in 1809, attended the school, and a statue of him stands in front of the library.

The Lion is an ancient coaching inn with a splendid ballroom. Among its famous 19th-century visitors were the singer Jenny Lind, the violinist Paganini, and Charles Dickens. The Battle of Shrewsbury (1403) was fought at Battlefield, 3 miles north of the town to the west of the A53.

Tong
A pretty village in undulating countryside, with some half-timbered houses. Dickens said it was this village he had in mind when writing the closing scenes of *The Old Curiosity Shop*. The early 15th-century red-sandstone church of St Bartholomew, known as the 'village Westminster Abbey', has a battlemented tower with a short spire, and a collection of fine monuments, many delicately carved in alabaster. They include those of Henry V's High Constable and Sir Richard Vernon, a 15th-century Speaker of the House of Commons.

Boscobel House, 3 miles east, is where Charles II hid after the Battle of Worcester in 1651. The famous 'Royal Oak' in the grounds is said to have grown from one of the acorns from a tree in which the King took refuge.

Wem
A small market town famous for its strong ales, and linked with the infamous Judge Jeffreys, who became Baron of Wem in 1685 and lived at Lowe Hall. This house, built in 1666, still has its original Jacobean interior. Much of the original town was burnt down in 1677, but a few delightful buildings remain, such as the black-and-white Old Hall and the 14th-century tower of the parish church.

In Arnold Bennett country

Boating On the Trent and Mersey Canal, and the Macclesfield Canal, at Alton Towers and Rudyard Reservoir.

Angling Coarse fishing on the Trent and Mersey Canal, Macclesfield Canal, Trentham Park Lake, Endon Brook near Cheddleton, Rudyard Reservoir and the Churnet below Leek; and trout on the River Manifold at Longnor, and in Tittesworth Reservoir near Leek.

Events Club Day in Leek is a Festival of Sunday Schools usually held the second Sat. in July. Endon has a well-dressing ceremony on Spring Bank Hol. Longnor has a Wakes Festival in Sept.

Places to see *Alton Towers*; grounds only: Easter to early Oct., daily. *Ford Green Hall*, Smallthorne: weekdays, except Tues. and Fri.; also Sun. afternoons. *Gladstone Pottery Museum*, Longton: weekdays, except Mon. Oct. to Mar., and Sun. afternoons. *Ilam Park* (NT): daily. *Leek Art Gallery*, Nicholson Institute: weekdays. *Spitfire Museum*, Stoke-on-Trent: weekdays.

Information centres Central Library, Bethesda Street, Hanley. Tel. Stoke-on-Trent 21242. 18 St Edward Street, Leek. Tel. Leek 385509. Gladstone Pottery Museum, Longton. Tel. Stoke-on-Trent 319232.

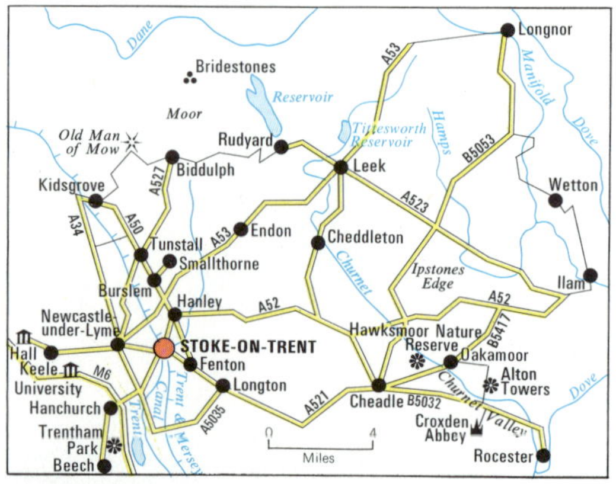

Rugged stone-walled moorland country, including a large part of the Peak District National Park, occupies the north-eastern corner of Staffordshire. The River Dane comes tumbling down to Three Shires Head, the meeting-place of Cheshire, Derbyshire and Staffordshire, then flows south-west through wild, little-travelled country along the boundary between Cheshire and Staffordshire.

A dramatic rock-formation called The Old Man of Mow is 2 miles west of Biddulph, and a nearby crag that is surmounted by a ruined stone tower gives splendid views across the Cheshire Plains. Just north-east, the lonely Biddulph moorland road cuts across a high plateau called Shepherd's Cross.

To the south and east of Leek, in the valleys of the Rivers Manifold and Churnet, is some of the loveliest countryside in England. Between the valleys are well-marked footpaths through woodland, and to the north are wide expanses of wind-swept heathlands where, centuries ago, the Romans mined copper and lead.

Industry dominates the area around Stoke-on-Trent, where the cluster of towns made famous as the 'Five Towns' of the novels of Arnold Bennett (1867–1931) form the Potteries. The Trent and Mersey Canal, which played such a large part in developing the Potteries and creating the Industrial Revolution, is today, after long neglect, coming back into its own, largely for pleasure craft. After flowing through the heart of the Potteries, the canal joins the River Trent.

UNIVERSITY CHAPEL *A chapel for all denominations is part of the University of Keele, established in 1962 and noted for courses which combine the Arts with social science training*

SHAM CASTLE *Close to The Old Man of Mow, a high crag on the Cheshire–Staffordshire border is capped by a ruined tower known as Mow Cop castle. It was built as a folly by Randle Wilbraham in 1760, and never served any purpose except to decorate the landscape*

Alton Towers

The turreted and castellated shell of what was once a vast 19th-century mansion built in Gothic style is surrounded by beautiful parklands that have become one of Staffordshire's great pleasure parks.

In the early 19th century, Charles Talbot, 15th Earl of Shrewsbury, transformed 600 acres of barren hillside by planting rare shrubs, trees and exotic flowers, and by adding lakes, Italianate fountains, conservatories and a Chinese pagoda. In 1831 his nephew John enlarged what had been a modest lodge into the mansion of Alton Towers.

The parks today include model and miniature railways and boating lakes. There is a memorial in the grounds to Charles Talbot, bearing the inscription 'He made the desert smile'.

To the north-west the River Churnet flows from bare, rocky hillsides into the lush, verdant lower Churnet Valley, where lanes and paths lead through dense woods, and there are attractive walks in every direction.

Biddulph
A small, well-planned industrial town set in the heart of lonely moorland. The parish church contains beautiful Flemish stained glass. Biddulph Old Hall, dated 1558, was badly damaged by Parliamentary troops during the Civil War but has recently been restored.

On Biddulph Moor, rising to over 1000 ft just east of the town, is the source of the 170 mile long River Trent, England's third-longest river after the Severn and the Thames. To the north are the Bridestones, a burial chamber in which it is said a Viking and his Anglo-Saxon wife were interred.

Cheadle
An old market town in the North Staffordshire hills, and a gateway to the richly wooded Churnet Valley. The 200-ft steeple of the Roman Catholic church, designed in 1846 by A. W. Pugin, one of the architects of the Houses of Parliament, is a landmark for miles around. There are picturesque half-timbered Elizabethan houses, and an ancient market cross.

Hawksmoor Nature Reserve, 2 miles north-east, was founded by the Staffordshire naturalist J. R. B. Masefield, a cousin of the poet John Masefield, and is now owned by the National Trust. Nature trails run through its 250 acres of moors, marshes and woodland, and provide a close view of birdlife.

Ilam
A village in the attractive Manifold Valley. Its church contains a carved Norman font, and there are two Saxon crosses in the churchyard. The River Manifold, joined by the River Hamps, disappears underground near Beeston Tor in dry weather and reappears in the grounds of Ilam Hall; Dr Johnson experimented with a marked cork to prove that they were the same waters.

William Congreve, the Restoration playwright, wrote *The Old Bachelor* while convalescing in Ilam. Old Steeplehouse Farm, half a mile north-west, gives views of the Manifold Valley.

Bones and teeth of early animals, including cave lions and cave hyenas, have been found in caves, such as Elder Bush Cave, along the Manifold Valley. Two attractive villages beside the Manifold gorge are Longnor and Wetton; the church at Longnor is notable for its memorial to a veteran of the Battle of Ramillies (1706), who is said to have lived to 112 years.

BENNETT AND HIS DOG

A cartoon of the novelist Arnold Bennett and his dog, drawn by Sir William Nicholson (1872–1949). Bennett was born near Hanley in 1867, and most of his famous novels, including *The Old Wives' Tale, The Card,* and *Clayhanger,* are set in the towns of the Potteries, which he immortalised as the 'Five Towns'

Kidsgrove
An industrialised town in the western foothills of the Pennines which owes its origin to Josiah Wedgwood, 'father' of the English pottery industry, who proposed the plan for the Trent and Mersey Canal to link the Potteries to the sea. His engineer, James Brindley, took 11 years to build a tunnel more than 1½ miles long through Harecastle Ridge in Kidsgrove, and the men who worked on the canal became the town's first inhabitants. The tunnel, now disused, still exists.

The town's coal mines and blast furnaces have been succeeded by the electronics and computer industries.

Newcastle-under-Lyme
Although the town has vast, sprawling collieries, ironworks and some potteries, it is set in rural countryside among woods and pleasant little villages.

Keele, 3 miles west, once an administrative centre of the powerful Knights Templar, has a modern university, its contemporary buildings grouped around the old Keele Hall.

Madeley Manor, another ancient home about 2 miles west of Keele, has become a College of Education. Izaak Walton stayed here with his host John Offley, to whom he dedicated his book *The Compleat Angler*.

Trentham Gardens and Park, 3½ miles south, were once the property of the Dukes of Sutherland, and are now Staffordshire's largest pleasure grounds. The gardens were mostly laid out by the architect Sir Joseph Paxton.

Only a length of wall in the Queen Elizabeth Park now remains of the 12th-century 'new' castle from which the town takes its name.

Rudyard
A delightful village with a pretty cluster of houses and gardens, set at the south end of lovely woods bordering Rudyard Reservoir. The reservoir was built to supply water to the Trent and Mersey Canal. There are good walks and picnic spots on the shore, and boating and fishing are permitted.

Rudyard Kipling, the novelist and poet, was named after the village, since it was here that his parents became engaged in the 1860's. Walks along the shore of Rudyard Reservoir lead to fascinating caverns, curious rock formations and Roman copper workings.

CORKSCREW FOUNTAIN *A spring 2 miles away feeds the Corkscrew Fountain in the grounds of Alton Towers. The gardens were laid out between 1814 and 1827*

Stoke-on-Trent
The names of Wedgwood, Minton, Copeland and Spode are known all over the world as incomparable examples of fine pottery and porcelain. All these wares are manufactured in this corner of north Staffordshire, where excavations prove that pottery has been made since long before the Roman occupation. The five towns of Tunstall, Burslem, Hanley, Longton and Stoke, made famous in Arnold Bennett's novels, amalgamated in 1910 together with a sixth town, Fenton, to form the one town of Stoke-on-Trent, now a city of 36 square miles. Many of the pottery firms have also merged, into a company called Allied Potteries.

It was in 1759 that Josiah Wedgwood, born in Burslem in 1730, set up his own business. The beauty of his pottery, after the brilliant Classical sculptor and designer John Flaxman had stamped his own creative genius on it, established a fashion for Wedgwood all over the civilised world. The industry grew to an importance which has never diminished. The Regency church in Stoke-on-Trent has a memorial to Wedgwood, and the Wedgwood Memorial Institute in Burslem commemorates the site of his first pottery factory.

Arnold Bennett's family lived from 1880 at 205 Waterloo Road, Cobridge, and Hanley was the home of Reginald Mitchell, designer of the Spitfire fighter plane, for most of his life.

At Smallthorne, near Burslem, Ford Green Hall, a fine Elizabethan timber-framed house, had associations with Izaak Walton and the early Quakers and now has a charming little museum.

The Staffordshire Potteries

The north Staffordshire towns which Arnold Bennett made famous in his novels are the traditional workshop of English potters. During the last 300 years, the craftsmen of Tunstall, Burslem, Hanley, Stoke, Fenton and Longton have made English pottery at its best: the finely shaped, handsomely decorated wares of Wedgwood, Minton, Spode and Copeland, which are sought after by collectors throughout the world.

It was not by chance that the Potteries came to north Staffordshire, for the towns had ample supplies of clay, as well as coal and water, on their doorstep. Fragments of pottery discovered in the area date back to Neolithic times (*c.* 2500–1900 BC), and excavations have uncovered later Roman and Saxon wares. Kilns found at Sneyd Green, Stoke, were proof that the 14th-century potters fired, or baked, their clay with local coal.

The early potters could not easily transport their fragile wares, and they tended to cater only for local needs. In the 1680's the Staffordshire potters were primarily engaged in making plain earthenware articles for ordinary household use; but for special occasions—such as coronations, birthdays or weddings—they produced boldly designed dishes, pots or mugs.

The art of the potter was given the impetus to greater refinement by the introduction to England in 1657 of a beverage made from infusion with hot water of the leaves of *Camellia sinensis*, an evergreen shrub from China. Within a few years, tea-drinking was fashionable among the rich; and the Staffordshire potters had the skill to meet a growing demand for high-quality pottery from which to drink it. By about 1690, the Elers brothers were making cups, saucers, teapots, tea-caddies and sugar bowls in stoneware, a hard, opaque pottery which was an improvement on the softer earthenware. Unlike earthenware, stoneware is non-porous and can be left unglazed.

The experience gained in these years prepared the way for the achievements of Josiah Wedgwood (1730–95). After learning his trade at Burslem, where he was born, Wedgwood set up as a master potter. Queen Charlotte, wife of George III, liked his cream-coloured pottery so much that it came to be known as 'Queen's Ware'. He later developed white relief work on a blue background—the style for which the name Wedgwood is best known.

During the later 18th century the building of canals helped north Staffordshire to remain the centre of this flourishing industry. China clay and other materials from the West Country enabled potters to produce further refinements, and wares could now be sent by waterway for export by sea to the Continent and to North America.

MERMAID PLATE *The early Staffordshire potters made domestic wares in red or brown clays, but they could also produce fine dishes like this one (c. 1670) by Thomas Toft. These were decorated in the 'slip-trailed' technique—the slip, or watered-down clay, being applied like icing on a cake*

CREAMWARE PLATE *In 1764 Wedgwood moved his business at Burslem to larger premises at Bell Works, and in 1765 he perfected his cream-coloured earthenware, which came to be known as Queen's Ware. Many of Wedgwood's pieces, like the plate above, were decorated with enamel transfer prints by Sadler and Green, a Liverpool firm*

CHANGING SCENE *The bottle-shaped brick ovens of the Potteries were among the great industrial landmarks of England, like the smoky mill chimneys of Lancashire. But today the Staffordshire skyline is vastly changed. All but a few 'bottle ovens' have gone—made redundant as electricity and gas replace the coal fires of the kilns. The few remaining are no longer used. A Spode factory oven still stands at Stoke and there is a huddle of disused ovens at Longton (above). Such relics as the Spode oven are preserved to remind the modern age of the Potteries' past; today the district is no longer seen through a filter of thick haze, being one of the smokeless zones of England*

WILLOW PATTERN *Josiah Spode, who became a master potter in 1770, made pottery printed from transfers in 'underglaze-blue'. His son, Josia II, perfected bone china. The Willow Pattern, used with variations since c. 1780, shows a mandarin pursuing his eloping daughter. As he overtakes her, she and her lover are changed into birds*

'BELL-LADY' *In the early 18th century, high-fired stoneware was glazed by throwing salt into the kiln. Later, Devon clays were used to whiten the body. Figures like this 'bell-lady' are attributed to Aaron Wood, a mould-maker of Burslem*

HUSSAR *Early creamware was made with the same clays as stoneware, but the firing temperature was lowered, resulting in an earthenware, to which a lead-glaze was added. This figure (c. 1745) is a type associated with John Astbury*

COLOURED TEAPOT *Lead-glazed creamware, coloured 'tortoiseshell' by high-temperature oxides, is mainly associated with the potter Thomas Whieldon who, c. 1740, was producing the full range of popular Staffordshire wares*

PINEAPPLE TEAPOT *Josiah Wedgwood opened his first factory at Burslem in 1759. Among his earliest wares were teapots in the form of cauliflowers and pineapples. Many were modelled by William Greatbach, Wedgwood adding the glazes*

BLACK VASE *In about 1767 Wedgwood produced his fine black unglazed stoneware, which he called 'basaltes'. This was used to reproduce wares being excavated at Herculaneum and Pompeii, which were thought to be Etruscan; hence 'Etruria', the name Wedgwood gave to his new factory*

NINE MUSES *The material commonly associated with Wedgwood is jasperware—stoneware decorated with white reliefs on blue, lavender, green, yellow or black. John Flaxman modelled the original for a fine vase depicting the Nine Muses. Wares of this type bear the mark* 'WEDGWOOD'

TOBY JUG *While Wedgwood was making more refined wares, earlier traditions were continued by Ralph Wood of Burslem and his son of the same name. The Toby jug was named after Toby Fillpot, 'a thirsty old soul' about whom a humorous ballad was published in the 1760's*

DRUNKEN PARSON *Finely modelled character studies such as 'The Vicar and Moses' (above), depicting a drunken parson whose clerk read the lessons, date from c. 1775. Many group 'portraits' of this type have been attributed to the partners Ralph Wood Jnr and Enoch Wood*

MINTON *Fine transfer-printed earthenware was made at Stoke from 1793 by Thomas Minton, who was trained as an engraver. In 1836 he was succeeded by his son Herbert. This Minton bowl and cover is a duplicate from a service presented by Queen Victoria to the Emperor of Austria*

'INNOCENCE' *White Parian ware was introduced at Copeland's factory in Stoke c. 1842. It was ideal for the miniature reproduction of marble sculpture. The figure above was made in 1847 from a reduced model by the sculptor J. H. Foley of his original figure called 'Innocence'*

FLATBACK *From the early 19th century many Staffordshire potters made simple earthenware groups which were sold for pence at fairs and markets. These flatbacks, usually made in a two-piece mould, with little modelling on the reverse, were popular in the Victorian era*

PÂTE-SUR-PÂTE *This style of popular and expensive decoration was achieved by building a thick layer of white clay on a coloured ground and then carving the clay as a bas-relief. The vase above bears the signature of M. L. Solon, who decorated it at the Minton factory c. 1890*

Woodland of Cannock Chase

Boating On the Rivers Penk, Sow and Trent. Sailing on the Trent and Mersey Canal, Shropshire Union Canal, Staffs. and Worcs. Canal. Boat hire at Burton upon Trent, Stafford and Stone.

Angling Coarse fishing on the Trent and Mersey Canal and on the Shropshire Union Canal; on the Sow at Stafford and the Penk at Penkridge.

Horse racing National Hunt meetings are held at Uttoxeter.

Events Burton upon Trent holds a market on Thur. and Sat. Dr. Johnson's birthday is celebrated at Uttoxeter on Sept. 19. The Abbots Bromley Horn Dance takes place on Mon. following the first Sun. after Sept. 4.

Places to see *Bass Museum*, Burton upon Trent: daily. *Blithfield Hall*: closed 1979. *Burton upon Trent Museum and Art Gallery*: weekdays. *Izaak Walton Cottage*, Shallowford: Thur. to Sun. *Shugborough* (NT): Mar. to Oct., Tues. to Fri. and Bank Hol. Mon.; also Sat. and Sun. afternoons. *Stafford Museum and Art Gallery*: Tues. to Sat. *Wedgwood Museum*, Barlaston: Mon. to Fri.

Information centre Town Clerk's Office, Town Hall, Burton upon Trent. Tel. Burton 45369. Public Relations Office, Borough Hall, Eastgate Street, Stafford. Tel. Stafford 3181.

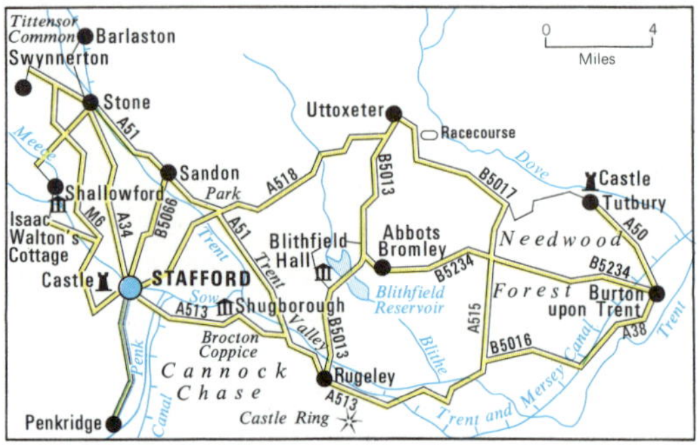

Although mid-Staffordshire contains the busy county town of Stafford and the great brewing industries of Burton upon Trent, it consists mainly of a broad belt of rich pastureland, divided into prosperous dairy farms, and crossed by canals and gently flowing rivers. Some of the most attractive scenery is to be seen from the towpaths alongside the Trent and Mersey Canal and the Shropshire Union Canal. The rivers include the Trent, the Dove and the unusually beautiful Blithe.

To the south lies Cannock Chase, 26 square miles of protected moorland and forest which was once a hunting ground of Plantagenet kings. The Chase rises to 800 ft at Castle Ring, and there are magnificent views across what is classified as one of Britain's Areas of Outstanding Natural Beauty. The remains of another former royal forest survive in the oaks and hollies of the vast Needwood Forest, between the Dove and the Blithe to the north-east. From the wooded parklands of Blithfield Hall, near Abbots Bromley, there are views of the glittering Blithfield Reservoir. South-west of Stone, between the Rivers Trent and Sow, is the village of Shallowford, once the home of Izaak Walton, author of *The Compleat Angler*. Walton gave his half-timbered cottage, with the River Meece flowing through the grounds, to the town of Stafford and it is kept as a memorial to him.

HADRIAN'S ARCH *The triumphal arch at Shugborough, a copy of Hadrian's Arch in Athens, was built for Thomas Anson in 1761 to commemorate the achievements of his brother, Admiral Anson*

BREWING AT BURTON *Though most beer is today mass-produced in huge vats, Bass beer is still brewed at Burton upon Trent in individual barrels as it has been since the 18th century*

Abbots Bromley
A delightful old town with typical Staffordshire half-timbered houses and an ancient church. The Bagot family lived here for 400 years before building their hall at Blithfield in the 15th century.

The town is famous for its annual Horn Dance in September. The dance, which has its origins in Anglo-Saxon times, is performed on the road by 12 dancers and musicians in Tudor costume. Six men balance ancient reindeer antlers on their shoulders; a seventh rides a hobby-horse; a 'fool' capers in multi-coloured motley; and with them are a boy with a bow and arrow, and a young girl. The dancers advance and retreat in stately fashion. Their dance is accompanied by an accordionist and a triangle player.

Burton upon Trent
A town known since the Middle Ages as the centre of British brewing, and pervaded by a scent of hops and malt. Michael Bass, who became Lord Burton in the 19th century, gave the town some of its finest buildings, among them the town hall and the churches of St Paul and St Modwen. There are three bridges with views of the Trent: the wide, modern bridge; the old wood and iron Ferry Bridge; and a footbridge which connects the market-place to Andressy Island, the site of the Ox Hay children's playground and gardens. Pleasant riverside walks provide vantage points for watching speedboat racing and sailing.

Cannock Chase
An oasis of forest land and heath on the doorstep of south Staffordshire's Black Country. It is the remnant of the vast hunting ground which covered much of Staffordshire in Norman times. There are miles of lovely walks through forest land, particularly glorious in spring and autumn. Brocton Coppice, to the north-west, still has some of the original great oaks remaining. Good viewpoints include the 600-ft Coppice Hill, from which the Clee Hills, 30 miles to the south-west in Shropshire, are often visible. The Chase has a large herd of fallow deer, descendants of those which escaped the arrows of the Plantagenets. Foxes and badgers abound, and lizards slither over rocks on the heathlands. Birdlife ranges from meadow-pipits to buzzards, and woodpeckers and nuthatches are common.

German and Commonwealth cemeteries on Cannock Chase commemorate the dead of two World Wars; the German cemetery includes the graves of the first Zeppelin crew shot down over Britain in the First World War.

Shugborough
A great white colonnaded mansion, set in beautiful grounds within a bend of the Sow as it joins the Trent. The house is the seat of the Anson family, Earls of Lichfield, and contains their magnificent collection of paintings and 18th-century furniture. The house, built in 1693 and enlarged in the 18th century, has been well restored by the National Trust. The beautiful gardens are reached by a bridge spanning a landscaped lake; they contain many 'Classical' monu-

THE HORN DANCERS OF ABBOTS BROMLEY—A MEDIEVAL CUSTOM LIVES ON

On the Monday following the first Sunday after September 4, dancers and musicians in Tudor dress perform a Horn Dance at Abbots Bromley to commemorate granting of hunting rights to villagers in Needwood Forest. The reindeer horns (above) date from the Anglo-Saxon period and never leave the parish

ments, and an elegant little Chinese House. This was designed by an officer of a ship commanded by Admiral Anson, whose defeat of the French in 1747 is commemorated by a triumphal arch.

Stafford
A charming county town on the River Sow, listed as a borough in the Domesday Book in 1086, and with a history dating back to before the Norman Conquest. St Mary's Church, standing in a 'Garden of Remembrance' for the dead of both World Wars, has a Norman font where Izaak Walton, who was born at 92 Eastgate Street in 1593, was baptised; there is also a bust in the north aisle inscribed 'Izaak Walton, Piscator'. The imposing central tower was built in the 13th century.

The Norman Church of St Chad has a fine chancel arch and nave arcades. There are some well-preserved houses dating from the 17th and 18th centuries; the oldest is the High House in Greengate Street, which sheltered Charles I and Prince Rupert for three nights in 1642. The Royal Brine Baths, opened in 1892, used brine extracted from salt deposits discovered in Stafford in the 19th century. The Baths have now been converted for freshwater swimming.

Stafford Castle, $1\frac{1}{2}$ miles south-west of the town, was rebuilt in the 19th century on the site of a 14th-century castle, but is now in ruins.

Stone
A pleasant, mellow old town with ruins of an ancient priory and some solid 18th and 19th-century houses in its long High Street. Admiral Jervis, who became Earl St Vincent after his naval victory at Cape St Vincent in 1797, is buried in the parish churchyard. Peter de Wint, one of England's greatest water-colourists, was born at Stone in 1784.

The River Trent and the Trent and Mersey Canal run parallel south of the town, and there are good views across the Trent Valley countryside. From Sandon Hall Park, 4 miles south-east along the canal, there are magnificent vistas of the Wrekin and the Clent Hills.

Swynnerton
An attractive village on high ground, surrounded by richly wooded country. There are a few well-thatched cottages, and the ancient blacksmith's forge, now a garage, looks out on to the main street, as does The Fitzherbert Arms, which dates from Jacobean times. The partly Norman Church of St Mary has a richly carved tower arch. An 8 ft high statue of Christ, believed to be late Norman, and found *c.* 1830 hidden in a family vault, is thought to have come from Lichfield Cathedral.

Tutbury
A picturesque town on the banks of the Dove, with a wide main street and a wealth of Tudor and Georgian houses. Its 15th-century half-timbered inn, The Dog and Partridge, was once a home of the Curzon family of Kedleston Hall in Derbyshire.

The priory church, built in 1100, is one of the finest Norman churches in the Midlands. Its west front, built 50 years later, has a magnificent doorway and seven arches with rich carving. The ruins of a once-imposing castle include three towers: one built by John of Gaunt in the 14th century; a south tower with a winding staircase and two chambers; and the high tower in which Mary, Queen of Scots was imprisoned for a time during 1568 and 1569.

Uttoxeter
An unspoilt market town, in which a Wednesday cattle market is still the main source of prosperity, as it has been since the town's first charter in 1251. There are some charming half-timbered houses round the market-place where Samuel Johnson, as a boy, steadfastly refused to work behind a bookstall belonging to his father, a Lichfield bookseller. When Johnson was an old man, he showed his regret by standing in the market-place for several hours of penance in the heavy rain. A plaque near the spot depicts the scene.

GOATS OF BLITHFIELD HALL *A unique herd of wild goats, called Bagot goats, is kept in the grounds of Blithfield Hall. The goats are named after the Bagot family, who were presented with the original herd by Richard II for giving him good hunting*

Birthplace of Dr Johnson

Boating On the Birmingham and Coventry Canal at Tamworth; the Staffs. and Worcs. Canal; the Trent and Mersey Canal.

Angling Coarse fishing on the Birmingham and Coventry Canal; the Trent and Mersey Canal; the Staffs. and Worcs. Canal; on the River Anker at Tamworth, the River Trent at Alrewas; Himley Park lakes, near Wolverhampton.

Events A parade, the Greenhill Bower, is held in Lichfield on Spring Bank Hol. Mon. Wolverhampton Music Festival is held in June.

Places to see *Bantock House Museum*, Wolverhampton, early porcelains and enamels: weekdays, Sun. afternoon. *Bilston Museum and Art Gallery*: weekdays. *Black Country Museum*, Dudley: mid-May to Aug., daily except Sat. *Chillingham Hall*, 8 miles north of Wolverhampton: May to mid-Sept., Thur. afternoon; also Sun. afternoon in Aug. *Dr Johnson's Birthplace Museum*, Lichfield: Tues. to Sat.; also Sun. afternoon, May to Sept. *Dudley Castle*: daily. *Dudley Museum and Art Gallery*: weekdays. *Letocetum* (NT), museum: weekdays, Sun. afternoon. *Lichfield Art Gallery and Museum*: weekdays. *Moseley Old Hall* (NT): Mar. to Oct., Wed., Thur., Sat., Sun. and Bank Hol. afternoons; Nov., Wed. and Sun. afternoons. *Oak House*, West Bromwich: weekdays; also Sun. afternoons May to Sept. *Tamworth Castle Museum*: weekdays, Sun. afternoons. *Wightwick Manor* (NT), near Wolverhampton: afternoons only (closed Feb.): Thur., Sat., Bank Hol. Sun. and Mon.; also Wed., May to Sept.

Information centres Tourist Centre, 21 Dam Street, Lichfield. Tel. Lichfield 52109. Council Offices, Church Street, Tamworth. Tel. Tamworth 3561.

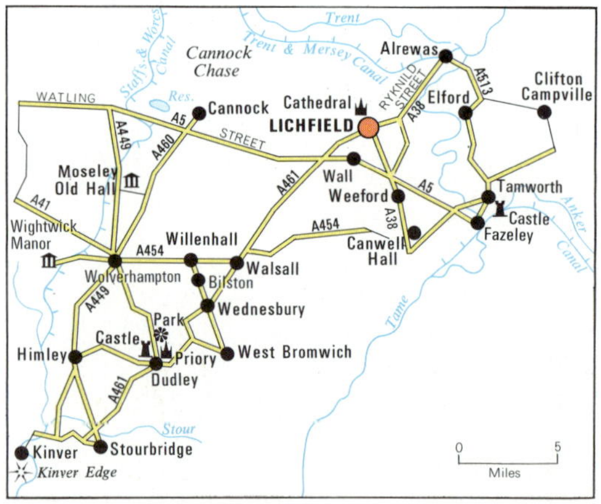

The limitless energy of the Black Country creates vast furnaces, their flames lighting up the night sky; activates great rolling mills, factories and mines; and makes a mammoth contribution to the national prosperity. Wolverhampton, at its centre, has been manufacturing locks and keys since the 16th century, and is today involved in almost every field of heavy manufacturing. Dudley rolls and smelts steel and iron; West Bromwich mainly makes springs; Willenhall turns out locks and keys by the million, as well as iron castings and steel strips; Walsall is England's centre for the manufacture of leather goods and fine saddlery; and Wednesbury is famed for manufacturing railway rolling-stock, steel tubes and metal pressings for the motor industry.

The Black Country is the result of Britain's 19th-century Industrial Revolution, but in spite of the scars which can still be seen in south Staffordshire, there is considerable pastoral, wooded and hilly country where not so much as a smokestack mars the landscape. Lichfield, to the east, is a charming small cathedral city and the birthplace of Dr Samuel Johnson. South-east, just below the route of the Roman Watling Street, a richly wooded area extends southwards to the Warwickshire border.

PENITENT DR JOHNSON *A piece of relief sculpture on the plinth of a statue of Dr Johnson in Market Square, Lichfield, recalls an incident when he was a young man. His father, who kept a bookshop in Breadmarket Street, asked him to look after a bookstall in the market at Uttoxeter. The proud Johnson refused, but in his old age he had a guilty conscience and did penance by standing in the market-place in the rain. The house in Breadmarket Street where Dr Johnson was born in 1709 is now a museum with many relics of his life, including manuscripts, letters and his walking stick. Townspeople honour his birthday, September 18, by gathering round the statue on the nearest Saturday to it. A statue of James Boswell, Dr Johnson's biographer, is also in Market Square. A third memorial in the square is to Edward Wightman, who became the last man in England to die at the stake when he was burnt there for heresy in April, 1612*

TOOLS OF THE LOCKSMITH'S TRADE

Locks and keys have been made in Wolverhampton and Willenhall for more than 400 years. Nowadays they are mostly machine-made in factories, but a few locksmiths still survive making mainly non-corroding brass locks to be fitted in ships and at ammunition stores

Alrewas
A beautiful, tranquil village with charming black-and-white thatched cottages, some dating from the 15th century. Its parish church was built in the 13th century, and the lofty arcades give grace and beauty to a fine interior.

Dudley
This ancient industrial town, in the newly created county of West Midlands, rises on ridges between 400 and 800 ft above sea level, and offers broad vistas, to the north over rolling Staffordshire hills, to the west over the Severn Valley, and to the south over the pasturelands of Hereford and Worcester. The ruins of Dudley Castle, with some walls 8 ft thick, date from the 13th century, and rise above magnificent woodlands. In a wooded valley below Castle Hill are the ruins of a Norman priory.

Also in the shadow of Castle Hill, at the Tipton end of the Dudley Canal Tunnel, is an open-air museum devoted to the life and industry of the whole of the Black Country.

The Dudley Canal Tunnel, which was recently re-opened, was an extremely busy waterway in the last century as it was part of the shortest route from the Black Country to the Severn. In one year, 1855, more than 41,000 boats went through it.

The dominating Church of St Thomas the Apostle, built in 1817, has a

'THE LADIES OF THE VALE' *The cathedral's three sandstone spires rise above Lichfield. The largest was destroyed by Cromwell's men during the Civil War, and later rebuilt*

graceful spire and above the marble altar is a carving of St Thomas by Samuel Joseph, who also has works in Westminster Abbey.

Wren's Nest Hill, 1 mile north-west of Dudley Castle, is a National Nature Reserve which also contains fossils of creatures at least 300 million years old.

Elford
A town on a curve of the River Tame. St Peter's Church was mostly rebuilt in the 19th century, but retains its 15th-century Perpendicular tower and its fine collection of tombs, mostly in the Howard Chantry Chapel. The earliest is the 14th-century alabaster table-tomb of Thomas de Arderne, a knight who fought at Poitiers, and his wife. On the sides of the tomb are 22 figures with angels bearing coats of arms. The church also has a collection of well-preserved shields, and a monument to the grandson of Sir John Stanley who was killed by a tennis ball in 1460.

A walk eastwards leads after 4½ miles to the small village of Clifton Campville, which has a medieval parish church notable for its tower and spire, old screens and carved stalls.

Kinver
A small border town surrounded by beautiful wooded countryside. Some fine old houses survive in the main street, and the parish church, standing high above the town, has good Norman as well as 14th and 15th-century features.

Steep paths lead to the top of Kinver Edge, a dramatic hill that dominates the town. Its 198 acres of heath and woodland are National Trust property. Halfway up is Holy Austin Rock, a huge sandstone formation with cave-like excavations, probably washed out by water over millions of years, and once used as dwellings by vanished tribes and hermits. From the summit, a perfect spot for picnics, can be seen four ranges of hills—the Clents, the Cotswolds, the Malverns and the Clees.

Lichfield
A rapidly modernising but still charming cathedral city, dominated by the cathedral's three graceful sandstone spires, known as 'The Ladies of the Vale'. The spacious Close is still a haven of peace in which gracious 14th and 15th-century houses, forming the Vicar's Close, surround a stretch of vivid green lawn.

The first cathedral was consecrated in AD 700 by St Chad, but the present building was mainly completed between 1195 and 1325. The cathedral's west front is rich with sandstone statuary, and five statues on the north-western tower and the bas-relief of Christ in Majesty above the central pillar are from the original cathedral. The 16th-century stained-glass windows in the Lady Chapel are among the best in England. They came from a dissolved Cistercian abbey in Herckenrode, in Belgium, early in the 19th century. In the cathedral library is one of the finest illuminated manuscripts in Europe. It includes the complete gospels of St Matthew and St Mark, and is called St Chad's Gospels, in memory of the missionary who became Bishop of Mercia in AD 669.

The house on the corner of Breadmarket Street where Samuel Johnson was born in 1709 is now a Johnsonian Museum. In the cobbled square is a statue of Dr Johnson, and on the other side of the square is a monument to James Boswell, his biographer. David Garrick, the actor, lived in Lichfield with his family, and in 1736 studied Latin and Greek under Samuel Johnson, who was then a schoolmaster at a grammar school. Another famous man born in Lichfield was Elias Ashmole, the antiquarian who left his priceless collection of antiquities to Oxford University. They are now in the Ashmolean Museum at Oxford.

At Wall, 2 miles south-west, is the excavated bath-house of a Roman posting station, Letocetum, on Watling Street. It is the most complete of its kind in Britain, and there is a museum.

Wolverhampton
The so-called 'Capital of the Black Country', now famous for its iron and brass foundries, possessed an important monastery before the Norman Conquest, and by 1258 was a thriving market town. Since the Second World War, many unattractive buildings of the Industrial Revolution have been removed by intelligent new planning and redevelopment. The Mander Centre and Wulfrun shopping precincts are a tribute to contemporary British architects, and there are fine parks, art galleries and museums. The large, mainly 15th-century parish church of St Peter, built of red stone, has a notable octagonal font and stone pulpit, and a carved lion on the balustrade of the lofty staircase.

On the Penn road to the south-west there is rural scenery and good walking country towards Himley, 6 miles away.

Moseley Old Hall, 4 miles north, is a fine Elizabethan house with many secret passages. Charles II hid there after the Battle of Worcester in 1651—the bed he slept in is on show. The hall, now owned by the National Trust, has a splendid collection of furniture, portraits, documents and treasures belonging to the Whitgreave family, who sheltered the king. The garden retains its formal 17th-century charm.

Wightwick Manor, 3 miles west, has a Jacobean appearance, though it was not built until 1887. Inside are some fine fabrics and wallpapers by William Morris, the 19th-century decorative artist. There is also some beautiful stained glass, much of it designed by C. E. Kempe. The house is rich in paintings by Rossetti, Burne-Jones, Ford Madox Brown, Watts, Ruskin and Millais. The gardens are laid out with terraces and pools, and some splendid Irish yews and golden holly trees.

WHERE TWO GUNPOWDER PLOTTERS WERE SHOT

When the Gunpowder Plot was discovered in November, 1605, two of the plotters, Robert Catesby and Thomas Percy, fled to Holbeche House, on the road from Himley to Stourbridge. They were caught and shot dead by the Sheriff of Worcestershire's men as they came out, apparently to give themselves up. At the same time a fire broke out and only a chimney (left) remained to be incorporated into the present rebuilt mansion

Derbyshire's tranquil corner

Angling There is coarse fishing at many places on the River Derwent, at Chellaston on the Trent, at Alvaston Park, Derby and Kedleston Hall.

Events The Derbyshire County Show is held at Elvaston Castle on Whit Mon. The Derbyshire Morris Men tour the county during the summer and stage dancing exhibitions.

Places to see *Derby Industrial Museum*, Silk Mill Lane: Tues. to Sat. *Derby Museum and Art Gallery*, incorporating a regimental museum, The Strand: Tues. to Sat. *Dale Abbey*, ruins, 4 miles north-east of Derby: daily. *Duffield Castle* (NT), ruins of castle which was destroyed in 1266: daily. *Ednaston Manor*, Brailsford, 8 miles north-west of Derby: gardens only; Wed. and Thur. afternoons; also Sun. afternoon mid-Apr. to Sept. *Kedleston Hall*: afternoons only: Easter Sun. and Mon.; late Apr. to Sept., Sun. and Bank Hol. Mon. and Tues. *Melbourne Hall*: afternoons only; Easter and Spring Bank Hol., Sat. to Tues.; early June to mid-Sept., Wed., Thur., Sat.; also Tues., July and Aug. *Sudbury Hall* (NT): Apr. to Oct., afternoons except Mon. and Tues., but open Bank Hol. *Transport and Grand Prix Museum*, Castle Donington: daily.

Information centres Reference Library, The Strand, Derby. Tel. Derby 31111. Public Library, Market Place, Ilkeston. Tel. Ilkeston 303361. The Library, Civic Way, Swadlincote. Tel. Burton upon Trent 217701.

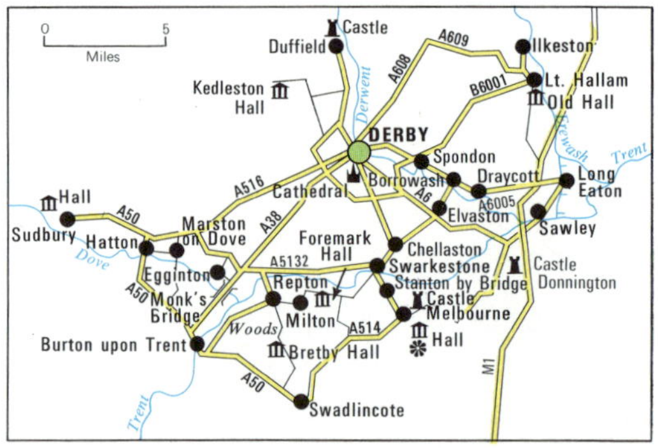

South Derbyshire lacks the rugged grandeur of the Dales and the Peak District further north, but it is fine walking country, with large areas of soft, undulating, pastoral scenery through which rivers meander lazily. To the west the River Dove, coming down from the Dales, winds along the Staffordshire border to meet the River Trent. Further east the Trent is joined by the Derwent, which flows through Derby.

The soil in this area is deep and rich, producing good crops of wheat and barley, much of which goes to the breweries at Burton upon Trent across the Staffordshire border. Clay found around Swadlincote is used for the town's pottery industry, an extension of the Staffordshire potteries.

The hub of south Derbyshire is the city of Derby. It is an ancient town; the Romans had a camp there, but it was influenced mostly by the Danes and its name comes from the Danish *deoraby*, meaning 'the place of the deer'. It was at Derby in 1745 that Bonnie Prince Charlie abandoned his advance on London. Today it is a busy, prosperous industrial centre famous for its railway works, Rolls-Royce factories and Crown Derby porcelain. There is an industrial belt that spreads along the county's eastern border, although many of Derbyshire's famous coalfields, important in the early stages of the Industrial Revolution, have now closed. Other industries have taken their place, yet the blackness of the 'Black Country' has not left any of the deep industrial scars seen in some parts of the neighbouring counties.

FROM CHURCH TO CATHEDRAL *James Gibbs retained the 16th-century tower when he rebuilt the parish church at Derby in 1725. The church, which became a cathedral in 1927, contains 18th-century wrought-iron work and a monument to 'Bess of Hardwick', the Countess of Shrewsbury, who died in 1607*

THE DERBY RAM

A statue in Derby's new shopping market illustrates an old Derbyshire folk song about 'the finest ram that ever was fed on hay'

Derby
As long ago as the Norman Conquest, Derby had a population of more than 2000 and no fewer than six churches. In 1717 England's first silk mill was established in Derby by Thomas Cotchet and John Lombe, who produced silk which became famous throughout Europe. Some of the city's finest 18th-century houses date from this period, and the wrought-iron gates of the silk mill still stand near the public library.

Industry expanded rapidly in the middle of the 19th century with the building of the Midland Railway's great locomotive and coach works, now run by British Rail. Derby is the home of Rolls-Royce. In one of the city's 20 parks, the Arboretum, stands a monument to the engineer Sir Henry Royce who, in partnership with the Hon. C. S. Rolls, the businessman, established the firm in Derby in 1908.

A great deal of old Derby still survives in this modern cathedral city. In Friar Gate, a street with some Georgian houses, is the ancient Church of St Werburgh which has a register recording the marriage in 1735 of Dr Samuel Johnson (1709–84) to Elizabeth 'Tetty' Porter. On St Mary's bridge across the Derwent is one of the few remaining bridge chapels in England. The oldest church, St Peter's, dates from Norman times, but most of the building is 14th century. The cathedral, until 1927 simply the parish church of All Saints, has a splendid tower built in Henry VIII's reign. It was restored in 1725 by James Gibbs.

The Derby and District College of Art and Technology, set in spacious grounds, and the Derby Museum and Art Gallery, are outstanding among Derby's modern buildings. Markeaton Park, largest of the town's many open spaces, has a fine boating lake.

Kedleston Hall, 4½ miles north-west, is a fine 18th-century mansion built in Classical style by James Paine and Robert Adam for the Curzons, who have lived at Kedleston for 850 years.

Ilkeston
A large town overlooking the attractive Erewash Valley. It has a busy market-place, thronged on market day by people from outlying villages. The coalfields stopped production in 1966, when the last coalfield was worked out. St Mary's parish church dates from 1150 and has a magnificent 14th-century screen.

At Little Hallam, half a mile south, is a beautiful 16th-century Jacobean half-timbered house called Old Hall.

Long Eaton
From Saxon times until the last century, Long Eaton was a small village. Today it is a busy industrial market town with a population of 32,000. Its prosperity grew with the lace industry, which still

flourishes. The town's parish church of St Laurence has a 14th-century chancel window with fine tracery.

There is a motor racing circuit, with a museum of Grand Prix cars, at Castle Donington, 4 miles to the south.

Marston on Dove

One of the most attractive old villages in this quarter of Derbyshire. The country around, watered by the quietly flowing Dove, is good for walking. The church has a bell dated 1366 in its 14th-century tower. A 2-mile walk along the river eastwards leads to Egginton, where the Dove is crossed by the beautiful 14th-century Monk's Bridge, built by the Abbot of Burton to carry traffic to the abbey.

Melbourne

Its name signifies 'a mill stream' which still flows through this small town, lying in undulating country south of the Trent. There are a few remains of a 14th-century castle in which the Duke of Bourbon was held for 19 years after being taken prisoner at Agincourt.

The town's most famous son was Lord Melbourne (1779–1848), Queen Victoria's first Prime Minister. His father owned Melbourne Hall, an elegant and graceful mansion which has none of the flamboyance often associated with stately homes. The house, now owned by the Marquess of Lothian, contains fine paintings, furniture and works of art. The beautiful formal gardens and lake were laid out by Henry Wise in the manner of Le Nôtre's gardens at Versailles. They include an ornamental pergola in wrought-iron, which is known as The Birdcage, and a 180 ft long yew tunnel.

Repton

One of England's most ancient towns, surrounded by hills and overlooking the River Trent; it was once the capital of the Saxon kingdom of Mercia. The crypt below St Wystan's Church, its roof supported by four twisted columns, is one of the best survivals of Anglo-Saxon architecture in the country. It was probably built before AD 975.

SEVEN SISTERS BRIDGE *The arched bridge over the Trent at Swarkestone, built in the 13th century, was restored in the last century*

WROUGHT-IRON MASTERPIECE *The Birdcage, a pergola at Melbourne Hall, was designed by Robert Bakewell in 1725*

About 200 years later a great priory was founded, but it fell into disrepair after the Dissolution of the Monasteries. On these ruins Repton School was built in 1557. The priory gateway is preserved, as well as the original priory guest hall, which now contains a library belonging to the school. One of the earliest brick buildings in the town is the Prior Overton Tower, built in 1438.

There is splendid walking country in Bretby Woods, 2 miles south-west. Bretby Hall, once the home of the Earls of Chesterfield, was rebuilt in the style of the Gothic revival in 1813. Benjamin Disraeli, when Prime Minister, was a frequent visitor to the house, which is now a hospital.

A fine Palladian house, Foremark Hall, is at Milton, 2 miles east. It is now a school but it is occasionally opened to the public during the summer.

Sudbury

One of the show villages of Derbyshire, built in warm, mellow red brick, mostly in the 17th century. Gabled cottages and houses edge the main road. The building of Sudbury Hall, originally the seat of the Vernon family, was started in 1613, and completed as late as 1695. It is a charming country house in the affluent manner of the Stuarts and has some fine plasterwork ceilings—a feature of the times—some excellent Laguerre murals, and carvings by Grinling Gibbons, the late 17th and early 18th-century sculptor and woodcarver. The Hall is now owned by the National Trust. In the grounds is All Saints' Church, which dates from the 12th century and has a window that was presented by Queen Victoria.

Swarkestone

A village noted for its graceful bridge which joins a ten-arch causeway leading to the village of Stanton by Bridge. The bridge was built in the 13th century and restored at the beginning of the 19th century. According to legend it was built by two sisters who had watched their lovers drown while they were trying to ford the Trent on horseback.

The lovely dales of Derbyshire

Angling There are trout and grayling in the Dove at Ashbourne and Hartington; trout, pike and coarse fish in the Derwent at Ambergate.

Boating Boats can be hired at Matlock Bath. There is good canoeing on the Derwent from Rowsley.

Events On Shrove Tuesday there is a pancake race at Winster, and at Ashbourne Shrovetide football is played between goals 3 miles apart. Well-dressing ceremonies at Tissington (Ascension Day), Wirksworth (Whitsun), Youlgreave (June), Bonsall and Barlow (both Aug.). Matlock Bath has Illuminations and Venetian Nights from end Aug. to early Oct.

Places to see *Bakewell Old House Museum*: Easter to Sept., afternoons. *Chatsworth*: Tues. to Sun., Apr. to early Oct.; Wed. and Sun., early Oct. to Dec.; also Bank Hol. Sun. and Mon. *Crich Tramway Museum*: Sat., Sun. and Bank Hol., Apr. to Oct.; also Tues., Wed., Thur., June to Aug. *Haddon Hall*: Apr. to Sept., Tues. to Sat.; also Bank Hol. Sun. and Mon. afternoons. *Hardwick Hall* (NT), 9½ miles south-east of Chesterfield: Apr. to Oct., Wed., Thur., Sat., Sun., Bank Hol. Mon. afternoons. *Heights of Abraham*, Great Rutland Cavern: Easter to mid-Oct., daily; Great Masson Cavern: Easter to Oct., Sun. and Bank Hol. weekends; Aug., daily. *Revolution House*, Chesterfield: Easter to Sept., daily. *Riber Castle Wildlife Park*, Matlock: daily. *Winster Market House* (NT): Apr. to Sept., Wed., Sat., Sun. and Bank Hol. afternoons.

Information centres Tourist Office, 13 Market Place, Ashbourne. Tel. Ashbourne 3666. The Pavilion, Matlock Bath. Tel. Matlock 55082.

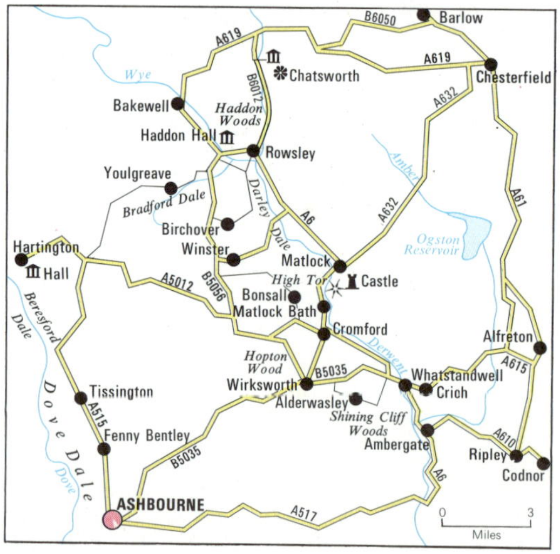

The high ridges of mid-Derbyshire are broken up by some of the most beautiful river-valley country in England, particularly along the course of the Rivers Wye, Derwent and Dove. The Wye flows from Bakewell through a beautiful green valley below Haddon Hall, then curves round Rowsley out of the Peak District National Park. Soon it joins the River Derwent which, further upstream, meanders through Chatsworth Park.

Further downstream there is pleasant scenery along the banks of the Derwent through Darley Dale and the Matlocks—a group of towns and villages, including Matlock and Matlock Bath, set among woodland and limestone cliffs. Around the Matlocks, the countryside is rich in history and archaeology, with fine old manor houses, Norman churches and stone circles. South of the Matlocks, the Derwent twists through wooded countryside offering a wide choice of walks in the National Trust's Shining Cliff Woods.

In the south-west is Dove Dale, the most famous and beautiful of the Derbyshire Dales. For much of its course the Dove runs through the National Park and forms a natural boundary with Staffordshire.

Chesterfield, an ancient town mentioned in the Domesday Book, is an important, but not grimy, industrial centre standing on the edge of large mining and industrial areas. It is probably best known to travellers by the twisted spire of its parish church.

The caves at Matlock and in the Wirksworth area were originally lead mines worked by the Romans; and limestone is still quarried as building stone, particularly at Hopton Wood.

Ashbourne
One of the most attractive market towns in Derbyshire, often called 'the gateway to the Peak', as it stands on the fringe of the Peak District National Park. In Church Street is the 13th to 14th-century Church of St Oswald, one of the most handsome parish churches in England, with a spire 212 ft high. The church is renowned for its 18th-century white marble sculpture of Penelope Boothby by Thomas Banks. She was the daughter of a local family and died aged five in 1791. The church also contains several monuments and effigies of the Cokaynes, a notable local family in the 15th and 16th centuries. Sir John Cokayne founded the grammar school in 1585, and the original stone-built Elizabethan building opposite the church is still used by boarders of the new grammar school. Ashbourne Hall, the home of the Cokaynes, although much altered, is now the county library.

Almost opposite the old grammar school is the 17th-century red-brick mansion where Samuel Johnson often visited his poet friend Dr John Taylor.

Bakewell
A valley town on the Wye surrounded by richly wooded hills stretching to high moorland. Its fine arched and buttressed bridge was built nearly 700 years ago, while the brown stone buildings, which have a warmth of colouring unusual in Peakland, mostly date from the 17th and 18th centuries. Outstanding are the Old Market Hall, Old Town Hall and Holme Hall, a mansion built in 1626.

Bath House is another brownstone building, built in 1697 for the Duke of Rutland. It is still fed by warm springs which were known in Roman times. The town's name comes from the Saxon *bad-quell* meaning 'bath well'.

Birchover
A village surrounded by magnificent rocky scenery. Beyond the village inn, The Druid, are Row Tor rocks, which include two 'rocking stones', one of which is estimated to weigh 50 tons. An 18th-century clergyman, Thomas Eyre, carved some of the rocks into seats. Just south of the village are two gritstone pinnacles separated by a 20-yd gap known as Robin Hood's Stride—mythically thought of as the giant stride of Robin Hood.

Chatsworth
This Classical mansion is one of the great stately homes of England. It was built in 1707 for the 1st Duke of Devonshire on to a much earlier building designed by his great great grandmother, Bess of Hardwick. The house still belongs to the Cavendish family, and its collection of paintings, sculpture, manuscripts and fine furniture is world

WELL-DRESSING—A DERBYSHIRE TRADITION

Flowers pressed into clay adorn wells at Litton (left), 6 miles north-west of Bakewell, Tissington (right), and other places during summer festivals

BAKEWELL TART *Known locally as Bakewell Pudding, this originated at the Rutland Arms when the cook, making a strawberry tart, spread egg mixture on top of the jam instead of using it in the pastry*

DOVE DALE *The River Dove, downstream from the 20 Stepping Stones, bubbles through a gorge known as Little Switzerland*

renowned. The splendid gardens were replanned in the 19th century by Sir Joseph Paxton, designer of the Crystal Palace, who planted rare coniferous trees, made the rock garden and added the Emperor fountain.

Crich

A village on a hill—its name comes from a word meaning 'hill'—with fine views. It is noted for its Tramway Museum, containing 40 trams of the 19th and 20th centuries, housed in a disused quarry. The exhibits include a Sheffield horse-drawn tram of 1874, in which visitors can ride, and a Prague tram brought from Czechoslovakia just before the Russian invasion of 1968. Just above the quarry, flashing 950 ft up, is the Beacon Light, a war memorial to the Nottingham and Derbyshire Regiment, the 'Sherwood Foresters'.

Dove Dale

A beautiful 2-mile stretch of the River Dove, flowing swiftly through a richly wooded limestone gorge, often called Little Switzerland. The most prominent feature is Ilam Rock, a tall pinnacle of limestone facing Pickering Tor, a similar pinnacle on the opposite bank. There are excellent views from Sharplow Point, also known as Lover's Leap, so called because a young girl is said to have jumped from it in despair over unrequited love. High in the hillside north of Lover's Leap are two caves, Reynard's Kitchen and Reynard's Cave. Spectacular rock formations along the gorge include Jacob's Ladder and the Twelve Apostles, and further downstream the 20 Stepping Stones link the Derbyshire and Staffordshire banks of the river. The Dove is famous for trout, and was fished by Izaak Walton.

Hartington

A small village centred round an open market-place, with attractive 18th and 19th-century buildings. This is a good centre for walking in Beresford Dale, to the west, which is followed by the upper Dove. Hartington Hall, built in 1350 and rebuilt in 1611, is a gabled house with fine oak panelling. It is now a youth hostel.

Matlock

A resort on the Derwent among woodlands and hills, with dramatic views of peaks and crags. The Heights of Abraham, 750 ft above the town, are said to have been named by an officer who fought under General Wolfe, because of their resemblance to the heights scaled in the capture of Quebec.

Matlock was a spa in Victorian times and is today a popular inland tourist resort. The Lido has two swimming-pools, and the Derwent Gardens have been transformed into a nocturnal fairyland.

From Matlock Dale there are easy paths up to the formidable-looking peak of High Tor, 380 ft above the dale. Riber Castle, now a ruined landmark with four tall corner towers, was built by John Smedley, a textile manufacturer, in 1862. It is now the site of a nature reserve for wildlife from both Britain and the Continent.

Rowsley

A typical Peak village with a fine 17th-century stone manor house, converted into the Peacock Hotel in 1828. The village is a good walking centre. Across the Wye Bridge the road leads westwards to Haddon Woods, and across the Derwent paths wind to the moors.

Haddon Hall, 1½ miles west, is one of the best-restored English medieval manors. It has romantic associations because of the elopement in 1558 of John Manners with Dorothy Vernon, during her sister's wedding party. Restoration was completed in the 1930's, and there are beautiful terraced gardens.

Wirksworth

A small town of stone houses and narrow streets, famous for its annual Whitsun well-dressing ceremony. It was once a lead-mining centre, dating from Roman times; and in Moot Hall, built in 1814, is a 16th-century bronze dish, used as a standard measurement of the lead produced by the miners.

In the 13th-century church is the lid of an Anglo-Saxon coffin, believed to be 9th-century work. There is also a wealth of early Christian carving. George Eliot set much of her novel *Adam Bede* in and around the town.

Youlgreave

An ancient hilltop village set in some of Derbyshire's best limestone scenery, on the edge of Bradford Dale. The name is from the Saxon, meaning 'yellow grove'. Old Hall, built in 1650, has a distinctly Cotswold look about it and the parish church has fine Norman work and a tower with eight pinnacles.

OLD TRAMS *Exhibits at Crich Museum span 80 years and include (left) Sheffield's last tram, which ran in 1960*

The Peak District

Angling All waters in the area are under private control, and permission must be obtained before trying the fine trout fishing on the Wye and Derwent.

Boating There are sailing clubs at Chapel-en-le-Frith, Whaley Bridge and Errwood Reservoir.

Events On May 29, Oak Apple Day, there is a procession at Castleton said to commemorate Charles II's escape after the Battle of Worcester. Well-dressing is a Derbyshire custom that takes place between Ascension Day and August at many places, including Litton, Tideswell, Hope, Ashford, Stoney Middleton, Buxton, Wormhill (near Buxton) and Eyam. Buxton has a summer programme of drama and music. In July is the Woodlands Love Feast, a religious ceremony that takes place close to the Ladybower Reservoir, near Bamford. Sheepdog trials are held at Longshaw early in Sept.

Places to see *Buxton Museum*, Terrace Road, local history: weekdays. Caves near Castleton—*Blue John Cavern*: daily; *Peak Cavern*: Easter to Sept., daily; *Speedwell Cavern*: daily; *Treak Cliff Cavern*: daily. *North Lees Hall*, Hathersage, believed to be the 'Thornfield Hall' of Charlotte Brontë's *Jane Eyre*: by appointment with occupants. *Peveril Castle*: daily, except Sun. morning Oct. to Mar.

Information centres Tourist Centre, The Crescent, Buxton. Tel. Buxton 5106.
Peak District National Park information centres: Bakewell (Tel. Bakewell 3227) and Edale (Tel. Hope Valley 70207).

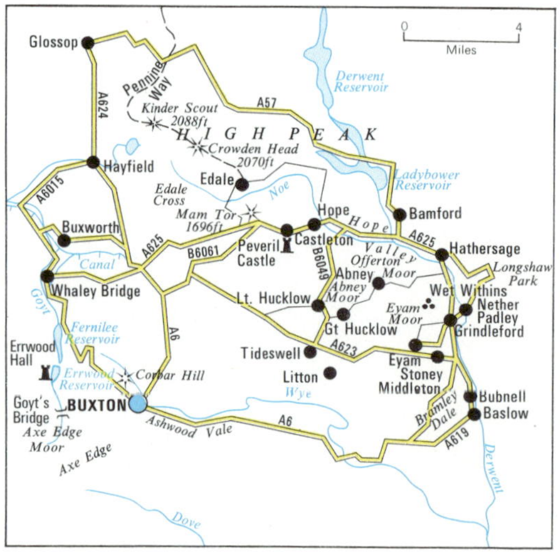

Some of Britain's most picturesque countryside is in north Derbyshire. High, rocky crags rise from rugged moorlands of heather and peat, cut by lushly pastured and wooded dales. A large part of the area is in the 540-square-mile Peak District National Park, Britain's first national park. Edale, in the heart of the area, is the start of the Pennine Way, a 250-mile track which runs along the Pennine Chain, the backbone of England, to the Scottish Border.

There are only two towns of any size in the area: Buxton, a spa and holiday resort, and Glossop, an industrial town near the Greater Manchester border. But there are many attractive stone hamlets, usually sited below the great 'edges'—the local name for the escarpments that tower over the valleys.

The Peak District is 'adventure country'—ideal for walking, scrambling, climbing and pot-holing. There are many underground caverns and natural tunnels, particularly in the central Castleton and Hope Valley areas, where the visitor will find a strange and magical world of stalactites and stalagmites.

CHALLENGING PEAK *The sheer face of Froggatt Edge, 3 miles north*

RIVAL TO BATH *The beautiful Crescent at Buxton, which stands*

WATERWAY RESTORATION *The Buxworth arm of the Peak Forest Canal. This once-derelict section is being restored by the Inland Waterways Protection Society*

Abney
A typical Derbyshire hamlet, lovely but lonely, set in wild moorland country just below Abney Moor. A mile to the south is a picturesque gorge or 'clough' dominated by Abney Grange, once a residence of the Abbots of Welbeck. Abney Moor slopes south-west to Little and Great Hucklow, which are popular gliding centres.

Axe Edge Moor
A superb rise of moorland, just south of Buxton off the main road to Leek. These moors are fine walking country and on them rise four of Derbyshire's most beautiful rivers—the Wye, the Goyt, the Manifold and the Dove. A grassy track, starting half a mile past the disused railway track south of Buxton on the Leek road, leads over Axe Edge, some 1600 ft above sea level, with fine views. The track winds back to the Leek road, passing near the source of the Dove. The nearby Traveller's Rest is one of the highest inns in England, 1535 ft above sea level.

Baslow
One of the most beautifully sited villages in Derbyshire. Its ancient stone bridge, with three mellowed arches, spans a fine stretch of the Derwent. St Anne's Church has a pretty setting by the river, and its clock has the words 'Victoria 1897' on its dial instead of figures. Set on heather-clad moors just north of the village is the picturesque hamlet of

of Baslow, overlooks the Derwent Valley, and provides a formidable challenge to climbers

opposite the town's hot springs, was built in 1780–4 to compete with the glories of Bath

Bubnell, overlooking Bramley Dale. On a nearby height is a stone plinth, erected as a monument to Wellington.

Buxton
Although it is one of the highest towns in England, at 1007 ft, Buxton is sheltered by the even higher hills surrounding it. It is a spa town and owes its fame to the 5th Duke of Devonshire who, at the end of the 18th century, built the town's beautiful Crescent as a rival to fashionable Bath. The Devonshire Royal Hospital, opened in 1859, has a dome 156 ft in diameter, one of the widest in the world. Buxton's springs, charged with nitrogen and carbon gas, well up from great depths at a constant temperature of 28°C (82°F), just as they did in Roman times. The water, unlike most spa water, is pleasant to drink.

Spas have lost much of their appeal today, but Buxton is still attracting visitors because of its fine situation and the facilities it offers for every kind of sport, as well as concerts and drama. It has two golf courses, and there is an indoor spa-water swimming pool in The Pavilion, which is set in 23 acres of gardens and has also a theatre and concert hall.

Corbar Woods, only half a mile from the Crescent, offer pleasant walks, and there are splendid views from nearby Corbar Hill. Ashwood Dale is an attractive valley, about a mile from the town centre to the east. Lovers' Leap, in the dale, is a huge natural cleft in the limestone rock where, according to tradition, two runaway lovers on a horse leapt the chasm to avoid pursuit.

To the north-west there are splendid views of the Goyt Valley from the main road which zigzags its way down towards Whaley Bridge.

Castleton
A large village, magnificently sited at the western entrance to the Hope Valley, which sweeps down to Grindleford Bridge near the Yorkshire border. Above the village green, with its pleasant weathered stone houses, rise the imposing ruins of Peveril Castle, built in Norman times and recently restored. It is described in Sir Walter Scott's novel, *Peveril of the Peak*.

Under the castle is Peak Cavern, one of the finest of many underground caverns in the area. A lane alongside a fast-flowing stream leads to the gaping mouth of the cavern, which in turn leads to a number of natural rock chambers, including Devil's Cavern, Roger's Rain House, where water flows continuously down the walls, and the Orchestral Chamber, so called because it has remarkable acoustic properties.

Speedwell Cavern, which can be approached by boat, is under Winnats Pass, where a ceaseless rush of water falls into Bottomless Pit. Treak Hill Cavern, which has been imaginatively floodlit to create a fairy-tale grotto, is at the foot of Treak Cliff Hill, the only place in the world where the mineral Blue John is found. This is a translucent variety of fluorspar, banded in red, blue, purple and yellow, which has been prized for making ornaments since Roman times. Jewellery and small vases made of the stone can be bought at the cavern and in Castleton.

Mam Tor, 1696 ft, 1½ miles west, is also called the 'Shivering Mountain' because of the way erosion causes shale to fall into the valley below. On top are the remains of an Iron Age fort.

Edale
An unspoilt village by the River Noe, and a centre for exploring the Peak District. Much of the surrounding land is owned by the National Trust, and gorges lead upwards on to cliffs, crags and bleak moorlands known as the Kinder Plateau.

One walk leads west through Upper Booth to a slope called Jacob's Ladder, then past Edale Cross and northwards to Kinder Scout—at 2088 ft the highest point in the Peak District. The bare and lonely scenery is relieved by occasional dramatic waterfalls, such as Kinder Downfall. Much of the surrounding moorland is preserved for grouse shooting, and information about access to the rugged slopes during the season (August 12–December 10) can be obtained at the information centre in Edale.

Eyam
A village high up among the moors, surrounded by wide open spaces looking rather like the scenery of 'Western' films. A hill track across Eyam Moor climbs to 1200 ft above sea level and offers distant views of Axe Edge, Mam Tor and Kinder Scout. On the moor is a prehistoric stone circle, Wet Withins.

Eyam has a sad historical importance: the village was devastated in 1665–6, when a box of infected clothes brought the Plague there. Under the leadership of their rector, William Mompesson, the villagers cut themselves off from the world to stop the disease spreading. Five out of every six inhabitants died. The courage of Mompesson and his parishioners is commemorated every year by an open-air service held on the last Sunday in August. A number of houses from the plague years survive.

BLUE JOHN VASE

The rare mineral Blue John is mined near Castleton. This 19th-century Blue John vase is in London's Institute of Geological Sciences

Goyt's Bridge
The River Goyt, one of the prettiest rivers in the district, rises just south of the present site of Goyt's Bridge. The hamlet of Goyt's Bridge was submerged in 1967 by the completion of the Errwood Reservoir; the old packhorse bridge that was once used for smuggling salt between Cheshire and Derbyshire was rebuilt further upstream. To the west, the grounds of the ruined Errwood Hall are thickly planted with pines, rhododendrons and azaleas. Some of the Goyt Valley is controlled at the weekend in summer and vehicle access is confined to a minibus service.

Grindleford
A village at the eastern end of the Hope Valley and at the centre of a fine stretch of moorlands and woods, with some good walking in all directions. Longshaw Park, 2 miles north-east, is a National Park estate of more than 1000 acres. On the first Thursday, Friday and Saturday in September there are sheep-dog trials at Longshaw.

At Nether Padley, a mile north-east, the ruins of an ancient chapel have been restored in memory of two Roman Catholic priests, Nicholas Garlick and Robert Ludlam, executed in 1588.

From wooded hills to an inland 'isle'

Angling There is coarse fishing on the River Trent at Gainsborough, on the River Ryton and Chesterfield Canal at Worksop and on the River Idle at Misterton and East Retford.

Boating There is boating and sailing on the Rivers Trent, Ancholme and Humber near Scunthorpe.

Events A festival with parades is held during June at Scunthorpe. The Haxey Hood Game, resembling Rugby football but played with a hood, takes place on Jan. 6 at Haxey. It dates from the 13th century when the hood of a Lady de Mowbray was blown away and retrieved by 12 workmen. A hood is thrown into the crowd and the winner is the one who gets the hood into a local inn.

Places to see *Clumber Park* (NT): afternoons. *Epworth Old Rectory*: weekdays and Sun. afternoons. *Gainsborough Old Hall*: weekday afternoons; also Sun. afternoons Easter to Oct. *Normanby Hall*, Scunthorpe: Apr. to Oct., weekdays except Tues.; Nov. to Mar., Mon. to Fri.; also Sun. afternoon. *Scunthorpe Borough Museum and Art Gallery*: weekdays, Sun. afternoon. *Sherwood Forest Visitors' Centre*, Edwinstowe: daily. *Thoresby Hall*: afternoons only; Easter and Bank Hol. weekends; Easter to Sept., Wed., Thur., Sat. and Sun. *Worksop Museum*: daily except Thur. and Sun.

Information centres Central Library, Carlton Street, Scunthorpe. Tel. Scunthorpe 60161. Public Library, Memorial Avenue, Worksop. Tel. Worksop 2408.

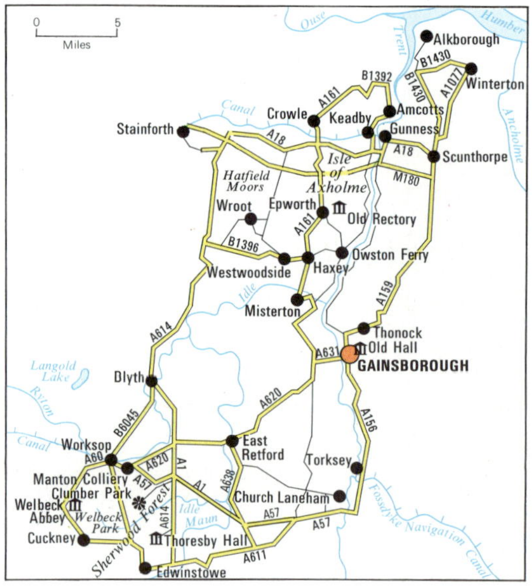

The calm and placid River Trent flows through wooded vales in Nottinghamshire, forming the county boundary with Lincolnshire, and then loops slowly through the low-lying flood plain of north Lincolnshire and Humberside to join the Humber Estuary below the village of Alkborough.

For the last 20 miles of its journey to the estuary, the Trent flows along the eastern edge of the curiously named Isle of Axholme. The name is believed to be derived from 'Haxey-holme', Haxey being a village in the area and the word *holme* being Scandinavian for an islet submerged in time of flood. The 'Isle' consists of 200,000 acres of flat agricultural land, drained in the 17th century by a Dutchman, Cornelius Vermuyden, and now providing good, rich land for market gardening and large-scale farming. The flat landscape is relieved by occasional belts of poplars.

The pattern of landholding in the Isle of Axholme is unusual. Even today there is preserved at Haxey the open-field system of strip-land farming dating back to before the Norman Conquest. A practice that originated in medieval times, peat cutting, is still carried on around Haxey and Westwoodside.

The Isle of Axholme is a place of pilgrimage for Methodists from all over the world, for the village of Epworth was the birthplace, in 1703, of John Wesley, founder of the Methodist Church.

Further south, near Worksop, the gentle wooded hills of 'The Dukeries' provide a complete contrast to the flat bleakness of the Isle of Axholme. These great estates in the north of Sherwood Forest are so called because they were originally owned by the Dukes of Norfolk, Portland, Newcastle and Kingston, and the Earls Manvers, Savile and Byron.

Alkborough
A bleak village of stone houses, clustered around an 11th-century church on a hill giving fine views of the Trent and Ouse where they join to form the Humber Estuary. There are pleasant walks through beechwoods. Julian's Bower, a curiously shaped maze cut into the ground west of the church, is believed to date back to the 12th century.

Blyth
The main road through this pretty village was once the old highway between London and York, but the village is now bypassed by the A1. The River Ryton meanders around three sides of the village. The church has a splendid nave, which is all that remains of an 11th-century Benedictine priory. The peaceful village green has an elm plantation and an ancient, beamed, stone-walled building, with a 700-year-old doorway.

Church Laneham
The River Trent is 41 miles from the mouth of the Humber as it flows through this village, but it is still tidal and is used occasionally by barges. The fine old church has an 11th-century doorway,

CLUMBER CHAPEL *The 180-ft spire of Clumber chapel overlooks the lake at Clumber Park. The chapel was built for the 7th Duke of Newcastle in 1886, at a cost of £30,000*

WHERE METHODISM BEGAN

John Wesley, founder of the Methodist Church, lived at the Old Rectory, Epworth (left). The house is preserved by the World Methodist Council and inside (right) is a bust of Wesley and a clock which belonged to him

WALK THROUGH THE BIRCHES *Clumber Park, near Worksop, was created in the late 18th century by the Dukes of Newcastle*

and from its 13th-century tower views extend as far as Lincoln Cathedral. At Torksey Lock, 1½ miles north, the Trent is joined by the Fossdyke Navigation Canal, the oldest canal in Britain, excavated by the Romans to link the Trent with the River Witham at Lincoln. Swans can often be seen in flight between the river and the canal lock at Torksey.

Edwinstowe
A pretty village on the River Maun, close to the older tracts of Sherwood Forest. There are some notable old oak trees here, including the Major Oak which is said to have sheltered Robin Hood. Cuckney, 5 miles north-west across woodland, is a pleasant wooded village with houses clustered around a pond on which there are mallards.

Thoresby Hall, 3 miles north of Edwinstowe, is one of the stately homes which give the name 'The Dukeries' to the area. The original hall, built in Thoresby Park in 1683 by William, 4th Earl of Kingston, was destroyed by fire in 1745. It was later rebuilt, but was demolished in the 19th century, when the present neo-Tudor house was designed for the 3rd Earl Manvers. It stands in 12,000 acres of parkland.

Epworth
The founder of the Methodist Church, John Wesley, was born in 1703 in the Old Rectory, where his father, Samuel Wesley, was the rector. The house was rebuilt in 1709 after a fire, and contains furniture associated with the Wesley family. American Methodists financed much of the restoration.

Samuel Wesley's tombstone is in the churchyard; his son once preached from it, after being barred from the church. The church contains the font where the family was baptised—John was the 15th of 19 children—and there is a large, stone Methodist church, built in 1889, near the centre of the town. Epworth's market cross was another early pulpit used by John Wesley.

Gainsborough
A busy market town and industrial centre on the east bank of the Trent, linked to Nottinghamshire on the opposite bank by a three-arched 18th-century bridge. Danish invaders, led by King Sweyn, father of Canute, ravaged the town during a series of plundering raids in the late 10th century. Sweyn was murdered in Gainsborough by one of the townspeople in 1014.

The town's oldest building, Old Hall, is one of the largest medieval houses in the country open to the public. The original building was destroyed in 1470 and rebuilt ten years later. Richard III stayed at the house in 1484 and it was also visited by Henry VIII and his sixth wife, Catharine Parr.

Today the river is a busy highway for the town's industries, which include flour milling, engineering and the manufacture of malt kilns, agricultural tools and road rollers. Some splendid 18th-century warehouses line the quayside. There is a well-wooded golf course at Thonock, 1½ miles north-east.

Scunthorpe
A large industrial town which was only a hamlet 100 years ago and owes its development to the local ironstone. Many Romano-British settlements have been found near by; a mosaic of the head of Ceres found at Winterton, 5 miles north, is in Scunthorpe Civic Centre.

Normanby Hall, 2 miles north, was built in 1829 and contains furniture and works of art of the Regency period. It stands in 40 acres of gardens.

Worksop
A town on the River Ryton, described as the gateway to 'The Dukeries'. It is on the edge of the Midlands coalfield, and Manton Colliery has some landscaped coal-tips. The town's most attractive building is the 14th-century gatehouse of the former priory of Radford. The nave in the Church of SS Mary and Cuthbert dates back to the 12th century and has some fine Norman work.

Clumber Park, 3 miles south-east, has forest walks, rhododendrons, picnic spaces and several Forestry Commission conifer plantations. Welbeck Abbey, 3 miles south of Worksop, is noted for its labyrinth of underground passages, which were added by the eccentric 5th Duke of Portland in the 19th century.

Wroot
A village in a desolate part of the Isle of Axholme, with Hatfield Moors to the north. The skyline is broken by rows of poplars. For two years John Wesley was curate here, when his father was Rector of Wroot and Epworth.

CLUMBER SPANIELS

This breed of spaniel took its name from Clumber Park, where the dogs were first bred for the Dukes of Newcastle as shooting dogs for the estate. The breeding produced dogs which remained silent during the chase—a characteristic which survives in them today

Nottingham and the Trent

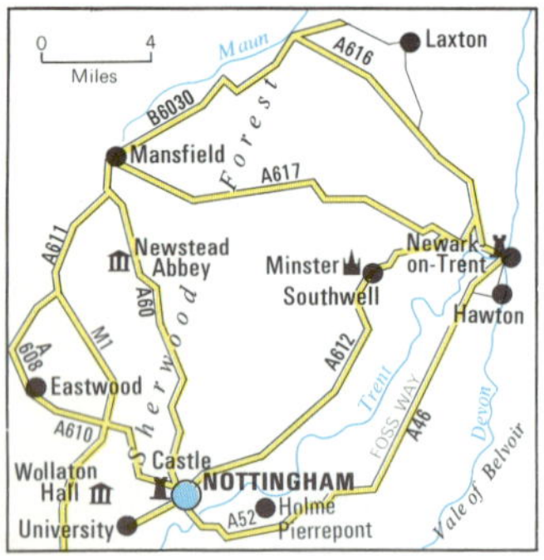

Water sports The National Water Sports Centre at Holme Pierrepont is 2 miles south-east of Nottingham.

Events Nottingham Festival is held for two weeks in June, and the Goose Fair, the largest fair in England, on the first Thur., Fri. and Sat. in Oct.

Places to see *Mansfield Museum and Art Gallery*: weekdays. *Newark Museum and Art Gallery*: weekdays except Thur. afternoons; also Sun. afternoons, Apr. to Sept. *Newstead Abbey*: afternoons, Easter to Sept. Nottingham: *Brewhouse Yard Museum*, *Castle Museum*, *Castlegate Museum of Costume and Textiles*: all daily. *Industrial Museum*, Wollaton Park: Sun. afternoons; also Wed. to Sat., Apr. to Sept., Thur. and Sat., Oct. to Mar. *Natural History Museum*, Wollaton Hall: weekdays and Sun. afternoons. *University Art Gallery*, Dept. of Fine Art: weekdays.

Information centres 18 Milton St., Nottingham. Tel. Nottingham 40661. Beast Market Hill, Newark-on-Trent. Tel. Newark-on-Trent 78962 (seasonal).

South Nottinghamshire is dominated by the historic and industrial city of Nottingham with its busy modern shopping centre, its university, theatres and sports grounds. In industrial terms the city means lace, tobacco, bicycles, leather, textiles and engineering—an environment brought vividly to life in Alan Sillitoe's novel *Saturday Night and Sunday Morning*. To the north-west, stretching towards Derbyshire, is the coalfield belt which featured in the novels of D. H. Lawrence, who was born at Eastwood in 1885, the fourth son of a miner.

Yet there is more to this part of Nottinghamshire than industry, collieries and slag heaps. The remains of Sherwood Forest, home of the legendary Robin Hood, lie to the north-east. The River Trent, meandering through its middle course, passes south of Nottingham and creates a broad, low-lying valley of mixed farming land which links Nottingham and Newark. The scenery is similar to that of the Wolds.

A modern road follows the Roman Foss Way across the county, between the Trent and the Vale of Belvoir. The fields alongside the road are often enormous, for modern agriculture has in places dispensed with hedgerows as an uneconomic use of space. Birdlife has suffered, but there are still plenty of lapwings among the hedgerows in the arable stretches.

TRIP TO JERUSALEM *The inn below Nottingham Castle was built in 1760 on the site of a much older brewhouse*

Eastwood

A horizon of pit-head machinery tells the casual visitor that this is a mining community; but the country all around is farmland. It was this striking contrast of farmland and collieries which set the scene for D. H. Lawrence's early books, notably *Sons and Lovers*. Lawrence (1885–1930) was born at 8a Victoria Street. The quiet rural beauty close to Eastwood deeply influenced his outlook, making him write, after much travel abroad: '. . . I am English, and my Englishness is my very vision.'

Hawton

The stately 15th-century tower of All Saints' Church can be seen above the trees from the Roman Foss Way. The church has one of the country's best 14th-century Easter sepulchres.

Laxton

One of the few villages in the country which still maintains the strip-farming practice of the Middle Ages. Under this system the arable land is divided into three great fields of more than 250 acres each. These are farmed on a three-year rotational basis; one field lies fallow each year, two are divided into strips shared among the farmers.

Mansfield

Before the discovery of coal, Mansfield was an ancient market town astride the tiny River Maun. The Romans had a camp there, and coins of several Roman Emperors have been found. Today, Mansfield is an industrial centre, surrounded by collieries and important for hosiery and footwear. The Sherwood Forest Golf Club, 3 miles east, lies among coniferous forest planted to shield the colliery slag heaps.

Newark-on-Trent

The town lies east and south of the canalised section of the River Trent that carries barge traffic beneath the greystone walls of Newark Castle. This castle, where King John died in 1216, was destroyed after withstanding three sieges in the Civil War for the Royalist cause. The west wall survives together with an exceptionally fine gate house built over three large arches. The town has a cobble-stoned market-place and two attractive 14th-century inns. The Queen's Sconce, on the southern outskirts, is the site of a fortification used by the Royalists in the Civil War; 'sconce' means an earthwork.

CITY OF LACE *Traditional patterns figure in Nottingham's modern lace. Twisted nylon threads make this 'flounce'*

GOOSE FAIR *The huge fun-fair held in Nottingham for three days every October has its origins in the principal hiring fair and autumn market of the Midlands, held in the city in medieval times. Each year 20,000 geese changed hands at the fair*

NEWARK CASTLE *The people of Newark rallied to Charles I in the Civil War, and this fortress on the Devon, under the command of Lord Bellasis, withstood three sieges. After Charles ordered its surrender, the castle was destroyed by the Parliamentarians*

Newstead Abbey

Henry II built Newstead Abbey for the Augustinians in 1170 as an atonement for the murder of Thomas à Becket. In 1540, after the Dissolution, it became the home of the Byron family and it remained their ancestral home until 1817. Now owned by Nottingham City Council, the abbey has 9 acres of gardens and lakes, and there are many Byron family treasures on display, including a table at which Lord Byron wrote part of 'Childe Harold'. Byron, who died in Greece, is buried at Hucknall Church, 3 miles south.

Nottingham

An ancient city with a turbulent history. Its growth was influenced by the Saxons, Danes and Normans, and the Domesday Book records that it was a flourishing trading community, with its own mint, in 1086. But it was due to the Industrial Revolution that Nottingham became the busy industrial centre it is today. Arkwright set up his first spinning machinery in Nottingham in 1771. In 1790 he used a steam engine to power his mill. Other industries followed, including lace-making, hosiery, light engineering, tobacco and bicycles.

For centuries, Nottingham's life has centred around the castle, built by William the Conqueror in 1068. It was destroyed twice during the reign of Stephen, and rebuilt. In 1212, King John hanged 28 Welsh boy hostages from the castle walls during a Welsh rebellion. It came under siege in the Civil War and was pulled down in 1651 by the Parliamentarians. A new castle was built by the Duke of Newcastle in 1674–9, and this was burnt down in 1831. It was a ruin until 1875 when the Corporation restored it. The castle is now the city's museum and art gallery, and the caves leading into the castle rock can be toured by appointment.

Other interesting buildings in the city include two old inns. The well-known Trip to Jerusalem, dating from the 18th century, was built on the site of an old brewhouse where, it is said, Crusaders stopped for ale. The Salutation Inn, built in 1240, was originally the guest house of a priory.

Nottingham is an important centre for music, the arts and sport. Trent Bridge, one of the five cricket grounds in the country where Test Matches are played, holds 40,000 people; Notts County, the oldest Football League club in the country, and Nottingham Forest both have grounds in the city; and at Holme Pierrepont, just beyond the city boundary, many international events take place on the 2000-metre lake of the National Water Sports Centre.

Nottingham University stands on a wooded site facing parkland in the south-west of the city. Close by is Wollaton Hall, built between 1580 and 1588 by Sir Francis Willoughby and occupied by the Willoughby family until 1925. Nottingham's Natural History Museum is now housed in the hall and its Industrial Museum in the outbuildings.

Southwell

A small town in an attractive belt of land where the soil is as red as that of Devon. Southwell Minster, built between the 12th and 14th centuries, is a superb Norman building, with magnificent twin towers on the west face. It is famous for its beautiful stone carvings of different types of foliage, including maple, oak, hawthorn and vine, which are known as 'The Leaves of Southwell'. These carvings by an unknown medieval sculptor, the earliest of their kind in England, adorn the columns in the Chapter House.

The 17th-century Saracen's Head is the town's oldest inn, where Charles I gave himself up to the Scots in 1646.

LEAVES OF SOUTHWELL *Buttercups are among the 'leaves' carved in the 13th century on the columns of Southwell Minster*

In search of Robin Hood

A 16th-century woodcut shows Robin as a ruffian, attacking and robbing a traveller

Robin Hood, England's most popular folk hero, is also the most elusive. He is the adopted son of two forests—Sherwood and Barnsdale—and is recalled by place names in at least ten counties. He has been called a forest elf, a god of witches, a sun-myth and a Scandinavian deity. But tradition insists that he was real, and even elevates him to a peerage—as Robert Fitzooth, rightful Earl of Huntingdon. He has also been called the last of the Saxon warriors to hold out against the Norman invaders, a leader of peasant uprisings and a rough-neck yeoman.

The people's hero

The Middle Ages saw the height of the legendary Robin's popularity, for minstrels and ballad-makers made him the ideal avenger of the people's wrongs. He was cheerful, just, chivalrous and God-fearing. Though an outlaw, he was always dignified and gracious. His sanctuary was the forest. His chief enemies were priests, officials in general and the Sheriff of Nottingham in particular. His band numbered more than 100 men. He lives in legend as a manly, hotheaded patriot; a master archer who could split a willow wand with an arrow at 400 paces; and an outlaw who loved his king (but shot his king's deer), harassed the corrupt clergy and protected the poor.

The ballad-makers gave Robin other special qualities. He had, for instance, the habit of not eating until some guest or adventure turned up. And he would recruit no man without first testing him in friendly combat. One man who almost brought this practice to an end was Friar Tuck, a jovial monk whose cell is said to have been at Copmanhurst, a grassy hamlet deep in the Nottinghamshire woods of Fountain Dale. When Robin first called to invite Friar Tuck to dinner, the monk buffeted the outlaw to his knees and tipped him into a stream. When Robin's henchman, Little John, appeared with his bow at the ready, the monk called up a pack of savage dogs trained to catch arrows in their mouths. Only when Little John began shooting two arrows at once, and so killed most of the dogs, did the Friar accept Robin's invitation.

Sources of the legend

The oldest surviving ballad about Robin Hood, 'A Lytell Geste of Robyn Hode', was printed in 1489, though the ballad itself probably dates from the last quarter of the 14th century—50 years or so after the supposed outlaw's death. In it Robin is a 14th-century outlaw who lived in the reign of Edward II (1307–27). He is a robber who steals from the rich and gives to the poor, a superb archer and a baiter of greedy churchmen.

Medieval ballads such as the 'Geste' provide the only records of Robin's life: they are the source of much of the legend and most of the scholarly argument that surrounds it. In the 18th century, a scholar called Joseph Ritson compiled a two-volume anthology of the literature on Robin Hood, called *Robin Hood, a Collection of all the Ancient Poems, Songs and Ballads now extant relating to that celebrated Outlaw*. Ritson's work is the basis of most modern versions of the Robin Hood story on television and in films and literature. He concluded that Robin Hood was an outlaw of noble descent, born *c.* 1160 in the reign of Henry II (1154–89), and definitely a Nottinghamshire man.

The case for a Robin of Barnsdale

Other scholars, and some of the ballad-makers, said that Robin's haunt was not Sherwood Forest, but Yorkshire's Barnsdale Forest, now a small wood 6 miles north-west of Doncaster.

Two places in Yorkshire claim to be Robin's birthplace: the city of Wakefield and the hamlet of Loxley, near Sheffield. The aged outlaw is said to have died in a timbered upper room of Kirklees Priory Farm—all that remains of a Cistercian nunnery near Huddersfield. Before he died, he struggled to the window and shot two arrows to mark his last resting place. The first fell in the River Calder and was carried off. The second landed 500 yds away in a thicket, where a tablet said to mark his grave now stands.

There is other evidence which supports the case for a Robin of Barnsdale. Local records show that *c.* 1285 a certain Robin Hood was born at Wakefield, the son of a Yorkshire forester. He took part in the Earl of Lancaster's 1322 uprising against Edward II.

Robin of Sherwood

But Nottinghamshire's Sherwood Forest is not likely to renounce its most famous son. In the 12th century, the forest stretched northwards for more than 20 miles from Nottingham and the Trent, and though only scraps of it survive today (the best parts are around Edwinstowe), they are rich in associations with Robin. In Sherwood legend, he married Maid Marian in the Church of St Mary at Edwinstowe and used the ancient Major Oak north of Edwinstowe as a meeting-place for his band of men. Maid Marian lived at Blidworth, about 9 miles north of Nottingham. So did Will Scarlet, one of Robin's men, who is reputedly buried in the village churchyard. Friar Tuck lived a mile west of Blidworth.

There are statues of Robin outside Clipstone's Archway Lodge, in the grounds of Thoresby Hall near Edwinstowe, and outside Nottingham Castle. There is a painting of him in the arcade of Nottingham Council House, and even the Council House's deep-toned bell is named after Little John, whose reputed grave is in the churchyard at Hathersage, Derbyshire.

But for all the places that claim connections with the outlaw, for all the ballads and broadsheets, plays and proverbs, mimes and rhymes, historians have found Robin Hood and his merry men as hard to track down as any Sheriff of Nottingham ever did.

SHERWOOD FOREST *According to one version of the Robin Hood legend, Robin and his outlaws hunted deer in Sherwood's glades, and hid in its fastnesses from the Sheriff of Nottingham*

Robin is elegant and Little John's name suits him in this 17th-century woodcut

An early 18th-century print makes Robin debonair and Little John enormous

In 1845, Robin is a Victorian heart-throb with a hero-worshipping Marian

In a 20th-century children's book Robin is a handsome, bearded robber

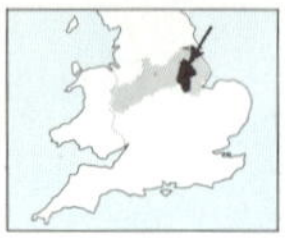

Lincoln's towering landmark

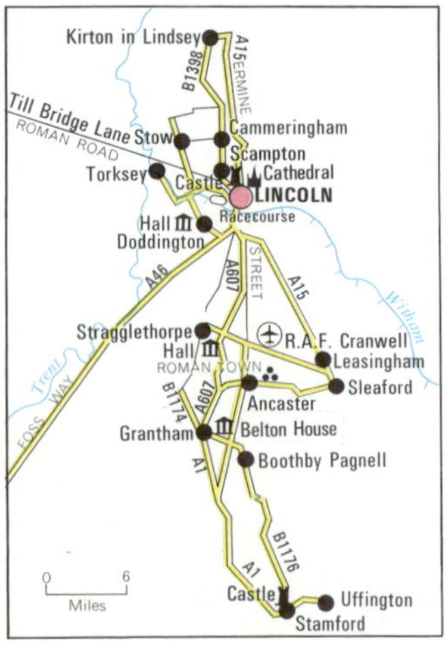

Angling There is coarse fishing on the River Witham from Grantham to Lincoln; on the River Trent; on the Fossdyke Navigation Canal at Lincoln; on the River Welland at Uffington and Stamford.

Boating Sailing and boating on the Fossdyke Navigation Canal.

Events Lincoln has a Music Festival in Mar., the Lincolnshire Show in June, and a Pleasure Fair in Sept.

Places to see *Aubourn Hall*, 6 miles south-west of Lincoln: June to Aug., Wed. afternoon. *Belton House*, 2 miles north-east of Grantham: Easter to early Oct., daily. *City and County Museum*, Lincoln: weekdays and Sun. afternoon. *Doddington Hall*: May to Sept., Wed. afternoon; also Sun. afternoon May, July and Aug. *Grantham House* (NT): Apr. to Sept., Wed. and Thur. afternoons. *Grantham Museum*: weekdays. *Lincoln Castle*: weekdays; also Sun. afternoon Apr. to Oct. *Lincoln Cathedral Library*: May to Sept., weekdays. *Lincoln Cathedral Treasury*: Easter to Sept., afternoons. *Museum of Lincolnshire Life*, Lincoln: weekdays, Sun. afternoon. *Royal Lincolnshire Regiment Museum*, Lincoln: Mon. to Fri. *Stamford Brewery Museum*: daily, except Mon. Dec. to Feb. *Woolsthorpe Manor* (NT), 7 miles south of Grantham: Apr. to Oct., Mon., Wed., Fri. and Sat.

Information centres Tourist Office, Bailgate, Lincoln. Tel. Lincoln 29828. St Mary's Hill, Stamford. Tel. Stamford 4444.

A narrow limestone ridge known as the Lincoln Edge runs from the Humber Estuary in the north, through Humberside, to Stamford in the south. Lincoln lies at the centre of the ridge, at the gap made by the River Witham.

The city dominates the region, and is itself dominated by the magnificent Cathedral Church of St Mary, visible from miles away on the main roads into the city. Two of these roads follow routes used by the Romans. The IXth Legion established the town of Lindum (Lincoln) in AD 48, at the junction of Ermine Street, leading to the north, and Foss Way, leading south-west as far as Exeter.

The local honey-coloured limestone is a building material which weathers well and is seen to advantage in cliff villages of the Lindsey and Kesteven areas and in the medieval parts of Lincoln. The countryside is mainly given over to agriculture, and farmers grow wheat, barley, sugar beet and especially potatoes, most of them for the crisp industry.

The flat land is ideal territory for airfields, and the RAF College at Cranwell is 13 miles south of Lincoln. During the Second World War, the 'Dambusters' of 617 Squadron flew from Scampton, 5 miles north of Lincoln, now a V-bomber base. Spitfires flew from Kirton in Lindsey, and in many places the landing-strips of former bases are breaking up only slowly, and forgotten runways still scar the land.

800-YEAR-OLD HOUSE *The Jew's House in The Strait, Lincoln, dates from c. 1170. It is now an antique shop, and one of the oldest houses in Britain still in use*

Ancaster
A village set in pleasant wooded country best known for its stone, quarried in medieval times to give Lincolnshire many of its churches. The quarries are 2 miles south of the village. Ancaster was important in Roman times, and traces of a 9-acre camp on Ermine Street can be seen. Finds of coins, pottery and mosaics from the site are in Grantham Museum.

Grantham
An ancient town which for years suffered from heavy traffic struggling through on the Great North Road, until a bypass was opened in the 1960's. It has some fine old coaching inns, and an attractive market square.

The beautiful 14th-century spire of St Wulfram's Church, rising to 281 ft amid a cluster of historic buildings, is a landmark for miles around. The church was built on the site of a Norman church, of which six pillars remain. A chained library, presented by a local rector in 1598, contains 83 books; the oldest volume is dated 1472. North of the church is the 15th-century grammar school, now King's School. Also near the church is Grantham House, originally 14th century, enlarged in the 16th century and extensively altered in the 18th century. It is now owned by the National Trust.

The Angel and Royal Hotel in the High Street has a 15th-century gateway and stands on the site of an earlier inn in which King John held court in 1213. The Beehive Inn in Castlegate has a unique 'inn sign'—a hive used by bees in a tree outside the inn.

Lincoln
The majestic, triple-towered cathedral standing on a 200 ft high limestone plateau overlooking the River Witham is at the centre of the city, surrounded by medieval buildings. The city grew up on this site because of its strategic position. The Romans built a camp here, and in 1068 William the Conqueror chose it as the site for a castle fortress. In modern times the city has become an important engineering centre.

The cathedral, rising to 271 ft, was built between the 12th and 14th centuries, and its honey-coloured stone seems to change colour in varying light. From the Observatory Tower at the south-east corner of the ruined Norman castle there is a bird's-eye view of the

ANCIENT AND MODERN *The parish church of Boothby Pagnell was built in the 12th century and has some fine Norman arches. The pews, roof, oak screen and much of the stained glass were completely renewed in 1897 as a gift from Mrs Cecil Thorold, who lived at nearby Boothby Hall*

west face of the cathedral. Lincoln has well-preserved Roman remains, including the splendid Newport Arch marking the north gate of the Roman settlement. The steep cobbled streets leading to the lower town are lined by medieval houses, many of them now antique shops.

Lincoln also has several Norman domestic buildings, including the Jew's House and the House of Aaron the Jew. These were built *c.* 1170 when the Normans were encouraging the Jews to finance trade.

North-east of the city centre there is a pleasant cricket ground, the Lindum. The old racecourse is now used only for occasional point-to-point races. The Fossdyke Navigation Canal, first excavated by the Romans and linking the River Witham to the Trent, has a towpath which provides pleasant walking as far as the Pyewipe Inn; 'pyewipe' is Lincolnshire dialect for the lapwing.

Doddington Hall, 5 miles south-west, is an Elizabethan manor house in mellowed brick. It contains a fine collection of china, tapestries and Stuart and Georgian furniture.

Scampton
A village of stone-walled cottages, nestling below Lincoln Edge, west of Ermine Street. The permanent ground of the Lincolnshire Show—held every June—lies to the south. There are pleasant walks along lanes to Cammeringham, north of Scampton airbase.

Stamford
An ancient town, built of mellowed local stone. The Romans had a camp here, the Saxons developed it further and the Danes made it the capital of the Fens. Later still the Normans built a castle, the traces of which can be seen today, on the site of the Danish stronghold. By the 12th century, Stamford was an important wool centre, and Stamford cloth was renowned throughout Europe. The wealth that came from wool paid for many of the 16th-century buildings in the town, which is notable for its pleasing mixture of different buildings—Georgian mansions, Queen Anne homes and Tudor houses.

In the eastern part of Stamford is the ruined chapel of St Leonard's Priory, dating mostly from the 12th century. In the wall of the old grammar school is Brasenose Gate; this was part of Brasenose Hall, which was occupied by rebellious Oxford University students who established halls of learning at Northampton and Stamford in the 13th century. By 1336 they had settled their differences with the university authorities and returned to Oxford. The 'brazen-nosed' bull from the Hall now decorates Brasenose College, Oxford.

The 13th-century St Mary's Church has an exceptionally fine 14th-century spire with four stone evangelists. All Saints' Church has a 13th-century nave and chancel and a separate tower and spire which were added in the 15th century; it also contains fine brasses.

MEDIEVAL MASTERPIECE *Lincoln Cathedral, with its fine west front, was built after an earthquake ruined an earlier church in 1185*

TENNYSON IN BRONZE *This statue of the poet Alfred, Lord Tennyson, by his friend G. F. Watts, was set up in Minster Yard, Lincoln, in 1905. Tennyson was born in 1809 in the rectory at Somersby, in the Lincolnshire Wolds, and there are memorials to him in Somersby Church*

Stow
This village can be approached from Lincoln by two Roman roads—Ermine Street as far north as Scampton and then Till Bridge Lane to the west. It is remarkable for its 11th-century Saxon and Norman church with a massive 15th-century tower. A carving of a dragon beneath the Early English font symbolises the defeated Devil. There is a fine Norman chancel in the church, which is known as the 'Mother Church of Lincoln'; it was once the cathedral of Lindsey, one of the three county councils into which Lincolnshire was divided—the others were Kesteven and Holland.

Stragglethorpe
An inelegant name for a tiny but interesting community down the west slope of the Lincoln Edge. At Stragglethorpe Hall is Britain's northernmost commercial vineyard—open on Saturdays in August—which has been built up to a vintage of more than 4000 bottles a year of Lincoln Imperial, a white burgundy-type wine. Until the Dissolution of the Monasteries, Britain had many vineyards, but the number dwindled to two, although more have been planted in recent years.

IN THE VINEYARD *Vines are sprayed against mildew at Stragglethorpe Hall on the slopes of the Lincoln Edge. This is the northernmost commercial vineyard in Britain; the grapes are left on the vines until after the first frosts, when they are picked and made into white wine*

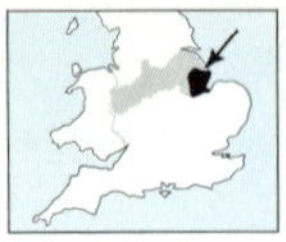

Fertile fenland of Britain's 'Holland'

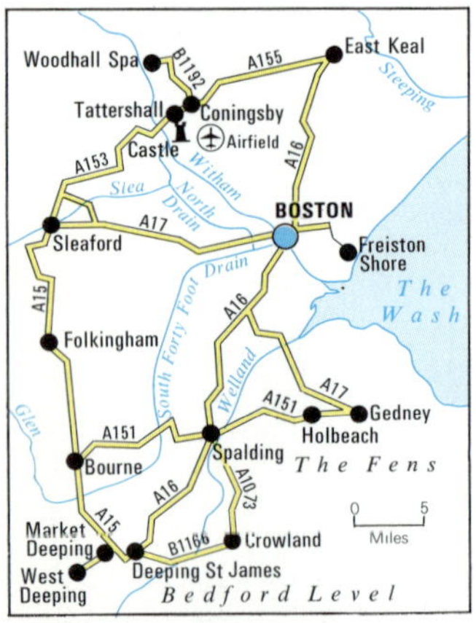

The flat fenland of Lincolnshire, only just above sea level, is largely and appropriately in a part of the county that, until recently, was an administrative division known as Holland. The triangulation points, giving heights above sea level, read monotonously in single figures. From the brow of the hill at East Keal on the A16, the whole panorama of the Lincolnshire fenland is spread out below. In the distance can be seen The Wash and the 272-ft Perpendicular tower of St Botolph's Church at Boston, graphically called the 'Boston Stump'.

The marshy land around The Wash, the refuge of Hereward the Wake, has been drained in sections over the centuries to create some of Britain's richest agricultural land. The Romans built the first sea wall along the north shore of The Wash, and the rivers which drain sluggishly into it—the Welland, the Steeping and the Witham—are all bounded by high man-made banks along their lower stretches. Every perspective in this completely flat land is two-thirds cloudscape, and the winds that sweep across The Wash in winter can be almost as cold and bitter as any weather experienced in Siberia.

The soil is varied within short distances but is generally rich. 'The darker the colour, the better the soil' is a local maxim. Forty well-farmed acres in the best areas can provide a good living for a family, and land for agriculture fetches a higher price here than in most other parts of the country. In spring, visitors drive round the tulip fields in Spalding.

Angling There is good coarse fishing for pike, bream and roach on the River Witham and on the North and South Forty Foots at Boston. Trout and coarse fishing on the Slea at Sleaford and on the Witham at Boston. Coarse fishing on the Welland at Spalding and Market Deeping.

Boating There is sailing and motor cruising on the River Witham at Boston; speedboat racing at Tattershall; and sailing on the Welland at Spalding.

Events Spalding Flower Parade is held early in May.

Places to see *Ayscoughfee Hall and Gardens*, Spalding: weekdays. *Boston Guildhall Museum*: weekdays, except Sat. afternoons Oct. to Apr. *Red Hall*, Bourne, Elizabethan gentleman's residence: Mon. to Fri. *Tattershall Castle* (NT): weekdays and Sun. afternoon, but closed afternoons Oct. to Mar.

Information centre Tourist Information Centre, Ayscoughfee Gardens, Spalding. Tel. 5468.

TATTERSHALL CASTLE *Windows in the keep bear the Arms of past owners*

Boston

The ancient town on the River Witham was a flourishing seaport in the 13th century, but its importance declined when the opening up of the New World diverted much of its trade to ports on Britain's west coast. The silting up of The Wash also contributed to Boston's decline as a port. But though the largest vessels cannot reach the town today, its quays still bustle with timber and banana boats.

The town and the land around are dominated by the 14th-century St Botolph's Church. The interior has a magnificent roof and fine carvings.

Boston has good buildings of the Middle Ages and other periods. South Street contains the 15th-century guildhall and the 18th-century Fydell House, the home of the Pilgrim College which has a room reserved for visitors from Boston, Massachusetts. The American Boston owes its name to emigrants from the town who sailed from Southampton in 1630, led by John Winthrop. The half-timbered Shodfriars Hall in the market place was built in 15th-century style only 100 years ago.

Bourne

This market town, once the refuge of Hereward the Wake, is known today for the BRM racing cars which were manufactured there. The town also services the agricultural community around it. Bourne's water is said to be among the purest in the country, and there are extensive watercress beds.

Sir William Cecil (1520–98), Lord High Treasurer to Elizabeth I, and created Baron Burghley in 1571, was born in a house which is now the Burghley Arms Hotel. The town was also the birthplace of Frederick Worth (1825–95), founder of the House of Worth in Paris, which became a centre of the fashion world. Only the 13th-century church remains of the Augustinian abbey founded in 1138.

TULIP TIME *More than half Britain's bulbs are grown around Spalding, and thousands of acres of spring flowers blossom at the end of April and the beginning of May*

LINCOLNSHIRE DUTCH GABLES

Houses gabled in Dutch style are a feature of the Fens. In the 16th century, the gables were 'crow-stepped'—with stepped and not sloping sides. Later these crow-steps were separated by curves, as in this 18th-century Lincolnshire house. The Dutch influence on Lincolnshire building-styles arose from trading links over the centuries

Coningsby

The Church of St Michael and All Angels in the village is notable for its early 17th-century, one-handed, red-faced clock. It is $16\frac{1}{2}$ ft in diameter, the largest one-handed clock in the world. The village is now dominated by an RAF jet-fighter base.

Folkingham

A village on the edge of the Fens and on the fringe of the limestone cliff. The A15 between Sleaford and Bourne turns into a square of splendid houses which retain the original atmosphere of this 18th-century coaching halt. On the site of a medieval castle is an old prison.

Freiston Shore
A village lying close to the sea amid rich agricultural land, intensively farmed for market produce. The sea wall is dotted with notices warning that the marshes are dangerous. The creeks also should be avoided, unless the visitor is prepared to swim to safety when the tide floods in quickly. There are well-worn, hard paths through the safe parts of the saltings. The marshes are excellent for bird-watching. In winter they echo to the clatter of thousands of redshanks and Brent geese, visiting The Wash after an Arctic summer. Snow buntings, along with the rarer Lapland buntings and Shore larks, may also be seen in winter.

Holbeach
A market town in the middle of the bulb-growing district. The church has a magnificent tower and spire. Between the town and sea wall there is a scatter of villages. One of these, Gedney, has a church with a 14th-century porch and 15th-century nave. There is a pleasant walk along the sea bank, but the sea itself is far out across a stretch of treacherous mud and marsh.

Sleaford
An ancient market town on the western edge of the Fens that takes its name from the river on which it stands. The 12th to 15th-century parish church of St Denys has splendid window tracery and some chained books. The Black Bull Inn has a carved stone dated 1689 showing bull-baiting, which was last practised in Sleaford in 1807.

Spalding
The River Welland flows under seven bridges through the centre of this splendid old market town. Spalding is the centre of an intensively farmed agricultural area and is the capital of 'Tulipland'. The countless tulips and daffodils provide a popular attraction for visitors who drive round the fields in April and early May to view a kaleidoscope of colour across some 10,000 acres.

The town is a happy mixture of old and new buildings. Among the oldest are the 13th-century Church of SS Mary and Nicholas, which has unusual double aisles, and the 14th-century White Hart Inn. The Gentlemen's Society, an antiquarian society founded in 1709–10 and including Sir Isaac Newton and Alexander Pope among its members, displays a bird collection in 15th-century Ayscoughfee Hall, and has a museum in Broad Street.

BOSTON STUMP *The octagonal tower of St Botolph's Church, rising 272 ft beside the River Witham at Boston, is a landmark for shipping in The Wash. The 'Boston Stump', as it is called, is visible for miles across the Fens and even from parts of Norfolk*

Tattershall
The flat land of the Fens and the flood plain of the River Witham provide views from all directions of Tattershall Castle. This 15th-century fortified house, now owned by the National Trust, is one of the most splendid examples of medieval brick building. Brick was only just becoming popular as a building material at that time. The square and massive medieval keep, built by the 3rd Lord Cromwell and restored this century, is one of the man-made landmarks of the Fens. From the keep there are magnificent views of the village, Lincoln Cathedral and the 'Boston Stump'.

West Deeping
This small village on the old Roman King Street is distinguished by a splendid watermill and an adjoining elegant Georgian facade. To the east, past Deeping St James with its partly-Norman priory church, is the fenland stretch known as the Bedford Level.

Woodhall Spa
The town has a pump room built in Victorian times after the discovery of medicinal water. The area is different from the Fens and has stretches of heather, pine and silver birch. The town's golf course is Lincolnshire's only course of championship standard.

The Lincolnshire Wolds

Angling There is trout and coarse fishing on the Rivers Bain and Waring at Horncastle. There is also coarse fishing, especially for big pike, in Revesby Reservoir, 4½ miles south-east of Horncastle.

Horse racing At Market Rasen.

Motor sports The Cadwell Racing Course, 4 miles south-west of Louth, has motor racing and motor-cycle racing during the summer. There is also cyclocross.

Forest walks The Forestry Commission have provided walks at Willingham Forest. They start from the picnic site 2 miles east of Market Rasen.

Events Louth holds a sportsman's week every July, covering all sporting activities including a gymkhana.

Place to see *Louth Naturalists, Antiquarian and Literary Society Museum*: Wed., Sat. and Sun. afternoons. *Watermill*, Alvingham, 2 miles north-east of Louth: Easter to Sept., Mon. and Thur. afternoons and 2nd and 4th Sun. afternoon of each month; also Bank Hol.

Information centres The Town Hall, Eastgate, Louth. Tel. Louth 2391. The Town Hall, Boston Road, Horncastle. Tel. Horncastle 3513.

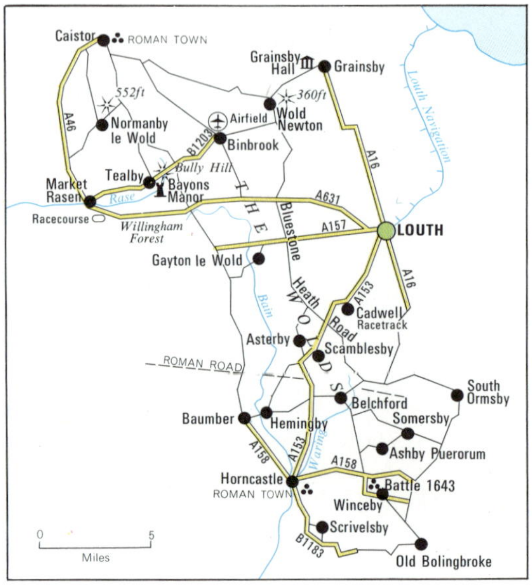

The 40-mile stretch of chalk uplands known as the Wolds belies the common belief that Lincolnshire is simply an extension of the flat East Anglian Fens. The Wolds contain rolling hills and deep valleys, quiet streams and hanging beechwoods, and the land rises to 552 ft near Normanby le Wold. The land is lightly populated, but there is heavy and prosperous investment in sheep and crop farming. In the north, farmers are concentrating increasingly on vegetables for the frozen-food factories around Grimsby. Peas are harvested to a tight schedule—often under floodlights on summer nights.

Apart from the main road to Skegness—and this is busy only in high summer—traffic is light. The minor roads offer lovely drives in pleasant countryside. Along the Bluestone Heath road, marking the crest of the scarp between South Ormsby and Gayton le Wold, pheasants can be seen at the roadside. Along the minor road between Baumber and Scamblesby, a superbly gabled house shows the Dutch influence on the county's architecture over the centuries. There are other links with the past. The route of a Roman road can be traced for 5 miles across the Wolds. It starts from the A153 to the north-west of Belchford and strikes west past Sotby Wood. The place names of towns and villages in the county recall the Danish invasions of the 9th century—the ending *-by*, for instance, is Danish for a settlement, and a *thorpe* was a farm belonging to a village.

Somersby, a village at the southern end of the Wolds, looking southwards to the enormous horizons of the Fens, is renowned as the birthplace of the 19th-century poet Alfred, Lord Tennyson. The vast distances and lonely horizons of the Wolds were to play their part in his poetry; in his 'In Memoriam' he recalled the

'Calm and deep peace on this high wold,
And on these dews that drench the furze.'

THE SPIRE OF LOUTH *The 300-ft spire of St James's Church at Louth, which stands like a beacon above the level marshlands of the Humber Estuary, was completed in 1515. The spire was built from stone brought 50 miles from the quarries at Ancaster; it reflects different colours as the light changes*

GRAZING LANDS *Sheep graze beside an old farm cart on the*

HARVESTING ROUND THE CLOCK

Large holdings and intensive farming methods make the Wolds one of England's most prosperous farming areas for wheat (below) and peas (right). The peas, destined for the frozen-food factories around Grimsby, have to be gathered at their peak condition, and harvesting goes on through the night under floodlights; farmers direct the drivers by short-wave radio

rolling chalk downlands of the Wolds near Louth; the area is fine sheep-rearing country

Caistor
The small market town was once a Roman settlement, the remains of which can still be seen. The Church of SS Peter and Paul is partly Saxon, and has a tower with Norman work in it.

Horncastle
One of the principal market towns serving this predominantly agricultural area. It lies in the valley of the River Bain at its junction with the River Waring. The walls of the Roman town, Banovallum, are partly preserved. The market-place is pleasantly leafy, but today's markets are not on the scale of the enormous ten-day horse fairs held annually until the last century. There are a number of pleasant brick houses and some old inns, including The Fighting Cocks, named after a popular sport in the days of the horse fairs. St Mary's Church, near the market-place, has some Civil War relics, such as pikes and scythes.

Louth
One of the most perfectly preserved Georgian market towns in England, and a good centre from which to tour the Wolds. The first view of Louth from the Lincoln road, coming over the hills from the west, is of the spire of St James's Church, which dates from 1515. This splendid soaring spire is made of Ancaster stone. The greatest wealth of Louth is in its variety of Georgian and early-Victorian architecture. The town has a complex street pattern and is best explored on foot. There is a variety of good brickwork, and Westgate is mostly Georgian.

There is a Georgian inn in Bridge Street, and an early publisher of Tennyson's poems had premises in the market-place. Monks' Dyke, now the name of a school, is a reminder of the Cistercian abbey which was sited a mile east of the town. A good golf course lies on rising land west of the town.

Old Bolingbroke
This is probably the finest Wold village, and certainly the most historic. Set in a south-facing pocket at the southern edge of the Wolds, it was the birthplace in 1366 of Henry IV, and mounds mark the site of the castle held by his father, John of Gaunt. In the Civil War the castle attracted the attention of Cromwell, as it was a Royalist stronghold in Parliamentary territory. A major clash between the two armies took place 3½ miles from the castle, near Winceby on the southern slopes of the Wolds, on October 12, 1643. From the main road there is a view north-east across placid fields of barley towards Slash Hollow, where the opposing armies met. Bolingbroke Castle was pulled down after the Parliamentarians' victory.

Scrivelsby
The now-demolished court in the fenced, 360-acre deer park at Scrivelsby was once the home of the Hereditary Grand Champion of England, who was granted feudal rights at the time of the Conquest. In medieval times it was his duty to arrive in full armour at Westminster at the time of a Coronation, and challenge anyone who disputed the king's right to the throne. The present Champion, who now carries the Royal Standard at Coronations, lives in the gatehouse.

Somersby
Tennyson, who was made Poet Laureate in 1850, was born in this little village in 1809. His father was the local rector; the rambling rectory is now a private house. Ashby Puerorum, 2 miles west, got the second part of its name, Latin for 'of the boys', because local land revenues were once used to support the boy choristers of Lincoln Cathedral.

Tealby
An attractive Wold village beside the River Rase. There is a steep climb to 480-ft Bully Hill, which has a beech clump clinging to its west face. The ruins of Bayons Manor, once the home of Tennyson's grandfather, lie just south of the village. Tealby is well looked after, with many good houses, expensively restored. To the east the road follows the river, although well up the side of its valley.

Wold Newton
In a valley between well-wooded shoulders of the Wolds, the village straggles along the road, seemingly submerged by its leafy surrounds. A lane to the east climbs to 360 ft, with lovely views north and east to the mouth of the River Humber. The land is well stocked with game; and pheasants, partridges and brown hares can often be seen. The lane then drops past Hawerby Farm down to Grainsby, on the edge of the Wolds, and leads through the gated parkland of Grainsby Hall. On the left, almost hidden by trees, is a church with a Norman tower.

GEORGIAN GEM *Westgate at Louth contains many fine 18th-century houses*

Port on a bracing coast

Angling There is coarse fishing on the Great Eau at Theddlethorpe All Saints, 3½ miles south of Saltfleet; on the River Steeping at Skegness and Spilsby, 7 miles south-west of Alford; on the Eresby Canal at Spilsby; and on the lakeside lido at Saltfleet. Sea fishing at Grimsby along the Humber and the foreshore to Tetney Lock; at Mablethorpe for flatfish and mackerel.

Boating There is offshore sailing at Cleethorpes, Grimsby and Humberston, 4 miles south of Grimsby. Dinghy sailing at South Beach, Ingoldmells, and at Saltfleet. Sailing and boating at Sutton on Sea and Mablethorpe.

Shipping There are regular summer passenger and car-ferry services from Immingham, 7 miles north-west of Grimsby, to Gothenburg, Sweden, on Fri. and on some Wed.

Places to see *Alford Windmill*: Spring and late Summer Bank Hol.; also 3rd Sat., June, July, Aug. *Burgh le Marsh Windmill*: daily. *Church Farm Museum*, Skegness: Apr. to Sept., daily. *Doughty Museum*, Grimsby: Tues. to Sat. *Gunby Hall* (NT): by written appointment with tenant. *Mablethorpe Animal and Bird Garden*: Easter to Oct., daily. *Thornton Abbey*: weekdays and Sun. afternoon.

Information centres Foreshore Office, North Parade, Skegness. Tel. Skegness 4821 (seasonal). Alexander Road, Cleethorpes. Tel. Cleethorpes 67472. Foreshore Office, Central Promenade, Mablethorpe. Tel. Mablethorpe 2496.

The long stretch of the Lincolnshire coast from Gibraltar Point to the mouth of the Humber is a land of sand-dunes and buckthorn, where the grey or mud-coloured North Sea often retreats so far across the foreshore as almost to disappear. The coast is flat and, since the disastrous floods of 1953, heavily embanked with concrete at danger points such as Sutton on Sea. The offshore gradient is so slight that even when there is a flood tide it is hard to find a good depth for swimming. Soil washed south from the Humberside coast has built up new stretches of dunes and salt-marsh at Gibraltar Point.

The holiday resorts—Cleethorpes, Mablethorpe and Skegness—come to life for the brief summer season of the East Coast. They have traditional ties with the industrial towns of the East Midlands, and succeed by offering raucous jollity and a holiday-camp atmosphere to their regular patrons. Large caravan sites have grown up along the coast in recent years. Behind the dunes lies marshland, flat but different in nature from the fen. This is rich pasture-land for Lincoln red cattle, and good farming land. The farmers often operate on such a large scale that two-way radios and closed-circuit television are their sophisticated aids. Three good windmills in working order at Alford, Burgh le Marsh and Waltham help to break the flat monotony of the marshland.

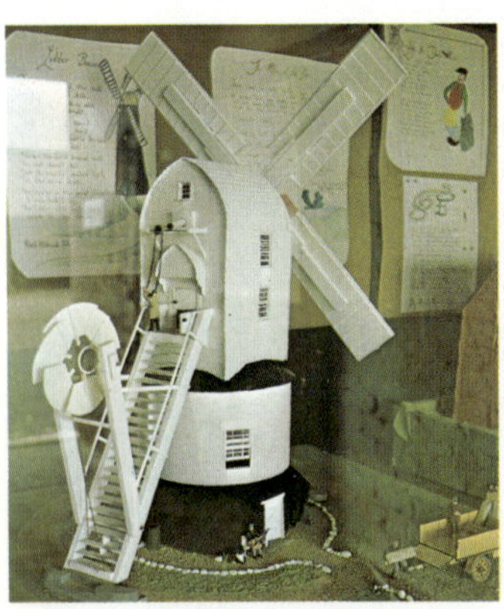

MODEL WINDMILL *Burgh le Marsh Windmill Museum, set up by a local school, contains models, prints and maps*

ALFORD MILL *Windmills are a feature of the Lincolnshire landscape. The five-sailed tower mill at Alford was built in 1837*

Alford
A pleasant small town with a five-sail windmill in full working order, though no longer used. West of the town, sheep graze on the gentle slopes of the Wolds, and there are pleasant lanes for walking between Ulceby, Skendleby and Claxby. Ulceby is a pretty village set in woodland, and has an attractive 18th-century manor house and brick church dating from 1826.

Burgh le Marsh
This village has a well-preserved tower windmill, in working order. The giant sails overshadow the surrounding houses. An outhouse adjoining the mill has been renovated by a local secondary school as a windmill museum. The village is notable for the discovery, in the 1930's, of a superbly worked pre-Bronze Age axehead, one of only five similar heads which have been unearthed in Britain. It is held by a local resident, an antiquary, who found it while digging in a chicken run. Cockpit Hill provides a fine view of the surrounding countryside.

Cleethorpes
A coastal resort whose wide promenade gives fine views of shipping entering the mouth of the Humber, and of distant Spurn Head, with its lighthouse and lifeboat station. Cleethorpes, just within the Humberside border, has a wide beach and the usual holiday facilities for visitors in the summer season. There are several fine houses in the suburbs and surrounding villages which reflect the wealth produced by Grimsby's fishing industry.

HOME FROM THE SEA *A trawler at the quayside at Grimsby, which until recently had a fleet of 260 ships. They can be away for weeks at a time following shoals of fish.*

SMOKED FISH *Haddock is cured by being smoked on rods for at least eight hours*

SEA LAVENDER *The flower grows widely on the Gibraltar Point salt-marshes*

Gibraltar Point
A nature reserve on the tip of the coast. Sandbanks and saltings stretching southwards into The Wash have been built up by eroded material from further north. A Field Centre is used by naturalists, and there are fine views on sunny days over the glittering waters of The Wash. There are three car parks, and many tracks through the dunes and grass. This is a centre for the study of bird migration; the ringing of migrants is part of the work of the station.

In spring the area is alive with the songs of thousands of larks. Careful watching may reveal kestrels searching for prey, or short-eared owls which quarter the saltings at dusk. Seals can often be seen on the offshore sandbanks at Dog's Head or Outer Knock.

Grimsby
The largest town on the coast, and one of the world's great fishing ports. Until the recent Icelandic cod war, there was a 24-hour movement of heavy lorries out of the town laden with frozen fish for the Midlands and the South; but that dispute has seriously diminished the activity of the port, and many of its trawlers are now laid up.

MEDIEVAL GRANDEUR *A bridge 120 ft long spans a moat to the fine 14th-century gatehouse of Thornton Abbey. The gatehouse, probably a guest house for the abbey, is an early example of a building faced partly in stone and partly in brick*

Gunby Hall
A National Trust property, but also a private residence, dating from 1700 and set on a mound at the head of a tree-lined drive. It has superbly panelled rooms and rich portraiture.

Mablethorpe
A holiday centre surrounded by bungalows and vast caravan sites. Good sands stretch southwards to Sutton on Sea, where there are more caravans and good bathing stretches.

Skegness
The posters on the railway station have, for generations, described the town as 'bracing'. Though the east winds can deter the less hardy visitor from the town's extensive beaches, Skegness has many attractions for the Midlands holidaymaker. There are plenty of seaside entertainments including donkey rides between the expansive dunes and the promenade, amusement arcades, a holiday camp and 34 acres of seafront gardens. There are two golf courses and, to the north, the town merges into Ingoldmells, which has excellent sands and large caravan parks.

Theddlethorpe St Helen
There is a National Nature Reserve here, and the banks of grass-covered dunes are an important conservation area for the natterjack toad—a small toad with a yellow stripe on its back, which does not hop, but runs. Along the coast to the north, past Saltfleet Haven to Donna Nook, the sea recedes so far that, at low tide, it all but disappears across an enormous expanse of ridged sand and mud which is very rich in shells. This can be a dangerous coast, because the unwary can find themselves lost in a sandy expanse if a mist comes in off the sea. The tide floods in quickly over this flat shore. A walk along the dunes is safer and more pleasant.

Thornton Abbey
The oil refineries lining the horizon to the north on Humberside are of the 20th century; but the great castellated gatehouse of the abbey is a monument to the ecclesiastical craftsmen of 600 years earlier. The remainder of the abbey, across a field to the east, is a well-tended ruin set off by trim lawns. The gatehouse, almost imperial in its solidity, retains superb carved figures on the west front and shows the great scale of the Augustinian abbey before the Dissolution. The dignified stone of farmhouses close by shows the use to which the pillaged ruins were later put.

Wainfleet All Saints
A former port, now 5 miles inland. South of the town the River Steeping winds between high banks to The Wash. William of Waynflete, a bishop of Winchester and founder of Magdalen College, Oxford, was born here *c.* 1395. In 1484 he left Magdalen College School, now a library, to the town.

NORTH-WEST ENGLAND

The counties that make up the north-west of England—Cheshire, Lancashire, the newly created Merseyside, Greater Manchester and Cumbria (Cumberland and Westmorland)—have always been different in character, even before the arrival of the Industrial Revolution which was to scar parts of the south, yet leave untouched vast areas of Cumbria. Differences in accent exist, too, for Cumbria, protected by its mountains, remained predominantly Celtic long after the Anglo-Saxon invasion had colonised much of Cheshire and Lancashire.

The area's greatest scenic distinction lies in the Lake District, set like a jewel among the Cumbrian Mountains. There are 16 major lakes, ranging in size from Windermere, 10½ miles long, to tiny Brothers Water, less than half a mile long. Towering above them are four mountains topping 3000 ft, including Scafell Pike, England's highest peak at 3210 ft. The mountains are separated by England's highest mountain passes, six of which carry roads climbing to over 1000 ft—including the 1489 ft high Kirkstone Pass. Footpaths climb higher still, reaching 2000 ft over Esk Hause, Sticks Pass and Nan Bield Pass.

LIMESTONE CIRCLE *Cheshire's flat sandstone land runs to Lancashire's Fylde plain. The Pennines' west flank of millstone grit and carboniferous limestone encircles the Lake District. Inside the ring are the granite outcrops of the Cumbrian Mountains*

The Lake District is a part of Cumbria to be relished slowly. The most popular centre for touring the lakes is Keswick, where in summer the roads are crowded with traffic streaming into Borrowdale. The roads to Buttermere over Newlands Pass, and to Lorton over Whinlatter Pass, avoid this bottleneck at the height of the tourist season and lead towards the quiet and majestic valleys of Ennerdale and Wasdale.

The remaining parts of north Cumbria convey the impression of a forgotten country. The western coast has industrial outposts which appear at Maryport, Workington, Whitehaven and Seascale like breakaway fragments of the south Lancashire scene. Around these towns, however, is the best coastline north of Blackpool. There are superb sands from Silloth to Millom and, inland, roads that cut across the hills offer glorious views. From Hartside Pass over the Pennine fells north-east of Penrith a third of north-west England, stretching beyond the Lake District to the Solway Firth, can be seen at a glance.

Damson blossom and dairy farming

Lakeland is surrounded by fertile country. There is dairy and stock-beef farming on the Solway plain and in the Vale of Eden, and orchards flourish in sheltered valleys—the Lyth Valley, west of Kendal, is a mass of damson blossom each spring. Further south, much of the agricultural landscape of Lancashire, and to some extent of Cheshire, is as man-made as the mills, factories and mines of the counties' industrial centres. To keep pace with the demands for produce, brought about by the Industrial Revolution of 100 years ago, peat bogs had to be drained in Merseyside and Greater Manchester, and pastures were improved in Cheshire. Today there is large-scale dairy farming on the Cheshire Plain and a variety of crops is grown in Lancashire and Merseyside. Potatoes grow around Ormskirk; tomatoes on the Fylde plain; asparagus at Formby; and market-gardening flourishes at Southport.

Lancashire is the most varied of the north-western counties. It has a windy moorland at its heart, and a great industrial tradition which grew first on cotton, 200 years ago, then on coal-mining, chemicals and engineering. In contrast, the fertile Lancashire plain has rural, wooded country, with sheltered hamlets and tiny villages around Pendle Hill. Further north is the rugged Bowland Forest and, beyond this, the green valley of the River Lune. Limestone hills rise north of Morecambe Bay, and the peninsula of Furness is rich in iron ore.

The white cliffs of south Cumbria

South Cumbria at once conveys an impression of great beauty. Most of the land is limestone, seen at its most striking south of Kendal, where cliffs flash white from Farleton Knott, a high and isolated grass-topped ridge flanking the M6 motorway. Similar ridges line the valley of the River Winster to the west, where hamlets stand on knolls above flat peatland, thick with foliage and flowers.

The more exposed limestone outcrops of Orton Scar, north of Kendal, have been plundered by the lorry-load to provide stones for rock gardens all over England. A rarer form of limestone, Coniston limestone, runs through south Cumbria from Shap, cutting across Kentmere, Ambleside and The Tarns. It can be best seen at Boo Tarn, near Coniston.

Throughout the North-West there is a profusion of architectural styles, with stonework in a variety of colours. Stately homes include Lyme Park, at Disley in Cheshire, one of the noblest English mansions, with an

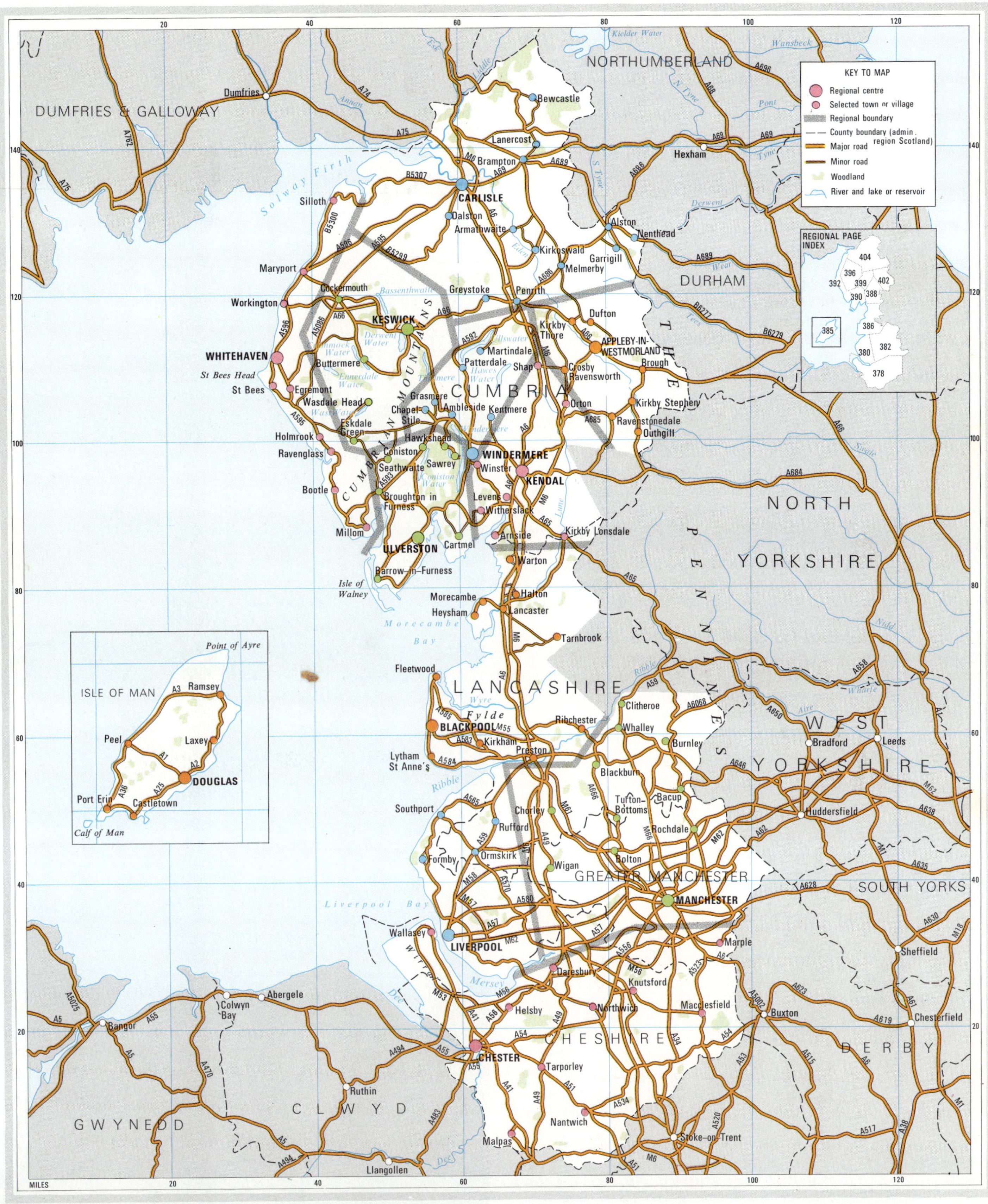
KEY TO MAP
Regional centre
Selected town or village
Regional boundary
County boundary (admin. region Scotland)
Major road
Minor road
Woodland
River and lake or reservoir
REGIONAL PAGE INDEX
404
396
392
399
402
390
388
385
386
382
380
378
DUMFRIES & GALLOWAY
NORTHUMBERLAND
DURHAM
CUMBRIA
CUMBRIAN MOUNTAINS
THE PENNINES
NORTH YORKSHIRE
LANCASHIRE
WEST YORKSHIRE
GREATER MANCHESTER
SOUTH YORKS
CHESHIRE
DERBY
CLWYD
GWYNEDD
ISLE OF MAN
Point of Ayre
Ramsey
Peel
Laxey
DOUGLAS
Port Erin
Castletown
Calf of Man
Dumfries
Bewcastle
Lanercost
Brampton
Hexham
CARLISLE
Silloth
Dalston
Armathwaite
Alston
Nenthead
Kirkoswald
Garrigill
Melmerby
Maryport
Cockermouth
Workington
Greystoke
Penrith
KESWICK
Dufton
Kirkby Thore
APPLEBY-IN-WESTMORLAND
WHITEHAVEN
Martindale
Buttermere
Patterdale
Shap
Crosby Ravensworth
Brough
St Bees Head
St Bees
Egremont
Wasdale Head
Grasmere
Orton
Kirkby Stephen
Chapel Stile
Ambleside
Kentmere
Ravenstonedale
Outhgill
Eskdale Green
Holmrook
Hawkshead
Ravenglass
Coniston
WINDERMERE
Seathwaite
Sawrey
Winster
KENDAL
Bootle
Broughton in Furness
Levens
Witherslack
Millom
Arnside
Kirkby Lonsdale
ULVERSTON
Cartmel
Warton
Barrow-in-Furness
Isle of Walney
Morecambe
Halton
Heysham
Lancaster
Morecambe Bay
Tarnbrook
Fleetwood
Fylde
Clitheroe
Ribchester
Whalley
BLACKPOOL
Kirkham
Burnley
Bradford
Leeds
Lytham St Anne's
Preston
Blackburn
Southport
Turton-Bottoms
Bacup
Chorley
Huddersfield
Rufford
Rochdale
Formby
Ormskirk
Bolton
Wigan
MANCHESTER
Liverpool Bay
Wallasey
LIVERPOOL
Marple
Sheffield
Daresbury
Knutsford
Abergele
Colwyn Bay
Helsby
Northwich
Macclesfield
Buxton
Bangor
Chesterfield
CHESTER
Tarporley
Ruthin
Nantwich
Malpas
Stoke-on-Trent
Llangollen
Solway Firth
Kielder Water
Wansbeck
Eden
Tees
Swale
Nidd
Ribble
Wyre
Wharfe
Aire
Mersey
Dee
Wirral
MILES

Elizabethan drawing-room which is hardly bettered anywhere in Britain. Equally attractive are the gracious houses such as Brantwood on the shores of Coniston. Black is the dominant colour in many a row of terraced cottages in the Lancashire valleys; a blackness not of industrial grime, but simply of years of weathering of yellow-gritstone walls. Blackened timbers and whitened plasterwork are the ingredients of the so-called 'magpie' houses which are a familiar sight throughout the Cheshire Plain. Blue and green slates cover the roofs of many Lakeland homes, contrasting with their whitewashed walls, while the sandstone areas of south Cumbria have villages of red-walled houses.

The main holiday centres of the North-West are Southport, Blackpool and Morecambe on the coast, and Keswick and Windermere in the Lake District. Blackpool is by far the largest, drawing huge numbers of day-trippers—especially for the autumn illuminations. Morecambe, with the M6 motorway coming almost into the town, is also crowded for the illuminations. By contrast, the Trough of Bowland, the fellsides above Tebay Gorge and the Cumbrian countryside north of Appleby-in-Westmorland are large and unspoilt tracts of lonely and lovely land which can all be reached easily from side turnings off the M6.

The scars begin to disappear

Many of the decaying buildings of industrial Lancashire and Greater Manchester, described by George Orwell as 'festering in planless chaos', have disappeared. Even the slag heaps, unkindly named 'the Wigan Alps', have been broken down and churned into the foundations of the M6 motorway; and there are plans to make ski-runs out of the slag heaps that remain above the disused coal-fields. The town centres themselves are also beginning to change. Wigan, Bolton, Blackburn and Burnley are all redeveloping their shopping areas as attractive pedestrian precincts; but at the same time they are retaining among the modern buildings the best of the old architecture, which is mainly Victorian.

The one unchanging facet of the North-West is the Lake District. Its protection as an area of unspoilt countryside has been assured by its designation in 1951 as a National Park—the country's largest, with 866 square miles of mountainous countryside. Its superb scenery is much the same today as it was more than 150 years ago when Wordsworth lived there and found inspiration among its hills and lakes.

A DRY, SUNNY SPRING IN LAKELAND

The Pennines create wide variations in the temperature and rainfall of the North-West, and high regions can be particularly wet, windy and bleak. The Lake District is at its sunniest and driest in the spring. The wettest parts of Cumbria have five times as much rain as London; but Manchester—despite its reputation as a rainy city—has 20 per cent less rain than south Cornwall. Blackpool averages more than 4 hours of sunshine a day

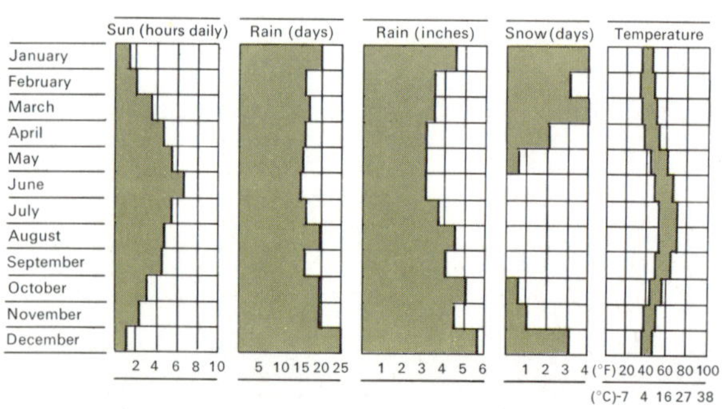

WORDSWORTH'S ULLSWATER *Ullswater, looking towards 2154-ft Place Fell, typifies the beauty of the lakes. It was here that Wordsworth saw 'a host of golden daffodils; beside the lake, beneath the trees, fluttering and dancing in the breeze'*

Across the Cheshire Plain

Boating Boats can be hired on the River Dee at Chester, and on the Shropshire Union Canal at Waverton and Macclesfield. Horse-drawn boat trips on the Chester Canal.

Places to see *Alderley Old Mill* (NT), Nether Alderley: Wed., Sun. and Bank Hol. afternoons, Apr. to Oct. *Beeston Castle*: daily, except Sun. morning Oct. to Mar. *Bramall Hall*, Bramhall: daily, except Thur. *Bridgemere Wildlife Park*, 6½ miles south-east of Nantwich: daily, Mar. to Oct. *British Heritage Centre*, Chester: daily. *Capesthorne*, 6½ miles north of Congleton: Sun. afternoon, Apr. to Sept.; also Wed. and Sat. afternoons from early May and Tues. and Thur. afternoons from late July. *Chester Heritage Centre*: Apr. to Sept., weekdays, Sun. afternoon; Oct. to Mar., afternoons except Wed. *Chester Zoo*, Upton: daily. *Department of Radio Astronomy*, Jodrell Bank: Easter to Oct., afternoons; Nov. to Easter, weekend afternoons. *Gawsworth Hall*: late Mar. to Oct., afternoons. *Grosvenor Museum*, Chester: weekdays, Sun. afternoon. *Guildhall Museum*, Chester: daily, except Wed. and Sun., May to mid-Sept. *Lady Lever Art Gallery*, Birkenhead: weekdays, Sun. afternoon. *Little Moreton Hall* (NT), 4 miles south-west of Congleton: Mar., Sat. and Sun. afternoons; Apr. to Oct., afternoons except Tues. *Lyme Park* (NT), 6½ miles south-east of Stockport: Apr. to Sept., Tues. to Sun. and Bank Hol. afternoons; Mar. and Oct., Sun. afternoon. *Tatton Park* (NT): park, daily except Mon.; house, afternoons except Mon., Apr. to mid-Oct.

Information centre Publicity Dept., Town Hall, Chester. Tel. Chester 40144.

Countryside like a vast park rolls across the Cheshire Plain outside the industrial centres. There are textile factories in Macclesfield and Stalybridge; a railway centre at Crewe; and, at Winsford, a salt mine which recalls the fact that millions of years ago this land was submerged by the sea. But the abiding impression of the plain is one of cattle moving lazily over grassy slopes thick with buttercups; of woodlands and meres; and of the typical black-and-white 'magpie' houses set among rhododendrons. The River Dee runs gently through this rich farmland, past the ancient city of Chester and out to the Irish Sea across a huge sandy estuary.

Wooded ridges were the sites of ancient British forts long before the Romans made Chester a key stronghold. These hilltops, scattered with traces of ramparts, give grandstand views. From Beeston Castle, near Tarporley, eight counties can be seen. And from a hilltop castle at Halton, near Runcorn, the mighty River Mersey winds below, on its way to the sea past the Wirral peninsula, where long stretches of sandy coastline and holiday resorts lie close to the cranes, grain elevators and oil-refinery tanks of Ellesmere Port and Birkenhead.

BRAMALL HALL *This 15th-century timbered house near Stockport was restored by the Davenport family in 1819*

ANCIENT AND MODERN *Ruined 13th-century Beeston Castle overlooks a modern mock-medieval castle in the Peckforton Hills*

CHESHIRE'S 'MAGPIE' HOUSES

Many box-framed 16th-century houses in Cheshire have their timbers darkened and their plaster painted white

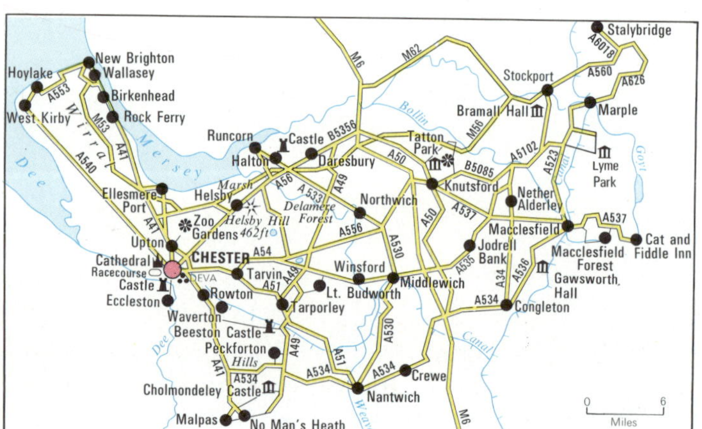

Chester
An ancient walled city on a sandstone spur north of the Dee. The Romans established their major camp of Deva here in AD 79 to protect the surrounding fertile land from Welsh tribesmen, sea pirates and other marauders. A Roman amphitheatre, measuring 314 ft by 286 ft, lies east of Newgate, and there are Roman remains, including a fine collection of coins, in the Grosvenor Museum in Grosvenor Street.

No other British city has such well-preserved enclosing ramparts; much of the original Roman wall survives, but many of the towers and gates were added in the Middle Ages. There is a 2-mile path round the crest of the red sandstone battlements. From King Charles's Tower, in 1645, Charles I is said to have watched the defeat of his forces at the Battle of Rowton Moor.

Chester's galleried streets, known as The Rows, date from the Middle Ages. Shops open on to balustraded walkways reached only by steps from the road. The city has some fine timbered inns, and a number of the half-timbered Tudor houses, notably Bishop Lloyd's House, God's Providence House, and Old Leche House, have rich carvings cut deep into age-blackened wood. The red sandstone cathedral, in St Werburgh Street, is mainly 14th century. It was a Benedictine Abbey until its dissolution in 1540, and the following year it became the cathedral for the new diocese of Chester.

THE ROWS *Medieval raised galleries in the centre of Chester form a traffic-free shopping precinct which can be reached from the busy road below by stairways*

Daresbury
The Rev. Charles Lutwidge Dodgson, better known as Lewis Carroll, the author of *Alice's Adventures in Wonderland*, was born here in 1832. The church, set among meadows and rhododendrons, has a bright red, blue and gold stained-glass window commemorating Alice, the Mad Hatter and other characters appearing in Alice's adventures.

Helsby
A village notable for the nearby viewpoint of Helsby Hill (462 ft) on which traces have been found of an Iron Age camp. The view to the west extends across Helsby Marsh to the broad sweep of the Mersey. The hill is used as a practice ground for climbers.

Knutsford
An attractive town with narrow streets and old black-and-white houses. Knutsford was the 'Cranford' of Mrs Gaskell's novel of that name. She was married in 1832 in the 18th-century parish church, and her grave is behind the 17th-century Unitarian chapel.

Tatton Hall, 2 miles north, built *c.* 1800, was the home of the Egerton family and houses a fine collection of furniture, pictures, china, silver and glass. It is surrounded by 54 acres of formal gardens and woodland laid out by Humphry Repton (1752–1818), and is one of the National Trust's most visited properties.

The giant radio telescope of Jodrell Bank looms 6 miles to the south. The Mark I radio telescope has a dish aerial 250 ft in diameter, weighing 2000 tons. The Concourse Building, opened in 1966, has an exhibition of radio astronomy, closed-circuit television demonstrations, and a model radio telescope, which visitors can operate.

Macclesfield
An old silk-manufacturing town full of character, from its steep streets to its 18th and 19th-century mills. Its oldest church, St Michael's, was largely rebuilt in the 18th and 19th centuries, but it still retains the battlemented look of its medieval origins and is reached, on one side, by 108 steps. Black-and-white timbered houses line hilly streets which look east over the green Bollin Valley towards the Peak District.

Gawsworth Hall, 3 miles south, is an attractive half-timbered manor house built mainly in the late 15th century. It was the home of Mary Fitton, Maid of Honour to Elizabeth I and the supposed 'Dark Lady' of Shakespeare's sonnets. The estate includes an orangery, a tilting ground and a large walled park.

Macclesfield Forest, 4 miles east, is a small village on the edge of the vast wild moorland of the same name. The crags and narrow valleys of these moors were once the haunt of highwaymen and brigands. The Cat and Fiddle Inn is 3 miles east in an isolated moorland setting, at 1690 ft.

Malpas
A small town of overhanging houses, hilly streets and half-timbered cottages, set in rich farmland. The 14th-century church of St Oswald has medieval stone carving, attractive stained glass and a superb 13th-century parish chest.

From No Man's Heath, north-east of the town, there is a fine view across the rhododendron-covered parkland of the 18th-century Cholmondeley Castle, a private mansion built in Gothic style.

Marple
The rocky, wooded ravine of the River Goyt forms the background to this delightful town, where houses cling to the river banks or perch on the hilltop. There are pleasant walks through woods, and across wild moors, with splendid views of the Derbyshire Peak District. The Peak Forest Canal crosses the River Goyt at Marple with the help of an aqueduct and 16 locks.

Nantwich
In this old salt-mining town on the River Weaver, black-and-white Tudor houses crowd together in quaint streets, the most notable of which is Welsh Row. The almshouses, built in 1638 by Sir Edmund Wright, are decorated with tiny carved figures. St Mary's Church has a fine octagonal tower that soars above silver birch trees. The 14th-century chancel has a remarkable stone-vaulted roof decorated with carvings.

Northwich
An important salt-producing town, in which some houses lean because of mining subsidence. At Anderton, just north of the town, a unique canal lift hoists vessels from the River Weaver Navigation to the Trent and Mersey Canal.

Tarporley
Rich farmlands and woods surround the spacious town. From the rose-filled churchyard of the medieval parish church there is a magnificent view of Beeston Castle, on the summit of the Peckforton Hills, 3 miles south. The ruined 13th-century castle sits on the top of a steep hill with terraced woods on one side, and overhanging rock on the other.

North of Tarporley is the 4000-acre Delamere Forest, with dense foliage and glistening patches of water such as Hatch Mere and Oak Mere.

Wallasey
The heart of the Merseyside playground on the Wirral peninsula. Miles of beaches, sand-dunes, promenades, piers and parks are connected to the busy shipbuilding and industrial centre of Birkenhead by docks and wharves.

WINDOW INTO SPACE *The Jodrell Bank radio telescope was built for Manchester University in 1957. Its 250 ft wide reflector receives radio impulses from Outer Space*

Liverpool – bustling port on the Mersey

Horse racing Grand National at Aintree, end Mar. or early Apr.

Angling There is coarse fishing on the Leeds and Liverpool Canal from Liverpool to Halsall, and in Liverpool Corporation reservoirs.

Events A large flower show is held at Southport at the end of August. There are several summer productions at the Open-Air Theatre in Calderstones Park, Liverpool. The Lord Mayor's Parade is held in Liverpool early in June, and there is a 2-day Police Horse Show later in the month. The Royal Liverpool Philharmonic Orchestra gives concerts at the Philharmonic Hall.

Places to see *Bootle Museum and Art Gallery*: daily, except Thur. and Sun. afternoons. *Knowsley Safari Park*: daily. *Liverpool Botanic Garden*, Harthill and Calderstone Parks: daily. *Martin Mere Nature Reserve*, 11 miles east of Southport: daily. *Merseyside County Museum* and *Planetarium*, Liverpool: weekdays Sun. afternoons. *Palm House Tropical Gardens*, Sefton Park: daily. *Pilkington Glass Museum*, St. Helens: Mon. to Fri.; also Sat. and Sun. afternoons. *Rufford Old Hall* (NT): Mar. to Dec., Tues. to Sun. afternoons, but closed Wed. in Mar. and Oct. to Dec. *St Helens Museum and Art Gallery*: weekdays. *Speke Hall* (NT): weekdays, Sun. afternoons. *Sudley Art Gallery*, Liverpool: weekdays, Sun. afternoons. *Walker Art Gallery*, Liverpool: weekdays, Sun. afternoons.

Information centre City Information Office, 187 St John's Centre, Elliot Street, Liverpool. Tel. 051–709 3631.

CATHEDRAL 'LANTERN' *The conical roof of Liverpool's huge Roman Catholic Cathedral is capped by a stained-glass lantern. The building, begun in 1933, took 34 years to complete*

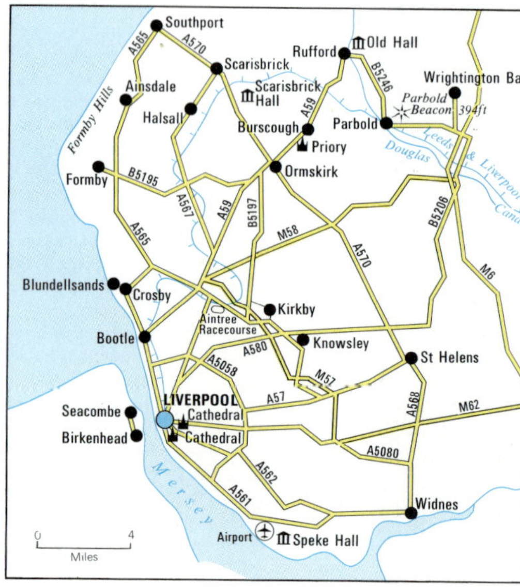

The northern bank of the River Mersey was first settled in the 1st century AD. By 1200 there was a fishing village on the Mersey, which was granted a charter by King John in 1207. Trading with the West Indies, and the slave trade, led to a surge of expansion in the late 17th and early 18th centuries, but it was not until the coming of the steamships in the 1840's that Liverpool began to take on its modern form. The steamships were introduced just as the Irish potato famine caused millions of Irishmen to emigrate. Tens of thousands got only to Liverpool.

Two tunnels under the Mersey connect Liverpool to Birkenhead. There is also a passenger ferry from the Pier Head landing stage in Liverpool to Birkenhead and Seacombe, and the best view of Liverpool's 7 miles of waterfront is obtained from one of these ferries. Dominating the busy scene is the Liver (pronounced Lie-ver) Building—the offices of the Royal Liver Friendly Society. Its two main towers are topped by 'Liver' birds, mythical birds from which the city is said to have taken its name. Underneath is the largest floating landing stage in the world, stretching for half a mile on 200 pontoons. The central docks are used by vessels bound for Ireland. Gladstone Dock, further north, commemorates the Victorian statesman who was born in Liverpool at 62 Rodney Street, which still has fine Georgian houses.

Liverpool's two modern cathedrals, both on high ground overlooking the city, are examples of two distinct kinds of ecclesiastical architecture. The Anglican Liverpool Cathedral, begun in 1904 by Sir Giles Gilbert Scott and completed in 1978, is built of red sandstone in Gothic style. It was damaged by bombs in the Second World War, and its fine peal of bells was first rung in 1951. Its aisles are unusual in being built as tunnels through the walls, and there is much fine stained glass. The Roman Catholic Metropolitan Cathedral was designed by Sir Frederick Gibberd and consecrated in 1967. The glass was designed by John Piper and Patrick Reyntiens. The building was originally designed by Sir Edwin Lutyens as a huge Classical domed building, but the war and soaring costs dictated the change of plan to a more contemporary design.

Liverpool is famed for its enlightened patronage of the arts. The Walker Art Gallery has a fine collection of European and English paintings, which includes Pre-Raphaelites. The Royal Liverpool Philharmonic Orchestra plays in the Philharmonic Hall, which was bought for the orchestra by the city. The University of Liverpool is expanding rapidly, and the Mossley Hill area will eventually become a university 'village' accommodating nearly 1500 students. Liverpool's poets, artists, writers and entertainers have made a lasting mark on the cultural life of the nation, particularly since the emergence of the Liverpool-born Beatles to international fame in the 1960's.

The city is famous for its sport, too. Goodison Park, Everton's ground, is one of the biggest football stadiums in Britain. Anfield, Liverpool's ground, has the famous 'Kop', where chanting fans pack the steep terraces behind one of the goals. Aintree Racecourse is the scene of the Grand National in the spring. Wild animals abound in the Knowsley Safari Park, which has lions, giraffes and a large herd of elephants.

A semicircle of industrial towns, including Crosby, Bootle, Kirkby, St Helens and Widnes, lies between Liverpool and the low-lying agricultural region beyond. This was marshland until it was reclaimed in the late 17th and early 18th centuries; now it is fertile farming land ideal for potato-growing.

LIVERPOOL PIERHEAD *A tug bustles along the Mersey through the seaport. The 295 ft high towers of the Royal Liver insurance com-*

THE FORMBY FORESHORE *Sandhills left by the receding sea extend for 7 miles along the coast from Formby to Southport. Much of the coast was bought by public subscription for the National Trust in 1967, and is rich in both plant and birdlife*

RUFFORD OLD HALL *The great hall of this 15th-century house, built by Robert Hesketh, has remained almost unaltered*

heart of Liverpool, Europe's busiest Atlantic pany's building dominate the waterfront

BIRD WHICH GAVE A CITY ITS NAME *A mythical 'Liver' bird, one of two on the towers of the Royal Liver building in Liverpool. Its name is thought to have come from the lyver seaweed in its mouth*

Formby
By 1910 the ancient seaside town of Formby had been completely buried under shifting sands. The sands are still accumulating as the sea recedes, and today a 2-mile stretch of lonely dunes, flanked by pines to hinder further movement, separates the new town from the sea. At Ainsdale, 3 miles north, is a National Nature Reserve.

Ormskirk
An important market town in the centre of rich farming land, largely covered by Lake Martinmere until the 18th century. The Perpendicular Church of SS Peter and Paul had a second tower added in 1540 to house the bells from Burscough Priory after its dissolution; the ruins of the 13th-century priory can still be seen 2 miles north-east of the town. There are some fine Georgian houses, notably in Burscough Street.

Scarisbrick Hall, 3 miles north-west, is an ornate neo-Gothic mansion built in the 19th century with turrets, gables and pinnacles dwarfed by a 100 ft tower. It is now occupied by a school and is not open to the public. The Scarisbrick family played a large part in draining the surrounding area in the 18th century.

Rufford
The Old Hall, a fine late-medieval manor house, contains a rare 15th-century carved screen, and one wing of the mansion houses a folk museum.

There are pleasant walks along the banks of the River Douglas. Parbold Beacon (394 ft), 3 miles south-east, overlooks the river, and from here the view extends over the farmlands and picturesque villages of the fertile Lancashire Plain. Wrightington Bar, 5 miles east, is an attractive village reached by narrow roads that were once the haunt of highwaymen.

Southport
A quiet family seaside resort with a particularly good sunshine record—an average of 5½ hours a day throughout the summer months. The broad, mile-long Lord Street, with its cafés, gardens, fountains and arcades, is a stately shopping street. The Church of St Cuthbert has a fine 18th-century font.

For over 100 years the retreating seas have given Southport an ever-widening expanse of sands, on which the 86-acre Marine Lake was constructed at the end of the 19th century. This large artificial boating lake and a sea-bathing lake are flanked by beautiful gardens. The long pier has its own railway.

Martin Mere Nature Reserve, eleven miles east of Southport, is a 360-acre site owned by the Wildfowl Trust where many migratory birds, including pink-footed geese, can be seen.

Speke Hall
The Hall, standing in a wooded park by the Mersey, is a magnificent 16th-century half-timbered house. Among its treasures, the great parlour contains a richly plastered ceiling and a fine carved chimney-piece, and the great hall is decorated with panels said to have been removed from Holyrood Palace.

Two yew trees in the garden are both more than 400 years old.

Port without a coastline

Boating Boats can be hired at Burnley for use on the Leeds and Liverpool Canal; the Burnley Embankment carries the waterway above Burnley rooftops. Boating on the lakes in Heaton Park, Prestwich and Platt Fields, Manchester.

Angling The Rivers Ribble, Mersey, Calder and Irwell are mostly polluted. In the Rochdale area there are coarse fish and trout in Hollingworth Lake, Littleborough, and in Buckley Wood Reservoir; coarse fish in Broadly Wood Reservoir and in the Rochdale Canal; trout in Hapton Reservoir, near Burnley, and Ogden Reservoir, Milnrow.

Events In Manchester there are two Walking Days, on Whit Sun. and on Spring Bank Hol. Mon., when religious processions march through the city. At Easter in Bacup, the Coconut Dancers, or 'Nutters', perform a traditional dance with wooden cups fixed to their hands, waists and knees.

Music Hallé Concerts are held fortnightly, on Wed. and Sun. from the end of Sept. to mid-May. The Hallé Proms are held every night for about a fortnight from the end of June.

Places to see *Astley Hall*, Chorley: afternoons. *British in India Museum*, Colne: May to Sept., Sat. and Sun. afternoons. *City Art Gallery*, Manchester: weekdays, Sun. afternoon *Gawthorpe Hall* (NT), Padiham: mid-Mar. to Oct., Wed., Sat., Sun. and Bank Hol. afternoons. *Hall i' th' Wood*: weekdays, except Thur.; Apr. to Sept., Sun. afternoons also. *Heaton Hall*: weekdays and Sun. afternoons. *Lewis Textile Museum*, Blackburn: weekdays. *North Western Museum of Science and Industry*, Manchester: weekdays. *Platt Hall*, Manchester, gallery of English costume: weekdays, Sun. afternoon. *Smithill's Hall*, Bolton: daily, except Thur. *Tonge Moor Textile Machinery Museum*, Bolton, including Crompton's 'spinning mule' and Hargreaves's 'spinning jenny': weekdays except Wed. afternoon. *Towneley Hall Art Gallery and Museum*, Burnley: Mon. to Fri. and Sun. afternoon. *Turton Tower*, Blackburn: Wed. and Sat. afternoons; also Sun. afternoon, Apr. to Oct. *Wythenshawe Hall*: weekdays and Sun. afternoon.

Information centres Information Office, Piccadilly Gardens, Manchester. Tel. 061-247 3694. Publicity and Public Relations Dept., Richmond Terrace, Blackburn. Tel. Blackburn 53277.

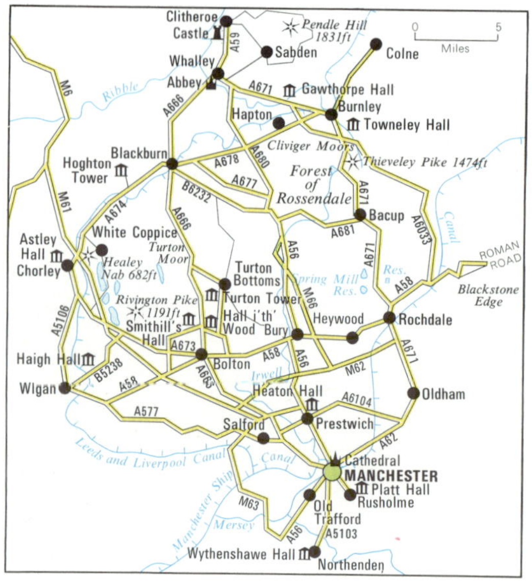

The origins of the key industrial and commercial city of Manchester are Roman: it was the site of Mancunium, a camp built by Agricola's legions on the banks of the River Irwell in AD 79, on their way from Chester to York.

Manchester's weaving tradition dates back to Flemish weavers in the 14th century, but it was little more than a large market town until the Industrial Revolution made it the main trading centre for Lancashire cotton. The proximity of coal for the steam-powered mills and the suitability of the climate for textile work helped the expansion. Late in the 19th century, industry shifted westward towards the ports, threatening to strand Manchester; but the completion of the Manchester Ship Canal in 1894 converted the city into an inland port and opened the way for the growth of other industries. Today Manchester is one of Britain's largest ports.

In recent years several changes have improved the quality of life in the city. In 1952 the first 'smokeless-zone' regulations in Britain were introduced in Manchester; today more than 26 square miles are covered. Exciting redevelopment schemes are going ahead in areas flattened by bombing in the Second World War. The Mancunian Way is an impressive flyover, nearly three-quarters of a mile long, that straddles the city centre from east to west. The old mill chimneys have been taken down, and slum-clearance operations are ridding the city of the 19th-century factories and workers' houses crammed chaotically together. Multi-storey buildings are taking their place, notably the 400 ft high Co-operative Insurance Society block and the towering Piccadilly Plaza building which incorporates a modern ground-level shopping centre. Near by are the great department stores of Market Street and Deansgate, and the fashion houses of King Street.

VICTORIAN SURVIVAL *Manchester Town Hall, designed in the Gothic style, is a monument to mid-Victorian prosperity*

The 15th-century Perpendicular Gothic cathedral is one of the city's showpieces. Its red Collyhurst stone was replaced with the harder Derbyshire stone in 1867, and the tower was rebuilt the following year. Removal of the side chapels during rebuilding gave the cathedral one of the widest naves in the country. The woodwork is particularly fine and includes an intricately carved rood screen and choir stalls. The imposing town hall was designed by Alfred Waterhouse and completed in 1877. It is elaborately decorated in Gothic style, and the 280-ft tower contains a carillon of 23 bells. Many of the 16th-century buildings in the Old Shambles were destroyed in the war, but the Wellington Inn survives.

The Free Trade Hall, bombed and rebuilt in the Palladian style, is the home of the Hallé Orchestra, whose distinguished conductors have included Sir John Barbirolli. The rotunda-style Central Library has a portico with Corinthian columns. The John

MANCHESTER SHIP CANAL *The 36 mile long canal was opened in 1894 to link the city's flourishing textile industry with the sea*

MANCHESTER REBORN *A towering office block dominates the city centre, which was redeveloped in the 1960's in areas flattened by bombing in the Second World War*

RENDEZVOUS *The Central Library is Manchester's best-known meeting place*

Rylands Library, built in 1899, is a fine Victorian Gothic building, and has a collection of 750,000 books, 3000 of which were printed before 1501. It also contains the St Christopher woodcut of 1423, the earliest dated Western print. Chetham's Library, founded in 1653, was the first free public library in Europe. The City Art Gallery, a Classical building designed by Sir Charles Barry, was opened in 1829 and specialises in the English school of painting.

Three halls set in public parks house the principal city museums. Heaton Hall, Prestwich, which was designed by James Wyatt and built in 1772, has a fine collection of period furniture, paintings and glass. Platt Hall, Rusholme, is a fine Georgian mansion and houses the Gallery of English Costume. Wythenshawe Hall, Northenden, is a half-timbered 16th-century manor house with a collection of Elizabethan furniture and 17th-century paintings and furnishings. The University, founded in 1880, is one of the biggest in the country. The county cricket ground at Old Trafford is a test-match venue, and Manchester is famed for its football, with Manchester United at Old Trafford and Manchester City at Maine Road.

The industrial centres of Lancashire and Greater Manchester lie in an arc spreading up to 25 miles north of Manchester; the important cotton-spinning towns of Bolton, Blackburn, Rochdale and Oldham are largest. But the area is not all industrial: the towns are wedged between ridges of sparsely populated flat-topped heights that run from north to south. The rivers and busy motorways share the valleys, while directly above them lie the unspoilt acres of the Forest of Rossendale, the Cliviger Moors, Turton Moor and Pendle Hill. Ancient pathways lead through wooded hillsides to 16th and 17th-century halls, Tudor farmhouses and old stone churches. Celtic outposts lie at the top of magnificent pikes, and give fine views of the countryside below.

Bacup
Rows of dark terraced houses present the typical urban landscape of the mill towns, and the blackened exteriors of mills and factories make striking silhouettes at sunset. The local Natural History Society's Museum is housed in a former inn built in the late 18th century.

The town is overlooked by flat-topped moors, rising to 1300 ft. These moors are part of the ancient Forest of Rossendale. Thieveley Pike, 1474 ft, stands $2\frac{1}{2}$ miles north of Bacup at the head of the valley of the River Irwell. Paths wind to the top where the Celts set up an earthwork; and below to the north stretch the wild Cliviger Moors.

Blackburn
The town's history of cotton weaving dates back to the 14th century, when it became the home of Flemish weavers. Rapid expansion came with the Industrial Revolution; full-scale working models of Hargreaves's 'spinning jenny' and Crompton's 'spinning mule', an improved version of the 'jenny', can be seen at the Lewis Textile Museum in Exchange Street. Old mills, some still in use, crowd round the Bolton Road locks of the Leeds and Liverpool Canal, and the crisp shapes of new multi-storey buildings can be seen from Witton Park and Corporation Park.

At Hoghton Tower, a fine 16th-century house on a hill 4 miles south-west, James I is reputed to have dubbed a loin of prime Lancashire beef 'Sir Loin' in jest, on a progress through the county in 1617. The house contains some fine 17th-century panelling.

Bolton
The birthplace of Samuel Crompton (1753–1827), the inventor of the 'spinning mule' which was to revolutionise the textile industry. The civic centre in Victoria Square has an art gallery, museum and aquarium. The Old Man and Scythe, a 13th-century inn in Church Gate, has associations with the Civil War. Lord Derby, who was executed by Cromwell in retaliation for a

HOME OF THE HALLÉ

The Free Trade Hall is the home of one of the country's leading orchestras, the Hallé, founded in 1858 by Sir Charles Hallé. Its principal conductors have included Hans Richter and Sir John Barbirolli

Royalist massacre in the town, spent his last hours there before his death. A new theatre, the Octagon, opened in 1967.

Hall i' th' Wood, 1½ miles north, is a fine half-timbered manor house, built in 1483. It was for a time the home of Samuel Crompton, and it now houses a folk museum. Smithill's Hall, 2 miles north-west, is one of Greater Manchester's oldest half-timbered manor houses. It was built in the 14th century and extended in Tudor times.

Burnley

Green and brown fells ring the dark gritstone buildings of this cotton-weaving centre. The town was hard hit in the depression years of the 1930's, but it fought back and a fine new town centre reflects its modern prosperity.

Towneley Hall, half a mile south-east, was the fortified home of the Towneley family from the 13th century until 1902. The present house dates from the 14th and 16th centuries; its dungeons and battlements remain, and it houses a museum and art gallery. Further south-east, the A646 cuts through the great rocky Cliviger Gorge. Three miles to the west, near Padiham, stands Gawthorpe Hall, an early 17th-century house restored in the 1860's.

Chorley

Cotton weaving, calico printing and engineering are the industries of this busy town. Henry Tate, the sugar magnate and founder of the Tate Gallery in London, was born here in 1819. Astley Hall, an Elizabethan mansion set in parkland beside a lake, has a splendid 17th-century facade, ornate plaster ceilings, Tudor carving, and a massive table for the game of shovel-board in the Long Gallery. The Hall also contains a fine collection of furniture, pottery, tapestries and pictures.

On the east, the town is overlooked by Healey Nab, which can be reached by ancient pathways defined by boulder walls. From the top, 682 ft high, the stark moors and deep valleys of Anglezarke and White Coppice can be seen to the east. This is ideal countryside to explore on foot. Rivington Pike, 4 miles south-east, is a popular viewpoint with a stone tower at its 1191-ft summit.

Clitheroe

A ruined Norman keep on a limestone cliff stands above the grey roofs of this pleasant market town, which was granted its charter in the 12th century.

Pendle Hill, 1831 ft, rises 4 miles to the east. Footpaths lead to the summit, from which spectacular views extend westwards to the Forest of Bowland, and to the flat Fylde Plain and the Irish Sea beyond. In 1652 George Fox had a vision on the summit which led him to preach and form the Society of Friends. Pendle Hill has also been associated with devil-worship; 19 of the witches tried at Lancaster Castle in 1612 were from the Pendle and Samlesbury area, and ten of them were sent to the gallows.

Rochdale

An important cotton-manufacturing town which was the birthplace of the Co-operative Movement. The depression of the early 19th century prompted a small group of local men to set up their own co-operative shop in 1844, and divide the surplus for the benefit of all. They formed the Rochdale Society of Equitable Pioneers. The original shop is now a museum.

John Bright, a 19th-century opponent of the Corn Laws, and Gracie Fields, the singer, were both born in Rochdale. On Blackstone Edge, 2 miles east, one of the best-preserved stretches of Roman road in the country runs across the Pennines into Yorkshire.

Turton Bottoms

A small village in spectacular walking country. Turton Tower is an impressive 12th-century house, to which an upper storey and half-timbered wings were added in the 16th century. The Ashworth Museum is housed in the upper storey of a large, well-preserved 15th-century tower. Humphrey Chetham, founder of a library and hospital in Manchester which now form the Blue Coat School, lived in Turton in the 17th century. The old inn in the High Street bears the Chetham arms.

Whalley

An attractive little town on the River Calder, notable for the remains of a 13th-century Cistercian abbey, founded by monks from Cheshire. The remains include part of the chapter house and a well-preserved 14th-century gateway. Stones from the original abbey can be seen in the walls of 16th and 17th-century churches, farms and houses in the neighbourhood. The parish church of St Mary was of Norman origin, but it is mainly 13th century; the fine canopied choir stalls with intricate misericord seats were taken from the abbey. The screened pews date from the 17th and 18th centuries. Three tall medieval crosses stand in the churchyard.

Wigan

Cooling towers, slag heaps and rows of back-to-back houses, described by George Orwell in *The Road to Wigan Pier*, are only one aspect of this important industrial town. It is one of the oldest boroughs of Lancashire—its charter was granted in the 13th century. The town was Royalist in the Civil War, and the site of a battle in 1651 is commemorated by a monument in Wigan Lane. Wigan Pier, a key loading-point on the canal to Liverpool, can still be seen.

Haigh Hall, 2½ miles north-east, is a mid-19th-century mansion set in a 200-acre park. It was formerly the home of the Earls of Crawford and is now owned by Wigan Corporation.

PAINTER OF THE LANCASHIRE SCENE

The constant theme of the painter L. S. Lowry, who was born in Manchester in 1887, has been the industrial landscape of Lancashire. This painting, *The Lake*, is part of the extensive collection in Salford Art Gallery

ASTLEY HALL *Many-paned windows ornament the 17th-century front of Astley Hall, Chorley, which contains ornate plasterwork*

The Isle of Man

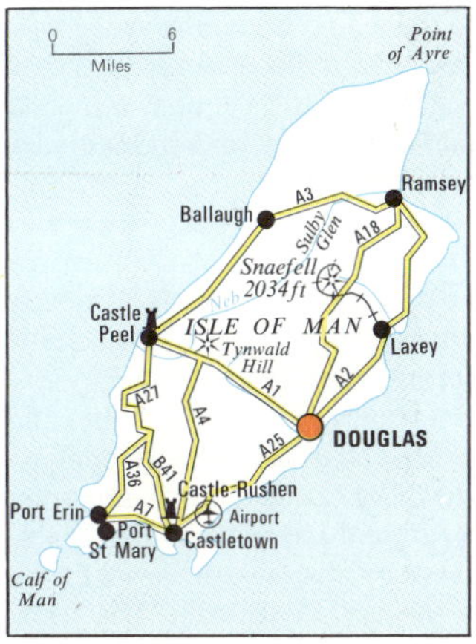

Angling Salmon and trout in Rivers Neb, Laxey, Sulby and Douglas; licences from Board of Agriculture and Fisheries, Douglas.

Events TT Races and Peel Viking Ceremony in June, Tynwald Ceremony in July, car rally and Grand Prix in Sept.

Places to see *Ballaugh Wildlife Park*: Easter, then daily mid-May to Sept. *Castle Rushen*: weekdays; also Sun. morning in summer. *Castletown Nautical Museum* and *Cregneish Folk Museum*: both mid-May to Sept., weekdays and Sun. afternoon. *Grove Rural Life Museum*, Ramsey: mid-May to Sept., Mon. to Fri., Sun. afternoon. *Manx Museum*, Douglas: weekdays. *Motorcycle Museum*, Snaefell: May to Sept., daily. *Peel Castle*: May to Sept., weekdays, Sun. afternoon. *Railway Museum*, Port Erin: May to Sept., daily.

Information centre 13 Victoria Street, Douglas. Tel. Douglas 4323.

THE MANX CAT

The tail-less Manx cat, peculiar to the Isle of Man, is thought to have been first bred about 300 years ago. Legend says that the original cat was a cross between cat and hare

The Isle of Man is a dot of green set in the middle of the Irish Sea, and England, Scotland, Ireland and Wales are all within view on a clear day. Its 227 square miles make it one of the smallest independent sovereign countries under the Crown. It was annexed by England in the 13th century, and is ruled by a Lieutenant Governor appointed by the Crown, but has its own parliament, the Tynwald, and its own laws and taxes. The native language of the island is a form of Celtic.

There are 500 miles of good, though lonely, roads. Even when motor cycles roar round the 38-mile motor circuit in June and September (when these roads are closed to public traffic), there is still solitude to be found on other byways thickly banked with gorse and heather. The northern plain has winding, thickly wooded lanes and picturesque villages. To the south is hilly country, bubbling with streams.

The climate is exceptionally mild, thanks to the Gulf Stream that encircles the island, and ideal for open-air activities. There are excellent walks at all levels, along wooded glen floors (Sulby Glen is the wildest) or on the heights; a mountain railway climbs Snaefell, and a road reaches 1300 ft up it. The clear sea beneath towering cliffs along much of the island's 100-mile coastline is ideal for scuba diving, and miles of silver sands offer perfect beaches for swimming.

The visitor driving north from Ronaldsway Airport should remember to salute 'the little people' when crossing tiny Ballona Bridge near Douglas. It is a well-observed local custom.

LAXEY *The 'Lady Isabella' water-wheel is the world's biggest*

Castletown
The island's former capital surrounds Castle Rushen, one of the finest medieval fortresses in Britain. Narrow streets crammed with quaint grey houses lead to a spacious beach at the edge of Castletown Bay. The Nautical Museum, in a 200-year-old three-storey boat-house, exhibits what is probably the country's oldest schooner-rigged yacht, the *Peggy*, built in 1791. Several fine walks lead to hills that are sometimes shrouded in mist; in Manx legend the mist is the protective cloak of Mannanan, an ancient god of the sea, and hides the island from would-be invaders.

Douglas
The island's capital and most popular holiday resort has a continental atmosphere. The promenade of the spacious 2-mile sea front is level with the sand; police in white helmets direct the traffic, and old-fashioned horse-drawn trams trundle gently along. On Prospect Hill stands the House of Keys, home of the Manx Parliament, the Tynwald, whose Scandinavian origins are earlier than those of Westminster.

Steam trains in summer connect Douglas with Port Erin.

The Manx National Museum, on the bluff above St Thomas's Church, contains many relics of the island's heritage. In Noble's Park the tail-less Manx cat is bred to preserve the species; a few cats are available for sale to visitors.

Laxey
This picturesque tidal harbour town on the east coast is dominated by 'Lady Isabella', the largest water-wheel in the world: $72\frac{1}{2}$ ft across and capable of raising 250 gal. of water a minute more than 1000 ft. The wheel, set in motion in 1854, was named after the wife of the island's Lieutenant Governor. It was used to keep the nearby lead mines free from water, and though the mines are now closed the wheel still turns. It is from Laxey that the electric train starts its 4-mile journey to the summit of Snaefell, the island's highest mountain.

Peel
An old-world fishing port noted for its Manx kippers, which are smoked on fires of oak woodchips. This natural harbour was once invaded by Vikings, and in commemoration a Viking Festival is held each June, when mock battles between Norsemen and Celts are re-enacted. Along the Douglas Road, $2\frac{1}{2}$ miles from Peel, stands tiny Tynwald Hill, shaped like a wedding cake. All new laws must be proclaimed from this hill in the English and Manx languages.

Port Erin
The crystal-clear water is ideal for scuba diving, and there are boat trips to the bird sanctuary on the Calf of Man, where many species of seabirds can be seen. The sanctuary is closed to visitors during the breeding season.

Port St Mary, 1 mile away across the narrow peninsula, is an equally charming resort with two bays. Old farming and fishing implements can be seen in the whitewashed thatched crofts of the Cregneish Open Air Folk Museum, and there is an aquarium at the Marine Biological Station.

Ramsey
The second-largest town on the island is sheltered by the northern tip of the hills that tower above. Robert the Bruce landed here in 1313 and snatched the island, for a time, for Scotland. In the 40-acre Mooragh Park, palm trees surround a 12-acre lake and give boating an exotic, tropical-lagoon flavour.

Holiday resorts of the Lancashire coast

Angling There is sea angling at Blackpool, Fleetwood and Morecambe. Salmon and trout in the River Lune at Lancaster and Halton.

Boating Sailing at Fleetwood, Morecambe and Lytham St Anne's. Regular regattas are held during the summer and autumn. Model yacht championships at Fleetwood in Aug.

Events The ancient custom of Egg Rolling takes place at Preston on Easter Mon. The Lancashire Art Exhibition is held at Preston in Mar A veteran car run to Manchester starts from Blackpool in June. Shows and bathing beauty contests throughout the summer at Blackpool, Morecambe and Fleetwood.

Places to see *Blackpool Zoo*, Stanley Park: daily. *Lancaster Castle*: Easter to Sept., daily. *Lancaster Museum*, with *Regimental Museum of King's Own Regiment*: weekdays. *Leighton Hall*, Yealand Conyers: May to Sept., Wed., Thur., Sun. and Bank Hol. afternoons. *Ribchester Museum*: weekday afternoons Feb. to Nov., but closed Thur. May to Aug. and Fri. in other months; open Sat. afternoon only Dec. and Jan. *Steamtown Museum*, Carnforth: daily.

Information centres Promenade, Blackpool. Tel. Blackpool 21623. Marine Road Central, Morecambe. Tel. Morecambe 414110. The Square, St. Anne's. Tel. Blackpool 725610.

DUNE FLOWER The Bloody Cranesbill, *Geranium sanguineum*, with a magenta flower, is found widely round Britain's coasts. Dunes in Lancashire are the home of a local variety with a paler pink flower

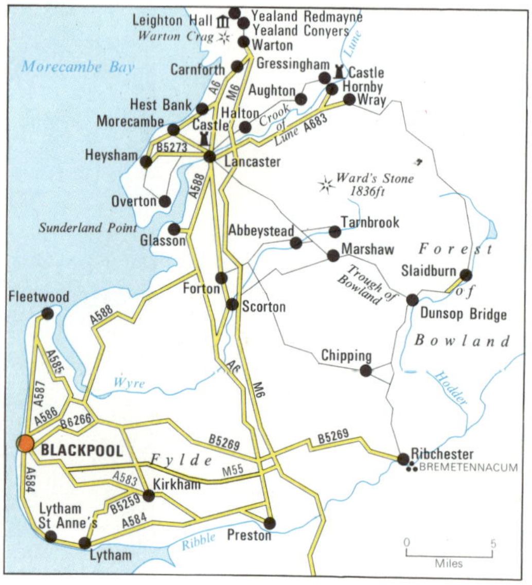

The 'lungs' of Lancashire lie between south Cumbria and the River Ribble, north of the county's densely populated and highly industrialised zones. The M6, running from north to south and closely following the route of an old Roman road, divides the area into two. The breathing space west of the motorway takes in 60 miles of sandy coastline; that to the east is wild moorland country with hills that rise to a height of 1836 ft, interspersed with wooded dales and beautiful river valleys.

The coastline 'lung' is the most popular resort area in the north of England. Since the mid-18th century it has provided for the recreational needs of people from the crowded centres of the North; today it draws visitors from all corners of the country. The prosperity of these resorts depends on their holiday trade, and they have poured millions of pounds into developing entertainment facilities. The sands and bathing are excellent in the south, around Lytham and Blackpool; and in the north there are magnificent views of the Lake District peaks across Morecambe Bay. The coastline is mainly low-lying, and certain roads near Fleetwood and Heysham are submerged at high tide. Northwards, the land rises to more hilly country.

East of the motorway, rugged fells rise to the Pennine Chain and the border with North Yorkshire. Pine and bracken fringe tumbling becks, and cattle grids lie across tiny valley roads. Old traders' routes cross the fells from Mill Houses, near Wray, to Slaidburn. The Trough of Bowland is a wild, heather-banked pass through which runs the only road to cross the lonely Forest of Bowland into North Yorkshire.

Blackpool

A lively, crowded, jostling resort, busiest during summer when the Lancashire factories and mills close down for their annual 'wakes', or holidays. The town began to develop as a recreational resort in the mid-18th century, and its popularity has grown with the years; now it has a resident population of 152,000 and attracts 8 million visitors during the summer season. The 6-mile promenade, well known for its spectacular autumn illuminations, is dominated by the 518-ft Blackpool Tower, which contains a fine aquarium, a zoo, a circus and a dance hall. There are four theatres in the town, and funfair thrills from dodgems to bingo are to be found along the stretch of the promenade known as the 'Golden Mile', and on the three piers. The trams on the sea-front are the only survivors of their kind in England.

By contrast, there are inland walks to Anchorsholme, 4 miles north, and the 300-acre Stanley Park has a rose garden, a boating lake and a golf course. The Grundy Art Gallery in Queen Street has a fine collection of works by 19th and 20th-century British artists.

Fleetwood

One of Britain's chief fishing ports, at the mouth of the Wyre Estuary. The peaks of the Lake District can be seen to the north across Morecambe Bay in clear weather, while the view to the east extends to cross the Lune Valley to the distant Pennines. The town has fine gardens, a marine lake and model yacht ponds. Trawlers can be watched returning to port at dawn from fishing grounds as far away as Iceland.

Halton

A peaceful village whose church retains a Roman altar and a 15th-century tower. In the churchyard stands an 11th-century carved cross. A mile upriver is the Crook of Lune, a beautiful wooded valley. Aughton, a picturesque village on a hillside, lies north-east; the thriller writer E. C. Lorac (1894–1958) lived here and often referred to the Lune Valley in her books, notably *Stillwater* and *Crook O' Lune*.

The road continues through the hidden hamlet of Gressingham, then crosses the Lune over a narrow bridge to

DEEP-SEA TRAWLERS *Fleetwood trawlers set out for fishing grounds around Iceland. The port also imports fruit from the Mediterranean and timber from Finland*

Hornby, whose castle keep can be seen for miles. The keep was erected by Sir Edward Stanley, who became Lord Monteagle after the Battle of Flodden Field in 1513. His coat of arms decorates the church tower in thanksgiving for his safe return from the battlefield.

Kirkham
A town with an attractive view over the Fylde plain; the name 'Fylde' applied to this low-lying area of Lancashire comes from the Old English *gefilde*, meaning a plain. Kirkham is now an agricultural centre and commuter area for Preston and Blackpool, but its history dates back to the Domesday Book. The Church of St John the Evangelist, built in 1845, was the first Roman Catholic church to be allowed a peal of bells after the Reformation. The bells are still rung today.

Lancaster
The county town takes its name from the Roman *castrum*, or camp, built beside the Lune on this site. The imposing medieval castle, with a Norman keep, on Castle Hill dominates the old grey city below. John of Gaunt, Duke of Lancaster and father of Henry IV, enlarged the castle, and Elizabeth I added fortifications as a defence against the Armada. It was a Parliamentary stronghold in the Civil War, and since the 18th century it has housed courts and a jail. The magnificent priory and parish church of St Mary, mainly Perpendicular in style but partly dating back to Saxon times, stands alongside; the wood-carving on its 14th-century choir stalls is some of the finest in Britain.

A tree-lined quay is a reminder of the days when the city was a port handling a bigger tonnage than Liverpool; the mid-18th-century Custom House, with its graceful Ionic columns, still has charm. The city has many fine Georgian houses. The Friends' Meeting House, standing on Meeting House Lane, dates from 1690 and the famous 18th-century divine George Whitefield often preached there. The high-domed Ashton Memorial was opened in 1909 in memory of the Williamson family, who gave the city the fine park in which the memorial stands.

Lytham St Anne's
A popular family resort with glorious sands and a promenade 1½ miles long ablaze with beautiful floral displays. Its fame lies chiefly in its four championship golf courses, including the Royal Lytham and St Anne's.

Morecambe and Heysham
Two ancient villages have merged into one lively resort which has a pleasure park, a Marineland with performing dolphins, and illuminations in autumn from the Battery to Happy Mount Park. There are spectacular views of the highest Lake District hills, and fine sunsets across Morecambe Bay. The remains of a pre-Conquest church, with graves carved out of rock, stand on a hill overlooking Heysham. The walk across Morecambe Bay at low tide from Hest Bank to Grange-over-Sands is a unique experience. It can also be hazardous, as there are three tidal rivers to ford, and walkers are permitted to cross only if accompanied by an official guide.

NORTHERN LIGHTS *From early September to late October, illuminations sparkle along 6 miles of Blackpool promenade, dominated by the famous 518 ft high tower*

SAILING ON THE BEACH *The British Sand Yacht Championships are held in May on Lytham St Anne's beach. The yachts are made of metal tubing and run on wheels*

Ribchester
An attractive village on the River Ribble, with a history dating back to the 1st century AD when it was the site of Bremetennacum, one of the largest Roman forts in England. A small museum next to the church contains objects found during excavations of the fort: Romano-British and Samian pottery, inscribed stones and a replica of a Roman cavalry helmet (the original is in the British Museum). Parts of the fort's granaries can be seen in the museum garden. During the Civil War, Ribchester was a Royalist outpost.

Sunderland Point
This piece of land, almost entirely surrounded by water, where the River Lune enters the Irish Sea, is reached across the saltings from the quaint village of Overton. The Point was a port in the 18th century, when ships crossed to the West Indies, and the first cargo of cotton to reach England was landed here. Nearby Snatchem's Inn can be cut off at high tide. Across the estuary is Glasson dock, part of the old port of Lancaster, at which modern pleasure craft now have moorings.

Tarnbrook
A beautifully wild valley under the windswept fellside of Ward's Stone, (1836 ft) on the upper reaches of the River Wyre. Motorists can leave the M6 near Forton Service Station and drive through ancient hunting-forest land to Abbeystead, 5 miles east. From here a road goes by Marshaw to Dunsop Bridge through the Trough of Bowland —the wild pass along which 20 'Lancashire witches' were taken from the Forest of Pendle in 1612 to be tried at Lancaster Castle; ten were hanged.

From Dunsop Bridge a road runs for 6 miles south-west through the haunting Hodder Valley to Chipping, a charming village with a rushing stream, fine chestnut trees and a rural factory where furniture is made. Scorton, a picturesque village set in excellent fell-walking country, lies 10 miles north-west.

Warton
Ancestors of George Washington, first President of the United States, came from this village. Other branches of the family lived in County Durham and Northamptonshire. Their coat of arms is set in the belfry wall of the restored 15th-century church. The Stars and Stripes flag is flown from the church on Independence Day, July 4. Yealand Conyers, 1 mile north, and Yealand Redmayne, 2 miles north, are two picturesque villages. Yealand Conyers has a Quaker Meeting House, built in 1692.

The gateway to Lakeland

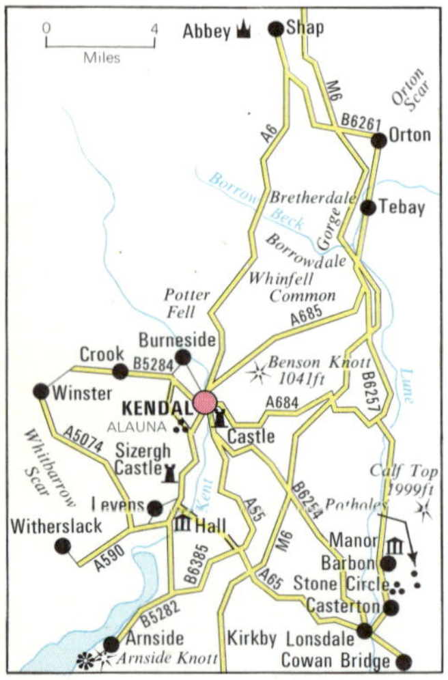

Events Kendal and district has two alternating biennial music festivals in May: the Mary Wakefield Music Festival (1981, 1983, etc.) and Lake District Music Festival (1980, 1982, etc.). The Kendal Gathering is held the first two weeks of Sept., with a torchlight procession the last Fri.

Places to see *Abbot Hall Museum of Lakeland Life*, Kendal: Mon. to Fri., also Sat. and Sun. afternoons. *Kendal Museum*: weekdays. *Castle Dairy*, Kendal, example of Tudor domestic architecture: weekdays. *Levens Hall*: Easter to Sept., Tues., Wed., Thur. and Sun. afternoons; gardens daily. *Shap Abbey*: weekdays and Sun. afternoons. *Sizergh Castle* (NT): Apr. to Sept., Wed. and Sun. afternoons; also Thur. afternoons July and Aug.

Caravan sites At Levens and Preston Patrick.

Information centre Town Hall, Kendal. Tel. Kendal 23649, ext. 253.

The M6 motorway, carving a great gully through the rocks of south Cumbria on its journey north, has not only changed the face of the countryside in this region, but has also brought a bright new future to Kendal. The completion of the motorway in 1970 meant that for the first time in its history Kendal no longer straddled a main route to Scotland.

The heavy lorries that pounded the streets throughout the day and night now roar along the sweeping motorway; and, with the disappearance of the noise and congestion attendant upon such through traffic, Kendal has been able to add tourism to its traditional boot and shoe and engineering industries. Here, in a superb riverside setting, is history, culture and architecture which the visitor can enjoy in tranquillity.

The motorway has brought another advantage: the region's hills and mountains, softened by rolling pasturelands and cornfields, are now within quicker, easier reach from the south. The remoter villages and fells are still unknown to the mass of the holiday crowds, though their winter weather is notorious. Snows come as early as October and can last on the highest summits until June; and the A6 is often blocked by snowfalls where it passes over Shap Fells.

KENDAL CASTLE *Only fragments remain of the Norman castle where Catharine Parr, last wife of Henry VIII, was born*

Arnside

This seaside town at the mouth of the River Kent was a busy port until the mid-1800's and the coming of the railway. It now attracts weekend sailors. Sea-washed turf near the town is sold for lawns and sports fields. A walk leads southwards to Arnside Knott, owned by the National Trust, which has rare flowers, lovely trees and, from its 522-ft peak, beautiful views across the sea.

Kendal

Known as 'the auld grey town' because of its many fine old houses and other buildings in grey limestone, Kendal was made a barony by Richard Coeur de Lion in 1189. In 1331 the Flemish established a woollen industry in the town, from which came its motto: *Pannus mihi panis*—wool is my bread.

The 14th-century ruined castle was the home of Catharine Parr, Henry VIII's sixth and last wife. It stands on a green hill where its overgrown moat and battlements create an impressive sight. Abbot Hall, an 18th-century mansion with period furniture, is an art gallery; a museum of Lakeland life and industry is in the stables. George Romney, the painter, was born in Kendal in 1734 and seven of his portraits hang in the town hall. Holy Trinity Church, one of the largest in England, was built in the 13th century and restored in the 19th century.

There are many lovely river walks by the Kent, on the south side of which, 1 mile from the town centre, is the site of the Roman fort of Alauna. Above the town, Serpentine Woods provide magnificent views of the valley.

Other interesting walks in the area are along Scout Scar, 2½ miles south-west, which gives views of Lakeland and the Yorkshire Dales; and to Benson Knott, a 1041-ft hill, 2 miles north-east. Potter Fell, above Burneside village, 2 miles north-west of Kendal, is a beautiful wilderness of bracken and heather.

Kirkby Lonsdale

One of the most beautiful towns in south Cumbria, set on a hill above the River Lune. Spanning the Lune, south of the town, is the Devil's Bridge, probably 13th century. The huge pool beneath the bridge is full of salmon and a favourite spot for aqualung divers. There is a lovely walk from the bridge along a footpath following the river for half a mile, and entering the town by stone steps leading up to the Norman St Mary's Church.

Among the town's fine buildings are the 17th-century Manor House and the 18th-century Fountain House. Underley Hall, a mile north, built in 1825, is a Roman Catholic seminary.

Casterton Girls' School, at the village of Casterton 1 mile north-east, was founded in 1823. It was formerly at Cowan Bridge, 2 miles south-east, and the Brontë sisters were pupils there. Half a mile north of Casterton is a circle of 20 prehistoric stones. Barbon, 3 miles north of Kirkby Lonsdale, lies beneath fells

THE PATH TO RUSKIN'S VIEW *An avenue of trees at Kirkby Lonsdale leads to The Brow, where a view of the Lune Valley was praised by John Ruskin as 'one of the loveliest scenes in England'*

DEVIL'S BRIDGE *The origins of this ancient stone bridge over the River Lune at Kirkby Lonsdale are obscure enough to have given rise to a legend that it was built by the Devil in one night*

SIZERGH CASTLE *This stronghold north-east of Levens has been the seat of the Strickland family for 700 years. Its main tower was built in 1360 as a shelter against Scots raiders*

where beacon fires were lit in the days of the Spanish Armada. Barbon Manor, built in 1862, is the seat of Lord Shuttleworth. Above the manor is the 1999-ft peak of Calf Top. There are many potholes 2½ miles to the south-east of Barbon. The best known among them are Bull Pot and Cow Pot.

Levens
Levens Hall is the largest Elizabethan mansion in south Cumbria. It is set in 100 acres of parkland, through which flows the Kent, and incorporates part of a 14th-century tower, built for protection against the Scots. The gardens were designed by a Frenchman called Beaumont between 1701 and 1704.

At Lyth Valley, to the north-west, daffodils and damson-tree blossom bring a splash of colour every spring.

Sizergh Castle—one of the most impressive castles in the county—is 1½ miles north-east of Levens. It has been the seat of the Strickland family for 700 years. The castle contains fine paintings, ceilings, panelling and furniture. There are pleasant walks on the fellside above the castle.

Orton
A secluded village with attractive stone houses and a spacious green. The Old Hall, built in 1604, is largely intact. George Whitehead, co-founder of the Society of Friends, was born in Orton *c.* 1636. There are good walks on the fell of Orton Scar, 1½ miles north.

Tebay, a long greystone village, 3 miles south, is also a good starting point for fell walks. Lune Gorge, stretching south from the village, is almost matched in its majesty by the magnificent gorge that has been artificially created through nearby cliffs to take the long, wide sweep of the M6 motorway.

Shap
A dour village near which the A6 road is often blocked by snow in winter. Just south of the railway bridge, a minor road leads west for a mile to the remains of Shap Abbey, *c.* 1200. Much of the masonry was pilfered to build cottages and farm walls, but the early 16th-century tower that remains is impressive. In the grounds of Shap Wells, a hotel built in 1850, 3½ miles south of Shap, is a charming statue (1842) of Queen Victoria as a young girl. It was the work of a mason from Lowther, a hamlet 6 miles north of Shap.

Superb walking country stretches on each side of the A6 around Shap, and motorists can park in valleys that strike off the road. South Cumbria's Borrowdale, for example, 7 miles south of Shap, is a fascinating peaty valley, and the surrounding Bretherdale, Roundthwaite and Whinfell commons are full of wildlife and rugged beauty. At High Borrow Bridge, just west, the Duke of Cumberland's forces routed those of Bonnie Prince Charlie in 1745.

Winster
Trees form archways over the twisting minor roads around this trim and lovely village. Most of the houses are 18th century or earlier. Throughout the area are rocky knolls and moss-banked waterfalls overlooking fields and tarns. Crook, a hamlet 3 miles east, is equally attractive.

Witherslack
The 17th-century church and school were gifts from John Barwick, a local man who was made Dean of St Paul's in 1661. The 3½ mile long limestone Whitbarrow Scar that strikes northwards is a spectacular crag with slopes covered in holly, hawthorn, wild strawberries and rock-roses. On the rocky common spreading out at the top, footpaths and stone stiles lead into a wooded world of crab-apple trees, rose hips, juniper, bracken, gorse and bramble.

ORNAMENTAL TREES *Box, holly and yew are shaped by the topiarist's art in the grounds of Levens Hall*

Wordsworth's valley

Angling There are salmon, sea trout and trout in the River Leven at Ulverston, and in the River Duddon at Broughton in Furness. There are brown trout in five reservoirs at Barrow-in-Furness, and trout, char, perch and pike in Coniston Water.

Events Ulverston has two annual 'hiring' fairs in May and Nov. Cark-in-Cartmel is the centre for the Lakeland Rose Show on the first weekend of July. There is also a 4-week exhibition of the work of local artists at Grange-over-Sands in July. Grange is the setting for the 9-mile Cross Bay Swim to Morecambe in late summer.

Places to see *Barrow-in-Furness Museum*: weekdays. *Brantwood*, Coniston Water: Apr. to Sept., daily except Sat. *Cartmel Priory Gatehouse* (NT), Hawkshead: Mar. to Dec., daily. *Furness Abbey*: daily, except Sun. morning Oct. to Mar. *Graythwaite Hall*: gardens; Apr. to June, daily. *Hawkshead Courthouse* (NT): Easter, then May to mid-Oct., afternoons except Mon. and Thur. *Hill Top* (NT), Near Sawrey: Apr. to Oct., weekdays, except Fri., Sun. afternoon. *Holker Hall*, near Cark: Easter to Sept., daily except Sat. *Lake Windermere Heather Garden*, Far Sawrey: early May to Oct., Sun. afternoon. *Ruskin Museum*, Coniston: Easter to Oct., daily.

Information centres The Centre, Ulverston. Tel. Ulverston 52299. Victoria Hall, Grange-over-Sands. Tel. Grange-over-Sands 4331 (seasonal).

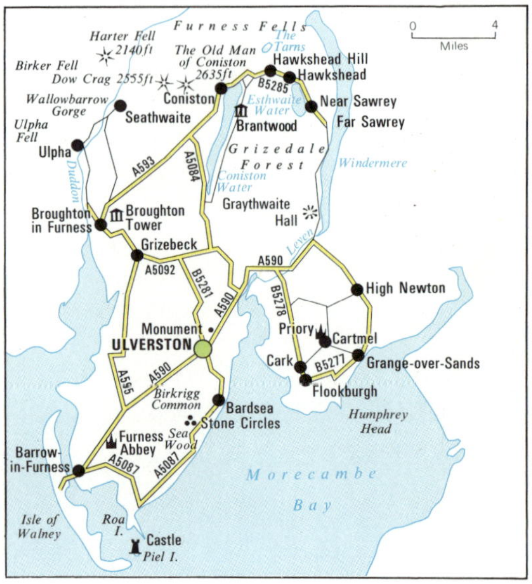

FELLS OVER CONISTON *Coniston village nestles in a tranquil setting*

Lakeland's south-west corner, formerly in Lancashire but now merged with Cumbria, has its own individuality. The dialect differs—authoress Beatrix Potter, who lived in the region for many years, described the local speech as the most musical she had ever heard. And the landscape differs—there are red-sandstone buildings around Barrow-in-Furness, white limestone outcrops among the sheeplands of the Furness Peninsula, and some of Britain's biggest slate quarries at Broughton in Furness.

But alongside this stony ruggedness there is a more gentle scenery. The picturesque Duddon Valley, which unfolds northwards for 8 miles from the Duddon Estuary, has waterfalls, fern-covered hillsides and birch woodlands. The valley inspired Wordsworth to write 34 sonnets about it. The little lake of The Tarns, north-east of Coniston, is one of the most beautiful in the whole Lake District.

South-west Cumbria's major lake is Coniston Water; here Donald Campbell made many attempts on the world waterspeed record and was killed in January 1967, when *Bluebird* crashed at 310 mph.

Two peninsulas jutting south into Morecambe Bay again provide contrasts. Westwards, at Barrow-in-Furness, are the towering cranes of a busy shipbuilding industry; eastwards is the seaside resort of Grange-over-Sands, while at nearby Humphrey Head white cliffs interrupt an otherwise flat coastline.

CROSS AND GATEHOUSE *Near Cartmel's 18th-century market cross is a priory gatehouse, dating from c. 1330*

Barrow-in-Furness
A mainly industrial town where ships and nuclear submarines are built. The town's parish church, bombed during the Second World War, has superb new windows. North-east of the town are the magnificent red-sandstone ruins of Furness Abbey, founded in 1127 and in its time one of the most powerful religious houses in the North. Among the remains are late-Norman arches.

Three 'islands' lie off the coast: the 9 mile long Isle of Walney, mainly residential but with a number of footpaths by the side of beautiful beaches; Roa Island, on the tip of a long headland; and Piel Island, half a mile away, which can be reached only by boat.

Piel's one building—apart from a superb ruined castle—is an inn whose landlord has the title of King of Piel. He has the power to confer the rank of Knight of Piel Island on visitors. The ceremony involves dubbing them with a sword and pouring beer over them.

Broughton in Furness
A small and attractive market town overlooking the Duddon Estuary. Broughton Tower is a 14th-century pele tower rebuilt *c.* 1750. A statue in the market square commemorates John Gilpin, a local man who gave the land on which the square is built. The town is an ideal centre for walks, with lovely woodlands full of rocks, bracken and streams, and wild, hilly country near Grizebeck, $2\frac{1}{2}$ miles south-east.

Broughton is also the gateway to Ulpha Fell. Four miles north, the steep S-bend, turning off north-west at the Traveller's Rest Inn, leads to a wonderful high mountain plateau with walks over Birker Fell and Ulpha Fell and views northwards of the highest lakeland peak, Scafell Pike.

Cartmel
A cathedral 'city' in miniature, with a magnificent priory church founded in 1188 by William Marshal, 1st Earl of Pembroke. Among the priory treasures are superb stained glass, carved misericords on the choir stalls and a first edition of Edmund Spenser's *Faerie Queene*. The 14th-century gabled gatehouse was once part of the priory; an 18th-century market cross is near by.

The best walking country in the area is above High Newton, 3 miles north-east, where woods line the roadsides and small hills are covered in bracken, hawthorn and holly.

Grange-over-Sands, 2 miles east of Cartmel, is sometimes called the Torquay of the North because of its warm spring temperatures—the highest in northern England. The town has a long promenade with excellent views across the bay to Morecambe, 9 miles south.

Along the top of the cliffs at Humphrey Head, 3 miles south, is a grassy ridge where the hawthorns have been bent almost flat by the winds. On the west side of the headland is Holy Well, an active mineral spring. A hole known as

beneath the Furness Fells, with The Old Man of Coniston (left) rising to 2635 ft

THE CHARM OF LAKELAND *The Tarns, near Coniston, is one of the prettiest of all Lakeland's lakes. It provides magnificent views of the surrounding mountains, including the Langdale Pikes, Red Screes, Fairfield and the Helvellyn range*

STORY-BOOK WORLD OF BEATRIX POTTER

Hill Top, at Near Sawrey, was the home of the writer of children's tales, Beatrix Potter. She was born in 1866 in London and her first book, *The Tale of Peter Rabbit,* was published in 1902, after she moved to Lakeland. Beatrix Potter illustrated her stories herself from her observation of the local countryside; the mouse is from *Appley Dapply's Nursery Rhymes*

Grand Arch in the face of the cliff gives a rocky climb to the top of the headland.

A tasty flat fish known as fluke can be caught at Flookburgh, a village 2 miles north-west of Humphrey Head.

Coniston

The atmosphere of a past mining industry is still retained in the tourist village situated half a mile from the head of Coniston Water. All round is superb scenery and the village is an ideal centre for scaling The Old Man of Coniston, at 2635 ft the highest peak in this area, and for climbing on Dow Crag. John Ruskin, who is buried at Coniston Church, lived at Brantwood, on the east shore of the lake, from 1871 until his death in 1900. The village museum contains some of his drawings, and models of geological structures in the area. The disused copper mines 1 mile north-west of Coniston attract many visitors. Care is needed when exploring the old tunnels and pit-heaps.

Coniston Water, $5\frac{1}{4}$ miles long, has excellent shoreside walks. There is a memorial to Donald Campbell, killed on the lake in 1967 when attempting a new world waterspeed record.

Two miles north-east of Coniston is the half-mile long, tree-lined lake many people consider the prettiest of all in the Lake District—The Tarns. It was originally three smaller lakes, but a dam that was built about 50 years ago joined them together.

Hawkshead

Tree-covered hills and picturesque stone cottages make this village one of the Lake District's leading beauty spots. The village, near the head of the $1\frac{1}{2}$ mile long Esthwaite Water, is overlooked by the Norman Church of St Michael which contains the private chapel of the Sandys family. Edwin Sandys, Archbishop of York, was born at Esthwaite Hall in 1516. In 1585 he founded the local grammar school where Wordsworth was a pupil. The school is now a museum and contains the desk on which Wordsworth carved his name. Ann Tyson's cottage, where Wordsworth lodged, is just off the main street. The Courthouse contains a museum of Lakeland industry.

The 1 mile long footpath from Hawkshead to Hawkshead Hill, west of the village, gives splendid views of nearby mountain ranges, and there are beautiful walks in the Grizedale Forest.

Sawrey

Divided into Far Sawrey and Near Sawrey, this beautiful village on the west side of Windermere has many old cottages set among trees and gardens of flowers. Beatrix Potter, the writer, lived at Hill Top, behind the Town Bank Arms in Near Sawrey, in the early 1900's. She married a south Cumbrian solicitor, William Heelis, and became a successful sheep farmer. When she died in 1943 she bequeathed her house and much of the surrounding land she owned to the National Trust. All around the village are lovely walks through copses and across fields.

Seathwaite

The modern church occupies the site of an old chapel whose vicar for more than 60 years was Robert Walker—made famous by Wordsworth's writings as the hard-working preacher who raised a family of eight children on a stipend of less than £50 a year.

The minor road through Seathwaite follows the river, and there are many grassy places beside small waterfalls for picnics. Wallowbarrow Gorge, half a mile to the west, is spectacular in flood.

The Walna Scar track that strikes out eastwards half a mile north of the village gives a mountainous 5-mile walk to Coniston. A mile north of Seathwaite are Forestry Commission woodlands, blending with the 2140-ft Harter Fell peak to provide an alpine setting.

Ulverston

The huge stone tower on the summit of Hoad Hill is a replica of Eddystone Lighthouse. It is a memorial to Sir John Barrow, founder of the Royal Geographical Society and for 40 years Secretary to the Admiralty, who was born in the town in 1764. There are many interesting walks in the area.

Bardsea, on the coast 3 miles south, is a charming village of greystone houses with an 18th-century inn and an excellent golf course. The sea winds have made the trees in Sea Wood, fringing the coast, lean over at an angle. On Birkrigg Common, 1 mile west, are prehistoric stone circles and a temple ruin known as Druid's Circle.

West Cumbria's green coast

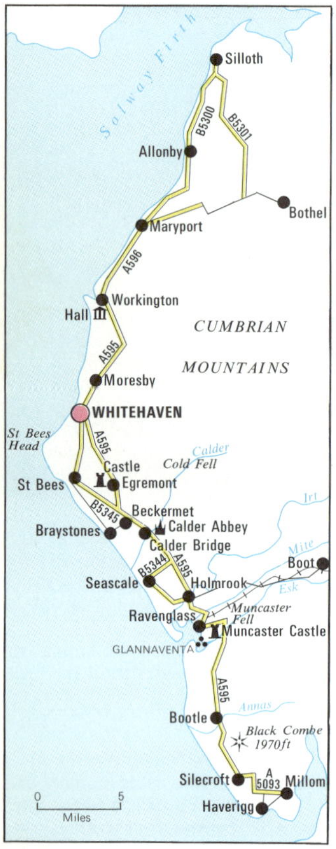

The Cumbrian coast, stretching 60 miles northwards from Millom to just beyond Silloth, has broad stretches of sand and spectacular sea views, towns of great character and inland walks in delightful valleys. Yet many people think of this region as flat and uninteresting—a judgment no doubt based on the scars left by industry.

In some places the industrial life, which originally grew from west Cumbria's coal and other minerals, has now died out; and even where it thrives, the smoking chimneys and cooling towers are so scattered that they rarely obtrude for long on the scenery.

In addition, the two main industrial centres of Workington and Whitehaven have kept the best of the old architecture in restyling their town centres. The panoramic view of Whitehaven from the bypass high above the town reveals an elegant blend of old and new.

Further north, the coast road from Maryport to Silloth follows the splendid sands of the Solway Firth. Inland, too, the region has much to offer. The countryside has superb walks and glorious views into the lakeland valleys eastwards; and Black Combe mountain, towering to 1970 ft across the south-west tip of Cumbria,has many delightful valleys to explore. On a clear day, there is a view from the mountain's summit of 14 English and Scottish counties, the Isle of Man, Snowdon, and the Irish Mountains of Mourne. And if any final evidence is needed that the Cumbrian coast is a land of pleasant greenness, the sea-washed turf from Silloth has such a rich quality that it is used on bowling greens all over the country.

ACROSS THE FIRTH *Spray bursts on the Silloth coast. Across the*

Sailing Clubs at Haverigg, Seascale and Whitehaven.

Angling There are salmon and sea trout in the Rivers Esk, Mite, Irt and Calder; tickets obtainable in Ravenglass, Bootle and Calder Bridge. Sea fishing for plaice and cod is possible from boats or from the shore, especially at Whitehaven and below St Bees Head.

Nature reserves Ravenglass Gullery (permit from Cumbria County Council, The Castle, Carlisle). St Bees Reserve (RSPB) and Easkmeals Reserve, near Ravenglass: both daily.

Events Whitehaven Civic Hall and Sports Centre is open all the year. Rosehill Theatre at Moresby has a winter season of music and drama.

Places to see *Egremont Castle*: daily. *Muncaster Castle*, Ravenglass: late Mar. to Oct., Sun., Tues., Wed., Thur. afternoons; gardens, afternoons except Fri. *Ravenglass and Eskdale Railway*: late Mar. to Oct., daily; limited service rest of year.

Information centre Market Place, Whitehaven. Tel. Whitehaven 5678.

Bootle
Beautiful countryside surrounds the village, which has attractive stone bridges crossing the River Annas. The bracken-lined flanks of Black Combe soar 2½ miles to the south-east. The peak, easily climbed by a path from the village, gives magnificent views. On the coast, 1½ miles west, are inviting stretches of sands.

Egremont
A small industrial centre in attractive surroundings with a ruined castle dating from 1130. Lowes Court, on the wide main street, is an art centre where paintings by local artists can be bought.

Just outside the village of Beckermet, 3 miles south, is Yeorton Hall, once the home of Hugh Gaitskell, the former Labour Party leader. From the village, a pleasant 1-mile walk leads south-west to Braystones, where there is a sandy beach and safe bathing.

From Calder Bridge, another attractive village 1½ miles south-east of Beckermet, tracks cross the bracken and heather wastes of Cold Fell, a wild moorland area. The ruins of the 12th-century Calder Abbey, built by the Savignac monks from Furness Abbey, are in a delightful setting by the River Calder, and there are striking views in the surrounding area of the Calder Hall atomic power station and the Windscale reactors.

Holmrook
A pretty village by a good fishing river, the Irt, with wonderful views of Muncaster Fell. There are easy walks on bracken-covered land. Boulders in the area are stained red where sheep have rubbed dye from their coats.

Irton Church, 1 mile north-east, is built on a site where an early crusader was buried. There are striking views through the church windows of the Wasdale peaks to the north-east.

MINIATURE RAILWAY *Volunteers help to run the 7 mile long Ravenglass and Eskdale miniature railway. The century-old line was originally used to carry minerals*

choppy waters of the Solway Firth rise the mountains of Galloway in Scotland

Seascale, 3 miles north-west of Holmrook, has excellent sands and coastline walks and the breakers are ideal for surfing. To the south is the Ravenglass Gullery Nature Reserve, Europe's largest black-headed gull colony. Permits to visit the reserve are given by Cumbria County Council.

Maryport
In the 18th century the lord of the manor, Colonel H. Senhouse, developed the village into a coal port, naming it after his wife, Mary. Today, much is wild and overgrown. The pits are closed and the docks, silting up, are used only by small fishing boats and by weekend sailors. But it is a fascinating spot, full of narrow streets, with a maze of walks around the docks and on to the harbour walls, where small boys cycle out along the piers to fish for mackerel.

Millom
The iron and steel that was once smelted in this town made it a miniature Sheffield. But this industry has now ceased and the town has a sad, neglected appearance. There is, however, beauty surrounding it. Black Combe, 4 miles north-west, makes an impressive backcloth and there are superb sands from Haverigg, 1 mile south, to Silecroft, 3 miles north-west, and beyond.

Ravenglass
A seafaring village on the estuary of three rivers—the Esk, the Mite and the Irt. The Ravenglass and Eskdale miniature railway, which has engines named after Lakeland rivers, runs daily services along Eskdale from Ravenglass to Dalegarth and back. A few minutes' walk south of Ravenglass is the site of the 4-acre Roman fort of Glannaventa, whose red-sandstone walls, covered with ivy, are almost 13 ft high.

The excellently preserved Muncaster Castle, built *c.* 1200 with 19th-century reconstructions, is 1 mile east of the village. The castle, which is open to the public, is the seat of the Pennington family. Its collection includes a glass cup with gold and enamel gilding known as 'The luck of the Muncaster', which was presented to the family by Henry VI, who took refuge there after being defeated at Hexham in 1464. Legend says that the family will prosper as long as the cup remains unbroken. The castle has beautiful gardens and is surrounded by hills and woods.

St Bees
Until the mid-1960's this was a quiet seaside village. Now it is developing as a flourishing resort with caravan sites, cafés, gift-shops and a night club. The original Church of SS Mary and Bega (*c.* AD 651) was destroyed by the Danes and refounded in the 12th century; the restored church is a splendid sandstone building. There was once a Benedictine nunnery on the site. Legend says that when St Bega, an Irish princess, asked the lord of the manor for land on which to build it, she was mockingly offered all the land covered by snow on midsummer's day. When St Bega awoke that day, there was snow covering a 3-mile stretch of land, which was then given to her for the nunnery.

St Bees School was founded in 1587 as a grammar school by a local man, Edmund Grindal, who was appointed Archbishop of Canterbury in 1576. It is now a public school.

Both north and south of the village are superb headland walks along the top of cliffs that are popular with rock-climbers. The 323-ft St Bees Head is topped by a 99 ft high lighthouse.

Silloth
Excellent sands, backed by grassy dunes, line the coast around the harbour; but the tide comes in fast and it is not wise to walk too far out at low tide. Across the Solway Firth are glorious views of Scotland, a mountain panorama dominated by the 1866-ft peak of Criffel.

Whitehaven
A town of great character developed in Wren style in the 17th and 18th centuries by the Lowther family. St James' Church, the Friends' Meeting House, the lighthouse and the new quay are all 18th-century. In the town centre many old buildings have been retained under a conservation scheme. Lowther Street, in particular, has some elegant old houses alongside the modern civic hall.

The harbour is worth visiting to see the ships that bring phosphate rocks from North Africa for the works on the hill above the sea, where detergent chemicals are made, and the last coal-fired dredger working in Britain. In 1778, John Paul Jones, the privateer who had become notorious for his exploits in the American War of Independence, attacked the harbour, set fire to one ship and spiked the battery guns.

At Moresby, 2 miles north of Whitehaven, is the attractive Rosehill Theatre, which is used for chamber music and drama. It was founded by a local silk-mill owner, Sir Nicholas Sekers, in 1959, and the interior was designed by Oliver Messel, the theatrical designer.

Workington
The town owes its modern growth to coal and steel, but traces of the Roman fort of Gabrosentum overlooking the harbour recall its importance in earlier times, too. Elegant Georgian houses line the cobble-stoned Portland Square. At Workington Hall, built in 1379, Mary, Queen of Scots stayed for a night in 1568 when fleeing to England after the Battle of Langside. St Michael's Church, rebuilt in 1887, has fragments of 8th-century crosses, and a large Norman arch.

A MODERN SKYLINE *The cooling towers of the Calder Hall atomic power station frame the Windscale atomic research centre. Calder Hall's reactors were the first in the world to be used to generate electricity on a commercial basis*

How Lakeland was formed

Some 500 million years ago the land that was to become the Lake District was a trough full of sediment under a muddy sea. In the immensity of time it has taken to become one of England's most celebrated pieces of landscape, its shape and character have swung from one extreme to another. Vast volcanic eruptions buried it under 2 miles of ash and lava about 450 million years ago. It has been mountain range, clear sea, swamp and desert. Only in the last million years, since Ice-Age glaciers gouged out its valleys and created the lakes, has it taken on anything like its present form.

The history of Lakeland is written in its rocks. Buckling under the pressures caused by movement of the Earth's crust, layers of rock have twisted from the horizontal to the almost vertical. Wind, rain, ice and frost have eroded the surface, revealing rocks from successive ages lying alongside one another.

The lakes themselves are the most recent geological addition to Lakeland landscape, and they may also be the first feature to change. Slowly, river-borne sediment is filling the basins carved out by glaciers. In 40,000–50,000 years' time, there may be no lakes left.

THREE FACES OF LAKELAND *The oldest rocks in Lakeland, called Skiddaw Slates, were formed from the debris that piled up on the Ordovician sea-bed from about 500 million years ago. Slopes built on Skiddaw Slates, such as snow-capped Saddleback (below), north-east of Keswick, are usually smooth, for the rocks weather evenly. By contrast, the jagged rocks of Scafell (top right), called Borrowdale Volcanics, record the violence of volcanoes which erupted 450 million years ago. In Silurian times, 440–395 million years ago, the sea reclaimed Lakeland; and erosion of the sediment once on the Silurian sea-bed gave rise to the gentle landscape around Hawkshead (below right)*

SMOOTH HILLS OF SKIDDAW SLATES

DISTRIBUTION OF ROCKS

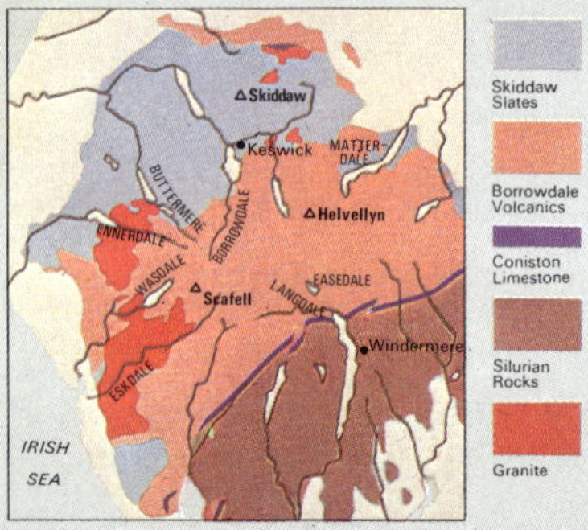

STAGES IN THE BUILDING OF LAKELAND

Varied scenery on the surface of Lakeland is a clue to the geological complexity underneath. Three processes, alternating over millions of years, have shaped the area's scenery: the accumulation of sedimentary rocks during periods of relative calm; the folding of these rocks by movements of the Earth; and constant erosion at the surface. The diagrams (right) show in simplified form five main stages in the development of the landscape of the Lake District

ORDOVICIAN PERIOD
(500–440 million years ago)
A tranquil period when sediment (Skiddaw Slates) piles up at the bottom of a shallow sea is followed by volcanic eruptions which bury the area under ash and lava (Borrowdale Volcanics). The cones build up above sea level

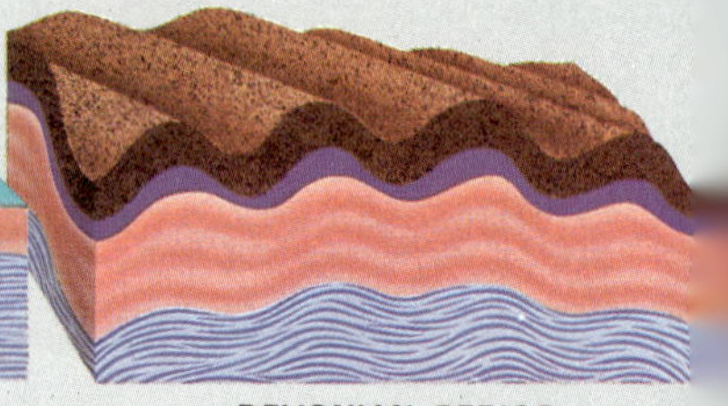

DEVONIAN PERIOD
(395–345 million years ago)
After the Ordovician Period the area lies unde the Silurian sea, and new rocks (first Conisto Limestone then other Silurian Rocks) pile up Earth movements in Devonian times buckle the rocks and throw up the Caledonian mountains

ICE-AGE CORRIE

Many Lakeland rivers have their source in tiny lakes or tarns high in the mountains, such as Small Water (left) at the head of a stream feeding Haweswater Reservoir. These lakes lie in small rock basins called corries, which were probably shallow hollows deepened by erosion during the Ice Age. Snow lying in the corrie built up and then packed tight, becoming a small glacier. Frost shattered the bedrock, and the glacier swept the debris away

GLACIER VALLEY

As glaciers pushed down through the river valleys during the Ice Age, they tended to cut them into a U-shape, as in Langdale Valley (left). Glacier valleys are relatively straight, and their sides are smooth, for the ice planed off rocks that lay in its path. When the glaciers finally melted about 10,000 years ago, some water overflowed to the south and some, trapped behind dams of debris in the valleys, helped to form the lakes

VOLCANIC ROCKS AND CRAGS

GENTLE LANDSCAPE BUILT ON SILURIAN ROCKS

CARBONIFEROUS PERIOD
(345–280 million years ago)
A warm, coral-rich sea drowns the eroded mountains, and a new layer of limestone builds up. Pressure from below folds the older rocks. Eventually the sea silts up and the area becomes marshland, with great ferns on its mudbanks

PERMIAN PERIOD
(280–225 million years ago)
The Carboniferous Rocks and all the rocks beneath them are thrown up in an arch by another great phase of mountain building. Erosion wears down the mountains and the area becomes an arid and wind-blown desert

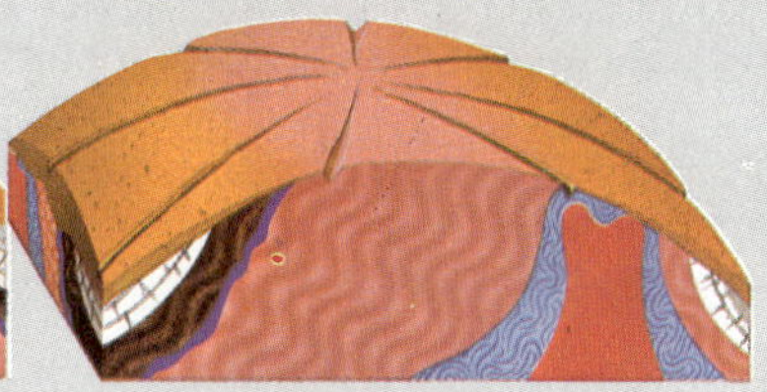

MIOCENE EPOCH
(26–7 million years ago)
Ripples from distant Earth movements raise the rocks into a dome. Erosion, mainly by Ice-Age glaciers, carves present-day Lakeland from the dome. The rivers still radiate from what was the dome's centre, near Scafell (right)

RADIAL PATTERN OF RIVERS

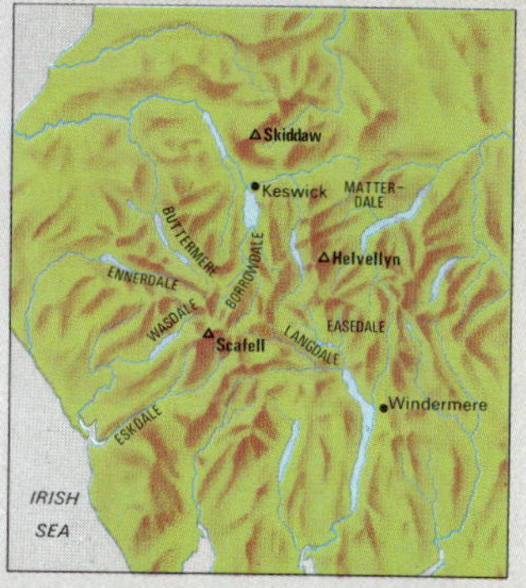

THE EFFECTS OF EROSION

The weather is continually changing the shape of Lakeland, and frost is one of the most potent forces. Water fills cracks in the rocks, then expands when it freezes. The rocks shatter, and rock fragments known as scree build up below and gradually form steep scree slopes. The scree slopes on the south-east shore of Wastwater (left), Lakeland's deepest lake, drop about 1700 ft from Illgill Head to the water at an angle of 35–40 degrees

THE LAKES AND MAN

Since Lake Thirlmere was first tapped for water in 1890, Man has joined Nature as a potent force changing the face of Lakeland. The area is one of northern England's most valuable sources of slate and granite, and quarries pock-mark the landscape. The lakes provide many northern towns with water. The dam at Haweswater (left), the reservoir behind it and the coniferous woods near by are all man-made features of Lakeland

Peaks of western Lakeland

Angling Salmon, sea and brown trout in the River Derwent and Bassenthwaite Lake. Coarse fish also on Derwent Water.

Nature trails A trail in Skelghyll Wood starts at Stone Steps, 1 mile south-east of Ambleside. White Moss Common trail starts from the foot-bridge 2½ miles north-west of Ambleside. Johnny Wood trail starts at Seatoller. Launchy Gill trail starts from the stile on the west shore of Thirlmere; Swirls trail starts from the car park on the east shore.

Events Keswick Theatre Festival lasts throughout the summer.

Places to see *Fitz Park Museum and Art Gallery*, Keswick, containing Southey, Wordsworth and Walpole manuscripts: Easter to Oct., weekdays. *Lingholm*, Keswick: gardens only; Apr. to Oct., weekdays. *St Herbert's Island*, Derwent Water: rowing boats can be hired at Keswick. *Wordsworth House* (NT), Cockermouth: Apr. to Oct., daily except Thur. afternoon and Sun.

Information centres Council Chambers, 50 Main Street, Keswick. Tel. Keswick 72645 (seasonal). Lake District National Park Information Service, The Moot Hall, Keswick. Tel. Keswick 72803 (seasonal).

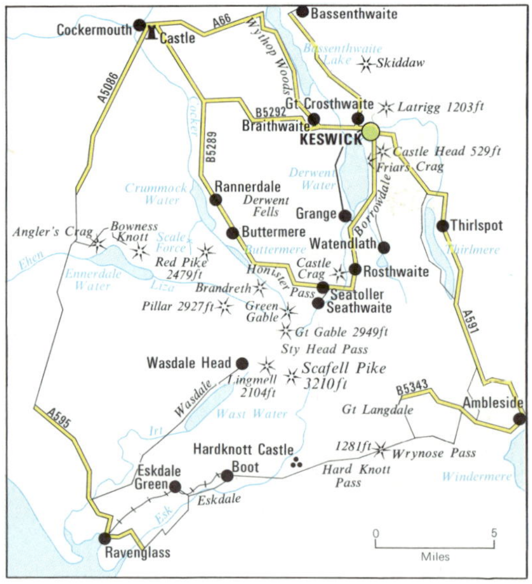

England's highest point, the boulder-strewn Scafell Pike, towers 3210 ft among the crags of the wildest and most majestic part of Lakeland. The Wastwater Hotel is a meeting-place for climbers. In the summer, long lines of walkers can be seen picking their way up stony hillsides to the top of Scafell Pike, from which the view embraces the lakes of Windermere, Derwent Water and Wast Water, and the peaks of Great Gable and Pillar.

Nestled beneath the bold austerity of the crags are eight major lakes with superb, tree-lined walks, and rich green valleys where the scent of bracken and the sound of gurgling waterfalls offer physical and mental relaxation after a climb among the magnificent hills.

The region, too, has the wettest place in England—at Seathwaite in the Borrowdale Valley, where the annual rainfall can be more than four times the London average. But visitors should not be deterred. May, June and September are the driest months, and it is in spring and autumn that the scenery is at its best—lush and green in spring, flecked with autumn tints from September until its vivid climax of colour in October.

ACROSS THE JAWS *The stone bridge at Grange crosses the Derwent at a narrow point known as the Jaws of Borrowdale. Rising behind Grange village are the Derwent Fells*

WHERE SOUTHEY LIES *Robert Southey (1774–1843) is buried in Great Crosthwaite churchyard. In the church is an effigy of the poet, with an inscription by Wordsworth*

THE IMPOSING FACE OF GREAT GABLE *The view from Lingmell, to the south, shows the pyramid shape which has given 2949-ft Great Gable its name. Despite its formidable appearance, Great Gable is one of the many Lakeland peaks which can be scaled in an afternoon by any reasonably active walker, provided he wears suitable clothes and boots and exercises proper care. The gentlest paths, such as those illustrated on the right, ascend the north slope of the mountain. Only experienced climbers should attempt to scale the south face, where a route starts from Wasdale Head, in the valley between Great Gable and Lingmell, and the top is reached by climbing to the left of the Great Napes—the rocky outcrops just below the summit. Lingmell, 2104 ft, is on one of the routes from Wasdale Head to the summit of Scafell Pike, England's highest mountain*

AN EASY WAY UP GREAT GABLE

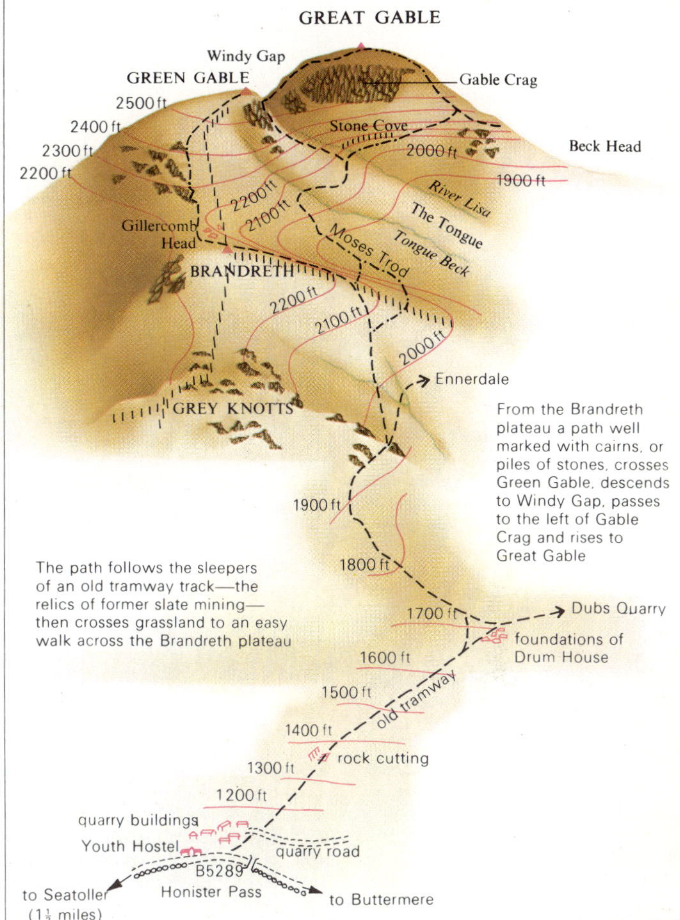

The ascent from Honister Pass is a good route for walkers who arrive by car. They can park at the pass, 1100 ft above sea level, from which a 3-mile walk leads to the top

Borrowdale
Fine walks lead from the steep-sided valley which runs 5 miles south from Derwent Water to the village of Seathwaite. Sourmilk Gill waterfall pours down the hillside west of Seathwaite to the Slabs, used by climbers as practice slopes. The path southwards leads to the 1600-ft Sty Head Pass, where footpaths from Borrowdale, Wasdale, Eskdale and Great Langdale meet.

The route passes the 2949-ft Great Gable, one of the highest and best-known mountains of the area, and continues to the hamlet of Wasdale Head. This is a richly satisfying walk, though a challenge in wet weather.

Near Rosthwaite, 2½ miles north-east of Seathwaite, is the Bowder Stone, a rock weighing almost 2000 tons that has fallen from the crags and appears to be delicately balanced on one edge. A ladder can be climbed to the top. There are splendid walks along the banks of the River Derwent, whose lovely green pools mirror birch trees. Beside the river is the 900-ft Castle Crag, the summit of which—reached by a fairly easy 20-minute walk—provides a superb view of Derwent Water.

Buttermere
A beautiful valley, in which the 1¼ mile long Buttermere Lake is hemmed in by high mountains. It is possible to walk right round the lake—through pine trees, bracken, and at one point through a tunnel in a cliff. The eastern road approach to Buttermere is over the fierce-looking 1176-ft Honister Pass, which has 1-in-4 gradients. At its western end a footpath through Warnscale Bottom follows a spectacular route between the 1900-ft Hay Stacks and the axe-edged 2126-ft Fleetwith Pike.

The village of Buttermere, north of the lake, has a tiny church built in 1841. From the church a lane leads south to Sourmilk Gill waterfalls (the same name, but different falls from the one in Borrowdale). From here a further path leads to Red Pike, a 2479-ft peak that is one of Lakeland's finest viewpoints. Five lakes can be seen from the top.

Crummock Water is a beautiful 2½ mile long lake north-west of Buttermere. To the south, the 100-ft Scale Force is the highest Lake District waterfall. To the north, the wild valley of Rannerdale is only a ten-minute walk from the B5289 road. This remote valley is a paradise for walkers.

Cockermouth
One of the oldest towns in west Cumbria, and the birthplace in 1770 of William Wordsworth. His home, Wordsworth House, is open to the public. There is also a ruined castle, dating from 1134, complete with a dungeon. Buses make a 15-mile circuit of Bassenthwaite Lake. Fletcher Christian, leader of the mutiny on the *Bounty*, was born in 1764 at Moorland Close, a farmhouse 1½ miles south of Cockermouth.

LAKE DISTRICT COTTAGE

Slate roofs are a common feature of Lakeland houses. They can vary in colour from grey, blue-grey and rust brown to the bright green of slates quarried at Borrowdale. The rubble walls of the houses, which are set on a base of rough-hewn stones with little mortar, are sometimes hung with slates, but more often the walls are plastered over, then whitewashed

Ennerdale
Seven miles of fell, forest and water combine to make Ennerdale one of the wildest and most attractive valleys in the Lake District. It is the only one not accessible by car—the motor road stops by Bowness Knott, half a mile from the north bank of Ennerdale Water. But there are excellent footpaths north, south and west of the lake shores, with views of the 811-ft Angler's Crag rock that towers to the north of the lake.

Three miles east of the lake is the 2927-ft Pillar mountain. Its famous crag, mentioned in Wordsworth's 'The Brothers', presents a challenge to climbers.

Eskdale Green
Pine trees and rhododendrons flank the road in this pretty village, which has lovely walks along the banks of the River Esk. At the hamlet of Boot, 2½ miles east, an iron girder crossing the river once supported a bridge on the 'Owd Ratty' railway line. The railway was built by a man called Ratcliffe in the 1870's to carry ore from the mines at Boot. The major part of this line is now the Ravenglass and Eskdale miniature railway, which runs through nearly 7 miles of dale scenery from Dalegarth Station, just south of Boot, to Ravenglass.

Hard Knott Pass
Extremely sharp bends, 1-in-3 gradients and the narrowness of the pass make this the most difficult road in the Lake District. The pass reaches a height of 1291 ft and provides many spectacular views. At its western end are the ruins of a Roman fort, Hardknott Castle.

Wrynose Pass, 1281 ft, continuing the road eastwards, gives sweeping views over the surrounding hills. Just below the summit is the Three Shire Stone, at the point where Lancashire, Cumberland and Westmorland met.

SAILS BELOW THE HILLS *Bassenthwaite Lake, with Skiddaw rising in the east and Wythop Woods fringing its western banks, is ideal for sailing. It has steady breezes instead of the fierce winds which funnel through mountain passes and sweep across some lakes*

Keswick
A moot hall built in 1813 is in the middle of the main square, and the 18th-century Greta Hall north of the square was the home of the poet Robert Southey. His tomb is in the churchyard at Great Crosthwaite, north-west of the town.

The walks around Keswick are superb. Castle Head, a 529-ft hill half a mile south, gives a glorious view of Derwent Water and Bassenthwaite Lake; 1203-ft Latrigg, a mile north-east, provides a higher, wider panorama; and Friar's Crag, a headland on Derwent Water's eastern shore, was said by the writer John Ruskin to be one of Europe's best scenic viewpoints.

Derwent Water is the widest of the lakes—1¼ miles across. St Herbert, a disciple of St Cuthbert, had a hermitage on the island in the lake in AD 685. The surviving ruins are of a later building.

Two miles south of Keswick, a minor road turns off the B5289 to Watendlath, snugly set amid green fields, dark hills and the waters of a tarn, and used by Hugh Walpole as the setting for his novel *Judith Paris*. The road to Watendlath passes through attractive country, including the beauty spot of Ashness Bridge.

Thirlmere
The best views of the 3¾-mile lake, now a reservoir, are from the minor road on the west side. Two climbers' crags border the lake—Castle Rock of Triermain, near the King's Head Inn at Thirlspot on the east side, and 1520-ft Raven Crag at the north-west corner.

Wasdale Head
British rock climbing began here in the 1880's on Great Gable and Scafell (pronounced Scawf'l, or Scaw-fell). The church in this wild village is one of the smallest in England and its cemetery has several graves of rock climbers.

Wasdale Head is a centre for climbing Scafell Pike, 3210 ft, England's highest peak. It is a safe mountain to climb, provided the recognised routes are followed. Perhaps the easiest of these, marked by piles of stones, starts a mile south, above Wast Water, and crosses Lingmell Gill. The summit can be reached in about three hours.

WHERE JOHN PEEL WENT HUNTING

John Peel (1776–1854) might have remained no more than a local character in the village of Caldbeck, 8 miles north-east of Bassenthwaite, if a friend had not brought him renown by writing 'D'ye ken John Peel' to the tune of a traditional Cumbrian song. Peel, painted (left) by an unknown artist, was more than 6 ft tall. He kept his own pack of hounds so that he could always go hunting, on horseback or on foot. His gravestone (right) is in Caldbeck churchyard

LAKELAND PLANT Touch-Me-Not *(Impatiens noli-tangere)*, an annual plant suited to moist conditions, is commonly seen in the Lake District

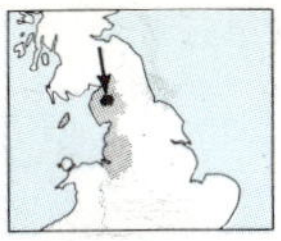

Helvellyn and the central lakes

Angling Brown trout and coarse fish in Lakes Windermere and Grasmere, Rydal Water and Esthwaite Water; brown trout and salmon in Rivers Gilpin, Kent and Leven.

Boating Pleasure trips on Ullswater from Glenridding, Howtown and Pooley Bridge; on Windermere from Bowness, Lakeside and Waterhead during the summer season.

Pony trekking Centre at Troutbeck.

Events Motor-boat races on Windermere from Broad Leas, every Sat., May to Sept. The drama season at the Grasmere Theatre is from May to July. Rush-bearing ceremonies at Ambleside, first Sat. in July and at Grasmere, first Sat. in Aug.

Places to see *Brockhole National Park Centre*, 2 miles north-west of Windermere: daily, mid-Mar. to mid-Nov. *Clappersgate* and *White Craggs Gardens*, Ambleside: daily, *Dove Cottage* and *Wordsworth Museum*, Grasmere: weekdays, Easter to Oct. *Rydal Mount*: daily, but closed mid-Jan. to Feb. *Townend* (NT), Troutbeck: Apr. to Oct., afternoons except Sat. and Mon., but open Bank Hol. Mon.: Mar., Wed. afternoons.

Information centres Lake District National Park Information Centre, Bank House, High Street, Windermere. Tel. Windermere 4561; and Old Courthouse, Ambleside. Tel. Ambleside 3084 (seasonal). Cumbria Tourist Board, Windermere. Tel. Windermere 4444.

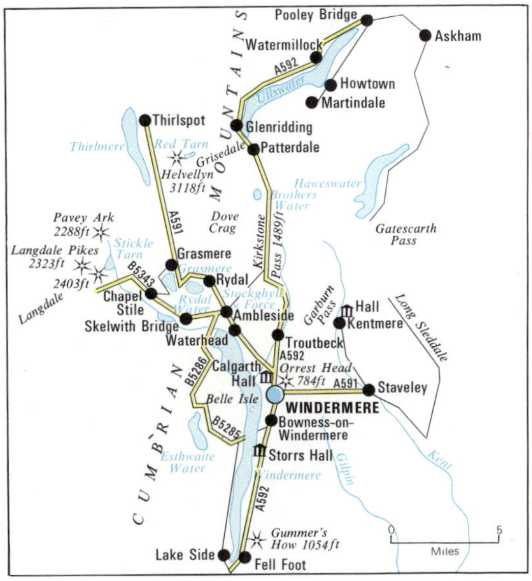

Central Cumbria, containing as it does almost every feature of mountain scenery, is to many visitors the loveliest and most satisfying part of the Lake District. It has the two largest lakes, Lake Windermere, more than 10 miles long, and Ullswater, 7 miles long; the most popular of all the peak climbs, Helvellyn; fertile valleys and lofty fells; noisy mountain streams; and a rich literary heritage.

It is small wonder that the region's roads in summer are crowded with cars and caravans, and its villages and towns packed with hikers and hill-climbers. But there are countless paths which the visitor can take to escape the holiday routes. They lead to high and lonely places, where all that can be heard is the bleating of the hardy Swaledale sheep.

The landscape is virtually unchanged from the days when William Wordsworth explored the hills and dales from his homes at Grasmere and Rydal Mount. Fellow writers, attracted by the beauty of the hills, visited him there. They included Sir Walter Scott, Charles Lamb and Samuel Taylor Coleridge.

Ambleside

A resort at the centre of the Lake District, and always crowded with walkers. Guides can be hired here, along with rope and tackle, for rock-climbing expeditions. Bridge House, a 17th-century rough-stone structure built as a summer-house, is now a National Trust information centre.

Every July the 19th-century Church of St Mary the Virgin observes the custom of rush-bearing, when children parade through the streets carrying rushes and flowers—a tradition handed down from the Middle Ages when rushes were used as carpets in churches.

Among many delightful fellside walks around Ambleside is one to Stockghyll Force—a beautiful waterfall set among woods 1 mile to the east. The route is signposted behind the Salutation Inn at the centre of the town. From Waterhead, just south, boat trips can be taken on Lake Windermere, including $1\frac{1}{4}$-hour trips along the full length of the lake to Lake Side in the south.

Chapel Stile

There is a mountaineering atmosphere about this hamlet. Here is the last petrol pump and the last shop before entering the Langdale Valley—which has a magnetic attraction for lakeland climbers.

The Langdale Pikes mark the head of Langdale, $2\frac{1}{2}$ miles west, and the Old Dungeon Ghyll Hotel is an excellent vantage point for watching helmeted climbers scaling rock faces. Behind the New Dungeon Ghyll Hotel, an easy but spectacular walk by the side of the Dungeon Ghyll waterfalls leads to Stickle Tarn. Over this circular mountain lake towers the precipitous 2288-ft Pavey Ark, an impressive and memorable sight.

From Stickle Tarn the footpath continues west to the main part of the Langdale Pikes, crowned by the magnificent 2323-ft Pike o' Stickle and the 2403-ft Harrison Stickle. Both these peaks can be covered quite easily during a single day's walking.

Grasmere

Dove Cottage, at the southern end of this village, was the home of William Wordsworth from 1799 until 1808. The house, and a museum near by that contains manuscripts and Wordsworth relics, are open to the public. The poet was buried in 1850 in St Oswald's churchyard, where his grave is marked by a simple stone.

Grasmere Sports—England's equivalent of the Highland Games—are held in Grasmere every year on the Thursday nearest to August 20. The games, which normally attract over ten thousand visitors, include Cumbrian wrestling, fell-racing to the top of Butter Crags and back, and hound-trailing, in which hounds follow an artificially laid

SNOW-COVERED PIKES *The Langdale Pikes rise steeply from the green floor of Langdale. The two crags of Harrison Stickle, 2403 ft (left) and Pavey Ark, 2288 ft, look challenging, but both can be easily 'scaled' in a day by the active walker. Mill Ghyll, in the dip, runs from Stickle Tarn at the foot of Pavey Ark*

FELL RUNNING *A cross-country race over the fells is one of the highlights of the Grasmere Sports, which have been held every year in mid-August since 1852*

RYDAL WATER *In 'The Prelude' Wordsworth recalls how one summer evening, as a boy, he stole a boat: 'Straight I unloosed her chain, and slipping in, pushed from the shore'*

trail across country at speeds of up to 20 mph. Rydal, 3 miles south-east, has a church dating from 1824. A path starting behind the church gives lovely views of Rydal Water, sheltered by Rydal Fell. Wordsworth lived at Rydal Mount for 33 years. The house is open to the public during the summer.

Kentmere

The 16th-century Kentmere Hall, now a farm, was the birthplace in 1517 of Bernard Gilpin, a parson whose evangelistic travels earned him the nickname of 'The Apostle of the North'. The fells surrounding Kentmere are among the loveliest in the Lakes—easy to reach, easy to walk, and all graced with solitude. A mile west of the village, the 1475-ft Garburn Pass, a bridleway linking Kentmere and Windermere, gives a superb view into Troutbeck Valley.

Kirkstone Pass

This is the highest pass in the region open to motorists, and it links Windermere to Patterdale. It reaches 1489 ft at its summit near the Kirkstone Pass Inn, with a gradient of 1 in 4 in places. The road from Ambleside starts with a minor road stretch, aptly named The Struggle. It joins the road from Windermere at the inn and is then only moderately steep and sufficiently wide for cars to pass. On the descent to Patterdale, rugged fells sweep down towards the small lake of Brothers Water, an idyllic scene which can be admired from a car park which lies to the west of the road. Also to the west is the towering black bulk of Dove Crag, a rock face 2603 ft up in the hills. The crag is one of the most exacting climbs in Britain.

Long Sleddale

A narrow, sheltered valley, 7 miles long, with green fields and woods and deep pools hidden in lonely ravines. Cars can travel most of its length by taking the left-hand fork off the A6, 4 miles north of Kendal. At the valley head, the road becomes little more than a rough track, and ahead loom the two tall crags of Buckbarrow and Goat Scar. A 2-mile mountain track leads over the 1950-ft Gatescarth Pass to the southernmost point of Haweswater Reservoir.

Haweswater is the most isolated of all the lakes, accessible by road only from Shap in the east or Askham in the north. It was originally only 2½ miles long, but a dam, completed in 1940, turned the lake into a 4½ mile long reservoir, submerging the village of Mardale which used to be at its head. The ruins of Mardale's Holy Trinity Church, demolished in 1936, can be seen through the waters; local legend says that the church bells can still be heard when the waters are whipped by strong winds.

Martindale

The two churches of this village just south of Ullswater—St Martin's, built in 1633, and St Peter's, built in 1880—are among the loneliest in Britain. This is wild and mountainous country, worth visiting for its rugged solitude. The best approach is along the winding road that runs down the south bank of Ullswater, reached by turning off the A592 just north of Pooley Bridge.

Patterdale

An attractive tourist village surrounded by mountains where St Patrick, the patron saint of Ireland, is said to have preached, and baptised converts. His holy well is at the roadside 1 mile north of the town. There are steamer trips along the 7-mile Ullswater, which is in a delightful setting; and there are many footpaths including shoreline walks through woods and hills on the eastern bank of the lake.

The village is an excellent base for climbing 3118-ft Helvellyn—the third-highest peak in the Lake District and the most popular climb. It can be tackled by any fully equipped and hardened hiker, but a head for heights is needed along the 1 mile long ridge of Striding Edge. The approach is along the Grisedale Valley and starts from a side-turning off the A592, near the police station at Patterdale. The walk to the summit is a distance of about 3 miles.

An easier climb to the summit, avoiding Striding Edge, can be made from the west. The footpath starts from Thirlspot on the A591 on the east bank of Thirlmere. This route is also about 3 miles long, taking 2 hours.

The view from the summit is breathtaking. On a clear day, almost every fell in Lakeland can be seen, as well as the Pennines to the east and the mountains of Scotland which lie 60 miles away to the north-west.

Windermere

This popular tourist centre is surrounded by easily reached vantage points which give glorious views of the countryside and the lake. Orrest Head, a 784-ft hill north of the town, provides one of the finest panoramas. The top can be reached in a few minutes by following the zigzag path beginning opposite the station beside the Windermere Hotel.

Another easy climb is to the top of Biskey How, a 300-ft hill just east of the Windermere suburb of Bowness, which has quaint, narrow streets, a 15th-century church with some good stained glass, and beautiful views across the lake. Bowness is the headquarters of the Royal Windermere Yacht Club.

Lake Windermere has 14 islands, including the privately owned Belle Isle which covers 30 acres. There is water-skiing from Waterhead at the north end of the lake.

The A592 which goes along the east side of the lake cuts well inland in many places, but there are still some excellent viewpoints. Among the best of these is the 1054-ft peak of Gummer's How, 6 miles south of Windermere, which can be reached by taking the side road at Fell Foot. There is a climb of about half a mile to reach the top.

LAKELAND WATERFALL *A mountain beck tumbles 70ft down rocks at Stockghyll Force waterfall, near Ambleside*

LAKESIDE PEACE *Boats can be hired at Windermere, which is a popular centre for rowing and sailing. Lake Windermere, more than 10 miles long, is England's largest lake, and lies in a valley gouged out by glaciers in the Ice Age a million years ago*

HELVELLYN FROM THE AIR *The 3118-ft mountain is the most popular climb in the Lake District. It can be approached from Patterdale along Striding Edge (foreground), above Red Tarn, but an easier ascent is from Thirlspot on the western side of Helvellyn*

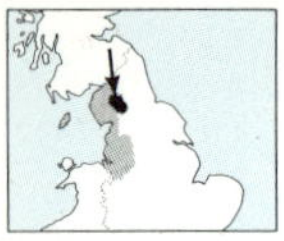

Along the Vale of Eden

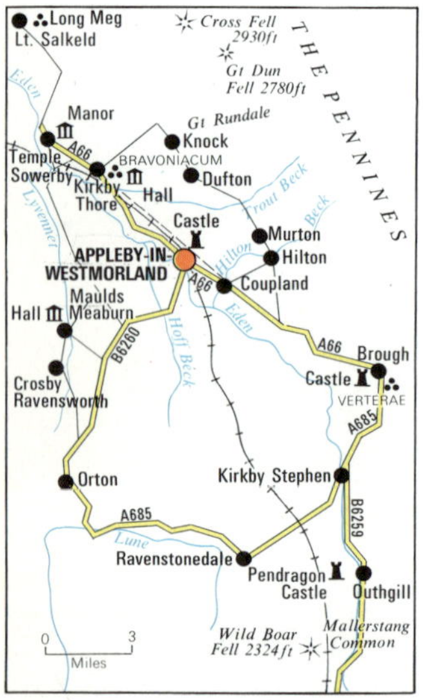

Angling There is salmon, trout and grayling fishing on the River Eden at Temple Sowerby and Kirkby Thore. There are brown trout in the Eden at Appleby; and salmon, sea trout and brown trout at Ravenstonedale on the tributaries of the River Lune.

Walking The fells are excellent for walking, with centres at Appleby, Crosby Ravensworth, Dufton, Kirkby Stephen and Outhgill.

Nature trail The Woodland Trail at Appleby-in-Westmorland passes more than 20 tree species; open from Easter to Oct. Guides are provided at the start of the trail, near Appleby, or from Eden Field Club, The Mill Cottage, Murton-cum-Hilton. There is also an urban trail round Appleby: details from information centre.

Golf There is a course at Brackenber Moor, 2 miles east of Appleby.

Swimming Appleby has an open-air heated swimming-pool.

Events Appleby-in-Westmorland has a Gipsy Fair on the second Wed. in June, and a fortnight's Festival in early July. Sulky trotting races (horse-and-carriage races) take place on Spring Bank Hol. Mon. and the Tues. before the Gipsy Fair.

Places to see *Acorn Bank* (NT), Temple Sowerby, gardens: Apr. to Oct., daily except Mon. *Brough Castle*: weekdays, Sun. afternoons. *Lowther Wildlife Park*, 7 miles west of Kirkby Thore: Apr. to mid-Oct., daily.

Information centre Moot Hall, Appleby. Tel. Appleby 51177 (seasonal).

The River Eden in the eastern part of Cumbria flows through a fertile valley; its waters are an anglers' paradise and on it lies the attractive 'place of the apple tree'—Appleby-in-Westmorland. A Roman road follows the river and deep, green-sided valleys bite into the heart of the Pennine mountains.

To the north, in striking contrast, are the mountain areas of Cross Fell and Great Dun Fell, cloud-capped, brooding summits almost 3000 ft high, beneath which lie the colourful sandstone villages of this agricultural and least-known corner of east Cumbria.

Through the middle of the region snakes the notorious 'Long Drag' railway—the 73-mile Settle to Carlisle stretch of the old Midland Railway, which cuts through the top of rocky summits and burrows deep into long, dark tunnels. Its path through the wilds was hewn out between 1869 and 1875 by gangs of Irish labourers living in shanty towns alongside the route.

The shanty towns have now disappeared and many of the stations have closed. But it is still England's highest railway line and, costing £47,500 per mile of track (about £750,000 at today's values), it is the most expensive stretch of railway ever laid in Britain.

CASTLE OF 'THE BUTCHER' *The 11th-century Brough Castle was*

Appleby-in-Westmorland
A castle dominated by a late-Norman keep stands at the top of Boroughgate, a main street closely packed with interesting houses on each side. The castle was restored in 1653 by the indomitable Lady Anne Clifford, Countess of Dorset, Pembroke and Montgomery, a noted opponent of Cromwell. Her passion for building is imprinted on the town. St Anne's Hospital was founded by her in 1651 as an almshouse—the white seats erected for the inhabitants can be seen in the cobbled courtyard; St Michael's Church in Bongate was restored by her; and at each end of Boroughgate is a cross with her motto: 'Retain your loyalty, preserve your rights.'

The partly Norman St Lawrence Church—rebuilt in the 17th century by Lady Anne—contains her tomb. The town's grammar school, which originally stood near the church, had among its pupils the brother of George Washington, first President of the United States.

The town is an excellent centre for walking—by the Eden and along the streams of Hoff Beck to the west, Hilton Beck to the east and Trout Beck to the north. Appleby Fair in June is famous for horses and a meeting-place for gipsies from all over Britain.

Hilton, 4 miles east, reached by turning off the A66 at Coupland, has a picturesque approach across a common and past fields where horses graze. There is an Army firing range near Murton, 1 mile north of Hilton, and walking on the fells is prohibited when a red flag is flying.

Brough
The remains of a castle, built by William II and restored in the 17th century by Lady Anne Clifford, stand on the site of Verterae, a Roman fort. The village also has a medieval church, St Michael's. There are walks on nearby fells, and although some lovely woods and hills are used by the Army as a firing range, it is safe to walk on them provided that the red flags are not flying. Deer can often be seen among the trees, high on green slopes.

Crosby Ravensworth
The Church of St Lawrence, a 12th-century building encircled by old trees, is one of the finest churches in east Cumbria—a 'cathedral' in miniature. The splendid fells surrounding the village have many Iron Age burial mounds, Roman relics and ancient settlements. There are ideal spots for picnics and walks just off the B6260 from Orton to Appleby.

At Maulds Meaburn, 1 mile north in the remote Lyvennet Valley, is Meaburn Hall, built in 1610, the birthplace in 1672 of the essayist Joseph Addison, creator of Sir Roger de Coverley.

Dufton
Squat sandstone houses are set round a spacious green in the village, which is an ideal starting-point for exploring some fascinating countryside. From just north of the village, a track leads to the summit of the 2930-ft Cross Fell, 6 miles away, while a narrow road leads off towards Knock village and Great Dun Fell. This

APPLEBY-IN-WESTMORLAND *Assizes were originally held in the 16th-century Moot Hall (left), which is now the meeting place of the Town Council*

the home of the 13th Baron Clifford (1435–61), nicknamed 'The Butcher' for his cruelty in the Wars of the Roses. It was restored in the 17th century but again fell into ruins

road ceases to be public at a point about 1½ miles beyond Knock, and from that point the 2780-ft peak can be reached only on foot along a bridle path or the Pennine Way.

At Great Rundale—a wild and lovely valley stretching east from Knock—there are old mine workings where amateur geologists may find glassy barytes crystals (used in the manufacture of paint) as large as a man's fist and extremely heavy. Knock village has red cottages and narrow roads between high sandstone walls. In summer, the surrounding fields are full of flowers; in autumn, the hedgerows are covered with nuts and rose-hips, tinted gold.

Kirkby Stephen

The 13th-century Church of St Stephen is approached through a stone portico built in 1810 by a naval purser, John Waller. Wool used to be spun on the open-air gallery of the house facing the church. The town has several Georgian houses including Winton Hall, built in 1726. Wharton Hall, *c.* 1559, was one of the seats of the Whartons—a family associated with Kirkby Stephen and Kirkby Thore for many centuries.

Around the town there are a number of beautiful walks; and, to the south, the fells that lead to Sedbergh give glorious views across the massive scenery of the Pennines.

Kirkby Thore

A former meeting-place for two Roman roads across the fells and the site of the Roman fort of Bravoniacum. The medieval St Michael's Church was partly built of stones from the fort. Kirkby Thore Hall, to the east, was for 13 generations another seat of the Whartons. Lowther Castle, 7 miles west, was the home of the Earls of Lonsdale until 1936. It is now only a shell, but its 3000-acre grounds contain a wildlife park with deer and wallabies.

Temple Sowerby, set at the foot of fells 2 miles north-west, is sometimes known as the 'queen' of east Cumbrian villages. Acorn Bank, a red-sandstone manor house, was built in 1730.

ROOFLESS SHELL *Little but the front façade now remains of Lowther Castle, which was built early in the 19th century on the site of an earlier castle*

SACRED CIRCLE *A ring of stones called Long Meg and Her Daughters, near Little Salkeld, is believed to have been used for worship in the Bronze Age*

Mallerstang

The parish is named after the Welsh *moel*, or 'bare hill' and the old Norse *stong*, or 'boundary mark', and lies in a lonely but lovely valley close to the Yorkshire border. The Norman Pendragon Castle was razed by the Scots in 1541 and restored by Lady Anne Clifford in 1660. The remains include a fortified pele tower.

The skyline is dominated by the 2324-ft mountain of Wild Boar Fell and all around is superb walking country, with views of the Settle to Carlisle railway crossing the 1169-ft Aisgill summit.

Ravenstonedale

A beautifully wooded village near the source of the River Lune. The 18th-century Church of St Oswald has a three-tiered pulpit with a seat in it for the parson's wife. The village was the birthplace of Elizabeth Gaunt, the last woman to be executed in England for a political offence. She was burnt at Tyburn in 1685 for sheltering a follower of the rebel Duke of Monmouth.

Tumbling streams of the western Pennines

Angling Salmon and trout fishing on the River Eden, with grayling in upper reaches; trout on the River Caldew; salmon and sea trout on the Rivers Irthing and Gelt.

Canoeing On the Eden around the Nunnery Rapids and through Wetheral Gorge.

Horse racing At Carlisle.

Hound trailing Regular meetings from Mar. to Oct. throughout the area. The trail followed by the dogs is laid with a rag soaked in a mixture of aniseed and paraffin.

Events Cumberland Agricultural Show is held at Carlisle in mid-July and Carlisle Great Fair in late Aug.

Places to see *Brougham Castle*, 1½ miles south-east of Penrith: daily, except Sun. morning Oct. to Mar. *Carlisle Castle*: daily except Sun. morning Oct. to Mar. *Carlisle Museum and Art Gallery*: weekdays; also Sun. afternoon in June, July and Aug. *Lanercost Priory*: weekdays and Sun. afternoon. *Penrith Castle and grounds*: daily. *Roman wall and fort*, Birdoswald: daily.

Flying Carlisle Airport, 7 miles north-east of city, for charter flights and private flying.

Information centres Old Town Hall, Green Market, Carlisle. Tel. Carlisle 25396/25517. Robinson's School, Middlegate, Penrith. Tel. Penrith 4671 (seasonal).

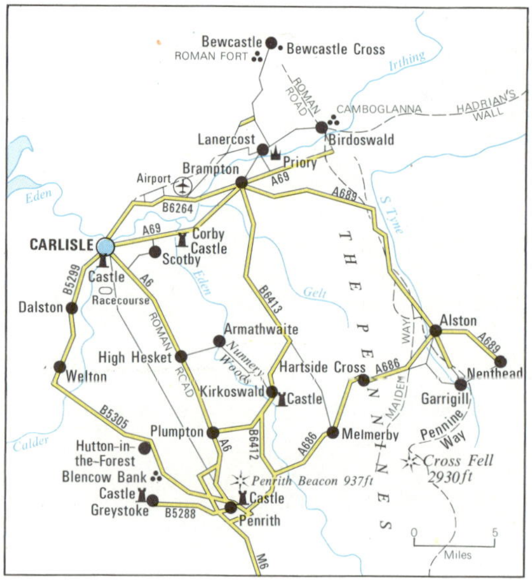

From the Border farmlands above Carlisle, where Roman auxiliaries used to patrol Hadrian's Wall, a stretch of peaceful countryside rises gently towards the Pennines to the south-east. It is a region of ruggedness and solitude. The area, especially in the north, is off the main tourist track. Most tourists make for the lakes, away to the south-west.

The countryside round Carlisle—the ancient and frequently-fought-over capital of north-west England, and many times raided by the Scots—is rich in historical associations and remains. Hadrian's Wall guarded the remote northern frontier of the Roman Empire, and fragments still stand. There are many prehistoric sites and there are castles, like the one begun in the 14th century at Penrith.

Streams tumble down the western side of the Pennines to join the Eden. The mountains form a lonely landscape, especially around Nenthead and among the hairpin bends of the road from Hartside Cross to Alston; but villages dot the landscape and save the region from being a complete wilderness.

Alston
Drystone walls border sloping fields, and the surrounding countryside is dotted with woods. The town, claimed to be the highest market town in England, commands sweeping views of the Pennines and the South Tyne Valley. It is built along a steep cobbled street, with side-streets of stone houses. Near the church stands a black-and-white timbered house of 1691. Two miles north is Clarghyll Hall, built in 1679.

Armathwaite
An attractive village clustered round its bridge over the River Eden. The 17th-century chapel of Christ and St Mary was built by Richard Skelton, lord of the manor. His ancestor John Skelton, a poet favoured by Henry VIII, is thought to have been born in the riverside castle, where the surviving tower has been incorporated into a Georgian mansion. Near by are walks through the Nunnery Woods beside the Eden.

Bewcastle
A historic village near the site of a Roman fort which was an outpost of Hadrian's Wall. The site covers 6 acres. Four ruined pele towers stand within about 2 miles of the village—at Crew Castle, Woodhead, High Grains and Low Grains. Bewcastle Cross, in the village churchyard, is a 1300-year-old cross with Runic inscriptions. The head of the cross is missing.

Birdoswald
The site of a 5-acre Roman fort known as Camboglanna, the largest fortress in the immediate vicinity of Hadrian's Wall. Parts of the walls, gateway and towers of the fort can be seen, as well as remains of the Wall itself.

Brampton
A handsome sandstone town near a tributary of the River Irthing. The church was built in 1874 by the Earl of Carlisle. The ruins of the original Norman church, built on the site of a Roman fort, are a mile west. A quarry near the River Gelt, about 2 miles south-west, still bears inscriptions scratched by Roman workmen.

Carlisle
This city, known in the Borderlands as 'Carel', was frequently raided by the Scots throughout its stormy early history, and was last captured during the Jacobite rising of 1745. It was once a Roman camp, Luguvalium, the wall of which still runs north of the city.

Carlisle, a busy commercial and industrial centre, has kept some of its ancient identity as the foremost agricultural centre of the north of England. There are several fine streets, such as Lowther Street, English Street and Victoria Place. A church begun in 1130 became Carlisle's cathedral in 1133, and a tower was added *c.* 1401. It is an imposing building, mainly of red sandstone with its earlier parts in greystone.

Carlisle has a market cross of 1682, and a castle which was begun under William II, added to by David I of

BEWCASTLE CROSS *The patterned 7th-century cross in Bewcastle churchyard is one of Britain's finest Anglo-Saxon relics*

BORDER FORTRESS *Carlisle Castle has watched over England's frontier with Scotland since 1092, when William II built it on the site of an ancient British camp*

MEDIEVAL SALMON TRAPS *Across the River Eden at Corby Castle are stone-and-wood salmon traps built by Benedictine monks in the 12th century. The traps are still used today*

Scotland after he captured it in the 12th century, and later still extended by Henry VIII. The keep contains the museum of the former Border Regiment, whose regimental march was 'D'ye ken John Peel'. Mary, Queen of Scots stayed in a building that stood near the keep. Other buildings of interest are an 18th-century town hall and a civic centre opened in 1964.

Dalston
Fine walks through fields and woods radiate from this attractive village, which is huddled round a green and a church, rebuilt in 1750. The B5299 through the nearby village of Welton leads towards superb fells where turf, heather and sheep come close to the roadside.

Garrigill
A homely village, off the holiday routes, at the foot of the Pennines. Stone houses, one shop, a small church of 1790 and a handsome Congregational chapel of 1757 are set around a spacious green near the South Tyne River. A lane parallel with the river leads south and becomes a track, part of the Pennine Way, climbing through wild moorland to the summit of Cross Fell—at 2930 ft the highest point in the Pennines.

Greystoke
A village with a medieval church and a Victorian castle, incorporating an earlier castle that had been re-fortified in 1353 by the 2nd Baron Greystoke. In the late 18th century the 11th Duke of Norfolk built three unusual farms near here: Fort Putnam and Bunkers Hill, both designed like forts; and Spire House, resembling a church. Two nearby cairns, Blencow Bank and Leadon Howe, mark Bronze Age burial sites.

Kirkoswald
An attractive village built of red sandstone. The 15th-century church has a Victorian tower standing 200 yds away, replacing an 18th-century wooden tower. The castle, now in ruins, was occupied for 500 years. The outstanding building is the College, seat of the Featherstonhaugh family since 1613, and previously the home of 12 priests from the collegiate church. A portrait of Charles I was presented by Charles II to mark services rendered by Sir Timothy Featherstonhaugh to the Royalists.

Lanercost
A few cottages stand round a famous red-sandstone priory, founded *c.* 1166 and repeatedly damaged by the Scots between 1296 and 1346. The ruined nave in its secluded spot near the Irthing was restored to form the parish church where services are held weekly—by candle and lamplight after dark. The river is spanned by a beautiful medieval bridge, with two arches and a protective base called a cutwater.

Melmerby
A sandstone village at the foot of the Pennines, its green planted with clusters of trees. The 17th-century Melmerby Hall is a private residence. Melmerby is in the path of what can sometimes be an 80-mph gale from Cross Fell, known locally as the Helm Wind, which may strike even when the air 6 miles away is scarcely moving. The Romans built a road here, the Maiden Way, which can be followed across the fells. In places it is 20 ft wide and reveals traces of the original paving.

Nenthead
The village was built during the 19th century as a model village for the miners working in the lead and zinc mines, which have long been derelict. Set 2000 ft up among the Pennines, Nenthead claims to have the highest church, chapel and vicarage in England. Here the 18th-century civil engineer John Smeaton built an underground canal. But the chief attraction is the grandeur and silence of the high moorlands.

Penrith
An attractive red-sandstone market town, now bypassed by the M6. A 14th-century castle is still splendid although in ruins. The parish church of St Andrew was mainly rebuilt in the 18th century but it retains a massive red-sandstone tower which is believed to be Norman, fragments of 15th-century glass, and 17th-century fittings. Views from Penrith Beacon, which stands 937 ft high, extend into Scotland.

THE HOWARD LIONS *Stone lions on the roof of 17th-century Corby Castle, near Carlisle, are part of the Arms of the Howard family, owners of the castle since 1611*

NORTH-EAST ENGLAND

Northumberland, Durham and Yorkshire were once part of the great Saxon kingdom of Northumbria, and they have shared a history as turbulent as that of any region in Britain. Many ties between the counties have endured through the centuries. Their combined resources of iron ore, coal and engineering skill played a key role in Britain's Industrial Revolution. But despite this, their wild hills remain unscarred and form one of the largest tracts of unspoilt countryside in England.

The heart of the North-East is the broad, lowland corridor which carries the main rail and road routes from London and the Midlands to the Scottish border. York is the great city of this lowland country. It stands on a site between two rivers and was chosen first by the Romans as a place that could be easily defended, then by the Norman conquerors as the capital of the North. It became a walled city—a city dominated by its great Minster, a market centre and a hub of commerce and the arts.

The Pennines, stretching from Derbyshire to the northern parts of Northumberland, form the western ramparts of the lowland corridor. Among them is some of England's finest walking country. Pen-y-ghent and Ingleborough Hill are characteristic of the flat-topped limestone hills which stand out as familiar hikers' landmarks above miles of open moorland. In Northumberland, the Pennines merge with the Cheviots, where the remote summits command inspiring views of Scotland. Roads threading their way through valleys do no more than skirt the hillside edges, and the best way to savour the attractions of the Pennines is to walk. The huge moorland expanses of grass, heather and peat—looking much as they have done since the beginning of history—are the haunt of grouse, curlew and the splendid, swift-flying Emperor moth. It is possible to walk for a morning, a day, even a whole weekend, and meet only a lone shepherd. His speech is likely to have a Scandinavian lilt, for many Pennine hill-folk are descended from Norwegians.

ENGLAND'S 'SPINE' *The massive Pennine range, the central hills of England, stretch the full length of the North-East, ending in the Cheviot Hills on the Scottish border. East of the Vale of York are the North York Moors and the Yorkshire Wolds*

The beauty of waterfalls and abbey ruins

There is also a softer natural beauty among the rugged landscapes, in the treasury of Alpine flowers left behind by the Ice Age around Teesdale-head in Durham. In the valleys below are the splendours of waterfalls, such as Cauldron Snout and High Force on the River Tees and, in the beautiful Yorkshire Dales, the spectacular Hardrow Force near Hawes in Wensleydale and the cataracts at Aysgarth, lower down the dale. There is historic beauty, too, in the remains of monastic buildings that are scattered all over the North-East. North Yorkshire's Fountains Abbey, founded in 1132, is the best known; Bolton Abbey, in a wooded gorge beside the River Wharfe, has the most romantic setting.

An added richness of the North-East lies in its castles and great houses, which show an increasing emphasis on fortification the nearer they are to the Scottish border. For Northumbria is frontier country, and the wild wastes of the Northumberland moorland were once a no-man's-land between England and Scotland. Hills which now echo only to the cry of the curlew were once alive with the clash of swords in the fierce, hand-to-hand fighting of the Border wars; and the mist-laden dawns were a cover for the wild tribes who crossed the Border to raid, pillage and murder among the landowners of the south. In Roman times, straight, paved roads led through the North-East to the furthest outposts of the Roman Empire, and to the great wall built by Emperor Hadrian from the Tyne to the Solway to keep out the unsubdued northern tribes. The finest surviving section of the wall is at Housesteads, near Hexham; two well-preserved Roman roads are on Wheeldale Moor, near Goathland, and at Blackstone Edge, on the Greater Manchester border west of Ripponden.

In the Dark Ages that followed the Roman withdrawal, Anglo-Saxon people from across the North Sea settled thickly all over Northumbria, naming their farms and villages in a distinctive way with words ending in *-ton* (an enclosure), *-ing* (place of), *-worth* (homestead), and *-field*. Then, in the 9th and 10th centuries, Northumbria was raided by the Danes, who brought names ending in *-by* (a settlement), *-toft* (a house site) and *-thorpe* (a farm). There were also invaders from Norway, who brought with them the word *dale* (a valley). Following the Norman conquest, William the Conqueror's merciless harrying of a rebellious North laid most of the land waste from the Humber to the Tweed.

The revolution that transformed the North-East

The rebirth of the North-East followed the union of the Crowns of Scotland and England in 1707. The land was successfully farmed and became the scene of many innovations—shorthorn cattle were first bred there, and experiments were carried out with new crops, rotations and machinery. Later came the Industrial Revolution, which transformed those areas which had coal into vast mining and industrial complexes. Ship-building, glass-making, chemical and iron works sprang up along the banks of the River Tyne. Ships for the first modern Japanese Navy were built on Tyneside between 1880 and 1905, and an iron and steel town

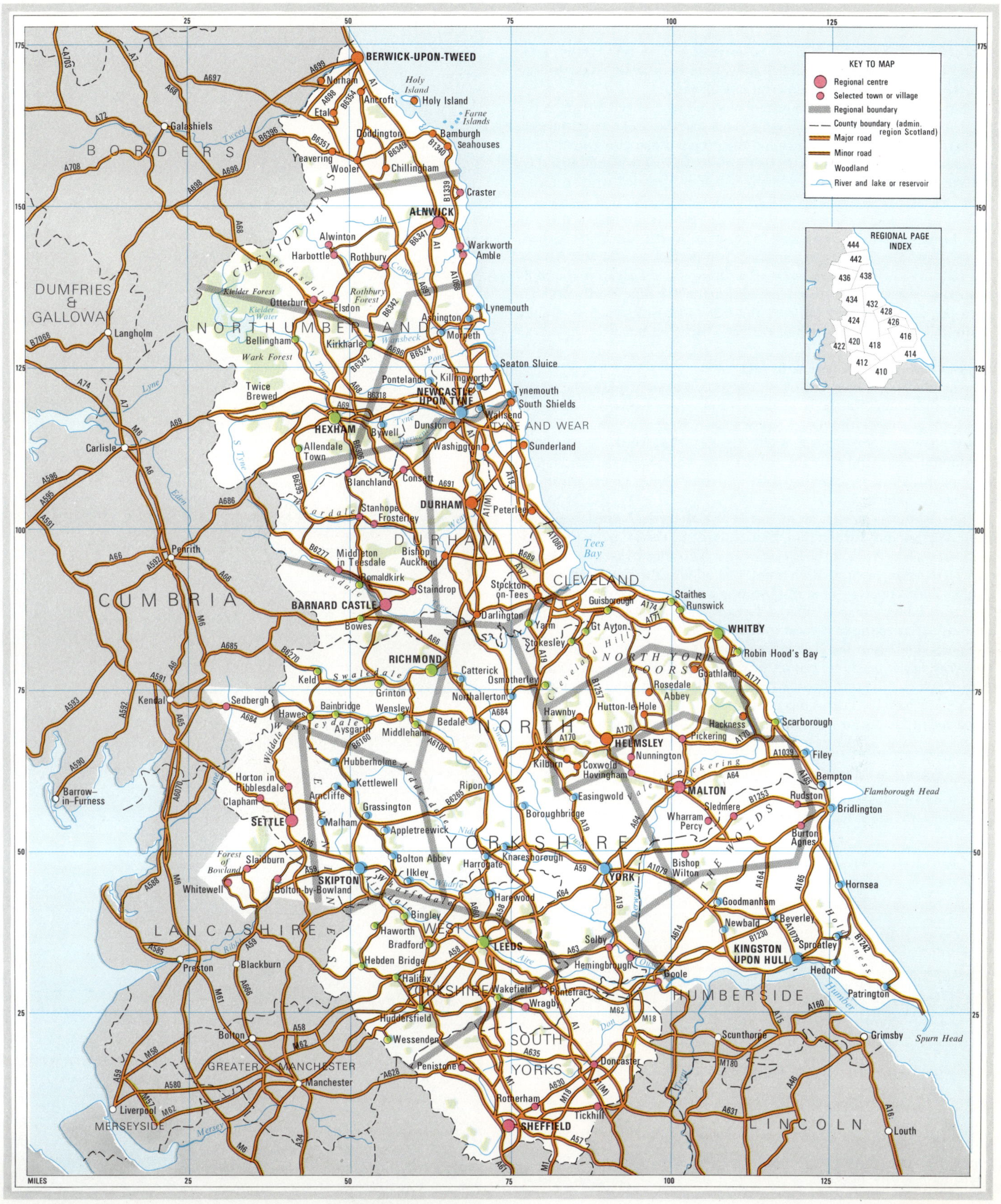
KEY TO MAP
Regional centre
Selected town or village
Regional boundary
County boundary (admin. region Scotland)
Major road
Minor road
Woodland
River and lake or reservoir
REGIONAL PAGE INDEX
444
442
436
438
434
432
428
426
424
420
418
416
414
422
412
410
BERWICK-UPON-TWEED
Norham
Holy Island
Ancroft
Etal
Farne Islands
Galashiels
Doddington
Bamburgh
Seahouses
BORDERS
Yeavering
Wooler
Chillingham
Craster
ALNWICK
CHEVIOT HILLS
Alwinton
Harbottle
Rothbury
Warkworth
Amble
DUMFRIES & GALLOWAY
Kielder Forest
Otterburn
Elsdon
Rothbury Forest
Kielder Water
Lynemouth
Ashington
Langholm
NORTHUMBERLAND
Morpeth
Bellingham
Kirkharle
Wark Forest
Seaton Sluice
Twice Brewed
Ponteland
Killingworth
Tynemouth
NEWCASTLE UPON TYNE
South Shields
Wallsend
HEXHAM
Bywell
Dunston
TYNE AND WEAR
Carlisle
Allendale Town
Washington
Sunderland
Blanchland
Consett
DURHAM
Peterlee
Stanhope
Frosterley
Weardale
DURHAM
Tees Bay
Penrith
Middleton in Teesdale
Bishop Auckland
Romaldkirk
CLEVELAND
Staindrop
Stockton on-Tees
Staithes
Runswick
CUMBRIA
BARNARD CASTLE
Guisborough
Bowes
Darlington
Yarm
Gt Ayton
WHITBY
Stokesley
RICHMOND
Robin Hood's Bay
NORTH YORK MOORS
Cleveland Hills
Keld
Swaledale
Catterick
Osmotherley
Goathland
Grinton
Rosedale Abbey
Kendal
Sedbergh
Northallerton
Hawes
Bainbridge
Wensley
Hawnby
Hutton-le-Hole
Hackness
Aysgarth
Wensleydale
Bedale
Scarborough
Middleham
NORTH
HELMSLEY
Pickering
Hubberholme
Nunnington
Filey
Kilburn
Coxwold
Hovingham
Vale of Pickering
Bempton
Horton in Ribblesdale
Kettlewell
Ripon
MALTON
Flamborough Head
Barrow-in-Furness
Arncliffe
Easingwold
Rudston
Clapham
Sledmere
Bridlington
Grassington
Boroughbridge
SETTLE
Malham
Wharram Percy
THE WOLDS
Burton Agnes
Appletreewick
YORKSHIRE
Forest of Bowland
Slaidburn
Bolton Abbey
Knaresborough
Harrogate
Bishop Wilton
Whitewell
SKIPTON
Ilkley
Bolton-by-Bowland
Wharfedale
YORK
Hornsea
Harewood
Goodmanham
Bingley
WEST
Newbald
Beverley
LANCASHIRE
Haworth
Holderness
Bradford
LEEDS
Selby
Sproatley
Preston
Blackburn
Hebden Bridge
KINGSTON UPON HULL
Hemingbrough
Hedon
Halifax
Goole
Wakefield
Pontefract
Patrington
YORKSHIRE
HUMBERSIDE
Wragby
Huddersfield
Bolton
Wessenden
SOUTH
Scunthorpe
Grimsby
Spurn Head
GREATER MANCHESTER
YORKS
Penistone
Doncaster
Manchester
Liverpool
Rotherham
MERSEYSIDE
Tickhill
SHEFFIELD
LINCOLN
Louth
MILES
25
50
75
100
125
175
150

grew at Middlesbrough, which at the beginning of the 19th century consisted of two farmhouses. Woollen mills were built in the West Riding valleys, and Sheffield became a great city of steel.

The variety of history is nowhere more clearly reflected than in the people of the North-East. Though welded together in an unmistakable northernness of speech and manner, the people of the cities, towns and dales each have their own distinctive dialects and ways of life. But they all have a genuine interest in a visitor's welfare, coupled with an informality of manner; for this is the least class-conscious part of England.

Many men and women from the North-East have contributed to the Arts. In literature, the Venerable Bede, John Wyclif, the Brontës, J. B. Priestley and the Sitwells; in music, Frederick Delius, who was Northumbria's most original composer; in painting, Lord Leighton, the mid-Victorian artist who specialised in Classical themes. The North-East has given the country Border ballads, and many folk songs such as 'Bobby Shafto', 'The Lass of Richmond Hill' and 'Blaydon Races'.

Where Captain Cook learnt to sail

People of the North-East also played an important early role in the world of communications. In the late 1500's, Christopher Saxton, of Tingley, near Leeds, became the first English map-maker; the pioneers of the railway, George Stephenson and Timothy Hackworth, came from Northumberland; and Captain James Cook, who completed the map of the modern world by charting Australia and New Zealand, learnt his seafaring on Whitby boats.

Superb beaches stretch for mile after mile along the Northumberland coast and around Bridlington Bay. Inland, a visitor may walk the medieval walls of York or the Elizabethan walls of Berwick-upon-Tweed, visit a Georgian town at Richmond, and admire the medieval stained glass in York Minster—or simply relax at a variety of resorts that range from tiny fishing villages, such as Craster, to Scarborough, one of the most visually striking east-coast towns.

Sports flourish in the North-East. Almost every town and village in Yorkshire has at least one cricket field and every other person seems to be an expert on the game. Football has a large following, while throughout County Durham the lure of pigeon racing has added a new feature to the landscape in the pigeon lofts that can be seen almost everywhere.

DRIER WEATHER IN THE LEE OF THE PENNINES

The low-lying coastal and inland regions of North Yorkshire, protected from south-westerly winds by the Pennines, are the driest parts of the north of England. York has only 24·7 in. of rain a year, and Hull 25 in.—less than most southern parts of England. The coastal regions of Northumberland and Durham also have a dry climate. Humberside and much of the Vale of York have high summer temperatures, which can reach 31°C (88°F) on the hottest days

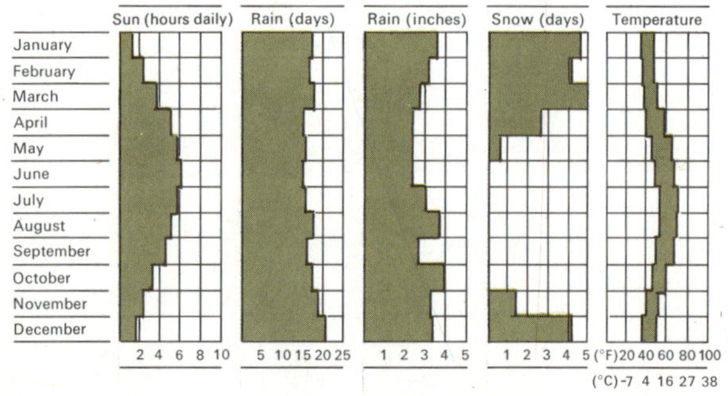

THE GREEN DALES *A farm nestles beneath the slopes of the Pennines at Widdale, 5 miles south-west of Hawes in the Yorkshire Dales National Park. The miles of drystone walls that stretch to the skyline were begun in the 18th century*

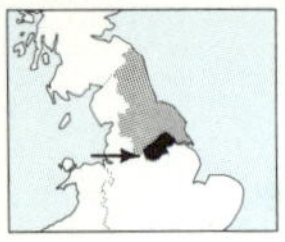

Steel city below the moors

Angling There is coarse and trout fishing at Goole and elsewhere on the River Ouse. Trout can also be caught in the following reservoirs: Damflask, 5 miles west of Sheffield; Morehall and Underbank, 8 miles north-west of Sheffield.

Events There is a Lord Mayor's Parade in Sheffield at the beginning of June. Rotherham has its annual 'Stattis' fair during the last weekend in Oct., celebrating the anniversary of the city receiving its Statutes.

Places to see *Abbeydale Industrial Hamlet*, Sheffield: daily. *Bishop's House*, Meersbrook Park, Sheffield: Wed. to Sun. *Conisbrough Castle*: daily, except Sun. morning Oct. to Mar. *Cusworth Hall*, South Yorkshire Museum, 1½ miles west of Doncaster: weekdays, Sun. afternoon. *Doncaster Museum and Art Gallery*: weekdays, Sun. afternoon. *Graves Art Gallery*, Surrey Street, and *Mappin Art Gallery*, Weston Park, Sheffield: both weekdays and Sun. afternoon. *Nostell Priory* (NT): afternoons; May to Sept., daily except Fri.; Apr. and Oct., Wed., Sat., Sun. *Pontefract Museum*: weekdays. *Roche Abbey*: daily, except Sun. morning Oct. to Mar. *Rotherham Museum*, Clifton Park: weekdays except Fri., Sun. afternoon. *Sheffield City Museum*, Weston Park: daily. *Shepherd Wheel*, Sheffield: Wed. to Sun.

Information centre City and Tourist Information Service, Town Hall, Sheffield. Tel. Sheffield 734760.

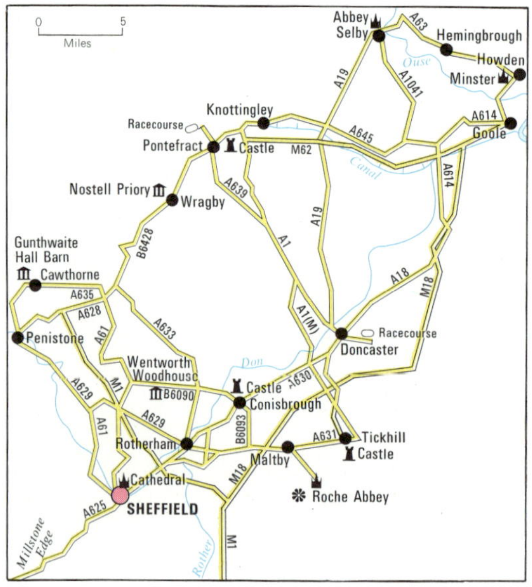

For at least seven centuries, knife blades have been made in Sheffield. The steel and cutlery industry first grew up in Sheffield because there was iron-ore near at hand; there were great forests to provide charcoal for smelting; there were fast streams to power the forges; and there was millstone grit for the grindstones. Today, though few of these factors are still relevant, Sheffield has retained its importance —partly because of its coal, which revolutionised the industry, but mainly through the craftsmanship bred through generations of skill with steel.

It is hard to find beauty among the steelworks that dominate this industrial Yorkshire scene. Yet Sheffield is favoured in a way that few other cities are. To the west, its boundaries stretch far into the moors on the borders of Derbyshire.

Eastwards, the River Don gradually shakes free of factories, and flows on towards the River Humber landscape, though there are still pockets of industry. Doncaster, apart from its fame as the scene of the St Leger horse race every September, is a centre for coal and engineering. But the slag heaps are set in rural lowlands, and the cooling towers of power-stations rise, like huge milk bottles, out of meadows and fields. There is greenery in plenty here in the South Yorkshire border country.

CONISBROUGH CASTLE *The 90 ft high buttressed keep, 5 miles*

NEW-LOOK CITY *Woodside is one of nine great post-war housing developments which have modernised industrial Sheffield*

Doncaster
A busy industrial town, with little left to recall its Roman and medieval history. There is some Georgian architecture, especially the Mansion House in the High Street and some houses in Hallgate and South Parade. The town has some fine 19th-century churches, among them the lofty parish church of St George facing the Don. The famous racecourse is on the east side of the town. The original 18th-century grandstand has Venetian windows, Tuscan columns and an Italianate tower.

Goole
One of Britain's furthest inland seaports, situated 42 miles from the North Sea, where the Don meets the Ouse. The rapid growth of Goole as a port dates from 1826, when docks were built and a canal cut from Knottingley. Today, coal is still the main cargo, drawn down the canal in 'Tom Puddings'—square containers like floating railway trucks. But many other cargoes are handled.

north-east of Rotherham, built c. 1185, is the oldest surviving circular keep in England

Hemingbrough
Monstrous power-station chimneys soar out of the flat fields. Contrasting with them is the tall, astonishingly slender spire of St Mary's Church, rising 120 ft above its 60 ft tower. Each century has contributed new treasures to the church since pre-Conquest days. The medieval woodwork is particularly fine. Howden, 5 miles south-east, also has a massive church, mainly 13th and 14th century. The original chancel and choir make a picturesque ruin east of the tower.

Millstone Edge
Nine miles south-west of Sheffield along the A625, there is a sudden spacious vista over Derbyshire's Hope Valley. The viewpoint is called, with justification, The Surprise. Lovely by-ways lead beneath the rugged scarp of Millstone Edge and across a wide sweep of unfenced moors along the borders of South Yorkshire and Derbyshire.

Penistone
This busy little market town divides its interests between agriculture and the steel industry. The church dates from the 13th century, and a former Cloth Hall and a Shambles date from 1768.

The barn at Gunthwaite Hall, 2 miles north, is a spectacular half-timbered building which has stood for nearly 500 years. It is of immense proportions; according to tradition, a young carpenter spent his 7-year apprenticeship making the wooden pegs that have held it secure for so long.

Pontefract
The castle has seen many tragedies. Richard II was murdered there in 1400; later, Roundheads and Royalists battled bitterly round its walls. Today, its ruins above the town rise out of well-kept flowerbeds, and there are lawn-tennis courts among the foundations. Below the castle, All Saints' Church, rebuilt in 1838, fills part of the ruins of an earlier church. A short walk from the castle along Micklegate and Horsefair leads to the 18th-century town hall and, beyond, to the wide market-place. Here are the butter cross (1734), St Giles's Church and some good examples of 18th-century architecture.

Several factories still make Pontefract cakes—the round liquorice sweets produced here since the 17th century; but the local fields of liquorice exist no more, and today the raw material comes mainly from plantations in Turkey. Pontefract's racecourse lies on the north side of the town.

Roche Abbey
Factory chimneys line the horizon south-east from Maltby, and farmlands spread between heaps of slag. Suddenly a lane narrows, burrows into bowers of green, and stops short at a stream by cliffs of white limestone. Here, in a grassy clearing, are the ruins of Roche Abbey, founded by Cistercian monks in 1147. The setting was landscaped in the 18th century by Capability Brown, as part of the grounds of Sandbeck Hall.

Rotherham
A busy industrial town at the confluence of the Rother and the Don. The bridge spanning the Don has a 15th-century chapel, one of only four such bridge chapels remaining in England. The 15th-century All Saints' Church, at the heart of the town, is one of the largest and finest churches in the county; the spire and the carved bench-ends and stalls are noteworthy. Wentworth Woodhouse, 4 miles north-west, is a great 18th-century mansion with a 600-ft frontage, one of the longest in England.

Selby
Canal barges once plied busily along the Ouse to the inland port of Selby. Nowadays the great mills that crush seeds for oils draw on Hull for their raw materials, and there is a Georgian calm about the town centre. The abbey, founded in the 11th century, looms massively over the main street. Few abbey churches in England so successfully survived the Dissolution, though there has been much rebuilding and restoration because of the collapse of the central tower in 1690 and a fire in 1906. An 18th-century wooden tollbridge across the Ouse is still used by cars.

NORMAN ABBEY *Selby Abbey, which dominates the main street of the town, was founded in the 11th century by the Benedictines, and survived the Dissolution. It has a splendid Norman doorway and some beautiful 14th-century stained-glass windows*

HISTORIC TITLE

The role of steel in Sheffield's life is marked by the name traditionally borne by one of the London–Sheffield expresses. The office of Master Cutler, now honorary, was created in 1624 to maintain order among Sheffield's cutlers.

Sheffield
Few cities in England have a finer setting than Sheffield, built in an amphitheatre of south Pennine slopes. The most interesting building is the parish church, made a cathedral in 1913. Stained glass adds mellow light to an interior in which later additions have been successfully grafted on to the 15th-century church.

For a city of its size, Sheffield has few early buildings of any note. Those of the 19th century include the Cutlers' Hall in Church Street with its Grecian façade, and there are some Georgian houses north of the cathedral, notably those in Paradise Square.

Sheffield's earliest industrial history is recalled at the Abbeydale Industrial Hamlet, $3\frac{1}{2}$ miles south-west. It comprises a restored 200-year-old scythe factory with all its equipment, including a furnace for producing steel in crucibles, and water-powered tilt-hammers and grindstones. Another relic of the past is the Shepherd Wheel at Endcliffe Park, $2\frac{1}{2}$ miles west of Sheffield—a late 18th-century cutlery grinding wheel.

Tickhill
The A1 passes a mile east of this little town where John of Gaunt (1340–99) was governor and where battles raged about the castle. Today, little stirs the calm of the wide streets which meet at the 18th-century market cross. The castle ruins are to the south-west and there is a friary at the west end of the town. The lovely parish church of St Mary attained its present grand proportions in the 14th century.

Wragby
The church of this tiny village stands within the grounds of Nostell Priory. Its collection of 16th to 18th-century Swiss painted glass is a major feature, a kaleidoscope of saintly and quaint scenes that fill the little church with an antique glow. Nostell Priory is a mansion built in the 18th century on the site of a vanished 12th-century Augustinian priory, and set in beautiful grounds.

Where wealth means wool

Angling There is good trout and coarse fishing on the River Aire at Bingley and Keighley, and on the Leeds and Liverpool Canal.

Events Bradford has an annual festival in Mar., which includes concerts by the Hallé Orchestra. There is a Bank Hol. gala in Leeds on late Summer Bank Hol. Mon. Leeds also has a fair on Woodhouse Moor in mid-Sept.

Places to see *Bankfield Museum and Art Gallery*, Halifax: weekdays, Sun. afternoon. *Bolling Hall*, Bradford, social and local history museum: daily. *Brontë Parsonage Museum*, Haworth: Jan. to early Dec., weekdays and Sun. afternoon. *Cartwright Memorial Hall*, Bradford, art gallery and museum: daily. *East Riddlesden Hall* (NT), 1 mile north-east of Keighley, manor house with medieval tithe barn: Mar. to Oct., afternoons except Mon.; also mornings, mid-July to mid-Sept. *Kirkstall Abbey* and *Kirkstall Abbey House Museum*: both weekdays and Sun. afternoon. *Oakwell Hall*, near Gomersal: Tues. to Sat.; also Sun. afternoon, Apr. to Oct. *Piece Hall, Halifax*, a textile museum: daily. *Redhouse*, Gomersal: Tues. to Sat.; also Sun. afternoon, Apr. to Oct. *Shibden Hall* and *W. Yorkshire Folk Museum*, Halifax: Mar. to Oct., weekdays and Sun. afternoon; also Sun. afternoon in Feb. *Temple Newsam*, Leeds: Tues. to Sun.

Information centres Central Library, Calverley Street, Leeds. Tel. Leeds 462453.
Central Library, Prince's Way, Bradford. Tel. Bradford 33081.

THE AIREDALE TERRIER

This breed, also called the Bingley terrier after the town of its origin, is the largest of the terriers. It was used by working men to make up scratch packs of individually owned pet dogs for weekend otter-hunting along rivers like the Aire. The Airedale is distinguished by its black-and-tan colouring

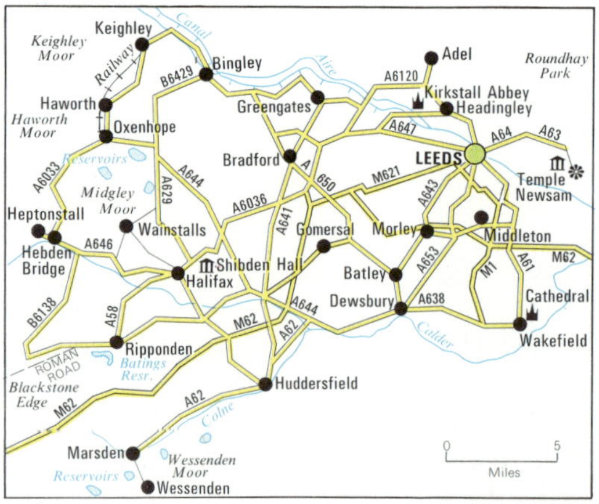

From time immemorial, sheep have grazed the moors of Yorkshire, and farmers and their families have spun and woven wool. With the introduction of machinery, the cottage-craft industry moved to mills which drew power from the fast-flowing Pennine streams and soft, lime-free water for the washing, carding and combing of the wool. With steam power, the main wool centres edged closer to the fuel sources of the coalfields, and crowded the valleys of the Rivers Colne, Calder and Aire.

So Bradford attracted the worsted trade away from Norwich, and grew into Britain's biggest wool market. Gradually, each division of the vast wool conurbation of West Yorkshire developed its own speciality: fancy worsteds in Huddersfield; tweeds in the Colne Valley; dress cloths in Bradford; and cheap, heavy woollen cloths in the districts of Dewsbury, Batley and Morley. Leeds became a world centre for ready-made clothing of all kinds.

The history of these times is written across the landscape. Forests of mill chimneys rise from the valley floors. On the moors, streams that once fed a scattered cottage industry now fill the reservoirs that supply vast urban populations.

MILL IN THE VALLEY *A wool mill is ringed by terraces of workers'*

Bingley
On the north-west side of Bingley, the Leeds and Liverpool Canal nears the eastern approaches of the Aire Gap. Within a quarter of a mile, between the Three Rise and Five Rise Locks, the water level is raised nearly 100 ft by a man-made staircase against the hillside. Once coal barges passed this way, but today the canal is used only by pleasure traffic. The towpath here is a favourite stroll, and a corner of the medieval village clusters around the 16th-century All Saints' Church.

Blackstone Edge
The road which runs across the moors of Blackstone Edge on the Greater Manchester border is the best-preserved section of Roman road in Britain. It makes a broad scar across this lonely stretch of moorland, rising to 1450 ft, and its stones have resisted the elements for more than 1800 years. The best approach to the road is from the A58, about 5 miles west of Ripponden and beyond the Bating's reservoir.

Bradford
From all directions roads drop down to the centre of the city, and here at the heart of the wool market is industrial scenery that may not attract but cannot fail to impress. It is a city born of the Industrial Revolution, from the flamboyant architecture of the Wool Exchange and the town hall to the unplanned labyrinth of streets burrowing between tiers of terraced houses. J. B. Priestley, the author, was born at 34 Mannheim Road in 1894. Bradford is ringed by former villages, now swamped by industrial growth. Greengates village, to the north-east, still has a 16th-century inn, The George and Dragon.

Halifax
The town's cloth trade dates back to the 15th century, and its oldest buildings are around the parish church of St John; they include the fine 18th-century Piece Hall in Thomas Street. But the town bears the stamp of the 19th century, notably represented by the town hall (the work of Sir Charles Barry, who designed the Houses of Parliament) and by the extravagant folly known as the

houses in a Pennine valley at Hebden Bridge

Wainhouse Tower. This octagonal tower, 253 ft high, was originally a dye-works chimney, and later topped by a pinnacle in the Renaissance style.

Shibden Hall, just east of the town, in a quiet park above a river, is a fine 15th-century mansion, now a museum. North of Halifax, greystone farms on rough moorland lie within 4 miles of the town centre. Lanes lead north-west through Wainstalls; further north, the moor rises eventually to 1400 ft, and reservoirs glisten in the hollows.

Haworth

Rooks cry raucously in the trees of the churchyard by the Brontës' famous parsonage, at the top of the steep main street. Industry stays in the valley below, and the air is fresh with the tang of the moors where Charlotte, Emily and Anne walked. The bleak ruin of High Withins on the moor was the setting for *Wuthering Heights*. At the Black Bull Inn in Haworth, which still stands, Branwell Brontë drank himself to death.

A favourite walk of the sisters leads for 2 miles west beyond the cemetery along Enfield Side to the Brontë waterfall, usually a mere trickle over moss-covered rocks. Here Charlotte came to mourn her sisters; here, too, she walked with her husband to see the stream in spate, and caught the cold which led to her death, in 1855.

The revived steam-hauled Worth Valley Railway runs for 5 miles from Keighley to Oxenhope, and back.

Hebden Bridge

An old bridge humps over the Hebden between dark grey houses. Mills clutter the valley floor, and wild moors loom above. Clinging to them, a mile up a steep lane north-west of the town, the hilltop village of Heptonstall is a lovely cluster of ancient weavers' cottages, with 13th-century church ruins alongside the 19th-century church.

Huddersfield

Connoisseurs of the industrial scene will admire the concentrated townscape below the moors. Among the many excellent Victorian buildings the railway station is outstanding. Designed by J. P. Pritchett in the Classical manner with long colonnades, and built in 1847–8, it is one of the finest railway buildings in England.

Leeds

The woollen trade predominates and has made Leeds the world centre for ready-made clothing; but its other industries include everything from clocks and chemicals to furniture, fish canning and ferro-concrete construction. Collieries creep close to the city boundaries, and so do farmlands.

There is an excellent art gallery; cricket at Headingley; drama at the Grand and the new civic playhouse; and one of Britain's leading universities. Leeds is also the home of one of the last remaining music-halls in Britain, the City Varieties. Grime coats many of its monumental Victorian buildings, the best of which include the Infirmary, Corn Exchange, the city market and the magnificent town hall. Yet not all is black. East of the town hall, the shops and office blocks of Headrow that were modern in the 1920's and 1930's now compete with complexes of concrete, brick and glass rising near by. Roundhay Park, formerly a royal hunting-ground, is the largest local playground. Middleton Railway, the oldest in existence, was built at Middleton Colliery in 1758. It is still worked by enthusiasts.

At Adel, once a village, now an affluent Leeds satellite, is one of the finest Norman churches in England. It has remained almost unaltered since the 12th century, and the detail in the south door and chancel arch is superb.

Kirkstall Abbey, 3 miles north-west, was a holy house that contributed much to the foundation of Leeds. In this 12th-century abbey, the Cistercian monks, who came here from Fountains Abbey, pioneered the exploitation of iron ore, tanning and potting, spinning and weaving, and set the pace for the growing town in the Middle Ages. The extensive remains are second only to Fountains Abbey in their completeness, and grounds leafy with sycamores slope down to the banks of the Aire.

Temple Newsam, 3 miles east of Leeds, is a mainly Jacobean house, though it was enlarged in the late 18th century. It is now a museum, rising grandly out of a 935-acre park. Once the Knights Templar had a flourishing farm here, but the lovely landscaping seen in the park today is the work of Capability Brown. Some 40,000 rose trees glorify a corner of the grounds. Parts of the west wing are Elizabethan.

Wakefield

Many Georgian houses reflect the prosperity of days when, before the rise of Leeds and Bradford, Wakefield was the centre of the clothing trade. The cathedral, founded in the 13th century, has the tallest spire in Yorkshire, 247 ft high. On the medieval bridge over the Calder is the best of only four bridge chapels remaining in England: a delicate, richly carved structure, originally from the 14th century, heavily restored in the 19th.

Wessenden

South-west of Huddersfield, the A62 edges away from industry along the Colne Valley. The mill chimneys become fewer, the hilltops greener. From Marsden, 7 miles south-west of Huddersfield, a lane leads south out of the valley. There are pastures, drystone walls and little grey farms, and after 2 miles the road ends at Wessenden, from which an attractive walk leads up to Wessenden Moor and the Pennine Way.

THE BRONTË SISTERS AND THEIR HOME

Patrick Branwell Brontë erased himself from the centre of the portrait he painted of his famous sisters—from the left, Anne, Emily and Charlotte. The Haworth Parsonage (right) where they lived is now the Brontë Museum

DEALING IN WOOL *The wool trade still employs most of Bradford's workers, and the Wool Exchange in Market Street, opened in 1867, attracts traders from all over the world*

The vanishing coastline

Angling There is coarse fishing on Hornsea Mere. Sea fishing at Bridlington, Filey, Hornsea and Flamborough. Bridlington has a sea-angling festival in Sept.

Boating Sailing at Hornsea, Filey and Bridlington. Boats for hire at Bridlington and Filey.

Events Bridlington has a regatta week in Aug. Hull has a Lord Mayor's Parade early in June, a two-day Show at the end of July, and a Fair that extends over eight days early in Oct.

Places to see *Bridlington Art Gallery and Museum*, Sewerby Hall: Easter to late Sept., Sun. to Fri., and Sat. afternoon. *Burton Constable Hall*: Easter, then May to mid-Oct., Sun. to Fri. afternoons. *Ferens Art Gallery*, Hull: weekdays. *Maister House* (NT), Hull: Mon. to Fri., except Bank Hol. *Skidby Windmill*, 4 miles south-west of Beverley: Sat.; also Sun. afternoon, May to Sept. *Spurn Head Nature Reserve*: daily. *Town Docks Museum, Transport and Archaeology Museum*, and *Wilberforce House*, Hull: all weekdays and Sun. afternoon.

Information centres Hull City Information Service, Central Library, Albion Street, Hull. Tel. Hull 223344. Information Centre, Garrison Street, Bridlington. Tel. Bridlington 73474. Town Clerk's Dept., The Hall, Lairgate, Beverley. Tel. Hull 882255. Council Offices, John Street, Filey. Tel. Scarborough 512204.

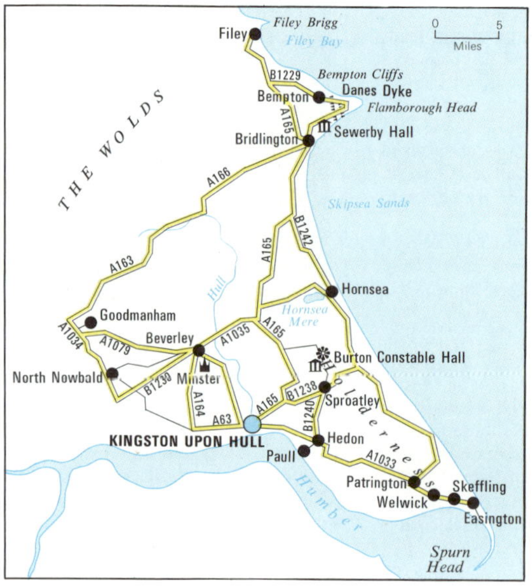

The coastline of Humberside is in a state of continuous movement, as the North Sea bites into low cliffs of clay, eroding them at the rate of 2–7 ft a year. Villages known to have existed in medieval times have disappeared completely under this perpetual attack. But there is profit, as well as loss, from the battering of the sea, for the sprawling hook of Spurn Head grows and changes shape almost annually.

The clay of Holderness, the lowland area east of the Yorkshire Wolds, was deposited over a foundation of chalk by the retreating ice sheets more than 10,000 years ago. The ice also left many small fresh-water lakes in its wake, but most of these have silted up, and today Hornsea Mere is the only remnant of the waters that once dotted the area. Artificial drainage and natural silting have combined to produce fertile soil from what were probably once great wastes of marshland; and today, in season, the flat expanses of Holderness are a golden patchwork of ripening wheat.

For the most part, farmlands reach to the edge of the cliffs, and the region's churches soar out of the red-brick villages whose livelihood comes from the surrounding fields, touched by the salt tang of the sea. On the broad Humber lies Hull, Britain's third-largest port, with its great fishing fleets and docks that extend some 7 miles along the river bank. Set in open country to the north of Hull, Beverley ranks as one of the more gracious towns in all England. Beyond Flamborough Head, chalk cliffs rise to some 300 ft to provide striking coastal scenery.

GOTHIC GLORY *Beverley Minster, begun in 1220 and completed two centuries later*

Bempton Cliffs

A road north from the White Horse Inn in Bempton village ends after a mile in a field-side track above a massive wall of flinty chalk rising some 300 ft straight out of the sea. Here is spectacular cliff scenery, providing the largest mainland breeding ground in England for sea-birds, among them guillemots, razorbills, kittiwakes and puffins. On the cliffs, too, is the only mainland gannet colony in Great Britain.

A clifftop footpath, suitable only for those with a good head for heights, continues south-east for about 4 miles to Flamborough Head, which is tipped by an 87-ft lighthouse. On the way it crosses Danes' Dyke, a massive defence earthwork, dating probably from the Iron Age, which cuts across the head-land west of Flamborough.

Beverley

With 14th-century St Mary's at the north end of the main street, and the twin-towered 13th-century Minster at the south, the glory of Beverley's ecclesiastical architecture competes with that of any town in Britain. Between the two lie market squares and narrow streets, distinguished by houses built during the prosperous days of the medieval cloth trade. The town is still the flourishing market centre for the area. Features of the Minster, Humber-side's most splendid Gothic church, are the 14th-century Percy Tomb, a monument to the Percy family of Northumberland, who also owned land in this region, and some magnificent wood-carvings. The 15th-century red-brick North Bar is the only survivor of the town's five medieval gates.

WHERE VIKINGS LANDED *The chalk nose of Flamborough Head, scene of a successful invasion by Vikings in the 10th century, is today colonised by thousands of seabirds*

Bridlington
A popular resort with bathing beaches and the usual seaside amusements. The old town, about a mile inland, is dominated by its priory church, founded in the reign of Henry I. The massive Bayle Gate, once a part of the priory buildings, is now a museum. Sewerby Hall, just north-east of the town, is a Georgian mansion with gardens and a park.

Filey
A great sweep of cliff and beach frames a small fleet of the distinctive fishing-craft known as cobles. The cliffs end beneath the headland in Filey Brigg, a ridge of rocks where breakers roar thunderously. Paths lead down to the Brigg, which is completely covered at high tide. The sands of the crescent-shaped Filey Bay curve round towards Flamborough Head 10 miles south. Holiday camps sprawl on the cliffs above Filey Bay.

Goodmanham
This quiet spot was one of the earliest sites of Christianity in Britain. The squat little Norman church, between the red-brick houses, is traditionally a successor of earlier sanctuaries which replaced a pagan temple. Coifi, the pagan high priest, was converted to Christianity by Paulinus in AD 627, with Edwin, King of Northumbria—an event which is commemorated in a modern stained-glass window in the church.

Hedon
The great church, known as the 'King of Holderness', dates from the 12th to 15th centuries, and has one of the finest towers in Yorkshire. Paull, 2 miles south-west, is a former fishing village looking out across the wide Humber to the flaring chimneys of Scunthorpe's steelworks. There are riverside inns and a little white lighthouse amid quayside houses; and ships pass close by.

Hornsea
This popular holiday town has a fine sandy beach, promenades, gardens and an amusement park. Behind is the original village, with old houses and narrow streets. From one of these an unsurfaced lane leads to Hornsea Mere, Humberside's largest freshwater lake, less than a mile from the sea. It is the only remaining lake of many formed in Holderness by the melting glaciers of the Ice Age. There is a sailing club at the Hornsea end, and boat trips are organised, but a nature reserve protects the deep shrubbery and tangled reeds at the western end, where wildlife abounds.

Hull
Kingston upon Hull is the city's official name. The River Hull joins the Humber here and has given rise to Britain's third-largest port after London and Liverpool. By the late 18th century, the old harbour at the mouth of this river was no longer sufficient. The first of a long line of new docks was built—and filled in 150 years later. Visitors stand on it when they admire the flowers in Queen's Gardens. The city is saturated in the traditions of the sea. Fishing fleets, cargo ships, oil tankers and, nowadays, streamlined modern car ferries, nose past Spurn Head, 21 miles south-east, and head for the forests of derricks and cranes along miles of Hull's dockland.

The docks grow almost annually to cope with a surging tide of cargo: wool from Australia and New Zealand for the West Riding mills, timber from Scandinavia, dairy products from Denmark, grain and seed for the flour mills and oil-extraction plants that punctuate the Hull horizons. Hull also has a Wilberforce Museum, in the house where the anti-slavery campaigner William Wilberforce (1759–1833) was born, and good transport and maritime museums.

SUMMER VISITOR

The Camberwell Beauty is common in summer and late autumn around Hull and other East Coast ports, but is rare inland. The butterflies do not breed in Britain but migrate across the North Sea or hatch out from eggs laid in timber imported from Europe. They may be seen in birch groves or near conifer plantations

North Newbald
The most attractive approach to the village is by the lane from Beverley, which follows a fold in the Wolds and drops to a delightful cluster of greystone and whitewashed cottages, with a stream running between banks bright with flowers. But the village's outstanding feature is its Norman church with four doorways, the most notable of which projects south of the nave.

Patrington
The church spire draws the eye for miles across flat farmland. The church, known as the 'Queen of Holderness', was built in the 14th century; it has the proportions of a small cathedral, and is one of the most splendid and spacious village churches in the North. The smaller villages of Welwick, Skeffling and Easington, strung out to the south-east along the rural Holderness road, also have medieval churches of interest.

Sproatley
The village straggles close to the main road in the flat, green heart of Holderness. To the north, avenues of trees, woods and glades add a new dimension to these wide horizons of ploughland. After a mile, an imposing entrance comes into view; cattle graze quietly in the pastures beyond and a drive leads to a beautiful Tudor structure in red brick. This is Burton Constable Hall, where even the pastures have a park-like quality, for they were planned by Capability Brown.

Spurn Head
The Yorkshire Naturalists' Trust owns this $3\frac{1}{2}$-mile sliver of land, in places only a few yards wide, curving in a great hook into the mouth of the Humber. It lengthens by about a yard a year, re-shaped by the silt carried down by the Humber and the debris of coastal erosion brought by the restless sea. For a small fee cars may be driven 3 miles to the lighthouse and lifeboatmen's houses, along a lane between tangles of sea buckthorn and marram grass. Beyond the lighthouse, walkers can continue for half a mile along the beach to the tip. Migrating birds converge for refuge here. Waders and terns can be found in this magnificent desolation.

SAILING CENTRE *Boats and wildlife share Hornsea Mere, a freshwater lake 2 miles long*

The Vale of Pickering

Angling Coarse fishing on the Derwent at Malton and 7 miles south-west, at Howsham. Trout in Pickering Beck at Pickering.

Events Pickering holds a two-day traction-engine and vintage-car rally in Aug. Malton has an agricultural show in mid-July.

Forest drive A 10-mile drive through the forests of Dalby and Bickley starts 1½ miles north of Thornton Dale.

Places to see *Beck Isle Museum of Rural Life*, Pickering: Easter to mid-Oct., daily. *Burton Agnes Hall*: May to mid-Oct., afternoons, except Sat.; also Easter Mon. *Castle Howard*: daily, Easter to Oct. *Flamingo Park*, Kirby Misperton Hall, 2½ miles south of Pickering: Easter to Sept., daily. *Gilling Castle*, 6 miles north-west of Malton: weekdays. *Kirkham Priory*: daily, except Sun. morning Oct. to Mar. *Malton Museum*: afternoons; also weekday mornings in summer months. *Nunnington Hall* (NT): Apr. to Oct., afternoons Wed. to Sun. and Bank Hol. *Pickering Castle*: daily, except Sun. morning Oct. to Mar. *Sledmere House*: Easter to mid-May, Sun. afternoon; mid-May to Sept., daily, except Mon. and Fri.; open Bank Hol.

Information centre North York Moors Railway, Pickering Station. Tel. Pickering 73791.

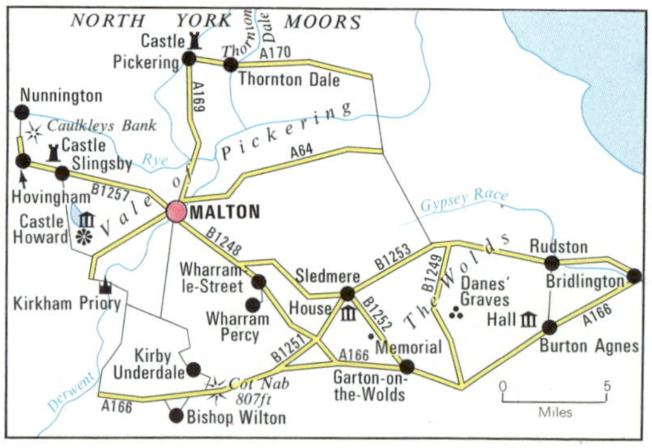

The Vale of Pickering is a broad trough of clay, separating the North York Moors from the Yorkshire Wolds. Once the vale drained eastwards into the North Sea. But during the Ice Age this outlet was obstructed and a wide lake formed, eventually eroding a new outlet westwards into the Vale of York through a passage where the ruins of Kirkham Priory now stand. So, because of an accident of geology, the waters of the River Derwent and its tributaries, rising within a few miles of the sea, travel some 50 miles in the opposite direction before spilling into the Ouse close to the Humber. In time, the valley floor silted up and marshlands thrived on the deposits that accumulated. The region, later drained, remains predominantly an area of damp pasture for cattle.

Most of the settlements, of which Malton is the major market centre, have found root on slightly higher, drained ground—on ancient deltas on the northern fringe; on the Howardian Hills, a barrier across the west of the vale; or on the slopes of the Wolds to the south.

The Wolds, a continuation of the chalk hills of Lincolnshire, undulate from the Humber northwards to the coast; they are smooth, rounded hills, rarely more than 600 ft high. Towards the east, their gentle slope is furrowed by the dry valleys of typical chalk country. The natural vegetation is wiry grass and gorse on light, shallow soil; but today both are rare. Brought under the plough by the needs of the Industrial Revolution and the far-seeing husbandry of families such as the Sykes of Sledmere, this former wasteland presents a satisfying scene of rolling cornland and sheep pastures, fringed by hedges and patched with woodland. The villages, mainly of red brick, and unpretentious in character, nestle attractively in folds between the cultivated hills.

CASTLE HOWARD *The palatial home designed by Sir John Vanbrugh*

HAUNTED HALL *The Elizabethan Burton Agnes Hall is said to be haunted by the daughter of its first owner. Her dying wish was that her skull be buried in the house*

Bishop Wilton
A village built on two sides of a wide green hollow where the Wolds sweep down to the Vale of York. The Normans began the church, which has a fine Romanesque chancel arch and doorway. Bishop Wilton is a good centre for walking on the gentle slopes of the Wold and for exploring the many, scattered prehistoric burial places.

Kirby Underdale, 2 miles north, is aptly named. A lane makes a long steep descent to a nook in the Wolds where a Norman church stands below the red-brick village.

Burton Agnes
Vicarage, church and hall make a magnificent group in one of the prettiest villages in the Wolds. The vicarage is white and sedate, and the part-Norman church hides behind an eerie tunnel of

TRIBUTE TO A BOXER *A memorial on Garton Hill, near Sledmere, to Sir Tatton Sykes, a 19th-century boxer and farmer*

for the 3rd Earl of Carlisle is the largest house in Yorkshire. A broad lake lies in its park

DEATH OF A KING *Medieval frescoes found under whitewash in Pickering Church include a scene (lower right) of the 9th-century martyr King Edmund being put to death*

yews. There is a very fine 15th-century alabaster tomb in the north aisle of the church. Beside the church rise the beautiful Elizabethan red-brick chimneys of Burton Agnes Hall. This building succeeded a simpler Norman manor house, part of which still exists. The Hall has a fine collection of Impressionist paintings. By the main road, ducks float on a little shrub-fringed lake. Traces of an extensive Iron Age cemetery—the so-called Danes' Graves—can be seen 5 miles to the west.

Hovingham

The church tower is Saxon, the Hall a stately example of 18th-century building, and the village, grouped round the green, presents an attractive scene. Slingsby, 2 miles south-east, has a romantically overgrown ruined 17th-century castle.

Kirkham Priory

Through a passage between the Yorkshire Wolds and the Howardian Hills, the Derwent finds its way into the Vale of York. Beside it, in the 12th century, Walter l'Espec founded an Augustinian priory. It was substantially enlarged in the 13th and 14th centuries, but what remains of its former splendour is today a calm ruin in a peaceful wooded valley. Above, the hillside blazes with the copper beeches of Kirkham Hall; below, a three-arched bridge spans the river at the foot of steep woodland. Within the broken priory walls, flowering cherry trees blossom in May.

Malton

A confusion of roads converges on this important market town above the River Derwent. It would be easy for the passing motorist to miss its centre, the old market square around a church dating from Norman times. There was a Roman fort at Malton, and finds from it are in the little museum at one corner of the market-place. Fridays and Saturdays are lively market days; the big livestock market is behind the square.

Castle Howard, 4½ miles south-west, is one of England's grandest houses, designed by Sir John Vanbrugh for the 3rd Earl of Carlisle, a member of the Howard family, and built between 1699 and 1726. Its immense façade, in a setting of magnificent parkland, is visible for miles around. The mansion contains a notable long gallery, some fine furniture and paintings, and the largest private collection in Britain of dress from the 17th century to the present day. In the grounds is a circular mausoleum designed by Nicholas Hawksmoor, Sir Christopher Wren's brilliant assistant, and a Temple of the Four Winds designed by Vanbrugh.

Nunnington

A pretty greystone village, off the main road, overlooked by the knoll of Caulkleys Bank, with an old church at the top and a 17th-century hall by the bridge over the River Rye at the bottom. From the church, there is an immense vista over the Vale of Pickering.

Pickering

A lovely town at the southern foot of the moors, commanding the broad vale. Its history goes back to 270 BC, when a Celtic settlement was founded there.

Legend has it that the tribe's king lost a ring in the river and that it was found in the belly of a pike. The town's name is said to be based on that incident, and its coat of arms includes a pike with a ring in its mouth.

The ruined 12th-century castle is on the north side of the town. The church, which contains 15th-century frescoes, stands above the main street.

Two miles to the east, the cottage gardens of pretty Thornton Dale village slope down to a clear roadside stream. Just out of the village to the north, a minor road winds its way up Thornton Dale valley to join a Forestry Commission road through beautiful forests, leading to the upper Derwent valley.

TRIBUTE TO A SON *Kirkham Priory, a ruin beside the River Derwent, was founded by a 12th-century judge, Walter l'Espec, after his son's death in a riding accident*

Rudston

Bronze Age man chose this hilltop as a sacred site, and Christianity followed suit; a Neolithic standing stone in the churchyard reaches as high as the nave roof of the Norman church. Below is the pretty village stream called the Gypsey Race. Known locally as the Woe Waters, the Race is believed to flow more strongly when a national disaster is imminent. This is said to have happened before the start of the First World War, and before the 1926 General Strike.

Sledmere

The park-like quality of much of the Wolds' farmland has its origins here. Sledmere House is the seat of the Sykes family, who invested their wealth in a virtual wasteland and began enclosing and taming the Wolds 200 years ago. The house has been rebuilt since the original was burnt down in 1911. The area is dotted with Sykes family monuments. One of these, 2 miles south-east on the road to Garton-on-the-Wolds, rises like a slender spire out of the fields, a landmark for miles.

Wharram Percy

One of England's lost villages from the Middle Ages, which has been discovered under the pastures in a cleft in the Wolds. The site, which is off the beaten track, can be reached from Wharram-le-Street, but the last part of the journey must be made on foot from Bella Farm. The roofless church is all that now stands above ground, but excavators have been following clues in the humpy pastures above to uncover the foundations of the village, which is believed to have died about 500 years ago.

Magnificent churches in the Vale of York

Events Harrogate has a Hallé Festival in June, the Great Yorkshire Show in July, and an International Festival in Aug.

Places to see *Aldborough Roman Museum*, Boroughbridge: daily, except Sun. morning Oct. to Mar. *Beningbrough Hall* (NT): May to Oct., afternoons. *Fountains Abbey*: Easter to Oct., daily; Feb., Mar. and Nov., Tues., Wed. and Thur. *Guildhall*, York: daily, May to Oct.; weekdays, Nov. to Apr. *Harewood House*: Easter to Oct., daily; Feb., Mar. and Nov., Tues., Wed. and Thur. *Merchant Adventurers' Hall*, York: weekdays. *National Railway Museum*, York: weekdays, Sun. afternoons. *Newby Hall*, near Ripon: afternoons only; Apr. and May, Sun.; June and Sept., Tues. to Thur., Sat. and Sun.; July and Aug., Tues. to Sun. *Treasurer's House* (NT), York: Apr. to Oct., daily. *Wakeman's House Museum*, Ripon: May to Sept., weekdays, Sun. afternoon; Oct. to Apr., Sat. *York Castle Museum*: daily. *York Heritage Centre*: weekdays.

Information centre De Grey Rooms, Exhibition Square, York YO1 2HB. Tel. York 21756.

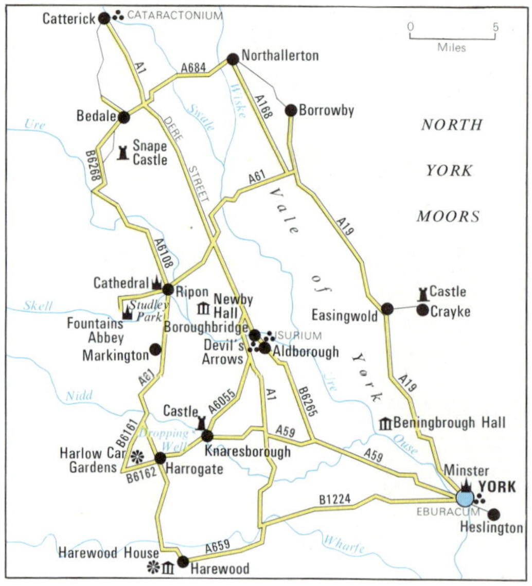

The Vale of York is a broad expanse of lowland dominated by one great river system. North of York, the Ure, fed by the Swale, becomes the Ouse, and on its way southwards is joined by the Nidd, Wharfe, Aire, Derwent and finally by the Trent, where it becomes the broad Humber. Being so well-watered, the vale is fertile. It is free from the smoke of industry and its horizons are uncluttered by the factory chimneys that rise like man-made forests away to the industrial south-west. Sandstone—a continuation of rock beneath the Midland Plain—forms the foundations, but thick overlays of more-recent deposits have given rise to a variety of farming. There is mixed farming on the predominant boulder-clay of the north, and rich ploughing land on the clay, sand and gravel soil deposited millions of years ago in the south. The wide, rolling farmlands are restful on the eye, yet the hills are never far away. The horizon is bounded to the west by the Yorkshire Dales, and to the east by the North York Moors or the gentler curves of the chalky Wolds.

The vale has been a main thoroughfare from time immemorial. Along it, prehistoric man at various times set up mysterious ceremonial circles and standing stones. Roman legions tramped up and down it; and the fortunes of Royalists and Roundheads ebbed and flowed there during the Civil War. Along a hard, dry ridge of limestone in the west of the vale, the A1 finds the same easy passage as the great Roman highway Dere Street before it. The limestone has been quarried to build some of Britain's finest ecclesiastical architecture, including York Minster, England's largest medieval cathedral, famous for its west front and magnificent stained-glass windows.

INTO THE PAST *Bygone days come alive at Castle Museum, York, where cobbled streets and reconstructed shop fronts represent periods from Tudor to Edwardian times. There is a replica of the hansom cab, whose designer, Joseph Hansom, was born in York in 1803*

Bedale
A wide cobbled verge gives a market-square width to Bedale's main street, where a market has been held since the 13th century. Old houses in brick and whitewash line the street in fine harmony. The mainly 13th and 14th-century church, with its interesting monuments, vaulted crypt and tower arch, is one of the noblest in North Yorkshire.

Snape Castle, 3 miles south, built in medieval and Tudor times and now partly in ruins, was the home of Catharine Parr, the last wife of Henry VIII.

Boroughbridge
A few hundred yards west of the town on the Roecliffe road are three massive stone monoliths dating from 2000–1500 BC. The largest stone is some 30 ft high. These standing stones of millstone grit, known as the Devil's Arrows, are a puzzling legacy from prehistoric man, for no one knows why these stones were dragged some 10 miles to their present site. One mile east of Boroughbridge, at Aldborough, are the remains of the extensive Roman town of Isurium.

Catterick
Although the name is widely associated with the ugly sprawl of its military camp to the west, Catterick itself is a delightful place of greystone houses clustering

ABBEY OF WEALTH *The floodlit ruins of 12th-century Fountains Abbey which, through the wool-trading skill of the monks, became the wealthiest Cistercian house in England*

around green lawns, with a brook babbling through and a pretty church. A few hundred yards away, traffic roars up the A1, passing above the site of a much earlier military camp—the Roman Cataractonium, of which traces remain.

Easingwold

It is easy to miss the cobblestones, copper beeches and mellow red brick of this little market town, for the A19 merely slices through its south-western fringe. The church, rebuilt in the 15th century, has a simple dignity.

Crayke, 3 miles to the east, is a hilltop village straggling steeply up to its church and 15th-century castle. There is a superb view from the top of the hill across the vale to York Minster.

Fountains Abbey

Benedictine monks from York came to this remote spot in 1132–3, adopted Cistercian rules and founded one of the most beautiful of all England's abbeys. By the early 16th century, the monks of the abbey had prospered through their involvement in the wool trade. Because of this prosperity, it was one of the first foundations to be sold by Henry VIII in 1540. The majestic medieval ruin is among the best-preserved in the country. There are two approaches to the abbey. A footpath leads for nearly a mile through the impressive grounds of Studley Park, 4 miles south-west of Ripon. A road reaches the abbey from the south-west, by a steep lane dipping down to a stream in the wooded seclusion of Skeldale.

Harewood

The village, planned with houses in terraces of dark grey stone, was rebuilt in the late 18th century outside the park of Harewood House, the home of the Earl of Harewood. House and village were designed by John Carr, and the interior of the house was ornamented by Adam and Chippendale.

Harrogate

This spa town is now also well known as a conference centre. Dignified Victorian architecture, banks of flowers and well-planned open spaces characterise the town, with 200 acres of grassland, called the Stray, probing into its very centre. Beyond the fine Valley Gardens are extensive pinewoods, laced with paths. Harlow Car Gardens, home of the Northern Horticultural Society and an outstanding centre for experimental gardening, are about a mile west of the town centre. From the escarpment of Birk Crag, just north of Harlow Car, broad views sweep west to the Dales.

Knaresborough

Georgian houses gaze sedately across narrow streets; and steep steps and alleys lead down to the River Nidd, which here curls round a sandstone cliff. Ruins of a 14th-century castle crown the clifftop, close to the market-place. On the opposite bank, paths lead through beechwoods to the damp and eerie Dropping Well. Water drops on to an overhang, forming a lime deposit, and is slowly petrifying a curious assortment of hats, toys, parasols and other objects strung above the rock face by the owners of the cave since the 19th century. In the nearby Mother Shipton's cave, the legendary prophetess was reputedly born in July 1488; her prophesies have often seemed remarkably relevant, even in the 20th century, for among them she predicted the development of aircraft. It remains to be seen, however, whether the

'World then to an end shall come
In Nineteen Hundred and Eighty One.'

Northallerton

The town is known as the 'capital' of North Yorkshire. By the market cross, an inn, The Old Fleece, is partly medieval; and fine old houses are grouped about the church, which has a pinnacled 15th-century tower.

The surrounding countryside and its villages are full of character. Borrowby, 5 miles south-east, is an example. Here, among rockeries vivid with flowers, greystone houses clamber towards a cross on a hilltop green which gives fine views across the vale.

Ripon

There is a fine sense of space in the cathedral, which is agreeably uncluttered by monuments. The building of the cathedral started in the 12th century on the site of an Anglo-Saxon church, from which a crypt survives beneath the present central tower.

The market square is a focal point for narrow, winding streets. From the central obelisk a forest horn is sounded, as in ancient times, at 9 o'clock at night by the town's official hornblower, the Wakeman. Ripon's most interesting secular building is the two-storey, timber-framed, 13th-century Wakeman's House on a corner of the market square. It contains a small museum.

PETRIFYING SPRING *Objects hung in Knaresborough's Dropping Well are solidified by lime in the water*

York

The Romans chose this dry site beside the Ouse for their fortress of Eburacum. Later, the Danes founded a colony here, and the Normans built their fortifications before prosperity came with the medieval wool trade.

The city's history is written in its streets. Four medieval gates lead in through walls, built on Roman foundations, that gird the old city for 3 miles. Most of the walls are intact and can be followed by a rampart walk. The Ouse flows through the city; narrow streets such as High and Low Petergate link crooked squares; and Georgian grace predominates in Micklegate and St Saviourgate. Across the short, narrow Shambles (from the Old English *shamel*, meaning a slaughterhouse) old timber-framed houses lean towards one another.

There are many small old churches, quaint and often glorious towers and the breathtaking spectacle of the Minster. It took, two-and-a-half centuries, from 1220 to 1470, to complete this poem in stone. Inside, a kaleidoscope of light explodes from windows of medieval stained glass that are among the art treasures of the world.

DEVIL'S ARROWS *The three monoliths at Boroughbridge are so named from the legend that they were part of a barrage shot by the Devil at some local cities*

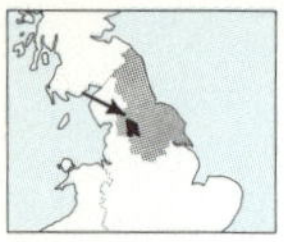

At the source of the Aire

Angling In the River Wharfe there are trout and grayling at Ilkley, Bolton Abbey and Grassington; trout at Kilnsey, 2 miles north-west of Grassington.

Walking The region forms part of Yorkshire Dales National Park and has many walks. It is possible to walk from Ilkley to Kettlewell on rough paths and tracks.

Nature trails On Ilkley Moor, starting from the Paddling Pool at the top of Wells Road via White Wells, Rocky Valley and the Tarn. The trail takes just over an hour. There is an all-seasons trail through Middleton Woods, 1 mile north-east of Ilkley, starting from the field-gate behind the Bathing Pool. This also takes about an hour.

Events Skipton has a music festival in Mar. and an exhibition of the work of Yorkshire artists in June. There is also a charity gala in June and the Craven Drama Festival in Nov. at Skipton. Ilkley is the centre for the Wharfedale Music Festival, held in May.

Places to see *Barden Tower*: daily. *Bolton Abbey*, priory ruins: daily. *Brimham Rocks*: daily. *Craven Museum*, Skipton: Apr. to Sept., weekdays, except Tues., and Sun. afternoon; Oct. to Mar., weekday afternoons, except Tues., and Sat. morning. *Malham Tarn* (NT): public access on foot only to south shore and large area of Low Trenhouse Farm (visitors must keep to the footpaths): daily. *Manor House Museum and Art Gallery*, Ilkley: daily. *Skipton Castle*: weekdays, Sun. afternoon.

Information centre Colvend, Hebden Road, Grassington. Tel. Grassington 752748 (seasonal).

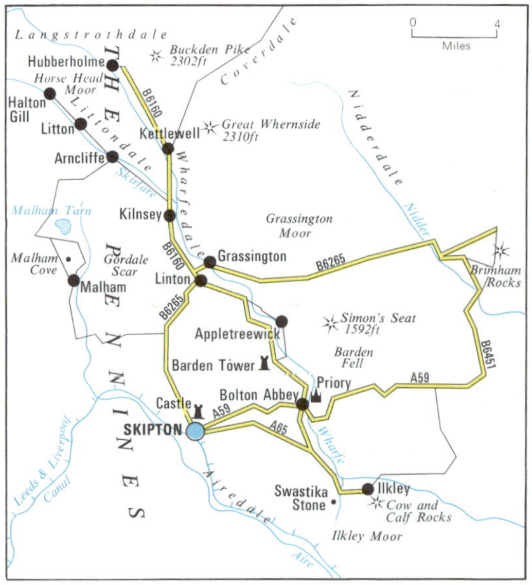

A desolate splendour reaches down from the Pennine heights merging into the quiet of the pastoral Eastern Dales, where the pace of life quickens on the fringe of industrial West Yorkshire. Most awesome of all is the massive natural limestone architecture of the scenery around Malham in upper Airedale. Towards the east, the limestone is overlaid by darker millstone grit, carpeted by sweeps of heather but breaking through in the dramatic outcrops which are among the sights of the area. Carvings on some rocks were left by strange pre-Christian cults.

These dales are the most accessible from West Yorkshire, and Wharfedale is accustomed to slow processions of traffic on sunny days. Yet remoteness remains in offshoots such as Littondale, or in the upper reaches of Nidderdale, and on the moors and felltops. Norman barons built their castles and the Church its religious houses, commanding the best routes through rich pastures along the valley floors. Restored or still in ruins, they are splendid buildings to see.

GORDALE SCAR *This ravine, at the head of which Gordale Beck plunges 300 ft in twin waterfalls, is part of the 22 mile long North Craven Fault, produced by earth movements during the Ice Age*

DOWN IN THE DALE *A stone bridge crosses Park Gill Beck at Kettlewell, a quiet upper Wharfedale village sheltering below the 2310-ft fell of Great Whernside*

Appletreewick

The place is as pretty as its name—a scattering of yeomen's houses in sunny gardens set between Wharfedale and the tawny moors. New tree plantations soften the lower slopes of Barden Fell to the south-east, and above rises Simon's Seat (1592 ft) best reached from the road to Bolton Abbey.

Arncliffe

There is a magnificent approach to the village over lonely moors from Malham into Littondale, one of the most peaceful and wooded of all the dales. The houses of Arncliffe, nestling among clumps of sycamores, are built of the characteristic greystone of the dales. The restored 12th-century church stands by a bridge near where the Cowside Beck joins the boisterous River Skirfare. Fine old stone barns stand in pastures overlooked by steep, wooded hills along the road towards Litton, which lies 2 miles north-west along the dale. This pretty village has quaint ancient houses and a good inn. Halton Gill, 2 miles further on, is a greystone huddle of 17th-century farms and one 'modern' 19th-century house near the head of Littondale, where a stream gushes down between steep pastures. Few tourists penetrate this far, and the pastoral peace is unspoilt. A footpath climbs north out of the dale across Horse Head Moor, and drops to Langstrothdale in about 3 miles.

Bolton Abbey
The 12th-century priory ruins stand among meadows, woods and waterfalls, a setting made famous by Landseer's painting *Bolton Abbey in Olden Time*. The nave, repaired and lengthened, is now the parish church. Half a mile north, the Wharfe is crossed by stepping stones. Roads and footpaths continue along this beautiful stretch of the river, leading after 2 miles to the ruins of the 15th-century Barden Tower, above one of the loveliest humpbacked bridges of the Dales. On the way, the paths pass The Strid, a gorge in which the Wharfe surges beneath limestone ledges. The name Strid comes from an Old English word meaning 'turmoil'.

Brimham Rocks
An outcrop of millstone grit on the moors high above Nidderdale and the Vale of York, moulded by weather and time into weird shapes. The outcrop covers about 50 acres, and from it the views extend far across the Vale of York to the ridges of the moors beyond.

Grassington
Upper Wharfedale's principal village has kept its charm. A medieval bridge, widened in later times, spans the Wharfe, and a small cobbled market square is the meeting place of narrow streets. Grassington Moor, north of the village, is covered with remains of lead mines—now long disused—which brought a boom to Grassington in the late 18th and early 19th centuries.

Linton, just across the river, is a delightful village with modest grey houses grouped around the village green. A tinkling beck is crossed by three bridges—a packhorse bridge, a clapper bridge, which takes its name from the long flat stones of which it is composed, and a modern bridge for road traffic. Gracefully dominating the scene is the imposing facade of Fountaine's Hospital, originally an almshouse for six poor women, but now for men also, founded in 1721 by Richard Fountaine.

NATURAL AMPHITHEATRE *Malham Cove's 240 ft high limestone cliff was created by earth movements in the Ice Age. Once water flowed in a valley above the cliff, but now it emerges from underground at the foot of the cove and flows south to join the Aire*

Hubberholme
A village set at the point where upper Wharfedale narrows at the entrance to Langstrothdale. The young river leaps over limestone ledges, and half a dozen summits topping 2000 ft loom above steep grass pastures to the east. A notable landmark is Buckden Pike, 2302 ft. The little church has a rare medieval rood loft, and beyond the humpbacked bridge is the George Inn, once the vicarage. The inn is the scene every New Year's Eve of the Hubberholme Parliament, at which the local vicar auctions the grazing rights of a plot of land in a ceremony that dates back 1000 years.

BOLTON ABBEY *The River Wharfe flows by the priory, which was founded in 1151. The nave, last restored in 1864, is now the parish church, but the remainder is in ruins*

Ilkley
The Wharfe flows beneath a gracious bridge dating from 1673 beside the main street of this spa town, the Roman Olicana. The bridge is now closed to motor traffic for its preservation. All Saints' Church has three Saxon crosses in the churchyard. The moors brood above. 'On Ilkla Moor baht 'at'—on Ilkley Moor without a hat—is an old folk song that has become the nearest thing to a Yorkshireman's national song.

A path above the wooded head of Hebers Ghyll, south-west of the town, leads to the 'Swastika Stone', a carved relic of the Bronze or Iron Age, from which views range across the whole valley below. South-east of the town, the moorland road passes close to Cow and Calf Rocks, a favourite practice ground for rock climbers. Westwards and southwards from here, paths continue across the moors to numerous stones with cup-shaped and ring-shaped carvings dating from the Bronze Age.

Kettlewell
One of the prettiest villages of upper Wharfedale, reached across a lovely old stone bridge. North-eastwards a minor road makes a stiff climb up the cleft between Great Whernside, 2310 ft, and Buckden Pike, dropping down into the North Riding by way of Coverdale to Wensleydale. Kilnsey Crag, by the roadside, 3 miles south of Kettlewell, attracts experienced rock climbers. Close to the Crag is the starting point of Mastiles Lane, which leads 5 miles west over the moors to Malham Tarn—a magnificent, if lonely, walk.

Malham
A village set in an amphitheatre of hills, the most rugged of North Yorkshire's limestone scenery. The gigantic limestone overhang of Malham Cove is 1 mile north of the village. A mile-long lane to the east, then a half-mile footpath, leads to the staggering cliffs of Gordale Scar, where waterfalls plunge down into a precipitous gorge.

Both sites can be combined in a 5-mile walk. There is a climb beside the waterfall of Gordale Scar, then a short scramble, and a path through the steep gorge to open moorland. The path then joins the road. After 1¼ miles it crosses a stream close to Malham Tarn, then turns south along the stream into a dry valley which opens out on to gleaming acres of water-eroded limestone at the top of Malham Cove. The easiest descent is down the west side of the cove.

Skipton
Roads converge from every direction on this busy market town at the eastern approach to the Aire Gap. The main Leeds–Liverpool Canal runs through the town, and is now used mainly by pleasure traffic. The great castle of the Cliffords stands behind the fine partly 14th-century Holy Trinity Church at the top of the busy High Street. Most of the castle is 14th–17th century, but one gateway of the original Norman castle built by Robert de Romille remains. Other features include a 50 ft long banqueting hall, a huge kitchen with roasting and baking hearths, a dungeon and a 'shell room', the walls of which are decorated with sea shells.

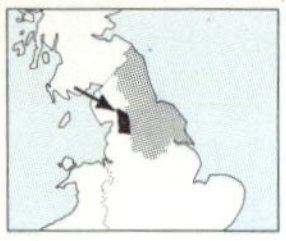

Under the lonely moors

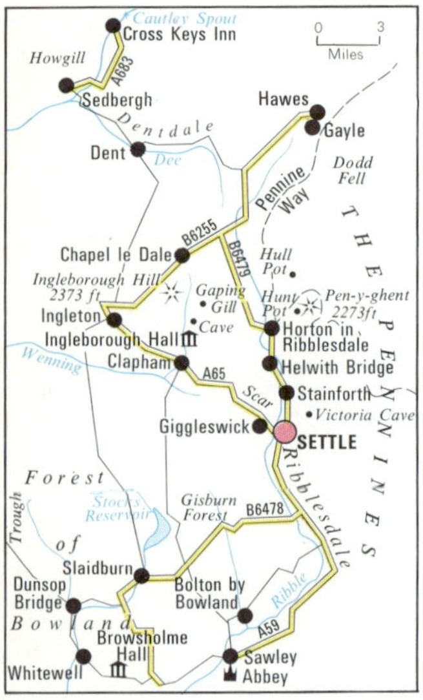

Events Settle has a six-day drama festival in early summer, and a Carnival Day in June or July.

Places to see *Browsholme Hall:* afternoons, mid-May to early June and mid-Aug. to early Sept. *Gaping Gill*: Spring and late Summer Bank Hols. *Ingleborough Cave*: Apr. to Sept., daily; also by arrangement. *White Scar Caves*, Ingleton: daily, subject to favourable conditions underground.

Information centre Yorkshire Dales National Park, Clapham via Lancaster. Tel. Clapham 419.

The Western Dales run down from some of the highest of the Pennines' moorland shoulders, and there is infinite loneliness beneath the bare brows at the dale heads. Passing down the dales, isolated farms give way to hamlets, then to villages on the valley floors, and finally to busy little towns that have developed beside the roads and railways cutting through England's mountain backbone.

Nearly 2 million years ago, the rocks that form this section of the Pennines cracked and the land slipped between the so-called 'Craven Faults' to form the Aire Gap—the only true gap, as opposed to a pass, through the Pennines. The major section of the South Craven Fault passes through Ingleton, Clapham and Settle, where it towers north-west of the town as the great roadside cliff of Giggleswick Scar. The Gap has contributed far more to the region than simply adding to the drama of its scenery. Invaders and traders have passed through since prehistory. Through it, too, road and rail routes have found an easy passage.

The rivers of the Western Dales include, in the south-west, the lovely Hodder, which passes through the little-known region of Bowland, a western bulge of the Pennines extending across the Lancashire border. Everywhere, except in the extreme north-west, limestone scenery predominates. Huge natural terraces of stone gleam against the fellsides, especially those of Ingleborough and Pen-y-ghent, and years of erosion have scoured out Britain's deepest potholes.

There has been quarrying along the lines of both the Craven Faults—especially in Ribblesdale. But remoteness is still the predominant quality, and this is the great attraction for walkers striding the moors from one dale head to another, or for potholers scrambling in the dank world beneath the moors.

A COUNTRY FOR POTHOLERS AND HIKERS

Man is dwarfed by the enormous main chamber of Gaping Gill, the largest limestone cave in Britain—big enough to contain York Minster. The yawning mouth, on the slopes of Ingleborough Hill, opens into the roof of the chamber. Water plunges 365 ft to the floor below (cross-section bottom right). The potholes lie near the Pennine Way (right), a footpath running 250 miles from Derbyshire to the Scottish border.

Pennine Way
Railway
above 2000 ft
1750–2000 ft
1500–1750 ft
1250–1500 ft
1000–1250 ft
750–1000 ft
500– 750 ft

DARK GIANT *Drystone walls, typical of the area, criss-cross the moorlands below Ingleborough Hill, seen from Chapel le Dale*

Bolton by Bowland
The lanes are tree-lined and there are two shady greens in this attractive, secluded village by Tosside Beck. Between the greens, the fine 13th-century church has a memorial to Sir Ralph Pudsey of Bolton Hall, his three wives and 25 children. A pleasant 2-mile walk follows the Beck to Sawley, with its ruined Cistercian Abbey.

Cautley Spout
An impressive waterfall, on the wild Cumbrian moorlands north of Sedbergh, descends 600 ft over the naked rock of Cautley Crag. Just beyond the Cross Keys Inn—its doorway is dated 1732, and teas are served under ancient beams—a footpath leads to the Spout.

Clapham
Clapham Beck chatters down from Ingleborough's flanks to form the centrepiece of this charming village. The banks of the beck are bushy with acacia and rhododendrons, and greystone

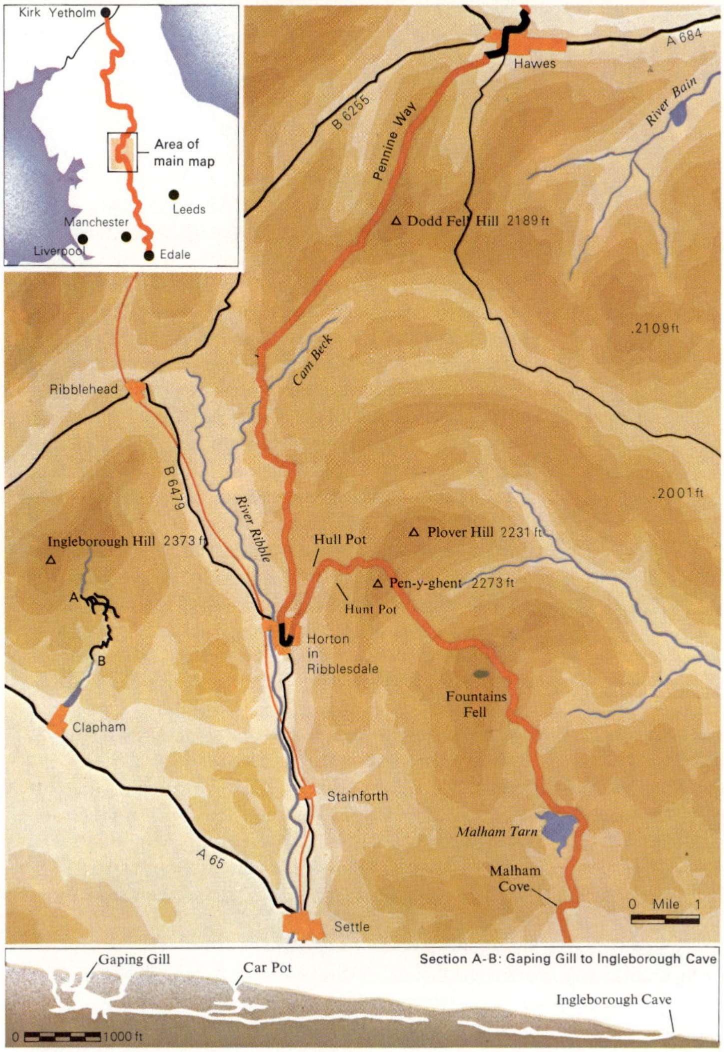

houses stand in bright little gardens. A path upstream leads to the grounds of Ingleborough Hall, now a school, with an exotic collection of bushes, trees and plants—many of them, including bamboo, from the East.

After $1\frac{1}{4}$ miles the path reaches Ingleborough Cave, extending for one-third of a mile beside rivulets and crystal-clear pools, and festooned with stalactites and stalagmites, beautiful and unusually varied in colouring and form.

A mile further up the path is Gaping Gill, the most dramatic of North Yorkshire's potholes. Water hurtles down in a single jet 365 ft to the floor. Visitors can usually go down by winch during the spring and August meets of the Bradford or Craven Pothole clubs; but it is dangerous to explore it without the company of experts.

Dentdale

One of the smallest of the dales, and utterly delightful. The little River Dee tumbles down the dale between trees and ferns, fed by many tributary becks. Here the countryside begins to take on the character of the nearby Lake District: dark grey rock looms over the valley west of Dent town; many farms and cottages are whitewashed, and hedges alternate with stone walls.

The town, with its cobbled main street, is a little gem, once a centre for knitting. A stone fountain on a corner is in memory of the geologist Adam Sedgwick, born at Dent in 1785. The railway station at Dent, now open only on special days, is the highest main line station in the country.

Horton in Ribblesdale

Great quarries scar the western fellsides from Helwith Bridge to Horton, and trains pass through remote pastures on the Settle–Carlisle route. Horton's architecture reflects it all: the yeomen's houses with dated doorheads, the workmen's cottages, and the Victorian terraces of the railway era. A huge limeworks towers above the railway station, and slate from other quarries—unusual in these parts—has brought variety to local gateways and stone walls. Geologists come to study the curiously twisted layers of rock, and walkers love the place for its access to the fells. Pen-y-ghent (2273 ft) overlooks the valley. Two fine potholes, Hunt Pot and Hull Pot, lie beneath the mountain's slopes. The Pennine Way passes between their mouths before descending to Horton and heading north again for Wensleydale.

Ingleborough Hill

Its distinctive shape makes Ingleborough a major landmark of North Yorkshire. It is best seen from lonely Chapel le Dale, a village that gives its name to an entire valley, gouged out by a glacier almost 2 million years ago, stretching north-east from Ingleton. The minor and many-gated road on the north side of the valley gives the best views. One of the shortest and easiest approaches to Ingleborough's summit is from just beyond the Hill Inn, 4 miles north-east of Ingleton. The climb leads across pastures to an immense natural terrace formed by acres of water-eroded limestone. Next comes a steepish ascent to the peaty moorland of the summit, reaching 2373 ft, where there are the remains of an Iron Age settlement.

Sedbergh

A town with a famous public school founded in 1525, an old bridge and a fine church, backed by fells that are geologically unusual. These fells, the Howgills, are composed of the same rock as those found in the southern Lake District, and are rounded in shape. Their sides are scarred with blue-black scree, their tops tawny with bracken and their flanks soft with springy grass.

Settle

Where the River Ribble flows through the Aire Gap, Settle has grown as a major market centre, to which farm folk flock on Tuesdays. It is a good walking centre at the heart of North Yorkshire's limestone scenery. Many bones, ranging from those of elephants and hippopotamuses to bones of Stone Age and Iron Age men, have been found in local caves, particularly Victoria Cave, 2 miles north-east of the town.

At Stainforth, $2\frac{1}{2}$ miles north, a precipitous lane, unsuitable for cars, descends to a secluded and beautiful packhorse bridge built in 1670; below it, the Ribble tumbles in waterfalls.

Slaidburn

Rolling green pastures and, beyond, bracken and heather heights, almost encircle this pretty village on the River Hodder in the heart of Bowland. The old church has an 18th-century three-decker pulpit. Gisburn Forest, north-east of the village, is an extensive mixed coniferous plantation sloping down to the eastern shore of Stocks Reservoir. The reservoir is an excellent bird-watching area, and the island rising from it is a low hill that once stood by the submerged village of Stocks.

Whitewell

A village of grey cottages in the lovely, wooded Hodder Valley. There are riverside walks, but the road also closely follows the river. It leads south into a thickly wooded ravine, and north through a more open valley to Dunsop Bridge, 2 miles away. Eastwards from Whitewell, the road climbs swiftly into limestone country to give views over the whole sweep of the valley. Then, in $2\frac{1}{2}$ miles, it leads to the fine 17th-century mansion of Browsholme (pronounced Brewsome) Hall, for centuries the home of the Parker family.

A road westwards from Dunsop Bridge leads to the 1000-ft Trough of Bowland, a lonely moorland pass on the Lancashire border, with wide views.

SHELVES OF LIMESTONE *A brook at Gayle, near Hawes, runs down a series of steps, formed by the natural weathering of limestone. From Dodd Fell, which rises to 2189 ft behind the village, the Pennine Way drops down through Gayle into Wensleydale*

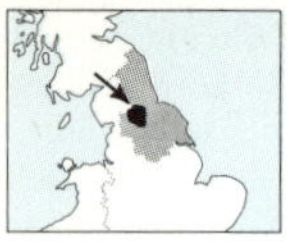

Castles and cascades among the Dales

Angling Trout and grayling in the River Ure at Middleham, Aysgarth, Bainbridge and Hawes, and in the River Swale at Richmond, Grinton and Keld.

Walking The whole region is ideal for walks, particularly around Richmond along old Roman routes to Bainbridge and Lancaster.

Events Richmond has a biennial 'Richmondshire' Festival with plays, concerts, art exhibitions, held in early summer (1979, 1981, etc.). At the annual 'First Fruits' harvest ceremony in the market-place at Richmond, wine is given to the farmer who produces the best sample of the new season's wheat.

Places to see *Bolton Castle*, Castle Bolton: daily, except Mon. *Bowes Castle*: weekdays, Sun. afternoon. *Easby Abbey*, 1 mile south-east of Richmond: weekdays and Sun. afternoons. *Georgian Theatre*, Richmond: daily during Easter weekend; May to Sept., afternoons when no performance at theatre. *Green Howards Museum*, Richmond: weekdays: also Sun. afternoons Apr. to Oct. *Jervaulx Abbey*: daily. *Middleham Castle*: weekdays, Sun. afternoons. *Richmond Castle*: daily, except Sun. mornings Oct. to Mar. *Yorkshire Museum of Carriages and Horse-drawn Vehicles*, Aysgarth Force: Easter to late Oct., daily.

Information centres Friary Gardens, Queens Road, Richmond. Tel. Richmond 3525 (summer). Swale House, Frenchgate, Richmond. Tel. Richmond 4221 (winter).

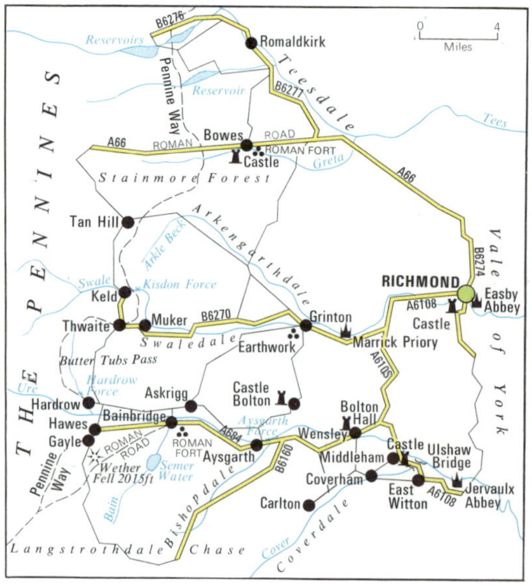

Upland moors sweep to a score of summits of more than 2000 ft in the Yorkshire Dales National Park. They are wild, often windswept—and infinitely appealing to those with a taste for solitude. Yet total stillness is rare, and the air is haunted by the cries of curlews, lapwings, gulls and golden plovers, and the raucous red grouse. Shaggy Swaledale sheep graze on the moors, surviving all but the fiercest winter storms; and smoke curls from the chimneys of some of England's loneliest farms.

Over a million years ago, ice flowing down the eastward tilt of the Pennines carved out the dales in their distinctive shapes. Wensleydale, watered by the Ure with its three spectacular waterfalls, is the broadest, most open and wooded of the Yorkshire valleys. Swaledale, sinuous between its steep hills, has a more secluded grandeur. Narrower tributary dales, such as Arkengarthdale, Coverdale and Bishopdale, burrow deep between the flanks of the fells. The hills are of limestone, capped here and there by millstone grit, and on them grow cotton grass and heather, flecked with bilberry and crowberry.

The slopes of the valleys are patterned with drystone walls. Castles and monastic ruins recall the Middle Ages. Almost every village and hamlet is dignified by sturdy greystone cottages and by Georgian houses from a later period of prosperity. The churches are intimate rather than grand, and in many churchyards sheep graze among the gravestones.

The Dales present a pastoral aspect today, but it was not always so. Moors and gill-sides still bear the man-made clawmarks of the lead mines. The industry declined rapidly in the 1880's with competition from foreign imports. Many families left, those who stayed re-adjusted to the fluctuating fortunes of farming, and the open moors regained their rural calm.

Aysgarth
A little east of the village, a lane plunges north past the church to Aysgarth Force, impressive waterfalls set in woods. The lane crosses one cascade by a beautiful old single-arched bridge, near a mill that is now a carriage museum. The lower falls are reached by signposted paths about a mile further on. Bolton Castle, 4 miles north-east, is a craggy relic of the 14th century. Mary, Queen of Scots was imprisoned there for six months after her flight to England in 1568, and the castle was besieged by Parliamentary forces during the Civil War. Surviving traces of medieval terraced fields are clearly visible to the west of the castle.

Bainbridge
The former centre of the once-great Forest of Wensleydale; a hunting horn is still blown from Bainbridge green each evening, a custom which dates back 700 years. The sound of the horn was intended to guide lost travellers to the village. Little grey houses face each other across this wide, steep green. Brough Hill, built out of glacial debris and topped by a Roman fort, heaves a great green shoulder out of the village. The River Bain flows down to Bainbridge from Semer Water, lying in the moors 2 miles south—nearly a mile long by half a mile wide, the largest natural lake in the dales. A mile up the lane towards Semer Water, a rough track, once a Roman road leading to Lancaster, forks right and runs across the wild moors for 5 miles before joining the Hawes–Buckden road.

Bowes
Along the straight scar of the Roman road across Stainmore Forest, now the A66, Bowes village huddles in a valley beneath its 12th-century ruined castle. The grave of 19-year-old George Ashton Taylor in the churchyard gave sad inspiration for the character of Smike in

HILLTOP RUINS *Richmond is dominated by the ruins of its Norman castle, overlooking the River Swale. It is one of the few surviving castles in England with 11th-century walls*

MARKET OBELISK *In the centre of Richmond's market-place stands an obelisk, erected in the late 18th century. The market is open on Saturdays*

Dickens's *Nicholas Nickleby*. Taylor was a pupil at Shaw's Academy, the original of Dotheboys Hall, the school in the novel, and now a café. Next to the church, a Norman keep, completed in 1187, stands on the site of a Roman fort. Two miles west along the main road, the Pennine Way leads to God's Bridge, a limestone shelf under which the River Greta has worn its way.

Grinton

In medieval times, the dead were brought in wicker biers from the far ends of Swaledale to the spacious churchyard of Grinton Church, the so-called 'Cathedral of the Dales'. This was first built by the Normans but most of the existing building is in Perpendicular style. Until the 19th century the moors above rang with mining activity. Today the village is still notable for its church, and for a three-arched bridge.

A minor road passes a prehistoric earthwork, probably dating from the Iron Age, a mile west of the village, then climbs high above the valley. It offers the longest and loveliest of all the views over Swaledale, before soaring over the moors to Askrigg in Wensleydale. Two miles south-east of Grinton are the remains of the 12th-century Marrick Priory, a former house for Benedictine nuns.

Hawes

This centre for touring upper Wensleydale lies higgledy-piggledy against the slopes, with a beck scurrying through. The setting of Hawes is more noteworthy than its individual buildings; there is a particularly attractive view of it on the road to Hardrow, about 1 mile across the valley to the north.

Hardrow (pronounced Hardraw) Force is a waterfall cascading 100 ft over a limestone ledge. A footpath passes behind the waterfall. The road to the north leads over Butter Tubs Pass. The Butter Tubs, though not the largest of the Pennine potholes, are certainly the closest to any road.

A wild road south of Hawes leads high out of Wensleydale, past the tiny cottages and waterfall of Gayle towards Langstrothdale and upper Wharfedale, with fine views of Ingleborough and other peaks. The rough track leading off the road to the east, 3 miles south of Hawes, follows the route of the Roman road leading to Bainbridge; the track passes within a few strides of the summit of Wether Fell (2015 ft).

Keld

A lovely greystone village, round which the fells crowd steep and close. Opposite the post office, a footpath joins the Pennine Way in a few hundred yards. South-eastwards the Way follows the contortions of the Swale through limestone cliffs, running alongside cataracts such as Kisdon Force, where the water tumbles in a never-ending roar. After 3 miles the road can be rejoined at Thwaite or Muker. Half a mile north-west of Keld, a minor moorland lane leads for 4 miles to Tan Hill Inn—one of England's highest (1732 ft) and loneliest inns, near a disused coal mine in the heather. Here, once more, the lane crosses the Pennine Way.

Middleham

Georgian houses surround the market-place, and the ruined castle has one of the largest keeps in England. Richard III acquired it in 1471, and his son, Edward, died there in 1484. Beyond the castle is the moor where, every morning, racehorses from a dozen local stables can be seen in training.

A mile south-east is Ulshaw Bridge, one of Wensleydale's loveliest bridges, built in 1674. Another mile further on, East Witton drowses round a rectangular green. Narrow lanes from Middleham and East Witton meet in the secluded valley of Coverdale, with its attractive village of Carlton; at The Foresters' Arms there are flagstones, a fine old fireplace in the bar and a Saxon burial mound right outside the kitchen.

AYSGARTH FORCE *A series of falls extend for half a mile along the River Ure*

GEORGIAN PLAYHOUSE *Richmond's Georgian Theatre is one of England's oldest theatres. It was built in 1788, closed 60 years later, and restored and re-opened in 1962*

Jervaulx Abbey, 6 miles south-east of Middleham, was a great Cistercian house, founded in the 12th century and among those dissolved by Henry VIII. The ruins, though less spectacular than those of Fountains and Rievaulx, have a quiet charm and enough has survived to enable the layout of the church and other buildings to be traced.

Richmond

One of Yorkshire's most attractive towns. From the top of the 11th-century castle keep there is one of northern England's finest views, across dales sweeping down to the Vale of York. On Saturdays the view includes, closer at hand, the coloured awnings of the stalls in the great rounded market-place. An island in this 20th-century bustle is the fabric of the medieval Holy Trinity Church, from which the curfew is rung each night. This former church now houses the Green Howards' regimental museum.

Romaldkirk

One of the prettiest villages to be found in upper Teesdale. Little greystone almshouses stand beside a noble 12th-century church, and there is a wide, irregular green. Lanes lead up to reservoirs high on the grassy plateau to the west; they are still moors, but the wildness seems to have been tamed here.

Wensley

This sleepy greystone village was once the principal market town in the dale. Its first charter was granted in 1202. The town's decline started after an outbreak of plague in 1563. The size and beauty of the church gives an indication of Wensley's bygone commercial importance; it rises beside the river like a little cathedral. Noteworthy are its Restoration font and cover, the early benches and box-pews and the 15th-century screen. Bolton Hall is the shell of a 17th-century house burnt out in 1902.

Relics of the past around the North York Moors

Angling There are trout and grayling in the River Derwent at Hackness, and in the River Rye at Helmsley, with trout only at Hawnby.

Walking The region is part of the North York Moors National Park and is ideal for walking. Goathland, Hawnby and Helmsley are good centres. There is a footpath from Helmsley to Rievaulx, and a track from Rievaulx to Hawnby.

Gliding The Yorkshire Gliding Club has its headquarters at Sutton Bank, 2 miles north of Kilburn.

Events The Ryedale Festival of Music and Drama is held in May each year at Beadlam, 2 miles east of Helmsley. The Ryedale Agricultural Show is held on the last Tues. in July at Kirkbymoorside, 5 miles north-east of Helmsley.

Places to see *Byland Abbey*: weekdays and Sun. afternoons. *Helmsley Castle*: daily, except Sun. mornings Oct. to Mar. *Rievaulx Abbey*: daily, except Sun. mornings Oct. to Mar. *Rievaulx Terrace and Temples* (NT): Apr. to Oct., Tues. to Sat. and Bank Hol. Mon.; also Sun. afternoons. *Ryedale Folk Museum*, Hutton-le-Hole, includes reconstructed cruck-framed house: Easter to Sept., afternoons; also mornings mid-July to Aug. *Shandy Hall*, Coxwold, Sterne museum: June to Sept., Wed. afternoons.

Information centre North Yorks. Moors National Park centres: Bondgate, Helmsley (Helmsley 657); Danby Lodge, Danby, Whitby (Castleton 654); Sutton Bank, Sutton, Thirsk (Sutton 426).

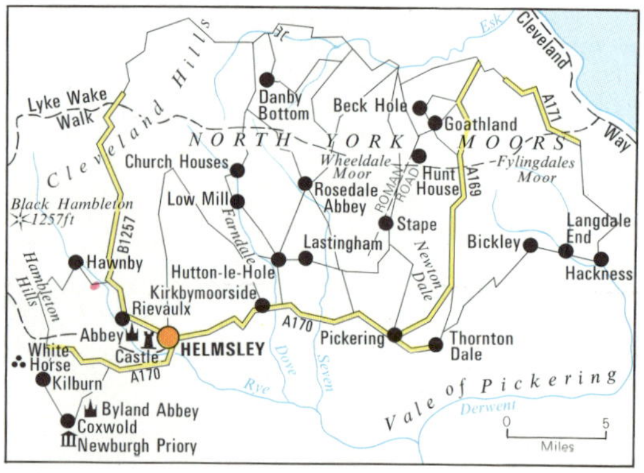

The blue distances of the North York Moors fill the high wedge between the North Yorkshire coastline and the Vale of York. Westwards they drop to the vale from the steep scarp of the Hambleton Hills, which reach 1257 ft at Black Hambleton. To the north-west they include the Cleveland Hills, from which the River Esk runs down through a lush valley to the sea at Whitby. The moors are mainly composed of sandstone, and the heather blooms magnificently from mid-summer into the autumn.

Out of the wild plateau, often rising to 1000 ft, other streams flow south in deep valleys to the Vale of Pickering. Little roads swoop between them; gradients of 1 in 4 are common, and even 1 in 3 is not rare. These are beautiful, secluded valleys, steep-sided, too narrow to encourage the growth of large settlements. Here and there, greystone villages cluster about a stream and sheep graze by the roadside while, higher up, lone farms brace themselves against winter storms.

Bronze and Iron Age circles and cairns of obscure purpose indicate the early presence of man on the moors, especially near Danby and on Shooting House Rigg. The Hambleton Road along the moors' western rim was prehistoric man's highway, later used by Romans, Normans and, above all, by the drovers. Today, walkers follow it along part of the 100-mile trail of the Cleveland Way. A Roman road can still partly be followed through the heather of Wheeldale Moor, south-west of Goathland. But those who follow the Lyke Wake Walk across the wild heart of the moors will find few other marks of man.

Coxwold

Laurence Sterne (1713–68), the author of *Tristram Shandy*, lived here at Shandy Hall, and preached in the 15th-century church whose octagonal tower rises at the top of the village. Grassy banks and cobbled verges line the steep main street, and greystone houses stand above. It is a picturesque place set at the point where the Vale of York begins to rise up to the Hambleton Hills. The ruins of Byland Abbey, 1½ miles north-east, are set in meadows against the wooded ridges of the moorland scarp.

Newburgh Priory, half a mile south-east, is a country mansion dating from Elizabethan and Georgian days, but incorporating some remains of a 12th-century Augustinian priory. According to tradition, Cromwell's body was brought here by his daughter after the Restoration, and is buried in a bricked-up vault which has never been opened.

Goathland

Sheep graze on the coarse grasses where the moors come right in among the greystone houses of this scattered little village. A lane leads 1 mile north-west to Beck Hole—a delightful hamlet, clasped in a wooded hollow. The whole area is fine walking country, and there are several waterfalls. South-west of the village, a lane leads 2½ miles to the hamlet of Hunt House; from it a sign-posted footpath leads to a remarkable stretch of Roman road which soars south over Wheeldale Moor for 3 miles to Stape, above Newton Dale.

The huge white globes on Fylingdales Moor, 5 miles south-east of Goathland, belong to the Fylingdales Early Warning Station, part of the defence network of the Western powers.

Hackness

A village, with a Hall and an 11th-century church with later additions, at the meeting place of several tributaries of the River Derwent. Becks rib this glorious country with tiny dales, converging on the main stream like the veins of a leaf. On one side are the moors, on the other the dark forest masses created by the Forestry Commission from once-wild moorland. These deep coniferous forests, broken by pastureland, change the character of the moors, and marked footpaths and nature trails give access to large areas of this miniature Switzerland. From Langdale End, 2 miles up the valley, the road climbs steeply to Bickley, from which a Forestry Commission road leads through the forests to Thornton Dale in the Vale of Pickering.

Hawnby

A cluster of greystone buildings on the upper reaches of the lovely River Rye. The little Norman church, which has some interesting carving round the north doorway, is half a mile to the west of the village, shaded by trees on the

HELMSLEY CASTLE *A double ditch surrounds the 12th-century castle, which fell into ruin after Sir Charles Duncombe bought it in 1689, then went to live in a mansion he built in the grounds. The mansion is now a school, but the castle is open to the public*

MAJESTIC RUIN *Rievaulx Abbey, surrounded by wooded hills, was founded in 1131 and is one of the earliest Cistercian buildings in England. Its chief glory is its choir, built c. 1225*

river bank. The lane continues north-westwards for another mile through woods as quiet as a cathedral, ending at Arden Hall, which was built on the site of a Benedictine nunnery. From here, a track leads over the bare moorland shoulders of the Hambleton Hills to an old north–south drove road and to Black Hambleton, 1257 ft high.

Helmsley

An attractive market town beneath the southern rim of the moors. The road drops down to red-roofed houses. Round the market square, creeper and wisteria twine round greystone houses, and cottage gardens back on to banks of daffodils by a brook flowing down to meet the Rye. A 12th-century castle ruin stands, craggy and broken, amid the well-kept lawns of Duncombe Park. It was probably built by Walter l'Espec, the founder of Rievaulx Abbey. This is a fine centre for walking; the Cleveland Way begins here along the marked foot-path to Rievaulx, north of the castle.

Rievaulx Abbey, 2 miles north-west, was founded in 1131, the first Cistercian house in the north of England, and one of the most magnificent monastic ruins in the country today. The name, pronounced 'Reevo', comes from Rye Vallis, or valley of the River Rye, above which the abbey ruins stand. There are fine views from the well laid-out Rievaulx Terrace, above the ruins to the east.

FAIR WINDS FOR GLIDING *Pilots of the Yorkshire Gliding Club take advantage of the currents when westerly winds sweeping across the plains are forced upwards by the 700-ft escarpment at Sutton Bank, 2 miles north of Kilburn*

Hutton-le-Hole

A showplace village, ringed by moors. Two becks meet here, chattering beneath little bridges alongside wide greens, and lanes wind past the old grey-stone cottages. The oldest building, Quaker Cottage, dating from 1695, is associated with John Richardson, a missionary to America, who became a friend of William Penn, the founder of Pennsylvania. Running 5 miles north-west is quiet Farndale, through which runs the River Dove. The river's upper reaches are a magnificent sight in April, when both banks glow with brilliant gold masses of wild daffodils. A riverside path follows the best section for $1\frac{1}{2}$ miles between Low Mill and Church Houses. Lastingham, $1\frac{1}{2}$ miles east of Hutton-le-Hole, has a beautiful church with an outstanding 11th-century crypt, built as a shrine for St Cedd.

Kilburn

A little village well known for its fine modern wood carvings, originally the work of Robert Thompson, the son of a local joiner, who died in 1955. The tradition he started is continued in his workshop which stands, surrounded by stacks of seasoning vats, next to the inn. It is both the village's focal point and the centre of its major industry. Examples of Thompson's own work, marked with a mouse, his trademark, are in the church. The White Horse, 314 ft long and 228 ft high, was cut into the turf above the village by the local schoolmaster John Hodgson and his pupils in 1857.

Rosedale Abbey

The main village in 7 mile long Rosedale, which has an attractive green with a little church close by. An inscription above its porch reads *omnia vanitas* (all is vanity). In the churchyard are a few stones of the 12th-century Cistercian nunnery, which gave the village its name. Southwards the valley narrows, and cool coniferous woods face the moors that drop close to the valley floor.

MARK OF A MASTER

Robert Thompson, a wood carver at Kilburn who died in 1955, used a mouse trademark, a tradition continued by craftsmen at his works

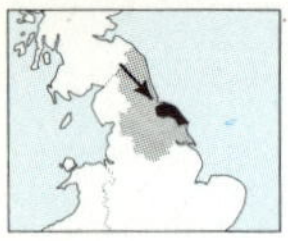

Coast of Captain Cook

Angling There is good coarse fishing on the Rivers Tees and Leven at Yarm, and sea-trout fishing on the Esk at Whitby. Sea fishing for codling at Whitby, Saltburn and Scarborough. There is good sea fishing from boat or harbour piers most of the year at Scarborough. There is an angling festival at Scarborough every Sept.

Boating There is sailing at Whitby and Scarborough, powerboat racing at Whitby throughout the season, and canoeing at Yarm.

Events Whitby has a Blessing of the Boats ceremony and a regatta in Aug. Scarborough has a summer Festival, and the Teesside International Eisteddfod is held at Middlesbrough in early Aug.

Places to see *Captain Cook Birthplace Museum*, Marton: weekdays. *Captain Cook Schoolroom Museum*, Great Ayton: weekday afternoons. *Mount Grace Priory* (NT): daily, except Sun. morning Oct. to Mar. *Ormesby Hall* (NT), 4 miles north-west of Great Ayton: Apr. to Oct., Wed., Sun. and Bank Hol. afternoons *Scarborough Art Gallery*, *Woodend Museum*, *Rotunda Museum* and *Londesborough Lodge*, folk life and history museum: all open weekdays; also Sun. afternoons Spring Bank Hol. to Sept. *Scarborough Castle*: daily, except Sun. mornings Oct. to Mar. *Whitby Abbey*: daily, except Sun. mornings Oct. to Mar. *Whitby Art Gallery* and *Museum*: both weekdays and Sun. afternoons.

Information centres Information Bureau, New Quay Road, Whitby, Tel. Whitby 2674. Information Centre, St Nicholas Cliff, Scarborough. Tel. Scarborough 72261.

Cleveland means 'cliff-land', and cliffs predominate both along the North Yorkshire coast and also inland, where the great scarp of the Cleveland Hills drops down to the lowlands south of the Tees. The ancient rock from which these hills were moulded has set the character of the region. From the ironstone in this chain of hills have grown the clamorous iron and steel industries of Teesside, and the mines that scar the steep coastal clefts north of Staithes. The waters of the streams run red because of the richness of the iron ore mined locally, especially round the old workings by Eston Nab.

To the north lies an area of mixed farming. Away from the industrial Tees, this is a warm rural landscape, punctuated by villages and market towns of mellow stone beneath the rim of hills and moors. Cleveland has bred great seafarers, the most famous of them being Captain James Cook. And from its green pastures has come one of the sturdiest and most versatile breeds of horse, the Cleveland Bay.

Walkers will find here marathon opportunities. The Cleveland Way, beginning in Helmsley, runs through the whole area, a total of nearly 100 miles; the Lyke Wake Walk, from Osmotherley to Ravenscar, covers 40 miles across wild heather moors.

THE BEACHCOMBERS *Children play at low tide in Staithes Harbour*

Great Ayton
Beneath the northern ridges of the moors lies one of Cleveland's prettiest villages. Captain James Cook went to school here. The school is now a museum, but the cottage where he lived was shipped stone by stone to Australia in 1934; an obelisk replaces it, hewn from rocks near Point Hicks, the first part of Australia sighted on Cook's voyage of discovery (1768–71). A monument to Cook on Easby Moor, south-east of Great Ayton, dominates the Cleveland skyline.

At Newton, 2 miles north-east, a path leads to the short, sharp scramble up Roseberry Topping (1057 ft), from which can be seen moorland heights, rural vales and the North Sea.

Guisborough
The red-roofed houses are of mellow stone, and in the broad main street stand a market cross and a 15th-century church. The craggy remnant of a 12th-century priory looks out to the spacious grounds of Guisborough Hall and the moors behind.

Osmotherley
John Wesley preached at a stone table by the old cross, in the centre of this lovely greystone village. The Cleveland Hills are to the east, and Hambleton's steep flanks to the south-east. From the top of the village, a track marked Moors Path shows that the Cleveland Way passes here. In about 1 mile, it joins the first section of the Lyke Wake Walk, named after a Cleveland dirge dating from ancient times when it was believed a dead man's soul had to pass over Whinny Moor. The walk crosses heather, bracken and bog nearly all the way on a 40-mile route to Ravenscar—a journey which has to be covered within 24 hours to qualify for membership of the Lyke Wake Club. The club's meeting place is at the Queen Catherine Hotel in the centre of Osmotherley village.

Mount Grace Priory, 1 mile north on a steep spur of the Cleveland Hills, is the best-preserved Carthusian house in England. It was founded by Thomas Holland, Duke of Surrey, at the end of the 14th century. The cells of the monks, who took a vow of silence, can be seen grouped round the cloisters.

Robin Hood's Bay
The narrow main street plunges giddily down to the sea, the little houses and shops crowding close. The sea has taken many houses; others are threatened. Once the inhabitants lived by fishing and smuggling, but today the interiors of the cottages have been modernised and the village attracts a tourist trade. The great bay sweeps 3 miles south, contained in a steep bowl of farmland. Ravenscar, on the southern headland, has a hotel standing on the site of a Roman lighthouse, and the views are magnificent.

Runswick
A village at the western end of a wide and sandy bay, between stark cliffs. Cottage gardens blaze with flowers barely beyond the reach of the sea. Kettle Ness, a headland east of the bay, is a fine viewpoint, with the remains of a Roman lighthouse.

Scarborough
Fishing village, seaside town, spa, historic site—Scarborough merges them all in a splendour of cliff scenery and sandy bays. Cockle stalls, bingo halls, amusement arcades and all the seaside fun of the fair make a garish assembly where Scarborough's oldest streets come down to the sea south of the headland. Embraced but not swamped by it all is the harbour where cobles and mules (traditional fishing vessels), drifters and trawlers nose in and out alongside the covered fish market.

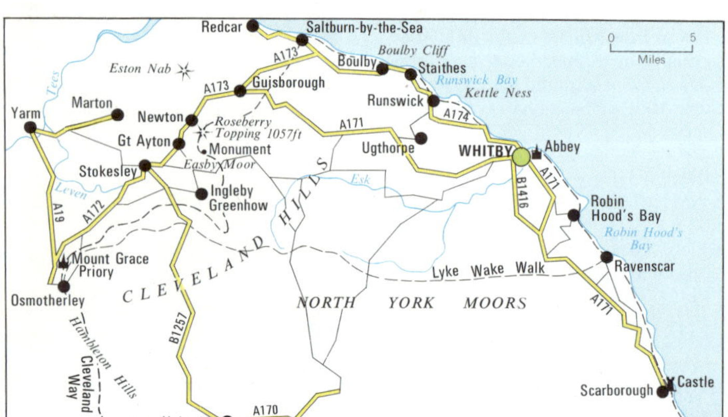

against a background of lofty cliffs

The headland is crowned by Scarborough Castle, a magnificent 12th-century relic, and gulls wheel and scream against the cliffs below. North of the headland, pastel-coloured hotels and boarding houses gaze out across a magnificent bay. The tempo has changed since Anne Brontë spent the last days of her life there—she was buried in the graveyard of St Mary's Church—but the town retains its appeal.

Staithes
Below the newer residential outskirts, the road is a narrow, precipitous coil down to the harbour of this ancient fishing village. Alleyways and steps make a maze of steep corridors between cottages that have become popular with weekend visitors. But there are still fishermen and nets, and exquisite views of cliffs dropping sheer into the sea. James Cook, employed here as a grocer's apprentice, lived in a pink cottage by the harbour, but the original shop has long since been washed away. Cowber Lane leads to England's highest perpendicular cliff, 700-ft Boulby Cliff, 2 miles west.

Stokesley
An attractive little market town on the River Leven. The tower and chancel of the church are 14th century, but the nave was rebuilt in 1771. Ingleby Greenhow, 5 miles south-east, has a Georgian church incorporating Norman fragments, with realistic animal carvings on the pillars of the nave.

Whitby
Colour, light, sound and smell are woven into the bright fabric of this fishing port and seaside resort. Above the town, on the high headland over the Esk, are the jagged sandstone ruins of Whitby Abbey. The first abbey at Whitby was founded in AD 657 by St Hilda on land given by Oswy, King of Northumbria, in thanksgiving for victory against the pagan King Penda of Mercia. It was at the Synod of Whitby, in AD 663, that the divided church in England finally accepted the authority and usages of the Roman Church, establishing, among other things, the method of determining the date of Easter. Later the Danes destroyed the abbey and the Normans rebuilt it, but their work, too, has gone; the ruins that stand today are 13th century. In the 7th century the abbey was the home of Caedmon, the first English Christian poet, and a cross commemorating him stands in the nearby St Mary's churchyard.

St Mary's, the parish church, has a Norman tower silhouetted against the open sky above the red roofs and steep alleys of Old Whitby. The approach to the church is by the 199 Church Stairs, giving a gull's eye view over the town.

West of the Esk there are sandy beaches, and along the river the nucleus of the old town crowds together in a jumble of narrow streets, where fishermen still mend their nets and little shops sell craftsmen's wares. On the Esk, the fishing fleets ride the harbour waters, from which William Scoresby (1760–1829), a noted navigator, left for the Arctic whaling grounds. Captain Cook, who sailed in the Whitby-built *Endeavour* in 1768 for Tahiti via Cape Horn, lived in the town as a young man. His house in Grape Lane is marked by a plaque.

Yarm
The Tees circles Yarm in a great loop, and its waters have often invaded the town's streets. Once Yarm was an important port and market town, and cobbled verges still give market-square proportions to the High Street, between a fine array of Georgian façades.

The town's market hall dates from 1710, and on its walls are two lines which mark the highest of the floods which have devastated the town. The first line marks the flood of 1771, when the waters rose about 7 ft. The second line, 4 ft high, dates from 1881.

The symbol of Yarm's great claim to fame is a plaque on the George and Dragon Inn, noting that there, on February 12, 1820, was held the promoters' meeting of the Stockton and Darlington Railway, the first public railway in the world. Shortly afterwards the railway reached Yarm, and the viaduct, which carries it high above the Tees for half a mile, still towers over the little town. From the High Street, Chapel Street leads east down to an octagonal chapel where John Wesley preached, while Church Wynd leads to a part-Norman church.

FISH FROM THE SEA AND JET FROM THE SHORE

The harbour at Whitby is ringed by a fishing village of steep alleyways and hillside cottages. The town that built Captain Cook's *Endeavour* has a modern shipyard which builds fishing boats and pleasure craft. The bracelet decoration (left) is carved from jet, which is still found along the cliffs near Whitby. Jet comes from wood which has been washed out to sea, fossilised and then subjected to the pressure of water and silt. This form of jewellery used to be popular in Victorian times.

SHELL-HIT ABBEY *The gaunt 13th-century ruins of Whitby Abbey stand on a headland. The east façade indicates the vast scale of the original building. Not all the damage is due to decay; in 1914 the abbey was shelled by the German Fleet*

When the Vikings came

Northumbria in the 7th and 8th centuries was a haven of Christian culture, where the arts flourished and men worked and worshipped against a background of security in this life and faith in the life to come. The Venerable Bede, who spent most of his life in a monastery at Jarrow, finished his *Ecclesiastical History* in AD 731, and at Lindisfarne Bishop Eadfrith compiled the richly illuminated *Lindisfarne Gospels*. This Golden Age was brought to a sudden end by the Viking invasion at the close of the 8th century. In 793, a fleet of Viking longships landed at Lindisfarne. 'In this year', states the *Anglo-Saxon Chronicle*, 'terrible portents appeared over Northumbria . . . and a little while after that the harrying of the heathen miserably destroyed God's church in Lindisfarne.'

Despite their spine-chilling reputation and fearsome names—Eric Blood-axe, Ivar the Boneless—these sea-roving Scandinavians brought some benefits. They ravaged the coasts of Europe; but they also founded Normandy, traded as far east as Russia and Baghdad, colonised Iceland and Greenland and discovered America five centuries before Columbus.

NORMAN PRIORY, LINDISFARNE *The monastery founded at Lindisfarne in the 7th century was destroyed by Vikings 200 years later. Later the Normans built this priory. The term Vikings (presumably from the viks or coastal creeks of their homeland) included all the Scandinavians. The first Viking raid on Lindisfarne was carried out by Norwegians, who also descended on Scotland, the northern islands and Ireland. In the 9th century Danish Vikings overwhelmed England's east coast and stayed as settlers. Swedish Vikings traded mostly through Russia (where they were called the Rus) and settled there. Some took part in the last Viking invasion of England in the 11th century*

THE LINDISFARNE GOSPELS *The Bishop of Lindisfarne produced this magnificent book, now in the British Museum, c.* AD *700. The page above shows St Matthew writing his gospel. The monks carried the book with them when they fled from Lindisfarne in 875, fearing another Viking raid. Ten years earlier, a large army of Danish Vikings had landed on the east coast and overrun East Anglia, Mercia and Northumbria. They were checked in Wessex by King Alfred and his Saxons at the battles of Ashdown (870) and Edington (878), after which the area settled by the Vikings, known as Danelaw, was established by treaty in 886. Fortified boroughs marked the Danelaw's frontier*

ST CUTHBERT'S COFFIN *When the monks fled from Lindisfarne, they took with them as many treasures as they could, piling many of them into this coffin containing the body of St Cuthbert, who had been Lindisfarne's bishop in the 7th century. The coffin is now in Durham Cathedral. After years of wandering, the monks finally settled in Durham*

ST CUTHBERT'S CROSS *During the Golden Age of Northumbrian art in the 7th and 8th centuries, a mingling of Celtic, English and European influences led local craftsmen to produce masterpieces such as this cross, now in Durham Cathedral, the* Lindisfarne Gospels *and the writings of the Venerable Bede. The Viking invasions brought the Golden Age to an end*

ENGLAND IN THE VIKING CENTURY

By the end of the 9th century, Anglo-Saxons held Northumberland, English Mercia and Wessex. The area settled by Danish Vikings was called the Danelaw. Viking raids ended when the Normans invaded from the south in 1066

VIKING RELICS *The cross (left) in the church of the Yorkshire village of Middleton dates from the 10th century and shows a Viking warrior laid out in his grave. The 11th-century Danish memorial stone (right) is in London's Guildhall Museum*

THE GOKSTAD SHIP

A typical Viking longship of *c.* AD 900, excavated in 1880 and now in an Oslo museum. It is over 76 ft long, yet its draught is only 3 ft, and its bottom planks are less than an inch thick. A replica sailed the Atlantic in 1893

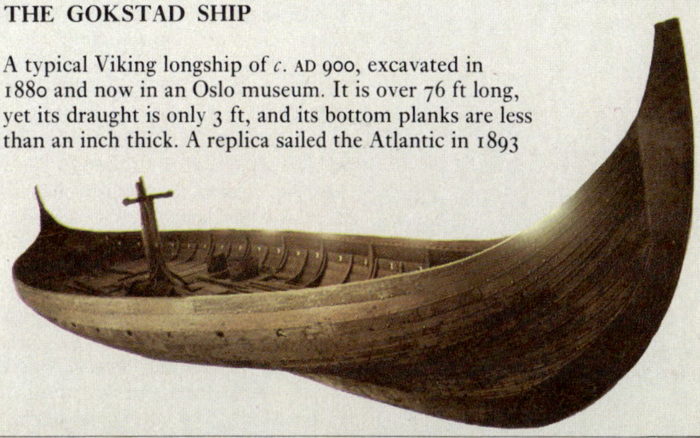

THE LINDISFARNE RAID *On this beach at Lindisfarne the Viking raiders are believed to have landed in* AD *793. The Vikings' ships, superbly functional in design, were the key to their triumphs. Their draught was shallow and they could land on any beach. The earliest raids, like those on Lindisfarne and Jarrow, were summer forays for plunder. But in 851 Danish Vikings wintered on the Isle of Thanet, and soon they had conquered eastern England. After a lull in the 10th century, armies of mercenaries from all over Scandinavia began to descend regularly on England from huge military camps in Denmark*

Industrial heartland around a majestic cathedral

Boating There are sailing clubs at South Shields, Sunderland and Hartlepool and rowing on the River Wear at Durham. Some canoeing from Yarm on the River Tees.

Events Durham has a Miners' Gala in July, a regatta in June and a carnival in Aug. Billingham has an International Folk Festival in Aug.

Places to see *Bishop's Park*, Bishop Auckland: daily. *Darlington Art Gallery*, Crown Street: weekdays. *Darlington Museum*, Tubwell Row: weekdays, except Thur. afternoon. *Durham Castle*: 1st 3 weeks Apr. and July to Sept., weekdays; other months, Mon., Wed., Sat. afternoons. *Durham Cathedral Treasury Museum*: weekdays, Sun. afternoon. *Durham Light Infantry Museum and Arts Centre*, Durham: Tues to Sat., and Sun. afternoon. *Gibside Chapel* (NT) afternoons only: Apr. to Sept., daily except Tues.; Oct. and Mar., Wed., Sat., Sun.; Nov. to Feb., Sun. *Gray Art Gallery and Museum*, Hartlepool: weekdays and Sun. afternoon. *Gulbenkian Museum of Oriental Art*, Durham: weekdays, Sun. afternoon. *Lambton Pleasure Park*, 2 miles north-east of Chester-le-Street: Mar. to Dec., daily. *Maritime Museum*, Hartlepool: weekdays. *North of England Open-Air Museum*, Beamish: daily, except Mon. Sept. to May. *Railway Museum*, North Road Station, Darlington: weekdays; also Sun. afternoon in summer. *Sunderland Museum and Art Gallery*: weekdays, Sun. afternoon. *Washington Old Hall* (NT): afternoons only: Mar. to Oct., daily, except Tues.; Nov. to Feb., Sat. and Sun. *Washington Waterfowl Park*: daily.

Information centre Tourist Information Bureau, 13 Claypath, Durham City. Tel. Durham 3720.

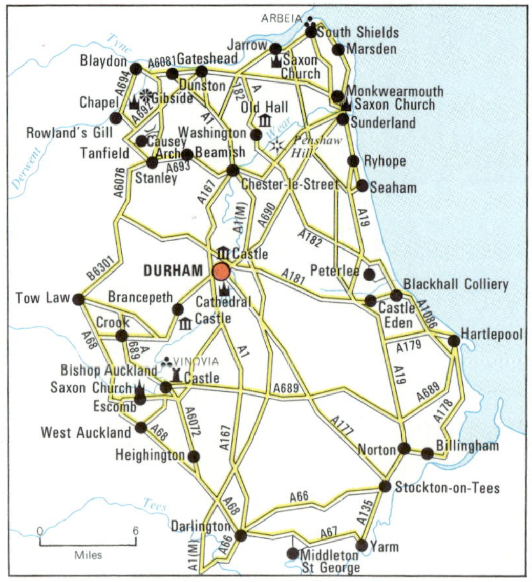

The A1 motorway, which leaves Scotch Corner 8 miles south-west of Darlington and bypasses the city of Durham to the east, separates this region into two distinct parts. Eastwards to the coast is the most heavily populated part of the county. An almost continuous built-up area, which grew with the Industrial Revolution on the heavy industries of ship-building and coal-mining, stretches along the coast from the River Tees to the Tyne estuary.

Yet in places the coastline has long, sandy beaches and low, rocky cliffs, around which seaside resorts have developed. Even though the new towns of Peterlee and Washington are encroaching on what little is left of the unspoilt inland region, the many wooded valleys that line the plateau towards the sea are being preserved as beauty spots.

At the heart of the region is Durham City itself, with its superb cathedral and castle towering proudly over the steep banks of the River Wear. The cathedral is a majestic sight which cannot fail to impress any lover of Britain's heritage.

Bishop Auckland
This town has been the country seat of the Bishops of Durham since the 12th century, and grew up round the gates of their castle, which is still the bishop's official residence. The castle, begun as a Norman manor house, stands in the 150-acre Bishop's Park, east of the town's market-place. The park, which has fine walks, neat lawns, beautiful trees, and two small streams, the Gauntless and Cordon Burn, running through it, is open to the public.

At Escomb, a mile west of Bishop Auckland, the village church is a gem—one of the best-preserved Saxon churches in the country. Its restoration to its original state dates from the 19th century. The big, square pieces of masonry in the lower parts of the walls were taken from the Roman camp of Vinovia, a mile north of Bishop Auckland at Binchester. The church key is at the house opposite the south door.

Causey Arch
A remarkable monument to the early days of mining spans Beamish Burn, a quarter-mile walk from the A6076, signposted just north of Stanley. It is a single-span stone bridge, the first of its kind to be built, dating from 1727. The bridge is 105 ft long, towers 85 ft above the stream and was used by coal wagons from nearby Tanfield. The designer, Ralph Wood, killed himself—for fear, it is said, that his bridge would collapse.

Darlington
This busy, bustling market centre is known as 'the birthplace of the railway'. George Stephenson's early steam engine *Locomotion* is on view on the main platform of Bank Top station. The town has Anglo-Saxon origins, and until the Victorian age of steam and iron was a centre for textile industries.

Heighington, 5 miles north-west, is perched on an escarpment 450 ft high and has a square, spacious village green—unusual in a county noted for its long, rectangular greens.

Durham
Here is one of the most visually attractive cities in Britain—a medieval treasure on the winding River Wear. The cathedral was begun in 1093 by Bishop William of Calais. It became a shrine for the body of St Cuthbert, whose tomb is still there. The Norman part of the building was completed by 1133.

It was the first church to use ribbed vaulting on a large scale, and has many other outstanding features—a richly ornamented interior, a magnificent screen behind the high altar, interesting tombs (including that of the Venerable Bede), 8th-century illuminated manuscripts, a 12th-century brass door-knocker that was used by law-breakers seeking sanctuary inside, and round pillars 27 ft high and nearly 7 ft in diameter. During the days of the Civil War, the Puritans used the cathedral to hold Scottish prisoners.

Durham Castle, built *c.* 1070, stands, like the cathedral, on the narrow neck of land that once guarded the approach to the city; it was originally the site of a Saxon church founded in AD 995. Around the cathedral and castle has grown the university, which now occupies most of the buildings in the old city centre, including the castle. The castle

DURHAM *The Norman cathedral stands on a 70 ft high rock surrounded on three sides by the River Wear*

GRITSTONE HOUSE

Many houses were built from Durham gritstone during the Industrial Revolution. The hard-wearing sandstone was also used to restore Durham Cathedral

BUSY TYNESIDE *Freighters crowd through the waters of the Tyne as they bring cargoes of iron ore to the cranes at South Shields. The docks stretch along 3 miles of waterfront*

is, however, still open to the public. Among the many modern buildings beyond the city walls is Dunelm House, the university students' union building which has become one of the city's showpieces. Beyond this building, the A690 leads eastwards past the Durham top-security jail to the old racecourse by the river, now a sports ground. Here, for one day every July, the area echoes from early dawn until late into the night to the sounds of brass bands and revelry, as members of miners' lodges throughout the county meet for the world-famous Durham Miners' Gala.

The trim village of Brancepeth, 4 miles south-west of Durham on the A690, is overshadowed by its reconstructed 12th-century castle, which is privately owned. A public footpath leads by the castle walls to the 13th-century Church of St Brandon, which is full of magnificent woodwork—carved pews, pulpit, altar rails and panelling.

Gibside

On the slopes of the River Derwent, 3 miles from its junction with the Tyne, is the Gibside Estate, one of the finest examples of Georgian landscaping in the county, carried out by Capability Brown. The estate, with its fine chapel, can be reached from the B6314 between Rowland's Gill and the A692.

Marsden

The short coastline of Tyne and Wear has a glorious stretch of sea shore, and a cliff walk at Marsden Bay looks down on caves and arches that have been carved out of the cliffs by the continuous pounding of the seas. Just offshore is Marsden Rock, a huge limestone mass cut by an archway under which boats can pass at high tide. The rock and the cliff ledges are nesting places for cormorants, kittiwakes, fulmars and gulls.

South Shields

This port at the eastern extremity of industrial Tyneside has extraordinary contrasts. On one side are the quays, warehouses and factories of its industrial life; on the other, attractive gardens and promenades provide holiday attractions. North of the town are the ruins of the Roman fort of Arbeia, built to guard the supply routes for the legions on the Roman Wall.

At Jarrow, 2½ miles west, the mainly Saxon St Paul's Church stands near the south entrance to the new Tyne tunnel. The church is part of the monastery where the Venerable Bede (673–735), historian and scholar, wrote his history of the English Church.

JARROW *St Paul's Church has relics of the Venerable Bede, who wrote his history of the Church at Jarrow Monastery*

Stockton-on-Tees

Now part of Teesside, this town has the broadest High Street in England where, every Wednesday and Saturday, an open-air market is held. In 1827, John Walker, a Stockton chemist, invented friction matches and sold them from his shop for two years before others exploited his idea commercially. Sir Christopher Wren helped to design the Church of St Thomas, completed in 1712.

Norton, to the north of Teesside, is an attractive village. The Church of St Mary has surviving Saxon tower arches and windows, and 14th-century effigies of a lady and knight.

Sunderland

Towering shipyard cranes compete with new blocks of offices and flats for the domination of the skyline around the town—the biggest in Tyne and Wear. The town is still largely dependent on the traditional industries of shipbuilding and coal-mining, whose boom days at the beginning of the century are nostalgically recalled in the fading façades of many old music halls around the town centre, which is itself surrounded with new building developments.

'LOCOMOTION' *Stephenson's early steam engine stands in Bank Top station at Darlington, the 'birthplace of the railway'*

North of the River Wear, at Monkwearmouth, is the magnificent Saxon relic of St Peter's Church, founded by Benedict Biscop in AD 674. Biscop was an Anglican nobleman who is believed to have been the first person to use glass windows and stone edifices in the construction of churches. He also founded St Paul's at Jarrow in AD 682. These two monasteries were the home of 600 monks.

At Ryhope, a little to the south, there is a splendid walk along a footpath on the cliffs, though it should be followed with care as the cliffs are rather crumbly.

Eight miles south, at Blackhall Colliery, miners' houses have a slate set in the wall by the front door. On this, the occupier would chalk up the time of the shift he was working so that the knocker-up would wake him on time.

Washington

Ancestors of George Washington lived in the 17th-century Washington Old Hall, which has been beautifully restored with the help of American funds. The village in which it is situated is now part of the new town of Washington which is planned to have a total population of some 80,000.

Penshaw Hill, 2 miles south-east, is worth visiting for the view of the surrounding coalfields. The hill is recalled in the Durham folk song about the Lambton worm which, says the song:

'. . . lapped his tail
Ten times round Penshaw Hill'.

High waterfalls of the west Durham moors

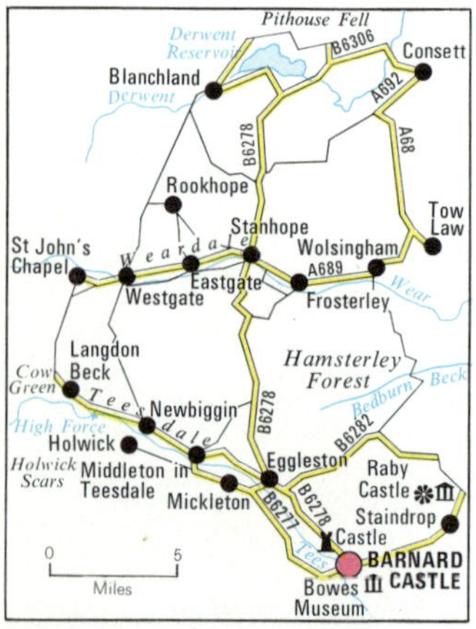

Some of the finest and most rugged scenery along the entire Pennine Chain is to be seen on the west Durham moors, which attract an increasing number of visitors each year. Motorists, hikers, skiers, campers—all come to the moors, prepared to brave weather which can be among the most hostile of any in England. Heavy rains in summer and fierce snowstorms in winter are carried by clouds that gather angrily over the high ridge of the Pennines to the west of the moors.

The moors are on a high tableland, rising to more than 2000 ft towards the west where they meet the striking fells of eastern Cumbria. The flat terrain and the wet climate combine to produce large areas of peaty, ill-drained moorland—conditions that can mean hard work for the ordinary walker, but which are ideally suited for providing water supplies. This explains the many reservoirs and dramatic waterfalls in the area.

Today's travellers will see evidence throughout the region—particularly in the south-east corner—of earlier adventurers who challenged the elements in their search for the coal, lead, silver and zinc that once lay rich in the limestone. Miners' cottages stand derelict; mining towns and villages are perched on nearly every hill, isolated from one another by steep slopes and difficult roads.

Most of the coal is now worked out and many settlements have the appearance of a dying past. But the picture for the visitor is far from grim. The older and more enduring fabric of rural life survives to delight the eye in farms and villages.

Rambling A Ramblers' Club at Barnard Castle organises walks.

Skiing Ski tows in Weardale and Teesdale are operated in the winter by Weardale and Teesdale Ski Clubs.

Sailing There is a sailing club on Derwent Reservoir.

Angling There is good trout fishing on several reservoirs in Upper Teesdale. A small stretch of the Tees at Barnard Castle is available to anglers. The River Wear is mostly preserved.

Pony trekking Stables and tuition at Middleton in Teesdale.

Events Stanhope Agricultural Society Show is held at Unthank Park, Stanhope, in early Sept. Weardale Agricultural Society Show and Fair is held at Vicarage Field, St John's Chapel, at the end of Aug. Wolsingham Agricultural Show and Fair, and Eggleston Agricultural Show, both take place in early Sept. The Whitsun Meet, at Demesnes Ground, Barnard Castle, on the Spring Bank Hol. includes a carnival and fair. A livestock and general market takes place at Barnard Castle every Wed. There is an Annual Exhibition and Show in Belle Vue Grounds, Consett, in early Aug.

Places to see *Barnard Castle*: daily, except Sun. mornings Oct. to Mar. *Bowes Museum*, Barnard Castle: weekdays and Sun. afternoons. *Old Lead Mines*, Killhope Burn, 6 miles north-west of St John's Chapel: daily. *Old Mill Wheel*, Killhope Burn, a water-mill with restored wheel: daily. *Raby Castle*: afternoons only; Easter weekend; mid-Apr. to late June, Wed. and Sun.; July to mid-Sept., Mon. to Fri.

Information centre Teesdale District Council, Galgate, Barnard Castle. Tel. Barnard Castle 38481.

Barnard Castle
A market town that is a useful base for exploring the upper dales of west Durham. The castle, now in ruins, guarded a crossing point on the River Tees and was rebuilt in 1112 by Bernard Baliol, ancestor of the founder of Balliol College, Oxford. The town has one of the best museums in the county—Bowes Museum, housed in an impressive mansion built in 1869 in the style of a French château. It has an excellent collection of paintings and European art, and one room is devoted to showing life in the district during earlier centuries.

At Mickleton, 6 miles north-west, visitors can see one of the results of this earlier way of life. A lay-by on the B6277 opposite the village gives a view over the long, narrow patterns of the surrounding fields which are the result of medieval strip cultivation. When low, the sun throws shadows across the fields, and the ridges made by teams of oxen pulling the plough can be easily seen.

Blanchland
Set on the River Derwent, this spot fully justifies its claim to be one of England's unspoilt villages. The village was planned in the early 18th century, and the building of its cottages followed the ground plan of monastic buildings founded in the 12th century by the White Canons, so named after the colour of the habits they wore. The church, gatehouse and monastic storehouse (now an inn) enclose a broad paved square. To ensure that the tranquillity of the setting is not spoilt, a car park has been built, restricting motorists to an area outside the monastic enclosure.

HIGH FORCE *The spectacular moorland waterfall drops 70 ft over steep cliffs, called the Great Whin Sill escarpment, in upper Teesdale. The falls, known to freeze in hard winters, are seen at their best after rain; a path from them leads on to the moors*

Consett
The panorama of the town's ironworks—a fascinating silhouette of chimneys, towers and smelters—is as impressive in its own stark way as the skyline of a battlemented city. The best view is from the A68 where the road rises north of the village of Tow Law. Iron has been smelted in the town since the 1840's, and more than a million tons of steel are now produced each year.

Derwent Reservoir
This 3½ mile long reservoir caters for anglers and yachtsmen as well as providing water supplies. There are a number of picnic sites and lay-bys. The best view of the reservoir is from the brow of the hill on Pithouse Fell, 3 miles north-east of Blanchland on the steep B6306 as it climbs towards Hexham.

At the bend of the road at Pithouse Fell there is a large quarry, where the weathering and iron-staining has made attractive patterns on the rock face.

Frosterley
This village has associations with almost every church in County Durham. From its quarries comes Frosterley marble, which polishes into a beautiful black marble, ingrained with small white fossil circles; it has been used for centuries for fonts, tombs and pillars in churches and cathedrals all over the world. There is an excellent example in St Michael's Church at Frosterley, built in 1866.

Hamsterley Forest
Routes have been laid out for motorists and for walkers to encourage them to explore this 5000-acre forest, one of the largest Forestry Commission areas in County Durham. Car parks and picnic spots are set in the open fields alongside Bedburn Beck. The timber from the spruce, pine, larch and hemlock trees is marketed for paper, chipboard, fencing and pit-props.

RABY CASTLE *The castle, near Staindrop, built by the Nevilles in the 14th century, had a hall in which 700 knights could meet. It was altered in 1765 and in the 19th century*

High Force

A footpath signposted opposite the High Force Hotel on the B6277 leads through pine and beech woodland to this 70-ft waterfall, one of the most celebrated features of rugged upper Teesdale. From the falls, a steep path leads to the top, where the scenery changes to bleak, open moorland.

Caldron Snout, 4 miles west, is the highest waterfall in England. Its tumbling Tees waters are a spectacular sight —a great cascade dropping 200 ft down a 450-ft staircase of rocks. In its wild setting it is a harder spot to reach than High Force, involving a 2½-mile drive along the side-road off the B6277 at Langdon Beck and a further mile walk.

The route passes the new Cow Green Reservoir where a nature trail has been laid out for visitors to examine some of the rarest alpine plants in the country. Throughout these regions it is advisable to wear warm clothing. The fells reach heights of more than 2000 ft and can be very cold even in mid-summer.

Middleton in Teesdale

This attractive town, set on the steep hillside above the River Tees, is an ideal centre for visiting the High Force and Caldron Snout waterfalls and the Durham Moors above them. From the late 17th century, Middleton was the centre of the district's lead mining, but most of the town's mining activity had ceased some 200 years later. Today, large quarries that can be seen westwards across the valley on Holwick Scars provide a hard rock used particularly in road building.

Staindrop

The unusually long rectangular village green is typical of mid-Durham. These greens are believed to have been extended over the years as land occupied by squatters' cottages was subsequently added to the original green.

At West Auckland, 5 miles north-east, is an even larger green dominated by a fine Tudor mansion.

Before reaching West Auckland, the A688 follows the eastern boundary of the ancient deer park of Raby Castle. From the road there is a view of deer over the stone wall, and several lay-bys have been provided for motorists. The moated and battlemented castle itself is mainly 14th century but with 18th and 19th-century alterations, and is open to the public on certain days during the summer months.

Stanhope

The giant stump of a fossilised tree that grew more than 250 million years ago stands by the churchyard wall as a monument to the origins of the village's former busy coal-mining life. The tree stump, 7 ft high, was removed in 1964 from a quarry near the village.

Stanhope is now a quiet holiday haven, set high in the moorland, and an excellent centre for walking. Footpaths lead to open moorland in all directions, and among the pleasant riverside walks is one leading to a medieval bridge a mile upstream.

At Rookhope to the north-west, the numerous disused lime quarries and kilns show the mining landscape as it used to be in the 19th century, when lead and silver were being mined. The mineral now being worked is fluorspar, used in smelting processes.

INDUSTRY AT CONSETT *The smoking chimneys of huge ironworks and steelworks form a dramatic background on the hills above Consett. The town, at 880 ft the highest in Durham, stands on the Derwent, and has been a centre of the iron industry since 1840*

FOSSILISED TREE *The tree stump in Stanhope churchyard, found in a local quarry, is more than 250 million years old*

Man-made forests on the Northumberland border

Boating Some canoeing and rowing at Hexham; sailing on Greenlee Lough and on Derwent Reservoir, 9 miles south-east of Hexham.

Angling Trout and coarse fishing on the River Tyne (some stretches are restricted). Trout, salmon and coarse fishing on the River North Tyne; on the River South Tyne, trout and occasional late salmon. Trout and a few grayling in the River Derwent. Trout in Derwent Reservoir and at Allendale Town in the River East Allen.

Nature trails At Lewisburn, Kielder, and Stonehaugh, 4 miles west of Wark.

Events The 'Baal' Fire Festival to celebrate the end of the old year is held at Allendale Town on Dec. 31. Bellingham has an Agricultural Show on the last Sat. in Aug.

Places to see *Border Forest Museum*, Kielder Castle, Kielder: weekdays and Sun. afternoons, Easter to Sept. *Chesters Museum*, Chollerton, Roman relics, fort and bath-house, and *Corstopitum Camp and Museum*, Corbridge, Roman tools and the Corbridge Lion sculpture: both daily, except Sun. mornings Oct. to Mar. *Housesteads Roman Fort and Museum* (NT): daily, except Sun. mornings Oct. to Mar. *Langley Castle*, Hexham: daily. *National Tractor and Farm Museum*, West Side, Newton, 3 miles east of Corbridge: Apr. to Sept., daily.

Information centres Manor Office, Hallgates, Hexham. Tel. Hexham 5225. National Park Information Centre, Once Brewed, Military Road, Bardon Mill (Easter to Oct. only). Tel. Bardon Mill 396.

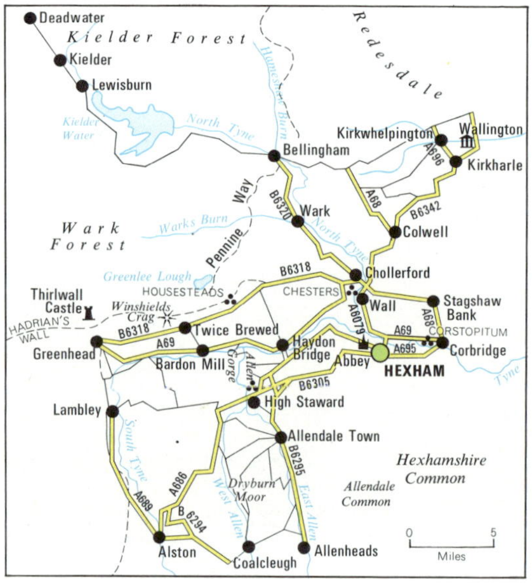

The Northumberland National Park, stretching north from Hadrian's Wall towards the Cheviot Hills, is one of the great remaining open spaces of Britain, covering nearly 400 square miles of high hills and open moorland. The park is bounded to the west by the 200 square miles of the Border Forest Park.

Kielder Forest, the largest of three separate forests forming the Border Forest Park, has been developed on land that 50 years ago was nothing more than barren moorland. Camping and picnic sites have been set up by the Forestry Commission and National Park authorities for visitors who come to enjoy the scenery.

From Roman times onwards, the dales south of Hadrian's Wall were explored by miners searching for lead, zinc and silver, and old mine shafts and derelict cottages can still be seen. Today, the area is becoming a popular playground for skiing enthusiasts.

For the walker, too, this is ideal country. It has the largest area of open moorland in the county at Allendale Common and contains the longest unbroken stretch of Hadrian's Wall.

Allendale Town

Once the centre of an important lead-mining area and now popular among trout fishermen and, in winter, skiers. It is perched on a steep cliff, 1400 ft above sea level, over the River East Allen, and the riverside walk below the town passes the mouth of the Beaumont Level, a large tunnel which was once the entrance to a lead mine.

The town celebrates the end of the old year with a ceremony dating back to pagan times during which men carry barrels of blazing tar on their heads to a bonfire in the market place.

The lanes to Hexhamshire Common offer excellent walks. Some are the original routes used to take lead ore by packhorse to smelters on Tyneside.

Around Coalcleugh, 8 miles south at the south-western extremity of the county, and at Allenheads, lies evidence of the former lead and coal-mining industries—derelict mines, tumbledown cottages and small farms that used to be leased out to the miners.

Allen Gorge

Steep banks, 250 ft high and covered with trees and sheltered riverside pathways, make this a magnificent place to explore. The best access point on the north side is from the minor road off the A69, 3 miles west of Haydon Bridge. The roads are steep and car parking is limited; but the scenery is worth the effort.

On the south side there is room to park by a disused railway station at High Staward on the A686, 8 miles south-west of Hexham. A footpath leads north for a mile, plunging into thick woodland with steep drops on either side, to the ruin of the Staward pele tower. Ahead is the route it once guarded—4 miles of the Allen Gorge, a majestic sight in any season and almost Alpine when cloaked in winter's snow.

Bellingham

A small market town that once had a thriving and reputable iron industry. Some of its metalwork was used in building the Tyne Bridge. A track to the north follows Hareshaw Burn to the foot of a waterfall at Hareshaw Linn. St Cuthbert's Well, reached by a path behind the churchyard, is said to have healing powers. The Pennine Way can be joined at Bellingham youth hostel.

Chesters

One of the great forts of the Roman wall occupies more than 5 acres in the grounds of an 18th-century mansion. It was the headquarters for a 500-strong cavalry regiment and has the remains of barracks, stables, the commandant's house and a regimental bath-house.

At Wall, a mile to the south, are fine examples of yeomen's houses with dates, religious inscriptions and the owners' initials carved in the lintels—a typical feature of building work carried out in the area in the 1640's.

A favourite picnic spot for motorists is Stagshaw Bank Common, 4 miles to the east, where the main A68 crosses General Wade's military road.

Corbridge

An attractive resort on the Tyne, 3 miles east of Hexham and near the Roman

ABBEY CARVINGS *Stone caricatures decorate the 15th-century Leschman Chantry in Hexham Abbey. They are thought to have been carved by students of Prior Leschman*

DESOLATE MINE *South of Bardon Mill is the chimney of an abandoned lead mine*

RAINBOW OVER REDESDALE *Spruce trees are a carefully controlled cash crop in Redesdale Forest, part of the Border Forest Park which forms Britain's largest area of woodland*

town of Corstopitum. St Andrew's Church has a fine Saxon tower and, inside, a Roman arch. A well-preserved example of a pele (peal) tower stands in the churchyard. These Border towers date from the 14th century and provided refuge from bands of marauding Scots.

Hexham

A centre both for visitors exploring the dales of south and west Northumberland and for local farmers. Sheep and cattle are brought from all parts of the North to the stockyards. In addition to Hexham Abbey, there is a 15th-century Moot Hall, or council chamber, and one of the finest open spaces in any town centre at The Seal—originally a monastic enclosure but now a public park.

A fine crypt is all that remains of a church completed in AD 678. A Saxon throne, or frith stool, in the chancel marks the centre of what used to be a circle of medieval sanctuary. It had a radius of a mile, within which fugitives from justice could claim the protection of the Church against civil authority. The church standing now was begun in the 11th century, and a massive staircase in the south transept once led to the monks' dormitory. The ornaments include Bishop Acca's Cross (AD 740).

Kielder Forest

The Forestry Commission has planted trees since the 1920's throughout more than 145,000 acres of what was once barren moorland. The spruce, larch, Scots pine and lodgepole pine are grown to supply timber for industry. They also provide shelter for roe deer, badgers, otters, red squirrels and foxes.

There are nature trails and tracks through the forest, and a 12-mile forest drive starts at Kielder.

Kirkharle

The mansions and parklands at Capheaton Hall and Wallington provide a gentle contrast to the solemn splendours of much of the county. The hamlet was the birthplace of Capability Brown, the landscape gardener, and some of his first attempts at turning untamed nature into a more gracious beauty were made in this area. A fine example of his work is at Wallington, a mile north-east of Kirkharle.

Kirkwhelpington, 2 miles north-west, is a small, compact village dominated by a mainly 13th-century church. There are pleasant walks from the village along the River Wansbeck. Charles Parsons, who invented the steam turbine, is buried in the village churchyard.

Twice Brewed

Of all the viewpoints along the Roman wall this is one of the most spectacular —and ideal for motorists. A car park on nearby Winshields Crag is right on the line of the wall so that visitors can easily explore the magnificent 3-mile stretch of desolate and rugged country leading east to Housesteads, where the remains of a Roman fort are considered to be the finest on the wall. The fort was built as a clifftop garrison for 1000 infantry. Outside the camp are the foundations of a large civil settlement.

FIRE FESTIVAL *On New Year's Eve the men of Allendale Town carry tubs of blazing tar to a bonfire in a ceremony dating back to pagan times which signals the end of the Old Year*

The changing face of bustling Tyneside

Boating There are sailing centres at Tynemouth, Blyth and Newbiggin-by-the-Sea, 2½ miles south of Lynemouth.

Angling A sea-angling festival is held at Whitley Bay in autumn, and an open championship at Tynemouth in Jan. Coarse fishing on the Rivers Wansbeck and Blyth.

Events The Newcastle Festival is held in Oct., and the Whitley Bay Drama Festival at the Priory Theatre in Apr. The Northumbrian Festival is at Morpeth in Apr., and the Highland Games at the Castle Ward Sports Centre, Ponteland, in June. Riding the Borough Boundaries takes place at Morpeth in Apr., and Walking the Bounds at Newbiggin-by-the-Sea in May.

Places to see Newcastle: *Bagpipe Museum*: Wed. to Sat. afternoons. *Keep Museum*: weekdays, except Mon. morning. *Laing Art Gallery*: weekdays and Sun. afternoon. *Plummer Tower*: weekdays. *Science Museum*: weekdays, Sun. afternoon. Newcastle University: *Hancock Museum*: weekdays and Sun. afternoon, Easter to Sept. *Hatton Gallery*: weekdays. *Greek Museum*: Mon. to Fri. *Museum of Antiquities*: weekdays. *Museum of Department of Mining Engineering*: Mon. to Fri. *Seaton Delaval Hall*, Seaton Delaval: May to Sept., Sun., Wed. and Bank Hol. afternoons.

Information centres Northumbria Tourist Board, Prudential Building, Pilgrim Street, Newcastle upon Tyne. Tel. Newcastle upon Tyne 28795. City Information Service, Princess Square, Newcastle upon Tyne. Tel. Newcastle upon Tyne 610691.

SEATON SLUICE *Channels were cut 60 ft into rock to make the harbour*

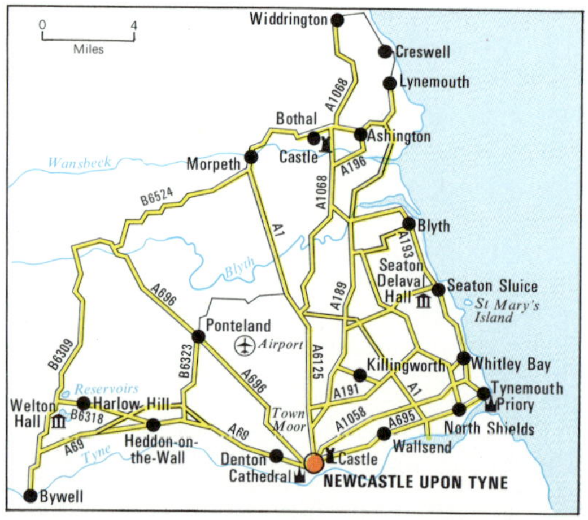

Much of the skyline of south-east Northumberland and Tyne and Wear is outlined with the symbols of the coal, iron and steel that made this region the centre of Britain's industrial greatness. Yet the landscape is predominantly rural and within sight of the collieries, with their rows of miners' houses, pit heaps and winding gear, are green pasturelands, farms and villages. The coastline has stretches of beaches that are among the finest in the country.

Today, the old industrial scars are disappearing as this corner of north-east England faces the challenge of modern industry. Elegant new housing estates and bright modern factories are rising where soot and grime once flourished. Dominating the region and leading the change is the great northern capital of Newcastle upon Tyne which, from humble beginnings as a Roman frontier station at a river crossing, has grown into a city with a population of more than a quarter of a million. Its bustling commercial life, its culture and, in places, the supreme dignity of its streets, attract visitors from all over the country. The Tyneside shipyards are world-famous.

Newcastle's ambitious rebuilding schemes now under way include a dramatic redevelopment of the city centre with flyover roads, shopping walkways linked by escalators, and new centres for cultural activities. In fashioning its future, Newcastle is determined to be rid of the cloth-cap image of its past.

VANBRUGH'S MASTERPIECE *A horse grazes in the grounds of Seaton Delaval Hall, a baroque 18th-century house regarded as one of Sir John Vanbrugh's finest works*

Ashington
This town, with a population of 26,000, was at one time known as the biggest mining 'village' in the world, but there are now modern estates where rows of miners' houses once stood. The centres of social life are still the working-men's clubs, which are notable for the impressive facades of their buildings. Despite the mainly industrial scene, the area is not without its beauty, particularly to the south along the banks of the River Wansbeck. Ashington is famous for its footballers, among them Bobby and Jack Charlton, who were born there and are the only brothers to have played together in an English international side.

Bothal, 2 miles west, is a pretty hamlet in a wooded gorge of the river, with a 14th-century castle and church.

Bywell
One of the most attractive of the many lovely villages on the edge of the coalfield area. In the 16th century, Bywell was a centre for ironwork. All that remains today are a few cottages, a market cross, a fortified manor house and two magnificent churches. St Peter's, originally Saxon, was once called the 'black' church, and 11th-century St Andrew's the 'white', because of the colour of the habits of the monks who founded them.

Killingworth
A central feature of this new town is a lake which has been thoughtfully adapted from an old coal 'flash'—a section of badly drained land caused through subsidence—for use as a sailing

TYNE CROSSINGS *Newcastle's five Tyne bridges are, from the top, the New Tyne Bridge (1928), Stephenson's two-tier High-Level Bridge (1849), the King Edward railway bridge (1906), Redheugh Bridge (1901) and the swing bridge (1876)*

centre. Many of the town's buildings have won awards for design. On the main road near the south entrance to the town is Dial Cottage, home of the railway pioneer George Stephenson, when he was brakesman and engineer at a nearby pit in the early 1800's.

Lynemouth

At the Creswell end of Druridge beach at Lynemouth, the winter gales sometimes expose the stumps of fossilised trees, still standing upright in the cliffs among the layers of sands and muds which swept over the primeval forests, making the coalfields. The nearby coal mine, which exploits seams stretching far out beneath the North Sea, is one of the most up-to-date mines of its kind in the country.

Morpeth

This busy market town, on a loop of the River Wansbeck, is a gateway to the moors, hills and coast. The town hall was designed by Sir John Vanbrugh in 1714, and an unusual 15th-century clock tower was once the town jail. The clock still strikes the curfew. There are a number of bridges crossing the river, as well as a path formed of stepping-stones, leading to pleasant riverside walks. A huge battlemented tower alongside the main A1 road is often confused by visitors with the town's Norman castle. The tower is, in fact, a police station, while the castle, now a private residence, is on a hill above the river.

Newcastle upon Tyne

Routes into the city by road and rail provide two contrasting views of this industrial and commercial centre of the North-East—one modern, one ancient. The main road route, over the New Tyne Bridge, is dominated by a towering office block, while railway passengers over Stephenson's High-Level Bridge see the massive 82 ft keep of the Norman Castle, built in 1172.

One of the best starting-points for exploring the city is the quayside. Steep flights of narrow steps between 17th-century timber warehouses lead into the castle enclosure, the keep and the Black Gate, built *c.* 1247. Beyond, at the junction of the market streets of Bigg Market, Cloth Market and Groat Market, is the medieval Church of St Nicholas, the fourth-largest parish church in England until it became a cathedral in 1882. Its spires, pinnacles and graceful lantern-tower make it an outstanding landmark.

In Victorian times Newcastle was given one of the finest town centres in England. This was due to the vision and enterprise of a builder, Richard Grainger, an architect, John Dobson, and John Clayton, the town clerk, who cleared away the congested centre of the city in the 1830's and built the graceful, broad throughfares of Grey Street and Grainger Street. It was Dobson who designed the impressive Central Railway Station, opened by Queen Victoria in 1850, which covers 17 acres and has 2 miles of platforms.

Equally impressive are the rebuilding projects being carried out today. The busy heart of the city, running from a magnificent new civic centre and the university to the old town hall, has supermarkets, multiple stores, cinemas, night clubs, a new library and the Laing Art Gallery.

For the outdoor enthusiast, the city has almost 1400 acres of open spaces, including the vast expanse of Town Moor to the north-west and the park of Jesmond Dene to the north-east. The surviving stretches of Hadrian's Wall, which once snaked 73 miles across the width of England, start in the outskirts of the city at Denton on the A69.

Ponteland

A fortified manor house in the village is now the Blackbird Inn, a name derived from the emblem of martlets that belonged to the de Valence family, lords of the manor in medieval times. Drinks are served in a tunnel-vaulted basement which is more than 600 years old and has a magnificent fireplace and a stone staircase leading down to it.

Seaton Sluice

Coal was once shipped from this charming little harbour, which took its name from a sluice built to clear sand deposited by the tides. The harbour was first built in the late 17th century by Sir Ralph Delaval, and improved in the 1750's. One mile inland is Seaton Delaval Hall, which was designed by Vanbrugh for the Delaval family in 1720.

Tynemouth

Beyond the broad High Street of fine 18th-century houses lie a moat and a ruined gateway leading into the remains of a priory. It was founded in the 11th and 12th centuries by Benedictines on the site of a 7th-century Anglo-Saxon monastery destroyed by the Danes in AD 865. The surviving ruins date from the 11th and 14th centuries. From the priory there are impressive views of the Tyne Estuary and the coastline, with its fine, sandy beaches.

Steep banks lining the River Tyne near North Shields provide excellent vantage points for viewing the busy river life and shipyards. The best view of the trawler fleets is obtained from near the High Light beacon.

Whitley Bay, 2 miles north of Tynemouth, is Tyneside's most popular seaside resort with fine sandy beaches, impressive hotels, a huge amusement park and facilities for golf, boating, swimming and sea fishing.

There is a pleasant walk along a causeway at the north end of the bay at low tide to St Mary's Island, which has quaint cottages, a lighthouse and small, rocky bays.

Wallsend

As its name implies, the town was the original eastern terminus of Hadrian's Wall. The liner *Mauretania*, which for 22 years held the record for the Atlantic crossing, was launched here in 1907.

Welton Hall

One of the finest farm groups in the county is situated just off the B6318, near the reservoirs west of Harlow Hill. Large barns and byres are built around an impressive 15th-century stone tower, beside the 17th-century manor house.

GOOD OLD DAYS *Music hall has been revived at Newcastle's Balmbras Theatre*

HADRIAN'S WALL

Hadrian, Roman Emperor AD 117–138, came to Britain in 122

The ruins of Hadrian's Wall form the most spectacular relic of Roman Britain. The mighty wall ran across the width of northern England for 73 miles, from Wallsend, near Newcastle upon Tyne, to Bowness-on-Solway on the Solway Firth. Its main purpose was to mark and protect the northern frontier of Rome's British province, and the north-west boundary of her Empire. The surviving portions, some nearly 14 ft high and made of great square stones, make an unforgettable impression as they undulate over the craggy spine of Britain, punctuated by the ruins of turrets, milecastles and forts, and paralleled by traces of ditches in front and behind. The wall, originally 15 ft high and topped by 6-ft battlements, was begun by Roman soldiers *c.* AD 120 by order of the Emperor Hadrian, and was manned largely by non-Romans recruited from all over the Empire. It was abandoned in 383

CARVINGS *Cloaked figures on a stone slab from Housesteads Fort are believed to depict either deities or local tribesmen*

LIFE IN A FORT *The remains of the buildings where grain was stored can be seen at Housesteads Fort, one of 17 big forts placed every 3–7 miles along the wall as quarters for the troops. Most forts were oblong in shape, with rounded corners. The central area was occupied by granaries, workshops and a headquarters building which included a place of worship. On either side of this section were stables and barrack blocks, each block housing a company of about 80 infantry or two 32-strong cavalry units. Inside, six or eight soldiers occupied a pair of rooms—an inner dormitory and a living-room fronting on to a veranda, under which the troops did their cooking. There were separate quarters for officers at the end of the block. The forts, whose garrisons varied in size from 500 infantry at Drumburgh to 1000 cavalry at Stanwix, were usually crossed by two main streets. Outside the ramparts were settlements of native huts, occupied by traders and camp-followers*

THE BUILDERS *An inscription from the fort at High Rochester, 16 miles north of Chesters, records the Roman builders' work*

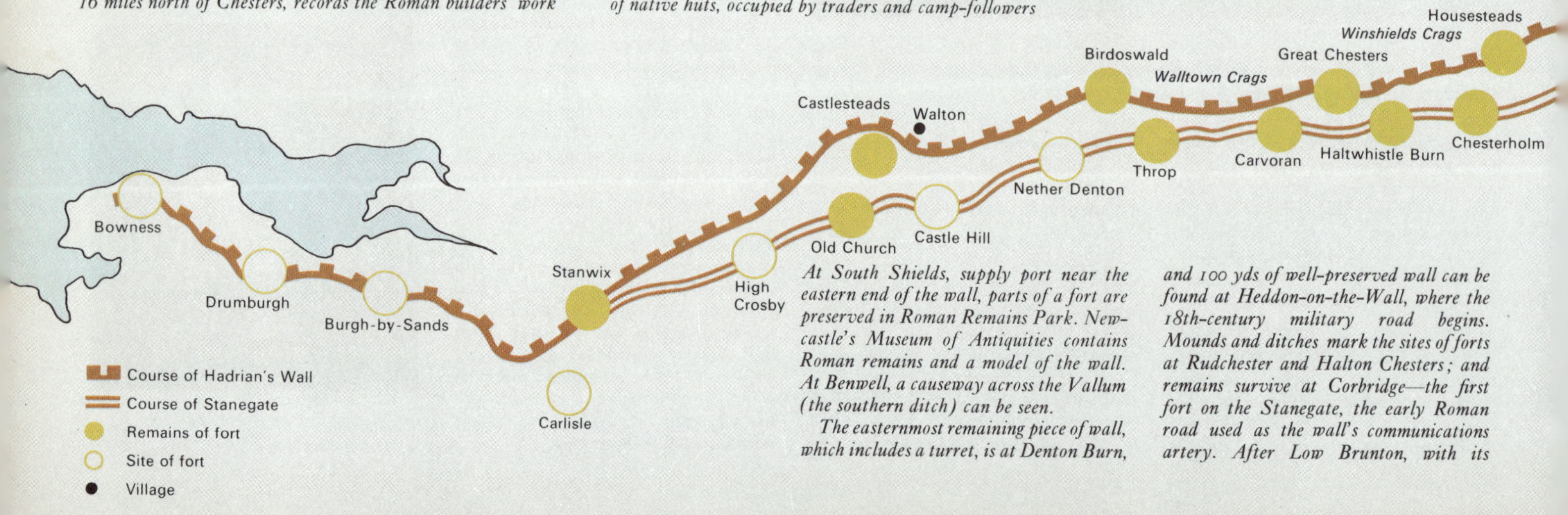

At South Shields, supply port near the eastern end of the wall, parts of a fort are preserved in Roman Remains Park. Newcastle's Museum of Antiquities contains Roman remains and a model of the wall. At Benwell, a causeway across the Vallum (the southern ditch) can be seen.

The easternmost remaining piece of wall, which includes a turret, is at Denton Burn, and 100 yds of well-preserved wall can be found at Heddon-on-the-Wall, where the 18th-century military road begins. Mounds and ditches mark the sites of forts at Rudchester and Halton Chesters; and remains survive at Corbridge—the first fort on the Stanegate, the early Roman road used as the wall's communications artery. After Low Brunton, with its

HOW RAIDERS WERE REPULSED *Tactically the wall was a trap, in which the defenders took the offensive. The wall was built along the crests of hills where possible, taking advantage of high ground. At every Roman mile (1620 yds) stood a milecastle, like the one whose remains adjoin the wall north of Haltwhistle (left). Hadrian's original plan was that infantry should sally forth from the milecastle's gates when alerted, and take attackers in the flank or the rear. To reach the wall, attackers had to cross the defensive northern ditch, which averaged 27 ft wide and 9 ft deep. Here, they were exposed to missile fire from the parapets. In* AD *122, when Hadrian visited Britain, he changed his plan, making cavalry responsible for the wall's defence*

SYMBOL OF POWER *A Roman coin carries the head of Hadrian on one side and on the other Britannia resting on stones said to represent the wall. Hadrian's Wall was a political symbol—a closed frontier between the 'barbarians' and the Romans. As well as being a fortification, it served as a customs barrier and an obstacle against any anti-Roman alliance between tribes north and south of the wall*

CHESTERS FORT *The forts along the wall contained soldiers' bath-houses, with steam rooms, baths and chambers where the men relaxed. These ruins of an extensive bath-house were uncovered at Chesters, where a cavalry regiment was stationed*

CORBRIDGE LION *This sculptured fountain-head and portion of a column were found at Corbridge, site of a fort and supply base, around which grew a town of about 35–40 acres. The lion and many other Roman remains can be seen in Corbridge Museum*

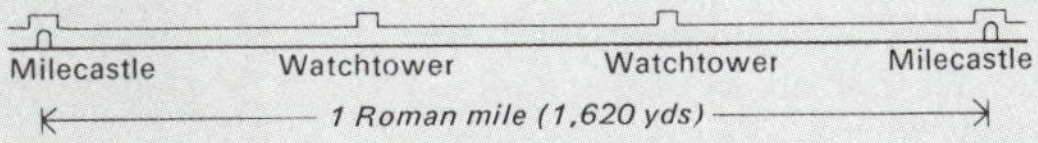

PASSING NEWS ALONG THE WALL *News of an attack could be signalled rapidly along the wall. Between milecastles were placed two turrets. These could be used as watchtowers and signalling posts, passing information to the milecastles, from which it was sent on to the major garrison forts if necessary*

MILITARY ROAD *After the 1745 uprising, part of the wall (as on the B6318 above) was destroyed to make a military road*

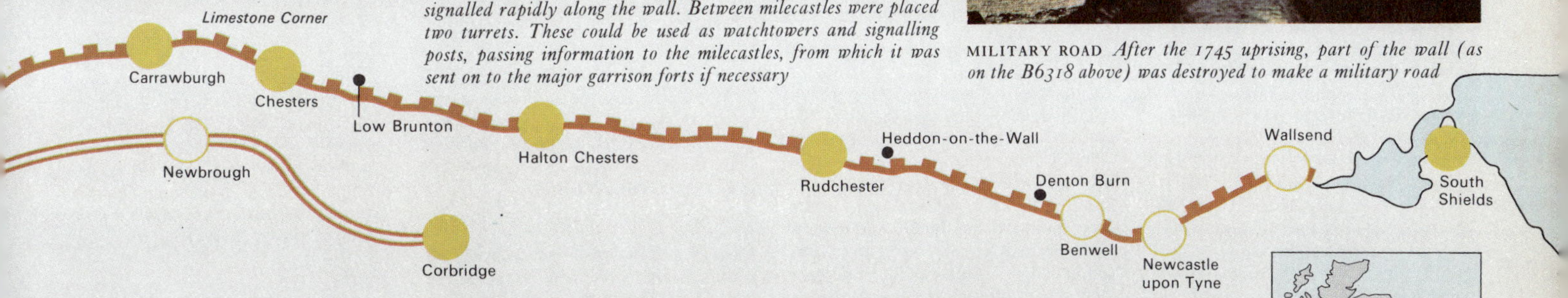

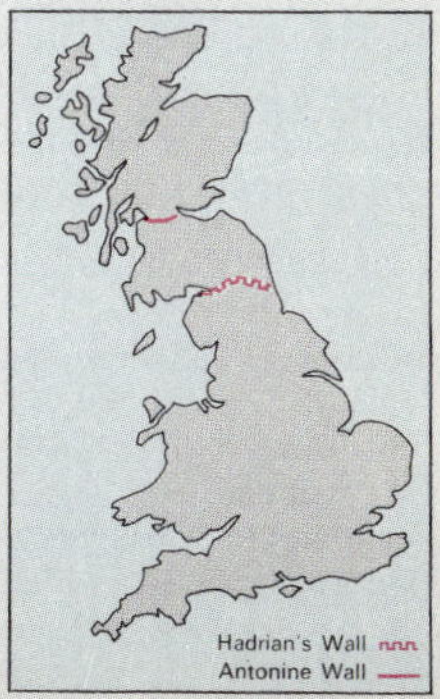

stretch of wall and turret, comes Chesters Fort, the remains of whose bridgehead, bath-house and other buildings are well preserved. At Limestone Corner the northern ditch had to be cut through solid rock, but work on it ceased in AD *122.*

It is along the central sector of the wall that the best-preserved remains are found. Carrawburgh contains a modern reconstruction of part of a Temple of Mithras. Housesteads is the most impressive of the remaining forts, with ramparts, gateways, granaries, latrines, headquarters and barracks plainly visible, and a nearby milecastle well preserved. At Chesterholm on the Stanegate, parts of the ramparts, gateways and central buildings remain. A fine section, winding over lofty hills to Winshields Crags, includes the highest point of the wall, 1230 ft above sea level. Past the milecastle at Haltwhistle Corner, north of Haltwhistle Burn, the wall goes on to Great Chesters where there are some fort remains. Hadrian's Wall proved more enduring than the turf Antonine Wall (right) built c. AD *143 further north, from the Forth to the Clyde*

Fortresses by the Coquet

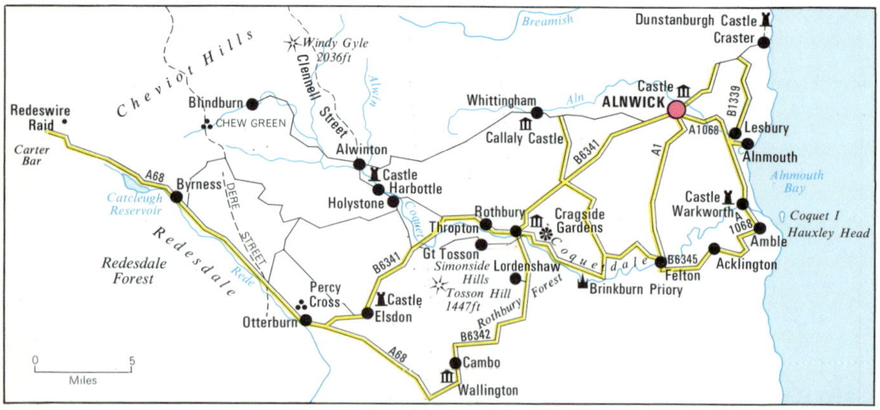

STONE GUARDIANS *Statues top the 14th-century barbican of Alnwick Castle, a stronghold of the Percy family since 1309*

Boating Sailing at Alnmouth and rowing boats for hire on the River Coquet at Warkworth.

Angling Salmon and trout in the River Coquet at Warkworth, Felton, Rothbury and Acklington; the River Breamish; and River Aln at Alnwick (some stretches preserved).

Events There is a Shrovetide football match between the parishes of St Michael and St Paul at Alnwick; the ball is piped to the field, and teams may number 150 each, with goals a quarter of a mile apart.
The Harbottle Agricultural Show is held on a Sat. in late Aug.
The Whittingham Games and fair are also held in Aug.

Places to see *Alnwick Castle*: May to Sept., afternoons except Fri. *Brinkburn Priory*: daily, except Sun. morning Oct. to Mar. *Callaly Castle*, Whittingham, 17th-century: Sat. and Sun. afternoons, late May to Sept. *Cragside* (NT), Rothbury: Spring to Sept., Tues. to Sun. afternoons; Oct., Sat. and Sun. afternoons. *Dunstanburgh Castle* (NT), 9 miles north-east of Alnwick: daily, except Sun. morning Oct. to Mar. *Howick Gardens*, 6 miles north-east of Alnwick: afternoons, Apr. to Sept. *Lady's Well*, Holystone: daily. *Otterburn Mill*: daily. *Wallington* (NT): Apr. to Sept., afternoons except Tues.; Oct., Sat. and Sun. afternoons. *Warkworth Castle*: daily, except Sun. mornings Oct. to Mar. *Warkworth Hermitage*, an ancient hermitage and chapel cut out of rock, reached by boat from the castle: weekdays and Sun. afternoons, Apr. to Sept.

Information centres Information Office, The Shambles, Alnwick. Tel. Alnwick 3120 (summer only). National Park Information Centre, Ingram. Tel. Powburn 248 (open Easter to Oct. only).

A beautiful salmon river, the Coquet, links Northumberland's past and present as it winds eastwards past priories and castles of a bygone age towards the North Sea coast where Northumberland's modern industrial life begins.

The Coquet rises in the Cheviot Hills, at a spot where the Romans built a camp (near today's Chew Green, 4 miles north of Byrness on the A68) to control the Border crossing of Dere Street. The river begins its journey in the sheep country of flat moorlands and open, grey dales and meanders through picturesque settings that are becoming favourite stopping places for fishermen, caravanners and campers. It then flows among grassy, rounded hills formed from lava rocks, then cuts through softer stone at a gorge just west of Alwinton, where Clennell Street, the old cattle-droving road over the Scottish Border, began.

Next it passes a gorge of hard, sandstone rocks at the Rothbury Fells, popular with climbers. The restful beauty of the river has helped to make Rothbury itself a favourite resort. Finally the Coquet makes its way through the coal and limestone regions of the coastal plains and out into the North Sea.

RIVERSIDE CHURCH *The church at Brinkburn Priory, on the banks of the River Coquet, was founded in the 12th century*

Alnwick
The main market town on the River Aln and an excellent centre for touring. Alnwick Castle, built on a 12th-century site and principal seat of the historic house of Percy, stood as a ruin for 200 years following the Border warfare and was restored in the 18th and 19th centuries by the Dukes of Northumberland. The symbol of the Percy family—a lion with straight, stiff tail—stands majestically on top of the Percy tenantry column, erected at the town's southern entrance in 1816 by 1000 grateful tenants after their rents had been reduced. A lay-by has been made for motorists on the steep north bank of the Aln, from which the view of the castle is almost identical to the one made famous in Canaletto's 18th-century painting which hangs in the castle.

Alnmouth, 4 miles south-east at the mouth of the river, has one of the oldest golf courses in England, laid out in 1869. This town, a seaport since 1200, is a growing centre for yachting.

Alwinton
English and Scottish wardens of the Middle March—the medieval defensive zone of the Border during 300 years of warfare—used to meet at the Rose and Thistle Inn when they had disputes to settle. Today, farmers from a wide area around meet in the hamlet every second Saturday in October on more friendly business—an annual agricultural show that provides a lively introduction to hill-country customs. The mainly 13th-century church is on two levels, the chancel being ten steps above the nave. Clennell Street, which was one of the early Border routes between England and Scotland, starts from Alwinton. It is a good day's walk—about a 15-mile round trip—needing stout boots and strong clothing, leading over fells and by forest to the Border at Russell's Cairn on top of Windy Gyle (2036 ft).

Amble
A small seaport, with sandy beaches ideal for bathing. There are plans to develop it as an industrial area as well as a holiday resort. Coquet Island lies 1 mile offshore and on quiet evenings during the breeding season the crooning of eider ducks can be heard. In the winter, south-easterly gales often disturb coal in seams covered by the sea a little way offshore, scattering small pieces of coal along the shores to the north. It is collected by the sackful by local people.

Brinkburn Priory

The church is all that remains of the priory founded by Augustinian canons *c.* 1135, but restoration in the 19th century has made this one of the best priory buildings in the county. Organ recitals are occasionally given and few lovelier settings for music could be imagined. The best view of the superb north doorway is from the top of the steep path beside the car park.

Carter Bar

A Border highpoint (1370 ft) that is a favourite stopping-place for enjoying the contrasting views of north and south. Scotland has the sunnier face, with lush green pastures, red ploughed fields and trim plantations. Half a mile to the north-east is the spot where, in 1575, the Scottish Jeddarts beat the Redesdale men in one of the last great Border battles—the Redeswire Raid.

The Catcleugh Reservoir, 4 miles south-east of Carter Bar, is the largest inland stretch of water in the county. The reservoir, developed in 1905, is more than a mile long and has a maximum depth of 78 ft.

Craster

A pleasant fishing village famous for its oak-smoked kippers. Whinstone, the very hard basaltic rock of the region, used to be shipped from the village until the local quarry closed in 1939. An easy but impressive 1½-mile coastal walk to the north can be taken to the ruins of Dunstanburgh Castle, standing on cliffs that rise 100 ft above the North Sea. The castle, which figured in three paintings by J. M. W. Turner, was begun in 1313 by the Earl of Lancaster. It has been decaying since the 16th century.

Elsdon

An isolated village that was once the Norman capital of Redesdale. Its houses are grouped around a 7-acre village green which has a pinfold—the northern term for a cattle or stray-animal pound. The village has a mainly 14th-century church, a parson's pele tower, and the earthworks of a Norman castle.

Harbottle

Almost hidden by the cottages in the village is a hump of rock and crumbling walls—all that is left of the once-great Norman castle, built *c.* 1160, that was the major stronghold in the defence of the Middle March. In the surrounding grasslands are the furrows and ridges of old ploughlands where crops were grown to support the Norman barons.

Otterburn

A town that earned itself a place in history with the Battle of Otterburn, fought 1½ miles to the north-west in August 1388. The battle, commemorated by the Percy Cross, resulted in the death of the Earl of Douglas, leading the victorious Scots against the English. The clash has inspired many ballads and legends, and is recounted in song in 'The Battle of Chevy Chase'. A wool industry survives in the village, and at Otterburn Mill, where a watermill is still in use, visitors can see tweeds being made.

BORDER TOWER *The fortified parsonage at Elsdon, on the right, was built c. 1400 on to a 14th-century pele tower, erected as a defence against Border raiders. It is a rugged structure with 8 ft thick walls, typical of many such Border towers*

Rothbury

There is an atmosphere of a Victorian watering place about the busiest market town in Coquetdale, with its stone houses and shops grouped along a steep sloping green on the north bank of the river. One mile to the east of the town is the Cragside Estate, home of the late Lord Armstrong (1810–1900), inventor of the Armstrong rifle-bored, breech-loading gun. Cragside, a 19th-century mansion, was one of the first houses in Britain to be lit by electric light. Its gardens are noted for their rhododendrons and artificial lakes.

Simonside Hills

The highest point of the Rothbury Fells, with Tosson Hill (1447 ft) the highest peak. A forest track climbs steeply over the hills by Lordenshaw, 2 miles south of Rothbury off the B6342, and leads to an excellent vantage point. The thin soil of the sandstone makes this a wild, heathery moorland, and the crags are popular with rock climbers.

Warkworth

The medieval castle was the 14th-century birthplace of Hotspur (Sir Henry Percy), who was slain at the Battle of Shrewsbury in 1403, when the Percys were defeated by Henry IV. For more than four centuries it was one of the most important castles in the north of England. Towering above the Coquet and wooded cliffs, it presents a dominating picture whether viewed from the medieval bridge, from the top of the village street, or from the river bank itself. The bridge has a rare medieval tower. The castle was mentioned by Shakespeare in *Henry IV*. The grassy slopes around the base of the walls are especially attractive in April when they are covered with daffodils. There is a sandy beach with good swimming 1 mile from the village.

CAMBO'S BEASTS *Heads of mythical beasts at 17th-century Wallington, near Cambo, came from London's Old Aldersgate when it was demolished in 1761. The mansion belonged to a merchant family, the Blacketts, whose ships used the carvings as ballast*

Border farmland south of the Tweed

Boating Sailing and water-skiing at Beadnell, sailing clubs at Berwick-upon-Tweed.

Angling Salmon and trout fishing on the River Tweed; coarse fishing at Berwick-upon-Tweed.

Events Blessing the Nets ceremony at Norham on Feb. 14 to open the salmon-fishing season. Seahouses has a May week early in the month, Wooler a carnival in July. The Tweedmouth Feast is in late July.

Places to see *Bamburgh Castle*: afternoons, Easter to Oct. *Farne Is.* (NT): Apr. to Sept., daily; access restricted mid-May to July. *Grace Darling Museum*, Bamburgh: Easter to mid-Oct., daily. *Lindisfarne Castle* (NT): Apr. to Sept., daily, except Fri.; Oct., Sat. and Sun. afternoons. *Lindisfarne Priory*: daily, except Sun. mornings Oct. to Mar. *Norham Castle*: weekdays and Sun. afternoons.

Information centres Castlegate Car Park, Berwick-upon-Tweed. Tel. Berwick 7187 (seasonal). Main Street, Seahouses. Tel. Seahouses 720424 (seasonal).

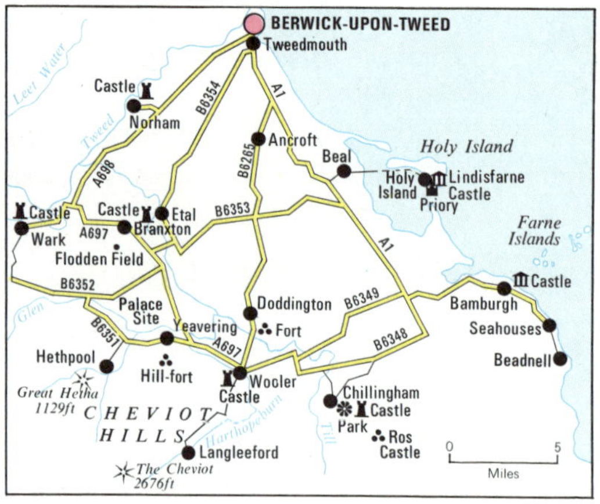

This northernmost tip of Northumberland is a comparatively empty corner of England. But what it lacks in the way of large villages it more than makes up for with its varied natural beauty. It has volcanic hills, a superb coastline of rocky cliffs, sand-dunes and the wildlife sanctuary of the Farne Islands. There is, too, a certain haunting quality amid the desolation, echoing a troubled and lawless past. This was once dangerous country, where English and Scottish armies went to war intermittently and local lords fought each other constantly for 300 years until the late 16th century. Grim reminders are everywhere. The great Tweedside fortress of Norham still stands on ghostly guard over the once-vulnerable east-coast route between the Cheviot Hills and the North Sea. Ruins of former castle strongholds can be seen in many small villages. Farms are often grouped around square, solid, stone-built pele towers, and many barns have 8 ft thick walls. All were part of the occupiers' attempts to defend themselves against raiding, pillaging and murder.

The landscape was transformed in the 18th century by the planting of woodlands and hedgerows enclosing large fields. Today the district is one of the most prosperous farming areas in the British Isles, producing high-quality barley and beef. Famous breeds of sheep, such as the Blackface and the Cheviot, roam the Cheviot Hills.

One of the outstanding attractions in this area is the wildlife sanctuary on the bare volcanic rocks of the Farne Islands, which can be reached from Seahouses. In the 7th century the islands were the retreat of Cuthbert, Bishop of Lindisfarne, one of many saints who helped to develop the region as one of the first Christian kingdoms in England.

A BRIDGE THAT HAS SPANNED THE TWEED FOR TWO CENTURIES

18TH CENTURY An engraving in the British Museum shows the Berwick-upon-Tweed of 1745 as a busy port and fishing town

20TH CENTURY Berwick's buildings have changed but its 15-arch bridge, built early in the 17th century, is still used today

Ancroft
The architecture of churches in the region reflects the turbulence of the days in which they were built. St Anne's at Ancroft is one of the best-preserved examples of a pele tower—or a 'parson's pele' as some towers are known. It is stubby and square, and appears to be a variation on a Norman church tower. But it is built like a fortress, with immense walls and a low, tunnel-vaulted room for the parson and his parishioners to shelter in during attacks.

Bamburgh
A popular, unspoilt resort that has a fine church, St Aidan's, mainly 13th century. Dominating this peaceful village is the enormous stone pile of Bamburgh Castle, once the seat of the first kings of Northumbria. The rocky fortress and the golden sands have been the setting for many films. In the village is a museum devoted to Grace Darling, the lighthouse-keeper's daughter who was born in Bamburgh in 1815. She rowed out with her father in September 1838 to rescue five people from the wrecked *Forfarshire* steamboat.

Berwick-upon-Tweed
The northernmost town of England was once a great port of Scotland, and it changed hands 13 times before finally becoming English territory in 1482.

A 2-mile walk leads round the top of the town's Elizabethan walls, starting

FLODDEN FIELD *Corn waves today where banners fluttered in September 1513, when James IV led the Scottish Army across the Tweed against an English force led by the Earl of Surrey. The Scots were routed and James was among many thousands killed*

from Meg's Mount where there are magnificent views inland along the winding River Tweed. The circuit then passes by the 15-arch stone bridge built by order of James I in 1611 to connect the town with Tweedmouth on the opposite side of the estuary. From there, it goes along the quayside, the shipyards and salmon fisheries and finally around the harbour mouth to the open ground fronting the North Sea. The route gives constantly changing views—a circuit looking out on almost rural calm around the busy heart of the town.

Chillingham
The 300-acre parkland that surrounds Chillingham Castle is the home of the country's only direct surviving herd of wild white cattle, descendants of the prehistoric wild oxen that used to roam the country's forests. The herd was cut off when the park was walled in 1220, and its isolation has saved it from outbreaks of foot and mouth disease elsewhere in Britain. There are some 50 cattle, and they can be visited by the public on guided tours every day except Tuesday. Ros Castle, owned by the National Trust, is an Iron Age fort on a 1036-ft hill $1\frac{1}{2}$ miles east of Chillingham. From here the coast can be seen to the east and the Cheviot Hills to the west.

Doddington
The two large farms and cottages that make up the village are grouped around a well-preserved pele tower—one of the last to be built on the Border in 1584. It is well worth a scramble up the steep slopes of the scarp of Dod Law, which overlooks the village, to view the panorama of the Cheviot Hills and to see the earthworks of an Iron-Age hill-fort on the Dod Law summit. A search of the moorland vegetation will reveal rock outcrops covered with strange carvings of cup and ring shapes, which are believed to date from the Bronze Age.

Etal
A village picturesquely different from most Northumbrian hamlets of similar size. It has an air of prosperity and has retained the neat, thatched roofs that were traditional in the area up to 200 years ago but which have generally given way to more austere red tiles and blue-grey slates. At the end of the village's only street are the remains of a 14th-century castle, ruined by the Scots before their defeat at the Battle of Flodden in 1513. Below the castle there is a salmon leap.

Flodden Field
A few hundred yards south of the village of Branxton is the scene of one of the bloodiest battles on English soil during which, according to various estimates, between 9000 and 16,000 Scottish and English soldiers were killed. A short, slippery footpath signposted on the narrow road by Branxton Church leads up through a cornfield to a simple monument inscribed 'To the brave of both nations'. It is said to mark the spot where James IV was slain during the fierce engagement in 1513. The victorious English soldiers were led by the Earl of Surrey.

Lindisfarne
Careful attention to the tide-table is recommended before driving the 3 miles from Beal across the causeway and sand-flats that link Lindisfarne, also known as Holy Island, with the mainland. Missionaries from Iona settled here in the 7th century but were driven out by the Danes in AD 875. The ruins of a Benedictine priory built in the 11th century and a small 16th-century castle are on the island. The limestone cliffs and sand-dunes of the north shore are a playground for the swarming bird life from the Farne Islands, and seals can often be seen offshore.

Norham
The great keep of the Norman castle, built *c.* 1160 high on the rocks above the Tweed, faced many a siege by Scottish armies, the most famous immortalised in Sir Walter Scott's poem 'Marmion'.

PELE TOWER *Villagers at Ancroft took refuge in a low, vaulted room in this square, thick-walled, 14th-century church tower during frequent Border clashes*

Seahouses
Weekend visitors help to turn this small fishing village into a lively resort. Just north of the village the National Trust owns stretches of dunes overlooking fine, sandy beaches. Boats from Seahouses take visitors to the Farne Islands, between 2 and 5 miles off the coast, where the barren slopes and cliffs, made up of fragments of the Great Whin Sill volcanic rocks, provide seabirds with ideal nesting sites. Cormorants, shags, kittiwakes, puffins, razorbills, gulls and terns breed in seclusion. The islands are also the only east-coast breeding ground of the grey seal. Beadnell, $1\frac{1}{2}$ miles south, is an ideal centre for sailing.

Wooler
A town on the fringe of the Cheviot Hills which makes a good base for hill-walking and fishing. South of the market-place is the mound of the Norman castle that guarded one of the highways to the south.

Five miles south-west, the farm at Langleeford is the starting-point for the easiest of the approaches to the flat summit of The Cheviot (2676 ft). The climb from the farm is dull and rather gruelling, but is worth while for the marvellous views in all directions from the top. Late autumn, when frosts have helped to harden the mud and peat, is the best time for walking on the summit.

Yeavering
Excavations during the late 1950's in a field by the River Glen revealed the existence of wooden halls and amphitheatres of the 7th-century capital of the Anglo-Saxon King Edwin, who permitted the monk Paulinus to convert the people of Northumbria to Christianity. A plaque has been erected by the roadside. On top of 1182-ft Yeavering Bell, to the south, is one of the largest Iron Age hill-forts of the Border country. The hill is believed to have been the capital of the local tribes at the time the Angles and Saxons conquered them.

THE HEROINE OF THE ISLANDS

Grace Darling was 23 when she rowed out with her father, the keeper of Longstone Lighthouse (left) in the Farne Islands, to rescue five people from a wrecked steamer in 1838. Her boat is in a Bamburgh museum

SCOTLAND

Scotland: a different nation still

Every year, thousands of visitors cross the almost unmarked border that lies across Britain between the Tweed and the Solway Firth. Some come for sport—golf, fishing, skiing, climbing—but most are in search of something less tangible. They seek the sense of a romantic past contained in the loneliness and beauty of one of the last great wildernesses in Europe. For this they go to the sea-lochs, the islands and the wild, silent mountain passes of the far North-West, an area evocative of old songs and long-departed heroes.

The Scots themselves do not see their country as a resting place of old traditions, but as a nation still, utterly different from the rest of Britain. They are so aware of their separate Scottishness that all over the world men of Scottish descent still bring inherited nostalgia to clan societies, and read Robert Burns in accents the poet never heard.

In the long, bitter struggle for independence, Scotland was never conquered, and when at last it became part of the United Kingdom in 1707 it was by treaty, even if many Scots regarded the Act of Union as a piece of abysmal treachery. Scotland retained its separate legal and ecclesiastical systems, and until well into the 20th century its separate system of free education was the most advanced and generous in Britain.

Biographies of Scots often begin with the story of a poor boy trudging to university carrying a sack of oatmeal which had to last him the year. Poverty, and the careful husbandry of meagre resources in a rigorous climate, have done much to shape the Scottish character. Presbyterian doctrine, with its emphasis on man's direct responsibility to God, had a particular appeal to the self-reliant people of the Lowlands.

Accents change within a few miles of crossing the frontier, and so do attitudes. Ruined forts, the relics of old frontier wars, stud the landscape on both sides of the Border, yet the Scots are more aware of the history and legends surrounding them than are the English. Statues on war memorials are depicted as wearing the bonnets of Scottish regiments, and the architecture of older buildings has little in common with English traditions. Often, as in Edinburgh's Old Town, the buildings show evidence of longer, closer contacts with the Continent than with southern Britain. The farmlands of the Central Lowlands are rich, but they are not like England's. There are fewer hedges, more walls, and often on the horizon there are mountains.

Independence of the Highland clans

The mountains are a constant reminder of that other Scotland which threatened the Lowlands for just as long, if not as effectively, as the English. Little more than 200 years ago, men who had to visit the Highlands on business affairs would make their wills before setting out, for the clansmen cared little for Lowland kings and laws. Only rarely did Lowlanders and Highlanders sink their differences, because the establishment of a common cause was almost impossible. The two parts of the country were divided not only geographically, but by language and interests as well. This division weakened Scotland throughout its history.

During the Dark Ages, Scotland, like the rest of Britain, was a melting pot for the roving peoples of northern Europe. Angles, Britons, Picts and Scots occupied different parts of the country, and had little in common except newly learnt Christianity and terror of the Norse raiders. It was this shared fear which finally brought Picts and Scots to unite under a single king, Kenneth MacAlpin, in AD 844. Both he and his successors

FEUDAL SCOTLAND *David I (left) who reigned from 1124 to 1153, is shown on an illuminated charter with his grandson, Malcolm IV, who succeeded him. David strengthened the feudal system and created 'Royal Burghs', in which merchants were given some self-government in exchange for export duties and rents*

RELIC OF A HERO *Robert the Bruce is said to have given this sword to Sir James Douglas in 1329, as a reminder of his dying wish that his heart should be buried in the Holy Land. Douglas died fighting the Moors in Spain in 1330 on his way to Palestine. Bruce's heart was later returned to Scotland and buried in Melrose Abbey*

BATTLE OF BANNOCKBURN *The battle which established Robert the Bruce on his throne was fought on June 23, 1314, for possession of Stirling Castle (at the top of this 15th-century drawing). He won against odds of nearly three to one. Edward II's army was hemmed between two bogs, and Bruce's infantry inflicted heavy casualties upon the packed ranks of the English knights*

THE LAWGIVER *James I, who reigned from 1406 to 1437, was the strongest of early Stuart kings, but spent the first 18 years of his reign as a hostage at the English court. He returned to Scotland in 1424, determined to stamp out the anarchy caused by his absence. A series of judicial executions disposed of the more turbulent nobles, and he pacified the Highlands with a mixture of diplomacy and superior generalship. Having restored law and order, he experimented with a Parliament on English lines, but Scotland was not yet sufficiently settled for this to be practicable. Instead, James I overhauled the chaotic financial system, and instituted many other reforms such as the establishment of inns in towns, the banning of football in favour of archery, and laws providing for a planned system of crop production. But active kings were seldom popular with the Scots nobility; in 1437 James was murdered in his bedroom closet, having put up a brave defence with the aid of fire-tongs. This memorial to him stands at Dryburgh Abbey*

UNTAMED HIGHLANDS (overleaf) *North-west Scotland contains some of the least-populated country in Europe. The mountains around Loch Alsh, on the coast of Ross and Cromarty, are formed of some of the world's oldest rocks, more than 2600 million years old. The loch itself was gouged out by glaciers in the Ice Age a million years ago* tried to push the kingdom to the south, but it was not until 1018 that Malcolm II, taking advantage of the defeat of the King of Northumbria by the Norsemen, extended Scottish dominion to the Tweed.

New-found unity received a serious setback when Malcolm III married Queen Margaret, a Saxon, in 1069. Margaret, a determined woman, persuaded Malcolm to adopt the feudal system of land holding, brought Celtic church practices into line with those of Rome, and alienated her husband's northern subjects by rejecting Gaelic as a court language in favour of Saxon and French. Though her son, David I, who reigned 1124–53, did much to further trade with Europe, he gave even greater encouragement to the Anglo-Normans, and granted lands to knights from England. These men and their descendants had a profound effect on Scottish affairs. Trade boomed in the Lowlands, the English language spread through the south and finally, through inter-marriage, the English Crown claimed overlordship of Scotland.

This was too much even for Scotland's weak king, John Baliol. He defied England's Edward I, who in 1296 invaded and laid waste the Lowlands. In 1297, the brilliant guerrilla leader William Wallace defeated the English at Stirling Bridge, but was later captured and executed by Edward, and English depredations continued. In this dark hour there emerged another leader, Robert the Bruce, who was crowned king in 1306. A man of strong personality, he united Lowlands and Highlands against the common foe, and won a decisive victory over the English at Bannockburn in 1314. 'We fight', said the Arbroath Declaration of 1320, 'not for glory, nor riches, nor honour, but only for that liberty . . .' Scotland, for a short time at least, was an undivided nation.

Bruce's daughter, Marjorie, married Walter, High Steward of Scotland, whose title became the name of his descendants—the long and ill-starred line of Stuart kings. Most of the early Stuarts died violent deaths when young, and their heirs succeeded to the throne as minors. This led to fighting among the Lowland nobles as they jockeyed for power, and the Highlands too were up in arms. James IV did much to restore order, and brought a measure of prosperity to the country. However, France, then at war with England, called upon Scotland's help under the terms of the 'Auld Alliance' of 1295, and in 1513 James invaded England. He died at Flodden, and another infant, James V, became king.

Neither James V's reign, nor that of his daughter Mary, Queen of Scots, was happy. Mary was one week old when she succeeded to the throne in 1542; she was married to the sickly French Dauphin at the age of six, and returned to her Scottish realm as a widow of 19.

Abdication forced by treachery

By 1561, much of the country was under the sway of the Protestant Kirk, and the aristocracy, including Mary's new husband Lord Darnley, equalled their treachery to the queen only by their treachery to one another. In 1567, Mary was forced to abdicate and she later fled to England, seeking the help of Elizabeth I. Elizabeth had none to offer; instead, she imprisoned Mary for 19 years, and finally executed her.

James VI, brought up to hate his mother, made only a formal objection to her execution. Besides, he was fairly certain that he would inherit the English Crown; and in 1603, when Elizabeth died, he succeeded her, as James I of England. The transfer of the court was a bitter blow to Scotland, though it kept its own government for another century. Then, in 1707, despite the protests of most of the people, the Scottish Parliament signed away its separate existence in exchange for religious tolerance, free trade with England, and heavy bribes. Dissatisfaction with the Union, and a wish to choose their own destiny, rallied Highlanders to the Stuart cause in 1715 and 1745. But these hopes were finally crushed by the English at Culloden on April 16, 1746, and Scottish independence had to exist only in men's minds until the recent moves towards devolution.

JAMES IV *This able monarch, who reigned over Scotland for 25 years, died at Flodden Field in 1513 in battle with the English under the Earl of Surrey*

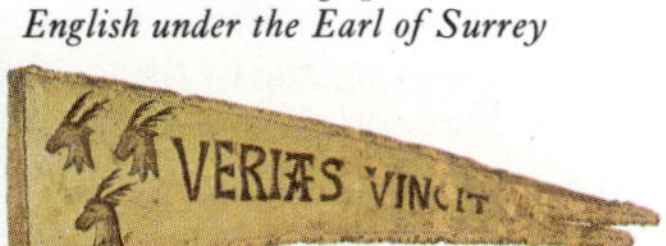

BLOODSTAINED BANNER *The banner of the Earl Marischal of Scotland, stained by the blood of the standard bearer at the Battle of Flodden in 1513. He died with the king and thousands of his countrymen. The English won because they made a better choice of ground, and because James IV attacked too early*

MARY, QUEEN OF SCOTS AND LORD DARNLEY *Their marriage was at first a love-match, but Darnley soon wearied the queen with his demands for equal power as king-consort. Jealous of the influence of Rizzio, the queen's secretary, he conspired to murder him. Darnley then betrayed his companions in an attempt to regain Mary's favour. Having alienated everyone, he was murdered in 1567. The extent of Mary's involvement in his death is one of the riddles of Scottish history*

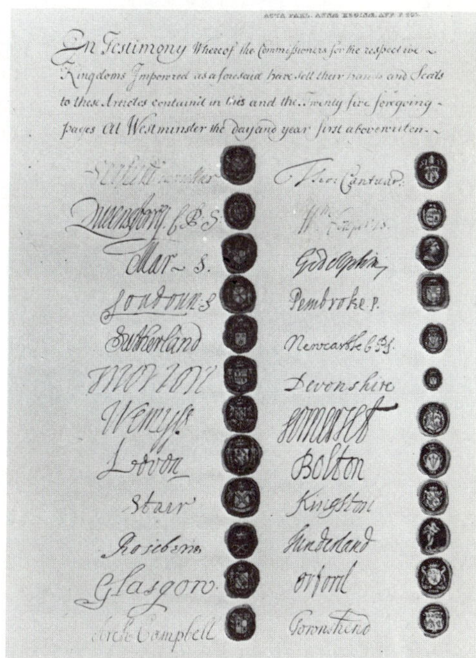
In Testimony whereof the Commissioners for the respective Kingdoms Impowered as aforesaid have sett their hands and Seals to these Articles contained in this and the Twenty five foregoing pages At Westminster the day and year first abovewritten.

Queensberry · Mar · Loudoun · Sutherland · Morton · Wemyss · Leven · Stair · Roseberry · Glasgow · Archd Campbell

Godolphin · Pembroke · Newcastle · Devonshire · Somerset · Bolton · Kingston · Sunderland · Orford · Townshend

TREATY OF UNION *Scotland's last Lord Privy Seal, the Earl of Seafield, described the 1707 Act of Union as 'Ane end of ane auld sang'. This treaty, signed by the Scots on the left and the English on the right, surrendered Scotland's political independence for 45 seats in the Westminster Parliament, free trade with England and the retention of legal and ecclesiastical freedom. The Act, though effective, was bitterly resented by most Scots*

SCOTTISH LOWLANDS

Traditionally, the southern half of Scotland is known as the Lowlands—a description which suggests flatness and a certain lack of variety. But the Lowlands, though not challenging the grandeur of the rugged North-West Highlands, are more hilly than most parts of England, and the climate, particularly in the central areas, can be as harsh in midwinter as that endured by any lonely hamlet in the Highland mountains. The dour and determined people of the Lowlands are typical of the Scots as the world tends to think of them, and the history of the Borderland between England and Scotland has been even more turbulent than that of the remote Highlands.

The change from Lowlands to Highlands, along a diagonal line from Dumbarton in the west to Stonehaven in the north-east, is a fairly abrupt one. Below the line, the land is often gentle and pretty—a rolling tableland of grassy hills and green dales. It is a countryside that is rich in farming and busy with sheep-rearing, yet it manages to support nearly all Scotland's industry and two-thirds of her population.

The western Lowland seaboard, mainly agricultural and unspoilt, also has the popular seaside and golf resorts of Strathclyde, including

HIGH 'LOWLANDS' *The midland valley between the Forth and the Clyde is the only lowland area in the literal sense of the word. The southern uplands rise to the Tweedsmuir Hills in the centre and the Pentland and Lammermuir Hills in the north-east*

Ardrossan, from which boats sail to the Island of Arran, 15 miles across the Firth of Clyde; Troon and its offshore bird sanctuary of Lady Isle; and Girvan, with lonely and rocky Ailsa Craig, a breeding place for birds, 10 miles out to sea. To the east, on the southern shore of the Firth of Forth, the fertile soils of eastern Lothian favour highly developed horticulture and agriculture. Just south of East Linton is one of the three Forestry Commission tree gardens in Scotland, where collections of rare specimen trees can be seen by the public; the other two are in Argyll. The two major cities of the Lowlands are Glasgow and Edinburgh—less than 50 miles apart in terms of travel, but a world apart in terms of their industry and architecture. Edinburgh is one of Europe's most beautiful capitals. It is built upon hills in a superb natural setting, overlooked by a mountain-in-miniature, Arthur's Seat, and with a 1000-year-old castle at its centre. In the 18th century, Edinburgh was the home of philosophers and wits, poets and scientists. They helped to bring a cosmopolitan atmosphere to the city that is still sustained each year by the Edinburgh International Festival of music and drama. Superb lonely countryside is within easy reach of the capital—south-west, the 16 mile long Pentland Hills, which Robert Louis Stevenson loved; south-east, the lonelier Moorfoot Hills.

From country town to shipyard city

Glasgow, with its satellite towns, forms the huge industrial heart of the Lowlands. It grew from being a pleasant burgh in pretty countryside into a great city—starting first in the 17th century as a major seaport to which sugar and tobacco were imported from America, then completing its development in the last 150 years with the establishment of steelworks and large docks and shipyards along the River Clyde. Today, Glasgow is Scotland's largest city and is the third-largest in population in the British Isles, after London and Birmingham.

Widespread redevelopment and reconstruction are transforming the quality of life in a city whose people have always been fortunate in one respect—there are few places in the western world where the grime and clamour of shipyard and steel mill can so quickly and easily be left behind for the delights of an inspiring and romantic countryside. To the north-west, only 15 miles away, is Loch Lomond; to the west, the Kintyre peninsula and the beginning of true Highland scenery.

The central Lowlands, which include Dumbarton, Kinross, Stirling and Clackmannan, formerly Scotland's smallest county, also offer a promise of the Highlands. Around ancient and busy market towns, the countryside begins to lengthen between them, the hills get higher, and pretty lochs and wooded rivers add their rippling beauty to the countryside. Despite the modern road bridges over the Forth and the Tay, Fife remains strangely independent of the rest of Scotland. The coalfields are being worked out, and the seaside villages are busier today with pleasure craft than with fishing boats. Only the ancient university town of St Andrews—world famous as the headquarters of golf, which was played there as long ago as the 15th century—and the rich farmland of northern Fife, retain their traditional character.

Land that inspired Sir Walter Scott

The great tourist attraction of the Lowlands outside Edinburgh is the Border country, consisting mainly of the districts of Roxburgh, Tweeddale, and Ettrick and Lauderdale, but also including parts of Berwick and Annandale and Eskdale. This is a land separated from England by the Cheviot Hills, of magnificent ruined abbeys—at Melrose, Jedburgh, Dryburgh and Kelso—of the mighty River Tweed, famous for its salmon fishing, and of beautiful hill scenery rich in the romantic stories of Border warfare that inspired many of the novels of Sir Walter Scott. His last and most famous home, Abbotsford House, is in the heart of the Border country.

Equally beautiful scenery is contained within the less-visited area of Dumfries and Galloway, in the west of the Lowlands. Here, in Stewartry and Merrick, the wild and lovely slopes of the mountain ranges—dominated by southern Scotland's highest peak, the 2770-ft Merrick—have earned themselves the name 'The Galloway Highlands'. This is the land of the red deer, of the thickly coated black and hornless

REGIONAL PAGE INDEX
478
472
484
468
482
470
466
454
486
462
458
456
460
KEY TO MAP
Regional centre
Selected town or village
Regional boundary
County boundary (admin. region Scotland)
Major road
Minor road
Woodland
River and lake or reservoir
HIGHLAND
GRAMPIAN
TAYSIDE
CENTRAL
FIFE
LOTHIAN
STRATHCLYDE
BORDERS
DUMFRIES & GALLOWAY
SOUTHERN UPLANDS
NORTHUMBERLAND
CUMBRIA
NORTH SEA
NORTH CHANNEL
Fort William
Oban
Perth
Dundee
ST ANDREWS
Cupar
Ceres
Crail
Fife Ness
Falkland
Kinross
Earlsferry
Elie
Kirkcaldy
Burntisland
Aberdour
Dunfermline
Culross
Callander
Bridge of Allan
Kippen
STIRLING
Fintry
Bannockburn
Bo'ness
Abercorn
Queensferry
Falkirk
LINLITHGOW
Kirkliston
EDINBURGH
Leith
Musselburgh
Prestonpans
Dirleton
Gullane
NORTH BERWICK
Dunbar
E. Linton
Haddington
Gifford
Eyemouth
Dalkeith
Roslin
Penicuik
Inveraray
Lochgoilhead
Rosneath
Helensburgh
Dunoon
Dumbarton
Greenock
Clydebank
GLASGOW
Cumbernauld
Paisley
Hamilton
Largs
Lanark
Biggar
PEEBLES
Stobo
Innerleithen
Traquair
Galashiels
Melrose
Stow
Duns
Coldstream
Kelso
Kirk Yetholm
Selkirk
JEDBURGH
Hawick
Irvine
Kilmarnock
Mauchline
AYR
Cumnock
Douglas
Leadhills
Sanquhar
Maybole
Girvan
Moffat
Thornhill
Lockerbie
Langholm
DUMFRIES
Ruthwell
Annan
Gretna
Carlisle
Penrith
Keswick
Kendal
New Abbey
Castle Douglas
Dalbeattie
Kippford
Southerness
Gatehouse of Fleet
KIRKCUDBRIGHT
Creetown
Newton Stewart
WIGTOWN
Glenluce
Cairnryan
Stranraer
Portpatrick
Port Logan
Drummore
Mull of Galloway
Port William
Garlieston
Whithorn
Burrow Head
Kilmory
Tarbert
Carradale
CAMPBELTOWN
Southend
Mull of Kintyre
Ailsa Craig
Arran
Bute
Islay
Jura
Colonsay
Oronsay
Mull
Rhum
Larne
Antrim
Belfast
Newry
Solway Firth
Firth of Clyde
Lowther Hills
Pentland Hills
Moorfoot Hills
Lammermuir Hills
Ochil Hills
Campsie Fells
MILES
30
60
90
120
150
180
210

Galloway cattle, of the golden eagle, and of wild goats with long, curly horns. Remote and tiny lochs dot the foot of the Merrick slopes where, around Loch Trool, spreads the 200-square-mile Glen Trool Forest Park, formed by the Forestry Commission in 1945.

The Galloway landscape has been a source of inspiration for many famous names in popular literature. S. R. Crockett based the 'Rathan Isle' of his novel *The Raiders* on Hestan Island at the entrance to Auchencairn Bay; Dorothy L. Sayers wove the countryside into *Five Red Herrings*; and much of the action of John Buchan's *The Thirty-Nine Steps* takes place around the Cairnsmore of Fleet, a lonely 2331-ft peak to the north-east of Creetown.

The Lowlands' historical links with the past are strongest in the cities and towns north of the central industrial belt. Dunfermline is an ancient capital with a beautiful old abbey in which Robert the Bruce is buried; and the town was the birthplace of James I in 1394 and of Charles I of England in 1600. James II was born at Stirling Castle in 1430 and James VI (James I of England) was christened and crowned there. The Scottish patriot William Wallace is commemorated by the 220 ft high Wallace Monument on Abbey Craig, north of Stirling Bridge. Perth, Scott's 'fair city', is all of that, and more—a prosperous market town, rich in the character of its streets and buildings.

Artistic talent from the Lowlands

In matters of the arts, the Lowlands have the edge over the Highlands. An intellectual maturity was reached in the 18th and early 19th centuries —Robert Burns, a Lowland farmer's son, and Sir Walter Scott, born in Edinburgh, are world-famous figures. The Scottish poet Allan Ramsay, a mining manager's son whose verse was to have considerable influence on Burns, was born at Leadhills. David Hume, the mid-18th-century philosopher, and James Boswell, friend and biographer of Samuel Johnson, were both born in Edinburgh.

The Lowlands have a splendid heritage in the visual arts, too—from the paintings of Sir Henry Raeburn, who was born at Stockbridge, Edinburgh, to the more domestic skills of textile-making, which have produced the linens of Dumfries and Galloway, Strathclyde's white needlework—a form of embroidery used in making table mats—and a wide array of woollen checks that are sold throughout the world.

THE LOWLANDS' SUNNY WEST COAST

Southern Scotland's most settled weather is between March and June. July tends to be cloudy and, in the west, August is generally wetter than in most other parts of Britain. The Firth of Forth, however, is a notably dry area—Inchkeith Island has 22 in. of rain a year, compared with Edinburgh's 24–27 in., Greenock's 62½ in., and an average for the whole of Scotland of 50 in. The coast north and south of Ayr, protected by hills, has an excellent sunshine record.

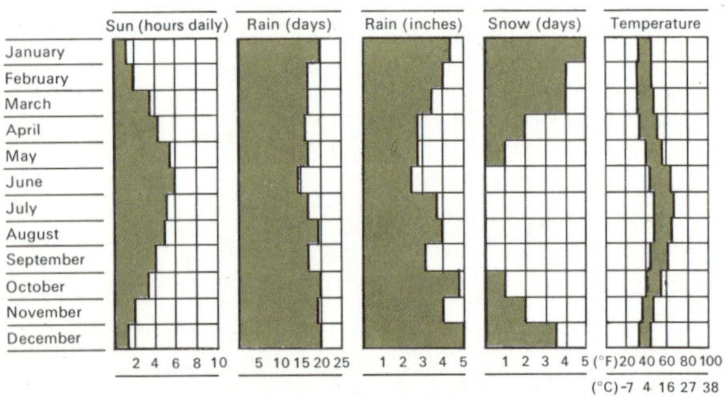

FOREST PARK *A rippling stream winds down from the hills at the head of Glen Trool Forest Park, established by the Forestry Commission in the Galloway uplands. Within the park is the 2770-ft peak of Merrick, southern Scotland's highest mountain*

The Border river valleys

Angling Trout fishing at Duns, Greenlaw, Hawick, Jedburgh, Lauder, Galashiels, Kelso, Coldstream and Melrose.

Events Common Riding, a festival of horse riding, is held at Hawick and Selkirk (both June) and Lauder (July/Aug.). There is a Mosstroopers Race Meeting at Hawick in June, and Melrose has a Festival in the same month. In July, Kelso has a Civic Week with pageant plays.

Places to see *Abbotsford House*: Apr. to Oct., weekdays and Sun. afternoons. *Bowhill*, 3 miles west of Selkirk: Easter and May to Sept., every afternoon. *Floors Castle*, Kelso: early May to Sept., Sun. to Thur. afternoons. *Hawick Museum and Art Gallery*, Wilton Lodge Park: weekdays; also Sun. afternoon Apr. to Oct. *Hermitage Castle*, 12 miles south of Hawick: weekdays, Sun. afternoon. *Mary, Queen of Scots' House*, Jedburgh: Mar. to Oct., daily. *Mellerstain*, Gordon: May to Sept., afternoons except Sat. *Melrose Abbey and Museum*: weekdays, Sun. afternoon. *Wilton Lodge Museum*, The Park, Hawick: weekdays; also Sun. afternoon, Apr. to Oct.

Information centre Borders Regional Council, Tourism Div., Newtown St Boswells. Tel. St Boswells 3301.

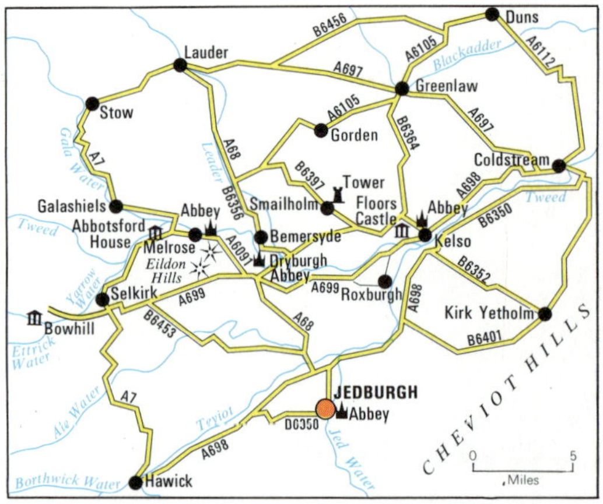

From the Cheviot Hills the russet and yellow moorlands and cool green pastures of the Scottish Borderlands stretch deep into Roxburgh, north-west into Ettrick and Lauderdale and north-east into Berwickshire. Through the valleys the Rivers Teviot, Yarrow and Jed flow to join the Tweed. These are rivers where the princely salmon and darting trout swim; and on the hillsides are the sheep from whose wool is made the tweed for which the Borderlands are famous throughout the world.

But in this peaceful land are the scars of a turbulent past—the gutted abbeys of Melrose, Jedburgh, Kelso and Dryburgh, laid waste by English invaders in raids from the 13th to 17th centuries. The English were not the only despoilers. For centuries the Border bandits known as reivers or mosstroopers fought out their own feuds, murdered and plundered, until the Borders were pacified by James II in the 15th century, when he overcame the powerful Border Earls.

The violence, the stories of medieval wizards, and the romance of the countryside inspired much of the writing of Sir Walter Scott, who lived at Abbotsford until his death. James Hogg (1770–1835), 'The Ettrick Shepherd', the son of a farmer, followed the tradition of the Border ballad writers in his poems of romance and local patriotism.

Each year the towns remember the stormy past with the Common Ridings—festivals in which local horsemen and women gallop over rough moors and hillsides. Rugby is the most popular sport and seven-a-side matches, which were first played at Melrose, are now popular wherever Rugby is played.

COLDSTREAM GUARDS

An 18th-century guardsman and his 20th-century successor. The Coldstream Guards were raised in 1650 by General Monk to serve in Cromwell's New Model Army

Coldstream
A small town where for centuries warring Scottish and English armies forded the Tweed. Each year a procession from Coldstream visits Flodden, 3 miles east across the border in England, where the Scots were defeated with great slaughter in 1513. The need to cross by the ford ended in 1766 when John Smeaton completed the present five-arched bridge. A plaque near the market shows the position of the house where General Monk raised the Coldstream Guards for Cromwell's Army in 1650.

Duns
Although little more than a village, Duns became the county town of Berwickshire after Berwick was declared a neutral town in 1551. The border was later revised to make Berwick a part of England. The monument on 700-ft Duns Law commemorates a camp made there in 1639 by General Leslie and his Covenanters before they marched on Newcastle. The Covenanters were supporters of the Scottish Reformed Church against Charles I's ecclesiastical policy. Duns Common Riding, or summer festival, goes on for a week. In the Burgh Chambers is the Jim Clark Museum, containing trophies won by the world champion racing driver who lived in Duns. He was killed in 1968.

Galashiels
A bustling tweed and woollen town amid green hills. Every June there is a pageant, the Braw Lad's Gathering, in which the history of the town is re-enacted. The town's motto 'Sour Plums', which can be seen on the municipal buildings, refers to a Border foray in the 14th century when a party of English raiders were slain while picking wild plums.

Hawick
The largest Border town, a market for sheepfarmers and a woollen-manufacturing centre since the 18th century. Hawick knitwear is exported all over the world. Wilton Lodge Museum has a section devoted to the history of the woollen trade. The Horse Monument in the High Street commemorates the callants, or youths, of the town who rallied to defeat an English raiding party at Hornshole in 1514, a year after Flodden. The event is also celebrated every June in the Common Riding, when horsemen ride the town's marches, or boundaries. Hermitage Castle, 12 miles south, was owned by the Earl of Bothwell, the lover of Mary, Queen of Scots, who rode 40 miles there and back from Jedburgh to visit him when he lay wounded.

Jedburgh
An ancient town, once the favourite residence of Scottish kings, now a good centre for riding, walking and climbing in the surrounding hills and moors. Jedburgh Castle, built in the 12th century, changed hands many times in the Border battles, and the Scottish Parliament had it destroyed in 1409 because the English seemed to be getting more advantage from it. The former county prison, built in 1823, is now on the castle site.

The abbey, founded by Prince David, later David I, in 1118, was repeatedly damaged by English invaders until in

THE ROMANTIC LAND OF SIR WALTER SCOTT

Scott (above right), born in Edinburgh in 1771, spent a great part of his adult life at Abbotsford House, his home near Melrose. His study (left) is preserved as he left it, with the desk at which he wrote many of his best-known novels. The Border country around Abbotsford was a major inspiration for Scott's romantic novels based on Scottish history. One of the novelist's favourite views, now known as Scott's View (far left), was from Bemersyde Hill, 2 miles east of Melrose, looking across the Tweed towards the Eildon Hills. Scott died at Abbotsford in 1832 and is buried in St Mary's Aisle in the ruins of Dryburgh Abbey (above)

1523 the Earl of Surrey ordered it to be burnt down—but even roofless and in ruins it is still magnificent. The Norman tower, which has been restored, the three tiers of arches which form the walls, and the tracery of the rose window in the west front make it one of the finest medieval buildings in Scotland. Mary, Queen of Scots' House, where the queen stayed in 1566, is now a museum, and relics of her there include a watch and a thimble-case.

Every February, on Shrove Tuesday, the 'Uppies', those born above the mercat cross, and the 'Doonies', those born below it, play handball through the streets of Jedburgh; the custom dates from medieval times. Jethart snails, a hard toffee, are a local delicacy.

Kelso

A market town with a wide, cobbled square, colour-washed buildings and lanes overlooking the Tweed. Scott described it as 'the most beautiful, if not the most romantic, village in Scotland'. The 12th-century abbey was the greatest in the Borders until it was destroyed by the Earl of Hertford in 1545, and now only a small part remains. The fine bridge, built by John Rennie in 1803, was his model for London's old Waterloo Bridge.

Floors Castle, seat of the Duke of Roxburgh, less than a mile north-west of Kelso, is a mansion designed by Vanbrugh in 1718 but greatly altered *c.* 1849. A holly tree in the grounds is said to mark the spot where James II was killed when a cannon blew up during a siege in 1460. Kelso is an excellent touring centre for the Cheviot Hills.

Kirk Yetholm

A Cheviot village at the northern end of the Pennine Way. A cottage still in the village was the 'palace' or headquarters of Scottish gipsies until the 'royal' line died out in 1883. The last gipsy queen, Esther Faa-Blyth, described the scattered village as 'sae mingle-mingle that ane micht think it was either built on a dark nicht, or sawn on a windy ane'—or, in other words, 'so topsy-turvy that one might think it was either built on a dark night or sown on a windy one'.

HERMITAGE CASTLE *The squat 13th-century fortress stands on the bleak moorland 12 miles south of Hawick. It was the home of the Earl of Bothwell, lover of Mary, Queen of Scots, whom he married in 1567 after the murder of her husband, Lord Darnley*

POET'S TOWER *The 16th-century Smailholm Tower, built on an outcrop of rock above Eden Water, was a favourite haunt of Sir Walter Scott, who lived near it during his childhood when he was sent to his grandfather's farm near Roxburgh*

CURFEW TOWER *Kelso's cobbled market square is dominated by its 18th-century court house, from which the curfew is still rung during the July Civic Week*

Melrose

A small town on the Tweed, sheltered by the Eildon Hills and in the centre of Sir Walter Scott country. Melrose Abbey was built for the Cistercian monks by David I in 1136 but was repeatedly ruined and rebuilt during Border wars and finally destroyed in English raids in 1543 and 1544. Enough remains of the nave, transepts and chancel to show how beautiful the abbey must have been. The heart of Robert the Bruce was to have been buried in the Holy Land, but Sir James Douglas, who was carrying it there, was killed in Spain fighting the Moors. According to tradition, he hurled the casket containing the heart at the enemy shouting 'Go first, brave heart'. Bruce's heart was later returned to Scotland and buried in Melrose Abbey.

Abbotsford House, Sir Walter Scott's home, is 2 miles west of Melrose. The novelist is buried in the ruins of the 12th-century Dryburgh Abbey, 5 miles south-east of Melrose. Also in the abbey is the tomb of Field Marshal Haig, the British Army's Commander-in-Chief in the First World War. Near the Haig family home, Bemersyde, is Scott's View, a favourite stopping point on the B6356 for views over the Tweed. Another fine viewpoint is Smailholm Tower, a 16th-century keep on a rocky outcrop, 7 miles east of Melrose. The tower was the setting for Scott's ballad 'The Eve of St John', written in 1800.

Selkirk

A hillside tweed-manufacturing town overlooking Yarrow Water. The explorer Mungo Park (1771–1806) was born near here; there is a statue of him in the High Street, and the town museum has some relics of his expeditions to Sumatra and the Niger. The museum also contains a flag said to have been captured at Flodden by the men, or 'souters', of Selkirk; the name, meaning shoemakers, recalls that Selkirk was once a shoemaking town. Selkirk is a good centre for exploring the lovely Yarrow and Ettrick Valleys.

Stow

A village with a 17th-century pack-horse bridge over Gala Water. A hilly road leads 5 miles north-east to Lauder, a small town which has a tolbooth, where dues were once collected from stallholders at the street fairs, and a 16th-century church with an octagonal spire.

The land of Annie Laurie

Water sports Sailing on Castle Loch, Lochmaben, with yacht races in the summer. Water-skiing on Mill Loch, Lochmaben.

Angling Salmon and trout in the Rivers Annan and Esk and in the Black Esk Reservoir. Trout in Kirtle Water and River Sark, and in Purdomstone Reservoir, Middlebie. Large pike and bream in Castle Loch, Lochmaben. Coarse fishing on Kirk and Mill Lochs, Lochmaben.

Events The ceremony of Riding the Marches (or boundaries) is held in Lockerbie in June, Langholm in July, and Sanquhar in Aug. The Festival of Good Neighbours is held in Dumfries in the first week of June.

Places to see *Bridge House Museum*, Dumfries: weekdays except Tues.; also Sun. afternoon, Apr. to Sept. *Burns House*, Dumfries: weekdays. *Burns Mausoleum*, Dumfries: by arrangement with Curator. *Caerlaverock Castle*: weekdays, Sun. afternoon. *Carlyle's House* (NTS), Ecclefechan: Easter to Oct., weekdays. *Drumlanrig Castle*: Easter and late Apr. to late Aug., afternoons. *Dumfries Museum*, Corberry Hill: weekdays except Tues.; also Sun. afternoons, Apr. to Sept. *Ellisland Farm*, 6 miles north-west of Dumfries; Burns's former granary, houses a collection of folk material: daily.

Information centres Tourist Information Centre, Whitesands, Dumfries. Tel. Dumfries 3862 (summer months only).

The history of the eastern part of Dumfries and Galloway is both turbulent and romantic; the region has bred fierce battles and lasting feuds, yet it has yielded some of the world's most touching ballads, including 'Annie Laurie'. Some of the most beautiful scenery of the Scottish Lowlands lies along the three parallel valleys of Nithsdale, Annandale and Eskdale, which run from the gentle Southern Uplands down to the wide, flat Solway Plain.

The River Nith, in its upper reaches, flows from Sanquhar down to Thornhill between ranges of shapely, green hills. A high, winding road leads north-eastwards out of the dale over the Mennock Pass to Scotland's highest villages, Wanlockhead, at 1380 ft, and Leadhills. Lead, gold and silver were once found in the surrounding Lowther Hills, and optimists still 'pan' for the precious minerals.

The River Annan flows down from the spectacular Devil's Beef Tub, a 500 ft deep hollow among four barren and wild hills which look, according to Sir Walter Scott in his novel *Redgauntlet*, 'as if they were laying their heads together to shut out the daylight from the dark hollow space between them'.

In Eskdale, the Black Esk and White Esk merge among moorland and forest to flow towards the Solway Firth near the English border. These were the former 'Debatable Lands', the Border lands that constantly changed hands between England and Scotland after prolonged feuds and raids in the 14th century.

WILD SLOPES *A gorge 8½ miles north-east of Moffat encloses the Grey Mare's Tail, one of Scotland's highest waterfalls, where the Tail Burn drops 200 ft to join Moffat Water*

Annan

A busy little town on the Solway Firth, with coastal shipping and shrimp fishing among its traditional activities. Just south of the town are the remains of the Solway Viaduct, opened in 1869 to carry iron ore across the Solway Firth from Cumbria. Badly damaged by a storm in 1881, the viaduct was repaired, but closed in 1921 because of lack of demand for the ore.

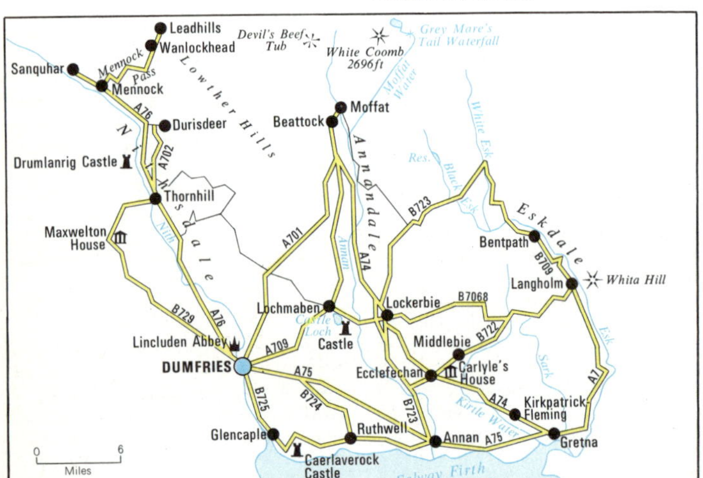

Dumfries

A town on the banks of the Nith, which is crossed by five bridges; the oldest is built of stone, with six arches dating from 1426. It is named Devorgilla's Bridge, after Lady Devorgilla who founded New Abbey, 5 miles south. The Mid Steeple was built in 1707 as muncipal buildings, courthouse and prison. The old Scots 'ell' measure of 37 in. is carved on the front of the building. A table of distances on the building includes the mileage to Huntingdon, in England, which in the 18th century was the destination for Scottish cattle drovers driving their beasts south for the markets of London.

BURNS MEMORIAL *A statue outside Greyfriars Church in Dumfries commemorates Robert Burns, who died in the town*

Robert Burns lived in Dumfries from 1791 until his death in 1796, and it was here that he wrote some of his most famous songs, including 'Auld Lang Syne' and 'Ye Banks and Braes of Bonnie Doon'. Burns is buried in a mausoleum in St Michael's churchyard. His home in Burns Street, formerly Mill Street, is a museum containing his manuscripts. The Town Museum, the Globe Inn and The Hole in the Wa' Tavern all contain Burns relics, and a statue of him stands in the High Street.

Lincluden Abbey, 1 mile north-west, was founded as a Benedictine convent in the 12th century. It later became a collegiate church, and the remains include fine stone-carvings and parts of the medieval domestic buildings.

Gretna

Gretna Hall, built in 1710, and the smithy at Gretna Green, still thrive on their fame as the first places over the Scottish border where, for a century, runaway young lovers from England could be married on the spot without parental consent. An English law of 1754 prevented clandestine marriages in England; but under Scots law, all a couple had to do was to declare in front of witnesses that they wished to become man and wife. In 1856 a law was passed requiring one of the parties to live in Scotland for three weeks before the marriage could take place. The blacksmith's shop still has the anvil over which couples were married. In 1940 the law was changed to stop the smith performing the ceremony.

Langholm

The chief town of Eskdale, nestling in the hills and famous for its woollens. On Whita Hill, just to the east, is a monument to General Sir John Malcolm (1769–1833), Governor of Bombay from 1827 to 1830, who was born near Langholm. Johnnie Armstrong, the 16th-century sheep rustler who plundered farms on both sides of the Border, lived at Gilnockie, $4\frac{1}{2}$ miles south-east. The restored defensive pele tower in which he hid after raids still stands. In 1529 Armstrong was finally trapped and executed at Caerlanrig, in Roxburgh.

TRAPPING SALMON *Fishermen waist-deep in the Nith near Glencaple use 'haaf' nets—from the Norwegian for 'heave'—to catch salmon*

At the point where the White Esk and the Black Esk meet, 8 miles north-west of Langholm, a Handfasting Fair used to be held every August from the 16th to the 18th century. At the fair, unmarried couples agreed to pair off for a year's trial marriage; at the time of the next year's fair they chose either to part or to marry.

Lockerbie

A town in Annandale notable as the scene of a battle in 1593 which ended one of the last great Border family feuds. The Johnstones routed the Maxwells, killing Lord Maxwell and 700 of his men. Many of the victims had their ears cut off with a cleaver—a method of mutilation which became known throughout the Border country as the 'Lockerbie nick'. Lochmaben Castle, $3\frac{1}{2}$ miles west, is claimed to have been a boyhood home of Robert the Bruce. Castle Loch, and the nearby Mill Loch, contain a rare fish called a vendace, about 7 in. long and having a heart-shaped mark on its head. Ecclefechan, 6 miles south of Lockerbie, was the birthplace of Thomas Carlyle, historian, critic and essayist. The cottage in which he was born in 1795 is maintained as a museum.

Moffat

An Annandale town which thrives as the centre of a sheep-farming area, symbolised by a statue of a ram in the wide High Street. Its popularity as a holiday resort grew from the discovery, in the mid-17th century, that the water from the town's wells had curative qualities. Among the distinguished visitors who came to take the waters was Robert Burns, who composed there the drinking song 'O Willie brew'd a peck o' Maut'.

North of Moffat, roads climb into spectacular hill scenery. One route leads to the Devil's Beef Tub, 5 miles north-west, a sheer-sided hollow in the hills, which is said once to have been used as a hiding-place for stolen cattle. Another route leads north-east along Moffat Water, past White Coomb (2696 ft) to Grey Mare's Tail, one of Scotland's highest waterfalls. The waterfall belongs to the National Trust for Scotland.

Ruthwell

The village is notable for its fine Runic cross, 18 ft high, which stands in a special apse in the village church. On it is carved, in Runic characters, a poem—the so-called 'Rood Lay' or 'Dream of the Cross'; it is written in the first person, as if the cross were speaking, and represents the earliest-known phrases in the English language. The poem is in the West Saxon dialect and may be by the Anglo-Saxon poet Caedmon.

Sanquhar

In this town in upper Nithsdale a granite monument marks the spot where the Covenanters formulated the two 'Declarations of Sanquhar' in 1680 and 1685, in their fight to defend Presbyterianism against the Stuarts.

Eliock House, at Mennock, 2 miles south-east, was the birthplace in 1560 of James Crichton, the man on whom J. M. Barrie based his play *The Admirable Crichton*. Crichton was renowned as the 'Marvel of Europe' for his physical and intellectual achievements. While still in his teens he could speak 12 languages fluently, and he became an expert horseman, fencer, dancer, singer and musician. He was killed in a street brawl in Mantua, Italy, when only 22.

Thornhill

A small town set in an attractive stretch of the Nith, and known as the 'ducal village' because of its long association with the Dukes of Queensberry and Buccleuch. North Drumlanrig Street is lined with lime trees planted by the 6th Duke of Buccleuch in the last century; a tall column set up in 1714 in the town centre supports a winged horse, the emblem of the Queensberrys.

Drumlanrig Castle, $3\frac{1}{2}$ miles north-west, was built for the 1st Duke of Queensberry *c.* 1680, but its high cost angered him so much that he spent only one night there and went to live at Sanquhar. The castle is now the seat of the Dukes of Buccleuch, and contains much fine woodwork.

The church at Durisdeer, 6 miles north, has fine 18th-century effigies of the 2nd Duke of Queensberry, who died in 1711, and his wife, sculpted in black-and-white marble by the Flemish sculptor John Nost. Beneath the effigies is a vault in which 12 of the Duke's family are buried. Maxwelton House, 5 miles south-west of Thornhill, was the home of Annie Laurie (1682–1764), immortalised by William Douglas, a rejected suitor for her hand, in the well-known love song written *c.* 1700. She eventually married another suitor, Alexander Ferguson.

SANDSTONE CASTLE *The late-14th-century Caerlaverock Castle, south of Dumfries, became a stronghold of the Maxwells, a powerful Border family, in the 15th century*

BRUCE'S CAVE. *This cave at Kirkpatrick-Fleming is said to be where a spider gave Robert the Bruce a lesson in perseverance*

Lochs and castles of an ancient Stewartry

Angling There are salmon, sea trout and brown trout in the Dee, Water of Fleet, Urr and Loch Ken (salmon fishing is at its best in Sept. and early Oct.). Coarse fishing for pike on Carlingwark Loch, Castle Douglas.

Swimming Good beaches west of Southerness and around the estuaries of the Urr, Dee and Fleet.

Events Sheep and cattle markets are held at Castle Douglas on Mon. Stewartry Art Society summer exhibition, Castle Douglas, mid-July to early Aug.

Forest drive The 10-mile 'Raiders Road' forest drive between Clatteringshaws Dam, 6 miles west of New Galloway, and Bennan, 5 miles south of New Galloway, is open daily, June to Sept.

Places to see *Broughton House Museum*, Kirkcudbright: Apr. to Oct., daily; Nov. to Mar., Tues. and Thur. *Dundrennan Abbey*: weekdays and Sun. afternoon. *MacLellan's Castle*, Kirkcudbright: daily. *Stewartry Museum*, Kirkcudbright: weekdays. *Sweetheart Abbey*, New Abbey: weekdays, Sun. afternoon. *Threave Castle*: weekdays and Sun. afternoon. *Threave Gardens* (NTS): daily.

Information centres Dumfries and Galloway Tourist Association, Harbour Square, Kirkcudbright. Tel. Kirkcudbright 30494. Summer only—Car Park, Dalbeattie. Tel. Dalbeattie 610117. Markethill, Castle Douglas. Tel. Castle Douglas 2611.

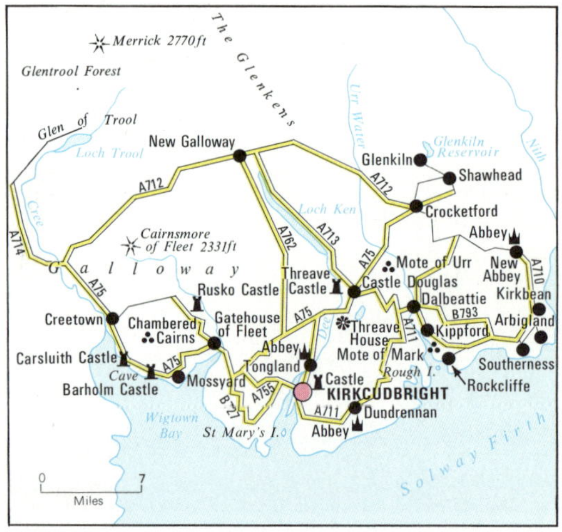

Stewartry, by its very name, recalls the distinction this district once possessed of having hereditary royal stewards as its lords. It contains three regions of very different character. In the north is a wild and desolate region known as The Glenkens, with lochs, jagged hills and waterfalls. This landscape gives way to rolling pastoral country, where the hardy Galloway cattle are raised. Finally, the coast of the Solway Firth has a gentler climate and brings back memories of smugglers and pirates.

There is still danger on these sandy beaches. The tide sweeps into the Firth as fast as a galloping horse, as the local saying goes, and only a foolhardy swimmer would ignore warning notices. There are gentler pleasures to be had in the compact Stewartry towns with their rows of 18th-century streets, and in walks among the ruined castles, mysterious earthworks and stone piles of prehistory which stud the land.

Since the days of the Picts, the people of Stewartry have kept a reputation for individuality. The rule of the Scottish kings was hardly effective there until the mid-15th century. Its mountains were a lair for Robert the Bruce in his days as a fugitive. The Covenanters, bound by covenant to defend the Presbyterian Church and combat Catholicism, died there in their hundreds. Memorials mark the scenes of their martyrdom, many of them carved by Robert Paterson, the eccentric wandering stonemason from whom Sir Walter Scott drew the central character of his novel *Old Mortality*.

Castle Douglas

The town was founded in the 18th century around the village and loch of Carlingwark, on the shores of which have been found traces of prehistoric crannogs—artificial island dwellings. A civic park has been created on the lochside. The town is set in rich farming land and holds a weekly cattle market.

Threave House, a Scottish baronial mansion house $1\frac{1}{2}$ miles south-west, has gardens open to the public, a school for gardeners, and a wildfowl refuge. On an islet in the River Dee west of the town is ruined 14th-century Threave Castle, once the sombre stronghold of the Black Douglases, so-called to distinguish the dark-haired branch of the family from another branch, the 'Red' Douglases. It is reputed that Mons Meg, the great cannon at Edinburgh Castle, was forged locally by a blacksmith named McKim and used by James II in 1455 to overcome Threave and its rebellious Douglas defenders. Over the doorway projects the 'gallows knob' from which the Douglases hanged their enemies. The castle was captured by the Covenanters in 1640 and dismantled.

Creetown

A sheltered and peaceful village, identified as the 'Porton ferry' of Sir Walter Scott's novel *Guy Mannering*. Five miles north is Cairnsmore of Fleet (2331 ft), which featured in John Buchan's spy novel *The Thirty-Nine Steps*. This is grand walking country with fine views. It is said that when Queen Victoria asked Thomas Carlyle what was the finest road in the kingdom, he replied: 'The coast road from Creetown to Gatehouse of Fleet.' The road runs for 18 miles with impressive seascapes on one hand and lush hedgerows and trees on the other, passing two ruined 16th-century castles, Carsluith and Barholm. At rugged Ravenshall Point, south of Barholm, is a cave used as a hiding place by Dirk Hatteraick, the smuggler captain in *Guy Mannering*. Up the Kirkdale Burn from Barholm are the 4000-year-old standing stones and chambered tombs of Cairnholy.

Dalbeattie

A town built of local granite in the wooded vale of the Urr Water. Quarries brought the town great prosperity, and the glistening grey stone was used all over the world. Today, granite chips are produced for road surfacing. The tower of Buittle Place, $1\frac{1}{2}$ miles west, was built in the 16th century from the old castle of Buittle or Botel, the birthplace in 1249 of John Baliol, vassal king of Scotland, known to his subjects as 'Toom Tabard' (Empty Coat). The 80 ft high Mote of Urr, $2\frac{1}{2}$ miles north, is a well-preserved Saxon or early Norman artificial mound within a fortified enclosure. Several of the local churches bear the name of St Constantine, who was a missionary in the area.

Dundrennan Abbey

The ruins of a rich Cistercian house founded in 1142. The small village of Dundrennan is partly built of stones from the abbey. Mary, Queen of Scots, after escaping from Loch Leven and being defeated at the Battle of Langside, spent her last night on Scottish soil at the abbey on May 16, 1568. She then entered England to seek help from Elizabeth I, who imprisoned her instead.

FOREST PARK *Loch Trool lies amid the 135,000 acres of the Glen Trool Forest Park. It was among these hills that Robert the Bruce fought the English for independence*

ISLAND CASTLE *The 14th-century Threave Castle stands on an islet in the Dee*

CASTLE HEARTH *A fireplace 8 ft across is part of the ruined hall at Threave Castle*

Gatehouse of Fleet

A former cotton town on the Water of Fleet, and the 'Kippletringan' of *Guy Mannering*. Burns composed 'Scots, wha hae wi' Wallace bled', on the moors near by and wrote it down in The Murray Arms at Gatehouse. On the road to Creetown is the well-preserved 15th-century tower of the McCullochs, with its sinister 'murder hole' over the entrance passage. Through this trap-door, boiling pitch was poured on to attackers. Rusko Castle, $4\frac{1}{2}$ miles north-west, was the 16th-century tower of the Gordons of Lochinvar, the family from which sprang the hero of Sir Walter Scott's poem 'Young Lochinvar'.

Glen Trool Forest Park

A 135,000-acre forest park of wild hills, lochs and waterfalls, culminating in the rugged heights of the Merrick (2770 ft), the highest mainland peak in southern Scotland. From these hills Robert the Bruce began his fight for independence, and a granite memorial beside Loch Trool recalls how he and his men defeated an English force in 1307 by hurling rocks at them.

Kippford

A small yachting and bathing resort. On the hill-walk to the neighbouring village of Rockcliffe is the Mote of Mark, a pre-Roman hill-fort overlooking the coast and a bird sanctuary on Rough Island. This was a smugglers' coastline; in the 18th century, wines and tobacco were smuggled into the inlets of the Solway Firth to escape increased import duties. The Customs service, of which Robert Burns was a member, was ineffectual.

Kirkcudbright

The Stewartry's most ancient burgh lies on the Dee Estuary. Its name means 'the church of Cuthbert'. In the old town graveyard are memorials to Covenanters and to Billy Marshal, the tinker king who died in 1792 aged 120, having, according to Scott, fathered four children after the age of 100. MacLellan's Castle, built in 1582, dominates the town. In the Earl of Selkirk's house on St Mary's Isle, Burns composed the much-quoted Selkirk Grace:

'Some hae meat and canna eat,
And some wad eat that want it:
But we hae meat and we can eat
And sae the Lord be thankit.'

North of the town is the ruined Tongland Abbey, one of whose abbots, John Damian, tried to fly from the battlements of Stirling Castle wearing wings of birds' feathers, in the presence of James IV. He landed in a manure heap.

Kirkcudbright is the centre of a lively group of weavers, potters and painters who work in the town's 18th-century byways. There is a museum of local antiquities, and Broughton House, bequeathed to the town by the artist E. A. Hornel, has a collection of his books and paintings. Visitors can play bowls, tennis or golf; and fishing, hill-climbing and bathing beaches are within easy reach.

New Abbey

This village is overlooked by the red-sandstone ruins of the Cistercian abbey founded in 1273 by Devorgilla, mother

VANISHING TRADITION *A weaver in Kirkcudbright spins wool on a traditional foot-operated wheel. Woollen goods are still made in the area, but spinning today is mainly done by machine*

of the vassal king John Baliol. Her husband, John Baliol the elder, had founded Balliol College, Oxford, and on his death Devorgilla became one of the richest women in Europe. She owned most of Galloway and had estates and castles in England as well as land in Normandy. She kept her late husband's embalmed heart in a silver and ivory casket by her side for 21 years until her death at the age of 80, when she and the casket were buried beside Baliol in front of the abbey altar. So the abbey gained its name of Dulce Cor, Latin for 'sweetheart', a word which has since become a part of the English language.

Southerness

A popular bathing resort with extensive sands and a golf links. Across the Firth can be seen the Cumberland coast and, on a clear day, the mountains of the Lake District, 30 miles away. Round the coast northwards at Arbigland stands the cottage birthplace of John Paul Jones (1747–92), honoured by Americans as the founder of their navy, but regarded nearer home as a pirate. He fought for France and was made a rear admiral in Russia. Kirkbean Church has a memorial font presented by the United States Navy in 1945.

CROW-STEPPED GABLES

The stepped projections on the sloping sides of gables, common in Scotland, are known as crow-steps, or corbie-steps. As well as being decorative, they provide protection against the weather at the point where the walls and roof meet. This style of gabling became popular throughout Europe during the Renaissance, and proved suited to the granite stones used for building the walls of houses in many parts of Scotland

Scotland's pastoral corner

Boating Yachting, regattas and dinghy racing at Whithorn, though the harbour is tidal, and on Loch Ryan. Boating at Stranraer, Garlieston and in Wigtown Bay.

Angling Trout fishing on the River Bladnoch; trout and salmon in the River Cree. There are several lochs between Stranraer and Newton Stewart where salmon or trout can be caught. On some lochs and rivers fishing is not allowed on Sun. Sea fishing at Stranraer at the head of Loch Ryan.

Ferries From Stranraer to Larne, Northern Ireland: four boats daily in each direction except Dec. 25 and 26 when there is one daily in each direction, and on Jan. 1 and 2 (two daily in each direction).

Events Pipe Band contest, Stranraer, first Sat. in June, and the Stranraer Show, last Wed. in July; Wigtown Show, first Wed. in Aug.

Places to see *Drumtroddan Standing Stones*, near Port William: daily. *Glenluce Abbey*: weekdays, Sun. afternoon. *Lochinch and Castle Kennedy Gardens*, near Stranraer: Apr. to Sept., daily, except Sat. *Logan Botanic Garden*: daily. *Portlogan Fishpond*: daily, except Tues. and Sat. *Whithorn Priory and Museum*: weekdays, Sun. afternoon. *Wigtown District Museum and Library*, Stranraer: Mon. to Fri., and Sat. morning. *Wren's Egg Stone Circle*, near Monteith House: daily.

Information centres Dumfries and Galloway Tourist Association, Newton Stewart. Tel. Newton Stewart 2549. Port Rodie, Stranraer. Tel. Stranraer 4502.

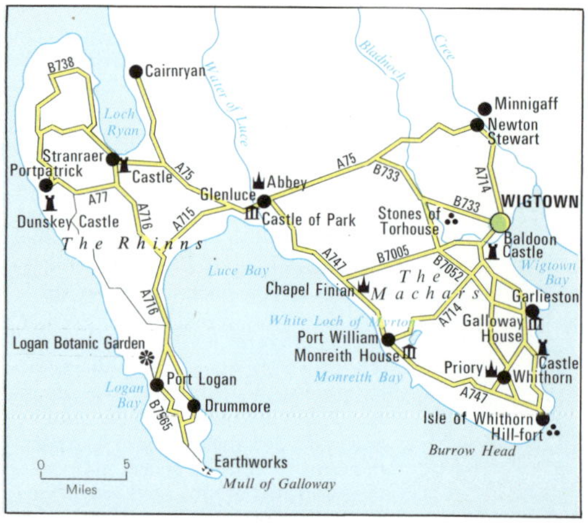

Modern civilisation has left almost untouched a rich store of beauty and relics of the past in the extreme west of Dumfries and Galloway. It is as though only the most discerning have been ready to search out this half-forgotten corner of Scotland, jutting into the Irish Sea. Those who do are amply rewarded. In the north are high moors, while The Machars peninsula in the south has farming land as rich as any in England.

The Gulf Stream washes the cliffs and sandy beaches, giving a gentle climate in which snow and fog are rare. Pastures support Blackface sheep, Ayrshire dairy cows and Black Galloway beef cattle. Most of the cattle on The Machars are Belted Galloways, with an unmistakable white body band.

The peaceful pastoral scene of this area which, with Stewartry to the east, formed the ancient district of Galloway, contrasts sharply with its history of bitter clashes for political and religious freedom. On all sides there are memorials to martyred Covenanters, the Presbyterian extremists.

Ruined castles recall Robert the Bruce's struggle for independence, and there are early relics of this corner's role as the cradle of Scottish Christianity.

LOGAN GARDEN *The sub-tropical gardens at Port Logan were*

STONES OF TORHOUSE *A circle of 19 standing stones near Wigtown, 60 ft in diameter, was erected in the Bronze Age*

MISSIONARY'S CHAPEL *The chapel on the Isle of Whithorn is dedicated to St Ninian, who brought Christianity to Scotland*

Cairnryan
This town of whitewashed cottages on the shore of Loch Ryan was an important war-time port. Troopships called here, and parts of Mulberry Harbour, the floating dock used in the D-Day invasion of Normandy in 1944, were assembled here. The Wig, a bay on the opposite shore of the loch, was a flying-boat base.

Drummore
A village on the lower prong of the double promontory of The Rhinns. From Drummore, the road leads to the Mull of Galloway at the tip of the prong. It is said that seven ancient kingdoms can be seen from it: Scotland, England, Ireland, Wales, the Isle of Man, Kyle

laid out more than a century ago

(Strathclyde), and Heaven. Traditionally, the Double Dykes across the neck of the Mull were earthworks left by the Picts. According to Robert Louis Stevenson's poem 'Heather Ale, a Galloway, Legend', the last Picts left were a father and son, who refused to tell the Scots invaders the secret of heather ale, the fabled Picts' drink. Rather than reveal it, the old man let the Scots hurl his son over the cliff, then threw himself over.

Garlieston

Pleasure craft use the harbour of this fishing village, which lies on a sheltered bay. One mile south is the 18th-century Galloway House, where the Earls of Galloway once lived. It is now a school.

On a clifftop 1½ miles further south is ruined Cruggleton Castle, the site of which is said to have been first fortified by the Norsemen. Near by is an early Norman church, restored in the 19th century by the Marquess of Bute.

Glenluce

A large village that lies on the Water of Luce as it nears its estuary in Luce Bay. Glenluce Abbey, 1 mile north-west, the ruins of a Cistercian house founded *c.* 1190, has intact a 15th-century vaulted chapter house. The border 'wizard', Michael Scott, is said to have lured the plague to the abbey in the 13th century and shut it in a vault. The lofty Castle of Park, a 16th-century mansion, overlooks the village from the brow of a hill across the river.

Newton Stewart

This attractive small town on the banks of the River Cree has a livestock market, and woollen mills where visitors can watch mohair rugs and scarves being made, which are on sale at the mill shop. Cree Bridge, granite-built in 1813 to replace one that was swept away by a flood, links the town with Minnigaff.

Port Logan

Rare plants and sub-tropical trees flourish in the walled Logan Botanic Garden, due to the Gulf Stream and a sheltered position. In Logan Bay is a tidal fish-pond built in the 18th century. The sea fish are tame and can be fed by hand when summoned by a bell.

Portpatrick

Until 1849 steamers sailed the 21 miles from Donaghadee in Northern Ireland to Portpatrick, which became a 'Gretna Green' for the Irish. Couples would land on a Saturday, have their banns called on Sunday, and marry on Monday. Gales and silting led to the harbour's neglect, and Stranraer replaced Portpatrick as a port. But, with its sandy bays and a climate that makes it one of the warmest places in south-west Scotland, Portpatrick is now popular as a holiday resort. The grim ruins on the clifftop to the south are those of Dunskey Castle, which was built *c.* 1510 by John Adair.

Port William

A holiday village on a sandy coast, founded by Sir William Maxwell in 1770. Monreith House, 1½ miles south-east, was built in 1799 as the home of the Maxwells. In the grounds stands a wheel-headed Celtic cross, possibly dating back to the 5th century. There is a bird sanctuary on the White Loch of Myrton, so called because legend says its water will whiten linen. On the shore of Monreith Bay, just south of Port William, is a restored chapel, Kirkmaiden-in-Fernis, on a site connected with an Irish princess, St Medan. A legend says that she landed there after floating across Luce Bay on a rock from the Mull of Galloway, where she had plucked out her eyes to discourage an ardent suitor. She bathed her face upon landing, and her sight was restored.

FORMER PORT *Portpatrick was a steamer port until its harbour declined last century*

Stranraer

The terminal of the 35-mile crossing from Larne in Northern Ireland. It has a marine lake, paddling pools, a rock garden and parks. In the centre of the town are parts of the 16th-century Castle of St John, which became a gaol, and in the late 17th century held Covenanters during Graham of Claverhouse's campaigns of religious persecution.

Whithorn

St Ninian, the son of a local chieftain, founded a monastery here in AD 397 and built his Candida Casa, or 'White House', probably the first Christian church in Scotland. In the 12th century Fergus, Lord of Galloway, built a priory: excavations in its ruins have revealed fragments of wall covered in pale plaster, believed to be from Ninian's Candida Casa. The ruins are entered through the Pend, a 17th-century arch on which are carved the Royal Arms of Scotland.

The modern town is airy and spacious. The museum contains ancient crosses and tombstones, including the 5th-century Latinus Stone, the earliest Christian memorial in Scotland. A moorland walk to the west coast, 2½ miles away, leads to St Ninian's Cave in Port Castle Bay, used by the missionary as a retreat. Crosses in the walls were possibly carved by his followers.

The Isle of Whithorn, 3 miles south-east, is where St Ninian landed *c.* AD 395, on his return from studying in Rome, to bring Christianity to Scotland. The ruins of a plain 13th-century chapel still stand, but there is no sign of any earlier church. On the point of the promontory are the remains of an Iron Age fort, and a late 17th-century tower.

Wigtown

This town is still a centre for The Machars peninsula, though its harbour is now silted up. The area is good for fishing and wildfowling. Two market crosses, an 18th-century one topped by a sundial and another which was erected in 1816, stand in the town's spacious central square. In 1685 two women Covenanters who were accused of attending the meetings of their sect were tied to stakes at the mouth of the River Bladnoch and drowned by the rising tide after refusing to give up their beliefs. A post marks the traditional site of their martyrdom. A monument to all the Covenanters stands on Windyhill, behind the town.

Three miles north-west, near Torhousekie Farm, are the Bronze Age Stones of Torhouse—19 standing stones in a circle. A mile south-west of Wigtown are the remains of Baldoon Castle, the setting for Sir Walter Scott's novel *The Bride of Lammermoor*.

SHORE CHAPEL *The remains of Chapel Finian are on the coast 5 miles north-west of Port William, and they are believed to date back to the 10th century*

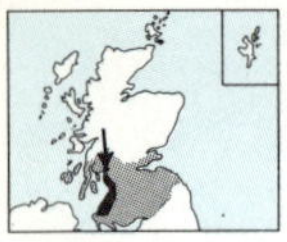

Landscape of Robert Burns

Angling Trout at Alloway and Greenock, in reservoirs near Girvan and on the River Stinchar.

Golf courses There are courses at Largs, Maybole, Prestwick, Troon, Girvan, Kilmarnock, New Cumnock, Turnberry and Skelmorlie.

Events Ayr has a music festival in Mar., and a sea-angling contest in July.

Places to see *Bachelors' Club* (NTS), Tarbolton, made famous by Burns: Apr. to Sept., daily. *Burns Cottage and Museum*, Alloway: weekdays, Sun. afternoon. *Burns Museum*, Kay Park, Kilmarnock: daily. *Burns Museum*, 28 Eglington Street, Irvine: by request. *Culzean Castle* (NTS): Apr. to Oct., daily; park open all year. *Dean Castle*, Kilmarnock: afternoons; also Sat. and Sun. mornings, mid-May to mid-Sept. *Loudoun Hall,* Vennel, Ayr: daily, July to Sept. *McLean Museum and Art Gallery*, Greenock: weekdays. *Souter Johnnie's Cottage* (NTS), Kirkoswald: Apr. to Sept., afternoons except Fri. *Tam o'Shanter Burns Museum*, Ayr: Apr. to Sept., weekdays; Oct. to Mar., weekday afternoons; also Sun. afternoon June to Aug.

Car ferries Ardrossan to Arran; Wemyss Bay to Rothesay; Gourock to Dunoon and Kilcreggan.

Information centres 30 Miller Road, Ayr. Tel. Ayr 68077. 15 Links Road, Prestwick. Tel. Prestwick 79234.

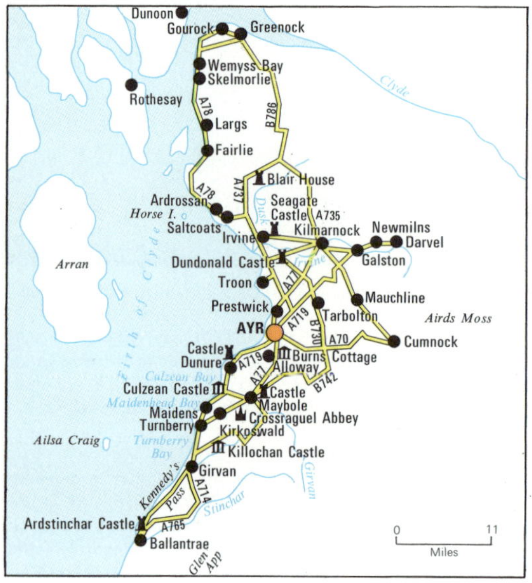

Southwards from Gourock, the holiday towns and steamer ports along the coast form a natural playground for the residents of the Clydeside shipbuilding towns. Where the hills come right down to the coast, to the north and south, there are cliffs and rocky coves; in between, broad bays are fringed with wide stretches of sandy shore. The coastline is sheltered to the east by a line of hills and to the west by the islands of Argyll, Bute and Arran, which can be seen across the Firth of Clyde. This protection, together with the warm currents of the Gulf Stream which surround the coast, gives a mild climate throughout the year.

This area is famous for its Ayrshire dairy cattle and early potatoes. The farming regions are backed by lofty hills where crystal-clear rivers, such as the Stinchar, wind through wooded valleys. Ruined strongholds overlooking river valleys and coastal bays are reminders of harsher times in Scottish history.

Robert Burns, Scotland's national poet, was born in Alloway on January 25, 1759, a date celebrated by Scotsmen all over the world as Burns Night. He drew much of his inspiration from the landscape. Towns and villages such as Alloway, Kirkoswald, Ayr, Mauchline and Tarbolton have been immortalised in his lyrics. Another famous Scot, Sir Alexander Fleming, who discovered penicillin in 1928, was born in Loudoun, Galston, in 1881.

BURNS COTTAGE *The gardener's cottage at Alloway in which Robert Burns was born in 1759 is now a museum*

Ayr
An attractive resort with excellent beaches and a fishing harbour. The town is notable for its connections with Robert Burns, who was born at Alloway, 2 miles south, in a thatched cottage which is preserved as a museum. The Brig o' Doon, mentioned in Burns's poem 'Tam o' Shanter', still spans the river—a simple arched bridge flanked by beautiful gardens.

Kirk Alloway, also mentioned in the poem, stands roofless not far away: the poet's father is buried in the graveyard. The 13th-century Auld Brig o' Ayr, Burns's '. . . poor narrow footpath of a street, Where two wheel-barrows tremble when they meet', was renovated in 1910. A Burns museum is housed in the thatched Tam o' Shanter Inn in Ayr High Street. The Auld Kirk of Ayr dates from 1654 when it replaced the 12th-century Church of St John.

Cumnock
An industrial and market town, surrounded by hills, in a mining district. Outside the town hall is a bust of James Keir Hardie, one of the founders of the Labour Party, who lived in the town when he was secretary of the Miners' Federation. Two miles north is Airds Moss, a barren expanse of moorland where Government troops defeated the Covenanters in 1680.

Girvan
A resort with sandy beaches and good fishing. A whisky distillery offers guided tours to visitors. Ailsa Craig, a 1110 ft high rock 10 miles off-shore, is a nesting ground for seabirds and provides the granite from which the stones used in the Scottish game of curling are made.

Killochan Castle, 3 miles north-east of Girvan, is the impressive 16th-century

KENNEDY'S PASS *The coast road south of*

SCENE OF TORTURE *Dunure Castle was the home of the 4th Earl of Cassillis, who in 1570 tortured the Abbot of Crossraguel by roasting to make him give up the abbey lands*

stronghold of the Cathcarts of Carleton in the valley of the Water of Girvan. Kennedy's Pass is the most dramatic part of the coastal road from Girvan to the resort village of Ballantrae, 12 miles south. Ballantrae, with its sand and shingle beaches, is on the fringe of some of the region's most attractive scenery. Near the bridge over the River Stinchar are the ruins of the 13th-century Ardstinchar Castle, an ancient stronghold of the Bargany Kennedy family.

Girvan follows a dramatic coastline

Greenock
An important industrial and ship-building town on the Clyde Estuary, and the birthplace in 1736 of James Watt, inventor of the steam engine. His statue stands in the Watt Library. A huge Cross of Lorraine on Lyle Hill, above the town, commemorates Free French sailors who died in the Battle of the Atlantic during the Second World War.

Gourock, 3 miles west along the Renfrew coast, is a well-known resort and yachting centre and an embarkation point for Clyde pleasure steamers.

Irvine
A manufacturing town and port which was Robert Burns's home from 1781 to 1782. The Burns Club was established in 1826 and is now a museum. The ruined 14th-century Seagate Castle was visited by Mary, Queen of Scots in 1563, and Marymass Week is held annually in the third week of August to commemorate the occasion.

Blair House, 6 miles north, is a fine 17th-century stronghold built by the Blair family around a 14th-century keep. The glen of Dusk Water, which flows through the grounds of the house, contains a cave with stalactites.

On the sandy dunes just north of Irvine is the Ardeer explosives factory; the site was chosen in 1873 by Alfred Nobel, the Swedish chemist, inventor of dynamite, and founder of the Nobel Prize. Today this is one of the main centres for the production of explosives in Britain. Saltcoats and Ardrossan, 6 miles north-west across a bay, have excellent sandy beaches and fine views across the Firth of Clyde. Horse Isle, a rocky nature reserve for seabirds, lies just off Ardrossan.

Kilmarnock
Johnny Walker, a grocer in King Street, started to blend whisky in Kilmarnock in 1820; today the whisky-bottling concern is the largest in the world. The town also has associations with Robert Burns. The first edition of his poems was printed here in 1786. Burns published these poems to raise the money to emigrate to Jamaica, but their success made him remain. A copy is housed in a museum inside the red-sandstone Burns Monument in Kay Park.

Dundonald Castle, $4\frac{1}{2}$ miles south-west, is a notable landmark high on an isolated hill. It was built by Robert II, the first Stuart king, who died there in 1390, as did Robert III in 1406.

East along the River Irvine from Kilmarnock are the three lace-making towns of Galston, Newmilns and Darvel, where Dutch and Huguenot immigrants settled in the 17th century.

Largs
Hills that rise to more than 1700 ft shelter this popular yachting resort. Day-long steamer cruises around the islands of the Firth of Clyde leave from its bay. Skelmorlie Aisle is all that remains of the 17th-century parish church; it has an elaborately painted wooden roof and fine carvings. A wide panorama of sea and mountains can be seen from the 50-acre Douglas Park, 600 ft above sea level. A round tower at Bowen Craig marks the naval victory of the Scots over King Håkon in 1263.

Mauchline
A farming town, noted also for making curling stones. Robert Burns began his married life there in 1788; his house in Castle Street is now a museum and his favourite 'howff', or inn, Poosie Nansie's, is little changed. Mossgiel Farm, 1 mile north-west, was rented by the poet and his brother in 1784, and a Burns memorial tower stands just to the east. From 1777 to 1784, Burns lived with his family at Lochlea Farm, near Tarbolton, 4 miles west of Mauchline. The village was enlivened at this time by the Bachelors' Club, a debating society founded in 1780 by the poet and his friends. The 17th-century thatched cottage where the members used to meet is now a museum.

Maybole
The former seat of the Earl of Cassillis, head of the powerful Lowland family of the Kennedys. The restored 17th-century Maybole Castle in the High Street was their town house. The ruined Collegiate church was founded in 1371, but later became the burial place of the Earls of Cassillis.

Crossraguel Abbey, 2 miles south-west, was a Cluniac house, founded in 1244. Its extensive ruins, notably the turreted gatehouse, the 240-box dovecot and the abbot's tower, date mainly from the 15th century.

Kirkoswald, 2 miles further south-west along the A77, is the village where Burns's character Souter Johnnie, Tam o' Shanter's crony, lived; his 18th-century thatched cottage is a Burns museum. The road continues to Turnberry and Maidens, sheltered resorts with sandy beaches and facilities for water-skiing and fishing. Culzean Castle was begun by Robert Adam in 1777 for the 10th Earl of Cassillis, around an older Kennedy stronghold. It is set in a 560-acre park, with cliff-top paths overlooking Culzean Bay.

Five miles north, on the way to the small fishing village of Dunure, is the 'Electric Brae', where an optical illusion, caused by the configuration of the surrounding countryside, makes the road appear to be descending, where in fact it is ascending.

ADAM MANSION *Culzean Castle, overlooking the Firth of Clyde, is one of the finest Adam houses in Scotland. It was begun by Robert Adam in 1777 for the 10th Earl of Cassillis in mock-Gothic style, incorporating the tower of an earlier Kennedy stronghold*

How Scotch Whisky is made

Scotch whisky was a by-product of traditional Scottish thrift. Frugal Scots farmers, rather than waste their surplus barley, mashed, fermented and distilled it, producing a drink at first called *uisge beatha*, Gaelic for 'water of life', and now simply called whisky. No one knows when the Scots learnt the art of distilling, though it may have been before they arrived from Ireland in the 5th century AD, for in Irish legend St Patrick taught the art. The first mention in Scottish records of a spirit distilled from grain does not occur before 1494, when the Exchequer Rolls record the provision of 'eight bolls of malt to Friar John Cor wherewith to make aquavitae'.

Today there are two kinds of Scotch whisky—the original malt whisky, made by the centuries-old pot-still process from barley that has been 'malted', or soaked and left to germinate; and grain whisky, made from maize as well as malted and unmalted barley, using the patent still process developed at the beginning of the 19th century. Most of the well-known brands of Scotch whisky are blends of many different grain and malt whiskies. The technique of blending was pioneered in Edinburgh in the 1860's, and a taste for the new, milder blended whiskies quickly spread to England and then to the rest of the world.

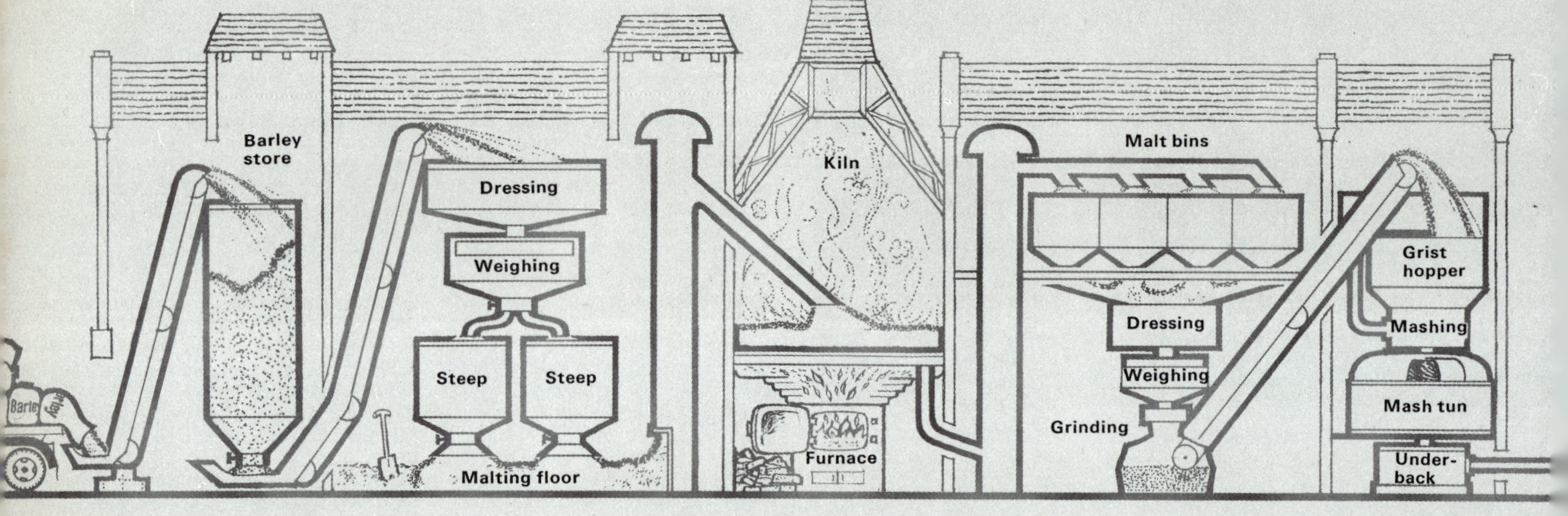

Barley store Barley is the raw material of the malt whisky distiller; but Scotch whisky is not necessarily distilled from barley grown in Scotland. For generations, the distillers in Glenlivet and Speyside used barley from the fertile fields of Moray and Banff. Today, with the world-wide demand for Scotch whisky, Scotland can supply only about one-third of the barley required by its distilleries, and most of the rest is grown in England.

The first process in making whisky is malting—turning barley into malt. Traditionally, the distiller does his own malting, though as the demand for whisky has grown, an increasing number of distillers have taken to buying ready-malted barley.

Malting begins when the distiller takes delivery of the barley, usually in September or October, soon after it has been harvested. The barley is in grain form, and must be ripe and dry, otherwise it may turn mouldy and make properly controlled malting impossible. It is stored in bins until ready for use, and then carried by elevators to the maltings

Maltings The barley is cleaned, weighed and soaked for two or three days in tanks of water called steeps. Then it is spread on the malting floor, where it germinates for 8–12 days, secreting an enzyme which makes the starch in barley soluble and prepares it for turning into sugar. The barley is regularly turned over (below) to control its temperature and rate of germination

Peat kiln The warm, damp, sweet-smelling barley is passed to the kiln for drying, which stops germination. It is spread on a base of perforated iron or wire mesh and dried in the heat of a peat fire (below). Distillery kilns have distinctive pagoda-shaped heads. An open ventilator at the top draws hot air from the peat fire through the barley. This gives it a smoky flavour which is passed on to the whisky

Malt storage The barley has now become malt—dry, crisp, peat-flavoured, different from the original barley in all but appearance. It is ready for the next stage in the process—mashing. It is stored in bins and then released (below) into a dressing machine, where it is cleaned. Then it is weighed to ensure that the right amount of malt is passed to the mill below, where it is ground

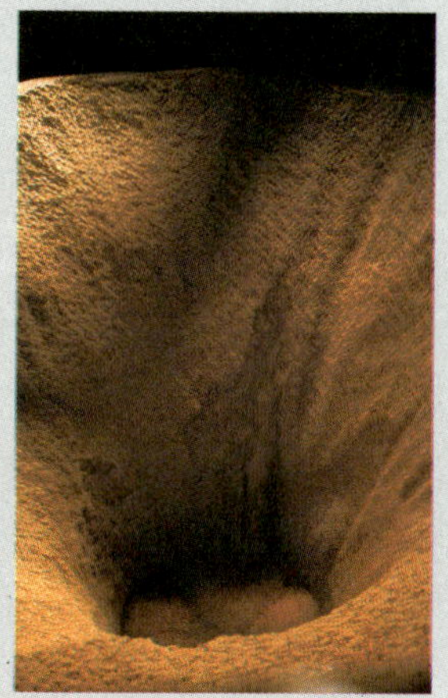

Mash house The ground malt, called grist, is carried up to the grist hopper and fed in measured quantities into the mash tun, an enormous vat able to hold several thousand gallons of liquid. In the mash tun the grist is mixed with hot water and left to infuse. This extracts the sugar content from the malt. The sugary water, called wort, is then drawn off through the bottom of the mash tun.

This process of mashing is repeated three or sometimes four times, and each time the water is at a different temperature. The first two extractions of wort pass to a container called the under-back. The liquid is clear, not yet alcoholic, and ready to go on to the next stage in the process—fermentation. The other extractions, because they are weaker, are drained back to the water tanks and used again when the next batch of malt is mashed.

Draff, the spent grain left in the mash tun after the wort has been drawn off, is taken by conveyor to the distillery's yard and sold as winter food for cattle. Usually draff accounts for about a quarter of the original malt

16th-century pot still For centuries, Scotch whisky has been made from malted barley mixed with yeast and water, then heated in pear-shaped containers called pot stills. The early Highland farmers who distilled their own whisky heated their pot stills in huge copper kettles over a peat fire (right). Smoke from the peat added to the whisky's flavour. Big modern distillers use basically the same technique. The vapour that rises in the still is condensed by cooling to make whisky. The shape of the still affects the vapour and so helps to give the whisky its taste

Highland water The legal definition of Scotch whisky is whisky made in Scotland, but even without this protection the drink would retain its individuality. Pure air and a cold climate, soft water from Highland burns, fine barley and fragrant peat combine with traditional skills and a centuries-old technique to produce a uniquely Scottish 'water of life'. The most important single influence on the taste of Scotch whisky is probably the Scottish water. This is why distilleries are often situated in narrow glens or in remote country near a tumbling stream

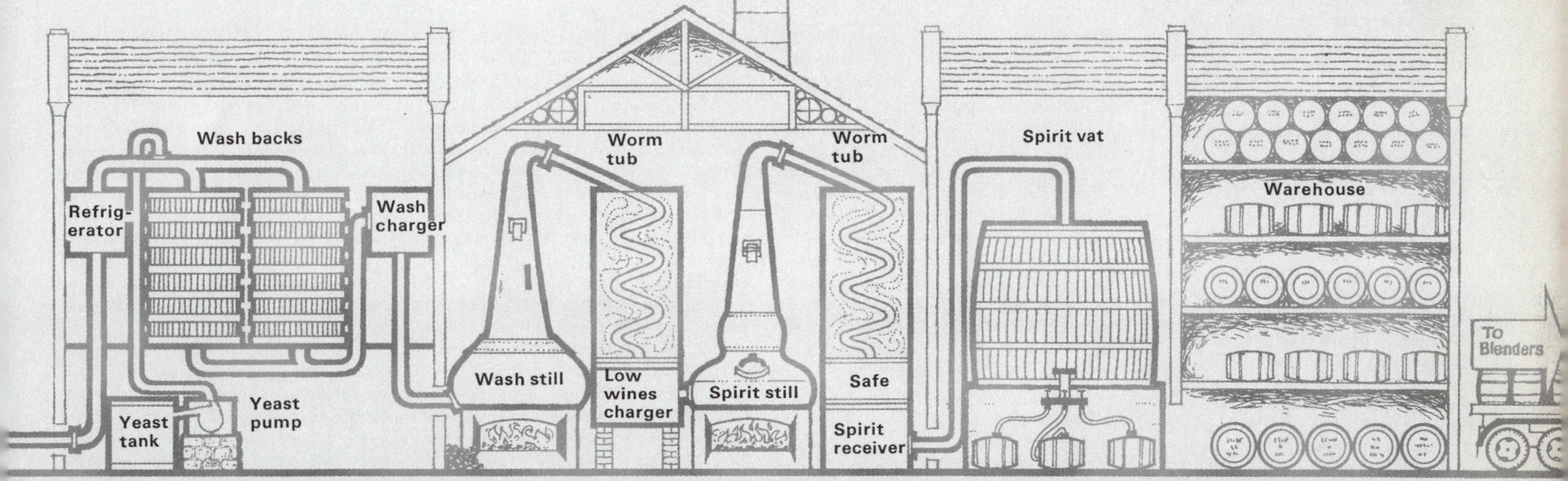

Illustration based on diagrams by The Scotch Whisky Association and The Distillers Company Ltd

Fermentation The wort is pumped from the underback into a refrigerator, for unless it is cooled the sugar would decompose and the heat would destroy the yeast used to ferment the liquid. As soon as the wort reaches a temperature of about 22°C (72°F), it is pumped into the washbacks, large vessels which hold from 2000 to 10,000 gallons of liquid. In a big distillery there may be as many as ten of these enormous vats.

Now yeast is added and fermentation begins. The yeast attacks the sugar in the wort and converts it into crude alcohol and carbon dioxide. The liquid starts to bubble as the gas rises to the surface. From the first gentle activity the process becomes gradually more furious, as the gas builds up and the yeast rises.

The distiller leaves a space of 3–4 ft between the liquid and the top of the washback. He uses mechanical stirrers, which skim the surface of the liquid, to prevent the yeast from rising too far. Before the distilleries were mechanised, this job was done by men who beat the surface of the liquid with sticks. Fermentation lasts for about 48 hours, sometimes less, and produces a clear liquid called wash containing low-strength alcohol and some unfermentable matter. All the carbon dioxide has escaped, and the wash is ready to be distilled

Distillation The wash is heated in copper stills (below) so that the alcohol becomes vapour and the unwanted residue is eliminated. The vapour rises and passes through a coiled tube or worm which is kept cool by running water. This condenses it back into a rough and as yet unpalatable liquid, known as low wines. The liquid is distilled again, then tested in the spirit safe by the stillman. If the spirit has reached an acceptable standard, it is collected in the spirit receiver; if not, it is re-distilled

Spirit store The whisky comes colourless and fiery from the spirit receiver. In the spirit vat it is diluted to about 110 degrees proof before being run into oak casks to mature (below). 'Proof spirit' means spirit of standard and approved strength. This standard was once determined by dampening gunpowder with the spirit and then applying a light to see if it would ignite. Today, 100 degrees proof spirit by British standards is spirit with 57·1 per cent of alcohol by volume, and 42·9 per cent of water

Maturing and blending Scotch whisky cannot legally be sold for consumption until it has matured in casks for at least three years. The time a whisky takes to mature depends on the size of the casks used, the strength at which the spirit is stored and the temperature and humidity of the warehouse. A good malt whisky may have been left in the cask for 15 years, or even longer. Air enters the oak casks and evaporation takes place. Eventually, the whisky loses its coarseness and becomes smooth and mellow.

There are more than 100 distilleries in Scotland and the whisky made in each has its own distinctive character. Some distilleries bottle part of their spirit and sell it as a single whisky; but most whiskies go to a blender. As many as 40 different single whiskies may be blended to make up the whisky that is eventually sold. After blending, the whisky is returned to casks and left for some months so that the different spirits can 'marry'.

When whisky comes from the distiller's spirit vat, it is a colourless liquid. In the casks, it gradually turns golden-brown. The blender, before putting his whisky on the market, may add a dash of caramel to perfect its colouring. He also dilutes it with water—70 degrees proof is normal for the home market and 75 degrees for general export

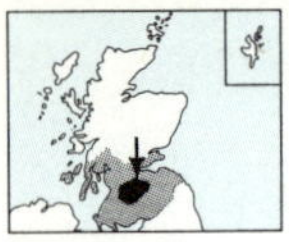

Gentle hills where the Clyde and Tweed rise

Angling There are trout in the River Tweed at Peebles and at Walkerburn, 2 miles east of Innerleithen (Apr. to Sept.), and salmon (mid-Feb. to Nov.). There are trout and grayling in the River Clyde at Lanark and Biggar.

Events The Beltane Festival, derived from a Celtic sun-worshipping ceremony, is held in Peebles in late June (Beltane originally meant a fire). A Fleming Queen (Mary Fleming was one of Mary, Queen of Scots' ladies-in-waiting) is crowned at Biggar in July. The Whuppity Scourie ceremony at Lanark on Mar. 1 is believed to be a relic of a pagan ceremony of chasing away winter.

Places to see *Dawyck House*, Stobo, ancient home of the Veitch and Naesmyth families, and of the Balfours since 1897; gardens only: mid-Apr. to Oct., afternoons. *Gladstone Court Museum*, Biggar: Easter to Oct., weekdays and Sun. afternoon. *John Hastie Museum*, Strathaven: Mon. to Fri. afternoons; also Sat. afternoon May to Sept. *Neidpath Castle*, Peebles: Easter to mid-Oct., weekdays, Sun. afternoon. *Traquair House*: mid-May to Sept., afternoons except Fri. *Tweeddale Museum*, Chambers Institute, Peebles: weekdays.

Information centre High Street, Peebles. Tel. Peebles 20138 (summer only).

Two of Britain's great rivers, the Clyde and the Tweed, rise within a mile of each other in the Southern Uplands of Scotland. The Tweed begins at Tweed's Well and the Clyde over the hills to the west; then for some miles the rivers run parallel before the Clyde turns north-west to the sea at Dumbarton and the Tweed north-east to Berwick. A third river, the Annan, rises in the same area and flows southwards. The Uplands are good walking country because, although the land rises in many places to more than 2000 ft, the slopes are gentle. Hills have descriptive names—'dods' are rounded summits, 'laws' are conical hills and 'rigs' are ridges. From their summits the walker can look eastwards over rolling green acres, or westwards down shallow vales towards Lanark.

Clydesdale is a rich valley devoted to growing fruit and vegetables; and sheep graze on the hills above the Tweed—providing the wool for the tweed cloth that has been woven in the small towns for two centuries.

Biggar
A town consisting largely of one long street along the valley of the Biggar Water. Only a tower remains of Boghall Castle, the home of Mary Fleming, one of the 'Four Marys' who were ladies-in-waiting to Mary, Queen of Scots; the others were Mary Seton, Mary Beaton and Mary Livingstone. Mary Fleming is remembered every July in the crowning of the Fleming Queen. There is a re-creation of a street of 19th-century shops in the Gladstone Court Museum—named after the family of William Ewart Gladstone, the Victorian Prime Minister, who came from the district.

Douglas
A coal-mining town on the Douglas Water, with a fragment of the 18th-century castle which was the model for Sir Walter Scott's *Castle Dangerous*. A new coal seam was opened beneath it in the 1940's and the undermining reduced it to ruins. An earlier castle on the site was the Douglases' stronghold; many of their warriors are buried in the partly 12th-century St Bride's Church. The tombs include those of 'the good Sir James of Douglas', who was killed by the Moors in Spain in 1330 while taking the heart of Robert the Bruce to the Holy Land, and of Archibald 'Bell the Cat', 5th Earl of Angus, who died in 1514. He was given the nickname after he killed Robert Cochrane, the low-born favourite of James III, in 1482.

Innerleithen
A village where Leithen Water meets the Tweed. Its first tweed mill was built in 1790, and the village became a tourist attraction 40 years later after Sir Walter Scott published his novel *St Ronan's Well*, in which he associated a local well, known until then as Doo's Well, with the 8th-century saint. The expulsion of the Devil by St Ronan is re-enacted every summer at the St Ronan Games.

Lanark
A town where David I built a castle in the 12th century. Nothing is left of the castle, but Lanark is still an important market town. New Lanark, 1 mile south, was founded as a socialistic experiment in 1784 by David Dale, a philanthropist, who built houses and cotton mills. His son-in-law, Robert Owen, became a partner in the mills and developed many welfare schemes for the workers, including a working day reduced to 10½ hours, a cost-price shop and schools for their children.

New Lanark looks over Cora Linn, which has a 90-ft waterfall, the most spectacular of the Clyde Falls. Cartland Crags rise to 400 ft, forming a chasm nearly a mile in length along the Mouse Water west of Lanark.

Leadhills
A ski resort and one of the highest villages in Scotland, 1350 ft above sea level. It gets its name from the lead mined in the Lowther Hills between the 13th and 19th centuries. Some gold was also found here, and it is believed to have been used in the crowns of Scottish kings. The poet Allan Ramsay was born at Leadhills in 1686; in 1741 he started a circulating library in Edinburgh, believed to be Britain's first.

Peebles
A quiet county town manufacturing tweeds and knitwear, and popular as a centre for salmon fishing on the Tweed. The bridge dates from the 15th century. The Chambers Institute, a library and museum, was given to the town by William Chambers (1800–83) and his brother Robert (1802–71), who were born in Peebles and published the first Chambers's dictionaries and encyclopedias. Among the town's historical remains are the ruins of Cross Kirk, built by Alexander II in 1261.

Neidpath Castle, built in the 15th century on a hill overlooking the Tweed, was held by the Earl of Tweeddale for Charles I in the Civil War until Cromwell's artillery battered its 11 ft thick walls and forced its defenders into submission. It was later restored and sold to the Queensberry family. The spendthrift 4th Duke, William Douglas Queensberry, known as 'Old Q', felled all the trees on the estate in the 18th century to raise money. He was denounced in a Wordsworth sonnet beginning 'Degenerate Douglas! Oh, the unworthy lord!'

St Mary's Loch
The green hills of the Ettrick Forest surround the 3 mile long loch whose beauty was praised by Wordsworth, Scott and by James Hogg, the 19th-century poet who lived at Ettrick, 6 miles south, and was known as the 'Ettrick Shepherd'. His statue is on a hill overlooking the loch. Dryhope Tower, now in ruins, was the home of Mary Scott, an ancestor of Sir Walter Scott. From Cappercleuch, on the northern shore of the loch, a single-track road follows the Megget Water to the isolated Talla Reservoir, giving fine hill views.

Stobo
A hamlet in the Tweed Valley, with a restored Norman church. Across the river is Dawyck House, a castellated mansion where Carl von Linné, the 18th-century Swedish naturalist who became famous for classifying plants and animals, visited his pupil Sir James Naesmyth. After the visit Naesmyth introduced many species of trees, including the larch, into Scotland.

ETTRICK SHEPHERD *This statue of James Hogg overlooks St Mary's Loch*

SALMON *Peebles' coat of arms has a motto: 'Against the stream they multiply'*

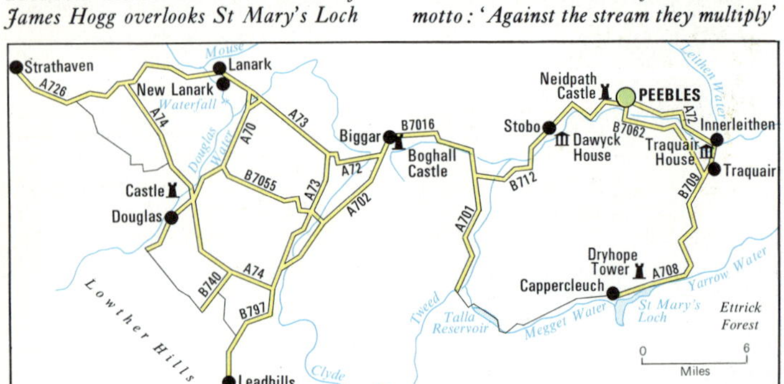

CROMWELL'S TARGET *The River Tweed winds past 15th-century Neidpath Castle, which was battered into submission by Cromwell's artillery in the Civil War and later restored*

Strathaven
A market town which became prosperous because of its silk industry in the Middle Ages. Dungavel House, once the shooting lodge of the Dukes of Hamilton, is a training centre for miners. West of the town is Lauder Ha', Sir Harry Lauder's home until his death in 1950.

Traquair
A hamlet on the Quair Water. Traquair House dates back to the 10th century and is one of the oldest inhabited houses in Scotland, although most of it was rebuilt in the 17th century. The mansion, with its little turrets and small windows, has sheltered 27 English and Scottish monarchs. William The Lion (1143–1214), when King of Scotland, held court in Traquair House and Mary, Queen of Scots stayed there in 1566.

There are two accounts of the house's Bear Gates, or Steekit Yetts. One version says that they were locked by the 7th Earl of Traquair after his young wife died in 1796, with orders that they should not be re-opened until an 8th countess entered the house—but the 7th was the last. Sir Walter Scott, however, said that the gates were closed after the Jacobite rising of 1745, and that they would not be opened until a Stuart once more ascended the throne.

THE LONG HISTORY AND THE STRONG ALE OF TRAQUAIR HOUSE

Traquair House is one of the oldest inhabited houses in Scotland. A thousand years of history lie behind the grey walls where 27 English and Scottish monarchs have stayed or held court. Mary, Queen of Scots visited Traquair in 1566, and Bonnie Prince Charlie stopped there in the rebellion of 1745. The house contains silver, glass, tapestries and embroideries from the 13th century, and relics of Mary

Beer was brewed in Traquair House for the staff and tenants of the estate for centuries. The strong ale, brewed in a 200-year-old copper, is now bottled and sold to visitors

Castles on a resort coast

Angling There is sea fishing from Dunbar and North Berwick. Trout in lochs and burns at Longformacus.

Places to see *Dirleton Castle and Gardens*: weekdays, Sun. afternoons. *Hailes Castle*: weekdays, Sun. afternoons. *Hamilton House* (NTS), Prestonpans: by appointment with tenant. *Inveresk Lodge Gardens* (NTS), Musselburgh: Mon., Wed., Fri.; also Sun. afternoons when occupied. *Lennoxlove*, Haddington: contents include the death mask of Mary, Queen of Scots: by written appointment. *Museum of Flight*, North Berwick: July and Aug., daily. *North Berwick Museum*: May to Sept., weekdays, Sun. afternoon . *Myreton Motor Museum*, Aberlady: Easter to Oct., daily: Nov. to Easter, Sat. and Sun. only. *Preston Mill* (NTS), East Linton: weekdays, Sun. afternoon.

Information centres Town House, High Street, Dunbar. Tel. Dunbar 63353. Quality Street, North Berwick. Tel. North Berwick 2197.

The country bordering the coast of eastern Lothian and Borders is a richly productive corner. Some of Scotland's finest agricultural land lies between the Lammermuir Hills and the coast, where fishing is still a thriving industry. Narrow, high-hedged roads and lanes thread among prosperous villages with broad greens. The farms are large, with cultivated acres running up to the foothills; and a characteristic feature of many large houses is an elaborate dovecot in the grounds, a relic of the Middle Ages when pigeons were a source of food.

The coast begins gently in the west with grassy dunes, but to the east becomes rocky then precipitous towards the 300-ft St Abb's Head. There are many sandy beaches with, almost invariably, golf courses behind them. The eastern part of Lothian has been called 'The Holy Land of golf', because it has a golfing tradition going back to the 16th century.

The Lammermuirs, gentle green hills that do not demand too much of the walker, offer panoramic views of the region. By-ways round the villages of Spott, Innerwick and Oldhamstocks give particularly rewarding views of the coast and the hills. An attractive drive starts from Garvald or from Gifford, winding through hills and over Moss Law (1346 ft) before descending to the Whiteadder valley.

TANTALLON CASTLE *The 14th-century castle, described in Scott's* Marmion, *is perched on cliffs above the Firth of Forth*

EYEMOUTH *The gardens of Gunsgreen House, which was an 18th-century smugglers' den, overlook the harbour*

Dirleton

A village with a 17th-century church and houses round a green. The massive sandstone Dirleton Castle was built in the early 13th century by the Norman De Vaux family, and Wallace's Scottish supporters held out here against Edward I's army in 1298. The castle was destroyed by Cromwell's troops in 1650 and was not rebuilt. The ruins contain a flower garden and a 17th-century bowling green, surrounded by yew trees, which is still in use.

Dunbar

A seaport and resort with a castle, now in ruins, where Mary, Queen of Scots stayed with Bothwell a few days before she surrendered to her rebellious nobles in 1567. The charming 17th-century Town House has a six-sided tower, and in the church, which was rebuilt in 1821, is an ornate marble monument to George Home, 1st Earl of Dunbar and Lord High Treasurer of Scotland, who died in 1611.

There is safe bathing from Belhaven Beach, 1 mile west, and from White Sands, 2 miles east. At Barns Ness, on the eastern edge of White Sands, fossils are abundant in the limestone cliffs.

East Linton

A village dominated by the ruins of 13th-century Hailes Castle, another of the places where Mary, Queen of Scots and Bothwell stayed in 1567 when fleeing from hostile Scottish lords. Traprain Law (734 ft), which rises south of the castle, was the site of a Celtic town, and an important hoard of native and Roman silver was found there in 1919. John Rennie, the designer of the old Waterloo Bridge in London, was born in 1761 at a mansion called Phantassie. A dovecot from the mansion is preserved near Preston Mill. The 18th-century mill, owned by the National Trust for Scotland, is the oldest working grain-mill operated by water in Scotland.

Eyemouth

A busy fishing town with cobbled streets, narrow 'pends', or archways leading to small courtyards, and 'wynds', narrow passageways between the buildings. Eyemouth was the scene of one of the worst fishing disasters in Scottish history in October 1881, when 129 men, almost the entire male population of Eyemouth, lost their lives in a storm. At Coldingham, 3 miles north-west of Eyemouth, are the ruins of an 11th-century Benedictine priory which was damaged in Border raids in 1216 and 1544. It was finally destroyed by Cromwell's troops in 1648. The parish church has been built into the ruins.

The 300-ft cliffs of St Abb's Head, 2 miles north-west of Eyemouth, have been the graveyard of many ships. The cliffs are honeycombed with caves, used by smugglers up to the 18th century. Fast Castle, a further 3½ miles west, was owned by the Home and Logan families and is now in ruins. Sir Walter Scott described it as 'Wolf's Crag' in *The Bride of Lammermoor*.

Gifford

An attractive village, with an avenue leading to Yester House, a fine Adam mansion built in 1745 and the home of the Marquess of Tweeddale. In the ruins of Yester Castle, 1½ miles south-east of the village, is a vaulted underground chamber known as Goblin Ha', which is said to have been built by a 13th-century local magician known as Hugo the Wizard. Gifford is a good centre for exploring the Lammermuir Hills. The new Cistercian abbey of Sancta Maria at Garvald, 4 miles north-east of Gifford, was begun in 1950.

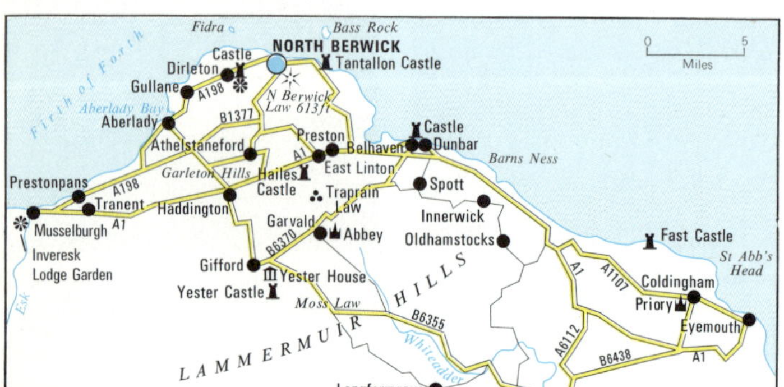

LAST SURVIVOR *Preston Mill, near East Linton, is the oldest working grain-mill in Scotland. The mill, dating from the 18th century, has two buildings—a conical kiln for drying grain and a barn containing machinery for grinding the corn. The machinery is driven by water from the mill-pond, beside which is a nesting-place for Muscovy ducks*

Gullane
A village, holiday resort and golfing centre. There are sandy beaches, and three public golf courses with magnificent views over the Firth of Forth. The championship course at Muirfield, half a mile north, is the headquarters of the Honourable Company of Edinburgh Golfers, founded in 1744 and the oldest golf club in the world. Visitors may play there only at the invitation of a member. Just south of Gullane is Aberlady Bay's 1439-acre nature reserve, the haunt of waders and wildfowl. The village of Aberlady was the port for Haddington until its harbour silted up in the 19th century. Its Myreton Motor Museum has a collection of old bicycles and motor vehicles dating from 1866.

Haddington
A gracious town with wide streets and a splendidly proportioned Town House, built by William Adam, father of the more famous Robert Adam, in 1748. An addition built 40 years later is now the Assembly Room and Council Chamber. The town was laid out as a long, narrow triangle in the 12th century and these boundaries can still be seen by following the line of High Street, Market Street and Hardgate.

Kinloch House is the gabled 18th-century town mansion of the Kinlochs of Gilmerton. The 15th-century St Mary's Church is known as the 'Lamp of Lothian' because of a lantern once on its tower. Until recent restoration, much of the church has lain in ruins since 1548, when the Scots and French besieged the English at Haddington.

At Athelstaneford, 2 miles north of Haddington in the Garleton Hills, a plaque marks the spot where a saltire, or Cross of St Andrew, is said to have appeared in the sky before the Picts and Scots decisively defeated a Northumbrian army—possibly led by the Saxon king, Athelstan—in AD 933.

Musselburgh
A fishing and manufacturing town at the mouth of the River Esk. Its three-arched 16th-century footbridge rests on Roman foundations. The town is celebrated for its golf course and has extensive market gardens, which developed the well-known Musselburgh strain of leeks. Every autumn, fishermen from Musselburgh hold 'Walks of Thanksgiving' for their catches.

North Berwick
One of the most popular east-coast resorts for swimming, sailing, golf and fishing. Behind the town is the 613-ft conical peak of North Berwick Law, crowned by a ruined watchtower and an arch formed from the jawbones of a whale. Just over a mile out in the Firth of Forth is 350 ft high Bass Rock. Gannets wheel endlessly round the rock and its satellite islands, which are all nature reserves. Boats from North Berwick Harbour make pleasure trips round the islands.

Tantallon Castle, 3 miles east, was built in 1375 and was the Douglas stronghold for centuries. It is on a headland with sheer 100-ft cliffs on three sides and a moat guarding the landward side. According to an old saying, an impossible task was 'like knocking down Tantallon or building a bridge to the Bass'. In fact Tantallon was knocked down. It withstood a siege by James V in 1528, but Cromwell's men under General George Monk reduced it to ruins in a 12-day bombardment in 1651. Extensive earthworks survive from the original castle defences.

Prestonpans
A manufacturing and seaside town, named after its salt pans. The salt industry was established in the town in the 12th century by the monks of Newbattle Abbey, and it became the exclusive supplier of eastern Scotland. Its monopoly was broken in 1707 when the Act of Union made it possible for salt to be imported into Scotland from England.

Prestonpans has a fine 17th-century mercat cross. There are several outstanding 17th-century houses: Hamilton House, dated 1628; Northfield House; and Preston House, of which only a portion remains. Bonnie Prince Charlie's troops had a swift success outside the town in 1745, defeating Sir John Cope's army in ten minutes.

DIRLETON CASTLE *The walls of the ruined castle rise straight from sheer rock*

Lothian landmarks in stone and steel

Events Riding the Marches and Common Riding take place at Linlithgow in June. Bo'ness Fair is held on a Fri., usually at the end of June or early in July. The Royal Highland Show is held at Ingliston in mid-June.

Places to see *Blackness Castle*: weekdays, Sun. afternoon. *Dalkeith Park*: Easter to Sept., daily. *Hopetoun House*: Easter; then daily late Apr. to Sept. *House of the Binns* (NTS): Easter; also May to Sept., afternoons except Fri. *Kinneil House*: weekdays, Sun. afternoon. *Linlithgow Palace*: weekdays and Sun. afternoon. *Roslin Castle*: Easter to Oct., weekdays.

Information centre The Vennel Car Park, Linlithgow. Tel. Linlithgow 4600 (summer only).

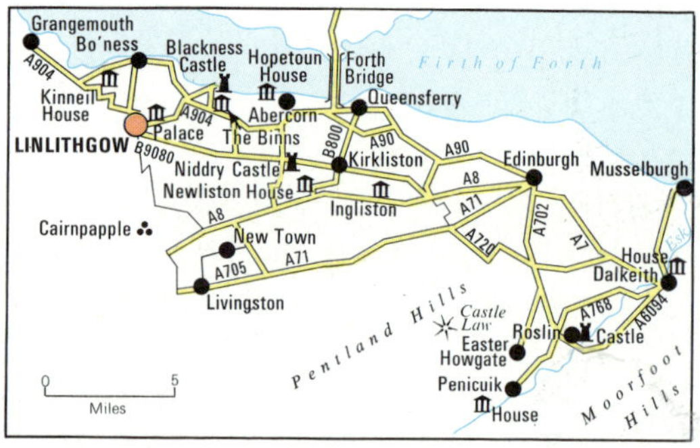

Western Lothian, an agricultural land with an industrial overlay, had its rich farming acres invaded by the apparatus of the oil-shale industry in the 19th century. Today the surviving farmland is concentrated mainly near the coast, while the landscape to the south is dominated by towering shale heaps, rising like red hills. The heaps have become useful as foundations for motorways, and some are even being landscaped. This is an area of ancient remains and modern achievements, including a New Town at Livingston and two bridges across the Firth of Forth. Some part of the steel railway bridge is always being repainted, so that 'painting the Forth Bridge' as a proverbial expression for an endless task is based on fact.

To the east is Edinburgh, with its medieval streets and later elegance that caused the city to be called 'The Athens of the North'. South of Edinburgh, the Pentlands and the Moorfoots, two of Scotland's most attractive hill ranges, offer infinite pleasure without hazard to the rambler.

The present district of Midlothian is only part of the former county of that name which won a place in political history. In the 'Midlothian Campaign' of 1879, Gladstone attacked the record of Disraeli's Government at a series of mass meetings during the first 'whistle-stop' tour by a party leader in Britain. Gladstone's by-election victory paved the way for the Conservatives' huge defeat in 1880.

FORTH BRIDGES *Britain's longest suspension bridge, completed in 1964, carries road traffic from Edinburgh and the Lowlands to the north; it towers 512 ft above the Firth of Forth, and is 1½ miles long. Beyond it is the cantilevered railway bridge, opened in 1890*

THE CRAFTSMAN WHOSE SKILL COST HIM HIS LIFE

The 15th-century chapel at Roslin (left) is notable for its elaborately carved Prentice Pillar, lit by a shaft of sunlight at the far end. An apprentice is said to have carved the pillar during the absence in Italy of his master mason. The tutor killed the lad in a jealous rage when he returned and saw his apprentice's skill. On the chapel walls are sculptured heads (above) of the mason, the boy and his weeping mother

Abercorn
A tiny hamlet on the shores of the Forth, notable for Hopetoun House, the seat of the Marquis of Linlithgow and one of Scotland's most splendid mansions. The central section was built by Sir William Bruce of Kinross between 1699 and 1703, and the wings were added by the famous architectural family of William Adam and his sons during the next 50 years. The mansion is situated amid parkland, with formal gardens in the style of Versailles surrounding the house. The Yellow Drawing Room, hung with damask, contains works by Rubens, Rembrandt and Titian. The Red Room is hung with silk, and the elegant furniture in the State Room was made by Thomas Chippendale, the famous 18th-century cabinet-maker.

Blackness Castle
The ruined 15th-century castle is often called Ship Castle because of its shape, with one oblong tower and one circular stair tower. The castle was used in the 17th century as a prison for Covenanters—Scottish Presbyterians who pledged themselves to maintain their chosen form of church government and worship. After the Act of Union in 1707, which merged the English and Scottish Parliaments, the castle was maintained as a strategic fortress.

The House of the Binns, dating from 1478, was once linked to Blackness Castle by an underground passage. In the 17th century it was the home of General Thomas Dalyell, who served in the Russian Army and, according to legend, consorted with the Devil. He raised the Royal Scots Greys at The Binns in 1681.

LINLITHGOW PALACE *On a knoll above the loch at Linlithgow stands the ruined palace which James I started to build in 1424. Mary, Queen of Scots was born there in 1542*

Bo'ness

Borrowstounness, to give the town its full name, was an important port in the 19th century but lost trade as Grangemouth, a few miles along the Firth of Forth, was developed. The eastern end of the Antonine Wall, a Roman fortification, lay here; one of the distance slabs, unearthed in 1868, has been set up at the east end of the town. Kinneil House, which dates from the 16th century, has good ceiling and wall decorations; six cartoons in the Parable Room illustrate the story of the Good Samaritan. In 1764, James Watt experimented with his steam engine in the house's park.

Dalkeith

An ancient milling and market town, given its charter in 1144. Electronics and diary-printing are two of the many prosperous new industries in the burgh, which has developed a fine modern town centre. Dalkeith House, which dates from the 12th century, was remodelled by James Smith in 1700 for the Duchess of Buccleuch; she was the widow of the rebel Duke of Monmouth, who was executed in 1685.

Kirkliston

A village with a 12th-century parish church. Its saddle-back tower, roofed like an ordinary house, rises above the village. The church is also notable for its carved Romanesque doorway. Newliston House, a small mansion built by Robert Adam between 1789 and 1792, is surrounded by trees which are said to have been planted by the 2nd Earl of Stair in the pattern formed by his regiment at the Battle of Dettingen. Niddry Castle, 2 miles west, was where Mary, Queen of Scots was taken by Lord Seton on the first night after her escape from Loch Leven Castle in 1568.

Ingliston, 1½ miles south, is the scene of the Royal Highland Show, Scotland's national agricultural show, held annually in mid-June.

Linlithgow

An ancient town, containing the fine ruins of a royal palace, which stands on a knoll above the lovely town loch. The palace dates from 1424, and James V and his daughter Mary, Queen of Scots were born there. The palace was destroyed by a fire, probably accidental, started by the Duke of Cumberland's troops in 1746.

Near the palace is the parish church of St Michael, dating from the 13th century but rebuilt after a fire in 1424. This is one of Scotland's finest churches. Its tower was topped by a crown steeple, but this was removed in the 1820's. A recent appeal fund provided a contemporary, and controversial, gold spire in the symbolic shape of a crown. The oldest bell dates from 1490, and tolled a knell for the defeat of the Scots by the English at Flodden in 1513.

Penicuik

This was for centuries Scotland's paper-making town, drawing power for the mills from the River Esk. It is now one of Midlothian's fastest-growing towns. Valleyfield Mill, founded in 1709, was used to house French prisoners captured during the Napoleonic Wars.

Penicuik House, built by Sir John Clerk (1676–1755), was a fine Queen Anne house, largely destroyed by fire in 1899. The stables of the ruins have been rebuilt by a descendant of Sir John to form a modern house. The poet Allan Ramsay, born in 1686, is commemorated by an obelisk in the grounds. Ramsay was an Edinburgh wigmaker who later became a bookseller. His best-known poem, 'The Gentle Shepherd', was published in 1725.

Queensferry

This small town, lying at the southern end of the two great Forth bridges, was named after Queen Margaret of Scotland, who was a regular traveller on the ferry that plied across the river for more than 800 years before the road bridge was opened in 1964. The queen used the ferry on her way from Edinburgh to her favourite home at Dunfermline in Fife. The Episcopal Church still uses a 15th-century Carmelite priory, and the Hawes Inn retains much of its character after nearly 300 years.

The 12th-century church at Dalmeny, a village with a tree-lined green 1 mile south of Queensferry, has a wealth of Romanesque carving and sculpture and is one of the finest churches of its period in Great Britain.

Roslin

A mining village on the Esk, below the ruins of Roslin (sometimes spelt Rosslyn) Castle, a 14th-century stronghold of Sir Henry Sinclair, 3rd Earl of Orkney. The dungeons and rooms can still be visited. Its 15th-century chapel was intended to be part of a Collegiate church, but was only partly built.

BRONZE AGE GRAVE *One of Scotland's most important prehistoric sites is on Cairnpapple Hill, 1000 ft above the Lowland plain. It consists of a cairn and a circle of upright stones 100 ft across, which mark the site of Bronze Age and Iron Age burials*

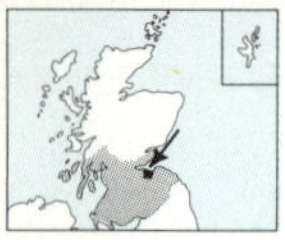

Scotland's beautiful capital

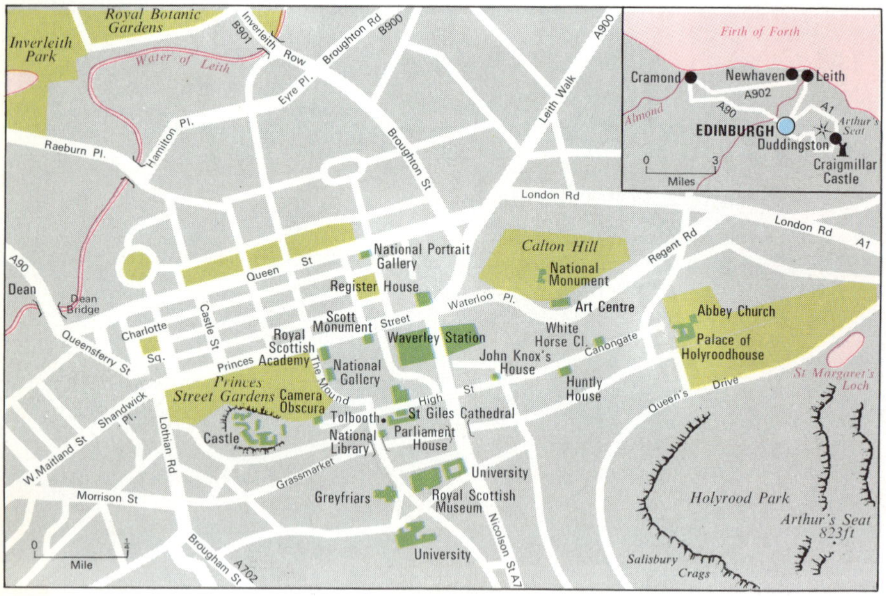

Events The Edinburgh International Festival of Music and Drama, the Film Festival and the Military Tattoo are held in late Aug. and early Sept. The Edinburgh Highland Games are held on Sat. preceding the Festival. The Royal Scottish Academy Art Exhibition is held from late Apr. to early Aug. Band Concerts and children's shows are held daily in summer in Princes Street Gardens. Beating the Retreat on Castle Esplanade is usually Wed. and Sat. evenings, May and June.

Places to see *Canongate Tolbooth*: weekdays. *Craigmillar Castle*: weekdays, Sun. afternoon. *Edinburgh Castle*: daily, except Sun. morning Nov. to Apr. *Georgian House* (NTS), Charlotte Square: Easter to mid-Oct., weekdays, Sun. afternoon; late Oct. to Jan., Sun. afternoon and Sat. *Huntly House*: weekdays. *John Knox House*: weekdays. *Lady Stair's House*: weekdays. *Lauriston Castle*: Apr. to Oct., daily, except Fri.; Nov. to Mar., Sat. and Sun. *Museum of Childhood*: weekdays. *National Gallery of Scotland*: weekdays, Sun. afternoons. *Nelson's Monument*: weekdays. *Palace of Holyroodhouse*: daily, except Sun. mornings Nov. to Apr. *Royal Botanic Gardens*: daily. *Royal Scottish Museum*: weekdays, Sun. afternoons. *Transport Museum*: weekdays, except Sat. afternoons. *Zoological Park*: daily. See also Galleries and Museums, p. 476.

Information centre
5 Waverley Bridge, Edinburgh.
Tel. 031–226 6591.

Most of Britain's ancient cities rose along river valleys. But Edinburgh, ringed by hills, was built on crags; and the tiny Water of Leith that flows through the New Town contributed little to the shape of the city. The centre is an area of broad plateaux, steep cliffs and deep canyons—an effect which is exaggerated by the height of the Old Town tenements whose crow-stepped gables loom against the sky. Steep, winding streets look down over roof-tops and up to soaring spires and the castle battlements, so that Scotland's capital seems more like Athens than a typical British city.

There is evidence of Iron Age occupation on Castle Rock, Calton Hill and Arthur's Seat, but medieval Edinburgh grew along the windy ridge that runs from the castle to the Abbey of Holyrood. Growth was restricted for a time by the King's Wall, built by James II in 1450, separating the city from the castle by the length of a bowshot. The city gate nearest to the castle was therefore called the Upper Bow, and that at the bottom of the High Street the Netherbow. The city soon expanded, however, and when the Flodden Wall was built during the panic after Scotland's defeat by the English at Flodden in 1513, it encompassed a larger area, taking in Greyfriars Church and the site of the present university, and stopping near the Nor' Loch. The drained loch's site is now occupied by Waverley Station and Princes Street Gardens.

The Flodden Wall shaped Edinburgh; for 250 years its citizens did not feel safe enough to build outside. Confined by the wall, they built upwards in a manner which made Edinburgh unique among European cities. The 'Lands', or tenements, nine, ten and sometimes as many as 14 storeys high, crowded noblemen and thieves, shopkeepers and artisans together in a warren of wynds, closes and courts.

This was old Edinburgh, the city of Mary, Queen of Scots and John Knox, of heroes such as Montrose, and villains such as Major Weir, a city dignitary who, after presiding over Montrose's execution in 1650, later confessed to a double life, in which he had combined respectability with vice and witchcraft.

The old city was often devastated by war, most terribly during the 'Rough Wooing' of 1544, when Henry VIII attempted to bully the Scots into a marriage between his son Edward and the infant Mary, Queen of Scots. Plague, too, blasted the city; in 1645, in one area, Mary King's Close off the High Street, not a single inhabitant survived. This close, which is much as it was when the last victims were removed, is now part of the City Chambers.

For much of its history, Edinburgh was a poor place, torn by civil and religious strife, preyed upon by a gangster nobility. It was a dirty city, chronically short of water, whose inhabitants emptied chamberpots from tenement windows with a cry of 'Gardyloo!'—a corrupt form of the French *gare l'eau*, 'mind the water'. But it was also a proud city, the home of the Scottish Parliament; when this was disbanded by the 1707 Act of Union, part of Edinburgh's spirit went too. Some, particularly large landowners, saw union with England

ANCIENT VANTAGE POINT *Edinburgh Castle perches on Castle Rock (above), possibly the site of an Iron Age fort. Paths winding below the castle (left) give sweeping views over the city*

and Wales as Scotland's way out of financial chaos. Most regarded the loss of Scottish independence with bitterness and dismay. Yet the Act of Union brought unexpected benefits to Edinburgh. Freed at last from the danger of invasion, and with new trade coming up the Forth to the Port of Leith, the city broke from its ancient walls.

The Nor' Loch was drained in 1760, and the North Bridge across the chasm was finished in 1772. Work soon began on the New Town, and it was Edinburgh's lasting fortune that it should coincide with the great period of Georgian architecture. The basic plan of squares and broad thoroughfares was James Craig's, and to him too goes the credit for building only on one side of Queen Street and Princes Street, leaving the opposite sides open as public gardens.

At first, the citizens were reluctant to move beyond the walls which had protected them for so long, and a bribe of £20 was offered to the first person to build a house in the New Town. This house, still standing in Thistle Court, began a spate of building which lasted through the last 30 years of the 18th century. The first public building was the Register House, the work of Robert Adam (1728–92), who also designed the university and the north side of Charlotte Square. But it is perhaps to his more austere successors that Edinburgh owes its title of 'Athens of the North'. Thomas Hamilton built the Royal High School at the foot of Calton Hill in 1829, modelling it on the Temple of Theseus in Athens; it is now an Art Centre. At the top of Calton Hill stands Charles Cockerell's Parthenon, a monument to Scots killed in the Napoleonic wars. It was never finished, but the tall pillars still stand magnificently over the city.

The early years of the New Town reflected the brilliance of Edinburgh's Golden Age. During the latter half of the 18th century and the first decade of the 19th, the city blossomed into one of Europe's leading cultural centres. It was the home of James Boswell, Robert Burns and Sir Walter Scott; of the philosopher David Hume and the political economist Adam Smith; of the painter Sir Henry Raeburn and the engineer Thomas Telford.

This promise of a Scottish revival was not quite fulfilled, just as work on the New Town, which continued into the 20th century, fell below the standards of the original planners. Nevertheless, the tradition remained strong enough to ensure that Edinburgh remained a capital in spirit far beyond its official role as the ecclesiastical and legal centre of Scotland.

EDINBURGH CASTLE The castle dominates all Edinburgh, with an air at once threatening and protective. Throughout its long history it has been equally ready to assume either role, depending on the sympathies of its occupiers.

The oldest part of the castle, and the oldest building in the city, is St Margaret's Chapel, dating in part from *c.* 1100. This tiny church, only 26 ft by 10 ft, commemorates the saintly Queen Margaret, sister of Edgar Atheling, king-elect of England after Harold died at Hastings. After the Norman Conquest, brother and sister fled to Scotland, where Margaret married Malcolm III in 1069. She reformed many aspects of the Scottish Church and State, and died in 1093, after hearing of the deaths of her husband and son at the Battle of Alnwick. St Margaret's Chapel has survived many perils. When Robert the Bruce captured the castle from the English in 1313, he destroyed every building, but ordered that the chapel should be left unharmed. After the Reformation in the 16th century, the chapel was used as a powder store by the castle gunners.

The massive cannon which stands at the chapel door is called Mons Meg. It was probably forged in Galloway *c.* 1455, and in its hey-day could hurl a 5 cwt stone ball about 1½ miles; however, it burst when it fired a royal salute to Charles II in 1680.

Behind the chapel lies Palace Yard, one side of which is taken up by the Scottish National War Memorial. This building, opened in 1927, has excited both admiration and dislike. It is a memorial to the 100,000 Scots who died in the First World War, and the theme is one of pride rather than sorrow. Every type of war service is depicted in bronze and stained glass, including that of the transport mules, the carrier pigeons and the mice and canaries used to detect gas in the Flanders trenches.

Opposite the memorial is the Great Hall, built by James IV early in the 16th century. It has a fine hammer-beam roof, and is now an armoury. The hall lies over the Casemates, vast vaulted rooms where prisoners of the Napoleonic Wars were kept; many of them carved their names, or pictures of ships and gallows, on the doors.

In a room in the Royal Palace on the east side of the Yard, Mary, Queen of Scots gave birth to James VI (later James I of England) in 1566. Doubts were cast on the child's legitimacy at the time, and these were revived in 1830 when what appeared to be a baby's skeleton was found behind the panelling in the room. Mary had no doubts; for as she bitterly told her husband Darnley, the child was so much his, she 'feared it would be the worse for him hereafter'.

The palace also contains the Honours of Scotland—the Scottish Crown Jewels, older than those in the Tower of London; some of them date from the 14th century. During the Cromwellian period they were hidden behind the pulpit of the village church of Kinneff in Kincardineshire. 'Cannones were dischargit' to celebrate their safe return to Edinburgh in 1662. Cannons are still discharged on Royal occasions in the city. In addition, since 1861 a gun has been fired each weekday at 1 p.m. from the Half Moon Battery on the castle ramparts as a time check.

The Castle Esplanade is used each autumn for the 3-week Military Tattoo, and has been the garrison's drilling ground for centuries. A plaque marks part of the Esplanade as Nova Scotian territory; it was ceded to Nova Scotia by Charles I so that baronets with titles in that land could be confirmed in them on Nova Scotian soil.

Outside the castle, on Castle Hill, is the Outlook Tower, whose Camera Obscura throws a bird's eye view of Edinburgh on to a table. Near by is Cannonball House, which has a cannon ball embedded in a gable; a legend says it was fired at a couple of clansmen during the 1745 rising. Opposite, a well marks the spot where, between 1479 and 1722, more than 300 women were burnt to death for witchcraft.

ROYAL MILE The name given to the ancient streets which run eastwards from Castle Hill to the gates of Holyroodhouse. They include the Lawnmarket, the High Street and the Canongate. Many of the houses and wynds date from the 17th century or earlier, and are laid out to a plan more ancient still.

The Lawnmarket, once called the Landmarket, was the place where country folk sold their produce; later, in the 18th century, it became a fashionable promenade. Lady Stair's House contains relics of Burns, Scott and Stevenson. David Hume, the philosopher, lived in Riddle's Court, and so did Bailie Macmorran, who was shot dead by a High School boy in 1595 for trying to break a schoolboys' strike. Deacon William Brodie, town councillor by day and burglar by night, lived in Brodie's Close.

The High Street is dominated by St Giles's, the High Kirk of Edinburgh, also known as St Giles's Cathedral. It was built in the 14th and 15th centuries, and altered during the 16th-century Reformation and by restoration in the 19th century. The dignified interior is enhanced by the Colours of famous Scottish regiments. John Knox was minister at St Giles's until his death in 1572, and preached his own fiery brand of Calvinism from the pulpit. Ironically, owing to the encroachment of Parliament Square on to the graveyard, he may now lie under the statue of Charles II, that most tolerant of monarchs. An event which foreshadowed the Covenant Wars occurred at St Giles's in 1637; an indignant woman, supposedly Jenny Geddes, threw a stool at the Dean for reading from the Anglican prayer book. The Marquis of Montrose is buried in the Chepman aisle.

Near the church, decorative cobbles mark the site of the Old Tolbooth, or prison, the 'Heart of Midlothian', which was stormed in the Porteous riots of 1736. Captain Porteous had ordered his troops to fire on an Edinburgh crowd that refused to disperse, and was condemned to death for murder. On hearing that a reprieve had been sent from London, the mob broke into the Tolbooth and hanged Porteous from a dyer's pole in the Grassmarket. Sir Walter Scott partly based his novel *The Heart of Midlothian* on these violent events. Near by is the mercat cross, for centuries the focus of city life. Here, in 1513, people gathered to hear of the death of James IV and 10,000 Scots at Flodden. Crowds gathered again in 1745 to hear Bonnie Prince Charlie proclaim his exiled father King James III. Here, too, was the market-place where Newhaven fishwives came to sell oysters, mussels, and the 'caller herrin'' (fresh herring) of the song of that title.

In Parliament House, behind Parliament Square, the last Scottish Government agreed to the Act of Union with England in 1707. According to an old song, many of its members were 'bought and sold for English gold'.

Just off the High Street, in Hyndford's Close, is the Museum of Childhood, containing toys, books and clothes made for and by children through the ages. At the end of the High Street is John Knox's House; though there is some doubt whether the preacher lived there, it contains relics of him. It was also supposedly given by Mary, Queen of Scots to her goldsmith. Beyond Netherbow Port is the Canongate, part of the separate burgh of Canongate.

FOUR FAMOUS CITIZENS AND TWO VILLAINS FROM

JAMES BOSWELL (1740–95) The fame of this local man rests on his biography of Dr Johnson

DAVID HUME (1711–76) The great philosopher was once refused a chair by Edinburgh University

ROBERT LOUIS STEVENSON (1850–94) The Edinburgh writer's novel *Dr Jekyll and Mr Hyde* was based on the character of Deacon Brodie

DEACON BRODIE Town councillor, executed for burglary in 1788

A LEADER OF THE ROMANTIC MOVEMENT

THE MONUMENT The 200-ft Gothic spire in Princes Street Gardens was built between 1840 and 1844 to commemorate Sir Walter Scott. There are 287 steps to the top

THE MAN Sir Walter Scott (1771–1832) was born in Edinburgh. His writings brought Scotland's past to life and established him as a leader of the Romantic literary movement in Europe

EDINBURGH'S PAST

SIR HENRY RAEBURN (1756–1823) The painter's portraits form a vivid record of the great men of his time

WILLIAM BURKE Body-snatcher and murderer, hanged in 1829

Many of the houses have been restored; White Horse Close contains a rare 17th-century building which was once the White Horse Inn, a staging post for coaches to London. Huntly House has a fine timbered front, and contains the most important of Edinburgh's museums of local history.

The letter 'S' is let into the ground at intervals across the road, marking the old sanctuary line of Holyrood Abbey. Once across that line, debtors were safe from pursuit. Passers-by would watch them being chased down the Canongate by bailiffs, and bet on the result. The right of sanctuary survived until 1880.

Robert Fergusson, the 18th-century poet, is buried in Canongate churchyard. When Burns came to Edinburgh in the 1780's, the grave was unmarked, and Burns—in debt, but tender-hearted as always—paid for a stone to be erected over the man whose verses he admired. Further evidence of Burns's tender heart is the single inscription 'Clarinda' on another stone. 'Clarinda'—Mrs Agnes Maclehose—was an Edinburgh woman with two children, and one of the poet's great loves. It was she who inspired one of his most haunting lyrics:

'Had we never lov'd sae kindly,
Had we never lov'd sae blindly,
Never met—or never parted,
We had ne'er been broken-hearted...'

HOLYROODHOUSE The palace, associated with the tragic history of the Stuarts, stands at the foot of the Canongate, and has for a background the dark crags of Arthur's Seat. It was begun as a palace *c.* 1500 by James IV, who enlarged an existing guesthouse of the nearby abbey which was founded in 1128; but most of the present structure was built for Charles II.

FORMER INN *A 17th-century building in White Horse Close, once an inn*

HIDDEN BYWAY *Upper Bow, one of the wynds—or narrow paths—which twist through ancient closes behind the main roads of Edinburgh's Old Town*

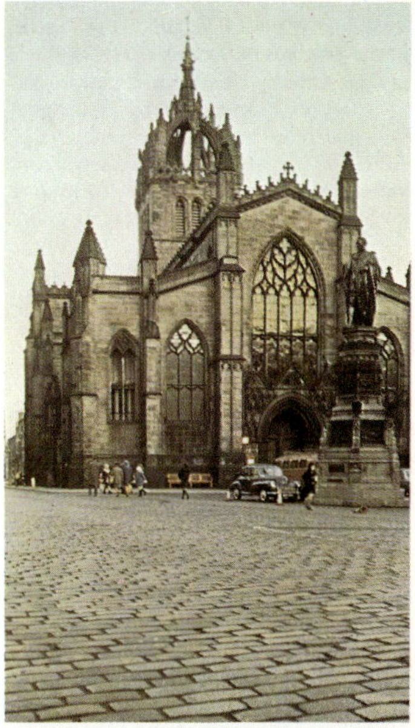

RARE STEEPLE *A 15th-century crown-shaped steeple tops St Giles's*

VANISHED PRISON *A heart-shaped pattern on the pavement near St Giles's marks the site of the 'Heart of Midlothian', a prison demolished in 1817*

A FOUNDER OF THE KIRK

JOHN KNOX (1505–72) Knox led the Protestant Reformation in Scotland. His writings include his *First Blast of the Trumpet against the Monstrous Regiment of Women*

KNOX'S HOUSE The reformer is believed to have lived in this 15th-century house in the High Street. It has a timber gallery, and is preserved as a museum

Many of the interiors were also commissioned by Charles, including the extraordinary Royal Portrait Gallery. Each one of the 110 Scottish kings and queens, depicted in 'large Royal postures', is the work of James de Witt, who painted the entire collection in two years, between 1684 and 1686, for the modest fee of £120 a year. It is doubtful if some of the subjects—Thebus I, for instance—were Scottish monarchs at all.

Leading from the picture gallery are the Audience Chamber and the private apartments of Mary, Queen of Scots—the scene of one of the best-documented murders in history. On a night in March, 1566, a gang of nobles, led by the queen's husband, Darnley, and the Earl of Morton, entered the queen's room by a private staircase and stabbed to death her friend and secretary, David Rizzio, in her presence. Rizzio's crimes seem to have been little more than his possession of a quick wit and the fact that the queen was fond of him; but Darnley was persuaded that he was her lover. The queen herself, pregnant at the time, was held at sword point by the Earl of Ruthven, who threatened to cut her 'into collops' if she stirred, while Darnley stood by, white-faced and stammering. In the following year, Darnley was strangled at his house at Kirk o' Field. The house, which stood on the site of the present university, was blown up on the same night.

Mary lived at the palace from 1561 to 1567, and it was here, in 1603, that her son, James VI of Scotland, learnt that he had also become James I of England, monarch of two kingdoms. A messenger rode the 400 miles from Elizabeth I's death-bed in Richmond Palace, Surrey, to Edinburgh in 62 hours.

Bonnie Prince Charlie held brief court here in 1745. He was defied by loyalist forces at the other end of the Royal Mile, for though he took the city without a fight, he never captured the castle. George IV visited Holyroodhouse in 1822, at the time when Britain was spellbound by Scott's novels and in love with all things Scottish. He attended a ball in full Highland regalia, but wearing pink silk tights. The State apartments, used by the Queen when in residence, contain rich tapestries and period furniture.

HOLYROOD ABBEY A picturesque ruin in the grounds of the palace. It was built as a penance by David I in 1128; legend says that the king went out hunting on a holy day and was attacked by a stag. About to be gored, he seized the stag's antlers; but the beast vanished, leaving in the king's hand a Holy Cross, or Rood. The abbey was built on the spot where the miracle occurred. For centuries, until the Reformation, it was a burial place of Scottish kings and queens. Many, too, were married there, including Mary, Queen of Scots.

The abbey's present ruinous state is due mainly to an over-heavy roof being placed on it in 1768, though it suffered depredation before that. It was one of the abbeys pillaged by the Earl of Hertford on his march through Scotland in 1544, and in 1688 it was plundered by a mob celebrating the accession of William of Orange. On that occasion, the vaults were opened and the Royal coffins broken into. Among the objects removed was the head of Lord Darnley, Mary's treacherous consort.

GREYFRIARS CHURCH The present church dates in part from 1612, when it was the first church to be opened in Edinburgh after the Reformation. It stands on the site of a monastery established by Dutch friars in the 13th century. The statue of 'Greyfriars Bobby', a terrier, crowns a fountain near the church. Bobby's owner was Jock Gray, a Border shepherd, who died in 1858 and was buried in the churchyard; Bobby watched over the grave for the remainder of his life, fed by the people of Edinburgh. Before he died, in 1872, he was adopted by the city and was buried at last beside his master.

It was in the churchyard, in 1638, that the first signatures were placed on the National Covenant, a solemn undertaking to resist the 'contrary errours and corruptions' of the Anglican faith forced upon Scotland by Charles I. National feeling and Protestant fervour for once united the Kirk, nobility and people, at least in the Lowlands. Religious wars were to mark Scottish history for the next half-century. Covenanting banners still hang inside the church, and in the churchyard can be seen the prison—then, as now, open to the sky—where 1200 Covenanters were held through the rigours of an Edinburgh winter in 1679. Their sufferings are commemorated by the Martyrs' Memorial near by. The churchyard also contains the graves of Captain Porteous and of the Earl of Morton, a Regent of Scotland during the minority of James VI. The Earl was executed in 1581.

SHOPS OF EDINBURGH'S OLD TOWN

HISTORY FOR SALE An antique shop sells curios of Scotland's past

TARTAN TRADE A traditional Highland figure adorns a kiltmaker's shop

SWEEP'S BRUSH A shop-sign recalls the city's smoky past as 'Auld Reekie'

SOUND OF SCOTLAND A firm of bagpipe makers flourishes near the castle

PRINCES STREET One of the great thoroughfares of the world, although individually its buildings have no particular architectural merit. The 'princes' after which it is named were the sons of George III. For many visitors, Princes Street is their first impression of Edinburgh, for the draughty steps from Waverley Station mount up to its eastern end. The north side of the street is a long array of shops, hotels and clubs; but it is the south side which gives Princes Street its particular character. Along the whole street, gardens fall steeply away into the canyon left by the draining of the Nor' Loch in the 18th century, while across the valley is the panorama of the Old Town and the castle. The West Princes Street Gardens contain the oldest Floral Clock in the world, built in 1903. It is 36 ft in circumference, and when the clock is filled with flowers—about 25,000 of them—the hour hand weighs 50 lb., and the minute hand 80 lb. Another landmark is the Scott Monument, a 200-ft Gothic spire whose architectural merits have been argued since its completion in 1844. Sir Walter Scott was born and educated in Edinburgh and spent much of his career there as a lawyer, publisher and author. His favourite home in the city was 39 Castle Street. Near its centre, Princes Street is linked to the Old Town by The Mound, which is really an enormous tip of debris thrown into the Nor' Loch when the New Town was being built in 1781.

GALLERIES AND MUSEUMS The National Gallery of Scotland, in Princes Street, opened in 1859, contains works ranging from the Renaissance to Cézanne, with many paintings by Scottish artists.

The Scottish National Portrait Gallery shares a building in Queen Street with the National Museum of Antiquities. The gallery contains Scottish portraits dating from 1550 to the present day. The museum depicts everyday life in Scotland from the Stone Age onwards, together with relics of famous Scots.

The Royal Scottish Museum, in Chambers Street, is the most comprehensive museum in Britain under a single roof. It has four main departments; technology, geology, natural history, and art and archaeology.

The City of Edinburgh Art Centre in Regent Road, opened in 1971, has a permanent collection of Scottish paintings. The Scottish National Gallery of Modern Art, built on the highest part of the Botanic Gardens, has a panoramic view of the city, and shows paintings and sculpture of the 20th century. The National Library of Scotland, founded in 1682, has over 2 million books and manuscripts. There is a permanent exhibition. All the galleries and museums are open on weekdays and Sunday afternoons. The library is open Monday to Friday, and Saturday afternoons.

EDINBURGH FESTIVAL For three weeks in late summer, Edinburgh hangs out flags, floodlights its gardens and ancient buildings, sends a hundred pipers skirling along Princes Street each morning, and plays host to nearly 100,000 people from all over the world. John Christie—founder of the Glyndebourne Opera in Sussex—conceived the idea of an international festival of music and the arts in 1947. Cambridge and Canterbury were both suggested as centres, but the final choice was Edinburgh. The first festival was held in 1947 and today Edinburgh has one of the most comprehensive international arts festivals in the world. Opera, ballet, concerts, theatre, and films are on the official programme. On the unofficial, but almost equally famous 'Fringe', young actors, folk singers and artists fill every small hall and cellar club. Scotland's particular contributions are the Highland Games, which precede the festival, and the spectacular floodlit Tattoo held on the Castle Esplanade.

DEAN VILLAGE A village on the Water of Leith, only five minutes from Princes Street. Many of the old houses and its arched bridge have been restored, while downstream the Dean Bridge, designed by Thomas Telford in 1832, soars 100 ft above the village. Near by, the Grecian-style temple of St Bernard's Well is built over a mineral spring, where in the 18th century fashionable citizens took the waters.

ARTHUR'S SEAT The summit of this 823-ft extinct volcano gives the best of all views of Edinburgh, particularly on the evenings—less frequent now than in the past—when the city wears a veil of blue smoke, recalling its nickname of 'Auld Reekie', or 'Old Smoky'. The title was supposed to have been conferred by a Fife laird, who regulated evening prayers to the hour when the distant city smoke grew thicker as housewives cooked supper. On the west side of Arthur's Seat are the cliffs known as the Salisbury Crags. At the foot of the hill are the Wells o' Wearie, said to have been named by people who trudged to them for water.

DUDDINGSTON VILLAGE A pretty village below Arthur's Seat. It has remains of prehistoric and Roman earthworks. Bonnie Prince Charlie's Highlanders camped there. The church has iron 'jougs', a collar for chaining criminals to the wall, last used *c.* 1850. The Sheep's Heid Inn is the oldest licensed premises in Scotland. Duddingston Loch is a wildfowl sanctuary.

HEART OF THE CITY *Shops and hotels line the north side of Princes Street, the city's elegant and spacious main thoroughfare. The south side of the street is fringed entirely by gardens*

VOLCANO WITH A VIEW *Salisbury Crags fringe the lower slopes of Arthur's Seat, an extinct volcano. The 823-ft summit of this dramatic landmark is easily climbed and offers magnificent views of the city and the surrounding countryside. Its name has nothing to do with King Arthur, but is probably a corruption of Archer's Seat*

GEORGIAN SCENE *A horse-drawn hire carriage harmonises with Charlotte Street in Edinburgh's New Town, which was built in the heyday of Georgian architecture*

HISTORIC STUART HOME *Holyroodhouse was the home of Mary, Queen of Scots for six years of her reign, and Bonnie Prince Charlie held court there in 1745*

Craigmillar Castle

This ruined 14th-century fortress on the outskirts of the city has its share of dark legend. The Earl of Mar, youngest son of James II, was bled to death here in 1479, on the orders, it is said, of his brother James III. Mary, Queen of Scots is believed to have met Bothwell here to plot the death of her husband, Darnley. She certainly visited the castle after Rizzio's death in 1566, but whether she had any direct hand in Darnley's murder has been a matter of historical argument ever since.

Cramond

A small village only 5 miles from Princes Street, on the attractive estuary of the River Almond. The church stands on the site of a Roman fort, Caer Almond, built by Antoninus Pius in AD 142. Recent excavations have produced coins, glass and other objects which can be seen in Huntly House Museum in Edinburgh, and a corner of the fort forms part of a garden in the village. Robert Louis Stevenson stayed at Cramond and described the village in his novel *St Ives*. The Old Bridge has associations with the Stuarts. James I crossed it on his way to Perth in 1436 and was warned by a soothsayer to go no further. He continued his journey, however, and was murdered in Perth. In the 16th century, James V was attacked by thieves on the bridge, and was rescued by Jock Howison, a miller. The king afterwards presented Howison with all the land around Braehead, but made the proviso that his descendants should always have a ewer of water and a basin ready to present to the sovereign. This condition was fulfilled at the last Coronation, when the miller's descendant presented Elizabeth II with a silver ewer and a bowl of rose water.

Leith

Edinburgh's seaport and a busy modern dock, situated where the Water of Leith enters the Firth of Forth. Leith was incorporated in Edinburgh in 1920.

The town was sacked by the English in 1544 and 1547. Mary, Queen of Scots landed here in 1561, when she returned from France where she had spent her childhood. She stayed in the home of a merchant, Andrew Lamb, which still stands, well-restored, in Water's Close, and is now a home for elderly people.

Newhaven

The original inhabitants of this little fishing village were Dutch, which may have had some influence on the picturesque costumes still worn by the fishwives. Since its foundation in 1500, Newhaven has supplied Edinburgh with fish. The hardships of fisher folk of earlier days is reflected in Lady Nairne's song 'Caller Herrin' ', written *c.* 1820:

'Wha'll buy my caller herrin'?
Oh, ye may ca' them vulgar farin'
Wives and mithers, sair despairin',
Ca' them lives o' men . . .'

The *Great Michael* was launched here in 1511; 240 ft long, it was then the largest ship afloat. It indirectly contributed to Scotland's defeat at Flodden (1513), since all the skilled gunners in the kingdom were employed on the ship.

Royal and ancient Fife

Angling There is trout fishing on lochs and reservoirs; trout and salmon in the River Eden; and mackerel and haddock along the coast.

Events Kirkcaldy has its annual Links Fair, or market, in Apr. The Byre Theatre, St Andrews, has a season of plays from Apr. to Dec. The Lammas Fair is held in St Andrews on the second Mon. and Tues. in Aug.

Places to see *Abbey of St Columba*, Inchcolm: weekdays and Sun. afternoons. *Aberdour Castle*: weekdays and Sun. afternoons. *Andrew Carnegie Birthplace Memorial*, Dunfermline: weekdays, Sun. afternoons. *Culross Palace*: weekdays, Sun. afternoons. *Falkland Palace* (NTS): Easter to Oct., weekdays, Sun. afternoon. *Hill of Tarvit* (NTS), near Cupar, 17th century: Easter to Sept., afternoons except Fri. *Kellie Castle* (NTS), Pittenweem: Easter to Sept., Wed. to Sun. afternoons; gardens daily in same months. *Loch Leven Castle*: weekdays and Sun. afternoons in summer. *Loch Leven Nature Centre*, Kinross: Apr. to Sept., daily except Fri. *The Palace*, Culross: weekdays, Sun. afternoon. *Ravenscraig Castle*, Kirkcaldy: weekdays and Sun. afternoons. *St Andrews Castle, Cathedral and Priory*: weekdays and Sun. afternoons. *Scottish Fisheries Museum*, Anstruther: Apr. to Oct., weekdays, Sun. afternoons; Nov. to Mar., afternoons except Tues. *The Study* (NTS), Culross: mid-Oct. to Mar., Sat.; also Sun. afternoons. *The Town House* (NTS), Culross: Easter to mid-Oct., weekdays and Sun. afternoons.

Information centre Publicity Officer, South Street, St Andrews. Tel. St Andrews 2021.

The region of Fife forms a peninsula some 20 miles wide between the Firth of Forth and the Firth of Tay. Its varied aspects include the rich agricultural valley of the Howe of Fife; one of Britain's most picturesque stretches of coastline, known as the East Neuk; Loch Leven, which attracts anglers from all over Europe; and a rich collection of historic buildings.

Perhaps Fife's greatest fame is as the home of golf, which has been played at St Andrews for at least 500 years. The game is said to have been brought to Scotland by traders from Holland, where people competed to strike a ball across frozen canals.

The Kingdom of Fife is so called because Dunfermline was the home of Scotland's kings from the days of Malcolm III, in the 11th century, until the Union of the Crowns of Scotland and England under James VI (James I of England) in 1603. In the past, Fife's isolated position kept it cut off from the rest of the Central Lowlands; but the opening of the two great road bridges over the Forth and the Tay, in 1964 and 1966, has ended this isolation, and the region is now established as a tourist area.

ST ANDREWS *The 'Royal and Ancient' was founded in 1754*

Aberdour
A resort with fine sands and a harbour popular with yachtsmen. It has a Norman church, St Fillan's, and a ruined 14th-century castle. On Inchcolm Island, 1½ miles off the coast, are the well-preserved ruins of the Abbey of St Columba. The abbey was founded in 1123 by Alexander I of Scotland, in gratitude for being sheltered after a shipwreck. On its choir wall are remains of medieval frescoes.

Burntisland
The port is notable for its parish church, St Columba's; it was built in 1592 and is square, with an octagonal tower added in the 18th century. It was at a meeting in this church in 1601 that the General Assembly proposed the Authorised Version of the Bible, which was published ten years later.

Ceres
An attractive village, with a green surrounded by old cottages and the medieval hump-backed Bishop's Bridge. The church above the village contains the tombs of the Earls of Crawford. On the last Saturday in June every year the village holds Highland Games, to commemorate the safe return of Ceres villagers from Robert the Bruce's victory over Edward II at Bannockburn in 1314. On a wall in the village is a 16th-century carving of a jovial-looking man holding a jug; he was the last Provost of Ceres, appointed in 1578.

Crail
The easternmost of the little fishing villages which huddle on the East Neuk's rocky coast. The red-tiled cottages which crowd round the harbour were once the haunt of smugglers; now they are occupied by artists. There is a fine 16th-century tolbooth, or toll-house, with a gilded copper salmon for a weathervane. The Collegiate church, mainly 13th century, contains an 8th-century carved cross.

Culross
The National Trust for Scotland has splendidly preserved this 16th and 17th-century town of red-tiled houses lining steep cobbled streets. Only the choir of the 13th-century abbey remains. The 'Palace', built between 1597 and 1611 by industrialist Sir George Bruce, retains its painted ceilings and walls, and terraced garden.

Cupar
This town provides a thriving market for the agricultural produce of the fertile Howe of Fife. Sir David Lyndsay gave the first performance of his 9 hour

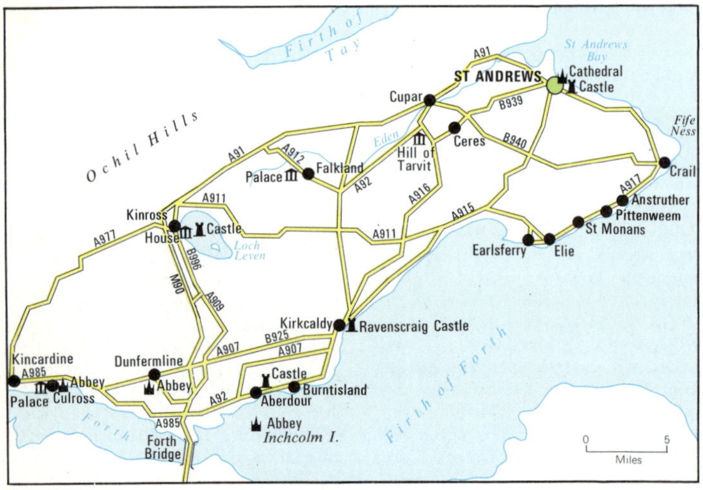

RED PARASITE The Red Broom-rape *(Orobanche alba)*, grows on Fife hill-sides near the coast and begins to flower in mid-summer. It is a parasite on the roots of wild thyme, and its blooms have a powerful scent

RUINED SPLENDOUR *The 12th-century Cathedral of St Andrews, seen from the tower of St Rule's Church. In the 17th century, stone was taken from the cathedral to build houses*

long play *Ane Satyre of the Three Estaits* there in 1535. This attack on the Church in Scotland has had several successful 20th-century revivals at the Edinburgh Festival.

Dunfermline
A flourishing textile-producing town, and the capital of Scotland for six centuries. Many kings of Scotland are buried there, including Robert the Bruce, and several monarchs were born there, notably two Stuarts, James I in 1394 and Charles I in 1600.

Dunfermline was also the birthplace, in 1835, of Andrew Carnegie, who emigrated to America and became an industrial millionaire and a great philanthropist, donating to the world nearly 3000 libraries. In 1903 he gave Dunfermline its beautiful Pittencrieff Park. The cottage where Carnegie was born is preserved as a museum.

Dunfermline Abbey was founded in 1072 by Queen Margaret, the wife of Malcolm III. Its foundations lie beneath the present nave, which is late Norman.

Elie and Earlsferry
Two resorts in one, on a sheltered, crescent-shaped bay. The resorts are noted for their fine golf courses, on one of which a trophy commemorating the great Scots golfer James Braid is played for annually. Braid, born in Earlsferry in 1870, won the Open Championship five times between 1900 and 1910.

St Monance, 2 miles east, is an attractive resort with some old houses. Pittenweem, 1½ miles further east, has a castle, Kellie Castle, mostly 16th century but partly dating back to 1360.

Falkland
A small town of picturesque old houses and cobbled streets. The 16th-century Falkland Palace was a favourite residence of Scottish kings until the death of James VI in 1625. Sir Walter Scott used it as the setting for part of his novel *The Fair Maid of Perth*. The Royal Tennis court, dating from 1539 and the oldest in Scotland, still exists.

Kinross
This small town on Loch Leven has a 17th century tolbooth with some fine decoration by Robert Adam. Not far away, still attached to the town cross, are the old 'jougs', an iron collar for wrongdoers. Kinross House is a fine late-17th-century house set in beautiful grounds between the town and the lochside. It was built by Sir William Bruce, architect of the Palace of Holyroodhouse in Edinburgh.

Loch Leven is famous for its delicious salmon trout; international trout-angling competitions are held there. It is also noted, in winter, for the sport of curling. On an island in the middle of the loch, which can be visited by boat in summer, stand the ruins of the 15th-century Loch Leven Castle. Mary, Queen of Scots escaped from it in 1568.

Kirkcaldy
An industrial town often known as the 'Lang Toun'—its main street is over a mile long. Two of Scotland's most famous men were born in Kirkcaldy: the economist Adam Smith (1723–90), author of *Wealth of Nations*, mostly written at Kirkcaldy; and the architect Robert Adam (1728–92). Ravenscraig Castle, built by James II in 1460, is a gaunt, impressive ruin.

St Andrews
A university city and summer resort on St Andrews Bay. The now-ruined cathedral was founded in 1161. Beside it stands St Rule's Church, built *c.* 1130; a spiral staircase leads to the top of the tower, which affords a splendid view of the city beneath. The ruined castle, founded in 1200 and rebuilt late in the 14th century, was destroyed in 1547. It stands on a rock overlooking the sea, and has a 24 ft deep, bottle-shaped dungeon, with a secret passage dug by the besieged garrison in a vain attempt to escape. St Andrews University, founded in 1410, is the oldest in Scotland. It incorporates a 17th-century library, in which the Scottish Parliament met in 1645. The Royal and Ancient Golf Club, founded in 1754, is the ruling authority on the game throughout the world. There are four golf courses on the coast north-west of the town. The Old Course is the oldest in the world; written records of its history go back to the 15th century. For a small fee, anyone can play on it—as on most golf courses in Scotland.

CHURCH BY THE SEA *The Old Kirk of St Monance, between Elie and Crail, has been a place of worship for 600 years. In stormy weather spray is flung right to the church door*

CLANS AND TARTANS

Scotland owes its clan system partly to an Englishwoman, Margaret, the Saxon Queen of Malcolm III. After their marriage in 1069, she introduced new fashions and new ideas to the Scottish court—and among the new ideas was the feudal system of land tenure. Until that time, most of the country had been divided into seven semi-independent tribal provinces. Under the feudal system, all land belonged to the king, who distributed it among his followers in exchange for allegiance and service. But a Highland chieftain could easily ignore a far-off Lowland king and, as time went by, the clan chiefs became minor kings themselves. They made alliances with other clans, had the power of life and death over their followers, and reckoned their strength in the number of swordsmen they could muster. The clansman's only allegiance was to his chief, both as battle leader and as head of the family. This unquestioning obedience helped to destroy the power of the clans in a single afternoon at Culloden on April 16, 1746.

SCOTTISH CHIEF *Alasdair MacDonnell of Glengarry (1771–1828) has been called the last of the great chiefs. He always wore full Highland dress, and was constantly accompanied by a guard of kilted clansmen. Many of the Glengarry MacDonnell clan emigrated to Canada c. 1800, and there, during the Anglo-American war of 1812, they became the last clan to be summoned into action by the fiery cross, the Highland symbol of war*

Tartans were originally badges of rank, then of districts, finally of clans. By c. 1700, most clans wore a distinctive tartan, though the patterns, or setts, were not always those by which they are distinguished now. A large number of the original setts were lost when tartans were banned for 36 years after Culloden, as an anti-Jacobite measure. Many of today's tartans date only from the 19th century, when the popularity of Sir Walter Scott's novels led to a romantic enthusiasm for the Highlands

MACKINTYRE *A widely scattered clan, some of whom were hereditary pipers to Clan Ranald, and others to the chiefs of Clan Menzies. Some were famous weavers, others foresters to the Lords of Lorn*

MACDONALD (DRESS) *MacDonalds were Lords of the Isles, and the most powerful of western clans. Lighter-patterned 'dress' tartans are strictly women's wear; men should wear* cath-dath*—the 'war colour'*

STUART OF BUTE (HUNTING) *The clan is descended from a son of Robert II (1316–90), the first Stewart king. The spelling 'Stuart', indicating Royal blood, was first used by Mary, Queen of Scots*

MACLACHLAN (DRESS) *This ancient clan has held land in Argyll since the 11th century. One chief fought in the Crusades; another was killed at Culloden while serving as aide to Bonnie Prince Charlie*

ANDERSON/MACANDREW *One of 26 clans of the confederated Clan Chattan, led by the chief of the Clan MacKintosh. This powerful federation was a constant threat to the king and the Lord of the Isles*

MACLEAN *Fighting against Cromwell at Inverkeithing (1651), seven brothers gave their lives to protect their chief, Sir Hector. 'Another for Hector!' is still one of the war cries of the Clan MacLean*

CAMPBELL (DRESS) *The rich, progressive Campbells were hated and feared by almost every other clan. They massacred the MacDonalds of Glencoe, and fought on the Government side in the '45 uprising*

MACLEAN (HUNTING) *The oldest documented tartan, whose colours are described in a charter given to MacLean of Duart in 1587. Hunting tartans are dark, and designed to camouflage the wearer*

CAMERON *A warrior clan whose battle cry was 'Sons of dogs, come here and get flesh'. The Camerons were loyal to the Stuart cause, and suffered some of the heaviest losses at the Battle of Culloden*

DISTRIBUTION OF PRINCIPAL CLANS IN 1600

Many clans still occupied these areas until the early 19th century, when they were evicted to clear the land for sheep-farming. Today, most Highland names occur throughout Scotland

MACGREGOR *'The nameless clan'—so called because when outlawed from 1603 to 1774 the clan was forbidden to use its own name. Landless for centuries, many MacGregors became bandits or mercenaries*

MACLEOD (DRESS) *The clan chief still lives in Dunvegan Castle in Skye, where the MacLeods' Fairy Flag is kept. The flag is traditionally supposed to make the MacLeods invincible in battle*

ROYAL TARTAN ('ROYAL STUART') *Now the personal tartan of the Queen, and once that of the Royal House of Stuart, whose last direct representative, the brother of Bonnie Prince Charlie, died in 1807*

Clydeside, cradle of great ocean liners

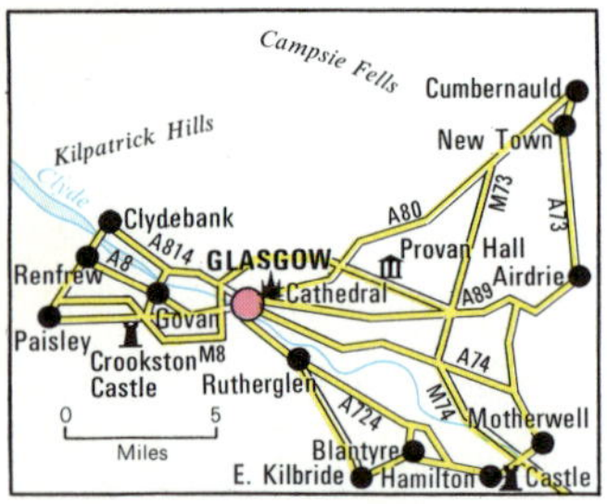

Angling There are roach and perch in the Forth–Clyde Canal and trout in reservoirs near Paisley.

Nature trails In the Glasgow parks of Kelvingrove, Dawsholm, Linn, Pollok, Rouken Glen, Rosshall and Springburn.

Music The Scottish National Orchestra gives weekly concerts during the winter in the City Hall and summer promenade concerts at the Kelvin Hall.

Places to see in Glasgow *Botanic Gardens*, Byres Road: daily. *Calderpark Zoo*: daily. *City of Glasgow Art Gallery and Museum*, Kelvingrove: weekdays, Sun. afternoons. *Fossil Grove*, Victoria Park, 230-million-year-old fossilised tree stumps: daily. *Hunterian Museum*: Mon. to Fri., also Sat. morning. *Museum of Transport*, Albert Drive: weekdays, Sun. afternoons. *Old Glasgow Museum*, People's Palace: weekdays, Sun. afternoons. *Pollok House*, Pollokshaws, 18th-century mansion: weekdays, Sun. afternoons. *Provand's Lordship*, Castle Street: weekdays.

Places to see around Glasgow *Bothwell Castle*, 8 miles south-east of Glasgow: weekdays, Sun. afternoons. *Crookston Castle*, visited by Mary, Queen of Scots and Darnley in 1565: weekdays, Sun. afternoons. *David Livingstone Centre*, Blantyre: weekdays and Sun. afternoons. *Hamilton Mausoleum*: daily. *Kilbarchan Weaver's Cottage* (NTS), 6 miles west of Paisley: May to Oct., Tues., Thur., Sat., Sun. afternoons. *Paisley Abbey*: weekdays. *Paisley Museum and Art Gallery*, High Street: weekdays. *Provan Hall* (NTS), Stepps: daily, except Tues. *Strathclyde Park*, 8 miles south-east of Glasgow: daily.

Information centre Information Bureau, George Square, Glasgow. Tel. 041–221 7371/6136.

Glasgow, the third most populous city in Britain, grew at a phenomenal rate during the Industrial Revolution, and little remains of its medieval glory as an ecclesiastical centre and seat of learning. The old city is buried beneath 19th-century Glasgow, whose citizens acquired qualities of fortitude and generosity forged in the bleakest of social conditions. The slums, the grimmest product of these conditions, are today giving way to new housing developments.

Traditionally, Glasgow was founded by St Kentigern—also called St Mungo—who built his church there in AD 543. In 1136, a cathedral was erected over his remains; and 1451 saw the birth of the university, the second to be established in Scotland.

Glasgow's commercial prosperity began in the 17th century, when its merchants set out to dominate the trade of the western seas. New World produce—tobacco, sugar and cotton—poured into the new Port Glasgow, 20 miles down-river, and up the deepened, widened Clyde to the heart of the city. The nearby Lanark coalfields provided power for Glasgow's 19th-century expansion in an era of iron and steel, heavy engineering and shipbuilding. Glasgow is still an industrial city, but perhaps the Glaswegian's greatest fortune lies in his surrounding countryside. The Campsie Fells and Kilpatrick Hills lie almost within the city, and the Trossachs, Loch Lomond and the Kyles of Bute are all within easy reach.

By the end of Victoria's reign, Glasgow's rapid expansion had engulfed many smaller towns, but buried in the suburban sprawl, or on its fringes, are older towns, such as Airdrie, Renfrew, Rutherglen and Paisley, whose roots are deep in the Middle Ages. Most of them are industrialised, but despite the shadow of their large neighbour, they have retained their independence and their local governments. Each is a separate entity, not only because of historical associations, but because of differing traditions of craftsmanship: Airdrie mined the coal that forged Motherwell's steel that built the ships of Clydebank.

OLD STYLE *Glasgow's Art Gallery and Museum in Kelvingrove Park was built in 1902 from the profits of the 1888 International Exhibition. Salvador Dali's* Christ of St John of the Cross *is one of its best-known paintings*

NEW STYLE *Glasgow's School of Art was the 1896 masterpiece of Charles Rennie Mackintosh, a pioneer of the modern style*

CATHEDRAL Glasgow has the only complete medieval cathedral on the Scottish mainland. It dates from the 12th and 13th centuries, and the spire and nave were added 200 years later. The site has been a holy place since the 6th-century church was built by St Mungo.

Until the Reformation, Glasgow Cathedral was a much-ornamented place of pilgrimage, but 16th-century Presbyterian zeal 'purged' it of all 'monuments of idolatry'. The building is best viewed from the Necropolis, a cemetery full of monuments to Glasgow merchants. Among them is the grave of William Miller (1810–72), who wrote 'Wee Willie Winkie'.

CITY CENTRE Central Glasgow is sooty-grey, and 150 years of smoke and grime overlies the once-creamy local stone. It is essentially Victorian, designed and built by Glasgow men, of whom the best-known is Alexander 'Greek' Thomson. His oddly successful mingling of Greek and Egyptian styles is best seen in St Vincent Street Church, in the terraces of Great Western Road, and in the 'Egyptian Halls' in Union Street.

The Renaissance style was equally popular—the City Chambers dominating George Square is a magnificent example. The biggest shops are located in Argyle, Sauchiehall and Buchanan Streets. Argyle Street is spanned by the 'Highlandman's Umbrella'—a railway viaduct which provided shelter for Scotsmen seeking work in the city.

CITY PARKS For an industrial city, Glasgow is fortunate in the number of its imaginatively laid out public parks. Linn Park, the loveliest of them, lies on the banks of the White Cart Water and has a nature trail and a children's zoo. Rouken Glen has more than 200 acres of attractive woods and parkland, including a boating lake.

Just outside Queen's Park is a monument commemorating the Battle of Langside in 1568, which ended the tragic reign of Mary, Queen of Scots.

CLYDEBANK CONTRASTS *Shipyards stand on what was farmland a century ago, and the countryside is still not far away*

PLANNING FOR THE FUTURE *Raised paths, keeping pedestrians clear of traffic, are a feature of Cumbernauld's model new town, begun in the late 1950's*

EXPLORER'S BIRTHPLACE *The room in the cottage at Blantyre where David Livingstone, the explorer, was born in 1813 is preserved as a memorial and museum*

GLASGOW CROSS This is the heart of old Glasgow, though only fragments of the past remain. The mercat cross itself is a replica, dating from 1929, of the medieval original. The 17th-century Tron Steeple, forming an arch over the pavement, is a remnant of St Mary's Church, burnt by drunken members of the local Hell Fire Club in 1793.

HAMPDEN PARK Glasgow is a place of fierce loyalties—religious, civic and national—and nowhere are these given greater expression than in the city's passionate devotion to soccer. Hampden Park, the biggest football stadium in Britain, with a capacity of 135,000, is owned by Queens Park F.C., the only amateur team still playing senior football. At international matches, the crowd's 'Hampden Roar' in support of Scotland can be heard a mile away.

But the greatest passions are aroused at a Rangers *v.* Celtic match among supporters of the two Glasgow teams. Celtic supporters are predominantly Roman Catholic, while those of Rangers are mainly Protestant.

MUSEUMS The Art Gallery and Museum in Kelvingrove Park is rich in work of the Dutch, modern French and Scottish schools, and the Mitchell Library in North Street has a Burns collection.

Glasgow's domestic history is illustrated at the People's Palace on Glasgow Green. It also has relics of the city's grocer-hero, Sir Thomas Lipton, whose yachts, all named 'Shamrock', made five unsuccessful attempts between 1899 and 1930 to win the America's Cup.

PROVAND'S LORDSHIP Glasgow's oldest domestic building, built in 1470 for the priest in charge of St Nicholas' Hospital. Today, it contains a fine collection of 17th-century furniture and paintings; it is also said to have sheltered several royal Stuarts.

Provan Hall, on the eastern fringe of the city, dates from the same period, and was built as the mansion house of the Laird of Provan. Its pepperbox tower, pierced for defence, and its corbie-stepped gable, make it one of the finest examples of the style of houses inhabited by minor lairds of the time. The hall now belongs to the National Trust for Scotland.

UNIVERSITY OF GLASGOW In 1451, Bishop Turnbull obtained Papal authority for the establishment of a university in Glasgow, and the first lectures were held either in the cathedral or in the Black Friars' monastery in the High Street. The High Street was the university's home for 400 years, and when it moved to its present Gilmorehill site in 1870, part of the old college facade was used to construct the lodge. This contrasts oddly with Sir George Gilbert Scott's Gothic pinnacles that overlook Kelvingrove Park and the Clyde shipyards. Though enormous by 19th-century standards, the university today is only the nucleus of a large number of institutions scattered throughout the city. It contains the Hunterian Museum, housing a superb collection of coins, manuscripts, early printed books, archaeological specimens, and paintings by Rembrandt, Rubens and Whistler.

Clydebank

Surprisingly, shipbuilding is not an old Clyde trade; at one time during the 16th century, Glasgow's only boatbuilder had to be bribed not to remain within the district. It was not until the 19th century that steam and steel provided the incentive to dredge and widen the river sufficiently to permit the launching of big ships. The town's most famous shipyard was John Brown's—cradle of the *Lusitania*, the *Queen Mary* and the *Queen Elizabeth* and *Queen Elizabeth II*.

Cumbernauld New Town

The Cumbernauld Development Corporation was established in 1956 to plan a new town for Glasgow's overspill population. Cumbernauld has become a model for town-planners all over the world. Shops, offices, hotels and entertainments are centralised into a multi-storey complex.

Hamilton

A rare example of an attractive industrial town, set in relatively unspoilt surroundings. It is the hereditary seat of the Dukes of Hamilton, though the palace has long been demolished and the Low Parks recently transformed into a multi-purpose recreational centre, Strathclyde Park. The mausoleum, planned by the 10th Duke and built between 1840 and 1855, is still to be seen; the interior is remarkable for its many-coloured marble construction and for its six-second echo.

Another ducal property, Chatelherault Lodge, stands near by. The lodge and the octagonal parish church were both designed by William Adam in 1732. The High Parks contain the ruins of 12th-century Cadzow Castle, and a herd of rare wild cattle, white with black markings. High Parks may be visited by appointment.

East Kilbride, 5 miles west of Hamilton, is one of Scotland's most impressive new towns. Its swimming pool, opened in 1968, was the first Olympic-size pool in the country.

Paisley

The town, which is the largest thread-manufacturing centre in the world, grew up around a Cluniac abbey founded in 1163; the nave is still in use as the parish church. The church incorporates St Mirren's Chapel, which contains an effigy, believed to be that of Marjory Bruce, daughter of Robert I. Parts of the abbey buildings are also included in the 17th-century Palace of Paisley, now restored as a war memorial.

The town's Museum and Art Gallery has a priceless collection of the famous Paisley shawls, whose 'pine' motif was introduced from Kashmir in 1770. Mass-production methods undersold British and continental rivals so effectively that Paisley's competitors have been forgotten.

Bonnie banks and Bannockburn

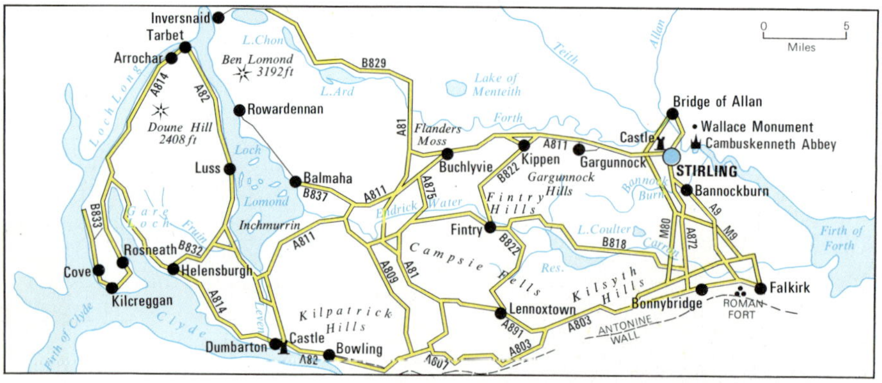

Angling Salmon, trout, pike and perch in Loch Lomond, Gare Loch, and in the River Leven. Trout and salmon in the Endrick Water, and in the River Teith. Trout in Lochs Ard, Chon and Coulter, Lake of Menteith and Allan Water.

Places to see *Bannockburn Monument* (NTS): daily, Apr. to Sept. *Dumbarton Castle*: weekdays and Sun. afternoon. *Rough Castle*, Roman fort, 1 mile east of Bonnybridge: daily. *Smith Institute*, Stirling: afternoons. *Stirling Castle*, including *Argyll and Sutherland Highlanders' Regimental Museum*: Apr. to Sept., weekdays, Sun. afternoon. *Wallace Monument*: daily.

Information centre Stirling Tourist Association, Dumbarton Road, Stirling. Tel. Stirling 5019.

On the narrow neck of land between the Firth of Clyde in the west and the Firth of Forth in the east are two places which symbolise Scotland for the visitor and for the Scotsman respectively—Loch Lomond and Bannockburn.

Loch Lomond, studded with islands and with a background of gentle hills in the south and harsh mountains in the north, has attracted visitors to Scotland for nearly two centuries. This tourist area extends across the Dunbarton hills in the west to Loch Long, where 13th-century Norse invaders landed and began a pillaging and wrecking tour of villages and islands. Now the loch bristles with the sails of yachts and dinghies from spring to autumn.

To the east, Stirling's massive castle high above the Forth looks down towards the battlefield of Bannockburn, where in 1314 Robert the Bruce put the English under Edward II to flight. The complete rout of the English forces secured Scotland's independence. Little remains of the Antonine Wall which the Romans built in AD 140, when Antoninus Pius was emperor, to keep out marauding Picts. The wall of turf and clay, together with a 12 ft deep ditch, ran 37 miles from near Bo'ness in the east to Bowling in the west, and linked 19 forts and signalling stations. Rough Castle, 1 mile east of Bonnybridge, is the best-preserved Roman fort on the wall, and other remains of the ditch can be seen at Watling Lodge, 1¼ miles west of Falkirk, and at Seabegs Wood, Bonnybridge.

Bannockburn
The battlefield on which in 1314 Robert the Bruce routed an English army three times larger than his own is just west of the town of Bannockburn. The 58 acres of the battlefield are owned by the National Trust for Scotland, and a rotunda, with panels describing the course of the battle, encircles the Borestone, in which the shaft of Bruce's standard is said to have been set. From the rotunda can be seen the Bannock Burn, the stream which was in front of the Scots' position; Gillies' Hill, from which 2000 Scotsmen descended to put to flight Edward II's already defeated English army; and Stirling Castle, 3 miles north. The equestrian statue of Bruce by C. d'O. Pilkington Jackson was unveiled by the Queen in 1964, on the 650th anniversary of the battle.

Bridge of Allan
A town and holiday resort on the Allan Water. It became a spa at the beginning of the last century, and Robert Louis Stevenson was among those who took the waters at the mineral spring at Airthrey, half a mile south-east. Stirling University is set in the Airthrey estate.

The Wallace Monument at Abbey Craig, 2 miles south-east, is a pinnacled tower commemorating Sir William Wallace, who rallied the Scots at the Battle of Stirling Bridge to defeat an English army under the Earl of Surrey in 1297 and became ruler of Scotland. A two-handed sword displayed in the tower is said to be his, though historians say this type of sword is not known to have been used by knights until the late 15th century. Wallace cleared the English out of Perth, Stirling and Lanark, but was defeated at Falkirk in 1298 and executed in London in 1305.

BRITAIN'S LARGEST LAKE *Ben Lomond, 3192 ft, towers beyond the waters of Loch Lomond, the largest lake in Great Britain*

WALLACE MONUMENT *The tower at Abbey Craig is a memorial to Scotland's medieval patriot, Sir William Wallace*

Dumbarton

A town on the River Leven where, when shipbuilding was its major industry, the famous *Cutty Sark* was built. From the 5th century until 1018 it was called Dunbreatan, Gaelic for 'Fort of the Britons', and was the centre of the independent kingdom of Strathclyde. A royal castle stood on Dumbarton Rock, a majestic 240 ft high rock commanding the river, until the Middle Ages. Little survives of the castle, but fortifications of the 17th and 18th centuries can still be seen. There is also a sundial given to the town by Mary, Queen of Scots when she stayed at the castle in 1548.

Falkirk

An important industrial centre where the Carron Ironworks were established in 1760 on the River Carron and produced 'carronades', or naval guns, which were used in Nelson's day. The works now produce light metal castings.

Fintry

A village between the Fintry Hills to the north-east and the Campsie Fells to the south. It lay in the centre of the ancient territory of Lennox which, in the Middle Ages, extended well into the regions now known as Central, Tayside and Strathclyde. The road south towards Lennoxtown gives fine views over the Campsies where dark basalt rocks protrude above the grass. The Loup of Fintry, 3 miles east, is a 90-ft waterfall.

Helensburgh

A resort on Gare Loch, popular for fishing, sailing and golf. It is a good centre from which to explore the wild hills and glens of Dunbarton. There are few roads, but the mountain scenery is magnificent, with the twin peaks of Doune Hill (2408 ft and 2298 ft) dominating the range. Helensburgh was the birthplace of John Logie Baird, the television pioneer.

Kippen

A village looking south towards the soaring Standmilane Craig. Although the hills are so close that little is seen of the winter sun, an enormous vine, known as the Kippen Great Vine, grew for 70 years in the village, producing 2000 bunches of grapes a year until it was removed in 1964 to make way for new houses. Gargunnock, $3\frac{1}{2}$ miles east, is a good centre for climbing the Gargunnock Hills, which rise to 1593 ft.

Buchlyvie, 5 miles west of Kippen, is on the edge of the Flanders Moss, which is partly rich agricultural land and partly a wild peat bog.

Agriculture was made possible by the enterprise of Lord Kames who, in the 18th century, had the idea of using water power to sluice away the peat in channels, which would uncover the rich soil beneath. The work took nearly a century to complete, for in some places the peat was 12 ft thick.

HOME OF THE KINGMAKER *Argyll's Lodging at Stirling, built in 1632, was the home of the Marquis of Argyll, the nobleman who crowned Charles II King of Scotland at Scone in 1651. It was a military hospital from 1799 to 1963, and is now a youth hostel*

HOME OF SCOTTISH KINGS *Stirling Castle, on a rock overlooking the Forth Valley, was a Scottish royal palace until 1603, when James VI became King of England*

Loch Lomond

The largest and one of the loveliest lochs in Scotland. Soft green hills slope away from its banks in the south and, further north, wooded mountains climb dramatically from its western and eastern shores. The loch is 23 miles long, ranges between half a mile and 5 miles wide, and is 630 ft at its deepest point. The south-east corner of the loch is a nature reserve.

The scenic attraction of Loch Lomond is partly due to its 30 islands. These islands also attracted Irish missionaries from the 5th century, who wanted their monasteries and nunneries to be secure from marauders. St Mirren is believed to have founded a monastery in the 6th century on Inchmurrin, the largest island, which is $1\frac{1}{2}$ miles long.

On the eastern side of the loch a twisting road follows the shore from Balmaha to Rowardennan, 7 miles north-west. From there a track, passing the majestic Ben Lomond (3192 ft) to the east, leads to the beautifully situated village of Inversnaid, 8 miles north. There are many attractive bays round the loch, filled with trout, pike and powan (a white fish found in Scottish lochs and Welsh lakes).

The song 'Loch Lomond' is said to have been composed by one of Bonnie Prince Charlie's captured followers on the eve of his execution in Carlisle Jail. The 'low road' of the song is the path by which the writer says his spirit will return to his native land after death quicker than his friend travelling to Scotland by the ordinary 'high road'.

Rosneath

A village and yachting centre on the Rosneath Peninsula. St Modan's Well is named after a 7th-century missionary who is said to have had his cell there. For centuries pilgrims came here to take the waters, said to have healing properties. Kilcreggan, 2 miles south-west, and Cove, 1 mile north-west of Kilcreggan, are popular sailing centres.

Stirling

An ancient town dominated by an imposing Renaissance castle standing on a sheer 250-ft crag. The present castle dates only from the 15th century, but earlier castles had been built on the site to command the routes across the surrounding Carse, or plain. The castle's Parliament Hall was built for James III (1451–88), and his son James IV added the fine gatehouse. James V built most of the royal palace in the early 16th century, and turned the castle into one of the most sumptuous in Scotland. James VI (James I of England) built the Chapel Royal for the christening of Prince Henry in 1594. Near the castle gates is the partly-15th-century Church of Holy Rude, where Mary, Queen of Scots was crowned in 1543.

The Smith Institute contains some 'Stirling heads', oaken roundels from the ceiling of the King's Presence Chamber in Stirling Castle.

Kintyre and the islands

CELTIC REMAINS *Tombstones in the churchyard at Kilmory, known as the Celtic slabs, date from medieval times*

Places to see *Auchindrain Farming Township Museum*: daily. *Brodrick Castle* (NTS), Arran: Easter to Sept., afternoons; gardens daily all year. *Crarae Lodge Gardens*, by Inveraray: daily, Apr. to Sept. *Inveraray Castle*: daily, except Fri., Apr. to early Oct. *Rothsay Castle*, Bute: weekdays, Sun. afternoon.

Steamers Regular steamer services connect the islands with each other and with the mainland at Ardrossan, Gourock, Tarbert and Wemyss Bay.

Information centres Mid-Argyll, Kintyre and Islay Tourist Organisation, Tourist Office, Campbeltown. Tel. Campbeltown 2056. Isle of Bute Tourist Organisation, The Pier, Rothesay. Tel. Rothesay 2151; and Pier Esplanade, Dunoon. Tel. Dunoon 3785.

The dramatic natural playground of western Strathclyde is cut up into peninsulas and islands by inlets of the sea, and crowned with bleak, savage mountains. Stretches of water are overlooked by the ruins of castles, and along the lochs and sea coast are holiday villages and towns, their gardens descending in terraces and their bays dotted with sails.

The mainland areas, the peninsula of Kintyre and the islands of Arran and Bute, are all easily accessible from the industrialised zone around Glasgow. Regular steamers serve the Inner Hebridean islands of Jura, Islay and Colonsay. The climate in this region is noticeably warmer than that of the Highlands, if slightly wetter, due to the Gulf Stream's influence.

A multitude of lochs and streams, with their salmon, sea-trout and brown trout, attract scores of amateur fishermen. Golden eagles live on the crags inland, deer browse in the glens, and grey Atlantic seals sun themselves on the sea rocks.

Boats of every description cruise in the calm, sheltered waters of the Kyles of Bute. In the remote interior, the occasional wildcat still stalks through the evergreen forests on the mountain slopes. The Argyll Forest Park, founded in 1936, stretches along the shores of Loch Long and across the Cowal peninsula almost to Loch Fyne.

INVERARAY CASTLE *The 18th-century castle, seen from a bridge*

Arran

Mountains, low hills, streams, glens and lochs earn the Island of Arran its description of 'Scotland in miniature'. The finest scenery is in the north, where lofty granite ridges are dominated by Goatfell (2866 ft). The surrounding wild areas of Glen Sannox to the north and Glen Rosa to the south are popular with walkers. There are many attractive sandy and rocky bays.

A good road encircles the island, and another crosses it from Brodick on the east coast, the chief port and holiday village, to the little resorts of Machrie and Blackwaterfoot on the west. Near Blackwaterfoot are Bronze Age cairns, and the King's Caves, which sheltered Robert the Bruce in the early 14th century. Picturesque Lochranza, or 'the loch of safe anchorage', is where Bruce landed from Ireland in 1306.

Three large bays lie in the shelter of the undulating east coast: Brodick Bay is dominated by a castle, built in 1456, which was once the home of the Dukes of Hamilton and is now owned by the National Trust for Scotland. Lamlash Bay is a haven for yachts, protected by the craggy Holy Island, on which is St Molais's cave, the cell of a hermit in the days of St Columba in the 6th century. Whiting Bay is another popular holiday centre. In the south of Arran, the landscape is more pastoral; the popular Arran cheese is made at Torrylin. The shore is sandy and the countryside is rich in standing stones of *c.* 2000 BC.

Bute

The 15 mile long island nestles at the foot of the hilly Cowal peninsula, from which it is separated by the beautiful stretch of water known as the Kyles of Bute. Cattle used to be made to swim across from Colintraive, on the mainland, to Rhubodach, on the island; now a car ferry makes the crossing. The north of the island is hilly; to the south the land is flat and more fertile. Rothesay, the principal town, is a resort and steamer port. The remains of its castle, surrounded by a deep moat, date from the 13th century. The castle was destroyed by Cromwell in the 17th century.

Campbeltown

The chief centre in the long peninsula of Kintyre. Its rocky beach provides good sea angling; and herring, white fish and lobsters are landed at the harbour. At the Old Quay Head stands Campbeltown Cross, a richly carved Celtic cross that dates from *c.* 1500.

Offshore is the island of Davaar, which can be reached across a bank of shingle. In a cave on the island, illuminated only by a shaft of light from a hole in the rock, is a Crucifixion scene, painted in 1887 and retouched by a local artist in 1956.

Carradale

A small Kintyre resort with a sheltered bay, facing the Island of Arran. The ruins of Aird Castle are near the pier, and an oval fort, its walls vitrified, or fused into a glassy substance by fire, stands at Carradale Point, a narrow peninsula which is sometimes isolated from the island at high water.

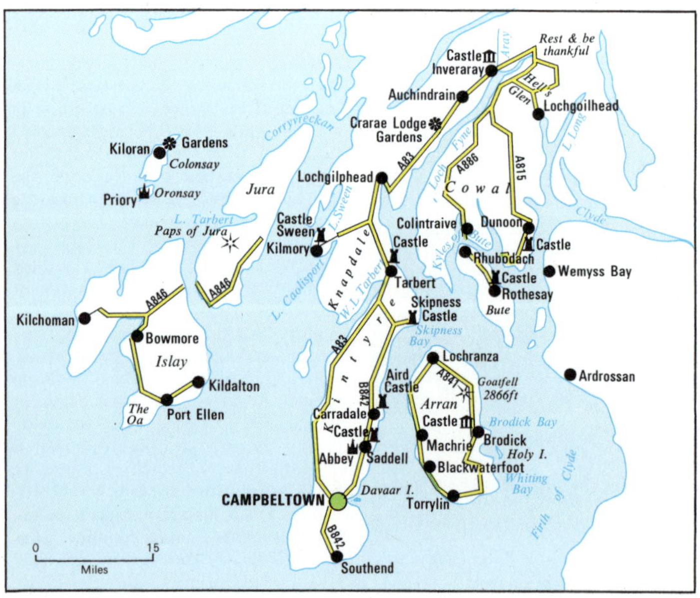

over the River Aray, was built for the 3rd Duke of Argyll by Robert Morris and William Adam

SKIPNESS *Remains of the Campbells' 13th-century castle overlook the bay*

SHELTERED VILLAGE *Tarbert lies at the foot of hills that almost enclose its harbour*

Saddell, 4 miles south, is a village on a bay, at the foot of Saddell Glen, with the remains of a 12th-century Cistercian monastery. The monastery is said to have been founded by Somerled, the first Lord of the Isles, from whom sprang the Clan Donald. Saddell Castle, south-east of the village, is a large battlemented tower dating from 1509.

Dunoon
A holiday town on the Firth of Clyde, with two fine bays and the ruins of a castle. Mary Campbell, Burns's sweetheart, 'Highland Mary', was born here, and she is commemorated by a statue on Castle Hill, overlooking the Clyde. The wild country of the Cowal peninsula behind the town includes the wooded slopes and charming waterfalls of Morag's Fairy Glen.

Innellan, 4 miles south of Dunoon, is a holiday village with villas looking across to Wemyss Bay. The weather is so mild that palm trees grow in some gardens. From Toward Point, 2½ miles further south-west, there are good views of the Clyde.

Inveraray
A beautiful white-walled town, hereditary seat of the Dukes of Argyll, whose castle has been the headquarters of the Campbell clan since the early 15th century. In 1644 the original village of Inveraray was burnt by the Royalist Marquis of Montrose. The 3rd Duke of Argyll built the new town and castle between 1746 and 1780. The castle was badly damaged by fire in 1975 but has since been restored.

At one end of the main street there is a tall Celtic burial cross from Iona. The parish church is divided by a wall that enables services to be held in Gaelic and English at the same time.

Inveraray faces Loch Fyne and is surrounded by some of the loveliest woods in Scotland. From the grounds of Inveraray Castle, a 5-mile walk up Glen Shira leads to the pretty Falls of Aray and to the home of the bandit Rob Roy, which is now a ruin.

At Auchindrain, 6 miles south-west of Inveraray, a museum of farm cottages evokes the rural life of the past. Crarae Lodge, 4 miles further south-west, has a fine woodland garden.

Islay
An island with fine beaches and bays, and good angling. Several Celtic crosses are dotted around the island, and those at Kildalton and Kilchoman are particularly finely carved.

The 200-year-old Killarow Church at Bowmore is circular—according to legend, so that the Devil would have no corners in which to hide. On the peninsula of The Oa is a monument to 650 American sailors lost from two ships wrecked on the rocky coast in 1918.

Jura
A rugged, mountainous island, reaching its highest points in the triple peaks, the Paps of Jura. Loch Tarbert divides the island almost in two.

From the northern tip of Jura can be seen and heard the whirlpool of Corryvreckan off the coast. Beaches and caves are dotted along the west coast, which is practically uninhabited. The island has a whisky distillery, but the main local industry is farming.

The small islands of Colonsay and Oronsay lie 8 miles to the west. They are separated by a narrow strait which can be crossed on foot for 3 hours at low tide. Colonsay House, at Kiloran, has sub-tropical gardens; Oronsay has the remains of a 14th-century priory.

Kilmory
A lobster-fishing centre on the narrow neck of land separating Loch Sween from Loch Caolisport. In the grounds of the Chapel of St Maelrubha is a collection of carved Celtic slabs. There are sweeping views across the water to the Paps of Jura. Castle Sween, 2½ miles north-east, is a 13th-century ruin.

Lochgoilhead
A Victorian township with fine views of the extensive range of hills, more than 2000 ft high, known as Argyll's Bowling Green, which form part of the vast Argyll Forest Park in the Cowal peninsula. The park, founded in 1936, stretches across the peninsula almost to Loch Fyne. Half a mile north of Lochgoilhead, two roads lead into spectacular mountain scenery. To the north-west is the rocky and lonely Hell's Glen, a forbidding pass crossing the hills to Loch Fyne. To the north-east is the Rest-and-be-thankful pass, at the northern limit of the mountainous Cowal peninsula.

Southend
A village with two sandy beaches, near Kintyre's southern tip. A grassy knoll near the ruined chapel of Keil, just to the west, is the traditional landing place in Argyll of St Columba (AD 521–97), who came from Ireland with his disciples to convert the Picts. A flat stone bears the carved prints of two right feet. They are known as 'St Columba's footprints', but they may have been carved to mark a place where pre-Christian chiefs took their tribal vows, for only 100 yds away stand the remains of a Druid altar.

Tarbert
A seaport village and herring-fishing centre on the tiny isthmus linking Knapdale and Kintyre, and dividing West and East Loch Tarbert. The ruined 14th-century castle was at one time a stronghold of Robert the Bruce. Steamers sail to Islay from West Loch Tarbert Pier.

SCOTTISH HIGHLANDS

Scotland means many things to the Scot, but to the non-Scottish holiday visitor it often means primarily the Highlands and Islands. Scotland's mountains would be lost in the foothills of the Andes or the Himalayas, but they yield nothing to the highest peaks in the world in terms of beauty, and their capacity to inspire awe. This is because they do not stand alone. They share the landscape with wild sea lochs that gouge deeply into the land; with icy streams that tumble through green and wooded glens; with the calm waters of great inland lochs; and, above all, with an ever-changing sky that gives rise to a variety of colour.

It is a lonely land. The Highlands and Islands cover about a quarter of Britain's land surface—but fewer than 1 in 50 of the population live there. Vast tracts of land have no roads. Only the walker and the camper have any chance of penetrating these solitudes.

Unlike the world's other great wildernesses, some of which have never known the hand of man, the Scottish Highlands, for all their loneliness, show many traces of human habitation. Every corner is a reminder of the past. There are crumbling crofts, recalling the enforced depopulation of the 18th and 19th centuries when the land was cleared of inhabitants to make room for large-scale sheep-farming. Ruined castles are reminders of the turbulent Middle Ages, while Iron Age forts and even Stone Age cave-dwellings survive from man's remoter past.

If man is largely absent today, wildlife is not. The Highlands are the last refuge of many mammals and birds found nowhere else in Britain. Golden eagles soar above the moors and crags, gannets plunge into the sea, and turkey-like capercaillies croak through the woodlands. The mammals of the Highlands include the wildcat, the pine marten, red deer and roe deer. Lochs and rivers teem with salmon and trout.

The Highlands and Islands are not all mountainous. Even on the rugged west coast there are many sheltered glens, where the land, warmed by the Gulf Stream, is green. At Poolewe in Ross and Cromarty, for instance, a large collection of sub-tropical plants thrives in the gardens of Inverewe, on a latitude further north than Moscow. Sutherland has some of the wildest and loneliest countryside in Britain, dominated by the rocky lunar landscape of the North-West Highlands. Caithness, by contrast, is largely flat and treeless, but the monotony of its interior is relieved by breathtaking seascapes along miles of its coastline. Further south, Easter Ross and the Black Isle are softer, greener areas, with many fertile farms. The lands bordering the Moray Firth and the lowlands of

LOCHS AND PEAKS *Great mountain ranges dominate northern Scotland. The Grampian Mountains, with the Monadhliaths and the Cairngorms, form a huge, continuous mass lying to the south and east of the Great Glen, which splits Scotland from the Moray Firth to Loch Linnhe. Beyond the glen to the north rise the North West Highlands*

SHETLAND ISLANDS
Herma Ness
Unst
Yell
Fetlar
Whalsay
Bressay
Foula
Scalloway
LERWICK
Sumburgh Head
Fair Isle
North Ronaldsay
Pierowall
Westray
Sanday
ORKNEY ISLANDS
Eday
Stronsay
Mainland
Finstown
Stromness
Kirkwall
St Mary's
Hoy
South Ronaldsay
Pentland Firth
Stroma
Duncansby Head
Cape Wrath
Durness
Bettyhill
Tongue
Thurso
WICK
Rhiconich
Scourie
Lochinver
Inchnadamph
Lairg
Brora
Golspie
Dornoch
ULLAPOOL
Dundonnell
Poolewe
Gairloch
HIGHLAND
NORTH WEST HIGHLANDS
Dingwall
Black Isle
Moray Firth
Lossiemouth
Banff
Fraserburgh
Buchan
Peterhead
Nairn
ELGIN
Forres
MORAY
NAIRN
Keith
Turriff
Huntly
Fyvie
Cruden Bay
INVERNESS
Grantown on Spey
Kinlochewe
Torridon
Applecross
LOCHCARRON
Plockton
Drumnadrochit
Monadhliath Mountains
Boat of Garten
Alford
Inverurie
ABERDEEN
Invermoriston
AVIEMORE
Coylumbridge
Cairngorm Mountains
GRAMPIAN
Glenelg
Fort Augustus
Feshiebridge
Kingussie
Newtonmore
Aboyne
Ballater
Banchory
KINCARDINE
Braemar
STONEHAVEN
GRAMPIAN MOUNTAINS
ANGUS
Dalwhinnie
Laurencekirk
Kinneff
Inverbervie
Clova
Edzell
Forest of Atholl
Blair Atholl
Killiecrankie
Kirkton of Glenisla
Tannadice
Brechin
St Cyrus
Montrose
Kinloch Rannoch
Pitlochry
Bridge of Cally
Kirriemuir
Forfar
Lunan
Glamis
Arbroath
L. Rannoch
Aberfeldy
Fortingall
Kenmore
Blairgowrie
Dunkeld
Sidlaw Hills
Monikie
Carnoustie
Broughty Ferry
L. Tay
Powfis
Easter Scone
DUNDEE
TAYSIDE
Killin
Comrie
PERTH
Firth of Tay
Balquhidder
Crieff
R. Earn
Abernethy
CENTRAL
Ochil Hills
FIFE
Fife Ness
Firth of Forth
CALLANDER
Aberfoyle
Port of Menteith
L. Lomond
Glasgow
STRATHCLYDE
BORDERS
Crinan
Colonsay
Jura
Islay
Sound of Jura
Firth of Clyde
OBAN
Firth of Lorn
L. Awe
L. Fyne
Mull
Ross of Mull
Iona
Staffa
Lochaline
Tiree
Coll
Ardnamurchan
Strontian
Fort William
Spean Bridge
Glenfinnan
L. Morar
L. Shiel
MALLAIG
Knoydart
Eigg
Muck
Rhum
Canna
Armadale
Broadford
Skye
Sligachan
Dunvegan
Uig
Raasay
L. Ness
L. Maree
L. Shin
LEWIS
STORNOWAY
Barvas
Arnol
Gt Bernera
Tarbert
Harris
Toe Head
Rodel
North Uist
Benbecula
South Uist
Eriskay
Barra
Berneray
WESTERN ISLES
OUTER HEBRIDES
INNER HEBRIDES
THE LITTLE MINCH
NORTH MINCH
A9
A82
A96
A87
A830
A835
A836
A838
A857
A859
A865
A970
A971
A968
A966
A882
A897
A837
A839
A832
A896
A890
A851
A86
A939
A940
A941
A95
A98
A952
A950
A975
A92
A947
A944
A980
A93
B974
A94
B955
B951
A85
A828
A849
A816
A83
A827
M90
A913
A811
A814
A809
A80
M80
M9
M8
A73
A8
A737
A736
A77
A78
A726
A74
A1
B7066
40
80
120
160
200
240
280
MILES
REGIONAL PAGE INDEX
526
524
522
520
518
508
510
504
502
514
500
498
492
496
494
KEY TO MAP
Regional centre
Selected town or village
Regional boundary
County boundary (admin. region Scotland)
Major road
Minor road
Woodland
River and lake or reservoir

eastern Grampian are rich farming areas. Picturesque fishing villages huddle along the coast in sheltered bays or on precipitous hillsides. Inland stand the Grampians—the highest and largest mountain mass in Britain. Tayside, south of the Grampians, offers a Highland landscape in miniature—heavily wooded, very green and prosperous. The pride of the Perth district is the area known as The Trossachs (meaning 'bristly country'), which is graphically described by Sir Walter Scott in *The Lady of the Lake* and *Rob Roy*. The Trossachs contain unparalleled views of mountain, loch, river and woodland and are dominated to the south by 2393-ft Ben Venue which overlooks the eastern end of Loch Katrine and the Pass of Achray.

Then there are the islands. The scenic beauty of Skye is enhanced by the romance which surrounds every inch of its ground. In the Outer Hebrides, the old Gaelic way of life survives with its language, its music and its crafts. The Orkneys and Shetlands were for centuries Viking strongholds, and their people and buildings are still more Norse than Scottish. There are hundreds of other islands, from tiny, remote St Kilda—a bird-watchers' paradise—to the great hump of Mull, where red deer roam the hills.

Northern Scotland has several holiday resorts, notably along the Grampian coast, and at Aviemore in the Cairngorms where an all-the-year-round holiday centre has been built. Elsewhere in the area more and more hotels, hostels, caravan sites, shops and restaurants are being provided every year, though the number of big hotels, shops and garages away from the few small towns is still limited. The Highlands are either bed-and-breakfast country—comfortable accommodation is available in many homes—or a place for the camper or caravanner. It offers most to the naturalist, the bird-watcher, the fisherman, the climber, the yachtsman and other lovers of the outdoor life. This is the last unspoilt quarter of Britain, where the visitor can get further 'away from it all' than is possible anywhere else on this crowded island.

Travel is never as easy as it seems. The hill that appears to loom round the corner may be 10 miles off as the crow flies and 50 miles by a single-track road that winds its way round hills and lochs. In many places, particularly in the North-West, Sunday is rigorously observed as The Lord's Day: ferries do not run, petrol is not available and, of course, no shops are open. Highland people are courteous and hospitable, but this is their land, and in it life is lived their way.

SNOW FOR THE WINTER SPORTSMAN

The Highlands have mixed weather. Glen Garry, in the west, has more than 200 in. of rain a year. On the sheltered Moray Firth, by contrast, many places have less than 25 in. a year. Temperatures compare favourably with those of the south of England. Dundee averages almost 15°C (59°F) during July compared with 16°C (61°F) for Falmouth in Cornwall. Winter visitors to the Highlands expect snow on the hills for skiing, and usually get it.

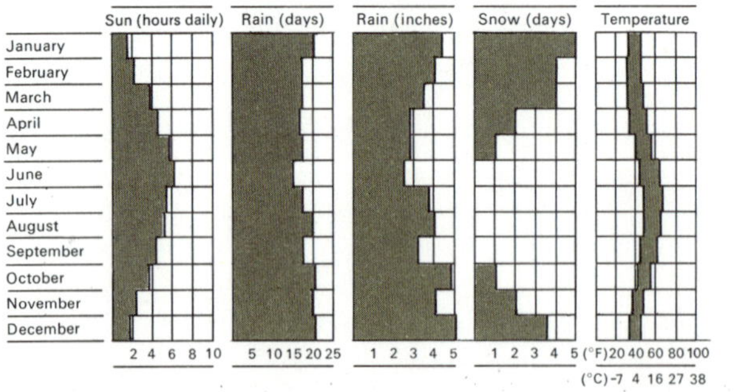

SNOW-CLAD GIANT *Britain's highest mountain, 4406-ft Ben Nevis, towers above the River Lochy, dwarfing the houses of Fort William that stand at its foot. The harmony between sky, mountain and water is typical of the scenery of the Highlands*

Glencoe and the lochs of north Argyll

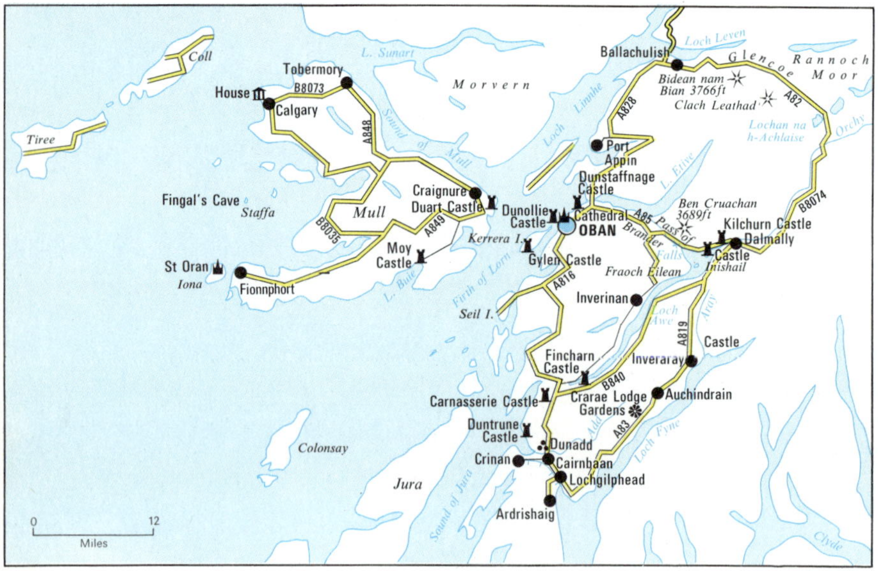

Angling There is good sea-angling throughout the area, especially from Oban and Tobermory.

Sailing At Oban and Tobermory.

Mountaineering Rock climbing on Ben Cruachan and Ben More, on Mull. Glencoe is also a good centre.

Nature trails At Inverinan and Dalavich, Loch Awe; Mull (forest trail), 1½ miles south-east of Tobermory; Glencoe (Signal Rock).

Events Highland Games are held at Tobermory in July. Oban is the scene of the West Highland Yachting Week, the first week in Aug., and of the Argyll Gathering, also in Aug.

Places to see *Auchindrain Farming Township Museum*: daily. *Crarae Lodge Gardens*: daily, Apr. to Sept. *Duart Castle*: Mon. to Fri., May to Sept.; also Sun. afternoon in July and Aug. *Glencoe* (NTS): Visitor Centre, daily, Easter to mid-Oct.

Ferries Oban to Craignure, Mull, cars and passengers: daily. Oban to Tobermory, Mull, passengers only: Mon., Wed. and Sat., May to Oct. Cruises Oban to Iona, early June to late Sept.

Information centres Mull and Iona: Tourist Information Office, 48 Main Street, Tobermory. Tel. Tobermory 2182. Mainland: Information Centre, Boswell House, Argyll Square, Oban. Tel. Oban 3122, 3551.

Northern Argyll is breathtaking in its mountain grandeur and steeped in clan and religious history. Its scenic richness ranges from the wild highland peaks of Glencoe, notorious for the massacre of 1692, to its jagged western coastline, more than a thousand miles long, and to the magic seascapes of the Inner Hebrides. Great sea lochs such as Loch Sunart, outer Loch Linnhe and Loch Etive are the haunts of gannets, divers and rare wading birds. Loch Awe, the largest of Argyll's inland lochs, is a paradise for salmon-fishing enthusiasts.

Oban is the great port for the Western Isles and a centre of Gaelic culture; it is the gateway to Mull, largest of the Inner Hebrides, and to the islands of Iona, the cradle of Scottish Christianity, and Staffa, where Fingal's Cave inspired Mendelssohn's overture.

Robert the Bruce, St Columba, Mary, Queen of Scots, Flora MacDonald—they are all woven into Argyll's history and legend. Everywhere are memories of the past, still kept alive today. In May and June the islands are at their flowery best and the nights are never inky dark. In September and October the hills of Lorn and Mull are a blaze of gold. And in winter the west coast days sparkle like crystal.

OBAN HARBOUR *Fishing boats lie on the waters of the harbour. On the hill behind stands the 19th-century McCaig's Tower, built by a local banker as a memorial to his family*

MORNING REFLECTIONS *Eighteenth-century houses on Tobermory quayside are reflected in the calm waters of the harbour*

Crinan
A yachtsman's haven on the Sound of Jura, overlooked by the early 11th-century Duntrune Castle, one of the oldest castles in Scotland still inhabited. Near Cairnbaan, 4 miles south-east, is the ruined hill-fort of Dunadd, once the capital of Dalriada, kingdom of the Scots. There are numerous Bronze Age stone circles in the vicinity, and Kilmartin churchyard, 5 miles north of Cairnbaan, has a carved cross dating from the 16th century. Carnasserie Castle, built in the late 16th century, was the home of John Carswell, the first post-Reformation Bishop of the Isles, whose translation of John Knox's Liturgy into Gaelic was the first book to be published in the language.

Crinan stands at the western end of the 9 mile long Crinan Canal, built between 1793 and 1801 to enable ships to reach the Atlantic from Loch Fyne, saving a sea voyage of 130 miles round the Kintyre Peninsula. Fishing boats, coasters and yachts still use the canal.

Glencoe
One of Scotland's wildest and most celebrated glens. It runs from Rannoch Moor to Loch Leven between some magnificent mountains, including the 3766-ft Bidean nam Bian.

Glencoe is also called the Glen of Weeping, for it was here, in 1692, that a company of soldiers under a Campbell commander massacred more than 40 MacDonalds who had received them hospitably for 12 days. The Campbells rose at 5 a.m. and, in the middle of a snowstorm, began the massacre. MacIan, the chief of the MacDonalds, was killed, but his two sons escaped to the hills with other survivors of the massacre. A monument to the murdered chief stands near the entrance to the glen.

There is a road through the pass, above which a rock platform called The Study gives a fine view. At its western end, Glencoe opens into Loch Leven. A bridge crosses the loch at Ballachulish.

Iona
On this tiny island St Columba established his abbey when he came from Ireland in AD 563 and sent his missionaries to convert Scotland to Christianity. Although he was buried there, his remains were later returned to Ireland. The reconstructed cathedral dates from *c.* 1200. Near by are the carved Celtic crosses of St Martin and St John. McLean's Cross, probably 15th century, stands on the road to St Oran's Cemetery, the oldest Christian cemetery in Scotland and the burial place of 48 Scottish kings, including Duncan, murdered by Macbeth in 1040. St Oran's Chapel is said to have been built by Queen Margaret in 1080.

Loch Awe
A curving and graceful loch, abounding in trout and salmon. It is 22 miles long and in most places only about a mile across; it acted for years as a natural moat protecting the Campbells of Inveraray from their enemies in the north. Along its banks and on its islands are many reminders of its fortified past. There is a ruined castle at Fincharn, at the southern end of the loch, and another on the island of Fraoch Eilean. The isle of Inishail has an ancient chapel and burial ground, and at the northern end of the loch are the ruins of Kilchurn Castle, built by Sir Colin Campbell in 1440. Near Dalmally, just north-east of Kilchurn Castle, is a monument to the Gaelic poet Duncan Ban Macintyre.

The vast bulk of Ben Cruachan (3689 ft) dominates Loch Awe at its northern end. On Ben Cruachan is the world's second-biggest hydro-electric power station, which pumps water from Loch Awe to a reservoir 1315 ft up the mountain. Below the mountain are the Falls of Cruachan, and the wild Pass of Brander, where Robert the Bruce routed the Clan MacDougall in 1308.

Mull
A beautiful island of moorland, forest and peaks. Duart Castle, a 13th-century stronghold of the Lords of the Isles, is now the home of the Chief of the Clan Maclean. Tobermory is the main centre and fishing port. Divers search for the treasure of the Spanish galleon *Florencia*, blown up in the bay in 1588.

The south of Mull has magnificent cliff scenery, and Moy Castle, on Loch Buie, has a water-filled dungeon. The wild countryside of Mull was the scene of many of David Balfour's adventures in R. L. Stevenson's novel *Kidnapped*.

RANNOCH MOOR *Snow-capped Clach Leathad, 3602 ft, is reflected in the still waters of Lochan na h-Achlaise, at the western end of Rannoch Moor. R. L. Stevenson, in his novel* Kidnapped, *described the 20 square miles of Rannoch Moor as being 'as waste as the sea'*

THE GLENCOE MASSACRE

In February 1692, Glencoe (right) was the scene of the notorious massacre of the MacDonald clan, who had failed to swear allegiance to William III and forswear the Jacobite cause by the time appointed by the government. Robert Campbell of Glen Lyon (above) led a company of troops to the glen where, after enjoying 12 days' hospitality, they butchered more than 40 of their unsuspecting hosts during the early hours of the morning

Oban
From Pulpit Hill there is a fine view across the Firth of Lorn and the Sound of Mull. McCaig's Tower, overlooking the town, is an unfinished replica of the Colosseum in Rome, built by a banker, John Stuart McCaig, in 1890 as a memorial to his family.

Near the little granite Cathedral of the Isles is the ruin of the 13th-century Dunollie Castle, seat of the MacDougall Lords of Lorn who once owned a third of Scotland. On the island of Kerrera, just offshore, stands Gylen Castle, a home of the MacDougalls, dating back to 1587. Dunstaffnage Castle, 3 miles north, was built mainly in the 13th century. It has round towers, and walls 10 ft thick, and was built for Alexander II's attack against the Norsemen when they held the Hebrides.

Seil Island, 15 miles south-west, is linked to the mainland by the Clachan Bridge. The bridge was designed by Telford in 1793 and is claimed to be the only bridge to 'span the Atlantic'.

Staffa
A small, uninhabited island, famous for its caves and basaltic formations, the result of volcanic action. Fingal's Cave, 227 ft long and 66 ft high, inspired Mendelssohn's 'Hebrides' overture. Smooth black columns of basalt rise from the sea like great organ pipes. Its original Gaelic name of An Uamh Bhinn, 'the musical cave', derived from the sounds of the sea echoing through its depths. Steamers go to Staffa from Oban, and landings can be made in calm weather.

The 'Fair City' of Perth, once Scotland's capital

Angling There is superb salmon fishing in rivers in the area, especially on the Tay, though some is preserved.

Pony trekking At Blair Atholl, Dunkeld and Spittal of Glenshee.

Events Perth Agricultural Show is held in Aug., Pitlochry Theatre Festival from mid-May to early Oct. The Crieff Highland Games are held in Aug., and the Pitlochry Highland Games in early Sept.

Places to see *Abercairny*, Crieff: gardens Wed., early Apr. to Sept. *Black Watch Museum*, Balhousie Castle, Perth: Mon. to Fri. *Blair Castle*: Apr., Sun. and Mon.; May to mid-Oct., weekdays and Sun. afternoons. *Branklyn Garden* (NTS), Perth: Mar. to Oct., daily. *Drummond Castle*, near Crieff: gardens Apr. to Sept., Wed., Sat. afternoons. *Dunblane Cathedral Museum*: late May to early Oct., daily. *Dunkeld Cathedral*: weekdays and Sun. afternoon. *Elcho Castle*: weekdays, Sun. afternoon. *Fair Maid of Perth's House*, Curfew Row, Perth: weekdays; also Sun. afternoon in summer. *Huntingtower Castle*, near Perth: weekdays, Sun. afternoon. *Meigle Museum*: weekdays. *Pass of Killiecrankie* (NTS): Visitor Centre: weekdays and Sun. afternoon, Easter to Sept. *Perth Museum and Art Gallery*: weekdays, Sun. afternoon. *Scone Palace*: May to Sept., weekdays, Sun. afternoon. *The Pinetum*, Scone: May to Sept., weekdays, Sun. afternoon.

Information centres Perth Tourist Association, Marshall Place, Perth. Tel. Perth 22900. Pitlochry Tourist Association, 28 Atholl Road, Pitlochry. Tel. Pitlochry 2215.

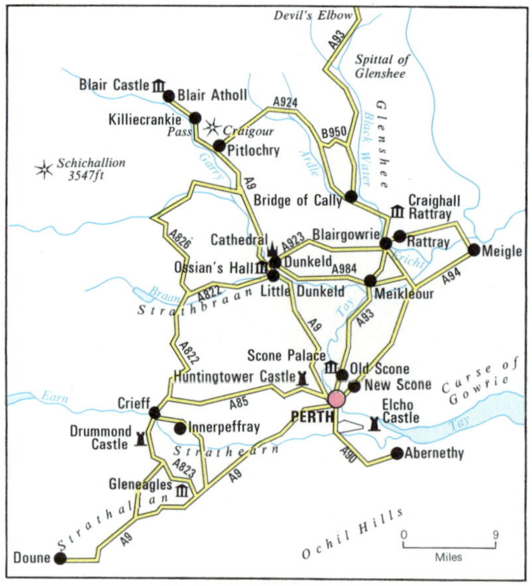

Sir Walter Scott wrote in his novel *The Fair Maid of Perth*, published in 1828, 'Amid all the provinces of Scotland, if an intelligent stranger were asked to describe the most varied and most beautiful, it is probable he would name the county of Perth . . .' Scott's praise is still justified. There are mountains and moors, hills and woods, lush farmlands, lochs and glens, and streams and rivulets in profusion.

The small, ancient city of Perth, once called St Johnstoun, is beautifully situated on the broad River Tay, the longest river in Scotland. North of the river stretches the Carse of Gowrie, the flat, fertile land that produces most of Scotland's strawberries. Neat villages alternate with charming small towns.

To the south-west, the world-famous Gleneagles golf courses spread like a green carpet over acres of undulating moorland between Strathearn and Strathallan. Evidence of an ancient past is abundant: there are Pictish forts, cairns, Roman remains and, at Scone, the site where Scottish kings were crowned on the famous 'Stone of Destiny'.

Abernethy
A village between the River Earn and the Ochil Hills that was once a Pictish capital and later a Roman base. A Roman fort has been excavated. The round 12th-century church tower is one of only two such towers on the mainland; the other is at Brechin in Angus.

Blair Atholl
A village on the River Garry, surrounded by magnificent Highland scenery. It stands at the meeting-point of several glens, where the Duke of Atholl built his castle in 1269. The imposing structure, in its fine sweep of parkland, was altered over the years, but restored in 1869 by John Bryce, the architect who was noted for his revival of the Scottish baronial style. The castle has a lovely tapestry room, Jacobite relics and a fine collection of armour.

WHERE A KING WAS KIDNAPPED *Huntingtower Castle, near Perth, was the scene, in 1582, of the kidnapping of James VI of Scotland by discontented Protestant nobles*

Blairgowrie
A compact little town and an attractive angling resort and touring base, as well as the centre of a prosperous strawberry and raspberry-growing region. The 19th-century Brig o' Blair over the swift-running River Ericht links Blairgowrie to Rattray. About 2 miles north the river runs between 200 ft high cliffs. Above the gorge stands Craighall, a 17th-century mansion still occupied by the Rattray family for whom it was originally built.

Meikleour, 4 miles south-west, is notable for its 90 ft high, 600 yd long beech hedge, planted in 1746 and bordering the modern Meikleour House.

Bridge of Cally
An attractive village on the River Ardle, which here meets the Black Water from Glenshee to become the River Ericht. Northwards, the road from the village climbs 1675 ft to the popular Glenshee ski slopes. On the way is the once-notorious Devil's Elbow (1950 ft), though its hazardous double bends have now been removed.

Crieff
A pleasant little hillside town overlooking beautiful Strathearn. At the entrance to the town hall an octagonal mercat cross stands within an iron railing, and by the 17th-century tolbooth are the old stocks. Across the road is a medieval cross of red sandstone, sculptured with interlaced Celtic knots, probably dating from the 10th century.

Innerpeffray, 3 miles south-east, is a straggling hamlet best known for its library, founded in 1680 by David Drummond, and one of the oldest libraries in Scotland. Its valuable collection includes several rare Bibles.

Drummond Castle, 2 miles south, was built by the first Lord Drummond in 1491. It survived bombardment by Cromwell, but was partly demolished in 1745. Only the square tower of the original building still stands, but there is an interesting collection of old armour.

Dunblane
A residential town with views over Allan Water, here spanned by a 16th-century bridge, and a cathedral with a Norman tower in the nave as well as some fine 13th-century Gothic architecture.

Dunkeld
A delightful, tiny cathedral town in the wooded valley of the Tay. Its beautiful ruined cathedral, set in lovely lawns, dates back to the 9th century, but only

TOWER REFUGE *Clergy took refuge in this tower at Abernethy during the 12th century*

FAIRY-TALE FORTRESS *Blair Castle, which belongs to the Duke of Atholl, was given its present castellated appearance in the 19th century, after being renovated in the mid-18th century. Comyn's Tower, with the flag, is a copy of the 13th-century original*

SCULPTURED STONE

This is one of 26 Pictish and early Christian stones, dating from the 7th to 10th centuries, in Meigle Museum

the 14th-century choir remains complete and restored, and this serves as the parish church. The wall of a house in the small peaceful square bears an early-18th-century upright 'ell', the old Scottish equivalent of a yard (37 in.). Across Telford's fine bridge is Inver, formerly Little Dunkeld and birthplace of Niel Gow (1727–1807), composer and player of reels and Strathspeys; his tomb stands in the churchyard.

In Strathbraan, about a mile south-west, is The Hermitage, formerly known as Ossian's Hall, a restored 18th-century 'folly' with splendid views of the river. Close by are the Falls of the Braan and a picturesque gorge.

Killiecrankie

A hamlet best known for the bloody battle which took place in 1689 at the head of the Pass of Killiecrankie, about 1 mile north. The battle was won for James VII of Scotland (James II of England) and the Jacobite cause by Graham of Claverhouse, Viscount Dundee—the 'Bonnie Dundee' of Scott's ballad—who defeated General Mackay but was killed in the moment of victory. A steep footpath descends to the narrow opening of the gorge, known as 'Soldier's Leap' after a trooper who jumped across the River Garry to escape the Royalist Highlanders. Much of the pass is owned by the National Trust for Scotland.

Perth

The 'Fair City', as it is known, was made a Royal Burgh in 1210, and fortified by Edward I of England in 1298. The city served as capital of Scotland for a century until, in 1437, James I of Scotland was murdered there and his widow and her young son, James II, moved the court to Edinburgh. Perth surrendered to Cromwell in 1651, and was occupied by Jacobite forces during the uprisings of 1715 and 1745.

St John's Kirk is one of the few buildings which remain from the city's medieval period. Here, in 1559, John Knox gave a famous sermon on church idolatry. Charles I, Charles II, and later Bonnie Prince Charlie attended services there. In North Port is the Fair Maid of Perth's House, restored in 1893 on the site of the house where, in 1396, lived Catherine Glover, the 'Fair Maid' of Sir Walter Scott's novel. It is now an antique and crafts shop. The Salutation Hotel, built in 1699, still has a minstrel gallery near the bedroom occupied by Bonnie Prince Charlie. The City Chambers are notable for late-19th-century stained-glass windows depicting scenes from Scott's *The Fair Maid of Perth* and other scenes of Robert the Bruce capturing the town in 1311.

The North Inch is a fine, spacious park in which stands a huge domed sports centre. At Huntingtower Castle, 2 miles north-west, a band of nobles, led by the Earl of Gowrie, kidnapped James VI (later James I of England) in 1582, and held him for a year to force him to change his ministers.

Pitlochry

A popular holiday resort in a beautiful setting of loch, river, mountains and woods. The Faskally Dam, on the River Tummel just outside the town, has a 'fish pass' where visitors in spring and early summer can watch salmon 'on the run' upstream past the hydro-electric power station. From the 1300-ft height of Craigouer, $1\frac{1}{2}$ miles north-west, once a beacon site, there is a splendid view of Schiehallion (3547 ft). The famous Festival Theatre at Pitlochry presents plays and concerts in summer.

Scone

The coronation place of Scottish kings; the last king to be crowned there was Charles II, in 1651. The Stone of Scone, or Stone of Destiny, was by tradition Jacob's pillow at Bethel. It is said to have been brought to Scone in the 9th century AD by Kenneth MacAlpin, the man who united Scotland after defeating the Picts at Scone. In 1297, Edward I took the Stone to London, where it has since remained beneath the Coronation Chair in Westminster Abbey—except for a brief period after it was removed in 1950. It was recovered in 1951.

Scone Palace, the home of the Earl of Mansfield, is a 19th-century castellated mansion built on the former site of the Abbey of Scone, founded in 1114 by Alexander I and destroyed by followers of John Knox in 1559. The palace houses a collection of china and ivory statuettes; in the park is preserved the old Cross of Scone.

MEDIEVAL CASTLE *Doune is one of Scotland's best-preserved 14th-century castles. It was the home of the 2nd Earl of Moray, hero of the ballad 'The Bonnie Earl of Moray'*

The romantic appeal of the Trossachs

Angling The Tay is one of the most important salmon rivers in Scotland. There are centres at Kenmore and Aberfeldy. There is also good fishing on most other waters.

Nature trails One trail starts at the Cobleland Caravan Site, Aberfoyle. Another, on Ben Lawers, is open from May to Sept.; turn left off A827 5 miles north-east of Killin.

Forest drive A 7-mile drive through Achray Forest starts 2 miles north of Aberfoyle and is open daily, except Tues., Easter to Sept.

Events Lochearnhead Highland Games are held in July.

Places to see *Ben Lawers Visitor Centre* (NTS): Easter to Sept., daily. *Blair Drummond Safari Park*: mid-Mar. to Oct., daily. *Doune Castle*: Apr. to Oct., daily, except Thur. in Apr. and Oct. *Doune Park Gardens* and *Veteran Car Museum*: Apr. to Oct., daily. *Museum of Scottish Tartans*, Comrie: weekdays and Sun. afternoon.

Information centres (summer only): Tourist Information Bureau, Leny Rd., Callander. Tel. Callander 30342. Tourist Information Centre, Main Street, Aberfoyle. Tel. Aberfoyle 352.

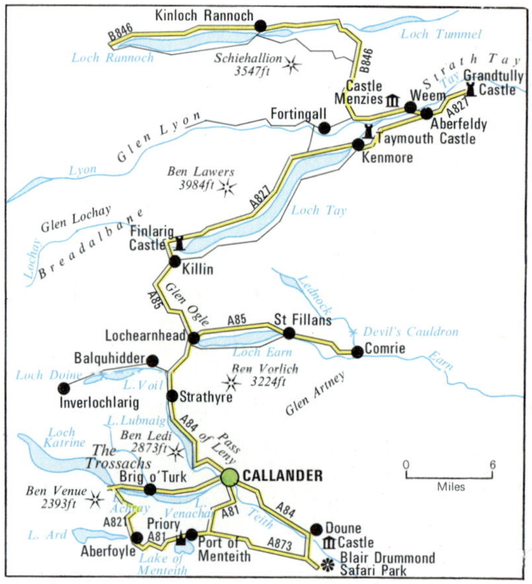

Three lochs—Katrine, Achray and Venachar—joined by small rivers, wind their way across the Central region. Between them and the Lowlands to the south is a stretch of country only 5 miles wide, with birch-covered mountains, dramatic crags, tumbling streams, moorland and glen. These are the Trossachs, an area which has often been called 'the Highlands in miniature'. This romantic appeal was stimulated when Sir Walter Scott's novel *Rob Roy* and his poem 'The Lady of the Lake' started a rush of tourists to the Trossachs early in the 19th century. The real 'Lady' was Ellen Douglas, and her 'Lake' was Loch Katrine. The places described in the poem can still be identified. Robert MacGregor, 'Rob Roy' (1671–1734), played a role in the Trossachs' history. Some regarded him as a Scottish patriot, a kind of Robin Hood who stole from the rich and gave to the poor; others saw him merely as a bandit and cattle rustler. Visitors to the Trossachs can imagine how easy it must have been for him to lie low there after his exploits. He is buried at Balquhidder.

Running from north-east to south-west across the Perth district is the Highland Boundary Fault—a deep fracture in the earth's crust where the rock, formed 300 million years ago, has not yet settled and there are still occasional earth tremors. Above ground, the line is followed by the sharp and dramatic change from the Lowlands to the Highlands. West Perth is walking and climbing country, while for the motorist there are magnificent drives through wooded glens or by the lovely lochs. Water from some of them is now piped to Glasgow or used in hydro-electric schemes, but this invasion of the Highlands has been made as unobtrusive as possible.

IN THE GLEN *The River Lochay, a good fishing river, winds east over the rocky floor of Glen Lochay in the Breadalbane hills west of Loch Tay*

Aberfeldy
A market town and holiday centre with a five-arched stone bridge over the River Tay, built in 1733 by General George Wade, to carry a military road. A monument south of the bridge marks the enrolment of the Black Watch, or Highland Regiment, into the British Army in 1739. The regiment, which had been raised in the area 15 years before, received its name because of its dark tartan uniform.

Grandtully (pronounced Grantly) Castle, 3 miles north-east in the sheltered valley of Strath Tay, was built in the 16th century and is the ancestral home of the Stewarts of Innermeath. The 16th-century St Mary's Church near by is noted for the finely painted heraldry on its wooden ceiling. Castle Menzies (pronounced Mingies), 1 mile north-west of Aberfeldy at Weem, is a gabled and turreted mansion built in 1571 and restored in 1957 as the chief seat of the Clan Menzies. An inn at Weem has a sign commemorating a visit there in 1733 by General Wade, 'Soldier and Engineer'.

Aberfoyle
A village which has grown rapidly since the 'Duke's road' was built by the Duke of Montrose in the 19th century to give easier access northwards towards the Trossachs. It is a good centre for touring, and the walker can explore the Menteith Hills, 1 mile north-west, the shores of the Lake of Menteith, and Loch Ard.

SALMON WATER *Loch Tay, 17 miles long, is one of the finest salmon-fishing waters in Britain. The River Tay flows from the loch's eastern end 70 miles to the North Sea*

Balquhidder
A village at the eastern end of Loch Voil and the burial place of Robert MacGregor, 'Rob Roy', who died in 1734. His wife Mary and two of his sons, Coll and Robert ('Robin Oig'), are buried beside him. Near the grave are the remains of a chapel where the Clan MacGregor met in 1589 and swore over the severed head of their enemy John Drummond, the King's Forester, that they would not give away the murderers, who were members of their clan.

North of Loch Voil are the Braes of Balquhidder, steep-sided valleys which are praised in a popular Scottish ballad by the 18th-century poet Robert Tannahill. A rough road and paths lead through the green braes to Loch Doine. Just beyond the loch, 5 miles west of Balquhidder, is a path to Inverlochlarig, the site of the now-vanished farmhouse where Rob Roy died.

Callander
A resort and tourist centre where the Rivers Teith and Leny meet, and a good starting point for tours of the Trossachs and Loch Katrine. Television has made Callander familiar as the 'Tannochbrae' of *Dr Finlay's Casebook*. From 2873-ft Ben Ledi, which overlooks the town from the north-west, the view on a clear day extends to Ben Lawers, 20 miles north, and to the Forth Bridge, 40 miles south-east.

A road north-west from Callander leads through the Pass of Leny, where the River Leny rushes through a narrow gorge. The road continues up the east bank of Loch Lubnaig to Strathyre, a quiet resort and walking centre.

Another road runs 6 miles west of Callander along the north bank of Loch Venachar to Brig o' Turk, a village of white-walled cottages set among steep, wooded hills. The village has long attracted artists, including John Ruskin and John Everett Millais who visited it in 1853. An early 19th-century bridge over the Finglas (or Turk) Water carries the main road on towards Loch Katrine, which has a pleasure-steamer pier at its eastern end.

Loch Katrine, which inspired Sir Walter Scott's poem 'The Lady of the Lake', is 9 miles long and 1 mile wide, but there is no road round it. A pleasure-steamer trip on the loch, or short walks from the pier to the Pass of Achray, with Ben Venue (2393 ft) rising to the south-west, give some idea of the rugged splendour of the Trossachs. Ellen's Isle, on Loch Katrine, is named after Ellen Douglas, the 'Lady of the Lake' in the poem. From the Middle Ages until the early 18th century, the MacGregors used the island to hide cattle they had stolen in raids on the Lowlands.

Comrie
A resort on the River Earn at the meeting-point of Glen Artney, to the south-west, and Glen Lednock, to the north. It is popular with climbers, and a particularly good walk is by a path up Glen Lednock to the Devil's Cauldron, where the River Lednock rushes down a narrow channel and through a hole in the rock. Comrie is on the Highland Boundary Fault, a 20,000 ft deep earth fracture which divides the Lowlands and the Highlands. Movement along the fault causes occasional earth tremors in Comrie, usually enough only to rattle windows; but a more severe tremor in 1839 cracked the walls of houses.

Fortingall
A village on the River Lyon, with thatched cottages and an ancient yew tree in the churchyard. It is claimed locally that the tree is 3000 years old, which is certainly an exaggeration; but it is recorded that the trunk was 56 ft in circumference in 1772. The trunk later split, and the remaining live stem is carefully tended. Wooded Glen Lyon stretches 30 miles west of Fortingall and is Scotland's longest glen.

GATEWAY TO THE HIGHLANDS *Callander, on one of the historic routes from Stirling to the Highlands, is expanding as a centre for driving and walking around the Trossachs, the Falls of Leny and Lochs Katrine and Venachar*

Kenmore
A resort at the eastern end of Loch Tay, which is popular with salmon fishermen. Taymouth Castle, 1 mile north-east, was built in the 19th century on the site of a 16th-century castle. It was a seat of the Earls of Breadalbane, and is now a college. Roads from Kenmore run west along the north and south banks of the 17 mile long loch. The best mountain views are from the southerly road, looking north across the lake to Ben Lawers (3984 ft), the highest peak in the Perth district. The National Trust for Scotland owns about 8000 acres around the mountain, and the largest number of varieties of Alpine plants in Britain grow on the lower slopes.

IN THE SNOW *Highland beef cattle, such as these in the hills near Loch Tay, are the hardiest and shaggiest British breed*

Killin
An all-year-round holiday resort for fishing on Loch Tay, walking, climbing or motoring in the surrounding mountains in summer, and skiing in the Ben Lawers range in winter. The ruins of Finlarig Castle, a former seat of the Campbells, are half a mile north.

Kinloch Rannoch
A village at the eastern end of the 10 mile long Loch Rannoch. The road encircling the loch gives a good view of Schichallion (3547 ft), 5 miles south-east of Kinloch Rannoch. Queen's View (753 ft), on the north bank of nearby Loch Tummel, was so named because Queen Victoria said she was impressed by the view west towards Schiehallion.

Lochearnhead
The red tropaeolum, or flame nasturtium, growing wild on the hills gives a bright summer background to the village. Lochearnhead is a centre for sailing and water-skiing on Loch Earn, and climbing in the surrounding mountains, or walking to the north up the wooded Glen Ogle towards Killin. A road runs round the loch, giving views southwards to the mountains, dominated by the 3224-ft peak of Ben Vorlich.

Port of Menteith
A small resort on the $1\frac{1}{2}$ mile long Lake of Menteith. Ferries from here visit Inchmahome, one of the three islands on the lake, where there are some well-preserved remains of a 13th-century Augustinian priory which was a retreat of Mary, Queen of Scots.

WILD FLOWERS *On Ben Lawers grow* Myosotis alpestris *(blue),* Silene acaulis *(pink) and* Sedum roseum *(yellow)*

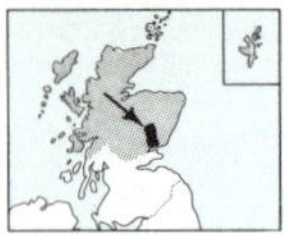

Dundee and the 'Silvery Tay'

Boating There is yachting on the Firth of Tay, with centres at Broughty Ferry and Dundee.

Angling Trout and pike in the lower reaches of the River Isla; its tributary, Dean Water, has large trout. Trout in Monikie and Crombie Reservoirs; Loch Glenogil and Loch Lee; Dean Water at Forfar.

Golf Visitors are welcome on Carnoustie's Championship course and the easier course of Burnside.

Places to see *Affleck Castle*: weekdays, Sun. afternoon. *Angus Folk Museum* (NTS), Glamis: May to Sept., afternoons. *Barrack Street Museum*, Dundee: weekdays. *Broughty Castle Museum*, Broughty Ferry: weekdays, except Fri.; also Sun. afternoon, July to Oct. *Claypotts Castle*: weekdays, Sun. afternoon. *Dundee Central Museum and Art Gallery*: weekdays. *Forfar Museum and Art Gallery*: weekdays. *Glamis Castle*: May to Sept., Sun. to Thur. afternoons. *Golf Museum*, Camperdown House, Dundee: weekdays, except Fri.; also Sun. afternoon, July to Sept. *J. M. Barrie's Birthplace* (NTS), Kirriemuir: May to Sept., weekdays, Sun. afternoon.

Information centre Dundee District Council, Civic Amenities Division, 15 Albert Square. Tel. Dundee 23141.

PICTISH CROSS *Animal carvings decorate this 8th-century Pictish stone in Aberlemno churchyard. A battle scene is on the reverse of the 6 ft slab*

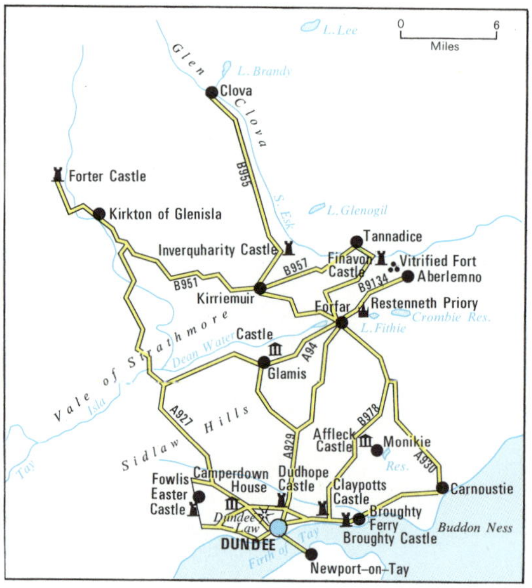

The heartland of Angus is the fertile Vale of Strathmore, dividing the towering eastern Grampians from the gentler Sidlaw Hills which lead down to the Firth of Tay. Steep-sided glens—the 'Braes of Angus'—cut their way through the northern hills, offering picturesque drives and rewarding climbs for the energetic.

The vale is a land of fine farms and a famous championship breed of beef cattle—the black Aberdeen Angus, noticeable for their lack of horns. The vale can be seen at its best from the battlements of Glamis Castle, the ancestral home of the Queen Mother's family and the place where Princess Margaret was born.

The city of Dundee, rich in history, rises augustly beside the Firth of Tay, which is crossed by the graceful 2-mile Tay railway bridge. The original Tay bridge was opened in 1878, but a year later it was blown down by a gale while a train was crossing, and 75 people were killed (the poet William McGonagall put the death roll at 90). The bridge, rebuilt in 1883–7, carries the main-line railway from Aberdeen to Edinburgh. The Tay road bridge linking Dundee with Fife and the south was opened in 1966.

ROAD LINK *Dundee climbs the slopes at the northern end of the 1¼ mile long Tay toll bridge, opened in 1966 to link the city directly with Fife and the south of Scotland. It is Britain's longest road bridge over a river, and cost £6,500,000 to build*

NAVAL VETERAN *The 46-gun frigate HMS* Unicorn, *launched in 1824, served the Royal Navy for 144 years as a frigate and training ship and is now preserved in Dundee Harbour*

Broughty Ferry
A popular holiday resort as well as a residential suburb of Dundee, built around the cottages of an old fishing village. Broughty Castle, a 15th-century tower on a rocky headland, was restored in 1860 and is now a museum featuring the past glories of the whaling industry. The 16th-century Claypotts Castle, once the home of James Graham of Claverhouse, is a well-preserved ruin with crow-stepped gables on its angle towers and a gunport in the kitchen.

Carnoustie
A holiday resort well known for its two golf courses—the Championship course, considered by professionals to be one of the leading courses in the world, and the Burnside. There are fine beaches with good bathing and attractive coastal walks. Southwards to Buddon Ness, a military training area, extend golden sand dunes, the result of the red sandstone of the area having been broken down by the weather and by the sea over thousands of years.

Clova
A hamlet in lonely Glen Clova, one of the loveliest of the Angus glens. The River South Esk tumbles down through rare plants and ferns on the rocky hills. A track leads 1½ miles northwards from Clova to Loch Brandy, set among the mountains at 2098 ft.

Dundee
A seaport on the Firth of Tay, notable for its jute industry. This originated as a by-product of the whaling industry for

RAIL LINK *The railway bridge across the Tay was opened in 1887 to replace the one which collapsed in 1879 as a train was crossing it*

which Dundee seamen were renowned in the 18th century. A Whaling and Fishing Company formed in 1756 supplied much of the oil for the city's lamps. In the early 19th century it was found that raw jute imported from India, when mixed with whale oil, could be woven into coarse fabrics used for various products from bags to carpets. The soil of the area around Dundee is particularly good for fruit growing, and the town also has a thriving jam industry, begun by Mrs Keiller, who started making the famous Dundee marmalade in 1797.

Dundee, made a Royal Burgh in 1190, has been the scene of several battles for Scottish independence. It was seized by the English in the 14th, 16th and 17th centuries. Early buildings that survive include the fine 15th-century Old Steeple of St Mary, all that remains of a great medieval church which was repeatedly sacked, and finally almost destroyed by fire in 1841. Cowgate Port, or Wishart Arch, is the only surviving gate of the old town walls. Dudhope Castle was the 15th-century home of the Scrimgeours; it was later owned by Graham of Claverhouse—the 'Bonnie Dundee' of Scott's ballad.

Dundee University, founded in 1881, was affiliated to St Andrew's University in 1897, but is now independent. The city has many fine schools and colleges, including the well-known Duncan of Jordanstowne College of Art. Camperdown House, a 19th-century mansion, houses a fascinating golf museum with exhibits covering the history of the game during three centuries. The City Museum and Art Gallery contains the oldest-known astrolabe, an instrument used in navigation, which dates from 1555. The Barrack Street Shipping and Industrial Museum illustrates the commercial and maritime life of the city through the centuries.

Dundee Law (571 ft), the highest point in the city, was once a volcano; the city's War Memorial is at the summit. The port of Dundee is still the focal point of the city's industrial life. The old-time whalers have gone, but jute-bearing merchantmen remain. The docks cover more than 35 acres and the shipyards, which built the polar exploration ships, Shackleton's *Terra Nova* and Scott's *Discovery*, are still busy.

Forfar

A town lying in the fertile Vale of Strathmore. Malcolm III is said to have held a Parliament here in 1057, at which he bestowed surnames and titles on Scottish noblemen. His castle was destroyed by Robert the Bruce, but the site is marked by a 17th-century octagonal turret, once the town cross. The town hall was designed by William Playfair (1789–1857); inside is kept the 'Forfar bridle'—an iron collar with a prong, used in medieval days to gag those about to be executed.

The ruined Restenneth Priory, 2 miles north-east, near Loch Fithie, has a tall, square tower, a 15th-century broach spire and some earlier work, mainly dating from the 12th century. Robert the Bruce's son is buried there.

Fowlis Easter

A village with a small church, St Marnock's, dating from 1453. It has medieval painted panels, a fine Sacrament House, and jougs—an iron collar for securing wrongdoers. There is also a bell dated 1508. Fowlis Castle was built in the early 17th century.

Glamis

A picturesque village famous as the site of Glamis Castle, the ancestral home of the Earl of Strathmore, father of the Queen Mother. The 14th-century castle, was rebuilt mainly in the 17th century in French-château style, and is said to be haunted. Shakespeare gave Macbeth the title of 'Thane of Glamis', though Macbeth's castle in the play was at Inverness. In 1715, the Old Pretender, the son of James VII of Scotland (James II of England) lodged at the castle.

The Queen Mother spent her childhood at Glamis, and Princess Margaret was born there in 1930. There are fine furnishings, paintings and armour, and in the beautiful grounds is a sundial with 84 dials. From the battlements of the castle are lovely views of the Vale of Strathmore. The village's restored cottages in Kirk Wynd house the Angus Folk Museum, illustrating domestic and farm life over the past 200 years.

Kirkton of Glenisla

An attractive village on the River Isla, in one of the most remote and peaceful glens of the eastern Grampians. Forter Castle, 4 miles north-west, is the ruined stronghold of the Ogilvie family.

DUNDEE'S OWN 'POET'

William McGonagall (1830–1902) of Dundee, noted for his bad verse, wrote of the Tay Bridge disaster: 'Beautiful railway bridge of the Silvery Tay, Alas I am very sorry to say, That 90 lives have been taken away, On the last Sabbath day of 1879'

Kirriemuir

An attractive small town called 'Thrums' in the novels of J. M. Barrie, who was born at 9 Brechin Road in 1860. The home of the creator of *Peter Pan* is now a Barrie Museum. The town is a good centre for exploring the hills to the north. Logie, a mainly 17th-century mansion with lovely gardens, stands about 1 mile south. Inverquharity Castle, 4 miles north-east, has a tower dating from the 15th century.

Monikie

A village notable for its fine battlemented 15th-century Affleck Castle. There is an exquisite little vaulted chapel and a very fine upper hall. The Panmure Monument, commemorating the first Lord Panmure of Brechin, stands on a hillside south of the town.

Tannadice

A small village on the River South Esk, in the Vale of Strathmore. Finavon Castle, 2 miles south-east, is a ruined 15th-century stronghold of the Crawford family. On the Hill of Finavon, to the south, are the remains of an Iron Age fort, its walls vitrified, or fused by fire, to form a glassy substance.

GLAMIS CASTLE *The 17th-century castle was designed for the Strathmore family in the style of a French château and built from locally quarried stone*

The Mearns coast

Angling Sea trout and brown trout in the North Esk at Edzell; salmon and trout in the South Esk at Brechin and in the Bervie Water at Inverbervie; trout in the Lunan, the Elliot at Arbroath, and also in the Carron at Stonehaven.

Events Angus Agricultural Show in July.

Places to see *Arbroath Abbey and Abbey Museum*: weekdays and Sun. afternoons. *Abroath Museum*, Signal Tower: weekdays. *Brechin Museum*: weekdays. *Dunnottar Castle*: weekdays, except Sat. in winter, and Sun. afternoon. *Glenesk Trust Folk Museum*, 10 miles north-west of Edzell: June to Sept., afternoons daily. *Montrose Museum*: closed 1979. *Muchalls Castle*, 4 miles north of Stonehaven: May to Sept., Tues. and Sun. afternoons. *St Cyrus Nature Reserve*: daily. *St Vigeans Collection*, St Vigeans; sculptured stones: weekdays.

Information centres 212 High Street, Montrose. Tel. Montrose 2000. Summer only—Information Office, 105 High Street, Arbroath. Tel. Arbroath 2609. Information Caravan, The Square, Stonehaven. Tel. Stonehaven 62806.

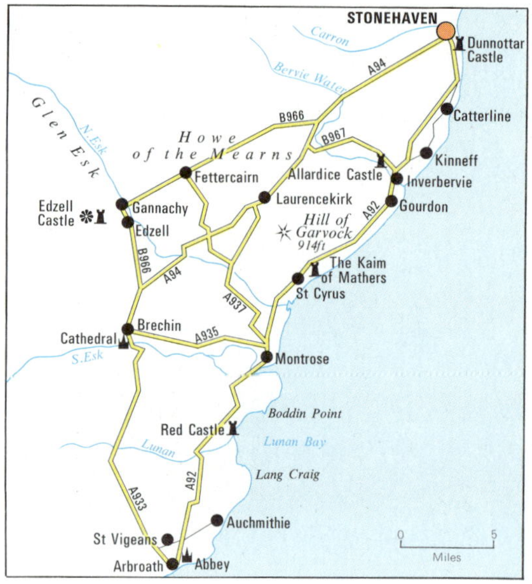

Along the coastline below Stonehaven, sandy beaches alternate with precipitous cliffs and sweeping bays with dunes, salt-flats or pebbles. The coast is punctuated by popular holiday resorts and little fishing villages, yet in many places fertile farmlands extend to the cliff edge.

Inland, and separated from the coast by the Garvock range, is the Howe of the Mearns. A 'howe' is a hollow or sheltered place; the name Mearns derives from two Gaelic words, *magh* and *innis*, meaning 'plain-of-the-islands', which described the Howe when it was desolate moorland dotted by ridges. This area of 50 square miles is now fertile, rolling farmland and woodland. Down Glen Esk, the River North Esk flows between heather slopes and pine and birch woods to enter the Howe of the Mearns at Gannachy. The wooded fells are splendid hiking country.

Fishing and farming are the traditional industries of the Mearns coast; spinning flourished in the 19th century but has now declined. East winds are prevalent, especially in spring and early summer, and bring frequent damp sea mists, known locally as 'haars'. Yet over the year the region has one of the best sunshine records in Scotland.

SCOTTISH DELICACY *The main catch of Arbroath's fishing fleet is haddock. The fish are hung by the tail on frames and smoked over wood-chip fires to make the famous Arbroath 'smokies'*

Arbroath
A resort and fishing port which is the home of the famous 'smokies'—haddock flavoured and browned by smoke from an oak fire. The pleasant smell of the smoking process pervades the streets. Indoor and open-air swimming pools augment the town's safe sea bathing.

Only ruins remain of Arbroath Abbey, where Scotland's Declaration of Independence was signed in 1320. A transcript of the document is in the town library. The abbey's circular window, known as the 'O of Arbroath', used to be lit up as a beacon to guide seamen. King William the Lion, founder of the abbey in 1178, is buried before the high altar, where the Stone of Scone was discovered in 1951 after it had been removed from beneath the Coronation Chair in Westminster Abbey.

To the north, red-sandstone cliffs are pierced by caves which can be visited on foot or by boat. Perched on top, overlooking the stack of Pint Stoup, is the village of Auchmithie, the 'Musselcrag' of Scott's novel *The Antiquary*.

Brechin
The streets of the old town, built mainly of the local red sandstone, rise steeply from the River South Esk. Next to the cathedral is an 87 ft high round tower dating from the 10th or 11th century. There is only one other tower like it on the Scottish mainland—in Abernethy, Tayside. Both towers were built to act as watchtower and place of refuge for the minister and for the safe-keeping of church treasures.

Edzell
A little inland resort, with the ruins of Edzell Castle near by. A 16th-century tower still stands, but the most notable feature is the walled garden, laid out by Lord Edzell in 1604. The town is approached through an arch which was erected in 1887 in memory of the 13th Earl of Dalhousie.

In the square of Fettercairn, 4 miles north-east, is the shaft of the Kincardine Town Cross of 1670, notched to show the width of the 37-in. Scottish measurement known as an 'ell'.

Inverbervie
A town strikingly situated on the south bank of a gorge through which Bervie Water reaches the sea. Beyond the river's mouth is a shingle bar of brilliantly hued pebbles. A memorial set up in 1969 honours Hercules Linton, the designer of the clipper *Cutty Sark*, who was born at 4 Market Square in 1836 and died in the same house 64 years later.

Allardice Castle, a mile up Bervie Water, was built *c.* 1662, and a mile further upstream is Arbuthnott House, another 17th-century building, with magnificent painted ceilings.

Gourdon, a mile south of Inverbervie, is a prosperous little fishing port. Women still bait the handlines, and the fish market attracts many visitors.

Kinneff
The Crown Jewels of Scotland were hidden behind the pulpit of Kinneff's parish church from 1652 to 1660. They had been smuggled out of Dunnottar Castle, after it fell to Cromwell's soldiers following an eight-month siege. Catter-

SMUGGLERS' SHORE *Waves lash the wild coast below the former smuggling village of Auchmithie, the 'Musselcrag' described in Scott's novel* The Antiquary

line, 3 miles north, is an artists' colony set attractively on a half-moon bay. It became the home of the late Joan Eardley, a member of the Glasgow School, who is noted for her townscapes featuring children. One of her paintings hangs in the bar of the Creel Inn—a gift to the people of this clifftop hamlet.

Laurencekirk
A town in the heart of the Howe of the Mearns, developed largely as a result of the patronage of Lord Gardenstone in the mid-18th century. He introduced loom weaving and encouraged the manufacture of snuff boxes. Both these trades have now died out, but the snuff boxes made by Charles Stivens are valuable collectors' items.

Overlooking the town on the highest point of the Hill of Garvock (914 ft) is the Johnstone Tower, erected in the early 19th century by James Farquhar from stones left over from the building of his own mansion.

Lunan Bay
The bay curves for almost 6 miles from Lang Craig, the end of the red-sandstone cliffs north of Arbroath, to Boddin Point. Dunes back the broad sweep of sand. The ruined Red Castle, a 13th-century fortification of King William the Lion, guards the mouth of Lunan Water. The small beach at Boddin Point and north to Montrose is a good area for finding semi-precious stones such as agate, which can be chipped out of the rock. The careful searcher may also find amethyst. Agate, cornelians, Cairngorm quartz, smoky quartz and jasper—the most common of the local stones—can be found among pebbles on the shore. People can keep the stones they find.

Montrose
A church steeple soars 220 ft above the elegant, gable-ended houses of the High Street, from which lead narrow, twisting closes, unchanged for 200 years and with no two alike. The Marquis of Montrose, the Royalist leader, was born in 1612 in a house at Castle Place, Old Montrose, now a government office.

Montrose is a popular sailing centre, as the town has water on three sides. The River South Esk flows through a 2 mile wide tidal basin, like an inland sea, behind the town. There is a fine beach, with a curve of sand 5 miles long. Pink-footed geese from the Arctic winter on the shores.

At ten o'clock each night the curfew bell, 'Big Peter', is rung from the steeple. It gets its name from Peter Ostens, who cast it in Rotterdam 300 years ago. A museum, in Museum Street, has many relics of Montrose's old seafaring days, and a collection of semi-precious stones which have been found locally.

St Cyrus
A National Nature Reserve has been set up in St Cyrus Bay. In its 227 acres flourish more than 300 species of plants, including the hairy violet and viper's bugloss. Insect life is equally rich. Breeding seals and eider ducks visit the bay and fulmars swoop around the cliffs.

Overhanging the sea is the ruined Kaim of Mathers, a stronghold built in 1424 by David Barclay of Mather.

ROYALIST STRONGHOLD *Dunnottar, near Stonehaven, was the last castle in Scotland to hold out against Cromwell's soldiers, surrendering in 1652 after an eight-month siege*

Stonehaven
A fishing port and a developing holiday town. Yachtsmen sail in its bay and there is good fishing in sea and river. The old town by the harbour has been well restored. The 17th-century tolbooth, successively a storehouse, a court and a prison, has been modernised and is a restaurant in summer. A plaque on a house at the southern end of Market Square marks the birthplace of Robert William Thomson (1822–73), inventor of the pneumatic tyre, the fountain pen and the dry dock. A veteran car rally is held in his memory each June.

Dunnottar Castle, $1\frac{1}{2}$ miles south, is a spectacular fortress on a rock by the sea. A path leads to the castle from the mainland. Much of the castle is 14th century and is well preserved; there are breathtaking views from the embrasures. In 1645 the Royalist Marquis of Montrose failed to dislodge the Earl Marischal of Scotland, a fierce Presbyterian Covenanter, from the castle. In the Civil War the castle was held by the Royalists, and the Scottish Crown Jewels were kept here until they were taken to Kinneff in 1652.

Robert Paterson, a wandering stonemason who tended the Covenanters' memorials in Dunnottar churchyard, was the 'Old Mortality'—Paterson's nickname—of Sir Walter Scott's novel.

Land of fairy-tale castles

Angling There are salmon and trout in the River Dee at Aberdeen, Banchory, Aboyne, Ballater and Braemar, in the River Don at Inverurie and Alford, and in the River Ythan at Fyvie.

Events Aberdeen has a two-week Festival in June, during which the Highland Games take place. Games also take place at Aboyne in the first week of Sept. and at Ballater in Aug. Braemar has the Royal Highland Gathering, a festival which is held on the first Sat. in Sept.

Places to see *Aberdeen Art Gallery*: weekdays and Sun. afternoons. *Balmoral Castle*, grounds only: May to July, weekdays; not open when Royal Family in residence. *Braemar Castle*: Easter to early Oct., daily. *Castle Fraser* (NTS): May to Sept., weekdays and Sun. afternoon. *Craigievar Castle* (NTS): May to Sept., afternoons except Fri. *Crathes Castle* (NTS): May to Sept., weekdays and Sun. afternoon. *Drum Castle* (NTS): May to Sept., weekdays, Sun. afternoon. *Haddo House* (NTS), near Methlick: June to Sept., weekdays, Sun. afternoon. *Kildrummy Castle*: gardens; weekdays, Sun. afternoon. *Leith Hall* (NTS): May to Sept., weekdays and Sun. afternoon. *Pitmedden Gardens* (NTS), Udny, 14 miles north of Aberdeen, gardens only: daily. *Provost Skene's House*, Aberdeen: weekdays.

Information centre Publicity Dept., St Nicholas House, Aberdeen. Tel. Aberdeen 23456.

Mountains and plains meet in Grampian's Aberdeen district. The flat-topped heights of the mountains, with snow-filled gullies and magnificent pinewood forests, fall eastwards to lush farmlands, where Aberdeen Angus cattle graze. Beyond the farmlands are sandy beaches and thriving fishing ports.

Two salmon rivers, the Don and Dee, converge from north-west and south-west upon Aberdeen. The city is built upon granite and out of granite, quarried from the 450 ft deep Rubislaw Pit, near Hazlehead Park in Aberdeen. Aberdeen's recorded history dates from the 12th century, and Robert the Bruce, in the early 14th century, was the city's greatest benefactor. Throughout the county are richly wooded valleys, lonely lochs and mountain roads, moors covered with purple and white heather and, above all, a magnificent series of castles. The area has more than 150 castle sites—most of them concentrated round the fertile valleys of the Don and Dee. Some are nothing but ruins, recalling turbulent centuries of Scottish history; others survive as massive stone forts still capable of withstanding a siege; others are fairy-tale structures, composed of castellated towers and conically roofed turrets. The best known of these is Balmoral, a private residence of the Queen, in a forest setting.

HIGHLAND VALLEY *Clunie Water cuts a broad valley through the Grampian Mountains on its way to join the Dee at Braemar*

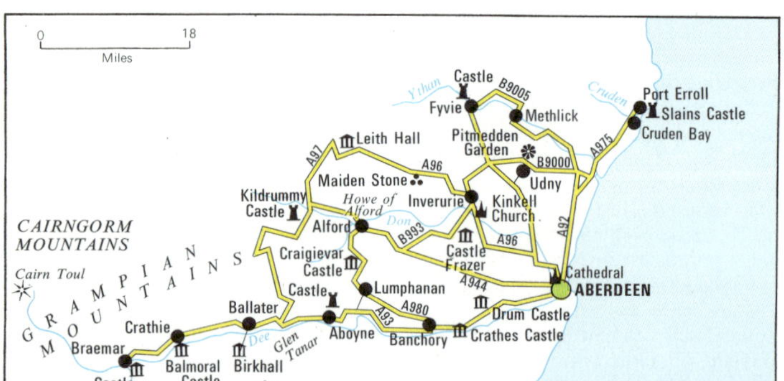

Aberdeen

Scotland's third-largest city derives its motto of 'Bon Accord' from the rallying cry of the Bruces: Robert the Bruce campaigned here against the Comyns, rival contenders for the throne of Scotland in the late 13th century. The city is built almost entirely of granite, which stands out clean and solid in the clear coastal light. Union Street, the broad central thoroughfare, is a fine example of the use of this local stone.

The Church of St Nicholas, just off Union Street, is divided by a 12th to 13th-century transept into the East and West Churches. Drum's Aisle, part of the transept, contains a fine medieval brass. Other treasures include a 17th-century portrait of Duncan Lidel, a mathematician and physician, in his laboratory, and a stone effigy of Sir Alexander Irvine, Captain Governor of Aberdeen from 1439 to 1442, and his wife. A 48-bell carillon is rung daily in summer. St Machar's Cathedral, in old Aberdeen, is a partly castellated 14th-century granite building. It has a 16th-century oak ceiling with heraldic motifs, and modern stained glass. The 17th-century Provost Skene's House in Guestrow houses a fine museum.

The 16th-century Provost Ross's House in Shiprow is one of the city's oldest houses. Aberdeen Art Gallery in Schoolhill has good representative English and French paintings, some Epstein bronzes and a Henry Moore sculpture. Aberdeen's municipal buildings incorporate the tower and spire of the Old Tolbooth, which was the scene of public executions until 1857. The Old Tolbooth still preserves the 'Aberdeen Maiden', said to have been the model for the French guillotine. In front of Aberdeen Grammar School is a statue of Lord Byron, a pupil there from 1794 to 1798. A statue of the 5th Duke of Gordon, Sir Walter Scott's 'Cock o' the North', stands in Golden Square.

Aberdeen University combines two medieval colleges—King's (1494) in High Street, Old Aberdeen, and Marischal (1593) in Broad Street. King's College still has its original crown tower and chapel. Marischal, rebuilt in 1844, has a soaring Perpendicular façade and is one of the finest granite buildings in the world.

Hazlehead Park, the city's largest park, has ornamental gardens, a nature trail and a maze. Inside Seaton Park are a Norman motte and a 17th-century fortified tower house.

Fishing plays a major part in modern Aberdeen's prosperity, and at the lively fish market the public can watch the fish being auctioned at 7.30 a.m.

Aboyne
Aboyne Castle, a Gordon stronghold just north of the village, has a history dating back to the 13th century, but the oldest surviving part is the west wing, rebuilt in 1671 and consisting of two towers and a keep.

South-west of the village is the long wooded valley of Glen Tanar, from which two good walking routes lead over the hills to Glen Mark. At Lumphanan, 5½ miles north-east, is Macbeth's Cairn, said to mark the site of Macbeth's last stand in 1057 before he was killed by Malcolm.

Alford
A market town on the Don, attractively situated in the centre of the fertile Howe of Alford. The Royalist Marquis of Montrose defeated General Baillie and the Covenanters in a Civil War battle here in 1645.

Craigievar Castle, 4 miles south on high ground above Leochel Burn, is a small, high-turreted, fairy-tale castle, practically unchanged since it was completed in 1626. Inside is a magnificent Renaissance ceiling, and an inscription over a bed reading 'Doe not vaiken sleiping dogs', the motto of the Forbes family, who built the castle.

The early-14th-century Kildrummy Castle, 7 miles west, was besieged in 1404 by the son of the Wolf of Badenoch and dismantled after the 1715 Jacobite Rising. The ruins, now extensively repaired, include two rounded towers and a chapel. There is an attractive Alpine garden laid out by Japanese designers in 1904.

Ballater
A busy holiday resort on Royal Deeside, surrounded by beautiful wooded hills, with the 3786-ft Lochnagar rising majestically to the south-west. Birkhall, a mile south, is an early-18th-century house, bought by Edward VII when he was Prince of Wales and now used by the Queen Mother.

Banchory
An attractive Deeside holiday village in beautiful wooded countryside. Lavender is grown here, and the factory where it is distilled into Dee Lavender Water can be visited. On the Brig o' Feugh, a narrow 18th-century bridge over a rugged gorge east of the village, an observation platform has been built from which, in spring, visitors can watch salmon leaping up the rapids.

Braemar
A Deeside resort village 1100 ft up in the Highlands, world-famous for its annual Royal Highland Gathering, held in September and usually attended by the Queen. The village is set among heather-carpeted hills, dominated to the west by the massive Cairn Toul (4241 ft). In 1715, the 6th Earl of Mar raised the Jacobite standard on a mound where the Invercauld Arms now stands. Braemar Castle, on a bluff overlooking the Dee, was built by the 2nd Earl of Mar in 1628; it was attacked and burnt in 1689 by Jacobites, and repaired in 1748. It has a round tower, a barrel-vaulted ceiling, and a massive iron gateway.

Balmoral Castle, 6 miles north-east, on a bend in the River Dee, was known in the 15th century as Bouchmorale, Gaelic for 'majestic dwelling'. Queen Victoria and Prince Albert bought it in 1853 and rebuilt it as a castle mansion in Scottish baronial style. It has been a royal residence ever since.

Crathie Church, just to the east, built of granite in 1895 and standing on a knoll, is where the Royal Family worship when in residence at Balmoral.

Cruden Bay
A resort with good beaches and a championship golf course. Bishop's Bridge, across the Cruden Water, is dated 1697. To the east stand the ruins of Slains Castle, built in 1664 by the Earl of Errol, Great Constable of Scotland. South-west of the castle is the fishing village of Port Errol. Bullers of Buchan, 2 miles north, is an immense rock amphitheatre carved out by the sea.

Fyvie
A pleasant resort village on the River Ythan, notable for the impressive fortified 15th-century Fyvie Castle, standing in wooded parkland. The four turret towers were named after their builders: Gordon, Meldrum, Preston and Seton. The Royalist Duke of Montrose was pursued here in 1644 by the Earl of Argyll, a Covenanter he later routed. Fyvie Castle is not open to the public.

Inverurie
A pleasant town on the Don, near which is the Bass, a 50 ft high mound, probably the site of an ancient stronghold. In the churchyard of the ruined Kinkell Church, 2 miles south, is the Brandsbutt Stone, which bears Pictish symbols and a Gaelic inscription. The Maiden Stone, 4½ miles north-west of Inverurie, is an early Christian monument. On it are carved a Celtic cross and Pictish symbols.

STATELY HOMES OF THE HIGHLANDS

Craigievar Castle (far left) is an extravaganza of turrets, gables and conical roofs. It has been continuously inhabited, without alterations, since it was built in 1626. Leith Hall (above) has been the home of the Leith family since 1650. Pitmedden Garden near Udny (left), is also 17th century

CUMBERLAND'S LODGING

Provost Skene's House, the home of a 17th-century provost, or mayor, of Aberdeen, has been restored as a museum. The Duke of Cumberland stayed there in 1746 before marching to Culloden where he defeated Bonnie Prince Charlie. A carved doorway of the house (right) was decorated in the 1670's. The provost's arms surmount a motif of grapes and vines, while roses and thistles garland the door

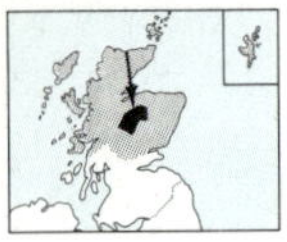

Lofty crags of the Cairngorms

Angling There are salmon and trout in the River Spey at Aviemore, Boat of Garten and Newtonmore.

Boating Sailing and canoeing on Loch Morlich and Loch Insh. There is a school on each loch.

Winter sports There are ski-schools at Aviemore Centre, Coylumbridge, Carrbridge, Newtonmore, Nethy Bridge and Kingussie.

Nature trails Trails are open all year round at Craigellachie, Aviemore (1 mile); round Loch an Eilein (2½ miles); Glenmore Forest (1¼–3 miles).

Events Kingussie and Newtonmore share the Clan Macpherson Gathering at the beginning of Aug.

Places to see *Clan Macpherson House and Museum*, Newtonmore: Easter to Sept., weekdays. *Highland Folk Museum*, Kingussie: weekdays, Sun. afternoons, Apr. to Oct. *Highland Wild Life Park*, Kincraig: daily, Mar. to Nov. *Landmark Exhibition* (Man and the Highlands), Carrbridge: daily.

Information centres Spey Valley Tourist Organisation, Main Road, Aviemore. Tel. Aviemore 810363. June–Sept. only, Information Centre, Perth Road, Newtonmore. Tel. Newtonmore 253.

HIGHLAND BIRDS

Ospreys nested and reared their young at Loch Garten in 1958 for the first time for 48 years

The golden eagle lives in eyries 1500–2000 ft up in the lonely Scottish Highlands

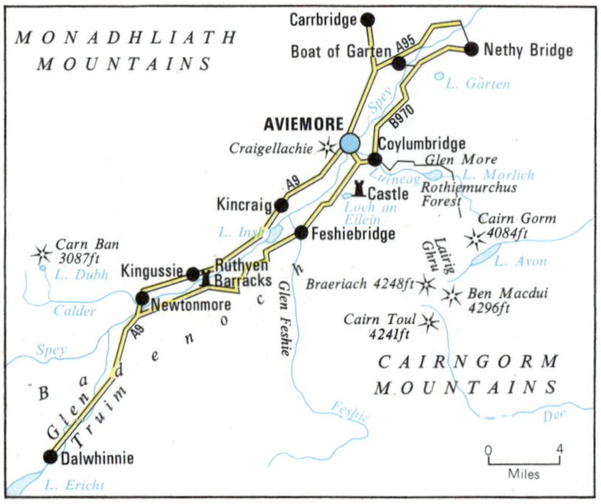

Between the valleys of the Rivers Spey and Dee the granite domes of the Cairngorms thrust upwards, across the southern Highland region and on into northern Grampian. Nine peaks in this magnificent wilderness are over 4000 ft and at least a dozen more top 3000 ft.

Glen More Forest Park, opened in 1948, begins at 1100 ft, 4 miles east of Aviemore, in the foothills of the Cairngorms. Thousands of pounds have been spent on cutting a good approach road into the mountains, and it is possible to ascend 3600 ft by road and chairlift, leaving a clamber of just over 400 ft to the 4084-ft summit of Cairn Gorm. The 12,500 acres of forest park, and the whole Cairngorm expanse, offer unparalleled mountain walks and the best skiing to be found anywhere in Britain.

There is fine walking, too, south-west along the Spey Valley through the district of Badenoch, the 'drowned land', which stretches from Loch an Eilein, near Aviemore, south-west to the outskirts of Dalwhinnie. Historically, Badenoch is Macpherson and Grant country. There are also many associations with Bonnie Prince Charlie and his cause, but the man whose exploits have left a shadow on the Valley's history is the Wolf of Badenoch. This notorious son of the Scottish King Robert II maintained a reign of terror in the late 14th century from fortresses at Ruthven and Loch an Eilein.

FOR EXPERTS ONLY *A tense moment for climbers on a buttress at*

Aviemore
A once unremarkable Speyside village, transformed in the 1960's by the building of a multi-million-pound all-the-year-round holiday complex. The Aviemore Centre is a massive concrete plaza with shops, restaurants, hotels, a theatre and concert hall, ice-rinks for skating and curling, a swimming-pool, a dry ski-slope, a go-kart track, bars and other recreational facilities. It lies at the heart of Britain's main winter-sports area, and there are many ski schools which also hire out all necessary equipment. The centre's bold modern architecture, which makes use of local granite and wood, harmonises with its setting at the foot of the historic rock of Craigellachie. This rock was the rallying place for the Clan Grant, whose war cry is 'Stand fast—Craigellachie'.

Boat of Garten
A village on the Spey, named after the ferry boat which was used before a bridge was built. On Loch Garten, 2 miles east of the village, the Royal Society for the Protection of Birds maintains an observation point from which visitors can watch the rare ospreys—large fish hawks—in their nesting area. The last ospreys in Britain had been killed off by 1910, but in 1958 a pair returned to Loch Garten, found the pike there plentiful, and stayed to nest. Since then they have returned every spring. They lay their eggs in late April or early May. The young hatch after five weeks and start to fly seven or eight weeks later, migrating to Africa in October. In 1970 the Loch Garten pair reared three young on the loch.

Coire an Lochain, in the Cairngorm range

The Cairngorms

These mountains take their name from Cairn Gorm (4084 ft) whose gently rounded shape makes it the least-dramatic mountain of the range. It is not even the highest; Ben Macdui (4296 ft), Braeriach (4248 ft) and Cairn Toul (4241 ft) are all higher. But Cairn Gorm has the most accessible summit. The road from Aviemore ends at a car park, from which chairlifts lead to a short distance from the top. At these heights, the weather can become sub-arctic in a matter of minutes. Even in summer, mist can settle in, or gales can spring up, or it can snow. So warm clothes, food, a map and compass should always be carried by anyone planning to walk in the mountains.

Ben Macdui, Braeriach and Cairn Toul are, like Cairn Gorm, easily scaled by the energetic. Their summits offer good views of Loch Avon, to the north-east, and glimpses of Caithness and the distant Atlantic. The climbing routes pass gigantic boulders, drifts of snow and spectacular waterfalls.

The main walking route through the Cairngorms is along the pass of Lairig Ghru, which links the Spey and Dee valleys. The route, 20 miles long, takes about nine hours in fine weather. It will test the most experienced walker, but it presents some of Europe's loneliest and most striking scenery as a reward.

More than 100 square miles of this rugged country make up the Cairngorms National Nature Reserve, the largest in Britain. In it grow Scots pines, junipers and birch trees, while alpine and Arctic plants, such as moss campion and creeping rhododendron, struggle to exist on the exposed open ground. Golden eagles, capercaillies, ptarmigan, deer and wild-cats all live here. Access to most of the area is unrestricted, though local lairds impose some restrictions on walkers and climbers in the grouse-shooting and deer-stalking seasons.

Coylumbridge

A tempting stopping-place on the way from Aviemore to the Cairngorm chair-lifts, with a hotel and sports complex of its own. On an island in Loch an Eilein, 2 miles south, are the ruins of a fortress of the Wolf of Badenoch.

Dalwhinnie

A village at the head of Glen Truim, and at the western end of the ancient Forest of Atholl, the threshold of the Cairngorms. The village name is a corruption of the Gaelic 'dell of the meeting'. On this desolate ground, highland chiefs and lowland barons met, parleyed, and often fought to the death. To the south-west stretches the lonely, hill-encircled Loch Ericht.

Feshiebridge

The village takes its name from the River Feshie, a tributary of the Spey, which runs down from the Cairngorms through the deep, wooded Glen Feshie.

CAIRNGORM STONES

Peat-coloured crystals found in the Cairngorms are used in jewellery

LONE TREE *A pine by Loch Morlich is a survivor of the once-vast Rothiemurchus Forest*

Insh Church, 1 mile west on the shores of Loch Insh, stands on a site used continuously for Christian worship since the 6th century. The present church dates from the 18th century. In it is preserved an 8th-century bronze Celtic hand-bell, which was once used to call people to worship at the site.

Kingussie

The so-called 'capital of Badenoch' has a number of hotels and a youth hostel. Its Highland Folk Museum, originally maintained by four Scottish universities, has a remarkable collection of items illustrating over two centuries of Highland customs. The district of Badenoch is known as 'the drowned land' because the Spey, even with its banks heightened and strengthened, can flood across the valley when the snows of a severe winter melt and send water cascading down from the mountains. But normally the slightest hint of sun makes the green of pine tree and meadow stand out against the tawny river bank and sandy scree, while the swift water bubbles blue over sparkling granite.

Loch Morlich

One of Scotland's most beautiful inland lochs, lying at an altitude of 1046 ft in the Glen More Forest Park. Around the loch, in what remains of the great Rothiemurchus Forest, reindeer roam free among the Scots pines and silver birches. At Glenmore Lodge, near the loch, the Scottish Sports Council runs courses for young people and youth leaders in climbing, sailing, canoeing, fly fishing and skiing. From Loch Morlich the River Luineag rushes through banks of majestic tall pines to the Spey Valley.

Newtonmore

A centre from which visitors, using highland ponies, can ride into the desolate Monadhliath Mountains. A track from the village climbs through wild and barren scenery, past the Calder River, to Loch Dubh and the massive Carn Ban (3087 ft), where eagles fly. A Clan Macpherson Museum includes the broken fiddle of the freebooting James Macpherson—a Scottish Robin Hood. Sentenced to death in 1701, he is said to have played the dirge 'Macpherson's Rant' on his fiddle as he stood on the gallows at Banff. He then offered the instrument to anyone who would think well of him. There were no takers, so he smashed it.

Ruthven Barracks

These barracks, now in ruins, were built in 1718 on the site of a castle of the Wolf of Badenoch. The barracks were captured by the Highlanders in the '45 uprising, and there they gathered after the rout of Culloden in April 1746. The last scene of the Rising took place there as the assembled chiefs waited for Bonnie Prince Charlie to raise his standard again. But the defeated prince sent them a message of farewell instead. The Highlanders then burnt the barracks, to prevent them falling into Government hands, while the prince became a fugitive.

GLEN MORE *Reindeer brought from Lapland in 1952 roam on the mountain slopes*

Skiing in Scotland

Britain's sporting year has been lengthened since skiing came into its own as a major sport in Scotland. The principal Scottish Highland skiing centres have built chairlifts and ski-tows which rival the amenities at traditional continental resorts. New hotels provide comfortable accommodation as well as après-ski entertainments.

Three main areas—the Cairngorm range above the Spey Valley, Glenshee and Glencoe—provide a perfect playground for downhill enthusiasts who want tows and chairlifts, so that they can get in as many runs as possible and cut out any arduous climbing. Other places offer good sport, but fewer concessions to comfort. The slopes of Beinn a' Bhuird above Mar Lodge can be reached from Braemar on Deeside. Strathpeffer and Dingwall are bases for Ben Wyvis in Easter Ross. A good access road ascends 2000 ft on the Green Lowther in Lanark, and there is easy road access also to Ben Lawers in Perth. A car is necessary for those who do not belong to ski clubs and are not entitled to use club transport, as runs are often a long way from hotels. Though the roads to the slopes are regularly snow-ploughed, it is a wise precaution to fit special tyres or chains.

At its best, Scottish skiing compares well with skiing on the Continent, though bitter winds and sudden 'white outs' caused by mist and blizzards can make it unpredictable. The season usually lasts from early December to the end of May—and, in some years, even later. During the first three months, high winds, short hours of daylight and sometimes bitterly cold weather contrast harshly with clear blue Alpine skies; but from March onwards the days lengthen and spring sunshine brightens the slopes. Reports of conditions at main resorts can be had from the Glasgow Weather Centre (Tel. 041-246 8091) or the Dial-a-Ski service (Tel. 031-246 8041). Further information may be obtained from the Scottish Tourist Board, 23 Ravelston Terrace, Edinburgh (Tel. 031-332 2433) or the Scottish Sports Council, 1 Colman Street, Edinburgh (Tel. 031-225 8411).

SCOTLAND'S MAIN SKIING CENTRES

In the Cairngorms, snow usually lies until late May or even June

Glenshee ski slopes are at their best in January and February

Glencoe has good nursery slopes and fast runs for experienced skiers

CAIRNGORMS (highest point 4296 ft)

Season and facilities Snow lies from November to late May and sometimes June. February and March are usually the best months for powder snow. The Cairngorms are most popular at Christmas and the New Year, though the weather is less severe at Easter. Local buses link centres with slopes, and ski clubs run services for members. Car parks 2000 ft up give access to chairlifts and tows capable of lifting over 5000 skiers an hour up to 3656 ft. There are easy, intermediate and difficult runs on Coire na Ciste, Coire Cas and White Lady, and good nursery slopes. Local cafés and restaurants include the Ptarmigan, which at 3656 ft is the highest restaurant in Britain, and has panoramic views over the surrounding countryside. Summer skiing is possible around the summit of Cairn Gorm itself, which is the starting point for high-level touring

Where to stay The £4,000,000 Aviemore Centre, 8 miles from the slopes, is a resort in itself. There are other Spey Valley resorts up to 20 miles from the slopes. Altogether, the area has more than 4000 beds, from hostels to luxury hotels. There are ski schools and ski shops, and equipment can be hired at most of the hotels, which also provide après-ski entertainments

How to get there The A9 trunk road from Perth to Inverness, and the main London to Inverness railway line, run through the valley. Coaches go direct from London, and there are trains from Edinburgh and Glasgow. Motorail services run from London to Perth or Aberdeen and from Stirling to Inverness. BEA fly to Inverness, leaving a further 30 miles to be covered by rail or road

GLENSHEE (highest point 3059 ft)

Season and facilities Runs are only about 2000–3000 ft high, and the season normally lasts from December until early in April. The low altitude is an advantage in January and February, when weather conditions in the loftier Cairngorms can make skiing difficult. The chairlift up the 3059-ft Cairnwell mountain starts from the west side of the A93 and serves the most testing of the Glenshee runs—the steep Tiger run—and an easy traverse to Cairnwell Burn, where a second lift leads to a pleasant ski run back to the main road. Good skiers can complete up to 30,000 ft of downhill running in a day. On the east side of the road, a draglift is useful for beginners. Experts can use it to get within walking or skiing distance of the Meall Odhar tow, which goes up to 3019 ft. There is a large area for beginners on the floor of the valley, beside the car parks and café

Where to stay Spittal of Glenshee is 6 miles south of runs. Blairgowrie, 23 miles away, is the closest centre of any size. Both places have ski schools and sports shops. Beds are available at hotels and farmhouses throughout the area, or at the Braemar Youth Hostel. Glenshee is popular for school parties from Scotland and over the Border, and for weekend visitors from Scottish cities

How to get there Slopes are on either side of the A93 from Perth to Braemar, 7 miles beyond the Devil's Elbow at the summit of the highest main road in Britain. Trains stop at Coupar Angus, Dunkeld and Perth. Hotels collect their guests from stations, as there are no local buses and arrange transport to the slopes. Motorail terminals are at Aberdeen, Perth, Stirling and Edinburgh

GLENCOE (highest point 3766 ft)

Season and facilities The snow is reliable from mid-December to late April, and there is exciting skiing on Meall a' Bhuiridh amid splendid scenery. When snow lies on the valley floor, beginners can find training areas there. A chairlift from the car park and café rises to a 2000-ft plateau. A 20-minute walk across the plateau leads to three tows—one for beginners on the nursery slopes, one climbing 400 ft to the Scottish Ski-Club hut, and the third going from the hut to the 3636-ft summit of Meall a' Bhuiridh. Hot snacks are provided at the hut. Chairlifts and tows run daily during holidays or at weekends; at other times they are hired out to charter parties only. A ski-school hires out equipment and gives instruction at the bottom of the chairlift. Experts who make full use of the tows can complete 20,000 ft of downhill skiing in a day

Where to stay Accommodation in the Glen is limited, apart from camping or beds in cottages or guest houses in Glencoe village (11 miles from slopes). Within a few minutes' drive of the chairlift is the Kingshouse Hotel, with après-ski entertainments, ski-hire facilities and instruction. Other hotels are at Bridge of Orchy (10 miles), Ballachulish (15 miles) or Tyndrum (19 miles)

How to get there Train services run to Bridge of Orchy, and hotels in the area arrange to pick up their guests from the station. A daily bus service covers the 81-mile route from Glasgow, and motorists out for a day's or weekend's skiing can drive to the terminal of the chairlift, where there is a car park, by turning up the half-mile access road from the A82 at Kingshouse Junction

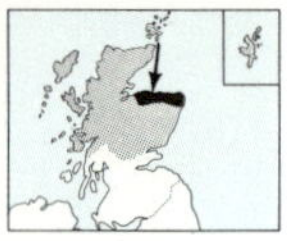

Speyside, 'Garden of the North'

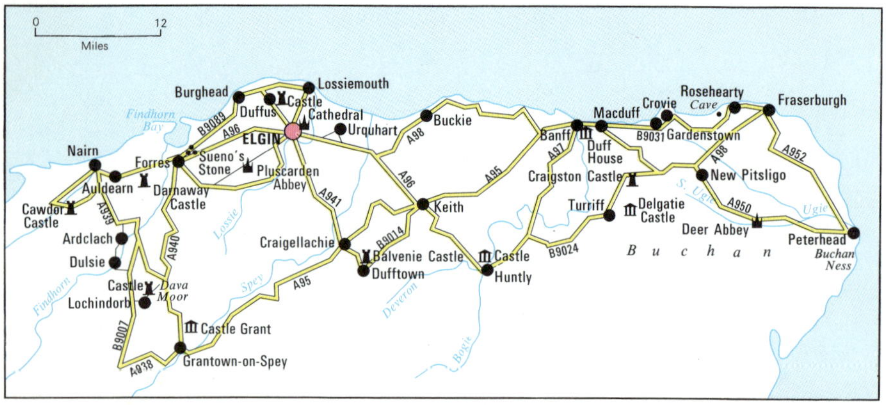

ALONG THE SPEY *The River Spey winds through woods 6 miles downstream from Grantown-on-Spey. The river is famous for its salmon fishing, for which Grantown-on-Spey is the centre*

Places to see *Balvenie Castle*: weekdays and Sun. afternoon. *Brodie Castle* (NTS), 6 miles east of Nairn: closed 1979. *Cawdor Castle*: daily, May to Sept. *Deer Abbey*: Apr. to Sept., weekdays, Sun. afternoon. *Elgin Museum*: mid-Mar. to mid-Oct., weekdays, but open Tues. in July and Aug. only; mid-Oct. to mid-Mar., Wed. and Sat. *Falconer Museum*, Forres: daily in summer. *Huntly Castle*: weekdays, Sun. afternoon. *Pluscarden Abbey*: by appointment. *William Grant Distilleries*, Dufftown: weekdays.

Information centres Summer only: High Street, Forres. Tel. Forres 2938. Saltoun Square, Fraserburgh. Tel. Fraserburgh 2315.

The Moray coast is sometimes called the Scottish Riviera. It is a pardonable exaggeration, for there are many beaches of firm sand, and the climate, if not sizzling, is dry and mild. The scenery is inviting: red-sandstone cliffs swooping on to beaches divided by rocky headlands. Macduff, Buckie, Peterhead, Lossiemouth and Fraserburgh are important fishing centres; Gardenstown and Crovie are attractive fishing villages in impressive cliff settings. Royal castles used to stand at Forres and Nairn.

Inland, the crops are good and the cattle feed well on green pastures. This district was known as the 'Garden of the North' long before tourist phraseology was invented. It attracted tourists of a special sort—Highland raiders who helped themselves to the farm produce and fat cattle. Today the district is famous for prime Scotch beef.

The coastal plain rises towards the foothills of the Cairngorms, taking in the 'malt country' where the water of the River Spey contributes to the quality of Scotch whisky. Apart from serving distilleries, the Spey is the third most important salmon river in Scotland after the Tay and the Tweed. It also yields sea trout and brown trout and is easily fished; the pools are well defined and readily accessible.

The north-east corner of this coastline, known as Buchan, comes to a climax at Buchan Ness, the easternmost point of Scotland. The people of Buchan speak a dialect called Buchan Doric, Old English in origin with French and Scandinavian additions.

CRAIGELLACHIE BRIDGE *The single-arched iron bridge over the Spey was designed by the Scottish engineer Thomas Telford, who built 1200 bridges in his native land*

Banff
A seaport and resort at the mouth of the River Deveron. Duff House, built by William Adam *c.* 1735, is the town's showpiece. The Biggar Fountain stands on the site of the former gallows where in 1701 James Macpherson, a Highland freebooter, played the fiddle as he was led to his execution.

Elgin
A market town and the tourist centre of Moray. The town is best known for its ruined 13th-century cathedral, which is one of the finest ecclesiastical buildings in Scotland. The cathedral and part of the town were burnt in 1390 by the notorious Wolf of Badenoch, the outlawed son of Robert II, Scotland's first Stuart king. Much of the original building still remains, including the fine choir.

In 1746, before Culloden, Bonnie Prince Charlie stayed at Thunderton House, built in 1650 and now a hotel. Pluscarden Priory, 6 miles south-west of Elgin, was founded in 1236 but also suffered at Wolf of Badenoch's hands in 1390. A small community of Benedictine monks began to rebuild it in 1948, and it was made an abbey in 1974.

Forres
A place mentioned in Shakespeare's *Macbeth* as the site of King Duncan's court. The town's museum contains a famous collection of fossils found in the local old red sandstone, and the witches' stone marks the place where three witches accused of causing the death of King Duffus were burnt in AD 965. From the Nelson Tower, erected in 1806 on top of the densely wooded Cluny Hill, there is a magnificent view of Findhorn Bay, 2 miles north. The Sueno's Stone, 1 mile east, is 20 ft high and made of sandstone. It bears remarkable carvings, but its origin is unknown. One theory is that it commemorates a battle won by the King of Denmark's son, Sueno, over Malcolm II in 1008. Just over 3 miles to the south-

PEARL FISHING ON THE SPEY

In summer the lower Spey is the centre of a pearl-fishing industry. The fishermen (left) scoop up mussels from the river bed, and 1 in 100 contains a pearl (above)

west of Forres is Darnaway Castle, the ancestral home of the Morays. The present castle dates from 1810, but it incorporates a hall where Mary, Queen of Scots stayed in 1564.

Fraserburgh
A holiday resort, fishing town and port dating back to the 16th century when it was founded under the name of Farthlie. It has a mercat cross dating from 1736. The quaintly named Wine Tower, probably 15th century, is Fraserburgh's oldest building. It stands above Scalch's Hole, a 100 ft long cave.

Rosehearty, 5 miles west, is a pretty fishing village. The cave of Cowshaven, west of the village, was the hiding place of the last Lord Pitsligo after he was outlawed for his part in the Jacobite Rising of 1745. Pitsligo Church, 8 miles south-west of Rosehearty, is noted for its richly carved gallery.

Grantown-on-Spey
A tourist resort popular with both anglers and skiers. Built predominantly in granite, it was founded in 1776 and was planned by Sir James Grant, a local landowner, as a centre for the Highland linen industry. Castle Grant, 2 miles north, is a fine mansion built between the 16th and 18th centuries.

Lochindorb, 7 miles north-west at the centre of the wild and lonely Dava Moor, has an island castle, now in ruins, which was one of the strongholds of the Wolf of Badenoch, who terrorised the Lowlands of Moray in the 14th century.

Huntly
An attractive market town at the point where the River Bogie joins the River Deveron, providing excellent fishing. Huntly Castle, the home of the once-powerful Gordons, is reached through a beautiful wooded park and it overlooks a gorge in the Deveron. On its upper storey the castle still has some of the original elaborate heraldic ornamentation, dating from the early 17th century.

Keith
The Auld Brig o' Keith, one of the two bridges that joins Keith to Fife Keith, dates from 1609. The newer bridge was built in 1770. The ruined Milton Tower was once the home of the Oliphant family. The Milton distillery, founded in 1785 and now called Strath Isla, is Scotland's oldest working malt-whisky distillery.

Dufftown, 10 miles south-west, is famous for its distilleries. The town was laid out by James Duff, 4th Earl of Fife, in 1817. Balvenie Castle, a mile north, is one of the largest and best preserved castles in north Scotland. It dates from the 14th century and its most notable feature is the two-leaved iron yett, or grille gate. The castle was owned first by the Comyns, then by the Douglases and finally by the Atholl family. It was visited by Edward I in 1304 and by Mary, Queen of Scots in 1562, and it was occupied by the English in 1746 during the Jacobite Rising.

Lossiemouth
A bustling and invigorating resort, where Ramsay MacDonald, Britain's first Labour Prime Minister, was born at 1 Gregory Place in 1866.

Duffus, $4\frac{1}{2}$ miles west, is the nearest village to Gordonstoun School, where both the Duke of Edinburgh and the Prince of Wales were pupils. Duffus Church, though ruined, has a fine 16th-century vaulted porch.

Burghead, $3\frac{1}{2}$ miles further west, is a fishing village. The Burghead Well, cut into the rock, was probably used as an early Christian baptistry. On Old Yule Night, January 11, the locals keep up the old custom of Burning the Clavie. A blazing *clavie*, Gaelic for basket, filled with tar is carried round the town to ward off evil spirits.

Nairn
A holiday resort offering fine sands, golf and fishing, and surrounded by attractive wooded countryside. Cawdor Castle, $4\frac{1}{2}$ miles south-west, was built by the Thane, or local chief, in 1390. It was altered in the 16th and 17th centuries, but it still has a drawbridge and keep. The richly wooded Findhorn Valley lies 8 miles south of Cawdor. Dulsie Bridge, a beautiful single-arched 18th-century bridge, spans the Findhorn over a spectacular gorge where there is a salmon leap.

Ardclach, 8 miles south of Nairn, has a church whose two-storey belfry, built in 1655, stands apart from the church, at the top of a hill.

Peterhead
A busy seaport and boat-building town at the mouth of the River Ugie, and only 3 miles from Buchan Ness, Scotland's most easterly point. Development of North Sea oilfields has made Peterhead one of the most important service ports in the north-east. The North Sea pounds at its exposed harbour, one breakwater of which was built by convict labour in the 1880's from granite quarried just south of Buchan Ness.

The remains of Deer Abbey, a Cistercian monastery founded in 1219, stand at Old Deer, 10 miles west of Peterhead. The abbey is beautifully situated on the banks of the River South Ugie. The monks of an earlier Celtic monastery on the site produced the famous 9th-century *Book of Deer*, now in the University Library, Cambridge.

Turriff
A thriving market town, mentioned in the 9th-century *Book of Deer*. A ruined church has a double belfry, built in 1635, which still survives. In 1639 the town was the scene of the Trot of Turriff, the first serious skirmish in the Bishops' War, when a band of Covenanters under the Master of Forbes were defeated by a Royalist force. Delgatie Castle, 2 miles north-east, is the home of the Clan Hay. It was built in the 14th to 16th centuries and has fine painted ceilings. Mary, Queen of Scots visited it—her portrait hangs in her room. Craigston Castle, $4\frac{1}{2}$ miles north-east, is an early 17th-century building.

STILLNESS AT NIGHT *Trawlers lie at the quayside in Fraserburgh Harbour, whose history goes back to the 16th century when it was built by Alexander Fraser*

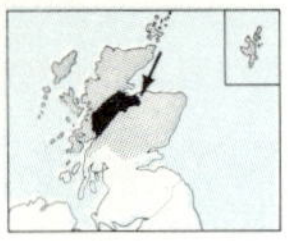

Ben Nevis and the Great Glen

Angling There are salmon and trout in the Great Glen, particularly at Fort William and Drumnadrochit.

Nature trails Culloden Forest Trail starts at Smithton, 3 miles east of Inverness.

Pony trekking At Drumnadrochit and Fort William.

Coach and steamer tours There are day tours from Oban to Iona. Daily cruises from Inverness via the Caledonian Canal to Loch Ness and from Fort William.

Events From June to mid-Sept. there are pipe-and-drum bands and Highland and country dancing on weekdays at the Northern Meeting Park, Inverness. There are Highland Games at Inverness in July, at Glen Urquhart, Glenfinnan and Fort William in July and Aug.

Places to see *Culloden* (NTS): site daily; Visitor Centre: Easter to mid-Oct., daily but closed Sun. morning June to Aug. *Museum and Art Gallery*, Castle Wynd, Inverness: weekdays. *Queen's Own Highlanders Museum*, Fort George: daily. *Urquhart Castle*, Drumnadrochit: weekdays and Sun. afternoons. *West Highland Museum*, Fort William: weekdays.

Information centres Fort William and District Tourist Organisation, Travel Centre, Fort William. Tel. Fort William 3581. Inverness and Loch Ness Tourist Organisation, Church Street, Inverness. Tel. Inverness 34353.

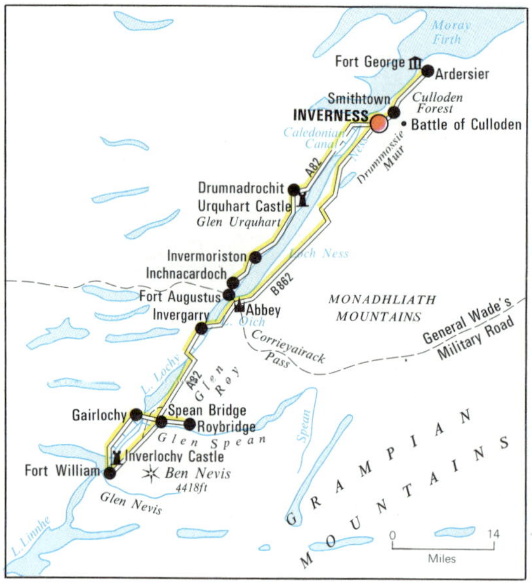

The Caledonian Canal is a magnificent relic of 19th-century engineering. Opened in 1847, it was a wonder of its time, providing sailing boats which passed between the Irish Sea and the North Sea with a fast and safe alternative passage to the stormy route around the north of Scotland. But the introduction of larger steamships made the canal out of date, and fishing boats and pleasure steamers are its main users today. However, the 60½-mile waterway, with its 22 miles of canal, remains an impressive monument to its designer, Thomas Telford.

The canal runs along the Great Glen, linking Lochs Linnhe, Lochy, Oich and Ness and the Moray Firth. Geologically, the glen is a fissure which divides the north-west of Scotland from the south-east.

The impressive mass of Ben Nevis dominates the south-west end of the glen, whose rivers are wild, and hustled onwards by waterfalls. Good roads run from end to end of the glen, partly following the line of General Wade's Military Road, built in the early 18th century to open up the Highlands and subdue the clans.

Ben Nevis
Britain's highest mountain, at 4418 ft. Glen Nevis, round the mountain's western and southern flanks, is one of the loveliest Scottish glens. From Achintee Farm, 2½ miles from Fort William, on the eastern bank of the River Nevis, a stony 5-mile path leads to the mountain's summit. A car was driven up this route in 1911, but the track is now only a narrow footpath. Walkers should take extreme care; accidents occur on Ben Nevis every year. Only very experienced climbers should tackle the precipitous cliffs on the mountain's northern flanks.

Culloden
A cairn marks the site on Drummossie Muir where the hopes of Prince Charles Edward Stuart, Bonnie Prince Charlie, were finally crushed at the Battle of Culloden in 1746. Leanach Cottage, around which the battle raged, still stands, and was inhabited until 1912. A path from Leanach Cottage leads through the Field of the English, where the 76 men of the Duke of Cumberland's forces who died during the battle are said to be buried. Some 1200 of Bonnie Prince Charlie's army of 5000 Highlanders were killed. The main reason for such slaughter was an opening English cannonade, followed by the tactics of the redcoats when the clansmen charged. Instead of attacking the Scotsman immediately in front of him, each English soldier bayoneted the exposed side of the Scotsman to the right. On the Highlanders' burial ground, simple headstones erected in 1881 distinguish the various clans which took part in the battle.

Drumnadrochit
A centre for angling, pony trekking and hill-walking, lying at the eastern end of the fertile Glen Urquhart. The ruined Urquhart Castle, one of Scotland's largest castles, stands 1½ miles to the south-east, on a promontory overlooking Loch Ness. The Chiefs of Grant owned the castle in 1509, and most of the existing building dates from that period. In 1692, the castle was blown up by the Grants to prevent it from becoming a Jacobite stronghold.

Fort Augustus
A popular angling centre, whose fort was built after the 1715 Jacobite rising and named after Augustus, Duke of Cumberland. General Wade enlarged it in 1730. In January 1745 the fort was captured by Bonnie Prince Charlie's forces, who held it until after the Battle of Culloden. A Benedictine abbey and a Roman Catholic boys' school now stand on the site of the old fort.

General Wade linked Fort Augustus with Speyside by a 22-mile Military Road, climbing to 2500 ft over the great Corrieyairack Pass. The road, completed in 1731, descends into the Spey Valley in steep zigzags; Bonnie Prince Charlie took this route in 1745 with his Highland army. Today it has been reduced to little more than a track.

Fort George
The fort, built in 1748, is an irregular polygon with six bastions. It is still a military garrison and houses the regimental museum of the Queen's Own Highlanders. Ardersier, a mile to the south, is a secluded little fishing community on the Inner Moray.

THE GENIUS OF THOMAS TELFORD

Thomas Telford (above) was born in 1757 at Glendinning in Dumfries. He began his engineering masterpiece, the Caledonian Canal, in 1803; although opened in 1822, it took 44 years to complete and the 29 locks along its course are still solid and smooth in operation. The Laggan Locks (above, right) link the canal to the entrance of Loch Lochy

GIANT ABOVE THE GLEN *Ben Nevis, towering above Fort William, is a granite mass more than 500 million years old. It can be climbed by a path starting near the town*

SECRET PORTRAIT *The picture of Bonnie Prince Charlie at Fort William can be seen only when reflected on to a curved and polished surface. The artist is unknown*

Fort William
An important touring centre for the Western Highlands, situated at the foot of Ben Nevis. The original earth-and-wattle fort was built in 1655 by General Monk, 1st Duke of Albemarle. It was rebuilt in stone in 1690 by order of William III, after whom it was named. The Jacobites failed to capture the fort both in 1715 and in 1745, and it continued to be garrisoned until 1855, after which it was demolished.

The West Highland Museum in the High Street contains the famous secret portrait of Bonnie Prince Charlie, which can be seen only if the picture is reflected on to the curved surface of a polished cylinder. There is also a reconstructed croft kitchen. The ruined 13th-century Inverlochy Castle, once the home of the Comyns, stands 2 miles north-east.

Invermoriston
A small town on the west bank of Loch Ness. A cairn near Ceannacroc Bridge marks the place where, in 1746, Roderick Mackenzie, one of Bonnie Prince Charlie's bodyguards, was killed by English troops. Mackenzie bore a striking resemblance to the prince, and said as he was dying, 'You have murdered your prince'. The soldiers, in their eagerness to get the £30,000 ransom for the prince, believed him, and the search was abandoned until the mistake was discovered. By this time, the prince had made good his escape.

Another cairn commemorates John Cobb, who died in 1952 while attempting to break the world waterspeed record on Loch Ness.

Inverness
An attractive and historic town on the River Ness. On Craig Phadrig are the remains of a fort where the Pictish King Brude is believed to have been visited by St Columba in AD 565. King David built the first stone castle in Inverness *c.* 1141. The Clock Tower is all that remains of a fort, or sconce, erected by Cromwell's army between 1652 and 1657. The 16th-century Abertarff House has an ancient spiral staircase; the house is now the headquarters of An Comunn Gaidhealach, the Highland Association which preserves Gaelic language and culture.

The Gothic-style Town House, built in 1878–82, was the scene of the first Cabinet meeting ever held outside London. It was called in 1921 by Lloyd George, holidaying in Scotland, to deal with a letter he had received from Eamon de Valera. In front of the Town House is the mercat cross incorporating the Clach-na-Cudainn, or 'stone of tubs', on which women rested their tubs on their way from the river. The 19th-century St Andrew's Cathedral has fine carved pillars.

Loch Oich
A short but attractive loch on which the Caledonian Canal reaches 105 ft above sea-level, its highest point. On the west side of the loch, near its southern tip, is the Well of the Heads, erected in 1812 by MacDonnell of Glengarry to commemorate, as one story has it, the decapitation by the family bard of seven brothers who had murdered the two sons of a 17th-century chief of Clan Keppoch, a branch of the MacDonnell Clan. The seven heads were washed in the well before being presented to the chief of the MacDonnells at Glengarry.

Spean Bridge
A hamlet in Glen Spean whose bridge, built by Thomas Telford in 1819, spans the turbulent River Spean as it flows westwards to Loch Lochy from the sandy and woody shores of Loch Laggan. At Gairlochy, 4 miles further west, the Caledonian Canal is raised to the level of Loch Lochy by two locks. The waters of the River Lochy have been diverted into the Spean over the Falls of Mucomir.

Roybridge lies 3 miles east at the south end of Glen Roy, notable for its 'parallel roads'—the former shore-lines of lakes formed in periods of glaciation, ending some 10,000 years ago.

INVERNESS *The 'capital of the Highlands' takes its name from the River Ness; 'Inver' is Gaelic for river mouth. On the right are St Mary's Gaelic Church and the High Church*

The riddle of Loch Ness

Whatever it is that stirs in Loch Ness, it is no newcomer. An inscription on a 14th-century map of the loch tells vaguely but chillingly of 'waves without wind, fish without fins, islands that float'. The description has seldom been bettered by the hundreds of witnesses who have testified to the creature's existence.

'Monster' sightings are not limited to Loch Ness: Lochs Awe, Rannoch, Lomond and Morar have all been said to contain specimens. The Loch Ness Monster owes its greater fame to the opening of a main road along the north shore of the loch in 1933. Since then, distant views of 'four shining black humps', 'brownish-grey humps', 'a wave' that shoots across the loch at 20 mph, have kept visitors flocking to the loch.

People who have seen the phenomenon more closely say that it is 'slug-like' or 'eel-like', with a head resembling a seal's or a gigantic snail's, while the long neck is embellished with a horse's mane. Its length has been estimated at anything between 25 ft and 70 ft, and its skin texture is 'warty' and 'slimy'. Close observers too, particularly Mr George Spicer and his wife who saw it jerking across a lochside road in 1933, have declared it 'fearful' and 'an abomination'.

So far, the creature has presented itself only in tantalising glimpses. To believers it has been an unknown fish, a giant slug and a plesiosaurus, which was (or is) a fish-eating dinosaur. Unbelievers are equally imaginative. They suggest that the 'monster' is really a mat of rotting vegetation propelling itself by released gases; waterfowl such as red-throated divers swimming in line ahead; a group of otters playing 'follow my leader'; even the remains of a First World War Zeppelin that appears periodically on the surface of the loch. In Gaelic folklore there is no mystery; the animal is an *Each Uisge*, one of the fearsome water-horses which haunt almost every sheet of dark water in the Highlands.

It is not surprising that such waters, cupped in savage hills, should produce legends. Loch Ness is part of the Great Glen, a geological fault that slashes across Scotland like a sword-cut. The loch itself is 24 miles long, about a mile broad and has an average depth of 400 ft.

Loch Ness has one direct outlet to the sea, the shallow River Ness, and it is fed by eight rivers and innumerable streams, each of which pours the peaty soil of the hills into the loch. Consequently, the water is dark. Divers working with powerful arc lamps 50 ft below the surface have been unable to see for more than 10 ft around them. Legends of caves said to be the home of a colony of monsters have yet to be disproved; these are supposed to be situated beneath the rocky ruins of Urquhart Castle.

Stories of a 'beast' in Loch Ness date back at least to the 6th century. It is recorded in Adamnan's biography of St Columba that in AD 565 the saint prevented a River Ness water monster from eating a Pict. According to another legend, the beast towed St Columba's boat across the water, and was granted perpetual freedom of the loch.

Such benevolence does not sound like the normal behaviour of the Gaelic water-horses. Sometimes these would appear on lochsides in the guise of milk-white Shetland ponies, bridled and saddled; and if a child attempted to ride one of them, it would carry him into the water.

Over the past 40 years, sightings have been claimed by more than 1000 people. Most of the sightings were in bright sunlight in conditions of flat calm, and several of the witnesses were trained observers—soldiers, doctors, seamen and water-bailiffs. Though many of the sightings were from a distance, witnesses have been convinced they were looking at a large animal, most of whose body was hidden beneath the water.

If it exists, it is most unlikely that the Loch Ness monster is a single animal. A prehistoric creature, living alone in Loch Ness, cut off from others of its kind, would have to be millions of

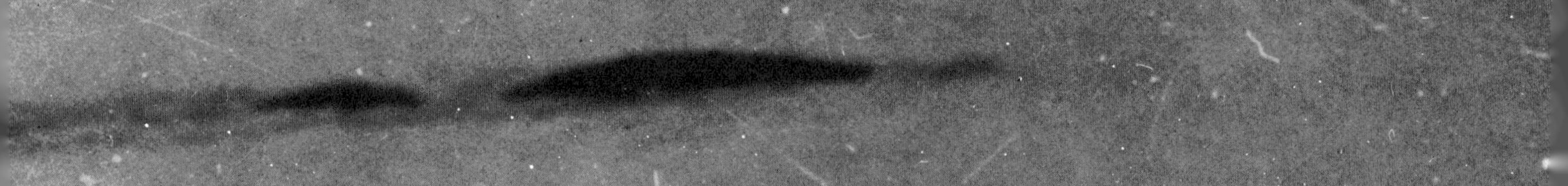

ON A SUMMER'S DAY *In the summer of 1955, Mr P. McNab saw something in the loch. He took this picture just as the 'object' which had disturbed the water was diving*

THREE HUMPS IN THE WATER *This was the sight that made Mr L. Stuart, working at the loch for the Forestry Commission, reach for his camera on July 14, 1951*

MYSTERY AT DAWN *Mr Peter O'Connor took this photograph by flashlight at 6.30 a.m. on May 27, 1960. He has named what he saw 'Nessiesaurus O'Connori'*

years old. For the species to survive there must be quite a large colony; discrepancies in reported sizes could be accounted for by the presence of adults and young. The colony theory is also supported by nearly simultaneous sightings in different parts of the loch.

According to naturalists, the chances of the creature being a reptile are remote. Though Loch Ness never freezes, its temperature never rises above 6°C (42°F) and this would be too cold for any known species. Also, reptiles breathe air, and would have to surface more frequently than the monster appears to. Fish, too, would seem to be ruled out, if legends and accounts of the animal's shore-going activities this century are to be believed. This leaves the invertebrates, and certainly many of the descriptions would fit an enormous worm or slug. But there is no evidence that a backbone-less creature of such bulk has ever existed on this planet.

Though most zoologists deny the possibility that a large and unknown animal might be living in Loch Ness, it is remarkable that reports of creatures in other Scottish lochs, and in lakes in Ireland, Norway and British Columbia, should be so similar in detail. Meanwhile, the mystery continues; and it is perhaps more exciting than any final scientific solution.

THE CAMERA'S EVIDENCE

The ruins of Urquhart Castle brood over the loch, and (left) a mysterious shape disturbs the surface of the water. Photographic experts examined the negatives of this and the other three photographs and agree that there are no signs of tampering

COMING UP FOR AIR? *Mr R. Wilson, a London surgeon, took this picture from the lochside in the spring of 1934*

Over the sea to Skye

Angling Sea fishing off the coast of Skye. There is salmon, sea and brown-trout fishing on Hinnisdal River, at Uig, on Loch Sligachan, the Snizort and Staffin Rivers, and around Ardvasar.

Boating Boats can be hired at Ardvasar, Portree and Isleornsay.

Pony trekking Ponies can be hired at Struan.

Events The Skye Provincial Gaelic Mod, a festival of song, is held in June at Portree. Also at Portree are the Skye Highland Games, usually on third Thur. in Aug. Piping competitions are held at Portree and Dunvegan Castle in Aug.

Places to see *Colbost Folk Museum*, Dunvegan: daily, Easter to Oct. *Dunvegan Castle*: mid-June to Sept., weekdays; Easter to May, and first three weeks in Oct., weekday afternoons. *Glenfinnan Monument* (NTS): mid-Apr. to mid-Oct., daily. *Skye Cottage Museum*, Kilmuir: Easter to Oct., daily.

Ferries Main car ferry from Kyle of Lochalsh to Kyleakin: daily. Glenelg to Kylerhea car ferry: June to Sept., weekdays. Mallaig to Armadale, car and passenger service: weekdays. Uig to Tarbert, Harris and Loch Maddy, North Uist: weekdays.

Information centre Meall House, Portree. Tel. Portree 2137.

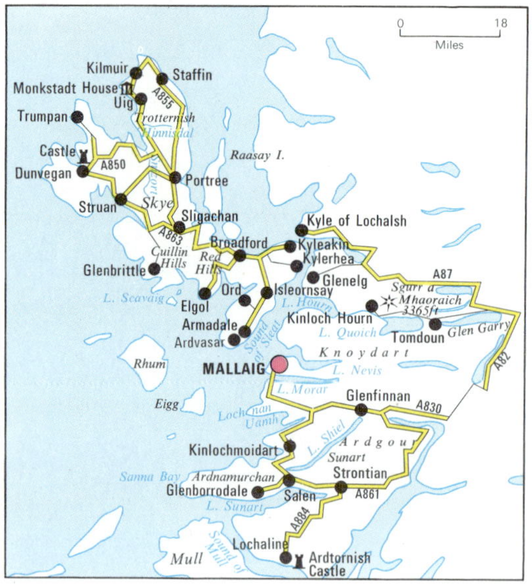

Skye is saturated with 4000 years of myth and history, expressed through tales of bravery and of magic—tales which the islanders bring to life by showing the castles, weapons and other relics of their heroes. The island's richest store of legend is that associated with its brief encounter with Prince Charles Edward Stuart, Bonnie Prince Charlie, when he was a fugitive from the English after the Battle of Culloden in 1746. The Prince also has many associations with the mainland, across the Sound of Sleat. He raised his father's standard at Glenfinnan, and it was at Loch nan Uamh that he landed from France, and later departed. The area contains some of the most spectacular scenery in the Highlands. Skye is 50 miles long, but no part is more than 6 miles from the sea.

There are adequate roads to Skye's many places of interest. Much of the mountainous mainland, however, is served by poor roads—and the district of Knoydart has virtually no roads at all. The few people who live there are served by hill tracks or, if they live on the coast, by sea. The countryside remains, in fact, much as the Prince must have seen it.

THE BLACK CUILLINS *Skye is dominated by the peaks of the Cuillin Hills, seen from Rubh 'an Dunain near Glenbrittle*

Ardnamurchan
The name is Gaelic for 'point of the great ocean', and the tip of the untamed peninsula is the westernmost point on the British mainland—23 miles further west than Land's End. A winding road leads to a lighthouse; the keeper will show visitors round. Sanna Bay, 2 miles north-east of the lighthouse, has pure white sand. The road, which starts at the hamlet of Salen, passes massed banks of rhododendrons at Glenborrodale, which are magnificent in June.

Armadale
A village in a prosperous farming area known as the 'garden of Skye'. Isleornsay, 6 miles north-east, has a sheltered anchorage used by yachtsmen. Ord, 6 miles north of Armadale on the west coast of Sleat, offers spectacular views of the Cuillin Hills.

Broadford
A meeting point for roads from the ferry ports of Armadale, Kylerhea and Kyleakin, and a convenient touring centre for Skye. The granite domes of the Red Hills overlook the village. Beinn na

MEMORIALS OF THE '45 *The monument of a kilted highlander at Glenfinnan (left) marks the spot where Bonnie Prince Charlie unfurled his father's standard on August 19, 1745, at the start of his attempt to recover for his father what an inscription near the monument calls 'a throne lost by the imprudence of his ancestors'. Seven men were with him when he landed from France at Loch nan Uamh, which runs into the open sea 12 miles west of Glenfinnan. While the clans rallied at Glenfinnan the prince and the seven men stayed at nearby Kinlochmoidart. Seven beech trees were planted in a meadow at Kinlochmoidart to commemorate the 'seven men of Moidart' who were among the Prince's most faithful companions. Six trees still stand in line (above); one tree blown down in a gale in the 1960's was replaced by a young sapling—the third tree from the left*

Caillich (2400 ft), 2 miles west, has on its top a large cairn under which lie the remains of a 13th-century Norwegian princess, who said she wanted the winds of Norway to blow over her grave.

Elgol, 10 miles south-west, is the village from which Bonnie Prince Charlie left for the mainland. From Elgol, boats cross Loch Scavaig to Loch Coruisk. The loch was painted by Turner and many other artists.

Dunvegan
A village which grew up round Dunvegan Castle, seat of the chiefs of the Clan MacLeod, who have lived there continuously for 700 years. The castle, much modified from the 15th to the 19th centuries, was once accessible only by boat; but now the moat has been bridged, and the castle is open to the public. Among its treasures are a lock of Bonnie Prince Charlie's hair, MacLeod family portraits by Ramsay and Raeburn, the four-pint drinking-horn which Rory More, the 13th MacLeod Chief, could empty at a draught, and the Bratach Sith, or Fairy Flag.

Tradition says that a fairy gave the flag to William, the 4th Chief, in the 14th century. The faded square of yellow silk, with red spots, is today kept under glass. The flag is said to have three magical properties: flown on the battlefield, it will ensure a MacLeod victory; spread on his marriage-bed, it will endow the MacLeod chief with children; unfurled at Dunvegan, it will charm herring into the loch.

The gift was made on condition that the flag should be used only in emergencies—when the MacLeods faced defeat, when the life of the sole heir was in danger, or when the clan was threatened with extinction. Twice the flag was flown in battle, and twice the MacLeods won—at the Battle of Glendale in 1490, and at Trumpan in 1597.

Trumpan, 9 miles north, still has the remains of the church which was set on fire in 1597 by MacDonald raiders while the congregation, all MacLeods, were inside at worship. Only one woman survived. The MacLeods of Dunvegan rushed to the spot and attacked the raiders after flying their Fairy Flag. Only two MacDonalds escaped death.

Glenfinnan
A hamlet at the head of Loch Shiel, where Bonnie Prince Charlie raised his father's standard on August 19, 1745. A round tower with a statue of a kilted highlander at the top marks the spot. St Finnan's Isle, in the loch, was for centuries the burial ground of the MacDonalds, who built a chapel there in the 16th century.

Knoydart
A district lying 'between heaven and hell'—the names given by the Gaels to the deep sea lochs of Nevis and Hourn. There are virtually no roads into the area. Kinloch Hourn, a hamlet in a hollow at the head of Loch Hourn, is as near as any road approaches Knoydart—and even then it involves a 20-mile drive from Tomdoun in Glen Garry along the often precipitous shore of Loch Quoich, round the shoulder of Sgùrr a Mhaoraich (3365 ft), then down a 1 in 6 hill through a 'lunar' landscape before reaching Kinloch Hourn. From the slopes of Sgùrr a Mhaoraich there is a fine view down the chasm of Loch Hourn, Scotland's most fiord-like inlet, flanked by sheer rocky walls.

Lochaline
A village in whose churchyard is a stone dating from the 16th century or earlier bearing one of the earliest-known likenesses of a kilted Scot. There are breathtaking views down the Sound of Mull to the ruins of Ardtornish Castle, the 14th-century stronghold of the Lords of the Isles. The ruins can be reached by ferry across the mouth of Loch Aline.

Mallaig
The western end of the songwriter's 'Road to the Isles', and today a large herring port. Loch nan Uamh, 8 miles south, is where Bonnie Prince Charlie arrived on the Scottish mainland on July 25, 1745, and left, never to return, on September 19, 1746. Loch Morar, 4 miles south-east is more than 1000 ft deep—the deepest inland water in Britain. It is said to harbour a monster which appears whenever a death is imminent in the Clan MacDonald.

BELL WITHOUT A BELFRY *The bell that calls worshippers to the Roman Catholic church at Glenfinnan stands on the ground. It was made in Dublin in 1878 and bears a design of an Irish wolfhound*

Portree
Skye's capital, sheltering at the mouth of a pretty loch, is a town of white-washed houses and hotels and is an ideal centre for touring the island.

Sligachan, 9 miles south of Portree, and Glenbrittle, a further 7 miles south-west, are centres for climbing the dramatic Cuillin Hills.

A car ferry from Sconser, 13 miles south of Portree, links Skye with the Island of Raasay.

Strontian
An attractive village at the head of Loch Sunart which gave its name to the element strontium, found there in the 18th century. Glen Strontian runs inland between the mountains of Sunart and Ardgour to the Ariundle Forest Nature Reserve.

Uig
A village on Trotternish, the largest Skye peninsula, and the ferry port for Harris and Uist, in the Outer Hebrides. Monkstadt House, 1½ miles north, is where Flora MacDonald brought Bonnie Prince Charlie, disguised as her maid, after their journey 'over the sea to Skye' from the isle of Benbecula.

In Kilmuir churchyard, 5 miles north, Flora MacDonald lies buried, wrapped in a sheet used by the Prince. A Celtic cross marks her grave.

The '45 Uprising

Bonnie Prince Charlie

Charles Edward Louis Philip Casimir Stuart (1720–88) lives in history as Bonnie Prince Charlie, the gallant youth who staked everything on his bid to win a kingdom. He was born in Rome, baptised a Roman Catholic and created Prince of Wales by his father, the Old Pretender. After his defeat at Culloden, Charles lived for another 42 futile years, a pathetic hanger-on in the courts of Europe. In the bitterness of defeat he took to drink, though he never lost hope of a Stuart restoration. His wife, Princess Louise of Stolberg, left him after six years to live in a convent. The 'lad born to be king' died in Rome, a broken-down, aged rake, tended by his natural daughter, Charlotte

One of the world's great romantic legends began on a July day in 1745, when Bonnie Prince Charlie landed on Scottish soil to try to win the throne of Britain for his father, the son of the deposed James II. Just seven men landed with the prince. It was a desperate and foolhardy adventure, but in less than a month more than 1000 Highland clansmen had rallied to his cause. Within two months this wild, undisciplined force, now grown to 2000, had routed a Government army under Sir John Cope at the Battle of Prestonpans, and the prince was holding court in Edinburgh.

By December 4, the prince's army had reached Derby, only 127 miles from London, throwing George II's Government into panic; the royal yacht was standing by to take the king to Hanover. But the king had 30,000 men in the field, against 5000 homesick Highlanders. Overruled by his generals, the prince retreated to Scotland. He won one more victory, at Falkirk on January 17, but at Culloden Moor, on April 16, 1746, his Highlanders, outnumbered 2 to 1, were crushed by an army commanded by King George's son, the Duke of Cumberland.

In the next five months the romantic legend grew, as Cumberland, who earned the nickname 'Butcher', relentlessly hunted the prince all over the Highlands and Islands. The prince had a £30,000 price on his head (worth more than half a million pounds in today's money), but he was never betrayed. Time and again the loyal men and women of the clans risked their lives to hide or protect him. The most famous of these was Flora MacDonald, who took the fugitive prince 'over the sea to Skye' disguised as her maid. Two months later, after more wanderings had stretched his endurance to breaking point, he left Scotland on a French ship.

George the Second

By contrast with the generous, impulsive prince who tried to take away his throne, George II (1683–1760) was a man of narrow interests, obsessed with petty details and small economies, and much given to counting his money, coin by coin. He spoke with a heavy German accent, and had little to endear him to Englishmen beyond the fact that he was an ardent Protestant. But that was enough. In the panic and patriotic fervour caused by Bonnie Prince Charlie's victory at Prestonpans, the Hanoverian king suddenly became popular. The actors at the Drury Lane Theatre added a new song to their programme on September 28, 1745. It was 'God Save the King'

The Battle of Culloden

The last charge of the clans against the guns and bayonets of Cumberland's redcoats. The Scots, half-starved and exhausted, lost 1200 men at Culloden, the English only 76

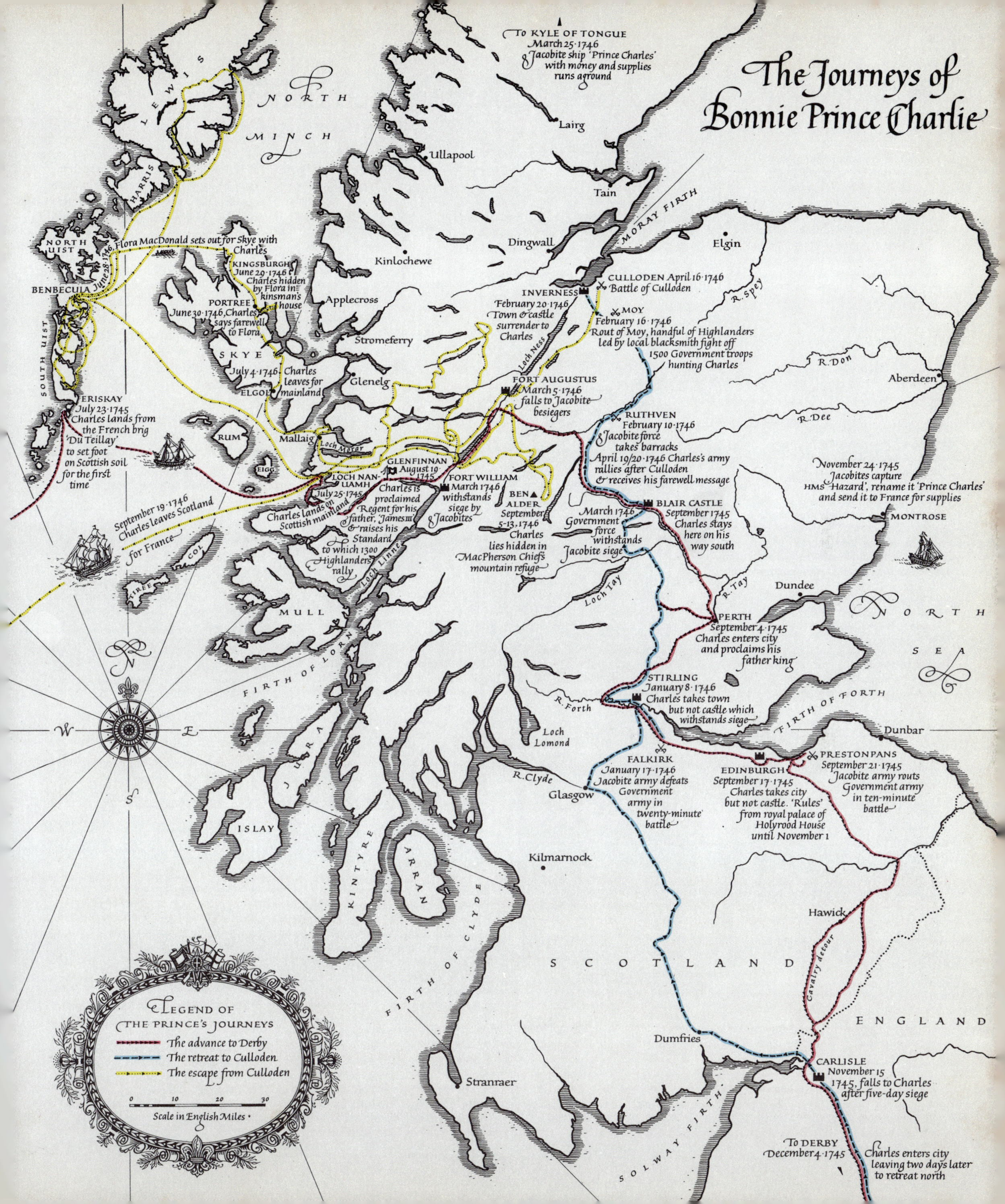

The Journeys of Bonnie Prince Charlie
TO KYLE OF TONGUE March 25·1746 Jacobite ship 'Prince Charles' with money and supplies runs aground
LEWIS
NORTH MINCH
HARRIS
NORTH UIST
BENBECULA
SOUTH UIST
June 28·1746 Flora MacDonald sets out for Skye with Charles
KINGSBURGH June 29·1746 Charles hidden by Flora in kinsman's house
PORTREE June 30·1746 Charles says farewell to Flora
SKYE
July 4·1746 Charles leaves for mainland
ELGOL
ERISKAY July 23·1745 Charles lands from the French brig 'Du Teillay' to set foot on Scottish soil for the first time
RUM
EIGG
Mallaig
Loch Morar
LOCH NAN UAMH July 25·1745 Charles lands on Scottish mainland
September 19·1746 Charles leaves Scotland for France
COL
TIREE
MULL
GLENFINNAN August 19·1745 Charles is proclaimed Regent for his father, James III & raises his Standard to which 1300 Highlanders rally
FORT WILLIAM March 1746 withstands siege by Jacobites
BEN ALDER September 5-13·1746 Charles lies hidden in MacPherson Chief's mountain refuge
Loch Linnhe
FIRTH OF LORN
JURA
ISLAY
KINTYRE
ARRAN
FIRTH OF CLYDE
Ullapool
Lairg
Tain
Dingwall
Kinlochewe
Applecross
Stromeferry
Glenelg
MORAY FIRTH
Elgin
INVERNESS February 20·1746 Town & castle surrender to Charles
CULLODEN April 16·1746 Battle of Culloden
MOY February 16·1746 Rout of Moy, handful of Highlanders led by local blacksmith fight off 1500 Government troops hunting Charles
Loch Ness
FORT AUGUSTUS March 5·1746 falls to Jacobite besiegers
RUTHVEN February 10·1746 Jacobite force takes barracks April 19/20·1746 Charles's army rallies after Culloden & receives his farewell message
R. Spey
R. Don
R. Dee
Aberdeen
November 24·1745 Jacobites capture HMS 'Hazard', rename it 'Prince Charles' and send it to France for supplies
MONTROSE
BLAIR CASTLE September 1745 Charles stays here on his way south
March 1746 Government force withstands Jacobite siege
Loch Tay
R. Tay
Dundee
PERTH September 4·1745 Charles enters city and proclaims his father king
NORTH SEA
STIRLING January 8·1746 Charles takes town but not castle which withstands siege
R. Forth
FIRTH OF FORTH
Loch Lomond
Dunbar
FALKIRK January 17·1746 Jacobite army defeats Government army in twenty-minute battle
EDINBURGH September 17·1745 Charles takes city but not castle. 'Rules' from royal palace of Holyrood House until November 1
PRESTONPANS September 21·1745 Jacobite army routs Government army in ten-minute battle
R. Clyde
Glasgow
Kilmarnock
SCOTLAND
Hawick
Cavalry detour
ENGLAND
Dumfries
Stranraer
SOLWAY FIRTH
CARLISLE November 15 1745, falls to Charles after five-day siege
TO DERBY December 4·1745 Charles enters city leaving two days later to retreat north
N
W
E
S
LEGEND OF THE PRINCE'S JOURNEYS
The advance to Derby
The retreat to Culloden
The escape from Culloden
0 10 20 30
Scale in English Miles

Ancient strongholds in the remote Highlands

Angling There is excellent salmon, brown-trout and sea-trout fishing on rivers and lochs throughout the area.

Walking Beinn Eighe National Nature Reserve has two nature trails, both starting from Loch Maree: the Coille na Glas Leitire trail, which is 1 mile long, and a mountain trail which is 5 hours of rough walking. National Trust of Scotland estates at Torridon, Balmacara and Kintail Forest are good centres for walks, climbs and botanical expeditions.

Events Plockton sailing regatta is held in the last week of July and first week of Aug.

Places to see *Beinn Eighe National Nature Reserve*: Visitor Centre: daily. *Dun Telve, Dun Troddan*, Iron Age brochs in Gleann Beag: daily. *Eilean Donnan Castle*, with *MacRae Museum*: Easter to Sept., weekdays. *Falls of Glomach* (NTS), Kintail: daily. *Strome Castle*, Loch Carron: daily. *Torridon Visitor Centre and Deer Museum* (NTS): daily in summer.

Ferries Kyle of Lochalsh to Kyleakin, Isle of Skye: daily. Glenelg to Kylerhea: daily, May to Sept.

Information centre Wester Ross Tourist Organisation, Achtercairn, Gairloch. Tel. Gairloch 2130.

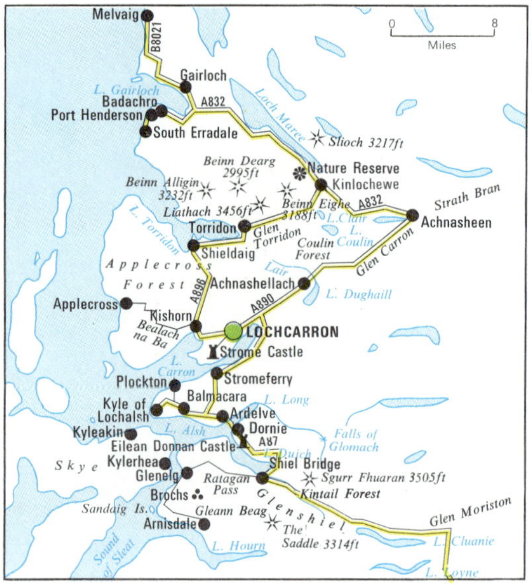

North of Fort William the traveller is venturing into the great wild outback of Britain. For almost 150 miles there are no towns and only a few small villages. But as the roads get narrower the countryside becomes more magnificent; the road linking Torridon and Shieldaig gives some of the most spectacular mountain views in Scotland.

Scattered through the wilderness are reminders that men have been there before—a highland chieftain's castle, such as Eilean Donnan, or the ruins of a Pictish stronghold, such as Dun Troddan. Reminders of more modern occupation are the national nature reserves: because of research work, movement within their boundaries is restricted.

There are hotels in Gairloch, Badachro, Kyle of Lochalsh, Kinlochewe, Lochcarron and Shieldaig, on Loch Torridon; and many houses offer bed and breakfast. Locally baked bread can still be obtained in a few places.

The AA maintains a Highland Patrol to assist stranded motorists.

Applecross

A quiet, remote village on the shore of the peninsula from which it takes its name. The only road to the village is from Kishorn, 10 miles east. It zigzags round hairpin bends into the wild grey landscape of the Applecross mountains, often alongside sheer drops of hundreds of feet. The road reaches a gradient of 1 in 4 as it climbs from sea level to 2054 ft at Bealach na Bà, the Pass of the Cattle, making it one of the highest roads in Britain. Magnificent views can be enjoyed from the summit. St Maelrubha, one of the Irish missionaries who brought Christianity to Scotland, founded a monastery at Applecross in AD 673 and a carved stone north of the village marks his grave.

Gairloch

A superb setting on Loch Gairloch with fine views to the Outer Hebrides, along with fine fishing and good bathing from sandy beaches, have made the village a popular holiday resort. It also has one of the few golf courses in north-west Scotland. The surrounding villages—Badachro, Port Henderson, South Erradale and Melvaig—offer hotels and lodgings for tourists.

Within the parish of Gairloch, which is one of the four largest in Scotland, there are 23 peaks rising to a height of 2000 ft or more: five of them are more than 3000 ft high.

Glenelg

A sleepy hamlet reached by an unclassified road from Shiel Bridge. The twisting climb over Ratagan Pass (1116 ft) is rewarded by a fine view of the mountain range known as the Five Sisters of Kintail, which is dominated by Sgùrr Fhuaran, 3505 ft.

In summer, a car ferry crosses the Sound of Sleat to Skye; it was from Glenelg that Dr Johnson and James Boswell crossed to Skye in 1773. In Gleann Beag, 2 miles south-east, stand two of the best-preserved Iron Age brochs on the Scottish mainland—Dun Telve and Dun Troddan. Brochs are stone towers with double walls, probably built more than 2000 years ago by the Picts for protection against raiders. The minor road south from Glenelg passes north of Loch Hourn to Arnisdale, 6 miles south. Sandaig Islands are a scatter of rocks in the Sound of Sleat, where there is a white lighthouse.

Kinlochewe

A base for hill-walking, climbing and fishing at the head of Loch Maree, which is dominated by its guardian mountain of Slioch 'The Spear' (3217 ft). To the

HUNTERS ON THE SLOPES OF BEINN EIGHE

The Beinn Eighe National Nature Reserve, with 3188-ft Ben Eighe in the background, is the hunting-ground of the pine marten (left) and the wildcat. Both animals rely on speed and agility to catch prey up to the size of squirrels: the pine marten can leap 14 ft

PINEWOOD PLANT The rare one-flowered wintergreen, *Moneses uniflora*, grows in pine forest of north-west Scotland. Its single white drooping flower appears from June to August, and has a smell similar to that of lily of the valley. The only other places in which it can be found are central Europe, Japan and North America south-east the steep funnel of Glen Docherty leads to the isolated hamlet of Achnasheen, 10 miles away, between Glen Carron and Strath Bran.

West of Kinlochewe stretches the Beinn Eighe National Nature Reserve, founded in 1951 as the first nature reserve in Britain. It covers more than 10,000 acres and preserves a large remnant of the ancient Caledonian pine forests. The reserve takes in part of Loch Maree, the Coire Mhic Fhearchair—a magnificent corrie, or mountain hollow below Ben Eighe—and has picnic and camping sites.

Kintail Forest

A profusion of mountains, lochs, glens and rivers makes this one of the most magnificent scenic areas of Scotland. It is reached from the south by the A87 from Invergarry. This road cuts over the hills by Loch Loyne to the western end of Glen Moriston. From there it runs alongside Loch Cluanie and on through the wild beauty of Glenshiel, flanked by the mountain range of the Five Sisters of Kintail on the east and The Saddle (3314 ft) on the west.

The road continues to Dornie, where three lochs meet—Lochs Duich, Alsh and Long. Here stands Eilean Donnan Castle, one of the most popular of all Scottish subjects for painters and photographers. A MacKenzie stronghold dating from 1220, it was blown up by an English man-o'-war in 1719, when it was being used as a base for a Jacobite rising. The MacRae family, who held Eilean Donnan as hereditary constables for the MacKenzies, rebuilt the castle in 1932 at a cost of £230,000.

A 14-mile drive east from Dornie leads to the 370-ft Falls of Glomach—one of the highest in Britain. The route lies along the west shore of Loch Long, then through Glen Elchaig; finally there is a rough climb on foot.

Kyle of Lochalsh

A busy shipping village, from the northern approaches to which there are superb views of the Cuillin Hills, almost 20 miles away on the island of Skye. It is the main ferry-stage for Skye, whose shores are only a few hundred yards across the Kyle Akin water.

Loch Carron

A loch strewn with islands, and narrowing to less than half a mile at Stromeferry. The ferry itself was replaced in 1970 by a road along the south side of the loch. Ruined Strome Castle overlooks the loch and offers fine views of Skye. The castle, a former MacDonnell stronghold, was blown up by the MacKenzies in a clan feud in 1603.

Lochcarron, on the north-west shore of the loch, is notable for its locally woven ties and tartans. Achnashellach, 8 miles north-east, looks over Loch Dùghaill and down a broad glen. North of the village, pedestrians can take the 7-mile hill track and follow the tumbling River Lair to Loch Coulin, Loch Clair and Glen Torridon. The views of Beinn Eighe (3188 ft) and Liathach (3456 ft) are breathtaking.

CLIMBERS' PLAYGROUND *Draped in icicles, the cliffs above the 2054-ft pass of Bealach na Bà in the Applecross peninsula provide a variety of testing winter climbs*

JACOBITE STRONGHOLD *Eilean Donnan Castle, built by Alexander II of Scotland in 1220 on an island at the meeting point of Lochs Duich, Alsh and Long, was bombarded by the English warship* Worcester *in 1719 when it was held by Jacobite sympathisers. The ruin was rebuilt in 1932 by the MacRae family, and is now a clan war memorial and museum*

Loch Maree

One of the most beautiful inland lochs in Scotland, set amid wild mountain scenery, with the great mass of Slioch dominating its south-eastern end. Druids once worshipped on tiny Isle Maree, one of many islets that dot the loch's waters. The islets are now in the care of the Nature Conservancy, from whom permission must be obtained before landing.

Plockton

White houses line a sheltered bay at the mouth of Loch Carron and look over to the Applecross mountains. Erbusaig Bay, 4 miles south-west, has a beach where branches of coral can be found.

Torridon

A village at the heart of some of Scotland's most magnificent wild scenery. Beinn Eighe, Liathach, Beinn Alligin (3232 ft), and Beinn Dearg (2995 ft) cluster round the village, north of Upper Loch Torridon. The mountains, lining both sides of the valley, are formed of red Torridonian sandstone and the horizontal rock strata give the slopes a distinctive banded appearance.

GLEN TORRIDON *Some of Scotland's wildest scenery lies along Glen Torridon. Across Loch Clair is a headland of pines, remnants of the primeval Caledonian Forest; beyond are the snow-capped peaks of Liathach, 3456 ft (left), and Beinn Eighe, 3188 ft*

Wilderness of Sutherland

Angling There is excellent salmon, sea-trout and brown-trout fishing throughout the area.

Nature Trails There is a nature trail at Knockan Cliff, 14 miles north of Ullapool, and a forest garden and trail at Lael Forest, Lochbroom.

Events Assynt Games and flower show, Lochinver, mid-Aug. International sea-angling championships, Ullapool, early Aug.

Places to see *Ardvreck Castle*: daily. *Calda House*, ruins of Seaforth stronghold burnt down in the 18th century: daily. *Corrieshalloch Gorge and Falls of Measach* (NTS): daily *Handa Bird Sanctuary* (permission from Warden at Tarbet): boats from Tarbet. *Inverewe Gardens* (NTS), Poolewe: daily. *Inverpolly National Nature Reserve*: daily. *Lochbroom Highland Museum*, Ullapool: Easter to Oct., weekdays.

Ferries Ullapool to Stornoway: twice daily except Sun. Keodale Ferry, linking Durness to minibus service to Cape Wrath: daily. Kylesku Ferry, from Kylestrome to Unapool: daily (phone Kylestrome 222 for verification in bad weather).

Information centres Sutherland Tourist Organisation, The Square, Dornoch. Tel. Dornoch 400. Summer only—Information Centre, Ullapool. Tel. Ullapool 2135.

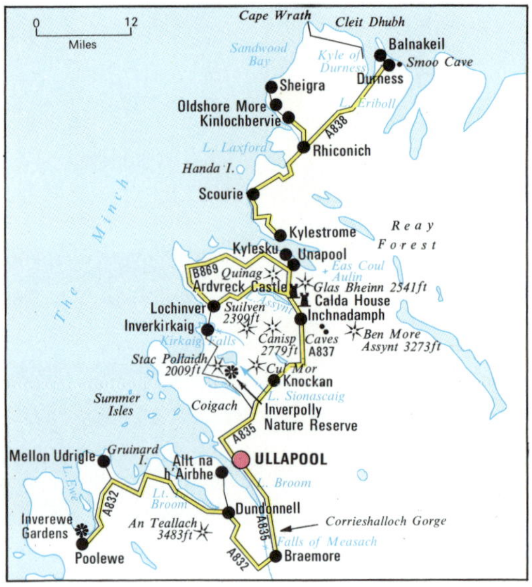

The great reaches of land stretching out towards Cape Wrath have a forbidding appearance. There are few roads and fewer signs of human life. The bulk of the land is Sutherland, a district which suffered desperately in the early 19th century during the Highland clearances, when landlords drove thousands of people from the land to make way for sheep and, later, deer. Sutherland has never fully recovered from that sad episode. It is by far the most sparsely populated area in Britain; only 12,000 people live in its 1.1 million acres—fewer than 7 people to the square mile, compared with the average of 586 for Britain as a whole.

Sutherland's wide, wild acres offer some of the most spectacular scenery in mainland Britain—the highest cliffs and the highest waterfall; weirdly shaped mountains, formed of rock more than 600 million years old; innumerable rivers and lochs; a rugged coastline softened by great sandy beaches; and wild stretches of moor and forest. All this lies beneath a sky in which sun and cloud are constantly changing, giving the landscape an infinite variety of colour.

Here, too, is a haven for wildlife. Inland are golden eagles, wildcats, pine martens and deer; seabirds and seals live along the shore; and the lochs and rivers teem with salmon and trout. There are a number of good hotels, one superb caravan site and a good supply of friendly bed-and-breakfast accommodation. But the camper has the best of it, for he can move freely across this huge north-western thrust of mainland towards the sea, and find solitude in one of the few great wildernesses still remaining in 20th-century Europe.

SMOO CAVE *On the wild north coast of Sutherland, a mile east of Durness, a vast cavern cuts into the limestone cliff. Visitors can enter on foot the outer chamber, which stretches for 203 ft.*

Cape Wrath

The extreme north-west point of the Scottish mainland is named after the Viking word *hvraf*, a turning point; this was where the Vikings turned south on their way to the Hebrides, which they held from the 9th to the 13th century. The cape is isolated and its hinterland untamed. One road from the cape lighthouse runs 10 miles east across the peninsula to connect with a pedestrian ferry across the Kyle of Durness. In summer a minibus service runs several times a day between the ferry and the lighthouse. The road passes within 2 miles of the cliffs at Cleit Dhubh—the highest on mainland Britain, rising 850 ft from the sea.

Dundonnell

A climbing centre near the head of Little Loch Broom, beneath the towering peaks of 3483-ft An Teallach. The mountain's name means 'the forge'—from the smoke-like mists which wreath its peaks. Near by is the tiny Loch Toll an Lochain, 2000 ft high and set amid spectacular scenery, flanked by a ridge of white quartzite slabs. The loch can be reached on foot from Dundonnell.

At Braemore, 8 miles south-east of Dundonnell, the Falls of Measach plunge 150 ft into Corrieshalloch Gorge. The mile-long gorge is owned by the National Trust for Scotland.

Durness

A trim crofting community which is also a tourist centre with good trout and salmon fishing. Balnakeil, 1 mile north-west, is a craft village where pottery and paintings are produced. Balnakeil Church, built in 1619, has a monument to the Gaelic poet Rob Donn Calder, sometimes called the 'Burns of the North', who died in 1778. In the limestone cliffs a mile east of Durness is the Smoo Cave, which is entered under a 'Gothic' arch 33 ft high and 130 ft wide. The first chamber, 203 ft long, can be visited by boat but two inner chambers are for experienced potholers only. Two miles further on, the road turns south to skirt Loch Eriboll, in which the rare Atlantic grey seals breed during the last four months of the year.

Gruinard Bay

One of the loveliest bays in Scotland, where rocky coves are interspersed with pink, sandy beaches. Gruinard Island, in the middle of the bay, was used as a germ warfare testing ground in the Second World War; it is still infected with anthrax and landing is prohibited. From Mellon Udrigle, near the western tip of the bay, there are fine views of the mountains of Coigach, 12 miles north-east across the island-studded waters.

SCOTLAND'S 'MATTERHORN' *The 2399-ft peak of Suilven (on the right), near Lochinver, is known as the Matterhorn of Scotland because of its dangerous cliff faces. Suilven is part of the remnants of a sandstone layer on top of the oldest rocks in Britain, which date back more than 2600 million years*

KIRKAIG FALLS *Sutherland is dotted with lochs and lovely waterfalls. The tumbling waters of the Kirkaig Falls lie on the River Kirkaig between Fionn Loch and Inverkirkaig*

Inchnadamph

A village at the centre of an area notable for its caves and underground streams. Ben More Assynt (3273 ft), is 4 miles south-east of Inchnadamph and on the lower slopes south of the village are the Allt nan Uamh caves, in which human bones 8000 years old have been found. A mile north of the village, on the shore of Loch Assynt, are the ruins of Ardvreck Castle, a MacLeod stronghold, where in 1650 Neil MacLeod arrested the Marquis of Montrose. Montrose was found sheltering in a hut at Assynt after an abortive invasion attempt on behalf of the exiled Charles II. He was handed over to the government by Neil MacLeod and was later executed at Edinburgh.

The road to Unapool, 10 miles north, passes the seven peaks of Quinag. Energy rather than mountaineering skill is all that is needed to climb to the ridges joining the peaks. On the other side of the road is Glas Bheinn (2541 ft), the source of Britain's highest waterfall, Eas Coul Aulin, which has a sheer drop of 658 ft—more than four times the height of Niagara Falls. The fall can be reached by boat on Loch Glencoul from Kylesku Ferry, or on foot from the road below Glas Bheinn.

Lochinver

A fishing village at the head of Loch Inver and a good centre for exploring the district of Assynt. There are some 300 small lochs in the area, and in Glencanisp Forest, 4 miles south-east, stands 2399-ft Suilven.

Poolewe

A small village in a protected position at the head of lovely Loch Ewe. The garden of Inverewe, 1 mile north, houses a wide variety of plants ranging from alpine to sub-tropical. The garden was created from barren land just over 100 years ago, and it survives in a latitude that is further north than Moscow's because the area is warmed by the Gulf Stream.

Rhiconich

A hamlet on the northern edge of the huge Reay Forest—once the hunting-grounds of the chiefs of the Clan MacKay. Kinlochbervie, 4 miles north-west, is a busy fishing port with two harbours and is a popular centre for walkers and anglers. At Oldshore More, 2 miles further north-west, is a fine bay where King Håkon IV of Norway anchored his fleet when he tried to invade Scotland in 1263. He was defeated soon after at Largs.

The road ends at Sheigra, 2 miles beyond Oldshore More, but a peat track leads on for another 4 miles to the beautiful Sandwood Bay.

Scourie

This crofting village is also a popular fishing resort. It lies on a sheltered, sandy bay 9 miles north-west of the Kylesku Ferry, which crosses the width of Loch a' Chairn Bhain. Handa Island, 2 miles north-west, was once inhabited by 12 families who appointed their own queen—the oldest widow in the community—and their own parliament. The tradition died when the potato famine of 1846 forced them to leave the island. It is now a bird sanctuary, inhabited by puffins, razorbills, kittiwakes, fulmars and gannets. Loch Laxford, 6 miles north-east of Scourie, has good salmon fishing during the season.

Ullapool

A small fishing port in Ross and Cromarty founded in the late 18th century and today a leading centre for sea angling. Its wide streets are named in both Gaelic and English. The Lochbroom Highland Museum, with its items of local origin and connection, is housed in one of Ullapool's original buildings. A passenger ferry links Ullapool with Allt na h'Airbhe, on the opposite shore of Loch Broom. In the outer loch, 12 miles north-west of Ullapool, are the Summer Isles, which are as attractive as their name. They once supported a community of inshore fishermen, but the herring shoals diminished and only one is still inhabited.

The Inverpolly National Nature Reserve, 10 miles north, covers 27,000 acres of mountain and loch, river and moor, crag and cliff. Few people live there, but it is the haunt of wildcat, pine-marten, golden eagle and deer. There is superb fishing in many of the lochs, particularly Loch Sionascaig. The mountains include the curiously shaped Stac Pollaidh (2009 ft) whose summit rocks present the outline of a fairy-tale castle. Knockan, 14 miles north-east of Ullapool, is the starting point of a 50-mile motor trail which runs through much of the reserve and over the Sutherland border into the rocky land of Assynt.

LONELY LAND OF THE ROVING DEER

Deer roam free in the wilderness of northern Scotland. The roe is smaller than the red deer and the buck has small branched antlers with at least six, and sometimes eight or more, points. The red deer has much wider branched antlers and a longer tail. In Scotland the deer are used to living outside their normal wooded haunts and herds can often be seen roaming the high moorlands

North to John o' Groat's

Angling There is sea fishing at Brora, Cromarty, Dunnet, Keiss, Lybster, Scrabster and Wick; salmon and trout fishing in lochs and rivers.

Sailing There are clubs at Dornoch, Thurso, Fortrose, Tain and Invergordon.

Sand yachting At Dunnet Bay.

Events Thurso Highland Games take place in early July, Dornoch Highland Games and Invergordon Highland Games in Aug. There are gala weeks at Tongue (early July) and Golspie (early Aug). Pipe bands play every Sat., from June to Sept., in Thurso and Wick.

Places to see *Caithness Glassworks*, Harrowhill, Wick: weekdays except Sat. afternoon. *Castle of Mey*: gardens: certain days in July and Aug. *Castle of Old Wick*: all year, except when neighbouring rifle range is in use. *Dounreay Atomic Energy Exhibition*: daily, May to Sept. *Dunrobin Castle*: May to Sept., weekdays, Sun. afternoon. *Hugh Miller's Cottage* (NTS), Cromarty: weekdays, May to Sept.; also Sun. afternoon June to Sept. *Sutherland Wool Mills*, Brora: Mon. to Thur.; also Fri. morning. *Thurso Museum*: weekdays.

Steamer services Scrabster to Stromness, Orkney, daily.

Information centres Caithness Tourist Organisation, Whitechapel Road, Wick. Tel. Wick 2596. Sutherland Tourist Organisation, The Square, Dornoch. Tel. Dornoch 400. Tourist Organisation, Information Centre, Muir of Ord. Tel. Muir of Ord 433.

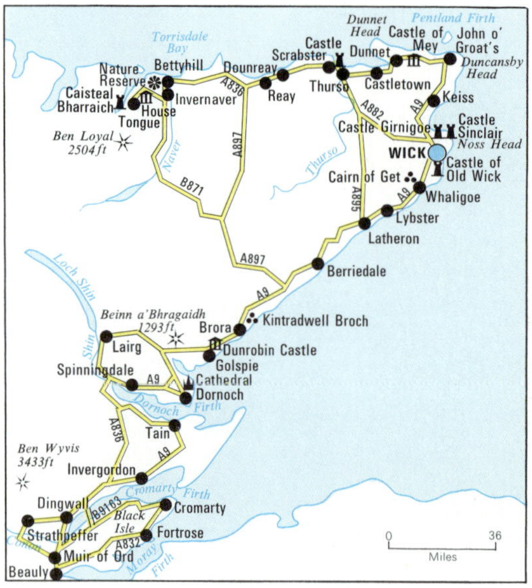

The countryside from the Black Isle northwards through the Highland region to the great undulating plateau of Caithness is wild and remote enough to have remained largely unspoilt. The seascapes are unforgettable. The North Sea, lashing the rocky eastern coast, has left its mark in dramatic cliffs and coves separated by natural arches or isolated pillars of rock. To the north there is a spectacular view from Duncansby Head across the Pentland Firth. In the west, Ben Loyal is a many-peaked landmark.

Stone circles and other prehistoric remains are plentiful, particularly round the Latheron valley on the south-eastern coast of Caithness. Vast tracts have remained almost uninhabited since the early 19th-century Highland clearances, and in 1959 the northern edge of this untamed area was chosen as the site of an atomic reactor, at Dounreay.

Britain's far northern corner is not entirely a wilderness. Easter Ross is mainly fertile low-lying land, encircled by sandy-shored firths; and all along the coast, attractive fishing villages and towns such as Brora, Golspie and Dornoch are becoming popular resorts. Even in the wilds of Caithness, determined reclamation of peat bogs has produced many acres of good agricultural land. The flagstones quarried at Thurso, and used to line roads and fields, give the region a distinctive character.

ROYAL SPA *Strathpeffer, now a tourist centre, was a mineral-water spa popular with European royalty in the 19th century*

NORTHERN TIP *The lighthouse on Dunnet Head, the most northerly point of the mainland, gives views to the Orkneys*

Bettyhill
The village, at the mouth of the River Naver, was founded by Elizabeth, Marchioness of Stafford, for crofters evicted during the Highland clearances to make room for sheep and deer. It is now a holiday resort offering good fishing, swimming and many other sports. At Torrisdale Bay, just north-west, there is a bird sanctuary; and Invernaver Nature Reserve, to the west, has a wide range of wildlife and plants, including some rare Alpine plants.

Black Isle
A fertile peninsula with patches of young forest. It is named the 'Black Isle' because it is seldom whitened by snow. Cromarty, at the north-east tip, has fine beaches. The cottage in which the geologist Hugh Miller was born in 1802 is now

STEPS TO THE SEA *From the village of Whaligoe, perched on the cliffs on the east coast of Caithness, 365 precarious steps lead to the fishing boats in the small harbour below*

a geological museum. Fortrose, an ancient town facing the Moray Firth, has a sheltered bay for yachting; there is also a chapter house and the vaulted crypt chapel of a ruined 13th-century cathedral. Nigg Bay is an attractive sheltered part of Cromarty Firth, with a scattering of pretty hamlets around its shores. Rosemarkie, near Fortrose, has another fine beach.

Brora

A thriving golf and fishing resort on the river of the same name. There is magnificent mountain and moor scenery, and sandy bays indent the rocky coast. There are many Pictish remains in the surrounding area, and 6 miles north is the Kintradwell broch, a drystone tower used as a fortification by the Picts between 200 BC and AD 50.

Castle of Mey

The 16th-century seat of the 4th Earl of Caithness, formerly known as Barrogill Castle, was saved from demolition in 1952 when the Queen Mother bought it as a summer home.

Canisbay, 3½ miles east, has a 15th-century church in which a slab on the south wall, dated 1558, is said to mark the grave of John de Groat, a member of the Dutch de Groot family whose octagonal house once stood at John o' Groat's, about 3½ miles north-east. The Queen Mother attends services at Canisbay Church when in residence at the Castle of Mey.

Dingwall

A town in Easter Ross, near the mouth of the River Conon. The town arms, a starfish, are displayed on a tolbooth (originally a booth for collecting tolls), dating from 1730. In front of this is the shaft of a former mercat cross, and beside it an iron gate of the old town jail. Strathpeffer, 6 miles west, is a good centre for touring the Easter Ross countryside, which is dominated by the 3433-ft summit of Ben Wyvis.

ANTLERS ON THE WALL *Deerstalking has been a sport in the hills behind Berriedale for centuries, and antlers of red deer shot locally festoon the village smithy*

Dornoch

A pleasant holiday resort that offers safe bathing from miles of golden sands, good fishing, and a famous golf course, charming views over the Dornoch Firth and a spacious main square. The 13th-century cathedral was largely destroyed by fire in 1570 but restored in the 18th–20th centuries; it is a landmark for miles. As many as 16 Earls of Sutherland are buried there. Inside, at the west end, there is a fine statue by Chantrey of the 1st Duke of Sutherland, and in the nave is an effigy of Sir Richard of Moray. He was the brother of Bishop Gilbert de Moravia, the founder of the cathedral, who was killed by the Danes at the Battle of Embo near the town in 1248.

The last woman to be judicially executed for witchcraft in Scotland was burnt in Dornoch in 1722. She was an old woman accused of turning her daughter into a pony, and a rough stone marks the site of her execution.

Golspie

A busy fishing town and an attractive holiday resort. The inscribed Gaelic stone on the old bridge is the rallying point for the Clan Sutherland. Spacious moors make a lofty background, rising to Beinn a' Bhragaidh (1293 ft), on which stands a statue by Chantrey of the 1st Duke of Sutherland, set up in 1834. Dunrobin Castle, just north-east, dates partly from the 12th century, and was once the home of the Dukes of Sutherland.

Lairg

A resort and market village at the east end of Loch Shin, popular with anglers, archaeologists and travellers in search of wild and beautiful countryside. About 3 miles south, among pretty woods, are the spectacular waterfalls of the River Shin, the site of a major salmon run. The Shin Valley Hydro-electric Scheme is one of the largest in the country. On the west side of the river is an Iron Age stone circle, and others are to the north.

THE HIGHLAND COTTAGE

The cottage is built with rubble walls and a slate roof, which have largely replaced earlier peat roofs tied down by stone-weighted ropes. The loft is used for storing fodder

Tongue

An attractive angling and climbing centre in Sutherland, north of the many-peaked Ben Loyal, and on the inland curve of the Kyle of Tongue. Ruined Caisteal Bharraich, once the home of an 11th-century Norse king, was a Mackay stronghold. Tongue House, a pleasant 17th and 18th-century building north of the village, is the seat of the Dukes of Sutherland.

Thurso

A fishing resort through which the River Thurso wends its way to Thurso Bay. The attractive locally quarried flagstones are much in evidence. The ruins of St Peter's Church date from the 16th century, and there are some fine 17th-century houses. The Thurso Museum has a plant and fossil collection and a small Runic cross. The remains can be seen of Thurso Castle, seat of the Sinclair family. Harold's Tower, 2 miles east of the town, is the Sinclair burial place, built over the grave of Earl Harold, the ruler of Caithness, who died in battle in 1196. Ten miles west of Thurso is the Dounreay Atomic reactor.

Wick

An ancient town with a large harbour, and an important sea-fishing centre. North and south of the town enormous rocks cap the rugged cliffs, and wreckage from storms at sea can often be found at their foot.

About a mile south of Wick, on a rock projecting into the sea, is the 14th-century Castle of Old Wick, known to seafarers as the 'Old Man of Wick'. The Cairn of Get, 6 miles south-west, is a Neolithic burial chamber in which several skeletons, leaf arrowheads and ornaments were found during the course of excavations in 1866.

From Noss Head Lighthouse, 3 miles north-east, there are spectacular views of the ruins of Castle Sinclair and Castle Girnigoe, across Sinclair's Bay; both were destroyed in 17th-century clan wars.

The 'Long Island' of the Outer Hebrides

Angling Salmon, sea trout and brown trout are plentiful on all the islands. There is salmon and trout fishing at Lochboisdale and Lochmaddy on South and North Uist; Leverburgh and Tarbert on Harris; Stornoway on Lewis. Also sea angling at Stornoway, where the Western Isles Open Sea-Angling Championships are held in Sept.

Events The Lewis Provincial Mod, a festival of folk music and poetry, is held at Stornoway in June. In late July there are Highland Games on South and North Uist and a Gala Week on Harris.

Places to see *Black House Museum*, Arnol: weekdays. *Carloway Broch*: daily. *Flora MacDonald's Birthplace*, Milton, South Uist: daily. *Kiessimul Castle*, facing Castlebay, Barra: May to Sept., Wed. and Sat. afternoons; access by ferry from Castlebay. *South Uist Cottage Museum*, Benbecula: weekdays.

Ferries There are regular services from Ullapool on the mainland to Stornoway, Lewis; and from Oban to Lochboisdale, South Uist and Castlebay, Barra. Also from Uig on Skye to Tarbert on Harris. Regular inter-island services run between Tarbert and Lochmaddy on North Uist, via Uig on Skye.

Roads The roads on Lewis and Harris are good. On North and South Uist and Barra they are narrow, with passing-places.

Information centre Western Isles Tourist Organisation, South Beach Quay, Stornoway, Isle of Lewis. Tel. Stornoway 3088.

SOAY SHEEP

The only truly wild sheep in Britain are the goat-like Soay on Hirta, the principal island in the St Kilda group. They were brought to the neighbouring islet of Soay in prehistoric times

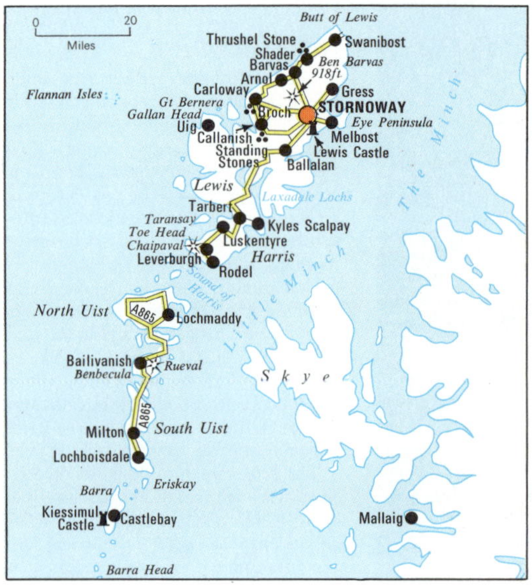

The Western Isles, more familiar as the Outer Hebrides and referred to locally as 'The Long Island', are a wild and rugged collection of islands stretching 130 miles from the Butt of Lewis to Barra Head. Their long sandy beaches are sometimes gold and sometimes silver-white from crushed shells, while the seaboard waters, abounding in trout and salmon, are shades of Caribbean blues and greens.

Westwards, the shores are pounded by the full force of the Atlantic, deeply slashed by sea lochs and studded with pretty islets. Rocks eroded into many shapes thrust through the wind-blown soil.

On Lewis, the largest of the islands, 30 miles long and 28 miles across at its widest point, there are a hundred scattered villages, most of them on the coast. The islanders' simple cottages are often painted in bright colours. The Butt of Lewis Lighthouse stands on rugged sea cliffs while, inland, small lochs dot the rolling peat moors. The crofters cut the peat with special spades, the women and children stacking it for winter fuel. Trees are rare, and pasture on the seaside *machair*, or wide beach, is limited; fishing and weaving are still the main industries.

On Harris, which is joined to Lewis, the landscape changes to bare hills and grand, dramatic peaks, some over 2000 ft high. North Uist, across the Sound of Harris, has so many *lochans*, or small lakes, that it is almost more water than solid earth. A 40 mile long road encircles the twisting shoreline in the north and passes a wealth of prehistoric standing stones, chambered cairns and brochs, or cylindrical drystone towers, dating back to the early Iron Age. South Uist has lochs on the west and mountainous hills on the east, divided by a road running the length of the island.

Gaelic is the first language of the majority of the islanders. Street names are sometimes bi-lingual, and Gaelic songs are still sung in the *ceilidhs*, the impromptu gatherings for singing and story-telling.

Arnol

A village on Lewis with a museum in a *tigh dubh*, the traditional black house of the islands. Its thick, drystone walls have tiny doors and windows, as protection against the harsh weather.

Carloway, 4 miles south-west, is the site of one of the best-preserved Iron Age brochs in the Hebrides; it stands 30 ft high on a hilltop, and it is possible to climb between its double walls.

The standing stones at Callanish, 9 miles south, are one of the most important of Scotland's prehistoric relics. They date from *c.* 2000 BC.

Barvas

A Lewis township reached by a moorland road from Stornoway, 12 miles south-east, which passes countless *lochans* and is overlooked by Ben Barvas (918 ft). About 4 miles north lies Shader, site of the Thrushel Stone, a tall prehistoric monolith. From Swanibost, 10 miles north, there is a view of the Eye of the Needle, a wild cape of rock pinnacles and cliffs near the Butt of Lewis. It was in this area that the first experiments were made in reseeding and reconstituting the barren moorland to make pastureland, a practice which today is widespread throughout the islands.

Benbecula

A tiny island between North and South Uist, vulnerable to wild winds from the sea. Rueval hill is a conspicuously high point in a fretwork of lochs, bays and islands. Most of the thousand people on Benbecula live in the principal community of Bailivanish, near the airfield which was made during the Second World War. It was from Benbecula that in 1746 Bonnie Prince Charlie, dressed as Flora MacDonald's maid, escaped in a rowing boat to Port Kilbride on Skye.

Eriskay

A charming island between Barra and South Uist, with a fame disproportionate to its size, arising from historical events two centuries apart. In 1744 Bonnie Prince Charlie first set foot on Scottish soil on Eriskay; and in 1941 the SS *Politicia* ran aground off the island carrying a large cargo of whisky. Compton Mackenzie's novel *Whisky Galore* was based on the subsequent events.

Today's population of 300 are mainly crofters and fishermen. Eriskay has its

LUSKENTYRE SANDS *These beaches lining a deep inlet on the Sound of Taransay are one of the beauty spots of Harris. They are sheltered by the offshore island of Taransay*

BARRA *The steamer from Oban arrives at Castlebay, a former McNeil stronghold and Barra Island's chief link with the mainland*

own strain of pony, and is frequently visited by colonies of seals. It is said that the pale pink sea convolvulus which blooms on the island was first planted by Bonnie Prince Charlie during his days of hiding here. The gentle sadness of the Gaelic melody 'The Eriskay Love Lilt' conveys the island's character.

Great Bernera
An island in Loch Roag, joined to the mainland of Lewis by a road bridge. The waters are a rich source of lobsters. Gallan Head, a bleak moorland promontory, looks out over 20 miles of sea to the Flannan Isles. A lighthouse was built on the islands in 1900 and during a gale soon afterwards all three lighthouse keepers on duty vanished.

Lochs
A parish on Lewis south-west of Stornoway, so called because the proportion of water to land is even higher here than elsewhere in the islands. There are hamlets on grassy knolls, where crofters grow potatoes in 'lazy beds'—rows of banked-up soil with their own drainage system. At Ballalan, at the head of lovely Loch Erisort, the road crosses moorland which was once the hunting-ground of the Earl of Seaforth, Chief of the Mackenzies; small red deer still roam wild.

RITUAL STONES *The ring of standing stones, one of them nearly 16 ft high, at Callanish on Lewis, may have been set up for sun-worship rituals nearly 4000 years ago*

Rodel
A village on Harris notable for its restored cruciform St Clement's Church, built on a hill overlooking the Little Minch and the Sound. The church, which dates from 1500, was built by the 8th MacLeod chief as a chapel, and has a fine MacLeod tomb built in 1528. It also has a sculptured square tower and a carved arch. It was restored by the Countess of Dunsmore in 1873.

St Kilda
The westernmost group of islands in the British Isles, lying 45 miles west of North Uist. By 1930 it became almost impossible to make a living here, and the St Kildans were evacuated to the mainland. The islands now belong to the National Trust for Scotland and are an undisturbed sanctuary for great colonies of gannets, fulmars and puffins. The St Kilda cliffs rise to nearly 1400 ft and are the highest in the British Isles.

Stornoway
The largest town in the Outer Hebrides and the unofficial 'capital' of Lewis. Stornoway is an important fishing port, the centre of the Harris tweed industry, and a popular sea-angling resort. The 2 mile long natural harbour has made it the centre of the Hebridean herring industry, and there is also a large lobster pond. Tweed-weaving is still a cottage industry, but spinning and finishing of the cloth is carried out in five Stornoway mills. Lewis Castle, facing the harbour, was presented to the town by Lord Leverhulme, who bought the island just after the First World War but failed in his attempt to modernise its industries by turning the crofters into fish-cannery workers. The castle, built in 1844, is now a technical college; its surroundings include the largest wooded park in the Outer Hebrides.

The Eye Peninsula consists of low-lying moorland extending for 8 miles into The Minch. There are fine deserted beaches at Braighe Sands, near the airport at Melbost, and at the east end of the sands is the ruin of Ui Chapel, containing several MacLeod tombs. Broad Bay, north-east of Stornoway, has excellent beaches, and the cliffs round here contain some interesting caves, notably Seal Cave at Gress, which can be reached by hired boat. Here, too, is the ruined church of St Aula (Olaf), the only Hebridean church dedicated to a Norse saint.

Tarbert
The biggest village on Harris, standing on a narrow isthmus between lochs. Its name means a narrow neck of land across which 'boats may be dragged'. A scenic road runs eastwards, ending at Kyles Scalpay, overlooking Scalpay Island, which is excellent for fishing. Cairns on the road to Luskentyre mark prehistoric funeral routes.

Toe Head
A peninsula on Harris stretching into the Atlantic, and a haven for seabirds. From Chaipaval hill the views of the Cuillins of Skye and the hills of North Uist are unforgettable. Outcrops of rock break up the sandy coastline through Scarista and past Borve Lodge, once Lord Leverhulme's home. Near the attractive village of Luskentyre is Loch Fincastle, a loch stocked with salmon.

HEATHER ROOF

Some houses on the stormy Atlantic coast of Scotland have a thatch of heather held in place by ropes, which are weighted with stones

The Orkneys and Shetlands

Angling Shetlands: good fishing for sea and brown trout. Orkneys: good trout fishing in all lochs.

Events Lerwick has the 'Up-Helly-Aa' Festival in Jan. Kirkwall has Ba' Games on Jan. 1 and Dec. 25, and a County Show early in Aug.

Places to see in the Orkneys *Bishop's Palace*, Kirkwall: weekdays and Sun. afternoon. *Earl's Palace*, Kirkwall: weekdays, Sun. afternoon. *Maes Howe*, ancient burial ground, on Kirkwall–Stromness road: weekdays and Sun. afternoon. *Orkney Natural History Museum*, Stromness: weekdays. *Skara Brae*, Stone Age village: weekdays, Sun. afternoon. *Tankerness House Museum*, Kirkwall: weekdays.

Places to see in the Shetlands *Broch of Mousa*, Isle of Mousa: May to Sept., weekdays. *Jarlshof*: weekdays, Sun. afternoon. *Lerwick County Museum*: weekdays, except Thur. afternoon.

Ferries There are services to the Orkneys and the Shetlands from Aberdeen and Scrabster.

Information centres Shetland Tourist Organisation, Alexandra Wharf, Lerwick. Tel. Lerwick 3434. Orkney Tourist Organisation, Information Centre, Kirkwall. Tel. Kirkwall 2856.

On a map, the Orkneys and Shetlands resemble a ragged path of stepping-stones reaching north-east from the Scottish mainland. It is a well-strewn path. There are 65 islands in the Orkneys, 30 of them inhabited; and there are 100 more Shetland islands, although only 15 are inhabited. Muckle Flugga, in the Shetlands, Britain's most northerly point, is more than 170 miles from John o' Groat's. It is more northerly than parts of Alaska, but its climate is softened by the Gulf Stream.

The Orkneys and Shetlands were settled by Norsemen in the 9th century, and for 500 years were ruled by Norway or Denmark. They passed to Scotland in 1468–9, when Christian I of Norway pawned them in lieu of a dowry on his daughter's marriage to James III. The biggest island in both the Orkneys and the Shetlands is called Mainland.

Most of the 18,300 population of the Orkneys get their living from farms, which are generally small but are worked intensively. The Shetlands, 50 miles further north, lie at the centre of rich fishing grounds, and fishing supports many of their 17,800 people. The highest point on the Shetlands, Ronas Hill, is 1475 ft, while the highest in the Orkneys is Ward Hill, 1570 ft, east of The Old Man of Hoy.

Both the Orkneys and Shetlands abound with relics of history. Shetland has more prehistoric sites than any other area of its size in Britain. Walking, angling and spotting rare birds are rewarding diversions. In June in the Shetlands, the sun never stays long below the horizon and the night is only twilight, or, as the Shetlanders call it, 'simmer dim'.

SCULPTED BY THE SEA *Yesnaby Castle, off the west coast of th*

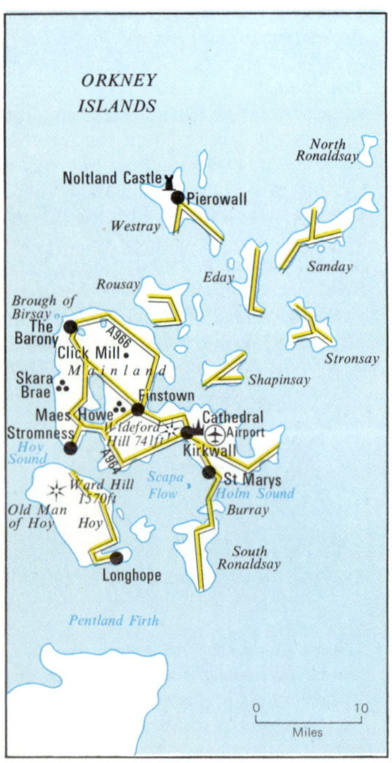

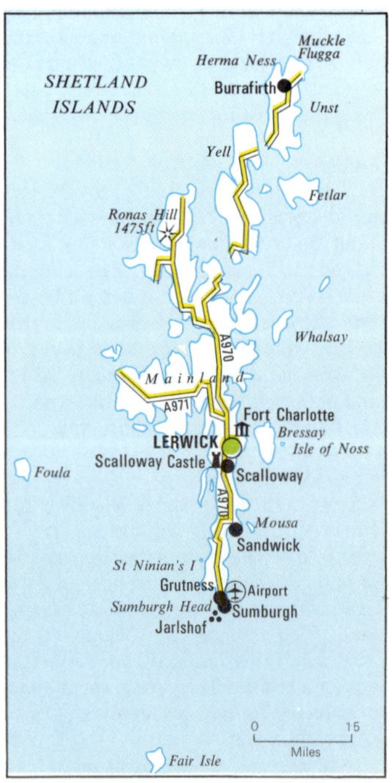

Fair Isle

The most remote inhabited island in Britain, lying 23 miles from the nearest land, midway between the Orkneys and the Shetlands. Ornithologists, who have an observatory on Fair Isle, have recorded more than 300 species of birds, ranging from the Alpine swift to the osprey. A hostel with room for 24 people was added to the observatory in 1969 and will accommodate tourists, when not occupied by ornithologists. The 50 islanders fish, farm, do coastguard duties and operate the weekly boat to Grutness in the Shetlands. The women of the island still knit in the intricate Fair Isle patterns, which are probably of Norse origin.

Finstown

A sheltered village on the Bay of Firth, with one of the few woods of mature trees in the Orkneys. Maes Howe, 3 miles to the west, is the finest Stone Age tomb in Britain. It dates from 2000 BC, and consists of several chambers built of huge stones and covered by a mound 26 ft high and 120 ft across. Cuween Hill Cairn, 1 mile south of Finstown, is another chambered tomb of similar age.

Click Mill, 6 miles north-west, is the only watermill designed to a Norse pattern still working today. It has a wheel that lies horizontally instead of in the usual vertical position.

Kirkwall

The capital of the Orkneys and a busy harbour town of narrow, twisting streets and high-gabled greystone houses clustered round the red and yellow sandstone mass of St Magnus's Cathedral. The cathedral was founded in 1137 by Earl Rognvald, the Norse ruler of Orkney, in memory of his uncle and predecessor, Magnus, who was murdered by a rival earl in 1115. The canonised remains of both rulers are sealed in pillars in the cathedral. St Magnus's skull was discovered during renovations in 1919. It was split across as though by an axe—just as the murder of Magnus is described in a Norse saga.

Near by is the Earl's Palace, built for the 2nd Earl of Orkney, Patrick Stewart, who was tried in Edinburgh and hanged in 1614 after his reign of tyranny. The palace walls are complete but roofless. Tankerness House, a town house of 1574, has been restored and houses a

Orkney island of Mainland near Skara Brae, is a rock stack eroded by sea and wind

STROMNESS *Since Viking days Stromness has been valued as a safe harbour, and today it is a terminal of the ferry linking the Orkneys with the mainland. In the 19th century, ships of the Hudson Bay Company called here to take on crew before crossing to Canada*

museum and art gallery. Kirkwall claims to have the oldest public lending library in Scotland, dating from 1683. Wideford Hill (741 ft), a mile west of the town, gives views south over the Pentland Firth to the mountains of Sutherland and to Fair Isle, more than 60 miles away to the north.

Lerwick

The capital of the Shetlands and the northernmost town in the British Isles, standing on Mainland, the Shetlands' largest island. Its picturesque harbour bustles with fishing boats from many lands. Some old merchants' houses have lodberries—loading piers built out over the harbour. Ships used to sail up to the lodberries' doors and unload straight into the merchants' premises. Fort Charlotte, built in 1665 to guard the harbour, was burnt by the Dutch in 1673, but later repaired.

On the last Tuesday in January, Lerwick celebrates the old Norse festival of 'Up-Helly-Aa'—the fire festival—to mark the beginning of the end of the long winter nights. The climax of the ceremonies is the burning of a 30 ft long replica of a Viking long ship. The island of Bressay, half a mile offshore, shelters Lerwick Harbour. It has spectacular cliffs, from one of which protrudes the Giant's Leg—a pillar of stone standing in the sea, but attached to the cliff at its top. The Isle of Noss, a few hundred yards east of Bressay, is a bird sanctuary.

Mousa

This uninhabited island, half a mile from the Shetland village of Sandwick, has the most complete Iron Age broch, or fortress tower, surviving anywhere. It stands 43 ft high, with 20 ft thick double walls of drystone masonry surrounding a courtyard 22 ft in diameter. Stairs inside the walls lead to galleries.

Pierowall

An attractive Orkney village on Westray, the most fertile of the northern isles. The 16th-century Noltland Castle, half a mile west, is the finest surviving 'Z-plan castle', so-called because it consists of a central building with wings jutting out from opposite corners.

North Ronaldsay, most northerly of the Orkneys, lies 17 miles north-east of Westray. Its 300 inhabitants maintain a 6 ft high wall round the island, just above high-water mark. This wall keeps the island's sheep off the limited land available for agriculture, leaving them to feed on seaweed on which they thrive, producing fine wool.

St Marys

A yachtsman's haven in the Orkneys on the Holm Sound. Running south from the village are the Churchill Barriers—250,000 tons of concrete blocks that were sunk in 1939 to carry a road linking Mainland to the islands of Lamb Holm, Glims Holm, Burray and South Ronaldsay. Sir Winston Churchill, then First Lord of the Admiralty, ordered the barriers to be built to block the eastern approach to the naval base of Scapa Flow. A German U-boat had slipped through and sunk the battleship *Royal Oak*, with the loss of more than 800 men.

Scapa Flow is 80 square miles of sheltered water surrounded by the southern Orkneys. The second largest of these, after Mainland, is Hoy, whose western cliffs rise to more than 1000 ft. The Old Man of Hoy is a 450-ft pillar of rock rising out of the sea; it was first climbed in 1966.

Longhope, a village of small white houses in southern Hoy, was the base of the Longhope lifeboat, whose crew of 8 died in 1969 going to the rescue of the Liberian tanker *Irene*, which had called for help while running short of fuel in mountainous seas. The *Irene* later came to rest in a rocky bay on the neighbouring island of South Ronaldsay, and all her 17-man crew were rescued.

St Ninian's Isle

A peninsula of Mainland in Shetland, 14 miles south of Lerwick. Here the British missionary St Ninian founded a chapel in the 5th century. In 1958, students excavating the chapel site found a hoard of beautifully worked silver bowls and ornaments, which are now in the National Museum of Antiquities in Edinburgh.

Scalloway

Once the capital of the Shetlands, when the Parliament met on an island in the loch. It stands on a bay sheltered by islands, and its houses are clustered around the well-preserved remains of the castle built by the 2nd Earl of Orkney, Patrick Stewart, in 1600. His cruelty to his tenants, for which he was eventually deposed, is remembered in the legend that blood was mixed with mortar in the building of the castle.

Stromness
The Orkneys' second town, standing on a sheltered bay in Hoy Sound. Its fishermen export lobsters and crabs by air to London and the Continent. Many of the picturesque harbourside houses have their own piers. Inland are narrow, stone-flagged streets with no footpaths. There is a museum with a display of boats and model ships.

Skara Brae, 6 miles north, is a 4000-year-old Stone Age village. First engulfed by sand and then uncovered by a storm, the village has been excavated to reveal a narrow street of beehive-shaped houses, a market-place and a potter's shop. Beds and tables inside the houses are all made of stone. The Barony, 6 miles further north, is a large village in an area of rich farmland, near to rocky scenery and trout lochs.

Sumburgh
The site of the Shetlands' airport, near which, on Sumburgh Head, is Jarlshof—a site where man has lived for 4000 years. The earliest inhabitants were Stone Age men of *c.* 2000 BC. There are extensive Bronze Age and Iron Age remains as well as those of a Viking village and a 16th-century mansion. By contrast there is a modern hotel, and Sumburgh Head lighthouse beams out over the Roost, a dangerous current. The sandy Bay of Quendale and the dramatic cliffs of Fitful Head (928 ft) are near by to the north-west.

Unst
The most northerly of the Shetland islands. Burrafirth, to the north, is on one of the loveliest inlets in the Shetlands, and has many caves. The peninsula of Herma Ness is a nature reserve, where great skuas, gannets, kittiwakes and puffins abound.

Yell
The second-largest island in the Shetlands supports a population of about 1000 who live by crofting on the peat-covered rocks, and by fishing. Fetlar, an island just east of Yell, breeds some of the finest Shetland ponies.

SEAL WATERS

The common seal is found in small herds on the Shetland and Orkney coasts, particularly in June and July. It is called tangfish in northern Scotland—from '*tang*', Shetland for seaweed, because of the seal's liking for low water where weeds cover rocks

JARLSHOF *On this 3-acre site on the Shetlands' Mainland, traces have been found of settlements of many periods. The earliest dates back 4000 years. In the foreground are Pictish ruins dating from c.* AD *800. Beyond are the remains of the 16th-century Laird's House, the model for Scott's Jarlshof in* The Pirate

HANDICRAFTS OF THE ISLANDS

SHAWL Shetland knitting at its best—a lace-styled shawl made of finest wool from the neck of the sheep

SILVERCRAFT These hand-wrought brooches are based on Norse originals found in excavations

IRONWORK A poker handle is bent into the shape of a ram's head, which is a traditional Shetland design

CARDIGAN Authentic Shetland knitwear is undyed. The colours are those of the sheep's wool

SHETLAND PONIES *Generations of breeding have produced these small, tough ponies, only 42 in. high at the shoulder when fully grown. They were formerly in demand as work ponies for pits and crofts, but are now sold as pets throughout the world*

THE OUTDOOR LIFE

Useful addresses for the holidaymaker

Angling

All inland water in Great Britain belongs to some person or organisation, and an angler must have permission from the owner of any water he intends to fish. A fee is usually payable.

In Scotland, the owner's permission is all that the angler needs. But in England and Wales all freshwater fishing is controlled by ten regional water authorities, and the angler usually needs an official licence from the appropriate authority.

A licence is always needed for salmon and trout. In most areas a licence is needed for coarse fish, too. No licence is required for sea fishing except on estuaries, where a water-authority licence must be obtained to fish for sea trout. Licences are obtainable from the water authorities themselves, fishing-tackle shops, hotels and clubs in the area.

At the time of publication, the cost of a salmon licence varies from £8 a season, or £2 a week, to 50p a season. Most authorities charge about £1 for a season's coarse fishing.

Water authorities in England and Wales set size limits to prevent immature fish being taken. These vary from authority to authority, but any fish smaller than that stipulated must be put back. There is no size limitation in Scotland.

A minimum close season, during which the taking of fish is banned in order to allow breeding, is also fixed by the water authority. Actual dates for trout and salmon vary from area to area, but the close season is roughly from the end of October until April or May.

There is a statutory close season for coarse fishing in England and Wales, from March 15 to June 16, but none in Scotland.

Addresses of water authorities from which information and licences can be obtained:

Anglian: Diploma House, Grammar School Walk, Huntingdon, Cambridgeshire PE18 6NZ.
Tel. Huntingdon 56181
Great Ouse House, Clarendon Road,
Cambridge CB2 2BL. Tel. Cambridge 61561
Rivers House, Springfield Road, Chelmsford, Essex CM2 6JN. Tel. Chelmsford 64721

North West: Liverpool Road, Great Sankey, Warrington WA5 3LP. Tel. Penketh 4161
New Town House, Buttermarket Street, Warrington WA1 2QG. Tel. Warrington 53999
Chertsey Hill, London Road, Carlisle CA1 2QX.
Tel. Carlisle 25151

Northumbrian: Northumbrian House,
Regent Centre, Gosforth,
Newcastle upon Tyne NE3 3PX.
Tel. Gosforth (Newcastle upon Tyne) 843151
Nevilles Court, Nevilles Cross, Durham DH1 4SX.
Tel. Durham 3456
Trenchard Avenue, Thornaby, Stockton, Teesside TS17 0EQ. Tel. Stockton 62216

Severn-Trent: Abelson House,
2297 Coventry Road, Sheldon, Birmingham B26 3PR. Tel. 021-743 4222
64 Albert Road North, Malvern WR14 2BB.
Tel. Malvern 61511
Meadow Lane, Nottingham NG2 38N.
Tel. Nottingham 865007

South West: 3-5 Barnfield Road,
Exeter, Devon EX1 1RE.
Tel. Exeter 50861
There is also an angling phone-in information service at this address on Exeter 31666.

Southern: Guildborne House, Worthing,
W. Sussex BN11 1LD. Tel. Worthing 205252
Eastleigh House, Market Street, Eastleigh SO5 5WA.
Tel. Eastleigh 614622
78 College Road, Maidstone ME16 8JG.
Tel. Maidstone 55211

Thames: New River Head, Roseberry Avenue, London EC1R 4TP. Tel. 01-837 3300
Nugent House, Vastern Road, Reading.
Tel. Reading 593333
The Grange, Crossbrook Street, Waltham Cross EN8 8LX. Tel. Waltham Cross 23611

Wessex: Techno House, Redcliffe Way, Bristol BS1 6NY. Tel. Bristol 25491
2 Nuffield Road, Poole BH17 7RL.
Tel. Poole 71144
Bridgwater House, King's Square, Bridgwater TA6 3AE. Tel. Bridgwater 57333

Yorkshire: West Riding House, 67 Albion Street, Leeds LS1 5AA. Tel. Leeds 448201
Castle Market Building, Exchange Street, Sheffield S1 1GB. Tel. Sheffield 26421
PO Box 201, George Street, Bradford,
W. Yorkshire BD1 5PZ. Tel. Bradford 23093

Welsh National Water Development Authority:
Highfield, Priestley Road, Caernarfon LL55 1HR.
Tel. Caernarfon 2247
Tremains House, Coychurch Road, Bridgend CF31 2AR. Tel. Bridgend 2217
19 Penyfai Lane, Furnace, Llanelli SA15 4EL.
Tel. Llanelli 57031

Camping and Caravanning

Camping is no longer confined to hardy adventurers. The modern tent is often a large structure of several rooms, and a variety of lightweight portable equipment, most of which can be hired, soon turns it into a comfortable holiday home for the family.

While it is still possible for the camper to 'get away from it all', many prefer to use organised camp sites which have facilities for bathing, laundering and shopping. There are a number of such sites in the National Parks and Forest Parks. Details of those in a National Park can be obtained only from the local office of the committee or board responsible for the park. Advanced booking is necessary at some sites, especially during peak holiday periods.

A modern trailer or motor caravan can sometimes offer comforts that are comparable with those of a hotel, particularly when its facilities are backed by those of a good caravan site.

About 1000 sites have been approved by the Automobile Association and are listed in their *Guide to Camping and Caravanning*. Addresses:

The Automobile Association,
Fanum House, Basingstoke RG21 2EA.
Tel. Basingstoke 20123

Camping Club of Great Britain and Ireland,
11 Lower Grosvenor Place, London SW1W 0EY.
Tel. 01-828 1012

Caravan Club,
East Grinstead House, East Grinstead RH19 1UA.
Tel. East Grinstead 26944

Forestry Commission, 231 Corstorphine Road, Edinburgh EH12 7AT. Tel. 031-334 0303

National Caravan Council,
43 High Street, Weybridge KT13 8BT.
Tel. Weybridge 51376

Canals and Rivers

Britain has about 3000 miles of canals and navigable rivers which are being used increasingly for pleasure cruising. One attraction of some of these waters is their remoteness, as they meander round the countryside usually far from road and rail routes, and another is the way they slow down the tempo of modern life; 15 miles a day is good going on a canal. About half the country's inland-waterways system is State-owned and controlled by the British Waterways Board.

Leisure-seekers are catered for by scores of firms which hire out self-drive motor cruisers accommodating from 2 to 12 people. Charges for a 2-berth cruiser range from £40 to £80 a week, according to season. For a 6-berth cruiser, the range is £70-£200. Canal cruisers are easy to handle, and a short demonstration by the owner is all the novice needs.

There are also larger 'hotel' boats, which have comfortable cabins, dining rooms and bars, and carry a full staff. Addresses to contact:

British Waterways Board, Melbury House,
Melbury Terrace, London NW1 6JJ.
Tel. 01-262 6711

British Waterways Board
Pleasure Craft Licensing Officer,
Willow Grange, Church Road, Watford,
Hertfordshire WD1 3QA. Tel. Watford 26422

Inland Waterways Association,
114 Regent's Park Road, London NW1 8UQ.
Tel. 01-586 2556

Association of Pleasure Craft Operators,
Norbury Junction, Stafford ST20 0PN.
Tel. Woodseaves 578

Canoeing

The canoe is the cheapest and most versatile of all craft. A handyman can build one and put it on the water fully equipped for about £100. A canoe can float in 4 in. of water or it can cross the Atlantic, a feat accomplished by Dr Hans Lindemann in 1957.

Canoeists can explore places inaccessible to other boats. There is, however, no general right of public access to any non-tidal waters. Parts of the Thames, Severn and Wye and some other waters are exceptions, but to be sure he is not trespassing, the canoeist should seek permission from the owner of the water. A licence is needed to canoe on canals controlled by the British Waterways Board.

There are more than 100,000 canoeists in Britain. More than half go touring—usually along canals, lakes and rivers, though occasionally round the coast. The others are canoe-sport enthusiasts, who race weirs and other turbulent waters.

Beginners can learn how to handle a canoe by joining a club belonging to the British Canoe Union, or by taking a course run by the Sports Council. Organisations that will be of assistance:

British Canoe Union,
Flexel House, High Street, Addlestone, near
Weybridge KT15 1JV. Tel. Weybridge 41341

British Waterways Board
Pleasure Craft Licensing Officer,
Willow Grange, Church Road, Watford,
Hertfordshire WD1 3QA. Tel. Watford 26422

Camping Club (Canoe Section),
9 Glebe Road, Sandy, Beds. SG19 1LS.
Tel. Sandy 80712

Sports Council, 70 Brompton Road,
London SW3 1EX. Tel. 01-589 3411

Children's holidays

Many organisations specialise in arranging holidays for unaccompanied children. Most of these holidays are based on outdoor activities. Organisations specialising in these holidays are:

British Trust for Conservation Volunteers,
(Conservation work camps for 16-year-olds and over)
10–14 Duke Street, Reading RG1 4RU.
Tel. Reading 596171

Council for British Archaeology,
(Details of digs and expeditions) 112 Kennington Road, London SE11 6RE. Tel. 01-582 0494

Council for Colony Holidays for School Children,
(Country and seaside holidays for children, 8–14)
Linden Manor, Upper Colwall, Malvern, Hereford and Worcester WR13 6PP. Tel. Colwall 40501

Cyclists Touring Club,
Cotterell House, 69 Meadrow, Godalming,
Surrey GU7 3HS. Tel. Godalming 7217

Field Studies Council,
(Residential courses in natural history)
9 Devereux Court, London WC2R 3JR.
Tel. 01-583 7471

Forest School Camps,
(Camps under canvas for children, 6½–17)
23 Station Avenue, Walton-on-Thames
KT12 1NF. Tel. Walton-on-Thames 45271

Outward Bound Trust, 360 Oxford Street,
London W1N 9HA. Tel. 01-491 1355

Scottish Sports Council,
1 St Colme Street, Edinburgh EH3 6AA.
Tel. 031-225 8411

Scottish Youth Hostels Association,
9 Glebe Crescent, Stirling FK8 2JA.
Tel. Stirling 2821

Sports Council,
(Courses in a wide range of sports; lower age limit 17)
70 Brompton Road, London SW3 1EX.
Tel. 01-589 3411

Wildlife Youth Service,
(Natural history, camping)
Marston Court, Manor Road, Wallington,
Surrey SM6 0DN. Tel. 01-669 4995

Yorkshire Field Studies,
Larpool Hall, Whitby, North Yorkshire YO21 1AA.
Tel. Whitby 2737

Youth Hostels Association, Trevelyan House,
St Albans, Hertfordshire AL1 2DY.
Tel. St Albans 55215

Climbing

Climbing, like other adventurous activities, is becoming more popular every year. But it is not a pastime to be undertaken lightly. It can be dangerous; about a dozen climbers are killed in Britain every year.

The safest way to start climbing is to attend one of the many beginners' courses held in Britain. A week's tuition organised by the Sports Council costs about £50. The British Mountaineering Council has about 200 affiliated clubs, many of which arrange courses for beginners. Courses are also run by some local education authorities, the Youth Hostels Association and the Scottish Sports Council. Addresses:

British Mountaineering Council,
Crawford House, Precinct Centre, Booth Street East,
Manchester M13 9RZ. Tel. 061-273 5835

Scottish Sports Council,
1 St Colme Street, Edinburgh EH3 6AA.
Tel. 031-225 8411

Sports Council,
70 Brompton Road, London SW3 1EX.
Tel. 01-589 3411

Youth Hostels Association, Trevelyan House,
St Albans, Hertfordshire AL1 2DY.
Tel. St Albans 55215

Gardens

Many of Britain's finest gardens are open to the public. Some, including many of those owned by the National Trust, open regularly for a large part of the year, while others open only at specific times during the summer, usually in aid of charity. Details of about 1750 gardens open during the summer are available from:

Gardeners' Sunday Organisation,
White Witches, Claygate Road, Dorking,
Surrey RH4 2PR. Tel. Dorking 4053

National Gardens Scheme,
57 Lower Belgrave Street, London SW1W 0LR.
Tel. 01-730 0355

Scotland's Gardens Scheme,
26 Castle Terrace, Edinburgh EH1 2EL.
Tel. 031-229 1870

Motor sport

A motor-sport event of some kind takes place in Britain every week of the year. There are 14 different types of competition for cars—ranging from circuit races to local car-club rallies—and five major classes of motor-cycle competition.

Circuit racing is further sub-divided into eight groups, the most important of which includes the Formula 1 racing cars, which compete in the Grand Prix races of the world championship series. Formula 1 cars are single-seater racing cars with 3-litre engines. America has two Grand Prix races a year, other countries one. The British Grand Prix takes place in July at either Silverstone (in odd-numbered years) or Brands Hatch (even-numbered years).

Racing circuits in regular use are:
Brands Hatch, near Farningham, Kent
Cadwell Park, near Horncastle, Lincolnshire
Castle Combe, near Chippenham, Wiltshire
Croft Autodrome, near Darlington, Co. Durham
Donington Park, near Leicester
Ingliston, near Edinburgh
Longridge, near Blackpool
Lydden, near Canterbury, Kent
Mallory Park, near Leicester
Oulton Park, near Tarporley, Cheshire
Silverstone, near Towcester, Northamptonshire
Snetterton, Norfolk
Thruxton, near Andover, Hampshire

Other popular events include hill climbs, auto-cross, sprints and drag racing. In hill climbs, matched cars race uphill one at a time against the clock. Auto-cross competitors race on a track laid out in a field, while sprint competitors race against the clock over a measured, flat course. In drag racing, specially built cars with huge rear wheels and enormous engines developing up to 1300 brake horsepower sprint over a quarter-mile course that they cover in six seconds from a standing start. The Royal Automobile Club is the organising body for motor sport in Britain.

The motor-cycle racing year reaches its climax in the International Tourist Trophy Races held on the Isle of Man early in June. Races are also held at many of the leading circuits. Other motor-cycle competitions include cross-country 'scrambles', grass-track races; and trials—either time-trials, individual races against the clock, or observed trials in which the competitor must not stop or put his feet on the ground. The Auto-Cycle Union is the governing body for motor-cycle sport. The addresses of the principal motor sport organisations are:

Auto-Cycle Union, 31 Belgrave Square,
London SW1X 8QQ. Tel. 01-235 7636

Royal Automobile Club,
Motor Sport Division, 31 Belgrave Square,
London SW1X 8QH. Tel. 01-235 8601

Nature Reserves

Several organisations will give information and encouragement to those with an interest in wildlife and natural history. These include the Government-established Nature Conservancy Council, which is responsible for nearly 300,000 acres of nature reserves; and the Forestry Commission, whose 3 million acres provide habitats for a wide range of plants and animals. County trusts are represented nationally by the Royal Society for the Promotion of Nature Conservation. The National Trust owns or controls nearly 500,000 acres of land in England and Wales. The National Trust for Scotland owns more than 84,000 acres.

Council for Nature,
(National body for local natural-history groups)
Zoological Gardens, Regent's Park,
London NW1 4RY. Tel. 01-722 7111

Forestry Commission, 231 Corstorphine Road,
Edinburgh EH12 7AT. Tel. 031-334 0303

National Trust, 42 Queen Anne's Gate,
London SW1H 9AS. Tel. 01-222 9251

National Trust for Scotland,
5 Charlotte Square, Edinburgh EH2 4DU.
Tel. 031-226 5922

Nature Conservancy Council,
19 Belgrave Square, London SW1X 8PY.
Tel. 01-235 3241

Royal Society for the Protection of Birds,
(Bird sanctuaries and observatories) The Lodge,
Sandy, Bedfordshire SG19 2DL. Tel. Sandy 80551

Scottish Wildlife Trust, 8 Dublin Street,
Edinburgh EH1 3PP. Tel. 031-557 1525

Society for the Promotion of Nature Conservation, The Green, Nettleham,
Lincoln LN2 2NR. Tel. Lincoln 52326

Wildfowl Trust, Slimbridge, Near Gloucester,
Glos. GL2 7BT. Tel. Cambridge (Glos.) 333

Riding

It is estimated that nearly two million people in Britain regularly ride horses for recreation. Every year more and more go on trekking holidays, and the number of riding schools approved by the British Horse Society is now more than 400.

The highlights of the show-jumping year are the Royal International Horse Show in July and the Horse of the Year Show in early October, both at Wembley. Other events include All-England shows at Hickstead, W. Sussex, at Easter and in July and August; the Royal Windsor Show in May; the British Timken Show at Duston, Northamptonshire, in late August; the Greater London Horse Show at Clapham Common on the late summer Bank Holiday weekend; and the Olympia International Show in December.

Horse trials are held at Badminton, Gloucestershire, in April; at Tidworth, Hampshire, in May; at Bramham Park, near Tadcaster, N. Yorkshire, in August; at Burghley, near Stamford, Lincolnshire; and Wylye, near Salisbury, in September.

There is a race meeting somewhere in Britain almost every weekday of the year. Useful addresses:

British Horse Society,
(Approved riding schools and advice on buying and caring for horses)
British Equestrian Centre, Stoneleigh, Kenilworth,
Warwickshire CV8 2LR. Tel. Coventry 27192

Show-jumping information is obtainable from the **British Show-Jumping Association,** whose headquarters is also at the British Equestrian Centre.

Ponies of Britain, (Pony-trekking holidays)
Brookside Farm, Ascot, Berkshire SL5 7LU.
Tel. Winkfield Row 2508

Racing Information Bureau,
(Flat and National Hunt Racing)
42 Portman Square, London W1H 0JE.
Tel. 01-486 4571

Sailing

There are more than 500 official sailing centres along Britain's vast coastline and on numerous lakes, reservoirs and rivers. More than 500,000 boating enthusiasts are already using them, and the number is constantly growing.

Many of these part-time sailors belong to clubs, of which more than 1500 are affiliated to the Royal Yachting Association. For sailing round the coast it is not essential to join a club, since the sea is free and open to all; but clubs have facilities such as moorings, club houses, launching slips—and other people around to help anyone in trouble.

Inland, however, it is virtually essential to join a club. Sailing rights on any stretch of inland water are usually restricted to members of a club. The pressure on inland clubs is heavy, and many have waiting lists.

Instruction in sailing can be obtained at more than 400 teaching establishments recognised by the Royal Yachting Association, and all affiliated clubs teach their own members. For the beginner, sailing need not be expensive, and boats can be hired at some centres.

Further advice can be obtained from:

Royal Yachting Association,
Victoria Way, Woking, Surrey GU21 1EQ.
Tel. Woking 5022

Sail Training Association
Bosham, Chichester, W. Sussex PO18 8HR.
Tel. Bosham 572429

Walking

There are more than 100,000 miles of footpaths and bridleways in England and Wales, and thousands of miles more in Scotland. The paths take the walker into the heart of the countryside, opening up large areas of Britain that can be seen in no other way. County councils are in the process of surveying paths in their areas; and as surveys are completed, paths are being marked on the 1¼ in. to 1 mile Ordnance Survey maps.

The Countryside Commission have established Long Distance Footpaths such as the 250-mile-long Pennine Way, which runs from Edale in Derbyshire to Kirk Yetholm in Borders; Yorkshire's 93-mile Cleveland way; the 167-mile Pembrokeshire Coast Path; Offa's Dyke Path, running for 168 miles through the Welsh Marches; the 80-mile South Downs Way and the 141-mile North Downs Way; the 85-mile Ridgeway Path from Overton Hill to Ivinghoe Beacon; and the South-West Coast Path, which hugs the coastline for 515 miles between Minehead and Poole.

Long-distance walking—especially hill-walking—calls for careful preparation: good boots, warm waterproof clothing, an emergency food supply, a compass, maps and a whistle to blow in case of accident.

The Forestry Commission provide information centres and marked trails through their Forest Parks. Several hundred Nature Trails—routes that pass through areas where particular plants and animals can be seen—are dotted throughout the country. Further information can be obtained from:

Countryside Commission,
(National Parks and Long Distance Footpaths)
John Dower House, Crescent Place,
Cheltenham GL50 3RA. Tel. Cheltenham 21381

Forestry Commission, (Forest Parks)
231 Corstorphine Road, Edinburh EH12 7AT.
Tel. 031-334 0303

Nature Conservancy Council,
(Nature Reserves, Nature Parks and Nature Trails)
19 Belgrave Square, London SW1X 8PY.
Tel. 01-235 3241

Ramblers' Association, (General information and advice) 1/4 Crawford Mews, York Street, London W1H 1PT. Tel. 01-262 1477

Law and the Holidaymaker

Trespassers cannot be prosecuted simply for trespassing, for it is not a crime. Trespass is, however, a civil wrong, and the landowner is entitled to order the trespasser to leave at once and to use reasonable force to remove him if he will not go. He is also entitled to get a court order to stop the trespasser repeating the trespass, and to sue for any damage sustained.

To walk on private land is a trespass unless the landowner has given permission or there is a public right of way. If a right of way is not passable, a walker is entitled to walk round the obstruction, even if this means walking on growing crops—though the detour must be no longer than is absolutely necessary. Going round a field, instead of through crops adjoining a path, may be more considerate, but it constitutes a trespass and a walker could be fined for damage caused. Camping on private or public land without permission is a trespass. Campers not using a proper camping site must seek the landowner's permission.

In addition to the law governing behaviour in the countryside, there is a 'Country Code', based on common sense, courtesy and consideration. The main points of the Code are: guard against all risk of fire; keep dogs under control; fasten all gates; keep to paths across farm land; avoid damaging fences, hedges and walls; leave no litter; safeguard water supplies; protect wildlife, plants and trees; go carefully on country roads; respect the life of the countryside.

Automobile Association Offices

Information and advice on all aspects of motoring is available to Automobile Association members from the following AA offices throughout England, Wales and Scotland. Telephone numbers in bold figures are for breakdown and information services only, and are available 24 hours a day, except where times are otherwise stated. Correspondence should be addressed to the Regional Headquarters. The zones follow the arrangement of the *Illustrated Guide to Britain* and do not represent the administrative regions of the AA.

SOUTH-WEST ENGLAND
Exeter Fanum House, Bedford Street.
Tel. Exeter 32121, **32121**
Plymouth 10 Old Town Street.
Tel. Plymouth 28004, **69989**
Truro 10 River Street. Tel. Truro 2283, **76455**
SOUTHERN ENGLAND
Basingstoke Head Office, Fanum House.
Tel. Basingstoke 20123, **56565**
Bournemouth Fanum House, 47 Richmond Hill.
Tel. Bournemouth 25751, **25751**
Southampton Fanum House, 11 The Avenue.
Tel. Southampton 36811, **36811**
SOUTH-EAST ENGLAND
Brighton 10 Churchill Square.
Tel. Brighton 24933, **24933**
Dover Fanum House, Russell Street.
Tel. Dover 203580
Guildford Fanum House, London Road.
Tel. Guildford 72841, **72841**
Maidstone 8 Colman House, King Street.
Tel. Maidstone 55353, **55353**
SOUTH MIDLANDS
Birmingham 134 New Street.
Tel. 021-550 4858, **021-550 4858**
Bristol Park Row. Tel. Bristol 298531,
298531; Park Row (Regional Headquarters).
Tel. Bristol 297272
Coventry 19 Cross Cheaping.
Tel. 021-550 4858, **021-550 4858**
Halesowen Fanum House, Dogkennel Lane
(Regional Headquarters). Tel. 021-550 4721
Leicester 132 Charles Street.
Tel. Leicester 20491, **20491**
Northampton 67 Abington Street.
Tel. Northampton 37411, **66242**
HOME COUNTIES
Oxford 133/134 High Street.
Tel. Oxford 46578, **40286**
Reading 45 Oxford Road.
Tel. Reading 581122, **581122**
Slough 57 High Street. Tel. Slough 28757, **28757**
LONDON
General, home travel information: Tel. 01-954 7373
Legal, technical, overseas travel, insurance:
Tel. 01-954 7355. 24-hr. breakdown: Tel. **01-954 7373**
City Regis House, King William Street.
Tel. 01-626 9993
Hammersmith 162 Fulham Palace Road.
Tel. 01-385 3677
Stanmore Fanum House, The Broadway.
Tel. 01-954 7355, **01-954 7373**
Teddington Fanum House, 7 High Street
(Regional Headquarters). Tel. 01-977 3200
West End Fanum House, 5 New Coventry Street.
Tel. 01-954 7355
EASTERN COUNTIES
Cambridge Janus House, 46/48 St Andrews Street.
Tel. Cambridge 63101, **63101**
Chelmsford 205 Moulsham Street.
Tel. Chelmsford 61711, **61711**
Norwich 126 Thorpe Road.
Tel. Norwich 29401, **29401**
WALES
Cardiff 7 Wood Street.
Tel. Cardiff 394111, **394111**
NORTH MIDLANDS
Nottingham Fanum House, 484 Derby Road.
Tel. Nottingham 77751, **77751**
Stoke-on-Trent 32/38 Stafford Street, Hanley.
Tel. Stoke-on-Trent 25881, **25881**
NORTH-WEST ENGLAND
Cheadle Fanum House, Station Road, Cheadle
Hulme (Regional Headquarters). Tel. 061-485 6188
General, home travel, 24-hr. breakdown:
Tel. **061-485 6299.**
Chester Mercia Square, Frodsham Street.
Tel. Chester 20438, **20438** (0700-2300 hours)
Liverpool Derby Square.
Tel. 051-709 7252, **051-709 7252**
NORTH-EAST ENGLAND
Hull 27 Carr Lane. Tel. Hull 28580, **28580**
Leeds 95 The Headrow. Tel. Leeds 38161, **38161**
Newcastle upon Tyne 13 Princess Square.
Tel. Newcastle 610111, **610111**
Sheffield 2 Fargate.
Tel. Sheffield 28861, **28861**
York 6 Church Street. Tel. York 27698, **27698**
SCOTTISH LOWLANDS
Edinburgh Fanum House, 18/22 Melville Street.
Tel. 031-225 8464, **031-225 8464**
Glasgow Erskine Fanum House, Erskine Harbour
(Regional Headquarters). Tel. 041-812 0144
269 Argyle Street. Tel. 041-812 0101, **041-812 0101**
SCOTTISH HIGHLANDS
Aberdeen Fanum House, 19 Golden Square.
Tel. Aberdeen 51231, **51231** (until 2300 hours)
Dundee 124 Overgate.
Tel. Dundee 25585, **25585**

INDEX OF PLACES

Page numbers in roman figures indicate the main description of a place, which is often accompanied by a photograph on the same page. Page numbers in italics denote other references or illustrations. Subjects of regional interest which are given special treatment are listed separately on p. 543

A

B

C

D

E

F

G

H

I

J

K

L

M

N

O

P

Q

R

S

T

U

V

W

Y

Z

INDEX OF REGIONAL SUBJECTS

A list of subjects of special regional interest which are given extended treatment in the book, either in illustrated panels on gazetteer pages or in double-page features

Animals

Birds

Building styles and materials

Insects

Butterflies:

Moths:

Local industries, food and crafts

People

Plants

ACKNOWLEDGMENTS

Many people and organisations assisted in the preparation of this book. The publishers wish to thank all of them, particularly

Dr P. J. Adams; Paul Atterbury; Derek Bayes; Mary Berry; The Trustees of the British Museum; The Trustees of the British Museum (Natural History); The British Tourist Authority, especially its library staff; Jenny Campbell; Marjorie Caton-Jones; A. C. Cooper Ltd; Department of the Environment; The Distillers Company Ltd; David Divine; Fairey Surveys Ltd; R. B. Fleming & Co Ltd; The Forestry Commission; Ian Gilchrist; Jeremy Grayson; Terry Hardy; Robert Harding; Highlands and Islands Development Board; Christina Hole; Nigel Holmes; Frances Howell; Barry Johnson; Ann Kings; Judy Lehane; Librarians throughout Britain, who helped in the checking of the material; The Loch Ness Phenomena Investigation Bureau; Macmillan & Co. Ltd and Mrs George Bambridge, for permission to include a stanza from 'A Smuggler's Song' by Rudyard Kipling; Richard Marshall; Tom Stalker Miller; The Ministry of Agriculture; The National Fruit Trials Farm, Faversham; The National Trust; Michael Newton; Ordnance Survey; Charles Pickard; The Royal Horticultural Society; Alec Samuel; Scotch House Ltd, Knightsbridge; The Scotch Whisky Association; Tom Scott; E. H. Shackleton; David Sharp; The Society of Authors and Jonathan Cape Ltd, for permission to use two verses from A. E. Housman's Collected Poems; Alan Sorrell; Summit Art Ltd; Basil Taylor; Hazel Thurston; Wales Tourist Board; Sheila Waters; Martin Weaver; *Westmorland Gazette*, for permission to use a map from A. Wainwright's *Pictorial Guide to the Lakeland Fells*; Anne Winterbotham; M. Wood, B.Sc., Dip. Cart.; W. J. Wright.

The publishers also wish to thank the following people and organisations for permission to reproduce photographs belonging to them or showing their property

Aerofilms Ltd; K. M. Andrews; Ardea; Associated Newspapers; Peter Baker; Barnaby's Picture Library; Arthur Bayntun; Bentley Wild Fowl Trust; Birmingham Art Gallery; Black Star; The Bodleian Library, Oxford; Bowles Outdoor Pursuits Centre; Brassey's Institute Library; Brighton Museum; The Trustees of the British Museum; The Trustees of the British Museum (Natural History); B.P.C. Publishing Ltd; David Brook; R. Bull; Camera Press; The Dean of Christ Church, Oxford; Peter Clayton; J. Cleare; The Company of Watermen and Lightermen; Master and Fellows of Corpus Christi College, Cambridge; Gerry Cranham; Curtis Brown Ltd, for permission to reproduce an illustration from *Wind in the Willows* © 1959 E. H. Shepard; The Daily Telegraph Ltd; F. Dalgety; Nicholas Davidson; J. M. Dent & Sons Ltd for permission to reproduce an illustration from *The New Forest*; Department of the Environment; R. Desmond; C. M. Dixon; The Dyson Perrins Museum, Worcester; John Edenbrow; The Mary Evans Picture Library; The Faculty of Advocates, Edinburgh; Ford Motor Company; S. A. Fox; Neville Fox-Davies; John R. Freeman & Co Ltd; Henry Grant; Susan Griggs; V. K. Guy; Tom Hanley; John Hillelson Agency/Magnum Photos; Michael Holford Library; Eric Hosking; Alan Hutchinson; The Institute of Geological Sciences; Ipswich Museum; Jarrold & Son; Jeu de Paume, Paris; A. F. Kersting; Keystone Press Agency; Edna Knowles; University of Leicester; London Express; The London Museum; J. McInnes; P. A. McNab; Mander & Mitchenson Collection; The Mansell Collection; J. March-Penney; Ministry of Defence; Monitor Press Features Ltd; The National Portrait Gallery; Neue Pinakothek, Munich; Museum of Antiquities of the University and the Society of Antiquaries of Newcastle upon Tyne; The Trustees of the National Gallery of Scotland; Nürnberger Museum; P. O'Connor; Oxford University Press, for permission to reproduce an illustration by Victor C. Ambrus from *Robin and his Merry Men* by Ian Serraillier; Petworth Collection; Ursula Pfistermeister; John Phipps; Picturepoint Colour Library; Pix Photos; Axel Poignant; Paul Popper; W. A. Poucher; Radio Times Hulton Picture Library; Rainbow Colour; *Réalités*; Colin Richardson Printers Ltd; Christopher Ridley; George Rodgers; Royal Botanic Society; The President and Council of the Royal College of Surgeons; Tom Sage; St Albans Museum; Dr J. K. St Joseph; Salford City Art Gallery; Scala, New York/Florence; Philippa Scott; The Scottish National Portrait Gallery; Brian Seed; The Trustees of Shakespeare's Birthplace, Stratford-upon-Avon; Brian Shuel; Skyport Fotos; D. K. Smart; Society of Antiquaries; S.P.A.D.E.M.; Spectrum Colour Library; City Museum and Art Gallery, Stoke-on-Trent; Stud & Stable, Newmarket; The Sulgrave Manor Board; Homer Sykes; Syndication International; Thames & Hudson; Transglobe; Trans-World; Tre Tryckare AB; The Unicorn Preservation Society; Universitetets Oldsaksamling, Oslo; Verulamium Museum; The Victoria and Albert Museum; Peter Way Ltd; Tom Weir; Thomas Wilkie; D. P. Wilson; Reg Wilson; Woodmansterne Ltd; Roger Worsley.

The publishers acknowledge their indebtedness to the following books which were used for reference

All About King Arthur by G. Ashe (W. H. Allen); *The Anglo-Saxon Chronicle* edited by D. Whitelock (Eyre & Spottiswoode); *Archaeology of the Anglo-Saxon Settlements* by E. T. Leeds (Oxford University Press); *Battlefields of Western Europe*, edited by D. Chandler (Hugh Evelyn); *Battles of the '45* by Buist & Tomasson (Batsford); *Bedfordshire* by Laurence Meynell (Robert Hale); *A Biographical Dictionary of English Architects 1660–1840* by H. M. Colvin (John Murray); *The Blue Guide to England and Wales* (Benn); *Bonnie Prince Charlie Maps* (Bartholomew); *The Borough Town of Stratford-upon-Avon* by Levi Fox (Corporation of Stratford-upon-Avon); *Breckland* by Olive Cook (Robert Hale); *Britain's Heritage* (Automobile Association); *The Broads* by R. H. Mottram (Robert Hale); *The Buildings of England* by Nikolaus Pevsner (Penguin); *Castles and Kings* by P. E. Cleator (Robert Hale); *Chambers's Biographical Dictionary* (Chambers); *Chambers's Encyclopaedia* (Newnes); *Cinque Ports* by Montague Burrows (Longmans Green); *The Columbia Encyclopedia* (Columbia University Press); *The Commoners' New Forest* by F. E. Kenchingston (Hutchinson); *The Companion Guide to London* by David Piper (Collins); *Companion into Durham* by J. E. Morris (Methuen); *Companion into Northumberland* by S. Moorhouse (Methuen); *The Complete British Butterflies in Colour* by E. Mansell and L. Hugh Newman (Ebury Press and Michael Joseph); *The Concise British Flora in Colour* by W. Keble Martin (Michael Joseph and Ebury Press); *A Concise History of Scotland* by Fitzroy MacLean (Thames & Hudson); *Curious Cornwall* by B. Trevail (Tor Mark Press); *Devon* by W. G. Hoskins (Collins); *Devon & Cornwall* by Ronald Duncan (Batsford); *The Dictionary of National Biography* (Oxford); *Discovering English Customs & Traditions* by Margaret Gascoigne (Shire Publications); *The East Midlands and the Peak District* by G. Dury (Nelson); *Encyclopaedia Britannica* (Encyclopaedia Britannica Ltd); *England and Wales* by Arnold Fellows (Oxford); *England's Markets* by Mary Cathcart Borer (Abelard-Schuman Ltd); *The English Castle* by H. Braun (Batsford); *English Coast Defences* by G. Clinch (G. Bell); *The English Lake District* by F. J. Monkhouse (Geographical Association); *English Medieval Castles* by R. Allen Brown (Batsford); *Everyday Life in the Viking Age* by Jacqueline Simpson (Batsford); *Everyman's Dictionary of Literary Biography* (J. M. Dent); *The Fens* by Alan Bloom (Robert Hale); *The Fens and West Norfolk* by Trevor A. Bevis (Bevis); *Festivals and Events* (British Petroleum); *The Field Guide to the Mammals of Britain and Europe*, by F. H. Van den Brink (Collins); *Gazetteer of the British Isles* (Bartholomew); *The Geological Column* (Manchester Museum); *Georgian London* by J. Summerson (Pelican); *The Golf Course Guide* by Donald Steel (Collins); *The Great Invasions* by L. Cottrell (Evans); *The Great Orm of Loch Ness* by F. W. Holiday (Faber & Faber); *Greater London* by Christopher Trent (Phoenix); *Guide to English Parish Churches* by John Betjeman (Collins); *Hadrian's Wall* by A. R. Birley (H.M.S.O.); *Haydn's Dictionary of Dates* (Haydn & Vincent); *The Highlands and Their Legends* by O. F. Swire (Oliver & Boyd); *A History of Scotland* by R. Mitchison (Methuen); *Illustrated Road Book of England and Wales* (AA); *Illustrated Road Book of Scotland* (AA); *Kent History Illustrated* by Frank W. Jessup (Kent County Council); *London: The Unique City* by Steen Eiler Rasmussen (Jonathan Cape); *London, An Illustrated History* by Ivor Brown (Studio Vista); *London Perceived* by V. S. Pritchett (Chatto & Windus and Heinemann); *The Making of the English Landscape* by W. G. Hoskins (Hodder); *Nairn's London* by Ian Nairn (Penguin); *A New Dictionary of British History* by S. H. Steinberg (Arnold); *Nicholson's Guide to the Thames* (Robert Nicholson); *North England* by A. E. Smailes (Nelson); *The Observer's Book of Larger Moths* by R. L. E. Ford (Warne); *The Orchard and Fruit Garden* by E. Hyams and A. A. Jackson (Longmans); *The Oxford Companion to English Literature* (Oxford); *The Oxford Dictionary of English Place Names* by Eilert Ekwall (Oxford); *Pageant of Lakeland* by A. H. Griffin (Robert Hale); *The Pattern of English Building* by Alec Clifton Taylor (Batsford); *The Peak District* by K. C. Edwards (A. C. Dent); *Pears Cyclopedia* (Pelham); *The Penguin Guide to London* by F. R. Banks (Penguin); *The Pennine Dales* by Arthur Raistrick (Eyre & Spottiswoode); *Portrait of the Lakes* by Norman Nicholson (Robert Hale); *Portrait of the New Forest* by B. Vesey Fitzgerald (Robert Hale); *Prehistoric Annals of Scotland* by Daniel Wilson (Macmillan); *Prince Charlie* by Compton Mackenzie (Dobson); *Properties of the National Trust* (National Trust); *The Rainbow—A Portrait of John Constable* by Andrew Shirley (Michael Joseph); *Reference Atlas of Greater London* (Bartholomew); *Royal Pageantry, Customs and Festivals* (Purnell); *Scotch Whisky* by David Daiches (Deutsch); *Shakespeare: A Pictorial Biography* by F. E. Halliday (Thames & Hudson); *Shakespeare in His Time* by Ivor Brown (Nelson); *Shakespeare: The Poet and His Background* by Peter Quennell (Weidenfeld & Nicholson); *The Shape of History* by D. Turnbull (Macmillan); *The Shell Guide to Britain and Northern Ireland* (Ebury Press and George Rainbird); *The Shell Guide to England* (Michael Joseph); *The Shell Guide to Scotland* (Ebury Press & Rainbird); *The Shell Guide to Wales* (Michael Joseph); *The Travellers Guides*, edited by Sean Jennett (Darton, Longman & Todd); *The Viking* (C. A. Watts); *The Vikings* by Holger Arbman (Thames & Hudson); *Where to Fish* by H. F. Wallis (Harmsworth Press); *Whitaker's Almanack* (Whitakers); *Yorkshire—East Riding* by J. Fairfax-Blakeborough (Robert Hale); *Yorkshire—West Riding* by Lettice Cooper (Robert Hale).

Paper, printing and binding by:

SIR JOSEPH CAUSTON & SONS LTD, EASTLEIGH; FRED A. CHURCHILL & PARTNERS LTD, SOUTHAMPTON; WINTERBOTTOM PRODUCTS LTD, SALFORD; SCHWITTER LTD, ZURICH; SOCIETE ROYALE HOLLANDAISE, MAASTRICHT; HAZELL, WATSON AND VINEY LTD, AYLESBURY